T0189616

Lecture Notes in Computer Science 9567

Commenced Publication in 1973
Founding and Former Series Editors:
Gerhard Goos, Juris Hartmanis, and Jan van Leeuwen

More information about this series at http://www.springer.com/series/7409

Qiaohong Zu · Bo Hu (Eds.)

Human Centered Computing

Second International Conference, HCC 2016
Colombo, Sri Lanka, January 7–9, 2016
Revised Selected Papers

 Springer

Editors
Qiaohong Zu
Wuhan, Hubei
China

Bo Hu
Fujitsu Laboratories of Europe Ltd.
Middlesex
UK

ISSN 0302-9743   ISSN 1611-3349 (electronic)
Lecture Notes in Computer Science
ISBN 978-3-319-31853-0   ISBN 978-3-319-31854-7 (eBook)
DOI 10.1007/978-3-319-31854-7

Library of Congress Control Number: 2016937939

LNCS Sublibrary: SL3 – Information Systems and Applications, incl. Internet/Web, and HCI

Printed on acid-free paper

This Springer imprint is published by Springer Nature
The registered company is Springer International Publishing AG Switzerland

Preface

HCC 2016, the Second International Conference on Human-Centered Computing was held during January 7–9, 2016, in Colombo, Sri Lanka. HCC is the successor of two international conference series on pervasive computing and Web society, which are seeing an increasing trend of merging topics and research foci. One of the conference series, known as the International Conference on Pervasive Computing and Applications (ICPCA), was organized between 2006 and 2013 as a major forum for pervasive computing, smart devices and spaces, wireless/mobile technologies, and sensor networks. In 2014, ICPCA joined forces with SWS to promote awareness of how pervasive technologies impact on the modern societies as well as on humans' everyday lives. HCC sets the vision of human-centric intelligent society and serves as a platform for exchanging innovative concepts and fostering collaborations.

The first HCC event was held successfully in Phnom Penh, Cambodia, during November 27–29, 2014. Built on the experience and feedback from the previous event, HCC 2016 again solicited and organized papers according to the following four categories: infrastructure and devices, service and solution, data and knowledge, and community. This categorization was also reflected in the arrangement of conference technical sessions.

HCC 2016 received 211 full-paper submissions. Every submitted paper went through a rigorous evaluation. Each paper was peer-reviewed by at least two members of the Program Committees and/or selected additional reviewers. While the decisions were made outright for many submissions, around 30 submissions were subject to author rebuttal and a second-round "meta-review" owing to disagreement in the initial reviews. Based on these comments and recommendations, the Program Committee co-chairs made acceptance decisions and classified the accepted papers into two categories:

Full papers: 58 papers passed the most stringent selection and were selected for oral presentation.

Short papers: 30 additional papers were selected for poster presentation.

Workshop papers: HCC 2016 also presented 20 papers from the doctoral workshop to encourage the exchange of concepts and ideas among research students and new researchers.

It has been another year of hard work and selfless contributions. The conference Steering Committee and Organizing Committee would like to express our gratitude to several individuals and organizations. We are grateful to all members of the Technical Program Committee and conference Advisory Board. The most significant task fell upon their experienced shoulders — it was their hard work that enabled us to identify a set of high-quality submissions reflecting the trends and interests of the related research fields. Our special thanks also go to the external reviewers, student volunteers, and local support team, who played a key role in making HCC 2016 a successful event. We are also grateful to Springer's editorial staff for their hard work in publishing these proceedings in the LNCS series.

Finally, we thank most of all the authors of the submitted papers for their continuous contribution and support.

February 2016   Qiaohong Zu
                                                                                        Bo Hu

Organization

General Conference Chair

Yong Tang   South China Normal University, China
Ning Gu   Fudan University, China

Steering Committee

Zongkai Lin   ICT, CAS, China
Bin Hu   Lanzhou University, China
Vic Callaghan   University of Essex, UK
Bo Hu   Fujitsu Laboratories of Europe Limited, UK
Ning Gu   Fudan University, China
Qiaohong Zu   Wuhan University of Technology, Chinaa

Organizing Committee Co-chairs

Bo Hu   Fujitsu Laboratories of Europe Limited, UK
Qiaohong Zu   Wuhan University of Technology, China
Tun Lu   Fudan University, China

Secretariat

Jizheng Wan   Coventry University, UK

International Advisory Committee

Alcaniz Mariano   Human Lab, Technical University of Valencia, Spain
Atilla Elci   Aksaray Üniversittesi, Turkey
Hai Jin   Huazhong University of Science and Technology, China
Callaghan Vic   University of Essex, UK
Ning Gu   Fudan University, China
Greiner Russ   University of Alberta, Canada
Greunen Darelle van   NMMU, South Africa
Gutknecht Jürg   ETH Zurich, Switzerland
Daqing He   University of Pittsburgh, USA
Holzinger Andreas   TU Graz, Austria
Bin Hu   Birmingham City University, UK
Kuan-Ching Li   Providence University, Taiwan
Zongkai Lin   ICT, CAS, China

Lindner Maik   SAP Research, USA
Junzhou Luo   Southeast University, China
Malyshkin Victor   Russian Academy of Science, Russia
Majoe Dennis   ETH Zurich, Switzerland
Reynolds Paul   France Telecom, France
Riss Uwe   SAP Research, Germany
Dingfang Chen   Wuhan University of Technology, China
Junde Song   Beijing University of Posts and Telecommunications,
                              China
Salvadores Manuel   Stanford University, USA
Terada Tsutomu   Osaka University, Japan
Shaojun Wang   Wright State University, USA
Tingshao Zhu   Chinese Academy of Science, China

Program Committee Co-chairs

Xianghua Ding   Fudan University, China
Yong Ming Kow   City University of Hong Kong, SAR China
Gihan Dias   Moratuwa University, Sri Lanka

Program Committee

Nidhal Bouaynaya	Qi Tian	Zhen Liu	Xiaoli Ni
Baomin Xu	Qiang Gao	Zhili Sun	Huping Xu
Bin Wang	Ronghui Liu	Zhiping Yang	Sobah Abbas
Bin Hu	Shaohua Huang	Zhongzhi Shi	Petersen
Changsheng Xu	Shufen Liu	Baoan Song	Ayman
Dajun Zeng	Tao Jiang	Baobin Li	Abdel-Hamid
Dan He	Tiejun Ma	Guihua Yang	Ralf Ackermann
Deyuan Chen	Tiejian Luo	Guofeng Deng	Matthew Adigun
Guoray Cai	Wei Qu	Jianping Wang	Marco Aiello
Haibo He	Weidong Wang	Jinshan Wang	Natasha Alechina
Hanqing Lu	Weiming Hu	Kan Shi	Sherif Ali
Jie Tang	Weiqiang Wang	Li Lei	Aggela Antoniou
Jingzhi Yan	Wenbin Gao	Ling Hou	Angeliki Antoniou
Kuanchang Gao	Xiaojun Wang	Liyou Yang	Juan Carlos
Lehua Cheng	Yalou Huang	Qianping Wang	Augusto
Li Cheng	Ying Liu	Rong Hu	Roberto Barchino
Maoqiang Xie	Ying Zhao	Rui Zheng	Plata
Marek Reformat	Yong Shi	Shuying Bai	Paolo Bellavista
Michael Mackay	Yongzhong Sha	Tao Zhou	Adam Belloum
Ming Li	Yunhua Hu	Tieer Shi	Simone Braun
Minglun Gong	Yuxi Li	Tong Zhang	Luis Carrico
Peng Gao	Zhaoli Song	Wenyong Qu	Alan Chamberlain

Dingfang Chen
Tianzhou Chen
Yiqiang Chen
Luke Chen
Lizhen Cui
Aba-Sah Dadzie
Mohsen Darianian
Marco De Sa
Matjaz Debevc
Luhong Diao
Monica Divitini
Talbi El-Ghazali
Henrik Eriksson
Yan Fu
Xiufen Fu
Shu Gao
Mauro Gaspari
Elena Gaura
Wasif Gilani
Peng Gong
Bin Gong
Horacio
  Gonzalez-Velez
Chaozhen Guo
Jose Gutierrez
Hong He
Fazhi He
Matthias Hollick
Andreas Holzinger
Masahiro Hori
Changqin Huang
Magnus
Ingmarsson
Diego Lopez de
  Ipina
Mike Jackson
Wenbin Jiang
Zongpu Jiang
Weijin Jiang
Lourdes Jimenez
  Rodriguez
Hai Jin
Matjaz Juric

Masoud Koleini
Romain Laborde
Luigi Lancieri
Victor Landassuri-
  Moreno
Bo Lang
Angelos Lazaris
Tobias Ley
Hua Li
Zongming Li
Keqiu Li
Shaozi Li
Wenfeng Li
Xiaofei Liao
Lizhen Liu
Shijun Liu
Hong Liu
Xiyu Liu
Lianru Liu
Yongjin Liu
Junzhou Luo
Chuangui Ma
Cuixia Ma
Huadong Ma
Yasir Malkani
Victor Malyshkin
Rene Mayrhofer
Paul McCarthy
Fiona McNeill
Mohamed Menaa
Marek Meyer
Martin Peter
  Michael
Pirjo Moen
Mounir Mokhtari
Maurice Mulvenna
Jenny Munnelly
Mario Munoz
Tobias Nelkner
Heiko Pfeffer
Sabri Pllana
Thomas Ploetz
Klaus Rechert

Uwe Riss
Andreas Schrader
Xubang Shen
Nianfeng Shi
Meilin Shi
Guangya Si
Beat Signer
Mei Song
Meina Song
Junde Song
Ralf Steinmetz
Gatziu Grivas
  Stella
Surong Sun
Xianfang Sun
Yuqing Sun
Tashihiro Tabata
Wenan Tan
Yong Tang
Xianping Tao
Shaohua Teng
Coral Walker
Yunlan Wang
Hongan Wang
Qianping Wang
Yun Wang
Hans-Friedrich
  Witschel
Gang Wu
Sibusiso Xulu
Toshihiro
  Yamauchi
Chenglei Yang
Laurence T. Yang
Yanfang Yang
Zhimin Yang
Chen Yu
Lei Yu
Xianchuan Yu
Xiaosu Zhan
Yong Zhang
Gansen Zhao
Tingshao Zhu

Jianyong Zhu
Zhenmin Zhu
Qiaohong Zu
Thomas
Jiagen Jin
Yuanda Cao
Weimin Zheng
Shufen Liu
Yongwei Wu
Guangwen Yang
Puyong Wang
Qiuhua Tang
Qingkui Chen
Liping Gao
Bo Yang
Jiantao Zhou
Guoxiang Yao
Lixi Li
Ruizhi Sun
Changyou Zhang
Jianbo Xu
Xiaochun Yang
Yichuan Jiang
Yijie Wang
Jinglan Yang
Weili Wu
Bo Jiang
Yingzhang Guo
Xiaoping Li
Jianguo Li
Dongning Liu
Xiangwei Zheng
Chao Yang
Shiying Li
Judy Chen
Daniel Pargman
Yun Huang
Hansu Gu
Patrick C. Shih
Jude Yew
Bryan C. Semaan
Qianying Liao
Alex Mitchell

Scholar-Centered Computing: Research and Practice

(Keynote)

Yong Tang

School of Computer Science,
South China Normal University,
Guangzhou City, Guangdong 510631, China
http://www.scholat.com/ytang

Social Network System (SNS) is a typical kind of application for Human Centered Computing (HCC), which is changing the life style of people. However, nowadays most of the popular social network websites are for general purposes. Along with the wide application of SNS, the specific demands in many domains or professional groups. For example, doctors and patients need to communicate about medical records, teachers and students need to communicate with course material, researchers need to cooperate with each other based on academic information. So there are more and more social network systems developing especially for special domain.

SCHOLAT, designed by our team, is a kind of vertical social network system to meet the demands of most teachers, researchers and students for their collaboration in education and research. Four main functions of SCHOLAT are below:

Academic assistant As the primary function, SCHOLAT firstly is an academic assistant for managing personal information. Each user has a storage space for saving personal information, such as biography, publications and so on. SCHOLAT also provide some tools including Scholar-Calendar, Online-disk, CV-Creator and System Recommendation to assist users to work. For example, Online-Disk can be used to manage the attachment file of personal information, such as PDF file of publications, scanning file of certification and so on.

Social network for scholars SCHOLAT is a social network system oriented for scholars, especially for teachers and students in universities. Users can create an academic circle to communicate, to share personal news and academic information. SCHOLAT also provides two popular communication tools for Chat and Mail between users.

Collaborative platform SCHOLAT is a cooperative platform for research and education. Users can create a group for cooperative work. Now, there are two kinds of SCHOLAT groups, one is for group research called S-Team, the other is for collaborative education called S-Course.

Domain-specific search engine SCHOLAT also is an academic search engine and news portal. Visitors can retrieve academic information and look for news, such as research papers, notices of position for Post Doc, and so on.

In this talk, I would like to discuss the research and practice of human centered computing based SCHOLAT. I will mainly focus on the design of system architecture, and demonstrate the usage through case studies and the big data applications in SCHOLAT. Last, I will propose the concept of SCHOLAT+ research, applications and services.

Contents

A Virtual Machine Data Communication Mechanism on Openstack

Jie Chen[1,2(✉)], Saihong Xu[1], Haiyang Zhang[1], and Zunliang Wang[1,2]

[1] School of Computer Science, Beijing University of Posts
and Telecommunications, Beijing 100876, People's Republic of China
chenjie52388@163.com
[2] Science and Technology on Information Transmission and Dissemination
in Communication Networks Laboratory, Shijiazhuang, China

Abstract. This article analyzed the advantages and disadvantages of current data communication mechanism among multiple virtual machines. Combining the characteristics of the cloud platform openstack, this paper puts forward a method to make the communication of virtual machines more efficient by using para-virtualization. Through the shared memory we can break down the communication barriers among the virtual machines and reduce the number of data copy times in the process of data transferring. Experiments show that the communication efficiency of multiple virtual machines gets higher.

Keywords: Communication of multiple virtual machines · Para-virtualization · Shared memory · KVM · Virtio

1 Introduction

Nowadays, the service provider around the world is adopting virtualization and cloud computing technology to deploy and deliver virtual network services, namely network function virtualization (NFV). Deploying services in virtual machines makes the deployment cost less and efficiency higher. And how to communicate among virtual machines more efficiently is becoming the focus of attention.

The continuous development of virtualization technology makes the dependencies of network function and its hardware eliminated. Just as the virtual network function (VNF) of NFV, it decouples the software and hardware. The most direct benefit is that we can create multiple independent virtual machines on the same set of physical hardware. These virtual machines can provide different functions. At present, the most popular and mature virtualization technologies include KVM, Zen, etc.

At the same time, the cloud computing has a rapid development in recent years. Cloud computing has become one of the hottest technology. It will combine a variety of software and hardware to constitute a powerful computing platform which can provide customers with various services through the network. It includes infrastructure as a service (IaaS), platform as a service (PaaS) and software as a service (SaaS). We can manage and schedule the computing resources using these technologies. NFV for the usage of cloud computing mainly concentrates in the IaaS layer. Here we consider openstack. We can use it to deploy virtualized environment quickly, and can create

© Springer International Publishing Switzerland 2016
Q. Zu and B. Hu (Eds.): HCC 2016, LNCS 9567, pp. 1–11, 2016.
DOI: 10.1007/978-3-319-31854-7_1

multiple interconnected virtual machines, namely VNF. And users can quickly deploy applications on the virtual servers.

With the mature of virtualization and cloud computing technology, the virtual machine is widely used today. Enterprise uses a set of physical resources to create many virtual machines, not only for their own use, but also providing services to others, such as economical cloud hosting now. These cloud hosting its essence is a series of virtual machines. This paper mainly studies the data communication mechanism of virtual machines based on openstack.

2   The Communication Scenarios

2.1   Communication Scenarios

Network function virtualization (NFV) has an application scenario, which is IP Multimedia System (IMS). The IMS system contains many entities. For the sake of simplicity, here we only consider the MRF. MRF is mainly completed for many calls and multimedia conferencing. MRF consists of MRFC (Multimedia Resource Function Controller) and MRFP (Multimedia Resource Function Processor). They complete the media flow control and load function respectively. In some improvements of IMS system such as NCSP [1], there will be an extra MRMS (multimedia resource management system) entity. The MRMS implements the management function of the whole system as shown in Fig. 1.

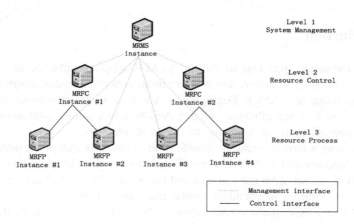

Fig. 1. MRF

2.2   Communication Requirements

In the multimedia resource management subsystem, MRMS is the manager of the MRF. It has two big functions: First, it provides query and modify function for the subsystem's software information of MRF; Followed by operation maintenance function, it is the main function of MRMS subsystem, providing query function, configuration function, operation function, authentication and so on.

The function mentioned above involves a large amount of data communication. In addition, in 3 GPP's IMS architecture, for MRFC and MRFP, MRFC is responsible for interacting with call session control server, receiving the control requirements for the media dealing from the application layer. And then process the received control requirements. Call MRFP to deal with media stream. These media stream includes audio, video, and signal data. So the data to be interacted is very large. Finally MRFP gives treatment results back to MRFC. We can see the process between MRFC and MRFP existing large amounts of data communication.

In such a scenario, we create many virtual machines to act as MRMS, MRFC and MRFP based on the same set of hardware. Facing a large amount of data communication in these virtual machines, the problem we need to solve is to make the communication as efficient as possible.

3   The Methods of Communication

Nowadays, there is many ways of data communication among virtual machines. Here we list some and compare them.

3.1   Pipeline

Pipeline is the most basic method of IPC. Usually a pipeline created by a process, and then the process calls fork to create a child process. Then the father process and the son process can use the pipeline to communicate. After calling pipe to create a pipeline, it will receive two file descriptor. One for writing, another is used to read. Due to the anonymous pipeline is half duplex, if we want to undertake two-way communication, we will have to build another pipeline.

3.2   Fifo

Also known as the named pipeline, FIFO is represented by a special file. It is longer limited to kinship between processes. For the communication among many virtual machines, the approach taken is to create a public FIFO to upload the data. And then to the public FIFO there is a monitoring process, the monitoring process takes the data from the pipeline. For every virtual machine in need to establish a dedicated FIFO, the monitoring process use it to transfer the data obtained from the public pipeline.

3.3   Message Queue

The message queue method uses the communication mechanism of processes. Through the public system message queue to exchange data among two or more processes, this way realizes the reliable message receiving and dispatching mechanism. Message queue technology is a kind of technology for the exchange of information among distributed applications. Message queue can reside in memory or on disk. Queue stores messages until they are read by applications. Through the message queue, the applications can perform independently. They don't need to know the position of each other.

3.4   Shared Memory Channel

In a large amount of data communication scenario, many people use shared memory way, which has the advantage of high efficiency. Shared memory is part of the physical memory shared by multiple processes. It is the fastest method for processes to share data. A process writes the data to the shared memory region, then all other processes who shared this memory area can soon see its contents. They exchange data through the shared memory region.

In all communication methods above, using pipeline is the worst. Because its half duplex communication mode is not convenient. Bidirectional communication need to build two pipeline which takes more resources; Using FIFO scheme with fewer pipelines is its advantage, but there is one drawback that it needs to maintain a mapping table, to record one-to-one correspondence relationship between the user ID and a dedicated FIFO. So the resource consumption is also big; Compared with the former two, message queue greatly simplifies the program logic relationship and dynamic mapping table is omitted which reduced resource consumption. But there is also a problem that the message queue is system level resources. It will not automatically shut down and the message will not disappear. Remaining messages in the queue accumulated to a certain degree will cause the performance loss of the system; The shared memory way, in terms of resource consumption, communication efficiency and flexibility are better than the front several ways. Because the virtual machines are based on openstack, the virtual machines ard based on the same set of physical hardware. Through the way of the Shared memory communication between them is possible, so the proposed method has also adopted the shared memory way. But the most primitive method of shared memory channel can't solve the problem of data communication among multiple virtual machines. It is that it can't solve the application scenario of multiple virtual machines communication problems. Because it needs to maintain a large number of shared memory region, the consumption of resources is too big. On the basis of openstack using the original shared memory model doesn't work. So this paper proposes a method of communication among multiple virtual machines on openstack, it can allocate shared memory for target virtual machine to read or write, and we can map dynamically in the building of a link. That can reduce a large amount of shared memory resource consumption when maintaining the system.

4   Design and Implementation

Openstack supports almost all kinds of hypervisors. The openstack we considered here is based on KVM, which is usually the default hypervisor. So the virtual machines created by openstack are a series of KVM virtual machines. However, the inter-domain communication of virtual machines based on KVM is cumbersome in the processing procedure. It needs to copy data repeatedly which impacts on the performances greatly.

Most of the behaviors of transmitting and receiving data packets in the network I/O process of a virtual machine client are simulated by the QEMU program in the host user mode, which equivalents to transfer data between host processes. So we can use the characteristics of host's Linux system to design and implement a communication mode based on shared memory. In order to implement the communication mode of shared memory among the virtual machines, we need para-virtualization programming interface virtio to implement equipment to offer direct network access based on shared memory. This method can reduce data copy times in inter-domain communication and improve communication efficiency.

4.1 Shared Memory

The above-mentioned virtual machines are created on the same physical machine. So we can use shared memory approach to implement the data communication among these virtual machines. The advantage of shared memory is high efficiency, suitable for the usage in a large number of data communication.

The method adopted in this paper is mapping the shared memory region when multiple virtual machines need inter-domain communication. The advantage of this method is that we can allocate a shared memory area and each virtual machine can dynamically map to it during the establishment of the link. So there is no need to maintain a large number of shared memory areas. This solves the synchronization issue of a large amount of data among multiple virtual machines. For the scenarios previously mentioned, this is a good solution. Greatly improve the efficiency of data transmission among virtual machines, and the response becomes faster.

For this shared memory architecture, it can be put into two parts in design. First, in order for scalability, each time creating a virtual machine, when need to communicate with other virtual machines, allocate a block of memory mapped into its address space, all virtual machines each correspond to a block of memory. Make these blocks of memory to form a circular linked list. When given two virtual machines need to synchronize data, we can find the corresponding block belongs to the peer virtual machine according to the circular linked list, and inform this virtual machine's memory address, both at the same time can write each other's virtual machine information to the corresponding memory of the peer side, which can greatly enhance the efficiency of data synchronization; Second, apply additional block of memory, so that all virtual machines are mapped into this block, this block of memory's size varies according to different scenarios. For the global data that all virtual machines need to synchronize, we can synchronize through this shared memory. Model is shown in Fig. 2.

4.1.1 The Communication Model

This section describes how to use the shared memory model in the whole process of communication. Based on the same set of physical hardware, the communication among virtual machines can be called domain communication. The domain communication refers to the communication happens on some clients which are on the same physical machine. The communication model is divided into two parts: the VM agent and Scanner agent. As is shown in Fig. 3.

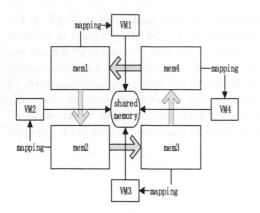

Fig. 2. Shared memory model   **Fig. 3.** Communication model

The agent at the bottom, its main job is to get all virtual machines' information using the API of openstack, such as virtual machine's IP and Mac address, so that the virtual machine can get the target machine's information when in need. The communication model among the virtual machines take the page as the basic unit of the Shared memory, through a series of pages constituting the block of memory to share [2]. In the communication model, most of the work is done by client virtual machines' agent. Its main task is to:

(1) Get the mac address of target virtual machine
(2) Query the underlying agent to get the id of target virtual machine
(3) Confirm whether the target virtual machine on the same physical machine
(4) Establish the shared memory communication.

4.1.2   The Process of Creating Shared Memory
Then we will list all kinds of communication scenarios among vm1, vm2 and vm3:

(1) Point-to-point Communication (vm1, vm2). According to the aforementioned shared memory structure and communication model, first vm1 agent send a query request to share layer agent to detect whether vm1 and vm2 is in the same physical machine. At the same time, the bottom agent tell vm2 that vm1 want to communicate with it with vm1's information appended. Then according to the information to allocate a piece of memory mem1 and mem2 respectively. Then vm1 write data to mem2 and vm2 write data to mem1. So can greatly improve the communication efficiency.
(2) The Communication of Multiple Virtual Machines (vm1,vm2 and vm3). Similar to the above process, the process of vm1 launched communication is as follows. First, vm1 through the agent to take a request of communication, then sharing layer agent determines the communication belongs to multiple virtual machines communication. Then determine whether all virtual machines are located in the same physical machine. If it is, apply for a large block of memory, again according to the relevant information of each virtual machine, the memory mapping to their corresponding

process address space. And then inform each virtual machine the environment is ready, you can communicate with each other.

(3) The Comparison with Other Communication Model. First, the communication method this paper presents compared with other not shared memory communication mode, greatly improves the efficiency of the communication among the virtual machines, according to the actual situation to use the characteristics of the virtual machines on openstack; Second, compared with other Shared memory communication mode, this model not only solves the point-to-point communication between two virtual machines, it can also act as a more effective communication mode among multiple virtual machines, hoping to provide certain reference for a more perfect and efficient communication mechanism among the virtual machines.

4.2 Full Virtualization

Linux full virtualization solution contains hardware virtualization technology mainly for the extension of the X86 architecture. Full virtualization runs faster than hardware emulation, but performances less than bare machine, because the hypervisor takes up some resources. The great advantage of full virtualization is the operating system without any modification. The only limitation is that the operating system must be able to support the underlying hardware. From the point of the full virtualization, the whole process of using KVM is that the bottom of the hardware which supports x86 virtualization extensions (such as AMD and Intel VT- the SVM technology) loads the KVM kernel module of the Linux kernel as a virtual machine manager. Then use KVM tools to load the client operating system and use QEMU to simulate virtual equipment and process the I/O requests.

After intercepting I/O instructions, KVM will redirect and simulate the I/O instructions. These operations are implemented by QEMU, a slightly modified software. QEMU simulates card, memory, bus and other hardware components, supplying a complete I/O model for the clients. Managing the memory by maintaining the mapping between the client's physical address and the host's physical address. In addition, QEMU will also provide virtual device interface for each client, using these to process the received requests, the specific process not described in detail here. I have to say, although the whole KVM virtualization architecture is simple and it takes full advantage of the performance benefits of Linux system, but in terms of virtual network implementation, it is far too complicated, especially low in performance when going on domain communication among virtual machines.

4.3 The Interface Virtio

KVM supports full virtualization and para-virtualization technology. Using full virtualization technology, the domain communication efficiency among virtual machines performs poorly. So it is hoped that through the para-virtualization mechanism to achieve better I/O performance. Para-virtualization similar to full virtualization is a popular virtualization technology. Here we use it to implement shared memory mechanism. It uses the Hypervisor (virtual machine management program) to share and access the underlying hardware, and the guest operating system has integrated the code of virtualization. Using para-virtualization mechanism KVM can achieve better I/O performance. At present, a general efficient I/O para-virtualization mechanism has been adopted by KVM, implemented by para-virtualization programming interface virtio. Virtio is a para-virtualization model suitable for multi-platform. The architecture of virtio is illustrated in Fig. 4.

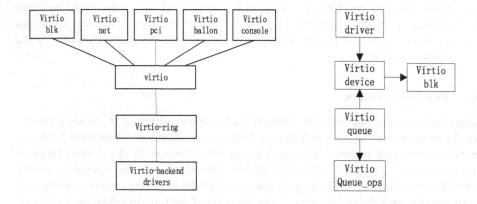

Fig. 4. Architecture of virtio   **Fig. 5.** Architecture

Virtio drivers are designed to be similar to the universal drivers and operating structures, as shown in Fig. 5. Virtio para-virtualization driver is divided into front driver and backend driver. It defines two layers to support the communication from the guest operating system to the hypervisor. The virtio_driver is in the top and it represents front-end drivers in the guest operating system. The devices matched with the drivers are encapsulated by the virtio_device in the guest operating system. Each virtio driver corresponds with back-end virtio device and back-end equipment is responsible for handling the requests from the interaction of front and end. Virtio_device get functions of receiving, dispatching and configuration by using the data buffer of virtio_queue object. Finally, each virtio_queue object references the virtqueue_ops object and the latter defines and deals with the underlying queue operations of the hypervisor drivers.

In the present of KVM virtual machines, the corresponding virtual bus, virtual block devices and virtual network devices have been implemented using virtio. According to the test results, the network throughput is improved about three times.

4.4   Implementing Virtual Devices

In view of the shared memory method mentioned above, the device model is realized using the programming interface virtio. The front and back-end I/O use 3.5 virtual queue to be responsible for receiving, sending the packages and the acess to control area. Besides, there is a structure, which is used to save the data descriptors taken from the virtio_queue. Each virtual machine uses the inter domain channel to communicate, which uses the interfaces of descriptors buffer to communicate with the virtual device virtio_inter. Data processing flow is to add buffer descriptors to the virtqueue or remove from it to transfer the requests. When the data packet is written to the shared memory channel, the client will call virto_inter_receive method to receive the data. Calling process is shown in Fig. 6.

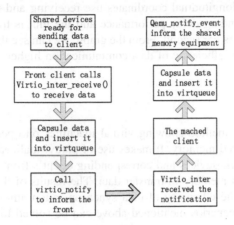

Fig. 6. Process

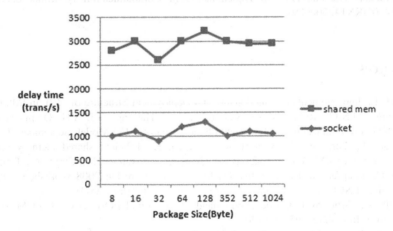

Fig. 7. Results

5 The Performance Analysis

In this section, we test the communication efficiency among multiple virtual machines, and analyze the test results with system ubuntu 14.10, I5 processor and Hz 2.53 G. The main contrast is the two cases: First, the throughput and transmission delay of communication of multiple virtual machines through the socket and other conventional methods to transfer a large amount of data; Second, get the communication results of multiple virtual machines through the shared memory method. The results are shown in Fig. 7 above.

From the Figure we can get that the way of shared memory reduce a large amount of data copy and transmission times, which can reduce the response time delay. As shown in the figure, the horizontal coordinates represent the size of the data packet and the unit is Byte. The longitudinal coordinates use receiving and transmission rate on behalf of the corresponding delay performance and the unit is tranction/s, that is the number of sending times per second. From the graph, we can see that the way of shared memory does make the efficiency of data communication higher and the delay lower.

6 Conclusion

This paper proposes a method showing virtual machines on openstack how to communicate with the shared memory. It makes use of paravirtualized I/O model virtio to simulate virtual network devices and corresponding client's front-end driver, utilizing the approach of shared memory to transfer data. The results of the test show that this method can improve the efficiency of data synchronization among virtual machines. The problems of the scenarios mentioned above can be solved to a large extent.

Acknowledgement. This work was supported by the open project of Science and Technology on Information Transmission and Dissemination in Communication Networks Laboratory (ITD-U14002/KX142600009).

References

1. Chen C.L.: Improvements in Functionality and Deployment Structure of MRF in IMS (2012)
2. Shengge, D.I.N.G., Ruhui, M.A., Alei, L.I.A.N.G., Haibing, G.U.A.N: Optimization for Inter-VMs Communication on KVM with Para-Virtualized I/O Model, September 2011
3. Diakhate, F., Perache, M., Namyst, R., Jourdren, H.: Efficient shared memory message passing for inter-VM communications. In: César, E., Alexander, M., Streit, A., Träff, J.L., Cérin, C., Knüpfer, A., Kranzlmüller, D., Jha, S. (eds.) Euro-Par 2008 Workshops - Parallel Processing. LNCS, vol. 5415, pp. 53–62. Springer, Heidelberg (2009)
4. Russell, R.: Virtio:towards a de-.factio standard for virtual I/O devices. J. ACM SIGOPS Oper. Syst. Rev. **42**(5), 95–103 (2008)
5. Kivity A., Kamay Y.L., Laor, D. et al.: KVM: the Linux virtual machine monitor. In: Proceedings of the Linux Symposium, Ottawa, Ontario, pp. 225–230 (2007)
6. Shengzhao, L., Qinfen, H., Limin, X. et al.: Optimizing network virtualization i kernel—based virtual machine. In: Procedings of the 1st IEEE Internal Conference on Information Science and Engineering (ICISE 2009), pp. 282–285. IEEE Computer Society, Washington DC (2009)
7. Chert, G.I., Lai, T.H.: Constructing parallel paths between two subcubes. IEEE Trans. Comput. **41**(1), 118–123 (1992)

8. Stankovie, J.A.: Implication of classical heduling results for real-time systems. IEEE Comput. **28**(6), 16–25 (1995)
9. Bellard, F.: QEMU, a fast and portable dynamic translator. In: Proceedings of the 2005 USENIX Annual Technical Conference (USENIX 2005), Marriott Anaheimm, April 2005. USENIX Association, Berkeley, CA, USA (2005)

Green Energy Forecast Based on Improved Grey Model for Green Base Stations

Jianbin Chuan[1], Yifei Wei[1(✉)], Yi Man[1], Mei Song[1], Siyuan Sun[2], and Xiaojun Wang[3]

[1] School of Electronic Engineering, Beijing University of Posts and Telecommunications,
Beijing 100876, China
jianbin_chuan@163.com, {weiyifei,manyi}@bupt.edu.cn
[2] China United Network Communications Corporation, Shanghai, China
[3] Dublin City University, Dublin, Ireland

Abstract. With the increasing scale of mobile network, the proportion of energy consumption of network in global is rapidly growing. Particularly, in order to estimate available energy in each node to intelligently optimize the base station by combining with the state of load, an improved grey model is put forward for green energy forecast in smart green base station (GBS), so that the smart GBS can be self-sufficient in energy under the premise of ensuring the quality of communication. In the paper, according to the weather conditions in a certain region, and combined with the solar energy harvesting system, the energy harvesting trend can be forecasted from an improved grey model which based on grey system, and then compared with the real data to prove the validity and practicability of the model.

Keywords: Smart green base station · Green energy · Energy harvesting system · Grey model · Solar energy

1 Introduction

Current research on green base station (GBS) mainly focuses on the power consumption and energy efficiency. Literature [1] puts forward to selectively close the base station with low traffic volume to reduce the energy consumption, but the base station will be accompanied by the emergence of the coverage of the problem. To solve this problem, The method of cell scaling is presented by paper [1, 2] which can dynamically adjust the coverage area of the cell to achieve the reasonable utilization of the system resources according to the network and load conditions, and also prove that the reasonable cell scaling scheme is an effective green access scheme. The power consumption of base station is divided into the static power consumption of the system and the dynamic network energy consumption in Ref. [3], and the optimal scheme is given in the time domain, spatial domain and frequency domain respectively as well. Paper [4] proposes a kind of energy saving mechanism in the case of limited battery capacity from the perspective of information theory. Further, in the case of limited battery capacity, paper [5] consider the dynamic energy arrival queue as a binary time channel without noise, and then puts forward an auxiliary random variable save-and-transmit scheme by

© Springer International Publishing Switzerland 2016
Q. Zu and B. Hu (Eds.): HCC 2016, LNCS 9567, pp. 12–22, 2016.
DOI: 10.1007/978-3-319-31854-7_2

combining Anantharam–Verdu's bits through queues and Shannon's state-dependent channels with causal state information available at the transmitter. Reference [6, 7] present that the directional glue-pouring algorithm is the optimal scheme for offline energy management for throughput maximization. Literature [8] puts forward a data packet transmission model associated random importance value for online energy management for general reward maximization. In the case of clear known of the battery status, the paper [9] presents a great potential energy saving method is Markov Decision Processes. In addition, energy efficiency optimization can be calculated through Policy Iteration Algorithm or some Heuristics Algorithm in Reference [10]. For the case of unknown battery status, the authors in [10] proposes the above methods are no longer probation, but some suboptimal policies can be obtained under the condition of full acknowledge of the past history of harvesting status. Besides, based on practical implement of solar energy as energy supply for base station, Literature [11] demonstrates the feasibility of full GBS.

In summary, GBS optimization is mainly limited in energy saving and energy efficiency improvement in the past, or based on the model which require to fully acquire the battery or energy harvesting statues in advance. Yet it only can find some rough suboptimal policies without known the energy status. As a whole, it is especially meaningful to fully acquire the development trend of energy status to do some forward prediction and then to do related forward optimization.

In this paper, a forecast algorithm based on an improved grey model (GM) of energy harvesting is proposed in the GBS with the supply energy of solar to forecast the energy trend to dynamically optimize the network to fulfill the energy supply of GBS itself under the condition of ensuring the quality of communication.

2 Network Models

With the continuous development of green base station technology, the future green wireless networks will become reality, as shown in Fig. 1, is a kind of future green wireless networks scenario. The model uses hierarchical management architecture. There are a number of micro GBS in a macro GBS, and also there are several green relay station as the supplementary of some micro GBS.

By selecting optimization strategy intelligently which based on status and trend of the energy and load of network, Resource Management Center's main function is to ensure the network's robustness, and to achieve energy saving and energy efficiency. And so as to other Resource Manager. The model is shown in Fig. 2. In architecture of this scenario, the green energy (GE) supply system refers to the solar power supply module. GE management system is mainly responsible for the monitoring and forecasting of the energy state of the solar power supply module, which provides reference for the intelligent strategy selection system. Control System is mainly responsible for monitoring the change of strategy so as to apply the new strategy through the network management system to the network to achieve the purpose of control network. Network management system is mainly responsible for monitoring and prediction of the network state, which provides reference function for monitoring and forecasting of network

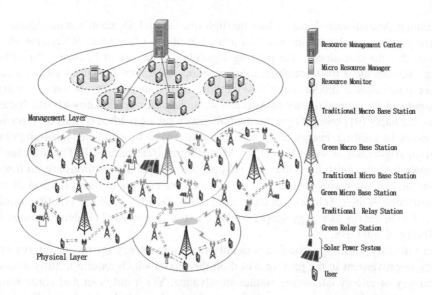

Fig. 1. Future wireless network with green base stations (Color figure online)

energy consumption, and provides the control interface to control the consumption status and forecast function, which provide reference function for strategy evaluation system and intelligent strategy selection system. The strategy evaluation mechanism is automatically completed by the corresponding algorithm. Strategy optimization mechanism can be machine learning, artificial intelligence, and also human analysis. Based on the state and forecast function of GE and network energy consumption, strategy storage system responsible for storage and management of the strategy. Intelligent strategy selection system responsible for choosing the best strategy from strategy storage system for control system.

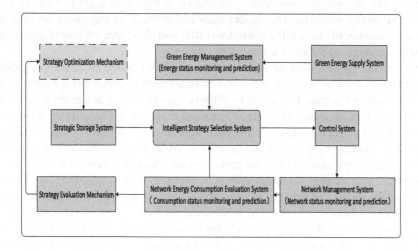

Fig. 2. Resource management model

Usually, the network optimization strategy is different under different circumstances. The optimization strategies of energy harvesting based on energy harvesting in various scenarios, such as Markov Decision Processes, queuing theory, information theory, water injection algorithm, etc., are summarized in paper [10]. However, the energy consumption function of the network obtained by energy consumption evaluation system must be matched with the energy state function obtained by the GE management system, as shown in Fig. 3.

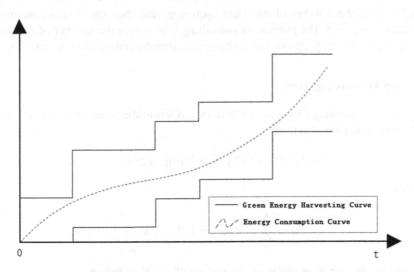

Fig. 3. Constrained energy consumption model

3   Green Energy Forecast

Solar energy is influenced by light intensity and temperature. The algorithm is improved as follow. Firstly, the primary data is processed by smooth processing equation. Secondly forecast model is built by using grey system. Thirdly, it will correct the forecast deviation through residual correction based on cosine function and then find the sequence rules through periodic extension for residual corrected sequence. Finally, in order to obtain the performance of the model, the log data are predicted so that it can be compared with the real data.

3.1   Smoothing Process of Primary Sequence

A primary time sequence as follow:

$$x^{(0)} = [x^{(0)}(1), x^{(0)}(2), \cdots, x^{(0)}(n)], \ n \geq 4 \tag{1}$$

Smooth processing equation as follow:

$$\tilde{x}^{(0)}(k) = \frac{x^{(0)}(k-1) + 2x^{(0)}(k) + x^{(0)}(k+1)}{4}, \; k = 1, 2, \cdots, m \tag{2}$$

Specifically, the beginning and end of the sequence can be calculated as follow:

$$\tilde{x}^{(0)}(1) = \frac{3x^{(0)}(1) + x^{(0)}(2)}{4}, \; \tilde{x}^{(0)}(m) = \frac{x^{(0)}(m-1) + 3x^{(0)}(m)}{4} \tag{3}$$

In (3), m is the number of raw data sequence, and then the forecast number of sequence is $n - m + 1$. The purpose of smoothing is to reduce the number of data mutations caused by the subjectivity and contingency, thereby reduce the interference.

3.2 Grey Forecasting Model

Applying Accumulating Generation Operator (AGO) to the input sequence $x^{(0)}$, a new sequence is generated as follow:

$$x^{(1)} = [x^{(1)}(1), x^{(1)}(2), \cdots, x^{(1)}(m)], \; n \geq 4 \tag{4}$$

Where

$$x^{(1)}(k) = \sum_{i=1}^{k} \tilde{x}^{(0)}(i), \; i = 1, 2, \cdots, m \tag{5}$$

Assuming the albinism differential equation of $x^{(1)}(k)$ as follow:

$$\frac{dx^{(1)}}{dt} + ax^{(1)} = u \tag{6}$$

Where, a is the development parameters of the model, and reflect the development trend of $x^{(1)}$ and the original sequence, u is the model coordination coefficient, and reflect the transformation relationship between data. Assuming $P = \begin{pmatrix} a \\ u \end{pmatrix}$, and according to the least square method, we can get the equation as follow:

$$P = (Q^T Q)^{-1} Q^T H \tag{7}$$

Where

$$H = \begin{pmatrix} x^{(0)}(2) \\ \vdots \\ x^{(0)}(m) \end{pmatrix}; \; Q = \begin{pmatrix} -\frac{1}{2}[x^{(1)}(1) + x^{(1)}(2)] & 1 \\ \vdots & \vdots \\ -\frac{1}{2}[x^{(1)}(m-1) + x^{(1)}(m)] & 1 \end{pmatrix} \tag{8}$$

The solution of (6) is an exponential function and the initial condition for $x^{(1)}(1)$ is $x^{(1)}(1) = \tilde{x}^{(0)}(1)$. Then, $x^{(1)}(k+1)$ can be obtained for $k = 1, 2, \cdots, m$ as follow:

$$x^{(1)}(k+1) = [\tilde{x}^{(0)}(1) - \frac{u}{a}]e^{-ak} + \frac{u}{a} \tag{9}$$

Prediction model can be obtained through accumulated subtraction operation on original series $x^{(0)}$ as follow:

$$\hat{x}^{(0)}(k) = (1 - e^a)(\tilde{x}^{(0)}(1) - \frac{u}{a})e^{-a(k-1)} \tag{10}$$

Fitting sequence of the original sequence $\hat{x}^{(0)}$ is obtained when $k = 1, 2, \cdots, m$, and the forecasted sequence is derived when $k = m+1, m+2, \cdots, n$.

3.3   Residual Correction Based on Cosine Function

Usually, the positive and negative residual of primary sequence alternately appear in the model that result in the deviation of model. However, the residual can be compensated by using the periodicity of cosine function, and the residual correction function is defined as follow:

$$\begin{cases} \delta_1^{(i)} = \cos(2\pi \times \frac{i}{n}) \\ \delta_2^{(i)} = \cos(4\pi \times \frac{i}{n}) \\ \quad\vdots \\ \delta_k^{(i)} = \cos(2k\pi \times \frac{i}{n}) \end{cases} (i = 0, 1, 2, \cdots, n) \tag{11}$$

Where, i is the location of correcting data, and δ_k is the corresponding correction function, k is the length of correction sequence. Correction function can effectively improve the accuracy of forecasted sequence through a larger k, but, with the increasing of k, the amount of calculation increases rapidly as well. So it necessary to choice an appropriate k.

The residual value is calculated as follow:

$$\delta(i) = \hat{x}^{(0)}(i) - x^{(0)}(0), \ i = 1, 2, \cdots, m \tag{12}$$

Assuming that the residual value of each data of forecasted sequence can be expressed by the correction function, and then we get the function as follow:

$$\begin{cases} \widehat{\delta}(1) = \lambda_1\delta_1^{(1)} + \lambda_2\delta_2^{(1)} + \cdots + \lambda_i\delta_i^{(1)} \\ \widehat{\delta}(2) = \lambda_1\delta_1^{(2)} + \lambda_2\delta_2^{(2)} + \cdots + \lambda_i\delta_i^{(2)} \\ \quad\vdots \\ \widehat{\delta}(m) = \lambda_1\delta_1^{(m)} + \lambda_2\delta_2^{(m)} + \cdots + \lambda_i\delta_i^{(m)} \end{cases} \tag{13}$$

And then

$$\widehat{\delta} = \lambda\Delta = \{\lambda_1, \lambda_2, \cdots, \lambda_k\} \begin{cases} \cos(2\pi \times \frac{1}{n}), \cos(2\pi \times \frac{2}{n}), \cdots, \cos(2\pi \times \frac{i}{n}) \\ \cos(4\pi \times \frac{1}{n}), \cos(4\pi \times \frac{2}{n}), \cdots, \cos(4\pi \times \frac{i}{n}) \\ \vdots \\ \cos(2k\pi \times \frac{1}{n}), \cos(2k\pi \times \frac{2}{n}), \cdots, \cos(2k\pi \times \frac{i}{n}) \end{cases} \tag{14}$$

Generally, (14) is no solution, but based on the minimum squared error of primary residual and corrected residual, the solution can be found by using least square method as follow:

$$\lambda = (\Delta^T \Delta)^{-1} \Delta^T \delta \tag{15}$$

And (15) is restricted by the condition as follow:

$$\min[\widehat{\delta}(i) - \delta(i)]^2 \tag{16}$$

So the fitted value of residual is obtained as follow:

$$\widehat{\delta}(i) = \lambda_1 \delta_1^{(i)} + \lambda_2 \delta_2^{(i)} + \cdots + \lambda_k \delta_k^{(i)} \tag{17}$$

Finally, the residual correction of original forecast based on cosine function is derived as follow:

$$\widehat{x}^{(0)}(k) = \widehat{x}^{(0)}(k) + \widehat{\delta} \tag{18}$$

3.4 Periodic Extension for Residual Correction Sequence

Aimed at digging out the rules hided in data and much more closing to real data, a new method that applies the periodic extension to the forecast result which has been through residual correction by cosine function is put forward in this section, and specific method is as follows.

Step 1: Obtaining deviation,

$$x'(k) = \tilde{x}^{(0)} - \hat{x}(k) \tag{19}$$

Step 2: Calculating the mean generating function of $x'(k)$ by using (20),

$$\bar{x}_l(i) = (\sum_{j=0}^{m_l-1} x'(i+jl))/m_l, \ i = 1, 2, \cdots, l, \ 1 \le l \le L \tag{20}$$

Where, m is the length of smooth processed sample sequence, $m_l = [m/l]$ is the maximum integer which is less than m/l, and $L = [m/2]$ is the same, so mean generating function is calculated as follow:

$$\begin{cases} \bar{x}_1(1)\ \bar{x}_2(1)\ \bar{x}_3(1)\ \cdots\ \bar{x}_L(1) \\ \quad\ \bar{x}_2(2)\ \bar{x}_3(2)\ \cdots\ \bar{x}_L(2) \\ \qquad\qquad \bar{x}_3(3)\ \cdots\ \bar{x}_L(3) \\ \qquad\qquad\qquad\ \ddots\qquad \vdots \\ \qquad\qquad\qquad\qquad\quad \bar{x}_L(L) \end{cases} \tag{21}$$

And $f_l(k)$, the periodic extension function of $\bar{x}_l(i)$, is derived by using the method as follow:

$$f_l(k) = \bar{x}_l(k),\ k = i[\bmod(l)],\ k = 1, 2, \cdots, m \tag{22}$$

Step 3: Extraction advantage period,

According to the basic principle of analysis of variance, it can be detected whether or not these is period l hiding in $x'(k)$ by the function as follow:

$$F^{(l)} = (m - l)S^{(l)}/((l - 1)S) \tag{23}$$

Where

$$S^{(l)} = \sum_{i=1}^{l} m_i(\bar{x}_l(i) - \bar{x})^2,\ m_i = m/i,\ \bar{x} = (\sum_{i=1}^{M} x(i))/m \tag{24}$$

$$S = \sum_{i=1}^{l} \sum_{j=1}^{m} (x(i + (j - 1)l) - \bar{x}_l(i))^2 \tag{25}$$

Equation (23) is satisfied with the distribution of F with the freedom $(l - 1, m - l)$. For a given confidence level in advance, if $F^l > F_\alpha(l - 1, m - l)$, it can be confirmed that l is the distinct period of $x(k)$.

Step 4: Acquisition periodic deviation correction sequence $x''(k)$, the periodic deviation correction sequence, is defined as follow:

$$x''(k) = x'(k) - f_l(k) \tag{26}$$

By repeating step 3 and step 4 for $x''(k)$, more obscure sequence rules will be found.
Step 5: The final forecast based on periodic deviation correction,
The value of the same time in different periods is superimposed as:

$$f(k) = \sum_{i=1}^{l} f_i(k) \tag{27}$$

Approximately, $x'(k)$ can be taken by $f(k)$, the final forecast result based on periodic deviation correction is obtained as follow:

$$\bar{x}(k) = \hat{x}(k) + f(k) \tag{28}$$

4   Simulation and Analysis

In order to obtain the improved grey model, the primary GM is processed by two consecutive steps that one is named as residual correction based on cosine function and the follow is periodic extension for residual correction sequence, which had discussed above. The main task of this section is the simulation of the improved model and then discussing the results.

Experimental data, coming from a polycrystalline silicon solar panel with 50 W power and 20 V open circuit voltage, is the record of current I of every 20 min for five days. For convenience, t is replaced with the number collection points.

On small scale, selecting 5 consecutive points of the first day to forecast the value of sixth points dynamically, and then repeating the process until all the points are predicted, finally, comparing with the real data of first days, as shown in Fig. 4.

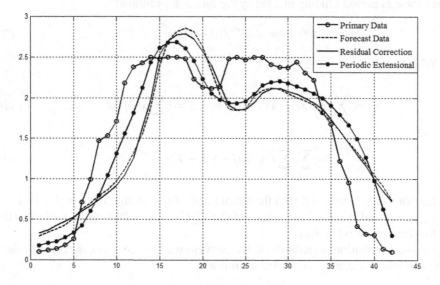

Fig. 4. Forecast results on small scale

The Primary Data curve is drawn out from the real data of first day. Forecast Data is the result of primary GM, obviously, not only the curve has a large fluctuation, but there are more bump point. Residual Correction curve, which is the residual correction result of forecast data curve based on cosine function, is very smooth. Periodic Extensional curve is the periodic extensional result of residual correction data, it makes the rules hided in data much clearer. There is no doubt that the improved grey model much more accurate.

The forecast results for next three days which based on the data of first five days is shown in Fig. 5.

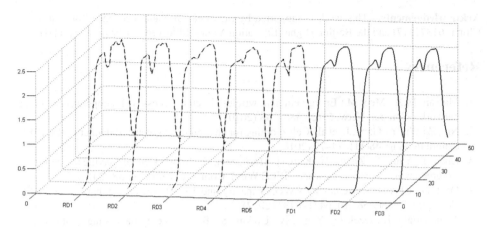

Fig. 5. Forecast results on large scale

RD1 to RD5 is the real data of the first five days and FD1 to FD3 is the forecast results of next three days. It obvious that the forecast results strongly depend on the original real data., though the shape of the forecast results of next three days are very similar to that of the original real data of first five days, it has its own feature as well, i.e. the forecast results above maintain the stability of the fixed points, and highlight the development trend of the unstable points. So it necessary to obtain more data to get much accurate forecast results.

In summary, by smoothing the primary data, correcting the residual of forecast result, and periodic extension of the correction result, the primary Gm is improved and it can weaken the deviation caused by the systematic and random error and highlight the regularity hided in data. Although the forecast results are slightly lagging, it is very close to the trend of development and total amount of the energy. On the other hand, the forecast results based on large scale and mass history data can meet the development and variation trend of the real data to some extent in the case of no obvious change of the external environment which both proved the outstanding performance of the model.

5   Conclusion

In this paper, we propose a full GBS model which depends on solar energy, and improve the accuracy of the forecast of solar energy by using an improved GM. The practice results show that the forecast data is highly close the real data in the absence of unexpected circumstances. However, this prediction is strongly dependent on real data. In order to improve the accuracy of forecasting results, the amount of sample data should be increased. In view of the model of the solar energy forecast, a more effective solution is to add the dynamic real-time forecast to the model, and then combine with the former forecast result based on former sample data to correct the deviation to improve the accuracy of the forecast dynamically. But the cost is an increase of the system overhead and energy consumption. So it is significance to make a comprehensive evaluation before the practical implement of the model for obtaining optimization.

Acknowledgements. This work is supported by the National Natural Science Foundation of China (61372117) and the Beijing Higher Education Young Elite Teacher Project (YETP0439).

References

1. Marsan, M.A., Meo, M.: Energy efficient wireless internet access with cooperative cellular networks. Comput. Netw. **55**(2), 386–398 (2010)
2. Niu, Z., Wu, Y., Gong, J., et al.: Cell zooming for cost-efficient green cellular networks. IEEE Commun. Mag. **48**(11), 74–79 (2010)
3. Chen, T., Yang, Y., Zhang, H., Kim, H., Horneman, K.: Network energy saving technologies for green wireless access networks. IEEE Wirel. Commun. **18**(5), 30–38 (2011)
4. Ozel, O., Ulukus, S.: Achieving AWGN capacity under stochastic energy harvesting. IEEE Trans. Inf. Theory **58**(10), 6471–6483 (2012)
5. Tutuncuoglu, K., Ozel, O., Yener, A., Ulukus, S.: Binary energy harvesting channel with finite energy storage. In: Proceedings of IEEE ISIT, July 2013, pp. 1591–1595 (2013)
6. Orhan, O., Gunduz, D., Erkip, E.: Throughput maximization for an energy harvesting system with processing cost. In: Proceedings of IEEE ITW, September 2012, pp. 84–88 (2012)
7. Xu, J., Zhang, R.: Throughput optimal policies for energy harvesting wireless transmitters with non-ideal circuit power. IEEE J. Sel. Areas Commun. **32**(2), 322–332 (2014)
8. Michelusi, N., Stamatiou, K., Zorzi, M.: On optimal transmission policies for energy harvesting devices. In: Proceedings of ITA, pp. 249–254 (2012)
9. Michelusi, N., Stamatiou, K., Zorzi, M.: Transmission policies for energy harvesting sensors with time-correlated energy supply. IEEE Trans. Commun. **61**(7), 2988–3001 (2013)
10. Ulukus, S., Yener, A., Simeone, O., Zorzi, M., Grover, P., Huang, K.: Energy harvesting wireless communications: a review of recent advances. IEEE J. Sel. Areas Commun. **33**(3), 360–381 (2015)
11. Valerdi, D., Zhu, Q., Exadaktylos, K., Xia, S.: Intelligent energy managed service for green base stations. In: 2010 IEEE GLOBECOM Workshops, pp. 1453–1457, December 2010

Emotion Detection from Natural Walking

Liqing Cui[1,2], Shun Li[1,2], and Tingshao Zhu[1,3,4]([✉])

[1] Institute of Psychology, Chinese Academy of Sciences (CAS),
Beijing 100101, China
cuiliqing1990@sina.com, xiaofo284@gmail.com,
tszhu@psych.ac.cn
[2] National Computer System Engineering Research Institute of China,
Beijing 100083, China
[3] Key Lab of Intelligent Information Processing, Institute of Computing
Technology, CAS, Beijing, China
[4] Institute of Computing Technology, Chinese Academy of Sciences,
Beijing 100190, China

Abstract. Emotion identification, which aims to determine a person's affective state automatically, has immense potential value in many areas, such as action tendency, health care, psychological detection and human-computer (robot) interaction. In this paper, we propose a novel method for identifying emotion from natural walking. After obtaining the three-axis acceleration data of wrist and ankle recorded by smartphone, we run a moving average filter window with different length w, then cut actual data into slices. 114 features are extracted from each slice, and Principal Component Analysis (PCA) is used for feature selection. We train SVM, Decision Tree, Multilayerperception, Random Tree and Random Forest classifiers, and compare the accuracy of emotion identification using different datasets (wrist vs. ankle) on different models. Results show that acceleration data from ankle has better performance in emotion identification than wrist. Among these models, SVM has the highest accuracy of 90.31 % for identifying anger vs. neutral, 89.76 % for happy vs. neutral, and 87.10 % for anger vs. happy. The model for identifying anger/neutral/happy yields the best accuracy of 85 %-78 %-78 %. The results show that we could identify people's emotional states through the gait of walking with high accuracy.

Keywords: Sensor mining · Emotion identification · Smartphone · Accelerometer · Sensor

1 Introduction

Nonverbal signals can provide additional cues for identifying a person's emotion and intention, which can be used to improve human-machine interaction, health state detection, etc. Traditionally, emotion detection is based on facial expressions, or linguistic and acoustic features in speech, which inevitably encounter high complexity in image or audio. Psychological studies on visual analysis of body movement found that human movement differ from other movements, which is the only visual stimulus we

Q. Zu and B. Hu (Eds.): HCC 2016, LNCS 9567, pp. 23–33, 2016.
DOI: 10.1007/978-3-319-31854-7_3

have experienced of both perceiving and producing [1]. In this paper, we propose a method of identifying human's emotion from natural walking. According to the date collection, we acquire the accelerometer data of person's wrist and ankle by built-in sensors. Nowadays, smartphone has already become an indispensable communication tool in daily life. It always integrates many powerful sensors, such as light sensors, acceleration sensors, gravity sensors, etc. Some of these sensors, with substantial computing power and high precision in small sizes, can not only complementarily make the phone more intelligent, but also provide new opportunities for data acquisition and mining.

In this paper, we use the acceleration sensor in smartphone to acquire accelerometer data of natural walking. To collect such data, participants are instructed to attach two smartphones to wrist and ankle separately, then walk several minutes naturally. Raw accelerometer data recorded by smartphone consists of gravity component. To acquire actual motion accelerometer data, we eliminate gravity component. After actual data is preprocessed by moving average filter window with different length w, it is cut into slices by sliding slice window. We extract 114 features from each slice, including time-domain, frequency-domain, power and distribution features. We use Principal Component Analysis (PCA) for feature selection. We evaluated the performance of different models, including SVM, Decision Tree, Random Forest, Multilayerperception and Random Tree, and tried to find the best model.

This work has a wide range of applications. It can generate daily, weekly or monthly emotion profile reporting how the emotion changes over time. Besides, this work can also be used for personal health by offering a timely feedback like having some exercise or entertainment.

The rest of this paper is organized as follows. Section 2 summarizes related work about identification of emotion by walking. Description of database, data preprocessing and feature extraction are presented in Sect. 3. Section 4 describes the results of the trained models and the performance of trained models for experiment. In Sect. 5, we discuss our methods and summary our work. Finally, the paper ends with a conclusion in Sect. 6.

2 Related Work

In psychology, there are several theories about emotion category. Ekman's basic emotions, including anger, disgust, fear, sadness and surprise, and the dimensional pleasure-arousal-dominance (PAD) model are widely used in automatic emotion recognition [7]. The PAD model spans a 3-dimensional space with the independent and arousal and dominance. An affective state is described as a point within this state space. By showing body joints on black background, the observers were able to recognize the gender or a familiar person by walking [6]. Montepare et al. found that people can identify emotions from gait [12]. Specifically, people can recognize sadness and anger much easier than pride. Pollick quantified expressive arm movements in terms of velocity and acceleration, and confirmed that velocity and acceleration are important in recognizing emotions. Crane and Gross illustrated that emotion recognition is not only depended on gesticulatory behavior, but also associated with emotion-specific changes in gait kinematics [5]. They have identified several activity features, including velocity, cadence, head orientation, shoulder and elbow range of motion, as significant parameters which are affected by emotions [5].

In fact, emotion states change rapidly even in a short walking, not even mention the complex activities within body movement. Janssen investigated the recognition of four emotional states by artificial neural nets. Karg applied Principal Component Analysis (PCA), Kernal PCA (KPCA) and Linear Discriminant Analysis (LDA) into kinematic parameters of person-dependent recognition and inter-individual recognition and had improved accuracy rates. In [9], PCA is used for features selection, and the best accuracy is achieved by Naive Bayes with 72 % for the four emotions which are sad, neutral, happy and angry during natural walking.

A general survey of analytical techniques for clinical and biomechanical gaits analysis is given in [3, 4]. It mainly refers to classification of clinical disorders, though the methods for feature extraction can be also taken for psychological gaits analysis. Dimension reduction techniques such as KPCA improves recognition of age in walking. The performance comparison of Principal Component Analysis (PCA) and KPCA is discussed in [2]. Martinez and Kak found that PCA can perform much better on small size of training sets [11].

In this paper, we extract relevant time-domain, frequency-domain, power and distribution features from kinematic acceleration data set to identify human emotion. We collect actual accelerometer data from wrist and ankle to build emotion identification models, and compare the identification accuracy with different moving filter windows(w).

3 Methods

The proposed emotion identification method based on three-axis acceleration sensor and gravity sensor embedded in smartphone comprises the following three steps: (1) data acquisition and pre-processing, (2) feature extraction, and (3) training and testing. At the last step, we train several classification models and evaluate their performance.

3.1 Participants

To identify emotion from natural walking, 59 healthy young adult participants (female = 32) were recruited from University of Chinese Academy of Sciences (UCAS). This study is supported by Institute of Psychology, Chinese Academy of Sciences (approval number: H15010) and written informed consent were obtained from all subjects prior to their participation. Our project employed two SAMSUNG I9100G and one SAMSUNG Tab as platform (Android operation system is used, because we can develop APP on Android system in smartphone and Tab to access raw data from accelerometer sensor and gravity sensor, and record time series).

The experiment was conducted on a fixed rectangle-shaped area (length: about 6 m, width:0:8 m), marked on the floor with red lines. After signed the consent form, each participant wore one smartphone on one wrist and the other on one ankle, and stand in front of the starting line. Once the participant was ready, the host started two APPs to start recording, and used one Tab to record the time stamp during the whole experiment. The participant was asked to walk naturally back and forth in demand area for about two minutes. Then the host stopped subject walking and recorded the end time by the Tab. Each participant was asked to report her/his current emotion state with a score from 1 to 10. For the first-round experiment, the emotion score of anger was recorded. For the second-round, happy score was acquired instead. Then the participant watched one emotional film clip [8] for emotion priming. After finishing watching the clip, the participant was asked to walk naturally back and forth again in demand area for about one minute, just as did before. Each participant was asked to report his/her current anger score and recall the anger score after watching film clip. To avoid any influence on emotional priming, we didn't ask participant to report her/his emotion score immediately after finishing the clip.

The second-round experiment was conducted after at least three hours (if the internal is too small, the participant's emotion arousal might be influenced by the first clip). The procedure is the same as the first-round experiment except that the participant watched the happy film clip [8], and report her/his happy emotion state on a scale of 1 to 10. We acquired the activity acceleration data from the smartphones, and the time stamp data from the Tab. Then we cut and aggregate activity accelerometer data of each participant from smartphone according to the time stamp recorded by the Tab.

3.2 Data Preprocessing

We acquired two groups of sensor data, one is for wrist and the other is for ankle. Each group includes raw accelerometer data set (SensorLa) and gravity data set (SensorGra). One sample raw data of X-axis from ankle is shown in Fig. 1.

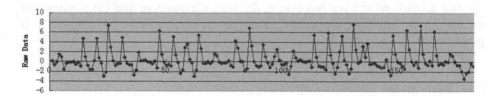

Fig. 1. One raw accelerometer data of X-axis from ankle

According to time stamp recorded, we cut every participant's walking data into two parts (before and after the clip). Every part contains one minute's raw accelerometer data. For the first two minutes' walking, we just used the last one minute's data before the film clip, for the participant might walk more steadily than that in the first minute. The actual accelerometer data we want to acquire is equal to SensorLa-SensorGra. Since noise and burrs may exist in the data, we run preprocessing on above actual accelerometer data, by moving average filter window as below:

$$Output[i] = \frac{1}{w} \sum_{j=0}^{w-1} Input[i+j]$$

The filter uses a series of raw discrete time signal as input, and outputs average signal for each sampling point. The size w is adjustable as well. In this paper, we just try to set w = 3, 5 just as did in [10]. Figure 2 presents the ankle wave signal with respect to w = 3, and the undulating signal become smoother than raw data shown in Fig. 1.

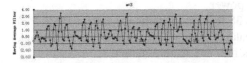

Fig. 2. One raw accelerometer data of X-axis from ankle is processed of X-axis from ankle is processed by moving average filter window w = 3

Fig. 3. one raw accelerometer data of X-axis from ankle is processed by moving average filter with w = 5

For w = 5 as shown in Fig. 3, the signal becomes more smoother than that of w = 3 in Fig. 2.

It is very obvious that w plays a key role in data preprocessing. But if w is too high, it may eliminate some minor changes in the data. Though it could make wave smoother, it also might throw away the key undulatory information of the data. Therefore, we just set w 3 and 5 for any further preprocessing. Since frequency is 5 Hz, few minutes can accumulate hundreds of pieces of records, it is a big work to deal with these records and extract features timely. We use sliding slice window to cut data of each part into slices. The size of sliding window may be quite different, which is set to 128 in this paper, and the coverage ratio is 50 %, as shown in Fig. 4.

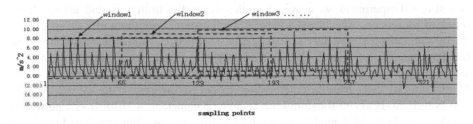

Fig. 4. Sliding slice window to cut accelerometer data

3.3 Feature Extraction

Participants walking have great differences in behavioral patterns, including gesture gait and speed. Besides, the length of different participants' data is various. In this paper, we extract time-domain feature, frequency-domain feature, power feature and distribution feature from each slice. Time-domain feature is directly computed from the data. Distribution feature includes each axis's standard deviation, kurtosis, skewness and correlation coefficient (every two axes). Standard deviation reflects the degree of dispersion within one slice. Kurtosis shows the at or sharp degree of top of frequency distribution curve. Skewness coefficient describes the characteristics of deviating symmetry degree for certain distribution. Frequency-domain feature includes the front 32 amplitude coefficients of FFT (Fast Fourier Transformation). Each amplitude coefficient represents the size of the corresponding low frequency signal. As for power feature, Power Spectral Density (PSD) is the power per unit of bandwidth. Means of PSD is the size of average power per unit of bandwidth. Standard deviation of PSD shows the degree of dispersion in terms of power.

In summary, each axis of slice produces 38 features. Totally, we extract $1*(38*3)$ features from each data slice, and extract features from all slices from one participant, then we aggregate all these feature matrices into one feature matrix.

To avoid important features with small values being ignored while model training, we run Z-score normalization for all features. After that, high dimension of feature vector's computational complexity increases, and information become much more redundant. In order to reduce the dimension of feature vectors, and acquire the best description of the different behavior and the best classification characteristics, dimension reduction is an essential step.

4 Results

For train sets we get from wrist and ankle with different $w(w = 3; 5)$ in the two rounds of experiment, for the first-round, we labelled each sample with 'neutral' or 'anger' after PCA, then we trained models in Weka. Similarly, for train sets got in the second-round, we labelled each with 'neutral' or 'happy', then trained models.

4.1 Anger Emotion Identification

In first-round experiment, we acquired accelerometer data from wrist and ankle. After a series of procession, we utilized kinds of classification algorithms to train models in Weka with default parameters and standard 10-fold cross validation, including SVM (model parameters: -S 0 -K 2 -D 3 -G 0.0 -R 0.0 -N 0.5 -M 40.0 -C 1.0 -E 0.001 -P 0.1 - seed 1), J48 (model parameters:-C 0.25 -M 2), Random Tree (model parameters: -K 0 - M 1.0 -V 0.001 -S 1), Multilayerperception (model parameters: -L 0.3 -M 0.2 -N 500 - V 0 -S 0 -E 20 -H a) and Random Forest (model parameters: -I 10 -K 0 -S 1 num-slots 1). Decision Tree (J48) model is explained easily and fast, but Random Forest can inspect impact between features. For SVM, it not just outstrips Multilayerperception in linearity and nonlinearity, but also has a good performance to deal with high dimension data.

The results of identification with w = 3 on wrist and ankle are shown in Table 1.

Table 1. The classification accuracy in different models when w = 3

Joint	SVM	DT	RF	MLP	RT
Wrist	90.03 %	56.25 %	62.21 %	63.92 %	58.81 %
Ankle	90.31 %	71.31 %	64.49 %	59.38 %	59.94 %

DT : Decision Tree.
RF : Random Forest.
MLP : Multilayerperception.
RT : Random Tree.

The results show that emotion priming by watching video clips really works. And the emotional arouse, shown by the change of their reported emotion scores, have significant influence on their gaits. In addition, both wrist and ankle have a relatively higher accuracy by SVM than other models. Meanwhile, the identification accuracy from ankle is higher than wrist. A possible reason is that the activity of hands is more complex than ankles when walking. There is much noise which is not easily filtered out from data.

In fact, when we set w = 5, the results we obtained change dramatically, as shown in below Table 2. The results show that for w = 5, the evaluation results of most above models have a little higher accuracy than the results of w = 3 except for SVM. The accuracy of wrist is still lower than ankle. We come to the same conclusion when w is 3.

Table 2. The classification accuracy in different models when w = 5

Joint	SVM	DT	RF	MLP	RT
Wrist	84.61 %	54.99 %	59.54 %	58.97 %	52.99 %
Ankle	87.46 %	74.07 %	65.81 %	–	62.68 %

– : invalid.

4.2 Happiness Emotion Identification

In second-round experiment, the way we obtained accelerometer data is the same as we did in the first-round experiment. After data preprocessing, we run several classification algorithms to train models in Weka. The classification results is shown in Table 3 with w = 3.

Table 3. The classification accuracy in different models when w = 3

Joint	SVM	DT	MLP	RT
Wrist	89.76 %	61.49 %	58.51 %	61.19 %
Ankle	87.65 %	67.46 %	61.49 %	62.39 %

From above results, we can find that the funny clip arouse participants' emotion and their gaits have a significant difference, which makes it easy to differentiate the gaits before and after emotion priming. Just as shown in Table 1, ankle performs better to identify emotion than wrist on all models. The ankle accuracy reaches 87.65 % on average. Similarly, w has a great influence on classification accuracy in second-round experiment, as shown in Table 4.

Table 4. The classification accuracy in different models when w = 5

Joint	SVM	DT	RF	MLP	RT
Wrist	83.73 %	63.68 %	58.20 %	51.94 %	62.69 %
Ankle	87.65 %	85.07 %	70.45 %	54.32 %	60.60 %

Table 4 demonstrates that w does influence emotion identification to some extend. Comparing with other models, SVM has the best accuracy of 87.65 %.

4.3 Emotions Identification

We aggregated data sets after emotion priming in both first-round experiment and second-round experiment, and respectively labelled them as 'anger' and 'happy'. The accuracy of classification is shown in Tables 5 and 6.

Table 5. Anger-happy classification accuracy in different models when w = 3

Joint	SVM	DT	RF	RT
Wrist	70.83%	63.34%	–	–
Ankle	78.00%	74.49%	63.34%	56.60%

Table 6. Anger-happy classification accuracy in different models when w = 5

Joint	SVM	DT	RF	RT
Wrist	65.98 %	63.05 %	54.25 %	54.25 %
Ankle	87.10 %	85.34 %	67.16 %	66.86 %

From above two tables, it is obvious that there is significant difference between person's gaits under different emotions. Besides, SVM always performs better on ankle, reaching 87.10 % to identify anger or happy with w = 5 than accuracy when w is 3. In Tables 7, 8 and 9, anger-neutral-happy emotion confusion matrix for SVM shows that neutral emotion is easiest to be identified. When w = 5, Table 10 shows that anger is easiest to be identified.

Four confusion matrixes show that the affective state happy is easier to be misclassified as anger. Similarly, anger is also easier to be misclassified as happy.

Table 7. Anger-neutral-happy confusion matrix when w = 3 for wrist

Affect	Anger	Neutral	Happy	Acc
Anger	136	7	32	78 %
Neutral	18	151	7	86 %
Happy	43	8	115	69 %

Table 8. Anger-neutral-happy confusion matrix when w = 3 for ankle

Affect	Anger	Neutral	Happy	Acc
Anger	126	10	39	72 %
Neutral	10	152	14	86 %
Happy	31	10	125	75 %

Table 9. Anger-neutral-happy confusion matrix when w = 5 for wrist

Affect	Anger	Neutral	Happy	Acc
Anger	121	18	36	69 %
Neutral	25	135	16	77 %
Happy	57	17	92	55 %

Table 10. Anger-neutral-happy confusion matrix when w = 5 for ankle

Affect	Anger	Neutral	Happy	Acc
Anger	148	5	22	85 %
Neutral	18	131	21	78 %
Happy	17	20	129	78 %

5   Discussion

In this paper, we use PCA for feature selection, and try different machine learning algorithms in Weka for training and testing different models. We build models with different parameter settings, and run 10-fold cross validation for evaluation.

We extract 114 features from accelerometer data, then train models to identify person's emotion based on participant's gait. The experimental results presented above are quite interesting and promising, which demonstrates that there exists significant difference of walking under different emotion. Different w values have an significant effect on the accuracy of identification. We find that when w becomes greater, the sequence is smoother in time-domain. But if w is too big, it may ignore any tiny changes and lead to the performance of the models decrease. Otherwise, small w loses an evident moving smooth performance. When w is 3 or 5, ankle has a better performance for emotion identification than wrist, with the accuracy of 90.31 % in first-round experiment and 89.76 % in second-round experiment. We infer that wrist has complex additional movement when people walk. Besides, two emotion states identification (anger-happiness) is relatively easy, whose accuracy reaches 87.10 %. For identifying anger/neutral/happy, the best accuracies for each state are 85 %-78 %-78 %.

In our work, we find SVM works the best, reaching 90.31 %. In our experiment, since we obtain person's actual wrist and ankle accelerometer data, there is less noise involved. Due to that, all features that we extract capably represent one person's gait characteristics. The results are much more credible as well.

6 Conclusion

This paper proposes to identify human emotion by natural walking. To do so, we obtained motion data by using accelerator sensors in smartphone attached to wrist and ankle. After data preprocessing, we extract 114 features from each slice.

We test four learning models in Weka with default parameters and standard 10-fold cross validation, including SVM, Decision Tree, Random Tree and Random Forest. Among them, SVM classifier works best to identify personal affect.

The results of different trained models indicate that ankle data is more capable to reveal human emotion than wrist, with the best accuracy of 90.31 %. The preprocess technique plays a key role in determining the performance of the model, especially the size of slice window. Both anger and happy can be recognized from human's characteristics of natural walking, which reaches an accuracy of 87.10 %. For identifying anger/neutral/happy, it yields the best accuracy of 85 %, 78 % and 78 %.

However, further considerations and improvements are required. That includes how the size of sliding slice window influences the performance of identification, and whether it can also improve model's accuracy. We also intend to investigate how to void the overlap of neighboring values between two adjacent filter windows, and we will try more advanced machine learning algorithms.

Acknowledgments. The authors gratefully acknowledges the generous support from National High-tech R&D Program of China (2013AA01A606), National Basic Research Program of China (2014CB744600), Key Research Program of Chinese Academy of Sciences (CAS) (KJZD-EWL04), and CAS Strategic Priority Research Program (XDA06030800).

References

1. Beale, C.P.R.: Affect and emotion in human-computer interaction
2. Cao, L., Chua, K., Chong, W., Lee, H., Gu, Q.: A comparison of PCA, KPCA and ICA for dimensionality reduction in support vector machine. Neurocomputing **55**(1C2), 321–336 (2003)
3. Chau, T.: A review of analytical techniques for gait data. Part 1: fuzzy, statistical and fractal methods. Gait Posture **13**(1), 49–66 (2001)
4. Chau, T.: A review of analytical techniques for gait data. Part 2: neural network and wavelet methods. Gait Posture **13**(2), 102–120 (2001)
5. Crane, E., Gross, M.: Motion capture and emotion: affect detection in whole body movement
6. Cutting, J., Kozlowski, L.: Recognizing friends by their walk: gait perception without familiarity cues. Bull. Psychon. Soc. **9**(5), 353–356 (1977)

7. Ekman, P., Friesen, W.: A new pan-cultural facial expression of emotion. Motiv. Emot. **10** (2), 159–168 (1986)
8. Song, J., Guozhen Zhao, Y.X., Sun, X., Ge, Y.: A chinese emotional film clips database
9. Karg, M., Jenke, R., Kuhnlenz, K., Buss, M.: A two-fold PCA-approach for interindividual recognition of emotions in natural walking. In: MLDM Posters, pp. 51–61 (2009)
10. Ma, L.: Sensor-based activities recognition on mobile platform. Master's thesis, Harbin Institute of Technology (2013)
11. Martinez, A.M., Kak, A.: PCA versus LDA. IEEE Trans. Pattern Anal. Mach. Intell. **23**(2), 228–233 (2001)
12. Montepare, J., Goldstein, S., Clausen, A.: The identification of emotions from gait information. J. Nonverbal Behav. **11**(1), 33–42 (1987)

Hybrid Resource Provisioning for Workflow Scheduling in Cloud Computing

Long Chen[1,2], Yucheng Guo[1,2], Xiaoping Li[1,2(✉)], and Rubén Ruiz[3]

[1] School of Computer Science and Engineering, Southeast University,
Nanjing 211189, People's Republic of China
xpli@seu.edu.cn
[2] Key Laboratory of Computer Network and Information Integration,
Southeast University, Ministry of Education, Nanjing 211189, China
[3] Grupo de Sistemas de Optimización Aplicada,
Instituto Tecnológico de Informática, Ciudad Politécnica de la Innovación,
Universitat Politécnica de Valéncia, Edifico 8G, Acc. B.,
Camino de Vera s/n, 46021 Valéncia, Spain
rruiz@eio.upv.es

Abstract. In cloud computing, cloud service providers always provide two resource provisioning manners to cloud consumers, reservation and on-demand. Costs can be reduced using these two manners. In this paper, we consider deadline constrained cloud workflow scheduling problem with total resource renting cost minimization by integrating the two manners. An integer programming model of the problem is constructed. A malleable earliest and finish time heuristic is proposed for the problem under study. Experimental results verify the effectiveness of proposed algorithm on instances with different scales and resources with different discounts.

Keywords: Workflow scheduling · Resource provisioning · Cost minimization · Cloud computing

1 Introduction

Complex workflow applications are widespread in scientific experiments and business analysis. Cloud computing provides high quality computing and storage resources for workflow applications [3]. Two resources provisioning manners are usually offered by Cloud Service Providers (CSP): the long-term reservation and the short-term on-demand. With the long-term reservation, users can get resources from CSP with a significant discount. However, they possess the resource during the entire renting period, which usually leads to poor resources utilization. The short-term on-demand enables users to rent and release computing capacity according to their demands. The average unit cost of the short-term on-demand is usually higher than that of the long-term reservation. The hybrid resource provisioning method of the two manners reduces the average unit cost and improves the flexibility of resources. Figure 1 shows the workflow scheduling with the hybrid

© Springer International Publishing Switzerland 2016
Q. Zu and B. Hu (Eds.): HCC 2016, LNCS 9567, pp. 34–46, 2016.
DOI: 10.1007/978-3-319-31854-7_4

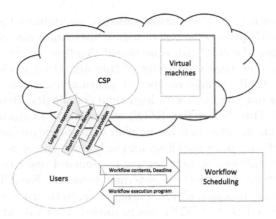

Fig. 1. Workflow scheduling with the hybrid resource provisioning manner.

resource provisioning manner. First, users send parameters of workflows (deadlines, tasks, runtimes) to the workflow scheduling module. The module generates scheduling plans according to the parameters. Each plan includes two parts: the workflow scheduling sequence and the cloud resource renting plan. Users rent resources and schedule tasks based on the scheduling plan. Resources are rented from the CSP using the long-term reservation and/or the short-term on-demand.

In this paper, we consider the deadline constrained cloud workflow scheduling problem to minimize the total resource renting cost using hybrid resource provisioning manners, which is NP-hard. To the best of our knowledge, no attention has been paid on this problem. The malleable earliest-finish-time heuristic is proposed for the problem under study. First, the task allocation sequence is created based on priorities. In terms of free time periods, reserved and/or on-demand resources are allocated to the tasks in the sequence. New sequences are discovered by a variable neighborhood search.

The rest of the paper is organized as follows. Related works are described in Sect. 2. Section 3 gives the mathematical model for the considered problem. In Sect. 4, we describe the proposed method and illustrate it using an example. Computational results are presented in Sect. 5, followed by conclusions and future works in Sect. 6.

2   Related Works

Workflow scheduling has been studied for many years. Recently, malleable task (tasks can be executed on multiple machines) scheduling in parallel [2] is a hot topic, which first determines the number of machines available for the malleable tasks. Makespans and renting costs minimizing are two common objectives of workflow scheduling problems.

Resources are limited on grids. HEFT [11] and CPA [13] are effective algorithms for workflow scheduling with makespan minimization. Singh et al. [12] used genetic algorithms to map tasks to resources with the objective of minimizing both the renting cost and makespan. Resources are limited and available between different time windows.

In cloud computing, resources are assumed to be unlimited and available all the time. Yu et al. [15] proposed a genetic algorithm to minimize the renting costs, which can minimize the cost with constrained deadline or minimize makespan with limited cost. The time complexity of this algorithm is closely related to the service scale. While a large number of alternative services were provided, the algorithm was not good and with high time complexity. Byun et al. [4] proposed a Balanced Time Scheduling (BTS) algorithm to minimize resource rent costs. The algorithm assumes that the number of hosts are unchanged during the implementation of the entire workflow, and only one type of resource is considered. BTS did not take into account renting on-demand resources either. All the resources are obtained through the long-term reservation. Even if a resource uses only one unit of time, it is paid all the renting time. In their later work [5], a new algorithm Partitioned BTS (PBTS) was proposed, which divides the workflow implementation process into sections according to the total amount of resources. Chaisiri et al. [6] proposed a new algorithm OCRP to optimize the resource provision cost in cloud computing. OCRP considered both reserved and on-demand resources. Tasks are supposed to be independent with known resource requirements. However, for the actual workflow scheduling problem, tasks are precedence constrained. The resource renting method and the resource requirements interact with each other. Abrishami et al. [1] proposed a method to assign workflow tasks to different resources in IaaS clouds. Juan et al. [8] considered to allocate resources to scientific computing workflows with multi-objective in Amazon EC2. Both resource renting cost and makespan were considered. However, they did not consider the problem with different resource provisioning methods.

In summary, there is no work considering both malleable tasks and hybrid resource provisioning though they can reduce the cost for the implementation of the workflow significantly, which is considered in this paper.

3   Mathematical Model

A workflow application can be represented by an activity-on-node Directed Acyclic Graph (DAG) $G(V, E)$, in which $V = \{v_0, \ldots, v_n\}$ is the set of tasks in G. $E = \{(v_i, v_j)|v_i \in V, v_j \in V, i < j\}$ defines the precedence relationships between tasks, which indicates that v_i must be finished before v_j starts. Each node v_i represents a task. v_i is processed on several Virtual Machines (VM). As the computing capacity of a virtual machine is usually in proportion to the price, only homogeneous resources are considered in this paper (i.e., different capacities can be normalized). The processing time of task v_i on a single virtual machine is P_i. All tasks are classified into two types: malleable tasks (the set is denoted as $\mathbb{M}$) and rigid tasks (the set is denoted as $\mathbb{R}$), i.e., $V = \mathbb{M} \cup \mathbb{R}$. A malleable task can be allocated to malleable virtual machines, i.e., it has multiple execution modes. Each malleable task could be executed by different numbers of machines with different processing times. Let $v_i \in \mathbb{M}$ be a malleable task. If m_i virtual machines are allocated to v_i, the processing time p_i is calculated by $p_i = \lceil P_i/m_i \rceil$, which is varying with the scheduling process. However, the number of virtual machines m_i allocated to a rigid task v_i ($v_i \in \mathbb{R}$) are fixed.

The execution mode and the processing time $p_i = \lceil P_i/m_i \rceil$ of a rigid task keep unchanged once they are determined. Tasks v_0 and v_n are dummy nodes, which represent the start and the end of the workflow. Processing times of the two dummy nodes are 0. Let D be the deadline of the workflow application.

Both of the two resource provisioning manners are adopted to rent resources for workflows. Let H be the total amount of rented resources, H^r represents the amount of long-term reserved resources and H_t^0 denotes the amount of short-term on-demand resources at time t. C_r and C_0 are the unit costs of a virtual machine with the long-term and the short-term resource provisioning. The ratio of C_r to C_o means the discount of a resource. i.e., $discount = C_r/C_0$. The total renting cost of resources includes both the reserved cost and the on-demand cost. The considered problem can be mathematically modeled as follows:

$$\min(f_n \times H^r \times C_r + \sum_{t=0}^{f_n} H_t^0 \times C_0) \tag{1}$$

s.t.

$$x_{iht} = \begin{cases} 1 & v_i \text{ is processing on the VM } h \text{ at time } t, \ \forall i \in \{0,\ldots,n\}, \\ & \forall h \in \{1,\ldots,H\}, \ \forall t \in \{0,\ldots,D\} \\ 0 & \text{others} \end{cases} \tag{2}$$

$$y_h = \begin{cases} 1 & h \text{ is an on-demand machine}, \ \forall h \in \{1,\ldots,H\} \\ 0 & h \text{ is a reserved machine}, \ \forall h \in \{1,\ldots,H\} \end{cases} \tag{3}$$

$$m_i = \sum_{h=1}^{H} \sum_{t=0}^{D} x_{iht}, \ \forall v_i \in \mathbb{M} \tag{4}$$

$$p_i = \lceil P_i/m_i \rceil, \ \forall i \in \{0,\ldots,n\} \tag{5}$$

$$s_i = \sum_{t=0}^{D} \frac{1}{m_i} \sum_{h=1}^{H} t \times x_{iht}, \ \forall i \in \{0,\ldots,n\} \tag{6}$$

$$s_i + p_i \leqslant s_j, \ \forall (i,j) \in E \tag{7}$$

$$f_n \leqslant D \tag{8}$$

$$\sum_{t=s_j}^{s_j+d_j} \sum_{i=0}^{n} x_{iht} = 1, \ \text{if } x_{jhs_j} = 1 \ \forall j \in \{0,\ldots,n\}, \ \forall h \in \{1,\ldots,H\} \tag{9}$$

$$H_{t_i}^0 = \sum_{h=1}^{H} \sum_{i=0}^{n} \sum_{t=t_i-d_i+1}^{t_i} x_{iht} y_h, \ \forall t_i \in \{0,\ldots,D\} \tag{10}$$

$$H^r = \sum_{h=1}^{H} (1 - y_h) \tag{11}$$

The binary variables $x_{iht} = 1$ in Eq. (2) means the task v_i is processed on the VM h at time t. The y_h in Eq. (3) takes 1 if the VM h rents resources using the on-demand manner. Equation (4) defines the number of VMs allocated to each mallable task. The processing time and start time of each task are determined by Eqs. (5) and (6). Formulas (7) and (8) specify the precedence and deadline constraints of the workflow. Equation (9) ensures that the execution is consecutive and non-preemptive. The number of reserved and on-demand resources are calculated by Eqs. (10) and (11).

Because of the discounts of the long term reservation, most tasks are allocated to the long-term reserved resources. Some other resources are rented using the short-term on-demand manner to improve the resource utilization.

4 Proposed Heuristic

Rule-based heuristics are common methods for workflow scheduling problems [13]. In this paper, we propose the malleable earliest finish time method (MEFT) for the considered problem which is composed of three components: initial schedule construction (ISC), variable neighborhood search (VNS) and schedule reconstruction (SR).

4.1 Initial Schedule Construction

ISC constructs an initial schedule using three procedures: reservation resources presetting, task sequencing and schedule constructing.

To preset the number of long-term reserved resources, the upper and lower bounds are calculated first. The lower bound is defined as the minimum amount of required resources to accomplish all the tasks with the deadline satisfied assuming all the resources are fully loaded and the precedence constraints between tasks are not involved. If the utilization rate of a resource is less than its *discount*, the on-demand manner obtains a cheaper cost than the reserved manner according to Formula (1). The upper bound is defined as the maximum amount of required resources with the resource utilization rate equal to the *discount*. The two bounds are defined as follows:

$$H_{\min}^r = \lceil \textstyle\sum_{v_i \in V} P_i \div D \rceil$$

$$H_{\max}^r = \lceil \textstyle\sum_{v_i \in V} P_i \div D \div discount \rceil$$

The reserved resource presetting process starts from the resources with the lower bound. The reserved resources H^r are initialized as $H_{\min}^r$. Suppose the reserved resources with the maximum amount are allocated to malleable tasks, i.e., $p_i = \lceil P_i/H_i \rceil$, $\forall v_i \in M$. The earliest start time est_i of v_i is calculated according to the critical-path based method given in [7]. If the earliest start time est_n of v_n is greater than the deadline D, no feasible schedule can be obtained using the current amount of reserved resources H^r. We increase H^r and try again until a feasible schedule is found or the upper bound $H_{\max}^r$ is reached.

Based on the obtained long-term reserved resources H^r, a sequence of tasks is determined by their priorities which are recursively defined as $rank_u(v_i) = P_i + \max_{v_j \in succ(v_i)} \{rank_u(v_j)\}$ with $rank_u(v_n) = 0$, where $succ(v_i)$ is the set of all successors of v_i. If there is more than one task processed in parallel, the task with the biggest processing time is set the highest priority. Therefore tasks on the critical path are allocated as early as possible. An initial sequence is obtained by sorting tasks by the increasing order of their priorities.

Tasks are scheduled according to the task sequence using the free time period-based schedule construction strategy. Resources are denoted by matrix $R = (r_{ij})_{D \times H^r}$ in which the column represents the time slots and the row represents the virtual machines, e.g., $r_{ij} = 1$ indicates that virtual machine j is occupied at time slot i. The execution of a task is denoted by a sub-matrix with all elements being 1. For example, the sub-matrix $R[i', \ldots, i''; j', \ldots, j'']$ indicates that the activity starts at time slot i' and finishes at time slot i'' and virtual machines j' to j'' are occupied during this period. The free time period is denoted as a sub-matrix with all elements being 0, which is a continuous period with a number of available resources. For example, the virtual machine is free during the time period between the finish time of the first task and the start time of the second task if a virtual machine is mapped to two tasks. If some other machines are also free during this period, a new free time period is constructed by combining the free time and those on the machines. All possible free time periods are found between the earliest start time of the current task and the latest finish time of the scheduled tasks. The process is given in Algorithm 1. All free time periods are sorted in the increasing order of the start times. The tasks are allocated to the free time periods. For a rigid task v_i, it is tried to be allocated from the first free time period. If v_i cannot be allocated to the current time period, there are two cases: no sufficient time or no sufficient resource. The first case implies that the time length of the period is less than that of the task processing time p_i. The current time period is unavailable and the next time period is explored. For the

---

Algorithm 1. Free Time Slot Searching

---

1 **Input:** resource matrix $(r_{ij})_{D \times H^r}$, the earliest start time Est_i of task v_i, the latest finish time t_{last} of allocated tasks.

2 **Output:** Free time period list $idleList$.

3 **begin**

4      $idleList \leftarrow \varnothing$;

5   **for** $(t = est_i; t < t_{last}; t \leftarrow t + 1)$ **do**

6   **for** $(h = 0; h < H^r; h \leftarrow h + 1)$ **do**

7   **if** $(r_{th} == 0)$ **then**

8   Check all the free time periods starting from r_{th};

9   Add the free time period to $idleList$;

10   Take the time period after t_{last} as a big free time period;

11   Add the big free time period to $idleList$;

12   **return** $idleList$;

---

second case, the least amount of short-term on-demand resources is calculated. The current free time period would be wasted if it is not allocate to v_i. Let the wasted workload be V and the workload of v_i is w_i. It is economical to rent some on-demand resources if $V \times discount > (w_i - V)$. The current task v_i is allocated to the current time period. For a malleable task, the allocation of resources is more complex because of the change of required resources. If resources of the current time period are available for the task, the maximum amount of resources is allocated to the task to make the task finish as early as possible. Otherwise, the maximum economical on-demand resources are rented. After all tasks are allocated, new free time periods followed to them are checked. If there are still some new free time periods, the processing times of the tasks are extended to reduce the amount of rented resources.

4.2　Variable Neighborhood Search

Usually, the cost of the inial schedule obtained by ISC is not the cheapest. It is natural to propose a variable neighborhood search (VNS) to adjust the task sequence, which exerts a great influence on the performance of the MEFT. An insertion operator $I(a, b)$, $(1 < a < n, 1 < b < n, a \neq b, b - 1)$ is adopted to change the order of tasks. The task at the position a is removed and inserted to position b in the sequence without violating the precedence constraints between tasks. Each insertion operator changes a task sequence $\bar{s}$ to a new one $\vec{s'}$. In addition, we define the r-insertion neighborhood $N_r(\bar{s})$ is the neighborhood set performing insertion operator r times on $\bar{s}$. Therefore $N_1(\bar{s})$ is the set of $\vec{s'}$ with only one insertion operator. Suppose the insertion operator is performed at most K times, i.e., $1 \leq r \leq K$.

Algorithm 2. Variable neighborhood search

---

1 **Input:** task sequence $\bar{s}$.
2 **Output:** task sequence $\vec{s'}$.
3 **begin**
4 $\quad$ $r \leftarrow 0$;
5 $\quad$ **repeat**
6 $\quad\quad$ $r \leftarrow r + 1$;
7 $\quad\quad$ **for** $(i = 0; i < \lambda; i \leftarrow i + 1)$ **do**
8 $\quad\quad\quad$ Randomly select $\vec{s'}$ from $N_r(\bar{s})$;
9 $\quad\quad\quad$ Calculate the cost $C(\vec{s'})$;
10 $\quad\quad\quad$ **if** $(C(\vec{s'}) < C(\bar{s}))$ **then**
11 $\quad\quad\quad\quad$ $\bar{s} \leftarrow \vec{s'}$;
12 $\quad\quad\quad\quad$ $r \leftarrow 0$;
13 $\quad\quad\quad\quad$ break;
14 $\quad$ **until** $r \leqslant K$;
15 $\quad$ **return** $\vec{s'}$;

The VNS starts from an initial sequence s. λ solutions are compared for each scale of neighborhood $N_r(\bar{s})$. In every time, a new task sequence is obtained. The above free time period-based schedule construction strategy is adopted to construct a new schedule. If the cost of the new schedule is cheaper than the previous one, the new task allocation sequence is set as the new start point. If no more optimal solution can be found after the K-insertion VNS for a start point, the algorithm stops. The process is described in Algorithm 2.

4.3   Schedule Reconstruction

The obtained schedule is reconstructed by reallocating tasks with on-demand resources after the VNS. These tasks are chosen with certain probability ω to be reallocated to the reservation resources. If a better new solution is obtained, the current solution is replaced by the new one. If all the tasks with on-demand resources have been reallocated, the schedule reconstruction (SR) procedure terminates. SR aims at destroying structures of solutions by allocating some tasks with cheaper resources to reduce the total renting cost. Surely, the utilization rate of the resources could be decreased during the process. The SR increases the diversification of the search and increases the probability of finding better solutions with multiple iterations.

4.4   An Example

To illustrate the process of the proposed MEFT, an workflow example with 7 tasks is shown in Fig. 2. Let the processing time P_i for each task on a single virtual machine be 3, 1, 2, 2, 2, 2, 2 respectively. v_3 and v_4 are malleable tasks with malleable resources and variable processing times. The other tasks are rigid tasks requiring rigid resources, in which v_5 and v_6 require two virtual machines while the remaining rigid tasks require only one virtual machine. Let the deadline of the workflow be 9 and the *discount* of the long-term reserved resources be 0.8.

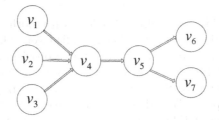

Fig. 2. An example of workflow instance.

The algorithm starts with the least long term reserved resources ($H^r = 2$). The priority of each task is calculated first to determine the initial task sequence, which are (1, 3, 2, 4, 5, 6, 7) in this example. v_1 is allocated first. Since there is only one whole free time period, v_1 is allocated to the time period 1, 2, 3 of virtual machine 1. v_3 is allocated next. The time period 1, 2, 3 of virtual machine

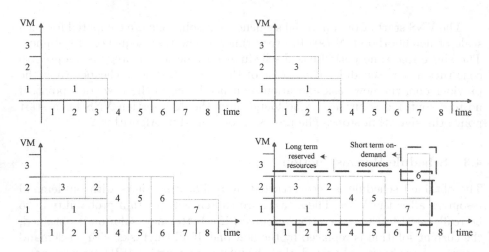

Fig. 3. Task scheduling process and result of MEFT.

2 is the earliest free time period. v_3 is allocated to the time period 1, 2 of virtual machine 2. The next task v_2 is allocated to the time period 3 of virtual machine 2. Since v_4 is a malleable task and can be processed in parallel, it is allocated to the time slot 4 of virtual machine 1 and 2 concurrently. Task v_5, v_6, v_7 are allocated next. Details are shown in Fig. 3. Since no on-demand resources are used in the schedule, the SR procedure is not performed. After several iterations of VNS, a new sequence (1, 3, 2, 4, 5, 7, 6) is found. Tasks are reallocated according to this sequence. While allocating v_6, the time slots 6 and 7 of virtual machine 2 are free which forms a free time period. The discount 0.8 meets the criteria for on-demand resource renting. A new virtual machine is rented for v_6 and v_6 is executed on virtual 2 and 3 concurrently.

5   Experimental Results

The considered workflow scheduling problem with both malleable tasks and hybrid resource provisioning has not been studied yet. The closest problem is that considered in [4] with only reserved resource provisioning and the number of reserved virtual machines minimization. BTS was proposed for the problem. In this paper, we adapted BTS (we call it ABTS in this paper) for the problem under study in two aspects: BTS does not allocate each task to a specific virtual machine. The schedule of BTS considers only the start time and the number of virtual machines for each task. In ABTS, tasks are allocated to a specific virtual machine after BTS gets a schedule. The task with the longest processing time is allocated to the virtual machines with the smallest index in order to minimize the renting cost of on-demand resources. If the utilization rate of a virtual machine is less than *discount* when calculating the resource renting cost of ABTS, the cost of this virtual machine is computed using the on-demand manner. Otherwise, the cost is computed according to the reserved manner.

The proposed MEFT is compared with ABTS in this paper. All the compared algorithms are coded in Java and executed on the same virtual machine with Intel i5-3470 CPU (4 cores, 3.1GHz) and 1GB memory of RAM. Workflow instances are randomly produced by Rangen [9,10] (benchmark of project scheduling problem), in which the number of tasks n takes value from $\{10, 20, 50, 100, 200\}$, 20 instances are generated for each size of the workflow. The number of resources is 1 and the network complexity is set as 1.8. The processing time of each task is randomly generated from the uniform distribution $U(10, 100)$. The deadline factor of each workflow instance is set as $\theta = 1.2$ according to [14], which means $D = Est_n \times 1.2$ for each instance.

The relative percentage deviation (RPD) is adopted to evaluate the performance. Let C_i^F denote the cost of instance i obtained by algorithm F, F^* be the best algorithm for instance i. RPD is defined as:

$$RPD = \frac{C_i^F - C_i^{F^*}}{C_i^{F^*}} \times 100\% \tag{12}$$

Three parameters of MEFT are calibrated: the scale of neighborhood $K \in \{3, 5, 8, 10, 12\}$, the number of solutions for each scale $\lambda \in \{6, 8, 10, 12, 14\}$ and the reconstruction probability $\omega \in \{0, 0.1, 0.2, 0.3, 0.4, 0.5, 0.6, 0.7, 0.8, 0.9, 1\}$.

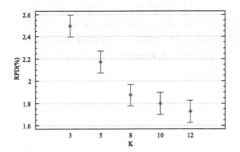

Fig. 4. Means plot with 95 % Tukey HSD confidence intervals for parameter K.

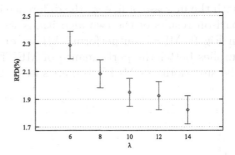

Fig. 5. Means plot with 95 % Tukey HSD confidence intervals for parameter λ.

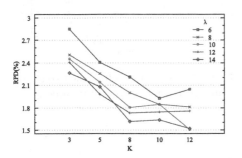

Fig. 6. Interactions with 95 % Tukey HSD confidence intervals between K and λ.

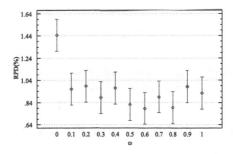

Fig. 7. Means plot with 95 % Tukey HSD confidence intervals for parameter ω.

The multi-factor analysis of variance (ANOVA) technique is adopted to analyze the performance of the algorithms with different parameter values. RPD is used as the response variable. First the three main hypotheses (normality, homoscedasticity, and independence of the residuals) are checked. Since all the three hypotheses are close to zero, they are acceptable in this analysis.

Figures 4 and 5 show the means plot with 95 % Tukey HSD confidence intervals for parameters K and λ respectively. With the increase of K and λ, RPD of MEFT decreases because more solutions are searched. However, more CPU time is required. Furthermore, interactions between K and λ with 95 % Tukey HSD confidence intervals are shown in Fig. 6. Figure 6 implies that MEFT gets the best performance when K and λ take value of 12 and 10 respectively. For the reconstruction probability ω, the means plot with 95 % Tukey HSD confidence intervals is shown in Fig. 7. Figure 7 means that MEFT gets the worst solution when $\omega = 0$ (no reconstruction). MEFT gets the best result when $\omega = 0.6$.

By setting the three parameters as 12, 10 and 0.6, MEFT is compared with ABTS. Instances with different size ($n \in \{10, 20, 50, 100, 200\}$) and different discount value ($discount \in \{0.4, 0.5, 0.6, 0.7, 0.8\}$) are randomly generated. The means plot with 95 % Tukey HSD confidence intervals of the compared algorithms with different instance sizes is shown in Fig. 8. Figure 8 illustrates that MEFT is better than ABTS on all instances. When $n = 10$, the RPD difference between MEFT and ABTS is 15.2 %. However, the difference becomes smaller with the increase of n, e.g., the difference is about 4.5 % when $n = 200$. The comparison results of the two algorithms with different $discount$ values are shown in Fig. 9. MEFT outperforms ABTS for all $discount$ values. Smaller $discount$ implies better the performance of MEFT. When the $discount$ becomes bigger, the superiority of MEFT becomes less significant.

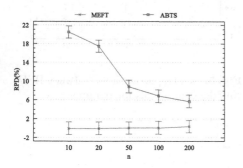
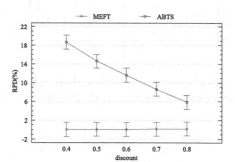

Fig. 8. Comparison result of the two algorithms with different instance size.

Fig. 9. Comparison result of the two algorithms with different $discount$ values.

6   Conclusion and Future Work

In this paper, the resource renting problem for workflow applications with hybrid resource provisioning was considered, which is closer to real cloud computing scenarios. Based on both long-term reservation and short-term on-demand resource renting manners, a mathematic model was established. A new heuristic MEFT was proposed and compared with the adapted BTS. Experimental results showed that MEFT outperforms ABTS when the scale of instances and the *discount* are not big. The differences between MEFT and ABTS become smaller with the increase of the scale of instances and *discount*.

Scheduling problems with multiple types of virtual machines in the cloud will be studied. More real scenarios including data locality and data transfer time between virtual machines are also worth considering.

Acknowledgment. This work is supported by the National Natural Science Foundation of China (Grants 61572127, 61272377) and the Specialized Research Fund for the Doctoral Program of Higher Education (20120092110027). Rubén Ruiz is supported by the Spanish Ministry of Economy and Competitiveness, under the project "RESULT - Realistic Extended Scheduling Using Light Techniques" (No. DPI2012-36243-C02-01) financed with FEDER funds.

References

1. Abrishami, S., Naghibzadeh, M., Epema, D.H.: Deadline-constrained workflow scheduling algorithms for infrastructure as a service clouds. Future Gener. Comput. Syst. **29**(1), 158–169 (2013)
2. Bardsiri, A.K., Hashemi, S.M.: A review of workflow scheduling in cloud computing environment. Int. J. Comput. Sci. Manag. Res. **1**(3), 348–351 (2012)
3. Buyya, R., Yeo, C.S., Venugopal, S.: Market-oriented cloud computing: vision, hype, and reality for delivering it services as computing utilities. In: 10th IEEE International Conference on High Performance Computing and Communications, HPCC 2008, pp. 5–13. IEEE (2008)
4. Byun, E.K., Kee, Y.S., Kim, J.S., Deelman, E., Maeng, S.: BTS: resource capacity estimate for time-targeted science workflows. J. Parallel. Distrib. Comput. **71**(6), 848–862 (2011)
5. Byun, E.K., Kee, Y.S., Kim, J.S., Maeng, S.: Cost optimized provisioning of elastic resources for application workflows. Future Gener. Comput. Syst. **27**(8), 1011–1026 (2011)
6. Chaisiri, S., Lee, B.S., Niyato, D.: Optimization of resource provisioning cost in cloud computing. IEEE Trans. Serv. Comput. **5**(2), 164–177 (2012)
7. Demeulemeester, E., Herroelen, W.S.: Project Scheduling: A Research Handbook, vol. 49. Kluwer Academic Publishers, Norwell (2002)
8. Durillo, J.J., Prodan, R.: Multi-objective workflow scheduling in Amazon EC2. Cluster Comput. **17**(2), 169–189 (2014)
9. Kolisch, R., Sprecher, A.: PSPLIB - A project scheduling problem library: or software-orsep operations research software exchange program. Eur. J. Oper. Res. **96**(1), 205–216 (1997)
10. Kolisch, R., Sprecher, A., Drexl, A.: Characterization and generation of a general class of resource-constrained project scheduling problems. Manag. Sci. **41**(10), 1693–1703 (1995)
11. Radulescu, A., Van Gemund, A.J.: A low-cost approach towards mixed task and data parallel scheduling. In: International Conference on Parallel Processing, pp. 69–76. IEEE (2001)

12. Singh, G., Kesselman, C., Deelman, E.: Application-level resource provisioning on the grid. In: Second IEEE International Conference on e-Science and Grid Computing, e-Science 2006, p. 83. IEEE (2006)
13. Topcuoglu, H., Hariri, S.: Wu, M.y.: Performance-effective and low-complexity task scheduling for heterogeneous computing. IEEE Trans. Parallel Distrib. Syst. **13**(3), 260–274 (2002)
14. Yamashita, D.S., Armentano, V.A., Laguna, M.: Scatter search for project scheduling with resource availability cost. Eur. J. Oper. Res. **169**(2), 623–637 (2006)
15. Yu, J., Buyya, R.: Scheduling scientific workflow applications with deadline and budget constraints using genetic algorithms. Sci. Program. **14**(3–4), 217–230 (2006)

Novel Hotspot Information Analysis System Using Automatic Information Extraction

Mo Chen[1(✉)], Deyu Yuan[2], Chen Zhang[3], Gang Du[3], and Xiangyang Gong[1]

[1] Beijing University of Posts and Telecommunications,
No. 10 Xitucheng Rd., Haidian District, Beijing 100876, China
15101135127@139.com
[2] People's Public Security University of China, Beijing 100038, China
yuandeyu@gmail.com
[3] China Mobile Group Design Institute Co., Ltd., Beijing, China
zhangchen@cmdi.chinamobile.com

Abstract. There is large amount of information available on the Internet, which introduces difficulties in capturing and analyzing hotspot information. In this paper, we propose a novel hotspot information analysis system with automatic information extraction using the technologies of internet crawling, similarity elimination and abstract generation. System verification results show that, compared to the traditional solutions based on manual extraction and analysis, the proposed method are more capable of realizing the automated information extraction and analysis, thus improve the efficiency of hotspot analysis.

Keywords: Massive information acquiring · Automatic information extraction · Hotspot analysis

1 Introduction

In recent years, human society has entered a new era of information technology represented by computer technology and modern communication technologies. In this era, broadband Internet, mobile networks and a variety of mobile terminals are increasingly being used in people's work and life, which make the communication between people more smoothly [1].

China has as many as 613 million Internet users, and the amount of annual increase has reached 61.5 million, making China the country with the largest number of people using the network in the world [2]. Data shows that the number of mobile users has reached the scale of 356 million, accounting for 58 % of the user population, compared to the same period of last year, an increase of about 58 million people. The size of the web database has been increasing at very fast rate [3]. Mobile Internet usage is constantly improving, the way people communicate involved in multi-faceted approaches and media such as the website, SMS (Short Message Service), MMS (Multimedia Messaging Service), e-mail, WAP (Wireless Application Protocol), mobile terminals and desktop [4].

© Springer International Publishing Switzerland 2016
Q. Zu and B. Hu (Eds.): HCC 2016, LNCS 9567, pp. 47–57, 2016.
DOI: 10.1007/978-3-319-31854-7_5

Modern information technology has brought great convenience to people's work and life [5]. With the rapid development of information technology and mobile communication technologies such as the smart mobile terminals, the information resources have been rapidly expanded [6]. However, these information resources are filled with large number of useless information and even harmful information. The harmful information rapidly spread in various ways, disrupting and causing many hazards to people's daily life and the human society [7]. How to extract and analyze massive hotspot information has become a challenging project [8–12]. The main content of this paper is to design and implement a massive hotspot information analysis system that can capture and analyze hotspot information in the specified network. The designed massive hotspot information analysis system consists of two parts: the massive information acquiring module and hotspot information analysis module. The massive information acquiring module crawl the information from the specified network, de-noise and convert them into formatted data, while hotspot information analysis module is responsible for data screening and analysis.

The rest of this paper is organized as follows. In Sect. 2, we describe the system architecture of the designed massive hotspot information analysis system. In Sect. 3, the detailed design and implementation of massive hotspot information analysis system is presented. System verification and test of the proposed system is analyzed and demonstrated in Sect. 4. Finally, we give the conclusions in Sect. 5.

2 System Architecture of Massive Hotspot Information Analysis System

In this paper, we design a massive hotspot information analysis system, which consists of the massive information acquiring module and hotspot information analysis module. The overall architecture of the system will use three layer design scheme, which will be shown in the following sections.

2.1 System Network Architecture

Considering the requirements and features of massive hotspot information analysis system, the framework adopted the B/S (Browser/Server) architecture. In B/S mode, the user operates the system and obtains the information through the browser. The advantage of this architecture is that it is not limited to a specific operating system, and avoids the time consumed in the client download, install and update procedure. Because the client and server do not need a large amount of data transmission, the B/S architecture can accomplish the presentation of data statistics and analysis conclusions for the console. The system network architecture is shown as Fig. 1.

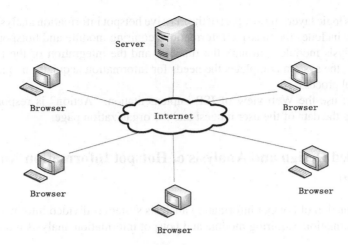

Fig. 1. System network architecture

2.2 System Hierarchical Architecture

The overall architecture of the system adopts three layers scheme. As shown in Fig. 2, the whole system is divided into three layers, data access layer, business logic layer and UI (User Interface) layer.

1. Data access layer: in charge of the operations of increase, delete, modify and find for data in the database, and to read, modify and save the physical files (xml files and index files). This layer is responsible for the corresponding needs of business logic layer and calling the database to operate.

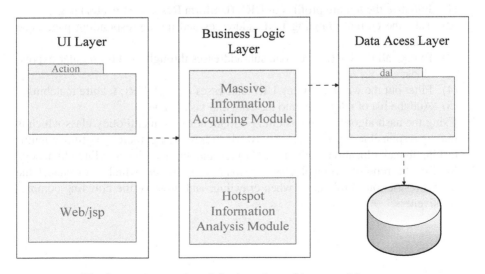

Fig. 2. Implementation of the three tier architecture of the system

2. Business logic layer: the key part of the massive hotspot information analysis system, it mainly includes the massive information acquiring module and hotspot information analysis module. Through the function and the integration of the two above modules, the system completes the needs for information acquisition, analysis and statistical process.
3. UI layer: use the Web view of JSP implementation. "Action" is responsible for receiving the data of the user request and the organization page.

3 Detailed Design and Analysis of Hotspot Information Analysis System

The main function of hotspot information analysis system is divided into two parts: the massive information acquiring module and hotspot information analysis module.

3.1 Detailed Design and Implementation of Massive Information Acquiring Module

The role of massive information acquiring module is to obtain structured information from the network. It consists of information crawling sub-module and information washing sub-module.

3.1.1 Information Crawling Sub-module

In order to meet the demands of massive data analysis, information crawling sub-module integrated open source web crawler Heritrix.

1. Define the Extractor classes for screening the worth crawling pages, the main process is as follows:
   (1) Initialize the feature profiles of URL (Uniform Resource Locator) pages;
   (2) Take the current crawling URL addresses and the corresponding page code string;
   (3) Extract all the URL page code sub-addresses through the http regular expressions;
   (4) Filter out the worth crawling URL addresses through URL feature matching;
   (5) Add the list of addresses into the crawling task queue.
2. Using the hash algorithm to customize ElfQueueAssignmentPolicy class which is mainly responsible for the hash of network address string, thereby optimize multi-tasking thread allocation methods of Heritrix and improve the crawling efficiency.
3. Modify the reptiles protocol class PreconditionEnforcer, which will cancel the access restriction in robots.txt when crawling, and improve the crawling comprehensiveness.

3.1.2   Information Washing Sub-module

Information washing sub-module can clean the crawled pages into structured data and store the structured data into a local file. The main process of this sub-module is shown as follows:

1. Acquire the files in the root directory by traversal recursive algorithm, preliminary screen the file through file name to obtain a valid html page addresses and get screened incremental pages based on the cleaned log file.
2. Get the file types according to the file directory features (micro-blog, news, internet website information), invoking the corresponding cleaning class to clean the html code file, and generate the List objects of Content information interface.
3. Call Content interface class contentsToXml method to map Content object list to xml format data, and store the data in the specified path in xml format.
4. Update the cleaned log files, including the last cleaning time, the number of added cleaning files.

The flow chart of information washing sub-module is shown as Fig. 3.

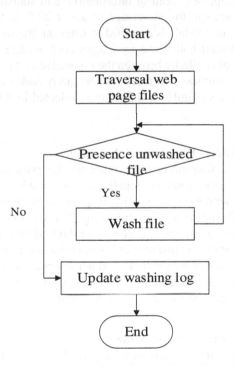

Fig. 3. Flow chart of information washing sub-module

3.2 Detailed Design and Implementation of the Hotspot Information Analysis Module

The main role of the hotspot information analysis module is to analyze data, which includes screening, similarity eliminating, electronic address extraction, keyword generation and abstract generation.

3.2.1 Screening Sub-module

Screening sub-module deletes the unwanted parts by acquiring the concerns of demand side. According to the demand for the theme concerned, the system designs concern vocabulary files which saved keywords of topic the user concerns, and different keywords are separated by newline, the initialization filter sub-module read the keywords into memory by reading documents.

3.2.2 Similarity Eliminating Sub-module

Website content often appears identical information, and statistical data derived that identical information account for an average of about 20 % in the same day. So the similarity eliminating sub-module is designed to filter out the same or similar content of a text document. Although both the vector space model and the edit distance algorithm can calculate a degree of similarity between the respective text comparisons, however, both the methods are insufficient to meet the constantly added new mass data in the operation of the system, so SimHash algorithm is selected in this system as the core algorithm.

3.2.3 Electronic Address Extraction Sub-module

Electronic address extraction sub-module completes the extraction of phone, website address and other relevant information from the text. The publisher's electronic address information such as telephone number often displays in the form of a picture on the publisher profile. While the costs of pattern recognition for image are often very high and the accuracy is low, meanwhile, it needs constant adjustment and maintenance. Through a large number of examinations of information in the platform, it can be seen that, in fact, more than half of the publisher contact information will appear in the text. Thus summarized the common features of electronic addresses and then used a text pattern matching to extract the required electronic address.

3.2.4 Keyword Generation Sub-module

Keyword extraction sub-module can extract keywords from the body text. In order to achieve the keyword extraction algorithm which is compliance with the system requirements and complete the system needs to generate keywords, the information entropy-based keyword extraction algorithm is used in this system.

The concept of information entropy is used in the system to calculate information entropy of the probability of different conjunctions after the word appears in a paper. The larger the information entropy of the probability for different conjunctions after a word is, the more average that there are different words after the word is. Experiment results show that more average the case is, the smaller the chance is when the word behind it is the same.

Through lots of experiments on text segmentation and information entropy calculation of various points of the "probabilities of word behind the different conjunctions", it can be obtained that most of the information entropy for a long text articles (the number of words is greater than 140) which can be used with word combinations behind the appearance of the same word are within 2, so we set the information entropy parameter threshold as 2.

3.2.5   Abstract Generation Sub-module

Abstract generation sub-module generated the abstract from the message body text. The abstract generation algorithm used in this system improved the cluster-based digest algorithms. In this algorithm, clusters are no longer partitioned, but clause is considered as the unit of keyword. The specific procedures are as follows:

1. Cut the chapter into multiple clauses;
2. Calculate significance score of clauses according to number of keywords and the participles;
3. Rank the significance score of clauses in descending order and select three clauses with the largest information;
4. Rank the three clauses according to the order of appearance in the article, and generate the abstract of the article finally.

4   System Verification and Test

The system's Web page interface is simple, elegant, clear and user-friendly. Sketch of the Web page interface is shown as Fig. 4.

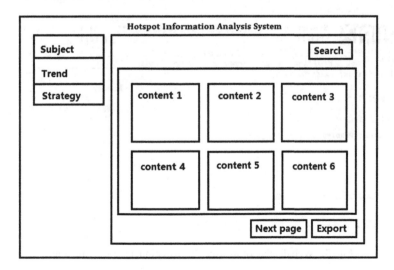

Fig. 4. Web page interface

The description of experimental conditions and the test environment is divided into three parts: the hardware configuration, software parameters and crawling parameter settings, specific settings are shown in Table 1.

Table 1. Simulation parameter settings

Parameter	Value
Start period of information crawling sub-module (s)	3600
Start period of hotspot information analysis module (s)	3600
Hamming distance threshold of similarity eliminating	3
Maximum number of connections participle for keyword extraction	3
Information entropy threshold for keyword extraction	2.0
The maximum number of keyword extraction	4
The maximum number of clauses for abstract generation	3

Hotspot information analysis system adopts B/S architecture, therefore we need two computers: one as a server, one as a client. All devices are in the same subnet. The configuration parameters of the system are shown as Table 1.

Test Conditions: website source for test is a classified information network, such as the second-hand housing information website.

Test Flow Description: use Firefox browser and enter the URL http://localhost:8080/ FakeWeb/pages/tool7/07hot.jsp.

1. Running massive information acquiring module.

   Massive information acquiring module completes the crawling task of 70 lists of second-hand housing pages in 58 City as shown in Fig. 5:

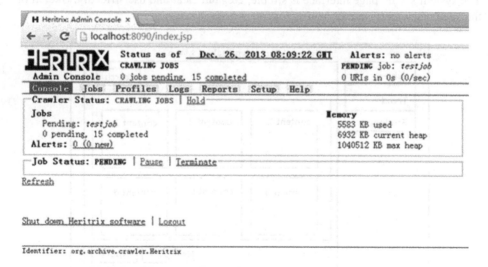

Fig. 5. Web display of massive information acquiring module

After the information crawling task is completed, the user can enter the specified folder to view the crawling results as shown in Fig. 6. Since 58 City retains the previous 70 list information of second-hand housing sites, the pages of each list is 50, so a total of 3500 Web page files are crawled in this task. The related information is shown in Fig. 6.

Fig. 6. Screenshot of crawling results

2. Running the cleaning sub-module and hotspot information analysis module.
   The system can run cleaning sub-module and hotspot information analysis module periodically. The system will handle 3500 Web page files incrementally, and stored the results in xml files. The console output process is shown as Fig. 7.

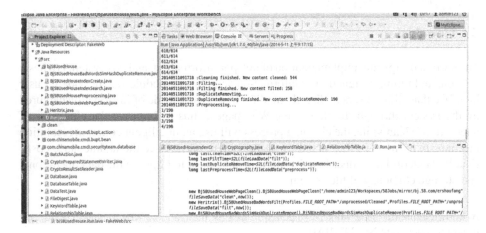

Fig. 7. Console output process

Click on the left button of "Trend" to enter the trend display page as shown in Fig. 8, we can see on the last half of page the five hotspot keywords of the total (keywords number of hits of information) over a period of time (optional week, half a week, one month, half a year). Click on one of these keywords to view the chart of heat formation for this keyword over the last period of time (six months if the display data is monthly).

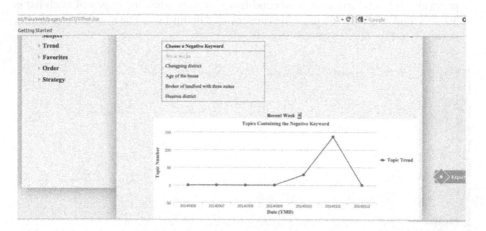

Fig. 8. Page of the trend

The functional and performance tests of hotspot information analysis systems are presented, and the results show that the achieved system function realized the expected demand with stable performance, and well done in a variety of different test environments. Condition of try running is also good enough.

5   Conclusion

The current design and implementation of hotspot information analysis system is a basic version, and future designation in information acquisition module will provide UI user interface that allows users to directly modify the network-wide of information captured by the system through the interactive Web pages, thus to improve the efficiency of interaction. Meanwhile, the cleaning process will use an intelligent common resolution mechanism to improve the versatility of the system and reduce the maintenance costs. Finally, Hadoop-based distributed systems will be used to improve the data operational and storage efficiency of the system.

Acknowledgment. This work is supported in part by the National Key Technology Support Program under grant No. 2012BAH41F03.

References

1. Martinez, J., Tintin, R.: Modern use of ICTs as tools for support in social research. In: 2015 Second International Conference on eDemocracy & eGovernment (ICEDEG), pp. 67–72. IEEE (2015)

2. Proenza, F., Girard, B., Proenza, F.: Problematic Internet Use among Internet Café Users in China. MIT Press (2015)
3. BrightPlanet.Com: The deep Web: surfacing hidden value. http://brightplanet.com. Accessed Dec 2012
4. Yang, S.Z.: The marketing chain in the mobile Internet era. In: 2011 International Conference on Machine Learning and Cybernetics (ICMLC), pp. 1058–1061. IEEE (2011)
5. Wei, W., Qian, L.: The profound effect of modern Information Technology revolution on network economy society. In: 2011 IEEE 3rd International Conference on Communication Software and Networks (ICCSN), pp. 299–301. IEEE (2011)
6. Inoue, A., Nagahata, R., Ishii, Y., et al.: Mobile internet-access behavior analysis. In: 2012 13th ACIS International Conference on Software Engineering, Artificial Intelligence, Networking and Parallel/Distributed Computing, pp. 766–770. IEEE Computer Society (2012)
7. Jin, H., Cui, B., Wang, J.: Mining mobile internet packets for malware detection. In: 2014 Ninth International Conference on P2P, Parallel, Grid, Cloud and Internet Computing (3PGCIC), pp. 481–486. IEEE (2014)
8. Al-Saggaf, Y., Islam, M.Z.: Data mining and privacy of social network sites' users: implications of the data mining problem. Sci. Eng. Ethics **21**, 941–966 (2014)
9. Zhang, C., Zhang, J.: InForCE: forum data crawling with information extraction. In: 2010 4th International Universal Communication Symposium (IUCS), pp. 367–373. IEEE (2010)
10. Gao, K., Wang, W., Gao, S.: Modelling on web dynamic incremental crawling and information processing. In: 2013 Proceedings of International Conference on Modelling, Identification & Control (ICMIC), pp. 293–298. IEEE (2013)
11. Ragan, E.D., Endert, A., Sanyal, J., et al.: Characterizing provenance in visualization and data analysis: an organizational framework of provenance types and purposes. IEEE Trans. Visual. Comput. Graph. **22**, 31–40 (2016)
12. Zhao, X.J., Huang, F.F., Bo, L.I., et al.: Research on topic semantic information extraction for network news. Comput. Knowl. Technol. (2015)

Support Vector Machine Based on Dynamic Density Equalization

Hongle Du[1]([⊠]), Shaohua Teng[2], Lin Zhang[1], and Yan Zhang[1]

[1] School of Mathematics and Computer Application, Shangluo University,
Shangluo 726000, Shaanxi, China
dh15597@163.com
[2] Faculty of Computer, Guangdong University of Technology,
Guangzhou 510006, Guangdong, China

Abstract. In order to resolve the classifiers' over fitting phenomenon to enhance classification performance under imbalanced dataset, a dynamic density equalization algorithm is proposed for imbalanced data classification. According to the relationship between sample's densities of different class, the algorithm is hierarchical clustering. First, samples of majority class are divided into multiple particles according to K-mean clustering in the kernel space. Then, cluster for every particle according to the relation between particle density and minority class. Then, replace the particle with the sample that it has highest similarity with the center of particle. Reform the new training dataset and get the final classifier. The algorithm may resolve the problem of imbalanced dataset and improve the classification performance of SVM. Experiment results with artificial dataset and four groups of UCI dataset show the algorithm is effectiveness for imbalanced dataset.

Keywords: Support Vector Machine · Imbalanced dataset · K-mean clustering · Dynamical granulation

1 Introduction

Support Vector Machine (SVM) shows lots of unique advantages to solve the problem about the small sample, nonlinear and high dimensional pattern recognition problems based on structural risk minimization principle. The traditional SVM has better classification performance for balanced data set. But in imbalanced data set, hyperplane of traditional SVM will shift to minority class in order to ensure minimum cost of misclassification. In other words, it is over learning for sample of majority class and under learning for sample of minority class. This leads to higher classification error rate for minority class. But in practical applications, classification performance requirements for minority class are more than majority class. For example, in network intrusion detection, abnormal behavioral data (intrusion data) is minority class because of difficult collected and normal behavioral data is majority class. The losses of dividing the intrusion behavior into normal behavior are more than it of dividing the normal behavior into intrusion behavior. In order to improve classification performance of classifier, many researchers propose many solutions. These methods can be summarized into two categories: method

© Springer International Publishing Switzerland 2016
Q. Zu and B. Hu (Eds.): HCC 2016, LNCS 9567, pp. 58–69, 2016.
DOI: 10.1007/978-3-319-31854-7_6

based on dataset and method based on algorithm. The method based on dataset is to remove some samples of majority class or increase some samples of minority class by certain strategies to make the dataset equalization. The methods often used include data resample [1–6], Cost-Sensitive Learning [7, 8], kernel method' integration method, etc.

Literature [1] cluster for majority class with K-means cluster algorithm. Set the same number of cluster centers and minority class samples, and look the cluster centers as new data set. Use over-sampling for minority class samples with SMOTE algorithm in order to avoiding too sparse of the final training dataset because of too small samples of minority class. In literature [2] clustering consistency index was introduced to find the boundary minority samples. And K-nearest density was defined to calculate the number of synthetic new samples and to reject the noise samples. The new samples generated by this method are much more beneficial for classifier learning. In literature [3], the majority samples are clusters using kernel fuzzy C-Means clustering algorithm in kernel space for randomly resampling representative samples with cluster information, which can not only reduce the number of majority samples, but also make the SVM classification hyperplane biased toward the majority class. In literature [4], majority class samples are clustered by using spectrum cluster in kernel space for resampling representative samples with cluster information. The number of selected samples in each cluster is dependent on the size of each cluster and the distance of the cluster to the all minority class samples.

Based on the above analysis, dynamic density equalization Support vector machine (DDESVM) algorithm is proposed in this paper. In this algorithm, majority class samples are hierarchical dynamic clustered in kernel space. Firstly, majority class is divided into many sub classes by K-means cluster algorithm. Then calculate the density of every sub class. If the number and density of the sub class meet the specified conditions, calculate the K values according to the number and density of the sub class and minority class. Then the sub class is again divided into sub classes. Finally, take the similar samples with the class center in each sub class to form a new dataset. This algorithm calculates the density and clusters all in kernel space. In order to ensure the density of samples after resampling is similar to density of minority class samples, dynamic calculate the K for every clustering according to the density relation between each sub class and minority class. Simulation results show that this method improves SVM classification performance on the imbalanced data, especially for minority sample classification accuracy.

2 Theoretical Analysis

2.1 Effect of Imbalanced Dataset for SVM

Imbalanced data refers to the number of samples of one class is more than the number of samples of other each class in a dataset. The maximum numbers of samples called majority class and the minimum numbers of samples called minority class. If the number of samples of one class in the dataset is very small (usually less than 10 %) is called a sparse class. Classification problem of imbalanced data is to construct the decision function by learning from imbalanced data. Traditional classification method will result in the majority class has higher recognition rate and minority class has lower recognition rate.

In order to observe the effect on classification hyperplane of SVM under imbalanced data, randomly generate uniform distribution samples of two classes as shown in Fig. 1. In Fig. 1(a), the first class is $U([0, 1] \times [0, 1])$ and sample number is 200. The second class is $U([0, 1] \times [1, 2])$ and sample number is 20. In Fig. 1(b), the first class is $U([0.8, 1] \times [0, 1])$ and sample number is 20. The second class is $U([0, 1] \times [1, 2])$ and sample number is 20. Obtain the decision Hyperplane by SVM training as shown in Fig. 1. In Fig. 1, the green line is Hyperplane. Cause the hyperplane drifting is not class number of samples but class density of samples.

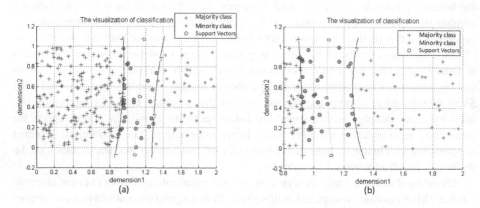

Fig. 1. The classification decision surface of different density

In imbalanced data, cause classification drifting to minority class is there is the same cost of two classed samples. In other words, there is the same penalty factor of two class samples. In this case, in order to ensure the classification interval as large as possible and the cost of misclassification as small as possible, obviously, hyperplane drift to minority class (the region of sample density small). This cause the over learning for majority class and under learning for minority class. Literature uses the different penalty factor for two classes. To reflect the importance of the minority class, minority class use a large penalty factor and majority class use a small penalty factor. However, in practical application, the importance of two class samples is difficult to measure. In other words, penalty factor is difficult to measure. In addition, the essence of the problem of imbalanced data is the density is not imbalanced. In this paper, the dynamic equalization algorithm is used to make the class density equalization, and the performance of the classifier is improved.

2.2 Sample Density in Kernel Space

To describe the density distribution of sample in kernel space, here are a few definitions of related concepts.

Definition 1. Given two samples x and y, then define the distance between two samples as follow:

$$d(x,y) = ||x - y|| \tag{1}$$

Where x and y are multidimensional vectors, and $||x||$ is second-order norm.

For linearly inseparable problem, it uses the non-linear map $\varphi : R^k \mapsto F$ to make the training samples map into feature space from input space. And it is linear classification in the feature space. Kernel function is $K(x,y) = \,<\phi(x), \phi(y)>$. The distance between two samples in kernel space is defined as follow:

$$d(x,y) = \sqrt{K(x,x) + K(y,y) - 2K(x,y)} \tag{2}$$

Set kernel function is RBF. That is $K(x,y) = \exp(-g||x - y||^2)$. g is an undetermined constant and will affect the final results. The general value of g is the reciprocal of the dimension. From the formula (5) can be obtained as follow:

$$
\begin{aligned}
d(x,y) &= \sqrt{K(x,x) + K(y,y) - 2K(x,y)} \\
&= \sqrt{\exp(-g||x - x||^2) + \exp(-g||y - y||^2) - 2 * \exp(-g||x - y||^2)} \\
&= \sqrt{2 - 2 * \exp(-g||x - y||^2)}
\end{aligned}
\tag{3}
$$

Each class can be considered as a hypersphere after dividing. Class center and class density are defined as follow:

Definition 2. Class Center: after dividing, i^{th} class G_i and it includes n_i samples. Then class center is expressed as:

$$C_i = \frac{1}{n_i}\sum_{m=1}^{n_i}\phi(x_m) = \frac{1}{n_i}\sqrt{(\sum_{m=1}^{n_i}\phi(x_m))^2} = \frac{1}{n_i}\sqrt{\sum_{m=1}^{n_i}\sum_{p=1}^{n_i}K(x_m,x_p)} \tag{4}$$

If kernel function is RBF, then i^{th} class center C_i is expressed as:

$$C_i = \frac{1}{n_i}\sqrt{\sum_{m=1}^{n_i}\sum_{p=1}^{n_i}\exp(-g||x_m - x_p||^2)}$$

According to above, the distance from sample x_j in class G_i to class center C_i is defined as:

$$
\begin{aligned}
D(x_j, C_i) &= \sqrt{K(x_j,x_j) + K(C_i,C_i) - 2K(x_j,C_i)} \\
&= \sqrt{K(x_j,x_j) + \frac{1}{n_i^2}\sum_{m=1}^{n_i}\sum_{p=1}^{n_i}K(x_m,x_p) - \frac{2}{n_i}\sum_{m=1}^{n_i}K(x_j,x_m)}
\end{aligned}
\tag{5}
$$

In order to make the class density equalization of majority class, the density of the sample is needed to calculate. The size of the class space in kernel space will be given. The class space is used to be described as a hypersphere that the radius is the maximum distance from one sample to class center. If present noise data, then cause the radius to be large. So it can't accurately describe the size of class space. In this paper, the average distance from the sample to the class center is used to describe the class space size.

Definition 3. Class space size: The sample x_{ij} represents the jth sample in i^{th} class. Then the size of class G_i is expressed as S_i that is m time's average distance from samples to class center.

$$S_i = m\frac{\sum_{j=1}^{n_i} d(\mu_i, x_{ij})}{n_i} = m\frac{\sum_{j=1}^{n_i} \sqrt{\frac{1}{n_i^2}\sum_{p=1}^{n_i}\sum_{q=1}^{n_i} K(x_p, x_q) - \frac{2}{n_i}\sum_{p=1}^{n_i} K(x_p, x_{ij}) + K(x_{ij}, x_{ij})}}{n_i}$$

The algorithm in this paper needs to calculate the ratio of two class density. So the value of m has no effect on the results. To simplify the calculations, here set the m = 1. Define the follow class density according to above definition of class space size.

Definition 4. Class density: The sample x_{ij} represents the jth sample in i^{th} class. Then class density ρ_i is the ratio of the number of class samples and the class space size. It is presented as follow:

$$\rho_i = \frac{n_i}{S_i} = \frac{(n_i)^2}{\sum_{j=1}^{n_i} \sqrt{\frac{1}{n_i^2}\sum_{p=1}^{n_i}\sum_{q=1}^{n_i} K(x_p, x_q) - \frac{2}{n_i}\sum_{p=1}^{n_i} K(x_p, x_{ij}) + K(x_{ij}, x_{ij})}} \tag{6}$$

If kernel function is RBF, then class density G_i is expressed as:

$$\rho_i = \frac{(n_i)^2}{\sum_{j=1}^{n_i} \sqrt{\frac{1}{n_i^2}\sum_{p=1}^{n_i}\sum_{q=1}^{n_i} \exp(-g||x_p - x_q||^2) - \frac{2}{n_i}\sum_{p=1}^{n_i} \exp(-g||x_p - x_{ij}||^2) + 1}} .$$

3   Dynamic Density Equalization Algorithm

3.1   Parameter Selection

There is a large amount of redundant information or information that is not helpful to the classification of samples in the majority class. These redundant information leads to the class density is not balanced and cause classification hyperplane drifting to minority class. Commonly used method is to delete redundant information through a certain strategy. For examples, DROP, CNN, cluster algorithm, etc. Above methods are under sampling according to number of class sample. When the redundancy is deleted, the relationship between the density of majority class and the density of minority class is not considered. So in this paper, a dynamic density equalization algorithm is proposed according to the relationship of class's density.

Only when the class sample density and minority sample density meet certain conditions, the class will be divided again. The condition of class is divided described as follow.

$$\begin{cases} n_i > 1 \\ \dfrac{\rho_i}{\rho_s} - 1 > \theta \end{cases} \tag{7}$$

Class density reflects the dense degree of the sample distribution. Sample equalization is to make the class density similar with density of minority class by dividing. Only when the class sample density and minority sample density meet certain conditions, the class will be divided. Construct a new training set with each subclass centers after dividing. So realize the density equalization of samples. Supposed a class is G_i, class density is ρ_i and density of minority class is ρ_s. Then the number of sub classes will be described as follow:

$$K_{lev-i} = \left\lfloor a * n_i * \frac{\rho_s}{\rho_i} \right\rfloor = \left\lfloor a * \frac{(n_s)^2 \sum\limits_{j=1}^{n_i} d(\mu_i, x_{ij})}{n_i \sum\limits_{j=1}^{n_s} d(\mu_s, x_{sj})} \right\rfloor \tag{8}$$

α is control parameter to control the degree of division and the number of sub classes. By formula (8) can be seen that the number of sub class is not only related to the number of the majority class samples and minority class samples, but also to the average distance from samples to class center.

3.2 Algorithm Description

The DDESVM algorithm is described as follows:

Input: training dataset. Majority class includes n samples and minority class includes m samples. And set the threshold θ.

Output: decision function.

Step 1. Calculate the density of minority class according to formula (6);

Step 2. For class G_i, if the number of samples is greater than 1, then calculate class density ρ_i (At the initial time, the density of the majority class is ρ_0).

Step 3. Calculate the relationship between the class density and minority class density. If formula (7) is satisfied, then calculate the number K_i of sub class according to the formula (8); otherwise, turn to divide another class.

Step 4. Cluster the samples of class G_i with K-means algorithm according to K_i and get K_i sub classes.

Step 5. Each sub class is divided for above K_i sub classes until all sub class do not meet formula (7).

Step 6. Take the sample that is nearest from class center for each sub classes. Construct the new dataset (new majority class) with above samples. Train and get classifier with new training dataset that includes new majority class and minority class.

4   Experiment and Data Analysis

4.1   Experimental Environment

In this paper, the experiment is completed based on Matlab 7.11.0 and the Taiwan Teacher's LIBSVM. Host is the Intel Core i7 2.3 GHz and 4G memory, operating system is Win7.

4.2   Performance Evaluation

The method of classification for balanced datasets, the used evaluation index is the classification accuracy. The evaluation index is based on the same error cost. Therefore, this evaluation index is not reasonable in imbalanced data sets. Literatures [16, 17] give the evaluation index for the imbalanced data. TP is the number of samples that is divided into normal in normal class. FP is the number of samples that is divided into normal in abnormal class. FN is the number of samples that is divided into abnormal in normal class. TN is the number of samples that is divided into abnormal in abnormal class. If the normal class is the majority class, the correct classification rate for the minority class is described as follow:

$$Se = TN/(TN + FP) \tag{9}$$

The correct classification rate for the majority class is described as follow:

$$Re = TP/(TP + FN) \tag{10}$$

The precision for the minority class is described as follow:

$$Pr = TN/(FP + FN) \tag{11}$$

According to above describe, F_v and G_m are defined as follow:

$$F_v = \frac{(1 + \lambda^2) * S_e * P_r}{\lambda^2 * S_e + P_r} \tag{12}$$

$$G_m = \sqrt{R_e * S_e} \tag{13}$$

Where λ reflect the importance P_r and R_e. F_v reflect the accuracy and precision of minority class samples. So it is able to reflect the classifier performance for minority class samples. G_m reflects the accuracy of minority class samples and majority class samples. So it is able to measure the classifier overall performance. This paper set $\lambda = 1$.

4.3　Artificial Data Set

4.3.1　Linear Separable Data

The experimental data of this section generate using artificial way. Randomly generated uniformly distributed samples of two classes. In training dataset, the first class is $U([0,1] \times [0,1])$ and sample number is 200, the second class is $U([0,1] \times [1,2])$ and sample number is 50. In test dataset, the first class is $U([0,1] \times [0,1])$ and sample number is 50, the second class is $U([0,1] \times [1,2])$ and sample number is 50.

Because of the above data sets are randomly generated, it has some chance. Therefore, the experimental results and the average of five results are given in Table 1. Here value of the control parameter is set to 1 and the kernel function is the Radial Basis Function. Support vector machine also use the Radial Basis Function. This Makes density calculations and support vector machine in the same space.

Table 1. Contrast the results (1)

No.	SVM			Cluster-SVM			DDESVM		
	AC	F_v	G_m	AC	F_v	G_m	AC	F_v	G_m
1	93	0.9209	0.9238	96	0.9603	0.9600	96	0.9603	0.9600
2	94	0.9362	0.9381	93	0.9375	0.9309	95	0.9494	0.9452
3	93	0.9170	0.9201	95	0.9533	0.9533	96	0.9613	0.9594
4	91	0.8971	0.9018	92	0.9259	0.9165	94	0.9434	0.9381
5	92	0.9170	0.9201	95	0.9551	0.9525	96	0.9613	0.9594
Average	92.6	0.9176	0.9208	94.2	0.9464	0.9426	95.4	0.9551	0.9524

Experimental data in Table 1 is the results after once dividing. Experimental results show that this paper algorithm is better than support vector machine algorithm and cluster-SVM algorithm. Figure 2 shows the classification renderings of experiment results of random time. It can be seen that the classification hyperplane is in the ideal position.

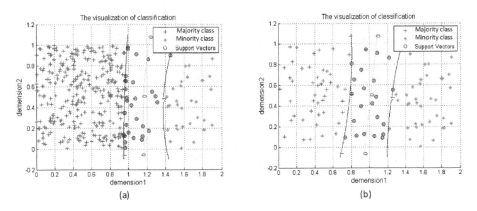

(a)　　　　　　　　　　　　　　　(b)

Fig. 2. The classification decision surface of DDESVM

4.3.2   Linear Inseparable Data

The experimental data of this section generate using two concentric circles $\begin{cases} x = \rho \cdot \cos \theta \\ y = \rho \cdot \sin \theta \end{cases}$, $\theta \in U[0, 2\pi]$. Uniformly distributed radio of the first class is $\rho \in [0, 6]$. The number of samples is 200. Uniformly distributed radio of the second class is $\rho \in [5, 10]$ and number of samples is 50. In test dataset, the number of two classes is 50. Here, the radial basis functions are selected and it is $K(x, y) = \exp(-g||x - y||^2)$. Figure 3(a), (b) are random two figures using the traditional SVM algorithm and this paper algorithm. You can clearly see hyperplane shifted to the majority class direction. Table 2 shows the random experimental results of five times. The different value of K and a will cause the very widely experimental results. The try method is used in this experiment to determine the values of K and a and get an optimal experimental results. How to choose the optimal K and a will be the main work of the next stage.

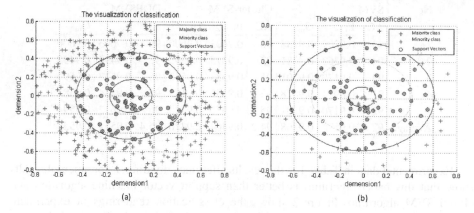

(a)   (b)

Fig. 3. The classification decision surface of DDESVM

Table 2. Contrast the results (2)

No.	SVM			Cluster-SVM			DDESVM		
	AC	F_v	G_m	AC	F_v	G_m	AC	F_v	G_m
1	81	0.7654	0.7874	94	0.9434	0.9381	98.5	0.9851	0.9850
2	76	0.6842	0.7211	92	0.9252	0.9173	98	0.9804	0.9798
3	85.5	0.8304	0.8426	94	0.9434	0.9381	95.5	0.9561	0.9547
4	72.5	0.6207	0.6708	92.5	0.9302	0.9220	97.5	0.9756	0.9747
5	79	0.7342	0.7616	94	0.9434	0.9381	95.5	0.9569	0.9539
Average	78.8	0.7270	0.7567	93.3	0.9371	0.9307	97	0.9708	0.9696

4.4   UCI Data Sets

The experimental data sets use five UCI data (Balance-scale, Contraceptive, Haberman, Hepatitis and Pima). From Tables 4 and 5, the algorithm has better performance when the density ratio of the majority of the class and the minority class is large. Experimental data of SVM, KSMOTE, BSMOTE-SVM, RU-BSMOTE-SVM and ODR-BSMOTE-SVM algorithms are derived from the literature. The experimental results of Cluster-SVM algorithm is based on the algorithm in the literature [1]. The experimental result of DDE-SVM is using this paper algorithm. Because the Cluster-SVM and DDE-SVM algorithms are based on K means clustering algorithm and it have randomness, so the experimental results of the two algorithms in Tables 4 and 5 are the optimal values (Table 3).

Table 3. Experimental data set

Dataset	Attribute	Number of majority class	Number of minority class	Ratio of majority and minority	Class number
Balance-scale	4	576	49	11.76	3
Contraceptive	9	629	333	1.89	2
Haberman	3	225	81	2.78	2
Hepatitis	19	123	32	3.84	2
Pima	8	500	268	1.87	2

Table 4. Contrast the results (1)

Algorithm	Balance-scale	Contraceptive	Haberman	Hepatitis	Pima
SVM	0.6145	0.5677	0.2909	0.6169	0.6195
KSMOTE-SVM	0.6513	0.5695	0.3616	0.6218	0.6534
BSMOTE-SVM	0.6475	0.5771	0.3013	0.6367	0.6372
RU-BSMOTE-SVM	0.6884	0.6023	0.4846	0.6271	0.6677
ODR-BSMOTE-SVM	0.7609	0.6035	0.5505	0.6421	0.6753
Cluster-SVM	0.6263	0.4881	0.4654	0.6013	0.6156
DDE-SVM	0.7237	0.6348	0.5766	0.6353	0.6861

Table 5. Contrast the results (2)

Algorithm	Balance-scale	Contraceptive	Haberman	Hepatitis	Pima
SVM	0.7374	0.6574	0.4260	0.7116	0.6928
KSMOTE-SVM	0.7650	0.6586	0.4891	0.7236	0.7273
BSMOTE-SVM	0.7633	0.6649	0.4373	0.7309	0.7007
RU-BSMOTE-SVM	0.8001	0.6847	0.6123	0.7309	0.7388
ODR-BSMOTE-SVM	0.9368	0.6869	0.6768	0.7426	0.7449
Cluster-SVM	0.6349	0.6692	0.5274	0.6667	0.6576
DDE-SVM	0.8641	0.7270	0.6611	0.7621	0.7641

4.5   Influence of Control Parameters on Results

In this paper, the algorithm needs to calculate the density of majority and minority class. Make the majority class equalization through dividing according to density and make the sample density of the two classes similar. Control parameter a is to control dividing speed and also affect the similar degree of the density. It is very importance. In order to intuitively see the effect of a value, experimental data of this section use the experimental in Sect. 3.2.1. Experimental results of different a show in Table 6. DDE-SVM algorithms are based on K means clustering algorithm and it have randomness, so the experimental results in Table 4 are the optimal values of many experiments.

As can be seen from Table 6, a value is smaller, and times to be divided are more. And the final sample density is more similar. The hyperplane drifting is smaller and the accuracy rate of classification is higher.

Table 6. Effect of a

a value	Number of sub class	Dividing number	Accuracy rate	F_v	G_m
1	47	1	93	0.9434	0.9381
0.5	49	3	95	0.9494	0.9452
0.2	48	3	95	0.9494	0.9452
0.1	49	4	96	0.9613	0.9594
0.05	48	6	96	0.9613	0.9594

5   Conclusion

In order to resolve the classifiers' over fitting phenomenon to enhance classification performance under imbalanced dataset, we start with the density equalization in this paper. Support vector machines need to be mapped to the kernel space for linear inseparable problem. So the density and clustering are carried out in the kernel space. Then resample according to the relationship between the densities of the classes. However, the method is not ideal for a small number of minority samples. Parameters optimization and the use the density equalization algorithm to over sampling for minority class will be the main work of the next stage.

Acknowledgement. This work was supported by the Shaanxi Provincial Natural Science Foundation (Grant No. 2014JM2-6122), Shanxi Provincial Education Department scientific research program funded projects (Grant No. 15JK1218) and the Science and Technology Foundation of Shangluo University (Grant No. 15SKY010).

References

1. Lin, S.Y., Li, C.H., Jiang, Y.: Under-sampling method research in class-imbalanced data. J. Comput. Res. Dev. **48**(7), 47–53 (2011)
2. Lou, X.J., Sun, Y.X., Liu, H.T.: Clustering boundary over-sampling classification method for imbalanced data sets. J. Zhejiang Univ. (Eng. Sci.) **47**(6), 944–950 (2013)

3. Tao, X.M., Hao, S.Y., Zhang, D.X.: Kernel cluset-based ensemble SVM approaches for unbalanced data. J. Harbin Eng. Univ. **34**(3), 381–388 (2013)
4. Zeng, Z.Q., Wu, Q., Liao, B.S.: A classfication method for imbalance data set based on kernel SMOTE. Acta Electronica Sin. **37**(11), 2489–2495 (2009)
5. Chen, S., Guo, G.D., Chen, L.F.: Clustering ensembles based classification method for imbalanced data sets. PR&AI **23**(6), 772–780 (2010)
6. Du, H.L.: Algorithm for imbalanced dataset based on K-Nearest Neighbor in kernel space. Chin. J. Front. Comput. Sci. Technol. **9**(7), 869–876 (2015)
7. Xia, Z.G., Xia, S.X., Cai, S.Y.: Semi-supervised Gaussian process classification algorithm addressing the class imbalance. J. Commun. **34**(5), 42–51 (2013)
8. Cao, P., Zhao, D., Zaiane, O.: An optimized cost-sensitive SVM for imbalanced data learning. In: Pei, J., Tseng, V.S., Cao, L., Motoda, H., Xu, G. (eds.) PAKDD 2013, Part II. LNCS, vol. 7819, pp. 280–292. Springer, Heidelberg (2013)

Research and Implementation of Neighbor Management Mechanism in Communication Level of General Routing Architecture Based on Quagga

Xiafei Dong[1,2(✉)], Yue Ma[1], Zunliang Wang[1,2], Saihong Xu[1], and Siyuan Sun[3]

[1] School of Computer Science, Beijing University of Posts and Telecommunications, Beijing 100876, People's Republic of China
ipaodong@gmail.com
[2] Science and Technology on Information Transmission and Dissemination in Communication Networks Laboratory, Beijing, China
[3] Beijing Branch, China United Network Communications Group Co. Ltd ("China Unicom"), Beijing, China

Abstract. This paper analyzes the current research situation of general routing protocol platform, and neighbors management mechanism in typical routing protocols. And, put forward a effective neighbors management mechanism in general routing protocol platform, based on the research of the functionality set required by existing routing protocols. In this paper, the experimental results show that this mechanism can be applied to the generalized routing protocol platform, meets the needs for routing protocol, and support the new routing protocol development based on the platform.

Keywords: General routing protocol platform · Neighbors management mechanism · Quagga

1 Introduction

In recent years, the hottest word in the computer science is "cloud computing". As the reconstruction of traditional computing model, cloud computing [1] plays the characteristics of "distributed" and "virtualization" incisively and vividly. In applications, infrastructure as a service (Iaas), platform as a service (Paas) and software as a service (Saas) applications such as flowers; In terms of network, traditional network architecture is also close to Limit Point. Applications require a variety of network services in the era of cloud. In order to satisfy the programmable network services, a variety of network architecture emerged. One of the most representative is the software defined network (SDN) [2], which is also combined with the concept of distribution and virtualization, and divided network services into application layer, control layer, forward layer and two layer protocols used to coordinate the application layer and control layer (north), control layer and forward layer (south). Thus, the purpose of SDN [3] meet "programmable" requirements in era of the cloud network with distribution and virtualization.

© Springer International Publishing Switzerland 2016
Q. Zu and B. Hu (Eds.): HCC 2016, LNCS 9567, pp. 70–80, 2016.
DOI: 10.1007/978-3-319-31854-7_7

In addition to SDN, there are other architecture is proposed, to solve the problems of the programmable network. General routing protocol platform is one of them. Unlike SDN, which think network structure is the restriction point of network topology provides programmable demand, general routing protocol platform consider that the seal of the traditional routing protocols, and the resulting repetitive construction and lengthy standardization process and closed routing architecture is the key. From this perspective, SDN is not really solve these problems, that programming of the application layer is not become simpler than traditional router. For example, RouterFlow provide a implementation of traditional routing protocol based on SDN. We have to do start with design of neighbor state machine, protocol data and routing calculation while develop a new routing protocol. Development cycle and the difficulty are both not reduced.

General routing protocol platform is a programmable open routing protocol platform, which allows routing protocols to consider less that has to be consider in traditional protocols but has nothing to do with the routing strategy. Such as data forwarding, neighbors management etc. For general platform, routing protocols are just applications running on it. Traditional routing architecture and general routing protocol platform architecture is shown in Fig. 1.

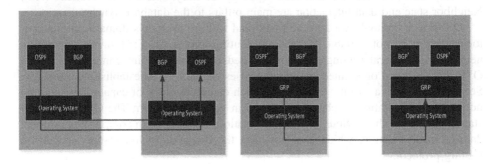

Fig. 1. Traditional routing architecture (left) and general routing protocol platform architecture (right)

General routing protocol platform provide the basis service interface for routing protocols, that routing protocols only need to care about routing calculation and other related business, which greatly simplifies the routing protocol design and implementation. So general routing protocol platform can be used in the development of new protocol verification, protocol service customization and even enterprise internal routing protocol development.

Different from traditional routing protocols, general routing protocol platform establish only one session between a pair of neighbors, which greatly save the system resources consumption. At the same time, protocol don't have to consider their neighbor, which simplifies the protocol standard and implementation. However, in order to meet many applications of protocols the general routing protocol based on general routing protocol platform, mechanism of neighbor management is particularly important.

2 Research Status

At present, the domestic and foreign research on general routing protocol platform is rare, a lot of technology standard has not been formed. Research on neighbor management of general routing protocol platform are much rarer. Neighbor management mechanism of traditional routing protocols, however, is quite mature, and many technology of them can be used for reference to the general routing protocol platform. Neighbor state machine is the main way of neighbor management. So that the neighbor management mechanism mainly includes the state machine definition and switch, connection establishment and management (optional). In mature traditional routing protocols, neighbor management mechanisms are similar but each has its characteristics.

2.1 OSPF [4] Neighbor State Machine

OSPF neighbor state machine include eight states as Down, Attempt, Init, 2-Way, Exstart, Exchange, Loading and Full [5, 6]. The state machine as shown in Fig. 2. OSPF is routing protocol based on a link-state (LSA), in which each router keeps the same link-state database (LSDB) described topology of fully autonomous systems (AS). Neighbor state and data interaction are main pillars to the database synchronization.

OSPF as commonly used in the traditional routing protocols domain routing protocol. But it is not suitable for general routing protocols. First of all, generally, neighbors in general routing protocol is based on point-to-point connections, while OSPF is not based on connection, which causes the lack of an establishment process; Secondly OSPF is a specific agreement, which causes the lack of capabilities required notice and consultation mechanism required in general platform; The OSPF neighbor state machine has the obvious protocol-correlation, that it contain complicated protocol data interactive action, which does not meet the demands of universality in general routing protocol.

2.2 BGP Neighbor State Machine

BGP is the most widely used inter-domain routing protocol. Its neighbors usually are not adjacent, so it can't through automatic discovery technologies such as multicast, but rather through configuration specified. By the same reason, message interaction of the BGP neighbor can only through point-to-point communication. In order to guarantee the reliability of the cross-domain message interaction, each pair of BGP neighbors establish a TCP connection. So the BGP neighbor state machine contains the session management process. The conversion process is shown in Fig. 3.

BGP create neighbor relationships according to the IP address of neighbor in configurations. In the beginning of the creation, state of all neighbor is Idle, which is the Initial state like Down state in OSPF. After that TCP connect request is sent to the neighbor and neighbor state goes into Connect. If the TCP connection is established successfully, neighbor goes into a temporarily state of Active. And then Open unsolicited messages, switch to Open Send state at the same time. Then the neighbor enter a state of time waiting for the Open message the counterpart sent. When it done, the neighbor enter OpenConfirm state and begin process of Open message authentication and negotiation ability. Finally, neighbor state machine goes into the steady state of Establish denotes session is ready, message interaction can be undertaken.

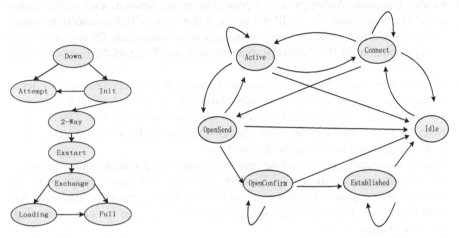

Fig. 2. OSPF neighbor state machine

Fig. 3. BGP neighbor state machine

As a result of the BGP neighbor state machine [7] protocol independence, it is closer to the general routing protocol platform from the function needed. However, there exist one drawback: it does not include the neighbor discovery process. This is due to the nature of inter-domain routing protocols of BGP. And general routing protocol platform provide the basis of service for all kinds of routing protocols. So it should have two mechanisms of neighbor discovery and configuration at the same time, and the state machine should also be compatible with two types of neighbors.

3 Neighbor Management

The functions of general routing protocol platform are different from any traditional routing protocols, so it is necessary to design a kind of neighbor management mechanism suitable for general routing protocol platform. Also, in order to do this, the first thing is to find out what kind of functions needs to be done by neighbor management mechanism.

3.1 General Routing Protocol Platform Feature Set

According the introduction, general routing protocol platform is essentially general part of the traditional routing protocols. It complete basic feature set for routing protocols that existed and created in future. This feature set should at least include the following functions.

(1) The neighbor management. Almost all routing protocols need to maintain their neighbors. In the general routing protocol platform, neighbors can be divided into physical neighbor and protocols one to the properties. Physical neighbor is physical adjacent neighbors, has nothing to do with the protocol; while protocol neighbor is related to the protocol.

(2) Establish Session. Although not all protocols require session, such as the traditional OSPF is based on the IP datagram, rather than a TCP connection, using session is relatively safe and easy to manage data interaction. Of course, it will weaken functions of the traditional protocol, such as relying on the function of the multicast.

(3) Message interaction. Message interaction is required by every protocol. General routing protocol platform of data transmission is not dependent on the session connection type, which can be through any type of connection (TCP, SSH, Netconf) to transmit data and can also be practical UDP such connection-less protocol, although we normally do not do so.

In addition, mature general routing protocol platform may contain more functions, such as the topology discovery, flooding, Qos, etc. The more general platform provide, the less protocol application needs to do. Ideally, the only need to do for routing protocol is calculating routing, he rest are all done by general routing protocol platform.

3.2 Neighbor Management Function Set

As mentioned in Sect. 3.1, neighbor management functions set includes the following parts:

(1) Discovery physical adjacent neighbors by sending multicast detecting packets (Hello) to each UP port.

(2) Establish Session to each physical neighbor and protocol one.

(3) Notice Abilities.

(4) Message interaction.

(5) State machine.

3.3 Neighbor Management Mechanism Process Description

3.3.1 Physical Neighbor Discovery

Like most traditional routing protocols, common routing protocol platforms' physical neighbor discovery based on multicast technology. Starting the platform router, all the ports with enabled IP are added to a specific IP group after start the platform router, and then from each port periodically sends probe packets Hello Packet carries its own port IP address to the specific IP group.

If the session setup fails, then router return to the initial state, waiting to be a new round neighbor discovery [8] process. After a session is established, two sides began the Capability Negotiation Process. Mutual transmit Capability Packets. Any error is able to make the session disconnected, looking forward to rediscover neighbors. Router received the Capability Packets select function set or version number information used to ensure that the other side can understand the after packets.

In addition, the physical neighbor relationships disconnection occur in the physical adjacency lift off due to the session disconnection, Keep-Alive Packets waiting time-out or other error conditions.

3.3.2 Logical Neighbor Management

In addition to physical adjacency neighbor, generic routing protocol also requires a logical neighbor management, including configuration neighbors and protocol neighbors. Configure neighbors specified by user interface or configuration file specifies; protocol neighbors are neighbors specified by upper layer protocol application. Both protocols are based on the neighbor address, with no discovery process. However, in order to ensure configuration consistency, it still need Hello to prior consultations. Session start to be established only after received the other side's Hello Packets. So besides sending Hello function (physical neighbor used multicast, logical neighbor used point-to-point), there are no difference between logical neighbor management and physical neighbor management.

Conditions of logical neighbor lifting due to the configuration changes or protocol need (or no longer need), besides session disconnected, Keep-Alive packets timeout, other errors. A logical neighbor relationship may be referenced in tables

Table 1. Neighbor state actions list

Events	Description
Start	Protocol start, triggered by configuration or command
RecvHello	Receive Hello message, Discover neighbors
HelloTimeOut	Wait for the Hello timeout
RecvOpen	Create session
OpenFailed	Create session failed
OpenSuccess	Create session successfully
RecvCap	Receive Capability Notice message
CapTimeOut	Wait for the Capability Notice timeout
BadCap	Ability negotiated failed
Closed	Close session
Stop	Protocol Down

Many ways, logical neighbor need to introduce the "reference counting", identifies the neighbor relationship account of current protocol. When releasing the neighbor relationship needs to determine neighbor reference count, only when the reference count equal to 0(no longer referenced) neighbor relationship really lifted, otherwise just decremented the count.

Table 2. Neighbor state list

States	Description
Idle	Initial state of Neighbors, shared by all neighbors
HelloSend	State after Hello sending, waiting for the Hello from counterpart. Shared by neighbors directed connect to the same interface
Open	State of create session
CapSend	State after Capability Notice sending, waiting for the Capability Notice from counterpart
Establish	Prepared

Table 3. Neighbor state machine table.

Current state	Events	Actions	Next state
Idle	StartTimer	Send Hello	HelloSend
	Others	Discard	Idle
HelloSend	RecvHello	Open Session	Open
	HelloTimeOut	Send Hello	HelloSend
	RecvOpen	Accept	Open
	Others	Discard	Idle
Open	OpenSuccess	Send Capability	CapSend
	OpenFailed	Clear Info	Idle
	Others	Clear Info	Idle
CapSend	RecvCap	Judge Capability	Establish
	CapTimeOut	Close Session	Idle
	BadCap	Close Session	Idle
	Others	Close Session	Idle
Establish	Others	Close Session	Idle

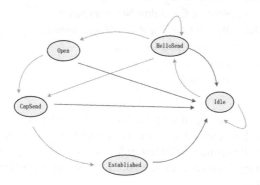

Fig. 4. Neighbor state machine graph

3.4 Neighbor State Machine Design

First, determine the set of events. Table 1 probably listed all kinds of events may occur during neighbor management process. These events will result in the switching operation and the corresponding state machine (Action).

According to the previous section, the status during neighbor discovery and management process can be determined. Table 2 lists these states and their descriptions. Table 3 and Fig. 4 illustrate a state transition diagram and its operations. Based on this description, it is easy to implement common routing protocol neighbor management system platform.

3.5 State Machine Based on a One-Way Session

The state machine in previous section is based on a full-duplex peer sessions such as TCP, but there are a lot of non-equivalence two-way or one-way session that can't work in accordance with the above state machine. Such as Netconf, SSH, HTTP. They are all client-server (c/s) architecture sessions, the server generally can't take the initiative to send a message to the client, which undermines the thought of full-duplex peer.

In general, what common routing protocol platform needs is a logical peer session, namely sessions entity has the same status that all can take the initiative to send messages and receive messages. C/S structure itself is unequal, the server generally can't take the initiate to make connections to the client, even some protocol server can't take the initiative to send a message, it can't be directly used for routing protocol neighbor session of general-purpose platform. A solution to this problem is to use a couple of sessions to simulate two-way conversation. These two sessions are logically equivalent to one pair of peer session. Because in this case, to coordinate the state of the session, Open state of the state machine in previous section will become complicated. At least it should be splited into two states: SendOpen and RevcOpen. At this point, SendOpen and RecvOpen represent the state of that a one-way connection is established. When two-way connections are established the status goes to CapSend; if connection fails in one direction, the other direction should be disconnected, the neighbor falls back to the Idle state waiting for rediscovery.

In addition, the second solution is to use long session and two-way dialogue, which require the support of session protocol. Many C/S structure sessions support long connection, such as HTTP (1. 1), SSH. Netconf. However, it is not enough that a long connection, the server must also be able to take the initiative to send a message to the client. Netconf is RPC-based, its server can't take the initiative to send messages to the client except Notification message, and we can't carry the data in the Notification either, it would become very strange. Thus Netconf can only use the way of pair-session.

As for the protocol such like HTTP(1.1) and SSH which can use peer sessions, you can just use only one non-equivalence session to simulate peer sessions. At this point the state machine does not need any changes, but both sides should select specific ways to receive and send messages in the realization, since two sides of the non-equivalence session use different ways to receive and send messages normally.

3.6   Add a Driver Layer for the Session

The neighbor session management based on the one-way session in previous section makes the development of common routing protocol platform become complicated. In many cases one routing platform does not support a specific kind of conversation, which leads to the change of state or conversational mode, eventually leading to the reconstruction of the entire platform. This problem can be solved by coupling: Creating the drive layer for the session management in session management. The drive layer provides an abstraction interface to establish a session, send messages, shut down the interface session and register the event handler that can accept connection, receive messages and accept close. Neighbor management module requires only a fixed state machine, and it is the drive layer that is responsible for the specific session implement. Different drivers for different types of sessions. In this way, the implement of neighbor state machine and session management implementation is not based on one specific session. Even the type of session has been changed, the neighbor state machine and session management don't need to do any change.

4   Instance

4.1   Instance System

In order to verify the effectiveness of the neighbor management mechanism in general routing protocol platform, this paper implements a general routing protocol platform based on the Quagga. The platform establish the driver layer for sessions as described in Sect. 3.6. The driver layer use Netconf connection and TCP connection. It exposes a simple registration, cancellation, send data interface and receive data event handlers to the upper level protocol. We implemented a simple protocol applications with function of sending and receiving data and writing routing information through the interaction with Zebra module. To test the effectiveness of the neighbor discovery and message interaction function.

4.2   Test Environment

Test topology is shown in Fig. 5.

4.3   Test Method

Through to the topology of the router start-stop, observe the neighbor discovery and message interaction is normal or not, to determine the effectiveness of the proposed function. This paper will use the Netconf and TCP session, in the process of testing randomly stop some port to test the robustness of the neighbor management. At the same time, in order to test performance of neighbor management based on general routing protocol platform, this paper also test time of neighbor discovery and session established. Which is between protocol start to neighbor sessions established.

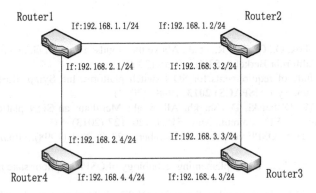

Fig. 5. Test environment topology

4.4   Results

As the result, neighbor management mechanism based on the two kinds of session of Netconf and TCP in general routing protocol platform is working properly. Neighbor discovery and session establish time contrast as shown in Fig. 6.

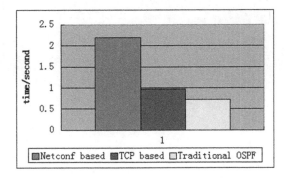

Fig. 6. Time consumption of neighbor management machine

5   Conclusion

This paper describes a kind of neighbor management mechanism applicable to general routing protocol platform, and presents its implementation based on Quagga. After tests, it works basically normal, and does not make more consumption than traditional routing protocols. Therefore it can be used as a standard mechanism model of general routing protocol platform in the future. However, details in the neighbor state machine have yet to be optimized, and function of the implementation of general routing protocol platform for test is simple and less efficient, that the mechanism can't be tested under a higher demand. These are the focuses of the next research work.

Acknowledgment. This work was supported by the National Natural Science Foundation of China (Grant No. 61471055).

References

1. Armbrust, M., Fox, O., Griffith, R., et al.: Above the clouds: a view of cloud computing. Eecs Dept. Univ. California Berkeley **53**(4), 50–58 (2009)
2. Hata, H.: A study of requirements for SDN switch platform. Int. Symp. IEEE Intell. Sign. Proces. Commun. Syst. (ISPACS) **2013**, 79–84 (2013)
3. Banikazemi, M., Olshefski, D., Shaikh, Ali, et al.: Meridian: an SDN platform for cloud network services. IEEE Commun. Mag. **51**(2), 120–127 (2013)
4. Moy, J.: RFC 2328: OSPF version 2, txt?number = 2328, 28:1 (1998). http://www.ietf.org/rfc/rfc2328
5. Zhou, J.L., Wang, Z.H.: The implementing technology of OSPF neighbor state machine. Mod. Comput. (2003)
6. Xiao, Y.J., Shi, R.H.: Design and realization of OSPF neighbor state machine based on TMS architecture. J. Changsha Telecommun. Technol. Vocat. Coll. (2005)
7. Rekhter, Y., Lougheed, K.: Border Gateway Protocol (BGP). Rfc T. J. Watson Research Center IBM Corp, vol. 19(8), pp. 3–4 (1990)
8. Qiu, X., Wu, C., Lin, X., et al.: InstantLeap: fast neighbor discovery in P2P VoD streaming. In: Proceedings of International Workshop on Network & Operating Systems Support for Digital Audio & Video. ACM (2009)

A General Rating Recommended Weight-Aware Model for Recommendation System

Haihong E, Yusheng Li[✉], Xuejun Zhao[✉],
Meina Song[✉], and Junde Song[✉]

PCN & CAD Center Laboratory, Beijing University of Posts
and Telecommunications, Xitucheng Road. 10, Beijing 100876, China
{ehaihong, liyuxing, zhaoxuejun,
mnsong, jdsong}@bupt.edu.cn

Abstract. In recommendation system, the ratings represent the users' preference and play an important role in recommending items to users. However, the ratings of items may be influenced by many factors, such as time (the latest ratings are more able to reflect the user's current preferences), user familiarity (the more familiar a user to an item, the more reliable of rating he gives). So ratings should have different recommended weights in different circumstances. However, current recommendation algorithms ignore this problem and use the ratings indiscriminately, this affecting the accuracy of the recommendation system. In this paper, we proposed a general rating recommended weight-aware model, which can fuse all kinds of recommended weights naturally for item recommendation. We design a new rating weight-aware probability matrix factorization model, which can assign recommended weight to every rating to obtain precise recommendations. We conduct comprehensive experiments using the real-world datasets. Experimental results show that the rating-aware recommendation model outperforms state-of-the-art latent factor models with a significant margin.

Keywords: Recommendation systems · Probability matrix factorization · Time span rating recommended weight-aware model · User familiarity recommended weight-aware model

1 Introduction

Recommender systems are powerful tools helping on-line users to leverage information overload by providing personalized recommendations [1]. Collaborative filtering (CF) and content-based techniques are two widely adopted approaches for recommendation systems. Collaborative filtering [2, 3] recommends items for a given user by referencing item ratings from other similar users, while content-based techniques [4] make recommendations by matching a user's personal interests (or profiles) with item content (e.g., item description or tags). Some research works have also discussed approaches that integrate both techniques for item recommendation [5].

© Springer International Publishing Switzerland 2016
Q. Zu and B. Hu (Eds.): HCC 2016, LNCS 9567, pp. 81–91, 2016.
DOI: 10.1007/978-3-319-31854-7_8

In recommender system, the ratings which users given to items play an important role in item recommendation. The rating usually is a five-point integer scale to express the degree of favorability to each item (normally, 1, 2, 3, 4 and 5 represent "hate", "do not like", "neutral", "like", and "love", respectively). Generally speaking, the ratings given by the people who are familiar with the items are more reliable. In our real life, when we want to get some advice, we not only consider the advice itself, but also consider the background of the person who provides the advice. For example, if the advice provider is an expert in the related fields, we will pay more attention to his opinion, otherwise, the advice is very little influenced by our decision. On the other hand, the impact of time on the ratings is obviously. Users' interest will change as time goes by, so the recent ratings can reflect the users' current interest better.

The above analysis shows that the time span and user familiarity have great impact on the ratings, the impact should be reflected by different recommendation weights: latest ratings and the ratings given by more familiarity user should have greater recommended weights. However, no emphasis has been placed on those problems in most recommender system works. Obviously, taking the ratings recommended weights into consideration in recommender system could improve the recommendation, however, it also bring many great challenges. The first challenge is how to model the time and user familiarity, so that each rating can get a recommended weight. After that, how to integrate the recommended weights to the recommendation model is another challenge.

To address those challenge, in this paper, we propose a new general rating recommended weight-aware recommendation model, and then apply this model to capture the effects of time span and user familiar on the recommended weights. We modified the PMF model to integration rating recommended weights. The experimental results on real-world dataset demonstrate the advantages of our model over competitive baseline algorithms on rating prediction.

2   Related Work

2.1   Tag Based Collaborative Filtering

Nakamoto, etc. [9] proposed a tag-based contextual CF by using the overlaps of tags. The authors constructed two models for combining CF and tagging systems at different stages in the recommendation process. However, the system may have problems if there is not sufficient reuse of tags for users. In Ji, etc. [10] the authors used tags to find similar users in order to form candidate tag set (CTS) for each user, and then they designed a novel approach of recommendation systems with collaborative tagging based on CTS. The authors [11] proposed to integrate tags in recommender systems by first extending the user-item matrix and then applying an algorithm that fuses two popular RS algorithms such that the correlations between users, items and tags can be captured simultaneously. They designed a generic mechanism that allowed tags to be integrated into standard CF. Bogers and Bosch [12] applied three different collaborative filtering algorithms in CiteULike for recommending scientific articles to users, and found that user-based CF performed best in CiteULike. A tag-based collaborative filtering (TBCF) was proposed, improving the effectiveness of neighbor selection based on semantic distance among tags assigned by different users, two users could be considered similar not only if they rated the items similarly, but also if they have similar cognitions over these items. WordNet was introduced to calculate the semantic similarity between two tags.

2.2 Time Based Collaborative Filtering

Some work is carried out to investigate time information in recommendations. The authors incorporated temporal information such as the user's purchase time and the item's launch time in order to increase recommendation accuracy. Two piecewise rating functions to compute the weights based on temporal information were proposed. The authors used exponential time decay function to compute time weights for different items according to each user and each cluster of items. Then used this time decay function in the phase of preference prediction in item-based collaborative filtering. However, in another important phase: similarity computation phase, the time affects is not reflected in compute the similarity between two users or items. The similarity between two users also changes as time goes by.

Unlike most of the above works which used tag or time information at different stages in the recommendation process to improve the recommendation accuracy, in this paper we modified the PMF algorithm to obtain a novel general model, this model is a rating recommended weight-aware model, which can be used to model any situation that affect the rating recommended weight.

3 Rating Recommended Weight-aware Model

In this section, we introduce our approach to incorporate recommended weight in a new probabilistic model for precise recommendation. We first introduce a general Rating Recommended Weight-aware Model (RRWM), then, further exploit this general model used on time span and user familiar.

3.1 General Rating Recommended Weight-aware Model

General rating recommended weight-aware model is a modified probabilistic matrix factorization model. Suppose we have M users and N items. Let $R \in \Re^{M \times N}$ be the user-item rating matrix and r_{ij} be the rating of user u_i for item i_j. $U \in \Re^{D \times M}$ and $V \in \Re^{D \times N}$ represent the D-dimensional user- and item-specific latent feature vectors, respectively (both U_i and V_j are column vectors in this paper). The conditional distribution over the observed ratings R is as follows:

$$p(R \mid U, V, \omega_{ij}, \sigma^2) = \prod_{i=1}^{M} \prod_{j=1}^{N} [N(r_{ij} \mid f(U_i, V_j, \omega_{ij}), \sigma^2)]^{I_{ij}} \tag{1}$$

where $N(x \mid \mu, \sigma^2)$ is the probability density function of the Gaussian distribution with mean μ and variance σ, and I_{ij} is the indicator variable that is equal to one if user u_i rated item i_j and equal to zero if otherwise. The function $f(x)$ is used to approximate the rating for item i_j by user u_i. w_{ij} is the recommended weight of the rating r_{ij}. By considering the rating recommended weights in recommendation, we define $f(x)$ as follows:

$$f(U_i, V_j, w_{ij}) = (1 + \alpha W(w_{ij}) \cdot g(U_i^T V_j)) \tag{2}$$

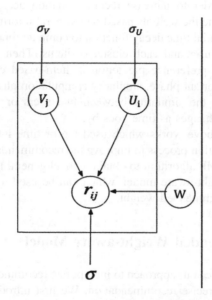

Fig. 1. Graphical model for RRWM

where $W(w_{ij})$ is a rating weight function that measures the rating recommended weight for the rating r_{ij}, is a parameter which controls the impact of the rating recommended weights. $g(x)$ is the logistic function $g(x) = 1/(1 + \exp(-x))$, which makes it possible to bound the range of $U_i^T V_j$ with the range [0, 1]. We also exploit the zero-mean spherical Gaussian prior on user and item latent feature vectors:

$$p(U \mid \sigma_U^2) = \prod_{i=1}^{M} N(U_i \mid 0, \sigma_U^2 I)$$

$$p(V \mid \sigma_V^2) = \prod_{j=1}^{N} N(V_j \mid 0, \sigma_V^2 I) \tag{3}$$

As show in Fig. 1, we obtain the following by using a Bayesian inference

$$p(U, V \mid R, w_{ij}, \sigma^2, \sigma_U^2, \sigma_V^2) \propto p(R \mid U, V, w_{ij}, \sigma^2)p(U \mid \sigma_U^2)p(V \mid \sigma_V^2)$$

$$= \prod_{i=1}^{M} \prod_{j=1}^{N} [N(r_{ij} \mid f(U_i, V_j, w_{ij}, \sigma^2))]^{I_{ij}} \times \prod_{i=1}^{M} N(U_i \mid 0, \sigma_U^2 I) \times \prod_{j=1}^{N} N(V_j \mid 0, \sigma_V^2 I) \quad (4)$$

U, V can be learned by maximizing the posterior or log-posterior over the user and item features with fixed hyperparameters (i.e. the observation noise variance and prior variance). By using Eq. (4), we can determine that the RRWM model is actually an enhanced general model of PMF that takes rating recommended weight into consideration. In other words, if we limit $\alpha = 0$, the RRWM model will become a PMF model. On the basis of Fig. 1, the log of the posterior distribution in Eq. (4) is expressed as follows:

$$\ln p(U, V \mid R, w_{ij}, \sigma^2, \sigma_U^2, \sigma_V^2) = -\frac{1}{2\sigma^2} \sum_{i=1}^{M} \sum_{j=1}^{N} I_{ij}(r_{ij} - f(U_i, V_j, w_{ij}))^2$$

$$- \frac{1}{2\sigma_U^2} \sum_{i=1}^{M} U_i^T U_i - \frac{1}{2\sigma_V^2} \sum_{j=1}^{N} V_j^T V_j - \frac{1}{2} [(\sum_{i=1}^{M} \sum_{j=1}^{N} I_{ij}) \ln \sigma^2 \quad (5)$$

$$+ MD \ln \sigma_U^2 + ND \ln \sigma_V^2] + C$$

Where C is a constant that does not depend on the parameters. Maximizing the log-posterior over user and item latent features is equivalent to minimizing the following sum-of-squared-errors objective function with quadratic regularized terms in Eq. (6):

$$E = \frac{1}{2} \sum_{i=1}^{M} \sum_{j=1}^{N} I_{ij}(r_{ij} - f(U_i, V_j, w_{ij}))^2 + \frac{\lambda_U}{2} \sum_{i=1}^{M} ||U_i||_F^2 + \frac{\lambda_V}{2} \sum_{j=1}^{N} ||V_j||_F^2 \quad (6)$$

where $\lambda_U = \sigma^2/\sigma_U^2$, $\lambda_V = \sigma^2/\sigma_V^2$ and $|| \cdot ||_F^2$ denotes the Frobenius norm. A local minimum of the objective function given by Eq. (6) can be obtained by performing gradient descent in U_i and V_j:

$$\frac{\partial E}{\partial U_i} = \sum_{j=1}^{N} I_{ij}((1 + \alpha W(w_{ij}))g(U_i^T V_j) - r_{ij})g'(U_i^T V_j) \cdot (1 + \alpha W(w_{ij}))V_j + \lambda_U U_i$$

$$\frac{\partial E}{\partial V_j} = \sum_{i=1}^{N} I_{ij}((1 + \alpha W(w_{ij}))g(U_i^T V_j) - r_{ij})g'(U_i^T V_j) \cdot (1 + \alpha W(w_{ij}))U_i + \lambda_V V_j \quad (7)$$

where $g'(\cdot)$ is the first-order derivative of the logistic function $g'(x) = \exp(x)/(1 + \exp(x))^2$. In order to reduce the model complexity, in all of the experiments we conduct in Sect. 4, we set $\lambda_U = \lambda_V$.

3.2   Time Span Rating Recommended Weight-aware Model

Generally speaking, the time when each user rated each item is different. The primary motivation behind this time span rating recommended weight-aware strategy is the fact that human interests drift as time goes by, which has been Demonstrated [6]. Most work on interest drifts uses either time window or forgetting functions to learn and track the changes of user's behavior as time passes. The exponential forgetting function is widely used in temporal applications to measure concept drifts to gradually discount the history of past behavior [7]. The exponential forgetting function is defined as follows:

$$W(w_{ij}) = \exp\{-\ln 2 * time(\mu_i, i_j) / hl_{\mu_i}\} \tag{8}$$

where $W(w_{ij})$ is the time weight denoting the degree a user's interests have declined to, $time(\mu_i, i_j)$ is a non-negative integer, it sets to be 0 if the rating day of item i_j is the last tagging day of a user u_i and sets to be 1 for the penultimate rating day of the same user, and so on, it remains the same for the same rating day. hl_{u_i} represents the half-life for each user, which adapts to each user's life circle. For users with a large hl_{u_i}, that is they have a long life span in rating behaviors, their interests will fall slowly; while for users with a small hl_{u_i}, that is they have a short life span in rating behaviors, their interests will fall quickly. When $time(u_i, i_j) = hl_{u_i}$, $W(w_{ij})$ falls to 1/2. For a given user, $time(u_i, i_j)$ is smaller when the rating time is closer to the recent rating time. Consequently, a higher time weight value will be given to a more recent rating, while an old rating will be assigned with a lower value. In this way, users' current interests could be detected by time span rating recommended weight strategy. Next, we use Eq. (8) to calculate the recommended weight values for each user ratings. Finally, replace the rating weight function $W(w_{ij})$ in Eq. (2) with formula (8). In this way, we can assign time span rating recommended weight to the general model to obtain a time span rating recommended weight model (tRRWM).

3.3   User Familiarity Rating Recommended Weight-aware Model

In a recommender system, items can be rated across multiple fields by users with varying degrees of familiarity. Hence, the ratings in a recommender system should have different recommended weights. Based on the assumption that a user is more likely familiar with the resources which the tags of high usage by him. We use tagging information to build the user-familiarity model and item feature vector model.

User-familiarity Vector: Suppose the tag set of user-marked items is $T = \{t_1, t_2, \cdots, t_L\}$, where L is the number of tags. We then define the user $\bar{u}_i$ familiarity vector $\bar{u}_i$ as follows:

$$\bar{u}_i = (\frac{s_i(t_1)}{n_{u_i}} \omega(t_1), \frac{s_i(t_2)}{n_{u_i}} \omega(t_2), \cdots \frac{s_i(t_L)}{n_{u_i}} \omega(t_L)) \tag{9}$$

n_{u_i} means total number of tags that the user u_i used. $s_i(t_k)$ means the times of the user u_i marked tag t_k. $s_i(t_k)/n_{u_i}$ means the proportion of the user u_i marked tags t_k to total tags. We use TF-IDF method to calculate weight $\omega(t_k)$, and the calculating formula is as: $\omega(t_k) = \log M/n_{t_k}$, here M is the total number of users, n_{t_k} is the total number of users who have used tag t_k, and this formula shows the importance of tag is proportional to the times of it appears of marked products, and is inversely proportional to the frequency of it appears in tags storehouse. $s_i(t_k)/n_{u_i}\omega(t_k)$ shows the importance of the tag t_k to the user u_i.

Item Feature Vector: Defining item i_j feature vector $\bar{i}_j$ is as:

$$\bar{i}_j = (\frac{s_j(t_1)}{m_{i_j}}\omega(t_1), \frac{s_j(t_2)}{m_{i_j}}\omega(t_2), \cdots \frac{s_j(t_L)}{m_{i_j}}\omega(t_L)) \tag{10}$$

m_{i_j} means the total number of tags assigned to item i_j, $s_j(t_k)$ means the times of item i_j assigned by tag t_k, $s_j(t_k)/m_{i_j}$ means the proportion of the item i_j marked by tag t_k to total tags. Similarly to user familiar vector, we use TF-IDF method to calculate weight $w(t_k) = \log N/n_{t_k}$, here N is the total number of items, n_{t_k} is the total number of items which have been assigned by tag t_k, shows the importance of the tag t_k to the item i_j.

We defined the user $\bar{u}_i$ familiarity degree to item $\bar{i}_j$ is:

$$W(\omega_{ij}) = \frac{\bar{u}_i \cdot \bar{i}_j}{X} \tag{11}$$

where X refers to the maximum value of the familiarity degree values.

Finally, we replace the rating weight function $W(\omega_{ij})$ in Eq. (2) with formula (11) as user familiarity recommended weight model and obtained the user familiarity rating recommended weight model (uRRWM).

4 Experimental Results and Analysis

4.1 Data Description

The experiments are based on one of the datasets given by the fifth ACM Conference on Recommender Systems (RecSys 2011). This dataset is an extension of the MovieLens dataset, which contains personal ratings, timestamp, tags, and tag assignments to movies. This data set contains 855598 ratings, 855598 timestamp and 9079 tags added to 10109 movies by 2113 users of the online movie recommender service MovieLens. The statistics of the dataset are summarized in Table 1.

Table 1. MovieLens Dataset Analysis

Users	2113	The number of users who used tags	2113
Movies	10109	The number of movies which assigned by tags	5908
Tags	9079	Average number of ratings by one user	405
Ratings	855598	Average number of tags assigned by one user	23
Timestamp	855598	Average number of tags assigned to one movie	8

4.2   Evaluation Metrics

The root mean square error (RMSE) is used to measure the prediction quality in comparison with the benchmark collaborative filtering methods, the RMSE is defined as:

$$RMSE = \sqrt{\frac{\sum_{i,j}\left(r_{i,j} - \hat{r}_{i,j}\right)^2}{N}}$$

where r_{ij} denotes the rating of item i_j by user u_i, $\hat{r}_{ij}$ denotes the corresponding rating predicted by the model, and N denotes the number of tested ratings.

4.3   Experiments Results

(1) Comparison Algorithm and Parameter Setting: The performance improvement of our algorithm is shown by comparing our algorithm with the top-performing recommendation algorithms, including Probabilistic Matrix Factorization (PMF) [8] and Singular Value Decomposition (SVD). Both of the two algorithms only use user-item rating matrix and uses the ratings indiscriminately for recommendations. For the PMF algorithm, we empirically specify the parameters as: $\lambda_U = \lambda_V = 0.05$. For tRRWM and uRRWM model, we used the same value for $\lambda_U = \lambda_V = 0.05$ and specify $\alpha = 5$. The dimension of the latent feature vectors D is 20.

(2) Performance Comparisons and Analysis: We use different amount of training data (99 %, 80 %, 50 %, 20 %, and 10 %) to test all the algorithms. For example, for the 99 % training data, we randomly select 99 % of the ratings from the MovieLens dataset as the training data to predict the remaining 1 % of ratings. The experimental results are shown in Table 2.

Table 2. MovieLens DataSet RMSE comparison

Training data	SVD	PMF	tRRWM	uRRWM
10 %	0.8531	0.7131	0.7058	0.7068
20 %	0.8337	0.7122	0.6811	0.6855
50 %	0.8142	0.7087	0.6042	0.6014
80 %	0.7989	0.7015	0.8534	0.5767
99 %	0.7881	0.6950	0.5780	0.5707

Table 2 shows that our rating weight-aware approach outperforms the other methods. On average, the tRRWM approach improves the accuracy by 22.88 % and 10.71 % relative to SVD and PMF, the uRRWM approach improves the accuracy by 23.16 % and 11.03 % relative to SVD and PMF, respectively. The improvements are significant, thus indicating the promising future of our rating recommended weight-aware recommendation approach.

We also notice that when many ratings are present in the training data sets, the more timestamp and user familiarity information will be used to improve recommendation performance. Hence, the proposed model will perform better than SVD and PMF when many ratings are observed.

(3) Impact of Parameter α: The main advantage of our recommendation approach is that it incorporates rating weights information, which helps in improving the prediction accuracy. In our model, parameter α balances the information from the ratings and rating recommended weights. If α = 0, we only mine the user-item rating matrix for matrix factorization; if α = inf we depend heavily on the recommended weights to predict the preferences of users. In other cases, we fuse ratings and rating recommended weights for probabilistic matrix factorization and to predict the ratings for active users.

Figures 2 and 3 show the effects of α on RMSE. We observe that the value of α has a significant effect on the recommendation results, thus indicating that fusing the rating

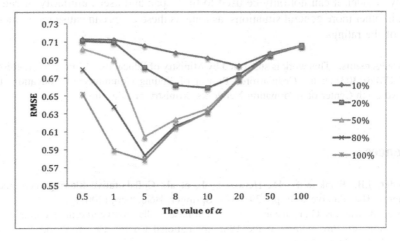

Fig. 2. The impact of parameter α in tRRWM model

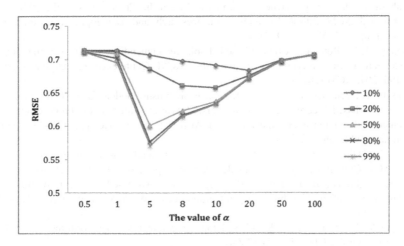

Fig. 3. The impact of parameter α in uRRWM model

recommended weights greatly improves recommendation accuracy. When α increases, the prediction accuracy also increases, however, after passing a certain threshold ($\alpha = 5$), the prediction accuracy decreases with the increasing value of α. This phenomenon coincides with the intuition that using the user-item rating matrix or over reliance on the recommended weights cannot generate a better performance than fusing these two resources together.

5 Conclusion

This research propose a probabilistic generative model, which naturally unifies the weights in the recommendation process. The experimental results show that the models proposed in this paper achieve a superior recommendation performance. Our model is a generative model, it can not only be used to time span and user familiarity, it can also be used in other more general situations, as long as these cases can cause recommended weighs of the ratings.

Acknowledgements. This work is supported by Ministry of Education - China Mobile Research Fund (MCM20130311); the Cosponsored Project of Beijing Committee of Education; Engineering Research Center of Information Networks, Ministry of Education.

References

1. Schafer, J.B., Frankowski, D., Herlocker, J., et al.: Collaborative filtering recommender systems. The adaptive web, pp. 291–324. Springer, Heidelberg (2007)
2. Sarwar, B., Karypis, G., Konstan, J., et al.: Item-based collaborative filtering recommendation algorithms. In: Proceedings of the 10th International Conference on World Wide Web, pp. 285–295. ACM (2001)
3. Wang, J., De Vries, A.P., Reinders, M.J.T.: Unifying user-based and item-based collaborative filtering approaches by similarity fusion. In: Proceedings of the 29th Annual International ACM SIGIR Conference on Research and Development in Information Retrieval, pp. 501–508. ACM (2006)
4. Mooney, R.J., Roy, L.: Content-based book recommending using learning for text categorization. In: Proceedings of the Fifth ACM Conference on Digital Libraries, pp. 195–204. ACM (2000)
5. Popescul, A., Pennock, D.M., Lawrence, S.: Probabilistic models for unified collaborative and content-based recommendation in sparse-data environments. In: Proceedings of the Seventeenth Conference on Uncertainty in Artificial Intelligence, pp. 437–444. Morgan Kaufmann Publishers Inc. (2001)
6. Lathia, N., Hailes, S., Capra, L.: kNN CF: a temporal social network. In: Proceedings of the 2008 ACM Conference on Recommender Systems, pp. 227–234. ACM (2008)
7. Cheng, Y., Qiu, G., Bu, J., et al.: Model bloggers' interests based on forgetting mechanism. In: Proceedings of the 17th International Conference on World Wide Web, pp. 1129–1130. ACM (2008)
8. Deshpande, M., Karypis, G.: Item-based top-n recommendation algorithms. ACM Trans. Inf. Syst. (TOIS) **22**(1), 143–177 (2004)

9. Nakamoto, R., Nakajima, S., Miyazaki, J., et al.: Tag-based contextual collaborative filtering. In: Proceedings of the 18th IEICE Data Engineering Workshop (2007)
10. Ji, A.-T., Yeon, C., Kim, H.-N., Jo, G.-S.: Collaborative tagging in recommender systems. In: Orgun, M.A., Thornton, J. (eds.) AI 2007. LNCS (LNAI), vol. 4830, pp. 377–386. Springer, Heidelberg (2007)
11. Tso-Sutter, K.H.L., Marinho, L.B., Schmidt-Thieme, L.: Tag-aware recommender systems by fusion of collaborative filtering algorithms. In: Proceedings of the 2008 ACM Symposium on Applied Computing, pp. 1995–1999. ACM (2008)
12. Bogers, T., Van den Bosch, A.: Recommending scientific articles using CiteULike. In: Proceedings of the 2008 ACM Conference on Recommender Systems, pp. 287–290. ACM (2008)

Survey on Android Applications Security

Chengzhou Fu, Chang Huang, Yong Tang$^{(\boxtimes)}$, Weiquan Zeng,
Dahao Wang, and Chengzhe Yuan

School of Computer Science, South China Normal University,
Guangzhou 510631, Guangdong Province, China
{fucz,2013022023,ytang,zengwq,
lzwdh2010,yuanchengzhe}@m.scnu.edu.cn

Abstract. Android plays a paramount role in mobile internet era and it is an extremely comfortable operating system to deploy in mobile devices. More and more security problems have been taken place on Android devices, and lead to leak users' privilege information. In order to survey the security situation of Android application, we have downloaded 1901 Android APK files from the application market for study. We present several schemas to protect Android applications and avoid others to invade smartphones.

Keywords: Android · Decompile · Smali · Permission · Memory tamper

1 Introduction

Nowadays, smartphone has become an import tool in people's daily life such as basic features, social activities, entertainments. Due to the important role of the devices, there will be many problems while using the wrong method. We should offer several effective schemas for Android users to avoid suffering a loss.

At the beginning, Android operating system (OS) seems to be the most secure OS in mobile devices. According to our research, we found that the view is not so correct. There are quite a few serious security information leaks.

In this paper, we talk about how to make the Android OS safer for users to operate and protect their information stored in smartphones. We come to this conclusion that Android is not security in some function, but we can improve the situation with some comfort methods and technologies.

First we discuss the Android permission model [1] in Sect. 3. In Sect. 4 we describe the Smali [2] code and decompile technology. Then we show the example to tamper the memory value of Android devices in Sect. 5. Finally we present the schema for information communication security in Sect. 6.

2 Android System Architecture

As we know, Android is developed based on the open source project. The project was bought by Google Inc. from the open source union in 2007. The Android OS architecture is shown in Fig. 1. Android code is opened to public, so many individuals or organizations develop the third-party systems such as CyanogenMod, MIUI, and Nubia UI.

Q. Zu and B. Hu (Eds.): HCC 2016, LNCS 9567, pp. 92–103, 2016.
DOI: 10.1007/978-3-319-31854-7_9

Android architecture [3] contains four layers. The application layer is on the top, and the other three layers including application framework, Android runtime, and Linux kernel respectively. Linux kernel [4] is an abstraction of the hardware and software. Android runtime's is a core component of DVM [5] (Dalvik virtual machine). Each Android process runs in a separate instance of DVM. Every application is assigned with a private Linux user ID called UID. This functionality allows Dalvik to run multiple applications in a separate process. Those applications run in a single process, which is requested to share a single UID. In addition, each of these applications has a separate ID.

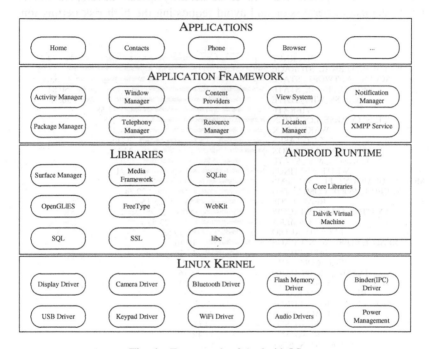

Fig. 1. Framework of Android OS

3 Permission Model

Android OS has become the most popular smartphone OS, more and more users choose the Android devices. This is a chance for Android technology developing, but meanwhile a challenge as well. The devices with that OS became a main target for hackers to invade.

Android platform has about 130 levels permission. Each application has its separate permissions configuration. The permission is based on three levels such as Normal, Dangerous and Signature: Normal level means that application can use the permission after applying; Dangerous level is a kind of permission which is harmful, it requires users' agreement when installed; Signature level needs to sign before accessing the permission.

According to our survey, we have summarized the permission condition from 1901 APKs which download from AppChina [6]. From Fig. 2, we can see the INTERNET permission is requested most frequently, which is more than 54 %. The result shows that most of the applications need to connect the network and communicate with other devices. There are also many applications apply for writing data to storage.

Particularly, the PHONE and SMS permission are extremely important to mobile devices. We found that 16.16 % of the applications require the CALL_PHONE permission. Both SEND_SMS and READ_SMS permissions are about 11 %. We suggest that mobile users may be careful when applications apply for those permissions. In view of the abuse of permission will cause security issues, developers should pay attention to the use of permission and avoid requesting the high risk permission.

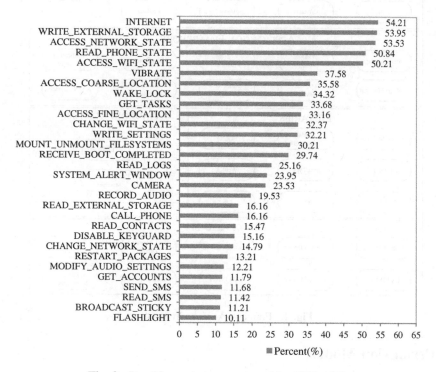

Fig. 2. Top 30 permissions requested by 1901 APKs

4 Smali Code and Android Decompile

For research the theory of the Android security environment and situation, we have developed a software platform to decompile the package of the Android applications which is based on the ApkTool [7] library. The screenshot of the software is shown in Fig. 3.

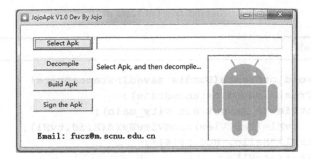

Fig. 3. Decompile tool screenshot

As Fig. 4 shows, the tool can convert the Dex file [8] to Smali code files. The Smali code can be tampered by intruders and then the tampering files will be repackaged to Android application files with the extension ".apk". That APK package can be installed to the devices the same as normal applications.

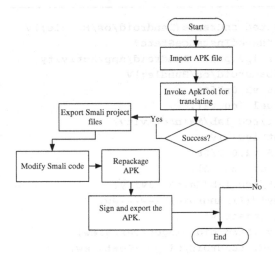

Fig. 4. Tamper and repackage the APK

If there is no schema to anti-tamper and the server will exchange information with the fake application. We can see what is highly dangerous while servers send the privilege message to the tampered application which runs in Android devices.

We have developed an application demo to introduce the way to modify the Smali code with decompiling tools. The *onCreate()* method of the main activity in Java class is shown in Table 1. Secondly, we translate the APK to Smali code is shown in Table 2. From the table we can see that the Smali code is just like assembly code, which was comprehended and able to tamper not particularly difficult by the invaders.

Table 1. Android Java onCreate method code

Android Java code

```
protected void onCreate(Bundle savedInstanceState) {
  super.onCreate(savedInstanceState);
  setContentView(R.layout.activity_main);
  TextView  tvHl=(TextView)findViewById(R.id.tvHl);
  String strHl="Hello, HCC 2016!";
  tvHl.setText(strHl);
}
```

Table 2. Android Smali code by decompile from APK

Android Smali code

```
.method protected onCreate(Landroid/os/Bundle;)V
  .parameter "savedInstanceState"
  invoke-super {p0,p1},  Landroid/app/Activity;
  ->onCreate(Landroid/os/Bundle;)V
  const/high16 v2,0x7f03
  invoke-virtual {p0,v2},
  Lcom/scholat/hcc_lab/MainActivity;
  ->setContentView(I)V
  const/high16 v2,0x7f08
  invoke-virtual {p0,v2},
  Lcom/scholat/hcc_lab/MainActivity;
  ->findViewById(I)Landroid/view/View;
  move-result-object v1
  check-cast v1,Landroid/widget/TextView;
  .local v1,tvHl:Landroid/widget/TextView;
  const-string v0,"Hello, HCC 2016!"
  .local v0,strHl:Ljava/lang/String;
  invoke-virtual {v1,v0},Landroid/widget/TextView;
  ->setText(Ljava/lang/CharSequence;)V
  return-void
.end method
```

As shown in Table 3, Vx values in the table denote a Dalvik register. Depending on the instruction, 16, 256 or 64 k registers can be accessed. Operations on long and double values use two registers (e.g. a double value addressed in the V0 register occupies the V0 and V1 registers).

Boolean values are stored as 1 for true and 0 for false. Operations on Booleans are translated into integer operations.

All the examples are given in Big-Endian format, "0F00 0A00" is coded as "0F, 00, 0A, 00" sequence. The Android opcode [9, 10] constant list is shown in Table 3.

Table 3. Partially Android Dalvik opcode

Opcode (hex)	Opcode name	Explanation	Example
6F	invoke-super	Invokes the virtual method of the immediate parent class.	6F10 A601 0100 invoke-super {v1},java.io.FilterOutputStream.close:()V // method@01a6 Invoking method@01a6 with one parameter v1.
15	const/high16	Puts the 16 bit constant into the topmost bits of the register. Used to initialize float values.	1500 2041 -const/high16 v0, #float 10.0 // #41200000 Moving the floating literal of 10.0 into v0. The 16 bit literal in the instruction carries the top 16 bits of the floating point number.
0C	move-result-object	Move the result object reference of the previous method invocation into vx.	0C00 -move-result-object v0
1F	check-cast	Checks whether the object reference in vx can be cast to an instance of a class referenced by type_id.	1F04 0100 -check-cast v4, HCCTest // type@0001 Checking whether the object reference in v4 can be cast to type@0001
1A	const-string	Puts reference to a string constant identified by string_id into vx.	1A08 0000 -const-string v8, "" // string@0000 Putting reference to string@0000.

As below, we give a sample to tamper the Smali code and repackage the Smali files to an Android application package. We tamper the value (const-string) "Hello, HCC 2016" to "Hello, CCF" in Smali file. After the operating, we install the APK to the virtual machine with Android OS. The screenshots are shown in Figs. 5 and 6.

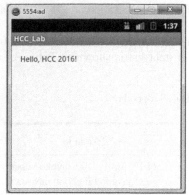

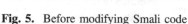

Fig. 5. Before modifying Smali code   **Fig. 6.** After modifying Smali code

We found that amount of the application APKs can be tampered the use of some technology. We download 1901 APKs from AppChina to support our study. We measured the percentage of APKs which were tampered successfully. The Fig. 7 shows that most of the Android APKs can be decompiled in a short time.

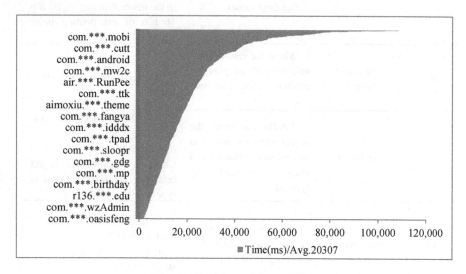

Fig. 7. Cost time of decompiling

For avoiding leaking the important information, we should protect the key code on security. In this section, we talk about a method of anti-decompile: writing core code in the Native Development Kit (NDK) file which is with the extension ".so". Using NDK technology, the core code is compiled into the dynamic library, and then invoke by Java Native Interface (JNI).

5 Memory Tampering

We have found that intruder can tamper the memory in Android [11] devices through proper tools easily such as Shaobing, Huluxia, and Bamenshenqi. Firstly, we try to find the address of the value which we desire to tamper, and we input the value what we should instead. Put the new value to address we have found before. As a result, we can see that the value which is shown of the screen has changed after we do the operations above.

Because there are so many equal values in memory, we might search so many addresses with one value at the first time searching process. If the count of value which we have found is too large for the tool to replace, we should try to change the value, and then find the address of the address again. After the operation, we can reduce the processing range, intending to tamper the value of memory more accuracy.

As the following screenshots in Fig. 8 and procedure in Fig. 9, the *Shaobing* tool running in Android device. At first, you may hook the application process to tamper. The tool will find the address in memory of the hooked application. After that, we input the new value to the filling box and press the *Modify* button, the tool will modify the memory to tamper the value which you want. As shown in Fig. 8, we tamper the price from ¥4998 to ¥19. If the server places an order without verifying, the hacker will buy the notebook at an inconceivable low price.

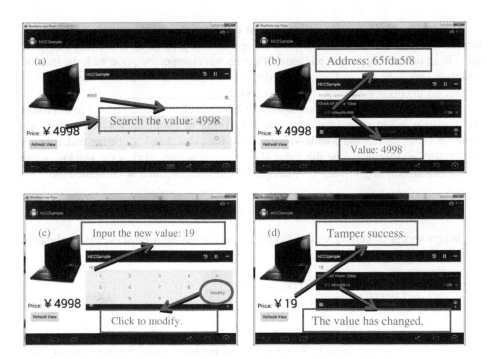

Fig. 8. Screenshots of tampering memory

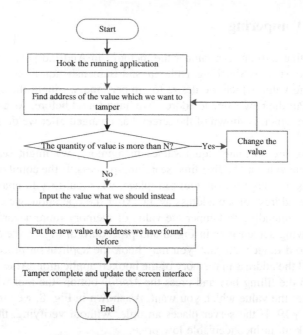

Fig. 9. Procedure of tampering memory

We can conclude that the android client can tamper the value easily according to our survey. This situation is so terrible for application product in commerce. Suppose there is an online shopping application. If the hackers tamper the price with the method which as shown above, and place an order at low price. There will be a huge negative impact on the normal operation of the software.

In this section, we present the implementation so-called Shadow-variable to protect the sensitive information from tampering. In order to avoid hackers to tamper the memory value, we use the double-value to store the value. Let V_{real} be the real value in application, and let V_{screen} be the value shown in the screen, $f(x)$ is the shadow value which calculation origin from x. A sample of the shadow value is computed as:

$$f(x) = \lfloor \sqrt{x^2 + x^3} \rfloor$$

When setting or getting values from memory in Android devices, the application must compare V_{screen} with V_{real}:

$$Convert_{Boolean} = \begin{cases} f(V_{real}) - f(V_{screen}) = 0 & T \\ f(V_{real}) - f(V_{screen}) \neq 0 & F \end{cases}$$

- If the $Convert_{Boolean}$ value is T, the value has not been tampered, we can judge the value as an original value;
- If the $Convert_{Boolean}$ value is F, the value has been tampered.

Here is the code for setting and getting value from mobile device memory as (Table 4):

Table 4. Java set-get code

Java set-get code

```
void setting(type value) {
    value_convert=Convert(value);
}
type getting(){
  if(Convert(value)==value_convert) {
   return value;
  }else{
   return NULL;
  }
}
```

6 Information Communication Security

Transferring the information between Android client and server is monitored easily if developers were not taking care of the security mechanisms. As Fig. 10 shows, we study how to transfer information security. Developers should encrypt the sensitive information on sending. Otherwise, if the whole information is encrypted, the process efficiency of application will be not so high. Consequently, we need to choose a strategy to process the information to keep it security.

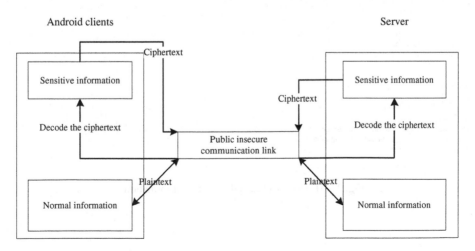

Fig. 10. Communication between Android client and server

In this section, we introduce the DES [12] (Data Encryption Standard) algorithm to exchange and store sensitive information. The DES was once a predominant symmetric-key algorithm for the encryption of electronic data. It was highly influential in the advancement of modern cryptography in academic world.

Here is the example for encrypting sensitive information. As you can see from Table 5, Java has a cipher class to implement the encryption and decryption algorithms. We set the key "HCCTest" and the cipher mode "DES".

Table 5. Encryption and decryption initialization code

Java code

```
Key key=getKey("HCCTest".getBytes("GB2312"));
Cipher en=Cipher.getInstance("DES/ECB/PKCS5Padding");
en.init(Cipher.ENCRYPT_MODE,key);
Cipher de=Cipher.getInstance("DES/ECB/PKCS5Padding");
de.init(Cipher.DECRYPT_MODE,key);
```

As shown in Fig. 11, after encrypting the data, it is still safe even if the information is stolen because hackers can hardly decipher encode text to original information. As we know, this operation will stretch the text and waste more bandwidth for transferring redundancy.

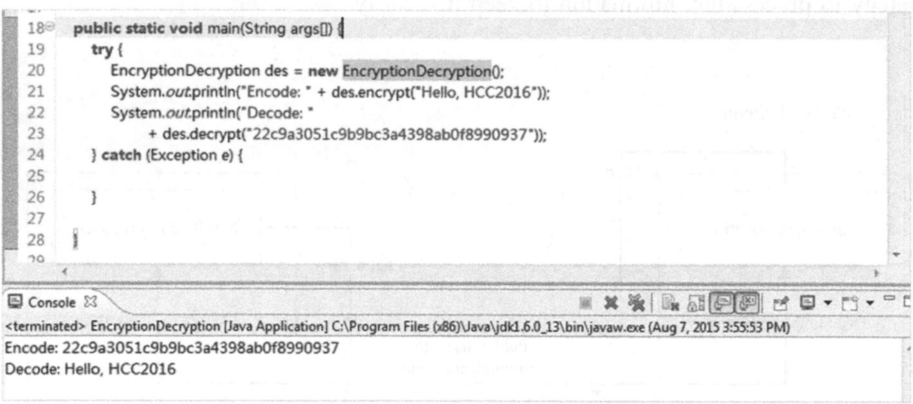

```
18⊝    public static void main(String args[]) {
19         try {
20             EncryptionDecryption des = new EncryptionDecryption();
21             System.out.println("Encode: " + des.encrypt("Hello, HCC2016"));
22             System.out.println("Decode: "
23                     + des.decrypt("22c9a3051c9b9bc3a4398ab0f8990937"));
24         } catch (Exception e) {
25
26         }
27
28     }
29
```

```
Console ⌗
<terminated> EncryptionDecryption [Java Application] C:\Program Files (x86)\Java\jdk1.6.0_13\bin\javaw.exe (Aug 7, 2015 3:55:53 PM)
Encode: 22c9a3051c9b9bc3a4398ab0f8990937
Decode: Hello, HCC2016
```

Fig. 11. Encode and decode the text information

7 Conclusion

On one hand, nowadays most of the devices are installed Android OS as primary system, and millions of applications have been developed so far. On the other hand, the security becomes a key problem of mobile users. We have presented a solution to improving the environment of Android OS security, which help developers to avoid invading from hackers and reduce loss. In the future, we will do in-depth research on the area and find more methods of protecting Android applications.

Acknowledgment. This work is supported by the National Nature Science Foundation of China (Grant No: 61272067, No: 61502180), the National High Technology Research and Development Program of China (863 Program, Grant No: 2013AA01A212), the Science and Technology Program of Guangzhou, China (Grant No: 2014J4300033), and the National Key Technology Support Program of China (Grant No: 2012BAH27F05).

References

 1. Vidas, T., Christin, N., Cranor, L.: Curbing Android permission creep. In: Proceedings of the Web 2.0 Security and Privacy 2011 Workshop, W2SP 2011, Oakland, CA (2011)
 2. Hoffmann, J., Ussath, M., Holz, T., Spreitzenbarth, M.: Slicing droids: program slicing for smali code. In: Proceedings of the 28th Annual ACM Symposium on Applied Computting, pp. 1844–1851. ACM, New York (2013)
 3. Gunasekera, S.A.: Android Apps Security. Apress, Berkeley (2012)
 4. Bovet, D., Cesati, M.: Understanding the Linux kernel. O'Reilly Media, Sebastopol (2005)
 5. Ehringer D.: The dalvik virtual machine architecture. Technical report, Google (2010)
 6. AppChina Market. http://www.appchina.com
 7. Winsniewski, R.: Android apktool: A Tool for Reverse Engineering Android apk Files. http://ibotpeaches.github.io/Apktool
 8. Enck, W., Octeau, D., McDaniel, P., Chaudhuri, S.: A study of android application security. In: Proceedings of the USENIX (2011)
 9. Bartel, A., Klein, J., Le Traon, Y., Monperrus, M.: Dexpler: converting android dalvik bytecode to jimple for static analysis with soot. In: Proceedings of the ACM SIGPLAN International Workshop on State of the Art in Java Program Analysis, SOAP 2012, pp. 27–38. ACM, New York (2012)
10. Gabor, P.: Dalvik opcodes. http://pallergabor.uw.hu/androidblog/dalvik_opcodes.html
11. Shabtai, A., Fledel, Y., Kanonov, U., Elovici, Y., Dolev, S., Glezer, C.: Google Android: a comprehensive security assessment. IEEE Secur. Priv. **8**(2), 5–44 (2010)
12. Liu, N.S., Guo, D.H., Huang, J.X.: AES algorithm implemented for PDA secure communication with Java. In: 2007 International Workshop on Anti-counterfeiting, Security and Identification, pp. 217–222. IEEE, New York (2007)

Green Precision Time Protocol Router Using Dynamic Frequency Scaling

Feng Guo[1]([⊠]), Mei Song[2], Yifei Wei[2], Luigi Sambolino[3],
Pengcheng Liu[1], Xiaojun Wang[1], and Martin Collier[1]

[1] School of Electronic Engineering, Dublin City University, Dublin 9, Ireland
{feng.guo2,pengcheng.liu3}@mail.dcu.ie,
{xiaojun.wang,martin.collier}@dcu.ie
[2] School of Electronic Engineering, Beijing University of Posts
and Telecommunications, Beijing, People's Republic of China
{songm,weiyifei}@bupt.edu.cn
[3] DITEN, University of Genoa, Genoa, Italy
luigi@tnt-lab.unige.it

Abstract. Time is the only reference frame among all the network devices over the Internet. Clock synchronization is crucial, especially in time sensitive networking scenarios that every time stamp matters. The Precise Time Protocol (PTP) standard enables precise clock synchronization in multicast capable networks. With hardware time stamping, the standard provides exceptionally tight clock synchronization with the accuracy within the nanosecond range. For this reason, the PTP enabled routers have been widespread in recent years. However, the performance is traditionally the primary concern in these routers without drawing enough attention on router power consumption. This work builds an energy efficient PTP router using dynamic frequency scaling towards green networking. Results indicate that, when in idle state, the proposed router can significantly reduce up to 16.89 % of the power consumption.

Keywords: Precise time protocol · Power consumption · Green networking · Energy efficiency · Dynamic frequency scaling

1 Introduction

The 21st century is in an era of information explosion. Information and communications technology (ICT) network devices have been adopted in every walk of life. However, in real networks, system clock on a network device may run at a significant different rate from other participating devices. This phenomenon can spark off several serious problems associated with clock skew, especially in time sensitive network applications that precise time coordination among all the participating network devices is mandatory.

In real networks, every aspect of managing, controlling, planning, securing and debugging involves an accurate time to initiate these actions and control the processes. Currently, the system clock in most of servers, workstations and other network devices is still manually set and barely checked afterwards. Once in operation, the system clock

© Springer International Publishing Switzerland 2016
Q. Zu and B. Hu (Eds.): HCC 2016, LNCS 9567, pp. 104–115, 2016.
DOI: 10.1007/978-3-319-31854-7_10

is usually maintained by a simple crystal oscillator time base in a battery-backed and clock-calendar device. The crystal oscillator tends to be imprecise, unstable and temperature sensitive. Due to clock drift, the system clock in this device may vary over time even though the clock has been accurately set beforehand. If such clock is maintained on its own, it's a long shot to keep clock synchronized among all the devices throughout the networks.

As network devices increasingly rely on existing local and global networks to communicate, appropriate mechanisms must be introduced to synchronize all the participating devices over the packet-switched and variable-latency data networks. To achieve real-time clock synchronization at high accuracy levels, many solution approaches have been proposed. Among these approaches, the Network Time Protocol (NTP) [1] has been the king solution of clock synchronization in distributed systems over decades. NTP is a networking protocol that synchronizes timekeeping among time servers and clients in distributed computing and networking. Based on peering and server/client model, NTP allows clock synchronization up to 10 milliseconds (ms) on wide area networks (WAN), and achieves up to 1 ms accuracy on local area networks (LAN) by exchanging time stamps using regular beacon packets. Defined in IEEE 1588, the Precision Time Protocol (PTP) [2] is designed for providing precise time coordination of LAN connected network devices requiring higher accuracies beyond those attainable using NTP. PTP enhances the accuracy of clock synchronization up to 100 microseconds (μs) with minimal network and local clock computing resources, and even achieves in the nanosecond (ns) region with hardware assistance.

Recently, PTP enabled routers have been widely used because many applications in telecommunications, automation tests and measurements require tight clock synchronization. With hardware assistance, the accuracy obtained from PTP is well beyond that achievable from standard software solutions. However, future ICT network equipments and infrastructures should integrate more energy-sustainable and eco-friendly features [3, 4]. Performance improvements should never be the sole battle field for networking manufacturers and designers [5, 6]. Instead, it should be holistically regarded as the first and the most essential metric in the entire family design metrics, along with power consumption, heat dissipation, reliability, security, etc.

This work incorporates a dynamic frequency scaling scheme [7, 8] into a PTP router, making it a more energy efficient Green PTP router (GPTP). The GPTP router is devoted at providing the same performance as the PTP router, but with the lowest possible power consumption for routing the same amount of traffic. This work is validated on the NetFPGA 1G board [9]. The NetFPGA board is used because that compared to the commercial routers, it provides sufficient flexibility to develop and experiment custom modules with reprogrammable and reconfigurable features, and supports a more accurate way to examine and quantify the power savings from green techniques.

The rest of this paper is organized as follows. Section 2 explores NTP and PTP which are networking protocols for clock synchronization. Section 3 addresses the architecture design of the GPTP on the NetFPGA board, describing the PTP on the NetFPGA, the frequency scaling design and the corresponding frequency control policies. Section 4 evaluates the GPTP router and compares the results with the PTP router. Section 5 concludes the paper.

2 Network Time Protocol and Precision Time Protocol

2.1 Network Time Protocol

The NTP can operate in unicast mode (point-to-point connection between a server and a client), or in broadcast mode (point-to-multipoint connection between a server and multiple clients) [10]. For both modes in NTP, the key for clock synchronization between servers and clients is through exchanging four time stamps. Taking NTP unicast as an example, as shown in Fig. 1 in NTP unicast mode, the four time stamps are the origin time stamp T_o at T_1 when the client's request packet departs the client, the receive time stamp T_r at T_2 when this request packet arrives at the server, the transmit time stamp T_t at T_3 when the server's response packet departs the server, and the destination time stamp T_d at T_4 when this response packet arrives at the client. With these four time stamps, the roundtrip delay and the clock offset can be calculated. The client clock finally utilizes the clock offset to adjust the time to agree with the server clock.

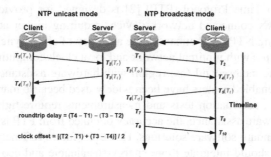

Fig. 1. Comparison between NTP unicast mode and NTP broadcast mode

Figure 1 also compares the differences between the unicast mode and the broadcast mode for NTP. In the unicast mode, the client pulls synchronization from the server. In the broadcast mode, the delay calculation is the same as the unicast mode. However, broadcast messages are initiated by the broadcast server and received by each broadcast client. Thus, compared with the unicast mode, the roles are reversed and the offset expression has an inverted sign.

2.2 Precision Time Protocol

The delay calculation in PTP is the same as that in NTP. The clock synchronization in PTP is achieved through exchanging four hardware generated time stamps in the data packets [11], which offers highly precise clock synchronization. Figure 2 presents an example of the messages exchanged between a PTP server and a PTP client. There are four messages involved Sync message, Sync follow up message, Delay request message and Delay response message.

The PTP broadcast mode is similar to the NTP broadcast mode, but using two messages to carry the broadcast time stamps, instead of using one single message in NTP. Thus, the four hardware generated time stamps in the PTP broadcast mode are slightly different from the four time stamps in the NTP broadcast mode. These four hardware generated time stamps are the origin time stamp T_o when the server starts with a Sync message at T_1, the receive time stamp T_r when the client records the Sync message at T_2, the transmit time stamp T_t when the client sends the Delay request message at T_5, and the destination time stamp T_d when the server receives Delay request message at T_6.

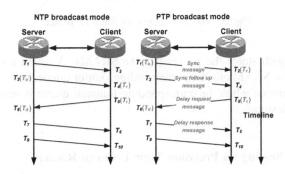

Fig. 2. Comparison between NTP broadcast mode and PTP broadcast mode

3 Green Precision Time Protocol Router

3.1 Precision Time Protocol on NetFPGA

The NetFPGA PTP router can be configured as a regular IPv4 router with PTP hardware time stamping feature. The router hardware implementation provides an exceptionally tight clock synchronization, which allows two NetFPGA PTP routers to be synchronized to a few 10 s of nanoseconds. For this router, each port can be configured as either a master to provide a highly accurate source of synchronization for PTP slaves, or a slave to synchronize to a PTP master. As shown in Fig. 3, the pipeline of the PTP router consists of eight receive queues, eight transmit queues and the user data path together with multiple modules. Both receive queues and transmit queues are divided into two groups: four MAC interfaces and four CPU DMA interfaces. The receive queues receive packets from I/O ports such as the Ethernet ports and the Peripheral Component Interconnect (PCI) over DMA, while the transmit queues send packets out of the I/O ports instead of receiving.

The pipeline in the user data path is 64 bit wide and all the internal module interfaces follow standard request grant First-In-First-Out (FIFO) protocol. In the user data path, the first module input arbiter decides which receive queue to service next, and pulls a packet from that receive queue and hands it to the output port lookup module. The output port lookup module is responsible for deciding which port the packet goes out of. After that decision is made, the packet is then handed to the output

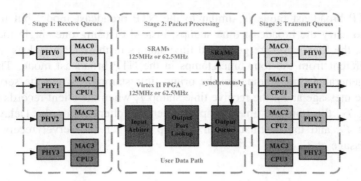

Fig. 3. The architecture of the PTP router

queues module which stores the packet into the SRAMs. A round robin arbiter reads the packet from the SRAMs to the corresponding output queue, and sends the packet out of the output queue when the corresponding transmit queue is ready to accept the packet for transmission.

3.2 Frequency Scaling on Precision Time Protocol Router

Since there are only 2 frequencies 125 MHz and 62.5 MHz provided in the NetFPGA PTP router, it is insufficient to examine and quantify the power savings from dynamic frequency scaling. For more finely tuned frequency switching, the GPTP router is designed and built to offer 23 grades of operating frequencies. This is accomplished by manipulating clock signals with the digital clock manager (DCM) available on the Virtex II FPGA. As shown in Fig. 4, a clock divider in the DCM provides advanced clocking capability which can generate new clock frequencies by dividing source clock frequency with allowed divisors. In the GPTP router, a wide range of 23 operating frequency options (125 MHz, 83.3 MHz, 62.5 MHz, 50 MHz, 41.7 MHz, 35.7 MHz, 31.3 MHz, 27.8 MHz, 25 MHz, 22.7 MHz, 20.8 MHz, 19.2 MHz, 17.9 MHz, 16.7 MHz, 15.6 MHz, 13.9 MHz, 12.5 MHz, 11.4 MHz, 10.4 MHz, 9.6 MHz, 8.9 MHz, 8.3 MHz and 7.8 MHz) are derived from the source clock 125 MHz by simultaneous frequency division with a set of divisors (1, 1.5, 2, 2.5, 3, 3.5, 4, 4.5, 5, 5.5, 6, 6.5, 7, 7.5, 8, 9, 10, 11, 12, 13, 14, 15 and 16).

For the NetFPGA PTP router, an inbuilt register in the register bus provides a switch to toggle the operating frequency of the core logic FPGA between 125 MHz and 62.5 MHz. However, the PTP router disallows switching the operating frequency of the core logic FPGA on the fly, due to the clock synchronization between the SRAMs and the core logic FPGA. When toggling the operating frequency of the PTP router between 125 MHz and 62.5 MHz, the frequency switching causes a board reset about 2 ms to restart the SRAMs and the core logic FPGA hardware with updated synchronous frequency, and re-mirror MAC addresses, IP addresses, routing table, and ARP table to the core logic FPGA hardware. All the buffered packets are lost during the board reset.

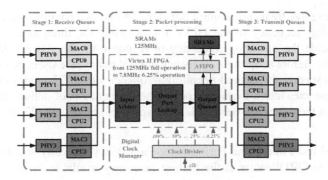

Fig. 4. The architecture of the GPTP router

Most applications are able to gracefully handle this board reset. When a user application realizes that packets are lost, the lost packets will be re-transmitted if the application is a file download, an email, or another none real-time application. The user probably won't ever perceive the board reset. However, if the application is a real-time conversation, a video conference or another real-time application that has a low tolerance for packet loss, the effect of board reset could be very noticeable to the user. The audio could be distorted and the video could show artifacts. The user may even suffer from connection lost if the packet loss is severe.

To eliminate the board reset problem, a custom module of asynchronous FIFO (AFIFO) is integrated between the SRAMs and the core logic FPGA. As shown in Fig. 4, the AFIFO module can isolate the SRAMs alone and keep them fully on at 125 MHz all the time, while the operating frequency of the core FPGA can be tuned among available frequencies in response to actual needs. The AFIFO allows safe data exchange between the SRAMs clock domain and the core FPGA clock domain, where the two clock domains are asynchronous to each other. The AFIFO involves a FIFO design where data is written into the FIFO to the SRAMs clock domain for load, and the data is read from the same FIFO to the core FPGA clock domain for extract.

3.3 Frequency Control Policy

Once frequency scaling capability is provided, appropriate frequency control policy must be implemented to choose the most desirable operating frequency to meet certain criteria. The frequency control policy is crucial in the GPTP router because it manages the operating frequency of the router, which in turn affects the power consumption and the performance of the router. To meet different demands under different application scenarios, five different frequency control policies are designed to balance the trade-off between power consumption and performance. Each control policy has a unique behavior, purpose and suitability in response to traffic load or user demands. The five implemented frequency control policies are: Performance-First Policy, Power-Saving-First Policy, User-Defined Policy, Dynamic-Frequency-Adaption Policy and Packet-Loss-Aware Policy.

Among these five frequency control policies, the first two control policies statically set the operating frequency of the GPTP router, while the three latter policies can dynamically scale the operating frequency in response to either traffic load or user specified inputs. Before adopting a frequency control policy, the users or the operators are allowed to specify the desired operating frequencies from 23 grades of supported operating frequencies into a frequency pool. The frequency pool defines the available frequencies that the router can be scaled. If not specified, by default, 23 frequencies are all available.

Performance-First Policy. The Performance-First Policy statically sets the operating frequency of the GPTP router at the highest frequency available from the frequency pool. This policy is to achieve the maximum performance out of the GPTP router by setting the operating frequency to the maximum level and staying at this level all the time. It does not attempt to provide any power saving features by default and it's suitable for constant heavy traffic load during rush hours. This policy is also the default frequency control policy in the original NetFPGA PTP router.

Power-Saving-First Policy. On the contrary, the Power-Saving-First Policy statically sets the operating frequency of the GPTP router at the lowest frequency available from the frequency pool. This policy is to keep the GPTP router running at the lowest operating frequency to obtain maximum power savings at the cost of the minimum performance. It should be used when the router constantly works at expected low traffic load. Otherwise, any unexpected network traffic burst can degrade the performance because the policy will never scale up the frequency, which may lead to significant packet delay and loss.

Dynamic-Frequency-Adaption Policy. The Dynamic-Frequency-Adaption Policy dynamically scales the operating frequency of the core logic FPGA processor among tunable frequencies available from the frequency pool in response to the traffic load. This policy consists of statistics monitoring and preset thresholds. The statistics monitoring involves a daemon design to indicate the current core logic operating frequency, count the amount of packets received in bytes for each receive queue and packets dropped in bytes for each output queue at 10 ms sampling period. The preset thresholds are to assess an associated traffic throughput threshold beyond which the router will begin to loss packets for each operating frequency as shown in Fig. 5. The policy periodically checks the amount of packets received in bytes for each receive queue and compares them with the preset thresholds. After comparison between these two values, it makes a decision to jump to the most appropriate frequency to maintain the required performance avoiding packet loss resulted from queue overflow.

For most scenarios, the Dynamic-Frequency-Adaption Policy can offer the best balance among performance, power consumption, heat dissipation and manageability. This is achieved at the cost of transition time overhead during the frequency switching. Frequently switching the operating frequency could introduce unnecessary transition time overhead such as extra network latency and power consumption.

Packet-Loss-Aware Policy. For the Dynamic-Frequency-Adaption Policy, the trade-off between performance and power consumption is mainly affected by the fixed preset thresholds. This policy is an elegant scheme if the incoming traffic does not

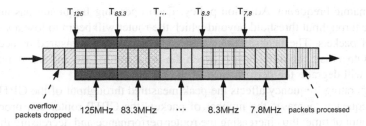

Fig. 5. Thresholds in Dynamic-Frequency-Adaption policy

change frequently and abruptly so that the router could switch the operating frequency smoothly. However, the operating frequency could frequently switch as a consequence of the instantaneous traffic fluctuating too frequently and abruptly, especially in the case that traffic load is close to a preset threshold. An effective policy should manage the router to operate at the lowest suitable frequency as much time as possible. Otherwise, unnecessary transition time overhead may outweigh the power savings from the frequency scaling scheme.

To eliminate this problem associated with the threshold-based policy, the Packet-Loss-Aware Policy is introduced. This policy adopts the same statistics monitoring daemon in the Dynamic-Frequency-Adaption policy to check the packet loss, but it has nothing to do with thresholds. The only criteria to switch to a higher frequency are when packet loss is detected, instead of jumping frequencies in the Dynamic-Frequency-Adaption Policy. If there are no packet loss for a period of time, the operating frequency steps down to the next available frequency. The scaling is following a level-by-level mechanism, which means that switching only appears between adjacent frequency levels regardless of fixed preset threshold so as to minimize the transition overhead for frequent fluctuations scenarios.

User-Defined Policy. The User-Defined Policy allows users to manually set an available operating frequency from the frequency pool. This policy also allows user-space programs to dynamically scale the operating frequency of the GPTP router. It is the most customizable frequency control policy and provides the flexibility for the users to design and experiment their own policies. If it's well customized by a user, it could be the best solution to balance the trade-off between power consumption and performance under certain circumstances.

4 Evaluations

4.1 Performance of the GPTP Router

To evaluate the impact of the operating frequency and the traffic characteristics on the performance of the GPTP router, the peak measured throughput is the most important metric to be measured. Different from the maximum theoretical throughput, the peak measured throughput is the throughput measured from a real implemented system. The peak measured throughput is crucial because it directly determines the preset threshold in the Dynamic-Frequency-Adaption policy. Each operating frequency has an associated traffic throughput threshold beyond which the router will begin to lose a significant number of packets. The peak measured throughput must be measured as accurate as possible. Otherwise, the difference between the input traffic load and inaccurate preset threshold will degrade the performance of the GPTP router.

The operating frequency affects the peak measured throughput of the GPTP router. Higher frequency increases the number of packets the GPTP router can process in a given amount of time, thus increasing the router performance and decreasing the packet delay time. The traffic characteristics could also affect the peak measured throughput. As indicated in the ECONET project deliverable D2.2 [12], the packet sizes of 64 Bytes, 576 Bytes and 1500 Bytes are typical packet sizes in real network links and the packet size profile peaks at 64 Bytes and 1500 Bytes. There are 23 grades of supported frequencies in the GPTP router. Each frequency has a unique peak measured throughput. Thus, the peak measured throughput of the GPTP router is measured under 3 different packet sizes and 23 different frequencies.

Figure 6 summarizes the peak measured throughput of the GPTP router under different packet sizes and different operating frequencies. Results show that higher operating frequency and larger packet size could lead to higher peak measured throughput. Due to less overhead on packet head processing, larger packet size typically means higher routing capacity for routers, or lower power consumption, or both. So it is advisable to use larger packet sizes whenever possible.

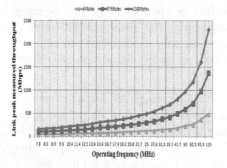

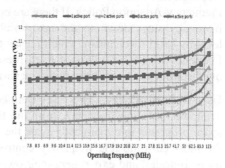

Fig. 6. Peak measured throughput of the GPTP router under different operating frequencies and different packet sizes

Fig. 7. Baseline power consumption of the GPTP router under different operating frequencies and different number of active ports

4.2   Power Consumption of the GPTP Router

To examine and quantify the power savings from dynamic frequency scaling on the GPTP router, baseline power measurements of the GPTP router is the first step to establish the entire power benchmarking process. The baseline power measurements of the GPTP router are the power measurements of router operating in idle state. In the idle state, the NetFPGA board is configured as the GPTP router but without routing any traffic.

In baseline power measurements, the four Ethernet ports of the NetFPGA hardware are activated one by one. The power consumption is measured at 23 different frequencies for the GPTP router. Figure 7 summarizes the baseline power consumption of the GPTP router under different operating frequencies and different number of active ports. The results reveal that the baseline power consumption of the router is proportional to the number of active ports, with approximately 1 W power consumption for each Ethernet port. The results also demonstrate that the baseline power consumption is proportional to the operating frequency.

4.3   Comparison Between PTP Router and GPTP Router

Figure 8 compares the baseline power consumption of PTP router and GPTP router at 125 MHz and 62.5 MHz. The GPTP router adopts different hardware design architecture from the PTP router, which leads to different baseline power consumption. The results indicate that under the same operating frequency at 125 MHz, the GPTP router consumes almost the same baseline power as the PTP router. However, at 62.5 MHz, the GPTP router consumes around 0.4 W (approximately 4 %) more baseline power than the PTP router due to different hardware architectures. For the PTP router, two SRAMs work synchronously with the core logic FPGA processor for writing and reading data at 125 MHz and 62.5 MHz. For the GPTP router, the core logic can be scaled among 23 different operating frequencies, but the two SRAMs are working asynchronously with the core logic and running constantly at 125 MHz, which leads to more baseline power than the PTP router at 62.5 MHz. Additionally, compared to the PTP router, the GPTP router integrates an AFIFO module, a clock divider in DCM. Each module contributes more power consumption.

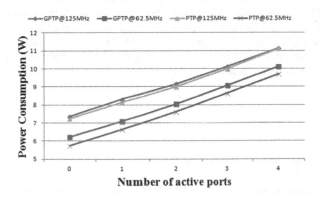

Fig. 8. Baseline power consumption of PTP router and GPTP router at 125 MHz and 62.5 MHz

One key point to be noted is that the power differences between the PTP router running at 125 MHz and 62.5 MHz come from the power difference in both the core logic FPGA processor and the SRAMs, whereas the power differences in the GPTP only come from the core logic FPGA processor because the SRAMs are always running at 125 MHz.

Table 1 summarizes the power consumption of the PTP router and the GPTP router in idle state. The PTP router is working with the Performance-First policy (PFP) at 125 MHz constantly even if no traffic is involved. However, with Power-Saving-First policy (PSFP), the GPTP router can switch to the lowest frequency at 7.8 MHz, consuming the lowest power consumption of 9.2471 W with the same QoS. Thus, in idle state, the power saving can be achieved at 16.89 %.

Table 1. GPTP router power saving in idle state

Type	Average power	Power saving
PTP with PFP at 125 MHz	11.1261 W	0 %
GPTP with PSFP at 7.8 MHz	9.2471 W	16.89 %

5 Conclusion

This paper adopts dynamic frequency scaling technique into the existing NetFPGA PTP router to reduce the power consumption of the router without compromising its performance. Different frequency switching policies and the scenarios in which each control policy can be used are discussed for the GPTP router. Experiments verify and quantify the energy savings from dynamic frequency scaling scheme. The results demonstrate that the built green module inside the NetFPGA PTP router significantly reduces the energy usage of the router hardware without noticeable performance degradation. Especially in the condition of low link utilization, energy can be saved with the same QoS.

Acknowledgements. This work is supported by the National Natural Science Foundation of China (61372117), the FP7 ECONET project (No. 258454), the Science Foundation Ireland (SFI) under the International Strategic Cooperation Award Grant Number SFI/13/ISCA/2845 and the China Scholarship Council (CSC). The authors would like to acknowledge our collaborators from Beijing Institute of Technology (BIT) and Hangzhou Dianzi University (HDU) for their contributions on the dynamic frequency scaling module.

References

1. Mills, D.: Internet time synchronization: the network time protocol. IEEE Trans. Commun. **39**(10), 1482–1493 (1991)
2. Eidson, J.: Measurement, Control, and Communication using IEEE 1588. Springer Science & Business Media, London (2006)
3. Bolla, R., Bruschi, R., Davoli, F., Cucchietti, F.: Energy efficiency in the future internet: a survey of existing approaches and trends in energy-aware fixed network infrastructures. IEEE Commun. Surv. Tutorials **13**(2), 223–244 (2011)
4. Luo, Y., Yu, J., Yang, J., Bhuyan, L.: Conserving network processor power consumption by exploiting traffic variability. ACM Trans. Archit. Code Optim. (TACO) **4**(1), 4 (2007)

5. Bolla, R., Davoli, F., Bruschi, R., Christensen, K., Cucchietti, F., Singh, S.: The potential impact of green technologies in next-generation wireline networks: is there room for energy saving optimization? IEEE Commun. Mag. **49**(8), 80–86 (2011)
6. Gunaratne, C., Christensen, K., Nordman, B., Suen, S.: Reducing the energy consumption of ethernet with adaptive link rate (alr). IEEE Trans. Comput. **57**(4), 448–461 (2008)
7. Fu, W., Song, T., Wang, S., Wang, X.: Dynamic frequency scaling architecture for energy efficient router. In: Proceedings of the Eighth ACM/IEEE Symposium on Architectures for Networking and Communications Systems, pp. 139–140. ACM (2012)
8. Bolla, R., Bruschi, R., Lombardo, C.: Dynamic voltage and frequency scaling in parallel network processors. In: 2012 IEEE 13th International Conference on High Performance Switching and Routing (HPSR), pp. 242–249. IEEE (2012)
9. Naous, J., Gibb, G., Bolouki, S., McKeown, N.: Netfpga: reusable router architecture for experimental research. In: Proceedings of the ACM Workshop on Programmable Routers for Extensible Services of Tomorrow, pp. 1–7. ACM (2008)
10. Mills, D., Martin, J., Burbank, J., Kasch, W.: Network time protocol version 4: Protocol and algorithms specification. Technical report (2010)
11. Yu, P., Yu, Q., Deng, H., Bao, X., Ma, Y., Guo, J.: The research of precision time protocol IEEE 1588. Autom. Electr. Power Syst. **33**(13), 99–103 (2009)
12. Bolla, R., Bruschi, R., Davoli, F., Di Gregorio, L., Giacomello, L., Lombardo, C., Parladori, G., Strugo, N., Zafeiropoulos, A.: The low energy consumption networks (econet) project. In: Sustainable Internet and ICT for Sustainability (SustainIT), pp. 1–5. IEEE (2012)

Research on the Deformation Technology of 3D Object for Natural Interaction

Yasong Guo[1(✉)], Wenjun Hou[2,3], Tiemeng Li[3], and Jiachen Fan[4]

[1] Automation School, Beijing University of Posts and Telecommunications,
Beijing, 100876, China
guoyasongabc@163.com

[2] Digital Media and Design Art, Beijing University of Posts and Telecommunications,
Beijing, China
hou1505@163.com

[3] Network System and Network Culture Key Laboratory of Beijing, Beijing, China
tiemeng2000@gmail.com

[4] School of Electronic Engineering, Beijing University of Posts and Telecommunications,
Beijing, China
406908388@qq.com

Abstract. Natural interaction is the inevitable trend of the development of human-computer interaction. The simulation of 3D object deformation in the virtual environment can bring more harmonious and friendly interactive experience to human. In this paper, a deformation algorithm based on weighted average normal for 3D object is proposed after the analysis of the existing 3D object deformation method. The algorithm is based on the weighted average normal of the triangular mesh of 3D object to determine the deformation direction of the mesh vertices and then simulate the deformation of 3D object. We invite 20 volunteers to participate in the 3D object deformation test based on LeapMotion. Most of them have a good interactive experience and they are satisfied. The result of the experiment shows that the algorithm is simple and easy to implement and has good effect of deformation.

Keywords: Natural interaction · 3D object · Weighted average normal · Deformation

1 Introduction

With the rapid development of computer technology and computer graphics technology, people's demand for the experience feeling in the process of human computer interaction is becoming higher and higher. The traditional method of human-computer interaction can not meet people's needs, and therefore more natural interaction is the inevitable trend of human-computer interaction development.

In natural interaction, the simulation of 3D object deformation in virtual environment can give people more harmonious and friendly interactive experience, so the deformation technology of 3D object becomes a hotspot of research. At present, there are four kinds of deformation technology of 3D object: Free-Form Deformation, Skeleton-driven

© Springer International Publishing Switzerland 2016
Q. Zu and B. Hu (Eds.): HCC 2016, LNCS 9567, pp. 116–126, 2016.
DOI: 10.1007/978-3-319-31854-7_11

Deformation, Physical-based Deformation and Surface-based Deformation. Compared to other deformation technologies, deformation technology based on the grid surface can be used to manipulate the grid surface of 3D object directly to realize deformation. So the deformation technology based on the grid surface is more in line with the requirements of natural interaction. So this paper will study the deformation technology based on the grid surface.

This paper presents a new algorithm of 3D object deformation based on weighted average normal for natural interaction. The algorithm is simple and easy to implement and has good effect of deformation. The algorithm uses the weighted average of the triangular mesh of 3D object to determine the deformation direction of the mesh vertices and then realizes the simulation of 3D object deformation.

2 Related Work

2.1 Natural Interaction

Natural interaction refers to the interaction between people and products, which allows users to use their own cognitive habits and their familiar life style. It is a very precise way to interact with products, and it is aimed to improve the naturality and efficiency of interaction. The rapid development of virtual reality and augmented reality provides a opportunity for the development of natural interaction. The domestic and foreign scholars have carried on the thorough research to the natural interaction technology of the virtual reality, augmented reality environment. Kaiser et al. [2] develop a multi-channel interactive system in virtual environment, and integrate the speech input and gesture input, and propose a system framework and development platform for multi-channel interaction in virtual environment. The Alice system developed by the Carnegie Mellon University's human computer interaction group [3–5] is a visual virtual environment creation tool, which allows users without programming experience to create their own cartoon stories through this system. Virtual reality technology has brought a good interactive experience, but it did not really achieve the requirements of natural interaction, and augmented reality technology can let people free hands, users can directly use the hand as an input device. For instance, user can use board with a mark affixed to interact with virtual objects [6], also can use gloves with mark affixed to manipulate virtual chess [7]. Kitehin Paul et al. [8] use gesture as the registration mark of virtual model in the scene, and realize the system that registers virtual model through hand identification, the system can register the virtual model in the hand. Compared with the previous technology which use the entity identification to carry out three-dimensional registration, the system is more real, natural.

Sun et al. [9] propose a 3D interaction algorithm for hand based natural behavior interaction in augmented reality, which uses a series of steps of hand detection, hand feature extraction and hand 3D structure reconstruction to get 3D structure of a bare hand and aligns the interaction information extracted from real world in virtual world to achieve hand based natural behavior 3D interaction. Wu [10] proposes the concept about natural interaction of virtual experiments, and constructed the theoretical model of interaction design of virtual experiments, and formulated the design principles of interaction design of virtual experiments combined with "availability", so as to guide the interaction design of virtual experiments.

2.2 3D Object Deformation Technology Based on Mesh Surface

Hsu et al. [11] present a method that allows a user to control a free-form deformation of an object by manipulating these control points. The core idea of this method is that the user selects a point from the mesh surface of the object, and moves it to the position of the post deformation, and then the system automatically reacts to the change of the FFD control points. This method does not need to consider the complexity of the algorithm, which greatly facilitates the user. Therefore, this method is a deformation technology based on the grid surface of 3D object. Then there are many researchers to improve the method.

Zorin et al. [12] propose a interactive multiresolution mesh editing technology. This method uses subdivision surfaces to get many levels of detail and the geometric differences in the middle are expressed by the displacement vector. Lee [13] also uses subdivision surfaces to express multiresolution mesh, but he uses the normal vector displacement to record the difference between the different resolution meshes. These two methods will produce obvious artificial marks after the completion of the deformation. In order to solve this problem, Marinov et al. [14] propose a multiresolution 3D mesh deformation technology based on GPU, and they use the method of normal vector displacement to to encode to express multiresolution mesh. Botsch et al. [15] use the deformation transfer technology to copy the deformation of the base mesh to the original mesh. In general, multiresolution mesh deformation can achieve a good result, but it is necessary to construct a multiresolution version of 3D object, which is a limit for 3D objects with complex geometrical structure or topological structure.

The deformation algorithm based on grid differential is also a deformation algorithm based on the grid surface. What the difference between it and the deformation algorithm based on multiresolution grid is that it uses non-global coordinate. This method has a good effect on keeping the local detail of 3D object. Sorkine et al. [16] propose the Laplace deformation technology, which uses the Laplace coordinate to define the energy minimization, and solves the least squares problem in the case of maintaining the Laplace coordinate, thus maintains the local details of the 3D object, as shown in Fig. 1. However, the drawback of the Laplace deformation technology is that it needs to solve a matrix which is proportional to the number of mesh vertices of a 3D object, and the computational complexity is high, so the deformation efficiency is very low.

Fig. 1. The impression drawing of the Laplace deformation technology [16]

Because the complexity of the algorithms above is high, it is not suitable for the requirement that proposed in this paper for natural interaction. Therefore, this paper proposes a simple algorithm based on weighted average normal.

3   Deformation Algorithm Based on Weighted Average Normal

In this paper, the research object is 3D object composed of triangular meshes, so the essence of deformation of 3D object is to realize the displacement of the mesh vertices. The three elements of force in physics are: magnitude, direction, the function point, place of application. The process of deformation is the process of force, then the 3D object's deformation must includes these three elements. In the deformation process, "magnitude" refers to the magnitude of the force imposed on the mesh point, "direction" is the direction of the displacement of the mesh points, "place of application" is the mesh vertices to carry out the displacement. This paper will focus on the deformation direction.

3.1   Weighted Average Normal

In 3D computer graphics, normal is often used for illumination calculation and mapping, so it can be used to simulate the real deformation direction. The normal of one mesh vertex is a straight line that passes through the vertex and is perpendicular to the tangent plane. The weighted average normal is weighted calculated by a vertex and its adjacent vertices. It is the displacement direction of these vertices. The calculation process is shown in Fig. 2.

(1) Set the radius of deformation, select the vertices: Deformation radius is used to define the region of deformation, that is, all the mesh vertices in the region are gonging to displace. For a 3D object, the deformation radius can be set according to the complexity of the triangle mesh or other requirement. Then, we choose the vertices according to the point of action and the radius of deformation, but the displacement of the vertices is different.

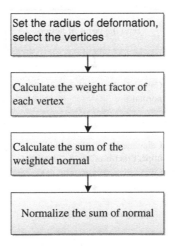

Fig. 2. The calculation process of weighted average normal

(2) Calculate the weight factor of each vertex: the so-called weight factor is the role of each vertex in determining the final deformation direction. According to the size of the distance between each vertex with the point of action, the weight factor of each mesh vertex is calculated, and the distance is closer, the weight factor is higher.

(3) Calculate the sum of the weighted normal: The normal of each selected mesh vertex is multiplied by their respective weight factor and then add together to get the sum of of the weighted normal.

(4) Normalize the sum of normal: Because we just need to know the displacement direction of the vertices, so we normalize the sum of normal, and finally we get the weighted average normal.

3.2   The Process of Deformation

Next we will detail how the algorithm based on the weighted average normal is applied to the deformation process. The deformation progress using the algorithm based on the weighted average normal is shown in Fig. 3:

(1) Find the point of action: In the real world, the deformation of the object needs to be in contact or collide with other objects. The same is true of the virtual 3D object, and it also needs to collide with other objects or rays as a prerequisite for deformation. After the collision, the collision point on the 3D object which is to be deformed is the point of action.

(2) Calculate the weighted average normal: According to the requirement to set the deformation radius, and then use the above method to calculate the weighted average normal.

(3) Calculate the displacement impact factor of the each vertex: In addition to the point of action and the direction, we also need to know the size of the vertex displacement to complete the process of deformation. The displacement impact factor is the

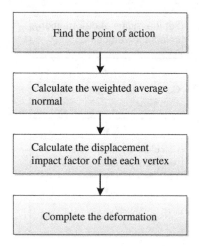

Fig. 3. The deformation process of 3D object using weighted average normal

degree of deformation of each vertex relative to the point of action, the value of which is 0~1. The displacement impact factor of each vertex is also related to the distance between the vertex and the point of action. The closer the distance is, the higher the deformation degree is. Here we use Gauss fuzzy algorithm to calculate the displacement impact factor, in order to make the surface smooth transition.

(4) Complete the deformation: Complete the displacement of the grid vertices in the weighted average normal direction, and realize the deformation.

4   Algorithm Instances

Unity3D is a cross-platform game development software developed by Unity Technologies, which can achieve three-dimensional video games, architectural visualization,

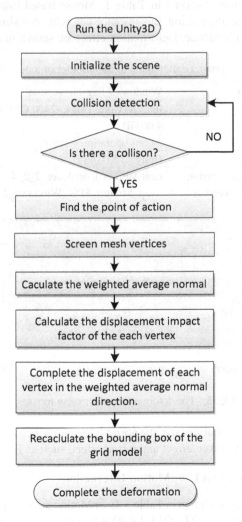

Fig. 4. The deformation process based on weighted average normal in Unity

real-time three-dimensional animation and other types of interactive products, and is a comprehensive professional game engine. Unity3D can be combined with a variety of intelligent hardware, so it is widely used in games, virtual reality and augmented reality, and other applications. So we use the Unity3D game engine as the development platform to implement the 3D object deformation algorithm based on the weighted average normal. In Unity3D, the implementation of the deformation algorithm based on the weighted average normal is shown in Fig. 4.

There are two instances in this paper, they use different interaction ways: one is to use the mouse, the other is use LeapMotion.

4.1   Deformation Based on Mouse Interaction

The system configuration is shown in Table 1. Mouse based interaction is the most common and most direct interaction, this instance can achieve a similar effect of virtual sculpture by dragging the mouse. Deformation effect are shown in Fig. 5.

Table 1.   The system configuration of the instance of mouse interaction

Windows version	Windows 7 flagship version
Processor	Intel(R) Core(TM) i5-2400 CPU @3.10gHZ
RAM	4.00 GB
System type	64 bits operation system
Unity3D version	Unity3D 5.0.0f3
LeapMotion plugin version	LeapMotion_CoreAsset_2_2_4
LeapMotion SDK version	Leap_Motion_SDK_Windows_2.2.5

A-Before deformation   B-Sunken effect   C-Raised effect

Fig. 5.   The deformation effect using mouse

For the three-dimensional surface, the normal directions includes positive and negative, so we can achieve sunken effect and raised effect, such as B and C.

4.2   Deformation Based on LeapMotion Interaction

The system configuration is shown in Table 2. LeapMotion is a somatosensory controller released by Leap in February 27, 2013. LeapMotion can accurately identify and trace the gesture, so that users can get rid of the mouse and use directly both hands to interact with virtual 3D object, so it is a more natural way of interaction. In this instance, through the LeapMotion to make both hands directly interact with the 3D object to achieve the deformation. Deformation effects are shown in Fig. 6.

Table 2. The system configuration of the instance of LeapMotion interaction

Windows version	Windows 7 flagship version
Processor	Intel(R) Core(TM) i5-2400 CPU @3.10gHZ
RAM	4.00 GB
System type	64 bits operation system
Unity3D version	Unity3D 5.0.0f3
LeapMotion plugin version	LeapMotion_CoreAsset_2_2_4
LeapMotion SDK version	Leap_Motion_SDK_Windows_2.2.5

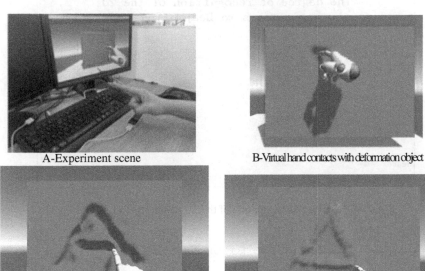

A-Experiment scene   B-Virtual hand contacts with deformation object

C-Sunken effect   D-Raised effect

Fig. 6. The deformation effect using LeapMotion

5 Instance Analysis

The same deformation algorithm is used in the two instances, but the interaction way using LeapMotion is more natural, so this paper only analyzes the interaction instance based on LeapMotion.

In the user experience experiment, we invite 20 volunteers to participate in the 3D object deformation test based on LeapMotion. The degree of recognition of the 20 volunteers to LeapMotion is shown in Fig. 7. The experiment requires each volunteer to complete writing "A" for six times, respectively, to record the time of each operation. Before the start of the experiment, each volunteer will be explained and trained, so that they can understand the process of the experiment and how to operate. After each person has done the experiment, they are asked to do a evaluation of the experience, there are five options, they are "very satisfied", "more satisfied", "general", "not satisfied", "very dissatisfied".

From the result of the experiment in Fig. 8, we can see that the operation is more skillful, the time is less to complete the task. The result of the survey in Fig. 9 shows that the proposed deformation algorithm in this paper can make the most of the users have a more natural and harmonious interactive experience.

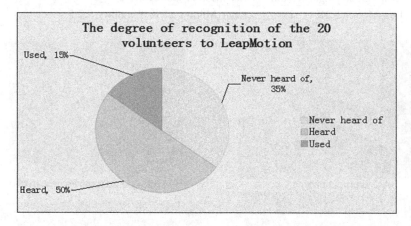

Fig. 7. The degree of recognition of the 20 volunteers to LeapMotion

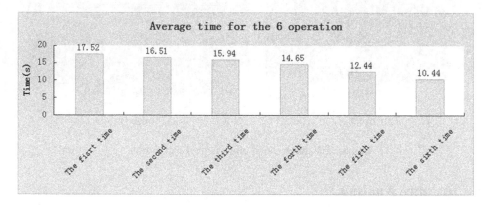

Fig. 8. Average time for the 6 operation

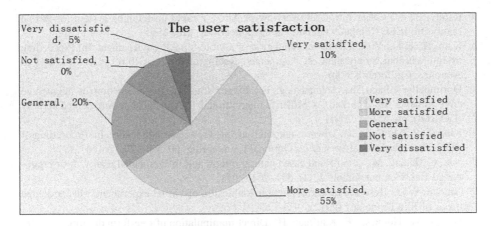

Fig. 9. The user satisfaction

6 Conclusion

Through the above two instances, we found that the deformation algorithm based on the weighted average normal has a more real deformation effect, and can achieve smooth deformation, and has better interactive experience. The next work of this paper can be divided into two parts: one part is the improvement of deformation algorithm, in fact, there are many ways to improve the algorithm, such as the screening algorithm of vertices, the calculation method of weight factor and so on. The other is to research the combination of LeapMotion, although we have could use LeapMotion to control the deformation of object, but can not determine the contact depth of the hand model and object, can not obtain the expectant accuracy.

Acknowledgment. We would like to thank all the people who have helped us in the course of our research, especially the 20 volunteers in the experiment, who let us know the advantages and disadvantages of our research, which are very helpful to our future research. In addition, our work is supported by Specialized Research Fund for the Doctoral Program of Higher Education (No. 20120005120005) and National Natural Science Foundation of China (No. 61303162).

References

1. Ye, Q.: The technology of 3D model deformation and its application. Master degree thesis of Zhejiang University of Technology (2013)
2. Kaiser, E., Alex, O., David, M., et al.: Mutual disambiguation of 3D multimodal interaction in augmented and virtual reality. In: Proceeding of the 5th International Conference on Multimodal Interfaces (ICMC 2003), Canada, pp. 12–19 (2003)
3. Stephen, C., Wanda, D., Randy, P.: Teaching objects-first in introductory computer science. In: SIGCSE (2003)
4. Mattew, C., Steve, A., Tommy, B.: Alice: lessons learned from building a 3D system for novices. In: CHI (2000)

5. Randy, P.: A brief architectural overview of Alice, a rapid prototyping system for virtual reality. In: IEEE Computer Graphics and Applications, May 1995
6. Kato, H., et al.: Virtual object manipulation of a table-top AR environment. In: Proceeding of International Symposium on Augmented Reality 2000 (ISAR00), pp. 111–119, Los Alamitos, California (2000)
7. Dorfinueller-Ulhaas, K., Schmalstieg, D.: Finger tracking for interaction in augmented environments. In: The 2nd ACM/IEEE International Symposium on Augmented Reality (ISAROI), pp. 55–64 (2001)
8. Kitehin, P., Martinez, K.: Towards natural fiducials for augmented reality. In: Proceeding of SPIE-The International Society for Optional Engineering, pp. 571–578 (2005)
9. Sun, C., Zhang, M., et al.: Hand based natural interaction in augmented reality. J. Comput.-Aided Des. Comput. Graph. 23(4), 697–704 (2011)
10. Xiaobo, W.U.: Research on natural interaction design of virtual experiment. Master degree thesis of Jilin University (2012)
11. Hsu, W.M., Hughes, J.F., Kaufman, H.: Direct manipulation of free-form deformations. In: Proceedings of the 19th Annual Conference on Computer Graphics and Interactive Techniques, pp. 177–184 (1992)
12. Zorin, D., Schroder, P., Sweldens, W.: Interactive multiresolution mesh editing. In: Proceedings of the 24th Annual Conference on Computer Graphics and Interactive Techniques, New York, pp. 168–259 (1997)
13. Lee, S.: Interactive multiresolution editing of arbitrary meshes. Comput. Graph. Forum 18(3), 73–82 (1999)
14. Marinov, M., Botsch, M., Kobbelt, L.: GPU-based multiresolution deformation using approximate normal field reconstruction. ACM J. Graph. Tools 12(1), 27–46 (2007)
15. Botsch, M., Summer, R., Pauly, M., et al.: Deformation transfer for detail-preserving surface editing. In: Vision, Modeling and Visualization, pp. 357–364 (2006)
16. Sorkine, O., Cohen-Or, D., et al.: Laplacian surface editing. In: Proceeding of the 2004 Eurographics/ACM SIGGRAPH Symposium on Geometry Processing, pp. 175–184 (2004)

Assessing the Visual Discomfort of Compressed Stereoscopic Images Using ERP

Chunping Hou, Guanghui Yue, and Lili Shen[✉]

School of Electronic and Information Engineering, Tianjin University, Tianjin, China
{hcp,yueguanghui,sll}@tju.edu.cn

Abstract. The 3D images are compressed before transmission and storage, as a result, visual discomfort happens. In this paper, we investigate the use of Event-Related Potentials (ERP) as a tool to evaluate the 3D visual discomfort caused by symmetric compressed 3D images. Experimental results demonstrate that presence of compressed 3D images with different compression ratio reliably elicits a measurable response in the brain. The amplitude and latency of P300 vary depending on the compression levels. In addition, the subjective evaluation results validate the reliability of ERP technique for 3D visual discomfort. Therefore, ERP can be used to evaluate the effect of visual discomfort caused by compression when viewing 3D images.

Keywords: Visual discomfort · ERP · 3D images · Compression

1   Introduction

Three dimensional (3D) display technology has been widely used by producing a strong sense of immersion compared to two dimensional (2D) display technology. Meanwhile, health and safety issues have attracted more and more attention. The 3D visual discomfort can caused by various reasons, such as the mismatch between the left and right images, excessive disparity, accommodation-vergence (AV) conflicts, and fast object motion [1, 2]. Hence, 3D visual discomfort evaluation has been an immediately addressed problem, such as eyestrain, nausea, headache, and neck pain.

Compared to the 2D images, 3D images occupy larger storage space and need faster transmission speed. To achieve it, images are compressed before storage and transmission. Modern compression technology can compress image from 1/10 to 1/50 [3]. However, higher compression ratio usually causes the information loss as well as the reduction of the image quality. As a result, visual discomfort happens.

Currently, two main methods are used in evaluating 3D visual discomfort, the subjective and objective measurements [4]. However, both measurements have disadvantages. Subjective perception is the most able to reflect the image and video viewing comfort. Thus, the subjective measurement is widely used in 3D viewing comfort. During the subjective measurement procedure, the stimuli are presented by various forms, such as single stimulus (SS) and double stimuli (DS). After viewing the stimuli, the participant should fill in a Simulator Sickness Questionnaire. To obtain a reliable

© Springer International Publishing Switzerland 2016
Q. Zu and B. Hu (Eds.): HCC 2016, LNCS 9567, pp. 127–137, 2016.
DOI: 10.1007/978-3-319-31854-7_12

result, it usually need a large number of participants. Due to the different perception with visual discomfort, different participants have various responses on the same stimulus. As a result, the subjective measurement is time-consuming and the results may have tendency to researcher's desire. On the contrary, the objective measurement is convenient by extraction image's features, such as peak-to-noise-ratio (PSNR), mean square error (MSE) and structural similarity (SSIM) [5–7]. To obtain more reliable result, more features need extracted. Then the extracted features are mapped to the subjective opinions using neural network, such as support vector Machine (SVM), back propagation (BP) [8]. The correlation coefficients reflect the performance of the extracted features effectively. However, for different types of distortion, the features, which are extracted for specific distortions, doesn't have the robustness and universality. It is high time to find a robust and universal 3D visual discomfort methods. As the development of neuroscience, more and more researchers are exploring new image and video visual discomfort assessment methods, such as eye blinking, ERP, and functional magnetic resonance imaging (fMRI) [9, 10].

In this paper, we attempt to evaluate the 3D visual discomfort caused by the symmetric compression of 3D images using ERP. The remainder of this paper is organized as follows. Section 2 introduces the related work on 3D visual discomfort assessment using ERP. In Sect. 3, the detail experiment information is introduced, including participants, stimuli, experiment procedure and data processing. Section 4 analyzes the experiment result and draw the conclusion about the experiment performance. Finally, Sect. 5 concludes this paper and demonstrates the future work.

2   Related Work

Electroencephalography (EEG), which arises from synchronized synaptic activity in populations of cortical neurons, is recorded on the ongoing human brain, and it is spontaneous electrical signals. ERP is extracted via repeatedly superimposing EEG and defined as the potential variations of the brain region under the special stimuli on perceive system. It reflects special mental activity and has been used for many fields besides neuroscience. Recently, researchers use it to evaluate the discomfort of 3D images and videos.

Murata *et al.* first used ERP technique for evaluating mental fatigue generated in the visual display terminal (VDT) work, and take P300 as the evaluation tool of mental fatigue [11]. With the rapid development of ERP technology, the characteristics of its rhythm, latency and amplitude have been proved by more and more researchers to evaluate the quality of the image and video. Chen *et al.* used rhythm characteristic, α, β, θ, δ, to compare the difference after watching 2DTV and 3DTV. Experimental results demonstrated that rhythm characteristic can be regarded as an effective method to evaluate the 3D visual discomfort. With the increasing of fatigue, high-frequency components reduced while low-frequency components increased. By constructing linear regression functions using extracted characteristic parameters and mean option scores (MOS), they detected each subject's data and further proofed the reliability of ERP-based 3D video discomfort assessment [12]. Zou *et al.* also took rhythm characteristic as an effective tool to detect the visual fatigue. The experiment result suggested that among nine types of EEG indices, α is the most promising indicator for detecting stereoscopic visual fatigue [13]. Bang *et al.* measured EEG signals, eye blinking rate (BR), facial temperature (FT) to evaluate the 3D visual fatigue [14]. Scholler *et al.* extracted EEG indices to evaluate the compressed video quality, experiment results demonstrated the amplitude P300 can treated as an efficiently tool to evaluate 3D image quality [15].

Different from previous studies, we focus on the amplitude and latency of the wave induced by compressed 3D image in special brain region. The amplitude and latency reflect the reaction strength and speed, respectively. ERP signal has high temporal resolution that can reflect the brain's response accurately. As the physiological characteristic, it doesn't change as human thoughts. In addition, 3D visual discomfort reflects a cognitive process involving unusual 3D focusing. Thus, ERP can be used as the objective assessment for 3D visual discomfort. Combined with the subjective assessment, it can be the excellent 3D visual discomfort assessment metric. In this paper, we use the ERP technology combined with subjective method to evaluate the symmetric compressed 3D images.

3 Experiment

3.1 Participants

5 right-handed subjects (mean age: 22.4 years) voluntarily participated in the experiment. All had normal or corrected-to-normal vision. No neurological disorders such as photosensitive epileptic seizures were reported. No one had professional experience in 3D visual discomfort or 3D quality evaluation and had no previous history of neurological nor psychiatric diseases and were free of any medication.

3.2 Stimuli

In this study, two 3D images (the original format is JPEG with resolution of 1920×1080 pixels) that represent the general scenes of life were used, namely peiyang and windmill. They were shown in Fig. 1. Note that the images are in side-by-side format. Each image has stereo display information both in and out screen. We changed the compression ratio of both views in four levels to induce the mismatch of binocular view. One is not changed as reference and the other three levels correspond to different compression ratio using the MATLAB function "imwrite". The compression ratios of the two pictures almost have no difference (for detail see Table 1), therefore, they have the same influence on experiment. For further analysis, we use the mean compression ratio of both 3D images.

Fig. 1. Experiment pictures (with side-by-side format), (up) peiyang, (bottom) windmill.

Table 1. Experiment pictures and compression levels

Name	Level	Compression ratio	Name	Level	Compression ratio	Mean value
peiyang	1	1:1	windmill	1	1:1	1:1
peiyang	2	1:0.62	windmill	2	1:0.60	1:0.61
peiyang	3	1:0.53	windmill	3	1:0.51	1:0.52
peiyang	4	1:0.45	windmill	4	1:0.43	1:0.44

Note that, in the compression ratio column, the first and second number respect compressed and original image, respectively.

3.3 Procedures

Participants that suit for the requirements for the experiment were trained to be familiar with the task before the experiment. After signing an informed consent document, participants were escorted to a dimly lit, sound-reduced testing room, and seated in a comfortable chair approximately 78 cm in front of a monitor. The pictures were presented on the 21 inch AOC 3D monitor (with a resolution of 1920 × 1080). The pictures covered 19.1° × 34.0° of visual angle. Stimuli were displayed using E-prime 2.0 software on a light grey background. The classical oddball paradigm was applied for the experiment, the level 1 occupied 60 % while other levels each occupied 13.3 %. Each trail consisted of three sessions. Firstly, one fixated white dot in the center of the screen appeared to attract subjects' attention. Secondly, the randomly selected 3D picture among the four levels was present for 600 ms. Finally, the white dot appeared again and the participant needed to judge if he or she was discomfort induced by the presentation of imperfect binocular image pairs. If the uncomfortableness happened, the participant should click the right button of the mouse, vice versa. Once the button was clicked, the next trail was triggered automatically. The experiment procedure was shown in Fig. 2. Each experiment had 486 trails. During the experiment, the participants were not allowed to saccade as well as looking up and down but the normal blink was permitted. Every 5 min the participant was manipulated for a 2 min rest. Also, if the participants felt uncomfortable seriously, he or she could stop the experiment automatically. The participants' behavior data (i.e. the button-press) was recorded by the E-prime 2.0 software in real time, while the EEG data was recorded by the Neuroscan 4.5 software synchronously.

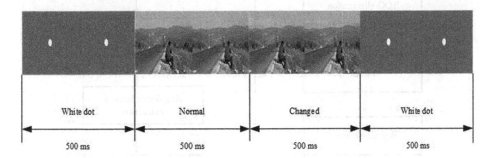

Fig. 2. Experiment procedure.

3.4 Electrophysiological Data Recording and Processing

EEG was recorded from 32 Ag-AgCl electrodes embedded in an elastic cap placed according to 10–20 system. Vertical and horizontal eye movement were monitored using four additional electrodes placed on the outer canthus of each eye and in the inferior and superior areas of the left orbit. Shampoo was used to remove keratin. Then, conductive liquid injection was necessary to ensure impedance of any electrode was below 5 KΩ. During EEG recording, all electrodes were referenced to the right mastoid reference (A2 electrode). AFz electrode that is in front of vertex was ground connection. EEG data was digitalized at 1000 Hz sampling rate, then filtered by the band pass between 100 Hz and 0.05 Hz to remove drifts and DC off-set, using the Neuroscan SyAmps2 amplifier.

The stored EEG data was immediately offline analyzed using Neuroscan 4.5 software. The procedure of ERP extraction was shown in Fig. 3. First, the EEG preview was implemented to reject the failed EEG data that drifted more serious. Secondly, the effect of electrooculogram (EOG) was removed. Thirdly, the EEG data was segmented by the range of −100 to 600 ms. As the stimuli presented time was longer than 700 ms, so the EEG segments were not overwrite the next stimulus baseline. The time range of −100 to 0 ms was taken as the baseline which was used to modify the EEG data. Then the corresponded epoch for each level was extracted using the epoch range, and filtered in 0.5 to 35 Hz after classifying superposition individually. For each group, all trials were averaged to increase the signal-to-noise ratio and extract ERPs from the spontaneous EEG. Finally after eliminating the unqualified data, the remaining data was used for the group average. ERP component between 300 to 320 ms after stimulus appearing was extracted. The extracted ERP component includes two parts, namely latency and amplitude. The amplitudes of electrodes in specific brain region were further used to statistical analysis.

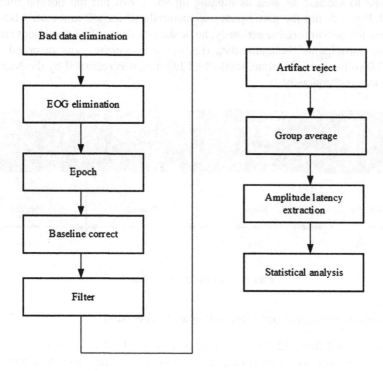

Fig. 3. Procedure of ERP extraction

4   Results

4.1   Behavior Data

Figure 4 shows each participant's detection rate using psychometric functions. The detections, d_r, is defined as the ratio between the right click number and the total click number of each level. It was expressed as:

$$d\_r = \frac{N_r}{N} \tag{1}$$

where N_r and N represent the right and total click numbers, respectively.

As expected, the detection rate increases as the compression ratio increasing, since obvious visual discomfort or incoordination appears. As depicted in Fig. 4, it is obviously that the detected incoordination or discomfort increases faster when the compression level setting is between 2 and 3 (corresponding to the compression ratio 1: 0.61 and 1: 0.52, respectively). In other words, participants hardly perceived the visual discomfort when the compression level beyond 2.

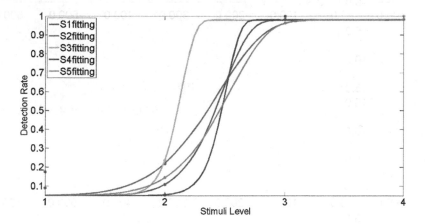

Fig. 4.   Detection Rate of all participants fitting using psychometric functions

4.2   ERP Results

ERP has two notable features, both amplitude and latency are constant in all epoch. The amplitude reflects the brain reaction strength while the latency is typically interpreted as a measurement of the speed of task reaction [16]. P300 is usually obtained in oddball paradigm, where the stimuli are presented with different probabilities in a random order. P300 surfaces as a positive deflection in voltage with a latency (delay between stimulus and response) of roughly 250 to 500 ms [17], it reflects the task difficult and appears in most brain region with the maximum amplitude in parietal lobe.

In this experiment, the P300 component elicited at frontal, parietal and central electrodes look very similar. It is elicited best on parietal lobe and ERPs. Taking the CPZ and PZ electrodes as examples, the mean amplitude is different among the different compression levels, as shown in Fig. 5. From the level 4 to level 1, the mean amplitude reduces, respectively. Meanwhile, the bigger compression ratio corresponds to the shorter latency. The reasonable explanation is that as a kind of advanced cognitive component, the peak amplitude of P300 decreases with task difficulty while latency becomes longer [18]. More information is lost as the compression ratio increases. As a result, the 3D image produces a bad stereoscopic effect, thus inducing visual discomfort and easy identification. In addition, it is easier to identify the worse one, thus requiring less processing time. The amplitude and latency characteristics when viewing 3D pictures mentioned above are valuable principles for 3D visual discomfort assessment. For further analysis of this principle, we apply statistical analysis on amplitude.

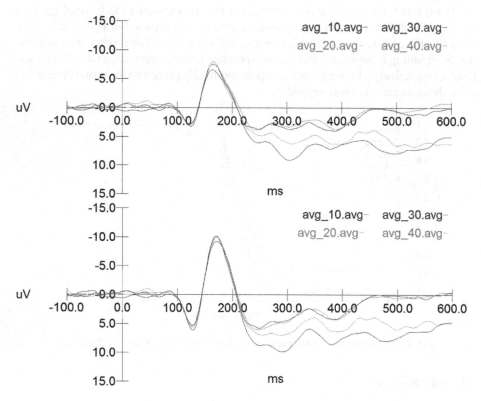

Fig. 5. ERP recorded on CPZ (top) and PZ (bottom) electrodes. The avg_40, avg_10, avg_20, avg_30 correspond to the level 1, 2, 3, 4, respectively.

Electrophysiological data time-locked to the presentation of the 3D stimulus showed the classical succession of visual ERP waveforms in response to various visual events. Table 2 was the statistical results of the mean amplitude using analysis of variance (ANOVA), as the freedom was more than one, the Greenhouse–Geisser correction was used. As mentioned above, the P300 is widely distributed in parietal lobe, central lobe as well as the perimeter zone. Eight electrodes located in these region were analyzed.

Aside from differences in amplitude recorded between the Level 4 and Level 1, the Level 4 and Level 3 ($p < 0.05$), there were no other significant effects on the P300 amplitude on CPZ and FCZ electrodes. Similarly, only significant effects appeared between Level 4 and Level 1, the Level 4 and Level 2 ($p < 0.05$) on PZ, C3 and CZ electrodes. On CP4 and C4 electrodes, the Level 4 and Level 1 had significant effect ($p < 0.05$). From the statistical analysis, the ERP amplitude of P300 differed among the different compression levels. In addition, the amplitude did not differ from the Level 2 and Level 1 ($p > 0.05$), further indicating that the less information loss induced by compression did not contribute substantially to discriminate. As the compression ratio increasing, more information is loss. As a result, the amplitude differed from the Level 4 and Level 1, Level 4 and Level 2 ($p < 0.05$). It indicated that the larger compression ratio causing visual discomfort was sufficient for the discrimination.

Table 2. ANOVA results of mean amplitude per electrode, standard deviation in brackets.

Electrode	Level 1	Level 2	Level 3	Level 4
PZ	3.583(0.892)	4.384(0.627)	6.289(1.175)	8.664(0.716)*,**
CPZ	3.136(0.450)	3.654(1.019)	6.187(0.719)*	8.944(0.706)*,***
CZ	2.486(0.552)	3.218(0.658)	5.615(1.033)	9.405(1.124)*,**
FCZ	3.136(0.450)	3.654(1.019)	6.187(0.719)*	8.944(0.706)*,***
CP3	4.204(0.369)	4.498(0.677)	5.973(1.070)	8.753(0.423)*,**
CP4	3.035(0.281)	3.647(1.093)	4.985(0.362)	7.223(0.231)*
C3	3.377(0.498)	3.704(0.495)	5.478(1.230)	8.756(0.703)*,**
C4	2.450(0.400)	3.069(0.933)	4.519(0.487)	7.716(0.887)*

* Significant from Level 1 (p < 0.05), ** Significant from Level 2 (p < 0.05), *** Significant from Level 3 (p < 0.05).

4.3 Subjective Assessment Results

Before the ERP experiment, 16 participants participated in the subjective assessment experiments with the same stimuli. The subjective categorical judgement method of SS was used with a five-point grading scale (1: extremely uncomfortable, 2: uncomfortable, 3: mildly uncomfortable, 4: comfortable, 5: very comfortable) [19]. Before the experiment, the participants were trained for 50 trails to enhance the comprehension of different compression levels. The 3D images processed by compression with different levels were randomly presented to participant for 5 s, and the participant should evaluate the visual discomfort using the five-point grading scale. Participants were stopped to rest for relieving accumulated fatigue every 10 min. The subjects were allowed to immediately stop if they felt difficult to continue due to excessive visual fatigue. According to the screening methodology recommended by ITU-R BT. 500-11, no outliers were detected. All the subjective scores were averaged and formed the mean option score (MOS). As expected, the lower scores correspond to larger compressed degree of 3D images, as shown in Fig. 6.

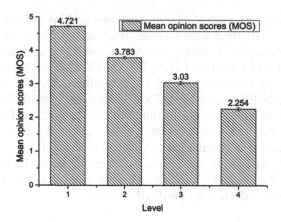

Fig. 6. Mean opinion scores (MOS), bars indicate the standard errors of the means

5   Conclusion and Future Work

The presence of 3D images' compression elicits the response in the brain, which is measurable with ERP. The effect varies with the compression ratio setting and can be observed at parietal lobe best. We have shown that the ERP technique can be applied to evaluate the 3D visual discomfort as an objective measurement in this paper. The amplitude features of P300 component extracted in EEG signals reflect the brain reaction to difficult of task. We firstly use it to evaluate the visual discomfort caused by symmetry compressed 3D images. The amplitude is in agree with the behavior data and MOS. As the amplitude increases and the detection rate increases, the latency gets shorter and the MOS decreases. That is to say, the subjective assessment validates the ERP methods and ERP technique can be used as an objective measurement to evaluate 3D visual discomfort caused by symmetry compressed 3D images.

In future work, we want to find out how precisely and reliably differences in visual discomfort caused by distorted 3D images can be determined by ERPs. Meanwhile, as the fMRI has high space resolution and can precisely trace the source where the visual discomfort happens, we attempt to further explore the brain source that produces 3D visual discomfort. Meanwhile, the ERP has high temporal resolution, the combination of fMRI and ERP can be used to assess the 3D visual discomfort. Compared to 2D images, the 3D visual discomfort is induced by various factors, such as excessive disparity, fast objects' motion and various stereoscopic distortions that yield binocular asymmetries [20]. We will evaluate the 3D visual discomfort caused by above factors using ERP technique in the future. The analysis methods will not limit to the amplitude and latency characteristic and aim to use source energy and rhythm characteristics.

Acknowledgements. This work was supported by the National Science Foundation of China under Grant 61302123, and by National Major Project under Grant 91320201 as well as Doctoral Education Department Foundation under Grant 20130032110010.

References

1. Hoffman, D.M., Girshick, A.R., Akeley, K., Banks, M.S.: Vergence-accommodation conflicts hinder visual performance and cause visual fatigue. J. Vis. **8**(3), 33 (2008)
2. Du, S.P., Masia, B., Hu, S.M., Gutierrez, D.: A metric of visual comfort for stereoscopic motion. ACM Trans. Graph. **32**, 1–8 (2013)
3. Wallace, G.K.: The JPEG still picture compression standard. Commun. ACM **34**(4), 30–44 (1991)
4. Tam, W.J., Speranza, F., Yano, S., Shimono, K., Ono, H.: Stereoscopic 3D-TV: visual comfort. IEEE Trans. Broadcast. **57**, 335–346 (2011)
5. Huynh-Thu, Q., Ghanbari, M.: Scope of validity of PSNR in image/video quality assessment. Electron. Lett. **44**, 800–801 (2008)
6. Tagliasacchi, M., Valenzise, G., Naccari, M., Tubaro, S.: A reduced-reference structural similarity approximation for videos corrupted by channel errors. Multimedia Tools Appl. **48**, 471–492 (2010)
7. Wang, Z., Lu, L., Bovik, A.C.: Video quality assessment based on structural distortion measurement. Signal Process. Image Commun. **19**, 121–132 (2004)
8. Park, J., Oh, H., Lee, S., et al.: 3D visual discomfort predictor: analysis of disparity and neural activity statistics. IEEE Trans. Image Process. **24**(3), 1101–1114 (2015)
9. Scholler, S., et al.: Toward a direct measure of video quality perception using EEG. IEEE Trans. Image Process. **21**, 2619–2629 (2012)
10. Kim, D., et al.: FMRI analysis of excessive binocular disparity on the human brain. Int. J. Imaging Syst. Technol. **24**, 94–102 (2014)
11. Murata, A., Uetake, A., Takasawa, Y.: Evaluation of mental fatigue using feature parameter extracted from event-related potential. Int. J. Ind. Ergon. **35**, 761–770 (2005)
12. Chen, C., et al.: Assessment visual fatigue of watching 3DTV using EEG power spectral parameters. Displays **35**, 266–272 (2014)
13. Zou, B., Liu, Y., Guo, M., et al.: EEG-based assessment of stereoscopic 3D visual fatigue caused by vergence-accommodation conflict. J. Displ. Technol. **11**(12), 1076–1083 (2015)
14. Bang, J.W., Heo, H., Choi, J.S., et al.: Assessment of eye fatigue caused by 3D displays based on multimodal measurements. Sensors **14**(9), 16467–16485 (2014)
15. Scholler, S., Bosse, S., Treder, M.S., et al.: Toward a direct measure of video quality perception using EEG. IEEE Trans. Image Process. **21**(5), 2619–2629 (2012)
16. Duncan, C.C., et al.: Event-related potentials in clinical research: guidelines for eliciting, recording, and quantifying mismatch negativity, P300, and N400. Clin. Neurophysiol. Official J. Int. Fed. Clin. Neurophysiol. **120**, 1883–1908 (2009)
17. Picton, T.W., et al.: Guidelines for using human event-related potentials to study cognition: recording standards and publication criteria. Psychophysiology **37**, 127–152 (2000)
18. Gajewski, P.D., Falkenstein, M.: Effects of task complexity on ERP components in Go/Nogo tasks. Int. J. Psychophysiol. Official J. Int. Organ. Psychophysiol. **87**, 273–278 (2013)
19. Aflaki, P., Hannuksela, M.M., Gabbouj, M.: Subjective quality assessment of asymmetric stereoscopic 3D video. Signal Image Video Process. **9**, 331–345 (2013)
20. Tam, W.J., Speranza, F., Yano, S., et al.: Stereoscopic 3D-TV: visual comfort. IEEE Trans. Broadcast. **57**(2), 335–346 (2011)

Optimization of Charging and Data Collection in Wireless Rechargeable Sensor Networks

Cheng Hu$^{(\boxtimes)}$ and Yun Wang

Key Lab of Computer Network and Information Integration,
MOE Southeast University, Nanjing 211189, China
{chhc,yunwang}@seu.edu.cn

Abstract. *Wireless Rechargeable Sensor Networks* (**WRSN**s) can significantly prolong the lifetime by employing a mobile charger to replenish the depleted energy of the sensor nodes. This paper considers the scenario that the mobile charger cannot maintain full operation of the WRSN. In this case, the first and foremost problem is how to allocate the insufficient energy to the sensor nodes and decide their corresponding data sensing rates. The objective is to maximize the utility of data collection, which concerns data fairness as well as data amount. To address this problem, we first formulate and simplify its optimization form. Then based on two observations, we propose the BalanceFlow scheme, which coordinates data sensing of the sensor nodes with charging of the mobile charger. Numerical results show that, the BalanceFlow scheme achieves near optimal utility compared with the optimization results.

Keywords: Wireless rechargeable sensor networks · Charging scheme · Data collection · Utility maximization

1 Introduction

Wireless Rechargeable Sensor Networks (**WRSN**s) have been gaining tremendous attention from the research community in recent years. In a typical WRSN, a *mobile charger* (**MC**) is employed to wirelessly recharge the batteries of the sensor nodes through techniques of wireless power transmission such as magnetic resonant coupling [1], and the sensor nodes are implanted with receiver chips as small as 3.4×3.56 mm^2 [2]. In this way, the lifetime of the WRSN can be significantly prolonged compared with traditional no-charging WSNs. Such paradigm also has two main advantages over energy-harvesting WSNs: WRSNs are more controllable and predictable in energy supply, and WRSNs are easier and more flexible in deployment.

Recent research on WRSNs focuses on designing charging schemes of the **MC**, in order to maintain the WRSN working continuously, while minimizing the charging cost [3–7]. These works implicitly assume that the **MC** is able to accomplish the charging mission of the WRSN, i.e., make sure that no sensor node will exhaust its energy. This condition is hardly true in unattended environment, where **MC**'s own battery can only be replenished by harvesting environmental energy, such as solar energy. Consequently, the energy provided by the **MC** cannot support full operations of all the sensor nodes. To accommodate these scenarios, researchers propose best-effort charging schemes to

© Springer International Publishing Switzerland 2016
Q. Zu and B. Hu (Eds.): HCC 2016, LNCS 9567, pp. 138–149, 2016.
DOI: 10.1007/978-3-319-31854-7_13

prolong the lifetime of the WRSN. Nevertheless, since the **MC** can harvest certain amount of energy regularly, the WRSN will never really "die". Thus a more important thing than prolonging the lifetime is how to maximize the network utilization during its design life. The network utilization can be a function of total data collected [4, 6], or can be measured by other criteria such as charging throughput and target monitoring quality. In this paper, we aim to maximize data fairness as well as data amount. Specifically, we define the utility function as the summation of the logarithm of total data generated by each sensor node.

Therefore, this paper addresses the *Insufficient Charging Problem* (**ICP**) described above. As the **MC** cannot support full operations of a WRSN, we degrade the data generation of the sensor nodes. Firstly, we observe that averaging data sensing rates of the sensor nodes can achieve high fairness, and allocating more energy to the sensor nodes with smaller energy-consuming coefficients (which will be explained later) can obtain more data. Then we propose the BalanceFlow scheme, which coordinates the data generating of the sensor nodes with the charging behaviors of the **MC**, to balance data fairness with data amount, and thus to maximize the network utilization.

The main contributions of this paper are summarized as follows. (1) We propose and reduce the optimization formulation of the **ICP**, so that it can be efficiently solved by a solver for convex problem. (2) Based on two key observations stated above, we propose the BalanceFlow scheme, which can obtain near optimal results compared with the optimization solution. (3) We conduct numerical simulations to evaluate the performance of the BalanceFlow scheme, and to make comparison with existing solutions. The results also reveal that data fairness is more important than available energy provided by the **MC** with respect to utility gain.

The remainder of the paper is organized as follows. Section 2 introduces the latest related work. Section 3 presents model assumptions and the research problem. The BalanceFlow scheme is proposed in Sect. 4, and evaluated through numerical simulations in Sect. 5. Section 6 concludes the paper.

2 Related Work

Recent advances in techniques of wireless power transmission and smart mobile vehicles have enabled a rapid development of WRSNs in the last few years. Many researchers assume that the MC can be fully replenished at a service station by replacing its battery or through DC charging. Xie et al. [3] let the MC periodically travel along the shortest Hamilton cycle throughout the WRSN to wirelessly charge each sensor node's battery. In this way, they constructed a renewable energy cycle by solving an optimization problem, with the objective of minimizing the overall energy consumption. Guo et al. [5] fully considered the influence of imbalanced energy consumption in WRSNs, and proposed an OnDemand charging scheme, which can be easily applied to address the ICP. Hu et al. [4] studied the problem of joint wireless energy replenishment and mobile data gathering for WRSNs. The target was to maximize the overall network utility in terms of data gathered by the MC. Zhao et al. [6] designed an adaptive solution that jointly selects the sensors to be charged and finds the optimal data gathering scheme, such that network utility can be maximized while maintaining perpetual operations of the network.

These works implicitly assume that the MC is able to accomplish the charging mission. To establish a definite boundary, Hu et al. [7] proposed an efficient decision condition to decide whether such condition holds in a WRSN, and suggest to degrade the charging service level when it fails. In this case, Peng et al. proposed a GreedyPlus scheme to maximize the minimum lifetime of all the sensor nodes, so as to maximize the lifetime of the WRSN. As for other criteria of the WRSN, Li et al. and Ren et al. aimed to maximize the charging throughput of the MC, i.e., maximize the number of charged sensor nodes during each charging cycle, while Dai et al. and Wang et al. aimed to maximize the target monitoring quality in the WRSN.

We, however, are interested in the data collected, and try to maximize the data fairness as well as data amount. This shares the same target in many research on energy-harvesting WSNs. Liu et al. considered time-varying energy conservation constraint, and proposed distributed scheme to timely compute the data sensing rates and routes, in order to maximize the summation of the logarithm of the data sensing rate of each sensor node. Zhang et al. strived to optimize data gathering by jointly considering data sensing and transmission. They first designed a balanced energy allocation scheme for each sensor to manage its energy use, and then proposed a distributed sensing rate and routing control algorithm to jointly optimize data sensing and transmission, while guaranteeing network fairness. In these works, sensor nodes independently harvest energy and thus can estimate their energy budgets. In WRSNs, however, the sensor nodes share a pool of energy that provided by the MC, giving rise to the energy allocation problem.

3   System Model and Problem Formulation

Consider a 2D WRSN composed of n homogeneous rechargeable sensor nodes $\mathbb{N} = \{N_1, N_2, \cdots, N_n\}$, one sink node (denoted by N0), and one MC. Each sensor node is powered by a battery with capacity ES. The battery can be wirelessly recharged by the MC. Since the charging efficiency is high, we omit the charging duration. The data sensing rate of each sensor node Ni is at most g_i^{max} $(1 \leq i \leq n)$. At any time t, the data sensing rate of Ni is $g_i(t) \leq g_i^{max}$. The sensor nodes send their sensed data to the sink node through a fixed tree-shaped route, which is rooted at the sink node. Denote the parent node of Ni by δ_i, the ancestor nodes of Ni by Δ_i, the children nodes of Ni by $C_i = \{c_i^1, c_i^2, \cdots, c_i^{n_i}\}$, and the offspring nodes of Ni by ∇_i. Then we have the following flow balance constraint at Ni:

$$\sum_{j \in C_i} f_{j,i}(t) + g_i(t) = f_{i,\delta_i}(t), \quad 1 \leq i \leq n, \tag{1}$$

where $f_{j,i}(t)$ is the flow rate from Nj to Ni at time t. Let $r_i(t) = \sum_{j \in C_i} f_{j,i}(t)$ representing the data received by Ni at time t, and $s_i(t) = f_{i,\delta_i}(t)$ denoting the data sent by Ni at time t. We adopt the energy model in [3], in which sensor nodes only consume energy in sending and receiving data. Then (1) implies that if the energy level of sensor node Ni falls below 0, or Ni cannot establish a data link to the sink node, Ni switches to a state of sleeping. Although Ni does not generate data or transmit data in the sleeping state, it can receive energy from the MC, and may consequently turn into a state of working. The energy consumption of Ni can be approximated by:

$$p_i(t) = \rho \cdot r_i(t) + \beta_i \cdot s_i(t), \quad 1 \leq i \leq n, \tag{2}$$

where ρ is the energy consumption for receiving per unit of data, and β_i is the energy consumption of N_i for sending per unit of data. In [3], $\beta_i = \left(\beta_1 + \beta_2 \cdot d_{i,j}^{\alpha} \right)$, where β_1 and β_2 are const coefficients, $d_{i,j}$ is the distance between N_i and N_j, and α is the path lose index. Note that the energy consumption of the sensor nodes is maximal when the sensor nodes sense data at their maximal rates. The maximal energy consumption rate of N_i is denoted by p_i^{max}.

The network utilization is defined as the summation of the Log of total data generated by each sensor node, which can be used to guarantee the fairness of data sensing rates.

$$U(x) = \sum_{i=1}^{n} \log(1 + x_i), \quad x_i = \int_t g_i(t), \quad 1 \leq i \leq n, \tag{3}$$

where x_i is the total amount of data generated by N_i.

Suppose that the **MC** can harvest energy from ambient energy, such as solar energy, and it can recharge the sensor nodes only when it has harvested enough energy. Denote E_M as the energy threshold that the **MC** can conduct charging, and let Γ be the period that the **MC** can harvest E_M energy. In reality, the amount of energy harvested by the **MC** during Γ may float around E_M. Nevertheless, the **MC** can keep const energy supply by storing extra energy to a backup battery, or overdraw energy from the backup battery when the energy harvested is insufficient. Without losing the essence of the problem, we carefully omit the moving time and moving energy of the **MC**. Then it implies that the sensor nodes can share E_M energy in each period Γ. Specifically, we consider the situation that the **MC** cannot maintain full operation of the WRSN, which is complementary to works like [3–7]. Formally speaking, we assume that

$$E_M < \sum_{i=1}^{n} p_i^{max} \cdot \Gamma. \tag{4}$$

Since the **MC** cannot overcharge the batteries of the sensor nodes, we have the following charging constraints:

$$\sum_{i=1}^{n} \gamma_i \leq E_M, \tag{5}$$

$$e_i(t) + \gamma_i \leq E_S, \quad 1 \leq i \leq n, \tag{6}$$

where t is the time when the **MC** charges N_i, $e_i(t)$ is the residual energy of N_i at time t, and γ_i is the amount of energy transferred to N_i. Furthermore, we let the **MC** conduct charging at the beginning of each round, and each sensor node can be charged at most once in each round.

Therefore, the problem under study is formulated as follows.

$$\text{Maximize} \quad U(x),$$
$$\text{s.t.} \quad (1)(2)(4)(5)(6).$$
(7)

4   The BalanceFlow Scheme

4.1   Reformulation of the Optimization Problem

Since the MC cannot guarantee full operation of the WRSN according to (4), the data generation of the WRSN has to be degraded. There are three possible ways of degradation: (a) ensure operational of a subset of sensor nodes, and let the other nodes sleep; (b) let the WRSN fully operational as long as possible, and sleep until next charging period; (c) let each sensor node generate data at a lower rate, so as to work all the time. The first way performs bad since its fairness is poor, and thus $U(x)$ is low. The second way and the third way can be mathematically equal, i.e., they can achieve the same value of $U(x)$. Nevertheless, when the data is highly related to its sensed time, the third way is more rational. Thus we adopt the third way and subsequently simplify the formulation of (7).

Based on the third degradation way, the data sensing rate of Ni is set to a const value gi $\left(1 \leq i \leq n, \; g_i \leq g_i^{max}\right)$. Consequently, the energy consumption rate of Ni is also fixed to $p_i \leq p_i^{max}$. To make sure that all sensor nodes work all the time, their depleted energy should be timely replenished, i.e.,

$$p_i \cdot \Gamma = \gamma_i.$$
(8)

Combining (5) with (8), we have

$$\sum_{i=1}^{n} p_i \cdot \Gamma \leq E_M.$$
(9)

Combining (1), (2) with (9), we have

$$\sum_{i=1}^{n} \omega_i \cdot g_i \leq E_M, \quad \omega_i = \left(\beta_i + \sum_{j \in \Delta_i} (\rho + \beta_j)\right) \cdot \Gamma, \quad 1 \leq i \leq n.$$
(10)

We name ω_i as the energy-consuming coefficient of Ni, which reveals the actual energy consumption of the whole WRSN for forwarding per unit of Ni's data to the sink node in each charging period. Let $G = [g_1, g_2, \cdots, g_n]^T$, $\Omega = [\omega_1, \omega_2, \cdots, \omega_n]$, then the inequality in (10) can be rewritten as $\Omega \cdot G \leq E_M$. Let $G_{max} = [g_1^{max}, g_2^{max}, \cdots, g_n^{max}]^T$, and I denote the $n \times n$ identity matrix, then it satisfies that $I \cdot G \leq G_{max}$.

Since $e_i(t) \geq 0$ in (6), plug (8) into (6) we have $p_i \cdot \Gamma \leq E_S$. Combine it with (1) and (2), we have

$$\left(\beta_i \cdot g_i + (\rho + \beta_i) \cdot \sum_{j \in C_i} g_j \right) \cdot \Gamma \leq E_S, \quad 1 \leq i \leq n. \tag{11}$$

Let $\Lambda = [\Lambda_1^T, \cdots, \Lambda_n^T]^T$, $\Lambda_i = [\lambda_i^1, \cdots, \lambda_i^n]$, $\lambda_i^j = \begin{cases} \beta_j, & j = i \\ \rho + \beta_j, & j \in C_i \\ 0, & \text{otherwise} \end{cases}$, and $E = [E_S, E_S, \cdots, E_S]^T$, then (11) is equivalent to $\Lambda \cdot G \leq E$.

Therefore, the optimization problem presented in (7) equals to

$$\begin{aligned} \textbf{Maximize} \quad & U(x), \\ s.t. \quad & A \cdot G \leq b, \quad A = \begin{bmatrix} \Omega \\ I \\ \Lambda \end{bmatrix}, \quad b = \begin{bmatrix} E_M \\ G_{max} \\ E \end{bmatrix}. \end{aligned} \tag{12}$$

Since $\log(G)$ is strictly concave, and the constraint $A \cdot G \leq b$ is linear, the formula (12) is a concave optimization problem. To solve this problem one can use CVX, a package for specifying and solving convex programs. However, in a WRSN, the sink node usually does not have powerful processors to solve the problem (12). Therefore, we propose a simple heuristic scheme, named BalanceFlow scheme, to address the problem.

4.2   The BalanceFlow Scheme

The BalanceFlow Scheme is developed based on two observations. (a) Given the total data sensing rate of all the sensor nodes, the utility function can take higher value if the data sensing rates of the sensor nodes are more balanced. It implies that one can force each sensor node generates data at the same rate, and the rate can be derived from the energy constraints above. Unfortunately, it is not the optimum choice since (b) forwarding data of different sensor nodes to the sink node consumes different amount of energy. In other words, the energy transferred to different sensor nodes makes difference in improving the value of the objective function U(x).

Remind that ω_i, the energy-consuming coefficient of Ni, reflects the actual energy consumption of the whole WRSN for forwarding per unit of Ni's data to the sink node in each charging period. We thus propose the following heuristic rule to determine the data sensing rate of each sensor node: Sensor node Ni generates data at a rate inversely proportional to its energy-consuming coefficient ω_i. Specifically, let $g_i \propto 1/\omega_i$, and $\sum_{i=1}^n g_i \cdot \omega_i = E_M$, then we have

$$g_i = \frac{E_M}{n \cdot \omega_i}.$$ (13)

When applying this heuristic to derive the data sensing rates of the sensor nodes, the remaining issues are how to deal with the situations that (a) the derived data sensing rate of Ni is larger than g_i^{max}, and (b) the total energy consumption of Ni during Γ is larger than ES. In these situations, the data sensing rates of Ni or Ni's offspring nodes should be lowered. Consequently, the energy originally consumed to forward these data is saved, and thus can be allocated to other sensor nodes. We greedily assign the saved energy to the sensor nodes in ascending order of their energy-consuming coefficients.

Formally speaking, if Ni decreases its data sensing rate by di, the amount of energy saved is $save = d_i \cdot \omega_i$. These energy can be allocated to Nj if (a) Nj is not sensing data at its maximum rate, i.e., $g_j < g_j^{max}$; (b) Nj's parent node can receive more data, i.e., $ar_{\delta_j} > 0$; (c) the energy consumption of Nj during Γ is less than ES, i.e., $\rho \cdot r_j + \beta_j \cdot s_j < E_S$. In condition (b), ari stands for the augmented data sensing rate of Ni. If ari > 0, Ni's data receiving rate can be increased by ari. Obviously, it is no larger than its ancestor nodes' augmented data sensing rates, i.e., $ar_i \leq ar_j$ $(j \in \Delta_i)$. At the same time, it will not cause Ni consuming energy larger than ES during Γ, i.e., $\rho \cdot (r_i + ar_i) + \beta_i \cdot (s_i + ar_i) \leq E_S$. Based on these rules, we propose the BalanceFlow scheme in Algorithm 1 to decide the data sensing rates of all the sensor nodes.

Algorithm 1 (BalanceFlow). Decide the data sensing rates of the sensor nodes.

Require: $\mathbb{N}, \{C_i\}, \{\Delta_i\}, G_{max}, E_S, E_M$;
Ensure: $G, U(x)$;
01: estimate the energy-consuming coefficients $\{\omega_i\}$ using (10);
02: calculate the initial value of $\{g_i\}$ using (13);
03: sort $\mathbb{N}$ by their route levels and energy-consuming coefficients;
04: calculate the initial value of $\{r_i\}$ and $\{s_i\}, 1 \leq i \leq n$;
05: **for** $N_i = N_1$ to N_n **do**
06:    **if** N_i's energy consumption during Γ exceeds E_S **do**
07:       scale down the data sensing rates of the entire subtree rooted at N_i;
08:       add the unused energy to *save*;
09:    **end if**
10:    **if** $g_i > g_i^{max}$ **do**
11:       $g_i = g_i^{max}$;
12:       add the unused energy to *save*;
13:    **end if**
14: **end for**
15: **for** $N_i = N_1$ to N_n **do**
16:    **if** N_i can augment ag_i **do**
17:       assign as much energy to N_i as possible;
18:       update sending and receiving rates of N_i's ancestor nodes;
19:    **end if**
20: **end for**
21: $U(x) = \sum_{i=1}^{n} \log(1 + g_i \cdot \Gamma \cdot \kappa)$;

Firstly, the initial data sensing rates G of the sensor nodes are estimated according to (10) and (13) (lines 1–2), and the initial data sending and receiving rates of the sensor nodes are calculated accordingly (line 3). Note that the sensor nodes are numbered in ascending order of their route levels (the route level of a sensor node equals to its hop number to the sink node), and in ascending order of their energy-consuming coefficients when their route levels are the same. Then G is adjusted based on the rules presented above (lines 5–21). The algorithm checks each sensor node N_i if its energy consumption during Γ exceeds E_S; if so, it scales down the data sensing rates of the entire sub-tree rooted at N_i (lines 6–9). Then it checks if g_i is still larger than g_i^{max}; if so, it simply sets $g_i = g_i^{max}$ (lines 10–13). The energy saved by decreasing the data sensing rates is stored in the variable *save*. Subsequently, the algorithm checks each sensor node N_i if it can augment its data sensing rate, and assign as much energy to it as possible (lines 15–20). Once N_i's data sensing rate is increased, its ancestors' data sending and receiving rates should be adjusted. The algorithm terminates if *save* is used up, or no more sensor node can augment its data sensing rate. Finally, the utility of the WRSN is calculated in line 21, where κ is the total charging rounds. It can be readily proved that the time complexity of the algorithm is $O(n \log(n))$.

5 Numerical Results

We evaluate the performance of the BalanceFlow scheme through numerical simulations. To this end, we randomly generate WRSNs over 1000×1000 m^2 square area. The sink node is located at the center of the area. The WRSN applies the minimal energy routing scheme, and the communication range of each sensor node is 200 m. Initially, the residual energy of the sensor nodes is 0, which is the stable status under the condition that the MC cannot maintain full operation of the WRSN. By default, we set $\alpha = 4$, $\beta 1 = 50$ nJ/b, $\beta 2 = 0.0013$ pJ·m^4/b, ES = 10 kJ [3], $g_i^{max} = 100$ kb/s $(1 \leq i \leq n)$, $\Gamma = 86400$ s (or roughly one day), $\kappa = 18000$ (or roughly 50 years).

For comparison, we select the OnDemand scheme [5] and the GreedyPlus scheme. The OnDemand scheme greedily charges the sensor nodes with least residual energy; the GreedyPlus scheme maximizes the minimum lifetime of all sensor nodes. In these schemes, we let the sensor nodes sense data at their maximum rates. In fact, these two schemes correspond to the first two degradation ways presented in Sect. 4.1. We also use CVX to solve (7) (labeled as the Optimization scheme), and regard its result as the upper bound of the problem.

We firstly range the network size from 50 nodes to 300 nodes, and range E_M from 10 kJ to 50 kJ in each sized WRSN, to evaluate the utility gained by these schemes. Each data is averaged over 5 simulations. The results are shown in Fig. 1, the left Y-axises depict the utility of the OnDemand scheme, while the right Y-axises show the utility of other schemes. Generally speaking, the utility of all the schemes increases as E_M increases, and the utility of the OnDemand scheme is far less than that of other schemes. This is because the OnDemand always charges the sensor nodes with least residual energy, and thus the sensor nodes around the WRSN are most frequently charged due to the energy-hole phenomenon [5]. Consequently, the data collected by

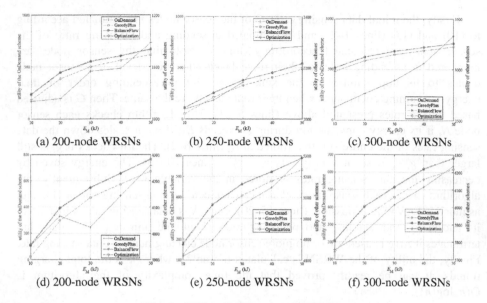

(a) 200-node WRSNs   (b) 250-node WRSNs   (c) 300-node WRSNs

(d) 200-node WRSNs   (e) 250-node WRSNs   (f) 300-node WRSNs

Fig. 1. Utility of different scale WRSNs

the OnDemand scheme is extremely unfair: most data is generated by the sensor nodes around the sink node, and only a little data is generated by the outer sensor nodes. Compared with the OnDemand scheme, other schemes are much fairer in data sensing. Specifically, the GreedyPlus scheme aims to unify the lifetime of all the sensor nodes. Since the maximum data sensing rates of the sensor nodes are the same, the GreedyPlus scheme is the fairest among these 4 schemes. The BalanceFlow scheme and the Optimization scheme unify the actual energy consumption of each sensor node, which balances fairness with energy efficiency. Informally speaking, in these two schemes, more energy is assigned to the sensor node that locates nearer to the sink node, and thus more data can be collected. As a result, the utility of the GreedyPlus scheme is lower than that of the BalanceFlow scheme and the Optimization scheme, while the Optimization scheme only slightly outperforms the BalanceFlow scheme.

To verify the inference above, we also display the total data gathered by these schemes in Fig. 2. In general, the total data of these schemes increases as E_M increases; the OnDemand scheme collects the most data in all cases, followed by the BalanceFlow scheme, the Optimization scheme, and the GreedyPlus scheme. The OnDemand scheme actually assigns most energy to the sensor nodes nearer to the sink node, whose energy-consuming coefficients are the smallest. This explains why the OnDemand scheme collects the most data. In contrast, the GreedyPlus scheme assigns more energy to outer nodes, so that they can work as long as inner nodes. Since the energy-consuming coefficients of the outer nodes are much higher, the total collected data is much less. The BalanceFlow scheme and the Optimization scheme balance data fairness with data amount, thus their results are in between the other two schemes.

Another interesting observation of Fig. 2 is that the BalanceFlow scheme gathers significantly more data than the Optimization scheme in 50-node and 100-node

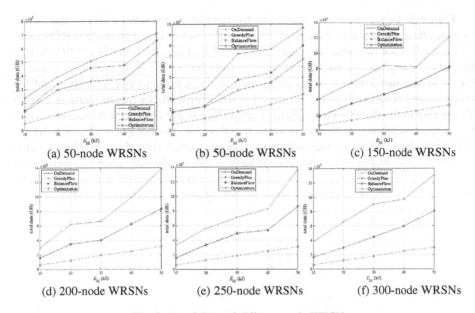

(a) 50-node WRSNs   (b) 50-node WRSNs   (c) 150-node WRSNs

(d) 200-node WRSNs   (e) 250-node WRSNs   (f) 300-node WRSNs

Fig. 2. Total data of different scale WRSNs

WRSNs, while collecting much the same data as the Optimization scheme in larger scale WRSNs. This is because in small scale WRSNs, based on (13), the energy assigned to the sensor nodes with least energy-consuming coefficients exceeds it battery volume, or makes the sensor nodes' data sensing rates higher than the upper bound. Consequently, the BalanceFlow scheme greedily reassigns the saved energy to other sensor nodes that can augment their data sensing rates according to Algorithm 1. While the Optimization scheme optimizes the data sensing rates of all the sensor nodes in order to maximize the network utilization. Therefore, the data collected by the BalanceFlow scheme is much more than that of the Optimization scheme in small sized WRSNs. As for large scale WRSNs, the reassignment process is seldom carried out, thus the total data collected by these schemes is almost the same.

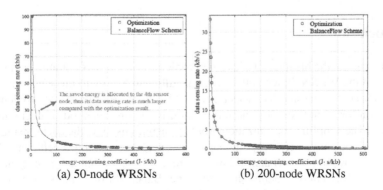

(a) 50-node WRSNs   (b) 200-node WRSNs

Fig. 3. Data sensing rate vs. energy-consuming coefficient of each sensor node

Figure 3 demonstrates the viewpoint by comparing the data sensing rates of the Optimization scheme with those of the BalanceFlow scheme in a 50-node WRSN and a 200-node WRSN (in these two cases, E_M = 30 kJ). The blue curve is the fit curve of the data sensing rate vs. energy-consuming coefficient of the Optimization scheme. In Fig. 3(a), the top 3 sensor nodes sense data at the maximum rate 100 kb/s, and the saved energy is assigned to the 4th sensor node. Therefore, it generates data at a much higher rate in the BalanceFlow scheme than it does in the Optimization scheme. Since its energy-consuming coefficient is much less than the other sensor nodes, it turns out that the BalanceFlow scheme collects significantly more data than the Optimization scheme. While in Fig. 3(b), the reassignment is not conducted, since the initial data sensing rates obtained by (13) are valid. It can be seen that the data sensing rates of the two schemes are almost identical, so as the utility and the total data (see Fig. 4).

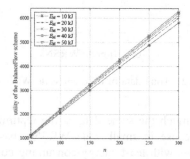

Fig. 4. Utility of the BalanceFlow scheme varying n

Finally, we explore the most important parameter that influences the utility gain. To this end, we show the utility gain of the BalanceFlow scheme in different scale WRSNs and with different value of E_M. Obviously, the key factor is the size of the WRSN, which approximately follows a linear relationship with the utility gain. In comparison, the available energy E_M only has trivial impact on the utility gain. This also verifies the importance of fairness in data sensing rates of the sensor nodes.

6   Conclusion

This paper studies the Insufficient Charging Problem: when the **MC** cannot guarantee full operation of the WRSN, how to allocate the insufficient energy to the sensor nodes and decide their corresponding data sensing rates. We firstly formulate the problem in an optimization form, and simplify the formulation based on a method of degrading data generation. The simplified optimization problem inspires us to set the data sensing rate of each sensor node inversely proportional to its energy-consuming coefficient. Consequently, we propose the BalanceFlow scheme, whose computation complexity is $O(n \log(n))$. Simulation results show that the BalanceFlow scheme achieves near optimal utility compared with the optimization solution, which significantly outperforms existing charging schemes. At the same time, the BalanceFlow scheme collects relatively large amount of data among all the evaluated schemes. The simulation results also reveal that data fairness is the key point to utility gain.

Acknowledgements. This research work is partially supported by the NSF of China under grant No. 60973122, and the 973 Program in China.

References

1. Kurs, A., Karalis, A., Moffatt, R., Joannopoulos, J.D., Fisher, P., Soljačić, M.: Wireless power transfer via strongly coupled magnetic resonances. Science **317**(5834), 83–86 (2007)
2. NXP Semiconductors. http://www.nxp.com
3. Xie, L.G., Shi, Y., Hou, Y.T., Sherali, H.D.: Making sensor networks immortal: an energy-renewal approach with wireless power transfer. IEEE/ACM Trans. Netw. **20**(6), 1748–1761 (2012)
4. Hu, C., Wang, Y., Zhou, L.: Make imbalance useful: an energy-efficient charging scheme in wireless sensor networks. In: Zu, Q., Vargas-Vera, M., Hu, B. (eds.) ICPCA/SWS. LNCS, vol. 8351, pp. 160–171. Springer, Heidelberg (2014)
5. Guo, S., Wang, C., Yang, Y.: Mobile data gathering with wireless energy replenishment in rechargeable sensor networks. In: Proceedings of INFOCOM, pp. 1932–1940 (2013)
6. Zhao, M., Li, J., Yang, Y.Y.: A framework of joint mobile energy replenishment and data gathering in wireless rechargeable sensor networks. IEEE Trans. Mob. Comput. **13**(12), 2689–2705 (2014)
7. Hu, C., Wang, Y.: Schedulability decision of charging missions in wireless rechargeable sensor networks. In: IEEE International Conference on Sensing, Communication, and Networking, pp. 450–458 (2014)

Single Link Routing Protocol for Wireless Sensor Network

Haolei Huang, Yong Zhang[✉], Da Guo, Yifei Wei, Juan Chen, and Xuyan Bao

School of Electronic Engineering, Beijing University of Posts and Telecommunications,
Beijing 100876, China
{huanghaolei,yongzhang,guoda,weiyifei}@bupt.edu.cn
499769923@qq.com, blxmyx@foxmail.com

Abstract. In this paper, we have proposed a single link routing protocol for wireless sensor network for the pre-deployed nodes in areas such as Fire Protection and Wildlife Surveillance. In our routing protocol, the single link was taken into consideration, which always appeared by the lack of device energy, the bad environment or sleep/wake of nodes themselves. To solve the problem caused by that condition, we have proposed one method of detecting unidirectional links by the Neighbor Matrix described in our paper. Once we have maintained the whole routing information of the pre-deployed nodes, the whole network could be accessible by every available path, of course, single link is included; yet the single link is only available when transmission is from the upstream node to the downstream node. This manner not only solves the shortage of traditional one, but also improves the transmission rate and efficiency of the network. From the simulation results, the proposed scheme can achieve remarkable performance improvements in terms of network efficiency, network delivery and end-to-end delay when compared with the traditional one.

Keywords: Neighbor matrix · Wireless sensor network · Network delivery · End-to-end delay · Network efficiency

1 Introduction

The traditional wireless sensor network routing protocols (TWSN) were widely used in many two-way link routing protocol networks, while in reality the topologies of the network are influenced by some other external factors, such as energy of nodes, wake/sleep and so on, these make the bad situation possible. Considering the existing unidirectional links may increase the overhead of the network, in this paper, we have proposed a new scheme of detecting the unidirectional links.

There have been many researchers focusing on single links occurred in the networks. Reference [1] introduces two new medium access control protocol called MLMAC-UL and ECTS-MAC that are able to transmit data over unidirectional links and receive acknowledgement messages for them using a neighborhood discovery protocol. Reference [2] focuses on node activity scheduling and its benefits brought by a cross layering approach. Reference [3] intends to realize the high channel utilization in wireless sensor network where nodes have different communication ranges. Reference [4] is attempted to design an efficiency key establishment scheme for sensor network with considerable

© Springer International Publishing Switzerland 2016
Q. Zu and B. Hu (Eds.): HCC 2016, LNCS 9567, pp. 150–159, 2016.
DOI: 10.1007/978-3-319-31854-7_14

amount of unidirectional links. Reference [5] presents a virtual coordinate assignment protocol to assign virtual coordinates to that have no geographic information in wireless sensor networks with unidirectional links. Reference [6] is investigated the effects of reverse path length in WSNs (wireless sensor networks) with unidirectional links induced by transmission power heterogeneity on network lifetime through a novel mixed integer programming framework.

However, the above algorithms are not involved in the routing algorithm that the single link is determined directly of static nodes pre-deployed in advance, due to all kinds of requirement of fast transmission, lower overhead and higher efficiency; One algorithm of checking unidirectional links becomes an urgent demand.

In this paper, we have investigated one scheme of single link routing protocol for wireless sensor network with three main parts: Single Link Detection part, Error Routing Definition and the Execution Procedure, in Single Link Detection part, we have proposed Distinguishable Single Link Neighbor Matrix (DSLNM), Non-Distinguishable Single Link Neighbor Matrix (NDSLNM) and Common Neighbor Node (CNN); for Error Routing Definition part, mainly are Neighbor Node Error Routing (NNER) and Non-Neighbor Node Error Routing (NNNER); in the Execution Procedure part, we have described the whole operation process of this scheme.

The rest of this paper is organized as follows: Sect. 2 shows the algorithm; Sect. 3 presents simulation results; Sect. 4 concludes the paper; the last section is the sincere acknowledge.

2 Single Link Routing Protocol

Before we are getting to know the single link routing protocol, let us take a look at something about Graph Theory. In order to facilitate the description and modeling, the wireless sensor network is abstracted as a directed graph G (V, E), the vertices of the graph are corresponded with the nodes of the network, and directed arcs are like the directed links of the networks. For example, directed graph <Vi, Vj> and <Vj, Vi> are quoted to indicate the link between Vi and Vj, while they are not the same link. In this directed graph, <Vi, Vj> represents the link from node Vi to node Vj, whereas, <Vj, Vi> is just the opposite.

From Fig. 1, one figure of the wireless sensor network structure, we can see that two-way arrow arcs represents bidirectional links where the two nodes can communicate with each other in it; while single links represented in one unidirectional way may also occur by some other factors. Considering the emitting power of the network after the long time energy consuming, it may be the situation depicted in Fig. 1 where the whole network is divided into two parts by the node G: nodes A, B, C, D, E and F constitute the subnet 1, while nodes G, H, I and J constitute the subnet 2.

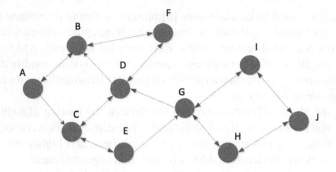

Fig. 1. Wireless sensor network structure

The existing routing protocols of wireless sensor network routing algorithm are most for the two-way links. From Fig. 1, though there is a single link from node A to node C, the communication between the two nodes cannot be completed directly, in fact, it is realized by using the multi hop between the nodes, A-B-F-D-C. In this way, it not only brings the high-time-delay, but also increases the overhead of the network. As we can see from Fig. 1 that node G is the key node of the two subnets, in terms of using the traditional bi-directional link routing protocol, the whole network is divided into two small parts. Thus one new routing protocol which can complete problem of unidirectional transmission not only connects the original split networks, but also enhances the connectivity and efficiency of the networks.

2.1 Single Link Detection

(1) **DSLNM and NDSLNM.** The network nodes periodically send IOHELLO messages and receive IOHELLORP messages, and the according to the routing information received from the neighbor nodes, information tables and neighbor routing information are updated. All the neighbor routing information formats of network nodes are the same, mainly are {node ID, node Address, Node of Last Hop, Status}. In the neighbor routing information, the status values are only 0 and 1; 0 represents link failure, 1 represents normal link, besides, the status values of nodes themselves are 1 for convenient purpose in information tables. In this way, we can get the neighbor routing information of each node. We take node A and node C as an example, here:

Neighbor routing information of node A: [1 1 0 0 0 0 0 0 0 0], and neighbor routing information of node C: [1 0 1 1 1 0 0 0 0 0]. Routing information exchange between nodes periodically, after several periods, the nodes can know the whole topology of the network. At a certain moment, just as the topology depicted in Fig. 1, we can get its neighbor matrix (constituted by neighbor routing information of each node), see Fig. 2:

$$A = \begin{bmatrix} 1 & 1 & 0 & 0 & 0 & 0 & 0 & 0 & 0 & 0 \\ 1 & 1 & 0 & 1 & 0 & 1 & 0 & 0 & 0 & 0 \\ 1 & 0 & 1 & 1 & 1 & 0 & 0 & 0 & 0 & 0 \\ 0 & 0 & 1 & 1 & 0 & 1 & 1 & 0 & 0 & 0 \\ 0 & 0 & 1 & 0 & 1 & 0 & 0 & 0 & 0 & 0 \\ 0 & 1 & 0 & 1 & 0 & 1 & 0 & 0 & 0 & 0 \\ 0 & 0 & 0 & 0 & 1 & 0 & 1 & 1 & 1 & 0 \\ 0 & 0 & 0 & 0 & 0 & 0 & 1 & 1 & 0 & 1 \\ 0 & 0 & 0 & 0 & 0 & 0 & 1 & 0 & 1 & 1 \\ 0 & 0 & 0 & 0 & 0 & 0 & 0 & 1 & 1 & 1 \end{bmatrix}$$

Fig. 2. Non-distinguishable single link neighbor matrixes

In Fig. 2, values 0 and 1 constitute the whole matrix, no matter how the neighbor information change, the value of main diagonal still remain value 1 just as depicted in neighbor routing information part. 0 represents link failure, 1 represents normal link in the matrix above. In addition, each row represents the link connection of one node to all the other nodes in the network. To check the single links from the whole network, values 2 and 3 are added to the information table. Value 2 means link valid from the beginning to the end; value 3 is just the opposite, exchange routing information in this way, matrix of Fig. 2 updates to another type (Fig. 3):

$$B = \begin{bmatrix} 1 & 1 & 2 & 0 & 0 & 0 & 0 & 0 & 0 & 0 \\ 1 & 1 & 0 & 3 & 0 & 1 & 0 & 0 & 0 & 0 \\ 3 & 0 & 1 & 1 & 1 & 0 & 0 & 0 & 0 & 0 \\ 0 & 2 & 1 & 1 & 0 & 1 & 3 & 0 & 0 & 0 \\ 0 & 0 & 1 & 0 & 1 & 0 & 2 & 0 & 0 & 0 \\ 0 & 1 & 0 & 1 & 0 & 1 & 0 & 0 & 0 & 0 \\ 0 & 0 & 0 & 2 & 3 & 0 & 1 & 1 & 1 & 0 \\ 0 & 0 & 0 & 0 & 0 & 0 & 1 & 1 & 0 & 1 \\ 0 & 0 & 0 & 0 & 0 & 0 & 1 & 0 & 1 & 1 \\ 0 & 0 & 0 & 0 & 0 & 0 & 0 & 1 & 1 & 1 \end{bmatrix}$$

Fig. 3. Distinguishable single link neighbor matrixes

There exist 4 states: 0, 1, 2 and 3, among them, 0 still means link failure, 1 means normal bidirectional link; While 2 means the normal unidirectional link from local node to its neighbor one, 3 is just the opposite. As depicted in former part in defining value 2 and value 3, we mark time T as one hop transmission time between two nodes. Reply time t exceeds time T; the links are regarded as unidirectional link automatically. From the matrix, we can easily know the connection of the links and the distribution of unidirectional links.

As we know that the neighbor matrix is useful in viewing the unidirectional link to select the optimization path, but the problem is that the matrix can be obtained for a long time by routing information exchange. In order to improve the efficiency, CNN has been proposed with the mechanism of transferring unidirectional-link-information between two nodes via the common neighbor node.

(2) **CNN.** Δ Network: composed by three neighbor nodes there exists two bidirectional links and one single link.

Before we are getting to know the whole network, we have defined three kinds of nodes, see:

Value 1: core nodes
Value 2 or 3: edge nodes
Value 0: death nodes.

In order to maintain the whole network and make a further understanding of the network efficiency, we should know the main distribution of three kinds of nodes. As we know that the Δ networks (backbone networks) are constituted by the core nodes, grasping the backbone networks is to grasp the entire network; edge nodes constituted the added networks, which can be one supplement to backbone ones, especially in leading to optimize short path; death nodes are the ignored part whether their data transmission or packet.

As we know that it is easy to check the bidirectional links, thus we first should check nodes in them by using the traditional method. After the value 1 is presented in the neighbor matrix, and then nodes (A–J) are selected from the first row to the last one in a successive order way to check the existence of bidirectional ways among the other nodes apart from nodes themselves, here, we mark i is the selected one, which belongs to one node of A to J; if there exists two or more nodes with a value of 1, the other nodes apart from node i in row i are send packets mutually in one single link routing way; if the nodes with a value of 2 or 3 last time, the nodes should send packets again this time; if the nodes with the value of 0, the nodes are regarded as link failure directly.

Of course, the process of updating should be recorded, indeed, the routing information of isolated nodes should be sent to core nodes near them to make a backup.

Here, we just take an example to illustrate that theory, when node B receives the IOHELLO message from node D, the routing information of node D is added to neighbor routing form of node B, structure of it is {ID of node D, Address of node D, node D, backup, 1}; while reversed communication is failure (maybe caused by link interruption or the limited energy of node B), routing information of node B is {ID of node B, Address of node B, null, 0}. The single link is detected between node B and node D by using common neighbor node F in contrasting the routing forms received from node B and node D, and then updates the information of node B and node D. Node B {ID of node D, Address of node D, node D, 2}; Node D {ID of node B, Address of node B, null, 3}.

2.2   Error Routing Definition

Error routing: One failure link between two nodes caused by decrease of emitting power or sudden disorder. Error Routing Definition is quoted to check out all the failure links to diminish the overhead of the network by Neighbor Node Error Routing and Non-Neighbor Node Error Routing.

(1) **NNER.** In unidirectional link wireless sensor networks, the nodes send IOHELLO messages to their neighbor nodes to check the connection. Format of IOHELLO (Table 1):

Table 1. Format of IOHELLO

Source address	Destination address	Version	Number

Version of IOHELLO message is determined by the sending time, Number consists of 0 and 1, 0 means the Number of the IOHELLO message sent by first time, 1 indicates Number of IOHELLO message sent by the second time with the same version of the first time. When node B has received IOHELLO message sent by node A, then node B will reply one IOHELLORP message with the format below (Table 2):

Table 2. Format of IOHELLORP

Source address	Destination address	Version	Number

When the source node has received the IOHELLORP messages from destination node, only the IOHELLORP of bigger Number (same with Version of IOHELLO) are accepted. If source node can receive the messages of IOHELLORP within specified time (two periods), normal link exists; if source node receives message of IOHELLORP over 2 periods, bidirectional link fails; if source node has not received messages of IOHEL-LORP within 1 period, message of IOHELLO is continued again from source node to its neighbor node with the same Version, Number 1, within 1 period source has not received message of IOHELLORP, link fails and updates the routing form; single link is formed under the situation that source node receives message of IOHELLORP with same Version, different Number from its neighbor node in continuous periods and then routing table is updated.

(2) **NNNER.** Support single link wireless sensor network (SWSN) is one demand routing protocol link the traditional sensor network, only specified route which has been used is saved. When source node needs the communication with destination node, first, it checks its routing table, if succeed, checks the effectiveness of the link by using LHELLO from source node to destination node; if fails, starts route discovery (Table 3).

Table 3. Format of LHELLO

Source address	Num 1 address, ..., Num N address	Destination address	Number of hop	Version

Source node is replied with LOHELLORP from destination node once it receives LHELLO. Format of LHELLORP (Table 4):

Table 4. Format of LHELLORP

Source address	Num 1 address, ..., Num N address	Destination address	Number of hop	Version

If source node receives LHELLORP from destination with the same Version in transmission delay, the link is valid, while if source node does not receive it, the link may be considered a failure link, and then route discovery is started, routing table is updated.

2.3 Execution Procedure

According to the above analysis and design, the algorithm procedure:

Step 1: Parameter initialization. Initial the total number of nodes n (n means the valid nodes), each node can get routing information from the other n-1 nodes and we mark it the number 1, here, we mark each node from itself the number 1 as well. So we can get matrix $A = n \times n$. If any one node i belonged to n can get routing information from another one j (node i does not equal to node j) belonged to n as well, on the contrary, it is not so, here we mark i = 2; similarly we mark i = 3 (node j can get routing information from node i, node i cannot get information from node j).

Set the conditions of stopping the iteration:

$$m <= n / \sum_{k=1}^{n} \theta_k N_k \qquad (1.1)$$

$$i <= n/l \qquad (1.2)$$

$$\theta_T = \sum_{k=1}^{n} \overline{\theta}_k t_k / T \qquad (1.3)$$

Note: m means numbers of 0 from $\forall x \in [A, J]$; $\theta_k \in (0, 1)$, $\theta_k \propto e$; e represents the energy; $N_k \propto n$; $l \propto m$; i represents the numbers of satisfying formula 1.2; θ_T represents the practical use efficiency, t_k represents the real use time, T represents use time in theory, $\overline{\theta}_k$ means the average of θ_k.

Step 2: broadcasting the routing information in a manner of DSLNM to get the matrix A.
Step 3: if formula 1.1 is not established; go to step 8.
Step 4: if formula 1.1 holds.
Step 5: if formula 1.2 is not established; go to step 8.
Step 6: if formula 1.2 holds.
Step 7: execute the formula 1.3; go to step 9.
Step 8: self-broadcasting the routing information by using the CNN method, check value 1 (main diagonal is excluded) of the local routing information; go to step 2.

Step 9: stop and output the outcome, analysis the energy consuming compared with position of previous pre-deployed nodes.

3   Simulation Analysis

In order to demonstrate the performance of scheme, we evaluate the performance of proposed scheme with neighbor matrix in terms of delay and the efficiency. As a comparison, not considering the single links, the delay and efficiency of traditional wireless sensor network are evaluated. The formulae below are given to calculate the end-to-end delay and the network efficiency of the two different networks; besides, the parameters are set in Table 5:

$$NE = ND/NW \qquad (1.4)$$

NE: network efficiency; ND: numbers of messages received by destination nodes; NW: numbers of messages sent from the whole network.

End-to-end delay: the time interval of messages (or their copies) sent from source nodes till the successful receiving by destination nodes.

Table 5. Simulation Parameters

Parameter	Value
Numbers of nodes in network	50
Maximum circle radius	100 m
Maximum communication radius	200 m
Packet size	512 k
Network bandwidth	2 M
Simulation duration	700 s

Figure 4 shows the network efficiency of two routing schemes respectively. Comparing performance of the two different routing schemes when circle radii change from 10 m to 100 m with a 10-meter-step, besides, the energy of nodes drop randomly with a 50-meter-step from the original 200 m (if the radiation radii exceed 50 m). It is obvious that network efficiency deceases as the distance of nodes increase and some energy of nodes decrease. However, the proposed scheme outperforms the other one. The reason is: the existing unidirectional links occurred in the network can be used to complete the communication of information; while the traditional one is split by the unidirectional links.

Figure 5 shows the end-to-end delay of the two routing schemes respectively. In this simulation, comparing the performance of two schemes like the manner in Fig. 1, it is observed that end-to-end delay of each scheme increases within 50 m. The reason stays the same with simulation of network efficiency. In addition, we could find that the end-to-end delay of proposed scheme is slightly less than the traditional one, however, when radius exceeds 62 m, the delay of proposed one is more than traditional one holds the

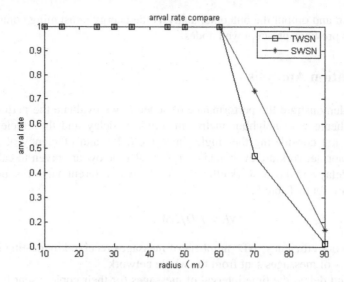

Fig. 4. Simulation of network efficiency

view that unidirectional links are used to transmit data, while the failure bidirectional links between this two nodes are not so.

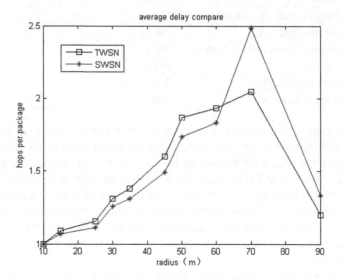

Fig. 5. Simulation of end-to-end delay

4   Conclusion

In this paper, an efficient neighbor matrix has successfully been proposed for detecting the unidirectional links existing in the wireless sensor network. Under the assumption of incommunicable areas, we compromise the complexity and performance of the detecting method to put forward a local network routing information in the static node network where the nodes could be pre-deployed in advance. The neighbor matrix combines with the common neighbor node are presented to get the information table in a manner of IOHELLO and IOHELLORP. The failure link is deleted in the manner of neighbor node error routing and non-neighbor node error routing. As we know that the routing information of the network means the connectivity after we have gotten the local routing form, in the meantime, the local routing form also means the direction of data transferring in a much shorter path by using the unidirectional links.

From the simulation results, the presented scheme can achieve significant improvements in the end-to-end delay, network efficiency and network delivery. To summarize, we believe that the presented scheme is an excellent routing detecting algorithm in terms of its application in the static nodes of wireless sensor networks.

Acknowledgment. This work was supported by the National Natural Science Foundation of China (No. 61571059).

References

1. Mank, S., Karnapke, R., Nolte, J.: MLMAC-UL and ECTS-MAC two MAC protocol for wireless sensor networks with unidirectional links. In: Sensor Technologies and Applications, pp. 623–629 (2009)
2. Minet, P., Mahfoudh, S., Chalhoub, G., Guitton, A.: Node coloring in a wireless sensor network with unidirectional links and topology changes. In: Wireless Communications and Networking Conference (WCNC), pp. 18–21, April 2010
3. Kanzaki, A., Hara, T., Nishio, S.: On TDMA slot assignment protocol considering the existence of unidirectional wireless links in ad hoc sensor networks. In: Mobile Data Management, pp. 10–12 (2006)
4. Zhang, Y., Gu, D.: Reliable key establishment scheme exploiting unidirectional links in wireless sensor networks. In: Embedded and Ubiquitous, pp. 17–20, December 2008
5. Lin, C.-H., Liu, B.-H., Yang, H.-Y., Kao, C.-Y., Tsai, M.-J.: Virtual-coordinate-based delivery-guaranteed routing protocol in wireless sensor networks with unidirectional links. In: INFOCOM 2008, pp. 13–18, April 2008
6. Batmaz, A.U., Tavli, B., Incebacak, D., Bicakci, K.: The impact of link unidirectionality and reverse path length on wireless sensor network lifetime. In: Communications (ICC), pp. 9–13, June 2013

Evaluation of Cognitive Awareness Based on Dual Task Situation

Wenjun Hou[2,3], Yi Ding[1(✉)], Xiangang Qin[4], and Yi Yang[4]

[1] Automation School, Beijing University of Posts and Telecommunications,
Beijing 100876, China
dingyicareer@163.com
[2] School of Digital Media and Design Art,
Beijing University of Posts and Telecommunications, Beijing, China
hou1505@163.com
[3] Network System and Network Culture Key Laboratory of Beijing, Beijing, China
[4] China Academy of Electronics and Information Technology, Beijing, China
1229537579@qq.com

Abstract. This paper investigated cognitive awareness based on dual task situation. We present a set of evaluation index and designed an experimental task to measure cognitive awareness under dual task situation. We also utilized this method to evaluate task performance in four monitor display ways, including single monitor and dual monitor. Task performance as well as psychological workload was discussed by E-prime, Tobii Glass and NASA-TLX. The result showed that single monitor embedded with a semitransparent window can improve cognitive awareness compared with dual monitor design.

Keywords: Dual task · Cognitive awareness · Ergonomics evaluation · Information display · Monitor

1 Introduction

With the increasing complexity of operational tasks in human-machine interactive environment, dual task or multi task situation requires more cognitive load, especially in scenarios with mission switching frequently (Grudin 2001) [1]. This put forward higher requirements for interface design. The traditional HMI assessment is mostly for single task situation, less covering dual task situation. However, compared to single task situation, dual task situation has some special features, conflicts such as attention, workload, visual limitations and perceived competition become more obvious (Wickens et al. 2006) [2]. These changes need to be paid attention by designers.

In order to reduce psychological workload for dual task, traditional design preferred to use two or three monitors in order to separate display area for each task. Some studies suggested that it can promote multi task performance by providing users with independent operation area, as it can reduce interference to help user focus attention, (Grudin 2001) [1]. However, such design also has some drawbacks practically, for example, when tasks switch frequently, increased spatial distance of user's eyes and body movements could be an extra workload. In addition, some studies showed that information

© Springer International Publishing Switzerland 2016
Q. Zu and B. Hu (Eds.): HCC 2016, LNCS 9567, pp. 160–171, 2016.
DOI: 10.1007/978-3-319-31854-7_15

perception on dual-monitor inclined to leave important information outside the vision field, resulting in the lower success rate of warning message capture (Bezerianos 2006) [3]. Besides, information perception has become a battlefield superiority and an important part of the information-based combat capability [16].

Therefore, we believe that it's meaningful to investigate people's perception performance during dual task which can apply to information display design. In this paper, we presented a dual task design using behaviour analysis and experimental measurements to evaluate four kinds of monitor design. We assessed the impact of different design on the operator's task performance and cognitive load. It also provided a reference for the information layout design based on dual task situation.

2 Determine Evaluation Index

Signal detection theory believed that observer needed to distinguish between two states: there is a signal or no signal, which is the basis for many practical scenarios, (Holldands and Neyedli 2011) [5]. We can design a task with fixed signal probability while using people's reactive time and hit rate to determine their performance, which can be used to reflect signal perceived sensitivity. Wolfe et al. believed that viewing time can be regarded as a resource demand index, the longer the viewing time, the higher the workload [7]. For dual task design, by recording the operator's eye viewing time, we can calculate the resource requirements under dual task situation. Besides, attention theory is also considered by us, which is, target subjected to a variety of certain attributes and the interference homogeneous may increase search accuracy [8] (Duncan and Humphreys 1989). Therefore, task design is considered with the above principles to help the operator perform the secondary task as well as maintaining high performance in the primary task.

In conclusion, we designed an experimental method to objectively evaluate participants' performance level based on above theory. The evaluation index, including: correct rate, reactive time to reflect incentive sensitivity; eye viewing time to reflect effort. Besides, we also use subjective evaluation method by utilizing NASA-TLX.

3 Dual Task Design

For dual task, participants need to perform the search task in the small monitor persistently and detect the random alarm signal on the big monitor during the experiment. The search task is the primary task, while signal detecting task is the secondary task. In order to prevent subjects encountering task conflict, participants were informed before the experiment to accord priority to the primary task. Our purpose is to make a comparison between four monitor positions, as well as determining alarm information perception level on the big monitor.

3.1 Material

Based on the E-prime platform programming, the material contains two parts: the keyboard to input and two monitors (a big and a small) to display. Material for small monitor is 36 letters (10 mm × 10 mm with default color black), P and R divided equally in 6 rows and 6 columns, the screen background color is white. During the experiment, a random letter will turn into red every other second, participant need to respond accordingly: If there is a red "P", then enter "1" in the keyboard, if there is a red "R", then enter "2". Material for the big monitor is a big map with several obstacles (green triangle, 10 mm × 10 mm). In order to compare people's information awareness level, nine target alarm signals are divided into nine parts, with equal probability. During the experiment, a random target alarm may flash for one second, and if the user perceives green flashing, tap "space" in the keyboard. The time interval between two tasks is at least one second, with signal gravity equals 72:27. Primary and secondary tasks appear randomly, preventing users from expectation (Figs. 1, 2 and 3).

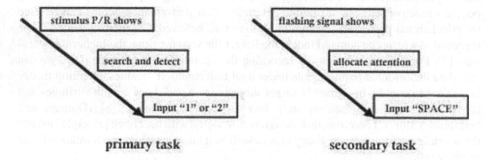

Fig. 1. Primary and secondary task flowchart

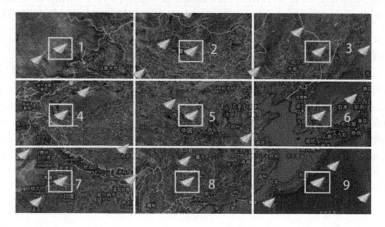

Fig. 2. Flashing information on big monitor. (Color figure online)

P   R   P   P   P   P
R   R   P   R   R   R
P   P   R   R   P   P
R   R   P   P   R   R
P   P   R   P   P   P
R   P   R   R   R   R

Fig. 3. Target information on small monitor. (Color figure online)

3.2 Subjects

Sixteen Chinese students of Beihang University (8 males and 8 females) with ages varying from 20 to 25 participated in the experiment. The participants all had normal vision or corrected-to-normal vision, right-handed and had no operational experience before (Fig. 4).

Fig. 4. Experimental scene

3.3 Variable

Two factors have been verified in the experiment. One factor is the relative position of two monitors, including left - right, middle - middle, right - left, internal. Another factor is the flashing signal's position on the big monitor. The dependent variable was reaction time and the accuracy rate.

3.4 Environment

The experiment is carried out at Beihang behavioural and human factors laboratory, normal indoor lighting conditions. Laboratory equipment is: (1) Think Station host, intelXeonE3-1230 CPU; (2) Two displays, large screen size is 27 in., with a resolution of 1920 × 1080, small screen size is 10 in., with a resolution of 1024 × 768; (3) Two keyboards, for responding input. Tasks are prepared with E-Prime2.0, which also presents experimental materials and records reaction time and accuracy rate. We use Tobii Glass as eye tracking device to collect eye tracking data and use Tobii Studio for eye tracking analysis.

4   Discussion

A total of 4720 responses were collected as experimental data samples, which came from E-DataAid. The data was then imported in SPSS software for analysis.

4.1   Primary Task

For the main task, four relative positions of two monitors were the main factor considered. Reaction time for accurate response was recorded. Accuracy was calculated according to the total correct response.

(1) Reaction Time.   Individual subject's mean RTs for four design ranged from 632.24 to 675.72 ms, as indicated in Fig. 5. Further examination of RTs were made with analysis of variance (ANOVA). The results showed significant effect ($F(3) = 24.948$, $P < 0.05$). By pairwise comparison, we can figure out a significant difference in design 4 comparing with the other three design. The result indicates that the small screen embedded in the big screen can make subjects respond faster.

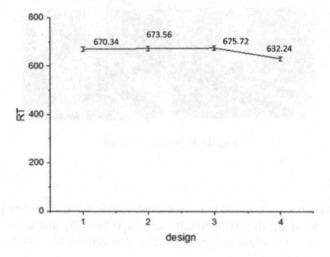

Fig. 5.   Reaction time on four monitor design

(2) Accuracy.   As showed in Fig. 6, mean accuracies ranged from 0.86 to 0.93, indicating that practice before recording was useful and subjects' main task performance maintained well. Further examination of RTs was performed with analysis of variance (ANOVA) with significant effect ($F(3) = 9.442$. $P < 0.05$). In pairwise comparison, we can find a significant difference in design 4 comparing with the other three design.

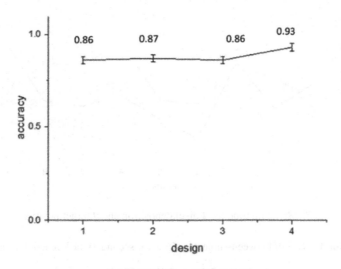

Fig. 6. Accuracy rate on four monitor design

4.2 Secondary Task

For the secondary task, two kinds of factors should be considered: four relative positions of two monitors and nine positions for the target. Reaction time for accurate response was recorded. We also calculate total miss response.

(1) Reaction Time. As there are two factors considered, we complied between-subjects effect and found that relative display position achieved significant effect level (F (3) = 3.230, P < 0.05), while target position didn't achieve significant effect (F (8) = 1.465 p > 0.05). By the interaction analysis, there is an interaction effect (F (24) = 1.575 p < 0.05) between the two variables. These results show that reaction time can vary significantly considering target position for different monitor position.

As Fig. 7 shows, the figure data trends can be found that in most locations, reaction time applied left > middle > right > single, despite 3 positions (1, 3, 9). Additional analysis of variance shows that only design 4 has a significant effect (F (8) = 3.33, P = 0.01). As showed in Fig. 7, left central area (4, 5, 7, 8) shared the best perception vision field (Table 1).

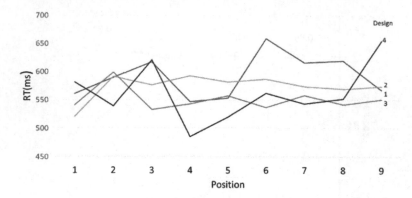

Fig. 7. Reaction time for 4 display position and 9 target position

Table 1. Test of between-subjects effects for secondary task reaction time

Tests of Between-Subjects Effects

Dependent Variable:RT

Source	Type III Sum of Squares	df	Mean Square	F	Sig.
Corrected Model	1038766.606	35	29679.046	1.732	.006
Intercept	2.491E8	1	2.491E8	14538.175	.000
design	166065.185	3	55355.062	3.230	.022
position	200851.030	8	25106.379	1.465	.166
design * position	647975.364	24	26998.974	1.575	.040
Error	13366925.08	780	17137.083		
Total	2.790E8	816			
Corrected Total	14405691.68	815			

a. R Squared = .072 (Adjusted R Squared = .030)

As for design 4, by comparing the information layout in a single-screen, we found that target in the embedded window is mostly easily ignored. Later interview showed that subjects inclined to regard this area as the primary task area, and flashing target was in conflict with their psychological expectations, so the reaction time appeared the longest. The result suggests that overlapping area is not adapted for showing dual task information, though this area is mostly within the vision field, subject's reaction time increases a lot (Fig. 8).

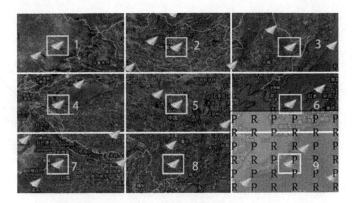

Fig. 8. Task operating area of a single screen design

(2) Analysis of Miss Response. Miss rate corresponds to the situation of missing the flashing target. By between subject effect analysis, small monitor position had a significant effect ($F (3) = 5.084$, $P < 0.05$). Target position had a significant effect ($F (8) = 8.656$ $P < 0.05$). Interactive effect between two factors is not significant ($F (24) = 1.484$ $p > 0.05$).

Figure 9 shows the miss rate for four monitor relative positions. Result indicates that design 4 has the lowest miss rate, which is significantly lower than the other three design. Figure 11 shows that position (5, 7, 8) has the lowest miss rate, which is in consistence with quick response area (Fig. 10).

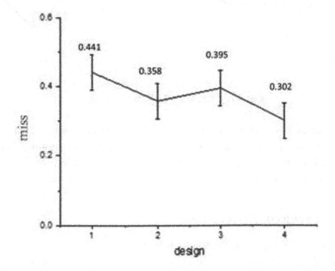

Fig. 9. Miss rate for secondary task

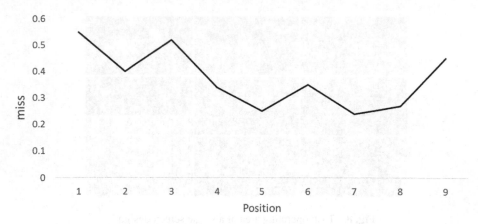

Fig. 10. Miss rate for different positions on the monitor

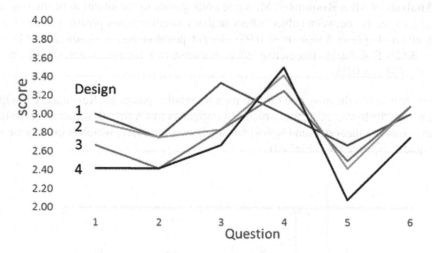

Fig. 11. Result for TLX questionnaire

After integrating two factors, we come to conclusion that single-monitor has the best information detecting performance. For nine positions, the overlapping field as well as the furthest field to the main task has the worst perception performance (position 1 and position 9). Warning message should be avoided at these locations.

4.3   Results of Subjective Mental Load

Based on NASA-TLX questionnaire, which included six questions covering issues of mental workload, physical load, load time, overall performance, depressed level, overall effort. As Fig. 11 suggested, design 4 has the lowest mental load.

4.4 Results of Eye Movement Analysis

Tobii glass was calibrated before the experiment, data was recorded and analysed afterward. As subjects' head movements would result in change of screen background, we select a period of record for qualitative analysis. Seen from heat map, subjects mostly focused on the small monitor, which reflected the primary and secondary tasks design.

Through statistical analysis, it can be seen from Fig. 13 that people assigned more time to the secondary task on single-monitor. We can deduce that single monitor design has lowest workload, leaving more cognitive resources to secondary task (Fig. 12).

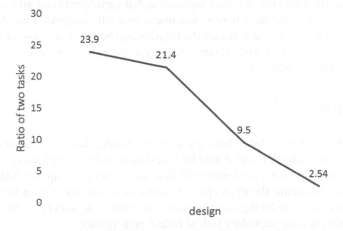

Fig. 12. Ratio of viewing time for two tasks (primary task/secondary task)

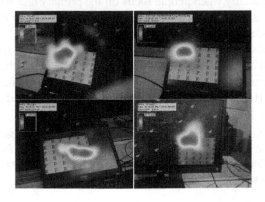

Fig. 13. REM hot zone

5   Discussion

In this study, the effect of monitor position and target position for dual task was examined under quantitative experimental design. We utilized a set of evaluation index to compare primary and secondary task performance under these four display positions. Results demonstrated that small window embedded in the large monitor had the best performance and less cognitive load. The experimental results also demonstrated layout for target information, which gives suggestions for target position design. For dual task, longer RTs is mostly in consistence with higher miss rate, which gives us indications for the layout design for target information, that is, the overlapping field and the field far away from the main task should be avoided. We've also found that performance would be better when the relative position of the small screen and large screen was left-right, which is in consistent with the user's visual scanning law. Through eye movement data acquisition and analysis, we've found that subject's attention is concentrated on the small screen mostly. However, it seems significant that participants can allocate more time for the secondary task when there's only one screen with embedded window.

Further research work could consider the relationship between the ratio of primary and secondary task and task performance to determine better appearance time for flashing information of dual task.

6   Conclusion

The results of this study provided following useful ergonomics design recommendations for HMI design and evaluation and should help designers to develop effective information display, in order to give users lower workload while encountering the dual task.

Based on signal detection theory, we put forward a set of evaluation index to compare dual task performance, including reaction time for both task, accuracy rate for the primary task, miss rate for secondary task to reflect performance.

The result shows that the single-monitor has advantages over dual-monitor under some occasions, especially when people focus on the primary task while leaving attention for secondary task. And embedded window in the big monitor can be a method to leave subjects an independent operational area.

Evaluation results also indicate the information layout design for dual task information. For small window, information displayed right is better than left. As for big monitor, the overlapping field as well as the farthest field to the small window has the worst perception performance. Warning message should be avoided at these locations.

Acknowledgment. We would like to thank all the people who have helped us in the course of our research. In addition, our work is supported by Specialized Research Fund for the Doctoral Program of Higher Education (No. 20110005110016) and Beijing Science and Technology Popularization of Special Projects (2015).

References

1. Grudin, J.: Partitioning digital worlds: focal and peripheral awareness in multiple monitor use. In: 2001 CHI Conference, vol. 3, no. 1, pp. 458–465 (2001)
2. Wickens, C.D., Dixon, S.R., Ambinder, M.S.: Workload and automation reliability in unmanned air vehicles. In: Cooke, N.J., Pringle, H.L., Pedersen, H.K., Connor, O. (eds.) Human Factors of Remotely Operated Vehicles, pp. 209–222. Elsevier, Amsterdam (2006)

3. Bezerianos, A., Dragicevic, P., Balakrishnan, R.: Mnemonic rendering: an image-based approach for exposing hidden changes in dynamic displays. In: Proceedings of the UIST 2006, pp. 159–168 (2006)
4. Moray, N.: Monitoring behavior and supervisory control. In: Boff, K.R., Kaufman, L., Thomas, J.P. (Eds.) Handbook of Perception and Performance, vol II, pp. 40-1–40-51. Wiley, New York
5. Hollands, J.G., Neyedli, H.F.: A reliance model for automated combat identification systems: implications for trust in automation. In: Stanton, N. (ed.) Trust in Military Teams, pp. 151–182. Ashgate, Farnham (2011)
6. Navon, D.: On the economy of the human processing system. Psychol. Rev. **86**, 254–255 (1979)
7. Wolfe, J.M., Horowitz, T.S., Kenner, N.M.: Rare items often missed in visual searches. Nature **435**, 439–440 (2005)
8. Duncan, J., Humphreys, G.W.: Visual search and stimulus similarity. Psychol. Rev. **96**, 433–458 (1989)
9. Cheal, M., Lyon, D.R.: Attention in visual search: multiple search classes. Percept. Psychophys. **52**(2), 113–138 (1992). University of Dayton Research Institute, Higley, Arizona
10. Truemper, J.M., et al.: Usability in multiple monitor displays. Database Adv. Inf. Syst. **39**(4) (2008)
11. Rogers, R., Monsell, S.: Costs of a predictable switch between simple cognitive tasks. J. Exp. Psychol. Gen. **124**(2), 207–231 (1995)
12. Bi, X., Balakrishnan, R.: Comparing usage of a large high-resolution display to single or dual desktop displays for daily work. In: CHI 2009, 4–9 April, Boston, Massachusetts, USA (2009)
13. Marcus, N., Mikael, D.: A study on user's preference on interruption when using wearable computers and head mounted displays. In: 3rd IEEE International Conference on Pervasive Computing and Communications (PerCom 2005) (2005)
14. Hutchings, D.R.: Display space usage and window management operation comparisons between single monitor and multiple monitor users. In: AVI 2004, 25–28 May 2004, Gallipoli (LE), Italy (2004)
15. Sheng, Z., Chuanjin, L.: A computer model of [A] information perception and processing process simulation based on the theory of multi-source attention 22(9), pp. 87–89 (2004)
16. Nan, J., Liang, D.: Information perception - the premise and the leading of the battlefield information superiority and the leading. Chin. Electron. Sci. Res. Inst. J. **6**(3), 221–226 (2013)

Research on Dynamic Generation of Digital Emergency Plan Based on Variable Structure Petri Net

Weidong Huang[✉], Yafei Ouyang, and Banglan Ding

Nanjing University of Posts and Telecommunications,
Wen Yuan Road No.9, Nanjing 210023, Jiangsu, China
huangwd@njupt.edu.cn

Abstract. The dynamic generation mechanism of digital emergency plan is an effective solution to deal with the complex changes of time and space environmental information. This paper described the generation templates and generation system dynamic of digital emergency plan, introduced the object-oriented Petri net method and constructed the generation system model based on variable structure Petri net. Then we did an analysis on the earthquake disaster digital emergency plan generation system through an example, built a digital emergency plan generation model based on population scene. Besides, we validate and analyze the model from two aspects. On the one hand, we validate the digital plan generation on the current situation with an example, on the other hand we demonstrate the dynamic change of the generation system model through the example. The experimental results show that the additional role of digital emergency plan real-time generated for decision body making emergency decision is stronger.

Keywords: Petri net · Emergency plan · Variable structure · Dynamic

1 Introduction

In recent years, the theory and application of the practice of emergency management has a thorough research and exploration, on the one hand, the introduction of the digital emergency plan, from frame structure including the organization system, operation mechanism, emergency safeguard, supervision and management, etc., it has systematic and standardized description and builds a variety of semantic model to simulate the different problem domain adaptive expression. On the other hand, due to the characteristics of unconventional emergencies, the distributed character, heterogeneity, timeliness and high-dimensional complexity etc., emergency plan how to respond to changes in the environment, and how to realize the logical deduction and dynamically generated, thereby it achieves environmental adaptability, This aspect of the study is just the rise [1, 2].

Dynamically generated digital plans try to take advantage of computer technology and network technology, according to the disposal process of the emergency, on the basis of instant messaging in this development, it forms a comprehensive, specific and

© Springer International Publishing Switzerland 2016
Q. Zu and B. Hu (Eds.): HCC 2016, LNCS 9567, pp. 172–182, 2016.
DOI: 10.1007/978-3-319-31854-7_16

targeted strong, intuitive and highly efficient emergency plan, using the result feedback and scene dynamic information to correct the emergency plan, and achieving effective dynamic disposal [3].

2 The Dynamically Generated Mechanism Analysis of the Digital Emergency Plan

The dynamically generated mechanism research of the digital emergency plan mainly explore how to deconstruct the framework, structural elements and structural feature of emergency plan, according to the dynamic and complex changing environment information of time and space in unconventional emergency special constraint conditions. Based on the evolution of the situation, it analyzes rules and the mechanism of dynamic evolution in the process of emergency response, and studies how to track, evaluate, modify and adjust according to action plan of simulate or real situation [4, 5].

2.1 The Digital Emergency Plan Generates Template Structure

The essence of digital emergency plan determines the scope and variety of objects in the generation process of unconventional emergency system. The production of digital plans happens after the outbreak of the event, its essence is generated according to event scene evolution corresponds to a series of real-time replying implementation of activities. The content structure of a replying implementation of activity can be resolved with fragmented as the target, operation, characters, receptor four parts.

'Target' refers to the goal of the activity implementation, is the emergency demand fragment extracted from the scenario evolution. Combined with the scenario evolution model, target can be linked to the internal state of the scene object, in particular, 'target' of replying implementation of activities is defined as change a certain scene object's state. There is a direct link between the 'change' and the 'target', namely, the "operation" of the implement activities. 'Operation' is the key of replying implementation of activities, not only associated with 'target', also has information transfer relationship between the 'character' object and 'recipient' object. 'Character' is the division of the person or organization of different responsibility or ability, is the executor of the 'operation'. 'Character' of information content comes from the organization system and emergency protection of two parts in the emergency plan structure. 'Recipient' refers to the executive of the activities, it can be an object of unconventional emergency system, also can be the object of a particular attribute. Such as bearing object communication system, power supply system, earthquake monitoring data and so on [2].

Dividing the structure of the implementation of activities, the active content can be abstracted into several knowledge fragments and the link between the various pieces of knowledge. The essence of the generation of real-time replying implementation of activity is the reorganization of knowledge fragments. The link between replying real-time activity system and event evolution scenarios is achieved by knowledge fragments of the 'target', a series of replying implementation of activity based on the scenario evolution and real-time production constitute the digital emergency plans (Fig. 1).

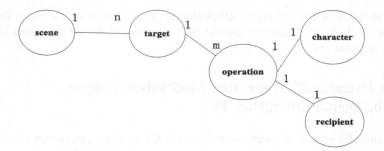

Fig. 1. Structure template for digital emergency plan

2.2 The Dynamic Analysis of Digital Plan Generation System

The core process of the generation of the digital emergency plan is based on the divided structure of knowledge fragments reorganization to reply implement activities, its system dynamics is caused by the characterization of the structure of the change of knowledge fragment reorganization of scenario evolution [6]. The relationship between the scene and the target is $1 : n$, it represents that a scenario object can be associated with n target object, in the same way, the relationship between the operation and the target is $1 : m$, it represents that a target can be associated with m operation object, And operation and character, operation and recipient are one-to-one relationship. Five classes of object of system are respectively the scenario object, the target object, the operation object, the character object, and recipient object. According to the scene that represents the laws of evolution and development trend, we make sure that all target of replying implement activities, associated combination operation, character, recipient and others knowledge fragments, this process is the generation of digital emergency plan.

We introduce the method of object-oriented Petri net, we can define system S as $S = (O, R)$ $(O = (O_i, i = 1, 2, \cdots, I))$, O_i is the object-oriented Petri net model of entity object. I represents the total number of objects. R represents the relationship of information transfer between each object. In systematic Petri net model, O and R determines the structure of the system in general, the dynamic characteristics of the system is mainly showed by the structural changes in the system, that is to say, the change of the system components O and R.

(1) Increase or decrease of O in the system. To study the increase or decrease in process of system objects, it is necessary to define system firstly: after k times changes of system S_k: $S_k = \{O_k, R_k, \sum_k, L_k, M_{k,0}\}$; for status identification $M_{k,s}$, increase object O_k^{ad}, reduce object O_k^{re} and color set that increase $\sum_k^{ad}$ or decrease $\sum_k^{re}$ of the $k+1$ times changed system, we can launch:

After the $k+1$ times change of the system $S_{k+1} = (O_{k+1}, R_{k+1}, \sum_{k+1}, L_{k+1}, M_{k+1,0})$, exists:

$$O_{k+1} = \left(O_k - O_k^{re}\right) \cup O_k^{ad};$$

$$R_{k+1} = \left(R_k - R_k^{re}\right) \cup R_k^{ad};$$

$$\sum\nolimits_{k+1} = \left(\sum\nolimits_k - \sum\nolimits_k^{re}\right) \cup \sum\nolimits_k^{ad};$$

$$M_{k+1,0} = M_{k,s} - M_{k,s}^{re} + M_{k,s}^{ad}; G_{k+1} = \left(G_k - G_k^i\right) \cup G_k^{ad}$$

In the formula, G_k^i is the rejecting isolated gate change of the transitive relation of O_k^{re}, G_k^{ad} is the adding gate change of the adding O_k^{ad}. Thus, need to make the following changes in input and output logic relationship: $\forall g \in G_{k+1}$:

$$\left[\begin{array}{l} L_{k+1}\left(\cdot g^{k+1}\right) = \vee/\wedge \left(\left(\cdot g^k - \cdot g^{kre}\right) \cup \cdot g^{kad}\right), \\ L_{k+1}\left(g.^{k+1}\right) = \vee/\wedge \left(\left(g.^k - g.^{kre}\right) \cup g.^{kad}\right) \end{array}\right], \cdot g^k \text{ and } g.^k \text{ respectively represent the}$$

output and input information database that connect with gate g through output and input connecting arc before the change, $\cdot g^{kre}$ and $g.^{kre}$ respectively represent the removed output and input information database that connect with gate g, along with the changes in the O_k^{kre} object through former output and input connecting arc, $\cdot g^{kad}$ and $g.^{kad}$ respectively represent the adding output and input information database that connect with gate g, along with the increase in the O_k^{kad} object through output and input connecting arc when is changing.

(2) The changes of R between different OPN. The information transfer relationship between different OPN can be divided into two parts, which can be divided into increasing information transfer relationship set and reducing the information transfer relationship set, we can get the increasing information transfer relationship set R_k^a, reducing the information transfer relationship set R_k^r, and R color set that increase $\sum_k^a$ or decrease $\sum_k^r$ of the $k+1$ times changed system, we can launch:

After the $k+1$ times change of the system $S_{k+1} = \left(O_{k+1}, R_{k+1}, \sum_{k+1}, L_{k+1}, M_{k+1,0}\right)$, exists:

① $R_{k+1ij} = \left(R_{kij} - R_{kij}^r\right) \cup R_{kij}^a = \left(OA_{k+1ij}, G_{k+1ij}, IA_{k+1ij}, E_{k+1ij}\right)$ $(i,j = 1,2,\cdots,I_k, \ i \neq j)$

In the formula, $OA_{k+1ij} = \left(OA_{kij} - OA_{kij}^r\right) \cup OA_{kij}^a$, OA_{kij}^a and OA_{kij}^r represent the increase and decrease output connecting arc by the object O_{ki} from OM_i to G_{kij};

$IA_{k+1ij} = \left(IA_{k+1ij} - IA_{kij}^r\right) \cup IA_{kij}^a$, IA_{kij}^a and IA_{kij}^r represent the increase and decrease input connecting arc of IM_i from the object G_{kij} to O_{ki}; E_{k+1ij}, there are two ways to sure, one is the change of the expression of content, expressed as $E_{k+1ij} = \left(E_{kij} - E_{kij}^{rm}\right) \cup E_{kij}^{am}$, the other is the addition or removal of an expression, expressed as: $E_{k+1ij} = \left(E_{kij} - E_{kij}^r\right) \cup E_{kij}^a$;

$G_{k+1ij} = \left(G_{kij} - G^r_{kij}\right) \cup G^a_{kij}$, G^a_{kij} and G^r_{kij} respectively represent the increased and isolated gate change between O_{ki} and O_{kj}.

② $\sum_{k+1} = \left(\sum_k - \sum_k^r\right) \cup \sum_k^a;$

③ $G_{k+1} = \bigcup_{i,j=1,i\neq j}^{I_{k+1}} G_{k+1ij};$

④ Input and output logic functions as follows:

$$\forall g \in G_{k+1} : \left[\begin{array}{l} L_{k+1}\left(.g^{k+1}\right) = \vee / \wedge \left((.g^k - .g^{kr}) \cup .g^{ka}\right), \\ L_{k+1}\left(g.^{k+1}\right) = \vee / \wedge \left((g.^k - g.^{kr}) \cup g.^{ka}\right) \end{array}\right], \text{ in the formula, } .g^k \text{ and}$$

$g.^k$ respectively represent the output and input information database that connect with gate g through output and input connecting arc before the change, $.g^{kr}$ and $g.^{kr}$ respectively represent the to be eliminated output and input information database that connect with gate g, along with the output and input connecting arc, $.g^{ka}$ and $g.^{ka}$ respectively represent the adding output and input information database that connect with gate g through output and the input connecting arc.

⑤ $O_{k+1} = O_k - O^i_k$ $(O^i_k \subset O_k)$, in the formula, O^i_k represents a set of objects that are isolated from the change in the transfer relationship in the system, $\forall O_{ki} \in O^i_k : \left[(R_{kij}, j = 1, 2, \cdots, I_k, j \neq i) = \Phi\right];$

⑥ $I_{k+1} = I_k - I^i_k$, in the formula, I^i_k represents the number of isolated objects;

⑦ $M_{k+1,0} = M_{k,s} - M^i_{k,s} - M^r_{k,s} + M^a_{k,s}$, in the formula, $M^i_{k,s}$ is the identification of the O^i_k, isolated object. $M^r_{k,s}$ and $M^a_{k,s}$ respectively represent Tokheim that adds or reduces after the change of system.

In the process of the analysis of the specific system changes, it can be said that a change, it may also be involved in the two types of structural changes. Therefore, we need to use the above two algorithms to modify structure of OPN-CS, in this case, we firstly analyze the change of information transmission, and then use the algorithm to increase or decrease.

3   The Generation of the Construction of System Model Based on Variable Structure Petri Net

The unconventional emergency scenario evolution model is a hierarchical network structure, and there is a complex relationship of situational factors between the level and inside the level, and the correlation between different scenarios in the object-oriented Petri net model is represented and implemented by the gate changes. The digital emergency plan generation system in the model construction is also used for the object oriented theory, the main structure of the system is modular storage and object classification. The generation of digital emergency plan based on scenario evolution needs to study the dynamic characteristics of the system, and the introduction of the Petri net modeling theory is based on the above analysis.

The architecture of digital emergency plan generation system includes five kinds of object modules, such as scene, target, operation, character and recipient. The system presents a hierarchical structure, and the objects in the hierarchy are independent and have no relation to the objects in the hierarchy. There is no cross-level information transmission relationship between objects. As the node elements in the scenario evolution model, the information transfer relationship between the scene objects in the generation system is characterized by hierarchical network structure. This can be known, the generation system of digital emergency plan, based on the scenario evolution, is the hierarchical network structure. In this article, the model is constructed to build the model of the generation process of the digital emergency plan, which is based on the scenario, on this basis, the formation of hierarchical network structure is related to the scene objects, we complete the generation of digital emergency plan based on the scenario evolution through the two steps [7].

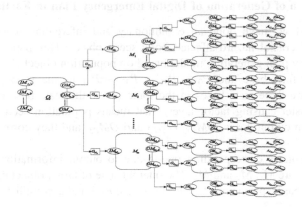

Fig. 2. The variable structure Petri net model of digital emergency plan generation system based on scene

The variable structure Petri net model of digital emergency plan based on a scene object in the scenario evolution model are as shown in Fig. 2. From left to right are the scene object S_i, the target object M, the operation target C, character object R and recipient object A. In the figure is the variable structure Petri net model of generation system based on scene $Q_i (i \in N_s)$, among them N_s is the total number of the scene objects in emergent events. The initial model of the system is $S_0 = (O_0, R'_0, \sum_0, L_0, M_{0,0})$ and $O_0 = (Q_0, M_0, C_0, R_0, A_0)$, $R'_0 = \left(R'_{Q_0 M_0}, R'_{M_0 C_0}, R'_{C_0 R_0}, R'_{C_0 A_0} \right)$, $G_0 = (G_{Q_0 M_0}, G_{M_0 C_0}, G_{C_0 R_0}, G_{C_0 A_0})$, $M_{0,0} = (MM_{0,0}, SM_{0,0})$.

The number of input information base is l and the number of output information base is n in the scene object Q_i. (The output information base between scene objects that has information transfer relationship with others has not been listed in the figure). Every output information base has a output arc relevant to target object M, and transferring information to target object M through door transition G_M and a input arc.

For target object M, every target object can has relevant to a number of $n_i (i = 1, 2, \ldots \ldots, m)$ operation target. Among them m is the number of target object M based on scene S_i. Target object M has a number of $\sum_{i=1}^{m} n_i$ output information bases. Every output information base has a output arc that points operation target C and transferring information to operation target C through door transition G_{C_M}.

For operation target C, every operation target has a information transfer relationship of one-to-one with character object R and recipient object A. Character object R receive information from operation target C through door transition $G_{R_{C_M}}$ and recipient object A receive information from operation target C through door transition $G_{A_{C_M}}$.

4 Application Analysis

4.1 The Design of Generation of Digital Emergency Plan in Earthquake

In the paper [8] we have done an evolutionary and inferential analysis of to the population P of crucial hazard-affected body scene object. This paper constructed a digital emergency plan generation model based on population object P. We choose P_{34} as the route of final base and $P_0 \rightarrow P_{31} \rightarrow P_{32} \rightarrow P_{34}$ as the scene of generation system. There are three state bases in the route (P_0 is the state base comprehensive affected by disaster causing factor layer), that means population scene object P has three information output bases, OM_{P1}, OM_{P2} and OM_{P3}, and they correspond to some target object.

The target objects corresponding one-to-one to output information bases OM_{P1}, OM_{P2} and OM_{P3} are M_1, M_2 and M_3. The internal state of target object can be summed up to three state bases, provision P_{M_i1}, performance P_{M_i2} and accomplishment P_{M_i3}, and among them $i = 1, 2, 3$.

The three states of target object, provision, performance and accomplishment correspond to three kinds of operation target, and provision information will be delivered to resource mobilization operation target (C_1), performance information will be delivered to performance operation target (C_2), accomplishment information will be delivered to report operation target (C_3).

Operation target C_1, C_2 and C_3 will build one-to-one correlation to character object R_1, R_2, R_3 and recipient object A_1, A_2, A_3. What need to explain is that the internal state of operation target should contain the most basic begin and end state. This paper mainly analyze the generation process of plan, ignoring considering the end state of operation target and only study information transition between operation target with character object and recipient object under the begin state.

The establishment of character object is mainly according to the national earthquake emergency plan system and the content of emergency guarantee part. The character object R associated with population scene object P can be summarized as salvage team (community volunteer team, regional rescue team, national earthquake rescue team, the local garrison troops, neighboring earthquake rescue team), Medical and rescue team (the local emergency medical teams, local hospital backup medical team, the army medical team nearby), Earthquake field emergency team (provincial seismological bureau on-site emergency team, China seismological bureau on-site emergency team, neighboring seismological bureau on-site emergency team), The field emergency command center, government departments and so on. Recipient object is determined by the operation object, such as recipient object related to search and rescue operation object is buried population.

From the analysis to the generation system process, we can find that the correlation structure of population scene P and target object M_1, M_2, M_3 are similar. We can combine the similar structure and use a PN model to indicate and use different colors to differ different personalities in the same kind of factor. This paper use E_1, E_2, E_3 to indicate the quality of three kinds of target object. We define the variable structure Petri net model of digital emergency plan generation system based on the population scene object P: $S_0 = \{O_0, R'_0, \sum_0, L_0, M_{0,0}\}$. And among them, $O_0 = (P_0, M_0, C_0, R_0, A_0)$, $R'_0 = (R'_M, R'_C, R'_R, R'_A)$, $G_0 = (G_M, G_C, G_R, G_A)$, $\sum_0 = \{E_1, E_2, E_3, J_1, J_2, J_3\}$, $M_{0,0} = (MM_{0,0}, SM_{0,0})$, $L_0 = \{[L(.G_M), L(G_M.)], [L(.G_C), L(G_C.)], [L(.G_R), L(G_R.)], [L(.G_A), L(G_A.)]\} = \{[OM_P, IM_M], [OM_M, IM_C], [OM_{C_1}, IM_R], [OM_{C_2}, IM_A]\}$. The digital emergency plan generation model based on population scene is as shown in Fig. 3.

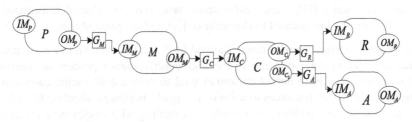

Fig. 3. The variable structure Petri net model of digital emergency plan generation system based on population scene

4.2 The Case of Digital Emergency Plan Generation in Earthquake

We have described the generation process of digital emergency plan in earthquake and built a digital plan generation model based on the population scene. On this basis, this section will validate and analyze the model from two aspects. On the one hand, we validate the digital plan generation on the current situation with an example, on the other hand we demonstrate the dynamic change of the generation system model through the example.

(1) The case of digital emergency plan generation in earthquake. According to the meaning of state bases P_{31}, P_{32}, P_{34} in the population scene object evolution case, we make an explain to the meaning of the above define number: OM_{P1} shows personnel buried information, OM_{P2} shows personnel injury information, OM_{P3} shows personnel death information, the abstract OM_P to the three kinds of output information base shows personnel emergency state information; G_{M_1} shows send out the information of searching and rescuing buried personnel, G_{M_2} shows send out the information of curing injured personnel, G_{M_3} shows send out the information

of insulating dead personnel, the abstract G_M to the three kinds of door change shows send out the information of dealing with personnel emergency state; IM_{M1} shows the request information of searching and rescuing buried personnel, IM_{M2} shows the request information of curing injured personnel, IM_{M3} shows the request information of insulating dead personnel, the abstract IM_M to the three kinds of input information base shows the request information of dealing with personnel emergency state; $G_{C_{M_1 1}}$ shows send out the provision information of searching and rescuing buried personnel, $G_{C_{M_1 2}}$ shows send out the performance information of searching and rescuing buried personnel, $G_{C_{M_1 3}}$ shows send out the accomplishment information of searching and rescuing buried personnel, $G_{C_{M_2 1}}$ shows send out the provision information of curing injured personnel, $G_{C_{M_2 2}}$ shows send out the performance information of curing injured personnel, $G_{C_{M_2 3}}$ shows send out the accomplishment information of curing injured personnel, $G_{C_{M_3 1}}$ shows send out the provision information of insulating dead personnel, $G_{C_{M_3 2}}$ shows send out the performance information of insulating dead personnel, $G_{C_{M_3 3}}$ shows send out the accomplishment information of insulating dead personnel, the abstract G_C to this kind of door change shows send out the information of dealing with personnel emergency state; OM_{C1} and OM_{C2} show send out the selected information of handler and the be operated to character object and recipient object.

The process of system performance showed in Fig. 3 is as shown in Fig. 4, and the practical implication corresponding to the above performance process is "personnel buried scene occur, ensure buried personnel goal to search and rescue, carry out the operation of mobilizing resources to achieve the goal, mobilize collection team by the field command center", realizing a generation of dealing with implementation activity and several such implementation activities form digital emergency plans in earthquake.

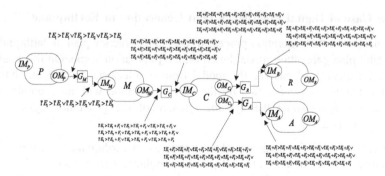

Fig. 4. The OPN-CS model of digital emergency plan generation system based on population scene

(2) The dynamic case of digital emergency plan generation system in earthquake. With the evolution of unconventional emergent events, scenario evolution system changes, then scenario evolution path inferenced also will change, this process is the origin of the dynamic change of digital emergency plan generation system. The structure change of the two kinds of model based on scene system after structure simplify mainly reflect the change of E_i in $\sum_0$ and the change of corresponding information transmit relation caused by the change of E_i. Next we will do an analysis to the structure change of the system by an example.

We let population scene P as study object, with time goes, at a time point:
$$y' = Max(z'_1, z'_2, z'_3) = Max(0.9, 0.9, 0.8) = 0.9, \mu'_{31} = \{\mu'_{311}, \mu'_{312}, \mu'_{313}\} = \{0.6,$$
$0.9, 0.8\}, \mu'_{32} = \{\mu'_{321}, \mu'_{322}, \mu'_{323}\} = \{0.6, 0.6, 0.9\}, \mu'_{33} = \{\mu'_{331}, \mu'_{332}\} = \{0.7, 0.9\}.$
According to the above algorithm, the scenario evolution path at this time is: ① The evolution path with P_{34} as goal base: $P_0 \rightarrow P_{31} \rightarrow P_{34}$ (0.486); ② The evolution path with P_{33} as goal base: $P_0 \rightarrow P_{31} \rightarrow P_{32} \rightarrow P_{33}$ (0.5103). Scenario evolution path and path value indicate that with time goes the possibility of personnel dead evolution becomes more and more big and the possibility of safe transfer becomes more and more small.

Along with the change of population scenario evolution path, at this time the digital emergency plan generation system based on population scene is S_1, which can show as $S_1 = \{O_1, R'_1, \sum_1, L_1, M_{1,0}\}$, among that $O_1 = (P_1, M_1, C_1, R_1, A_1)$, $R'_1 = (R'_{M1}, R'_{C1}, R'_{R1}, R'_{A1})$, $G_1 = (G_{M1}, G_{C1}, G_{R1}, G_{A1})$, $\sum_1 = \{E_1, E_3, J_1, J_2, J_3\}$, $M_{1,0} = (MM_{1,0}, SM_{1,0})$, $L_1 = \{[L(.G_{M1}), L(G_{M1}.)], [L(.G_{C1}), L(G_{C1}.)], [L(.G_{R1}), L(G_{R1}.)], [L(.G_{A1}), L(G_{A1}.)]\} = \{[OM_{P1}, IM_{M1}], [OM_{M1}, IM_{C1}], [OM_{C11}, IM_{R1}], [OM_{C21}, IM_{A1}]\}$.

The change of evolution path can direct affect the information transfer relation between population scene object P (O_1) and target object M (O_2), that is to say, the information transfer relation assemble that be shifted out is R''_1: $R''_1 = \bigcup\limits_{i,j=1, i\neq j}^{l_k} R''_{kij}$

$= R''_{012}$ $(R''_{012} \subseteq R'_{012})$. According to the algorithm of system structure transformation, we describe the process of the above information transfer as below:

① $R'_{M1} = R'_M - R''_1 = R'_{012} - R''_{012} = (OA_{112}, G_{112}, IA_{112}, E_{112})$, Among, $OA_{112} = OA_{112} - OA''_{012}, IA_{112} = IA_{012} - IA''_{012}$

② E^{rm}_{012} is the expression function content of output arc and input arc of shifting out P and M, door transition and input and output logic function do not change, so $G_1 = G_0, L_1 = L_0$;

③ The output arc and input arc in system have not increase or decrease, so do not exit the object assemble isolated by the content change of arc expression function, so $O_1 = O_0$;

④ $M_{1,0} = M_{0,0} - M''_{0,0}, M''_{0,0}$ is tochen shifted out of all object bases in the changing system.

5 Conclusion

Through the case analysis to scenario evolution application in earthquake, we can build Petri net model catering to object of scenario evolution in earthquake and choose the key recipient disaster object population P as example object of study, then we can obtain scenario evolution path of population P. Meanwhile, we do a confirmation to the structure change of the generation system model of digital emergency plan in earthquake based on scene by an example. We can foresee the additional role of digital emergency plan real-time generated for decision body making emergency decision is stronger.

Acknowledgement. Work described in this paper was funded by the National Natural Science Foundation of China under Grant No. 71171117. The authors would like to thank other researchers in Nanjing University of Posts and Telecommunications and Nanjing University for discussion.

References

1. Yanyan, W., Song, H., Chaoqing, Y., Changwei, H.: The flood risk and flood alleviation benefit of land use management in Taihu Basin. Shuili Xuebao **03**, 327–335 (2013)
2. Jiaxing, S., Chuang, L.: Research on parameterized reachability graph of Petri net models. J. Syst. Simul. **S1**, 38–43 (2007)
3. Baohua, Y., Zhigeng, F., Sifeng, L., Mingli, H.: Model of co-coupling in unconventional incidents based on GERTS network. Syst. Eng.-Theor. Pract. **05**, 963–970 (2012)
4. Johnston, M., Gilmore, A., et al.: Dealing with environmental uncettainty: the value of scenario planning for small to medium-sized entreprise (SMEs). Eur. J. Mark. **42**(11/12), 1170–1178 (2008)
5. Jiang, H., Huang, J.: The study on the issues of scenario evolvement in real-time decision making of infrequent fatal emergencies. J. Huazhong Univ. Sci. Technol. (Soc. Sci. Ed.) **1**, 025 (2009)
6. Bodwell, W., Chermack, T.: Organizational ambidexterity: inegrating deliberate and emergent strategy with scenario planning. Technol. Forecast. Soc. Change **77**(2), 193–202 (2010)
7. Kaakai, F., Hayat, S., El Moudni, A.: A hybrid Petri nets based simulation model for evaluating the design of railway transit stations. Simul. Model. Pract. Theor. **15**(8), 935–969 (2007)
8. Huang, W.D., Ding, B.L., Yan, L.: The design of dynamic response system based on digital emergency plan. Adv. Mater. Res. **605**, 1855–1860 (2013)

A Fast Clustering Algorithm for Massive Short Message

Ya Huang[1,2(✉)], Wenzhi Zhang[2], Haiyang Zhang[1], and Saihong Xu[1]

[1] School of Computer Science, Beijing University of Posts and Telecommunications,
Beijing 100876, People's Republic of China
[2] Science and Technology on Information Transmission and Dissemination in Communication
Networks Laboratory, Beijing, China
huangya0105@sina.com

Abstract. With the rapid development of mobile communication technology, the short message is playing a more and more important role in the daily life. Most of existing clustering algorithms are hard to be applied in dealing with massive short message due to the huge scale of data and similarity. This paper presents an efficient clustering algorithm by taking a special method to build feature string and a reasonable selection of cluster number. Experiments show that the clustering system based on this algorithm can depose millions of short message per hour with high precision and recall.

Keywords: Clustering · Feature string · Short message

1 Introduction

With the widespread use of mobile devices, especially smart phones, the mobile internet era has arrived. According to the report released by China Internet Network Information Center (CNNIC) in Beijing, the 35th "Statistical Report on Internet Development in China" [1] shows that up to December 2014, the scale of mobile phone users has reached 557 million, which continues to maintain steady growth. At the same time, the use of short message has penetrated into various fields. The social phenomenon of using short message to spread dissemination of pornographic and spam is increasing, which not only occupy the limited network resources, resulting in network congestion, but also has brought economic losses to a number of mobile phone users. Therefore to establish effective and accurate public opinion prediction model to research and analysis mass short message is very important. Short message has some common characteristics: a. Number of words is small, usually less than 140 characters, but a very large number of repetitions. b. Frequent use of network terms and acronyms, namely variation of the message. Therefore, short message text processing has to face these characteristics, and to promote the development of adaptive technology in order to cope with the reality of complex application requirements.

For dealing with massive short message data is very inconvenient, we need to make cluster analysis before other analysis procedure. At the same time this information which is carrying a wealth of user information becomes an information resource of great value. Therefore, the demand for this kind of data clustering will be more prominent. For

Q. Zu and B. Hu (Eds.): HCC 2016, LNCS 9567, pp. 183–192, 2016.
DOI: 10.1007/978-3-319-31854-7_17

example, by clustering short message, you can dig the hot spot information on the network and find the similar characteristics of mass short messages, then help operators to access and analyze messages effectively.

This article is organized as follows. We firstly introduce the relevant technical background, and then focus on explaining the rapid clustering algorithm for mass short message. Then, experimental evaluation on real short message data is conducted to prove the effectiveness and efficiency of the proposed method. Finally, we discuss the results obtained from our experiments and make some conclusions.

2   Background

The cluster analysis of short messages refers to the analysis process of dividing short messages collection into multiple classes (clusters) [2]. Clustering to divide the category is unknown which different classification, that clustering is a non-supervised learning method. Commonly used text clustering methods are hierarchical clustering method and point distribution clustering method [3, 4]. This section analyzes the two clustering algorithm in the application of short message clustering, and proposed an improved clustering algorithm to achieve short message clustering.

2.1   Hierarchical Clustering

Hierarchical clustering method [5] contains a bottom-up (aggregation) and top-down (division) two different implementations. Bottom-up implementation process: First each message as an independent category, and then according to certain rules will be the most similar plurality of message iteration aggregated into a class. Until the stop condition is met. Top-down implementation process is just opposite of bottom-up implementation process. The process of hierarchical clustering is shown in Fig. 1(a).

Hierarchical clustering method is one of the most commonly used clustering methods, Its advantage is that we can get the hierarchy of clustering and have high accuracy, and drawback is the algorithm efficiency is not high. Its time complexity and space complexity all is $O(n^2)$. When you merge it needs to compare the similarity of all classes globally to determine the best two similarly classes. So the calculation is too large, we cannot cope with the requirement of massive text clustering.

2.2   Point Distribution Clustering

The most famous point distribution clustering method is K-Means which is the most commonly used in the field of data mining and statistical. First, we need to select K data point as the initial cluster center. And then calculate the distance between each data point and each cluster center and assign to each category. Finally, according to distribution category, we recalculate the new cluster center. Repeating the above process until it reaches the termination condition. The general process of k-means algorithm is shown in Fig. 1(b).

The advantages of K-Means [6] is the process simple, low computational complexity and high efficiency. The disadvantage of this algorithm is needed to determine the clustering number in advance. For the initial selection of K value and K data points are also very sensitive. However, for the mass text messaging it is very difficult to give the number of clusters in advance and choose the initial cluster center, while iterative process also takes a long time, so the algorithm cannot be applied to the study.

In recent years a number of short text clustering algorithms have been proposed [7, 8], but ordinary clustering algorithm is not suitable for solving this problem. Common clustering idea is to set a certain threshold and put the similar characteristics text into one group, which is generally applicable to the category small. When category number is very large, the number of comparisons will grow rapidly, seriously affected the clustering efficiency. So for the mass text messaging, the amount of data is quite large, if you use common clustering algorithm, not only time consuming very large, and the clustering effect will be greatly affected. So this paper presents an improved clustering algorithm which quickly achieves significant short messages clustering.

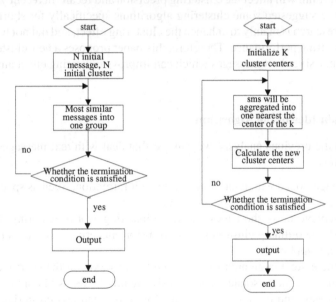

Fig. 1.   (a) Hierarchical clustering process (b) K-Means clustering process

3   Algorithm Design and Analysis

3.1   General Clustering Algorithms Failed

In this paper, the research data is mainly real users daily message text which provided by mobile operators. Because these messages are from real users, so a big difference to their vocabulary, and the proportion of professional vocabulary related is relatively low. Those short messages are different from the traditional text clustering, and it usually has the following features:

1. The form is not standard, more colloquial. Many messages have colloquial phrases, network popular words and some deformation fonts, etc.
2. The amount of data is very large, typically at least one million, and the similarity is high.
3. High real-time requirements. When an emergency occurs, the messages spread very quickly and update quickly.

According to the characteristics of the above short messages and by analyzing commonly used clustering algorithms described in the previous section, it can be found that common text clustering such as K-Means algorithm or hierarchical clustering algorithm, which in short message text clustering effect is poor. The common clustering algorithm is usually set a threshold value in advance. This is obviously only suitable for small amounts of data categories. For massive spam short messages, clustering on the number of categories must be very big. If you use the common clustering algorithm the efficiency is quite low. In addition, as the diversity of text messaging, using ordinary clustering algorithm will affect the clustering precision and recall. In recent years, some academics have suggested some clustering algorithms specifically for short messages [7], but their research is mainly to enhance the clustering effect, and did not have greatly improved clustering performance. Therefore, this paper proposes a new clustering algorithm for the massive short messages which can improve clustering effect and performance.

3.2 The Main Idea of the Algorithm

According to the previous analysis, we can see that deal with text messages has three main difficulties:

1. Text message doped with a lot of interference information, Such as special characters, network symbols, numbers, and so on.
2. How to achieve mass short message fast clustering worth exploring. Previously mentioned, the ordinary clustering algorithm for clustering large amount of information is not applicable.
3. Usually, there are a large number of isolated points exist in the short message [3]. At the same time these isolated texts usually are not the focus of our concern in the cluster analysis, and if a lot of time to deal with isolated text clustering algorithm will lead to inefficiency.

For the above difficulties, I early designed a clustering algorithm based on index. Its general idea is to participle the short message. Then, building a HashMap which KEY is word and Value is an array which short messages contain the corresponding word. Selecting three words in this short message and finding a set of messages containing these words. Finally calculating the similarity between them and determining the final similarity clustering. The advantage of this method is high accuracy of clustering. But with the amount of short messages to soar, the clustering efficiency fell sharply.

In order to solve the efficiency problem, we proposed a fast clustering algorithm for mass short message. Firstly, according to the characteristics of the text message is preprocessed. Then, experiments prove that this paper proposes a suitable feature string selection methods, and to extract the features of text string to build index system. Finally, by traversing short message and finding the feature list to determine the category of message, and ultimately obtained clustering results. The algorithm will delete the aforementioned isolated point during the clustering, thereby improving the efficiency of clustering.

3.3 Short Message Preprocessing

Short message preprocessing mainly to the conversion of some special characters, remove all interference information which may affect the clustering results. And finally to the clustering result can be directly analyzed. The specific steps are: First, to remove all interfering characters, such as punctuation, spaces, special characters, and so on. These characters are of no practical significance for the message, so get rid of them do not cause interference to the clustering results. Second, because the figures are not much practical significance for SMS, such as "Dear user 13500146807" and "Dear User 15914893488", although the figures are different, but generally meaning is the same, so the figures are all so removed. Third, remove the download address, such as the "to: wap.qwe312.com/2.apk" and "to: wap.lll328.com/12.apk".

After a series of pretreatment, the majority of the interference information can be removed.

3.4 Feature String Selection

Let $ST = \{w_1, w_2, w_3 \ldots w_n\}$ is a short message, w_i (where $i = 1, 2 \ldots n$) is the message of every word. According to the algorithm requirements, let feature string length is m, and $d_j = \{w_{j+1}, w_{j+2}, w_{j+3} \ldots w_{j+m}\}$ is a string. The effect and efficiency of experiment are there is a certain relationship with the choice of the feature string of length. If m is too large, the clustering result is that each cluster is relatively small, and m is too small, the result will not have the effect of clustering. In later experiments, we will compare the effect about the selected feature length for the experimental results, and ultimately select the most appropriate feature string length for this algorithm.

3.5 Algorithm Description

A general description of algorithm will be given below.
Input: short message text files which are preprocessed.
Output: short message text clustering results.

Step 1. According to a feature string selection rules, to build feature string FeatureMap. Key is a string of a fixed length; Value is the string frequency across all text messages files.
Step 2. For each message, according to the FeatureMap, gets a new FreqMap. Key is the frequency of feature text strings, and the Value is this message contains this frequency an array of feature text strings

Step 3. According to step 2 FreqMap, first to descending order of the length of the array Value, to get the maximum length of the array Value. If the length of the array Value is greater than three at the same time the corresponding feature string frequency is not equal to one, then select the first feature string of the array Value as this message clustering number.

Step 4. Loop execution step 2, step 3, until iterate over all message text. Clustering results are obtained then the program ends.

3.6 Select the Cluster Number

Traversal text message, obtained the frequency of all the characteristics string and its corresponding text message characteristics string. Finally, select the largest number of arrays which the characteristics string of the same frequency text message, set up its first character string for the cluster number.

When select cluster number, we can directly found that low frequency characteristics string to build variant library provides the real experimental data. The advantage of this way to select cluster number is, when text message similarly if there is only the difference of some words, no matter where the location of the difference, most of their character string is the same, so the clustering number is the same, this will not affect the cluster results.

3.7 Efficiency Analysis of Algorithms

The number of input short messages and the size of the generated feature strings Map affect the efficiency of the algorithm. The more the number of short messages, the greater the character string Map, the program is run for longer time. When build the frequency character strings Map, the algorithm processing time is mainly with the length of message and feature string, and the number of messages. If the number of short message is n, the time complexity of this step is $O(n * (L, m))$. When selecting cluster number, the algorithm processing time is mainly with the number of the different frequency characteristic strings and short messages. Now assume that the number of the different frequency character strings of each message is X and the short message is n, the time complexity of this step is $O(n * X * \log 2X)$. Because we deal with short message, so the size of the L, X and m relative to the short message number n is very small and can be neglected. After the above analysis, we have come to the time complexity of the algorithm is generally $O(n)$, than ordinary clustering algorithms (the time complexity is $O(n^2)$) much faster (Table 1).

Table 1. Time complexity of the algorithm

Build character string Map time complexity	Select time complexity of clustering number	Time complexity of this algorithm
$O(n*(L-m))$	$O(n*X*\log_2 X)$	$O(n)$

Where n is the number of short messages, m is characterized by length, L is the average length of SMS, X is the number of different frequency character strings of each message.

4 Experimental Results and Analysis

4.1 Experimental Environment and Evaluation Index

We implemented the entire algorithm in Java on a Linux operation system with memory of 8.0 GB, clocked Core quad-core 3.30 GHz. Experimental data sets are real mobile phone text messages which mobile operator provided. According to the characteristics of the short message, in order to ensure the correctness and effectiveness of the experimental results, we must preprocess messages through known variant libraries of mobile operators which involve removing some special characters and variant words, etc.

Experiments using the four evaluation index which is the most widely used in text cluster literature, namely precision, recall, purity, F-measure.

Precision refers to the number of SMS manual annotation of the same category accounted for the proportion of the sum of all the clustering results. Precision is defined as:

$$P(i,j) = \frac{Nij}{Ni} \tag{1}$$

Nij is the number of the artificial label class j in cluster i, Ni is the total number of short messages in cluster i.

Recall molecules equal precision, and denominator is the total number of messages manually labeled this category. Recall is defined as:

$$R(i,j) = \frac{Nij}{Nj} \tag{2}$$

Nj represents the total number of messages which manually labeled category j.

Purity is the weighted average of calculating the maximum precision of each category j, the higher the purity, the better clustering effect.

$$Purity = \sum \frac{Ni}{N} maxP(i,j) \tag{3}$$

N is the total number of short messages.

By comparing the size of the F-measure we can also see that the clustering results is good or bad. F-measure is defined as:

$$F = \frac{2 \times P \times R}{P + R} \tag{4}$$

P is the average precision and R is the average recall of clustering results.

4.2 Experimental Results

Experiment is divided into four parts: first, determine the character string of length; second, clustering results accuracy; third, algorithm efficiency; fourth, compared with other clustering algorithm.

Experiment 1: The experiment of determining the length of character string. We selected the thousands of short messages, by selecting different length of the feature string to create characteristics Map, then calculate the size of the Map, finally to choose the appropriate feature string length m. When generating feature string Map, in order to effectively use of memory, we remove what the frequency is one of characteristics string, because they have no sense of follow-up experiments. Set the size of the character string Map is S and remove the frequency is one of characteristics string Map is S1.

Table 2. Selected the length of characteristics string

m	3	4	5	6	7	8
S	1049850	1453650	1631306	1689739	1701844	1687480
S1	491638	586566	615539	616190	608256	595650

From Table 2, we can see clearly that with the increase of the length of character string, and the character string Map is growing, while the length of character string is equal to 6 to the maximum value. So algorithm selected the length of character string m is 6. The chart below more clearly reflects the relationship between the length of feature string and the size of feature string frequency Map (Fig. 2).

Experiment 2: The experiment of clustering results accuracy. We selected three groups of experimental data, each of them are 80 short messages. For each set of message data clustering, we use precision and recall index to analyze the correctness of the clustering algorithm and the effect of clustering.

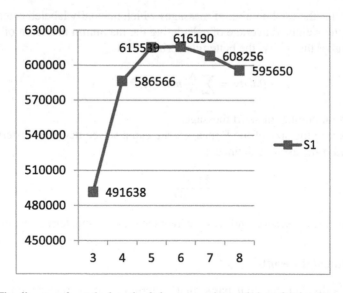

Fig. 2. The diagram about the length of character string and size of string frequency map

Table 3. Clustering results evaluation

Group	Number of messages	Precision	Recall	Purity	F-measure
1	80	100 %	94.3 %	95.0 %	97.1 %
2	80	100 %	100 %	100 %	100 %
3	80	97.4 %	92.3 %	98.8 %	94.8 %

We can see from Table 3 that three different sets of short messages which through the clustering algorithm to get its precision and recall rates are very high. Because the algorithm processing text data have the features of a lot of the same or similar situation, so the precision and recall rate is higher than ordinary text clustering results. From the experimental results it can be seen there were some errors in the clustering results. The cause of these conditions is mainly due to some messages Chinese words is very little which only a few words. Its length is shorter than the length of character string, thus causing the original message content in similar to gather two classes. Other reason is that some of the message is longer, but it's only a small part of the content is similar and most of the other content is different. It is also likely to put these different meanings messages together into a cluster. From the experimental results it can be seen that the algorithm for clustering the mass short message is correct and effective.

Experiment 3: The experiment of algorithm efficiency. This paper thesis is the mass short message fast clustering, so the efficiency of the clustering algorithm is the key of the algorithm is good or bad (Table 4).

Table 4. Clustering efficiency statistics

	Number of messages	Number of clusters	Execution time (s)
1	42316	4267	7
2	100000	11855	13
3	175898	20960	18
4	242316	32331	25
5	433582	57942	42
6	942316	108345	97
7	2084871	225742	269
8	2255087	231245	287

Through the experiments we can see that the clustering algorithm processing time is very fast. Processing more than 200 million spam messages takes only five minutes or so. The algorithm for mass short message clustering efficiency is very high.

Experiment 4: Clustering comparison. We choose the third group 80 short messages from experiment 2 as experimental data, and then compare this algorithm with hierarchical clustering algorithm and K-Means. We set the stop condition of hierarchical clustering and K-Means to 10 (that is the number of final cluster results). Comparison of the results shown in Table 5:

Table 5. Compared with other clustering algorithms

Algorithm	Experimental parameters	Number of clusters	Precision	Recall	Execution time (s)
Hierarchical clustering	Clusters = 10	10	91.5 %	89.6 %	6.53
K-Means	k = 10	10	86.9 %	87.3 %	10.28
This algorithm	m = 6	13	97.4 %	92.3 %	0.76

The Table 5 shows that the precision, recall, executing efficiency of clustering algorithm compared with traditional clustering algorithms are improved significantly.

5 Conclusion

In this paper, we mainly study on the rapid clustering of large-scale spam messages in real communication environment. Paper presented a clustering algorithm based on the message content character string matching and use Lucene search server clustering index. The experimental results show that the proposed algorithm for processing real spam messages clusters have a high execution efficiency and accuracy.

Acknowledgement. This work was supported by The open project of Science and Technology on Information Transmission and Dissemination in Communication Networks Laboratory (ITD-U14002/KX142600009).

References

1. http://www.cac.gov.cn/cnnic35fzzktjbg.htm (2014)
2. Hotho, A., Nürnberger, A., Paaβ, G.: A brief survey of text mining. In: LDV Forum, vol. 20, no. 1, pp. 19–62 (2005)
3. Peng, Z., Xiaoming, Y., Hongbo, X., Liu, C.: Incomplete clustering for large scale short texts. J. Chin. Inf. Process. **25**(1), 54–59 (2011)
4. Rajaraman, A., Ullman, J.D.: Mining of Massive Datasets, pp. 176–190 (2012)
5. Mocian, H: Survey of Distributed Clustering Techniques [EB/OL]. 1st term ISO report (2009)
6. Steinley, D.: K-means clustering: a half-century synthesis. Br. J. Math. Stat. Psychol. 59(May (34)), pp. 1–34 (2006)
7. He, H., Chen, B., Xu, W.R., Guo, J.: Short text feature extraction and clustering for web topic mining [EB/OL]. In: Proceeding of the 3rd International Conference on Semantics, Knowledge and Grid, pp. 382–385. IEEE, Washington D.C., USA (2007)
8. Zhou, H., Liu, J.: Study on mass chinese short message text density clustering. Comput. Eng. **11**, 81–83 (2010)

Research of K-means Clustering Method Based on DNA Genetic Algorithm and P System

Zhenni Jiang$^{(\boxtimes)}$, Wenke Zang, and Xiyu Liu

School of Management Science and Engineering,
Shandong Normal University, Jinan, Shandong, China
1179480219@qq.com, zwker@163.com, xyliu@sdnu.edu.cn

Abstract. This paper proposed a k-means clustering analysis method, which is based on DNA genetic algorithm and P system. DNA encoding is used to analyze the initial center of cluster and the P system is used to realize the clustering. The quality of the clustering is judged by the Euclidean distance of the corresponding cluster center, the rate of convergence and the image of the clustering result. Through selection, crossover, mutation and inversion, we can get the best center of the cluster. At the end of the paper, we take the simulation experience and the result shows the effect of this method is superior to the genetic algorithm of k-means clustering method. The simulation experiment is finished in the MATLAB 2014a and the experiment data is random generated.

Keywords: K-means · DNA genetic algorithm · P system

1 Introduction

Clustering is a rapidly developing area which contributes to research field including data mining, machine learning, spatial database technology, biology, marketing and so on [1]. Clustering analysis has become a vibrant research issue in data mining area owing to a mass of data store in database, and the clustering analysis method is a new multivariate statistical method, which aggregates things in to categories in accordance with certain properties of them. K-means algorithms is a common clustering algorithm based on partition, it uses average of data objects as clustering center, so clustering process is influenced by noisy data and initial clustering center. What's more, objects in the same cluster are similar to each other and objects from distinct cluster are different from each other. But the result of the algorithm may be trapped into local optimum [2]. To solve this problem, we propose a k-means clustering algorithm based on DNA genetic algorithm and P system.

The basic structure of DNA-GA is similar with the traditional genetic algorithm, except that the DNA genetic algorithm uses the DNA encoding, and gets the solution to the problem based on the encoding genetic manipulation to the individual [3]. Under certain conditions, the DNA-genetic algorithm can converge to the global optimal solution in search space, and apply it to the K-means clustering algorithm can overcome the shortcoming of easily plunged into local optimum and sensitive to initialization.

© Springer International Publishing Switzerland 2016
Q. Zu and B. Hu (Eds.): HCC 2016, LNCS 9567, pp. 193–203, 2016.
DOI: 10.1007/978-3-319-31854-7_18

P system is the biology model of membrane Computing introduced by Păun [4]. Roughly speaking, a P system consists of a membrane structure, in the compartments of which one places multisets of objects which evolve according to given rules in a synchronous nondeterministic maximally parallel manner [5, 7]. The paper combine the parallelism of P system and DNA genetic algorithm can improve the performance of K-means clustering algorithms. The main idea of this paper is to use DNA algorithm to find the initial cluster center and realize the clustering in the P system. This strategy is a new application of the combination of DNA genetic algorithm and P system.

2 Related Knowledge

2.1 K-means Algorithm

K-means algorithm is a kind of partition clustering algorithm, give the number of class k, using the principle of the closest distance, assigns the n objects to the k class. The result of clustering is express by the k clustering center, based on the given clustering objective function. What's more, objects in the same cluster are similar to each other and objects from distinct cluster are different from each other. The algorithm adopts the method of iterative update, and each iteration process is conducted to the direction of the objective function value to reduce.

Suppose there are N L-dimensional data points, which are expressed as $x_i(i = 1, 2, \ldots, N)$ for the clustering problem. Each data point $x_i(i = 1, 2, \ldots, N)$ is characterized by a vector of L values that is $x_{i1}, x_{i2}, \ldots, x_{iL}$, assuming that the above data are be divided into class k and k cluster centers are $c_1, c_2, \ldots, c_k$.

The criterion function of clustering is expressed by object function J:

$$J = \sum_{j=1}^{k} \sum_{xi \in Gi} \|x_i - c_j\|^2 \tag{1}$$

here, xi is the original sample point, c_j is the center of the class G_i.

The advantage of K-means algorithm is that quickly computation, smaller resource consumption. Besides K-means algorithm can process large data sets, and the algorithm is scalable and efficient. The K-means clustering algorithm process is as follows [6]:

(1) Choose k data objects representing the cluster center (k < n);
(2) Assign each data object of the entire data set to the cluster having the closest center;
(3) Compute new center for each cluster, by averaging the data objects belonging to the cluster, and calculate the value J of the criterion function at this time using formula (1);
(4) If at least one of the center has changed, go to step 2, otherwise go to step 5;
(5) Output the clusters.

2.2 DNA Genetic Algorithm

In the traditional genetic algorithm, the binary encoding is the most common one, which cannot express the wealth of genetic information and the computation model does not reflect the effect of genetic information for organism growth and development, especially the key role of DNA encoding mechanism. The basic structure of DNA-GA is similar with the traditional genetic algorithm, except that the DNA genetic algorithm uses the DNA encoding, and gets the solution to the problem based on the encoding genetic manipulation to the individual. DNA-GA evolves from the traditional genetic algorithm, and in addition to the advantages of traditional genetic algorithm, the DNA genetic algorithm has the following advantages:

First: Its encoding has greater improvement, suitable to express complex knowledge.

Second: Its allows the population to maintain a certain level of diversity in the case of low mutation probability.

Three: Its introduces complex gene-level operations, develops more effective genetic operators, such as inversion, separation, ectopic, etc.

DNA genetic algorithm uses the form of DNA encoding and the base string composed of four bases CGAT to represent the candidate solution to the problem. Then according changing the four bases into four numbers, namely 0, 1, 2, 3, thus turning a basic string into a quaternary numeric string, and mapped to the interval of the independent variable changes resulting integer. The accuracy of this encoding is determined by the length of the base string corresponding to each independence variable. Most of the DNA genetic algorithm operators are still simple crossover operators, mutation operators and inversion operators [8].

Crossover operator: for each selected for breeding, which part of the DNA strand interchangeable, to produce a new strand of DNA through the cross.

Single point crossover: for example: CGTAGCTGGAG GTACCCTGA 2:ACGTGTTGAAC CCGGTAACGA. Sequences 1 and 2 cross-operation: 1:CGTAGCTGGAG CCGGTAACGA 2:ACGTGTTGAAC GTACCCTGA.

Mutation operator: selected DNA chain base in the position of a gene mutation for another base. For example: the sequence ACGTGTTGAAC CCGGTAACGA mutation operation ACATGTCGAAC CGCGTACCGA.

Inversion operator: the inversion of the order of a certain period of the sequence in the individual. For example: ACGTGTTGAAC GGTACCCTGA inversion operation CAGTGTTGAAC GGTACCCTGA.

2.3 P System

P system is an abstracted membrane computing model according to the mechanism of cells processing chemical substances. According to the differences of the biochemical reaction of biological cells or tissues they simulate, they are divided into three categories: Cell-like P system, Tissue-like P system and Neural-like P system. Neural-like P system is focus of the membrane computing theory research, which the membrane system cells are made of neurons, and their thinking are derived from biological nervous system. Instead of considering a hierarchical structure, the membranes of tissue-like P system are placed at the node of a graph, and this variant takes inspiration from two biological phenomena:intercellular communication and communication between neurons. Cell-like P system simulates the structure and function of cells, and its basic elements include membrane structure, objects and rules. Membranes divide the entire system into different regions. The outermost membrane is called the skin membrane. If the interior of a membrane has no other membranes, it is called basic membrane, otherwise non-elemental membrane. Objects and rules exist in various regions. The implementation of rules has uncertainty and maximum parallelism. The basic membrane structure is shown in Fig. 1:

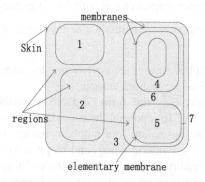

Fig. 1. The structure of membrane

In general, a P system with active membrane of degree m is construct:

$$\Pi = (O, \mu, w_1, w_2, \ldots, w_m, R_1, R_2, \ldots, R_m, i_0)$$

Where:

(1) O is an alphabet. Its elements are called objects;
(2) μ is a membrane structure of degree m,each membrane has a corresponding label;
(3) $w_i(i = 1,2\ldots m)$ is the multiset of objects in membrane i;
(4) $R_i(i = 1,2\ldots m)$ is the evolution rules of membrane i.

3   K-means Clustering Algorithm of DNA-GA and P System

3.1   Fitness Function

The fitness function is used to evaluate the fitness of individuals. For the K-means clustering of objective function, the smaller the objective function is, the better effect of clustering is [2]. The DNA genetic algorithm clustering analysis of fitness should be at maximum. So the paper use the negative objective function to define the fitness function.

$$J = \sum_{j=1}^{k} \sum_{xi \in Gi} \|x_i - c_j\|^2 \tag{2}$$

here, xi is the original sample point, c_j is the center of the class G_i.

And, the fitness function as follows:

$$F = -J. \tag{3}$$

3.2   DNA Encoding and Decoding

In this paper, the DNA encoding is used in the DNA genetic clustering. The cluster center is considered as the chromosomal DNA encoding, and a chromosome is considered as a string that consists of K cluster centers. As for Class K clustering analysis for the L-dimensional sample data, the chromosome structure that is based on the cluster center of the chromosome is:

$$S = \{x_{11}, x_{12}, \cdots, x_{1L}, x_{21}, x_{22}, \cdots, x_{2L}, x_{K1}, x_{K2} \cdots x_{KL}\}.$$

Every chromosome is DNA encoding with the length of K*L.

3.3   Population Initialization

The initialization process is to randomly generate an initial population. Select from the sample space of k individuals, whose values are determined by the users. Each individual means an initial cluster center. Repeat size chromosome initialization process until the initial population is generated.

3.4   Selection Operation

In the process of biological evolution, the species that have the strong ability to adapt to the living environment will have more opportunities to pass on to the next generation, while the opportunity for those species with poor ability is relatively small. Choices of operation are built on the evaluation of individual fitness, and its purpose is to avoid gene deletion and to improve the global convergence and computational efficiency. In this paper, we choose the roulette wheel selection.

3.5   Crossover Operation

The crossover operation is to sufficiently replace the individual part of the structure of the two paternal, to generate new individual operating. Its purpose is to produce new individuals for the next generation, and the crossover operation is a key part of the genetic algorithm. This article takes a one-point crossover.

3.6   Mutation Operation and Inversion Operation

Mutation operation has two purposes: first, the enhancement of local search ability of the algorithm; the second, the increase of the diversity of the population in order to change the performance of the algorithm and to avoid premature convergence. The mutation operator can produce populations of new genes. This article takes a random mutation operation. Inversion operation and mutation operations can generate new gene-rich genetic diversity and is more effective in preventing the genetic algorithm from the local optimum.

3.7   P Processing

Because of the P system can process the problem in a synchronous non-deterministic maximally parallel manner, so we combined the P system and DNA genetic algorithm to realize clustering can shorten the elapsed time successfully. In this paper, we used the P system to realized the clustering. The structure of P system is shown in Fig. 2:

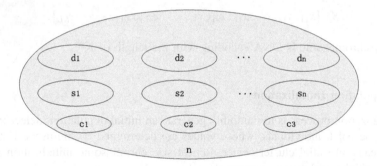

Fig. 2.   The structure of P system

After DNA genetic algorithm to give an initial k cluster centers, k centers were sent into membrane d_1 to d_n in k times.

Step 1: Every time, it should calculate the distance between the data point and cluster center, and mark the index of the cluster center. We using Euclidean distance to calculate the distance, and the formula is as follows:

$$d = \sqrt{(x_i - c_x)^2 + (y_i - c_y)^2} \tag{4}$$

Which, the (x_i, y_i) is the data point, and the (c_x, c_y) is the center point.

Step 2: The distance value corresponding input into the membrane s1 to s_n, until k cluster center successively entered. At the end, there is k data in every membrane s1 to s_n.

Step 3: We can get the minimum by compare the k data and output the data into membrane c_1 to c_k, which the index located. For example, the index of the distance of the data point d_3 and the first cluster center is 1, and this distance is the minimum in k distance value, so the data point d_3 is put into the membrane c_1.

Step 4: Eventually, all of the data points will be divided into k groups and recalculate the cluster center.

Step 5: Repeat the steps until the cluster centers no longer change.

Step 6: The data points in k membranes $c_1, c_2 \ldots c_k$ are the final clustering result.

4   Simulation Experiment

In order to verify the validity of the above algorithm, we use the matlab simulation experiment. For example, we use the fix $(\text{rand}(100, 2) * 100)$, and randomly generate 100 two-dimensional coordinates of range of [0,100]. The data distribution is shown in Fig. 3:

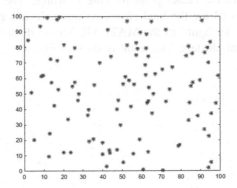

Fig. 3. Random data distribution map

We used the k-means clustering analysis of DNA genetic algorithm and divided the sample into three categories.

4.1   Using Matlab for K-means Algorithm Based on DNA Genetic Algorithm and P System (DGPKM)

4.1.1   Initial Data
Suppose the population size is 20, the maximum iterative algebra is 500, and crossover probability is 0.8. The mutation probability is 0.01 and the inversion probability is 0.01.

4.1.2   DNA Encoding and Population Initialization
The mapping used in this paper is 0123/CGAT, and the probability of 0,1,2,3 is 0.156, 0.157, 0.344, 0, 343. We makes the length of chromosome is 66. We may randomly set up a DNA sequence: ACTGTACGATG CCGATATCGTAG AGTGCACTATC ATAGTCGTACG GTTCGATACTG ACTGTCGTACG, which corresponds to the cluster center $(x_{11}, x_{12}, x_{21}, x_{22}, x_{31}, x_{32})$.

4.1.3   Selection, Crossover, Mutation and Inversion Operation

Based on chromosome sequence of DNA, we can calculate the value of the fitness of each chromosome according to the fitness function shown in Fig. 2.

In this paper, use the roulette wheel selection method to select the operation, and then have cross-operation. Cross option is to use a one-point crossover. Then have the mutation operation, with the random mutation operator. The last is the inversion operation, which changes the richness of the chromosome. And then we have the next generation of choice until you reach the maximum of iteration.

4.1.4   Operation Clustering Realized Based on P System

When we get the initial cluster center point, we divided the n data point into the d1 to d100 membrane. Three centers were sent into membrane d1 to d100 in three times and calculate the distance between the data points and the cluster center according to the process of the introduction in the chapter three. So we can get a new center point and repeat the process until the center point no longer change. The data points in three membranes c1, c2 and c3 are the final clustering result. In this paper, we output the clustering result with the figure in the MATLAB. We used three different colors to represent three different clusters. The result is show in Fig. 4:

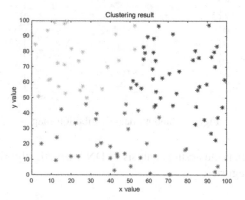

Fig. 4. The clustering result

4.1.5   Simulation Results

The output center point is (71.1268, 73.4807; 23.7190, 71.5122; 66.4748, 24.3633) and the changes of the optimal fitness function is shown in Fig. 5:

4.2   Using Matlab for K-means Algorithm Based on Genetic Algorithm

Matlab is used to analyze the K-means algorithm of genetic algorithm. After 500 iteration. The output center point is: (62.4817, 24.1817, 19.9805, 69.7606; 81.1920, 73.7665) and the changes of the optimal fitness function is show in Fig. 6:

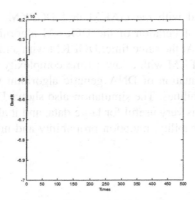

Fig. 5. DGPKM fitness function

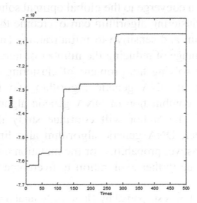

Fig. 6. GAKM fitness function

We have simulation and comparison between the genetic algorithm K-means clustering analysis and K-means clustering analysis based on DNA genetic algorithm and P system. Simulation at random for 10 times, 20 times, 30 times respectively and calculate the fitness function when they achieve the maximum iterations. At the same time, we compared the average number of iteration. They are showed in Table 1:

Table 1. DGPKM and GAKM compared result

	DGPKM		GAKM	
	Fitness	Iteration	Fitness	Iteration
10	−5.8884e + 04	250	−6.1534e + 04	408
20	−5.8341e + 04	270	−6.3002e + 04	372
30	−5.9420e + 04	248	−6.5085e + 04	340

Through the compared with the GAKM and DGPKM, we can find there is a reduction in the number of iteration of the DGPKM algorithm and we get a better fitness with the DGPKM. At the same time, DGPKM with a higher convergence speed than the GAKM, and DGPKM with a lower time complexity than the GAKM. All of this shows that the combination of DNA genetic algorithm with P system have the powerful computing capabilities. The simulation also shows DGPKM is superior than the GAKM. This thought is very useful for large data, and it also impact by the size of population, crossover probability, mutation probability and inversion probability.

5   Conclusion

This paper presents a combination of DNA genetic algorithm and P system to realized the K-means clustering analysis algorithm, which overcomes the slow convergence characteristics of local clustering analysis and realized the clustering in parallel way. DNA-genetic algorithm can converge to the global optimal solution in search space and apply it to the K-means clustering algorithm can overcome the shortcoming of easily plunged into local optimum and sensitive to initialization. The experiment show that the algorithm has its advantage of reducing the number of iterations and improving the clustering performance in solving the problem of clustering. The algorithm actually combines the advantages of DNA genetic algorithm and P system. As the data dimension increasing, the combination of DNA genetic algorithm and P system will have better performance. The author will continue study the processing of high-dimensional data. However, DNA genetic algorithm also limited by the change of population size, or the crossover probability, or the mutation probability, the number of iteration number. It need the further exploration to overcome this limitation.

Acknowledgment. This work was supported by National Natural Science Foundation of China (61170038), Natural science foundation of Shandong Province, China (ZR2011FM001), Technology development projects of Shandong province, China (2012G0020314), Soft science research project of Shandong Province, China (2013RZB01019), Jinan City independent innovation plan project in Colleges and Universities, China (201401202), Ministry of education of Humanities and social science research projects, China (12YJA630152), Social Science Fund Project of Shandong Province, China (11CGLJ22), outstanding youth scientist foundation project of Shandong Province, China (BS2013DX037), young star of science and technology plan project, Jinan (20120108), science and technology development project, Jinan (201211003), science and technology development project, Jinan (201305004).

References

1. Han, J., Kambr, M.: Data Mining Concepts and Techniques. Elsevier Inc., USA (2012). chap. 8
2. Feng, M., Wang, Z.: A genetic k-means clustering algorithm based on the optimized initial centers. Comput. Inf. Sci. **4**(3), 88 (2011)

3. Zang, W., Liu, X., Wang, Y.: Clustering analysis research based on DNA genetic algorithm. In: Zu, Q., Hu, B., Elçi, A. (eds.) ICPCA/SWS 2012. LNCS, vol. 7719, pp. 801–813. Springer, Heidelberg (2013)
4. Păun, G.: Computing with membranes. J. Comput. Syst. Sci. **61**(1), 108–143 (2000)
5. Escuela, G., Gutiérrez-Naranjo, M.A.: An application of genetic algorithms to membrane computing. In: Eighth Brainstorming Week on Membrane Computing, pp. 101–108 (2010)
6. Poteras, C.M., Mihaescu, M.C., Mocanu, M.: An optimized version of the k-means clustering algorithm. In: 2014 Federated Conference on Computer Science and Information Systems (FedCSIS), pp. 695–699. IEEE (2014)
7. Lingras, P.: Applications of rough set based k-means, Kohonen Som, GA clustering. In: Peters, J.F., Skowron, A., Marek, V.W., Orłowska, E., Słowiński, R., Ziarko, W.P. (eds.) Transactions on Rough Sets VII. LNCS, vol. 4400, pp. 120–139. Springer, Heidelberg (2007)
8. Huang, H., Zhong, Y., Nie, S.: The application of improved dna genetic algorithm in solving multi-objective optimization problem. In: Zhao, M., Sha, J. (eds.) ICCIP 2012. LNCS, vol. 289, pp. 459–467. Springer, Heidelberg (2012)

A Linkage Model of Non-circular Gear Shaping and Computer Simulation Processing

Bo Li$^{(\boxtimes)}$, Jun He, Dingfang Chen, Fangyan Zheng, Botao Li, and Hongxiang Zhang

Institute of Intelligent Manufacturing and Control,
Wuhan University of Technology, Heping Road No.1040, Wuchang District,
Wuhan 430063, Hubei, China
whlibo163@163.com, 1341717981@qq.com

Abstract. The non-circular internal gears and non-circular external gears of concave pitch curve can not be processed by gear hobbing currently. Gear shaping, compared with gear hobbing, is a more general method which can solve all the problems above. Unlike previous geometric algorithms, by using the normal vector of gear pitch curve and in combination with the processing feed of shape cutter in this paper, a three-axis linkage mathematical model of non-circular gear shaping based on the model of the envelope is obtained. At the same time, through MATLAB and Visual C++ mixed programming, a non-circular gear shaping system is developed according to the linkage model. Finally, with a pair of three order elliptic gears, and via the computer-aided manufacturing, the whole non-circular gear shaping processing in three-axis linkage CNC gear shaping machine is shown in this paper, and then proving the correctness of the linkage shaping model and the shaping method of non-circular gear.

Keywords: Non-circular gear · Gear shaping · Linkage model · Gear shaping system · Simulation processing

1 Introduction

The non-circular gear processing methods now are mainly gear hobbing and gear shaping, but there are many limitations in gear hobbing, such as can not to process non-circular internal gears and non-circular external gears of concave pitch curve [1], easy to undercut and so on. By contrast, gear shaping, which can process both non-circular external gears of concave pitch curve and internal gears, is a general method solving all the limitations above.

With the rapidly development of CNC processing technology, CNC gear shaping method has become one of the main gear processing. High processing efficiency, wide range and high precision, make it widely used in manufacturing non-circular gears today [2]. CNC programming system is an important part in CNC processing technology, and the existing non-circular gear shaping systems now are inefficient, error-prone and small suitable, so there is a very important significance in the study of non-circular gear shaping automatic programming system.

© Springer International Publishing Switzerland 2016
Q. Zu and B. Hu (Eds.): HCC 2016, LNCS 9567, pp. 204–214, 2016.
DOI: 10.1007/978-3-319-31854-7_19

Combining the structure of general three-axis linkage CNC gear shaping machine and the processing feed of shape cutter, and through using the normal vector of gear pitch curve, a three-axis linkage mathematical model of shaping non-circular gear is built [3, 4]. Finally, the cutting process is simulated in the form of computer graphic, and the process is implemented within a general three-axis CNC gear shaping machine, which proves the shaping model and the above shaping method.

2 A Linkage Model of Gear Shaping Containing Processing Feed

The principle of shaping non-circular gear by a shape cutter is to ensure the pure rotation between the pitch circle of shape cutter and the pitch curve of non-circular gear [5]. But when shaping a non-circular gear, instead of the pure mesh motion, the feed of the shape cutter should contain processing feed of shape cutter. And like the cylindrical gear manufacturing process, the non-circular gears shaping is also divided into several cycles, and the number of the cycles is co-determined by the shape cutter parameters and the processing capability of the CNC machine. The geometric relationship in non-circular gear shaping containing feed by a shape cutter as shown in Fig. 1. The pitch circle of shape cutter and the pitch curve of non-circular gear are no longer tangent with each other, and the distance between them is h_0. Now $\overline{O_1P} = h_o = r_0 + h$, h is the processing feed of each cycle, r_o is the radius of the pitch circle of shape cutter.

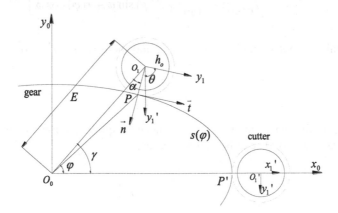

Fig. 1. Geometrical relatioship in shaping non-circular gear with feed

A fixed right angle coordinate system $x_0O_0y_0$ has been established in the rotary center of the non-circular gear. The pitch curve of non-circular gear defined as $r(\varphi)$. P' is the contact point between the pitch curve of the non-circular gear and the pitch circle of shape cutter with a polar angle $\varphi = 0$, and it is also the shaping starting point of shape cutter. P is the contact point when shape cutter moves to the position that the polar angle is φ. And the θ is the rotation angle of shape cutter from $\varphi = 0$ to $\varphi = \varphi$. The arc length of pitch curve of the non-circular gear at point P is $S(\varphi)$. With the pure rolling relationship, the rotating angle of shape cutter is:

$$\theta = \frac{S(\varphi)}{r_o} = \frac{\int_0^{\varphi} \sqrt{r(\varphi)^2 + r'(\varphi)^2} d\varphi}{r_o} \tag{1}$$

Supposing that $\overrightarrow{t}$ is the unit tangent vector of the pitch curve of non-circular gear at point P, the unit normal vector of pitch curve of non-circular gear at point P is $\overrightarrow{n}$. In addition, in the center of the rotary center of the shape cutter, a moving right angle coordinate system $x_1 O_1 y_1$ has been established, and the moving right angle coordinate center O_1 is the center of the shape cutter. The x_1 axis and y_1 axis directions are consistent with the unit normal vector $\overrightarrow{n}$ and the unit tangent vector $\overrightarrow{t}$ respectively.

The contact point P is

$$\begin{bmatrix} x_p \\ y_p \end{bmatrix} = \begin{bmatrix} r(\varphi) \cos \varphi \\ r(\varphi) \sin \varphi \end{bmatrix} \tag{2}$$

The unit tangent vector at P is

$$t = \frac{t_0}{|t_0|} = \frac{1}{\sqrt{r'(\varphi)^2 + r(\varphi)^2}} \begin{bmatrix} r'(\varphi) \cos \varphi - r(\varphi) \sin \varphi \\ r'(\varphi) \sin \varphi + r(\varphi) \cos \varphi \end{bmatrix} \tag{3}$$

Let the unit tangent vector $\overrightarrow{t} = [t_x \quad t_y]^T$, and there is $\overrightarrow{n} \cdot \overrightarrow{t} = \overrightarrow{0}$, so

$$\overrightarrow{n} = \begin{bmatrix} t_y \\ -t_x \end{bmatrix} \tag{4}$$

The center of the shape cutter O_1 is on the normal equidistant line of the pitch curve of non-circular gear, so O_1 can be represented as:

$$\begin{bmatrix} x_{O_1} \\ y_{O_1} \end{bmatrix} = \begin{bmatrix} x_P + r_o t_y \\ y_P - r_o t_x \end{bmatrix} \tag{5}$$

Thus the center distance between the cutter and non-circular gear is:

$$E = \left| \overrightarrow{O_1 O_0} \right| = \sqrt{r(\varphi)^2 + r_o^2 + \frac{2 r_o r(\varphi)^2}{\sqrt{r(\varphi)^2 + r'(\varphi)^2}}} \tag{6}$$

The polar angle of shape cutter at point O_1 relative to $x_0 O_0 y_0$ is:

$$\gamma = arctan(\frac{y_{O_1}}{x_{O_1}}) = arctan[\frac{r(\varphi)\sin\varphi - r_o t_x}{r(\varphi)\cos\varphi + r_o t_y}] \tag{7}$$

The angle between $\overline{O_0 O_1}$ and $\overline{P O_1}$ is:

$$\alpha = arccos(\frac{\overrightarrow{PO_1} \cdot \overrightarrow{O_0 O_1}}{|\overrightarrow{PO_1}| |\overrightarrow{O_0 O_1}|}) = arccos[\frac{(x_{O_1} - x_p, y_{O_1} - y_p)(x_{O_1}, y_{O_1})}{Er_o}]$$

$$= arccos \frac{r_o \cdot \sqrt{r(\varphi)^2 + r'(\varphi)^2} - r(\varphi)^2}{E \cdot \sqrt{r(\varphi)^2 + r'(\varphi)^2}} \tag{8}$$

Figure 2 shows the configuration of general three-axis linkage CNC gear shaping machine with the SINUMERIK system. X axis is the linear axis of the center distance between the cutter and the non-circular gears; C1 axis is the revolving axis of the non-circular gears; C2 axis is the revolving axis of the shape cutter. X axis, C2 axis and C1 axis are three linkage axes with nonlinear interpolation when the non-circular gear is shaped.

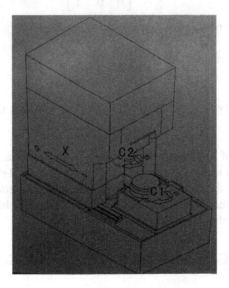

Fig. 2. The configuration of general three-axis linkage CNC shaping machine

So the position of each linkage axis containing feed of the shape cutter can be presented as follow:

$$
\begin{cases}
X(\varphi, h_o) = E = \sqrt{r(\varphi)^2 + h_o^2 + \dfrac{2h_o r(\varphi)}{\sqrt{r(\varphi)^2 + r'(\varphi)^2}}} \\[3ex]
C1(\varphi, h_o) = \gamma - \varphi = arctan\Big[\dfrac{r(\varphi)\sin\varphi + r_o t_x}{r(\varphi)\cos\varphi - r_o t_y}\Big] - \varphi \\[3ex]
C2(\varphi, h_o) = \theta - \alpha = \dfrac{\displaystyle\int_0^{\varphi}\sqrt{r(\varphi)^2 + r'(\varphi)^2}\,d\varphi}{r_o} - arccos\dfrac{r_o \cdot \sqrt{r(\varphi)^2 + r'(\varphi)^2} - r(\varphi)^2}{a \cdot \sqrt{r(\varphi)^2 + r'(\varphi)^2}}
\end{cases}
$$

$$(9)$$

According to the coordinate transformation [6], the transformation matrix between C1 axis and C2 axis is:

$$
M_{XA} = \begin{bmatrix} cos(C1) & -sin(C1) & 0 \\ sin(C1) & cos(C1) & 0 \\ 0 & 0 & 1 \end{bmatrix}
\tag{10}
$$

The transformation matrix between X axis and the base is:

$$
M_{OX} = \begin{bmatrix} 1 & 0 & X \\ 0 & 1 & 0 \\ 0 & 0 & 1 \end{bmatrix}
\tag{11}
$$

The transformation matrix between the base and B axis is:

$$
M_{BO} = \begin{bmatrix} cos(C2) & sin(C2) & 0 \\ -sin(C2) & cos(C2) & 0 \\ 0 & 0 & 1 \end{bmatrix}
\tag{12}
$$

According to the above relationship, the envelope equation of the shape cutter is:

$$
r = M_{BO} M_{OX} M_{XA} r_2
\tag{13}
$$

When the model of tooth profile generating method containing feed with shape cutter is established, by using computer programming to control the feed and the speed of three axes to realize the nonlinear interaction, the dynamic graphics simulation and shaping codes are obtained. And then non-circular gear can be shaped in CNC shaping machine tool with the shaping codes.

3 The Design of Computer Aided Non-circular Gear Shaping System

3.1 The Principle of Non-circular Gear Shaping System Design

For different types of non-circular gears, though the pitch curve of each is not identical, and the processing cycle is also very different, but the design parameters and processing parameters they need are roughly the same. Therefore, it is necessary to design a non-circular gear shaping program. Traditional non-circular gear shaping program mostly stay in manual programming, and there are some limitations such as low efficiency, a large amount of data, error prone and poor adaptability, also need specialized programming staffs [7], which greatly limit the non-circular gear shaping automatic processing development. In this case, it is of great practical significance to develop a simple and easy to operate shaping program.

The design of gear shaping program is a complicated numerical calculation process [8]. For this reason, by using the normal vector of gear pitch curve in this paper, an algorithm of the non-circular gear tooth profile based on the model of the envelope is obtained, which greatly simplify the non-circular gear shaping program.

The purpose of designing the non-circular gear program is through the computer aided design and manufacturing to calculate and process the basic parameters of the input non-circular gears, the dynamic graphics simulation and the shaping codes will be obtained finally. The principle is shown in Fig. 3.

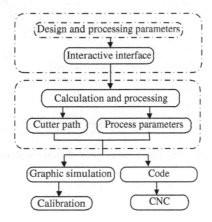

Fig. 3. The principle of the non-circular gear shaping program system

3.2   The Design of Non-circular Gear Shaping System

According to the principle of gear shaping program system, this paper uses the method of MATLAB and Visual C++ mixed language to write this program. MATLAB has a very strong numerical analysis, matrix calculation and graphics display, etc., but its execution speed is greatly limited for using the interpretation of language; The Visual C++ is suitable for system development, and it is simple and easy to operate, and the speed of implementation is relatively fast, but it is more complicated than MATLAB in engineering calculation. By using of Visual C++ and MATLAB mixed language to take greatly advantage of the two languages, the non-circular gear shaping system will be easier and more efficient.

According to the shape and design requirements of the non-circular gear, the gear shaping system firstly use MATLAB to determine the processing parameters of the axis of the shaping machine, and optimize them. Then, the parameters of the each axis are written in a specific format and by the Visual C++ through the serial port to transmit the shaping code to the CNC performs interpolation operation, realizing the non- circular gear shaping automation.

The main interface of the non-circular gear shaping program is designed by using the module design, which is composed of the input part, graphic simulation, code

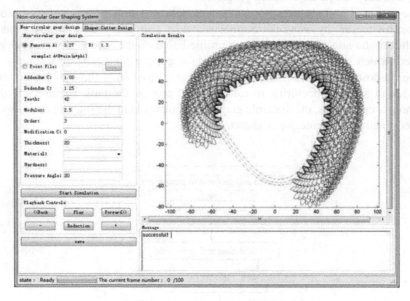

Fig. 4. The non-circular gear shaping system

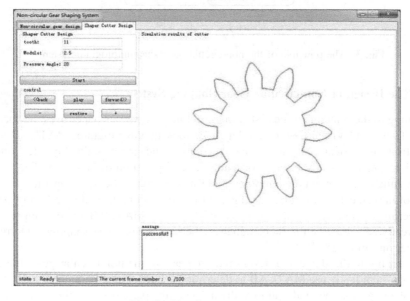

Fig. 5. The shape cutter system

generation and information display. The input part is divided into non-circular gear design parameters, shape cutter parameters and processing parameters. As shown in Fig. 4, it is a non-circular gear design parameter module. When the design parameters are input, and take processing parameters into account, the dynamic graphics simulation of shaping and the codes will be obtained. As shown in Fig. 5, it is the design system of shape cutter.

4   Example and Computer Simulation Analysis

4.1   Parameters of the Gears

Taking a pair of non-circular gears with three order sinusoidal gear ratio function as an example. And the parameters of the gears are shown as follows:
The pitch curve of drive gear is

$$r_1(\varphi) = \frac{a}{1 + i_{12}(\varphi)} = \frac{82.064}{2.0198 + 0.2 \sin 3\varphi} \tag{14}$$

The teeth number of drive gear is $z_1 = 42$, the pressure angle is $\alpha = 20°$, the module is $m = 2\ mm$, the addendum coefficient is $h_a^* = 1$, and the dedendum coefficient is $h_f^* = 1.25$. The tooth number of the shape cutter is $z_0 = 13$, the module of the shape cutter is $m_0 = 2\ mm$, and the pressure angle of the shape cutter is $\alpha_0 = 20°$.

According to the calculation, the center distance of this pair of gear is $a = 82.604\ mm$.

The pitch curve of the driven gear is:

$$r_2(\varphi) = a - r_1(\varphi) = \frac{165.753 + 16.413 \sin 3\varphi}{2.0198 + 0.2 \sin 3\varphi} \tag{15}$$

The tooth number of driven gear is:

$$z_2 = z_1 = 42. \tag{16}$$

4.2   Computer Simulation Analysis

When the relevant parameters of the non-circular gear are input into the gear shaping program, including m, h_a^*, h_f^*, z_1 and so on. By using the computer aided manufacturing system, the computer dynamic graphics simulation and local amplification graphics simulation of non-circular gear shaping (as shown in Fig. 6) and shaping codes (as shown in Fig. 7) are obtained. From the results of non-circular gear graphics simulation, the position relationship between the shape cutter and the non-circular gear could be seen intuitively, so that the improper design parameters and the undercut could be judged in advance. It has a good guide to the design and manufacturing of the non-circular gears.

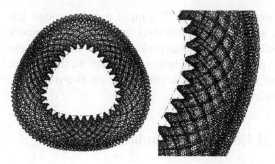

Fig. 6. The computer dynamic simulation

```
%Gear Shaping Codes
F301
G54 G01 G90 X 39.123 C1= 175.669 C2= 184.13
M01
M03 S301  M07
F21
G01 G90 X 34.123 C1= 175.669 C2= 184.137
G01 G90 X 33.924 C1= 175.693 C2= 184.161
G01 G90 X 33.724 C1= 175.718 C2= 184.186
G01 G90 X 33.525 C1= 175.743 C2= 184.211
G01 G90 X 33.325 C1= 175.768 C2= 184.236
G01 G90 X 33.126 C1= 175.793 C2= 184.262
```

Fig. 7. The gear shaping codes

When the shaping codes are input into the general three-axis CNC gear shaping machine with the SINUMERIK system, by setting reasonable processing parameters, the non-circular gears can be shaped automatically with the CNC gear shaping machine. The processing of the drive gear is shown in Fig. 8. Figure. 9 shows the finished drive gear and local amplification of the drive gear, the tooth profile of the finished gear looks the same as the corresponding enveloping surface shown in Fig. 6. As we can see, the shaping model and the above shaping method are correct.

Fig. 8. Processing of the drive gear

Fig. 9. The finished gear

5 Conclusions

In this paper, a three-axis linkage model of gear shaping containing processing feed is presented. Compared with the traditional geometric algorithm, this model is more simple, universal and easier to be realized on the computer. The correctness of this linkage model has been proved through the graphics simulation and gear shaping. Through the computer programming and graphics simulation technology, the improper design parameters would be judged in advance, which provides a direct basis for the design and manufacturing of non-circular gears. At the same time, through the combination of the automatic programming system and the general three-axis CNC shaping machine, the technology function of the general three-axis CNC shaping machine is extended, and the demand of the non-circular gear for the small volume, low-cost production is satisfied simultaneously.

Acknowledgment. This research is supported by Science and technology support program of Hubei Province under Grant No. 2014BAA024. The authors also would like to express appreciation to the anonymous reviewers for their helpful comments on improving the paper.

References

1. Li, J., Wu, X., Mao, S., et al.: Numerical computation of teeth profile of non-circular gear. J. Xi'an Jiaotong Univ. **39**(1), 75–78 (2005)
2. He, G., Hu, C., Sha, C., et al.: Mathematical model and graphics simulation of the shaping of elliptical gears. Mach. Des. Manuf. **6**, 8–10 (2004)
3. Shi, Y.: Research on Machining Methods of Non-circular Gears and Simulation of the Machining Process of Gear Hobbing. Dong Hua University, Shanghai (2013)
4. Hu, C., Ding, H., Yan, K., et al.: Linkage control model of non-circular gear hobbing process. Lanzhou: J. Lanzhou Univ. Technol. (1), 43–45 (2005)
5. Wu, X., Wang, G.: Non-circular Gear and Non-uniform Transmission Ratio, pp. 35–44. Mechanical Industry Press, Beijing (1997)

214   B. Li et al.

6. Zheng, F., Chen, D., Liu, Y.: A general algorithm for non-circular gear tooth profile. J. Mech. Transm. (04), 64–66 (2013)
7. Mo, Z.: Parametric Design of Non-circular Gears and Development of Automatic Programming System. Lanzhou University of Technology, Lanzhou (2013)
8. Yang, S.: Development of automatic programming system for CNC machining of non-circular gears. Combined Mach. Tools Autom. Process. Technol. (1), 84–88 (2008)

Measurement of Composite Error of Pitch Curve of Non-circular Gear Based on C++ and MATLAB

Bo Li[1], Hongxiang Zhang[1(✉)], Dingfang Chen[1], Tulian Xian[2],
Botao Li[1], Jun He[1], and Fangyan Zheng[1]

[1] Wuhan University of Technology, Heping Road No. 1040, Wuchang District,
Wuhan 430063, Hubei, China
{whlibol63,18771016792}@163.com
[2] Shenzhen Deren Electronic Co., Ltd., 33 Road, Guangming Streets,
Guangming New District, Shenzhen 518107, Guangdong, China

Abstract. In view of the present low efficiency of error measurement of non-circular gear, and the complicated problem of measuring operation, the measurement device of double-flank engagement is designed. The system which is used to measure composite error of pitch curve of non-circular gear is developed based on mixed programming of C++ and MATLAB. The system can observe the real-time measurement data of sensors and can be used to process the test data to obtain the errors automatically, so the efficiency and precision of measurement is greatly improved. The error of pitch curve is obtained through measuring elliptic gear, which verifies the device's feasibility on the principle and algorithm of measurement. The paper provides an efficient and feasible method for the automatic measurement of the error of pitch curve of non-circular gear.

Keywords: Non-circular gear · Pitch curve · Error-measuring system · Mixed programming · Sensor

1 Introduction

Non-circular gear has both variable transmission characteristics of cam and accurate transmission characteristics of gear, therefore, it has a wide range of applications in machinery manufacturing, heavy industry and light industry machinery. However, the measurement technology of the error of non-circular gears is far behind the processing technology, which restricts the development of the non-circular gears. Only a few scholars have studied the error measurement of non-circular gear so far. So it is of great significance to study the error measurement of non-circular gear. De-wei Tang put forward method of single-flank engagement and double-flank engagement to measure non-circular gear, both methods take a cylindrical gear as the master gear to measure non-circular gear. However, method of single-flank engagement needs to control the meshing center distance of two gears real-time, which is not easy to achieve because of the high demand for CNC system [1]. Method of double-flank engagement is easy to achieve, but De-wei Tang just put forward a measurement method, and did not make a

© Springer International Publishing Switzerland 2016
Q. Zu and B. Hu (Eds.): HCC 2016, LNCS 9567, pp. 215–225, 2016.
DOI: 10.1007/978-3-319-31854-7_20

more profound practical analysis [2]. Dong Guoqing proposed the concept of pitch curve radial composite error, and didn't do further analysis on the efficiency of measurement and calculation process [3]. Liu Haijun discussed the non-circular gear polar tracking measurement technology, but the paper didn't make analysis about radial composite error of pitch curve [4].

All the measurement methods mentioned above don't measure the composite error of pitch curve of non-circular gear efficiently, so it is necessary to design a new method to measure the composite error of pitch curve. This paper designs a measurement device and develops a measurement system, which can measure the composite error of pitch curve automatically and efficiently.

2   Principle of Measurement

The measurement method of non-circular gear is different from cylindrical gear. When a pair of cylindrical gears are meshing, the meshing point is on the straight line connecting the center points of two gears, the pitch circle of the gear is easily obtained. However, non-circular gear and cylindrical gear meshing, the mesh point P1 is often not on the straight line connecting the center points of two gears (as shown in Fig. 1). But the measurement method of non-circular gear can use the measurement method of cylindrical gear for reference. When cylindrical gear and non-circular gear are double-flank engagement, the both tooth surfaces contact, and non-circular gear's pitch curve and cylindrical gear's pitch circle appear pure rolling, there is a certain mathematical relationship between rotational angle of non-circular and rotational angle of cylindrical gear, if the relevant parameters are known, the data points of pitch curve of non-circular gear can be obtained. Compared with parameters of theoretical pitch curve, radial composite error of pitch curve can be obtained.

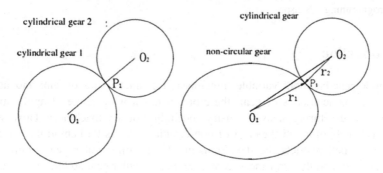

Fig. 1. The difference between two meshing conditions

Measurement device of radial composite error of pitch curve of non-circular gear uses standard cylindrical gear and non-circular gear to achieve variable center distance double-flank engagement. Measurement system is developed based on mixed programming of C++ and MATLAB. Measurement system can collect the data of sensors

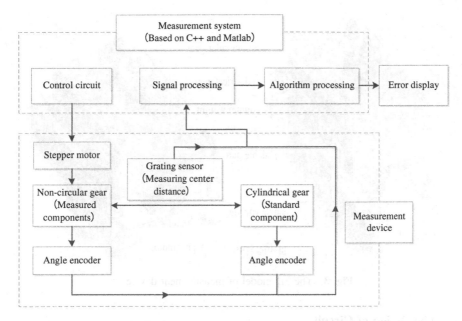

Fig. 2. The measuring schematic of composite error of pitch curve of non-circular gear

and can process the data automatically. When the standard cylindrical gear is engaged with non-circular gear, the data acquisition system measures the data of the rotational angle of cylindrical gear, the rotational angle of non-circular gear and the center distance of the two gears. According to the relationship between the rotational angle, the center distance and the pitch curve of non-circle gear, a reasonable mathematical model is constructed, and the error of the pitch curve is obtained via measurement system. The principle of measurement is shown in Fig. 2.

3   The Design of Measurement Device and Circuit

3.1   The Design of Measurement Device

According to measuring principle, the meshing of non-circular gear and cylindrical gear is a variable center distance transmission, grating sensor which is fixed parallel to the guide rail records the change of center distance, and angle sensors record the rotational angle of two gears. The 3D model of device is shown in Fig. 3. Non-circular gear is a driver gear, and cylindrical gear which can move along the guide rail under the variable center distance transmission is a passive gear. Stepper motor whose speed is controlled by measurement systems provides power for non-circular gear. Constant tension is provided by the counter weight to keep the two gears meshing.

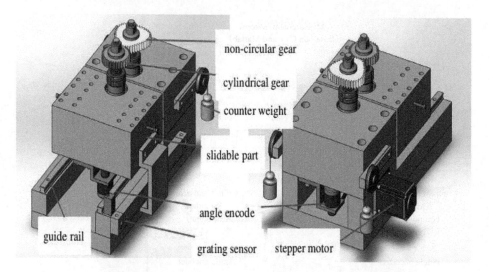

Fig. 3. The 3D model of measurement device

3.2 The Design of Circuit

Data acquisition circuit is mainly composed of the main chip, signal input circuit, signal output circuit and serial communication circuit.

Single chip microcomputer of STM32 series is used for the main chip, this single chip microcomputer is 32-bit single chip based on Cortex-MARM kernel with a flexible way of communication, powerful computing capability and efficient signal acquisition mechanism. STM32 microcontrollers is very suitable to be the main chip of lower computer for sampling data of sensor and communicating with host computer.

Signal acquisition input circuit mainly collects physical signal which is measured by grating sensor and angle encoders, after optoelectronic isolation, the signal is transmitted to the STM32 microcontrollers, after the preliminary data processing, the data is cached in single-chip microcomputer and it will be sent to the computer.

Signal input circuit is mainly to control the rotational speed of the stepper motor, so that the non-circular gear keeps an appropriate rotational speed in order to ensure that the sensor collects data without losing the frame.

Serial communication circuit can realize the data conversion between the computer USB interface and the universal serial port, which is convenient to transmit the measurement data to the computer.

The recording and controlling of the data acquisition need to be realized by software program. The program is based on the C language program written in Keil uVision4.

The factual picture of the data collection circuit board is shown in Fig. 4, by connecting with stepper motors, sensors and measurement systems, the function of data acquisition can be realized.

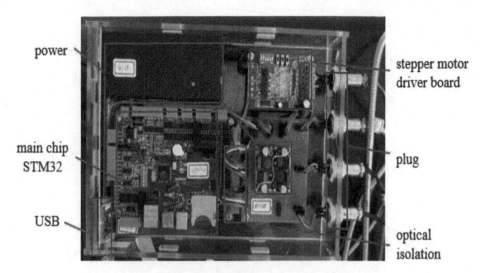

Fig. 4. The circuit board of data acquisition

4 Mathematical Model of Pitch Curve Measurement

The figure of conjugate geometrical relationship between a cylindrical gear and a non-circular gear is shown in Fig. 5. Supposing that the radius of the standard cylindrical gear is r_1, at a certain time, the rotational angle of the cylindrical gear is ϕ_1, the rotational angle of the non-circular gear is ϕ_2, and the center distance between two gears is A. ϕ_1 and ϕ_2 can be measured by the angle encoders, A can be measured by grating sensor [5].

The relationship between the polar diameter r_2 and the polar angle θ_2 of the non-circular gears can be obtained by constructing the algorithm, and the pitch curve equation of the non-circular gear is also determined.

Based on the inversion method to depict the initial position and reversal angle ϕ_2 of the meshing engagement position, the following equations can be obtained by Gear meshing theory [6, 7] and the differential geometry [8].

$$dr_2 - (A \sin \beta)d\theta_1 = 0 \qquad (1)$$

According to the angular relationship, following equation can be obtained:

$$tgv = \frac{r_1 \sin \beta}{A + r_1 \cos \beta} \qquad (2)$$

$$\theta_2 = \phi_2 - v + v_0 \qquad (3)$$

$$\theta_1 = \phi_1 - \beta + \beta_0 \qquad (4)$$

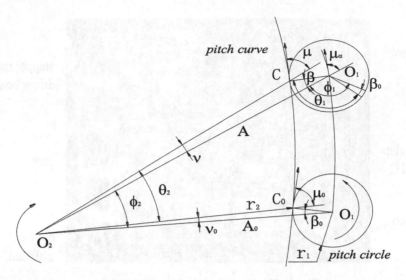

Fig. 5. The conjugate geometric relationships between non-circular gear and cylindrical gear

$$u_a = \frac{\pi}{2} - \beta \tag{5}$$

Supposing that the center distance equation of the two gears meshing is $A = f(\phi_2)$, The polar coordinates equation of the center of the cylindrical gear center O_1 is $\begin{cases} A = f(\phi_2) \\ \theta = \phi_2 \end{cases}$, and according to differential geometry:

$$\tan u_a = A/(dA/d\phi_2) \tag{6}$$

All kinds of above formulas are known as nonlinear differential equations, by using the method of numerical calculation [9], the polar diameter r_2 and the polar angle θ_2 can be calculated, it is actual pitch curves of the non-circular gear, combined with the equation of theoretical pitch curve, the error of pitch curve $\Delta r = r_2 - r_{2r}$ is obtained.

5   The Realization of Automatic Measurement

Send the data which is collected by measurement system to computer, in order to facilitate control, automatically calculate and display the measurement results, the interface of measurement system based on C++ language is developed in Microsoft Visual Studio development environment. The measured data needs to be solved by numerical method, however, it is not easy to work out via C++ programming, and MATLAB has a wealth of built-in libraries, solving numerical problems is easy to implement, Therefore, using MATLAB to implement the algorithm, writing programs

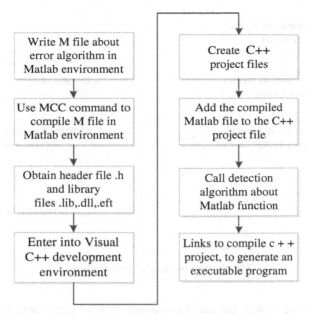

Fig. 6. The flow chart of mixed programming of MATLAB and C++

in MATLAB, then, compiled into an executable file for C++ calls, the use of mixed programming of C++ and MATLAB is easy to achieve the numerical solution of the measurement algorithm [10]. Mixed programming flow chart is shown in Fig. 6.

Before the measurement, initialize parameters on the interface of measurement system. The three sets of sensor data send by the lower computer can be displayed in real time on the interface of the measurement system (Fig. 7). After data acquisition is

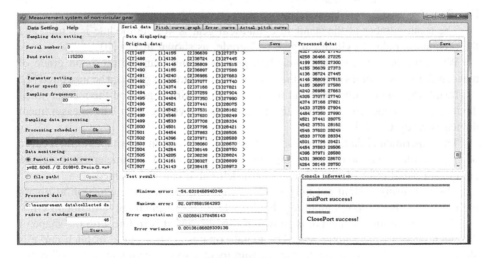

Fig. 7. The interface of measurement system

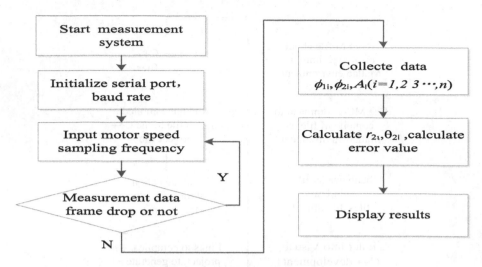

Fig. 8. The measurement flow chart

completed, push the button, the radial composite error of pitch curve of non-circular gear is obtained, the measurement flow chart is shown in Fig. 8.

6 Experimental Analysis and Description

Taking the three-order elliptic gear as an example, the elliptic gear is installed on the measurement device to measure the error of pitch curve. The elliptic gear is processed by CNC gear shaping machine (the highest precision grade of cylindrical gear processed by CNC gear shaping machine is 7 grade). Pitch curve equation under polar coordinate is $r = \frac{82.6045}{2.02 + 0.2\sin(3\varphi)}$, the number of teeth is 42, module is 2 mm, as shown in Fig. 9.

The tooth number of the standard cylindrical gear is 46, the module is 2 mm, and the precision grade of cylindrical gear is 5 grade, as shown in Fig. 10.

When the precision grade of standard gear is higher than the precision grade of measured gear two grades or more, the error of the non-circular gear can be measured [2].

Install the non-circular gear and the standard cylindrical gear on the measurement device, connect the circuit, open the measurement system, then, the measurement device is ready to work.

The experimental data is processed automatically to obtain the shape of pitch curve of non-circular gear, and then comparing with theoretical parameters and values, composite radial error of non-circular gear pitch curve can be obtained.

The measuring system not only supports inputting pitch curve equation to obtain the error, but also supports inputting the discrete points of pitch curve to obtain error.

The shape of the pitch curve is shown in Fig. 11, and it is in line with the shape of the pitch curve of the elliptic gear. The radial composite error curve of pitch curve is shown in Fig. 12. According to the measurement curve, maximum value of radial

Fig. 9. Three-order elliptic gear   **Fig. 10.** Standard cylindrical gear

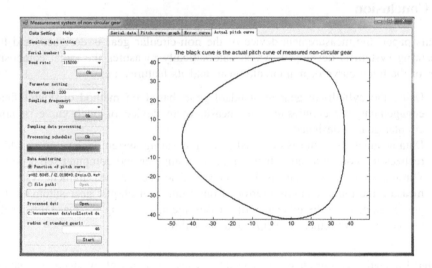

Fig. 11. The pitch curve of non-circular gear

composite error of pitch curve of non-circular gear is 82.09 μm, the minimum value is−54 μm. The curve of error is consistent with the shape of the curves in reference [6] when the cutter and the gear blank are installed off-center. The cause of actual error may be due to the result of combined action of a series of reasons such as off-center installation of work piece, off-center installation of cutter and the precision of machine. It needs further research.

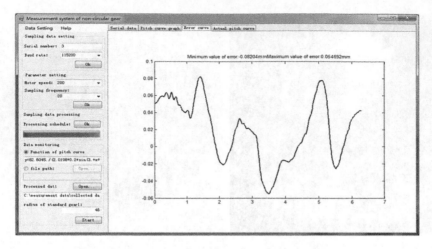

Fig. 12. The radial composite error curve of pitch curve

7 Conclusion

In this paper, the measurement device of the non-circular gear is designed, and the measuring system is developed, which automatically measures the radial composite error of the pitch curve of non-circular gear, and its features are:

(1) Using the cylindrical gear as standard gear, based on method of double-flank engagement, the composite error measurement device of pitch curve of non-circular gear is designed.

(2) Data acquisition circuit is designed and a measuring system is developed, which realizes the communication between lower computer and computer serial port.

(3) Through an example analysis, it is successful to use the measurement system to measure the radial composite error of pitch curve of elliptic gear automatically, greatly improving the efficiency of measurement, verifying the feasibility of the device on measurement principle and algorithm.

Acknowledgment. This research is supported by Science and technology support program of Hubei Province under Grant No. 2014BAA024. The authors also would like to express appreciation to the anonymous reviewers for their helpful comments on improving the paper.

References

1. Tang, D.-w.: A method of single-flank engagement to measure error of non-circular gear. J. Mech. Transm. **12**(10), 1098–1100 (2001)

2. Tang, D.-w.: Measuring error of non-circular gear on double flank contact tester. J. Mech. Transm. **21**(3), 35–38 (1997)

3. Dong, G.-Q., Xu, X., Tang, D.-w.: Preliminary study of precision index and comprehensive measurement method of non-circular gear. J. Mech. Transm. **23**(3), 37–40 (1999)
4. Hai-jun, L.: The Study on tracking and measuring non-circular gear of polar coordinates. Tianjin University, Tianjin (2010)
5. Dong, G.-q.: Study on precision index and measurement method of non-circular gear. Harbin Institute of Technology, pp. 24–33 (1998)
6. Wu, X.-T., Wang, G.-H.: Non-Circular Gear and Non-uniform Transmission Ratio, pp. 35–44. Mechanical Industry Press, Beijing (1997)
7. Wu, X.-t.: Gear Meshing Theory, pp. 23–30. Xi'an Jiaotong University Press, Xi'an (2009)
8. Xu, S., Ji, Y.: Differential Geometry, p. 02. Press of University of Science and Technology of China, Hefei (2013)
9. Chen, X.-j.: Numerical Analysis, pp. 45–51. Wuhan University of Technology Press, Wuhan (2013)
10. Liang, Z., Wang, J.-y.: Mixed Programming of MATLAB and C/C++. Posts and Telecom Press, Beijing (2008)

Research and Design on the Recognition System of Human Parasite Eggs Based on MapReduce

Feng Li[✉] and Xiaofang Hu

School of Computer Science and Communication Engineering,
JiangSu University, Zhenjiang 212013, JiangSu, China
lfengli@ujs.edu.cn, 21046139782@qq.com

Abstract. For the parasite eggs recognition method based on image has disadvantage in real-time and accuracy, this paper presents a shape recognition method combined with gray scale and colorimeter distribution features, and designs a recognition system of human parasite eggs based on MapReduce which takes advantage of the thought about parallel framework of MapReduce. Experiments show that the implementation of the recognition system has good accuracy and real-time.

Keywords: RGB · HSI · MapReduce · Human parasite eggs recognition

1 Introduction

Human parasitic diseases are dangerous to human health, pathogen detection is the focus to prevent them, and how to quickly and correctly identify parasite category is the key for the pathogen monitor. With the development of the modern medicine microscopic image processing technology, scholars have proposed many automatic identification methods of the human parasite eggs based on the image. Such as Johan Musaeus Bruun et al. [1] use the elliptic filter to detect the parasite eggs position and angle firstly, and then extract some relevant features based on this values, finally, adopt liner discriminant analysis to recognize the parasite eggs; Sommer C et al. [2, 3] extract five kinds of feature value from five different bovine parasitic nematodes eggs to study, and establish the earliest automatic identification system of the parasite eggs; Yang Ys et al. [4] build a four-dimensional feature space from seven kinds of human parasite eggs firstly, and then use neural network classifier to classify and recognize the parasite eggs based on the four kinds morphological characteristics; Ya-e Zhao [5] proposes an image segmentation method named eight direction boundary tracking method, and by extracting four kinds internal features: perimeter, area, density and circularity to recognize; She-xin Peng et al. [6] combine the image texture feature with perimeter, area, and roundness to recognize the parasite eggs. Above methods can be divided into two steps, extracting characteristics from parasite eggs and selecting a corresponding classification method. Among them the features extraction is the key step. However, in real life the parasite eggs have more sorts, shapes and sizes, even the same kind of parasite eggs maybe show some different forms in their different stages. More critical is

© Springer International Publishing Switzerland 2016
Q. Zu and B. Hu (Eds.): HCC 2016, LNCS 9567, pp. 226–237, 2016.
DOI: 10.1007/978-3-319-31854-7_21

that there often attached a large number of impurities around the target eggs which will affect us to locate and extract the parasite eggs, and even decline the identification accuracy. Therefore, Qi-yan Sun et al. [7] put forward a method based on the edge space distribution histogram to get the preliminary position of the parasite eggs, it can reduce the interference of impurities around the edge. However, this method is mainly based on the gray image to locate and identify the eggs, and it does not fully takes advantage of the color information of the sample images which will expense the recognition robustness.

Further more, considering the same kind of parasite eggs maybe show a different form at various stages, shape type segmentation will be an effective method to solve this problem and improve the recognition accuracy. Therefore, on the basis of the study of Qi-yan Sun [7], this paper proposes a new shape recognition method combined with gray and chromaticity distribution features, and further introduces a category break-down mechanism to improve the recognition accuracy. However, with the increase-ment of the category number, the recognition efficiency will also gradually decline in stand-alone identification system, and even the end users can not to bear. To solve this problem, this paper combines MapReduce framework [8] proposed by Google, designs and realizes a new recognition system of human parasite eggs based on MapReduce. Combining with the parasite eggs recognition algorithm and the parallel processing model MapReduce can improve the recognition efficiency effectively.

2 The Overall Design Framework of Human Parasite Eggs Recognition System

2.1 The Design Idea

For the edge space distribution histogram proposed by Qiyan Sun et al. [7], shape category subdivision is an effective way to improve the recognition accuracy, but in stand-alone identification system, with the increasement of the parasite eggs category, the identification efficiency will drop significantly. MapReduce programming model is a distributed framework of task parallelization, therefore this paper put forward a recognition system of human parasite eggs based on MapReduce.

2.2 System Structure

This system is divided into three layer architectures: presentation layer, business logic layer and data layer, as shown in Fig. 1.

Presentation layer: C/S: Extracting the templates information of the sample pictures interactively, and training the parameters of the templates information. B/S: Users submit the pending recognition image, and choose the recognition method (example recognition or automatic recognition), and show the recognition result. Example recognition is based on the specific template choosed by users, and automatic recog-nition is iterate through all templates.

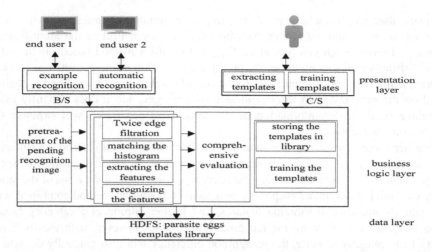

Fig. 1. System framework

Business logic layer: C/S: Training the templates parameters, such as similar size threshold, information entropy threshold, the filter window coefficient and so on. Putting the class templates into the library, and storing it in HDFS. B/S: Parasite eggs recognition process: Pretreating the pending recognition image, then processing the image parallely as shown in Fig. 1, finally, evaluating the Intermediate results comprehensively and getting the final recognition result.

Data layer: The templates library of the parasite eggs is stored in HDFS, according to the user's choice about the recognition method to extract the templates characteristics, and to match the pending recognition image. Finally, the matching result will be stored in HDFS and feedback to the user.

3   The Algorithm Implementation of the Human Parasite Eggs Recognition System

3.1   Definition of the Edge Space Distribution Histogram

In parasite eggs recognition process, because of the pending recognition image always have a lot of impurities, it is difficult to locate the parasite eggs area, so how to improve the robustness of the parasite eggs regional localization algorithm has become the key to the whole parasite eggs recognition algorithm. For which we learn the idea of Qiyan Sun et al. [7] and introduce the concept named the edge space distribution histogram.

The edge space distribution histogram is a description for the spatial distribution of the image edge pixels. Because the introduction of the edge space distribution histogram is to locate and recognize the parasite eggs edge area, so we divide the parasite eggs into several kinds according to their shapes firstly, for extracting the edge information better, each kind parasite eggs edge area can be fixed in a spatial distribution scope, as shown in Fig. 2(a), we call it class mask. In this basis divide the class mask into n regional blocks just like Fig. 2(b). We can define the edge pixels distribution of the areas as class mask's edge space distribution histogram, as formula (1):

$$\text{Hist} = \sum_{i=1}^{n} (T_i / \sum_{i=1}^{n} T_i) \tag{1}$$

T_i is the edge pixels of the ith regional block, n is the block number of the class mask and the class mask division is take the centroid of the region as center and equal angle.

On this basis, we can know that the class mask is the key for extracting the edge information. So the edge space distribution histogram template of each kind parasite egg can be defined as formula (2).

$$SP = \{M, Hist\}$$
$$M = \{B_0, B_1, B_2 \ldots B_{n-1}\} \tag{2}$$

SP is an edge space distribution histogram template, M is the class mask, Hist is the edge space distribution histogram, B_i is the ith regional block, n is the block number of the class mask.

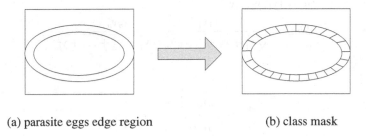

(a) parasite eggs edge region   (b) class mask

Fig. 2. Definition of the parasite eggs edge space distribution histogram

3.2 The Edge Space Distribution Histogram Matching

After establishing the edge space distribution histogram of each kind parasite egg, we can use the class mask and the edge space distribution histogram to match the related area of the pending recognition image to judge wether there are parasite eggs. If the similarity of this area is up to a certain value, it can be considered that it is a candidate area contained this kind parasite eggs. And then we can combine with other characteristics and identification methods for further judgement. Of course, we need to do image binarization before matching the edge space distribution histogram. But the parasite eggs distribution of the pending recognition image is random, that is to say, the parasite eggs distribution direction is random, as shown in Fig. 3(a). To extract the edge space distribution histogram of the pending recognition image, we can gradually rotate the class mask, but the method will lead a large amount of calculation. So we introduce a multi-angle class mask pre-storage mechanism, it means that each kind parasite egg template contains multi-angle class mask. Based on the above, the formula (2) can be described as formula (3).

$$SP = \{\{M_0, M_1, M_2 \ldots M_{n-1}\}, Hist\}$$
$$M = \{B_{(1,0)}, B_{(1,1)}, B_{(1,2)} \ldots B_{(1,n-1)}\} \tag{3}$$

M_i means the ith angle class mask, N is the equally divided angle number from 0 degrees to 360 degrees.

On this basis, using each angle class mask to extract the edge area of the pending recognition image, then calculating the edge space distribution histogram and getting the similarity compare to the template histogram. Finally, judging the similarity, if the max similarity meets the preset threshold, we can draw the conclusion that this area is a candidate area. The calculation process is described as formula (4). Sim_k is the similarity of the kth rotated angle, it is the max similarity, and the corresponding angle is the most similar angle, h_i is the histogram of the ith candidate area, h_t is the template histogram.

$$Sim = \max\{Sim_0, Sim_1 \ldots Sim_{N-1}\}$$
$$h_i = (x_1, x_2 \ldots x_n)$$
$$h_t = (y_1, y_2 \ldots y_n) \tag{4}$$
$$Sim_k = \frac{x_1 y_1 + x_2 y_2 + \ldots x_n y_n}{\sqrt{x_1^2 + x_2^2 + \ldots + x_n^2}\sqrt{y_1^2 + y_2^2 + \ldots + y_n^2}}$$

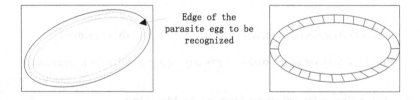

Edge of the parasite egg to be recognized

(a) parasite egg's edge distribution   (b)class mask

Fig. 3. Edge region of the pending recognition parasite eggs and the class mask

3.3   The Parasite Eggs Recognition Based on the Edge Space Distribution Histogram

Before recognition, we need to do sorts subdivision for the parasite eggs, because there are some differences in the form of the parasite eggs in different stages. Subdivision can not only extend the template library, but also improve the recognition accuracy. After completing the subdivision, two kinds templates based respectively on gray scale distribution characteristic and chromaticity distribution characteristic of each kind of human parasite egg should be established. The templates mainly contains the edge space distribution histogram, the width of the minimum square contained a parasite eggs named W, the information entropy named E, a duty ratio named O and the template training parameter information. According to the templates information can recognize the image, the specific recognition process as shown in Fig. 4.

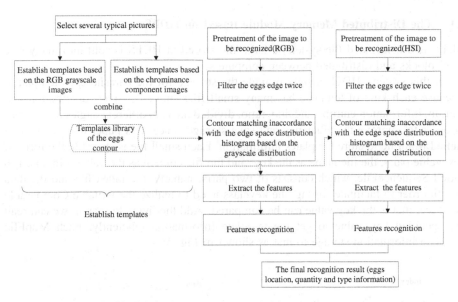

Fig. 4. Parasite eggs recognition process

W: Get the side length of the minimum square that can contain a parasite egg;

E: Get the information entropy of gray scale and chromaticity distribution characteristic depend on the edge space distribution histogram;

O: The ratio of the pixels number in external and internal region of the parasite eggs edge area, if the ratio is larger, maybe there are much impurities in the peripheral of the edge area, and we can be consider to remove it.

Pretreatment: Employing gray normalization or get the Hue component of the pending recognition image, canny edge detection, and binarization processing.

Twice filtration: Filtering the most impurity edge by the templates training threshold, filling the edge with ellipses, and get the candidate regions.

Extract characteristics: For recognizing the parasite eggs furtherly, this paper combined the edge space distribution histogram with other characteristics.

Feature recognition: Base on the training parameters, comparing the features information of the pending recognition image with the template information to determine wether this area contains parasite eggs, the type information and the location information of the parasite eggs.

4 System Modules

The System is mainly composed of the distributed file system HDFS and the distributed model MapReduce.

4.1 The Distributed Memory Module Based on HDFS

HDFS is a distributed file system, a large file stored in HDFS is split into many size fixed blocks and distributed between computers.

In this system, HDFS mainly provide the storage for the parasite eggs templates. Because each kind of template has many small files (the edge space distribution histogram, information entropy and duty ratio, divided areas in different angles and so on). In order to improve the efficiency and save storage space, this paper uses the format named MapFile to store templates information. Each small file is stored in the form of key-value pairs, the file name as the key, and the file content as the value. MapFile is a sorted SequenceFile, which consists of two parts, namely, the index file and the data file. In order to facilitate sorting, the keyclass need to realize the writable Comparable interface, that is the key value can be compared. Add the index to search, we can read the specified key value to get the template information efficiently. Each MapFlie template information storage format as shown in Fig. 5:

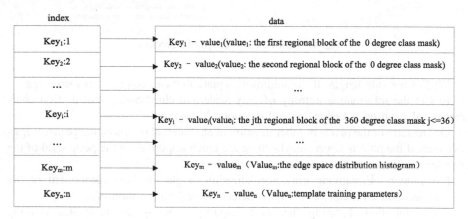

Fig. 5. Storage format of the template information

4.2 The Parallel Processing Module Based on MapReduce

MapReduce is a distributed parallel computing framework, taking advantage of the thought named "divide and rule". It distributes the operation with a large-scale data set to each nodes to complete the job together, and then combines each intermediate result to get a final result. The process can be abstracted as two functions: Map function and Reduce function. MapReduce accepts the two functions defined by user, and then the computing tasks will be carried out automatically and scheduled parallely in the cluster composed of a large number of computers.

Two processing stages of MapReduce:

Map: (K1,V1) → list(K2,V2)

Reduce: (K2,list(V2)) → list(K3,V3)

The realization of Map function and Reduce function:

Map function: The input data of Map task are many text files named after one or more template name, like template1 & template2 & template3, and the corresponding template path as the content, like path1 & path2 & path3. This paper uses the customized classes named WholeInputFormat and WholeRecordReader to realize the whole file to read, and get a key-value pair, the key is the MapFile filename and the value is the storage paths. The system will split the input data and assign them to each Map task, then use function Map to do contour matching, finally, store the intermediate result in local system. The intermediate result is in form of key-value pair, the key is the template name, and the value is a custom list class named CRectBufList which is used to save the recognition information includes the location information, type information of the parasite eggs and the related templates training parameters.

Reduce function: Reduce task is mainly to collect the intermediate results from each Map task, and filters them according to the location information to get the final result. The result of Reduce task will be stored in HDFS.

Combining with the above, the work diagram of how MapReduce to realize human parasite eggs recognition as shown in Fig. 6, the detailed processing of Map task and Reduce task as shown in Fig. 7.

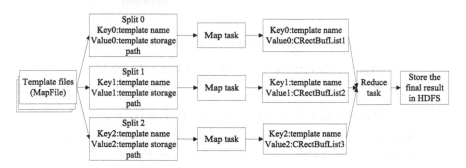

Fig. 6. Work diagram of the realization of human parasite eggs recognition based on MapReduce

5   Experimental Analysis

5.1   Introduction of the Experimental Environment

This experiment uses Java as the system development language, and builds a Hadoop cluster with five common computers. The cluster has one master node as Namenode and JobTracker, four slave nodes as DataNode and Tasktracker. Its configuration information is shown in Table 1.

234   F. Li and X. Hu

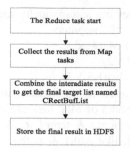

(1)The detail process of the Reduce task

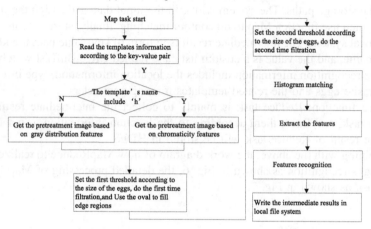

(2)The detail process of the Map task

Fig. 7. The detail process of Map task and Reduce task

Table 1. Configuration information of the Hadoop cluster

Node name	CPU/Memory Information of Nodes	Operating System
Master	Intel(R)Pentium(R)cpu 2.93 GHZ\2 GB	CentOS
Slave1	Intel(R)Pentium(R)cpu 2.93 GHZ\2 GB	CentOS
Slave2	Intel(R)Pentium(R)cpu 2.93 GHZ\2 GB	CentOS
Slave3	Intel(R)Pentium(R)cpu 2.93 GHZ\2 GB	CentOS
Slave4	Intel(R)Pentium(R)cpu 2.93 GHZ\2 GB	CentOS

5.2   The Analysis of System Identification Accuracy

The experiment selects ten kinds common human parasite eggs, each picture is 1600*1200 pixels. As shown in Table 2, R represents the recognition accuracy of the identification method based on the gray scale distribution characteristic, H&R represents the recognition accuracy based on the new identification method combined grayscale with chromaticity distribution characteristics. Ten parasite eggs are: ① Ascaris lumbricoides unFertilized eggs ② Ascaris lumbricoides Fertilized eggs ③ taenia ④ Trichuris trichiura Eggs ⑤ ova of clonorchis sinensis ⑥ hymenolepis diminuta ⑦ hymenolepis nana ⑧ ova of hookworm ⑨ Paragonimus westermani ⑩ fasciolopsis buski.

Table 2. The comparison result of the recognition accuracy

Species	①	②	③	④	⑤	⑥	⑦	⑧	⑨	⑩
Picture number	100	100	100	100	100	100	100	100	100	100
Correct recognition number R	84	96	95	94	98	98	91	89	95	94
Correct recognition rate R	84 %	96 %	95 %	94 %	98 %	98 %	91 %	89 %	95 %	94 %
Correct recognition number H&R	88	99	95	95	100	98	93	92	97	94
Correct recognition rate H&R	88 %	99 %	95 %	95 %	100 %	98 %	93 %	92 %	97 %	94 %

From Table 2 we can see that the new recognition method combined gray scale distribution characteristic with chromaticity distribution characteristic can improve the accuracy to some extend, and they can complement each other.

5.3 The Analysis of System Identification Efficiency

The experiment selects ten kinds common parasite eggs, each picture is 1600*1200 pixels. Before the experiment, we need to establish the templates for each kind parasite egg. This experiment tests and compares the recognition efficiency in a single node, double nodes, three nodes and four nodes as well as stand-alone mode. The experiment result is shown in Fig. 8.

Result shows that, under the condition of single machine, with the increasement of the templates number, recognition time presents nearly linear growth trend. Because the hardware resources is limited of the stand-alone system, when the number of templates up to a certain conditions, the identification process maybe unable to complete.

As seen from Fig. 8, the recognition efficiency of a single node is lower than that of stand-alone, because of the implementation of MapReduce program will take some time to initial, allocate tasks, and clear the job. This experiment takes four templates as a Map task, that is to say one Map task will match four templates. When the number of templates is 4, there is only one Map task, so the efficiency of stand-alone is higher than the other; when there are more than 8 templates, the number of Map task will be greater than 2, then the recognition efficiency will be better than stand-alone if there are more than 2 nodes; while there are more than 16 templates, the Map task number will be over the node number, that is some nodes may be have more than one Map task, the recognition efficiency will present nearly linear growth trend.

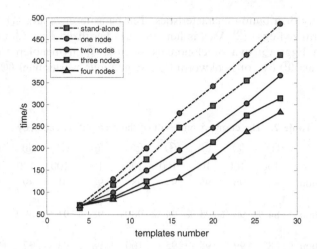

Fig. 8. Recognition efficiency based on different nodes number

6 Conclusion

On the basis of the existing research results on parasite eggs, we proposed a new recognition method that combine human parasite eggs recognition technology based on content and MapReduce distributed framework. This paper optimized the existing recognition algorithm, proposed a shape classification algorithm that combine gray scale and chromaticity distribution feature based on the subdivision of parasite eggs. This algorithm not only achieves to improve the accuracy of recognition, but also shorten the identification time. At the same time, Hadoop is a highly scalable storage platform that can span thousands of inexpensive computers operating in parallel with good scalability. Because of the limited resources available, this study consists of five nodes, With the increasing number of the templates, we can extend our Hadoop cluster nodes to achieve higher recognition efficiency.

References

1. Bruun, J.M., Kapel, C.M.O., Carstensen, J.M.: Detection and classification of parasite eggs for use in helminthic therapy. In: IEEE International Symposium on Biomedical Imaging. pp. 1627–1630. IEEE, January 2012
2. Sommer, C.: Digital image analysis and identification of eggs from bovine parasitic nematodes. J. Helminthol. **70**(2), 143–151 (1996)
3. Sommer, C.: Quantitative characterization of texture used for identification of eggs of bovine parasitic nematodes. J. Helminthol. **72**(2), 179–182 (1998)
4. ZYang Y.S., Park, D.K., Kim, H.C., et al.: Automatic identification of human helminth eggs on microscopic fecal specimens using digital image processing and an artificial neural network. IEEE Trans. Biomed. Eng. **48**(6), 718–730 (2001)

5. Zhao, Y.-E.: Automatic identification of human parasite eggs. China Stereology Image Anal. **2**(3), 135–138 (1997)
6. Peng, S.-X., Liao, S.-T.: Study on computer automatic recognition technology of parasite eggs. J. Hunan Normal Univ. (Medical Edition) **2**(2), 11–15 (2005)
7. Li, F., Sun, Q.-Y.: Study on the shape classification algorithm of human parasite eggs based on the features of image boundary. Comput. Sci. **39**(5), 261–265 (2011)
8. Li, J.-J., Cui, J., et al.: Survey of mapreduce parallel programming model. Acta Electronica Sinica **39**(11), 2635–2642 (2011)

Virtual Mapping of Software Defined Wireless Network Based on Topological Perception

Muxuan Li[✉], Xiaojuan Wang, Shifang Chen,
Mei Song, and Yue Ma

Department of Electronic Engineering, Beijing University of Posts
and Telecommunications, Beijing 100876, China
{13820963775, wj2718}@163.com,
{csf1207, songm, mayue}@bupt.edu.cn

Abstract. Software defined network (SDN) and network virtualization have been considered as promising technologies that relieve the rigid network problem. Most of current research efforts in SDN and network virtualization focus on wired network, but only limited work has been done on extending the technologies to wireless area. In this paper, we design an architecture of software defined wireless network (SDWN) based on MobileFlow forwarding engine (MFFE). Accordingly, we propose an algorithm based on virtual mapping, which reconciles wireless network and system model by introducing expansion coefficient. Benefitting from resource topological perception, our scheme introduces community division, which improves the efficiency and reliability of virtual network mapping. Extensive wireless-oriented simulation shows the feasibility of wireless network virtualization based on SDN.

Keywords: *Index terms*—SDWN · Virtual mapping · Resource topological perception · MFFE

1 Introduction

With the progress of modern communication technology and the mature Internet technology, the demands of services and applications become increasingly multifarious. However, the contradiction between the emerging technologies and traditional network architecture has become more and more fierce, which shows the defects of current mobile network. As a result, a revolutionary architecture is required to solve the contradictions mentioned above. Software defined network (SDN) [1, 2], a new network architecture, abstracts the control plane, forward plane and application plane of network equipment and makes the network control be isolated from physical network topology. Network virtualization [3], key technology of constructing the future network, is regarded as an effective scheme to overcome the rigid network.

Introducing SDN as well as network virtualization into architecture design [4] greatly ease the ossification in the field of wired networks. With the growing types of users and increasingly multifarious service, academia and industry lead a new trend that extends SDN and network virtualization to mobile and wireless networks [5].

© Springer International Publishing Switzerland 2016
Q. Zu and B. Hu (Eds.): HCC 2016, LNCS 9567, pp. 238–249, 2016.
DOI: 10.1007/978-3-319-31854-7_22

Recently, some network innovations based on SDN and virtualization have been proposed to design the wireless architecture. In [6], based on SDN paradigm, the author decouples the control plane and data plane in evolved packet core (EPC) architecture. Accordingly, the mobile network architecture is designed, which supports wireless devices to access. The core cogitation is substituting MobileFlow forwarding engine (MFFE) with wireless interface for wired OpenFlow switches, and integrating the control function of all the devices into MobileFlow controller (MFC). In [7], SDN is introduced into frameless network architecture (FNA). The paper aims to increase capacity by network architecture evolving. In particular, the traditional base station (BS) is separated with central processing entity (CPE) and antenna element (AE) to perform network virtualization. OpenFlow controller (OFC) and resource pool (RP) server are used as the centralized control entity to support the decoupling of control plane and forward plane in SDN. In addition, the paper proposes the concept of virtualized radio resource pooling (VRRP) and the mobile-oriented service slicing. In [8], the paper proposes virtualization scheme and allocation algorithm of wireless access network in wireless mesh network. The premise of the algorithm is that access node should adopt dual antenna structure based on orthogonal frequency-division multiplexing (OFDM). Each virtual access network can operate independently by allocating subcarriers on each link. Channel allocation algorithm may ease the interference among wireless links. The paper promotes the overall network performance by enhanced-genetic algorithm as well as proves the feasibility of virtual access networks.

Virtual mapping algorithm is the core issue of architecture design. Nonetheless, wireless networks have specific constraints, such as link reliability, heterogeneous access nodes, high transmission delay and strong interference. In addition, request of user in wireless scenario is capacity instead of bandwidth. As a result, it does have difficulties in not only linking up the relationship between wired bandwidth and wireless capacity, but also allocating limited resources of spectrum. More critically, virtual mapping itself is a NP-hard problem. As we investigated before, the architecture of wireless network is difficult to access heterogeneous network and hard to reach the algorithmic level. On these grounds, we design an architecture of software defined wireless network (SDWN) based on virtualization. The architecture allows operators to modify and innovate network architecture in a form of software definition. Moreover, by introducing unified forwarding entity, a number of networks with different protocols can coexist in the same physical network topology. It turns out that the architecture facilitates deploying our wireless system model and algorithm based on resource topology perception, we further introduce expansion coefficient γ to convert wireless spectrum into wired bandwidth. Consequently, the simulation results show that our scheme achieves the implementation of wireless network virtualization based on SDN.

The remainder of this paper is organized as follows. SDWN architecture based on virtual mapping is described in Sect. 2. In Sect. 3, we present system model and involved parties. An algorithm based on resource topological perception is elaborated in Sect. 4 with two components: node mapping and link mapping. Section 5 gives simulation setup and result to evaluate the performance. Finally, we come to a conclusion of this paper.

2   Wireless Access Network Virtualization Architecture

SDN abstracts devices with computing resources into nodes and abstracts bandwidth as well as spectrum into links. The existing virtual network is mainly in view of core network. Our scheme maps switches and routers to resource pool through control unit, and then finds a proper path by optimization algorithm. In this paper, we consider the proliferation of mobile users and research on network virtualization of wireless access.

Resources should be allocated appropriately to each network in the process of virtual access network mapping. Virtual networks should be isolated with each other and we adopt orthogonal frequency division multiple access (OFDMA) as communication technology in physical layer to guarantee the isolation among virtual access networks. OFDMA divides bandwidth into orthogonal and non-overlapping subcarrier set. Consequently, users are independent of each other. Figure 1 depicts the wireless access network virtualization architecture based on SDWN.

The architecture contains infrastructure plane, control plane and application plane. In wireless access network of infrastructure plane, following the separation of controlling and forwarding of SDN, BS is divided into antenna element (AE), base station processing element (BPE) and base station control element that is abstracted into control plane. AEs are in charge of sending and receiving signals while BEs are used to forward data from/to BS. Access network and core network are connected by serving gateway (S-GW) and PDN gateway (P-GW). MFFE with radio interface, can monitor each step of packet forwarding based on flow table received from control plane. All the devices in this plane are forwarding equipments. The plane is regarded as the carrier of requests for user equipment (UE) and data transmission.

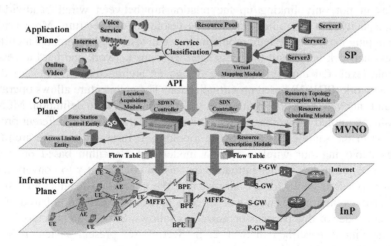

Fig. 1.   Wireless access network virtualization architecture based on SDWN

Control plane is mainly in charge of abstracting request from application, extracting characteristic and generating constraints. Bearing all the control entities, control plane is split logically into SDWN controller of access network and SDN controller of core network. The two parts are coordinated to control the entire network, and then send the instruction signal to physical devices–MFFEs in the form of transmitting flow tables.

Application plane is on the top of the architecture and classifies the services according to application type. By calling data from resource pool, the system completes virtual mapping that follows "Centralized Management and Distributed Control". Eventually, this plane abstracts application through application programming interfaces (APIs). It makes it possible for UE to develop a wide variety of applications without concerning the physical topology, as the architecture blocks the equipment details of underlying network.

In network virtualization, the separation of controlling and forwarding prompts three roles to complete the corresponding business. Infrastructure Provider (InP), corresponds to infrastructure plane of the architecture, presides over deploying and maintaining the physical devices. InP provides a unified programmable interface while blocking the underlying infrastructure for upper planes. Physical resources are sliced into multiple virtual slices for service provider. Service Provider (SP), corresponds to application plane, deploys protocol and takes responsibility to operate and manage the virtual networks. SP forwards request to virtual network provider after generating virtual request based on the service. Mobile Virtual Network Operator (MVNO), corresponds to control plane, searches and combines virtual resources among InPs to meet the needs of SPs. As an intermediary role between the InP and SP, MVNO simplifies the matching process.

3   System Model

Wireless access networks are divided into K layers, and each layer represents different type of networks, such as Macrocell, Microcell and Femtocell. Each layer of network differs in power, location and density. Signal to interference plus noise ratio (SINR) of the user is given in formula (1):

$$SINR_m^{(i)}(P) = \frac{p_m^{(i)} \cdot h_m^{(i)} \cdot \left\| x_m^{(i)} \right\|^{-\alpha}}{I_m^{(i)}(P) + \sigma^2} \tag{1}$$

In which

(1) $p_m^{(i)}$ denotes the transmitted power of No. i layer BS-m and $P = \{p_m^{(i)}, m \in \phi_i, 1 \leq i \leq k\}$.

(2) $h_m^{(i)}$ is fading from AE to UE, which obeys independent identically distribution with μ mean.

(3) $\left\| x_m^{(i)} \right\|^{-\alpha}$ presents standard path loss function while $\alpha \geq 2$ is the index of path loss.

(4) σ presents a constant additive noise power.

(5) $I_m^{(i)}(P)$ denotes the interference of user which comes from each layer. So it can be written as:

$$I_m^{(i)}(P) = \sum_{j=1}^{K} \sum_{m \in \phi_j \setminus x_m^{(i)}} P_m^{(j)} \cdot h_m^{(j)} \cdot \left\| x_m^{(j)} \right\|^{-\alpha} \tag{2}$$

4 Algorithm Based on Resource Topology Identification

Network virtualization in wired scenario considers constraints of node and link on the basis of user's virtual request, so as to achieve resource allocation optimization of the coexistence of multiple virtual networks. With the characteristics of limited spectrum resources, poor reliability of link and strong interference, wireless network virtualization should take channel quality into consideration. Virtual network mapping meets the capacity requirement of wireless user by allocation orthogonal subcarriers. In this way, the virtual networks can independently operate and develop. According to Shannon Theory, wireless bandwidth can be written as:

$$W_v = \frac{C_v}{\log_2[1 + SINR_m^{(i)}(P)]} \tag{3}$$

Where C_v presents capacity requirement of wireless user.

In wireless access network, if a single subcarrier bandwidth is w_0, and W_v presents required bandwidth of virtual access network, the number of subcarriers allocated to this virtual network should be as follows:

$$n = \left\lceil \frac{W_v}{w_0} \right\rceil \tag{4}$$

By combining formula (3), n can be written as:

$$n = \left\lceil \frac{1}{w_0} \cdot \frac{C_v}{\log_2[1 + SINR_m^{(i)}(P)]} \right\rceil \tag{5}$$

When virtual requests arrive, the resource allocation strategy of physical network can be seen from Fig. 2. As shown in the figure, H ∼ M are wired nodes and the rest present wireless nodes. The number denotes attributes of the node, with the symbol "/" spacing resources that the node owns and remaining resources. In addition to central processing unit (CPU) resources of all the nodes in box of solid line, spectrum resources of links that connected to the wireless node are in dashed frame. The number of wired link denotes bandwidth attributes. In other words, wireless physical link owns bandwidth and spectrum resources, while wired link only has the attributes of bandwidth. With our thoughts of resource topological perception, the physical nodes can be divided into two communities according to the location.

We describe the physical network by weighted undirected graph $G_s = (N_s, L_s)$, where N_s and L_s denote physical node set and physical link set respectively. Graph $G_v = (N_v, L_v)$ is used for describing the virtual network, in which N_v and L_v denote virtual node set and virtual link set respectively.

The system releases the resources of virtual requests and updates remaining resources after node and link mapping. However, the complexity of wireless link makes the actual allocation of bandwidth different from the bandwidth required. Expansion coefficient γ should be added in resources updating.

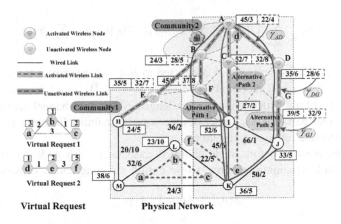

Fig. 2. Virtual mapping resources allocation strategy

We divided underlying network into two communities according to the connectivity of physical nodes. Internal nodes within one community joint tightly, while the connectivity between the two communities is poor. In this case, our virtual mapping algorithm is based on resource topology identification. Assuming that the endpoints of the virtual path are mapped respectively to physical nodes from different communities, there are little backup links for link mapping as the poor connectivity if the link would fail. Consequently, the system has to return the virtual request. Therefore, the endpoints of the path should be mapped into the same community in the process of node mapping. In the following subsections, we will study how the system maps the node and link, so as to meet the requests of virtual networks.

4.1 Node Mapping

Selecting target node concerns not only attributes of node, but also that links connected to the node to be mapped. Node resources are consist of CPU capacity and location, which are written as $cpu()$ and $loc()$ respectively. Resources of links that are connected to the node are bandwidth, where $B()$ and $W()$ represent wired and wireless link respectively.

Define factor of node mapping $g_a^i = 1$ if n_v^i is mapped to n_s^a, else $g_a^i = 0$, where n_s^a is physical node a, and n_v^i is virtual node i.

Define CPU ability of node is the remaining CPU resources and it can be written as:

$$A_N(n_s) = cpu(n_s) - \sum_{\forall n_v \in N_v \to n_s} cpu(n_v) \tag{6}$$

Define average bandwidth ability of node is the remaining bandwidth resources of m links which connected to the node to be mapped and it can be written as:

$$A_L(n_s) = \frac{1}{m} \sum_{\forall l_s \in L_v \to n_s} \left\{ \lambda[B(l_s) - \sum_{\forall l_v \in L_v \to l_s} B(l_v)] + (1-\lambda)\gamma_{l_s}[W(l_s) - \sum_{\forall l_v \in L_v \to l_s} W(l_v)] \right\} \tag{7}$$

Where "$A \dashv B$" represents that A connected to B. $\lambda = 1$ represents the physical link is wired link while $\lambda = 0$ represents wireless link. $\gamma_{l_s} \in [1, +\infty)$ is expansion coefficient of wireless link, which related to link length, SINR and channel quality. In other words, the former part of $A_L(n_s)$ describes the wired remaining link resource while the latter is the wireless remaining resource.

As we demonstrate before, node ability is associated with node remaining CPU resource and link remaining resource, so we define mapping ability of node as:

$$T(n_s) = A_N(n_s) \cdot A_L(n_s) \tag{8}$$

In the view of resource topology identification, we define connectivity of nodes as:

$$\delta(n_s^m, n_s^n) = \frac{1}{2}(S_m \cdot S_n + 1) \tag{9}$$

Where $S_m = 1$ if m belongs to *Community*1, else $S_m = -1$ if m belongs to *Community*2. In this way, we can quantitative measure whether the two nodes to be mapped in the same virtual network are in the same community.

We adopt greedy algorithm in node mapping, which means that in each virtual request, we first map the node requesting the maximal CPU in order to obtain more revenue. What is more, in the case of satisfying some constraints, that node will be mapped to the physical node with the best mapping ability. The objective function and constraints of node mapping are as follows:

Objective function:

$$\text{Maximize}_{T(n_s^a), \forall n_s^a \to n_v^i} \tag{10}$$

st.

$$cpu(n_v^i) \le A_N(n_s^a), \forall n_s^a \to n_v^i \tag{11}$$

$$\sum_{n_v^i \in N_v} g_a^i \leq 1, \forall n_s^a \in N_s \tag{12}$$

$$\sum_{n_s^a \in N_s} g_a^i = 1, \forall n_v^i \in N_v \tag{13}$$

$$g_a^i \in \{0, 1\}, \forall n_s^a \in N_s, \forall n_v^i \in N_v \tag{14}$$

$$\delta(n_s^a, n_s^b) = 1, \forall n_s^a \rightarrow n_v^i, \forall n_s^b \rightarrow n_v^j \tag{15}$$

Formula (10) denotes the objective function of the virtual node mapping. The system firstly provides alternative nodes according to the location of user, and then allocates optimal physical node to virtual network based on formula (10). Constraint of node resources are given in formula (11), which means CPU capacity the physical node owns must meet the demand of that in virtual network. Formula (12) presents that for the same virtual request, a physical node can carry one virtual node at most, while formula (13) presents that for the same virtual request, a virtual node can only be mapped to one physical node. Formula (14) constrains g_a^i as a binary factor. The endpoints of the link mapped to the same community are confined in formula (15).

4.2 Link Mapping

After node mapping based on greedy algorithm, the physical network should offer physical path consisting one or some physical link to map the virtual link. Underlying network provides some alternate paths based on the mapped nodes and selects an optimal path according to bandwidth request as well as objective function.

Define the link mapping coefficient $f_{ab}^{ij} = 1$ if l_s^{ab} belongs to mapped path of l_v^{ij}, else $f_{ab}^{ij} = 0$, where l_s^{ab} denotes the physical link between physical node a and b. l_v^{ij} is the virtual link between virtual node i and j.

In the virtual network mapping, revenue refers to the benefits operators that physical network belongs obtain by receiving a virtual request.

As the revenue only related to the served resource from mapped virtual request in virtual network, including served CPU for node and served bandwidth for link, we further define virtual mapping revenue as:

$$R(G_v) = \alpha_R \sum_{n_v \in N_v} cpu(n_v) + (1 - \alpha_R) \sum_{l_v \in L_v} B(l_v) \tag{16}$$

However, the cost depends on both virtual request and physical network, the cost of virtual mapping can be defined as:

$$C(G_v) = \alpha_C \sum_{n_v \in N_v} cpu(n_v) + (1 - \alpha_C)[\sum_{l_v^{ij} \in L_v} \sum_{l_s^{ab} \in L_S} \lambda f_{ab}^{ij} \cdot B(l_s^{ab}) + (1 - \lambda) f_{ab}^{ij} \cdot \gamma_{l_s^{ab}} W(l_s^{ab})] \tag{17}$$

Where α_R and α_C are used to balance the weight between CPU and bandwidth in $R(G_v)$ and $C(G_v)$ respectively. In other words, the operator can balance the weight between node and link by adjusting this parameter. We use the ratio $\eta = \frac{R(G_v)}{C(G_v)}$ to evaluate the network mapping. K-shortest path (KSP) algorithm is adopted in link mapping, which means that in the case of satisfying some constraints, we prefer the path with the least links in order to reduce cost. The objective function and constraints of link mapping are as follows:

Objective function:

$$\text{Maximize } \eta \tag{18}$$

st.

$$f_{ab}^{ij} \cdot B(l_v^{ij}) \le \lambda B(l_s^{ab}) + (1 - \lambda)\gamma_{l_{ab}} W(l_s^{ab}), \forall l_s^{ab} \in L_s, \forall l_v^{ij} \in L_v \tag{19}$$

$$\sum_{l_s^{ab} \in L_s} f_{ab}^{ij} - \sum_{l_s^{ab} \in L_s} f_{ba}^{ij} = \begin{cases} 1 & if \ g_a^i = 1 \\ -1 & if \ g_a^j = 1 \\ 0 & otherwise \end{cases}, \forall n_s^a \in N_s, \forall l_v^{ij} \in L_v \tag{20}$$

$$f_{ab}^{ij} \in \{0, 1\}, \forall l_s^{ab} \in L_s, \forall l_v^{ij} \in L_v \tag{21}$$

Formula (18) is the objective function of virtual network mapping. η reflects the utilization of physical resources as well as the relationship between revenue and cost after achievement of a virtual mapping. Constraint of link resources is given in formula (19). Spectrum capacity that the physical links own must meet the demand of bandwidth of virtual link. Formula (20) is constraint of connectivity. Formula (21) constrains f_{ab}^{ij} as a binary factor.

5   Simulation

5.1   Simulation Setup

Consider an underlying network with seven AEs and UEs deployed inside based on PPP model. The density of AEs and UEs are set to be 0.2 and 0.35 respectively. The carrier frequency and effective transmission of UE are 2 GHz and 9 MHz respectively. We set the power profile of [0,46 dBm] for each AE. Each channel has a bandwidth of 20 kHz while the path loss fading obeys exponential power delay profile with index $\alpha = 2$, and the noise figure is 5 dB. To simplify the virtual mapping, α_R and α_C are both set to be 0.5.

Based on GT-ITM, which is widely used in topology generation, the simulation generates the underlying topology network and virtual network request. The underlying network randomly generates 100 nodes within the range of (25×25), and the connection probability of each pair of nodes is 0.5. CPU resources of each physical node and available bandwidth of each link both follow Uniform distribution between 50 and 100.

The unit cost of CPU resources and bandwidth obey Uniform distribution of [1, 3]. Moreover, the location information of physical nodes obeys Two-dimensional Uniform distribution.

Virtual network requests arrive with Poisson process with [4, 14] mean and their lifetimes obey Exponential distribution with 1000 s mean. The number of virtual nodes obeys integral Uniform distribution of [5, 15] and the location of each virtual node obeys integral Two-dimensional uniform distribution. The connection probability of each pair of nodes is 0.5. CPU request of each virtual node and bandwidth request of each virtual link follow integral Uniform distribution of [0, 20] and [0, 50] respectively. Limitation of distance between virtual node and physical node obeys integral Uniform distribution of [1, 10]. Set of available physical nodes can be generated according to the location and distance limitation.

5.2   Network Mapping Performance

In this subsection, we evaluate the performances of our algorithm with different number of mapped virtual networks and nodes in each network. We take the ratio $\eta = \frac{R(G_v)}{C(G_v)}$ as the optimizing index in our performance evaluation. In Figs. 3 and 4, the different results show how the number of mapped virtual networks and nodes in each network effects revenue (R) and cost (C).

Figure 3 demonstrates that the revenue of virtual mapping will increase along with the number of virtual networks growing. In addition, the number of nodes in each network can also achieve higher The result lies in the more virtual networks request, the more revenue can get from the service provider. For a single virtual network, the quantity of nodes is also proportional to the revenue. By leasing resource and deploy virtual network rational, service provider satisfy the user who acquire high level of quality of service (QoS).

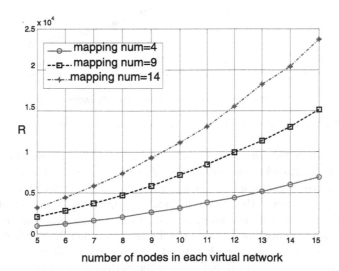

Fig. 3. Impact of the number of nodes and mapped networks on revenue

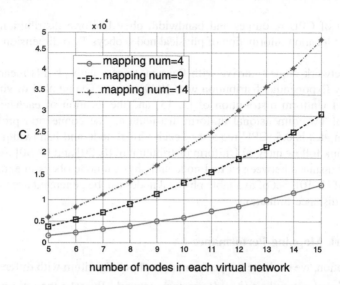

Fig. 4. Impact of the number of nodes and mapped networks on cost

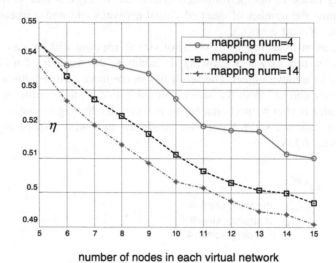

number of nodes in each virtual network

Fig. 5. Impact of the number of nodes and mapped networks on η

Figure 4 testifies that the cost of virtual mapping will increase along with the number of virtual networks growing. The number of nodes in each network can also achieve higher cost. This result lies in the more virtual networks request, the more physical power consume. The power include the deployment of virtual network, control signal consumption, forwarding power, resource storage and so on.

Figure 5 shows the relationship between the ratio of η and the number of mapped virtual networks and nodes in each network. As the figure shown, increasing the number of nodes in each network will worsen the performance of objective function.

As the more nodes in a virtual network, the less available physical nodes there are, which could degenerate the rationality of allocation. η will decrease with the increasing of number of mapped virtual networks. As more virtual networks share the limited resources and the complexity of constraints adds, the performance of objective function decreases. Note that there are a couple of flat parts of the red line (mapping number = 4). The result lies in that the resources relatively adequate because of the small quantity of mapped virtual networks. The performance of η will not degrade in a significant way when adding a couple of nodes in a single network. The results of the simulation confirm the feasibility of our algorithm.

6 Conclusion

In this paper, the study of SDN and network virtualization is further extended to SDWN. From the perspective of system architecture evolution, the architecture of wireless access network virtualization based on SDWN is proposed, which achieves the separation of controlling and forwarding. By introducing expansion coefficient, wireless networks can be integrated into the algorithm, which is in view of resource topological perception. In addition, the results of the simulation show the performance of the revenue and cost and the factors that achieve higher resource utilization.

Acknowledgment. This work was supported in part by the National Natural Science Foundation of China under Grant No.61372117.

References

1. Gelberger, A., Yemini, N., Giladi, R.: Performance analysis of software-defined networking (SDN). In: IEEE International Symposium on Modeling, Analysis & Simulation of Computer & Telecommunication Systems, pp. 389–393. IEEE Computer Society (2013)
2. Xiao, P., Qu, W., Qi, H., et al.: The SDN controller placement problem for WAN. In: IEEE/CIC International Conference on Communications in China, pp. 220–224. IEEE (2014)
3. Herker, S., An, X., Kiess, W., et al.: Path protection with explicit availability constraints for virtual network embedding. In: IEEE International Symposium on Personal Indoor & Mobile Radio Communications, pp. 2978–2983. IEEE (2013)
4. Yang, M., Li, Y., Jin, D., et al.: OpenRAN: a software-defined ran architecture via virtualization. ACM Sigcomm Comput. Commun. Rev. **43**(4), 549–550 (2013)
5. Soliman, M., Nandy, B., Lambadaris, I., et al.: Exploring source routed forwarding in SDN-based WANs. In: IEEE International Conference on Communications, pp. 3070–3075. IEEE (2014)
6. Pentikousis, K., Wang, Y., Hu, W.: Mobileflow: toward software-defined mobile networks. Ommnaon Magazn **51**(7), 4453 (2013)
7. Xiaodong, X., Huixin, Z., Xun, D., et al.: SDN based next generation mobile network with service slicing and trials. Wirel. Commun. Over Zigbee Automot. Inclination Meas. China Commun. **11**(2), 65–77 (2014)
8. Ouni, A., Rivano, H., Valois, F.: Wireless mesh networks: energy - capacity tradeoff and physical layer parameters. In: IEEE International Symposium on Personal Indoor & Mobile Radio Communications, pp. 1845–1849. IEEE (2011)

Investigation on Mobility Model in Opportunistic Network

Ruonan Li[1], Yong Zhang[1(✉)], Da Guo[1], Zhaohua Chen[2], and Chunping Hou[3]

[1] ICN & CAD Center, Beijing University of Posts and Telecommunications, Beijing, China
{liruonan,yongzhang,guoda}@bupt.edu.cn
[2] Company Information DEPT, China Telecom Hainan Branch, Hainan, China
18907552883@189.cn
[3] Tianjin University, Tianjin, China
hcp@tju.edu.cn

Abstract. Opportunistic Network as a novel networking, taking advantage of meeting opportunities of mobile nodes, completes the message transmission from the source node to the destination node through the way of each hop. Mobility model decides how the nodes move and is used to analyze network performance with various protocols, such as routing protocols, data dissemination protocols, etc. Currently many mobility models are proposed by researchers. To evaluate these mobility models, an analysis method is proposed. So we propose a method by analyzing mobile distance to assess node mobility models. This paper firstly introduced the commonly used mobility models based on ONE simulation platform, and then a calculation method of node mobile distance is put forward. Next, it was simulated and discussed that we have considered the nodes mobility features by mobile distance. Finally, we use the node contact duration and node inter-contact time as a validation, to make an evaluation for node mobility model.

Keywords: Opportunistic network · Mobility model · Node mobile distance · Node mobility features

1 Introduction

With the rapid development of wireless smart devices and mobile Ad-hoc network, opportunistic network can effectively communicate under the condition without using any fixed network infrastructure or without an end-to-end complete link, which has attracted wide spread attention in recently years. Opportunistic network takes advantage of meeting opportunities to forward messages, so we have to figure out the encounter patterns of mobile devices, while researching the encounter characteristics of mobile devices firstly should make it clear the nodes mobility features.

The location and speed of the node usually can be described for mobility model. But based on real mobility traces, humans have location preferences and they visit nearby locations more frequently compared to far-away locations, also speed at which humans move increases with distance to be traveled [1]. Therefore, we should analyze the node mobile distance when considering the encounter characteristics of mobile nodes. Through the mobile distance we can make a discussion about the nodes mobility features in order to draw the relevant conclusions for node mobility model.

© Springer International Publishing Switzerland 2016
Q. Zu and B. Hu (Eds.): HCC 2016, LNCS 9567, pp. 250–261, 2016.
DOI: 10.1007/978-3-319-31854-7_23

In this paper, based on the traditional node encounter characteristics, a calculation and research on node mobile distance have been made and then mobile distance has been simulated by ONE simulation platform, finally the contact duration and inter-contact time can be exploited to make the further validation. The main contributions are as follows:

- We point out the importance of node mobile distance and propose the analysis method of mobile distance when considering the characteristics for meeting nodes.
- A simulation about mobile distance using ONE simulation platform has been made so that we can analyze the node mobility features.
- The contact duration and inter-contact time verify node mobility features on the basis of mobile distance, to make a comprehensive research direction when selecting an appropriate model for opportunistic network.

2 Related Work

2.1 Mobility Model

Mobility Model provides the node movement way and plays an important role in mobile network. The ONE simulator mainly offers six mobility models: (a) Random Way point (RWP); (b) Map Based Movement (MBM); (c) Shortest Path Map Based Movement (SPMBM); (d) Map Route Movement (MRM); (e) External Movement (EM); (f) Working Day Movement (WDM) [2]. In these six models, RWP is the most basic movement model, which has significant reference in random mobility models. It is typical representative that MBM, SPMBM and MRM are based on map in the mobility models, and there is an enormous proportion of mobility models in ONE simulation platform. Among the three models, a node can randomly select the next map point, and you can easily simulate the road topology by importing the real world map. EM and WDM models are the basis of humans' real life. EM is a model that can be imported external real data or some experimental projects, which provides the real basis for the practical application of network simulation. WDM model [3] has considered the real activity rules of human beings (such as office work during the day, mall shopping after work, at home to sleep at night, etc.). At the same time, people also are free to choose transportation (walking, buses, cars, etc.). So this mobility model is more authenticity.

2.2 Encounter Characteristics

In the mobility model of opportunistic network, the contact duration and inter-contact time are the important performance evaluation indicators which often are discussed by us. The contact duration is the time interval from a node when it enters into the scope of communication with each other to the time when they leave the range of communication of each other. The inter-contact time is the time interval from the time when one node leaves the communication range of each other to the time when another node enters into the communication range of time. In the research of the opportunistic network, the contact duration and inter-contact time as important indicators are simulated according to the human movements.

1. The contact duration reflects that two nodes can transmit data to each other during the meeting [4].
2. The inter-contact time reflects the frequency of two nodes to transmit data to each other [4].
3. The contact duration follows power-law distribution [5].
4. The inter-contact time follows power-law distribution, also some laws show that the inter-contact time follows power-law distribution with an exponential factor trailing [6].

As we all know, based on the real scenario of human life, the movement of one node has its own preference and characteristics of the group. The focus of this paper is not only to verity the distributions of meeting time, but guess node mobile distance also follows power-law distribution by reference to the distributions of the contact duration and inter-contact time. The node mobile distance, is the actual moving distance of one node when the node enters the communication range of another node. For the real scenario of human movements, we consider the characteristics both time and space during the meeting, which are the essential factors.

3   Node Mobile Distance

3.1   The Algorithm of Mobile Distance

Node mobile distance is the actual distance of a node when the node moves to meet with another node [7]. Based on the ONE simulation platform, in order to facilitate to capture data for the calculation method of the mobile distance, we assume that a node is the source node, when the source node enters the communication range with the first relay node, return the source node actual distance, and then we define the mobile distance as the moving distance when a node encounters with another. The Table 1 is the algorithm of mobile distance.

Table 1. The algorithm of mobility mobile distance

The Algorithm of Mobile Distance
1.   Move from S to $P_{(x,y)}$ along a straight line at the limited speed
2. $v = [v_{min}, v_{max}]$
3.   Superposition of distance dis before the update the simulation time
4. $dis \tan ce = dis + +$
5.   Until the node S encounters P
6.   Return a list of every $dis \tan ce$ of the node S

Node S sends Message to others, then the message is forwarded to the next hop $P_{(x,y)}$ through the copy, and the node S stays in the meeting position $P_{(x,y)}$ for some time. In the journey of arriving at the destination $P_{(x,y)}$, due to the moving of nodes, the node to obtain real-time distance (*dis*) is changed [8]. When a node S encounters with another node $P_{(x,y)}$, it will return the location (*loc*) of the node S and then we can make the distance (*dis*) during the simulation time differential accumulation, to get distance (*dis* tan *ce*) as the mobile distance from the spots movements for the source node S, which all nodes of the position areas are within the moving speed $v = [v_{\min}, v_{\max}]$.

3.2 The Calculating of Mobile Distance

It is computed based on all the location of every node for mobile distance. We can define current time i, current location *loc* as a flag, and return the distance from the current node to the destination node d_i. Then we define next time j, this location *loc* for another flag, and return the distance from the node to the destination node d_j. So there is a distance interval Δd, then

$$\Delta d = \left| d_i - d_j \right| \ (i > 0, j > 0) \tag{1}$$

Each updated simulation time, it will make such a calculation and output for the distance interval Δd, since the simulation time is 0.1 s, and the simulation speed Δv is relatively small, so the speed can be made integration approximately equivalent to make differential accumulation for the short distance Δd_k. Then,

$$L = \int_0^t \Delta v dt = \sum_{k=0} \Delta d_k \tag{2}$$

In the mobility models of opportunistic network [7], a node chooses an associated cell as next goal based on distance it will have to travel with some distribution laws, so we set above parameters to describe the node mobile distance. Then we will make an algorithm achievement based on ONE simulator and then make a simulation for every mobility model by setting the scene for each model.

4 Evaluation Standard

4.1 The Complementary Cumulative Distribution Function

The complementary cumulative distribution function (CCDF), is a function of continuous, all is greater than a value, and its occurrence probability, which is the probability density function integral, which can complete description of a real probability distribution of random variable X. The complementary cumulative distribution functions are defined as follows:

$$F(a) = P(x > a). \tag{3}$$

4.2 Goodness of Fit

Goodness-of-fit (R^2) refers to the fitting degree of regression line on the sample observations. The statistical magnitude for goodness of fit is the square of r_{xy}, the correlation coefficient, which is also called determination coefficient.

$$r_{xy} = \frac{\sum (X_i - \overline{X})(Y_i - \overline{Y})}{\sqrt{\sum (X_i - \overline{X})^2 (Y_i - \overline{Y})^2}} \tag{4}$$

$$R^2 = \frac{\sum (Y_i - \overline{Y})^2 - \sum (Y_i - \hat{Y}_t)^2}{\sum (Y_i - \overline{Y})^2} = \frac{\sum (\hat{Y}_t - \overline{Y})^2}{\sum (Y_i - \overline{Y})^2} \tag{5}$$

Where R^2 is equal to the proportion of regression sum of squares in total sum of squared residuals, with the range from 0 to 1. While R^2 is closed to 1, showing that the actual observed point is closer to sample line, and it is better of the fitting degree for the observed value. While R^2 is closed to 0, which indicates that the actual observed point is further to sample line, so it is not satisfied. Therefore, we will make an evaluation standard considering both CCDF and R^2.

5 Simulation Results

There will be six mobility models to be used ONE simulator to simulate experiment scenario, we got results for mobile distance, contact time and inter-contact time.

5.1 The Mobile Distance

We simulated and got the result of the complementary cumulative distribution function (CCDF) for mobile distance for each mobility model by setting the scenario parameters in ONE simulator. The following are the simulation results of six mobility models (RWP, MBM, SPMBM, MRM, EM, WDM) as well as some possible fitting functions for mobile distance as shown in Fig. 1.

First, it is RWP model, whose mobile distance is possible fitting function $F(\Delta s) = 0.9477 * s^{-0.4085}$ and goodness of fit $R^2 = 0.8965$. We can find that the probability of meeting nodes follows a power-law distribution obviously. With the increasing of time, the probability takes a sharp decline.

Secondly, it is MBM model, whose mobile distance is possible fitting function $F(\Delta s) = 0.9017 * s^{-0.4638}$, and goodness of fit $R^2 = 0.9341$. When mobile distance is over 3000 m the probability of meeting node is low and almost unchanged. Therefore, we think it power-law distribution that MBM model follows.

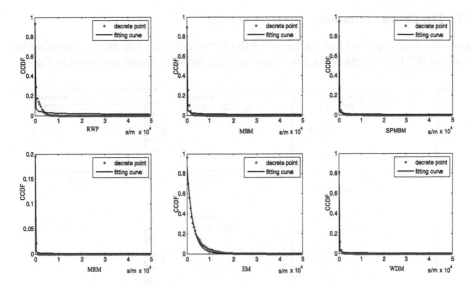

Fig. 1. CCDF of mobile distance for six mobility models

Thirdly, it is SPMBM model, whose mobile distance is possible fitting function $F(\Delta s) = 0.9546 * s^{-0.5358}$ and goodness of fit $R^2 = 0.9854$. The goodness of fit is so high that shows that mobile distance of SPMBM follows a strong power-law distribution. When mobile distance is less than 2000 m the probability of meeting node has drastically reduced, while the distance is more than 2000 m the probability curve of meeting node gradually become gently and almost close to zero.

Fourthly, it is MRM model, whose mobile distance is possible fitting function $F(\Delta s) = 0.1954 * s^{-0.5959}$ and goodness of fit $R^2 = 0.9906$. Because of the limited transportation (only bus or subway, etc.) the probability of meeting is very low, the maxim of which is nearly close to 0.2 and the probability is quickly closed to zero with the distance increasing.

Fifthly, it is EM model, whose mobile distance is possible fitting function $F(\Delta s) = 0.8758 * \exp(-0.0003728 * s)$ and goodness of fit $R^2 = 0.9875$. Referring to external data from Cambridge Haggle project and the hosts are about between forty and fifty, the simulation results show the strong exponential distribution law. When mobile distance is less than 5000 m the probability of meeting has drastically reduced, while the distance is between 5000 m and 15000 m the probability slowly decreases then when the distance is more than 15000 m the probability of meeting is gradually closed to zero. So, when the nodes are not so many we think it exponential distribution. The exponential distribution shows a more slowly attenuation.

Finally, it is WDM model, whose mobile distance is possible fitting function $F(\Delta s) = 0.8187 * s^{-0.5420}$ and goodness of fit $R^2 = 9840$. In the simulation of WDM model, we can find that when mobile distance is less than about 2000 m the probability of meeting node has taken a sharp decline, while the distance is more than 2000 m the probability of meeting is observably closed to zero. Also, it follows a strong power-law distribution.

5.2 The Contact Duration

Also, we simulated and got the result of the complementary cumulative distribution function (CCDF) for the contact duration for each mobility model as shown in Fig. 2.

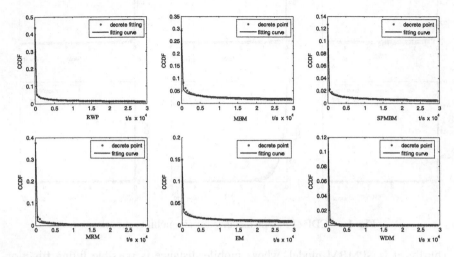

Fig. 2. CCDF of contact duration for six mobility models

In Fig. 2, we can make a fitting curve for the contact duration. First is RWP model, and its contact duration is possible fitting function $F(\Delta t) = 0.4386 * t^{-0.3473}$ and goodness of fit $R^2 = 0.9998$. Second is MBM model, and its contact duration is possible fitting function $F(\Delta t) = 0.2969 * t^{-0.2695}$ and goodness of fit $R^2 = 0.9813$. Third is SPMBM model, and its contact duration is possible fitting function $F(\Delta t) = 0.1277 * t^{-0.3055}$ and goodness of fit $R^2 = 0.9968$. Fourth is MRM model, and its contact duration is possible fitting function $F(\Delta t) = 0.3777 * t^{-0.4647}$ and goodness of fit $R^2 = 0.9911$. Fifth is EM model, and its contact duration is possible fitting function $F(\Delta t) = 0.1507 * t^{-0.2615}$ and goodness of fit $R^2 = 0.9907$. Finally is WDM model, and its contact duration is possible fitting function $F(\Delta t) = 0.1193 * t^{-0.5761}$ and goodness of fit $R^2 = 0.9965$.

All of the six mobility models follows power-law distribution law. Because of the different movements, the probability of meeting shows different results. When the contact duration becomes longer, the probability of meeting will get smaller, even quickly closed to zero. Besides, the long contact duration may cause the fact that the message transmitted is aborted or dropped. So the contact duration plays an import role in choosing an appropriate mobility model.

5.3 Inter-contact Time

Also, we simulated and got the result of the complementary cumulative distribution function (CCDF) for the inter-contact time for each mobility model as shown in Fig. 3.

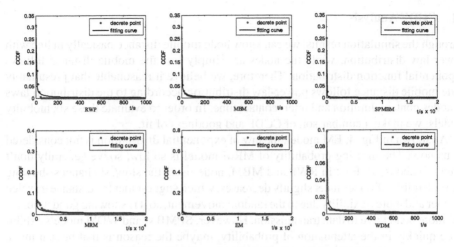

Fig. 3. CCDF of inter-contact time for six mobility models

We can find that RWP model, the possible fitted function is $F(\Delta t) = 0.3154 * t^{-0.7622}$ and goodness of fit is $R^2 = 0.9334$. MBM model, the possible fitted function is $F(\Delta t) = 0.2999 * t^{-0.7935}$ and goodness of fit is $R^2 = 0.9980$. SPMBM model, the possible fitted function is $F(\Delta t) = 0.2528 * t^{-0.6576}$ and goodness of fit is $R^2 = 0.9932$. MRM model, the possible fitted function is $F(\Delta t) = 0.3612 * t^{-0.4246}$ and goodness of fit is $R^2 = 0.9577$. EM model, the possible fitted function is $F(\Delta t) = 0.7382 * t^{-0.6961}$ and goodness of fit is $R^2 = 0.9997$. WDM model, the possible function is $F(\Delta t) = 0.09733 * t^{-0.7017}$ and goodness of fit is $R^2 = 0.9861$.

Above all, we can find whether contact duration or inter-contact time follows power-law distribution. So that the mobile distance mainly follows power-law distribution is convincing and reasonable. The contact duration decides on the possibility of two nodes which can transmit data to each other during the meeting. The inter-contact time reflects the frequency of two nodes to transmit data to each other. It is obvious that the probability of meeting node is very low and almost closed to zero when the time interval increases. Some mobility model has low meeting probability even from the start, which shows its inherent attribute. Consequently, it is of importance for us to choose a favorable model.

6   Specific Analysis

This paper firstly focuses on the properties of mobility models, such as mobile distance, contact duration and inter-contact time by taking into account of the complementary cumulative distribution function and goodness of fit. To sum up, we will analyze the two performances to evaluate the six mobility models.

6.1   CCDF Analysis

Through the simulation results, we can know node mobile distance basically in line with power-law distribution, while the nodes are simply less the mobile distance follows exponential function distribution. Therefore, we believe it reasonable that presumably node mobile distance follows power-law distribution according to the distribution laws of nodes contact duration and inter–contact time. In order to evaluate these six mobility models, we make a comparison of CCDF and goodness of fit.

As shown in Fig. 4, EM model, the law of exponential distribution is not considered by us now. The meeting probability of MRM model is so low, so we generally don't intend to choose it. First in RWP and MBM, node takes the slowest changes showing the probability of nodes meet slightly decreases, which suggest that the distance traveled broader and more flexibility due to the random movement, so it is showing good mobility and more conducive to data transmission. However, SPMBM and WDM models exhibit more quickly in the attenuation of probability, maybe the reason is that human move more regular rather than random. So when considering the human regular or real traces, we can choose SPMBM and WDM models, as for which one can be decided according to the specific requirements.

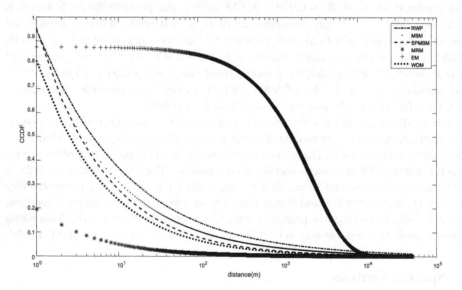

Fig. 4. The comparison of six kinds of models for mobile distance

Then, we have discussed the mobility model laws about exponential distribution. First, we guess maybe it is the reason that the distance or the node number is a factor influenced on distribution law. EM model tells me that numbers of nodes play an important role. So, we also make a compassion to figure out whether the distance has an impact on distribution law. This is a case from **WDM model** in Fig. 5.

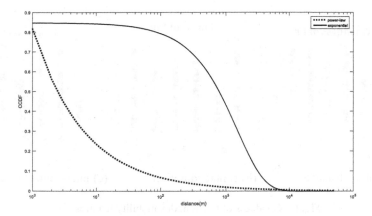

Fig. 5. The different distributions of WDM mobile distance

When the distance is within 2000 m, I make a simulation and fit a function so that I can get a result that the WDM distance follows $F(\Delta s) = 0.8476 * \exp(-0.0006772 * s)$ and $R^2 = 0.9944$. For other models, they are the similar laws, which show mobile distance depends on the distance and the numbers of hosts. Thus, mobile distance follows power-law or exponential law.

In addition, simulation result confirms that Complementary Cumulative Distribution Function (CCDF) of mobile distance for RWP, MBM, SPMBM, MRM and WDM models matches with their CCDF of contact duration and inter-contact time based on real traces, the power-law distribution.

6.2   Goodness of Fit Analysis

We can know that each model basically follows power-law distribution through the CCDF, and Fig. 6 (a) is a column graph, the goodness of fit of mobile distance which in these six models is so high and almost closed to one, showing that they are all fit very well, especially SPMBM, MRM, EM and WDM. So it is a verification again that SPMBM and WDM are more follows human moving regular matching with EM, the external data that based on real traces. However, MRM model which has the low meeting probability is not suitable for us.

By the contrast in Fig. 6 (b), different mobility models follow power-law distribution for the contact duration. The power-law fitting coefficients of MBM model is smaller than the other models, indicating that MBM model has weaker power-law characteristics, so we should not consider MBM model. The RWP, SPMBM and WDM model all have wonderful goodness of fit, which can be selected for the appropriate next hop to have helped more favorable.

In Fig. 6 (c), all mobility models follow power-law distribution, but obviously MBM model, SPMBM model, EM model and WDM model fit better, indicating that inter-contact time has an important impact on choosing a good model. Compared to these mobility models, EM is based on real data, so the probability is better. However, the

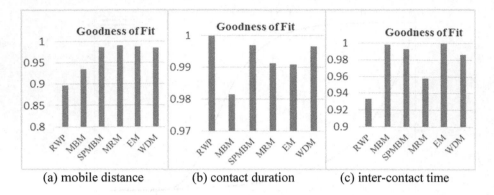

(a) mobile distance	(b) contact duration	(c) inter-contact time

Fig. 6. Goodness of fit for nodes mobility features

SPMBM model shows good distribution characteristics than others. The time interval is shorter, the success of forwarding message will become higher.

7 Conclusion

Through the analysis of six mobility models based on ONE simulation platform in opportunistic network, we can draw the following three conclusions.

- The mobile distance for most node mobility models follows power-law distribution. If the nodes are relatively few or the distance is relatively short, then it will show the law of exponential function.
- The mobile distance, contact duration and inter-contact time are all of importance on choosing an appropriate mobility model. Considering the three factors synthetically, we can draw a conclusion that SPMBM model is the best, also we can choose WDM model if you prefer to consider humans activity.
- When making the research on some certain encounter characteristics, we can consider the goodness of fit as a simple filter firstly to choose better mobility models.

Of course, I have to admit that this paper also has some limitations. I have simulated many times for mobile distance, and actually the fitting function is not only one. I hope that there are more people in the future can continue my thoughts to make more in-depth research on mobile distance for more mobility models in opportunistic network.

Acknowledgements. The authors would like to thank the reviewers for their detailed reviews and constructive comments, which have helped improve the quality of this paper. This work is supported by the National Natural Science Foundation of China under Grant No.61372117 and No.61171097.

References

1. Narmawala, Z., Srivastava, S.: Improved heterogeneous human walk mobility model with hub and gateway identification. In: Chatterjee, M., Cao, J.-n., Kothapalli, K., Rajsbaum, S. (eds.) ICDCN 2014. LNCS, vol. 8314, pp. 469–483. Springer, Heidelberg (2014)
2. Zhen, W., Xin-hua, W., Jing-qi, S.: Extending research for ONE simulator of opportunistic network. Appl. Res. Comput. **29**(1), 272–277 (2012)
3. Wu, F., Chen, T., Zhong, S., et al.: A bargaining—based approach for incentive-compatible message forwarding in opportunistic networks. In: IEEE International Conference on Communications (ICC), pp. 789–793 (2012)
4. Gang, C., Yun-yong, Z., Yong, Z., Mei, S.: Period dividing opportunistic networks mobility model based on human realistic scenarios. J. Commun. (JOC) **34**(Z1), 182–189 (2013)
5. Rhee, I., Shin, M., Hong, S., Lee, K., Kim, S.J., Chong, S.: On the levy-walk nature of human mobility. IEEE/ACM Trans. Netw. (TON) **19**(3), 630–643 (2011)
6. Chaintreau, A., Hui, P., Crowcroft, J., Diot, C., Gass, R., Scott, J.: Impact of human mobility on opportunistic forwarding algorithms. IEEE Trans. Mob. Comput. **6**(6), 606–620 (2007)
7. Karagiannis, T., Boudec, J.Y.L., Vojnovic, M.: Power law and exponential decay of inter-contact times between mobile devices. Microsoft Research, pp. 1377–1390 (2007)
8. Hui, P., Crowcroft, J., Yoneki, E.: Bubble rap: Social-based forwarding in delay tolerant networks. IEEE Trans. Mob. Comput. **10**(11), 1576–1589 (2011)

Research on the Performance of Shipboard Command and Control System Based on DDS

Shufen Liu[1,2], Qijia Gu[3], Zongpu Jia[2], Yikun Zhang[1(✉)], and Xinyong Wang[1]

[1] College of Computer Science and Technology,
Jilin University, Changchun, China
liusf@mail.jlu.edu.cn,
{equalparadise,chufengs}@163.com
[2] College of Computer Science and Technology,
Henan Polytechnic University, Jiaozuo, China
Jiazongpu@126.com
[3] System Engineering Research Institute of China
State Shipbuilding Corporation, Beijing, China

Abstract. For the adaptability of DDS (Data Distribution Service) to the demand of communication support for shipboard command and control system, this paper presents a series of evaluation criteria and methods to evaluate the performance. Through the analysis of the performance evaluation criteria, we show that DDS can be applied to the shipboard command and control system, and support communication of the next generation system.

Keywords: DDS · Adaptability evaluation · Performance · Shipboard command and control system

1 Introduction

DDS (Data Distribution Service) is a platform independent middleware specification. It is based on publish/subscribe model. The data model is the center to complete the loose coupling between publisher and subscriber. DDS can complete packing and unpacking messages. All DDS communication nodes are location transparent. Dynamic exit or addition of subsystem will not cause shock. User nodes only need to declare the publish/subscribe message.

DDS is a message middleware specification, developed and maintained by OMG (Management Group Object) [1, 2]. DDS is based on the publish/subscribe message transmission model. The system nodes only need to subscribe to information of their interests or publish information that they possess, but do not care about the specific information of other nodes. So it achieves the anonymous data transmission, and all nodes are transparent [1, 3]. This is similar to the newspaper subscription: for users, the newspaper and press are location transparent. Conversely, the users' locations for the newspaper are also transparent. The coupling between the users and the newspaper I very weak, through the newspaper name (it may be a subscription code). In DDS,

Q. Zu and B. Hu (Eds.): HCC 2016, LNCS 9567, pp. 262–272, 2016.
DOI: 10.1007/978-3-319-31854-7_24

the counterpart of the newspaper name is the Topic (subject). Publisher/subscriber is based on the same Topic to complete the adaptive discovery and matching. At the same time, DDS also provides a rich set of QoS (Quality of Service) strategies [4]. By adjusting the configuration of the QoS strategy, it can achieve different transmission control.

According to the logic structure of the shipboard command and control system, the prototype system is constructed by using multiple computers in the laboratory, and the performance of the system is evaluated. By measuring the delay, jitter, throughput, and maximum transmission rate of the system to evaluate the performance of DDS, we demonstrate that it can meet the requirements of the performance of shipboard command and control system.

2 Performance Evaluation

For a communication system, delay, jitter, and throughput are typically chosen as the criteria of performance evaluations. The smaller the delay is, the better the real-time performance is, and so is the adaptability to the communication environments that enforce strong requirements on the real-time performance. If the system has large jitter, even though the average delay is small, it is also disastrous for the shipboard command and control system. If delay is suddenly increased for some critical message, the consequences could be catastrophic. Throughput represents the communication system's capability to process messages.

2.1 Delay

In a communication system, the message transmission delay includes many aspects, including the physical media transmission delay $D_{c-delay}$, network buffer delay $D_{n-delay}$, the message processing delay of the network protocol layer $D_{a-delay}$, delay message due to packet routing and addressing $D_{r-delay}$. Specifically, the network delay can be represented as:

$$D = D_{c-delay} + D_{n-delay} + D_{a-delay} + D_{r-delay} \tag{1}$$

In the actual delay measurement, the message roundtrip method is usually used to obtain the specific delay. Specifically, the sender sends a message, and receiver receives the message and returns the original message. The consumption time of the process divided by two is a half of the communication delay. In order to make the delay data more accurate, we use the following statistical methods. For a message, we measure its delay N times, and take their average value as the final delay measurement as follows:

$$D_{avg(n)} = \frac{1}{n} \sum_{i=1}^{n} D_i \tag{2}$$

In the above equation, $D_{avg(n)}$ is the average delay of n times of measurement, and D_i is the delay of the subscription and publication of data i.

2.2 Jitter

The stability of the communication system is characterized by the jitter. Lower jitter shows that the communication of the system is more stable, and the communication delay can be better predicted. The main reason for the jitter is the jitter of the network processing or the jitter of the physical transmission media. In this paper, the larger jitter indicates the delay of system couldn't be predicted in the worst case. Small jitter is the premise of real-time performance and stability of a communication system.

In general, the ratio between the standard deviation of delay and the average value of the delay is used as the system jitter and is defined as:

$$\sigma = \sqrt{\left(n \sum_{i=1}^{n} D_i^2 - \left(\sum_{i=1}^{n} D_i\right)^2\right) \Big/ n(n-1)} \tag{3}$$

$$J = \sigma / D_{avg(n)} \times 100\,\%. \tag{4}$$

2.3 Throughput

The throughput of a communication system can be considered as the demonstration of the ability to handle the messages. The higher the throughput is, the better the message processing capability is. To measure the throughput, a set of messages are sent in the speed of v messages per second. If all messages are received, then increase the speed. Otherwise, it means some packages are lost due to lack of capability to process such large messages. In this case, messages are sent with a lower speed. The critical maximum transmission rate is obtained by constantly adjustment s of the speed to get the final maximum speed v_{max}. Assuming at this point, the message size is s, then the throughput of the communication system is:

$$T_s = v_{max} \times s. \tag{5}$$

3   The Methods and Results of Performance Evaluation

In this section, we measure the various criteria for evaluating the performance of DDS, including delay, jitter, throughput, the impact of number of subscribers to the delay, and the maximal message transmission rate, etc. In addition, we analyze the trend of these criteria [5, 6].

3.1   The Delay and the Impact of Subscriber's Number on Delay

We select subject sender A and receiver B from a machine deployed with the system and perform DDS messaging sending and receiving and measure the message delay according to the different lengths of the messages. Then we select sender A deployed with the system and multiple subscribers (4 in our case) for the same experiments.

Specific Requirements. The message sizes are 40 byte, 100 byte, 200 byte, 500 byte, 1 KB, 2 KB, 5 KB, 10 KB, 20 KB, and 50 KB, respectively. Network adapter is a 100 Mbps network adapter. For various sizes of messages, the transmission interval is 10 ms. We collect at least about 1000 samples and take the average of its delay (the unit is microsecond).

Measurement Method. For a single subscription, the machine A sends messages and records the sending time. Then machine B receives and forwards the message back immediately. When machine A receives the forwarded message, it again records the receiving time. The difference between the sending time and receiving time is about twice the sending delay time (the delay data generated by the experiment have been converted to one way delay time).

For multiple subscriptions, machine A sends messages and records the sending time. The first machine that receives the message forwards it back immediately. The machine A receives forwarded messages, which is distinguished by receiver machine number, and records the receiving time. All the time difference value is about twice the delay time (the delay data generated by the experiment have been converted to one way delay time). The network adapter is 100 Mbps.

Results Record. The measurement results are recorded in the form of horizontal and vertical coordinates: the horizontal coordinates are the message sizes, measured in byte, while the vertical coordinates are the delay time, measured in microsecond. Results are shown in Fig. 1.

3.2   Jitter

The jitter can be calculated based on the delay measurements in the previous section.

Results Record. The measurement results of jitter are recorded in the same form as the delay: the horizontal coordinate are the message sizes, measured in byte while the vertical coordinate are the ratio of the delay jitter. Results are shown in Fig. 2.

3.3   Throughput

We select a machine deployed with the system as the subject publisher, and the other machines as the subscribers. Only one subject is sent and will be received. On the sending machine, the system changes the sending frequency continuously. It sends 10000 DDS messages to make sure that the receiver receives the message. Constantly changing the length of the message, we record the total time taken for sending 10000 DDS messages.

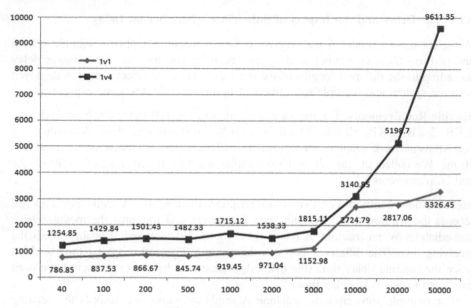

Fig. 1. The delay statistics

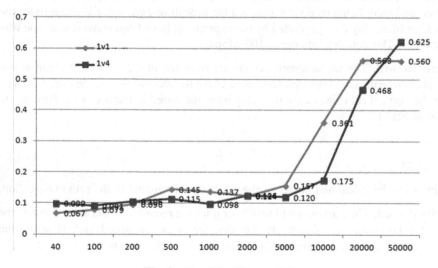

Fig. 2. The delay jitter statistics

Specific Requirements. The message sizes are 40 byte, 100 byte, 200 byte, 500 byte, 1 KB, 2 KB, 5 KB, 10 KB, 20 KB, 50 KB, respectively. Two kinds of network devices are used for measurement: the first one is a 100 ms network adapter while the second is 1000 Mbps.

Measurement Method. With message sizes, the system sends 10000 samples continuously, and records the total time (the unit is seconds). Three identical operations are performed for each sample size and the results are recorded. We use the following formula to calculate the throughput:

Throughput = Sample size * 10000/the average time of 3 times/1024/1024.

Experimental Results. The measurement results are recorded in the form of horizontal and vertical coordinates. Horizontal coordinate is the message size s measured in byte; the vertical coordinate is the bandwidth occupancy with unit in MB/s. Results are shown in Fig. 3:

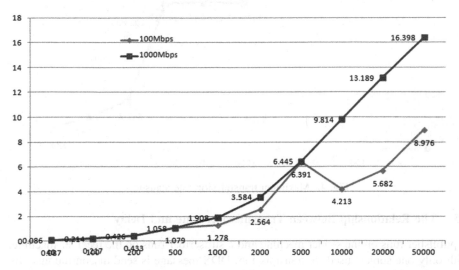

Fig. 3. Throughput statistics

3.4   The Maximum Message Transmission Rate

Here the settings are the same as Sect. 3.3. On the sending machine, the system sends DDS messages continuously without interruption, and the receivers receive messages. Constantly changing the lengths of the message, the maximal number of messages that can be successfully sent is used as the maximum message transmission rate.

Specific Requirements. The message sizes are 40 byte, 100 byte, 200 byte, 500 byte, 1 KB, 2 KB, 5 KB, 10 KB, 20 KB, 50 KB, respectively. The two kinds of network adapter are 100 Mbps and 1000 Mbps, respectively.

Measurement Method. With different message sizes, the system sends 10000 samples continuously and records the total time (the unit is seconds). Again, three measurements are recorded per message length. We use the following formula to calculate the maximum message transmission rate:

Message Rate = 10000/the average time of 3 times.

Experimental Results. The measurement results are recorded in the form of horizontal and vertical coordinates. The horizontal coordinates are the message sizes, measured in byte, while the vertical coordinates are the message rates measured in (a/s). Experimental results are shown in Fig. 4:

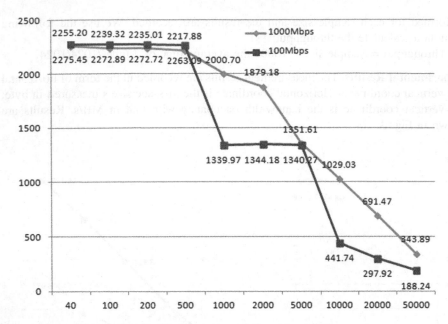

Fig. 4. Maximum transmission rate statistics

3.5   The Relationship Between Transmission Rate and Delay

A publisher runs on the sender machine and a subscriber runs on the receiver machine, with only one subject used for transmission. DDS message is send discontinuously by the sender with the packet size 200 Byte. Make sure the receiver receives the messages. In order to change the sending rate, we change the sending interval constantly and record the delay of different message rate.

Specific Requirements. The transmission intervals are 1 ms, 10 ms, 20 ms, 50 ms, 100 ms, 1000 ms, respectively. The same two network adapters are used.

Experimental Results. The measurement results are recorded in the form of horizontal and vertical coordinates. Horizontal coordinates are the sending intervals measured in MS; the vertical coordinates are the delay time measured in microseconds, as shown in Fig. 5.

4   Analysis of the Performance Evaluation

This paper analyzes the trend of the performance in the various evaluation criteria, and points out the range of the condition parameters in the specified criteria.

4.1   Analysis of Delay Evaluation Results

When the sample size is over 10000 bytes in one-to-one transmission, there is a phenomenon of packet loss. With the increase of message size, message loss is more serious.

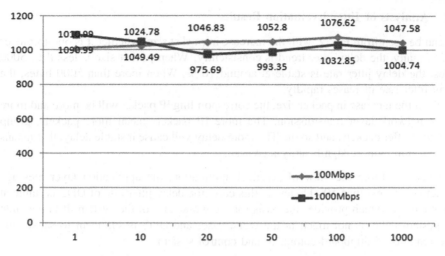

Fig. 5. The impact of transmission rate on the delay

No package loss is observed with other small samples sizes. With the 100 Mbps adapter, the 10 K's effective rate is 58 % (total sample is 2103, effective sample is 1229), 20 K's effective rate is 37 % (total sample is 1744, effective sample is 643), and 50 K's effective rate is 28 % (total sample is 1436, effective sample is 402).

In the case of one-to-many transmission, the packet loss is very rare. Even if the loss happens during large data transmission, the loss rate is less than 2 % (100 Mbps network adapter). The phenomenon is related to the recognition algorithm. When multiple machines subscribe data, one single response from one subscribers will result in no package loss.

When the sample size is less than 5000 bytes, the delay is basically similar. Based on Fig. 5, the changing trend is stable. The delay is under 2000 microseconds and the increasing is not obvious. But when the sample size was increased to 10000 bytes, in both the one-to-one and one-to-many transmissions, the change trend of the performance is consistently. The delay will have a more substantial increase. With the increase of sample size, the trend of the delay also increases linearly.

Using network analysis tool Wireshark, we show that, without changing the default QoS policy, each packet which is one-to-many transmission will arrive in the form of peer to peer. Therefore, the results show that when increasing the number of subscribers (peer to peer send), the delay will grow with a small amplitude.

Conclusion: From the view of practical application, the size of data packet which is usually in the application layer is less than 4 K (typically less than 1 K). In this case, the delay of DDS for the development is smooth and sufficient to satisfy the requirements of real-time communication in the shipboard command and control system.

4.2   Analysis of Jitter Evaluation Results

As can be seen from Fig. 2, with the increase in packet size, whether it is one-to-one or one-to-many, the delay jitter trend is consistently. When packet size is less than 5000 bytes, the delay jitter rate is stable at around 10 %. When more than 5000 bytes, the delay jitter rate increases rapidly.

With the increase in packet size, the corresponding IP packet will be more and more in the network layer transmission. The more IP packets mean more packets, group packets, buffer packets, and so on. The more delay will cause instable delay, that means the jitter rate will be significantly increased.

Conclusions: From the view of practical application, the application layer message packet size is less than 5000 bytes. In this case, the delay jitter rate of DDS is stable at around 10 %, which provides the basis for the worst case of the system. It proves that the system delay is not much in the worst case, and DDS is sufficient to satisfy the requirements of shipboard command and control system.

4.3   Analysis of Throughput Evaluation Results

According to the statistics shown in Fig. 3, the change in the throughput of the 100 Mbps adapter and 1000 Mbps adapter is similar. In other words, when DDS transmits the large byte data (without considering the packet loss), it will have larger bandwidth occupancy rate and increase the sending time.

For 100 Mbps network adapter, when the packet size is 10000 bytes, due to the bandwidth limit of the network adapter at this time, the throughput will fall. When the packet size is 10000 bytes, the amount of packet transmission in the unit time will drop. However, the package is not large, the transmission of the unit time is reduced, which affects the throughput and results in decrease. For 1000 Mbps network adapter, there is no such problem.

Conclusion: When the data timeliness requirements are not high, and the data quantity is large, it is suitable to use DDS to transmit large data packets to increase the bandwidth utilization. Because the larger the data packet is, the better overall trend of the DDS throughput is.

4.4   Analysis of Maximum Message Transmission Rate Evaluation Results

According to Fig. 4, the maximum transmission rate of DDS is almost constant and high level in the sample size of 500 bytes. When it is more than 1000 bytes, the 1000 Mbps adapter and the 100 Mbps adapter show different message transmission rates.

From the overall trend, for the 100 Mbps network adapter, the sample size less than 500 byte shows a similar message transmission rate. The sample size between 500 and 5000 byte have a consistent sending rate and are less than 500 bytes message transmission rate. When it is more than 10000 byte, message sending rate decreases significantly.

For 1000 Mbps network adapter, when the sample size is less than 500 bytes, the message transmission rate is the same. With the increase of the sample size, message transmission rate is linear decreased.

Conclusion: When the data timeliness requirements are high, the smaller data format should be used DDS to transmit data packets. It can improve the transmission rate and satisfy the real-time requirements of the communication.

4.5   Analysis of the Influence of Transmission Rate on Delay Evaluation Results

According to Fig. 5, obviously, when the selected package is not large, in the selection of several transmission frequency, the delay tends to be stable (1.1 ms delay), and even almost no change.

Conclusion: Combined with the analysis of delay, it is found that the DDS is able to maintain a low transmission delay performance for the common packets size and sending frequency, and delay is stable, which can satisfy the requirements of the delay stability of the ship command and control system.

5   Conclusion

In this paper, we use specialized RTI DDS to implement the underlying communication layer, measure the characterization of performance evaluation criteria and analyze the change trend of these criteria along with some communication factors. Through the analysis, the results show that the DDS can support the communication business and satisfy the needs of the performance. It can simplify the development and deployment of the next generation of shipboard command and control system by using DDS as a message middleware.

References

1. Pardo-Castellote, G.: Omg data-distribution service: architectural overview. In: Proceedings of the 23rd International Conference on Distributed Computing Systems Workshops, 2003, pp. 200–206. IEEE (2003)
2. Schlesselman, J.M., Pardo-Castellote, G., Farabaugh, B.: OMG data-distribution service (DDS): architectural update. In: Military Communications Conference, MILCOM 2004, vol. 2, pp. 961–967. IEEE (2004)
3. Wang, N., Schmidt, D.C., van't Hag, H., et al.: Toward an adaptive data distribution service for dynamic large-scale network-centric operation and warfare (NCOW) systems. In: Military Communications Conference, MILCOM 2008, pp. 1–7. IEEE (2008)
4. Mazouzi, M., Hasnaoui, S., Abid, M.: Challenges and solutions in configuring, rapid developing and deploying of a QoS-enabled component middleware. In: Proceedings of the 2008 IEEE conference on Design and Test Workshop, IDT 2008, 3rd International Conference, pp. 221–224 (2008)

5. Moon, S.B., Skelly, P., Towsley, D.: Estimation and removal of clock skew from network delay measurements. In: INFOCOM 1999, Proceedings of the Eighteenth Annual Joint Conference of the IEEE Computer and Communications Societies, vol. 1, pp. 227–234. IEEE (1999)
6. Schmidt, D.C., Huston, S.D.: C++ Network Programming vol 2: Systematic Reuse with ACE and Frameworks. Addison-Wesley (2002)

Research and Implementation of Cache Node Backup Strategy in Distributed Caching System

Wenlin Liu[1,2(✉)], Haiyang Zhang[1], Saihong Xu[1],
Yue Ma[1], and Siyuan Sun[3]

[1] School of Computer Science, Beijing University of Posts
and Telecommunications, Beijing 100876,
People's Republic of China
jzcslw15@163.com
[2] Science and Technology on Information Transmission and Dissemination
in Communication Networks Laboratory, Beijing, People's Republic of China
[3] Beijing Branch, China United Network Communications Group Co., Ltd,
Beijing, People's Republic of China

Abstract. This paper studies the mutual backup strategy of cache nodes in the distributed caching system, and proposes a new dynamic adaptive mutual backup strategy for the cache nodes by analyzing the specific application scenarios and requirements. Experimental results show that the proposed method supports the hot switch of the distributed caching system, can improve the availability and scalability of the system, and realize the functions of load balance and fault tolerance of the system.

Keywords: Distributed caching system · Backup strategy · Load balancing

1 Introduction

In recent years, with the rapid development of Web2.0 website, these websites' demand for high concurrency and real-time performance is becoming higher and higher, so the high performance distributed memory caching system has been applied on a large scale. The usage of cache can effectively improve the application's speed of accessing data, reduce the response time of the user's request, and ease the pressure of the background database. The distributed caching system in this paper is mainly divided into application interface layer, local cache layer and database interface layer. Application interface layer provides the APIs for upper business, including the functions of reading, writing, deleting data and so on. The database interface layer encapsulates the interface of accessing the background database, and the local cache layer realizes the core functions of the distributed caching system. It mainly includes memory management module, cache synchronization mechanism, lock mechanism, and some core data structure definition and so on.

When data loss happens in a cache node or a cache node is not available, it generally will not affect the upper business, the upper application program can directly

© Springer International Publishing Switzerland 2016
Q. Zu and B. Hu (Eds.): HCC 2016, LNCS 9567, pp. 273–283, 2016.
DOI: 10.1007/978-3-319-31854-7_25

obtain data from the background database when the cache is not hit. But with the increase in business volume and the amount of users, cache should bear most of the pressure of data access, so when the cache fails, the database will not be able to withstand the huge pressure of data access and crashes.

Therefore, in distributed caching system, the availability can be improved by the means of hot backup. When a cache server fails in the system, the request of data access can be switched to its hot standby servers. In the scheme of hot backup between cache nodes, the mutual backup strategy is a problem worthy of study. Good mutual backup strategy can improve the availability and scalability of the distributed caching system, and guarantee the high performance.

This paper proposes a new mutual backup strategy between cache nodes in a distributed caching system, which is dynamic adaptive mutual backup strategy.

2   Scene Description

In order to improve the speed of accessing data, the distributed caching system needs to be in the same virtual machine with the upper business, and compiled together with it by the means of API.

The distributed caching system has a great relationship with the upper business. In order to improve the availability, the upper application needs the function of hot switch provided by the distributed caching system, that is, when a cache node fails, it should send the request of accessing data to its backup node instead of the background database, which can guarantee the quick response of the caching system. It is also needed that this system can achieve the corresponding backup strategy when the upper business has different needs, such as specifying the number of backup nodes and the location of the backup nodes.

The mutual backup strategy studied in this paper can dynamically plan the number of backup nodes and the location of backup nodes and can deal with the case of adding a new node or a node failing flexibly, so that the backup data can be distributed on each node in the cluster. This strategy can also make full use of the existing machine resources and ensure the high reliability, high availability and high scalability of the distributed caching system.

3   Research Status

Currently, the popular distributed memory caching system has redis, memcached and so on. Memcached is an open source distributed memory caching system, which was once synonymous with distributed caching. Due to its excellent performance and simple design, it is widely used by a large number of websites. In recent years, the development of non-relational database is very fast, and related products are emerging, redis is one of the representatives. Redis supports more extensive operations, some new features such as master-slave synchronization, which can be used as a high performance distributed caching system. Different system uses different backup strategy according to its own characteristics.

3.1   The Backup Strategy of Memcached

From the point of design, the server nodes of memcached do not communicate with each other, so that the cluster can have no limit to the level of expansion, and its distributed is ensured by the client's routing algorithm: the consistent hashing. Memcached itself is a large scale high performance distributed caching system, without data redundancy backup. There is no official or authoritative solution about the backup strategy of memcached. There are generally two common ideas.

3.1.1   The Backup Strategy of N+x

In the distributed caching system composed of memcached, there are N memcached servers, which share x backup servers. When x equals to N, the backup strategy of N+x reduces to double nodes backup strategy, namely every memcached server has two nodes: master node and slave node, after the failure of the master node, the data access request will be switched to its slave node; when the master node works normally, the two nodes can synchronize data quickly. It can be considered as a small probability event when the master node and its backup node fail simultaneously. Double nodes backup strategy is designed to be simple. Its disadvantage is that it cannot make full use of the system resources provided by each machine and increase the cost of hardware. N+x backup strategy is improved from double nodes backup strategy. Each node configured with a backup node consumes too much of machine resources, it is better to let n nodes share x backup nodes (x is less than N). This greatly reduces the cost of hardware, but when the size of the cluster continues to increase, it is also needed to increase the number of backup servers, hardware costs are still high.

3.1.2   The Backup Strategy of Caching Proxy Server

Using the caching proxy can prevent single point of failure and improve the availability of the caching system. The memcached server is connected to the caching proxy server, and the cache proxy server is connected to the memcached client. The caching proxy server can be connected to multiple memcached servers and synchronize their data. If a memcached server fails, the data will not be lost, the caching system is still able to work; if a caching proxy server fails, the memcached client can send the request to another caching proxy server, the caching system is still able to work. As shown below:

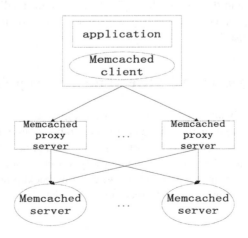

This backup strategy is safe and reliable, but the architecture of the whole system is somewhat complex, and the increase in the number of nodes in the cluster will also lead to a corresponding increase in the cost of hardware.

3.2 The Backup Strategy of Redis

Redis is a non-relational database, but also can be used as a distributed memory caching system. Redis is powerful and has a flexible and diverse backup strategy.

3.2.1 The Backup Strategy of Master and Slave

Redis provides the function of copy to achieve automatic synchronization of the database. The user can make a server copy another server by executing the SLAVEOF command or setting the slaveof option. A master can have multiple slaves. After the master-slave relationship is determined, the whole replication process is automatically performed, without programmer's intervention. When master encounters a single point of failure, any of its slaves can continue to provide services.

This backup strategy is scalable, and the synchronization process is transparent to the programmer, reducing the burden on the programmer. However, each redis master server is equipped with one or more slave servers, which makes the number of nodes in the cluster too much.

3.2.2 The Persistent Backup Strategy of Redis

Redis supporting persistence means that redis can synchronize data in memory to disk. Redis provides two kinds of persistence mode, which are RDB and AOF. RDB can save the state of the database to a RDB file at a point in time, the RDB file generated by the function of RDB persistence is a compressed binary file, which can restore the database state. AOF persistence records the state of the database by keeping the write commands executed by the redis server. When the redis server is restarted, the database state can be restored by loading and executing the commands stored in the AOF file.

RDB and AOF all save the state of the redis to the physical hard disk, when the redis is restarted, it can restore the data in redis by loading RDB and AOF files. However, during the failure of redis, the application can not directly access data from RDB and AOF files, and the data in the cache has a certain timeliness, when redis is restored, the previous hot data may not be hot data any more. So this backup strategy is not suitable for this distributed caching system.

4   Analysis of Dynamic Adaptive Mutual Backup Strategy

The main idea of the dynamic adaptive mutual backup strategy is to use the existing cache nodes in the system to backup data to each other, without adding additional machines. Each cache node, in addition to its own hot data, also back up the data of other nodes, which can make full use of the memory resources of each machine. When a node fails, the upper business can quickly switch to its backup node, and it does not affect the upper application program to read and write data from the cache.

4.1   The Design of Dynamic Adaptive Mutual Backup Strategy

The main idea of this strategy is as follows:

All of the nodes in the cluster are stored in an array, which is composed of a ring. In a clockwise direction, the data in the first node is backed up to the second and third nodes (if the specified number of backup is 2); the data in the second node is backed up to the third and fourth nodes, and so on. The data in the last node is backed up to the first and second nodes.

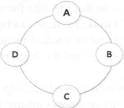

As shown above, if the system has four nodes: A, B, C, D, saving the nodes in the array in order, A is the first node, D is the last node. If the specified number of backup is 2, then the data in node A will be backed up to B and C nodes, the data in the node B will be backed up to the C and D nodes, and so on.

After the backup is completed, the data on each node is shown in the following table:

A	B	C	D
C'	A'	A'	B'
D'	D'	B'	C'

Each column in the table indicates the data in a node after the completion of the backup. Take the first column as an example: the data in the cache node A, besides its own data, but also the data stored in C and D nodes.

This strategy does not need to specify the backup relationship among the nodes in advance, but generates the backup strategy automatically according to the law above. At the same time, it can also be flexible in case of adding a new node and a node failing.

4.2   Adding a New Node

When a new node is added to this system, the upper LB module detects it, and updates the array containing the information of all nodes in the system. The new node's info will be added to the end of the array. The backup strategy of such a system will be dynamically changed. After adding a new node E:

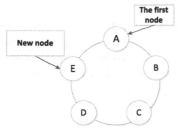

After the backup is completed, the data on each node is shown in the following table:

A	B	C	D	E
D'	A'	A'	B'	C'
E'	E'	B'	C'	D'

Through observation, it can be seen that the data from C to A needs to be migrated to the new node E. The data from D to B also needs to be migrated to the new node E, while the data of new node E needs to be backed up to A and B. So the impact of adding a new node is the last two nodes and the beginning two nodes in the array of node's info.

When new nodes are added in the distributed caching system, the dynamic adaptive mutual backup strategy can work normally and ensure the scalability of the system. After the dynamic adjustment, the amount of data is consistent in each node, and the load is balanced.

4.3   Node Failure

When a node fails, the LB module can detect this situation and the backup strategy of this system will also be adjusted. When the adjustment is finished, the information of this node will be removed from the array of info.

If C node fails, after data migration is completed, the data on each node is shown in the following table:

A	B	D	E
D'	A'	A'	B'
E'	E'	B'	D'
		C'	C'

The data from A to C will be migrated to the node D, the data from B to C will be migrated to the node E. The impact of a node failure is the front two nodes and the rear two nodes. At the same time it can be observed that the data of the node C has been kept in the D and E nodes, so the system can send the data access request of node C to the node D and E, instead of the background database.

4.4   Fault Node Recovery

After the recovery of a fault node, the upper LB module detects this situation, and then adds the node's information to the end of the array. One more step to do in this situation is to remove the backup data from other nodes when the node warms up (load data from the background database). The following dynamic adjustment is same as adding a new node.

5   Implement of Dynamic Adaptive Mutual Backup Strategy

cachenodeinfo: An array including info of all nodes in this distributed caching system.
datamigration(data, nodeA, nodeB): data migration module, migrating data from the node A to the node B, if the data is NULL, then it will empty the data of node A in node B.

findnode(ip, cachenodeinfo): find the location of the node in the cachenodeinfo array.

def databackup(): // Data backup operation

\# Calculate the time interval from the last backup to the present

timeinter = nowtime - lasttime;

\# If the interval is greater than the time interval specified in the configuration file, a backup operation will be performed

if (timeinter < config.backupinterval) return;

\#find the location of its own node in the array.

index = findnode(ip, cachenodeinfo);

backup1 = (index+1) % cachenodeinfo.size;

backup2 = (index+2) % cachenodeinfo.size;

\#start data backup: incremental backup (newdata represents the updated data since the last backup).

datamigration(newdata,index,backup1);

datamigration(newdata,index,backup2);

def   addnewnode(newnode):

\# If this node is the node of fault which recovers, then call the recovernode function

if(isrecovernode(newnode)){

      noderecover (newnode);

      return;

}

\# Otherwise, this node is a new node.

cachenodeinfo.addback(newnode);

\# Adding a node only affects its front two nodes and rear two nodes

prevtwo = newnode − 2;

prevone = newnode − 1;

nextone = (newnode+1) % cachenodeinfo.size;

nexttwo = (newnode+2) % cachenodeinfo.size;

myself = findnode(ip,cachenodeinfo);

if(myself == prevtwo){

\#Back up the data of prevtwo to the new node

      datamigration(myself.alldata, myself, newnode);

\# At the same time, delete data from prevtwo to the nextone node

     datamigration(NULL, myself, nextone);

}

if(myself == prevone){

\# Back up the data of the prevone to the new node.

      datamigration(myself.alldata, myself, newnode);

\# At the same time, delete data from the prevone to the nexttwo

     datamigration(NULL, myself, nexttwo);

}

```
        return;
        def   nodefail(failnodeip):
        failnode = findnode(failnodeip, cachenodeinfo);
        # Make a mark on the failed node in the array of information
        cachenodeinfo.mark(failnode);
        prevone = (failnode+cachenodeinfo.size – 1)% cachenodeinfo.size;
        prevtwo = (failnode+cachenodeinfo.size – 2)% cachenodeinfo.size;
        nextone = (failnode+1) % cachenodeinfo.size;
        nexttwo = (failnode+2) % cachenodeinfo.size;
        myself = findnode(ip,cachenodeinfo);
        if(myself == prevone){
                datamigration(myself.alldata,myself,nexttwo);
        }
        if(myself == prevtwo){
                datamigration(myself.alldata,myself,nextone);
        }
        return;
        def   noderecover(recovernode){
        # remove the fault mark
        cachenodeinfo.removemark(recovernode);
        prevone = (recovernode + cachenodeinfo.size–1) % cachenodeinfo.size;
        prevtwo = (recovernode + cachenodeinfo.size–2) % cachenodeinfo.size;
        nextone = (recovernode + 1) % cachenodeinfo.size;
        nexttwo = (recovernode + 2) % cachenodeinfo.size;
        myself = findnode(ip, cachenodeinfo);
        if(myself == prevone){
                datamigration(myself.alldata,myself,recovernode);
                datamigration(NULL,myself,nexttw);
        }
        if(myself == prevtwo){
                datamigration(myself.alldata,myself, recovernode);
                datamigration(NULL,myself,nexton);
        }
        return;
```

6   Verification of Mutual Backup Strategy

On a host, four virtual machines are launched, named as A, B, C, D, and the distributed caching system is started on the four nodes. Different data is written to different nodes. According to the backup strategy described in this paper, the data written into the A node will be backed up to the B and C, as the same way, the data written into the B node will be backed up to C and D, etc. Thus, it is normal to verify the mutual backup strategy by writing test program to read the data. In normal case, start the cache, and write (ka1, kb1), (va1, vb1), (kc1, vc1), (kd1, vd1) to four nodes respectively. Data are as follows:

Node	Data
A	ka1,va1
B	kb1,vb1
C	kc1,vc1
D	kd1,vd1

If the dynamic adaptive mutual backup strategy is normal, the data in each node will be the same as the following table:

Node	Data(itself)	Data(backup)
A	ka1,va1	(kc1,vc1) (kd1,vd1)
B	kb1,vb1	(ka1,va1) (kd1,vd1)
C	kc1,vc1	(ka1,va1) (kb1,vb1)
D	Kd1,vd1	(kb1,vb1) (kc1,vc1)

Write test procedure, read data of each node in A, B, C, D. The results are as follows:

Operation	Result
getall(A)	(ka1,va1) (kc1,vc1) (kd1,vd1)
getall(B)	(kb1,vb1) (ka1,va1) (kd1,vd1)
getall(C)	(kc1,vc1) (ka1,va1) (kb1,vb1)
getall(D)	(kd1,vd1) (kb1,vb1) (kc1,vc1)

By the results of reading data, it can be found that the mutual backup strategy works correctly.

Add a new node E, and write data (ke1, ve1), according to the dynamic adaptive mutual backup strategy, the data in each node will be shown as the following table:

Node	Data(itself)	Data(backup)
A	ka1,va1	(kd1,vd1) (ke1,ve1)
B	kb1,vb1	(ka1,va1) (ke1,ve1)
C	kc1,vc1	(ka1,va1) (kb1,vb1)
D	kd1,vd1	(kb1,vb1) (kc1,vc1)
E	ke1,ve1	(kc1,vc1) (kd1,vd1)

Read data from each node using the test program, and the results are as follows:

Operation	Result
getall(A)	(ka1,va1) (kd1,vd1) (ke1,ve1)
getall(B)	(kb1,vb1) (ka1,va1) (ke1,ve1)
getall(C)	(kc1,vc1) (ka1,va1) (kb1,vb1)
getall(D)	(kd1,vd1) (kb1,vb1) (kc1,vc1)
getall(E)	(ke1,ve1) (kc1,vc1) (kd1,vd1)

By the results it can be found that when a new node is added, the dynamic mutual backup strategy works correctly.

When a node fails, such as C node, the node data will be as follows:

Node	Node(itself)	Data(backup)
A	ka1,va1	(kd1,vd1)(ke1,ve1)
B	kb1,vb1	(ka1,va1)(ke1,ve1)
D	kd1,vd1	(kb1,vb1) (kc1,vc1) (ka1,va1)
E	ke1,ve1	(kc1,vc1) (kd1,vd1)(kb1,vb1)

Using the test program to read data from each node, the results are as follows:

Operation	Result
getall(A)	(ka1,va1) (kd1,vd1) (ke1,ve1)
getall(B)	(kb1,vb1) (ka1,va1) (ke1,ve1)
getall(D)	(kd1,vd1) (kb1,vb1) (kc1,vc1) (ka1,va1)
getall(E)	(ke1,ve1) (kc1,vc1) (kd1,vd1) (kb1,vb1)

By the results it can be seen that the mutual backup strategy works properly.

The fault node C recovers, then according to the dynamic mutual backup strategy, the data of each node should be as follows:

Node	Data(itself)	Data(backup)
A	ka1,va1	(kd1,vd1) (ke1,ve1)
B	kb1,vb1	(ka1,va1) (ke1,ve1)
C	kc1,vc1	(ka1,va1) (kb1,vb1)
D	kd1,vd1	(kb1,vb1) (kc1,vc1)
E	ke1,ve1	(kc1,vc1) (kd1,vd1)

By writing the test program to read data in each node, the results are as follows:

Operation	Result
getall(A)	(ka1,va1) (kd1,vd1) (ke1,ve1)
getall(B)	(kb1,vb1) (ka1,va1) (ke1,ve1)
getall(C)	(kc1,vc1) (ka1,va1) (kb1,vb1)
getall(D)	(kd1,vd1) (kb1,vb1) (kc1,vc1)
getall(E)	(ke1,ve1) (kc1,vc1) (kd1,vd1)

By the results it can be seen that the dynamic adaptive mutual backup strategy works normally.

Through the above four tests, it can be seen that the actual results are consistent with the theoretical results. Dynamic adaptive mutual backup strategy in distributed caching system works correctly.

7 Conclusion

This paper analyzes and designs a dynamic adaptive mutual backup strategy from the specific application scenarios of the distributed caching system, it can improve the availability, so that the caching system has a certain fault tolerance and the load balance of the system is guaranteed, too. Then the strategy is implemented and verified. All in all, in the distributed caching system, the dynamic adaptive mutual backup strategy is simple and convenient and can guarantee the high reliability and good performance of the system.

Acknowledgment. This work was supported by the National Natural Science Foundation of China (Grant No. 61471055).

References

1. Qiu, Z.-W.: Based on the distributed cache redis system architecture research. Netw. Secur. Technol. Application **10**, 50–54 (2014)
2. Li, W.-X., Yang, X.-H.: Storage model based on distributed cache for message oriented middleware. Comput. Eng. **36**(13), 93–95 (2010)
3. Xiao, Y.-Y., Liu, Y.-S.: Global consistency fuzzy backup strategy for distributed real-time main memory database. Comput. Sci. **33**, 151–154 (2006)
4. Tudorica, B.G., Bucur, C.: A comparison between several NoSQL databases with comments and notes. In: Roedunet International Conference (RoEduNet), vol. 10(1), pp. 1–5 (2011)
5. Ma, Y.-X.: Characteristic analysis based on redis database. Internet Things Technol. **3**, 105–106 (2015)
6. Huang, J.-H.: The Design and Implementation of Redis. China Machine Press, Beijing (2014)
7. Redis cluster tutorial. http://redis.io/topics/cluster-tutorial

The Behavior Analysis of Product Negative Word-of-Mouth Spread on Sina Weibo

Yachu Liu and Yinghong Ma[✉]

College of Management Science and Engineering,
Shandong Normal University, Jinan, China
{lyclucky, msesdnu}@sina.com

Abstract. Now Weibo has become a new product information communication style and plays an increasingly important role in user's cognitive behavior. Besides, the online word of mouth is formed by user experience and idea. So in order to clarify Weibo WOM spread mechanism, we need to research the negative word of mouth spread behavior, and take some right solution for merchants. This article gathered negative product information and date from Sina Weibo, analyze the network model and use WeiboEvents analysis tool to research their network structure, get the spread characteristic. We expect it could take some help for the future develops on Weibo WOM.

Keywords: Word of mouth · Complete network · Small world characteristic · Spread behavior

1 Introduction

With the popular of Internet application, mobile terminal services, and social networking service application (online social networks, OSNs), now Sina Weibo, Renren, Facebook, Flickr, etc. have become the main platform for people to exchange, access and issue information. Users on OSNs sharing information and communicate with each other by unidirectional or bidirectional friends links. They are no longer audiences to receive information, but to actively participate in the network, to become producers of information, shares and disseminators.

Academic study of OSNs has a long time. Researchers initially focused on its static topology [1]. In terms of user behavior, Schneider et al. adopt network layer retrospective method, defining user conversation to study interactive behavior [2].

Based on user relationships, Weibo is a platform with information sharing, dissemination and access. Through WEB, WAP and a variety of clients, users can set up individual communities and achieve real-time information sharing.

Weibo as a kind of information transmission media, Since on-line in August 2009, Weibo has shown an unstoppable trend to be quickly accepted by public. The CNNIC published "The 35th times of China Internet network development state statistics report" [3] on February 3, 2015, showed that as of December 2014, micro-blog user scale has 249 million in China. Now, no matter government, stars, or common people, they have been accustomed to publish speech on Weibo. With its high degree of customer experience, transmission speed, the low technical threshold and cost, has

Q. Zu and B. Hu (Eds.): HCC 2016, LNCS 9567, pp. 284–295, 2016.
DOI: 10.1007/978-3-319-31854-7_26

become the focus of network marketing in the future. The vast number of users makes Weibo as an emerging market for companies.

Weibo users are both producers and consumers of information. With the seamless connectivity of mobile platform and Internet, the application of social networking service, and the transmission mode of network information has been greatly changed. So research Weibo network is helpful for us to learn the propagation characteristics of social network, use and control the spread of information, and it has provided a theoretical basis for corporate marketing and public opinion monitoring.

Usually, when users interested in some product information which published by their concerned objects, they can point to praise, comment or forward to their own homepage. With forwarding, a message can be presented to next level and increase the message visibility. With relevant product information published and propagate, it could form a positive and negative word of mouth, and users form a first impression with the product accordingly.

Weibo word of mouth research in China was started from 2011, the study mainly involves the form of product information, its value [4], marketing strategy [5], and the negative effects of Weibo information.

Foreign research was mainly by Ehrlich and Shami (2010) [6], they suggested that the Weibo negativity information about product often spread faster than positive. Aviles et al. (2011) [7] deemed that the Weibo has topic tag function. Park et al. (2011) empirically confirmed that the influence extent of audience and the trust will influence its spread on Twitter. Yu et al. (2012) [8] found out that the audience on the Sina Weibo is easier to forward kinds of information.

From above, most scholars research the topic unilaterally, such as effect, significance. Few of them use data analysis from the user's point to examine the attitudes held by ordinary users, and the valuence of public praise.

We use complex network analysis method on Sina Weibo, obtained data sets related to product information, and then build relational network and information dissemination model with visualization tool called WeiboEvents. Besides, we used SPSS and Matlab to analysis the property of the network, concluded that the network has both scale-free and small-world phenomenon. Since users forwarded Weibo could promote the dissemination of information and the spread is based on network, we constructed Weibo information transmission model on the basis of previous studies. In order to build the model, we center on the blogger who has published Weibo, through a cascade of communication to simulate the dynamic changes and access path information dissemination.

This paper is structured as follow. First, analyze the topological properties of Weibo network. Next, analyze a piece of authenticated user's negative Weibo with product information and get an idea of its effect. This part we study its main propagation path, forward number and exposure range. In Sect. 4, we search product information in different areas, infer the difference of concern degree and acceptance degree. This is benefit for us to understand the background of negative WOM. Finally we discuss the strategy of negative WOM spread about products on Weibo.

2 Topological Properties Analysis of Weibo Network

Dissemination of information between Weibo users mainly rely on user relationship, called "concern - be concerned" and "forward – dialogue". According to the complex network theory, we build network with users as nodes, and the relationship between users as edges.

Define the Weibo relation network as $G(V, E)$, V is node set, and E is edge set. If user A followed user B, then we got an arc from A to B. Use the Sina Weibo API interface, we got data with 70,220 nodes. The average of in-degree and out-degree are 21.01 and 21.30. Use Matlab to calculate the distribution of node-degree, cluster coefficient and average path length. Use origin to draw the cumulative degree distribution graphs, such as Figs. 1 and 2.

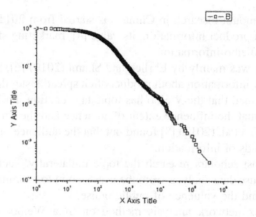

Fig. 1. The cumulative in-degree distribution of Weibo user forwarding network

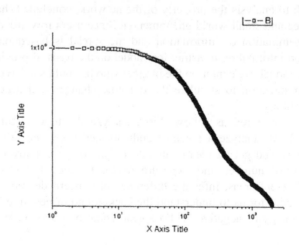

Fig. 2. The cumulative out-degree distribution of Weibo user forwarding network

The horizontal x axis is the number of the degree K in Weibo network, and the vertical y axis takes the percentage.

The distribution according to $p(\tau) \propto \tau^{-\gamma}$, in-degree $\gamma = 1.05$, out-degree $\gamma = 1.12$. This indicates that Weibo user concern network has scale-free characteristic and fat-tails.

Take any node i, k_i as the directly connected node number of i, E_i as the edge number connected with i. So there could exist $C_{k_i}^2$ edges. Define the cluster coefficient of node i as

$$C_i = \frac{E_i}{C_{k_i}^2} = \frac{2E_i}{k_i(k_i - 1)}.$$

The average path length means the average of the shortest length with any two nodes in the network. It could reflect network tightness. d_{ij} takes as the geometric distance from node i to j, P is the evolution probability.

$$l(p) = \frac{1}{\frac{1}{2}n(n+1)} \sum_{i \geq j} d(p)_{ij}.$$

Use Pajek, the cluster coefficient is 0.23, and the average path length is 4.6. The smaller average path length and the greater cluster coefficient indicate that Weibo network has typically small world characteristic.

3 Weibo with Product Information Spread Characteristics

Word-of-mouth is a form which transmits information through human verbal communication. Customer word-of-mouth research around the world has get the attention of scholars for a long time, customer satisfaction, customer loyalty and customer complaints is a main keywords in the field of customer word-of-mouth research. The Internet word of mouth (IWOM) refers that customers share their opinion about a product, service, brand or company via the Internet (such as forums, social networks, timely information, etc.).

Positive Weibo WOM information can attract more customers for the enterprise, but negative WOM information will also become the barriers in the development of enterprises.

Traditional communication methods, each unsatisfied customer may complain for 10 relatives or friends to spread negative impact on the enterprise, and there is a third in the ten friends or relatives will convey the negative information to the other 20 people. After two spread stages, the number of potential impact would reach 77. Today with Internet, the media channel has been increasingly developed. So how far negative information can be passed, and how many people can be effect is a new problem. This paper was studied based on this background.

When user's attention release Weibo with negative product information, the user usually does not take prize, the formation of negative WOM reflect on content and forwarding number.

3.1   Negative Word-of-Mouth About Product Information

In order to reveal the negative product information transmission characteristic, this paper selected a piece of representative Weibo published by "People's Daily" (concern number 1164, fans 38780702) at 9:50 on November 10, 2013. The content was the vacuum packing of Juewei and Zhou Black Duck has e. coli exceed bid. The Weibo has drawn widely attention once published. As of 17:43 on June 27, 2015, it received 10437 times forward and 2199 times comment.

This paper use WeiboEvents to research its visualization and describe the forward process. First, Figs. 1, 2 and 3 shows the transmission and diffusion process. We find out that with time goes, the forwarding number has a power law growth trend. The forward number rose sharply at the first 6 h, and then the speed has gradually slowdown. This is connected with celebrity often draw more attention than ordinary. Two days later, it reached the decay stage. This indicates that the life of Weibo is short. Ordinary information spread of Weibo undergoes six stages as latent, growth, spread, outbreak, decay and death.

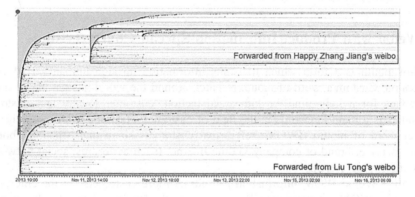

Fig. 3. Weibo diffusion trend - sail structure view

Set the expand threshold as 50, means that we only analysis users who was forwarded number at least 50. Figure 4 is the ring view.

According to Weibo forwarded number, summary the transmission node. The basic information of part nodes has shown in Table 1.

Although the authenticated user plays important role in the spread of information, but in forwarding nodes, authenticated user accounts for only 3 % of the total amount. This suggests that the cognitive subject of Weibo information is still a normal user.

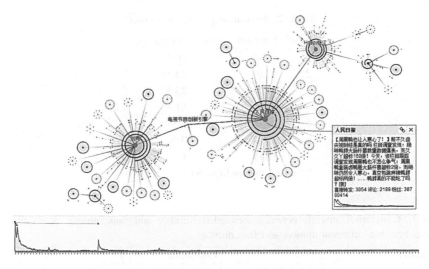

Fig. 4. Weibo diffusion trend - ring view

Table 1. Node forward quantity list

User name	Fans number	Forward number	Forwarded number
People's Daily	38780414	1	3054
Liu Tong	18641967	1	1555
Happy Zhang Jiang	5664658	1	818
Is CCTV finance true	465044	2	204
Nanchang railway	3505949	1	65
Li Xiaobei LBB	44	1	55
Y_yuhannen	36	1	55
Sunshine orange	161	1	53

In forwarding level, Table 2 shows forward hierarchy proportion. Expectations for this case, the average path length are 2.1. So in Weibo negative information transmission process, information publisher is the spread core and this is similar to traditional WOM. Besides, through the hierarchy of the proportion is easy to conclude that the forwarding behavior isn't endless. With the level increase, the percentages continuously decrease. The percentage almost to zero when forwarding level reach 6.

Meeyoung and Haned et al. (2010) researched that there is no direct relationship between high in-degree of user and large forwarding number on the Twitter platform. However, in this case, we analyzed the correlation between forwarding number and fans number with 101 nodes. In Table 3 we conclude that the correlation coefficient is 0.988, and the correlation is significant at the 0.01 level. On the analysis of the comments and fans, there has correlation between them and the correlation coefficient is 0.911. This means that the comment is also an important factor in the study of the IWOM (internet word of mouth).

Table 2. Forwarding level percentage[a]

Level	Forward number	Percentage
1	3054	40 %
2	1739	23 %
3	1926	25 %
4	809	11 %
5	109	1 %
6	19	0 %
Total	7656	1

[a] Expand threshold is 50

Table 3. Correlation analysis between forwarded number and fans number & Correlation analysis between comment number and fans number

Correlation		Forwarded number	Fans number	Correlation		Fans number	Comment number
Forwarded number	Pearson correlation	1	.988[**]	Fans number	Pearson correlation	1	.911[*]
	Sig. (2-tailed)		.000		Sig. (2-tailed)		.000
	N	101	101		N	101	101
Fans number	Pearson correlation	.988[**]	1	Comment number	Pearson correlation	.911[*]	1
	Sig. (2-tailed)	.000			Sig. (2-tailed)	.000	
	N	101	101		N	101	101

[**]. Correlation is significant at the 0.01 level (2-tailed).

Each level exist potential impact group, who have read the information but didn't take any operate on it, called Potential Impact User. They have effect for information diffusion below the line. Message Exposure Range refers to the total amount that who has read the Weibo or carried out a certain operation on it.

Due to the large amount of data for the selected sample, we estimate it as follow. Use another Weibo visualization tool called "Weiboreach", analyze 10 authenticated users and statistic their message exposure range. We found that the exposure rang is about 1.134 times to the number of total fans. The 10 authenticated users have 63410712 fans, so the exposure estimate about Weibo published by "People's Daily" was 71907747. Single look from exposure, this Weibo has spread very extensive.

In single weibo spread process, the forwarded or comment number of each forwarding node has positive correlation with its fans amount. Product negative IWOM transmission path graph is a topology network, and it has nodes with good information transmission which stay on the core position, while ordinary users are receiver. Over 6 levels, the forwarding percentage approach to 0, so the network has more obvious boundaries.

In summary, the original node in negative WOM communication process plays the most significant role, and it is unfavorable for the continued marketing.

3.2 Multi-Field Product Information Weibo Spread Characteristics

The above section has analyzed the spread characteristics about single product information Weibo, next we statistic negative product information published from March to June, 2015. We analyze forwarding number and comment number in different field. As ordinary Weibo's active period is short, so our sample is good to avoid active Weibo.

Use keyword targeting method to search negative WOM information from Sina database, and we got 2532 pieces Weibo which contained keywords "product, bad". After screening, total 278 pieces has pertinent to the topic. Classify the sample according to the industry, we have Table 4.

Table 4. Frequency table of sample with different industry

Classification	Frequency	Percentage	Mean of forwarded number	Mean of comment number	Std. deviation of comment number
Digital Product	94	33.81	4.61	11.16	29.69
Appliance	27	9.71	2.33	5.37	9.85
Food	24	8.63	5.63	8.33	13.09
Clothes	10	3.6	3.3	4.7	5.08
Home Building Materials	7	2.52	2.29	3.29	4.86
Vehicles & Spare Parts	11	3.96	4.71	9.43	16.53
Office Supplies	3	1.08	2.5	4.5	3.54
Daily Supplies	10	3.6	1	2	2.21
Entertainment	7	2.52	0.17	1	2
Beauty	17	6.11	3.12	9.06	18.1
IT Finance	49	17.63	2.39	3.33	4.02
Chemical Machinery	2	0.72	5.5	3.5	3.54
Service	17	6.11	0.94	5.53	8.08
Total	278	100	2.96	5.48	

From Table 4, Digital Product has the most prone with negative WOM, accounted for 33.81 % of the total sample size, namely electronic digital products is the hard-hit area to generate negative WOM. Also, IT finance is the second area to generate negative WOM. This indicates that these areas have much more topics, such as products qualities, management question, while users pay more attention on it.

Exclude an outlier; we analyze the means of forwarded number about 277 pieces Weibo in different industry. The results showed that food negative information has the largest forwarded number, reached 5.63 averages. Vehicles & Spare Parts ranked second, its negative WOM forwarded number has 4.71 averages. Digital products ranked third with 4.61. Meanwhile, these three categories also has large comment number mean, which all ranked top four. This is relationship with the frequent incidents about food safety, the vehicle as a means of transport, and electronic equipment for daily application equipment has integrated into the lives of people.

Since the samples showed quite different frequency in different industries about the willingness for customers to spread negative WOM, therefore, we need to take consistency test. Such as Table 5.

Table 5. Negative WOM spread preference in different industry

Test statistics	
	Frequence
Chi-Square	1.615^a
df	9
Asymp. Sig	.996

[a] 10 cells (100.0 %) have expected frequencies less than 5. The minimum expected cell frequency is 1.3

Therefore, on the Weibo platform exists the phenomenon that customers in certain industries are more willing to spread a negative WOM. We may consider that Weibo user presence information sensitivity in specific industries, especially for high-tech products. This requires that manufacturers should pay more attention on product negative IWOM and deal in probably way once problem occur.

In the same way, we find out that there was no sufficient evidence to prove the frequency of negative WOM in different industries related to the type of users. It means that ordinary user and authenticated user send negative information Weibo has no obvious differ for various industries. Or the sensitivity in different use is almost same. However, since the authenticated user universally has high concern degree, such users' remarks should cause manufacturers' attention.

3.3   The Number of Potential Impact

According to the sample statistical indicators distribution characteristics and statistic results, we predict the number that how many users can negative WOM Weibo directly and potentially affect in different industries.

The two measure indicators about the effect number of negative product information Weibo are forwarded number and comment number. Table 6 shows that

Table 6. Correlation analysis between forwarded number and comments number

Correlation		Forwarded number	Comment number
Forwarded number	Pearson correlation	1	.712**
	Sig. (2-tailed)		.000
	N	272	272
Comment number	Pearson correlation	.712**	1
	Sig. (2-tailed)	.000	
	N	272	272

**. Correlation is significant at the 0.01 level (2-tailed)

between forwarded number and comments number, correlation is significant at the 0.01 level, and the correlation coefficient is 0.712. Assume 0.712 is the forwarded number and comments number correlation coefficient of overall Weibo.

There may exist overlap between forwarding participants and commentators. The forwarded is easy to statistic by software, but how to deal with the overlap coefficient is difficult. This paper assume that there is a comment conversion factor α, used to measure people who has comment Weibo without forwarding. So the influence number by negative product information is

$$P = F + \alpha C$$

P is the direct influenced number, F is the forwarded number, C is the comment number, α is the comment conversion 0.712.

The direct influence number is the number who has responded directly. In negative product information area means the comment or forwarded node number. In different industry, the most widely direct influence number is 4, and the average is 6.

Besides, each level exist potential impact group, and the statistic method is different with one piece Weibo such as Chap. 3.1. Chapter 3.1 adopted the way to estimate the exposure rang, and this chapter we make potential impact number as directly affect number multiply with the average of each node's fans number.

$$I = P \times E(n)$$

I is the potential impact number, P is the direct influenced number, n is node's fans number.

Suppose each forwarded node has the same fans number with the origin publish node, then $E(n)$ is the average fans number with each origin node (Table 7).

In Table 7, appliance has the largest potentially affect number, and office supply is the second, digital product is the third. Such as Beauty has a large direct influence number, but it's potentially affect number is small. This is because Beauty has small percentage in authenticated user. Vehicles & Spare Parts has the similar phenomenon. Table 8 has illuminated that even has similar direct affect number between authenticate

Table 7. Contrast influence number table in different industry

Classification	Direct influence number	Fans number	Potentially affect number
Digital Product	12.56	5,416	68,025
Appliance	6.15	21,375	131,456
Food	11.56	3,571	41,281
Clothes	6.65	1,573	10,460
Home Building Materials	4.63	2,894	13,399
Vehicles & Spare Parts	11.42	230	2,627
Office Supplies	5.70	13,549	77,229
Daily Supplies	2.42	4,352	10,532
Entertainment	0.88	38,870	34,206
Beauty	9.57	125	1,196
IT Finance	4.76	6,793	32,063
Chemical Machinery	7.99	450	3,595
Service	4.88	332	1,620
Total	6.86	7,656	52,520

Table 8. Contrast table between affect number and user style

User	Authenticate user	Ordinary user	Total
Direct affect number	7.19	6.74	6.86
Fans number	46,474	868	7,656
Potential affect number	334,148	5,850	52,520

user and ordinary user, the former has over 50 times than the latter on fans number. So the former has almost 60 times than the latter on potential affect number.

4   Conclusion

Through the analysis about single Weibo negative WOM, we found that Weibo network has typically small world characteristic, forwarded number has obvious correlation with fans number, and so as comment number.

From multi-field product information Weibo, we concluded that a piece of negative WOM could directly influence 4 to 6 users, and potentially affect thousands of users. Users often pay more attention on technical negative information.

Thus, with the rapid growing internet, producer should pay more attention on product quality. When negative Weibo occurred, they could deal with the authenticate user properly.

These results only applied to Sina Weibo, and may has one-sidedness with the sample. How to statistic the influence about negative product WOM properly on different social platform is a new research direction.

Acknowledgments. This work was supported by the National Natural Science Foundation of China (No. 71471106), Specialized Research Fund for the Doctoral Program of Higher Education (20133704110003).

References

1. Mislove, A., Marcon, M., Gummadi, K.P., et al.: Measurement and analysis of online social networks. In: Proceedings of the 7th ACM SIGCOMM Conference on Internet Measurement, pp. 29–42. ACM, New York (2007)
2. Schneider, F., Feldmann, A., Krishnamur, B., et al.: Understanding online social network usage from a networking perspective. In: Proceedings of the 9th ACM SIGCOMM Conference on Internet Measurement, pp. 35–48. ACM, New York (2009)
3. CNNIC. The 35th times of China Internet development state statistics report, February 2015
4. Hu, Z.: The present situation and development trend of domestic blog advertising. Contemp. Commun. (5), 76–78 (2007)
5. Lu, J.: The microblogging propagation characteristics and the analysis of profit mode. J. Rev. (4), 58–62 (2010)
6. Schneider, F., Feldmann, A., Krishnamurthy, B., Willinger, W.: Understanding online social network usage from a network perspective. In: Proceedings of the ACM SIGCOMM Internet Measurement Conference, pp. 35–48. ACM Press, New York (2009)
7. Xu, T., Chen, Y., Fu, X., Hui, P.: Twittering by cuckoo: decentralized and socio-aware online microblogging services. In: Proceedings of the ACM SIGCOMM 2010 Conference, SIGCOMM 2010, pp. 473–474. ACM Press, New York (2010)
8. Diaz-Aviles, E., Siehndel, P., Naini, K.D.: Exploiting social #-tagging behavior in Twitter for information filtering and recommendation. In: 2011 Text Retrieval Conference (TREC), pp. 98–102. IEEE Press, Gaithersburg (2011)

A Node Localization Verification Model for WSN

Chunyu Miao[1,2], Guoyong Dai[1], Lina Chen[3], Hongbo Jin[1],
and Qingzhang Chen[1(✉)]

[1] College of Computer Science and Technology,
Zhejiang University of Technology, Hangzhou 310014, China
netmcy@zjnu.cn, daiguoyong@gmail.com,
qzchen@zjut.edu.cn
[2] College of XingZhi, Zhejiang Normal University, Jinhua 321004, China
[3] College of Mathematics, Physics and Information Engineering,
Zhejiang Normal University, Jinhua 321004, China
1013131850@qq.com

Abstract. Localization is one of the most important technologies in wireless sensor networks. Range-based localization methods are widely used in many applications. However, traditional RSS-based methods cannot work well in scenarios with unreliable anchors. A reputation scheme based distributed location verification model called UNDA is proposed to solve the unreliable node recognizing issue in such scenarios. UNDA combines direct reputation and third-party reputation to recognize unreliable anchor. Furthermore, a credibility-updating scheme is presented to make the third-party reputation more accuracy. Extensive simulation experiments indicate that the location verification algorithm has relatively high accuracy as well as low communication overhead, and the convergence of UNDA is rapid. The UNDA can be a used as an underlayer for traditional RSS-based localization algorithms to realize reliable localization.

Keywords: Wireless sensor networks · Localization · Location verification · Distributed reputation model

1 Introduction

Wireless sensor network (WSN) is a kind of ad hoc network. It is composed of a large number of battery-operated sensor nodes (we briefly call them sensor or node) with limited processing and communication capabilities [1]. With the proliferation of information technology like microelectronics, the usage of wireless sensor networks has gradually expanded from the military to various other fields, such as industry, agriculture, medicine, transportation, and so forth [2, 3]. The location of the sensor node is a pivotal context information for sensed data. Generally, the amount of sensor nodes is enormous, hence it is impractical to measure the location of each node ahead of schedule. Due to the high energy consumption and cost, it is prohibitive to equip each sensor node with global positioning system (GPS) and besides, GPS cannot be used in sheltered environment such as indoor scenarios. Therefore, we usually adopt some indirect method to estimate the locations of sensor nodes.

© Springer International Publishing Switzerland 2016
Q. Zu and B. Hu (Eds.): HCC 2016, LNCS 9567, pp. 296–309, 2016.
DOI: 10.1007/978-3-319-31854-7_27

In WSN, we call the location-aware nodes as anchors, and the others are normal nodes [4]. Normal nodes evaluate their locations by some mathematical methods using the locations of anchors as references. According to whether the localization process needs to measure the distance between nodes, the localization algorithms fallen into range-based localization algorithm [5] and range-free localization algorithm [6]. In general, range-based localization algorithms fulfill the localization by ranging the distances between nodes through their received signal strength indicator (RSSI), time of arrival (TOA) or angle of arrival (AOA) [7] and so on. Among them, RSSI-based ranging methods are of the most practical and applicable.

In traditional static wireless sensor networks, the use of anchor nodes with pre-defined location is pervasive to reduce the deployment cost. We assume that all nodes are stationary, so the predefined location information of all anchor nodes is reliable, but in practice, the nodes may move accidentally due to natural or human factors. They may also broadcast erroneous information because of malfunctions. Moreover, in a hostile environment, the anchors even may be compromised and deliberately provide incorrect location references. All this will cause great localization errors, which will degrade the quality of service (QoS) of the WSN. Therefore, in such scenario, we should consider the location verification to recognize the nodes with wrong location information.

In view of the scenario mentioned above, we propose a distributed lightweight node location verification model based on reputation scheme. A certain node determinates location reliabilities of its neighbors and find out the nodes with unreliable location information by integrating direct reputation and third-party reputations. Our contributions include: (1) a distributed location verification model is constructed to meet the requirement of reliable localization, (2) the proposed model provides relative high performance with low computational cost and communication overhead, (3) our proposed location verification model is ubiquitous, and it can be jointed with the ranging-based localization methods easily. The reminder of this paper is organized as follows: Sect. 2 gives a brief review to related work; problem modeling is given in Sect. 3; Sect. 4 provides a detailed description about the distributed reputation scheme; The location verification model is present in Sect. 5; Sect. 6 verifies the availability and the efficiency of the proposed algorithm by experiments, followed by conclusions and the future work in Sect. 7.

2 The State of the Art

At present, there are some works concentrating on reliable localization in WSNs, which can be divided into outlier tolerant schemes [8] and reliable anchor selection schemes [9]. The former are applicable in scenarios with small ranging disturbances. They mainly focus on mitigating the localization reference effects of unreliable anchors, but if there are large errors in the reference locations, the localization accuracy will be significantly degraded. Our research belongs to the latter, so we review the state of the art of this area below.

2.1 Reliable Localization Based on Anchor Filtration

With respect to the reliable localization using RSSI ranging, Beacon Movement Detection (BMD) proposed by Kuo et al. [10] is mainly used to identify the anchors whose location has been changed passively in the network. That is, constructing a BMD engine in the network to collect all the RSSI information, which can identify whether the location of anchors has changed within a certain tolerance range. Usually, this kind of centralized algorithm has heavy communication traffic and sink nodes or background computers with strong computing power are required as well, hence it is not suitable for large scale WSN networks. There are certain related works which verify the anchor location by introducing a hidden localization verification station [11], which is also a centralized algorithm. In [12, 13] rigidity theory is introduced to exclude outliers to provide reliable localization, however, rigidity theory requires pretty high ranging accuracy and it is computationally intensive. Garg et al. [14] proposed an anchor exclusion method by excluding the nodes who provided the largest gradient in the localization process to improve the reliability of localization, but they don't consider the reference effect of normal nodes, and the method is unsuitable for anchor sparse networks, and in addition, it is also computationally intensive. Reference [15] designs a reliable localization algorithm using a distributed reputation model, but they only take the observation of anchors into consideration result in poor performance in anchor sparse WSN. According to mutual observing information between neighbor nodes, Wei and Guan [16] formulated a probability model to implement location verification, which achieved relatively good results, but they didn't discuss the subsequent moved-node re-localization process. Literature [17] uses a RSSI-based distributed neighbor node scoring mechanism to identify drifted anchors, but it cannot be used in the case with compromised anchors.

2.2 Reputation Model

The concept of reputation is derived from social sciences and is used to denote credibility of certain object. Reputation scheme is widely adopted in various kind of node classification and data fusion thanks to its distributed and computational convenience. Sicari et al. introduced node reputation mechanism to improve the accuracy of data fusion. In [18], a relay node election scheme is proposed in mobile ad hoc network. It is used to recognize the selfish action of node to provide the optimal link-state protocol operating well. Srinivasan et al. present a distributed reputation model (i.e. DRBTS) to filter out the reliable anchors. It is the first time that reputation model is introduced to reliable localization. The main idea of DRBTS is anchor classifying based on integrating anchors' mutual observation. It reduces the influence arise from unreliable anchors in a concise manner, but the reputation scheme adopted by DRBTS is too simple to provide high robust and accuracy. He et al. similarly constructed an anchor reputation to recognize unreliable anchor including direct reputation only. Both of these reputation models mentioned above don't consider third-party reputation coming from normal nodes, so their performance in anchor sparse WSN is poor. As far as we known, we are the first ones to introduce a direct reputation and third-party reputation combined mode with comprehensive reputation update scheme for location verification.

3   Problem Presentation

The main notation used in this paper is listed in Table 1.

Table 1. Notation of variables

Variables	Meaning
m	Amount of anchor nodes
n	Amount of normal nodes
C_{anchor}	Real coordinate of anchor
C_{normal}	Real coordinate of normal node
C_e	Estimated coordinate of normal node
d_{ij}	Real distance between a pair of nodes
δ_{ij}	Ranging distance
$\hat{d}_{ij}$	Calculated pairwise distance based on estimated coordinate
Δ	Localization error
A_d	Collection of unreliable anchors
$Dij(t)$	Direct reputation
$Iij(t)$	Third-party reputation
$Cij(t)$	Recommended reputation
$S()$	Collection of direct neighbors
$Diff$	Reputation differential
STD	Reputation standard deviation
RTD	Relative reputation difference
α_j	Reputation weight
ω	Detection threshold

3.1   Problem Statement

According to whether a node knows its location in advance or not, WSN nodes fall into two classes: normal nodes and anchor nodes. Anchor nodes know their location, and normal nodes estimate their location based on the location of anchors through some mathematical method. The anchor cannot get its location by GPS in some shielded environments, so in general, the location is predefined manually. The localization accuracy of range-based methods is relatively high, and a distance measured via RSSI has no need for extra devices, so many works focus on RSSI-based ranging localization methods. In realistic static WSN, location of some nodes (including normal node and anchor) maybe changed due to natural or human factors. This mismatch between real location and nodes' knowledge leads a degradation of WSN's QoS. Several definition and assumption are present firstly.

Definition 1. Node Drifting: in some scenarios, there may be some nodes' locations that were moved passively, for example nodes moved by animals, and we call this kind of movement node drifting.

Definition 2. Anchor Drifting: some anchors broadcast wrong location reference because of location changing or malfunction, and we call this anchor drifting.

Definition 3. Malicious Nodes: Due to hardware malfunctions or for other reasons, some anchors broadcast wrong location reference information. Furthermore, in hostile environments, some anchors may be compromised to deliberately give other nodes wrong location references. We call these anchors malicious anchors.

We call drifted anchors and malicious anchors unreliable anchors because these anchors can cause a significant localization error. It should be noted that normal nodes can eliminate these effects by re-locating themselves periodically, but after drifting or being compromised, these anchors can produce large negative effects on normal nodes' localization process due to the location inconsistency between the claimed location and the real location of anchors. So, our objective is to recognize these unreliable anchors in such scenario.

The core issues and solution proposed in this paper are based on these assumptions listed below.

(1) All of the nodes in the network have the same communication radius, i.e., r, and the sensing model is an ideal circle.
(2) The pairwise ranging distances of (n_i, n_j) are unbiased, i.e. $\delta_{ij} = \delta_{ji}$.
(3) There are not collusions between these malicious anchors.
(4) All of the nodes can be drifted, but only the anchor nodes might be compromised.
(5) The proportion of unreliable nodes including drifted nodes and malicious anchors is lower than 50 %. Otherwise, we cannot recognize the unreliable nodes.

3.2   Problem Modeling

Let us assume that the total node number of a 2D deployed WSN is N. There are m anchors, denoted as $A = \{a_i : i = 1, \ldots, m\}$ and n normal nodes denoted as $S = \{s_i : i = 1, \ldots, n\}$, where $m + n = N$ and $m \ll n$. The coordinates of the anchors are $C_{anchor} = \{c_i : i = 1, \ldots, m\}, c_i = [x_i, y_i]$. The coordinates of the normal nodes are unknown, and we assume their coordinates are $C_{normal} = \{c_i : i = 1, \ldots, n\}$, $c_i = [x_i, y_i]$. C_r is collection of all nodes, i.e. $C_r = C_{anchor} \cup C_{normal}$. The pairwise distance of neighbor nodes is δ_{ij} which can be acquired by Eq. (1) in an ideal environment without noise-like errors is [7]:

$$\delta_{ij} = 10^{\frac{Rssi-E}{10n}} \tag{1}$$

where δ_{ij} denotes the pairwise distance, E and n are constants which are relevant to the antenna gain and environment. Using the measured distance, node n_i estimates its coordinates $C_e = [x_e, y_e]$ via a certain localization algorithm $f(\cdot)$. The real pairwise distance is $d_{ij} = ||c_i - c_j||; i, j = 1, \ldots, N$; Due to the measurement error, $\delta_{ij} = d_{ij} + d_{ij} \cdot noise_{ij}, noise_{ij} \sim \chi(0, \sigma^2)$ (normal distribution, mean is 0, variance is σ^2), results in $C_e \neq C_{anchor}$. According to C_e and C_{anchor}, we get the localization distance of a certain node denoted as $\hat{d}_{ij}$, $|d_{ij} - \hat{d}_{ij}| = \Delta$, where Δ is the localization error.

All of nodes may have drifted or been compromised after the whole network was deployed. Let us assume the proportion of drifted and compromised nodes is relatively small, that is, the number is p. These nodes denoted as $A_d = \{a_k : k = 1, \ldots, p, p \ll m\}$. The coordinates of anchors in collection A_d broadcast coordinates C'_{anchor}, which is different to their real coordinates C_{anchor}, i.e., $C_{anchor} \neq C'_{anchor}$. A larger localization error Δ will be introduced when the normal nodes re-estimate their coordinates using C'_{anchor}. We can design a location verification model $g(\cdot)$ to recognize unreliable anchors, i.e. $g(A) = A'_d$, where A'_d is output of $g(\cdot)$. Our objective is make A'_d approximate to A_d, i.e. $Min|A_d - A'_d|$.

4 Distributed Reputation Model

After the network was deployed and initial localization completed, each node calculates the reputation of its direct neighbor periodically to verify their location. The reputation R_{ij} is composed of direct reputation of node i to node j and the third-party reputation of node i to node j. Both of these two reputations' range are [0, 1). The location verification model is based on the calculation of reputation, so we first present the details of reputation calculation.

4.1 Direct Reputation

Definition 4. Direct reputation: The trust value of location between direct neighbor in WSN.

Let D_{ij} denotes the direct reputation of node i to node j. Every node calculates its direct neighbor's D_{ij} in each time slot. The calculation of direct reputation is based on ranging distance δ_{ij} and calculated pairwise distance $\hat{d}_{ij}$. D_{ij} in time slot t can be expressed as formula (2).

$$D_{ij}(t) = \begin{cases} 1 - \frac{|\delta_{ij}(t) - \min(r, \hat{d}_{ij}(t))|}{\delta_{ij}(t) + \min(r, \hat{d}_{ij}(t))} & node\ j\ was\ a\ direct\ neighbor\ of\ node\ i\ in\ last\ time\ slot \\ 0 & it\ is\ the\ first\ time\ that\ node\ i\ can\ hear\ node\ j \end{cases}$$

$$(2)$$

Although, there is an error item in δ_{ij}, it can represent relatively actual pairwise distance. According to formula (2), when a certain node yields a drift with relative large distance or there are some mismatches between actual location and broadcasted location, its direct reputation is decreasing. Formula (2) embodies the situation well that the smaller the pairwise distance is, the accurate of ranging distance is. Meanwhile, each node adopts the untrusted principal to new direct neighbor.

4.2   Third-Party Credibility

In WSN, each node has more than one direct neighbor due to the redundancy deployment. Let us assume node i and node j are a pair of direct neighbors, and $S_j(t)$ stands for the collection of direct neighbor of node j. Every single node in $S_j(t)$ can share its direct reputation for node j to other nodes as long as they broadcast the reputation to *2-hop* neighbors. For node i, after collecting reputations broadcasted by other nodes, it can calculate the third-party reputation of node j using formula (3).

$$I_{i,j}(t) = \frac{\sum C_{i,m}(t) \cdot R_{m,j}(t)}{\sum C_{i,m}(t)}, \ (m \in S_j(t) \cap m \neq i) \tag{3}$$

Where $R_{m,j}(t)$ stands for the reputation of node m to node j in time slot t,$C_{i,m}(t)$ denotes the recommended credibility of node m from perspective of node i in time slot t. $R_{m,j}(t)$ is defined as formula (4):

$$R_{m,j}(t) = D_{m,j}(t) \tag{4}$$

But, the calculation of $C_{i,m}(t)$ is relative complex, because we cannot get it from the perspective of node i directly. There is probably third-party reputation deterioration due to node drifting or unreliable anchor. As shown in Fig. 1, node $S5$ is drifted in time slot t, but the pairwise distance of node $S1$ and $S5$ is unchanged, so node $S5$ get a pretty high $D_{s1,s5}(t)$. While the distance change between node $S5$ and $S2(S4)$ leads a relative low direct reputation from S5 to S2(S4). Furthermore, because it is the first time that node $S5$ can hear node $S3$, the $D_{s5,s3}(t) = 0$. Finally, all of the reputations received by $S1$ from $S5$ to other nodes are essentially unreliable, but $S1$ trust $S5$ due to the relative high $D_{s1,s5}(t)$.

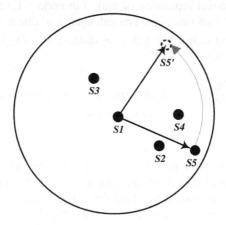

Fig. 1. Node drifting *vs* third-party reputation

In order to solve the problem mentioned above, we introduce Credibility updating scheme. Firstly, we need to calculate the node reputation difference Dif and relative reputation difference RRD using formulas (5) and (6) respectively.

$$Dif_{i(m,j)} = \sum_{k \in S(j)} |R_{k,j} - R_{m,j}| \Big/ |S(j)| \tag{5}$$

$$RRD_{i(m,j)} = Dif_{i(m,j)} / STD_j \tag{6}$$

Where $Dif_{i(m,j)}$ stands for reputation deviation form node m to node j, in node i's opinion. $|S(j)|$ denotes the cardinal of $S(j)$. STD_j represents the standard variance of reputation form all other nodes in $S(j)$ to node j. If the value of $RTD_{i(m,j)}$ is less than or equal to, node i considers the reputation of node m to node j is consistent with other nodes; otherwise, node i believes there is third-party reputation deterioration of node j. Updating process of $C_{i,m}(t)$ based on $RTD_{i(m,j)}$ is defined as formula (7).

$$C_{i,m}(t) = \begin{cases} C_{i,m}(t-1) + (1 - C_{i,m}(t-1))(1 - RTD_{i(m,j)}) & 0 < = RTD_{i(m,j)} < = 1, t > 0 \\ C_{i,m}(t-1)/RTD_{i(m,j)} & RTD_{i(m,j)} > = 1, t > 0 \\ D_{i,m}(t) & t = 0 \end{cases}$$

$$\tag{7}$$

The credibility updating scheme can degrade the negative effects aroused from node drifting and unreliable anchor in third-party reputation calculation.

4.3 Integrated Reputation

In time slot t, after node i got $D_{i,j}(t)$ and $I_{i,j}(t)$, the integrated reputation of node i to node j $T_{i,j}(t)$ can be calculated by formula (8).

$$T_{i,j}(t) = \alpha D_{i,j}(t) + (1 - \alpha)I_{i,j}(t) \tag{8}$$

Where α is reputation weight, its value determines the dependency level of direct reputation and third-party reputation. If the value of α is too large, and the node is moved itself, the performance of location verification will be declined; conversely, if the value of α is too small, the impact aroused from other nodes' Misjudgments is severe. The determination with respect to value of α is presented in Sect. 6.1 by simulation analysis.

5 Node Location Verification Model

We call this Location verification model UNDA (Unreliable Node Detection Algorithm). The main idea of UNDA is recognizing location unreliable nodes by each node's reputation in a distributed manner. After WSN deployed and initial localization completed, UNDA is conducted in each time slot. The procedure in each time slot is explained as follows:

Step 1: Each node calculates direct reputations (expressed as $D(t)$) of its neighbors.
Step 2: Each node broadcasts its $D(t)$ to 2-hop neighbors.
Step 3: After collecting $D(t)$, each node calculates relevant coefficient and integrated reputation of its neighbors.
Step 4: Each node proceeds location verification of itself and its neighbors based on a detection threshold ω.

Node who finds out itself drift can re-invoke certain location procedure using reliable anchors to calibrates its location. It should be noted that in the self-location verification process, node sets its reputation as 1, then utilizes the $RTD_{i(m,i)}$ to make judgement. If $RTD_{i(m,i)} > 1$, it determines the drift per se.

We give an example as illustrated in Fig. 2 (only part of the network is presented). Let us assume S6 is drifted (moved to S6') in time slot t and anchor B2 changes into unreliable anchor with a deliberately wrong location reference B2'. Assuming that the value of ω is 0.5. The two reputations of S1 and S3 to S6 are zero, because it is the first time that S1 and S3 can hear S6, that is $D_{S1,S6}(t) = 0$ and $D_{S3,S6}(t) = 0$. $D_{S4,S6}(t)$ is in the range of $(0,1)$ due to the changing of their relative location (0.6 for example). Although the value of $D_{S4,S6}(t)$ is greater than ω, but after integrating the third-party reputation $I_{S1,S6}(t)$ and $I_{S3,S6}(t)$ the $T_{S4,S6}(t)$ is less than ω significantly. Thereby, S4 recognizes S6 as drifted node successfully. In the same way, B2's neighbors can discover the mismatch between the actual location of B2 and its broadcasted location.

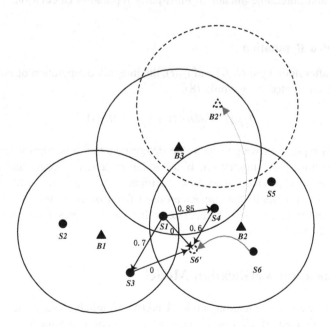

Fig. 2. Schematic diagram of location verification

6 Experiment Results and Analysis

Simulations are conducted in a square with 500 m × 500 m area. There are n normal nodes and m anchors that are deployed randomly. The interval of each pair of anchors is more than 5 m. The communication radius of each node is 50 m. After the deployment and the initial localization, there are p anchors changed to unreliable anchors, their location changes are more than 20 m, and among them, the proportion of compromised anchors is less than 45 %. Each experiment is conducted 20 times.

6.1 Determination of Detection Threshold

Some experiments with node various raining error are conducted to determine the value of ω. Where $m + n = 400$, and the proportion of m is 10 %. Both of the proportion of drifted node and the proportion of unreliable anchor are 20 %. Node ranging error is $[0.1*r, 0.3r]$, and stepsize is $0.1*r$. The recognition success rate (RS) and the recognition error rate (RE) are selected to evaluate the performance of our UNDA. The recognition success rate is a ratio of the number of nodes considered as unreliable to the number of actual unreliable nodes. The recognition error rate is a ratio of the number of nodes considered as unreliable nodes by erroneous judgment to the number of actual unreliable nodes. These two indicators are defined in formulas (9) and (10) respectively.

$$RS = |A_d \cap A'_d| / |A_d| \tag{9}$$

$$RE = |A_d - A'_d| / |A_d| \tag{10}$$

The simulation results are shown in Fig. 5. The RS decrease along with the ranging error increasing, while the RE increase obviously. The RS and RE are both increased with the increase of ω. While the ω is in the range of $[0.5, 0.7]$. The RS is increased significantly, and the RE is in a gently increase. To balance the false negative and the false positive, we set the ω as 0.7 in remainders of the experiments (Fig. 3).

6.2 Performance of UNDA

The algorithm in [17] is used to compare with our UNDA, because it also fulfills location verification in a distributed manner, and we call it NDD. However, by reason of the NDD adopts an idea that every node must participate in location verification initiatively, it cannot be applied in scenario with malicious anchor. Hence, there only is drifted node (including drifted anchor) in our experiments. There are a random number of drifted nodes per time slot, but the total amount of drifted nodes is fixed. Firstly, the number of drifted anchor is fixed (20 %) and the number of normal node varies from 100 to 400 with stepsize 50. The RS of these two algorithms increases as the node density increases, and the error rates of the two decline correspondingly. The reason is that the quantity of reference nodes is increased, but the recognition performance of UNDA is better than NDD as shown in Fig. 4. The reason is the recommended credibility updating scheme

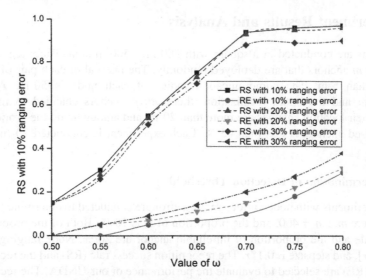

Fig. 3. Detection threshold *vs.* performance

introduced in UNDA can eliminate the negative effects of drifted nodes better. Whereas, each iteration of the NDD is a totally new process, so the performance cannot be improved along with the time accumulating. After that, the number of nodes is fixed as 400, and the amount of drifted anchors varies from 0 to 20. The performance comparison is shown in Fig. 5. Both of these two algorithms have relatively low success rate and relatively high error rate in the circumstance where the quantity of unreliable anchors is large. However, the performance of UNDA is relatively great. The reason also is the introduced recommended credibility updating scheme.

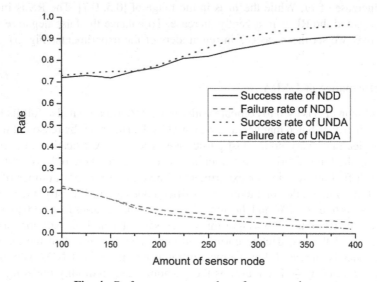

Fig. 4. Performance *vs.* number of sensor node

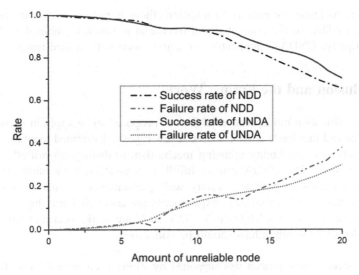

Fig. 5. Performance *vs.* number of unreliable anchor node;

6.3   Efficiency of UNDA

UNDA yields a better performance thanks to its credibility updating scheme which is a converging process of each node's knowledge about location of its neighbor. To verify convergence rate of UNDA, we count the number of being recognized as unreliable nodes in each time slot in the same scenario as Sect. 6.1. The amount of sensor node is set to 400, and the rate of drifted nodes and unreliable anchors is 30 %. The result is shown in Fig. 6. UNDA reaches the final consequence in time slot 3, and it has already yielded a pretty good performance in time slot 2. The reputation sharing process of UNDA is a limited broadcast, that is, in 2-hop range for each node. Let us assume the average network connectivity is N_c, the average communication overhead of each node

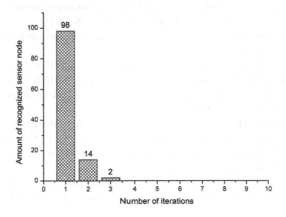

Fig. 6. Convergence performance of UNDA

is $O(N_c)$ due to linear correlation. In addition, there is not complex numerical computation in UNDA, so the computational overhead is small. Combined with its distributed property, UNDA is applicable for sensor node with limited resource.

7   Conclusion and the Future Work

A location verification model named UNDA is proposed to be apply in scenario with drifted nodes and unreliable anchors. UNDA leverages a distributed reputation scheme with comprehensive credibility updating mechanism to distinguish drifted nodes and unreliable anchors. The UNDA can be fulfill as a underlayer by other RSSI-based localization methods to provide a pretty well performance in such scenarios with location unreliable nodes. Extensive experiments are conducted and the results verify the performance and the availability of UNDA. In future work, location verification for range-free localization algorithms should be concerned.

Acknowledgments. This research was supported by Zhejiang Province Science Technology Department Public Welfare Technology Application Research Project (2015C33060), The National Natural Science Foundation of China (61379023) and Opening Fund of Zhejiang Provincial Top Key Discipline of Computer Science and Technology at Zhejiang Normal University, P.R. China (ZC323014074).

References

1. Akyildiz, F., Su, W., Sankarasubramaniam, Y., Cayirci, E.: Wireless sensor networks: a survey. Comput. Netw. **38**(4), 393–422 (2002)
2. Jang, W.S., Lee, D.E., Choi, J.H.: Ad-hoc performance of wireless sensor network for large scale civil and construction engineering applications. Autom. Constr. **26**(10), 32–45 (2012)
3. Hackmann, G., Sun, F., Castaneda, N., et al.: A holistic approach to decentralized structural damage localization using wireless sensor networks. Comput. Commun. **36**(1), 29–41 (2012)
4. Coluccia, A., Ricciato, F.: RSS-based localization via bayesian ranging and iterative least squares positioning. IEEE Commun. Lett. **18**(5), 873–876 (2014)
5. Safa, H.: A novel localization algorithm for large scale wireless sensor networks. Comput. Commun. **45**, 32–46 (2014)
6. Zhang, S., Liu, X., Wang, J., et al.: Accurate range-free localization for anisotropic wireless sensor networks. ACM Trans. Sens. Netw. (TOSN) **11**(3), 51 (2015)
7. Oliveira, L., Li, H., Almeida, L., et al.: RSSI-based relative localisation for mobile robots. Ad Hoc Netw. **13**, 321–335 (2014)
8. Zhong, S., Jadliwala, M., Upadhyaya, S., et al.: Towards a theory of robust localization against malicious beacon nodes. In: INFOCOM 2008, pp. 2065–2073 (2008)
9. Hwang, J., He, T., Kim, Y.: Detecting phantom nodes in wireless sensor networks. In: INFOCOM 2007, pp. 2391–2395 (2007)
10. Kuo, S.P., Kuo, H.J., Tseng, Y.C.: The beacon movement detection problem in wireless sensor networks for localization applications. IEEE Trans. Mob. Comput. **8**(10), 1326–1338 (2009)

11. Zeng, Y., Cao, J., Hong, J., et al.: Secure localization and location verification in wireless sensor networks: a survey. J. Supercomput. **64**(3), 685–701 (2013)
12. Yang, Z., Jian, L., Wu, C., et al.: Beyond triangle inequality: sifting noisy and outlier distance measurements for localization. ACM Trans. Sens. Netw. (TOSN) **9**(2), 26 (2013)
13. Yang, Z., Wu, C., Chen, T., et al.: Detecting outlier measurements based on graph rigidity for wireless sensor network localization. IEEE Trans. Veh. Technol. **62**(1), 374–383 (2013)
14. Garg, R., Varna, A.L., Wu, M.: An efficient gradient descent approach to secure localization in resource constrained wireless sensor networks. IEEE Trans. Inf. Forensics Secur. **7**(2), 717–730 (2012)
15. Srinivasan, A., Teitelbaum, J., Wu, J.: DRBTS: distributed reputation-based beacon trust system. In: 2nd IEEE International Symposium on Dependable, Autonomic and Secure Computing, pp. 277–283. IEEE (2006)
16. Wei, Y., Guan, Y.: Lightweight Location verification algorithms for wireless sensor networks. IEEE Trans. Parallel Distrib. Syst. **24**(5), 938–950 (2013)
17. Xia, M., Sun, P., Wang, X., et al.: Distributed beacon drifting detection for localization in unstable environments. Math. Prob. Eng. (2013)
18. Moati, N., Otrok, H., Mourad, A., et al.: Reputation-based cooperative detection model of selfish nodes in cluster-based QoS-OLSR protocol. Wireless Pers. Commun. **75**(3), 1747–1768 (2014)

Identification of Critical Variables for Soft Error Detection

Junchi Ma[1,2](✉) and Yun Wang[1,2]

[1] School of Computer Science and Engineering,
Southeast University, Nanjing 211189, China
bjbzmjc@126.com, yunwang@seu.edu.cn
[2] Key Laboratory of Computer Network and Information Integration,
Ministry of Education, Nanjing, China

Abstract. As process technology scales, electronic devices become more susceptible to soft error induced by radiation. *Silent data corruption* occurs without any symptoms and is the most severe result incurred by soft error. Duplication is the effective way to protect the program from soft error, but it has high overhead which is increasingly unacceptable for applications. Duplicating critical variables only can significantly reduce the overhead. This paper introduces an approach that identifying the variables which are critical to the execution of the program. We apply Dynamic Dependence Graph to analyze the propagation between instructions and find out the propagation path. The criticality of memory location is characterized and the criticality of each variable is then calculated. Fault injections show that with our approach the duplication achieves high detection rate with low overhead.

Keywords: Silent data corruption · Detection mechanism · Duplication · Soft error

1 Introduction

Radiation-induced errors caused by neutrons in cosmic rays or alpha particles in packaging material have provoked growing concerns [1]. The fault rate per device (e.g., latch, SRAM cell) in a bulk CMOS process is projected to remain roughly constant or decrease slightly for the next several technology generations. Thus, with the increase in the number of transistors on a chip and the reduction of chip sizes, fault rate will grow with Moore's Law [2].

The result of soft error is categorized into three kinds [1], *benign*, *detected unrecoverable errors* (DUE) and *silent data corruption* (SDC). *Benign* means the error is masked and DUE means the error is so serious that even it is detected the process cannot recover. When DUE occurs, the system is aware that the program is executed abnormally. Errors that incur wrong output of the program belong to SDC. Compared with *benign* and DUE, SDC is more insidious since it occurs without any symptoms. When SDC occurs, applications or even the entire spacecraft system can be affected, which may have catastrophic consequences. This paper focuses on eliminating SDC.

© Springer International Publishing Switzerland 2016
Q. Zu and B. Hu (Eds.): HCC 2016, LNCS 9567, pp. 310–321, 2016.
DOI: 10.1007/978-3-319-31854-7_28

In order to detect hardware faults, applying redundant hardware and software has been the usual solution. Owing to prohibitive overhead, detection mechanisms by hardware (like TMR [3]) are increasingly unacceptable for modern commodity systems. To alleviate the overhead, several software redundancy techniques have been proposed [4–7], which rely on duplication at instruction level. If the entire set of variables is duplicated, the resulting overhead can be unacceptable for some applications. Hence, trends have been set for adaptive and selective protection, which applies duplication to more susceptible variables.

A previous proposed technique to measure the criticality of the variables can be found in, which is based on the runtime analysis of variables' behavior. Instantaneous Criticality Function (ICF) is defined to represent the criticality of a variable at a given time. The criticality of variable across its lifetime is obtained by calculating the integral of ICF. ABM chooses critical variable by applying Dynamic Dependence Graph. Critical variable are variables with the highest fan-outs in the DDG. Errors in these variables are likely to propagate to many locations in the program.

Previous techniques find the variable that affects the execution of program. However, they are not geared towards the errors incur SDC. For SDC, the variable that involves output is more critical than others. A soft error will produce an SDC if there exists a propagation path to the output. Therefore, data propagation is used to analyze SDC causing fault.

In this paper, we propose an approach to identify critical variable for incurring SDC in the presence of soft errors. First, we analyze fault propagation of SDC using Dynamic Dependence Graph and find the entire propagation path. The criticality of memory location is then calculated backwards from those involve output. During the calculation, error masking is also considered to eliminate the paths that incur *benign*. Digital characteristics and semantic of the instruction is used to estimate the probability of error masking. The criticality of variable is calculated by averaging the criticality of memory locations involves the variable across its lifetime. Duplications are deployed to the critical variables and detection rate is evaluated by fault injections. Experiments show that our method achieves better detection rate for SDC than previous techniques.

Our main contribution is an algorithm to choose variables that are critical to the output of the program. The chosen variables should be paid special attention in the protection than other variables.

The remainder of this paper is structured as follows: firstly, the criticality of memory location and write and read operation are defined. Secondly, an algorithm for criticality calculation is given. Thirdly, the calculation of error masking parameter is characterized; the experimental results are then presented. Finally, the last section summarizes and concludes this work.

2 Model

We apply Dynamic Dependence Graph to analyze fault propagation. Dynamic Dependence Graph is a directed-acyclic graph that captures the dependencies among values produced in the course of program execution. The Dynamic Dependence Graph is defined as a tuple $G = (V, E)$. V is the set of instruction nodes, $V = \{i0, i1 \ldots in\}$.

Each instruction is given as a tuple I = (Os, Od, Pre, Suc). Os and Od denote the set of source and destination operand. Pre and Suc denote the set of predecessors and successors instructions in the DDG. E is the set of edges that denote dependencies between instructions, when ij reads the value produced by ik, there should be an edge $i_k \rightarrow i_j$.

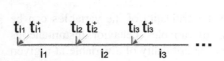

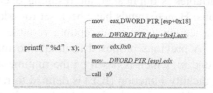

Fig. 1. Time system based on instruction execution

Fig. 2. An example of printf function

We also make a little change on conditional jump instruction in the DDG. Conditional jump influences the consequent block, thus the conditional jump node is set as the predecessor of nodes in the next block. Variable is stored in memory location and invoked by loading the value to Os. A tuple (u, t) denotes a memory location u at a given time t of the program execution. We use $v \triangleright (u, t)$ where $v \in \{$set of variable of the program$\}$ to denote that the variable v is stored in the memory location u at the moment t. The lifetime of a variable is defined as the time period in which the variable is allocated in memory.

The time system is based on the execution sequence of instructions. The index of instruction denotes the sequence number of execution. For example in Fig. 1, $i1$ is the first dynamic instruction. $t_{i_1}^+$ is the moment when $i1$ is about to be executed, and t_{i_2} is the moment just after $i1$ is executed.

The criticality of a memory location $\delta(u, t)$ is defined to estimate the effect on the final result when the memory unit u is corrupted at the moment t. And the criticality of variable $\delta(v)$ is defined by Eq. 1. $\delta(v)$ is calculated by averaging all the $\delta(u, t)$ that related to v across its lifetime.

$$\delta(v) = \frac{1}{|v.lifetime|} \int \delta(u,t)dt, \quad v \triangleright (u,t) \tag{1}$$

First of all, the final result is dominated by the printf, cout or other kinds of output function. To incur an SDC, the printed contents, which is the data of print function, must be corrupted. We consider the propagation to the instruction which write the destination operand of printf. Figure 2 shows an example of printf function. The mov instruction that load parameters of printf function is defined as set I_p. The underlined instructions which move parameters to the call stack of print function belong to I_p) is set to 1, where $u \in i_p.O_s \wedge i_j \in I_p$, as shown in Eq. 2. The value is just a baseline for other criticality, which is calculated by estimating the possibility that its error propagates to I_p.

$$\delta\left(u, t_{i_j}^{+}\right) = 1, \quad u \in i_p.O_s \wedge i_j \in I_p \tag{2}$$

To obtain $\delta(v)$, we need to calculate $\delta(u, t)$ where $t \in v.lifetime$. Supposing ik is the consequent instruction that reads or writes the memory location holding the valuable v after ij. We categorize the calculation into two situations depending on whether the operation of ij is read or write.

2.1 The Criticality of Write Operation

$$\delta(u, t) = \begin{cases} 0 & t_{i_j} < t < t_{i_{j+1}} \\ \sum_{i_k \in ij.suc} \delta\left(u, t_{i_k}^{+}\right).P\left(i_k | i_j\right) & t = t_{i_{j+1}} \end{cases} \tag{3}$$

Equation 3 computes the criticality of u as destination operand, where $u \in i_j$. $O_d \wedge u \in i_k.O_s$. During the execution of ij ($t_{i_j} < t < t_{i_{j+1}}$), the criticality of u during the execution is set to 0, since the old data is refreshed after the write operation and error cannot affect its successors. When u is corrupted after a write operation, all of its successors use the wrong value of u. Thus, error in u propagates through the successors. The criticality of u as destination operand equals to sum of the source operand of its successors' criticality. The execution probability $P(ik|ij)$ is also considered to leverage the often executed instruction.

Equation 4 calculates the criticality of period that after ij's execution and before ik's execution. The calculation is performed based on ik's operation.

1. ik reads u. $\delta(u, t)$ is set to $\delta\left(u, t_{i_{j+1}}\right)$ before the ik reads u, since erroneous u can propagate to ij's successors.
2. ik writes u. u is refreshed by ik, thus erroneous u will be masked and $\delta(u, t)$ is set to 0.

$$\delta(u, t) = \begin{cases} \delta\left(u, t_{i_{j+1}}\right) & t_{i_{j+1}} < t < t_{i_k} \wedge u \in i_k.O_s \\ 0 & t_{i_{j+1}} < t < t_{i_k} \wedge u \in i_k.O_d \end{cases} \tag{4}$$

2.2 The Criticality of Read Operation

Equation 5 computes the criticality of us as source operand, where $u \in i_j.O_s \wedge u_d \in i_j.O_d$. Error in the source operand doesn't always incur a wrong destination operand. We introduce Pm to denote the probability of error masking. If $Pm = 1$, i.e. error masking must happen, $\delta(us, t) = 0$ since error in us has no impact on u_d. Here we mainly consider error masking of some kinds of logical and branch instructions, i.e. *and, or, cmp* instructions and discuss it in subsequent section.

$$\delta(u, t) = \delta\left(u_d, t_{i_{j+1}}\right)\left(1 - P_m\left(i_j\right)\right) \quad t_{i_j} < t < t_{i_{j+1}} \tag{5}$$

Equation 6 calculates the criticality of period that after ij's execution and before ik's execution. We also categorize the calculation into two situations.

1. ik reads u. $\delta(u, t)$ is set to $\delta(u, t_{i_k}^+)$, since erroneous u can propagate to ik.
2. ik writes u. u is refreshed by ik, thus erroneous u will be masked and $\delta(u, t)$ is set to 0.

$$\delta(u, t) = \begin{cases} \delta(u, t_{i_k}^+) & t_{i_{j+1}} \leq t < t_{i_k} \wedge u \in i_k.O_s \\ 0 & t_{i_{j+1}} \leq t < t_{i_k} \wedge u \in i_k.O_d \end{cases} \tag{6}$$

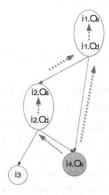

Fig. 3. Criticality computation diagram. The red dotted line points out the direction of iteration. The yellow node $i4$ belongs to Ip. (Color figure online)

2.3   The Algorithm to Calculate Criticality

The algorithm is shown in Algorithm 1. We traverse the path from Ip in the DDG. The algorithm has two phases. The first phase is from line 1 to 10, the nodes which have a path to Ip in the DDG are found and they are included in L. The criticality of nodes in L is calculated in the second phase.

The second phase starts from the node that belongs to Ip and it goes along the edge backward. For nodes in Ip, $\delta\left(u, t_{i_j}^+\right)$ is assigned 1. M includes the nodes that have been traversed, and is initialized as Ip. L contains the nodes that need to be traversed. Each time it pop a node in L, if the nodes' successors have already been calculated it's ready for calculation. The criticality of current node's destination operand and source operand are calculated by using the aforementioned equations. Then the node finishes calculation is put into M. The iteration continues until L is empty. As the last step, we calculate the criticality of variables in the program by Eq. 2.

An example is shown in Fig. 3, which shows a snippet of DDG. There are 4 nodes and $i4 \in Ip$. The calculation starts by setting $\delta\left(i_4.O_s, t_{i_4}^+\right) = 1$. The order of calculation should be $\delta\left(i_4.O_s, t_{i_4}^+\right) \rightarrow \delta\left(i_2.O_d, t_{i_3}\right) \rightarrow \delta\left(i_2.O_s, t_{i_2}^+\right) \rightarrow \delta\left(i_1.O_d, t_{i_2}\right) \rightarrow \delta\left(i_1.O_s, t_{i_1}^+\right)$. $i3$ is not traversed since no path to $i4$ is found from $i3$.

2.4   Estimation of Error Masking Parameter *Pm*

Un-ACE bits analysis aims to find the bits that don't influence the system output. In, all bits of NOP instructions, dynamic dead instructions, etc. are considered as Un-ACE bits. These bits are analyzed to have no impact on the output in this paper too. For example, dynamic dead instructions whose results are not used have no successors in the DDG, thus their criticality is not defined.

Algorithm 1. The algorithm to calculate criticality

Input: I_p
Output: $\delta(v)$
1: $M \leftarrow I_p$;
2: **while** $M \neq \varnothing$ **do**
3:     $i_j = M{:}pop$;
4:     **for all** $i_k \in i_j.Pre$ **do**
5:        **if** $i_k \notin L$ **then**
6:            $L = L \cup i_k$;
7:            $M = M \cup i_k$;
8:        **end if**
9:     **end for**
10: **end while**
11: **for all** $i_j \in I_p$ **do**
12:    $\delta\left(u, t_{i_j}^+\right) \leftarrow 1,\ u \in i_j.O_s \wedge i_j \in I_p$
13: **end for**
14: $M \leftarrow I_p$;
15: **while** $L \neq \varnothing$ **do**
16:     **for all** $i_j \in L$ **do**
17:        **if** $i_j{:}Suc \subset M$ **then**
18:           calculate $\delta(u,t)$ by Eq.3-6
19:           $L \leftarrow L \setminus i_j$;
20:           $M \leftarrow M \cup i_j$;
21:        **end if**
22:     **end for**
23: **end while**
24: **for all** $v \in \{$set of variables of the program$\}$ **do**
25:    calculate $\delta(v)$ by Eq.2.
26: **end for**

Error masking of some kinds of logical and branch instructions, i.e. *and, or, cmp* instructions is discussed in this section. For example, and x, 3(00000011) which means $x \leftarrow x\&00000011$. Error in the 7th-2nd bit of x is masked since the bits are 0, and no matter what is in these bits of x the result will be 0. Error masking often occurs in the program. It has been observed that about 40 % of all dynamic conditional branches don't influence the output. Therefore it is necessary to characterize error masking for criticality calculation.

In order to calculate *Pm*, data traces of instructions are extracted and masking bits of the destination operand of those instructions are identified. Here we analyze the type of unsigned integer and suppose that number of operand obeys uniform distribution. An unsigned integer has 32 bits, maximum value is $2^{32} - 1$ and minimum value is 0.

$f_0^k(a_1, a_2), f_1^k(a_1, a_2)$ are defined in Eqs. 7, 8, where $0 \leq a_1 < a_2 \leq 2^{32}$, $0 \leq k \leq 31$, and x_k denotes the kth bit of x. $f_0^k(a_1, a_2)$ counts how many times the kth bit is 0 from a_1 to $a_2 - 1$, and $f_1^k(a_1, a_2)$ counts how many times the kth bit is 1.

$$f_0^k(a_1, a_2) = \sum_{x=a_1}^{a_2-1} (1 - x_k) \tag{7}$$

$$f_1^k(a_1, a_2) = \sum_{x=a_1}^{a_2-1} x_k \tag{8}$$

Given $f_0^k(0, a_1)$ and $f_0^k(0, a_2)$, $f_0^k(a_1, a_2)$, $f_1^k(a_1, a_2)$ can be easily calculated by Eqs. 9, 10. The computation of $f_0^k(0, a)$ is discussed in Eq. 11, and the proof of Eq. 11 is given below.

$$f_0^k(a_1, a_2) = f_0^k(0, a_2) - f_0^k(0, a_1) \tag{9}$$

$$f_1^k(a_1, a_2) = a_2 - a_1 - f_0^k(0, a_2) + f_0^k(0, a_1) \tag{10}$$

$$f_0^k(0, a) = p_1 + p_2 + p_3 \tag{11}$$

$$p_1 = \left\lfloor \frac{a}{2^{k+1}} \right\rfloor . 2^k \tag{12}$$

$$p_2 = a\%2^{k+1} - a\%2^k \tag{13}$$

$$p_3 = \left(1 - \frac{p_2}{2^k}\right) . a\%2^k \tag{14}$$

Proof: The kth bit from 0 to $a - 1$ repeats in a cycle whose length is 2^{k+1}. Taking 0 to 8 as an example, the cycle length of 0th bit is 2, the cycle length of 1st bit is 4. The kth bit of the last number $a - 1$ is either 0 or 1. When ended with 0, the kth bit from 0 to $a - 1$ is $\underbrace{00...011...1}_{2^{k+1}} \underbrace{00...011...1}_{2^{k+1}} ... \underbrace{00...0}_{\leq 2^k}$; otherwise, the kth bit is $\underbrace{00...011...1}_{2^{k+1}} \underbrace{00...011...1}_{2^{k+1}} ... \underbrace{00...0}_{2^k} \underbrace{11...1}_{\leq 2^k}$.

In Eq. 11, p_1 equals the total number of zeroes in all cycles, for 2^k is the number of zeroes in one cycle and $\left\lfloor \frac{a}{2^{k+1}} \right\rfloor$ is the number of cycles. Furthermore, p_2 and p_3 calculate the number of residual zeroes out of cycles. Supposing the number of zeroes out of cycle is n_0. We just need to proof that $p_2 + p_3 = n_0$ in both situations (ending with zero or one).

Ending with 0. $n_0 = a\%2^{k+1} = a\%2^k$, $p_2 = 0$, $p_3 = a\%2^k = n_0$ ∴ $p_2 + p_3 = n_0$.

Ending with 1. $n_0 = 2^k$, $p_2 = 2^k$, $p_3 = 0$ ∴ $p_2 + p_3 = n_0 \square$

For logical instructions, *and, or, cmp* instructions are discussed below. $N(A)$ denotes the number of occurrence of event A.

1. and x, y

   and x, y instruction performs logic calculation that x bitwise-and y. Whenever $y_k = 1$ or $y_k = 0$, if $x_k = 0$, the result remains the same. $N(x_k = 0) = \sum_0^{31} f_0^k(x_{min}, x_{max} + 1)$ $\therefore P_m = \dfrac{\sum_{k=0}^{31} f_0^k(x_{min}, x_{max} + 1)}{32(x_{max} - x_{min} + 1)}$

2. or x, y

   or x, y instruction performs logic calculation that x bitwise-or y. whenever $y_k = 1$ or $y_k = 0$, if $x_k = 1$, the result remains the same. To conclude, $P_m = \dfrac{\sum_{k=0}^{31} f_1^k(x_{min}, x_{max} + 1)}{32(x_{max} - x_{min} + 1)}$.

Figure 4 shows the *Pm* of *and, or* instruction given *xmin, xmax*. We set the interval of x, i.e. *xmax* $-$ *xmin* $+ 1$, as 32. The *Pm* of *and* instruction decreases in general. Since the sum of the *Pm* of *and, or* instruction equals 1, the *Pm* of *or* instruction increases along the opposite trend of *and* instruction.

Cmp instructions are always followed by conditional jump instruction. Based on the conditional flag produced by cmp instruction, the conditional jump instruction takes a particular branch. We analyze the error masking by enumerating each type of the conditional jump instruction.

1. *ja*

   If $x > y$, it takes the next instruction, else falls through.

   (1) when $x \le y_{min} \le y$

       (a) $y_k = 0$, $y' = y + 2^k \ge x$

       (b) $y_k = 1$, $y' = y - 2^k \ge x \therefore y \ge x + 2^k$

   $$N(x < y_{min} \le y) = \sum_{x = x_{min}}^{min(y_{min}, x_{max})} \sum_{k=0}^{31} \left(f_0^k(y_{min}, y_{max} + 1) + f_1^k(max(x + 2^k, y_{min}), y_{max} + 1) \right)$$

   (2) when $y_{min} \le x \le y \le y_{max}$

       (a) $y_k = 0$, $y' = y + 2^k \ge x$

       (b) $y_k = 1$, $y' = y - 2^k \ge x \therefore y \ge x + 2^k$

   $$N(y_{min} \le x \le y \le y_{max}) = \sum_{x = max(y_{min}, x_{min})}^{min(x_{max}, y_{max} - 1)} \sum_{k=0}^{31} \left(f_0^k(x, y_{max} + 1) + f_1^k(x + 2^k, y_{max} + 1) \right)$$

   (3) when $y_{min} \le y < x \le y_{max}$

       (a) $y_k = 0$, $y' = y + 2^k < x \therefore y < x - 2^k$

       b) $y_k = 1$, $y' = y - 2^k < x$

   $$N(y_{min} \le y < x \le y_{max}) = \sum_{x = max(y_{min} + 1, x_{min})}^{min(y_{max}, x_{max})} \sum_{k=0}^{31} \left(f_0^k(y_{min}, x - 2^k) + f_1^k(y_{min}, x) \right)$$

   (4) when $y \le y_{max} < x$

       (a) $y_k = 0$, $y' = y + 2^k < x \therefore y < x - 2^k$

       (b) $y_k = 1$, $y' = y - 2^k < x$

$$N(y \le y_{max} < x) = \sum_{x=\max(y_{max}+1,x_{min})}^{x_{max}} \sum_{k=0}^{31} \left(f_0^k \left(y_{min}, \min(x - 2^k, y_{max} + 1) \right) + f_1^k (y_{min}, y_{max} + 1) \right)$$

$$\therefore P_m = \frac{N(x \le y_{min} \le y) + N(y_{min} \le x \le y \le y_{max}) + N(y_{min} \le y < x \le y_{max}) + N(y \le y_{max} < x)}{32(x_{max} - x_{min} + 1)(y_{max} - y_{min} + 1)}$$

2. jb

If $x < y$, it takes the next instruction, else falls through. Given space limitations, here we only show the results.

(1) when $x < y_{min} \le y$

$$N(x < y_{min} \le y) = \sum_{x=x_{min}}^{\min(x_{max}, y_{min} - 1)} \sum_{k=0}^{31} \left(f_0^k (y_{min}, y_{max} + 1) + f_1^k \left(\max(y_{min}, x + 2^k + 1), y_{max} + 1 \right) \right)$$

(2) when $y_{min} \le x < y \le y_{max}$

$$N(y_{min} \le x < y \le y_{max}) = \sum_{x=\max(y_{min}, x_{min})}^{\min(y_{max}-1, x_{max})} \sum_{k=0}^{31} \left(f_0^k (x + 1, y_{max} + 1) + f_1^k (x + 2^k + 1, y_{max} + 1) \right)$$

(3) when $y_{min} \le y \le x \le y_{max}$

$$N(y_{min} \le y \le x \le y_{max}) = \sum_{x=\max(y_{min}, x_{min})}^{\min(y_{max}, x_{max})} \sum_{k=0}^{31} \left(f_0^k (y_{min}, x - 2^k + 1) + f_1^k (y_{min}, x + 1) \right)$$

(4) when $y \le y_{max} \le x$

$$N(y \le y_{max} \le x) = \sum_{x=\max(x_{min}, y_{max})}^{x_{max}} \sum_{k=0}^{31} \left(f_0^k \left(y_{min}, \min(y_{max} + 1, x - 2^k + 1) \right) + f_1^k (y_{min}, y_{max} + 1) \right)$$

$$\therefore P_m = \frac{N(x < y_{min} \le y) + N(y_{min} \le x < y \le y_{max}) + N(y_{min} \le y \le x \le y_{max}) + N(y \le y_{max} \le x)}{32(x_{max} - x_{min} + 1)(y_{max} - y_{min} + 1)}$$

jae, jbe which considers the situation of equal could be analyzed in similar ways.

3   Experimental Results

The fault model we assume is a single bit flip within the register file or memory. Fault in the opcode is not considered, since it always causes illegal opcode exception rather than SDC. The injection is done by altering a randomly selected bit in the destination operand. It is also assumed that the control flow is protected using techniques like basic block signature. In our experiments, we employ the dynamic instrument tool Pin for fault injection. Pin is a dynamic binary instrumentation framework for the IA-32 and x86-64 instruction-set architectures that enables the creation of dynamic program analysis tools.

The benchmarks studied here are the Siemens suite of programs. The Siemens programs considered are schedule, schedule2 (which are priority schedulers), print tokens, print tokens2 (which perform lexical analysis) and tcas (which decides the action of aeroplane system). These are C programs consisting of a few hundred lines of C code and each is equipped with extensive test suite. The benchmarks only contain console output and their outcomes are printed by the function printf. The outcome is compared with that of fault-free execution. If any divergence is found, the execution is categorized as SDC. We do not consider faults from system calls and library function calls and faults in floating point registers.

Dependencies among instructions are obtained by recording the data log of each instruction. Each log contains the tag of instruction (sequence number of dynamic instruction, name of operand, etc.) and the value of operand before the execution and after the execution. The DDG is constructed by applying the scheme in.

$P(ik|ij)$ in Eq. 3 is evaluated by "-ftest-coverage -fprofile-arcs" option provided by gcc. All the test plans of the benchmark are implemented to get the complete profiling information of branch execution probability.

The effectiveness of the duplication is validated by fault injections. We apply our own tool developed in Pin to generate logs of the instructions that accesses those critical variables. The values of the critical variables are compared with that of the golden run. If the values are different, it denotes a successful detection. In addition, we don't compare variable that represents address, since in each execution the address allocated is always different.

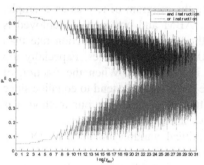

Fig. 4. *Pm* of *and, or* instruction

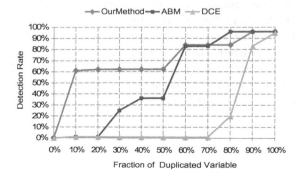

Fig. 5. Detection Rate of SDC via Variable Duplication

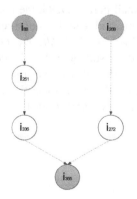

Fig. 6. DDG Example of tcas

Fig. 7. Comparison of Detection Rate with ABM and DCE

3.1 Detection Rate

Figure 5 shows the detection rate of SDC for different fractions of duplicated variables. The variables are sorted by their criticality and each fraction (10 %–100 %) of variables according to their rankings is duplicated. The total average detection rate for all benchmarks studied here is 84.6 %. Even the fraction of duplication reaches 20 %, the detection rate is pretty high, which reaches 71.8 %.

3.2 Comparison with Related Work

The average detection rate of DCE is 68.6 %, and that of ABM is 75.8 %. DCE applies Instantaneous Criticality Function (ICF) to represent the criticality of a variable at a given time. ICF changes when an instruction reads or writes the variable. For a read event, ICF increases by a constant β. For a write event, ICF remains constant. The criticality of variable across its lifetime is obtained by calculating the integral of ICF. ABM applies Dynamic Dependence Graph and the variables with the highest fan-outs are selected as critical variables.

Our method achieves higher detection rate because the propagation of SDC is analyzed and used to deploy duplication. We take the program of tcas as an example. The fault injection campaign of tcas with DCE, ABM and our method deployed is shown in Fig. 7, it could be found that our method has a higher detection rate than other two methods when duplicating the first 60 % critical variables. Especially top 10 %–50 %, the advantage is easy to observe in the figure. When the fraction of duplicated variable rises, the detection rates of the three methods tend to equalize since the duplication is gradually close to full-scale. It is clear that with our method it is possible to reach higher dependability using a low amount of redundancy.

To get insight to the duplication, the most critical variable obtained by DCE is *Positive_RA_Alt_Thresh[3]*. The variable is initialed at the beginning of the program, read many times and destroyed in the end. According to DCE, the variable has a long lifetime and its ICF increases each time when it is read.

The node which has highest fan-outs in the DDG is considered the most critical by ABM, and *Own_Tracked_Alt* is most critical in tcas. The most critical variable obtained by own method is *need_upward_RA*. Figure 6 presents a small part of DDG, the relationships among the three variable identified by each method can be observed. $(i_{88}.O_d, t_{89}) \triangleright Positive\_RA\_Alt\_Thresh[3]$, $(i_{268}.O_d, t_{i_{269}}) \triangleright Own\_Tracked\_Alt$, $(i_{355}.O_d, t_{i_{356}}) \triangleright need\_upward\_RA$. Furthermore, $i88$ and $i268$ are predecessors of $i355$ and there are some intermediate nodes between them. Error of $i88$ or $i268$ may not propagate to $i355$ since error masking occurs in the intermediate nodes. From the point of criticality obtained by our method, $\delta(i355, ti356)$ (0.80) is higher than $\delta(i88, ti89)$ (0.0017) and $\delta(i268, ti269)$ (0.00057).

4 Conclusion

This paper presents an approach that seeks to find the critical variable for the execution of the program. We use DDG to analyze the fault propagation between instructions. Each memory location is characterized first and their related variable's criticality is defined as the integral across its lifetime. Experimental results show that our approach achieves high detection rate when duplicating the critical variables.

Our approach can help to derive detectors for applications. Future work will involve integrating our approach into a compiler and automatically deriving the actual detectors for checking.

References

1. Mukherjee, S.S., Emer, J., Reinhardt, S.K.: The soft error problem: an architectural perspective. In: 11th International Symposium on High-Performance Computer Architecture, HPCA-11, pp. 243–247. IEEE (2005)
2. Racunas, P., Constantinides, K., Manne, S., Mukherjee, S.S.: Perturbation-based fault screening. In: IEEE 13th International Symposium on High Performance Computer Architecture, HPCA 2007, pp. 169–180. IEEE (2007)
3. Ernst, D., Das, S., Lee, S., Blaauw, D., Austin, T., Mudge, T., Kim, N.S., Flautner, K.: Razor: circuit-level correction of timing errors for low-power operation. IEEE Micro **24**(6), 10–20 (2004)
4. Hari, S.K.S., Adve, S.V., Naeimi, H.: Low-cost program-level detectors for reducing silent data corruptions. In: 2012 42nd Annual IEEE/IFIP International Conference on Dependable Systems and Networks (DSN), pp. 1–12. IEEE (2012)
5. Reis, G.A., Chang, J., Vachharajani, N., Rangan, R., August, D.I.: Swift: software implemented fault tolerance. In: Proceedings of the International Symposium on Code Generation and Optimization, pp. 243–254. IEEE Computer Society (2005)
6. Chang, J., Reis, G.A., August, D.I.: Automatic instruction-level software-only recovery. In: International Conference on Dependable Systems and Networks, DSN 2006, pp. 83–92. IEEE (2006)
7. Mitropoulou, K., Porpodas, V., Cintra, M.: DRIFT: decoupled CompileR-based instruction-level fault-tolerance. In: Cașcaval, C., Montesinos-Ortego, P. (eds.) LCPC 2013. LNCS, vol. 8664, pp. 217–233. Springer, Heidelberg (2014)

A High Dimensional Clustering Algorithm Based on Dynamic P System and Swarm Intelligence

Chenggong Qiu, Laisheng Xiang, and Xiyu Liu[(⊠)]

School of Management Science and Engineering,
Shandong Normal University, Jinan, Shandong, China
{chgqiu,xls3366,sdxyliu}@163.com

Abstract. The purpose of this paper is to propose a new clustering algorithm, which combines membrane computing with one of swarm intelligence algorithm: ant colony algorithm. The new algorithm is called DPSC algorithm, which can cluster high dimensional data through membrane coefficient, radius and conditional communication rules and rewriting rules. The whole process of DPSC algorithm is shown by 9 points with 5 dimensions, which indicates the feasibility of the algorithm. All the processes are conducted in membranes. The DPSC algorithm provides an alternative for traditional computing.

Keywords: Dynamic P system · Swarm intelligence · High dimensional data · Clustering algorithm

1 Introduction

Membrane computing is a new class of distributed and parallel computing devices initiated by Păun [1]. It abstracts computing models from the functioning of living cells. The advantage of this method is the huge inherent parallelism. There are three main classes of P systems investigated: cell-like P systems [2], tissue-like P systems [3], neural-like P systems [4]. New classes of P systems, computational power, application of P system, implementation of P system are four hot topics in membrane computing recently. Inspired by a variety of disciplines, different classes of P systems emerge. Researchers also study the computational completeness and effectiveness of P system, discusses the calculations of different membrane computing model [5].

Clustering, an unsupervised learning technique, is used in many fields, including machine learning, data mining, pattern recognition, image analysis, etc. There are many types of clustering, such as hierarchical clustering, density-based clustering, subspace clustering, etc. Large volume, high dimension and fast velocity are three main characteristics of data set today. Current clustering methods also include: Probabilistic model-based clustering, high-dimensional data clustering, graph and grid clustering, background knowledge-based clustering, limited spatial clustering and so on. Chen proposes TW-k-Means algorithm: a new two variable weights K-means algorithm. Hong gives a pairwise constraints MMC algorithm and so on [6, 7].

© Springer International Publishing Switzerland 2016
Q. Zu and B. Hu (Eds.): HCC 2016, LNCS 9567, pp. 322–331, 2016.
DOI: 10.1007/978-3-319-31854-7_29

Swarm intelligence is a soft bionic to biological populations. Individuals can be seen as simple single, but also allowed to have the ability to learn to solve specific problems. Currently, the studies on swarm intelligence, mostly starting from swarm intelligence rules, establish the appropriate model, the proposed algorithm. Algorithms are applied to solve practical problems. Ant colony algorithm and particle swarm optimization algorithm are two main algorithms in swarm intelligence. They are widely applied to combinatorial optimization, constrained optimization, multi-objective optimization, scheduling optimization, planning and task allocation, data classification, and other fields [8, 9].

Based on the above researches, this paper develops a clustering method based a novel dynamic P system, called DPSC, by combining the thought of ant colony algorithms with a novel P system in a proper way to solve clustering problems.

2 Dynamic P System with Membranes and Rules Parameters

A dynamic P system with membranes and rules parameters (of degree $m \geq 1$) is a construct of the form:

$$\prod = (O, C, H, e, r, \mu, \omega_1, \ldots, \omega_m, R, i_0)$$

Where, O is the alphabet of objects, C is the control conditions of rules, μ is a membrane structure with m membranes, labeled with elements of H, where H is a finite set of labels for membranes, $\omega_1, \cdots, \omega_m$ are strings over O. Here, we add two parameters for membranes: coefficient and radius. Radius denotes the size of membrane, which means membrane can only communicate with objects within radius. Coefficient is used in the process of membrane computing, which is only signed in skin membranes.

R is a finite set of rules of dynamic P system:

(i) object evolution rules:
$$[a \xrightarrow{C} v]_h^r$$

(ii) send-in communication rules:
$$a[]_h^r \xrightarrow{C} [b]_h^r$$

(iii) send-out communication rules:
$$[a]_h^r \xrightarrow{C} []_h^r b$$

(iv) membrane dissolution rules:
$$[a]_h^r \xrightarrow{C} b$$

(v) membrane division rules:
$$[a]_h^r \xrightarrow{C} [b]_h^r [d]_h^r$$

C is the controlling condition of rules, which can be set as time, velocity, concentration. For two single rules, $[a \xrightarrow{C} v]_h^r$ and $[a \xrightarrow{C_1} v_1]_h^r$, assume that C is the reactant time of rules and $C > C_1$, after C_1, a changes into v_1 and no v produced. Rule (i) is rewriting rule used in parallel in the region of membrane h with condition C. (ii) and (iii) are communication rules, where (ii) sends an object into a membrane. On the contrary, (iii) sends an object out of a membrane. If there are $a[]_h^r \overset{C_1}{\to} [b]_h^r$, $[b]_h^r \overset{C_2}{\to} []_h^r a$ and $C_1 > C_2$, assume that C is reactant velocity, then, the number of b in membrane h is more than that of a out of membrane h. (iv) is dissolution rule, which is a special rule in P system with active membrane, allowing membrane's dissolution in reaction. (v) is division rule, with which a membrane is divided into two membranes with possibly different labels and different electric charges; and the object a specified in the rule is replaced by possibly new objects b, c respectively in the two new membranes; and the remaining objects are duplicated in the process.

3   Design of the Hybrid Clustering Algorithm

We use the thought of ant colony clustering algorithm. The advantage of our algorithm is that we can get different clustering results simultaneously, which are caused by parameter α or ant number. The algorithm is designed by using the network membrane structure of a P system with α number of outer cells and each outer cell has membranes equal to n, α and n are set before calculation. To be specific, all outer cells and their child-membranes are placed inside one skin membrane of the dynamic P system in a common environment. The channels link each pair of child-membranes communicated. Each child-membrane independently evolves inside one outer membrane according to its own evolutionary mechanism and at the same time communicates with other cells through channels.

The objects in each cell are organized as multisets of integer-valued strings corresponding to patterns of clustering. The evolution rules, which are responsible to evolve the system, come from the use of transformation and communication rules of P systems and functions of swarm intelligence algorithm.

We set l numbers of coefficient α with l numbers of skin membranes, $n * l$ numbers of all patterns are put into l skin membranes for initialization. Then, each skin membrane does its own clustering. Benefit to the parallelism of membrane computing, l numbers of clustering execute simultaneously. Different skin membrane has different number of child-membranes, which is determined by membrane creation rules (similar to ant number of ant colony algorithm). In skin membrane, every child-membrane finds strings within its radius and calculates the group similarity. One string will be chosen and produce a membrane, then, rule parameter p_{in} determines whether the string will be sent into the new membrane. If there is a membrane with strings, rule parameter p_{down} determines whether the string will be sent out of the membrane. Rules will execute in this way until it reaches the iterations. Then, strings will be clustered in skin membranes. At last, strings who has the least distance to a same membrane with means will go into same membranes. The result can be read out by skin membranes.

The framework of the dynamic P system is shown in Fig. 1, which can be described as the following construct.

$$\prod = (O, C, H, \mu, \omega_1, \ldots, \omega_m, R, i_0)$$

Where, $O = \{\beta_{i(x,y)}, \omega_j, \theta_{ij}, g, \eta_{i(x,y)} | 1 \leq i \leq n, 1 \leq j \leq m\}$,

$C = \{P_{in}, P_{out}, P_{up}, P_{down}, M_{ji}\}$, $H = \{outer_1, \cdots, outer_{\alpha\_number}\}$

Rules are as follows:

$$[\theta_{ij}\omega_j\beta_{i(x_i,y_i)} \rightarrow \omega_j[\beta_{i(x_i,y_i)}]_j^r]_{o_\alpha}$$

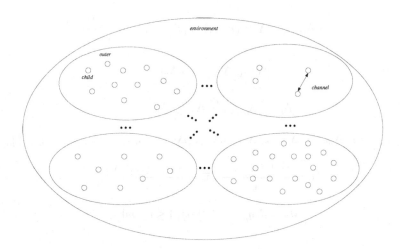

Fig. 1. Membrane structure for DPSC algorithm

$$[f(O_i) = \begin{cases} \frac{1}{s^2} \sum\limits_{O_j \in Neigh_{s \times s}} [1 - \frac{d(O_i,O_j)}{\alpha}], & f > 0 \\ 0, & f < 0 \end{cases}]_{o_\alpha}$$

$$[P_{in} = \begin{cases} 1 - \varepsilon, & f(O_i) \leq 0 \\ 1 - kf(O_i), & 0 < f(O_i) \leq 1/k \\ 0 + \varepsilon, & f(O_i) > 1/k \end{cases}]_{o_\alpha}$$

$$[P_{out} = random[0,1]]_{o_\alpha}$$

$$[\begin{cases} \theta_{ij}\omega_j\beta_{j(x_j,y_j)}[\beta_{i(x_i,y_i)}]_j^r \xrightarrow{P_{in}} [g\eta_{i(x_i,y_i)}\beta_{j(x_j,y_j)}]_j^r\omega_j \\ \theta_{ij}\omega_j\beta_{j(x_j,y_j)}[\beta_{i(x_i,y_i)}]_j^r \xrightarrow{P_{out}} \beta_{i(x_i,y_i)}\omega_j[\beta_{j(x_j,y_j)}]_j^r \end{cases}]_{o_\alpha}$$

$$[P_{down} = \begin{cases} 1-\varepsilon, & f(O_i) \geq 1/k \\ kf(O_i), & 0 < f(O_i) < 1/k \\ 0+\varepsilon, & f(O_i) \leq 0 \end{cases}]_{o_\alpha},$$

$$[P_{up} = P_{out} = random[0,1]]_{o_\alpha}$$

$$[\theta_{jk}\omega_j\beta_{k(x_k,y_k)}[g\eta_{i(x_i,y_i)}\beta_{j(x_j,y_j)}]_j^r \xrightarrow{P_{down}} \beta_{j(x_j,y_j)}[\beta_{k(x_k,y_k)}]_j^r\omega_j]_{o_\alpha}$$

$$[\theta_{jk}\omega_j\beta_{k(x_k,y_k)}[g\eta_{i(x_i,y_i)}]_j^r \xrightarrow{P_{up}} \beta_{j(x_j,y_j)}[g\eta_{i(x_i,y_i)}\beta_{k(x_k,y_k)}]_j^r\omega_j]_{o_\alpha}$$

$$[[\Delta_{(x,y)}]_j^r \rightarrow \Delta_{(x,y)}]_{o_\alpha}, \ \Delta = \{\eta_{(x,y)}\} \cup \{\beta_{(x,y)}\}, \ [s = \sqrt{(\frac{x_i-x_j}{x_i})^2}]_{o_\alpha}$$

$$[\Delta_{i(x_i,y_i)}\Delta_{j(x_j,y_j)} \xrightarrow{s} \Delta_{ij}]_{o_\alpha},$$

$$[\Delta_{i(x_i,y_i)}\Delta_{j(x_j,y_j)} \xrightarrow{ds} \Delta_{i(x_i,y_i)}\Delta_{j(x_j,y_j)}]_{o_\alpha}$$

$$[\Delta_{ij}\Delta_{jk}\ldots\Delta_{hm}\Delta_{mn} \rightarrow [\Delta_{ijk\ldots hmn}\Delta_{i(x_i,y_i)}\Delta_{j(x_j,y_j)}\Delta_{k(x_k,y_k)}\Delta_{h(x_h,y_h)}\Delta_{m(x_m,y_m)}\Delta_{n(x_n,y_n)}]_i]_{o_\alpha}$$

$$[\overline{x_i} = \frac{x_1+x_2,\ldots,x_l}{g}, \overline{y_i} = \frac{y_1+y_2,\ldots,y_l}{g}]_{o_\alpha}$$

$$[M_{ji} = d(\eta_{j(x,y)}, (\overline{x_i},\overline{y_i})), 1 \leq i \leq m]_{o_\alpha}$$

$$[\Delta_{i(x_i,y_i)} \xrightarrow{M_{ji}} [\Delta_{i(x_i,y_i)}]_i]_{o_\alpha},$$

$$[[\Delta_{i(x_i,y_i)}\Delta_{j(x_j,y_j)}\Delta_{k(x_k,y_k)}\cdots\Delta_{h(x_h,y_h)}\Delta_{m(x_m,y_m)}]_i \rightarrow \Delta_{ijkhm}]_{o_\alpha}$$

To clearly understand the P system based clustering algorithm, in what follows we describe its procedures step by step.

Step 1. Initialization: a membrane structure with l numbers of outer membranes with different α, is constructed. Outer membranes $1, 2, \ldots, l$ have one copy of patterns set $\{\beta_{i(x,y)}|1 \leq i \leq m\}$. One pattern $\beta_{i(x,y)}$ is sent to a child membrane jl in the help of ω_j by rule $[\theta_{ij}\omega_j\beta_{i(x,y)} \rightarrow \omega_j[\beta_{i(x,y)}]_j^r]_l$ among all $N_1, N_2, \ldots, N_l$ numbers of child-membranes at the same time, $1 \leq jl \leq N_l$. $N_1, N_2, \ldots, N_l$ numbers of child-membranes at the same time, $1 \leq jl \leq N_l$ are created by this rule as well. θ_{ij} ensures ω_j and $\beta_{i(x,y)}$ only can act in rule $\omega_j\beta_{i(x,y)} \rightarrow \omega_j[\beta_{i(x,y)}]_j^r$ once.

Step 2. Parameter setting: we have to preset four parameters for the algorithm: r, size, ds, n. r is the radius of child-membrane, size is the space for outer membrane, ds is a threshold setting for measure distance between two patterns and n is the iteration of membrane rules. Besides, $P_{up} = P_{out} = random[0,1]$, $f(O_i)$, P_{in}, P_{down}, s, $(\overline{x_i},\overline{y_i})$ are calculated by equation.

Step 3. Clustering process: after initialization, the system computes $f(O_i)$. If the child-membrane j does not have strings as $\eta_{(x,y)}$, then, the model calculates P_{in} and executes rules:

$$\begin{cases} \theta_{ij}\omega_j\beta_{j(x,y)}[\beta_{i(x,y)}]_j^r \xrightarrow{P_{in}} [g\eta_{i(x,y)}\beta_{j(x,y)}]_j^r\omega_j \\ \theta_{ij}\omega_j\beta_{j(x,y)}[\beta_{i(x,y)}]_j^r \xrightarrow{P_{out}} \beta_{i(x,y)}\omega_j[\beta_{j(x,y)}]_j^r. \end{cases}$$

As the definition of controlling condition of rules, P is seen as reactant velocity. If $P_{in} > P_{out}$, $\beta_{i(x,y)}$ changes into $\eta_{i(x,y)}$ and stays in membrane j. Otherwise, $\beta_{i(x,y)}$ is sent back to outer membrane. $\beta_{j(x,y)}$ is the next string being operating. On the contrary, if there are strings $\eta_{(x,y)}$ in child-membrane j, then, the model calculates P_{down} and exe-cutes rules:

$$\begin{cases} \theta_{jk}\omega_j\beta_{k(x,y)}[g\eta_{i(x,y)}\beta_{j(x,y)}]_j^r \xrightarrow{P_{down}} \beta_{j(x,y)}[\beta_{k(x,y)}]_j^r\omega_j \\ \theta_{jk}\omega_j\beta_{k(x,y)}[g\eta_{i(x,y)}]_j^r \xrightarrow{P_{up}} \beta_{j(x,y)}[g\eta_{i(x,y)}\beta_{k(x,y)}]_j^r\omega_j. \end{cases} \quad \text{If } P_{down} > P_{up}, \ \eta_{i(x,y)}$$

changes into $\beta_{j(x,y)}$ and go back to outer membrane again. Here, pattern i is rewritten into j. Otherwise, $\eta_{i(x,y)}$ stays in membrane j. $\beta_{k(x,y)}$ is the next string being operating. When the execution of rules reaches n, $[\Delta_{(x,y)}]_j^r \rightarrow \Delta_{(x,y)}$ begins to work. Rule to cluster patterns whose distance less than ds into a new produced membrane i by membrane division rules. Patterns are grouped into k numbers of membrane i. Then, a k-means based membrane computing process starts. Every membrane i computes its means distance. Then, rule sends string $\Delta = \{\eta_{(x,y)}\} \cup \{\beta_{(x,y)}\}$ to their least distance membrane.

Step 4. Termination condition: the system halts when there nothing changing, which is to say the membrane computing model is stable.

Step 5. Output: Δ_{ijkhm} is the output strings. We read it out from outer membrane. We can also read out other coefficient membranes' results and make a comparison at the same time.

4   Experiment and Analysis

We extract 9 points from three types of iris data set as a simple example in Fig. 2 to illustrate the process of DPSC. Each data has five attributes, in addition to a property is classified attributes, the rest of the statistical data is discrete data: (5.1,3.5,1.4,0.2,2), (4.9,3.0,1.4,0.2,2), (4.6,3.2,1.4,0.2,2), (6.6,2.9,4.6,1.3,3), (6.5,2.8,4.6,1.5,3), (6.2,2.9,4.3,1.3,3), (7.7,3.8,6.7,2.2,1), (7.9,3.8,6.4,2.0,1), (7.7,3.0, 6.1,2.3,1) (Fig. 3).

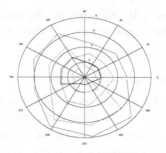

Fig. 2. Multidimensional visualization Radar

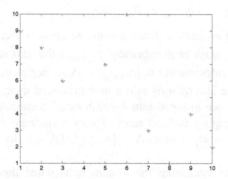

Fig. 3. Initial data distribution of the 9 points

$$[\theta_{95}\omega_5\beta_{9(1,9)} \rightarrow \omega_5[\beta_{9(1,9)}]_5^3]_{o_{0.2}},$$

$$[\theta_{11}\omega_1\beta_{1(10,2)} \rightarrow \omega_1[\beta_{1(10,2)}]_1^3]_{o_{0.2}},$$

$$[\theta_{32}\omega_2\beta_{3(5,7)} \rightarrow \omega_2[\beta_{3(5,7)}]_2^3]_{o_{0.2}},$$

$$[\theta_{53}\omega_3\beta_{5(7,3)} \rightarrow \omega_3[\beta_{5(7,3)}]_3^3]_{o_{0.2}},$$

$$[\theta_{74}\omega_4\beta_{7(2,8)} \rightarrow \omega_4[\beta_{7(2,8)}]_4^3]_{o_{0.2}}$$

$$\left[\left\{ \begin{array}{l} \theta_{11}\omega_1\beta_{1'(5.5,8)}[\beta_{1(10,2)}]_1^3 \xrightarrow{1} \\[2mm] [g\eta_{1(10,2)}\beta_{1'(5.5,8)}]_1^3\omega_1 \\[2mm] \theta_{11}\omega_1\beta_{1'(5.5,8)}[\beta_{1(10,2)}]_1^3 \xrightarrow{0.4525} \\[2mm] \beta_{1(10,2)}\omega_1[\beta_{1'(5.5,8)}]_1^3 \end{array} \right. \right]_{o_{0.2}},$$

$$\left[\left\{ \begin{array}{l} \theta_{32}\omega_2\beta_{3'(3.5,2)}[\beta_{3(5,7)}]_2^3 \xrightarrow{1} \\[2mm] [g\eta_{3(5,7)}\beta_{3'(3.5,2)}]_2^3\omega_2 \\[2mm] \theta_{32}\omega_2\beta_{3'(3.5,2)}[\beta_{3(5,7)}]_2^3 \xrightarrow{0.8921} \\[2mm] \beta_{3(5,7)}\omega_2[\beta_{3'(3.5,2)}]_2^3 \end{array} \right. \right]_{o_{0.2}}$$

$$[\left\{\begin{array}{l} \theta_{53}\omega_3\beta_{5'(0,1.5)}[\beta_{5(7,3)}]_3^3 \xrightarrow{1} \\ [g\eta_{5(7,3)}\beta_{5'(0,1.5)}]_3^3\omega_3 \\ \theta_{53}\omega_3\beta_{5'(0,1.5)}[\beta_{5(7,3)}]_3^3 \xrightarrow{0.0816} \\ \beta_{5(7,3)}\omega_j[\beta_{5'(0,1.5)}]_3^3 \end{array}\right]_{o_{0.2}},$$

$$[\left\{\begin{array}{l} \theta_{74}\omega_4\beta_{7'(1,9.5)}[\beta_{7(2,8)}]_4^3 \xrightarrow{0.9966} \\ [g\eta_{7(2,8)}\beta_{7'(1,9.5)}]_4^3\omega_4 \\ \theta_{74}\omega_4\beta_{7'(1,9.5)}[\beta_{7(2,8)}]_4^3 \xrightarrow{0.3231} \\ \beta_{7(2,8)}\omega_4[\beta_{7'(1,9.5)}]_4^3 \end{array}\right]_{o_{0.2}}$$

$$[\left\{\begin{array}{l} \theta_{95}\omega_5\beta_{9'(8,5)}[\beta_{9(1,9)}]_5^3 \xrightarrow{1} \\ [g\eta_{9(1,9)}\beta_{9'(8,5)}]_5^3\omega_5 \\ \theta_{95}\omega_5\beta_{9'(8,5)}[\beta_{9(1,9)}]_5^3 \xrightarrow{0.8045} \\ \beta_{9(1,9)}\omega_5[\beta_{9'(8,5)}]_5^3 \end{array}\right]_{o_\alpha}\cdots\cdots$$

$$[\Delta_{1(2,9.5)}\Delta_{2(2.5,8)} \xrightarrow{1.5} \Delta_{12}]_{o_{0.2}}$$

$$[\Delta_{1(2,9.5)}\Delta_{2(2.5,8)} \xrightarrow{3.5} \Delta_{1(2,9.5)}\Delta_{2(2.5,8)}]_{o_{0.2}}\cdots\cdots$$

$$[\Delta_{8(3,5.5)}\Delta_{9(3.5,2.5)} \xrightarrow{3.0} \Delta_{89}]_{o_{0.2}}$$

$$[\Delta_{8(3,5.5)}\Delta_{9(3.5,2.5)} \xrightarrow{3.5} \Delta_{8(3,5.5)}\Delta_{9(3.5,2.5)}]_{o_{0.2}}$$

$$[\Delta_{12}\Delta_{13}\Delta_{23} \rightarrow [\Delta_{123}\Delta_{1(2,9.5)}\Delta_{2(2.5,8)}\Delta_{3(3,10)}]_1]_{o_{0.2}}$$

$$[\Delta_{45}\Delta_{46}\Delta_{56} \rightarrow [\Delta_{456}\Delta_{4(6.5,8)}\Delta_{5(6.5,8.5)}\Delta_{6(7.5,7)}]_2]_{o_{0.2}}$$

$$[\Delta_{78}\Delta_{79}\Delta_{89} \rightarrow [\Delta_{789}\Delta_{7(2.5,4)}\Delta_{8(3,5.5)}\Delta_{9(3.5,2.5)}]_3]_{o_{0.2}}$$

$$[\Delta_{1(2,9.5)} \xrightarrow{0.6} [\Delta_{1(2,9.5)}]_1]_{o_{0.2}} [\Delta_{1(2,9.5)} \xrightarrow[\quad]{5.1} \Delta_{1(2,9.5)}]_2]_{o_{0.2}}$$

$$[\Delta_{1(2,9.5)} \xrightarrow{5.6} [\Delta_{1(2,9.5)}]_{0.3}]_{o_{0.2}}$$

$$\cdots\cdots$$

$$[\Delta_{9(3.5,2.5)} \xrightarrow{6.8} [\Delta_{9(3.5,2.5)}]_1]_{o_{0.2}} [\Delta_{9(3.5,2.5)} \xrightarrow{6.2} [\Delta_{9(3.5,2.5)}]_2]_{o_{0.2}}$$

$$[\Delta_{9(3.5,2.5)} \xrightarrow{1.6} [\Delta_{9(3.5,2.5)}]_3]_{o_{0.2}}$$

$$[[\Delta_{1(2,9.5)}\Delta_{2(2.5,8)}\Delta_{3(3,10)}]_1 \rightarrow \Delta_{123}]_{o_{0.2}},$$

$$[[\Delta_{4(6.5,8)}\Delta_{5(6.5,8.5)}\Delta_{6(7.5,7)}]_2 \rightarrow \Delta_{456}]_{o_{0.2}}$$

$$[\Delta_{7(2.5,4)}\Delta_{8(3,5.5)}\Delta_{9(3.5,2.5)}]_3 \rightarrow \Delta_{789}]_{o_{0.2}}$$

Above we choose the best result of clustering with an array of parameters to show its rules in detail. Indeed, we choose 5 numbers of different parameters to execute the example. Time complexity of ant colony algorithm is $O(N * M * R^2)$, for 5 numbers of experiments, time consuming is 373 s. However, DPSC only use 14.08 s to complete the computation (Table 1, Fig. 4).

5 Conclusion

A new strategy for the ant colony clustering algorithm using membrane computing is proposed in this paper. The P system is used to implement clustering. All the processes are conducted in membranes. The controlling conditions, membrane coefficient and radius play an important role in the action of membrane computing model. The whole process of the algorithm is shown by a 9 points test data set, which shows the effectiveness and feasibility of our algorithm.

Table 1. Clustering evaluation of the example (CN means containing clustering number; RN is right clustering number; CS is clustering shrinkage; CA is clustering accuracy)

CN	3
RN	3
CS	100 %
CA	100 %

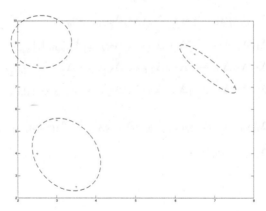

Fig. 4. Final clustering result of the 9 points

Although the process of the proposed algorithm is provided and an instance to prove its feasibility is presented, there are also many works needed to do for further study. In the future, we will continue researching the use of membrane computing techniques to cluster spatial data.

Acknowledgements. This research is supported by the Natural Science Foundation of China (No. 61170038, 61472231), Humanities and Social Sciences Project of the Ministry of Education of China (No. 12YJA630152), Outstanding Young Scientist Award Foundation of Shandong Province (No. BS2013DX037), A Project of Shandong Province Higher Educational Science and Technology Program (No. J15LN28).

References

1. Păun, G.: A quick introduction to membrane computing. J. Logic Algebraic Program. **79**, 291–294 (2010)
2. Păun, G.: Computing with membranes. J. Comput. Syst. Sci. **61**(1), 108–143 (2000)
3. Martin-Vide, C., Pazos, J., Păun, G., Rodriguez-Paton, A.: Tissue P systems. Theoret. Comput. Sci. **296**(2), 295–326 (2003)
4. Ionescu, M., Păun, G., Yokomori, T.: Spiking neural P systems. Fundamenta Informaticae **71**(2–3), 279–308 (2006)
5. Leporati, A.: Computational complexity of p systems with active membranes. In: Alhazov, A., Cojocaru, S., Gheorghe, M., Rogozhin, Y., Rozenberg, G., Salomaa, A. (eds.) CMC 2013. LNCS, vol. 8340, pp. 19–32. Springer, Heidelberg (2014)
6. Hernandez, N.H.S., Juayong, R.A.B., Adorna, H.N.: Solving hard problems in evolution-communication P systems with energy. In: CMC14, Chisinau, Moldova, pp. 181–198 (2013)
7. Chen, X., Xu, X., Huang, J., et al.: TW-k-means: automated two-level variable weighting clustering algorithm for multi-view data. IEEE Trans. Knowl. Data Eng. **25**(4), 932–945 (2013)
8. Zeng, H., Cheung, Y.-M.: Semi-supervised maximum margin clustering with pairwise constraints. IEEE Trans. Knowl. Data Eng. **24**(5), 926–940 (2012)
9. Cardona, M., Colomer, A., Peréz-Jiménz, M.J., Zaragoza, A.: Hierarchical clustering with membrane. Computing **27**, 185–204 (2013)

Petri Net Applied in Document Flow Management System

Chun Shan[1], Wei Zhang[2(✉)], and Shaohua Teng[1,2]

[1] Guangdong Polytechnic Normal University, Guangzhou, China
shanchun2002@126.com
[2] Guangdong University of Technology, Guangzhou, China
{weizhang, shteng}@gdut.edu.cn

Abstract. Document examination and approval system is a typical workflow system. Based on real OA (Office Automation) system, the Petri net modeling workflow is discussed in this paper. Three typical procedures are modeled by Petri net, which are delivering the document management, receiving the document management, and multi-level document examination and approval. Petri net modeling methods and technologies are showed. At the last, Petri net system activity, boundedness, and deadlock are discussed.

Keywords: Petri net · Workflow · Modeling · Receiving the document management · Delivering the document management · Multi-level document examination and approval

1 Introduction

Workflow is a concept for a regular work activity with a fixed program proposed. Through the work activities broken down into well-defined tasks, roles, rules, and procedures for implementation and monitoring, that is to improve the level of organization of production and work efficiency, workflow technology provides advanced tools for enterprises to better achieve business objectives [1].

In 1993, the International WfMC (Workflow Management Coalition) was established, a series of standards of the relevant term of workflow management systems involved, the architecture and application programming interfaces [2].

Workflow Management Coalition gives the following Workflow definition:

Definition 1 [3]: Workflow: Workflow refers to the whole or part of the business process supported by automated computer or semi-automated, in this process, documents, information or tasks according to certain rules of the transfer process, to achieve interoperability among members of the organization to achieve business the overall goal.

A workflow consists of a series of events and their relationship to each other, but also the process of starting and termination conditions and activities, and a description of each activity can be more broadly to all (workflow by computer software systems in practical situations management system) to control the process of its implementation is called workflow.

Q. Zu and B. Hu (Eds.): HCC 2016, LNCS 9567, pp. 332–343, 2016.
DOI: 10.1007/978-3-319-31854-7_30

Currently workflow has been widely applied to office automation software, including sending and receiving text, business management, planning approvals execution, petition, and project management.

Typical workflow application can actually depict an enterprise business process, which is composed of a series of activities. It can be plotted in the form of a flowchart, so you can get a clear visual impression of the workflow. It can be distinguished by Petri nets. In this paper, Petri net refers to the workflow. An enterprise and an institution's actual office systems are used to illustrate the Petri net modeling process and technology in document flow system.

2   Petri Net

Petri net is a mathematical and graphical description and analysis tool for the system [5]. A concurrent, asynchronous, distributed, parallel, uncertainty or randomness in information processing systems can be constructed by using the Petri net models.

Any system consists of two elements: present the state of the elements and indicates the change in status of elements. In Petri nets, the former with a library (place), the latter is represented by the changes (transition) [5–7]. Libraries store certain resources, each represented by a token. Changes are to change the role of the state, the token of libraries is to determine whether changes occur, the dependencies between them represented by the arc (arrows) is a Petri net. Its form is defined as follows:

Definition 2 [6]: Directed Network: three-tuple $N = (S, T; F)$ referred to the network is necessary and sufficient conditions are:

(1) $S \cap T = \varnothing$;
(2) $S \cup T \neq \varnothing$;
(3) $F \subseteq (S \times T) \cup (T \times S)$ ("$\times$" for Cartesian product;
(4) $dom(F) \cup cod(F) = S \cup T$, Among them

   $dom(F) = \{x | \exists y:(x, y) \in F\}$
   $cod(F) = \{y | \exists x:(x, y) \in F\}$
   $dom(F)$ and $cod(F)$ Respectively for the domain and range of F.

Definition 3 [5, 6]: Pre-set: set up $\forall x \in S \cup T$, order

   $*x = \{y \mid (y, x) \in F\}$
   $* x$ is called the pre-set of x.

Definition 4 [5, 6]: Post-set: set up $\forall x \in S \cup T$, order

   $x* = \{y \mid (x, y) \in F\}$
   $* x$ is called post-set of x.

Definition 5 [6]: Set up $N = (S, T; F)$ as a directed network, $\Omega 0 = \{0, 1, 2, \ldots\}$, $\Omega = \{1, 2, \ldots\}$, Then:

   $K: S \rightarrow \Omega \cup \{\infty\}$ The capacity function called N.

The capacity of a given function K, M:S $\to$ $\Omega 0$ Condition known as a logo of N is: $\forall$ s $\in$ S: M(s) $\leq$ K(s).

(1) W: F $\to$ Ω Called for the weight function of N, For (x, y) $\in$ F, W (x, y) = W ((x, y)) is called the right of (x, y).

Definition 6 [5–8]: Petri nets: Six-tuple PN = (S, T; F, K, W, M0) called Petri nets, if and only if:

(1) N = (S, T; F) for a directed network; called the base web of PN;
(2) K, W, M0 following the capacity function and on the right functions and identity of N. For PN initial identification;
(3) the rule is triggered:

    ① changes called enabled iff;
    ② under the M t is enabled changes can trigger changes in identity, logo design successor was raised for M', then

$$M'(p)=\begin{cases} M(p) + 1, p \in t^* - {}^*t \\ M(p) - 1, p \in {}^*t - t^*, \text{ known } M[t > M' \\ M(p), \text{others} \end{cases}$$

Theorem 1: Changes to trigger the rule: If the location changes each input t have at least one token, the changes are implemented.

Proof: Since each transition t of the input position has at least one token, the Change t needs to consume to meet the resource, whereby, with the proviso Changes already have occurred, Changes may be implemented.

Changes implemented means: Under the current system state changes occur prerequisite represent events.

3 Workflow and Petri Net Mapping

Work flow system applications, enterprises business process can be represented a workflow process. A process (workflow) is composed of many tasks that are executed and a series of condition that decisions the order of execution; Task is a logical unit of work, which can be executed as a resource when as a whole. According to WfMC definition, there are four basic workflow routing structure: order routing, branch routing, parallel routes, cycle routes. The rest of complex structures and processes are constructed by combining them.

The beginning of the library Petri nets are used to describe the beginning gofa business process. The end of the library Petri nets are used to describe the ending of a business process, business process tasks with Petri nets to represent changes, Petri nets routing decisions of the business process task simple mentation.

The following was four basic routing structure modeling of Petri net workflow.

3.1   The Basic Structure of Petri Net Modeling

Workflow has four basic routing structure, such as the order of the routing, branch routing, parallel routing, routing loop, they may be separately modeled as follows:

(1) The order of the routing. Figure 1(a) shows the task execution order of A and B, the Petri net in Fig. 1(b) is as shown. Order routing logic expresses the causal relationship between business process tasks. When task A executed, tasks B starts executing in the Fig. 1(a). C1 library represents the start of task, C2 library represents the post-condition of task A and the precondition of task B. Preconditions of activity is represented by the direct activity predecessor and the corresponding status flag; post-conditions activities indicate follow-up activities after the end of the current activities. Petri net modeling of order routing is done by adding a library located between two tasks, in order to achieve the task link, as shown in Fig. 1(b) as a showed.

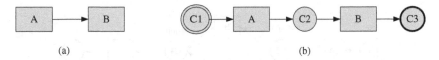

(a)   (b)

Fig. 1. (a) The order of the routing structure; (b) Order Petri net modeling task

(2) Parallel routing. Parallel Routing is shown as Fig. 2(a), tasks B and C are parallel tasks, which can be performed in any order. Petri nets by adding and-split (task A) and-join (task D) express this relationship. A task express parallel relationship of task B and C. Task D begins when activities of task B and task C end, that express the idea of synchronization.

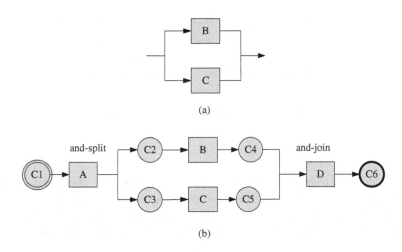

Fig. 2. (a) Parallel routing structure; (b) Parallel tasks Petri net modeling

(3) Branch route. Branch routing shown as Fig. 3(a). After the implementation of the task A, B or C is selected to perform, and then perform the task D. Figure 3(b) shows the Petri net modeling branch route. When libraries contain C2 token, tasks B and tasks C is ready at the same time, but executing the task B or task C, depends on the order of trigger. If task B triggered before task C, then task B perform, C is prohibited; otherwise tasks C perform, task B is prohibited. Then selecting Task B or Task C is not depended on Task A. Trigger mechanism of Task B and Task C are shown as Fig. 4, which has four different trigger types.

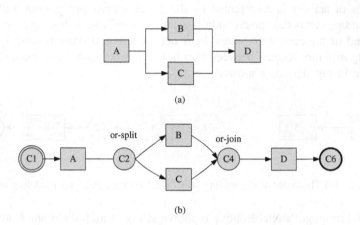

Fig. 3. (a) The structure of the branch routes; (b) Branch routing Petri net

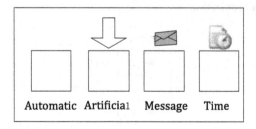

Fig. 4. Concurrent tasks four trigger type

Auto: automatic trigger type automatically triggers when the conditions meet.
Artificial trigger: those select tasks from the task list and execute them.
Message triggers: the task is triggered when an external message is received.
Time-Triggered: a controlling timer is set to trigger executing the task.

(4) Circulation route. Cycle routes is shown in Fig. 5(a), task B is executing the loop, task C2 is a control action, its role is to examine the results of the task B, and decide whether the token is transferred to the C3 or continue executing task B, if the token is moved back to C2, the cycle continues executing task B, if the token is moved to C3, then end the loop. The task B can no longer be executed, continue to implement the process.

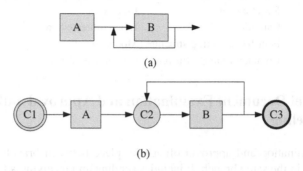

(a)

(b)

Fig. 5. (a) Routing loop; (b) Cycle route Petri net modeling

3.2 Workflow Modeling

From the modeling, a workflow is actually to execute a task, which defines the tasks that need to be performed, and the order and conditions of executing task. a workflow can be described as: work items is a task ready performed; running the work item is called activity; when the work is actually carried out, it changes into an activity.

Thus, the mapping between Petri net modeling and workflow elements is described in Table 1, shown as follows:

(1) a ready transition is refer to a work item;
(2) one or more transitions are refer to a task;
(3) executing a transition corresponds to an activity/process;
(4) building blocks (and-split, and-join, or-split, or-join) are used to model sequential, conditional, parallel, cycling routes;
(5) a condition corresponds to a library. This condition can be included forwarding transition conditions and post-dependency conditions;
(6) a library and directed arcs correspond to causal dependence;
(7) an "entrance" Starting library (no input arcs library) corresponds to the beginning point of the workflow;
(8) an "export" ending library (no output arcs of the library) corresponds to the end of the workflow.

Thus, in this paper Petri net is used to describe workflow. Mapping between workflow elements and a Petri net as for Table 1.

Table 1. The relationship of the workflow and Petri net

Workflow	Petri net
Starting workflow	Starting library
Ending workflow	End library
Task	Multiple changes
Work item	Ready changes
Activities/process	Changes implemented
Requirement	Library
Causality	Library/directed arc
Four basic routing structure	Modeling
Complex routing structures	Complex modeling

4 Multi-level Document Examination and Approval and Petri Net Modeling

Document examination and approval often take place between branches, among different members in the same branch. It includes sending and receiving a file, registering, marking, archiving. And this article focuses on receiving and sending a document and multi-level document examination and approval.

The following sending and receiving documents, and multi-level document examination and approval module is a practical application system of an enterprise or a branch. By extracting the public part of document flow, universal modules are modeled.

4.1 Receiving Process and Modeling

Receiving management means the process that is to read and process files about sending to a company, the company leadership or authority. It includes registering, running, undertaking, handling, and so on, but also querying, printing, archiving, and other functions. Receiving file includes the company's receiving, party's receiving, and other receiving types. Discussion of modeling ignores receiving type and details, and pay attention to commonly modeling of workflow. A modeling example of a business receiving file is used in the text, and Fig. 6 is a receiving file OA system of workflow modeling.

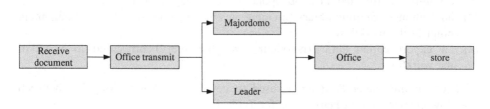

Fig. 6. Modeling of business receiving file workflows

Petri net modeling workflow is shown in Fig. 7, which includes six tasks: registering, corporately distributing, for director's office examining and approving, for leader examining and approving, returning to the office and archiving, in which director's office and leader examining and approving deal with in parallel or branch mode (here in parallel). Workflow starts from the library p1, and ends the library p8. Each process task represents a transition. p1 has a token that represents a document not processed. t1 consumes p1 resources when t1 takes place; t1 generates a new token in p2, t2 and then run. If two tokens are separately generated in p3 and p4, then t3 and t4 can execute immediately, after both run, t5 can run. T5 ensures the correct implementation of transitions of parallel tasks. p7 produces a document, after t6 takes place, enters into the last state p8.

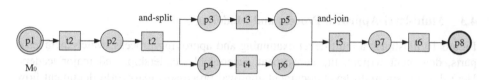

Fig. 7. Petri net modeling business receipt management workflow

4.2 Dispatch Process and Modeling

Sending document management refers to the management that the company sends out a file. Sending document subsystem includes drafting, reviewing, cooperatly approving, existing writings, dispatching, and archiving. Sending document management subsystem includes that the company dispatches a document, the department dispatches a document. These workflow processes are different, and they depend on the draft document file types and working man. In this paper, the "Company dispatching" is used for an example. Business sending document management workflow is shown in Fig. 8.

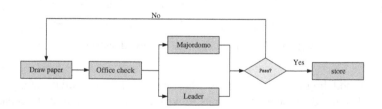

Fig. 8. Business sending document management workflow

Sending document management process is as follow: the user drafts up documents in the database, posting to the workflow process, the file transfers in the workflow process in the serial or parallel cooperate reviewing according to need. After the end of the flow process, a formal official document is produced, and returned to the drafters. The document can be look up at any time, printed and tracked table. Figure 9 is a document management workflow of Petri nets modeling, which shows the changes of the operation and status during workflow. In Fig. 9, t1 represents drafting a document, t2 represents modifies proof reading, t3 said Director's review, t4 said the leadership review, t5 said nuclear draft, t6 is signing and issuing, t7 said redrafting.

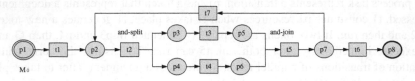

Fig. 9. Petri net modeling issued a document management workflow enterprise

4.3   Multi-level Approval Process and Modeling

Figure 10 illustrates a multi-level examining and approving process, which includes 4 parts, document writers, the department, responsible leadership, and major leaders. Here illustrates a multi-level document approval processes, real-world document flow may be different, and some simple, some may be more complicated. However, after careful analysis, they can be modeled by Petri nets.

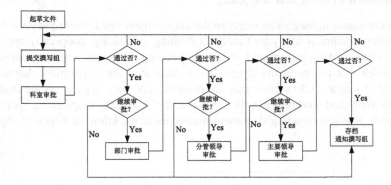

Fig. 10. Multi-level approval process documents

Petri net modeling in Fig. 10 is shown in Fig. 11. p1 is the initial state, pb for the final state, t1 drafts documents, t2 submits to writing group, t3 submits to department, t4 is department reviewing, t5 is whether to continue the examination and approval, t6 is responsible leader approving, t7 is whether to continue the examination and approval, t8 represents major leadership for approval, t9 is by No, ta returns modifying documents, tb archive/notification writing group.

4.4   Workflow Net Analysis

The following takes an analysis for receiving document, analyzes the workflow.

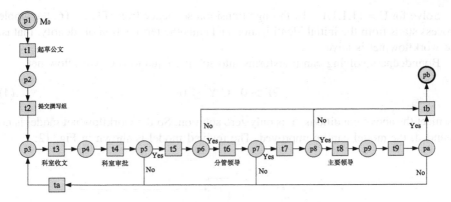

Fig. 11. Multi-level modeling using Petri nets document processes

Petri net in Fig. 7 starts initial marking M0, all possible states in the tree model are reachable. Based on this model, identify the workflow, including checking the workflow model is safe, bounded and no deadlock.

By applying invariant analysis method and Petri net theory, the model is analyzed for its performance.

In Fig. 7, when t2 produces two tokens, the network is no deadlock. But the workflow net activity can be though not multivariate analysis method to establish the following state equations to solve.

$$M = M0 + C U \tag{1}$$

Which set M0 = (1, 0, 0, 0, 0, 0, 0, 0); M = (0, 0, 0, 0, 0, 0, 0, 1) respectively for Initial identification and termination of the model, its associated matrix is C:

$$C = \begin{bmatrix} -1 & 0 & 0 & 0 & 0 & 0 \\ 1 & -1 & 0 & 0 & 0 & 0 \\ 0 & 1 & -1 & 0 & 0 & 0 \\ 0 & 1 & 0 & -1 & 0 & 0 \\ 0 & 0 & 1 & 0 & -1 & 0 \\ 0 & 0 & 0 & 1 & -1 & 0 \\ 0 & 0 & 0 & 0 & 0 & -1 \\ 0 & 0 & 0 & 0 & 0 & 1 \end{bmatrix} \tag{2}$$

Equation (1) changes into solving the following equation.

$$(1, 0, 0, 0, 0, 0, 0, 0)T + C U = (0, 0, 0, 0, 0, 0, 0, 1)T \tag{3}$$

Solve for U = (1,1,1,1,1,1), through transition sequence from T1,…, T6, the whole process starts from the initial identification and ends the termination of identity, that is, the workflow net is alive.

Boundedness solving can transforms into solving equations of workflow net.

$$\exists Y > 0, \ C \, Y \le 0 \tag{4}$$

To meet the above conditions, Y is only zero solution. So the workflow net model is no bounded, the model can be improved. The revived model is shown in Fig. 12.

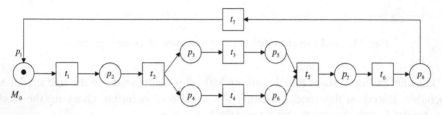

Fig. 12. Improved Petri net model

In this model, the process of adding a virtual task t7, receiving management process from starting to finishing is executed not only once, but the execution of the loop by solving the equation of state.

Y has an infinite number of non-negative solutions, the improved model is bounded. From the above analysis of Petri nets, the workflow model meet the definition of WfMC can transformed into Petri net model. By applying a mathematical simulation, Petri net workflow model can be solved, and get the requirements of the workflow model.

$$C = \begin{bmatrix} -1 & 0 & 0 & 0 & 0 & 0 \\ 1 & -1 & 0 & 0 & 0 & 0 \\ 0 & 1 & -1 & 0 & 0 & 0 \\ 0 & 1 & 0 & -1 & 0 & 0 \\ 0 & 0 & 1 & 0 & -1 & 0 \\ 0 & 0 & 0 & 1 & -1 & 0 \\ 0 & 0 & 0 & 0 & 1 & -1 \\ 0 & 0 & 0 & 0 & 0 & 1 \end{bmatrix} ; \ CY \le 0 \Rightarrow \begin{cases} -y_1 + y_7 \le 0 \\ y_1 - y_2 \le 0 \\ y_2 - y_3 \le 0 \\ y_2 - y_4 \le 0 \\ y_3 - y_5 \le 0 \\ y_4 - y_5 \le 0 \\ y_5 - y_6 \le 0 \\ y_6 - y_7 \le 0 \end{cases} . \tag{5}$$

5 Conclusion

This paper discusses the modeling techniques of Petri net in document approval system. By receiving document management, sending document management, and multi-level document approval process, three typical Petri net modeling workflow is described. Finally, receiving management is used to analyze the activity, boundedness and deadlock problems in the Petri net system.

Acknowledgments. This research was partly supported by Guangdong Provincial Science & Technology Project (Grant No. 2012B091000173, 2013B010401034, 2013B090200017, 2013B010401029), Guangzhou City Science & Technology Project (Grant No. 2012J5100054, 2013J4500028, 201508010067), and Key Laboratory of the Ministry of Guangdong Province project (Grant No. 15zk0132).

References

1. Kacmar, C., Carey, J., Alexander, M.: Providing workflow services using a programmable hypermedia environment. Inf. Softw. Technol. **40**, 381–396 (2006)
2. Hollingsworth, D.: The Workflow Reference Model. Workflow Management Coalition (1995)
3. Haves, J.G., Peyrovian, E., Sarin, S., et al.: Workflow interoperability standards for the internet. Internet Comput. **4**(3), 37–45 (2006)
4. Faustmann, G.: Configuration for adaptation a human-centered approach to flexible workflow enactment. Comput. Support. Coop. Work: CSCW **9**(3), 413–434 (2006)
5. Yang, W., Gu, T.: Software Engineering. Publishing House of Electronics Industry, Beijing (2009)
6. Yuan, C.: Petri Net Principle and Application. Publishing House of Electronics Industry, Beijing (2005)
7. Yuan, C.: Petri Net Application. Science Press, Beijing (2013)
8. Chen, X.: Colored Petri net applied in intrusion detection. Guangdong University of Technology (2011)

Mu-En: Multi-path of Entity Recommendation Based on Path Similarity

Meina Song, Xuejun Zhao[✉], Haihong E, and Cong Zheng

School of Computer Science, Beijing University of Posts
and Telecommunications, Beijing, People's Republic of China
mnsong@gmail.com,
{xuejunzhao,ehaihong,zhengcong}@bupt.edu.cn

Abstract. In the process of exploring the path of similarity in entity recommendation, the selection of nodes in the path selection process attracts more and more attention. However, single-node path composed by one attribute is valued as the path in the face of the entity with multiple attributes for current research work, with adopting the path in similarity and advanced algorithm. In this work, we investigate the entity attributes in recommender system based on the link prediction method methods; on the basis of path similarity, we analyze the specific single-node paths, and also design the multi-node path composed of multi attributes. Therefore, this study not only provides more profound recommender results based on path similarity, but also greatly widens the path selection and improves the recommender accuracy.

Keywords: Entity recommendation · Matrix factorization · Link prediction · Path similarity · Multi-node path

1 Introduction

Owing to dividing the data set into the link between entities and the entities that represent users, objects and their attributes in entity recommendation, amounts of experiments have been introduced into the research of the entities and links [1]; Besides, the most significant link is the user's rating on entity, most of which can be gathered by the research on matrix factorization (MF) [2]. Yet the user-entity score would be large and sparse, personalized recommendation has been improved by leveraging additional user or entity relation network, as the requirement of recommender accuracy and computer carrying ability.

In entity-link (and its attributes) network (EL network) [3], the main goal is to discover the connection between definite entities and related attributes, the above issue is normally handled in Link Prediction (LP) problem –predicting the emergence of links in a future network, based on certain network information [4].

The solution to the LP problem will lead to the further exploration of the EL network structure, and the result will work on entity recommendation [5]. Owing to the EL network divided into the homogeneous EL network composed of link with one attribute and the heterogeneous EL network composed of link with various attributes, and LP problem can also be discussed separately in these two EL network structures [4]. It has

© Springer International Publishing Switzerland 2016
Q. Zu and B. Hu (Eds.): HCC 2016, LNCS 9567, pp. 344–354, 2016.
DOI: 10.1007/978-3-319-31854-7_31

been found that the classification and related methods can be applied in the both network [5, 6]. However, in practice, as heterogeneous EL network maintains most of the entities and their attributes, researchers adopt the methods of Markov network, non-parametric Bayesian framework and the used homogeneous measure [7, 8]. With the advent of large-scale heterogeneous EL network, researchers have introduced the concept of path which is from the link of various attributes, to form the path of similarity. For example, the link formed by one attribute forms a single-node path, and that formed by various attributes forms a multi-node path. On this basis, the similarity of the entity and its attributes are obtained as path similarity to solve the LP problem, which is applied in the recommender system to describe the characteristics of entities' related attributes in heterogeneous EL network.

The path similarity for the relationships among entities (and their attributes) and MF method indicting user-entity ratings are integrated for more complete and accurate results. The introduction of associated entity attributes of the recommendation improves the recommender accuracy, and the diversity of attributes is not well reflected in the algorithm. In the case of various attributes in recommender system, the current algorithm can only simulate the optimization results of a variety of single-node paths for attributes to assume the similarity. In addition, the comparison between different single-node paths is not proposed at present.

Therefore, for the sake of solving these two problems, we propose Multi-path of entity recommendation based on Path Similarity (Mu-En), which provides a more concise and profound method for the recommender system.

Through the above work, the main academic results of this paper are as follows:

1. In the entity recommendation, the entities and their attributes are analyzed, based on the equivalence of the path, we design various entity paths.
2. In the selection of the scale for similarity, the single-node paths in the heterogeneous graph are compared, and the advantages and disadvantages are derived, which is the basis for exploration of the multi-node paths;
3. Researching on the intrinsic relationship of the various attributes, we introduce the multi-node paths in entity recommendation, associated with comparing results of the single-node paths. We contrast the multi-node path with the single-node ones, and conclude the multi-node paths being more excellent.

The rest of the paper is organized as follows. In the second section, we explain the related work. The third section explains the model in detail; besides, the experimental results are analyzed. We conclude this paper in 4.

2 Related Work

2.1 Introduction of Matrix Factorization (MF)

MF characterizes the numeric solution for users to figure out the unseen or blank user-entity ratings, as user-entity ratings are not always acquired and presented by the input source. In addition, MF has been a key technique to predict the user-entity ratings in recommender system, as the prediction accuracy and computation simplicity.

As the usage of MF method being more and more popular in the past years, MF method has been the fundamental technique for recommender system given the accuracy, practicability and conciseness of MF.

MF method relies on the matrix of users' ratings on entities and factorizes into user-specific matrix and entity-specific matrix which are represented by U and V, successively. U is the set of all users: $\{U_1, U_2, \ldots, U_I\}$, the index of U_i indicates the i-th ($i \in (1, I)$) user in U set; V is the set of all entities: $\{V_1, V_2, \ldots, V_J\}$; the index of V_j indicates the j-th ($j \in (1, J)$) entity in V set. In addition, R is high correspondence to the users' rating on entities, where the index of R_{ij} indicates the i-th user's rating on j-th entity in R set. Then the common way is to minimize the sum of squared-errors objective function with quadratic regularization term (λ).

$$\min_{U,V} \sum_{i=1}^{I} \sum_{j=1}^{J} (R_{ij} - U_i \cdot V_j)^2 + \lambda (\sum_{i=1}^{I} ||U_i||_F^2 + \sum_{j=1}^{J} ||V_j||_F^2). \quad (1)$$

2.2 Link Prediction (LP) Problem

In the course of the entity recommendation, the LP problem of entities V_1 and V_2 is predicted by the ratings on related attributes, and thus the target link $V_1 \rightarrow V_2$ is obtained. As the complexity of heterogeneous EL network, this paper will probe into entity attributes from the solution to LP. Heterogeneous EL network G, composed of a entity set V and a link set E, is equal to $G = (V, E)$ according to the concept of network graph.

Links among entities representing semantic description are usually invisible or vacant, even the most ordinary links that users rate on entities can not be an exception. We can transform these semantic descriptions into numerical ones to conduct the researches on LP problem. In the recommendation of single semantic properties, the simple and clear entity mapping function ϕ has been applied, which can reach one correspondence of the entities.

Entity correspondence function $\phi : V \rightarrow A$, V represents the collection of entities, A represents a collection of entities after function ϕ mapping. The mapping function implements the correspondence between the object sets.

Under the condition of multiple-attribute entities, the entity mapping function may not be able to completely outline the corresponding relationship of the various attributes when some attributes being relevant and the others being not. In the process of handling the problem, as many types of attributes are associated with various entities, the link mapping function φ is eagerly needed to express clearly.

Link mapping function $\varphi : E \rightarrow R$, E represents the link between entities, and R represents the link set after the function mapping. The corresponding relationship between the link sets under various attributes is realized by the mapping function. For example, genre-keyword relationship between genre and keyword is achieved by mapping movie-genre and movie-keyword in function φ.

Typically, multiple entities and their links included by the heterogeneous network, after the entity mapping function and the link mapping function, could interpret the similarity scale - path better. We can apply the entity path to depict the relationships in heterogeneous EL networks, like $Q_G = (P, R)$ after function mapping, the representation of the network is $P_1 \xrightarrow{R_1} P_2 \xrightarrow{R_2} \ldots \xrightarrow{R_l} P_{l+1}$, which defines the connection from entity P_1 to entity P_{l+1} through composite link $R = R_1 \rightarrow R_2 \ldots \rightarrow R_l$.

The mapping function and the entity approach discussed above have significantly implications for the LP problem, due to the path selection of heterogeneous EL network, and the most simple path adopts single attribute R_1 to connect the entities P_1 and P_{l+1}: $P_1 \rightarrow R_1 \rightarrow P_{l+1}$.

Entities P_1 and P_2 own attribute R_1, while attribute R_1 associates with attribute R_2, by the means of $R_1 \rightarrow R_2$ through link mapping function and reversibility of link, we can obtain the link relationship between V_1 and V_2 by multi-node path $P_1 \rightarrow R_1 \rightarrow R_2 \rightarrow R_1 \rightarrow P_2$ or $P_1 \rightarrow R_2 \rightarrow R_1 \rightarrow R_2 \rightarrow P_2$. Therefore, the experiments of single-node paths between $P_1 \rightarrow R_1 \rightarrow P_2$ and $P_1 \rightarrow R_2 \rightarrow P_2$ is obliged. And if the experimental result of the former is more excellent than the later, which indicts the link R_1 meeting actual requirements of heterogeneous EL network, the primary element is R_1, and the multi-node path is $P_1 \rightarrow R_1 \rightarrow R_2 \rightarrow R_1 \rightarrow P_2$; $P_1 \rightarrow R_2 \rightarrow R_1 \rightarrow R_2 \rightarrow P_2$ is deduced in the same way.

The above paths would be described in Table 1 and following introduction.

Table 1. Path in heterogeneous network.

Path	Semantic
P-R	Entity P own the attribute R
R-R	The connection among attributes belonging to R
P-R-P	Entities share the same attribute in R
P-R_1-R_2-R_1-P	The common attribute R_2 between entities in P could be connected by different attributes belonging to R_1

2.3   Similarity Algorithm

This paper focuses on the prediction of the links among entities in heterogeneous EL network, which is different from the traditional LP problem. The key of LP is to solve this problem by means of probability method, information entropy or similarity. This paper mainly focuses on the similarity of the path similarity (PAS).

PAS is created and applied to heterogeneous networks, so PAS is an important tool to analyze LP and a significant way to improve the recommender accuracy. Due to the assumption that the entity path is reversible, the PAS is defined on entities i and j.

$$S_{ij}^{(l)} = \frac{2 \times |P_{i \sim j}^{(l)}|}{|P_{i \sim i}^{(l)}| + |P_{j \sim j}^{(l)}|} \tag{2}$$

Among them, $P_{i \sim j}^{(l)}$ is the distance between entities i and j on entity path l, $P_{i \sim i}^{(l)}$ is the distance of i and itself on path l, $P_{j \sim j}^{(l)}$ is the distance of j and itself on entity path j.

The Eq. (2) indicates that the decision is made by two parts: the connectivity defined by the number of nodes on the entity path l between entities i and j and the visibility defined by the number of nodes on the entity path l of entity i or j.

3   Proposed Method

3.1   Model Description

While meeting kinds of links among various entities and their attributes in the heterogeneous network, the network will be classified into the entity rating network and entities (and its attributes) link network.

After the implementation of the MF algorithm, Mu-En will introduce the revision factor matrix S to revise on the item factor matrix V. The paths of selected similarity in this paper would consider the single-node path composed of one element. And then on the basis of results in single-node paths, we research on the multi-node path to choose the best path for similarity.

In the application of algorithm in this paper, we could consider the parameters in MF resulting in rating network and similarity resulting in link network, leveraging regularization coefficient and the parameters preventing over-fitting in MF.

3.2   Inference

On the purpose of primary destination-recommendation, the process of reasonable recommendation for each entity, first, generates relevant user's non numerical form or vacant ratings through matrix factorization (MF). But then the result solely relies on subjective ratings of users, thus ignoring the users or items and other entities own attribute. Therefore, the entity attribute is introduced into the analysis of recommender system, conducting more convincing experiments on recommendation.

Broadly speaking, Entity attributes play a huge role in entity recommendation. And due to deviation of the items, original variances can be corrected in a certain degree. Because the entity attribute can become the node of similarity path, the similarity algorithm (such as PAS) is introduced to solve the LP problem in recommender system. However, there is no enough attention on the selection of the similarity path where the attribute is the node. Therefore, while confronting of various movie attributes (such as genre or keyword) and handling LP problem, most algorithms can only adopt random projections, or simulate the optimization results from a variety of single element as the uniform scale of similarity, but not take full advantage of the links among multiple attributes to guide the LP problem; In addition, there is no comparison between the path similarity of single element, but indeed the pros and cons of the similarity will provide certain guidance to entity recommendation algorithm.

Typically, the entity attributes are normally introduced into similarity algorithm in the independent form. The recommendation process between the entity 1 and entity 2 is schematically shown the following Fig. 2, where attribute 1 is regarded as recommendation factor. After the similarity calculating, the recommender system can be worked out.

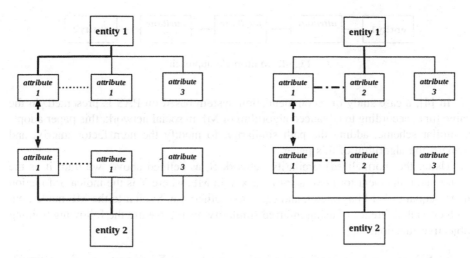

Fig. 1. Entity recommendation of single attribute

Fig. 2. Entity recommendation of multiple attributes

In the recommender approach as shown in Fig. 1, recommender path of entity-attribute- entity can be realized, due to participation of attribute 1. Such as the following Fig. 3, the entity attributes 1 will be recommended as the node in path of PAS, realizing recommendation of single-node path.

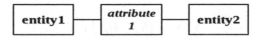

Fig. 3. Single-node path

However, the entity attributes are normally related to each other, not entirely independent. For instance, in Fig. 2, attribute 1 and 2 are the undertake relationship (or other related relationship), whether the two attributes are included by entities or not, then to a large extent, the attribute 2 of entity 1 and entity 2 can be connected to similar or even same attribute 1, and thus the multi-node path can be formed when path of similarity associating with various attributes in this case. Take the following Fig. 8 as an example, when entity 1 and entity 2 are in the course of the recommendation, after attribute 2 providing link to attribute 1, attribute 1 would be regarded as recommendation factor. The recommender system can work after the similarity of attribute 1 and 2.

In the recommender approach as shown in Fig. 2, the recommender path entity-attribute2-attribute1-attribute2-entity can be achieved, due to the recommender link between entity 1 and entity 2. Such as the following Fig. 4, while the entity 1 and 2 apply the similarity algorithm in the process of entity recommendation, the entity attributes 1 and 2 will be recommended as the nodes in path of PAS, realizing the recommendation of multi-node path.

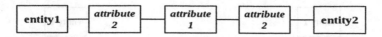

Fig. 4. Multi-node approach

In [4], a case study of recommendation system based on PAS is presented. In the same time, according to advanced algorithm of MF in social network, this paper adopts a similar scheme, adding the path similarity, to modify the item factor matrix, and realizes the algorithm of this paper.

Using the (normalized) similarity network S, as defined above, we train it as the additional refinement for item factor matrix V in MF, where Y is the indicator function that is equal to 1 if I has rated j, and equal to 0 otherwise. Similar to the MF model, but with crucial difference of using inferred similarity matrix, we use the following training objective function.

$$\min_{U,V,\Theta} \sum_{i,j} (Y \otimes (R_{ij} - U_i V_j))^2 + \lambda_0(\|U\|_F^2 + \|V\|_F^2) + \lambda_1 \sum_{j,k} S_{jk}\|V_j - V_k\|^2 + \lambda_2\|\Theta\|^2$$

$$s.t. U \geq 0, V \geq 0, \Theta \geq 0, S_{jk} = \sum_{l=1}^{L} \theta_l S_{jk}^{(l)}, \sum_{l=1}^{L} \theta_l = 1$$

$$(3)$$

According to Eq. 3, the algorithm applies the formulas 4, 5 to calculate the gradient, and then minimizes the objective function.

$$\frac{\partial H}{\partial U_i} = \sum_j Y_{ij} \otimes (R_{ij} - U_i V_j^T) \cdot V_j + \lambda_0 U_i \tag{4}$$

$$\frac{\partial H}{\partial V_j} = \sum_j Y_{ij} \otimes (R_{ij} - U_i V_j^T) \cdot V_j + \lambda_0 V_j + \lambda_1 \sum_{j \neq k} S_{jk} \cdot (V_j - V_k) \tag{5}$$

Therefore, for the sake of convenience and widely-adaptability, this paper adopts the composite link, makes a comparison of single-node paths, and obtains the pros and cons. Then, a comparison between the better single-node path and the multi-node path would be conducted.

3.3   Experimental Data Set

We adopt standard data set Movielens-100 k, which is a collection of data on Movielens website from the Grouplens research center. In Movielens-100 k data set, the range of the rating data is [1, 5]; Besides, data contains keywords as well as the movie genres, etc. For effectiveness of the data set, scholars of Grouplens research group will preprocess the data obtained from Movielens website, and they remove users with number of ratings of less than 20.

We adopt the rating data set Movielens-100 k and remove users' rating lower than 25, on the basis of original data set. The final rating data is as Table 2.

Table 2. Movielens-100 k data set

Data set	User	Movie	Genre	Keyword
Movielens-100 k	706	100023	18	342

In this paper, the accuracy and efficiency of the proposed algorithm, performance of the algorithm through the prediction accuracy of MAE (average absolute deviation) was assessed.

$$MAE = \frac{1}{T} \sum_{i,j} |\overline{R_{ij}} - R_{ij}| \tag{6}$$

Among them, T is the number of items rated by user U in the system, R_{ij} is the actual rating on item j of the user i, $\overline{R_{ij}}$ is the predicted ratings on items of recommender system.

In experiments based on the path similarity of this thesis, we adopt the ratio of test set in 40 %, 60 %, 80 %, besides, the dimension of Matrix factorization is 10, 20, 15. In addition to comparison of the single-node and multi-node paths, the algorithm is also compared with the classical algorithm PMF (probability matrix factorization) and the original model.

3.4 Experimental Data Set

For the convenience of algorithm analysis, we regard PMF, Original, Genre, Keyword, Keyword-genre-keyword as the abbreviation of probability matrix factorization, the original algorithm, movie-genre-movie algorithm, movie-keyword-movie algorithm, movie-keyword-genre-keyword-movie, respectively.

Experimental data is shown in Tables 3 and 4.

Table 3. The algorithm performance with the ratio of test set at 40 % and 60 %

Algorithm performance	40 %					60 %	
	d = 5	10	15	20	5	10
PMF	0.914	0.897	0.876	0.872	0.889	0.865
Original	0.894	0.862	0.868	0.834	0.867	0.842
Genre	0.915	0.887	0.864	0.847	0.879	0.856
keyword	0.882	0.873	0.865	0.852	0.857	0.849
Keyword-genre-keyword	0.873	0.861	0.846	0.843	0.857	0.856

Table 4. The algorithm performance with the ratio of test set at 60 % and 80 %

Algorithm performance	60 %		80 %			
	15	20	5	10	15	20
PMF	0.847	0.836	0.841	0.829	0.799	0.779
Original	0.837	0.816	0.810	0.805	0.785	0.783
Genre	0.841	0.824	0.823	0.813	0.807	0.795
keyword	0.839	0.823	0.815	0.798	0.774	0.769
Keyword-genre-keyword	0.837	0.812	0.808	0.796	0.781	0.775

First, the single-node path and the original algorithm are analyzed, and the data with test set is 40 %, 60 % and 80 %, as shown in Fig. 5. As the original algorithm would be the optimization of single-node path movie-genre-movie and movie-keyword-movie, we discuss properties of the original algorithm and single-node path algorithm together.

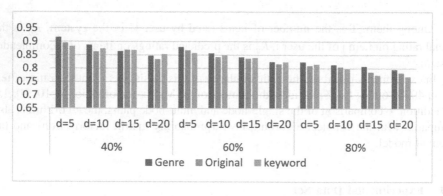

Fig. 5. Algorithm comparison of single-node path

Overall, the performance of two single-node path movie-genre-movie and movie-keyword-movie is good. Whether the size in dimension of matrix factorization and the test set is large or not, the prediction accuracy is high. While analyzing single-node paths, the effect of movie-keyword-movie is better than that of the movie-genre-movie, in a large degree, due to the data of keywords and genres is not in the same magnitude. Intuitively, the experimental result of original algorithm performs well as the original algorithm is the optimized results of single-node paths, but the effect of original algorithm cannot be out of the single-node range.

The previous comparison of the two single-node paths indicts the movie-keyword-movie better than the movie-genre-movie, so in the subsequent selection of multi-node path, the keyword would be the primary element in the path, and thus the multi-node path is movie-keyword-genre-movie-movie. The overall results of five algorithm in this thesis with the ratio of test set at 40 %, 60 %, and 80 % would be presented in Figs. 6, 7 and 8, respectively.

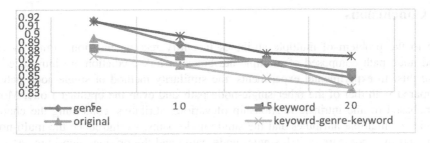

Fig. 6. Algorithm comparison of 40 % test set

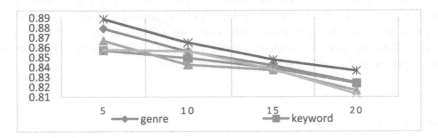

Fig. 7. Algorithm comparison of 60 % test set

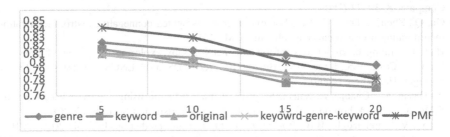

Fig. 8. Algorithm comparison of 80 % test set

By means of the algorithm comparison in various test set, it is obvious to notice the unified algorithms being better and better with the MAE decreasing on the single-node path and multi-node path, with the increase of the ratio in test set and the specific matrix factorization dimension. Besides, all algorithms are better than the PMF algorithm; Normally, in a single-node way, effect of movie-keyword-movie is better than original algorithm, although in the test set 40 % and 60 %, the situation would be inverse but a bit; In the unified case, the overall performance of the movie-keyword-genre-keyword-movie is better than single-node paths and the original algorithm, although the situation would be inverse but a bit.

4 Conclusions

Due to the problem of multiple attributes in entity recommendation, similarity and multi-node path composed of multiple attributes in link prediction are introduced to solve this. In experimental experiments, the similarity method of single-node path is compared with that of the other single-node path and even the optimized one. Moreover, based on the intrinsic relationship of various attributes, combining the characteristics of multiple attributes and the single-node paths, we introduce the multi-node path, and then compare it with single- node paths and the original algorithm. At last, the model can effectively evaluate entity link network and the entity rating network, experimental results show that the experimental results of user factor matrix and item factor matrix can simulate the behavior trend of users. The experiments indict multi-node path in Mu-En is better than the original algorithm and single-node paths in Mu-En in movielens-100 k. For the future work, we will extend the algorithm to more abundant data set, especially including more abundant entity elements, and carry out more experiments to verify the accuracy of the model.

References

1. Liben-Nowell, D., Kleinberg, J.: The link - prediction problem for social networks. J. Am. Soc. Inform. Sci. Technol. **58**(7), 1019–1031 (2007)
2. Koren, Y., Bell, R., Volinsky, C.: Matrix factorization techniques for recommender systems. Computer **8**, 30–37 (2009)
3. Gu, Q., Zhou, J., Ding, C.: Collaborative filtering: weighted nonnegative matrix factorization incorporating user and entity graphs. In SDM (2010)
4. Han, J.: Mining heterogeneous information networks by exploring the power of links. In: Gama, J., Costa, V.S., Jorge, A.M., Brazdil, P.B. (eds.) DS 2009. LNCS, vol. 5808, pp. 13–30. Springer, Heidelberg (2009)
5. Al Hasan, M., Chaoji, V., Salem, S., et al.: Link prediction using supervised learning. In: SDM 2006: Workshop on Link Analysis, Counter-terrorism and Security (2006)
6. Leroy, V., Cambazoglu, B.B., Bonchi, F.: Cold start link prediction. In KDD 2010 (2010)
7. Taskar, B., Wong, M.F., Abbeel, P., Koller, D.: Link prediction in relational data. In NIP 2003 (2003)
8. Ji, M., Sun, Y., Danilevsky, M., Han, J., Gao, J.: Graph Regularized Transductive Classification on Heterogeneous Information Networks. In: Balcázar, J.L., Bonchi, F., Gionis, A., Sebag, M. (eds.) ECML PKDD 2010, Part I. LNCS, vol. 6321, pp. 570–586. Springer, Heidelberg (2010)

Identifying Collusion Attack Based on Preference Similarity in Mixed Reputation Recommendation Model

Tengteng Shen[1(✉)], Wenan Tan[1,2], Yong Sun[1], and Li Huang[1,3]

[1] School of Computer Science and Technology,
Nanjing University of Aeronautics and Astronautics, Nanjing 211106, China
{qiudeluoye, sunyong_cug}@163.com
[2] School of Computer and Information,
Shanghai Second Polytechnic University, Shanghai 210209, China
wtan@foxmail.com
[3] School of Information and Electromechanical Engineering,
Jiangsu Open University, Nanjing 210017, China
huangli713@126.com

Abstract. Due to the emergence of a large number of new nodes in peer-to-peer network, the trust matrix is sparse and data is insufficient. Therefore, global trusts of peers are inaccurate which are computed by trust matrix iteration and the success rates of transactions become low. PSRTrust, a mixed trust model combining global trusts and local trusts based on preference similarities, is proposed to restore sparse trust matrix by Similarity Random Walk. It optimizes the unreasonable assumption, improves the power-law distribution, and identifies collusion attack by preference similarity. Mathematic analyses and simulation results show that the proposed model is more robust under general conditions that collusion attacks in an attempt to deliberately subvert the system, and the success rates of transactions are higher compared to the current trust model.

Keywords: Peer-to-peer · Trust · Sparse trust calculation · Preference similarity · Distributed hash table · Collusion attack

1 Introduction

A peer-to-peer (P2P) network, being a highly sharing and distributed network without center services, has many benefits over traditional Internet, such as Client/Server or Brower/Server. Peers in this network communicate directly with each other to exchange information they own, distribute tasks, or execute transactions. But the anonymous, open and dynamic natures of this network are vulnerable to malicious attacks. A variety of attacks on trust models are currently found, including the attacks of single malicious node or collusion attacks. And the collusion group consisting of many malicious nodes is more harmful when collaborating with each other. Whether the trust model can identify and isolate the collusion nodes or not, determines the validity and robustness of trust model. In order to avoid these security risks, establishing a reliable trust model is crucial [1].

© Springer International Publishing Switzerland 2016
Q. Zu and B. Hu (Eds.): HCC 2016, LNCS 9567, pp. 355–364, 2016.
DOI: 10.1007/978-3-319-31854-7_32

Trust model is an evaluation system, in which each peer is evaluated quantifiably based on historical transaction records [2, 3]. Generally, the trust model is divided into two categories, the personalized trust rating model and the global reputation model.

The former can predict trust rating between two peers, which have no transactions before, according to the recommendations of limited peers. It is easy and efficient due to the self-policing of each peer, but this predicted trust of peer is local and partial. This trust rating value could be obtained by applying different functions to consider all the history transactions' importance, data, and services quality, etc. Some typical approaches to calculate the local trust ratings are given in [6, 7]. VectorTrust [6] investigates the Most Trustable Path (MTP) of two peers using Bellman-Ford algorithm. Moreover, M-Trust [7] predicts the local trust combining Bellman-Ford algorithm with weighted average. These models need to leverage the existing interactions, which is influenced by the integrity of trust data. Therefore, this paper utilizes a robust approach, preference similarity, to the integrity of trust data.

The global reputation model defines a comprehensive evaluation for each peer in the network by considering all local trusts from other peers who have interacted directly or indirectly with this peer. Several global models are configurated in [9, 10, 11]. EigenTrust [9] aggregates local trusts between peers by having them perform a distributed calculation approaching the eigenvector of trust matrix over the peers. This model relies on an assumption, that is, the peer with higher global trust is more credible. But this assumption leads that most transactions occur in a few peers that have higher global trust. This not only makes a few peers with higher global trust under the heavy load and resources of other peers wasteful, but also neglects the selective preference of peers, which results in the inaccuracy of trust quantification and low success rate of transactions.

With a large number of new peers joining, the number of peers and resources in P2P networks is increasing. In the initial stage, the trust matrix is sparse, which records interaction evaluations between peers, so the trust data is incomplete and the trust quantification is reduced accordingly.

To solve the problems above, this paper proposes a mixed reputation recommendation model based on preference similarities in order to identify and isolate malicious collusions. This model presents Similarity Random Walk to predict indirect trust by combining with Random Walk strategy in literature [12], which alleviates the problem of sparseness to improve the quality of recommendation system. Moreover, this paper also puts forward rational improvement to the power-law distribution and the Chord protocol to realize the distributed storage and query of trust data.

2   PSRTrust System Construction

2.1   Model Definition

Definition 1. Preference Vector. The different peers have different preference to the evaluation indicators when evaluating various services. The evaluation indicators includes download speed, file quality, transmission speed, etc: $(\omega_{i1}, \omega_{i2}, \omega_{i3}, \cdots, \varphi_{ik})$, where $\omega_{ik} = 0, 1, 2, 3, 4, 5$; ω_{ik} represents the kth preference degree of peer i.

Definition 2. Preference Similarity. The different preference degree of evaluation indicators between peer i and peer j results in the different evaluation behaviors. The formulas can calculate the similarity, such as cosine similarity, generalized Dice coefficient method, etc. This paper selects the cosine similarity formula to compute the preference similarity among peers.

$$C_{ij} = \frac{\sum_{l=1}^{n} \omega_{il}\omega_{jl}}{\sqrt{\sum_{l=1}^{k} \omega_{il}^2}\sqrt{\sum_{l=1}^{k} \omega_{jl}^2}} \tag{1}$$

Definition 3. Preference Similarity Matrix $(C_{ij})_{n \times n}$.

Definition 4. Local Trust. The local can be divided into direct trust and indirect trust. The direct trust, D_{ij}, represents that peer i evaluates peer j according to the direct historical transaction records. The formula is:

$$\begin{cases} \frac{\max(S_{ij},0)}{\sum_j \max(S_{ij},0)}, \sum_j \max(S_{ij},0) \neq 0 \\ 0, \sum_j \max(S_{ij},0) = 0 \end{cases} \tag{2}$$

Where $S_{ij} = G_{ij} - F_{ij}$, G_{ij} represents the successful interactions with peer j based on peer i. To the contrary, F_{ij} indicates the unsuccessful interactions. And $D_{ii} = 0$. The indirect trust, T_{ij}, peer i predicts the trust rating of peer j by recommendations of other peers while peer i has no transactions with peer j before. The calculation formula is:

$$T_{ij} = \sum_{k \in R} D_{kj} \times G_k \times C_{ik} \tag{3}$$

where R is a node set who has interactions with peer j. D_{kj} is the direct trust between peer j and recommended node k in set R. C_{ik} is a preference similarity value between peer j and recommended node k in set R. G_k is the global trust of recommended node.

Definition 5. Trust Matrix. That is a direct trust matrix $(D_{ij})_{n \times n}$.

Definition 6. Global Trust. The global trust is a comprehensive evaluation given by all other nodes. The global trust vector is

$$G = (G_1, G_2, \cdots G_n)^T \tag{4}$$

where G_i is the global trust of peer i.

2.2 Similarity Random Walk (SRW)

In P2P network, the interactions among peers are random. On the basis of the definition of trust matrix, $\forall i \geq 1, j \leq n$, $0 \leq D_{ij} \leq 1$ and $\sum_{i=1}^{n} D_{ij} = 1$. Therefore, $(D_{ij})_{n \times n}$ is a stochastic matrix in which each row sum equals to 1. All global reputation values G_i for n nodes form a normalized reputation vector $G = (G_i)_n$ where $\sum_{i=1}^{n} G_i = 1$. The global trust vector is calculated by formula (5), given an arbitrary initial reputation vector $G^{(0)}$ and the threshold of small error ε. After a sufficient number of k iterations, the global reputation vector converges to the eigenvector of trust matrix G. This recursive process is motivated by the Markov random walk, which is widely used in ranking Web pages. Every iteration considers the local trust of all neighbors.

$$G^{(t+1)} = (D_{ij})_{n \times n} \times G^{(t)} \tag{5}$$

With a large number of new peers joining, the number of peers and resources in P2P networks are increasing. Comparing to the network scale, the trust matrix recording interaction evaluations between peers become sparse, which renders the incompleteness of trust data and the incompleteness of trust data. Due to this problem, the global trust obtained by iteration of trust matrix is inaccurate.

Definition 7. Reverse Trust Matrix of 0-1. $(N_{ij})_{n \times n}$ is a matrix on the basis of trust matrix where $N_{ij} = 0, 1$:

$$N_{ij} = \begin{cases} 1, D_{ij} = 0 \\ 0, D_{ij} \neq 0 \end{cases} \tag{6}$$

This paper proposes a similarity random walk strategy, which combines the idea of paper [12] with Markov random walk to accurately calculate global reputations. In each iteration, this paper takes the preference similarities among peers into account to restore the deficient trust matrix. The indirect trust matrix $(T_{ij})_{n \times n}$ can be computed by considering preference similarity according to formula (7). Then the repaired matrix of preference similarity $(S_{ij})_{n \times n}$ is calculated by formula (8) which is a normalized matrix. Eventually, the iteration computing aggregates by formula (9).

$$(T_{ij})_{n \times n} = (G_k \times C_{ik})_{n \times n} \times (D_{ij})_{n \times n} \tag{7}$$

$$(S_{ij})_{n \times n} = (T_{ij})_{n \times n} \& (N_{ij})_{n \times n} + (D_{ij})_{n \times n} \tag{8}$$

$$G^{(t+1)} = (S_{ij})_{n \times n} \times G^{(t)}. \tag{9}$$

2.3   Improvement of Power-Law Distribution

In EigenTrust and PowerTrust model, the hypothesis that the peer who has the higher global trust is more reliable, leads to the power-law distribution of feedbacks. In other words, the vast majority of transactions occur in a few peers that have higher global trust, which makes these peers under the heavy loads and resources of other peers wasteful. This assumption doesn't take different preferences of peers and local trusts into consideration which neglects individual choices.

This article adopts the strategy in Fig. 1 referring to the factors above. Firstly, this strategy takes personal interaction records of peer i into account. If peer i has

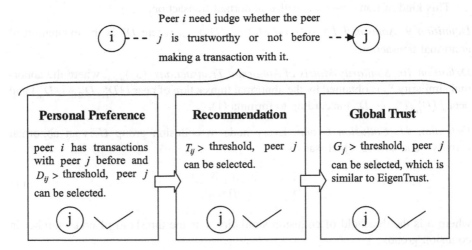

Fig. 1. Improvement of strategy

transactions with the peer j before and $D_{ij} \geq$ threshold, peer j is reliable and selectable. Moreover, peer i judges whether peer j is reliable or not by the recommendations of peers who are similar to peer i. If there is no interaction between two peers and no recommendation given by similarity peers, the following strategy is same to Eigen-Trust, that is to say, the global reputation of peer j is the ultimate standard.

3   Collusion Attacks

Collusion group is a combination of two or more malicious peers which supply a large number of fake transactions. Malicious peers in this group set high trust values among each other to get highlighted global trusts as trustworthy peers have and give low trust values to other good peers. The attacked targets of all peers in collusion group are consistent, that is to say, when some peers in collusion group attack targets, other malicious peers in collusion group also attack the target peers. Then the attacks of peers in collusion group to the same target are consistent. If some peers in collusion group aim to lower or increase the trust values of targets, the other peers in collusion group will adopt the same strategy. Therefore, the activities of malicious peers in collusion group are similar to each other. This paper uses the activities similarities among peers in collusion group to identify the collusion peers.

3.1   Definition of Collusion Attacks

Definition 8. Abnormal Transaction. The deviation between direct trust value D_{ij} and global reputation G_j is greater than abnormal threshold ω. The formula is:

$$\left| \frac{G_j - D_{ij}}{G_j} \right| > \omega, (0 \leq \omega \leq 1) \tag{10}$$

This kind of transactions is called abnormal transaction.

Definition 9. Abnormal Transaction Matrix. $(D^*_{ij})_{n \times n}$, where D^*_{ij} is the evaluation of abnormal transaction.

Definition 10. Similarity Matrix of Abnormal Transactions. $(S_{ij})_{n \times n}$, where the abnormal similarity S_{ij} is obtained by the abnormal transaction of peer i $(D^*_{i1}, D^*_{i2}, \cdots D^*_{in})$ and peer j $(D^*_{j1}, D^*_{j2}, \cdots D^*_{jn})$ according to formula (1).

Definition 11. Collusion Group. Every node in collusion group U is an abnormal activity node among which satisfy

$$\begin{cases} S_{ij} > \delta, (0 \le \delta \le 1) \\ |U| > \varepsilon, (0 \le \varepsilon) \end{cases} \tag{11}$$

where δ is the threshold of collusion similarity, ϵ is the threshold of node number in collusion group.

3.2   Collusion Detection

This paper implements the activities similarity among collusion group to identify the collusion attacks. Firstly, the attacked activities of malicious nodes are identified by leveraging the consistency of attacked targets and activities in collusion according to the Definition 8. This process filters trust matrix $(D_{ij})_{n \times n}$ to obtain abnormal transaction matrix $(D^*_{ij})_{n \times n}$, in which the majority of horizontal vectors are zero vector. Then the activity similarities S_{ij} among nonzero horizontal vectors of $(D^*_{ij})_{n \times n}$ is obtained by the formula in Definition 10. Eventually, the collusion group is identified by using the similarity matrix of abnormal transactions according to Definition 11. The strategy in this paper is specified in Algorithm 1.

Algorithm 1. The detection of collusion group.

```
For (peer iI R) {
  For (peer jI (R-1) & i<j)
    If (|Gj-Dij / Gj| > ω, (0 ≤ ω ≤ 1))
      Add Dij to the (D*i1, D*i2, ··· D*in);
For (peer iI R) {
  For (peer jI (R-1) & i<j) {
    If ((D*i1, D*i2, ··· D*in) ≠ 0⃗ & (D*j1, D*j2, ··· D*jn) ≠ 0⃗) {

      Sij = Σⁿl=1 DilDjl / √(Σᵏl=1 D²il)√(Σᵏl=1 D²jl) ;

      If (Sij > δ) {
        Add peer j into the similarity set of peer i U1;
      }
    }
  }
}
}
```

4 Experiment and Discussion

Our simulation experiment is performed by using Quantitative Trust Management (QTM), a simulation system. The PSRTrust model is implemented by Java code. Due to the similarity in computing global trusts between this model and EigenTrust, this paper makes contrast experiments among PSRTrust, EigenTrust and NoTrust.

In the simulation experiments of QTM, the P2P network is defined by parameters in Table 1. The mapping relations between nodes and files in P2P network is generated by the path file. And the mapping relations between nodes and requirements documents are also in this file. This paper make comparisons among different model by the success rate of transactions.

Table 1. Parameters in simulation experiments

Parameter	Basic definition	Default value
n	Number of peers	100
f	Number of files	200
t	Number of transactions	1000
p	Pre-trusted users	10
m	Purely malicious users	20
ε	Threshold for convergence	0.001

4.1 Sparse Trust Matrix Experiments

Two simulation experiments on trusty matrix sparsity have been conducted. First experiment is to study how trusty matrix sparsity affects success rate of trades between

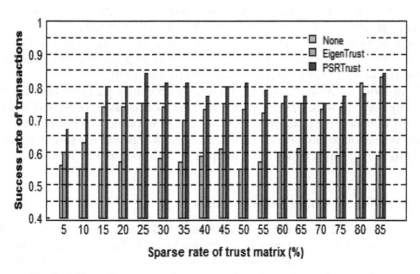

Fig. 2. Effect of sparse rate in trust matrix to success rate of transactions

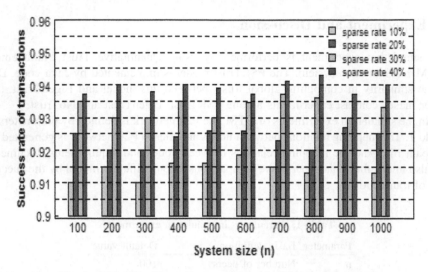

Fig. 3. Effect of system size to model with different sparse rates

nodes. The other studies if the performance of PSRTrust is stable with different sparseness in different networks.

As shown in Fig. 2, with sparseness ranges from 5 % to 55 %, because trusty matrix sparseness is too large and data of PSRTrust model are more complete than EigenTrust and NoTrust, then in the changing of sparseness, PSRTrust model has higher success rate. Compared with EigenTrust, the rate can be increased by 4 %–11 % and maximum success rate appears when sparseness is 25 %. With the increase of trust data and sparseness ranging from 60 % to 85 %, success rate gap between PSRTrust and EigenTrust becomes smaller, and finally the gap becomes very tiny.

In Fig. 3, with trusty matrix sparseness being 10 %, 20 %, 30 % and 40 %, PSRTrust performs differently in P2P networks with different scales. As the scale of networks becomes larger, with the same sparseness, trade success rate of PSRTrust model is almost the same from 0 % to 0.6 %. While with different sparseness, trade success rate of PSRTrust fluctuates between −0.01 and +0.01.

From above analysis, PSRTrust can relatively accurately predict default data with Similarity Random Walk strategy. Hence, its trade success rate is better with less trust data; and with more trust data, its success rate can be the same with that of EigenTrust model. Simulation results have shown that the scale of networks has smaller impact on PSRTrust model, which means it can be applied to large-scale P2P networks.

4.2   Effectiveness Against Collusion Attacks

Comparison of PSRTrust with EigenTrust and NoTrust is shown in Fig. 4. With EigenTrust model or without models, as the number of colluding nodes increase, gap trade success rate is small, which indicates that colluding nodes have larger effect on EigenTrustl. That is to say, EigenTrust doesn't use any strategy to prohibit the effect of

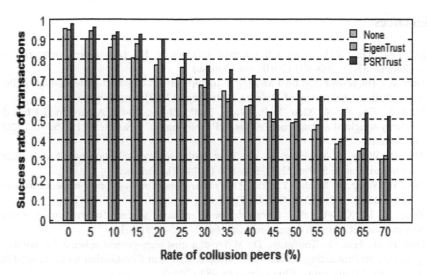

Fig. 4. Effect of collusion attack to success rate of transactions

colluding nodes. According to the similarity of attack objects and attack behaviors between nodes in colluding teams, the study conduct clustering analysis, identify and curb colluding nodes. When the rate of malicious nodes ranges from 0 to 20 %, success rate of the model keep above 90 %; when ranging from 20 % to 70 %, the gap is larger than 10 % between PSRTrust, EigenTrust and NoTrust, which means PSRTrust has a better success rate; when the rate is above 60 %, the gap becomes above 15 %. From the above analysis, PSRTrust model can better curb the effect of colluding nodes, and obviously improve the trade success rate between nodes.

5 Conclusions and Future Work

To treat incomplete trust data, using Similarity Random Walk, this paper constructs Preference Similarity Recommendation Trust (PSRTrust) model, and identifies malicious nodes by the similarity of malicious nodes in colluding teams. Simulation experiments have shown that the model can be applied to large-scale P2P networks. With incomplete trust data, the model can still performs well, and it can better restrict the attack of colluding teams.

Reward and punishment mechanism is another important part of P2P security mechanisms, which will severely punish malicious nodes. Future studies will be carried out in these aspects.

Acknowledgement. The paper is supported in part by the National Natural Science Foundation of China under Grant No. 61272036, the Fundamental Research Funds for the Central Universities under Grant No. NZ2013306, the Key Disciplines of Software Engineering of Shanghai Second Polytechnic University under Grant No. XXKZD1301, and the University Natural Science Foundation of Jiangsu Province under Grant No. 15KJB520005.

References

1. Li, Y.-J., Dai, Y.-F.: Research on trust mechanism for peer-to-peer network. Chin. J. Comput. **33**(3), 390–405 (2010). (in Chinese)
2. Dou, W.: The research on trust-aware P2P topologies and constructing technologies. Ph. D. thesis. National University of Defense Technology (2003). (in Chinese)
3. Li, J.-T., Jing, Y.-N., Xiao, X.-P., Wang, X.-P., Zhang, G.-D.: A trust model based on similarity-weighted recommendation for P2P environment. J. Softw. **18**(1), 157–167 (2007). (in Chinese)
4. Zhu, R., Wang, H.-M., Feng, D.-W.: Trustworthy services selection based on preference recommendation. J. Softw. **22**(5), 852–864 (2011). (in Chinese)
5. Dou, W., Wang, H.-M., Jia, Y., Zou, P.: A recommendation-based peer-to-peer trust model. J. Softw. **15**(4), 571–583 (2004). (in Chinese)
6. Zhao, H., Li, X.: VectorTrust: trust vector aggregation scheme for trust management in peer-to-peer networks. J. Supercomputing **64**(3), 805–829 (2013)
7. Qureshi, B., Min, G., Kouvatsos, D.: M-Trust: a trust management scheme for mobile P2P networks. In: Proceedings of the IEEE Trustcom 2010 in Conjunction with 7th IEEE/IFIP (EUC 2010), Hong Kong, China, pp. 476–483 (2010)
8. Hu, J.-L., Wu, Q.-Y., Zhou, B., Liu, J.-H.: Roubust feedback credibility-based distributed P2P trust model. J. Softw. **20**, 2885–2898 (2009). (in Chinese)
9. Kamvar, S., Schlosser, M., Garcia-Molina, H.: The EigenTrust algorithm for reputation management in P2P networks. In: Proceedings of ACM World Wide Web Conference (WWW 2003), May 2003
10. Zhou, R., Hwang, K.: PowerTrust: a robust and scalable reputation system for trusted peer-to-peer computing. IEEE Trans. Parallel Distrib. Syst. **18**(4), 460–473 (2007)
11. Xiong, L., Liu, L.: PeerTrust: supporting reputation-based trust for peer-to-peer electronic communities. IEEE Trans. Knowl. Data Eng. **16**(7), 843–857 (2004)
12. Wang, S.-C., Lin, S.-M., Lu, Y.-C.: Handling the incomplete data problem using Bayesian networks. J. Tsinghua Univ. **40**(9), 65–68 (2000). (in Chinese)
13. Ratnasamy, S., Francis, P., Handley, M., Karp, R., Shenker, S.: A scalable content addressable network. In: Proceedings of ACM SIGCOMM, August 2001
14. Stoica, I., Morris, R., Karger, D., Kaashoek, M.F., Balakrishnan, H.: Chord: a scalable peer-to-peer lookup service for internet applications. In: Proceedings of the 2001 Conference on Applications, Technologies, Architectures, and Protocols for Computer Communications, pp. 149–160. ACM Press (2001)
15. West, A.G., Lee, I., Kannan, S., Sokolsky, O.: An evaluation framework for reputation management systems. Dept. Comput. Inf. Sci. (2009)

An Improved K-medoids Clustering Algorithm Based on a Grid Cell Graph Realized by the P System

Wei Sun, Laisheng Xiang, Xiyu Liu$^{(\boxtimes)}$, and Dan Zhao

College of Management Science and Engineering, Shandong Normal University,
East of Wenhua Road No. 88, Jinan 250014, Shandong, China
{weizifighting, sdxyliu, 13793195081}@163.com

Abstract. When the data set is massive and dense, it can often be convenient that clustering all effective grid cells which contain many points. This study firstly divides the data points into different grid cells. Then, the study proposed a specific P system to compute the improved K-medoids. Clustering Algorithm based on a grid cell graph and extended the application of membrane computing. The study improve the K-medoids algorithm by selecting the k initial centers based on the gravitation between the effective grid cells which can greatly improve the quality of clustering. The study make the gravitation between two grid cells as the similarity. As we all known, the P system has the advantage of high parallelism and lower computational time complexity. This specific P system also can handle the big data based on the level of grid cells.

Keywords: Data mining · Clustering · Membrane computing · Grid cell algorithm · K-medoids algorithm

1 Introduction

Clustering is an important part in data mining which tries to find the structures of unlabeled data sets. As a result, the elements in the same cluster have higher similarities than those in different clusters. Clustering is to describe data sets more simply by using some interesting or meaningful clusters after got their distribution structures.

The K-medoids algorithm has the advantages of strong robustness and high accuracy. However, the K-medoids algorithm also suffers from some drawbacks. It is very sensitive to the initial centers. In this study we improved the K-medoids with grid cell graph. It selected k high density grid cell as initial centers to get over this drawbacks and combined the improved K-medoids clustering algorithm with a novel P system to immensely reduce the time complexity. Grid cell graph clustering algorithm can decrease time and space complexity for massive data sets. The algorithm first divide the clustering space into finite number of cells, and then perform the required operations on the grid-cell space.

Membrane computing, first introduced by Paun in 1998 [1] has been applied on many fields such as combinatorial problem, finite state problems and graph theory. It has the advantage of parallelism so it can lessen the time complexity and improve the process speed of massive data sets.

© Springer International Publishing Switzerland 2016
Q. Zu and B. Hu (Eds.): HCC 2016, LNCS 9567, pp. 365–374, 2016.
DOI: 10.1007/978-3-319-31854-7_33

This study firstly divides the data points into different grid cells. Then, the study proposed a specific P system to compute the improved K-medoids algorithm based on grid cell. This study improve the algorithm by selecting the k initial centers based on the gravitation between the effective grid cells. This study make the gravitation between two grid cells as the similarity. As we all known, the P system has the advantage of high parallelism and lower computational time complexity. This specific P system also can handle the big data based on the level of grid cells.

2   The Improved K-medoids Clustering Based on Grid Cell Graph

2.1   The Preprocess of Data

The Grid Cell is defined as follows: Grid cells can be obtained after partitioned the multidimensional ordered attribute space by using a multidimensional grid partition method. If the number of points in a grid cell is larger than a threshold parameter Min, then this grid cell is called an effective grid cell.

The data structure of grid cell g can be defined as [2]:

$$D(g) = (\text{Grid-Label, Grid-Position, Grid-Range, Point-Number, Points-set}) \quad (1)$$

In (1), Grid-Label is the key label of the grid cell.

Grid-Position is the center position of the grid cell. It is an m−dimensional vector expressed by $P = (p_1, p_2, \ldots, p_m)$.

Grid-Range records the region of the grid cell. It is an m−dimensional interval vector expressed by:

$$R = ([p_1 - r_1 / 2, p_1 + r_1 / 2), \ldots, [p_m - r_m / 2, p_m + r_m / 2)) \quad (2)$$

where $r_i(i = 1, 2, \ldots, m)$ is the interval length in the $i - th$ dimension of the grid cell. Point-Number records the number of points in the grid cell. Points-Set records the labels of points of the grid cell.

Procedure:

Step 1:   The number of effective grid cells EG(effective grid) is set to zero.

Step 2:   Suppose there are l effective grid cells after partitioned the m-dimensional ordered attribute space by using a multidimensional grid partition method basing on $Interval = (\gamma_1, \gamma_2, \ldots \gamma_m)$. If the number of points in a grid cell is larger than the threshold parameter Min, then this grid cell is regarded as an effective grid cell and the operation EG++ is executed. At last, some basic information of this effective grid cell is stored according to (1).

Step 3:   Finally, a set containing all effective grid cells can be obtained.

2.2   The Improved K-medoids Algorithm Based on the Grid Cells

The steps of the improved K-medoids algorithm based on the grid cells are as follows:

Step1:   Identify the k initial center points;

a. Firstly, calculate the gravitation as similarity between any two points.

$$F = \frac{Gm_i m_j}{w_{ij}^2} \tag{3}$$

In (3), G is a constant, m_i, m_j are the numbers of points in the grid cell i, j, w_{ij} is the distance between the center point of the grid cell i and j.

b. Count the number of points which is in the radius of any point $m_i + +$;
c. If the counts exceeds the given parameter Min, the grid cell is defined as an effective grid cell.
d. Select the highest density effective grid cell as the initial center of the first cluster, then find the effective grid cell which has the minimum gravitation to the first center point as the second initial center, and the third initial center is the effective grid cell which has the minimum total gravitation to the first and the second center points. And so on, until the k initial centers are determined [3];

Step 2:   Distribute the remaining data points to the clusters by the criterion of the maximum gravitation to the center of the corresponding cluster;

Step 3:   Randomly select a non-center point in each cluster;

Step 4:   Compute the total gravitation of changing the initial center by the selected point;

Step 5:   If the gravitation becomes large, turn the selected point to be the center point. Otherwise, the initial center point remains unchanged;

Step 6:   Repeat the steps 1 to 5 above until the k centers don't change anymore or we reach the maximum number.

The advantage of the density based K-medoids algorithm lies in taking the density of data points into consideration. As a consequence, the clustering result gains more accuracy.

3   A Specific P System for the Improved K-medoids Algorithm

3.1   Basic Concept of P System

According to different process of cells managing chemical substances, There are mainly three kinds of models are proposed: Cell-like P Systems, Tissue-like P Systems and Neural-like P Systems [4]. The rules in P system are executed uncertainly and maximum concurrently. P system van be divided into three types from the angle of kinds of rules: transition P system, P system with commution rules and P system with active membranes [16].

In this study, the Cell-like P System is applied. It imitates the function and structure of the cells, including the membrane structure, rules and objects. A membrane m with no lower neighbor is called elementary membrane and a membrane m with no upper neighbor is called a skin membrane [5]. Membranes divide the whole system into different regions [6]. Rules and objects exist in regions. The rules are executed in a nondeterministic and maximum parallel way (Fig. 1).

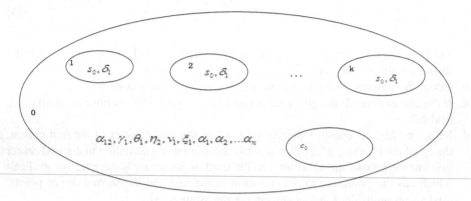

Fig. 1. The membrane structure of P system with improved K-medoids algorithm based on grid cell

$$\prod = (O, \mu, M_0 \ldots M_k, r_i, i_0) \tag{4}$$

The notation in (4) are:

O represents the objects in the P system. Each object is a $k * d$ dimensional vector. μ represents the membrane structure of the P system. M mean the initial objects on the membrane.

$M_0 = (\alpha_{12}, \gamma_1, \theta_1, \eta_2, \nu_1, \xi_1, \alpha_1, \alpha_2, \ldots \alpha_n)$ denotes the initial objects in membrane 0.
$M_1 = M_2 = \ldots = M_k = (s_0, \delta_1)$ denotes the initial objects in membrane 1, 2...k.
r symbolize the rules contained in the membrane. i_0 indicates the output region.

3.2   Different Rules in the P System

The rules in the region 0 of the P system:

$$r_1 = \{\gamma_i \alpha_i \beta_i^t \to \gamma_{i+1} A_{mi} \beta_{mi}^t | Min - 1 \le t \le n\} \cup \{\gamma_i \beta_i^t \to \gamma_{i+1} | 0 \le t < Min - 1\}$$
$$\cup \{\gamma_{n+1} A_{mi} \to A_{li} | 1 \le i \le n\}$$

$$r_2 = \{\beta_{1j_1}^{t_{j_1}} \beta_{2j_2}^{t_{j_2}} \ldots \beta_{lj_l}^{t_{j_l}} \to \beta_{1j_1}^{t_{j_1}-n} \beta_{2j_2}^{t_{j_2}-n} \ldots \beta_{lj_l}^{t_{j_l}-n} | 1 \le j_1, j_2 \ldots j_l \le n, Min - 1 \le t_{j_1}, t_{j_2} \ldots t_{j_l} \le n\}$$

$$r_3 = \{\beta_{1j_1}^{t_1}\beta_{2j_2}^{t_2}\ldots\beta_{lj_l}^{t_l} \rightarrow \beta_{1j_1}^{t_1+1}\beta_{2j_2}^{t_2+1}\ldots\beta_{lj_l}^{t_{ul}+1}| -n < t_1, t_2\ldots t_l < 0, 1 \leq j_1, j_2\ldots j_l \leq n\}$$

$$r_4 = \{A_{pj_p}\beta_{1j_1}^{t_1}\beta_{1j_2}^{t_2}\ldots\beta_{1j_l}^{t_l} \rightarrow O_{1j_p}, O_{1j_{p,\mathrm{int}1}}|t_p = 0, 1 \leq p \leq l\}$$

$$r_5 = \{\eta_t\theta_p A_{pi}O_{1j_1}O_{2j_2}\ldots O_{(t-1)j_{(t-1)}} \rightarrow \eta_t\theta_p A_{pi}O_{1j_1}O_{2j_2}\ldots O_{(t-1)j_{(t-1)}}F_{pj_1}^{\omega_{ij_1}}F_{pj_2}^{\omega_{ij_2}}\ldots F_{pj_{(t-1)}}^{\omega_{ij_{(t-1)}}}$$
$$|1 \leq j_1, j_2\ldots j_l \leq n, 1 \leq p \leq l, 2 \leq t \leq k\} \cup \{(\theta_p \rightarrow \theta_{p+1})_{\neg A_{pi}}|1 \leq i \leq n\}$$

$$r_6 = \{A_{pi}F_{pj_1}^{\omega_{ij_1}}F_{pj_2}^{\omega_{ij_2}}\ldots F_{pj_{(t-1)}}^{\omega_{ij_{(t-1)}}} \rightarrow A_{pi}F_p^{\omega_p^{t-1}}|2 \leq t \leq k, 1 \leq p \leq l, 1 \leq j_1, j_2\ldots j_l \leq n\}$$

$$r_7 = \{F_{pj_1}^{\omega_{1j_1}^{t-1}}F_{pj_2}^{\omega_{2j_2}^{t-1}}\ldots F_{pj_{(t-1)}}^{\omega_{lj_l}^{t-1}} \rightarrow F_{pj_1}^{(\omega_{1j_1}^{t-1}-1)}F_{pj_2}^{(\omega_{2j_2}^{t-1}-1)}\ldots F_{pj_{(t-1)}}^{(\omega_{lj_l}^{t-1}-1)}|2 \leq t \leq k\}$$

$$r_8 = \{A_{pi}F_{1j_1}^{t_1}F_{2j_2}^{t_2}\ldots F_{lj_l}^{t_l}\eta_t \rightarrow O_{ti}, O_{ti,\mathrm{int}}\eta_{t+1}|t_j = 0, 2 \leq t \leq k, 1 \leq p, i, j_1, j_2\ldots j_l \leq n\}$$

$$r_9 = \{A_{pi} \rightarrow \alpha_i|1 \leq p \leq l, 1 \leq i \leq n\}$$

$$r_{10} = \{(\xi_i\alpha_iO_{1j_1}O_{2j_2}\ldots O_{kj_k} \rightarrow \xi_i\alpha_iO_{1j_1}O_{2j_2}\ldots O_{kj_k}F_{ij_1}^{\omega_{ij_1}}F_{ij_2}^{\omega_{ij_2}}\ldots F_{ijk}^{\omega_{ijk}})_{\alpha_i}|1 \leq i, j_1, j_2\ldots j_l \leq n\}$$
$$\cup \{(\xi_i \rightarrow \xi_{i+1})_{\neg\alpha_i}|1 \leq i \leq n\}$$

$$r_{11} = \{\xi_iF_{ij_1}^{\omega_{ij_1}}F_{ij_2}^{\omega_{ij_2}}\ldots F_{ijk}^{\omega_{ijk}} \rightarrow \xi_iF_{ij_1}^{\omega_{ij_1}-M}F_{ij_2}^{\omega_{ij_2}-M}\ldots F_{ijk}^{\omega_{ijk}-M}|1 \leq i, j_1, j_2\ldots j_l \leq n\}$$

$$r_{12} = \{\xi_iF_{ij_1}^{\omega_{ij_1}-M}F_{ij_2}^{\omega_{ij_2}-M}\ldots F_{ijk}^{\omega_{ijk}-M}$$
$$\rightarrow \xi_iF_{ij_1}^{\omega_{ij_1}-M+1}F_{ij_2}^{\omega_{ij_2}-M+1}\ldots F_{ijk}^{\omega_{ijk}-M+1}|1 \leq i, j_1, j_2\ldots j_l \leq n\}$$

$$r_{13} = \{\xi_i\alpha_iF_{i1}^{\omega_1}F_{i2}^{\omega_2}\ldots F_{ik}^{\omega_k} \rightarrow \xi_{i+1}\alpha_{i,\mathrm{inj}}|\omega_j = 0, 1 \leq i \leq n, 1 \leq j \leq k\}$$

$$r_{14} = \{v_1^iv_2^j \rightarrow (\theta)_{in1}(\theta)_{in2}\ldots(\theta)_{ink}|1 \leq i \leq n, 0 \leq j \leq k\} \cup \{v_2^k$$
$$\rightarrow (\zeta_1)_{in1}(\zeta_2)_{in2}\ldots(\zeta_k)_{ink}\}$$

The rules in the region $i(1 \leq i \leq k)$ of the P system [7, 8, 11]:

$$r_1' = \{(\theta\delta_t\alpha_t \rightarrow \theta X_t N_t)_{\alpha_t}|1 \leq t \leq n\} \cup \{(\theta\delta_t \rightarrow \theta\delta_{t+1})_{\neg\alpha_t}|1 \leq t \leq n\}$$

$$r_2' = \{s_0N_t\alpha_iO_{jh} \rightarrow s_{0+F_{ti}-F_{hi}}N_t\beta_iO_{jh}|1 \leq t, i, h \leq n, 1 \leq j \leq k\}$$

$$r_3' = \{s_0N_tO_{jh} \rightarrow s_p\alpha_hO_{jt}\pi_1|s_p > s_0, 1 \leq t, h \leq n, 1 \leq j \leq k\}$$
$$\cup \{s_0N_tO_{jh} \rightarrow s_p\alpha_tO_{jh}\pi_2|s_p < s_0, 1 \leq t, h \leq n, 1 \leq j \leq k\}$$

$$r_4' = \{b_i \rightarrow \alpha_i|1 \leq i \leq n\}$$

$$r_5' = \{X_t \rightarrow \delta_{t+1} | 1 \le t \le n\}$$

$$r_6' = \{\pi_1^i \pi_2^j \rightarrow v_{1,out} | 1 \le i \le n, 0 \le j \le n\} \cup \left\{ (\pi_2^j \rightarrow v_{2,out})_{\neg \pi_1^i} | 1 \le i, j \le n \right\}$$

$$r_7' = \{\theta \delta_{n+1} O_{jh} \alpha_i \rightarrow \delta_1 O_{jh}(\delta_1 O_{jh} \alpha_i, out) \psi | 1 \le i, h \le n, 1 \le j \le k\}$$
$$\cap \{\zeta_t O_{th} \alpha_i \rightarrow (\zeta_t O_{th} \alpha_i)_{inC_0} | 1 \le t \le k, 1 \le i, h \le n\}$$

$$M = \frac{G t_{max}^2}{w_{min}^2} \tag{5}$$

In (5), t_{max} means the maximum numbers of points in the grid cells. w_{min} means the minimum distance between two grid cells. M represents the maximum gravitation between the two grid cells.

3.3 The Computing Process in the P System

This section introduces the whole computations and responses in the specific P systems. High priority rule is executed prior [9]. Firstly the rule r_1 is performed according to the priority relationship. The rule r_1 is applied to search for the high density grid cell. If the grid cell α_i is a high density grid cell, it is converted to A_{mi} which means the m-th high density grid cell is α_i. And β_i' is rewritten as β_{mi}' which means the m-th high density grid cell A_{mi} contains t points. Moreover, the subscript of the last high density grid cell indicates the total number of high density ones. Then, it initiates the process to single out the highest density grid cell center point by rule r_2, r_3 and r_4. First, let all the multiplicity of $\beta_{pj_p}^{t_{jp}}$ subtract n. Second, let all the multiplicity of $\beta_{pj_p}^{t_{jp}}$ increase until one of them is 0. This means the p-th high density grid cell A_{pj_p} is the highest density grid cell and it is converted to O_{1j_p} to represent the center point of cluster 1.

Meantime, O_{1j_p} is put into the membrane labeled 1. Then, it searches for the second initial center point. Beginning with A_{1i} (if A_{1i} exists), rule r_5 is applied to calculate the gravitation between A_{1i} and O_{1j_p} and generate object $F_{pj_1}^{\omega_{ij_1}}$ which means the gravitation between the first high density grid cell A_{1i} and the center point O_{1j_p} of cluster 1 is ω_{ij_1}. Object θ_p is used to control the circulation, thus the distance between the one of high density points and O_{1j_1} can be obtained by increasing the subscript of θ_p. Then, it apply rule r_6 to get the summation of the gravitation between A_{1i} and O_{1j_p} and generates $F_p^{\omega_p^{t-1}}$. By performing the rule r_7, all the summations of the gravitations between one high density grid cell and O_{1j_1} decrease until one of them becomes 0. This means the p-th high density point has the minimum gravitation from O_{1j_1}. Then, the A_{pi} is exactly the center point of cluster 2.

Concurrently, object η_2 is converted to η_3 and it goes to next loop to search for the high density grid cell which has the minimum gravitation to O_{1j_1} and O_{2j_2}. So on it finds the k initial center points. In the next phase, it will allocate the $n - k$ common points into the membranes according to the maximum gravitation between the grid cell and the center points. First, rule r_{10} calculates gravitation between the α_i and the k initial center point and produces $F_{ij_1}^{\omega_{ij_1}}$ to $F_{ij_k}^{\omega_{ij_k}}$. Then, rule r_{11}, it subtract the constant M. Next, the r_{12} makes the $F_{ij_1}^{\omega_{ij_1}-M}$ increase until one of them becomes 0 labeled j. This means the grid cell α_i is closest to the center point of cluster j. And the grid cell α_i is sent into the j membrane. In this way, the remained points are put into the membranes labeled 1 to k.

Since there is an v_1 in membrane 0, rule r_{14} is employed to produce object θ and send a θ to the membranes labeled 1 to k. As a result, rules in membranes labeled 1 to k are activated.

In membrane $t(1 \leq t \leq k)$, it starts with point a_1 (if a_1 exists). And a_1 is set as the new center point N_1. If a_1 doesn't exist, the subscript of object δ_t increases and it goes to the next loop directly. Then, according to rule r_2', it calculates the sum between the gravitation between the new center point M_1 and the remaining points and the gravitation between the initial center point and the remaining points. The sum is added to the subscript of object s_0. It is worth noting that point α_i is transformed to b_i to avoid calculating repeatedly. Next, it apply rule r_3' to determine whether the new center point can replace the original one O_{tj_t} by detecting the total sum value. If the sum increases, that is the subscript of s_p is larger than s_0, the new center point can replace the original one and N_t is converted to O_{tj_t} and meanwhile the original center point O_{jh} is transformed to a_h. Moreover, an object π_1 is produced to show it. Otherwise, the initial center point remains unchanged and this situation is implied by object π_2. And it restores s_0 to s_p. Then, b_i is converted to α_i. It executes rule r_5' to turn X_t for next cycle. In the following step, it performs r_5'. If there exists any π_1, it means the center point of this cluster has been refined and the points need to be reclassified. By r_7', the points of cluster in the respective membrane are put into the membrane 0 for next loop. In the membrane 0, rule r_{14} is applied to produce object θ to trigger next cycle when there is any v_1. Otherwise, it produce object ζ to membranes labeled from 1 to k. The rule r_7' is activated to send the final cluster in the corresponding membrane to output membrane C_0 once there is an object ζ. The P system will not halt if rules are always executed, then this calculation is invalid, and there is no result being outputted [10]. Eventually, the computation of the clustering with the specific P system is accomplished. The output membrane is used to save the final calculation result [13].

3.4   Experiment and Analysis

This section mainly introduced the experiments, which included the data sets and parameters in experiments, the process of experiment and the experiment results. In order to give a better interpretation of our P system model for the grid cell K-medoids clustering with initial centers optimized, we take an example to simulate the procedure of the P system. Experimental results were calculated for the iris data set from UCI Machine Learning Repository. In this study, we evaluate and compare the P system with the classical K-means algorithm and the classical K- medoids algorithm (Fig. 2).

Firstly, the P system need input Iris Data set $S = \{X_1, X_2, \ldots X_n\}$, the interval length vector *Interval* $= (\gamma_1, \gamma_2, \ldots \gamma_m)$ of grid cell, the threshold parameter Min of effective grid cell and the cluster number k. The study set $\gamma_1 = \gamma_2 = \ldots = \gamma_m = 0.2$, Min = 2 and the maximum execution numbers are 1000. And the P system eventually distributes the Iris data set into 3 clusters with the maximum gravitation. In P system, each membrane is considered as a parallel computing unit with high efficiency. In every operation the rules on the same membrane are applied in a maximally parallel manner until it halts. The P system halts, when the execution steps arrive the maximum numbers or the cluster centers do not change. The object stored in the skin membrane is regarded as the best cluster centers.

Through these experimental results, the conclusion is that the special P system with grid cell K-medoids algorithm has higher average correct rates compared with the classical k-means algorithm and the classical K-medoids. In a word, the special P system with grid cell K-medoids algorithm gets a better clustering partition and can handle with big data and greatly shorten the computing time (Table 1).

Table 1. The average performance of the three methods in clustering Iris data sets.

Method	Correct points	Correct rates
K-means	137	91.3 %
K-medoids	143	95.3 %
P system	148	98.7 %

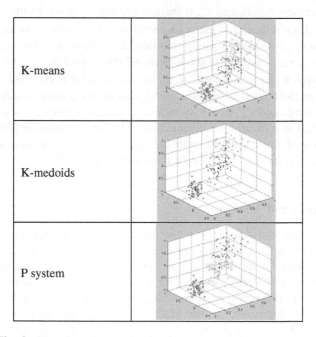

Fig. 2. The clustering result with three methods for iris data sets.

4 Conclusions

The paper presents a new P system with special membrane structure in the framework of the cellular computing with membranes. Membrane computing is a new biological computing method and P system has great parallelism which can immensely reduce the time complexity.

The P system combined with grid cell improved K-medoids algorithm which can help find the optimal cluster centers to improve the performance of the K-medoids algorithm and also can have the advantage of handle the big data. This study also proposed a novel method that used the gravitation between the Grid cells to represent the similarity of the two Grid cell.

Under the control of the membrane rules, the objects are distributed into different membranes in the P system. Membranes update the local best objects and the global best object synchronously until system reach the halt conditions. The experimental results verify the advantages of the proposed P system with the hybrid algorithm.

Acknowledgement. Project supported by National Natural Science Foundation of China (61170038,61472231), Jinan City independent innovation plan project in College and Universities, China (201401202), Ministry of education of Humanities and social science research project, China (12YJA630152), Social Science Fund Project of Shandong Province, China (11CGLJ22), outstanding youth scientist foundation project of Shandong Province, China (BS 2013DX037).

References

1. Păun, G.: Membrane computing. In: Lingas, A., Nilsson, B.J. (eds.) FCT 2003. LNCS, vol. 2751, pp. 284–295. Springer, Heidelberg (2003)
2. Chen, X.: Clustering based on a near neighbor graph and a grid cell graph. J. Intell. Inf. Syst. **40**(3), 529–554 (2013)
3. Ester, M., Kriedel, H., Sander, J., et al.: A density-based algorithm for discovering clustering clusters in large spatial database with noise. In: Proceedings of the 2nd International Conference on Knowledge Discovery and Data Mining, Portland, USA, pp. 226–231 (1996)
4. Mohammed, M.: An efficient density based improved K- medoids clustering algorithm. Int. J. Comput. Distrib. Syst. (2011)
5. Li, Q., Liu, X.: A K-medoids clustering algorithm with initial centers optimized by a P system. In: Zu, Q., Hu, B., Gu, N., Seng, S. (eds.) HCC 2014. LNCS, vol. 8944, pp. 488–500. Springer, Heidelberg (2015)
6. Paun, G.: A quick introduction to membrane computing. J. Logic Algebraic Program. **79**, 291–294 (2010)
7. Han, L., Xiang, L., Liu, X., Luan, J.: The K-medoids algorithm with initial centers optimized based on a P system. Inf. Comput. Sci. **11**(6), 132–144 (2014)
8. Pérez Jiménez, M.J., Romero Campero, F.J.: Attacking the common algorithmic problem by recognizer P systems. In: Margenstern, M. (ed.) MCU 2004. LNCS, vol. 3354, pp. 304–315. Springer, Heidelberg (2005)
9. Paun, G.: Computing with membranes. J. Comput. Syst. Sci. **61**, 108–143 (2000)

10. Zhang, G.X., Pan, L.Q.: A survey of membrane computing as a new branch of natural computing. Chin. J. Comput. **33**, 208–214 (2010)
11. Marc, G.A., Daniel, M., Alfonso, R.P., Petr, S.: A P system and a constructive membrane-inspired DNA algorithm for solving the maximum clique problem. BioSystems **90**, 687–697 (2007)
12. Paun, G., Rozenberg, G., Salomaa, A.: The Oxford Handbook of Membrane Computing. Oxford University Press, New York (2010)
13. Paun, G., Paun, R.: Membrane computing and economics: Numerical P systems. Fundamenta Informaticae. J. **73**(1), 213–227 (2006)
14. Pavel, A., Arsene, O., Buiu, C.: Enzymatic numerical P systems-a new class of membrane computing systems. In: 2010 IEEE Fifth International Conference on Bio-Inspired Computing: Theories and Applications (BIC-TA), pp. 1331–1336. IEEE (2010)
15. Jie, S., Liu, X.Y.: Density-based clustering by P system with active membranes on commodity recommendation in E-commerce websites. WSEAS Trans. Comput. **13**, 20–33 (2014)
16. Freund, R., Oswald, M., Paun, G.: Catalytic and purely catalytic P system and P automata: control mechnisms for obtaining computational completeness. In: 14th International Conference, CMC14, pp. 317–320 (2013)

Toward Gamified Personality Acquisition
in Travel Recommender Systems

Feben Teklemicael[1,2($\boxtimes$)], Yong Zhang[2], Yongji Wu[1,2], Yanshen Yin[1,2],
and Chunxiao Xing[2]

[1] Department of Computer Science and Technology, Tsinghua University, Beijing, China
[2] Research Institute of Information Technology, TNLIST, Tsinghua University, Beijing, China
{teklemicaelf10,yj-wu13,yys12}@mails.tsinghua.edu.cn,
{zhangyong05,xingcx}@tsinghua.edu.cn

Abstract. This paper proposes a novel method for user profiling in recommender systems (RS). RS have emerged as a key tool in information filtering. But despite their importance in our lives, systems still suffer from the cold-start problem: the inability to infer preferences of a new user who has not rated enough items. Up till now, only limited research has focused on optimizing user profile acquisition processes. This paper addresses that gap, employing a gamified personality-acquisition system based on the widely used Five Factor Model (FFM) for assessing personality. Our web-based system accurately extrapolates a user's preferences by guiding them through a series of interactive and contextualized questions. This paper demonstrates the efficacy of a gamified user profiling system that employs story-based questions derived from explicit personality inventory questions. The Gamified Personality Acquisition (GPA) system was shown to increase Mean Absolute Error (MAE) and Receiver Operating Characteristic (ROC) sensitivity in a travel RS while mitigating the cold-start problem in comparison to rating-based and traditional personality-based RS.

Keywords: User profiling · Personality · Five-Factor model · Item response theory · Recommendation system · Tourism

1 Introduction

The rapid growth of the tourism industry in recent years has provided online travel booking services and other entities with a massive amount of traveler data. As a result, travel sites that wish to provide useful recommendations are faced with the overwhelming task of mining through information. There is a great need for an accurate internal representation of users as a foundation for recommender services.

Recommender systems (RS) address the information overload problem by categorizing users' interests and providing personalized recommendations. In the past, predominant focus was placed on rating structures as a way of understanding users. This makes accuracy dependent on the engagement of the user when providing ratings. However, a trending solution is the employment of personality in the user modeling process. Personality Based Recommender Systems (PBRS) have served multiple

© Springer International Publishing Switzerland 2016
Q. Zu and B. Hu (Eds.): HCC 2016, LNCS 9567, pp. 375–385, 2016.
DOI: 10.1007/978-3-319-31854-7_34

purposes, including increasing recommender accuracy [12], providing a user-centric experience [9, 13] and eliminating the cold-start problem [12]. But despite the growing use of personality in RS we still observe decreased user engagement levels during the personality acquisition process [9, 11, 15].

Another recent trend is the inclusion of context in recommender systems. Authors Adomavicius and Tuzhilin in [1] have provided a detailed guide to Context-Aware Recommender Systems (CARS), while also emphasizing that the definition of context varies amongst disciplines. However, a widely used explanation is found in the works of Dey [8]: "Context is any information that can be used to characterize the situation of an entity," that is, the user whom the context influences. Because personalities do not exist in a vacuum, context is crucial to understanding real users' preferences.

We propose a gamified personality acquisition method that incorporates travel-related questions for context inclusion, increased accuracy and user engagement. We assume possible increased accuracy based on the works of, among others, Mishel et al., who discuss the role of the situation of as locus of control when assessing personality. During interaction with the personality assessment system—in psychology jargon often referred to as a "scale"—users are asked "what-if" questions: If you were in situation x while traveling, how would you respond?

In the next section we will discuss related works and highlight current methods of personality acquisition. Section 3 will detail our approach to the scale construction process and the Item Response Theory (IRT) we used as an evaluation metric, as well as our methodology in building our Gamified Personality Acquisition (GPA) system. In Sect. 4 we will discuss our results and conclusions. Lastly, we will conclude with future directions in Sect. 5.

2   Background and Related Work

2.1   Personality Model

Psychologists have constructed several instruments to measure personality. In contemporary science, one of the most widely accepted trait theories is the Five Factor Model (FFM), also known as Big Five. This psychological construct divides personality traits into five dimensions: Openness, Conscientiousness, Extraversion, Agreeableness, and Neuroticism (OCEAN) [5]. The revised NEO personality inventory (NEO PI-R) [5] consists of 240 items, which take participants approximately 45 min. to complete. Others, such as (NEO-FFI) [5], and (TIPI) [10], are made up of 60 and 10 items respectively. Though lengthier instruments demonstrate better psychometric quality, as identified in [10], long instruments may be impractical in certain research settings. In order to achieve a user-centric personality acquisition experience, whereby a participant's engagement level and accuracy are maintained or even increased, we decided to modify the Ten-Item Personality Inventory (TIPI) [10]. TIPI consists of 10 bi-polar items, each representing high and low poles of the Five Factor Model. The traits and respective adjectival descriptors can be found in Table 1.

Table 1. Ten-item personality inventory (TIPI)

Trait	High pole item	Low pole item
Extraversion	Extraverted, enthusiastic	Reserved, quiet
Agreeableness	Sympathetic, warm	Critical, quarrelsome
Conscientiousness	Dependable, self- disciplined	Disorganized, careless
Emotional stability	Calm, emotionally stable	Anxious, easily upset
Openness to experiences	Open to new experiences, complex	Conventional, uncreative

2.2 Personality Acquisition

Various branches of the computation field, such as Artificial Intelligence (AI), have focused on finding ways to extract users' personalities. Largely, these approaches can be divided into explicit and implicit methods. Explicit methods ask users to answer question sets from validated personality inventories used in the psychology domain. Implicit methods investigate users' personalities by observing a person's interactions with an interface or analyzing digital footprints such as social networks, blogs, comments, etc. [12]. For instance, the authors Walker et al. used personality markers in language to detect a user's personality. Thus user personality can be inferred by analyzing text (i.e. written essays) or conversations. This application [16] was built using WEKA machine learning models, which are trained on the Psychology Essay corpora designed by Pennebaker and King. The system gives a choice of four algorithms: linear regression, M5' model tree, M5' regression tree, and vector machines for regression. Researchers Wright and Chin [4] have also developed a similar tool; however, to our knowledge, it is not freely available. Additionally, Yokoyama et al. successfully developed a tool using Egogram as well as Multinomial Naïve Bayes to evaluate the personalities of bloggers. More recently, authors Shen, Brdiczka, and Liu succeeded in creating a system that analyzes personality from e-mail messages. Recent research further investigates the feasibility of both methods. The explicit method was also preferred by participants in a study conducted by Hu et al. [13], which compared personality quiz questionnaires to rating-based preference elicitation. These results were analyzed in terms of several criteria: perceived accuracy, user effort, and user loyalty.

Even though the inclusion of personality in the recommendation process has led to increased accuracy, researchers have also uncovered the need for an "entertaining personality quiz" [11] or "interactive and engaging" interface [9]. Thus far there have only been a few works focused on making this process more user-centered. In [7] the authors had partial success developing stories to assess the FFM. However, this is only one approach to keeping users engaged.

3 Methodology

We divide this section into two parts: (i) the approach to creating our contextualized scale and GPA, and (ii) the approach to building the personalized TravelRecommender based on GPA.

3.1   Gamified Personality Acquisition (GPA) System

Personality Scale Construction.   Our methodology comprises 4 steps.

Step 1: Articulate construct and context.

In the first step, we identified the TIPI as a base for our modified scale and therefore attempted to map the underlying construct (Big Five), thus assuming the dimensions listed in Table 1. The scale is designed to assess personality in the context of travel recommendations. In BestTripChoice, over 30 years of industry knowledge and academic research were used to establish a 15-question quiz that sorts travelers into "travel personalities" and generates a destination recommendation. Destination personality is a concept derived from brand personality. The behaviors of travelers used by Plog were used as inspiration to apply context to items as well as response options.

Step 2: Choose response format and initial item pool.

The response options in TIPI are in the form of a 7-point Likert scale (disagree strongly, disagree moderately, disagree a little, neither agree nor disagree, agree a little, agree moderately, and agree strongly). We therefore also mapped 7 response options to each item. The items (corresponding to a trait, i.e. extraversion) are represented in the form of a contextualized situation (e.g. "You sit outside at the hotel bar and are having something to drink; suddenly a crowd of people joins because it is happy hour"). The response options are in the form of an action-based response to that particular travel situation, depending on level of target trait (e.g. a response indicating a high degree of extraversion would be "I put down my book and join the crowd"). A partial contextualized scale can be found in Table 2.

Table 2.   Partial Contextualized Scale for Extraversion

7-Point Likert Mapping								
Dimension	Item	Disagree strongly	Disagree moderately	Disagree a little	Neither	Agree a little	Agree Moderately	Agree strongly
Extraversion	extra1 (extraverted enthusiastic)	I return to my hotel room asap	I hide in my book	I find a quite area around the bar	Neutral	I engage in small talk if irritated by others	I initiate small talk	I join right in and mingle

Step 3: Collect data from respondents.

We collected data using Amazon's Mechanical Turk workforce. This collaborative platform brings researchers and participants together efficiently and has proven effective and accurate in the social sciences [2, 3]. To ensure reliability of data, participants went through a rigorous qualification process that included an English proficiency test designed by Cambridge English.[1] To eliminate potential misunderstandings due to language and cultural differences, we only accepted adult workers from the United

---

[1] Cambridge English: www.cambridgeenglish.org.

States. According to the test makers, native proficiency can be assigned to test scores of 23 out 25. Given that this standard is based on British English versus American English, we set the threshold to slightly lower, at 20 out of 25. Additionally, attention check questions were input to insure participants were reading the questions. Finally, 549 participants were used to evaluate the psychometric quality of our scale.

Step 4: Examine psychometric properties and quality.

We used Item Response Theory (IRT) to evaluate the psychometric quality of our contextualized scale. There are two main parameters in the Graded Response Model (GRM) of IRT, shown in Eq. 1 below. Item discrimination (a) indicates the degree to which an item distinguishes between examinees with various levels of a target trait. An item's difficulty parameter (b) is on the same metric as the level of the trait (depicted as theta, Θ, on an arbitrary scale). This index marks at what trait level examinees have a 0.50 probability of endorsing a given response category versus any higher-level response category. Thus according to the analysis seen in Table 5, an examinee must have an extraversion (extra1) level of -1.289 to have a 50/50 chance of endorsing the first response category versus response categories 2–7.

$$P(Y \geq j|\theta) = \frac{\exp^{a_i(\theta - b_u)}}{1 + \exp^{a_i(\theta - b_u)}} \tag{1}$$

These parameters are graphically represented by Item Characteristic Curves (ICC) and Item information Curves (IIC) in Fig. 3. Information indicates to what degree the test is estimating a person's ability at each level. Thus the more information is present (i.e. the more peaks over a broader range of ability levels on the IIC), the more reliable the item/scale is. The scale construction led to successfully acquiring items to measure 60 % of the FFM. The other 40 % were completed with four items from the original TIPI.

GPA. We implemented the GPA System using the Unity3d Game Engine.[2] We chose to use a game engine to mimic game-like features to the extent possible without creating too much noise. A user more focused on "winning" than truthfully answering questions

Fig. 1. GPA start interface and sample question interface (from left to right)

---

[2] Unity3d: http://unity3d.com.

could compromise the integrity of the personality assessment. Unity3d is an open-source cross-platform game engine. It is currently one of the most popular game engines due to the support of the open-source community as well as sufficient availability of documentation. A sample interface of GPA is shown in Fig. 1 below.

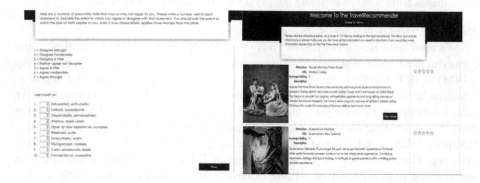

Fig. 2. GPA TIPI interface and rating-based interface (from left to right)

3.2 Personalized TravelRecommender Based on GPA

We evaluated the performance of GPA by integrating it into a collaborative filtering-based TravelRecommender using real-life data from Trip Advisor, the world's largest platform for travel-related reviews. We measured the effects of GPA on the recommender performance in terms of Mean Absolute Error (MAE) and Receiver Operating Characteristic (ROC) sensitivity. We additionally built a rating-based, as well as TIPI-based, preference elicitation interface to serve as a baseline for comparison (see Fig. 2). The recommendation process consists of two stages: The first stage entails a similarity estimation based on predetermined criteria, and the second stage is a prediction of a rating for a given item. We decided to employ similarity and prediction algorithms as seen in [12]. The method employs the Pearson correlation coefficient, which is one of the most commonly used similarity computations in RS research. While the authors compared rating-based to personality-based recommender systems, we modified their approach to adjust for our cases, adding a GPA-based case and using a different FFM personality assessment inventory as seen in Table 1. Lastly, we collected user preference data.

Data Collection. The personality-based TravelRecommender uses a data set obtained from Trip Advisor. We chose Trip Advisor as a data source because it is the world's largest travel site and displays various travel-related points of interest and reviews. According to Trip Advisor, the site has 315 million unique visitors monthly and provides 190 million reviews covering over 4.4 million accommodations, restaurants, and attractions. We aimed to obtain a broad spectrum of points of interest and therefore decided to utilize TA's guide for the "Best of 2014," selecting the top 10 cities for every continent. Due to time limitations, we also selected the top 100 attractions per destination and the first 200 reviews. The data statistics summary can be found in Table 3 below.

Table 3. Trip Advisor Data Statistics

Item	Count
Country	24
City	40
Attraction	12,022
Review	993,615
Author	390,115
Attraction per city	301
Review per attraction	83
Review per author	3

Personality Scoring Using Authors' Reviews. Given the novelty of using personality in RS, there is a corresponding lack of available data mapping user preferences to personality scores. Therefore, we employed the Personality Recognizer [16] mentioned in Sect. 2 to calculate personality scores of the authors/users from our Trip Advisor dataset. For research purposes, the personality-based TravelRecommender used static data, and therefore the calculation of personality scores was performed offline and stored in the database as well. This software employs the Linguistic Inquiry and Word Count program (LIWC)[3] and the MRC Psycholinguistic Database Machine Usable Dictionary (MRC).[4] LIWC is often used as a text analysis tool; it counts words and assigns them to the psychological categories defined in the LIWC dictionaries. MRC is a machine-usable dictionary designed by the University of Oxford for researchers of artificial intelligence and computer science, who need psychological and linguistic word descriptions. The Personality Recognizer outputs personality scores based on the FFM ranging from 1–7 for each domain. To ensure a reasonable word count for every author's personality assessment, we then separated out all reviewers having at least five reviews and computed their FFM personality scores using the Personality Recognizer. We also found that several were not written in English and thus excluded any authors who had a user name written in a non-Latin alphabet. Table 4 summarizes the new updated dataset.

Table 4. Data Containing Personality Scores

Item	Count
Word count	27,583,905
Number of authors with reviews count > 5	41,151
Average word count per author	670
Number of respective attractions	8,838

Participants. To evaluate the effects of GPA in our TravelRecommender, we invited the same (already screened) participants to experience our system. A total of 246 participants out of the 549 responded. After further filtering, i.e. selecting users who completed the GPE, TIPI and Rating-Based (RB) interface, we obtained results for 66 unique

---

[3] LIWC: http://liwc.net.

[4] MRC: http://ota.ox.ac.uk/headers/1054.xml.

participants. There were 39 female and 27 male participants with ages ranging from 22 to 66 (mean = 42.33, st. dev. = 14.54). Fourty-three percent of participants described themselves as traveling "a few times per year," while 28.9 % claimed to travel "at least once per year." A vast majority, 68.18 %, stated they had traveled abroad at least once.

4   Results

4.1   Item Response Theory

The ltm package in R was used to calibrate the items with the graded response model. Parameter estimates are shown in Table 4. The analysis for the extraversion domain shows difficulty scores ranging from -1.289 to 1.54, covering a relatively wide spectrum of the ability continuum. A scale that is targeted to assess a broad range of the ability level, according to [6], should range from -2 to 2 units of ability levels.

Overall, both items of the domain contribute to the reliability of the test. The peaks (where the test is most reliable) of the TIC are at approximately 4 for ability levels from -2 to 2, indicating that the scale provides a reasonably good amount of information for the extraversion domain and can be considered reliable for that trait level range. We can also see high discrimination values for extra1 and extra66, 3.907 and 1.436 respectively. Thus for both items in this dimension the scale is discriminating well between low- and high-level examinees of the trait. For space limitation reasons, the other domains are not discussed in depth; however, Table 5 can be referred to for interpretations. We must note that some of the items did not have sufficiently high discrimination values, resulting in an inability to assess the broad spectrum of the trait level. Thus we decided to construct the final scale with six story-based items and four from the original TIPI scale to ensure a solid measure of the FFM (seen in Table 5 as items starting with "t").

Table 5. Difficulty and Discrimination Parameters

	Extrmt1	Extrmt2	Extrmt3	Extrmt4	Extrmt5	Extrmt6	Dscrmn
extra1	−1.289	−0.761	−0.494	−0.389	1.136	1.554	3.907
extra66	−3.289	−0.859	−0.094	0.269	2.452	3.936	1.436
agree7	−2.28	−1.594	−1.225	−0.739	−0.002	2.32	1.853
tagree2t	−10.411	−6.712	−2.549	−1.634	0.028	2.539	0.408
tcons3	−2.604	−1.936	−1.59	−1.24	−0.508	0.662	4.316
tcons8	−3.489	−2.54	−1.178	−0.905	−0.199	0.806	1.436
emo9	−1.755	−0.991	−0.283	−0.272	1.276	1.717	3.036
temo4	−2.596	−1.506	−0.311	0.03	0.69	1.773	1.255
open5	−3.675	−2.315	−1.133	−0.936	0.356	1.413	1.165
open10	−3.164	−1.923	−0.783	−0.626	−0.082	1.057	1.342
	1 v. 2-7	1-2 vs. 3-7	1-3 v. 4-7	1-4 v. 5-7	1-5 vs. 6-7	1-6 vs. 7	

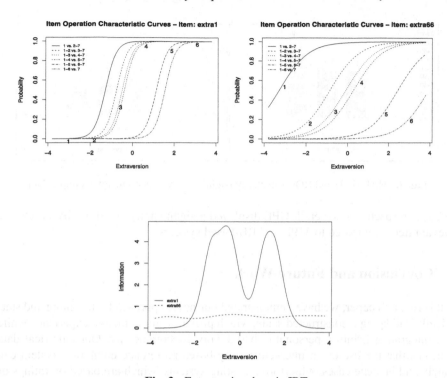

Fig. 3. Extraversion domain IRT

4.2 GPA-Based TravelRecommender

In the subsequent analysis, we will look at a sample of the collected data. The sample was chosen based on whether a participant completed all three cases and thus could provide a direct comparison. There were a total of 66 unique participants out of the 264 total who finished all stages.

Mean Absolute Error (MAE). Figure 4 displays the MAE values for the 66 unique participants in the sample described above. In this sample, GPE (MAE = 1.116) outperformed TIPI (MAE = 1.186) with a 5.93 % decrease. In this sample, the MAE for RB also performed significantly worse, showing an average absolute error of 1.84 stars in rating prediction. GPE as well as TIPI both exhibited a significantly lower prediction error over the traditional RB system, with increases of 39.36 % and 35.54 %, respectively.

Receiver Operating Characteristic (ROC) Sensitivity. ROC sensitivity is the sample's performance with respect to decision support: more specifically, its ability to retrieve true positives. Figure 4 displays the results with respect to ROC sensitivity. These clearly indicate that GPE (MAE = 0.616) outperforms TIPI (MAE = 0.576) and RB (MAE = 0.53). In this sample set there is a significant difference of 6.94 % and

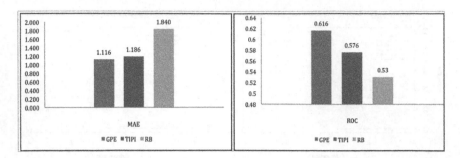

Fig. 4. MAE (left) and ROC sensitivity (right) of travel recommender sample data

16.23 %, respectively. Overall, GPE displayed a significantly better ability to retrieve relevant items compared to TIPI- and RB-based systems.

5   Conclusion and Future Work

In this research paper, we have demonstrated our novel approach to designing and statistically validating a constructed scale, which provides an interactive experience while also integrating it into a personality-based TravelRecommender. Our empirical data indicates that the use of an interactive story-based preference elicitation system can match, and in some cases outperform, existing systems, which are based on ratings or traditional personality questionnaires, in terms of accuracy metrics.

We intend to further explore the effects of having a scale that is comprised of 100 % story-based assessment, versus the present 60–40 % split. Based on the current results, we believe that we can improve usability by using only contextualized personality assessment items. Another avenue, which we plan to explore, is the inclusion of machine learning algorithms that adjust personality assessment questions based on the response given for one question. This would provide for an adaptive system that more accurately assesses various facets of a given domain. While the vast majority in the first survey (nearly 60 %) preferred the interactive questions, it would be interesting to explore personality acquisition in a more gamified manner that depends less on text and more on graphical cues instead.

Recommendation systems are designed for the user, and thus we must find ways to increase system likability and at the same time increase the likelihood that a user will consult it in the future.

Acknowledgments. We are grateful to RB, a doctoral student of quantitative psychology, for his assistance during the IRT analysis. This work was supported by the National High-tech R&D Program of China (Grant No. SS2015AA020102), National Basic Research Program of China (Grant No. 2011CB302302), Tsinghua University Initiative Scientific Research Program.

References

1. Adomavicius, G., Tuzhilin, A.: Context-Aware Recommender Systems. pp. 1–40
2. Berinsky, A.J., et al.: Evaluating online labor markets for experimental research: Amazon.com's Mechanical Turk. Polit. Anal. 20, 351–368 (2012)
3. Buhrmester, M., et al.: Amazon's Mechanical Turk: A New Source of Inexpensive, Yet High-Quality, Data? (2011)
4. Wright, W.R., Chin, D.N.: Personality profiling from text: introducing part-of-speech N-grams. In: Dimitrova, V., Kuflik, T., Chin, D., Ricci, F., Dolog, P., Houben, G.-J. (eds.) UMAP 2014. LNCS, vol. 8538, pp. 243–253. Springer, Heidelberg (2014)
5. Costa Jr., P.T., McCrae, R.R.: Revised NEO Personality Inventory (NEO-PI-R) and NEO Five-Factor Inventory professional manual. Psychological Assessment Resources, Odessa (1992)
6. DeMars, C.: Item Response Theory. Oxford University Press, Oxford (2010)
7. Dennis, M., et al.: The quest for validated personality trait stories. In: Proceedings of the 2012 ACM International Conference on Intelligent User Interfaces – IUI 2012, p. 273. ACM Press, New York (2012)
8. Dey, A.K.: Understanding and Using Context (2001)
9. Dunn, G., Wiersema, J., Ham, J., Aroyo, L.: Evaluating interface variants on personality acquisition for recommender systems. In: Houben, G.-J., McCalla, G., Pianesi, F., Zancanaro, M. (eds.) UMAP 2009. LNCS, vol. 5535, pp. 259–270. Springer, Heidelberg (2009)
10. Gosling, S.D., et al.: A very brief measure of the Big-Five personality domains. J. Res. Pers. 37(6), 504–528 (2003)
11. Hu, R., Pu, P.: Acceptance issues of personality-based recommender systems. In: Proceedings of the Third ACM Conference on Recommender Systems – RecSys 2009, p. 221. ACM Press, New York (2009)
12. Hu, R., Pu, P.: Enhancing collaborative filtering systems with personality information. In: Proceedings of the Fifth ACM Conference on Recommender Systems – RecSys 2011, p. 197. ACM Press, New York (2011)
13. Hu, R., Pu, P.: A comparative user study on rating vs. personality quiz based preference elicitation methods. In: International Conference on Intelligent User Interfaces (IUI) (2009)
14. Kittur, A., et al.: Crowdsourcing user studies with Mechanical Turk. In: Proceeding of the Twenty-Sixth Annual SIGCHI Conference on Human Factors in Computing Systems, pp. 453–456 (2008)
15. Konstan, J.A., Riedl, J.: Recommender systems: from algorithms to user experience. User Model. User-adapt. Interact. 22(1–2), 101–123 (2012)
16. Mairesse, F.: Personality Recognizer Software. http://people.csail.mit.edu/francois/research/personality/demo.html

The Study and Application on Multi-dimension and Multi-layer Credit Scoring

Luyao Teng[1(✉)], Wei Zhang[2], Feiyi Tang[1],
Shaohua Teng[2], and Xiufen Fu[2]

[1] College of Engineering and Science, Victoria University,
Ballarat Rd, Footscray, VIC 3011, Australia
luyaot@student.unimelb.edu.au,
feiyi.tang@live.vu.edu.au
[2] School of Computer Science and Technology,
Guangdong University of Technology,
Guangzhou 510006, Guangdong, China
{weizhang, shteng, xffu}@gdut.edu.cn

Abstract. Scoring of customer's credit is the basis of making an investment. Hence how to calculate scores, namely 'Credit Scoring', is an important and difficult task. Based on current methods, a credit scoring method composed by multi-layer analysis is proposed in this paper, which includes removing outliers, clustering, k-Nearest Neighbor. Especially, this method first separates outliers from data set, and then clusters by fuzzy and similarity in order to divide data into uncertain data and certain data. Here, we focus on analyzing the uncertain data to improve the accuracy of our credit scoring. At last, experiments are used to validate our method more efficient than other credit scoring methods.

Keywords: Credit scoring · Uncertain data · Clustering · Outlier · Multi-layer analysis

1 Introduction

Credit scoring is the set of decision models that help lenders in the granting of consumer credit. They decide who will get credit, how much credit they should get, and what strategies will enhance the profitability of the borrowers [1].

Credit scoring assesses the risk of lending about a particular consumer. Sometimes, some lenders will assess an individual as credit worthy and others will not. That may lead to the cases, some can get credit from all lenders and others who cannot [1].

It is extremely important for one or a company to have a higher level of credit score because:

- It indicates an individual or a company's competitive advantage, therefore a more acceptable loan may be offered.
- It is a crucial factor that the third-party institution recommends you or your business.
- And also buyers will favor to purchase from the company with higher credit scores even though the price may be higher.

© Springer International Publishing Switzerland 2016
Q. Zu and B. Hu (Eds.): HCC 2016, LNCS 9567, pp. 386–399, 2016.
DOI: 10.1007/978-3-319-31854-7_35

The multi-granularity and multi-layer analysis is used to build multi-layer model of credit scoring in this paper, in order to generate higher and more accurate scoring.

2 Related Works

Many credit scoring institutions and researchers all over the world have putted forward kinds of methods to score credit based on different scoring factors and perspectives. The methods of common credit scoring include: Binomial Expansion Technique (BET); Monte Carlo Simulation (MCS); Fourier Transform Method (FTM); Lognormal Method (LNM), etc.

Moody Investors Service [2] proposed a binomial expansion method in 1996 which provides credit scores for combining investment in a certain period of time. Davis [3] followed up on this idea and proposed an infectious default model. Jarrow et al. [4–8] firstly apply Markov model into credit scoring method. Monte Carlo Model has been widely utilized in assessing customer's credit for selling financial products. Ghamami et al. effectively improved Monte Carlo Model by adding credit risk pricing and measurement.

In addition, various machine learning methods are used in classification, such as SVM (Support Vector Machine), neural network, etc. Crook et al. proposed a marginal score curve, and then applied logistic regression method to analyze data. Bellotti et al. apply SVM to extract fundamental factors and attributes of credit scoring data. Chen et al. apply SOM (Self Organization Map) Neural Network in classifying customers. However, they only apply a single method for modeling. Twala applies multi-classifier to assess credit risk. He explores the predicted behavior of five classifiers for different types of noise in terms of credit risk prediction accuracy, and how such accuracy could be enhanced by using classifier ensembles. Benchmarking is utilized to compare with the performance of each individual classifier on predictive accuracy. Huang et al. proposed a hybrid model generated by genetic algorithm and SVM based on SVM and data mining approach. West et al. started with classic combination method in terms of Crossvalidata, Bagging and boosting; and then followed up with a neural network to test an ensemble method. Similarly, Wang et al. conducts a comparative assessment of the performance of three popular ensemble methods, i.e., Bagging, Boosting, and Stacking, based on four base learners, i.e., Logistic Regression Analysis (LRA), Decision Tree (DT), Artificial Neural Network (ANN) and Support Vector Machine (SVM). Experimental results show that the three ensemble methods can substantially improve individual base learners. In particular, Bagging performs better than Boosting across all credit datasets. Stacking and Bagging DT in those experiments, obtain the best performance in terms of average accuracy. More recently, Marqués proposed a two-level classifier ensembles for credit risk assessment while Danenas optimized classifiers based on SVM for credit risk by optimizing particle swarm algorithm, and applied it to real financial data for the experiment.

3　Credit Data and Assessment

The data is the most important in credit scoring, and making decisions can be always depended on analyzing data. A real data set of credit data from a bank is represented in the section in order to exhibit the structure of the credit data before we can analyze it.

3.1　Credit Data

The format of a financial data is as follows:

Customer_Banking (dob, nkid, dep, phon, sinc, aes, dainc, res, dhval, dmort, doutm, doutl, douthp, doutcc, Bad).

These attributes and descriptions are listed in Table 1.

Table 1.　Various attributes and descriptions

No.	Variable name	Description	No.	Variable name	Description
1	dob	Year of birth	9	dhval	value of home
2	nkid	number of children	10	dmort	mortgage balance outstanding
3	dep	number of other dependents	11	doutm	outgoings on mortgage or rent
4	phon	is there a home phone	12	doutl	outgoings on loans
5	sinc	spouse's income	13	douthp	outgoings on hire purchase
6	aes	applicant's employment status	14	doutcc	outgoings on credit cards
7	dainc	applicant's income	15	bad	good/bad indicator
8	res	residential status			

3.2　Credit Scoring Data Preprocessing

Because credit scoring comes from multiple data sources, collecting customer data is incomplete, noise, and inconsistent. Data preprocessing is used to improve the quality of the data. The data preprocessing is shown in the Fig. 1.

They include data cleaning, data integration, correlation analysis, redundancies and conflict detection, principal components analysis, and attribute selection. The data before data preprocessing are shown in Table 2, and the data after data preprocessing are given in Table 3.

Data cleaning is composed of discrepancy detection and data transformation iterates. Some transformations may generate more discrepancies. Some nested discrepancies may only be detected after others have been fixed.

Data integration merges data from multiple data stores. The semantic heterogeneity and structure of data pose great challenges in data integration. Careful integration can help to reduce and avoid redundancies and inconsistencies in the resulting data set.

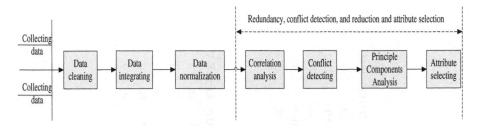

Fig. 1. Data preprocessing procedure

Data normalization or standardization are used to avoid dependence on the choice of measurement units of the data. In this paper, the data is transformed to fall into a range [0.0, 1.0]. Min-max normalization is used to perform a linear transformation on the original data.

Redundancies and correlation analysis include three steps, which are separately analyzing redundancy and correlation, checking tuple duplication, and detecting and resolving data value conflicts.

Attribute subset selection reduces the credit scoring data set size by removing irrelevant or redundant attributes. The goal of attribute selection is to find a minimum attribute set that analysis results generated by them is similar to the results obtained by using all attributes.

4 Credit Scoring Method

From different aspects and perspectives, credit scoring methods have been generated. But they do have some common features, and are discussed in this section.

4.1 Credit Scoring

Common credit scoring applies comprehensive factor to assess in terms of index of customer education background, finance condition, repaying capability, income level, and prospect expectation etc. Based on these factors a scoring calculating for a particular customer is taken as a reference to his/her credit scoring level.

The limitation of such system is obvious:

1. How to decide index weight is optional, scoring of customer finance often depends on personal bias.
2. Some particular factors are ignored, for example, a customer's credibility is always determined by its weakest factor but not the strong one. Thus average scoring veils the most risky point for a client.
3. Most of the factors and its weight are determined before the calculation, and gives the same criteria to all customers with coming from the different background.
4. The system can only process one by one, which is considerably inefficient.

Table 2. Some samples of customer credit data

DOB	NKID	DEP	PHON	SINC	AES	DAINC	RES	DHVAL	DMORT	DOUTM	DOUTL	DOUTHP	DOUTCC	BAD
19.0	4.0	.0	1	.00	R	.00	O	14464.00	4.00	.00	.00	.00	.00	.00
41.0	2.0	.0	1	.00	P	36000.00	O	.00	.00	280.00	664.00	.00	80.00	.00
66.0	.0	.0	1	.00	N	30000.00	N	.00	.00	.00	.00	.00	.00	.00
51.0	2.0	.0	1	.00	P	464.00	O	24928.00	8464.00	584.00	320.00	.00	60.00	.00
65.0	.0	.0	1	.00	P	15000.00	P	.00	.00	.00	.00	.00	.00	.00

Table 3. Normalized samples of customer credit data

DOB	NKID	DEP	PHON	SINC	DAINC	DHVAL	DMORT	DOUTM	DOUTL	DOUTHP	DOUTCC	AES	RES	BAD
0.1667	0.80	0.0	1	0.0000	0.0000	0.2228	0.0000	0.0000	0.0000	0.0000	0.0000	R	O	0
0.3958	0.40	0.0	1	0.0000	0.5556	0.0000	0.0000	0.0737	0.0237	0.0000	0.0286	P	O	0
0.6563	0.00	0.0	1	0.0000	0.4630	0.0000	0.0000	0.0000	0.0000	0.0000	0.0000	N	N	0
0.5000	0.40	0.0	1	0.0000	0.0072	0.3839	0.1323	0.1537	0.0114	0.0000	0.0214	P	O	0
0.6458	0.00	0.0	1	0.0000	0.2315	0.0000	0.0000	0.0000	0.0000	0.0000	0.0000	P	P	0

4.2   Modeling Credit Scoring

Since customers' credit data were collected from different data source, the data is huge and complicated. Before analyzing, we first divide the dataset into similar clusters; and then, apply hierarchy analysis to rate the data in each cluster. On the lower level, we sketchily analyze and filter data; while, in the higher level, we deeply analyze the remainder of data. In this paper, a multi-layer and multi-dimensional crediting scoring system is built, which combines separating outliers, clustering, decision trees, SVM, and ensemble classifier with multi-dimensional and multi-level analysis. In this process, fuzzy set and analyzing uncertain data is discussed. The detailed processes are shown as Fig. 2.

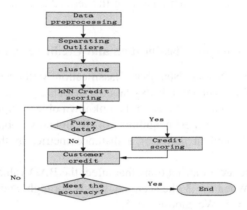

Fig. 2. Credit scoring flow chart

Dividing outliers are used to separate outliers from credit data, in order to decrease or avoid the influence of noise and abnormal data. Then clustering is used to divide remainder data into some clusters.

In all credit scoring, the data can always be grouped into two classes, certain data and uncertain data. In order to improve both efficiency and effectiveness of classification, we apply different methods to deal with certain data and uncertain data separately. For the former, a simple, efficient classification method is selected; for the latter, decision trees and multi-layer recursion deep analysis is applied.

Description of our process are as follows:

Step 1: Separating outliers;
Step 2: Clustering customer's credit data
Step 3: First round ranking
    Step 3.1. Modeling by kNN algorithm and fuzzy analysis of each cluster
    Step 3.2. Analyzing every cluster
    Step 3.3. Setting different classes for each object with a symbol 0 (Good), 1 (Bad), and Uncertain
Step 4: Applying deep learning regression analysis for uncertain data
    Step 4.1. Applying SVM and ensemble classifier to review all data

Step 4.2. Setting different classes with a symbol 0 (Good), 1 (Bad), and Uncertain

Step 4.3. Deciding whether accuracy is satisfied. If not, repeat Step 3 otherwise quit.

4.3   Separating Outliers

Outliers are data that deviate from normal data, and analyzing this kind of data usually needs expert's knowledge. In order to avoid confusion during analysis we need to find out all outliers and wipe them up before further analysis. In the data set, we detect 59 outliers and we build models upon analyzing the rest 1225 data.

4.4   kNN Nearest Neighbor Classification and Credit Scoring

The main idea of kNN Nearest Neighbor Classification Method is as follows. When given an unknown object (tuple), a kNN classifier searches the pattern space for the k training objects (tuples) that are closest to the unknown object (tuple). These k training objects (tuples) are the k "nearest neighbors" of the unknown object (tuple).

"Closeness" is defined in terms of a distance metric, in this paper, which is Euclidean distance.

In the paper, there are 14 attributions that affect the BAD value. We choose $k = 3$, 5, and 7, for a trial. When $k = 3$, the accuracy rate is not high, and their results are the same as $k = 7$ and $k = 5$. We choose $k = 5$.

In addition, we use Euclidean Metric to measure the distance between two samples, which is normally used to measure the similarity or dissimilarity between two data objects. The function is shown in formula (3):

$$d(i,j) = \sqrt[2]{(x_{i1} - x_{j1})^2 + (x_{i2} - x_{j2})^2 + \cdots + (x_{in} - x_{jn})^2} \qquad (3)$$

Where $i = (x_{i1}, x_{i2}, \ldots, x_{in})$ and $j = (x_{j1}, x_{j2}, \ldots, x_{jn})$ are two n-dimensional data objects.

Missing Value Handling: Eliminating the object with missing data.

Using kNN, the results can be divided into two group, right or error:

(1) error: including classified object that belongs to class 0 into class 1, and classified object that belongs to class 1 into class 0;
(2) right: including classified object that belongs to class 1 into class 1, and classified object that belongs to class 0 into class 0.

There are 1115 training data, which occupy 91 % of total dataset; and there are 110 testing data, have 9 % proportion to the total dataset. The number of data in dataset is 1225, and the accuracy rate of the result is 72.33 % from Table 4. In the table, frequency represents the number of data in the dataset; and valid percentage is the proportion occupied by usable data in the dataset.

Table 4. Prediction results about kNN algorithm

		Frequency	Percentage (%)	Valid percentage (%)	Accumulate (%)
result	error	339	27.67	27.67	27.67
	right	886	72.33	72.33	72.33
	total	1225	100.0	100.0	100.0

4.5 Analyzing Uncertain Data

In the experiment of kNN, we found that when $k = 5$, and there are 2:3 or 3:2 in the nearest neighbor, namely, 2 elements among 5 objects of the nearest neighbors belong to class 0, and others 3 belong to class 1; or 3 objects among 5 objects of the nearest neighbors belong to class 0, and 2 are class 1; we define the data sample as uncertain data, and the predicted values are defined in definition 1.

Definition 1: uncertain data: Let x be any clustering objects. If x only has 5 elements in the nearest neighbor, and in which only 2, or 3 objects belong to category 1, we identified that the sample x is uncertain data.

Definition 2: Credit Scoring: Let x be any clustering objects who include only 5 elements in the nearest neighbor, and x_1, x_2, x_3, x_4, and x_5 are 5 nearest neighbor of x, then, we define the customer's credit scoring class (CSC) in formula (4):

$$CSC = \begin{cases} 0 & \text{when there are 4 or above of } x_1, x_2, x_3, x_4, x_5 \text{ belongs to category 0} \\ 1 & \text{when there are 4 or above of } x_1, x_2, x_3, x_4, x_5 \text{ belongs to category 1} \\ u & \text{Others} \end{cases}$$

(4)

where, u represents the uncertain data, CSC represents the credit classification.

Predicting uncertain data by using kNN classifier is shown in Table 5. According to the definition 1 and 2, there are 401 uncertain data in the dataset, and 260 of these data are classified correctly, 141 are wrongly classified, and detailed description is shown in Table 6. For these uncertain data, the accuracy rate of kNN classifying is 64.84 %, which is smaller than 72.33 %, and it indicates that the accuracy rate can be improved by applying other ways.

4.6 Scoring Uncertain Data

From the last section, we generate 401 uncertain data. In this section, we focus on discussing how to classify these uncertain data by applying SVM and ensemble classifier.

SVM is used to classify 401 uncertain data in order to improve classification accuracy.

A Radial Basis Function (RBF) is a scalar function along the radial symmetry. It is often defined as a monotone function of the Euclidean distance between the point X

Table 5. Classifying the uncertain Data by kNN classifier

Real credit	Predict	0	1	Predict correction	Error absolute value
0	0	0.571	0.429	1	0.142
0	0	0.571	0.429	1	0.142
0	1	0.429	0.571	0	0.142
0	0	0.571	0.429	1	0.142
0	0	0.571	0.429	1	0.142
0	0	0.571	0.429	1	0.142
0	1	0.429	0.517	0	0.142
0	0	0.571	0.429	1	0.142
0	0	0.571	0.429	1	0.142
0	0	0.571	0.429	1	0.142
0	0	0.571	0.429	1	0.142
0	1	0.429	0.571	0	0.142
0	0	0.571	0.429	1	0.142
0	0	0.571	0.429	1	0.142
...	...	...	...	...	...

Table 6. Some of the uncertain data

DAINC	DHVAL	DMORT	DOUTM	DOUTL	DOUTHP	DOUTCC	RES2	AES2	BAD
0.4630	0.0000	0.0000	0.0000	0.0000	0.0000	0.0000	4.00	4.00	0
0.0072	0.3839	0.1323	0.1537	0.0114	0.0000	0.0214	11.00	6.00	0
0.2315	0.0000	0.0000	0.0000	0.0000	0.0000	0.0000	0.00	6.00	0
0.7407	0.6683	0.7260	0.2947	0.0000	0.0000	0.0000	11.00	5.00	0
0.4630	0.9621	0.8750	0.1368	0.0000	0.0600	0.0000	11.00	13.00	0

and the center point XC in the space. And it is called as k(‖x-xc‖). It is always a local function.

When deciding penalty parameters c and RBF kernel parameters g, a grid parameters optimization function is needed to determine them. In the grid searching, all the possible values of two tuple (c, g) are used to test, and a cross validation method is used to find the most accurate (c, g).

The k-fold cross validation method is used to analyze these 401 uncertain data, in which k is 10 in the text. In the beginning, these 401 data are divided into 10 subsets. In which, a sample subset is used as testing set, and others are used as training sets. Cross validations are repeated for 10 times, and each sample set is verified once. Ten testing results are used to compute an average, and finally an assessment is formed.

In this paper, the best parameters c = 2 and g = 64 are formed by the grid parameters optimization function. The results are shown in Table 7. At last, the average

Table 7. Given C = 2 and g = 64, prediction result of uncertain data

10 cross validation	Prediction accuracy (%)
k1	74.359
k2	79.4872
k3	79.4872
k4	71.7949
k5	82.0513
k6	64.1026
k7	79.4872
k8	74.359
k9	74.359
k10	70
Average	74.94874

accuracy of the experiments is about 74.95 %, it is far greater than 64.84 % in Sect. 5.2.

We randomly select 90 % data from the 401 uncertain data to create a training dataset (TrainD), and the rest 10 % data will be used to test the model, which we recognize as testing dataset (TestD). We use $TrainD_i$ to build classifier C_i and combine all base classifier into an ensemble classifier, the detailed processes are shown as following:

The basic idea is to build multiple classifiers from the original data and aggregate their predictions when classifying unknown examples [22]. In this paper, we construct n base classifiers by repeating n times. Firstly we divide the original data set D into 2 subsets TrainD and TestD, where TrainD is training set and TestD is the testing set. At first, an integrated learning method is initiated by using the training set TrainD. After learning, an integrated classifier is called to produce outputs as classifying unknown examples. The architecture of the integrated classifier is shown in Fig. 3. Building base classifier i, TrainD is divided into $TrainD_{i1}$ and $TrainD_{i2}$ (i = 1, 2, ..., n), in which $TrainD_{i1}$ is used to build basic classifier i, and $TrainD_{i2}$ is the testing set.

At last, we get C_2, ..., C_{n-1}, and C_n. C_+ classifier fusions prediction results of each base classifier and generates combination classification results of the model. Here, SVM is base classifier, the AdaBoost algorithm is used to apply building multi-classifiers. 3, 5, and 7 base classifiers are used to do experiments. The results are shown in Tables 8 and 9.

4.7 Credit Data Scoring

Credit scoring combines certain data scoring with uncertain data scoring. Thus, the credit scoring is as follows in the paper:

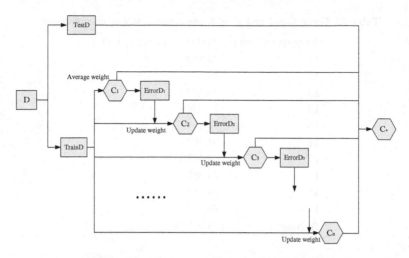

Fig. 3. The structure of the integrated classifiers

Table 8. Accuracy of different classifiers

Train samples	Base classifiers	AdaBoost
324	3	92.68 %
	5	92.68 %
	7	92.68 %

Table 9. Three times classification improvements of seven base classifiers

Samples	C11	C12	C13	C14	C15	C16	C17	F1	Final accuracy
324	63.41 %	70.73 %	68.29 %	68.29 %	68.29 %	68.29 %	68.29 %	68.29 %	92.68 %
	C21	C22	C23	C24	C25	C26	C27	F2	
	92.68 %	92.68 %	92.68 %	92.68 %	92.68 %	92.68 %	87.80 %	92.68 %	
	C31	C32	C33	C34	C35	C36	C37	F3	
	90.24 %	92.68 %	90.24 %	92.68 %	92.68 %	92.68 %	90.24 %	92.68 %	

(1) scoring certain data and its accuracy;
(2) scoring uncertain data and its accuracy;
(3) totaling whole credit scoring and its accuracy.

The credit scoring based on kNN and SVM can be divided into: scoring certain data by applying kNN and computing its accuracy, and scoring uncertain data by applying SVM and computing its accuracy.

Applying kNN analyzing certain data and computing the accuracy

(1) From Table 6 in Sect. 5.2, we have 886 data correctly classified in 1225 data, and there are two categories, Trust (CSC = 0) or Fail (CSC = 1);

(2) According to the definition 1 and 2, we have 401 uncertain data, and there are 260 data correctly classified by applying kNN classification method;

(3) After removing the uncertain data, there still are 626 data correctly classified.

Applying SVM analyzing uncertain data and computing the accuracy

(1) there are 401 uncertain data;
(2) after applying SVM, the average accuracy is 74.949 %
(3) 300 data are correctly classified.

There may be an excessive fitting problem by applying SVM analyze uncertain data, since the k-fold cross-validation is applied. Namely, the testing data are also involved in training set. This might be the reason that SVM has higher accuracy.

Computing the accuracy of whole data set

(1) There are 626 + 300 data correctly classified;
(2) The accuracy of the whole dataset is 75.59 %.

This indicates that the accuracy is improved by 75.59 − 72.33 = 3.26 %.

In the same way, we can get the accuracy of ensemble classifier.

In Table 9, we can find the information of classifying uncertain data by applying ensemble classifier. The accuracy of F1 is 68.29 %, thus there are 401 * 68.29 % ≈ 274 data classified in the right class, and this is higher than the classification accuracy of using kNN method only.

If using F2 and F3, the accuracy of classifying an uncertain data is 92.68 %, and the uncertain data correctly classified are: 401 * 92.68 % ≈ 371. It is significantly higher than using kNN method. However, the excessive fitting problem also exists in F2 and F3.

If using F1 to derive the whole dataset, the data correctly classified are: 626 + 274 = 900, and the accuracy is 900/1225 = 73.47 %.

5   Experiments and Analyzing Results

These experiments are made in the paper by using kNN classifier, SVM classifier, and ensemble classifier.

5.1   Data Set

Experiment's data came from a commercial bank. Original data can be shown in Table 2, while preprocessed data is in Table 3, which includes 1225 data with 14 attributes and 1 class tag.

5.2   Experiments

The results of the experiments are shown in Table 10.

From Table 10, we can find that:

Table 10. Comparing three classification methods

Classification method	Certain data	Uncertain data	Total amount	Accuracy	Description
	824	401			
kNN	626	260	886	72.33 %	
SVM		300	926	75.59 %	excessive fitting
Ensemble 1		274	900	73.47 %	
Ensemble 2		371	997	81.39 %	excessive fitting

1. When applying kNN algorithm in Sect. 5.2, 1115 of whole data (91 %) are used to play training data; 110 of whole data (9 %) are used as testing data; and the accuracy is 72.33 %, and it indicates 886 data correctly classified.
   Depending on definition 1 and 2, there are 401 uncertain data. Among these data, 260 are properly classified, and the accuracy is 64.84 %.
2. After applying SVM to analyze the uncertain data, we have an average accuracy at 74.95 %; within which, there are 300 data correctly classified. Thus, the data correctly classified by applying both kNN and SVM are 866 − 260 + 300 = 926, and the accuracy is 75.59 %
3. If using the ensemble classifier F1 based on SVM to analyze the uncertain data, the accuracy is 68.29 %. There are 274 uncertain data correctly classified, and total classification accuracy is 900/1225 = 73.47 %
4. If using the ensemble classifier F2 or F3 based on SVM to analyze the uncertain data, the accuracy is 92.68 %. There are 371 uncertain data correctly classified. Thus, when using kNN and ensemble classifier F2 or F3, there are 886 − 260 + 371 = 997 data correctly classified, and the accuracy is 81.39 %.
5. The problem of excessive fitting exists in SVM, F2 and F3. In addition, from F2 and F3 we find that the ensemble classifiers are steady state after training.

From all of above, we can conclude that ensemble classifier has the best effect in analyzing uncertain data. It is ineffective to apply only a classifier.

6 Conclusion

Accompany with big data emerging, analyzing massive data become a major problem. A multi-layer analysis method is proposed in this paper to improve the accuracy of credit scoring. It contains following steps: firstly separating outliers; clustering data into different clusters; and then modeling for each cluster and dividing data into certain and uncertain data. Since certain data are the majority of the data, they are analyzed and filtered by a simple analysis method. And then, we focus on studying the uncertain data by applying multi-layer recursion analysis method in order to generate a multi-layer decision-tree model for credit scoring. The experiment results show that the model proposed in the paper can produce more accuracy for credit scoring.

Acknowledgments. This research was partly supported by National Natural Science Foundation of China (Grant No. 61402118, No. 61104156 and No. 61370229), Guangdong Provincial Science & Technology Project (Grant No. 2012B091000173, 2013B010401034, 2013B090200017, 2013B010401029), Guangzhou City Science & Technology Project (Grant No. 2012J5100054, 2013J4500028, 201508010067), and Key Laboratory of the Ministry of Guangdong Province project (Grant No. 15zk0132).

References

1. Thomas, L.C., Edelman, D.B., Crook, J.N.: Credit Scoring and Its Applications. Society for Industrial and Applied Mathematics, Philadelphia (2002)
2. Moody's Investors Service. The Binomial Expansion Method Applied to CBO/CLO Analysis. Moody's, New York, 10007 (1996)
3. Davis, M., Lo, V.: Infectious default. Quant. Financ. **1**, 382–387 (2001)
4. Jarrow, R.A., Turnbull, S.M.: Pricing derivatives on financial securities subject to credit risk. J. Financ. **50**, 53–86 (1995)
5. Jarrow, R.A., Lando, D., Turnbull, S.M.: A Markov model for the term structure of credit risk spreads. Rev. Financ. Stud. **10**, 481–523 (1997)
6. Lu, S.L., Kuo, C.J.: The default probability of bank loans in Taiwan: an empirical investigation by Markov chain model. Asia Pac. Manag. Rev. **11**(2), 111–122 (2006)
7. Lu, S.L.: Comparing the reliability of a discrete-time and a continuous-time Markov chain model in determining credit risk. Appl. Econ. Lett. **16**(11), 1143–1148 (2009)
8. Canabarro, E., Duffie, D.: Measuring and marking counterparty risk. In: Tilman, L.M. (ed.) Asset/Liability Management of Financial Institutions: Maximising Shareholder Value through Risk-Conscious Investing, Euromoney Institutional Investor (2003)

Proactive Scheduling Optimization of Emergency Rescue Based on Hybrid Genetic-Tabu Optimization Algorithm

Wenan Tan[1,2(✉)], Quanquan Zhang[1], and Yong Sun[1]

[1] School of Computer Science and Technology,
Nanjing University of Aeronautics and Astronautics, Nanjing 210016, China
wtan@foxmail.com, zhangqq1202@outlook.com, syong@nuaa.edu.cn
[2] School of Computer and Information, Shanghai Second Polytechnic University,
Shanghai 210209, China

Abstract. With the objective of minimizing rescue loss, the paper is about proactive scheduling optimization. First, an optimization model is proposed. Priorities are assigned based on rescue activity's urgency level, and optimization objective function is constructed. The issue is strongly NP-hard based on which a genetic-tabu heuristic algorithm is designed. Finally an example demonstrates the feasibility and effectiveness of the research. The study can provide decision support for emergency rescue.

Keywords: Emergency rescue · Genetic algorithm · Tabu search · Proactive scheduling

1 Introduction

All kinds of safety accidents and natural disasters frequently occur, which has significantly impacted economic development and social stability. Timely and effective rescue activities can save lives and properties to maximum extent. In order to respond to emergencies, government and enterprises have made great efforts to establish and implement rescue plans. In view of emergencies' inherent uncertainty, it is difficult to carry out rescue plans [1]. Hence, scientific emergency rescue plans are important guidance for optimizing resource utilization and efficient implementation of rescue activities [2].

Based on historical data of the same kind and the uncertainty of rescue activities, proactive scheduling arranges emergency rescue activities and then develops rescue plans in advance [3, 4]. Combining the analysis of existing materials of similar emergencies with rescue objective, future rescue work can be legitimately predicted [5].

In this paper, according to data of past emergencies and the prediction of future events, resource-constrained emergency rescue plan is developed with the objective of minimizing rescue losses.

2 Problem Definition

For some emergency, its rescue process can be depicted as an AoN (Activity on Node) network in which every node represents rescue activity and directed edge represents

© Springer International Publishing Switzerland 2016
Q. Zu and B. Hu (Eds.): HCC 2016, LNCS 9567, pp. 400–408, 2016.
DOI: 10.1007/978-3-319-31854-7_36

logical relationship between activities. Rescue time of activity i is denoted as d_i. The amount of required resource is r_i. The total of resource is R. Without resource constraint, rescue plan $U^0 = (u_1^0, u_2^0, u_3^0, ..., u_n^0)$. Because of resource constraint, the amount of resource is constant at every unit interval. The original plan needs to be modified. Weight coefficient λ_i is assigned to every rescue activity. λ_i reflects relative losses of rescue activities if delayed for one unit time. In other words, the larger λ_i is, the more important the rescue activity i is. Relative losses for time delay is denoted as $\lambda_i(u_i - u_i^0)$. The objective of the study is to minimize loss of rescue plan.

3   Optimization Model

Optimization model of rescue plan is as follows.

$$\min Loss = \sum_{i=1}^{n} [\lambda_i(u_i - u_i^0)] \tag{1}$$

$$\text{s.t. } u_i = u_i^0, n \in F^T \cap P^T \tag{2}$$

$$u_j \geq u_i + d_i, i \in V_i \tag{3}$$

$$\sum_{i \in P^t} r_i \leq R \tag{4}$$

$$u_i \geq 0, i = 1, 2, ..., n \tag{5}$$

where F^T is the set of completed activities; P^T is the set of activities in progress; V_i is the set of activities that happen after activity i. (1) is objective function that minimizes rescue loss for time delay; constraint Eq. (2) defines start time of completed activities as that of original plan; (3) constrains logical relationship between activities; (4) means at a point the sum of resource required by all activities should not be larger than the total of resource; (5) is the domain of definition for decision variables.

4   Hybrid Genetic-Tabu Algorithm

Founder of tabu algorithm F. Glover has given the theoretical basis for the hybrid of genetic algorithm (GA) and tabu search algorithm (TS) [6]. In reference [6], he analyzed and compared GA and TS in a wide range. Every chromosome is treated as initial solution S^{ini} of tabu algorithm. Then a feasible solution S^{nei} is selected from neighborhood of S^{ini}. The process is repeated until optimal solution is found. Tabu list is used in tabu algorithm to increase the stability and enlarge the search scopes [7]. Aspiration criterion is if a tabooed move can result in a better solution, the ignoring the tabu.

The genetic-tabu algorithm (GTA) can avoid the local minimum while using traditional method. It uses TS to quickly search for local optimal solution of every chromosome generated from GA.

4.1 Encoding

GTA adopts symbolic coding method which consists of start time sequence.

Fitness function: the larger the value of objective function is, the lower its fitness is.

Initial population: in line with logical relationship of activities, an activity sequence is selected.

4.2 Selection

GTA uses following selection strategy: candidate solutions of every generation are sorted in descending order; the first individual is copied to the next generation; the other candidate solutions are selected according to its fitness. The larger the fitness is, the larger probability the candidate is selected.

4.3 Crossover

According to crossover probability p_1, the crossover operation is as follows.

Step 1 Select one chromosome from candidate set.

Step 2 Generate random numbers r_1 between 0 and 1, and judge if conduct crossover operation. If $r_1 < p_1$, go to Step 3, or copy the chromosome to next generation and go to Step 1.

Step 3 Generate random numbers r_2 and r_3 between 1 and n, exchange the values of them.

4.4 Mutation

Mutation probability is p_2. Mutation operation is as follows.

Step 1. Generate random number r_3 between 0 and 1, and judge if conduct mutation operation. If $r_3 < p_2$, go to Step 2, otherwise, keep the chromosome to the next generation.

Step 2. Generate random numbers r_4 and r_5 between 1 and n, reverse the order of r_4 and r_5.

4.5 Neighborhood

(1) When start time of some activity changes, ignoring resource constraint, use dynamic critical path method to compute time window in the set A^U of activities that haven't happened. (2) Select one activity randomly in A^U, which can satisfy logical and resource constraint.

4.6 Tabu List

When generating neighborhood points of current solution, countermovement is added to tabu list. And the first countermovement of tabu list is removed.

Specific steps of GTA are described as follows.

1. Initialize population.
2. Calculate fitness of every individual.
3. According to selection strategy, select chromosomes of next generation.
4. Conduct crossover operation with crossover probability p_1.
5. Conduct mutation operation with mutation probability p_2.
6. Filter chromosomes of this generation, exclude m candidate solutions and then according to fitness orders add m individuals, go to Step 4.
7. Conduct tabu search in new population.
    (a) Take every chromosome as initial solution of tabu search.
    (b) Calculate value of objective function $Loss^{ini}$ of initial solution S^{ini}. Define the total N of feasible solutions as the end condition of tabu search. Initialize tabu list, let $n = 0$.
    (c) Generate a neighborhood point S^{nei} of S^{ini}; compute the value $Loss^{nei}$ of S^{nei}; check if S^{nei} is in tabu list, if yes go to (e), otherwise, go to (d).
    (d) Let S^{nei} be current solution, and update tabu list. If $Loss^{nei} < Loss^{min}$, let $Loss^{min} = Loss^{nei}$, S^{nei} is optimal solution, n ++, go to (f), otherwise go to (f).
    (e) If $Loss^{nei} < Loss^{best}$, activate movement tabu status of this neighborhood point. Let S^{nei} be current solution, $Loss^{cur} = Loss^{min} = Loss^{nei}$, n ++, update tabu list and go to (f), otherwise go to (c).
    (f) Judge if $n >= N$, if yes, go to (g), otherwise go to (c).
    (g) Return optimal solution and its value of objective function $Loss^{best}$.
8. Judge if the number of iteration is equal to that of genetic algorithm, if yes, select minimum $Loss$ in current population and stop GTA, otherwise go to Step 3.

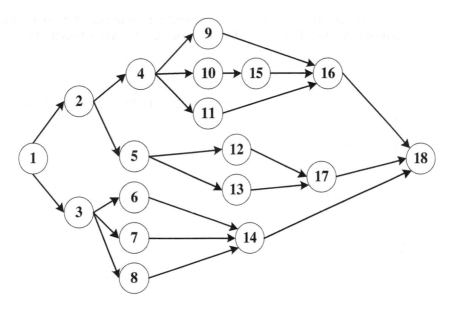

Fig. 1. AoN network

5 Experiments

According to some historical data, following table is established (Table 1).

Table 1. Activity indexes

No.	Duration	Weight	Resource
1	1	0	1
2	1	10	10
3	2	5	15
4	2	5	4
5	5	12	10
6	6	4	15
7	6	8	17
8	4	6	6
9	3	10	12
10	5	6	15
11	6	9	4
12	6	9	22
13	8	5	5
14	8	4	15
15	7	8	10
16	5	7	8
17	4	10	4
18	1	20	10

Ignoring resource constraint, every activity can performs at the start time computed by critical path method. And the loss is 0. Taking resource constraint into consideration

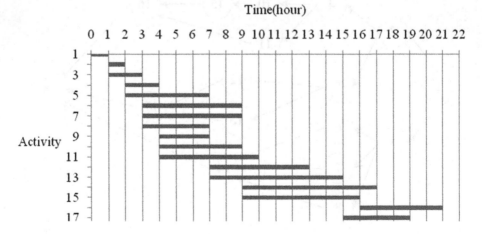

Fig. 2. Activity sequence without resource constraint

(in this example, total amount of resource is 55), it is probable that the sum of the amount of resources all activities required is larger than total amount. Then the original activity sequence should be adjusted. Adjusted activity indexes are shown in Table 2.

Table 2. Adjustment comparison of activities

No	Duration	Start time	Adjusted start time	Time change
1	1	0	0	0
2	1	1	1	0
3	2	1	1	0
4	2	2	2	0
5	5	2	2	0
6	6	3	10	7
7	6	3	3	0
8	4	3	3	0
9	3	4	4	0
10	5	4	9	5
11	6	4	4	0
12	6	7	7	0
13	8	7	13	6
14	8	9	14	5
15	7	9	9	0
16	5	16	16	0
17	4	15	15	0
18	1	21	21	0

With GTA, optimal solution can be obtained as follows.
(0, 1, 1, 2, 2, 10, 3, 3, 4, 9, 4, 7, 13, 14, 9, 16, 15, 21)

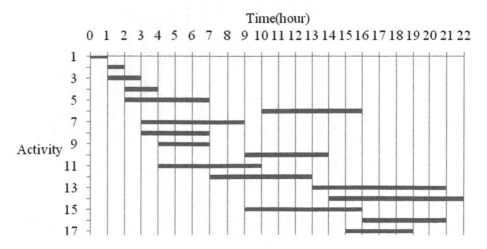

Fig. 3. Activity sequence with resource constraint

The loss of the plan is 88.

Figure 2 demonstrates the activity sequence without resource constraint of AoN network in Fig. 1. At time 4, there are seven activities (Activity 5, Activity 6, Activity 7, Activity 8, Activity 9, Activity 10, and Activity 11) that are active. However, total amount of resource needed is 79, larger than 55. Hence, with resource constraint, the activity sequence in Fig. 2 is infeasible. Similar situation happens at time 5, 6, 7, 8, 9 (Figs. 3 and 4).

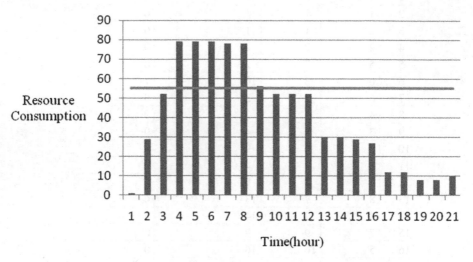

Fig. 4. Resource consumption without resource constraint (horizontal line represents resource upper limit)

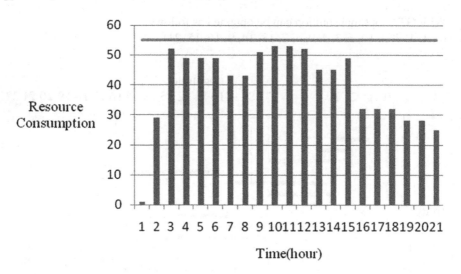

Fig. 5. Resource consumption with resource constraint (horizontal line represents resource upper limit)

After adjusting the execution sequence, at every time point, total resource needed is under 55 as shown in Fig. 5. For example, At time 4, execution sequence of seven active activities in Fig. 2 have been adjusted. In the new sequence, five activities are active at time 4. Activity 6 and Activity 10 have been postponed to time 9 and time 10 respectively. On the other hand, the sum of resources needed by the five activities is smaller than 55.

6   Conclusions

In this study, an emergency rescue plan with minimum rescue loss is constructed with the method of proactive scheduling optimization for rescue activities. With the definition of the problem, an optimization model is proposed. The model consists of an objective function and several constraint conditions. The genetic-tabu algorithm (GTA) is designed to calculate optimal solution for emergency rescue. GTA combines the advantages of genetic algorithm and tabu search algorithm. Finally an example is given to demonstrate the feasibility and effectiveness of GTA.

Without resource constraint, activities can perform at its initial start time computed by critical path method. However, in real life, resource constraint exists in most cases. Then, the original rescue plan needs to be adjusted. Activities are sorted according to their weights. Activities with higher priorities can perform before those with lower priorities. Then the loss can be minimized. This study can provide decision support for emergency rescue implementation.

Acknowledgement.   This paper was supported in part by the National Natural Science Foundation of China under Grant No. 61272036, and Key Disciplines of Software Engineering of Shanghai Second Polytechnic University under Grant No. XXKZD1301.

References

1. Jun, H., Wenguo, Y., Jianming, Z.: Research and major issues on emergency resource system. China Emerg. Manag. **2**, 10–13 (2009)
2. Jie, C., Xiaoguang, Y., Showyang, W.: Major issues in public incidents emergency management. China Emerg. Manag. **4**(2), 84–93 (2007)
3. Lambrechts, O., Demeulemeester, E., Herroelen, W.: A tabu search procedure for developing robust predictive project schedules. Int. J. Prod. Econ. **111**(2), 493–508 (2008)
4. Vonder, S.V.D., Demeulemeester, E., Herroelen, W.: Proactive heuristic procedures for robust project scheduling: an experimental analysis. Eur. J. Oper. Res. **189**(3), 723–733 (2008)
5. Schatteman, D., Herroelen, W., Vonder, S.V.D., et al.: A methodology for integrated risk management and proactive scheduling of construction projects. J. Constr. Eng. Manag. **134**(11), 1–28 (2008)
6. Elmaghraby, S.E.: Activity nets: a guided tour through some recent developments. Eur. J. Oper. Res. **82**(3), 383–408 (1995)
7. Glover, F., Kelly, J.P., Laguna, M.: Genetic algorithms and tabu search: hybrids for optimization. Comput. Oper. Res. **22**(93), 111–134 (1995)

8. Nowicki, E., Smutnicki, C.: A fast taboo search algorithm for the job shop problem. Manage. Sci. **42**(6), 797–813 (1996)
9. Ling, W.: Intelligent Optimization Algorithm with Applications. Tsinghua University Press, Beijing (2001)
10. Tan, W., Sun, Y., Li, L.X.: A trust service-oriented scheduling model for workflow applications in cloud computing. IEEE Syst. J. **8**(3), 868–878 (2014)
11. Xu, L., Ming, H.: Application of tabu search-parallel genetic algorithm for job-shop scheduling. Comput. Integr. Manuf. Syst. **11**(05), 678–681 (2005)

SSSP on GPU Without Atomic Operation

Feng Wang[1], Liehuang Zhu[1], and Changyou Zhang[2(✉)]

[1] School of Computer Science and Technology, Beijing Institute of Technology,
Beijing 100081, China
[2] Laboratory of Parallel Software and Computational Science,
Institute of Software, Chinese Academy of Science, Beijing 100190, China
changyou@iscas.ac.cn

Abstract. Graph is a general theoretical model in many large scale data-driven applications. SSSP (Single Source Shortest Path) algorithm is a foundation for most important algorithms and applications. GPU remains its mainstream station in high performance computing with heterogeneous architecture computers. Because of the high parallelization of the GPU threads, the distances of the vertices of the GPU are updated by atomic operations to avoid the read and write errors. Most atomic operations are unnecessary since the read-write conflicts are rare in large graph. However, without atomic operations the result accuracy can't be guaranteed. The atomic operations take large part of the running time of the program. To improve the performance of SSSP on GPU, we proposed an algorithm with data block iterations instead of atomic operations. The algorithm not only gets a high speed-up but also guarantees the accuracy of the result. Experimental results show that this SSSP algorithm gained a speedup of three times than the serial algorithm on CPU and more than ten times than the parallel algorithm on GPU with atomic operation.

Keywords: Graph · SSSP · Atomic operation · Data block iteration

1 Introduction

In the field of data analytics, graph is a vital kind of data structure and attracts more and more researchers' interest. Graph can be used to clarify complex problems and organize text information based on the logical relationship. Information can be easily acquired with the format of graph. Graph is defined on data represented in the form of a graph G = (V, E), with V the set of vertices and E the set of edges with weights. Generally the vertices represent the things and the edges represent the relationships. The Single-Source Shortest Path (SSSP) problem is a classical problem of graph. SSSP computes the weight of the shortest path from a special vertex (source) to all other vertices. SSSP can be widely used in computer science like network topologies, social relationship, traffic simulations and web searching.

The most well-known serial SSSP algorithm is Dijkstra algorithm [1]. With Fibonacci heap [2], the time complexity of serial Dijkstra algorithm is $O(|E| + |V|\log|V|)$. The Bellman-Ford algorithm, instead of greedily selecting the minimum-weight node not yet processed to relax, simply relaxes all the edges, and does this $|V|$-1 times. As the "Big Data Times" approaches, more and more problems can be simply represented by graph.

© Springer International Publishing Switzerland 2016
Q. Zu and B. Hu (Eds.): HCC 2016, LNCS 9567, pp. 409–419, 2016.
DOI: 10.1007/978-3-319-31854-7_37

However, the count of vertices and edges is too large. If we still use the serial algorithms, the time consuming is unpredictable large. So we have to turn to the parallel computation to accelerate solving SSSP.

The most prevailing way of parallel computations includes the use of GPU, whose many-cores can provide enough parallelization. To conveniently program on GPU, NVIDIA introduced CUDA in C/Fortran programming language [5]. The block of CUDA is collection of threads that can be run on each core of device currently. A grid is a collection of blocks assigned to multiprocessor.

One of the bottlenecks of GPU is that its atomic operation is time-consuming. However, to ensure the accuracy of the program, some global and share data must be locked with atomic operation. It costs notable running time to execute instructions with atomic operation. So, avoiding atomic operation is helpful to speed up SSSP on GPU. In this paper we adopt delta-stepping algorithm [4] to solve SSSP. Our program does all relax operations on GPU without atomic operation. We use data block iteration instead of the atomic operation.

The remainder of this paper is organized as follows: Sect. 2 introduces the related work on SSSP with GPU by others. Section 3 describes our algorithm in detail. Section 4 presents the experimental results of our algorithms. Section 5 analyses the performance. Section 6 summarizes the conclusions we have obtained and describe further works.

2 Related Work

Some GPU-based SSSP algorithms related researches have been detailed. The basic knowledge of GPU and CUDA is the foundation of GPU-based SSSP. Dijkstra algorithm is the typical serial algorithm and delta-stepping algorithm is a parallel algorithm. These works contributed to the further researches and constructed the basement of our algorithm.

2.1 CUDA-Based Program

GPU [5] attracts more and more interest in academic and industrial circle. However, the architecture of GPU degrades the flexibility of its algorithm. The great difference between CPU parallel program and GPU is that every thread on GPU occupies hardware resource alone without other kernels running simultaneously. In CUDA architecture, except the register, GPU memory can be distinguished into two categories. One is the share memory, which records variables for each block. Each thread in the same block shares this memory [5, 6]. Another is the global memory, which can be read and written by all threads. However, the time of reading and writing data in global memory is about 100 times than that of share one. Using these two kinds of memory reasonably will create significant speed-up performance.

In CUDA, it can perform the read-modify-write without being interrupted by other threads. The operations that satisfy this constraint are called atomic operation. They can be used to coordinate execution between concurrent threads. A kernel on a GPU, can suffer severe performance degradation when including an atomic operation. Marwa Elteir has shown that a single of memory access execution time increases significantly up to 69.4-fold with atomic operation. The atomic operation makes large latency in the program.

2.2 Parallel Algorithm of SSSP

To solve the SSSP problem in parallel, Meyer and Sanders proposed the Delta (Δ)-stepping algorithm [4]. Delta-stepping algorithm extracts a group of vertices in a finite section (bucket) and processes these vertices in parallel. Delta-stepping algorithm is added by the concept of a liner array: Bucket[]. Delta(Δ) is the width of the bucket and Bucket[i] is the vertices set $\{v \in V : v$ is queued and distance[v] $\in [i *\Delta,(i +1) *\Delta]\}$. For the weight of edge w, when w is higher than delta, the edge is a heavy edge. Otherwise it is a light edge. The light edges in a bucket need to be iterated many times until no vertex can be relaxed, while the heavy edges just need once. The algorithm proceeds as following:

(1) Initialization: The distances of all the vertices d[i] = ∞, expect the source vertex s, with d[s] = 0.
(2) Relax light edge: For every vertices v in the current bucket, if the edge w[v,v'] is a light edge and neighbor vertex v' distance d[v'] is higher than d[v] + w[v,v'], then relax vertex v': d[v'] $\leftarrow$ d[v] + w[v,v'].
(3) Update: After the current bucket clears all vertices. Insert the new relaxed vertices into the corresponding bucket.
(4) Iteration: If new vertices have been relaxed, the program backs to step 2.
(5) Relax heavy edges: For heavy edge e[v,v'], whose start vertex v is in current bucket, relax v', as the same as step 2.
(6) Come into the next bucket. If all the vertices have been relaxed, the algorithm is finished. Else turn to step 2.

2.3 Parallel GPU-Based Algorithm of SSSP

Dijkstra algorithm can be distinguished into two versions of parallelization on GPU. The first one is to parallelize the internal operations of the sequential Dijkstra algorithm. The second is to perform several Dijkstra algorithms through disjoint subgraphs in parallel. However, the first one's parallelization is too low, Hector and Yuri has realized it in on GPU [8]. In the second one some works are in vain sometimes. So the parallelization versions of Dijkstra algorithm can't get high speed-up.

Baggio has tested his delta-stepping implementation with atomic operations on CUDA. However, their achieve rates 8–17x times slower than Dijkstra's method. Since the atomic operation's launching and recycling takes large part of the running time and most atomic operations are unnecessary. So, avoiding using atomic operation can create speedup.

Pedro J. Matin has proposed to visit the vertex's all predecessors before relaxing the vertex. In the process of relaxing, the vertex is relaxed by every predecessor in serial, which has a great impact on the speed. For the low parallelization of Dijkstra algorithm and the leaping of large leaping of memory, the algorithm doesn't get a high speedup.

3 Program Description

3.1 Graph Presentation

N. Bell and M. Garland [7] discuss possible implementations, advantages and disadvantages of the formats of graph. Hectore [8] and Pedro select the CSR graph format to store their graphs. For CSR is space-efficient, requiring one array for every edge and another array for the edges' weights. In CUDA, it is proposed to avoid thread's jumping in memory to reduce latency [5]. In CSR, we get an edge's information from three different memory blocks. So, we use the edge-weight combined graph format, in which the edge array and weight array are combined into a neighbor information array. The edge's weight follows its end vertex in this array. Another array (start position array) records the vertices start position in the combined array. Figure 1(a) shows an example graph and Fig. 1(b) shows the resulting graph format we use for the example graph.

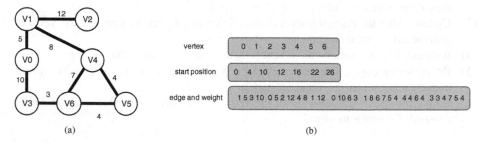

Fig. 1. An example of the edge-weight combined graph format we use.

3.2 Mapping CUDA Threads and Memory

3.2.1 Thread Allocation

In [8] and, the GPU's count of threads is equal to that of the vertices, and every thread is responsible to a vertex. In delta-stepping algorithm, many vertices are not in the current bucket. Using that many threads makes large latency. We can save threads by partitioning all vertices into blocks. Vertices' neighbor information in a block is successive, as is shown in Fig. 2(a). Threads can get the responding vertex's start position from start position array in Fig. 1(b). The edge-weight array is partitioned to a matrix as is shown in Fig. 2(b). A thread block is responsible for a column. If a vertex is in current bucket, the corresponding thread will try to relax its neighbors. After computing all the responsible vertices, the thread blocks finishes once bucket computing.

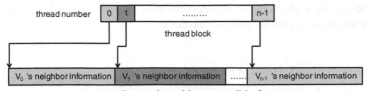

(a) Every thread is responsible for vertex

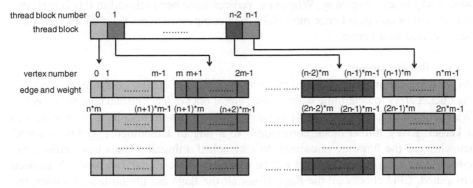

(b) Every thread block is responsible for a column of edge-weight data

Fig. 2. An example of data block map. The grid size is n, and block size is m.

3.2.2 Memory Dispatching

Considering that the number of the vertices is large and the distances to the source vertex are read and modified by the fathers' corresponding threads, the array distance[] keeping all the vertices' distance is located in global memory. The flag array Ismodified[], whose size is equal to the count of thread blocks, is transferred to host CPU. So the flag Ismodified[] array is also in the global memory. Every thread block has a flag "Isrelaxed" to record whether the threads in it have relaxed new vertices after finishing computing a data block. For it is only read and modified by threads in this block, it is in the shared memory. Another variable is the current bucket number, which is same to all threads. So it can be either a shared variable or a thread one.

3.3 Extension with Delta-Stepping

The most important design is the bucket. The original delta-stepping algorithm proposes to record the vertices of the current bucket in an array. Since GPU threads work in parallel, it is hard and time-consuming to record the vertices in an array. As we traverse all the vertices in the bucket computing, we just use the distance of vertices to compute which bucket they are in and flags Ismodified[] to record whether new vertices have been relaxed in this traversal. Not all flags are initialized value after a traversal, which means new vertices may be inserted into current bucket.

In original delta-stepping algorithm, it first relaxes all light edges of the current bucket in iteration and then relaxes the heavy edges after that. In our program, since threads traverses all the vertices in the bucket computing, it relaxes both kinds of edges in bucket iteration to save another time of traversal.

3.4   Computing Without Atomic Operation

In the process of bucket computing, we use one kernel for a computing once. A bucket need many times computing. When new vertices have been relaxed in this kernel, this bucket will be computed once more. GPU will compute next bucket after no vertex has been relaxed in a kernel.

3.4.1   Bucket Design

As we don't use an array to record the vertices relaxed in the last compute, we can't use the bucket array to determine whether the current bucket has finished computing as [4]. We use the flag array Ismodified[] to record whether new vertices have been relaxed in a kernel. Every thread block corresponds to a flag in Ismodified[]. Before a kernel launches, all the flags are initialized. In a kernel, if a thread relaxes new vertices, the thread block's corresponding flag will be modified. After all the data blocks have been computed, CPU checks all the flags. If not all the flags are the initialized values, the current bucket's computing has not completed, for new vertices have been relaxed in this kernel. If all the flags are the initialized values, the next kernel will come into next bucket.

3.4.2   Data Block Iteration

In the process of data block computing, the algorithm makes full use of the parallelism function. Every thread tries to relax the neighbors of the responsible vertex. Before computing a data block, one thread of the thread block initializes the share 'Isrelxed' flag. The flag is used to record whether new vertices have been relaxed in this data block computing.

In the process of data block computing, if a thread's corresponding vertex is in current bucket, it will try to explore its neighbors. When neighbor's distance is relaxed to a new smaller one, the threads modify their thread blocks' share flag 'Isrelaxed'. After all the neighbors of a data block have been explored, threads of this block are in synchronization. Then, a thread checks the shared flag. If the flag's value is not the initialized one, which means that some vertices' neighbors have been relaxed in computing, the thread block must come back to compute this data block again.

3.4.3   Avoiding Atomic Operation

Hectore [8] and Pedro J. Martin use atomic instructions that allow only one thread to update the same vertex's distance once, to avoid such concurrency inconsistencies as two vertices i and i' access the same vertex j and the worse value $d[i] + w(i,j)$ were finally left. The atomic operation turns numbers of threads to compete for access to a relatively small number of memory addresses. The launching and recycling of atomic operation will occupy lots of GPU clocks. And the execution in atomic operation is much time-consuming than the normal one. In the large graph, most atomic operations are unnecessary, since the vertices' count is much larger than the degree of graph and the read-write conflicts are rare in large graph. However, without atomic operations a vertex may be not relaxed to the smallest distance, and its following vertices distance accuracy can't be guaranteed.

In our algorithm, if a vertex is relaxed by a thread, the thread will be back to computing again since the thread block's share flag 'Isrelaxed' was modified computing. The neighbor's distance may not be relaxed to the smallest distance in the first computing. However, in the following computing, the thread which can relax the neighbor to the smallest distance will iterate relaxing it until it equals to the smallest distance.

Another advantage of our algorithm is that we relax more vertices in the data block iteration. In most graphs, the data is of well locality. The vertices are linked to the ones whose numbers are close to theirs, and the vertices in a local region are in the same bucket. If a vertex's neighbors are relaxed, it will be high possible that the vertex and its neighbors are in the same data block. In the next time's data block computing, the program relaxes the neighbors' neighbors.

An example is shown in Fig. 3(a). The red vertex is relaxed by thread block I and thread block II concurrently. Maybe the distances of red vertex is not the smaller after the first computing. Both threads will relax it again. After the second computing, the red vertex must be relaxed to the smaller distance of its both parents. Although write-after-read error may happen in the first computing, the distance will be guaranteed to be the smaller after the second computing.

The new relaxed blue vertex is relaxed to the current bucket in the first computing. And its corresponding thread is just in thread block I, as Fig. 3 (b) shows. The blue vertex's neighbors are also relaxed in the second computing. So, the thread block not only relaxes the red vertices to the shortest distance, but also relaxes the blue vertex's neighbors in the second computing.

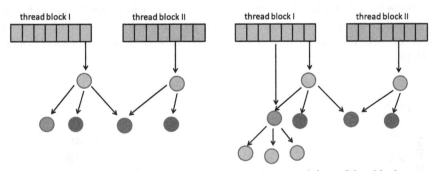

(a) the first time of data block computing   (b) the second time of data block computing

Fig. 3. An example of raise parallelism in the data block computing. (Color figure online)

4   Experiment and Results

The hardware condition of the experiment is illustrated in the following and the experimental results of different SSSP algorithms are compared to verify the performance enhancements of our algorithm.

4.1 Setup of Experiment

The performance results are obtained by using the same hardware. In our case we use Geforce GTX 480, 1401 MHz clock, 1536 MB memory with CUDA 6.0 toolkit, which runs on the UBUNTU Desktop 14.04.2. Regarding the host CPU machine, we use an AMD Phenom(tm) x4 960T Processor.

The experiment graph data is the New York City road network from with 264 K vertices and 733 K edges and Northwest USA road network with 1208 K vertices and 2820 K edges. The New York City's max length of the edges is 36946. The max degree of the graph is 8 and the average degree of the vertices is 5.55. In Northwest USA road network, the max length of the all the edges is 128569. The max degree is 9, and the average degree is 4.67.

We test our DBI (data block iteration) GPU implementation against two algorithms: (1) serial SSSP algorithm: Dijkstra with Fibonacci heap, (2) AO (atomic operation) GPU implements. We change the two GPU algorithms' block size and grid size to make deeper comparisons of these two implements.

4.2 Results

Delta is an important parameter in delta-stepping algorithm, so we show the running timings of two GPU implements under different values of delta.

Figure 4 shows the results of New York City road network with grid size of 346 and block size of 192. When delta is beyond 100 K, both algorithms are stable as the delta increases. When delta is 340 K, our DBI algorithm gets the shortest running time: 27.73 ms. AO gets its shortest running time of 355 ms when delta is 430 K. The largest distance of the vertices is no more than 500 K. So when delta is above 500 K, all the vertices are in the first bucket. From the Fig. 4, we can conclude that the algorithm of DBI is more than ten times faster than AO under the same value of delta in New York City road network. The running time of serial Dijkstra algorithm with Fibonacci heap is about 71 ms.

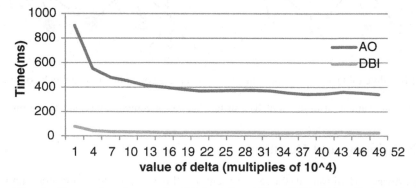

Fig. 4. The running time result of Delta-AO and Delta-DBI of New York road

Figure 5 shows the results of Northwest U.S.A road network with grid size of 256 and block size of 346. When delta is about 7 M, both algorithms get the highest speed: AO's running time is nearly 4486 ms, and the DBI's is nearly 465 ms. From the Fig. 5, we can conclude that the algorithm of DBI is also more than ten times faster than AO under the same value of delta. The running time of serial Dijkstra algorithm with Fibonacci heap is about 1421 ms.

Both experiments show that the implement of AO's running time is even larger than the Dijkstra algorithm with Fibonacci heap. While the highest speed of DBI is nearly three times higher than the speed of serial Dijkstra algorithm with Fibonacci heap.

As the two GPU implements, we change the grid size and block size to compare the results. In [6], it is proposed that the block size is the multiple of 32. The New York network results are shown in Tables 1 and 2 under delta of 340 K. The Northwest U.S. A network results are shown in Tables 3 and 4 under delta of 7 M.

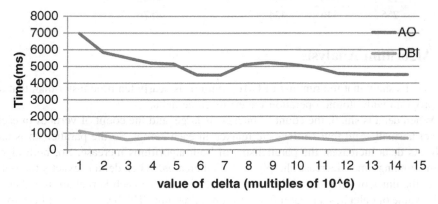

Fig. 5. The running time result of Delta-AO and Delta-DBI of Northwest road

Table 1. The results of DBI and AO implements when block size is 192 of New York.

Block size	Grid size	DBI running time (ms)	AO running time (ms)
192	173	30.98	482.39
192	346	27.73	458.67
192	692	28.05	470.17
192	1384	29.74	479.79

Table 2. The results of DBI and AO implements when grid size is 346 of New York.

Block Size	Grid size	DBI running time (ms)	AO running time (ms)
32	346	98.30	643.41
64	346	54.64	587.71
128	346	34.92	485.80
192	346	27.73	467.28
256	346	29.39	478.86

Table 3. The results of DBI and AO implements when block size is 192 of Northwest

Block size	Grid size	DBI running time (ms)	AO running time (ms)
256	173	507	5442
256	346	424	4576
256	692	471	4732
256	1384	494	4721

Table 4. The results of DBI and AO implements when block size is 192 of Northwest

Block Size	Grid size	DBI running time (ms)	AO running time (ms)
32	346	904	10148
64	346	724	7425
128	346	525	5390
192	346	444	4642
256	346	424	4576

5 Algorithm Analysis

The results show that the running of DBI programs is nearly ten time faster than that of the program with atomic operation under the same delta.

When delta is small, the count of buckets is large, and the count of vertices in each bucket is small. And few vertices are relaxed in each kernel. So the parallelism is not high. As delta increases, the parallelisms of both algorithms increase. So, both algorithms running times decrease sharply as delta increases. When delta is exactly the right value, the times of kernels and the average running time of each kernel are in balance, so the value of delta has a great influence on running time. The best values of both road networks are 340 K and 7 M respectively.

Marwa Elteir has explained that atomic operation is a split-phase in CompletPath not FastPath. Atomic operation in the kernel may force the complier to use the CompletePath for all loads and stores in the kernel. A single of memory access through CompletePath execution time increases significantly up to 69.4-fold with atomic operation. So, the atomic operation makes large latency in the program.

However, in the graph with large number of vertices, the degree is much smaller than the count of vertices, the rate of read-write conflicts is not high. In our both experimental graphs, when delta is at the best value, the rate of read-write conflicts is not more than 1.0 %. So, many atomic operations are unnecessary. But we can't distinguish which atomic operation can be omitted. Our DBI algorithm use data block iteration to avoid atomic operation. Experiments show that the average iteration time of DBI is about 4.4 in each kernel in New York network. Although we compute the data block many times, the time of computing the data block once is much lower than that with atomic operation. We also relax more vertices in the data block iteration. So, our DBI implement get a high speed-up.

6   Conclusion and Future Work

In this paper we have demonstrated the effectiveness of our method to solve the SSSP problem on GPU. The comparisons we have used have proved effective to achieve three times of speedup to the serial Dijkstra algorithm. Our main contribution is to show that atomic operations can be avoided to speed up in SSSP. The method of data block iteration can be not only implied in SSSP, but also can be used in other GPU algorithm to get speedup. Furthermore, there are some works to do in our future work.

First, we would like to avoid the multiple times of launching kernels of GPU. The aim of launching and recycling of kernels is to synchronize all the GPU threads. CUDA doesn't support synchronizing all the thread in instructions. Launching and recycling takes up large part of the running time of the program. Avoiding synchronizing threads by host CPU is a good way to create larger speed-up. Another possible improvement target is how to make full shared memory in algorithm. The vertex distance is located in global memory for that other thread can modify them. Different from the global memory data, the shared data can't be modified by other blocks' thread. However the shared memory data can be read and written 100 times faster than the global one. So how to use the shared memory is another improvement

Acknowledgement. This paper is supported by the Natural Science Foundation of China (61379048); Special Project of National CAS Union – The High Performance Cloud Service Platform for Enterprise Creative Computing; Special Project of Hebei-CAS Union (Hebei, No.14010015)–The Performance Optimization of Key Algorithms of Health Data Processing in Senile Dementia Analysis.

References

1. Dijkstra, E.W.: A note on two problems in connexion with graphs. Numer. Math. **1**, 269–271 (1959). http://dx.doi.org/10.1007/BF01386390
2. Fredman, M.L., Tarjan, R.E.: Fibonacci heaps their uses in improved network optimization algorithms. J. ACM (JACM) **34**, 596–615 (1987)
3. Bellman, R.: On a routing problem. Q. Appl. Math. **16**, 87–90 (1958)
4. Meyer, U., Sanders, P.: Δ-stepping: a parallelizable shortest path algorithm. J. Algorithms **49**, 114–152 (2003)
5. http://www.nvidia.com/object/cuda_home.html#
6. Sanders, J., Kandrot, E.: CUDA by Example: An Introduction to General-Purpose GPU Programming. Addison-Wesley, Upper Saddle River (2010)
7. Bell, N., Garland, M.: Implementing sparse matrix-vector multiplication on throughput-oriented processors. In: SC's 2009: Proceedings of the 2009 ACM/IEEE Conference on Supercomputing, pp. 18:1–18:11, November 2009
8. Ortega-Arranz, H., Torres, Y.: A new GPU-based approach to the shortest path problem. IEEE (2013)

ISS: An Iterative Scrubbing Strategy
for Improving Memory Reliability Against MBU

Hui Wang and Yun Wang$^{(\boxtimes)}$

Key Laboratory of Computer Network and Information Integration,
MOE, Department of Computer Science and Engineering, Southeast University,
Nanjing 210096, People's Republic of China
{huiwang_cs,yunwang}@seu.edu.cn

Abstract. As technology scales, multiple bit upsets (MBUs) have shown prominent effect, thus affecting the reliability of memory to a great extent. In order to mitigate MBUs errors, interleaving schemes together with single error correction (SEC) codes can be used to provide the greatest protection for advanced computer memories. In this paper, an algorithm of iterative scrubbing strategy (ISS) is proposed for the optimal interleaving distance (ID), which should be maximized under some conditions. The proposed algorithm should keep the complexity and the area overhead of designing ID as low as possible without compromising memory reliability. The key principle is to take advantage of the locality of MBU errors and to realize efficient scrubbing. The efficiency of the proposed approach will be compared with conventional strategy.

Keywords: Soft error · MBU · ISS · Interleaving distance

1 Introduction

Memory reliability is a critical issue for computer. CMOS technology has shrunken to a point where alpha particles from packaging materials and high energy neutrons from terrestrial atmosphere have started causing such malfunction at an increasing rate [1,2]. The common method addressing such problem includes error correction capabilities on memory by using per-word error correction codes (ECCs). However, extra-added bits increase the probability of suffering single event upset (SEU), because the number of storage elements is expanded. Nowadays, single error correction, double error detection (SEC-DED) and scrubbing techniques are the most common methods for protecting memory [3–5]. As technology scales, MBUs occur more frequently in memories, and contribute to more than 55 % of all the upsets according to recent research. MBU affects adjacent bits because the energetic particles have local impact [6,7]. The physical ID scheme is typically employed to protect memory structures [8–11], such as cache memory. Interleaving separates different bits of a logical word into different physical positions following a determined pattern.

A spatial MBU is a MBU induced by a SEU, where two or more physically adjacent bits are upset. By contrast, a temporal MBU is a MBU resulted

© Springer International Publishing Switzerland 2016
Q. Zu and B. Hu (Eds.): HCC 2016, LNCS 9567, pp. 420–431, 2016.
DOI: 10.1007/978-3-319-31854-7_38

from multiple SEUs over time. Both single-bit upset and multi-bit upset are very important for assessing the vulnerability of SRAM-based memory structure, such as instruction and data caches. Typical techniques for the protection of memories against temporal MBU include error correction codes and scrubbing [11–13]. Typical techniques for the protection of memories against spatial MBUs include interleaving, error correction codes, and scrubbing. By interleaving distance scheme, logical checkwords are added into physically dispersed locations of the memory, so that MBUs can appear as multiple single-bit upsets in different words, instead of a multi-bit upset in a single word. However, the larger the interleaving interval is, the more complex and costly a memory design will be. The larger column span a MBU covers, the lower the probability of MBU occurrence will present [14]. During the designing stage of a memory structure, the selection of the interleaving scheme is generally driven by the effectiveness of designing activities, such as power saving or power consumption, xy-ratio, pin-mapping, access time, floor-planning and column decoding [13,14].

In this paper, the approach of scrubbing is taken further by designing an iterative scrubbing sequence for a given memory. The selection of the interleaving interval is incorporated into the analytical model for the first time in this paper, while the failure probability is kept under a determined level. The rest of the paper is organized as follows. Section 2 presents the general background and motivation. The iterative algorithm and techniques are proposed in Sect. 3. Reliability analysis of the ISS algorithm and additional memory operations are shown in Sect. 4. Section 5 presents the simulation results. Section 6 concludes the paper.

2 Background and Motivation

2.1 Scrubbing Scheme

Several studies have been conducted to the reliability of memory by using protective mechanisms against soft errors, and an optimized scrubbing strategy was proposed in [16]. To protect the memory in microprocessor, ECC is often applied by designers in advanced memories, which typically provides single error correction and double error detection (SECDED). If the scrubbing interval is set as short enough, the occurrence probability of a temporal MBU is practically eliminated [12]. Scrubbing can be performed in a deterministic or a probabilistic model. Deterministic scrubbing, means that a memory word is checked periodically, when the word checking is produced through a cyclic, and constant process. Probabilistic scrubbing, such as exponentially-distributed scrubbing means that a memory word is assumed to be checked in an exponentially-distributed time period. As technology scales, MBU resulted from SEU will occupy the main position, especially when memories are used in hostile environments.

Although the process of SEU becoming MBU is avoided due to the design of interleaving, silent data corruption (SDC) may not be completely removed until the corrected data are written back through the entire memory at scrubbing time. When these SDC errors are accumulated, they will be detected unrecoverable

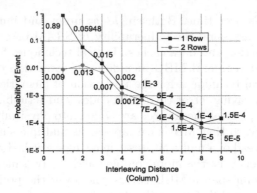

Fig. 1. Probability of different MBUs

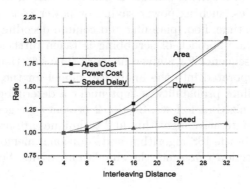

Fig. 2. Area cost, power cost, speed delay of different IDs

errors (DUE). For instance, a single spatial MBU may be treated as multiple SBUs because of the interleaving design. However, if these SBUs are not corrected in time, they will eventually become temporal MBUs, which cannot be corrected by SEC-DED strategy.

A methodology called SEC-DED-DAEC [15], is proposed for deriving an error correcting code through heuristic search, which adopts the same number of check bits as the conventional SEC-DED codes that are commonly used. By this method, the most likely adjacent double-bit errors can be detected and corrected, which will be adopted for scrubbing the memory in the iterative algorithm in this paper. Since the spatial MBU caused by a single event has the characteristic of clustering, the bits in a single MBU can be corrected as soon as any error bit is detected. It will be feasible under the condition that the MBU is segmented by ID and do not exceed the ability of correction.

2.2   Interleaving Distance

As the errors in a spatial MBU are physically close, this physical clustering of errors is due to the nature of the radiation particle hits, of which the errors are

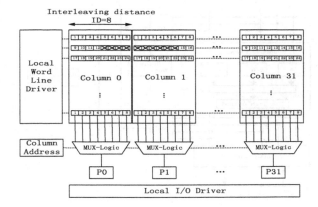

Fig. 3. An example of MBU spans 10 columns in memory

localized along the trajectory of the particles. The irradiation experiments show that if the energy and the type of particle are determinate, the angles of event will be the determining factor for MBUs. Ideally, the ID is determined as the maximum MBU size. However, the probability distribution of different MBUs sizes are not balanced [17], which is shown in Fig. 1. The latest experiment of the neutron induced in SRAM shows that the ratio of MBU to SBU increases by 46 % as the process technology node shrinks from 250 nm to 22 nm [18]. The power consumption, silicon area and delay of speed with different IDs are shown in Fig. 2. It shows that these performance indexes with ID = 32 are two times higher than those with ID = 4, and the costs of both area and power increase significantly with the ID while the speed is nearly the same. As choosing a square shape of the xy-ratio is the typical design practice, the larger size of ID is not suitable in design practices. Therefore, if smaller ID meets the reliability target of memory, it is more attractive and effective.

3   Iterative Scrubbing Strategy

In order to present the proposed iteration of scrubbing strategy and minimize the ID, the memory structure with ID described in [6] will be adopted, which is shown in Fig. 3. It denotes that an ID of 8 is adopted. The bits in the same group within an ID belong to the same bits in logic words, and the bits in a row are simultaneously enabled by the local word driver to be selected through row address decoding. An example of a spatial MBU is also shown in Fig. 3. In this case, a MBU spanning 10 columns has been shown.

Under certain assumptions, such as an exponential distribution, the $MTTF$ of various components comprising a system can be combined to obtain the $MTTF$ of the whole system. Therefore, the $MTTF$ of the memory which is made up of these two parts (e.g., $MTTF_{spatial}$ and $MTTF_{temporal}$) can be computed as a function of the partial $MTTFs$ as

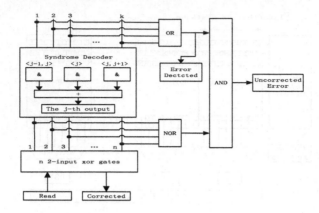

Fig. 4. The block diagram of SEC-DED-DAEC

$$MTTF_{system} = \frac{1}{\frac{1}{MTTF_{spatial}} + \frac{1}{MTTF_{temporal}}} \tag{1}$$

For the purpose of improving the reliability of memory system, two ways can be adopted, as raising the value of $MTTF_{spatial}$ or $MTTF_{temporal}$. The value of $MTTF_{temporal}$, which is approximated by:

$$MTTF_{temporal} = MTTF_{scrubbing} = \frac{2 \cdot M}{\lambda_{word}^2 \cdot T_s}, \tag{2}$$

and it can be improved by reducing the scrubbing cycle T_s [19], where λ_{word} is the error event arrival rate for the memory word, and M is the number of words in the memory. However, T_s cannot be too small. For performance and operational reasons, it is good practice to keep the scrubbing cycle within a reasonable range. In addition, scrubbing is not effective to achieve high system $MTTF$. Equation (1) has shown that a small percentage of decrease in $MTTF_{spatial}$ can degrade the $MTTF_{system}$, under the condition of fixed scrubbing interval. The reliability of memory suffering from spatial MBU can be given by

$$MTTF_{spatial} = \frac{1}{\lambda_{word} \cdot M \cdot p_{ID}}, \tag{3}$$

where λ_{word} represents the error event arrival rate for memory word, M is the memory size in words, and p_{ID} is the probability that an error event is a MBU of which the size exceeds the ID. In other words, as soon as such MBU occurs, an uncorrectable error occurs, and there a memory failure happens.

Scrubbing is a fundamental technique to avoid the accumulation of errors. The proposed scrubbing strategy adopts the principle described above to identify the most likely adjacent double-bit error cased by a spatial MBU, and the SEC-DED-DAEC codes are used to correct these disperse bit errors. When the occurrence of MBU is significant, the scrubbing strategy and scrubbing process is important for the reliability of memory. The newly proposed iterative scrubbing in this paper improves the scrubbing process which is describes in [16]. It not only doubles the mean time to failure, but also reduces the residence time of MBU in memory. In the proposed method, the scrubbing strategy is divided into two groups and each group is read sequentially. This scrubbing strategy replaces the traditional strategy, by which the words are read in sequential order. During the process of scrubbing, if a correctable error is detected, the nearby 8 bits are also checked immediately to clear the error in order to reduce the residence time in memory. The detail of ISS is shown in Algorithm 1, and the process of scrubbing is shown in Fig. 5. Once a bit error is detected, the adjacent 8 bits are also immediately checked, and whether a MBU has happened is determined through this immediate check. In Fig. 5, if the bit labeled 1 of the word 10 is upset, the bits labeled 1 of the word 1, 2, 3, 9, 11, 17, 18, 19 are also checked. Therefore, this scrubbing strategy can reduce the occurrence of temporal MBU, which significantly increases the mean time to failure of memory.

Algorithm 1. Algorithm of Iterative Scrubbing Strategy (ISS)

Data: Memory words and SEC-DED-DAEC codes
Result: Memory after scrubbing
1 Step of initialization;
2 **foreach** *each word $i \in [1, M]$* **do**
3   Compute the ECC codes using SEC-DED-DAEC for each word i;
4   Store these ECC codes in check digits corresponding to information digits of the word i;
5 **end**
6 Step of scrubbing;
7 **foreach** *word $i \in [1, M]$ of each round* **do**
8   **if** *Read memory word i, and it has single-bit error or double-bit error* **then**
9   **if** *The error pattern is single-bit error* **then**
10   Check the bits around the error bit and the scrubbing algorithm recurs on these eight bits;
11   **else if** *Error pattern is adjacent double-bit error* **then**
12   SEC-DED-DAEC codes are used to correct it, and the scrubbing algorithm recurs on these two adjacent bits;
13   **else**
14   The type of double-bit error can not be corrected;
15   **end**
16   **else**
17   More than two bit errord have happened, which cannot be corrected;
18   **end**
19 **end**

In order to present the algorithm more clearly, a basic process of the SEC-DED-DAEC codes should be described. The block diagram of SEC-DED-DAEC is shown in Fig. 4. There are k bits syndromes and n 2-input XOR gates. First of all, if a non-zero syndrome is detected, then the OR gate flags an error indication. In the next place, if any of single-bit upset (SBU) is encountered, the syndrome

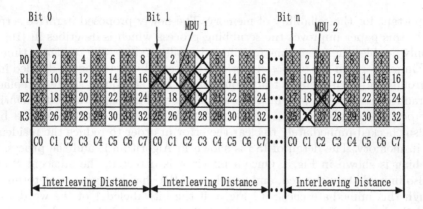

Fig. 5. An example of MBUs pattern with two events

decoder generates a 1 in the erroneous bit position. Once again, if the syndrome matches any of the adjacent double-bit errors, the syndrome decoder generates 1's at the erroneous adjacent bit positions. In the other cases, the syndrome decoder outputs zero. The outputs of the syndrome decoder are matched to generate the corrected words by using n 2-input XOR gates, which is also shown in Fig. 4. When an uncorrectable error is detected, the syndrome is checked to see whether it corresponds to an adjacent double-bit error through heuristic search algorithm. If that is the case, the words of which the bits are between the bits in error are also read and checked by SEC-DED-DAEC codes. The SEC-DED-DAEC codes take the input word and compute a number of parity bits that are stored with the original data (corresponding to the k bits), when the word is scrubbing, these k bits are recomputed and compared with the stored ones. The result of this computing process is called as the syndrome. If the syndrome is zero, there is no error occurring. If the syndrome is not zero, there may be three outcomes, namely, single-bit error, adjacent double-bit error, and others. Hence, if the syndrome corresponds to either single-error or adjacent double-bit error, the error will be detected and corrected. Otherwise, a failure will be announced. When there is a second SEU in the same row in which a large MBU occurs, there are combinations of these two events that can lead to an undetected failure, which is also illustrated in Fig. 5. The properties of the SEC-DED-DAEC codes are shown as follows: all the single-bit errors can be corrected by SEC codes, all the double-bit error can be detected by DED codes, and all the adjacent double-bit errors can be corrected by DAEC codes. The rest patterns of the errors are uncorrectable by using SEC-DED-DAEC codes.

4   Reliability Analysis

The method proposed in Sect. 3 is analyzed by the metric of mean time to failure ($MTTF$), which is commonly used to evaluate the reliability of memory system. The assumptions and metrics used in the analysis are shown below:

- The memory is protected with SEC-DED-DAEC codes for each word.
- The memory implements an interleaving scheme with ID equal to the half of maximum MBU size, and the ID should be rounded up to the closest power of 2. For instance, if the maximum size of MBU is 20, then ID = 16 will be chosen rather than ID = 32.
- Events are supposed to occur randomly, and the arrival rate of error events follows a Poisson distribution, with a probability of λ_{word}.
- Iterative scrubbing algorithm is implemented by using part of the available memory bandwidth, and also the write/read operations required are uniformly distributed over the scrubbing period.
- The error events that are caused by neutron or alpha particles are not correlated, and they can affect any part of the memory. The error type can be SBU or MBU, and the MBUs are clustered.

The proposed scrubbing algorithm can reduce the ID to the half of the maximum MBU size. $p_{failure}$ means a large MBU exceeds the ability that SEC-DED-DAEC can correct. Since we assume the pattern of MBU is clustered, then $p_{failure} \geq p[2 \cdot ID + 1]$, where $p[2 \cdot ID]$ refers to the probability that a MBU error spans exactly $2 \cdot ID$ columns. If λ_{word} is the error event arrival rate for the memory word, the $MTTF$ for failures caused by MBUs can be denoted by:

$$MTTF|_{MBU} = \frac{METF}{\lambda_{word} \cdot M},\tag{4}$$

where $METF$ is mean events to failure. Therefore, the $MTTF$ of failure caused by large MBUs can be then approximated by

$$MTTF|_{proposed} = \frac{1}{\lambda_{word} \cdot M \cdot \sum_{i=2\cdot ID+1}^{\infty} p[i]},\tag{5}$$

where $p[i]$ is the probability that an event causes i bit errors. The memory reliability used in traditional models is directly obtained as

$$MTTF|_{traditional} = \frac{1}{\lambda_{word} \cdot M \cdot \sum_{i=ID+1}^{\infty} p[i]}\tag{6}$$

In order to compare the traditional technique with the proposed strategy, the increase in $MTTF$ provided by the iterative scrubbing scheme is measured by computing the following ratio:

$$\frac{MTTF|_{proposed}}{MTTF|_{traditional}} = \frac{\lambda_{word} \cdot M \cdot \sum_{i=ID+1}^{\infty} p[i]}{\lambda_{word} \cdot M \cdot \sum_{i=2\cdot ID+1}^{\infty} p[i]} = 1 + \frac{\sum_{i=ID+1}^{2\cdot ID} p[i]}{\sum_{i=2\cdot ID+1}^{\infty} p[i]}\tag{7}$$

The ratio will be large when the average number of bit errors is large. The total $MTTF$ of the memory caused by SBU or MBU will be determined by two aspects. First one is direct failure caused by MBU when an event provokes the errors that exceed $2 \cdot ID$, and the other one is the accumulated failure caused by two independent events causing errors on the same word in memory.

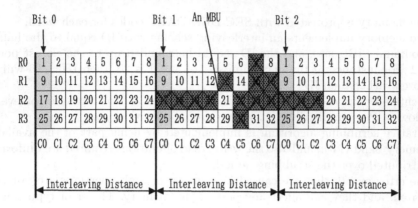

Fig. 6. An example of MBU pattern spanning 11 columns and 4 rows in memory

The improvement in the application of the proposed technique to alleviate the effect of large MBUs can be significant, for the occurrence of MBU is not balanced, and the value of $p_{failure}[k]$ decreases sharply as k increases. Therefore, as MBUs tend to increase with the development of memory technology, more benefits will be obtained from the proposed scheme.

5 Simulation Results

In this section, the theoretical analysis which has been presented in the previous section will be validated. A number of simulation experiments have been done, and the time to failure of 5000 simulations has been averaged to estimate the proposed method for improving the reliability of memory system. The proposed iterative scrubbing technique has been simulated and the reliability of memory has been presented by the mean time to failure ($MTTF$) for different configurations. The MBUs will be detected in one round and scrubbed effectively in each $\frac{T_{scrubbing}}{2}$. The traditional scrubbing strategy that is done continuously has also been simulated. As our assumption is that MBUs are all adjacent, these MBUs are assumed to be vertical, horizontal, diagonal, or any combination of them, which are the most common types of the MBUs in all scenarios. Thus, most large MBUs will be detected in one round and scrubbing effectively in each $\frac{T_{scrubbing}}{2}$, and can be corrected immediately. The reduction in the average time that an error stays in the memory system is compared with that of traditional scrubbing strategy, and the reduction factor (RF_{All}) of the memory system can be calculated by the equation as follows:

$$RF_{All} = \frac{\sum_{i=1}^{Max}\{i \cdot P_f(i) \sum_X [P(i,X) \cdot RF(i,X)]\}}{\sum_{i=1}^{Max}(i \cdot P_f(i))}, \qquad (8)$$

where $P_f(i)$ is the percentage of all the patterns with i-bit MBUs, $P(i,X)$ is percentage of i-bit MBUs that have pattern of error X, and the $RF(i,X)$ represents the reduction factor for the pattern X. For the MBU pattern in Fig. 6, the

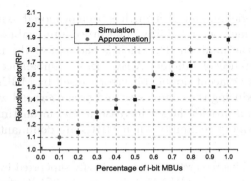

Fig. 7. Ratio of proposed scrubbing strategy for different percentages of MBUs

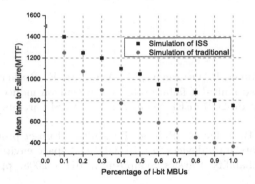

Fig. 8. MTTF of proposed scrubbing strategy for different percentages of MBUs, with $T_{scrubbing} = 0.1$, $\lambda_{word} = 0.001$, and $M = 32$ M words

reduction factor will be 2 for adjacent horizontal event, diagonal event, vertical event, or any combination of them. However, the average of the reduction factor for single-bit error will be 1, which means the iterative scrubbing scheme is suitable for the memories suffered from single-event upset with adjacent MBUs being dominant. The reduction factor of different percentages of MBUs for simulation and approximation is shown in Fig. 7. The ratio increases up to 2 when the percentage of the i-bit MBU is nearly 100 %, which also shows good agreement with the theoretical approximations and the simulation.

The $MTTF$ for different configurations of the ISS and the traditional scrubbing strategy is shown in Fig. 8. It shows that $MTTF$ decreases as the percentage of i-bit MBUs increases. The ratio of $MTTF$ increases up to two when all the error patterns are MBU, which confirms the increase in $MTTF$ provided by the ISS.

6 Conclusion

MBUs cannot be ignored or treated as negligible in designing reliable memory system. In this paper, an iterative scrubbing algorithm of memory that adopts

SEC-DED-DAEC codes and interleaving has been proposed to mitigate the effect of spatial MBU on memory reliability. The procedure enables the designers of memory to choose the minimal ID, which is the half of the maximize span of MBU, as the occurrence of different MBU sizes is imbalanced. The proposed strategy can correct adjacent double bit error caused by MBUs that exceed the ID by twice, thus reducing the complexity and area overhead when selecting the ID. This strategy can provide larger increase in the mean time to failure, and also improve the memory reliability when MBUs are dominant.

Acknowledgment. This research work was partially supported by 863 Hi-Tech Program in China under grant No.2011AA040502, and the 973 Program in China under grant 2009CB320705. We thank all of the anonymous reviewers of this work for their valuable comments.

References

1. Georgakos, G., Huber, P., Ostermayr, M., Amirante, E., Ruckerbauer, F.: Investigation of increased multi-bit failure rate due to neutron induced seu in advanced embedded srams. In: 2007 IEEE Symposium on VLSI Circuits, pp. 80–81. IEEE (2007)
2. Seifert, N., Gill, B., Foley, K., Relangi, P.: Multi-cell upset probabilities of 45nm high-k+ metal gate sram devices in terrestrial and space environments. In: IEEE International Reliability Physics Symposium, IRPS 2008, pp. 181–186. IEEE (2008)
3. Chen, C.-L., Hsiao, M.: Error-correcting codes for semiconductor memory applications: a state-of-the-art review. IBM J. Res. Dev. **28**(2), 124–134 (1984)
4. Cher, C.-Y., Muller, K.P., Haring, R.A., Satterfield, D.L., Musta, T.E., Gooding, T., Davis, K.D., Dombrowa, M.B., Kopcsay, G.V., Senger, R.M., et al.: Soft error resiliency characterization on ibm bluegene/q processor. In: ASP-DAC, pp. 385–387 (2014)
5. Park, A., Narayanan, V., Bowman, K., Atallah, F., Artieri, A., Yoon, S.S., Yuen, K., Hansquine, D.: Exploiting error-correcting codes for cache minimum supply voltage reduction while maintaining coverage for radiation-induced soft errors. In: 2014 IEEE Proceedings of the Custom Integrated Circuits Conference (CICC), pp. 1–4. IEEE (2014)
6. Lee, S., Baeg, S., Reviriego, P.: Memory reliability model for accumulated and clustered soft errors. IEEE Trans. Nucl. Sci. **58**(5), 2483–2492 (2011)
7. Reviriego, P., Maestro, J.A., Cervantes, C.: Reliability analysis of memories suffering multiple bit upsets. IEEE Trans. Device Mater. Reliab. **7**(4), 592–601 (2007)
8. Maniatakos, M., Michael, M.K., Makris, Y.: Vulnerability-based interleaving for multi-bit upset (mbu) protection in modern microprocessors. In: 2012 IEEE International Test Conference (ITC), pp. 1–8. IEEE (2012)
9. Baeg, S., Wen, S., Wong, R.: Minimizing soft errors in tcam devices: a probabilistic approach to determining scrubbing intervals. IEEE Trans. Circ. Syst. I Regul. Pap. **57**(4), 814–822 (2010)
10. Reviriego, P., Maestro, J.A., Baeg, S., Wen, S., Wong, R.: Protection of memories suffering mcus through the selection of the optimal interleaving distance. IEEE Trans. Nucl. Sci. **57**(4), 2124–2128 (2010)

11. Palframan, D.J., Kim, N.S., Lipasti, M.H.: Precision-aware soft error protection for GPUs. In: 20th International Symposium on High Performance Computer Architecture (HPCA), Proceedings, pp. 49–59. IEEE (2014)
12. Mukherjee, S.S., Emer, J., Fossum, T., Reinhardt, S.K.: Cache scrubbing in microprocessors: myth or necessity? In: 10th IEEE Pacific Rim International Symposium on Dependable Computing, Proceedings, pp. 37–42. IEEE (2004)
13. Baeg, S., Wen, S., Wong, R.: Sram interleaving distance selection with a soft error failure model. IEEE Trans. Nucl. Sci. **56**(4), 2111–2118 (2009)
14. Maestro, J.A., Reviriego, P., Baeg, S., Wen, S., Wong, R.: Mitigating the effects of large multiple cell upsets (mcus) in memories. ACM Trans. Des. Autom. Electron. Syst. (TODAES) **16**(4), 45 (2011)
15. Dutta, A., Touba, N.A.: Multiple bit upset tolerant memory using a selective cycle avoidance based sec-ded-daec code. In: 25th IEEE VLSI Test Symposium, pp. 349–354. IEEE (2007)
16. Reviriego, P., Maestro, J.A., Baeg, S.: Optimizing scrubbing sequences for advanced computer memories. IEEE Trans. Device Mater. Reliab. (T-DMR) **10**(2), 192–200 (2010)
17. Tipton, A.D., Pellish, J.A., Hutson, J.M., Baumann, R., Deng, X., Marshall, A., Xapsos, M.A., Kim, H.S., Friendlich, M.R., Campola, M.J., et al.: Device-orientation effects on multiple-bit upset in 65 nm srams. IEEE Trans. Nucl. Sci. **55**(6), 2880–2885 (2008)
18. Ibe, E., Taniguchi, H., Yahagi, Y., Shimbo, K.-I., Toba, T.: Impact of scaling on neutron-induced soft error in srams from a 250 nm to a 22 nm design rule. IEEE Trans. Electron Devices **57**(7), 1527–1538 (2010)
19. Saleh, A.M., Serrano, J.J., Patel, J.H.: Reliability of scrubbing recovery-techniques for memory systems. IEEE Trans. Reliab. **39**(1), 114–122 (1990)

A Distributed User Association Algorithm in Heterogeneous Cellular Networks

Junfu Wu[1]($\boxtimes$), Yinglei Teng[1], Mei Song[1], Deyu Yuan[2],
Baoling Liu[1], and Siyuan Sun[3]

[1] School of Electronic Engineering, Beijing University of Posts
and Telecommunications, Beijing, China
905518594@qq.com
[2] People's Public Security University of China, Beijing, China
[3] Beijing Branch of China United Network Communications
Corporation Limited, Beijing, China

Abstract. In this paper, we study the user association scheme in a heterogeneous network (HetNets), attempt to resolve the problem of interference avoidance and load balancing in HetNets. We formulate a logarithmic objective function, to reduce the utility of heavy load base station, and present a distributed load-aware association algorithm, which encourage users to associate the more lightly loaded stations. User will connect to low-power station (e.g., pico or femto cell), even if they offer a lower instantaneous SINR than the macro cell base station. We observe that users are stimulated by our scheme to associate with low-load, low-power base station. Simulation results support our expectations: in the proposed algorithm achieves a good load balancing between macro and femto cells, and increase the user average throughput. In addition, compare with Max-SINR algorithm, traditional algorithm, our distributed Load-Aware algorithm has a low complexity.

Keywords: Heterogeneous networks · User association · Load balancing · Distributed algorithm

1 Introduction and Related Work

Recently, heterogeneous networks are foreseen as the next generation network infrastructure. The existence of many new types of greener access nodes, just as femto, pico cell, is more economical and efficient than high-power macro-only cell system. Although, HetNets system brings new challenges to traditional network because of the conventional cellular network high-power macro-only cell system. These low-power BSs are deployed to the high-traffic zones. In order to make the load balancing, user should be attracted to the low-power BSs, which have low loaded and can provide a higher quality of communication, by offering more resource blocks than the macrocell BSs. So, a more balanced user association reduces the load on the macrocell, allowing low-power to serve more remaining users. We investigate many solution of this HetNets cell user association problem.

© Springer International Publishing Switzerland 2016
Q. Zu and B. Hu (Eds.): HCC 2016, LNCS 9567, pp. 432–442, 2016.
DOI: 10.1007/978-3-319-31854-7_39

In traditional macro-only cellular networks, there have many prior work on load balancing schemes. But HetNets is different with traditional networks in many ways, unequal coverage sizes and signal power result unequal loads. So, if users simply association with the BS which has a stronger signal. The difference in load in HetNets will be more complex, and the potential gains from load-aware association larger.

Recently, many approaches have been proposed to optimize traffic transfer strategies in cellular networks. The called "cell breathing" technique [1, 2] dynamically changes the coverage sizes depending on the load situation of the cells real-time. A popular approach is to achieve load balancing by abstracting the problem to a convex optimization. They make utility functions as network-wide proportional fairness [3], the utility functions is partial frequency reuse and load balancing [4], and the utility function is α-optimal user association [2]. It proposer a dynamic cell range expansion algorithm for load balancing. [6]

In this paper, we present a load-aware user association method and distributed algorithm in HetNets. This paper is organized as follows. In Sect. 2, we describe the considered system model and formulate the optimization problem. In Sect. 3, we propose a distributed load-aware association algorithm for the optimization problem. The performance of the proposed algorithms is analyzed and demonstrated in Sect. 3. Finally, we give the conclusions in Sect. 4.

2 System Model and Problem Formulation

2.1 System Model

In this section, we consider the user association of a femtocell network with femtocell subscribers and macrocell users randomly distributed around the femtocell BSs. As show in Fig. 1, the femtocell network is open access, both subscribers and public users can access the network and each user can receive its required bandwidth from the femtocell at its location.

In traditional cellular networks, the association scheme is max-SINR, user connect with the station has max SINR in Fig. 2(b). The coverage areas and signal transmitted power are almost the same among macrocells. However, in heterogeneous networks,

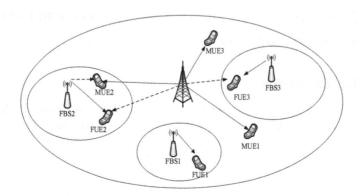

Fig. 1. System model

the different tiers have different (widely divergent) transmit powers, and macrocell is much larger than that of smaller BSs. There are deploying many low-power stations in a macrocell coverage area. If we also adopt traditional association scheme, just like Fig. 2(a)(b). We propose a load-aware scheme, it leads to more efficient resource utilization, by handover of load to underutilized small BSs, in Fig. 2(c).

We consider the downlink of a femtocell network, which consists of M macro base stations as $\mathbf{M} = \{1,\ldots,M\}$, F femto base stations as $\mathbf{F} = \{1,\ldots,F\}$.

We define the instantaneous communication capacity of unit physical resource block (PRB) as:

$$
r_{ij} = \begin{cases} \log_2(1 + \dfrac{p_{k,n}^f h_{k,n}^f}{wN_0 + \displaystyle\sum_{\substack{i=1;i\neq k; \\ n\in[1,N_i]}}^{F} p_{i,n}^f h_{i,n}^f + \displaystyle\sum_{j=1}^{M} P_0 h_{0,m}}), & UE\ i\ is\ associate\ with\ FBS\ j \\[4ex] \log_2(1 + \dfrac{P_{0,m} h_{0,m}}{wN_0 + \displaystyle\sum_{i=1;n\in[1,N_i]}^{F} p_{i,n}^f h_{i,n}^f}), & UE\ i\ is\ associate\ with\ MBS\ j \end{cases}
\tag{1}
$$

Where P_0, $p_{k,n}^f$ are the transmit power of MBS and Femto BSs respectively. h_{in} is the channel gain of user i on PRB n, w is the bandwidth of unit PRB, and N_0 is the thermal noise.

So, the capacity of downlink communication is:

$$
R_{ij} = w_{ij} \cdot r_{ij}
\tag{2}
$$

Where w_{ij} is the number of PBK which assign to user i associated BS j, we define BS set as $\mathbf{B} = \{MBS, FBS\}$, and user set as U. The optimal resource allocation solution is equal allocation, we denote user association indicators as $\{x_{ij}\}$:

$$
x_{ij} = \begin{cases} 1, & UE\ i\ is\ associate\ with\ BS\ j \\ 0, & other \end{cases}
\tag{3}
$$

Where $\sum_i x_{ij} = 1, x_{ij} \in \{0,1\}$. In the following, we maximize the total of users' corresponding data rate, and formulate the objective function.

2.2   Problem Formulation

In the traditional user association scheme, the solution of the optimization problem is to find the indicators $\{x_{ij}\}$ corresponding to the objective function, just like (6):

$$
\max \sum_j \sum_i x_{ij} R_{ij}
\tag{4}
$$

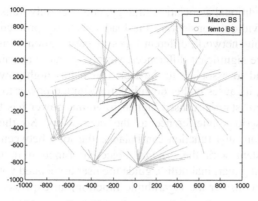

(a)   Best-Channel user association scheme

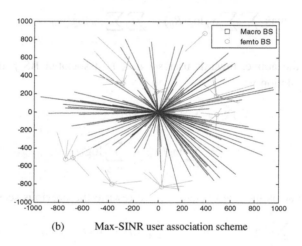

(b)   Max-SINR user association scheme

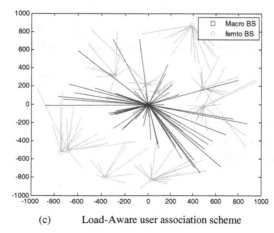

(c)   Load-Aware user association scheme

Fig. 2. Different user association scheme in HetNets

But this is the traditional association strategy, consider only transmission rate as the optimization goal, without considering the load balancing problem. Under the honeycomb heterogeneous network, different types of base station transmitted power and area covered all have significant differences, simply to rate maximization as the goal, makes the users tend to associate to the BSs which has high-power, or strong load capacity. Especially, it causes higher downlink transmitted power to the cell edge user, associated with macro station, caused higher downlink power has transmitted power. Especially causes serious interference to the near users. So this paper considers introducing a function, this function can balance the load between different types of base station, consistent with the original objective function monotonicity, rate of increase of diminishing marginal utility, guide the user associated with less load of base station. Clearly, we consider the logarithmic function, an expression of the objective function is:

$$\max \sum_j \sum_i x_{ij} \log(R_{ij}) = \sum_j \sum_i x_{ij} \log(w_{ij} \cdot r_{ij}) \qquad (5)$$

Analysis of the above, towards user set $u_j \in U$ associated BS j, the throughput function of base station is:

$$
\begin{aligned}
THR_j &= \sum_{i \in u_j} \log(w_{ij} \cdot r_{ij}) \\
&= \sum_{i \in u_j} \log(w_{ij}) + \sum_{i \in u_j} \log(r_{ij})
\end{aligned}
\qquad (6)
$$

The second part is the fixed value, and we rewrite the previous section as

$$\max_w \sum_{i \in u_j} \log(w_{ij}) = \max_w \log(\prod_{i \in u_j} w_{ij}) \Leftrightarrow \max_w \sqrt[n]{w_{1j}w_{2j}\cdots w_{nj}} \qquad (7)$$

Where the n denotes the number of users associated with BS j. As we know, the geometric mean is smaller than the arithmetic mean, so we have

$$\sqrt[M_j]{w_{1j}w_{2j}\cdots w_{nj}} \leq \frac{w_{1j}+w_{2j}+\cdots+w_{nj}}{M_j} \qquad (8)$$

Where the equality establish if and only if $w_{1j} = w_{2j} = \cdots = w_{nj}$. Therefore, to maximize (8), w_{ij} should be equal W_j/M_j.

The problem (7) can be rewrited as

$$\max \ F(x) = \sum_j \sum_i x_{ij} \log(\frac{W_j r_{ij}}{M_j}) \qquad (9)$$

The above problem is a NP problem due to the binary variable $x_{i,j}$. It can be solved through a brute force algorithm, but the complexity of the algorithm is inefficient. We consider a low- complexity algorithm. So, we relax the $x_{i,j} \in \{0,1\}$ to $x_{i,j} \in [0,1]$. In this case, x_{ij} can be interpretated the probability of UE i is associated with BS j [7].

Via the gradient descent method, the value of x_{ij} is updated along the direction:

$$x_{ij}(t) = x_{ij}(t-1) + \delta \bullet \Delta x_{ij} \tag{10}$$

Where δ is the iteration step size, Δx as:

$$\Delta x_{ij} = \frac{\partial F(x)}{\partial x_{ij}} = \log(\frac{W_j r_{ij}}{M_j}) - 1 \tag{11}$$

Then we sort x_{ij} values, the larger value of x_{ij} means higher association probability. Each UE can only be accepted by one BS at any time, once a UE accepted, the constraints should are checked. The detailed user association algorithm be described as:

Algorithm 1. Gradient Descent User Association Algorithm

---
(1) Initialize association matrix $x_{ij} = 0$, the set of user has associated

---
(2) *for* $u = 1, \cdots, Um$
    for $t = 1, \cdots, T$
      for $i = 1, \cdots, Um$

---
         while $M_j < W_j$
           for $j = 1, \cdots, N$(number of BS)
             $x_{ij}(t+1) = x_{ij}(t) + \lambda \cdot \Delta x_{ij}(t)$
        end
      end
      //Update the x_{ij} values.
        $\max x_{ij} = 1$ and $M_j = \sum_i x_{ij}$.
      end
    end
  end

---
(3) User association method
    $[I, J] = sort(x_{ij}, descent)$

In Fig. 1(a) show many users associate with macro BS, on the other hand, many small BSs server very few users with some even being idle. Compared with the association of Max-SINR association, the load-aware association in (8) moves traffic off congested macrocells and onto more lightly loaded small cells.

The primal formulation in (11) can be changed in an equivalent form as

$$\max \sum_j \sum_i x_{ij} \log(R_{ij}) - \sum_j M_j \log(M_j)$$

$$s.t. \ 0 \le x_{ij} \le 1 \tag{12}$$

$$0 \le \sum_j M_j \le Um$$

Where $Um = \sum_j M_j$ is the number of users in our model scene, W is the number of physics resource block which assign to single base station, $M_j = \sum_i x_{ij}$ is the number of user associated BS j. We bring in μ as the lagrange multiplier, the primal objective function is changed as:

$$\max \sum_j \sum_i x_{ij} \left(\log(R_{ij}) - \mu_j\right) + \sum_j M_j \left(\mu_j - \log(M_j)\right)$$

$$s.t. \ 0 \le x_{ij} \le 1 \tag{13}$$

$$0 \le \sum_j M_j \le Um$$

We define μ_j as the associated cost of BS j charge to users. Different types of base station can bid different price, in order to achieve the goal of balancing load of base station. So, we define $\sum_j \sum_i x_{ij} \left(\log(R_{ij}) - \mu_j\right)$ as user benefit, and $\sum_j M_j \left(\mu_j - \log(M_j)\right)$ is the system benefit.

The dual problems of (15) is thus:

$$\min_{\mu} \ \max_{x} \ \sum_j \sum_i x_{ij} \left(\log(R_{ij}) - \mu_j\right) + \sum_j M_j \left(\mu_j - \log(M_j)\right) \tag{14}$$

Can be rewrited as:

$$\min_{\mu} \ G(\mu) = U_x(\mu) + S_M(\mu) \tag{15}$$

where

$$U_x(\mu) = \max_{x} \ \sum_j \sum_i x_{ij} \left(\log(R_{ij}) - \mu_j\right)$$

$$s.t. \ 0 \le x_{ij} \le 1 \tag{16}$$

$$S_M(\mu) = \max_{x} \ \sum_j M_j \left(\mu_j - \log(M_j)\right)$$

$$s.t. \ M_j \le W_j \tag{17}$$

μ is update by $\nabla G(\mu)$. When the optimal solution of (14) and (15), is same, that is strong duality holds. Salter's condition is a simple constraint qualifications under which strong duality holds. The constraints in (14) are linear equalities and inequalities, and thus the Slater condition reduces (14) to feasibility. Therefore, the primal problem (14) can be equivalently a dual problem (16). And the problem (16) has a dual optimal μ as the primal optimal. Therefore, given the dual optimal μ, we can get the primal optimal solution by solving the decoupled problems (17) and (18) separately without coordination among the users and BSs.

We try solve these two sub-problem by a distribute algorithm, the distributed algorithm is given as follows:

Algorithm 2. A distributed algorithm

(1) Initialize variable.
(2)
for t= 1,...,T   **User terminal:**   Each user measures the SINR by using pilot signals from all BSs, and receives the value of μ_j broadcast by the BS at the beginning of the iteration.   User i associate BS j , if it satisfies thus: $$j = \arg\max_j (\log(R_{ij}) - \mu_j(t))$$
BS terminal: Each BS updates the new value of K_j and μ_j in two steps and announces the new multiplier μ_j to the system.   To obtain the maximizer of problem (17), we set its gradient to be 0 with the constraint $$M_j(t+1) = \min(W_j, e^{(\mu_j(t)-1)})$$ The   new   value   of   Lagrange   multiplier   is   updated   by   thus: $$\mu_j(t+1) = \mu_j(t) + \delta(t)\left(M_j(t) - \sum_i x_{ij}(t)\right).$$ Where $\delta(t)$ is a positive step sizes.
(3) End iteration until: The value of user association indicators is stable: $x(t+1) == x(t)$.

There is a nice interpretation of μ. The multiplier μ works as a message between users and BSs in the system. In fact, it can be interpreted as the price of the BSs determined by the load situation, which can be either positive or negative. If we interpret $\sum_i x_{ij}$ as the serving demand for BS j and K_j as the service the BS j can provide, then μ_j is the bridge between demand and supply, and Eq. (17) is indeed consistent with the law of supply and demand: if the demand I x_{ij} for BS j exceeds the supply K_j, the price μ_j will go up; otherwise, the price μ_j will decrease. Thus, when the BS j is over-loaded, it will increase its price μ_j and fewer users will associate with it, while other under-loaded BSs will decrease the price so as to attract more users. Moreover, the function of μ in distributed algorithm motivates rate bias scheme, which is discussed in Sect. 4.

3   Simulation and Analysis

In this section, we present the performance results of the proposed user association scheme and compare its performance to other schemes such as traditional algorithm.

To evaluate the performance of the two proposed algorithms, the 10 cell are simulated, include 1 macrocell and 9 femtocells. The macrocell in the center, 9 femtocells are symmetrically located along a circle with radius as 1 km, 200 users also randomly distributed in the macrocell area.

We first describe the parameter settings adopted in our simulation, and shown in Table 1.

Table 1. Simulation Parameter Settings

Parameter	Value
Frequency spacing of a PRB	180 kHz
Slot length T_s	0.1 ms
Thermal noise N_0	−174 dBm/Hz
Path-loss factor	2
Macrocell Transmit power	47 dBm
Path maximum Doppler shift	10 Hz

Simulation parameters are summarized in Table 1, which closely follows the latest standard proposed by 3GPP. In this paper, we assume the average channel power gain is only influenced by the path-loss model and antennas gains. A slotted time system is considered with the slot length to be 1 ms. Due to computational complexity, we consider two FBSs which are randomly located around the MBS in the femtocell network, each serving one FUE.

In order to show the efficiency of our proposed algorithm, we choose the traditional Max-SINR algorithm to compare with our distributed load-aware algorithm.

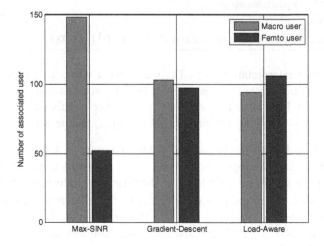

Fig. 3. Comparisons of average number of users in two tiers in system.

Figure 3 compares the load situations among different association schemes. The max-SINR association results is very unbalanced loads, the macro BS are over-loaded, while femto BSs server fewer users. With some even being idle. In the Gradient-Descent and our Load-aware association algorithm, the load is shifted to the less congested femto BSs.

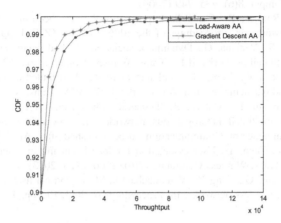

Fig. 4. CDF of throughtput of traditional gradient descent algorithm and load-aware association algorithm

Figure 4 compares the cumulative distribution function (CDF) of long-term throughtput between conventional algorithm and load-aware association algorithm. In HetNets, the CDF of GDA is 1. This picture provides strong evidence again that the load-aware association algorithm outperforms Gradient Descent scheme in providing the quality of services.

4   Conclusion

In this paper, we propose a load-aware user association schemes that achieve load balancing and distributed in HetNets through a dual optimization problem. Simulation results show that the proposed algorithm can achieve an optimal solution. The Load-Aware algorithm is still superior to the Gradient-Descent algorithm in algorithm complexity and performance.

Acknowledgment. This work is supported in part by the National Natural Science Foundation of China (Grants No. 61302081), the State Major Science and Technology Special Projects (Grants No. 2014ZX03004002).

References

1. Das, S., Viswanathan, H., Rittenhouse, G.: Dynamic load balancing through coordinated scheduling in packet data systems. In: Proceedings of the 2003 IEEE INFOCOM, vol. 1, pp. 786–796
2. Bejerano, Y., Han, S.J.: Cell breathing techniques for load balancing in wireless LANs. IEEE Trans. Mobile Comput. 8(6), 735–749 (2009)
3. Bu, T., Li, L., Ramjee, R.: Generalized proportional fair scheduling in third generation wireless data networks. In: Proceedings of the 2006 IEEE INFOCOM, pp. 1–12
4. Son, K., Chong, S., Veciana, G.: Dynamic association for load balancing and interference avoidance in multi-cell networks. IEEE Trans. Wireless Commun. 8(7), 3566–3576 (2009)
5. Kim, H., de Veciana, G., Yang, X., Venkatachalam, M.: Distributed α-optimal user association and cell load balancing in wireless networks. IEEE/ACM Trans. Netw. 99, 1–14 (2011)
6. Corroy, S., Falconetti, L., Mathar, R.: Dynamic cell association for downlink sum rate maximization in multi-cell heterogeneous networks. In: Proceedings of the 2012 IEEE International Conference on Communication, to be published after, April 2012
7. Ye, Q., Rong, B., Chen, Y.: User association for load balancing in heterogeneous cellular networks. IEEE Trans. Wireless Commun. 12(6), 2706–2716 (2013)
8. Kim, H., de Veciana, G., Yang X., Venkatachalam, M.: α-Optimal user association and cell load balancing in wireless networks. In: Proceedings of the IEEE, pp. 1–5 (2010)

NCFR: Network Coding Fair Routing for Multi-success-rate Wireless Sensor Networks

Lvju Wang, Chun Ma, Anwen Wang$^{(\boxtimes)}$, Jun Guo, Xiaoyan Yin,
Wei Wang, Binbin Xie, Xiaojiang Chen, and Dingyi Fang

School of Information Science and Technology,
Northwest University, Xi'an, China
LvjuWang0201@gmail.com, machun1989@hotmail.com,
wang_anwen@163.com, guojun@nwu.edu.cn,
scxiaoyanyin@gmail.com, vi_w@sohu.com,
{xjchen, dyf}@nwu.edu.cn

Abstract. Recently network coding has become a promising approach to improve the network throughput in wireless networks. However, the existing network coding-based routing protocols can't well work at improving the network throughput in wireless network with multi-success-rate and link asymmetry, which use low quality links for coding. In this paper, we use transmission count as link quality and provide a theoretical formulation for computing the transmission count of network coding in wireless network with multi-success-rate and link asymmetry. Then we advocate a simple route selection strategy (called: NCF-network coding fair routing) to maximize the network throughput and reduce delay by minimizing transmission count in this wireless network. NCF computes source-destination routes by optimizing initial routing paths resulting in more coding opportunities. The simulation results demonstrate that NCF improves coding opportunity leading to higher end-to-end throughout when compared to SPATH.

Keywords: Network coding · Multi-success-rate · Link asymmetry · The transmission count

1 Introduction

Network coding has received much attention recently due to increasing the utilization of both wired and wireless network, since introduced by Ahlswede et al. in 2000 [1].

We explain the basic idea how network coding improves the network performance in wireless network using the typical "Alice-Bob structure" and "X-structure". For "Alice-Bob structure" case (shown in Fig. 1), Alice wants to send a single packet (A) to Bob, while Bob wants to send a single packet (B) to Al-ice. Due to transmission range limitations, Alice and Bob are not able to exchange packet directly and must need the help of a relay node (R) to forward their packets. Using standard techniques of packet forwarding, node R needs to forward two packets to complete these end-to-end packet transfers. In comparison, using a simple form of network coding (as employed

© Springer International Publishing Switzerland 2016
Q. Zu and B. Hu (Eds.): HCC 2016, LNCS 9567, pp. 443–453, 2016.
DOI: 10.1007/978-3-319-31854-7_40

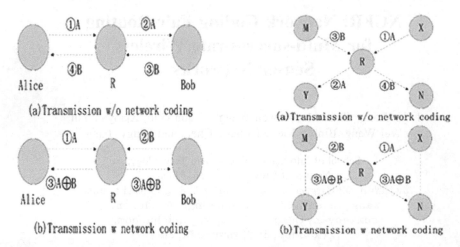

Fig. 1. "Alice-Bob structure" network coding

Fig. 2. "X-structure" network coding

in the COPE approach [2]), R transmits a new packet XORed A and B resulting in only three wireless transmissions instead of four wireless transmission using the following sequence: (i) Alice transmits packet A with Bob being the intended recipient; (ii) Bob transmits packet B with Alice being the intended recipient; and (iii) Node R transmits a new packet C with both Alice and Bob being intended recipients of this new packet. Alice has a copy of packet A, it can obtain packet B by performing an XOR of packet B and C. Similarly, Bob can obtain packet A. Wireless medium as broadcast nature allows such communication to be possible and there is a throughput improvement of 33 % in this example.

Similar coding gain can be achieved in "X-structure" with opportunistic listening (shown in Fig. 2), where there are two intended packet transfers as follows: from node M to node N, X to Y. Due to range limitations, both these paths go through the relay node R. Let us assume that M, X transmit their packets in sequence to R. When Node M transmits its packet to Node R, Node X and Y, in promiscuous mode, snoop on all packets communicated by its neighbors [3]. Similarly, when Node X transmits its packet to R, Nodes M and N snoop on this packet. Therefore, at the end of these two packet transmissions, if Node R were to transmit a single coded packet that XORs all of the two packets, then each node (N and Y) would be able to correctly decode their intended packets. Thus, the packet transfers are completed by using just three packet transmissions instead of four. Note that in the absence of coding, four packet transmissions would have been necessary.

From above figures we can see that, network coding can help to significantly improve the overall network throughput via decrease number of transmissions. However, we can also see that, the coding opportunities depend on the occurrences of Alice-Bob structure and X-structures in the transmission path. Therefore, performing gain can be obtained by taking coding opportunity into account when selecting the transmit routing [4]. Take the following example shown in Fig. 3(a). There exist two flows from the opposite direction, one flow (f1) from node A to node E with the path A → B → D → E, the other flow (f2) from node F to node B with the path F → E → C → B. Now supposed network coding is allowed, f2 change the path to F → E → D → B. This change offers coding opportunity on node D and improves the network throughput.

Katti et. al [2] introduced a practical method and efficient system named COPE, in which network coding was applied in order to improve wireless network throughput. In COPE, packets are XOR'ed together, and forwarded in a single transmission. The experimental results show that COPE increases network throughput. The prior works [3, 4] which decide transmission route taking network coding opportunities into consideration can achieve better performance. However, to the best of our knowledge, there is no work analyzing the unavailability of prior network coding-based routing and exploiting the network coding-routing to improve network performance in wireless network with multi-success-rate and link asymmetry. In this paper, we will explain the unavailability of prior work in this network using following example.

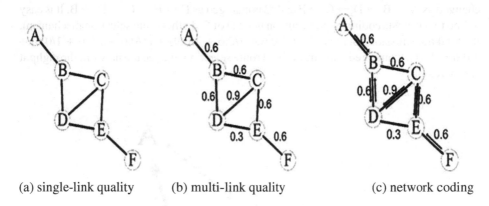

(a) single-link quality   (b) multi-link quality   (c) network coding

Fig. 3. Illustration of routing with network coding

2   Challenges in Multi-success-rate Wireless Network

When taking multi-success-rate into consideration, more coding opportunities are not necessarily mean higher throughput and the prior work will not make wise decisions. Look at the same topology with different success rate as shown in Fig. 3(c). The numbers on each edge denote the transmission success rate in this network.

In this example, there is the same topology and the same flows as Fig. 3(a). Without network coding, the optimal route should be f2 (F → E → C → B), under which the total ETX of the two flows are 11.7 $((1/0.6 + 1/0.6 + 1/0.3) + (1/0.6 * 3) = 11/7)$. Considering the network coding, the route is changed to get more coding opportunity. If the path F → E → D → B is selected, we can see there is coding opportunity in node D. However, here D can only broadcast using the maximum ETX of the two outgoing links when transmits the coded packet. Thus the total transmission count of the path is 11.7 $((1/0.6 + 1/0.6) + (1/0.6 + 1/0.3) + 1/0.3 = 11.7)$. In this example, network coding routings doesn't provide end-to-end throughput gain compared with traditional routing. The key reason is that the high transmission success rate can not be utilized sufficiently while the lowest success rate is used for the coded packet broadcasting and become the bottleneck for the overall wireless network performance.

Best of our knowledge, in all the existing network coding routing design, there is no any discussion on the multi-success-rate wireless network. This paper focuses on this scenario. To clearly explain the challenges in this wireless network, we will use ETX metric [5] to denote success-rate of transmission.

To solve this capacity waste problem and explore the performance by network coding, we consider using a network coding fair routing to increase the network coding opportunity. The general idea of this paper is: when the link quality between the source node and destination node are not so good (just like the link between node D and node E), namely in the scenario of existing diversity on the link quality, we choose the node which has better link quality between source and destination nodes as the Alternative Node (like node C in Fig. 3(c)) to promote the total capacity.

In the example in Fig. 3(c), we choose node C as the alternative node then f1 is changed as $A \rightarrow B \rightarrow D \rightarrow C \rightarrow E$ and f2 is changed as $F \rightarrow E \rightarrow C \rightarrow D \rightarrow B$. It is easy to find that it exists coding opportunity on node D or C. In this route selection mechanism, the total transmission count is 11.1 ((1/0.6 + 1/0.6 + 1/0.9) + (1/0.6 + 1/0.6 + 1/0.6) + 1/0.6 = 11.1). Compared with the original route selection, we see the network throughput are increased.

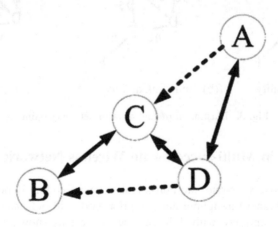

Fig. 4. Illustration of asymmetry in link

3   Challenges in Asymmetry of Link

In this part, we focus on the scenario with link asymmetry. The existing routing protocols assume that all nodes have the same transmission range and the wireless network has only symmetric links. However, because of different battery power, the difference of nodes' transmission range is unavoidable to cause some problem in link asymmetry which means that node A is within node B's transmission range, but not vice versa. However, best of our acknowledge the existing works using network coding don't consider the link asymmetry, then that's the second part we talk about.

In Fig. 4, the arrow on each edge denotes the dataflow that could happen, double arrow indicate nodes in the left and right of link could communication each other like the link between B and C, while the one-way arrow denotes that data transmission only happened from one node to another such as the link from node A to C. There exist two flows, one flow from node A to node B with the route A → C → B; the other flow from node B to node A with the route B → C → D → A under this transmission strategy, the ETX is 5. However, considering coding strategy, we add a node D then route 1 is changed as A → D → C → B, and route 2 still is B → C → D → A. Although the ETX under strategy 2 still is 5, there appeared coding opportunity in node C or D.

4 The Δ-Bound Tradeoff Strategy

In random topology based on the link quality, synthesizing above two scenario, we now provide a model whose degree of Diversity of Link-quality and Asymmetry of Link can be controlled trough a parameter Δ. We use Δ to express transmission success-rate then Diversity of Link-quality and Asymmetry of Link are thus special cases of Δ-Bound Tradeoff model. In particular, when Δ = 1, the model equals link quality is best. If Δ = 0, then it denotes the situation that node can't communication with another in link asymmetry scenario.

As mentioned in Introduction Section, it is obvious that changing the transmission paths proved by SPATH in multi-success rate wireless networks improves the network throughput by exploiting the benefit of network coding. In the rest of the paper, we provide a theoretical formulation for maximizing the transmission throughput of network coding.

NCFR computes source-destination routes by optimizing routing paths provided the NC Routing [4] resulting in less transmission count using high transmission success rate.

5 Related Work

Network coding has received much attention recently, since introduced by Ahlswede et al. in [1], whereafter a lots of works mainly focus on the construction about network coding [6–8]. Sachin Katti et al. [2] proposed a COPE strategy which aimed at increasing the capacity using encoding the packets. Sengupta et al. [3] proposed a network coding aware routing under the traditional and opportunistic listening environment. Zhang J et al. [4] proposed cooperative network coding routing to analyse the reach the maximum through-out. Rui Prior et al. [9] designed a network coding protocol for enhancing the reliability and speed of data gathering in smart grid communications. Alireza Keshavarz-Haddad et al. [10] explored limitations of the benefit of network coding in multihop wireless networks. Xingcheng Liu et al. proposed a network coding-based cooperative communications scheme (NCCC) to achieve a good reliability performance in WSNs.

Different from previous work relying on the transmission quality isomorphism environment, NCF Routing consider the problem of link-quality diversity and link asymmetry which is select the local optimum transmission counts routing to achieve the preferable throughout under the constraint of link quality.

6   Notation and Modeling Assumptions

As mentioned in Introduction Section, we can clearly see that under multi-success-rate wireless networks, transmission route should be re-selected so as to exploit the benefit of network coding. In this paper, we will provide a theoretical formulation for maximizing the transmission throughput in multi-success-rate wireless networks. To achieve this target, in this section, we will define the notations needed for problem formulation.

6.1   A. Network Topology Graph

The wireless network topology, given by the nodes and the links corresponding to pairs of nodes within a direct communication range, is modeled as a graph $G = (N, E)$. Each node in the network can be a source or destination of traffic. We let $e = (i, j)$ represent a directed link in the network from node i to node j. The success-rate of transmission on a link will be denoted by $T(e) = T(i, j)$.

The sets of incoming and out-going edges at node i are denoted by $E^-(i)$ and $E^+(i)$ respectively. The transmitting node for link will be denoted by $t(e)$ and its receiving node by r(e). We use d_{ij} to denote the distance between node i and node j; l_i denote the transmission range. Thus $d_{ij} < l_j$ mean transmit successfully, or $d_{ij} > l_i$ indicate failed. In our model, we use the success rate as the significant index to select the best routing with the lowest transmission counts. And then we use the $t(p_{e_j})$ to express the success rate on the link of p_{e_j}.

6.2   Δ-Bound Trade-off Network Coding Fair-Routing Protocol (NCF)

We now formulate the problem of minimum transmission counts with network coding. We assume that in a wireless network, there already exist several K flows. For each flow k, $1 \leq k \leq K$, the routing path is P_K, the transmission counts for this flow is $T(k)$. Now H new flows are injected into the network, for each flow h, $1 \leq h \leq H$, the traffic is from the source node $s(h)$ to the destination node $d(h)$. Assume for each path $h \in R$, if it is selected, then $f_h(P) = 1$, else $f_h(P) = 0$. Let $1/t(P_{e_j})$ denote transmission count of the link e_j, in which the $t(p_{e_j})$ denotes the transmission success rates. We use $T_i^{\{e\}}, \forall e \in E^+(i) \in N$ to denote the transmission counts on the link e, then $t(h)T$ denotes the transmission counts for routing the flow h in the network, λ is a fractional variable. For a link $e = (i, j, k)$, e denotes its reverse link $e = (k, j, i)$.

The target of the below optimization problem is to minimum the transmission counts. We use the sign function to constraints the opportunity of network coding under the asymmetry links. More specifically,

Minimum

$$\sum_{h=1}^{H} t(h)T \tag{1}$$

Subject to

$$\sum_{P \in \Re^h} f_h(P) = 1, \forall 1 \le h \le H, f_h(P) = 0, 1 \tag{2}$$

$$T_i^{\{e_1,e_2\}} \le \sum_{K=1}^{k} \sum_{\bar{e}_1 e_2 \in P} \sum_{j=1}^{3} 1/t(p_{e_j}) + \prod_{j=1}^{3} \operatorname{sgn}\left[t(p_{e_j})\right] \times \sum_{h=1}^{H} \sum_{\bar{e}_2 e_1 \in p} f_h(p)\left[\sum_{j=1}^{3} 1/t(p_{e_j})\right], \forall e_1, e_2 \in E^+(i), i \in N \tag{3}$$

$$T_i^{\{e\}} \le \prod_{j=1}^{3} \operatorname{sgn}\left[t(p_{e_j})\right] \times \sum_{h=1}^{H} \sum_{e \in P, s(h)=i} f_h(p)\left[\sum_{j=1}^{3} 1/t(p_{e_j})\right] + \sum_{k=1}^{k}\left[\sum_{e \in P, s(h)=i} \sum_{j=1}^{3} 1/t(p_{e_j})\right.$$
$$+ \sum_{e_1 \in E^-(i)} \sum_{K=1}^{k} \sum_{e_1 e \in P} \sum_{j=1}^{3} 1/t(p_{e_j}) + \sum_{h=1}^{H} \sum_{e_1 e \in p} f_h(p)\left[\sum_{j=1}^{3} 1/t(p_{e_j})\right] - T_i^{\{e,\bar{e}_1\}}\right], \forall e \in E^+(i), i \in N \tag{4}$$

- Constraints (2) denote the routing selection constraints which means a flow demand only has one path.
- Constraints (4) show the remaining transmission counts in the original unicast links.

7 Approximation Algorithm

In this section we will explain the main idea to minimize transmission count as follows. Basically, what we need is to find a initial routing decision for a demand under multi-success-rate wireless network. Then we use local search algorithm in all cross nodes to find network coding opportunities and minimize transmission count. If there is a coding opportunity by re-select the path in the node and the transmission count of the new local path decreases, we will use the new path instead of the initial path.

7.1 Initial Routing Solution

The initial routing decision is made by an independent routing protocol. In the multi-success-rate wireless network, we use the ETX-based shortest path routing strategy as the initial solution.

7.2   Optimal Local Path

A local path re-select algorithm is proposed to optimize the initial routing decision by decreasing transmission count. The algorithm basic idea is when a node is cross node, the node search coding opportunities, get an available local strategy set and use an available local strategy that has minimum ETX as new local paths instead of initial local paths. This algorithm is explained by Algorithm 1. For clearly explaining the algorithm, we use ni;nj denote the ETX of the link from node ni to nj, E denote total ETX of the initial local paths, $E(S)$ denote the total ETX of a local path strategy S with network coding, $L(v)$ denote an available local strategy set of node v, and $l(v)$ denote a strategy that have minimum ETX in $L(v)$.

Algorithm 1. Optimal local path

1: if node v is cross node then

2:    $L(v) = \emptyset$;

3:    compute E of two local flows: $p_1 \to v \to n_1$, $p_2 \to v \to n_2$;

4:    for each v's neighbour node a_i do

5:       if $\alpha_{a_i,v} < \alpha_{p_2,v}$ then

6:          there is a local choice strategy $S1_i$: $p_1 \to a_i \to n_1$, $p_2 \to a_i \to v \to n_2$;

7:       $E(S1_i) = max\left(\alpha_{p_1}, a_i, \alpha_{p_1}, v\right) + max\left(\alpha_{p_2}, a_i, \alpha_{p_2}, n_1\right) + max\left(\alpha_{a_i}, n_2, \alpha_{a_i}, v\right)$;

8:       if $E > E(S1_i)$ then

9:          $L(v) = L(v) + S1_i$;

10:       end if

11:    end if

12:    if $\alpha_{v,a_i} < \alpha_{v,n_2}$ then

13:       there is a local choice strategy $S2_i$: $p_1 \to a_i \to n_1$, $p_2 \to v \to a_i \to n_2$;

14:       $E(S2_i) = max\left(\alpha_{p_1}, a_i, \alpha_{p_1} n_2\right) + max\left(\alpha_{p_2}, a_i, \alpha_{p_2} n_1\right) + max\left(\alpha_{a_i}, n_2, \alpha_{a_i} n_1\right)$;

15:       if $E > E(S2_i)$ then

16:          $L(v) = L(v) + S2_i$;

17:       end if

18:    end if

19:    end for

20:    get $l(v)$ and use $l(v)$ as new local paths;

21: end if

The algorithm identify three scenarios: (1) low transmission success rate in-going link in cross node (Fig. 5(a)); (2) low transmission success rate out-going link in cross node (Fig. 5(b)). In Algorithm 1, for $max(\alpha_{p_2,v}, \alpha_{p_2,n_1}) + max(\alpha_{p_1,v}, \alpha_{p_1,n_2}) + max(\alpha_{v,n_2}, \alpha_{v,n_1})$, the first two parts denote that the maximum ETX of flow link and snoop link is used.

We have deliberately chosen a wireless network topology in Fig. 5(a) to detailedly explain the algorithm. There are two demands, demand $h1$ from node $s1$ to node $d1$ and demand $h2$ from node $s2$ to node $d2$. We can get two ETX-based shortest paths, p_1 $(s1 \rightarrow A \rightarrow C \rightarrow F \rightarrow d1)$ and $E \rightarrow C \rightarrow D \rightarrow B(s2 \rightarrow E \rightarrow C \rightarrow B \rightarrow d2)$ for the demands. There are two different direction flow in node C as a flow cross node. For exploiting the coding opportunity and minimizing transmission count, we attempt to re-select local path of p_1 and p_2 by traversing all available local path within two hop range of C. We find a node D that is neighbour of C. Although the ETX of the initial local path p_{c1} $(A \rightarrow C \rightarrow F)$ is less the new path p'_{c1} $(A \rightarrow D \rightarrow F)$'s ETX and p_{c2} $(E \rightarrow C \rightarrow B)$ is less p'_{c2} $(E \rightarrow D \rightarrow C \rightarrow B)$, the sum ETX of two new local path p'_{c1} and p'_{c2} is less than the sum EXT of the two initial local path p_{c1} and path p_{c2} due to a network coding opportunity in node D. So, we get two new paths: path p'_1 and p'_2 by p'_{c1} and p'_{c2} instead of p_{c1} and p_{c2} respectively due to decrease transmission count.

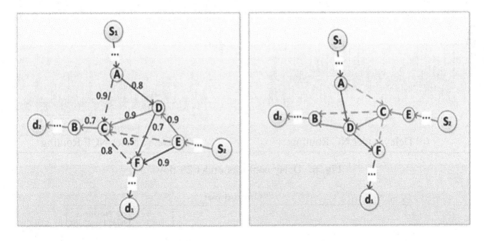

Fig. 5. Three identifiable scenarios

(a) Re-select scenario 1: low transmission success rate in-going link in cross node. Two initial local paths: $A \rightarrow C \rightarrow F$, $E \rightarrow C \rightarrow B$, The cross node: C. An available local strategy: $A \rightarrow D \rightarrow F$, $E \rightarrow D \rightarrow C \rightarrow B$.

(b) Re-select scenario 2: low transmission success rate outgoing link in cross node. Two initial local paths: $A \rightarrow C \rightarrow F$, $E \rightarrow C \rightarrow B$. The cross node: C. An available local strategy: $A \rightarrow D \rightarrow F$, $E \rightarrow C \rightarrow D \rightarrow B$.

8 Simulation Results

In this section, we evaluate the performance of two routing schemes on randomly generated network topology using Java. The positions of the nodes were chosen randomly in a square of side 100 units. The transmission success rate can be chosen randomly, according to IEEE802.11a standard.

Evaluation 1-Delay analysis under the increase of number of packets: Fig. 6 show the delay comparison under 20 flows. The source node and sink node of each flow were chosen randomly. We can draw the conclusion that NCF Routing has less communication delay comparing with NC Routing from the Fig. 6.

Evaluation 2-Throughput analysis under the increase of number of packets: We build the Δ-Bound NCF Routing in the second part and want to maximum the network throughput by minimum the transmission count. In this part we want to simulate the throughput and analyse how the NCF Routing change the performance.

Figure 7 show the same scenes with Fig. 6. From Fig. 7, we can clearly see that the NCF Routing has the better throughput than NC Routing under 20 flows. By computation

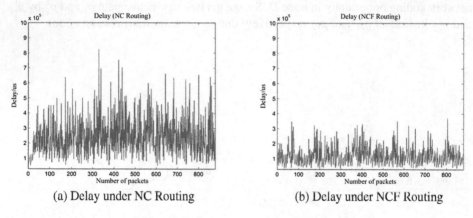

(a) Delay under NC Routing   (b) Delay under NCF Routing

Fig. 6. Delay contrasts under 20 flows

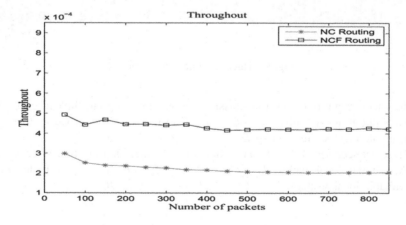

Fig. 7. Throughput contrasts under 20 flows

we could find the throughput of NCF Routing is 108.96 % times that of the NC Routing. The significant difference was led by the number of flows increase then chance of network coding rose.

Above all, NCF Routing shows the better performance than NC Routing with the more intensive of data flows. And under the more number of nodes and packets the advantage would become more and more obvious.

9 Conclusion

The paper presents NCF Routing, a routing selection strategy that leverage network coding under the problem of link-quality diversity and link asymmetry. The main idea is to select the local optimum transmission counts routing to achieve the preferable throughout under the constraint of link quality. Future research on more accurate models of transmission counts should make NCF Routing a ubiquitous routing selection approach.

Acknowlegment. This work was supported by the NSFC (61202198, 61373177, GX1403), the Industorial Public Relation Project of Shaanxi Technology Committee 2011K06-07, 2011K0609, 2012K06-17 Industrialization Project of Shaanxi Educational Department 2011JG06, the CPSF under Grant No.2012M521797, the International Cooperation Foundation of Shaanxi Province, China under Grant No. 2013KW01-02, and the International Postdoctoral Exchange Fellowship Program 2013 under Grant No. 57 funded by the office of China Postdoctoral Council.

References

1. Ahlswede, R., Cai, N., Li, S.-Y.R., Yeung, R.W.: Network information flow. IEEE Trans. Inf. Theory **46**(4), 1204–1216 (2000)
2. Katti, S., Rahul, H., Hu, W., Katabi, D., Médard, M., Crowcroft, J.: XORs in the air: practical wireless network coding. In: ACM SIGCOMM Computer Communication Review, vol. 36, pp. 243–254. ACM (2006)
3. Sengupta, S., Rayanchu, S., Banerjee, S.: Network coding-aware routing in wireless networks. IEEE/ACM Trans. Networking **18**(4), 1158–1170 (2010)
4. Zhang, J., Zhang, Q.: Cooperative network coding-aware routing for multi-rate wireless networks. In: IEEE INFOCOM 2009, pp. 181–189. IEEE (2009)
5. De Couto, D.S.J., Aguayo, D., Bicket, J., Morris, R.: A high-throughput path metric for multi-hop wireless routing. Wirel. Netw. **11**(4), 419–434 (2005)
6. Chou, P.A., Wu, Y., Jain, K.: Practical network coding (2003)
7. Dougherty, R., Freiling, C., Zeger, K.: Insufficiency of linear coding in network information flow. IEEE Trans. Inf. Theory **51**(8), 2745–2759 (2005)
8. Koetter, R., Médard, M.: An algebraic approach to network coding. IEEE/ACM Trans. Networking (TON) **11**(5), 782–795 (2003)
9. Prior, R., Lucani, D.E., Phulpin, Y., Nistor, M., Barros, J.: Network coding protocols for smart grid communications. IEEE Trans. Smart Grid **5**(3), 1523–1531 (2014)
10. Keshavarz-Haddad, A., Riedi, R.H.: Bounds on the benefit of network coding for wireless multicast and unicast. IEEE Trans. Mob. Comput. **13**(1), 102–115 (2014)

Energy-Saving Power Allocation Scheme for Relay Networks Based on Graphical Method of Classification

Yifei Wei[(⊠)], Hengyu Lai, Xia Gong, Da Guo, and Chunping Hou

School of Electronic Engineering, Beijing University of Posts
and Telecommunications, Beijing 100876, People's Republic of China
weiyifei@bupt.edu.cn, lindagongxia@163.com,
hcp@tju.edu.cn

Abstract. With the development of mobile communication, there is a lot of research concentrating on cooperative relaying. However, the previous studies mainly focus on the transmission performance. In this paper, we considered a two-hop relay cooperative network, and proposed an energy-saving power allocation scheme based on graphical method of classification, so as to solve the problems of nonlinear constraints in the network scenario. As the scheme figures show, the proposed scheme can greatly reduce the difficulty of solving the problem, and from the simulation results, it can be concluded that the proposed scheme has realized the goal of energy-saving, and it improved the quality of service (QoS) at the same time.

Keywords: Energy-saving · Cooperative relay network · Power allocation · Graphical method of classification

1 Introduction

In the mobile communications, due to the channel noise and time variability, data from the source nodes may not always be transmitted to the destination terminal. When the destination couldn't receive the information correctly, based on the traditional method, the sender would need to increase the transmission power to overcome the channel noise [1]. But with limited energy, the transmission power of mobile terminals can't achieve too much [2], and it may be result in much more wasting of limited energy. As it demonstrated in [3], replacing the radio base station (RBS) with the femtocell RBS or macrocell RBS can make more contribution to the energy saving, other than increasing the transmission power of the RBS directly. Furthermore, by designing new resource allocation algorithm and using of cooperative multi point technology, energy efficiency have been achieved in heterogeneous networks [4]. Using the random geometry method, the energy consumption of the relay auxiliary network is studied in literature [5], and further, energy efficiency model of the network is established to evaluate energy consuming as well. Obviously, in order to save energy, a relay is often needed to forward the message as it does in this paper. Through the cooperative transmission of relays, the destination node received two separated information, and restored the

© Springer International Publishing Switzerland 2016
Q. Zu and B. Hu (Eds.): HCC 2016, LNCS 9567, pp. 454–464, 2016.
DOI: 10.1007/978-3-319-31854-7_41

original information by merging two of the received same information, which is taking use of spatial diversity [6]. Although the signal to noise ratio (SNR) of the two separate signals is not large enough, through the merging, the receiving SNR of the information is considerable. If the energy distribution of the source nodes and relay nodes are reasonable, the total transmitting power can be reduced greatly, thus achieving the goal of save energy [7, 8].

But not in all conditions that using relay can save energy. Therefore, before the source node sends the information, it is needed to estimate whether it can achieve energy-saving by using relay nodes. Most previous studies of cooperative relay networks are aimed to improve the performance and quality of service. In this paper, taking the transmission performance into account, we proposed an energy-saving relay selection scheme based on the guarantees of QoS.

2   System Model

In this paper, we consider a two-hop relay network in which a secondary source node S have transmission need to a secondary destination node D. Due to the long distance of direct transmission, relay node R is considerable to transmit the information between S and D. Provided that the communication channels are flat fading over each band. As shown in Fig. 1, the channel gain coefficients of a source node to a destination node, a source node to a relay node and a relay node to a destination node are respectively h_{sr}, h_{rd}, h_{sd}.

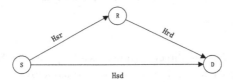

Fig. 1. Two-hop relay model

Provided that the signal that the source node sent is x, the transmitting power of source is p_s, while the transmitting power of relay node is p_r, and the channel noise is Gauss white noise whose mean value is 0 and variance is N0, so the received signal of the destination node and relay node are:

$$y_{sd} = \sqrt{p_s}h_{sd}x + N_{sd} \tag{1}$$

$$y_{sr} = \sqrt{p_s}h_{sr}x + N_{sr} \tag{2}$$

Where y_{sd} is the information that the destination node received from the source node, y_{sr} is the information that the relay node received from the source node. h_{sd} and h_{sr} are the channel gain coefficient of the source node to the destination node and the source node to the relay node.

In the cooperative relay scheme with AF communication mode, the amplification coefficient is:

$$\beta = \frac{\sqrt{p_r}}{\sqrt{p_r |h_{sr}|^2 + N_0}} \tag{3}$$

Then the information which the destination node received from the relay node is:

$$y_{rd} = \beta h_{rd} y_{sr} + N_0 \tag{4}$$

A more accurate description is:

$$y_{rd} = \beta h_{rd} h_{sr} x + N'_{rd} \tag{5}$$

where

$$N'_{rd} = \beta h_{rd} h_{sr} N_{sr} + N_{rd} \tag{6}$$

The variance of N'_{rd} is

$$N'_0 = (\beta + 1) N_0 \tag{7}$$

Due to the receiver merging the two channel signals through maximum ratio combining (MRC) method, the SNR can be expressed as:

$$\gamma = \gamma_1 + \gamma_2 \tag{8}$$

Where γ_1 is the SNR of direct channel, while γ_2 is the SNR of the received information forwarded by relay, they are expressed as below,

$$\gamma_1 = \frac{p_s |h_{sd}|^2}{N_0} \tag{9}$$

$$\gamma_2 = \frac{1}{N_0} \frac{p_s p_r |h_{sr}|^2 |h_{rd}|^2}{N_0 + p_s |h_{sr}|^2 + p_r |h_{rd}|^2} \tag{10}$$

Therefore, the received SNR of using cooperative relay technology to transmit is:

$$\gamma = \frac{p_s |h_{sd}|^2}{N_0} + \frac{1}{N_0} \frac{p_s p_r |h_{sr}|^2 |h_{rd}|^2}{N_0 + p_s |h_{sr}|^2 + p_r |h_{rd}|^2} \tag{11}$$

3 Energy-Saving Power Allocation Strategy

3.1 Algorithm Analysis Based on Graphical Method of Classification

In previous studies, the most classical power allocation algorithm is based on optimal performance, and the basic idea is to use the total SNR of cooperative relay transmission as a measure of transmission performance and QoS. Assuming that the sum transmission power of the source node and the relay node is fixed, consider how to allocate emission power of a source node and a relay node to make the total SNR maximize. We can get the objective function:

$$MAX\{\gamma\} \tag{12}$$

The constraint condition is:

$$p = p_s + p_r \tag{13}$$

With the known parameters of h_{sd}, h_{sr}, h_{rd} and N_0, this problem is an optimal problem of linear constraint function, and can be solved by using the Lagrange multipliers method.

Because the scheme is proposed based on the network performance, so it pursuits the maximal SNR under the constraint of total power consumption. But if it aimed to saving energy, it is a reverse problem of the above allocation algorithm. So the problem is that based on a certain constraints of SNR, obtain the minimum total power consumption of the network, the objective function can be expressed as below,

$$MIN\{p\} \tag{14}$$

The constraint function is:

$$\frac{p_s|h_{sd}|^2}{N_0} + \frac{1}{N_0}\frac{p_s p_r |h_{sr}|^2 |h_{rd}|^2}{N_0 + p_s|h_{sr}|^2 + p_r|h_{rd}|^2} = \gamma \tag{15}$$

The problem looks like an equivalent transformation of the above one, and should be solved in Lagrange multiplier method, but the fact is not the case. The constraint condition of power allocation strategy that based on the optimal performance is a linear problem, and it is relatively easy to handle by using Lagrange multiplier method. The constraint condition of power allocation strategy based on the optimal energy consumption is a nonlinear problem. If dealing with Lagrange multiplier method, it is complicated. And there are probabilities of no solution cases, so the method is not convenient to analyze the practical problems. In order to analyze this problem more intuitive, the constraint function and objective function are shown in Fig. 2.

From the Fig. 2, we can find out the relationship between the objective function and the constraint condition. For the power allocation strategy of optimal energy consumption, the dashed line is the objective function, and the hyperbola present the constraint condition, the solution of the problem is to find out the intersection point of the linear equation x + y = c and the hyperbolic equation in the first quadrant, and the parameter c of the linear equation is minimal. It can be seen from Fig. 2 that when the tangency point is in the first quartile, C is the smallest. So the essence of the problem is to find a tangent of the hyperbola. In particular, when the hyperbolic parameter changes, there may couldn't find an intersection in the first quadrant, as shown in Fig. 3.

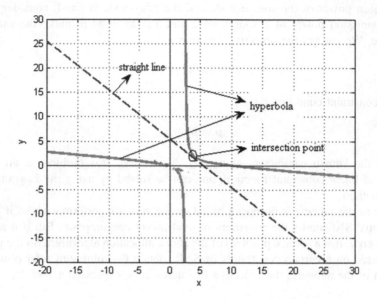

Fig. 2. SNR constraint and power allocation (the intersection is in the upper y axis)

If the intersection point of the hyperbola and dashed line is in the fourth quadrant or second quadrant, then there is no solution of the problem. The cases also correspond to the no solution conditions of the Lagrange multiplier method. From a practical point of view, the transmission power provided by device couldn't be negative, so in this time, how should the source node allocate the transmit power? In fact, every point on the hyperbola is an x and y allocation scheme. In solving the problem shows in Fig. 3, we just need to find a point on the hyperbola, the sum of horizontal and vertical coordinate values of the point is the minimum. It can be seen from the figure that the intersection point of hyperbola and x axis is required. The reason is very simple, the curvature of every point of the hyperbola along the negative direction of x axis is increasing, so the smaller x is, the more x + y. Therefore, when y = 0, x + y is the minimum value, and the value is equal to x. That is to say that it give up the cooperative relay scheme at the time, and only allocate the transmit power to the source node.

3.2 Algorithm Description

In this paper, we make use of a new method to solve the problem, as is called graphical method of classification.

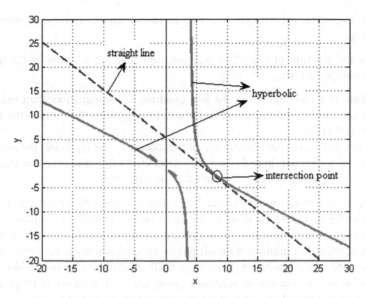

Fig. 3. SNR constraint and power allocation (the intersection is in the lower y axis)

The basic idea of the graphical method of classification shows below:

1. Mathematical modeling, provided that the objective function is linear.

$$p = p_s + p_r \tag{16}$$

The constraint conditions are:

$$\frac{p_s|h_{sd}|^2}{N_0} + \frac{1}{N_0} \frac{p_s p_r |h_{sr}|^2 |h_{rd}|^2}{N_0 + p_s|h_{sr}|^2 + p_r|h_{rd}|^2} = \gamma \tag{17}$$

$$p_s > 0 \tag{18}$$

$$p_r > 0 \tag{19}$$

Finding the intersection point of hyperbola and dashed line through the graphical method of vector equation. From Eqs. (16) and (17), we can get a quadratic equation with one unknown parameter of p_s

$$
\begin{aligned}
&(|h_{sd}|^2|h_{sr}|^2 - |h_{sd}|^2|h_{rd}|^2 - |h_{sr}|^2|h_{rd}|^2)p_s^2 \\
&+ (|h_{sd}|^2|h_{rd}|^2 p + |h_{sr}|^2|h_{rd}|^2 p \\
&+ |h_{sd}|^2 N_0 - \gamma|h_{sr}|^2 N_0 + \gamma|h_{rd}|^2 N_0)p_s \\
&- \gamma|h_{rd}|^2 N_0 p - N_0^2 \gamma = 0
\end{aligned}
\tag{20}
$$

Let the hyperbola and straight line only have one intersection point, namely they are tangency.

2. Discuss the solution of classified problem, and find the solution of the quadratic equation of p_s in (20).

   - If there is a real solution in the first quadrant of the equation, then find out the solution, and calculate p_s and p_r by substituting the solution into the formulas (16) and (17);
   - If there isn't a real solution in the first quadrant of the equation, the intersection point of x-axis and hyperbola is the solution. At this time, we can calculate p_s and p_r by Substituting $p_r = 0$ into the formula (16).

In fact, the situations above also can be explained. When the channel conditions of the source to the relay and the relay to the destination are much better than that of the source directly to the destination, the cooperative relay is suitable for transmission. In this situation, there is a minimal transmit power allocation scheme between relay node and source node on the condition of a certain SNR. And if the channel condition of the relay node to the destination is relatively poor, the best solution is to give up the cooperative relay technology, and adopt the direct way to transmit data.

4 Simulation Results and Analysis

We simulated the energy-saving power allocation algorithm, and compared it with the average power allocation algorithm and the previous power distribution scheme based on optimal network performance.

Provided that the simulation scenario is an ad hoc network with Rayleigh fading channels and Gaussian white noise, and there are a source node, a destination node, and some relay nodes randomly distributed in the network. The noise mean is 0 and variance equal to 1 of the channels in the network.

Each relay utilize various channels parameter to find out their optimal power allocation scheme according to the optimal power allocation algorithm describes above, and compare this scheme with the equal power allocation algorithm and the power distribution scheme based on optimal performance.

The parameters of power allocation algorithm based on optimal energy-saving and optimal performance is the same, the difference is that the objective function and constraints exchanged. The average power allocation algorithm is relatively simple, the source node and the relay node can be assigned the same power on the condition of total power constraint, the simulation results shown in Fig. 4.

Figure 4 shows the relationship of Symbol Error Rate (SER) and transmission power under the condition that the channel gain coefficient is $h_{sd}/h_{sr}/h_{rd} = 1 : 3 : 7$. The lower SER of three power allocation algorithms, the power consumption is higher. When the SER of the three algorithms is equal, energy-saving power allocation strategy requires a minimal total transmit power. Thus, in order to save energy, energy-saving power allocation strategy is the best choice.

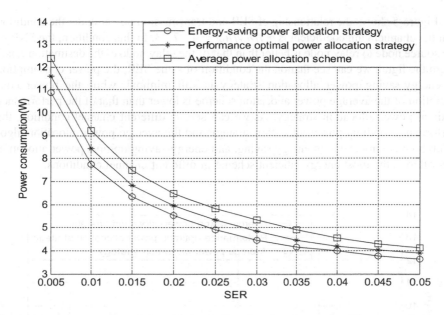

Fig. 4. Power consumption of three kinds of allocation algorithm under different restrictions of SER $(h_{sd}/h_{sr}/h_{rd} = 1/3/7)$

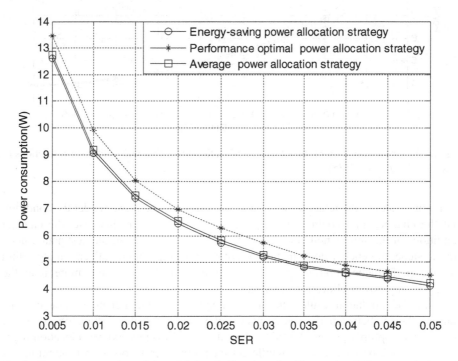

Fig. 5. Power consumption of three kinds of allocation algorithm under different restrictions of SER $(h_{sd}/h_{sr}/h_{rd} = 1/7/3)$

Figure 5 shows the relationship of SER and transmission power under the condition that the channel gain coefficient is $h_{sd}/h_{sr}/h_{rd} = 1 : 7 : 3$. In this condition, the SNR of the source node to relay node is better than that of the relay node to the destination node. From the figure we can see that on the condition of same SER, the power consumption of energy-saving power allocation strategy is still minimal, while the power consumption of the average power allocation scheme is lower than that of the performance optimal power allocation strategy. As we can see, in different channel condition, the performance optimal power allocation strategy and the average power allocation algorithm both are not stable in energy saving, and energy-saving optimal power allocation algorithm is the most energy efficient scheme in different channel conditions.

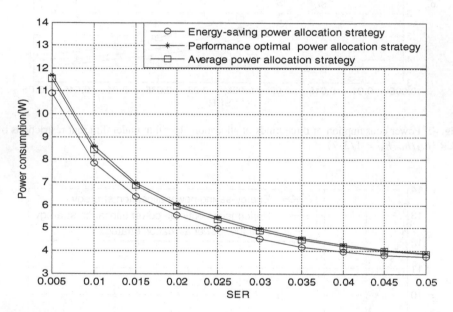

Fig. 6. Power consumption of three kinds of allocation algorithm under different restrictions of SER $(h_{sd}/h_{sr}/h_{rd} = 1/5/5)$

Figure 6 shows the relationship of SER and transmission power under the condition that the channel gain coefficient is $h_{sd}/h_{sr}/h_{rd} = 1 : 5 : 5$. In this case, the channel conditions of the source node to relay node and the relay node to the destination node are the same, the energy consumption of both the average power allocation algorithm and the performance optimal power allocation algorithm are both more than the energy-saving power allocation algorithm.

From the simulation result of the above, it can be found that changes in the channel gain coefficient between the source node, relay node and the destination node, the performance optimal power allocation algorithms and average power allocation algorithm have their own advantages in different scenarios over the power consumption, but compared to the energy-saving power allocation strategy, both are inferior. Thus,

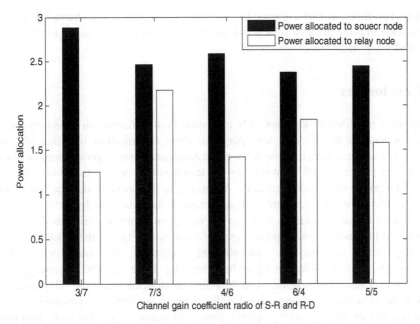

Fig. 7. The energy-saving power allocation histogram of S-R and R-D in different channel gain coefficient rate

regardless of the channel state changes, the power consumption of the energy-saving power allocation strategy is the lowest compared with the other two strategies. Comparing the three figures, it can be seen that if the channel state of the source node to the relay node is better than that of the relay node to the destination node, the power consumption is less.

Figure 7 is the power distribution histogram of energy-saving power allocation algorithm when the channel gain coefficient of source node to relay node and relay node to the destination node is different. It can be seen from the figure, no matter what the channel coefficient ratio is, the power distributed to the source node is more than that distributed to relay nodes in the power distribution scheme. It also can be concluded that the smaller channel coefficient ratio is, the more power allocated to the source node are, and the greater channel coefficient ratio is, the transmit power allocated to source node and relay node are tend to be more balanced. This is because that the signal sent from the relay nodes are dependent on the received signal from the source node, only in the guarantee of that the relay node can receive signal correctly, the signal forwarding could be meaningful.

On the other hand, the signal transmitted from the source node is sent to the relay node and the destination node, thus the source node needs to provide a diversity gain, and the relay node provides the second diversity gain, so that the destination node can get two diversity gains after the merger of the two signals. Therefore, the source node should be allocated more transmitting power. Especially in the situation that when the channel state of source node to relay node is bad, the power assigned to the source node could be two times of that assigned to the relay nodes. And if the channel state of the source node to relay node is quite good, the transmission power assigned to the source node and relay node are almost equal.

5   Conclusions

Cooperative relay technology not only can improve the transmission performance by using cooperative diversity, it also played a great contribution in terms of saving energy. In a wireless network, the main evaluation parameter of power consumption is transmitting power, so taking minimize the transmission power as the objective, we proposed a power allocation algorithm. According to the problem that the source node is pretty difficult to obtain the channel coefficient of the source node to relay node and relay node to the destination node, regarding the green communication as the goal, we put forward the energy-saving relay selection strategy. By taking the advantage of that the relay nodes are easy to gain channel coefficient, and combined with the energy-saving power allocation algorithm, the relay node provide the energy-saving optimal power allocated scheme. And then the source node select the relay node, thus find out the most energy-saving relay. Finally, through the simulation analysis, it can be found out that the energy-saving optimal power allocation algorithm is the best one in energy-saving compared to the other power allocation algorithm.

Acknowledgment. This work was supported by the Beijing Higher Education Young Elite Teacher Project (YETP0439), and the National Natural Science Foundation of China (No. 61571059).

References

1. Yuan, G., Zhang, X., Wang, W., Yang, Y.: Carrier aggregation for LTE-advanced mobile communication systems. IEEE Commun. Mag. **48**(2), 88–93 (2010)
2. Li, G.Y., Xu, Z., Xiong, C., Yang, C., Zhang, S., Chen, Y., Xu, S.: Energy-efficient wireless communications: tutorial, survey, and open issues. IEEE Wirel. Commun. **18**(6), 28–35 (2011)
3. [30] 3GPP TR36.913. Requirements for Evolved UTRA (E-UTRA) and Evolved UTRAN (EUTRAN) [S] (2011)
4. Chen, T., Yang, Y., Zhang, H., Kim, H., Horneman, K.: Network energy saving technologies for green wireless access networks. IEEE Wirel. Commun. **18**(5), 30–38 (2011)
5. Soh, Y.S., Member, S., Quek, T.Q.S., et al.: Energy efficient heterogeneous cellular networks. IEEE J. Sel. Areas Commun. **31**(5), 840–850 (2013)
6. Sendonaris, A., Erkip, E., Aazhang, B.: User cooperation diversity, Part I-System description. IEEE Trans. Commun. **1**(11), 1927–1938 (2003)
7. Huang, R., Feng, C., Zhang, T.: Energy efficient design in AF relay networks with bidirectional asymmetric traffic. In: Proceedings of WCNC Workshop, Paris, pp. 7–11 (2012)
8. Sadek, A.K., Su, W., Liu, K.J.R.: Multinode cooperative communications in wireless networks. IEEE Trans. Sig. Process. **55**(1), 341–355 (2007)

Sensitive Information Protection of CAD Model Based on Free-Form Deformation in Collaborative Design

Yiqi Wu[1,2], Fazhi He[1,2(✉)], Weidong Li[2,3], Xiantao Cai[1,2], and Xiaoxia Li[2,3]

[1] School of Computer Science, Wuhan University, Wuhan, People's Republic of China
fzhe@whu.edu.cn
[2] Faculty of Engineering and Computing, Coventry University, Coventry, UK
[3] College of Science, Huazhong Agricultural University, Wuhan, China

Abstract. How to protect the sensitive information of CAD model is becoming a challenging issue in collaborative product development (CPD). This paper proposed a free-form deformation (FFD) based method to protect the sensitive information in feature-based CAD model. With the advantages of FFD from computational mathematics and computer graphics, we can indirectly transform FFD lattice parameters that drive the original sketch parameters, and finally encrypt and deform the original CAD model. In this way, not only the sensitive information can be hidden by partial deformation, but also the range and direction of deformation can be easily controlled by collaborative parterres in a flexible and robust manner. The case study and experiments demonstrate the proposed idea and method.

Keywords: Free-form deformation · Collaborative design · CAD model · Encryption

1 Introduction

In the Collaborative product development (CPD) environment, the enterprises internal resources could be integrated and optimized as the market resource. The design group share information and communicate with each other across region as they are in a virtual enterprise. These bring not only the enhancement of design efficiency and product quality but also the cost reduction [1–3]. In this development mode, the production requirement is disintegrated into multi sub requirements by the original equipment manufacturer (OEM) and then they are distributed to different parts suppliers for a collaborative development.

On one hand, to achieve the successful collaborative design, designers and developers cross regions, enterprises and departments have to share and interoperate the design data to realize and analyze the design and maintain the consistency of it [4–6].

On the other hand, represented by CAD model, the digital model contains a lot of important sensitive data with intellectual property such as the configuration of design

© Springer International Publishing Switzerland 2016
Q. Zu and B. Hu (Eds.): HCC 2016, LNCS 9567, pp. 465–474, 2016.
DOI: 10.1007/978-3-319-31854-7_42

parameters, the customized defined features, and the external shape of specific surface and so on. These sensitive data is in the CAD model in the manner of sensitive modeling features which embodies the design idea and knowledge, and is the carrier of development ability and core competitiveness of the enterprises in the supply chain. In this situation, the lack of sensitive information protection for CAD model will cause significant risks in CPD including but not limited to the data stolen of storage in server, leakage in network transmission, uncontrollable spread of clients. And all these risks become more prominent with the era of cloud computing, cloud storage and big data. The enthusiasm of enterprises to participate in the CPD will be weakened for these risks and how to prevent them has become a main technical barrier in collaborative design.

Aiming at these CAD model security problems, this paper proposed a sensitive information protection method by model deformation. The rest of this paper is organized as follows. In Sect. 2, related work of collaborative design and CAD model security is briefly reviewed. The idea and procedure of the proposed method in this paper is introduced in Sect. 3. Section 4 discusses the implementation cases of feature based CAD model encryption. Finally, in Sect. 5 summaries the contributions of the paper and indicates some future works.

2   Related Work

While the network gives convenience to collaborative work, it also brings security risks to the private sensitive information of each collaborative partner. The sensitive information of CAD has to be protected because the security risk has become a main obstacle of collaborative design implementation [7]. Generally speaking there are two kinds of approach for information security: information authorization and information hiding [8]. According to related work of integrating general information security method into collaborative CAD information protection, there are two categories of approaches: first one deals with the framework of the collaborative system, such as access control; the second one is to deals with the CAD models directly, such as multi-resolution methods and model encryption methods.

The encryption method for feature-based CAD model is currently lacking. Moreover, the flexible encryption method for partial sensitive information of a CAD model is lacking. Cai proposed a multi-granularity partial encryption method which uses a encryption matrix to encrypt parameters of the sketch of feature based CAD model and then improved this method to a customized encryption one for collaboration in cloud manufacturing environment [9, 10].

This paper proposed sensitive information protection method for parametric feature-based CAD model. This method hides sensitive information by partial model deformation. The concept of sketch control point is introduced. The sketch control point is adopted as the minimum operation granularity of encryption subjective to facilitate the encryption. Further, a free-form deformation based sketch encryption method is proposed which can provide the necessary restriction of direction and range of the deformation. The deformed model can be restored to original shape.

3 CAD Model Encryption Based on Model Deformation

In collaborative design, the safety of model information sharing is reflected in two aspects: preventing sensitive information leakage to intruder during the transmission process and protecting private sensitive information while sharing models to other collaborative partners. The purpose of this paper is to satisfy these two requirements in collaborative design by encrypting the sensitive part of a model.

3.1 Deformable Sketch Elements and Sketch Control Point

3.1.1 Sketch Based Modeling Procedure

The basic modeling process of common parametric CAD system is: first, create the sketch of the model based on sketch parameters; then, based on the created sketch, select modeling features and adjust feature parameters to finish the modeling process. For example, to create the hole feature in Fig. 1 (c), the sketch of the hole needs to be designed first by setting the center location and radius parameters on the top surface of the boss which is the datum plane (Fig. 1.a); then use the extruded cut feature and set the depth parameter of the extrusion to obtain the required hole (Fig. 1.b).

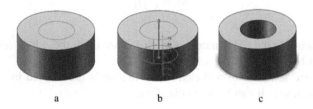

a   b   c

Fig. 1. Parametrical modeling: a. create sketch; b. set feature parameters; c. complete model

CAD systems provide plentiful basic shape tools of sketch. Various sketches for practical modeling can be created by using these sketch elements.

The sketch can be classified into 2D sketch and 3D sketch according to the space location of sketch. 2D sketch is created on a selected datum plane and 3D sketch is created in space.

3.1.2 Concept of Sketch Control Point

When using these sketch elements to create a sketch, some points with geometry means can be retrieved by APIs of the CAD systems. These points control the position and shape of the sketch by their coordinates. We name these points as the sketch control points. For example, Fig. 2 shows some of the sketch elements of SolidWorks 2014. The light blue points are the retrieved sketch control points from the sketch. They are the vertices of the rectangle, the center of the circular, control points of the spline, endpoints of the long/short axis and center of the ellipse respectively.

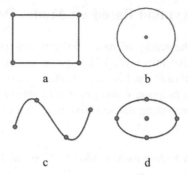

Fig. 2. Sketch control points of some basic sketch elements: a. rectangle; b. circular; c. spline; d. ellipse

3.2   Model Deformation by Sketch Parameters Modification

The parametrical feature-based CAD model is consisted of a set of features which represents the shape and design semantics. The modeling process can be formalized as:

$$M = \bigcup_{i=1}^{n} f_i \tag{1}$$

M is the feature-based CAD model, the ith feature in all the n features of the mode can be denoted by f_i.

The shape and semantic of a sketch based feature is determined by its sketch and the feature parameters. It can be formalized as:

$$f(s) = G(\bigcup_{j=1}^{m} s(p_s), p_f) \tag{2}$$

f is the feature of the model, s denotes the sketch of the feature f, p_s and p_f represent the parameters of the sketch and the feature respectively. The sketch control points can be retrieved from the sketch. The shape of the sketch is controlled by parameters of the sketch and the sketch control points. So the sketch can be detailed described as:

$$S = G(\bigcup_{i=1}^{n} C_i, P_s) \tag{3}$$

S is the shape of the sketch, C_i is the ith sketch control point in the sketch and P_s is the parameters of the sketch, such as the length and the angle.

According to Eqs. (1), (2) and (3), when the parameters of the sketch control points are modified, the position and shape of the sketch are changed. The position and shape of the feature are modified along with the deformation of the sketch. Finally, the CAD model is deformed. When the parameters of the sketch control points are modified back to original value, the model would be deformed to the original shape.

The feature is the minimum modeling unit of a parametrical model. No matter the modeling features, sketches of features or sketch control points are independent if there is no constraint added, which means it is possible to deform part of the model when other area of the model remains unchanged. The security protection method proposed in this paper can encrypt part of the model with the fine granularity of sketch based modeling feature.

3.3   Procedure of Deformation Based Encryption

The proposed model encryption method hides sensitive information by deformation of sensitive partial CAD model. The deformation is caused by modifying parameters of sketch control points. The parameters of sketch control point are represented by 2D/3D coordinates of the point.

The procedure of the model encryption includes four steps:

1. Information partition: To the CAD model with sensitive information, select the sensitive part which is represented by sketch-based modeling features;
2. Sketch retrieval: Retrieve the sketches of the selected part;
3. Sketch encryption: Use a certain sketch deformation method to encrypt the sketch;
4. Partial model encryption: The sensitive part of the model can be encrypted by using the deformed sketch to recreate features.

The sensitive part of the model in step 1 needs to be selected manually by the designer. All the information and parameters retrieval and modification in the procedure are applied by APIs of CAD systems.

After the encryption of the sensitive model part, the designer of the original model can send the encrypted model to collaborative partners. Then the model can be further modified. Then modified model with encrypted part can be decrypted by the original model designer.

Therefore, the above mentioned CAD model encryption method can fit the requirement of model information security in collaborative design from the following aspects:

1. The encryption result is still a correct CAD model and the model can be further modified;
2. In the encrypted model, the sensitive part of the model is deformed distinctly. The sensitive information can be hidden successfully;
3. The encrypted model can be decrypted to original shape.

3.4   FFD Based Sketch Control Points Encryption

The key process of the proposed model encryption is used an appropriate method to achieve the reversible transform for the coordinates of sketch control points. This paper introduces an encryption method based on free-form deformation (FFD), which is a commonly used technology in the area of computer graphics.

3.4.1   Generation of the Encryption Deformation Lattice

To each sketch of the features in the sensitive part of the model, an encryption control lattice should be generated. That is, for a model M, if the sensitive part M' contains (j-i + 1) features represented as (fi, fi + 1, ... , fj-1, fj), the encryption control lattices (Li, Li + 1, ... , Lj-1, Lj) are created for the sketch control points in each sketch (si, si + 1, ..., sj-1, sj) of the features respectively.

The encryption lattice is a parallelepiped for 3D sketch. Set the edges of the lattice are parallel to the axis of the Cartesian coordinate respectively. All the sketch points should be inside of the lattice. That is to say, to all the sketch control points (x_1, y_1, z_1), (x_2, y_2, z_2), $\cdots$, (x_n, y_n, z_n) and the diagonal vertices of the lattice $(x_{Lmin}, y_{Lmin}, z_{Lmin})$ have the relationship of:

$$
\begin{aligned}
&x_{Lmax} > x_{max}, y_{Lmax} > y_{max}, z_{Lmax} > z_{max}; \\
&x_{Lmin} < x_{min}, y_{Lmin} < y_{min}, z_{Lmin} < z_{min} \\
&x_{max} = \max(x_1, x_2, \cdots, x_n), y_{max} = \max(y_1, y_2, \cdots, y_n), z_{max} = \max(z_1, z_2, \cdots, z_n) \\
&x_{min} = \min(x_1, x_2, \cdots, x_n), y_{min} = \min(y_1, y_2, \cdots, y_n), z_{min} = \min(z_1, z_2, \cdots, z_n)
\end{aligned}
\tag{4}
$$

Based on the same idea, the lattice of a 2D sketch is a rectangle. All the 2D sketch points should be inside of the lattice. The diagonal vertices of the lattice is (x_{Lmax}, y_{Lmax}) and (x_{Lmin}, y_{Lmin}). Hereinafter, this paper takes the 3D sketch control points as the object to introduce the FFD based sketch control point encryption method. The method for 2D sketch is based on the same idea only decreases one dimension when generating the control lattice and doing encryption calculation.

Taking the 3D sketch control point encryption as an example, first create the local coordinate system in the parallelepiped. Then a sketch control point $C(x, y, z,)$ has the parameter coordinate (s, t, u) in this system and it can be represented as:

$$
s = \frac{x - x_{Lmin}}{x_{Lmax} - x_{Lmin}}, t = \frac{y - y_{Lmin}}{y_{Lmax} - y_{Lmin}}, u = \frac{z - z_{Lmin}}{z_{Lmax} - z_{Lmin}}
\tag{5}
$$

Use planes to dissect the parallelepiped uniformly in three directions of the coordinates and get l, m, n sections of the parallelepiped in each direction respectively. The vertices of the parallelepiped and the intersection points between the parallelepiped dissection planes consist the encryption lattice control points, denoted as $P_{i,j,k}$, in which $i = 0, 1, \cdots, l; j = 0, 1, \cdots, m; k = 0, 1, \cdots, n$. The coordinate of $P_{i,j,k}$ is:

$$
P_{i,j,k} = (x_{Lmin} + \frac{i}{l}(x_{Lmax} - x_{Lmin}), y_{Lmin} + \frac{j}{m}(y_{Lmax} - y_{Lmin}), z_{Lmin} + \frac{k}{n}(z_{Lmax} - z_{Lmin}))
\tag{6}
$$

Thereby, the 3D encryption lattice is created.

3.4.2   Calculation of Sketch Control Point Coordinates Transformation

According to the FFD, when the control point $P_{i,j,k}$ is moved to $P'_{i,j,k}$, the coordinate of the sketch control point X is transformed and it can be denoted as $X_{encryption}$. The local parameter coordinates (s, t, u) remains unchanged, so its transferred Cartesian coordinates can be calculated as:

$$X_{encryption3D} = \sum_{i=0}^{l} \sum_{j=0}^{m} \sum_{k=0}^{n} P'_{i,j,k} B_{i,l}(s) B_{j,m}(t) B_{k,n}(u) \tag{7}$$

$B_{i,l}(s), B_{j,m}(t), B_{k,n}(u)$ are Bernstein polynomials of l, m and n degree. By using this equation, when the coordinates of the encryption lattice control points are modified, the Cartesian coordinates of the sketch control points are changed which means they are encrypted.

The decryption can be achieved by using Eq. (8), which means when the encryption control lattice is deformed back to the original shape. The encrypted model in it will be deformed to its initial shape as well.

$$X_{decryption3D} = \sum_{i-0}^{l} \sum_{j-0}^{m} \sum_{k-0}^{n} P_{i,j,k} B_{i,l}(s) B_{j,m}(t) B_{k,n}(u) \tag{8}$$

The encryption key of 3D sketch control points is the set of encryption lattice control points after the deformation:

$$C_{encryption} = \left\{ P'_{i,j,k} | i \in [1, 2, \cdots, l], j \in [1, 2, \cdots, m], k \in [1, 2, \cdots, n] \right\} \tag{9}$$

The decryption key is the set of encryption lattice control points with initial coordinates:

$$C_{decryption} = \left\{ P_{i,j,k} | i \in [1, 2, \cdots, l], j \in [1, 2, \cdots, m], k \in [1, 2, \cdots, n] \right\} \tag{10}$$

Likewise, the 2D sketch control points encryption can be implemented by using equation:

$$X_{encryption2D} = \sum_{i=0}^{l} \sum_{j=0}^{m} P'_{i,j} B_{i,l}(s) B_{j,m}(t) \tag{11}$$

The decryption calculation is:

$$X_{decryption2D} = \sum_{i=0}^{l} \sum_{j=0}^{m} P_{i,j} B_{i,l}(s) B_{j,m}(t) \tag{12}$$

The encryption and decryption key is shown as Eqs. (13) and (14) respectively:

$$C_{encryption2D} = \left\{ P'_{i,j} | i \in [1, 2, \cdots, l], j \in [1, 2, \cdots, m] \right\} \tag{13}$$

$$C_{decryption2D} = \left\{ P_{i,j,k} | i \in [1, 2, \cdots, l], j \in [1, 2, \cdots, m] \right\} \tag{14}$$

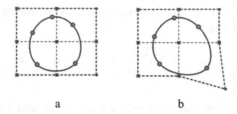

Fig. 3. Sketch encryption based on FFD: a. original sketch; b. encrypted sketch

The encryption results shown in Fig. 3 indicate that the range and direction of sketch deformation have positive correlation with those of the encryption lattice control points. So, the encryption result can be constrained by the encryption lattice intuitively which means the validity of encrypted model can be guaranteed.

4   Case Studies and Analyses

4.1   Case Studies

Some case studies are made to testify the effectiveness and validity of the proposed method. Some parametrical feature based CAD model for academic research and industry are used as experimental subjects. The implementation of the method is based on the secondary development for SolidWorks 2014 and CITIA V5 R21. The development environment is VS2008.

The encryption results of CAD models are shown in Fig. 4. From the results, models or partial models are deformed visibly and properly. The encrypted models remain parametrical ones so that they can be shared to other collaborative partners and modified by them. All the encrypted models can be decrypted to original shape.

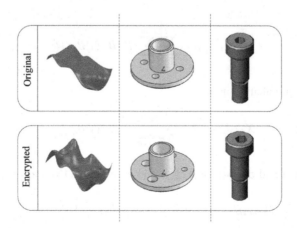

Fig. 4. Case study: partial encryption for CAD models

By using the sketch control point encryption method based on FFD, because the deformation range and direction are constrained by the encryption lattice, the validity of the encryption is easy to ensure.

4.2   Analyses

4.2.1   Summary of Encryption Calculation and Time Complexity Analysis

According to Eq. (7), the time complexity of encryption for one point is $O(n^3)$. In the whole encryption process, all the sketch control points need to be encrypted. So the time complexity of this method is $O(n^4)$.

It should be noted that although the l, m, n in Eq. (7) can be any positive integer, in the practical application of sketch encryption method based on FFD, the value does not have to be very large to get an encryption result. In the cases of this paper, the value of l, m and n is 3 respectively. On the other side, the number of the sketch control points in a model is not large. Therefore, although the complexity of this method is $O(n^4)$, Current computer operation ability can satisfy the computing requirement absolutely.

4.2.2   Security Analysis

From the description of the encryption method, we can see that to decrypt the encrypted model to original shape, the only decryption key is needed.

The decryption key is set of the lattice control points with initial coordinates. The control points can be set in any place as long as it satisfies the restraint of Eq. (4). So the parameters space of the key is large enough to avoid the cracking.

What's more, when using the proposed method, a wrong key can decrypt the model to a certain shape as well. In this situation, intruders cannot find out if it is the correct model with the original shape. Unless the designer offers the key, there is no way to find out what is the real design idea of the designer. Thereby the reliability of this security protection method is guaranteed.

5   Conclusion and Future Work

In order to face the challenging issues of information security in CPD, this paper present a FFD based encryption method to protect the sensitive information of CAD model. The contributions of the proposed method are summarized as follows. Firstly, FFD based encryption is applied on the feature based CAD model. Therefore, this method is superior to the geometry model method in process of CPD. Secondly, the FFD based encryption method can deform and encrypt the different parts of CAD respectively. In this way, the encrypted CAD mode can be send to different users without leakage of the sensitive information in collaborative design. Furthermore, an indirectly encryption method based on FFD is proposed. Therefore, the collaborative partners can easily control the deformation range and direction in a very flexible and very robust way.

Future work of this paper can include but not limited to: to adopt better encryption calculation, to extend the method into heterogeneous CAD system and to extend this method for assembly information security in collaborative design.

Acknowledgment. This paper is supported by the National Science Foundation of China (Grant No. 61472289 and 61303215) and Hubei Province Science Foundation (Grant No. 2015CFB254)

References

1. Zhang, D., He, F., Han, S.H., et al.: Quantitative optimization of interoperability during feature-based data exchange. Integr. Comput. Aided Eng. **23**(1), 31–51 (2016)
2. He, F., Han, S.H.: A method and tool for human–human interaction and instant collaboration in CSCW-based CAD. Comput. Ind. **57**(8), 740–751 (2006)
3. Cheng, Y., He, F., Cai, X., et al.: A group Undo/Redo method in 3D collaborative modeling systems with performance evaluation. J. Netw. Comput. Appl. **36**(6), 1512–1522 (2013)
4. Jing, S., He, F., Han, S., et al.: A method for topological entity correspondence in a replicated collaborative CAD system. Comput. Ind. **60**(7), 467–475 (2009)
5. Cai, X., Li, X., He, F., et al.: Flexible concurrency control for legacy CAD to construct collaborative CAD environment. J. Adv. Mech. Des. Syst. Manuf. **6**(3), 324–339 (2012)
6. Liu, H., He, F., Zhu, F., et al.: Consistency maintenance in collaborative CAD systems. Chin. J. Electron. **22**(1), 15–20 (2013)
7. Hauck, S., Knol, S.: Data security for Web-based CAD. In: Proceedings of the 35th Annual Design Automation Conference, pp. 788–793 (1998)
8. Rutledge, L.S., Hoffman, L.J.: A survey of issues in computer network security. Comput. Secur. **5**(4), 296–308 (1986)
9. Cai, X., Li, W., He, F., et al.: Customized encryption of computer aided design models for collaboration in cloud manufacturing environment. J. Manuf. Sci. Eng. **137**(4), 040905 (2015)
10. Cai, X., He, F.Z., Li, W.D., et al.: Encryption based partial sharing of CAD models. Integr. Comput. Aided Eng. **22**(3), 243–260 (2015)

Keywords Popularity Analysis Based on Hidden Markov Model

Liang Xue[1,2(✉)], Zunliang Wang[1,2], Wenzhi Zhang[2],
and Haiyang Zhang[1]

[1] School of Computer Science, Beijing University of Posts
and Telecommunications, Beijing 100876, People's Republic of China
524125611@qq.com
[2] Science and Technology on Information Transmission and Dissemination
in Communication Networks Laboratory, Beijing, China

Abstract. This paper first analyzes the existing methods for identifying popular keywords. By studying the methods on how to define the popular keywords with their occurrence frequency, a new approach to analyze the keyword popularity will be proposed. The paper first built a new model based on the Hidden Markov Model, then introduced several parameters who impacts the feature of the model and described how the model works. Using the Stirling formula and the Viterbi algorithm to simplify the calculation. Adjusting the model's parameters by comparing the experimental results and the output of the system. Finally, obtained a higher accuracy, effective keyword popularity analysis system.

Keywords: Hidden markov model · Keyword popularity analysis · Occurrence frequency · Probability distributions

1 Introduction

With the information plays an increasingly important role in people's daily life, tracking certain keywords has become one of the urgent demand in many of today's systems. In order to monitor the trend of public opinion, Department of Public Safety may focus on the activity of some sensitive word in a short term on the Internet. Operators may need to filter spam messages efficiently in a period, so they always track the keywords which represent the spam messages. Even ordinary Internet users often needs to have the knowledge that how frequently some certain keywords will occur in some periods.

Currently, based on this demand, there already have some keywords popularity or public opinion analysis systems. To analyze the public opinion, the common practice is to monitor the target keyword's occurrence time and record the time slot between each adjacent occurrences, compare the slots' difference to build a model. Analyzing the length of the time slot to recognize whether the keyword meets the standards which defines a popular keyword. However, this practice would be very difficult to implement because it is hard to obtain the raw data, even if we have already got the raw data, it is not conducive to the subsequent calculation process, this leads to a consequence that

© Springer International Publishing Switzerland 2016
Q. Zu and B. Hu (Eds.): HCC 2016, LNCS 9567, pp. 475–486, 2016.
DOI: 10.1007/978-3-319-31854-7_43

the final result requires a relatively large amount of computation, but this relatively "heavy" operation did not bring any significant accuracy improvement of the system.

Suppose a target keyword has already be given, how to efficiently analyze the keyword to find out in which period it shows a burst of occurrence, and in which period it does not have this feature has become a barrier that lots of research needs to break through.

HMM (Hidden Markov Model) is a common method for analyzing changes in different states. It is manifested by analyzing a number of attributes of the target to finalize the process. However, HMM model also has a very fatal flaw. It is through the Viterbi algorithm traceback procedure to determine the hidden state of the system, but there has a dimension barrier in Viterbi algorithm. When the number of the output dimensions getting large, calculation process will involve more states transitions. As the output dimensions constantly upgrading its scale, the computation of the algorithm will increase exponentially and soon fall into the incalculable state. But, fortunately, whether the keyword is popular or not, there are only two hidden states (hot, non-hot), so HMM model is a solution of the popular keyword determination and a lightweight tool to use. This paper will be accomplished by using the HMM model analysis system.

2 Research Status

Currently, there has not a particularly large number of domestic and international research focus on popularity analysis for keywords field. But for text flow and message flow, there has some relatively mature theoretical systems, keywords popularity analysis have many similarities with them, some of the techniques and ideas can be borrowed to complete the keywords popularity analysis. For text stream, mail flow analysis, the system usually divided into the following steps.

2.1 Infinite State Model

Let the $n + 1$ length of message sequence reach the system in the length of time T: If the message within this time completely uniform spaced, so they reach the interval between the size of $\hat{g} = T/n$. If the burst strength increases, the interval will become smaller and smaller. To track this burst, we should focus on the infinite state automaton, making every interval can mapping to a particular hidden state. The so-called infinite state automaton refers to a model with the parameter t_0 which is the time gap between two adjacent occurrence, this model treat the hidden state which is the next member of the sequence arrival time as t_1, since the next member may coming soon ($t_1 = 0$), or may never come ($t_1 = \infty$), so this hidden state's range is infinite, call such a model for the name infinite state machine model.

2.2 Hidden Markov Model

Hidden Markov model is a statistical model. It is used to describe an implicit parameter during the Markov process. The sticking point is to determine the hidden parameters from the parameters can be observed. Then use these parameters to make further analysis.

Hidden Markov model is a kind of Markov chain, but can be calculated by the observation of the vector sequence. HMM is a double random process, a certain number of states of hidden Markov chains and a random function set.

In a simple Markov model, the state is directly visible to the observer, and therefore the state transition probabilities are the only parameters in the model. In a hidden Markov model, the state is not directly visible, but output, dependent on the state, is visible. Each state has a probability distribution over the possible output tokens. Therefore the sequence of tokens generated by an HMM gives some information about the sequence of states. Note that the adjective 'hidden' refers to the state sequence through which the model passes, not to the parameters of the model; the model is still referred to as a 'hidden' Markov model even if these parameters are known exactly.

2.3   Calculate the Minimum Cost State Series

Through a given message set, it can be used to generate a hidden Markov model, and find a possible state sequences. Given n + 1 pieces of information and their exact arrival time. This determines n message arrival interval $X = (x_1, x_2, ..., x_n)$. Bayesian process can be used to determine the state sequence $q = (q_1, q_2, ..., q_n)$ of conditional probability. Each state sequence q has an objective equation f based on X, the purpose is to find a state sequence q to make this objective equation f getting its maximum value. State sequence is the result to be analyzed.

3   Keyword Popularity Analysis

Different from analysing the message flow and text flow, in the research of keywords popularity anlaysis, the system tend to pay its attention on whether the word in the given message set is a hot word rather than every breakdown state. In addition, based on the demands of network statistics and the difficulty to get the raw data, the message set is often rendered in such a form that the statistical data is recorded by the number of occurrences of certain words in a particular interval.

Based on the foregoing facts, in order to analyze the keyword popularity problem, there will be three problems. What model need to be established? How to analyze the model? And how to enumerate the intermediate results?

3.1   Finite State Machine Model

3.1.1   Determine the Hidden State

Given a keyword and a information set in a certain time range, suppose this keyword can only have two states in a short period of time: "hot" and "non-hot", this just can be used to represent the 0 and 1 states. The first step to build the model is to give each period a state variable S, its value can be only chosen from S_0, S_1 which the S_0 state indicates a non-hot state, and the S_1 state indicates a hot state. Since these two states are not visible to the system, we call them "hidden state".

This modeling approach is constructed with a two-state probabilistic automaton (A). When A is in state S_0, keywords appear at a lower frequency. When A is in state S_1, keywords appear at a higher frequency. Whether the keyword is hot depends on the state it currently located.

3.1.2 Poisson Distribution Hypothesis

In the foregoing, what the system mostly concerned about is the probability distribution the keyword obeyed no matter which state the keyword currently is. Only after getting the probability distribution can we analysis the system.

In the actual case, if an event, e.g., a telephone exchange receives a call, the number of the passengers of a bus stop, the scale of a radioactive substance emitted particles, etc. appears randomly and independently at a fixed average instantaneous rate λ (also known as density), then the appearing number of this event in a unit time (area or volume) obey the Poisson distribution P (λ) (Fig. 1).

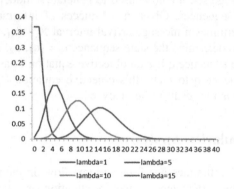

Fig. 1. The poisson distribution

Poisson distribution's parameter λ is the average frequency of occurrence during a certain time (or area) of random events. Poisson distribution adapted to describe the number of times which a random event occured in a period of time. Expectation and variance of the Poisson distribution are both λ.

$$R(x = k) = \frac{\lambda^k}{k!}\, e^{-\lambda}, k = 0, 1 \ldots$$

How many times a random event occured in a period time makes the input data of the system. Poisson distribution fit this statistical method perfectly, so naturally, assume the keyword analysis system obey the Poisson distribution.

λ is the only parameter that determines the whole Poisson distribution. In the case that the keywords' frequency of occurrence has been determined, the only way to distinguish different states is to check the parameter λ.

Through the existing data to extrapolate which distribution the random event obeyed is the common method in parameter estimation. In the discrete random variable parameter estimation, point estimates are general approach, which estimate the sample means as the population mean. Here the input data mean λ_0 will be treated as the state S_0's parameter and the other parameter λ_1 as the state S_1's mean which $\lambda_1 = \theta\lambda_0$, $\theta \in [1, +\infty)$.

3.1.3   Noise Reduction

When analyzing the input data, there will be such a situation, namely the keywords occurs alternately in high-frequency and low- frequency. If there is no distinguishment, the final results of the analysis are likely to exhibit S_0, S_1 alternately as the same. If a keywords has already stayed in some state, a slight fluctuations in a certain range which is considered as a normal fluctuation in the state is suggested. That means the keyword tends to maintain its current status instead of promiscuously switching, in other words, keyword has this feature that it will hold its "status' inertia".

Define the instability which described above with a new name "noise." In order to eliminate the noise as much as possible without affect the result too much in the same time, the keyword will pay a cost when converts into another state, so it is more likely to maintain its current state. That is why there has another parameter called state holding probability $p \in (0,1)$, its meaning is that each time when the keyword converts its current hidden state into the other one, the process always goes with a cost. For example, suppose the current time is i−1, the keyword is in S_0 and S_1 state's probabilities when the system gose to the next time i are as follows:

$$S_i^0 = R^0(k_i)p$$

$$S_i^1 = R^1(k_i)(1 - p)$$

Or:

$$S_i^n = R^n(k_i)\alpha$$

The meaning of α is, if the previous state and the current state is inconsistent, $\alpha = (1-p)$; otherwise $\alpha = p$. k_i represents the occurrence frequency of the keyword in the i-th time intervals, $R^n()$ represents the poisson distribution in state n. With the value of p gets bigger and bigger, the conversion between different status becomes more and more difficult, so the stability of the final result will be improved with this process. However, dealing with the parameter p must be very carefully, because when p is too large, the state can no longer be converted, the hidden state of the keyword will stays in one situation consistently which will lose the analysis' significance.

In addition, parameter θ to some extent also affect the probability of the state transition. Because the state transition is impacted not only by the state holding parameter, but also by the poisson distributions itself. With the increase of parameters θ, the transition between the hidden states will get difficult likely and the result will also present a stable trend. That means parameter p and θ codetermines the stability of the analysis result. Fortunately these two parameters can be flexibly configured, they can be trained by existing samples and adjusted at any time until the system get the most appropriate parameter values.

To sum up, in order to eliminate noises between different states, machine A with probability 1–p change its status and with probability p to maintain the current status, and all these conversions will happen independently to each other.

3.2   Generate the Status Chain

3.2.1   The Objective Function

Suppose the system has already got the appropriate value of p and θ, further more, every hidden state chain's probability needs to be calculated. The system's aim is to find out a maximum probability chain which is the exactly output of the HMM.

To get the probability of a hidden state chain, first step is to traverse the input data set, calculate the probability of the frequency which the keyword occurs in state S_0 and S_1. Since every time the conversion happens independently, the probability of the hidden state chain is the multiplicative of the result that the keyword frequency probability multiplied by the state holding probability (p) or state converting probability (1–p).

Starting with the initial state, calculate the probability if the keyword is in state S_0 or S_1. Define that the initial state of the system is with probability q in S_0 state, with probability 1–q in the S_1 state. During the first time interval, the hidden state chain's tail is in state S_0 and S_1 with probability:

$$S_1^0 = R^0(k_1)q$$

$$S_1^1 = R^1(k_1)(1 - q)$$

Then calculate the probability of the system when it is in state S_0 and in state S_1. Suppose the current time is i–1, the system is in S_0 state. The probability of the hidden state chain's tail equals S_0 is W_0, and suppose that when system goes to the time i, the system will convert into state S_1, then the probability of the hidden state chain took place in time i is:

$$W_i^1 = W_{i-1}^0 R^1(k_i)(1 - p) = W_{i-1}^0 S_i^1$$

Known the initial state and the recurrence functional in any conditions, use the method of mathematical induction can easily get the solving formula to calculate any hidden state chain probability of the system:

$$W = \prod_{i=1}^{m} S_i^n$$

m represents the total number of the hidden state, namely the scale of the input data set. For purposes of calculation, taking the logarithm on both sides at the same time, get:

$$T = \ln W = \sum_{i=1}^{m} \ln S_i^n = \sum_{i=1}^{m} (\ln R^n(k_i) + \ln \alpha)$$

T is the objective function which the system is seeking for. How to find a hidden state chain that have the maximum value among all the hidden state chains is the core issue in keyword popularity analysis system.

3.2.2   Seek Maximum

Even the simplest example like 0–1 automaton model, if measured data in dates during a month, the scale of the calculations involved is as much as 2^{31}. Moreover, in the actual case, the unit of time may be hours or minutes, the length of the statistical interval may be a year or even decades. Obviously, the solution that enumerate all the hidden state chain, compared with each other, and then pick up the largest one doesn't have the practical feasibility.

A general approach to find the optimal solution in a huge solution space is the dynamic programming algorithm. So, if a state transition equation can be found to preserve the intermediate results when every time the system steps forward, then the maximum value of the objective function will be easily obtained.

Whenever the system advanced from the current moment to the next moment, the hidden state transfer path has the following four possible ways (Fig. 2):

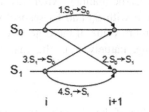

Fig. 2. Possible paths of hidden markov chain

Under the current moment, state S_0 can be maintained from the previous moment's state S_0, or it can be converted from the previous moment's state S_1, S_1 is in a similar way. Thus, find the following two state transition equations:

$$f_0(i) = Max(f_0(i-1)p, f_1(i-1)(1-p))$$

$$f_1(i) = Max(f_0(i-1)(1-p), f_1(i-1)p)$$

p represents state holding probability. $f_n(i)$ represents the ith moment's intermediate results which means the maximum probability of the hidden state chain ending with state S_n at time i. Everytime the system advanced to the next time, it will calculate four values: the product of the probability that system converts to the state S_1 from state S_0 and the probability that the previous moment's intermediate results in state S_0; the product of the probability that system maintains the state S_0 from the previous moment and the probability that the previous moment's intermediate results in state S_0; the product of the probability that system converts to the state S_0 from state S_1 and the probability that the previous moment's intermediate results in state S_1; the product of the probability that system maintains the state S_1 from the previous moment and the probability that the previous moment's intermediate results in state S_1. Divide the four results into two groups by the current state of the system S_0 and S_1. Bring these four values into the corresponding state transition equation by group for comparison, update the current moment's intermediate results with the output results from the equation.

In the above case, if the current moment's intermediate results shows that the two paths are from the previous S_0 to current S_1 and from the previous S_1 to current S_0. Add these two paths to the end of each hidden state chain and updates the intermediate results, as shown below (Fig. 3):

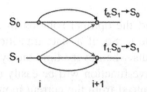

Fig. 3. Two chosen paths from the state transition equations

The rest can be done in the same manner. After traverses all the input, two hidden state chain will be found ending with S_0 and S_1 respectively. The results of the state transition equation is the maximum value of the objective function. Compare these two results and pick the larger one, namely it is the maximum value of the objective function.

3.2.3 Backtracking

After getting the maximum value of the objective function, there is still one final step needed. Backtracking the hidden state chain which makes the objective function gets its maximum value.

Backtracking process needs to know the details at each step when seeking the maximum value of the objective function. For example, the system needs to know from which previous hidden state that the current hidden state got its value. So, use an extra matrix to record the specific information of the hidden state chain every time the system advanced to the next step. Suppose the system has m states and the total number of the steps is n. Naturally, a m * n matrix can be used to record every specific situation during the analysis process.

In this paper, considering the machine A has only two state (S_0, S_1), a two-dimensional array is be chosen to hold the record correspondingly. Just reverse traverse this two-dimensional array and sort out the record, then the hidden state chain path can be got, the sequence of S_0, S_1 which is generated during this process is the result of the keyword popularty analysis system.

3.3 Optimization

When calculating the objective function T, the value of R() and the logarithm of α are the two numbers need to be calculated. Since α which has only two possible values is the input parameter of the system, it is easy to obtain. But when it comes to the logarithmic calculation of the poisson distribution, there will be a huge amount of work. Every step requires four times of the logarithmic calculation. In addition, poisson distribution calculation process will involve factorial operation. It will exceed the upper bound of integer in most operating system when the factorial operation just comes to 20. To the keyword popularity analysis system, most keywords in any website appears Hundreds of thousands of time every day. So, how to optimize the computing is one of the problems in our system need to be solved.

Before starting the process of the calculation, the equation can be transformed into another form:

$$\ln R(k) = \ln \frac{\lambda^k}{k!} \, e^{-\lambda} = k \ln \lambda - \ln k! - \lambda$$

It can be easily found that the key to reduce the computational quantity is to find a simplest way to get ln(k!).

Stirling's formula has important applications in mathematical analysis, number theory, probability theory and other related fields. It is a mathematical formula used to compute the approximation of the factorial of n. In general, if n is too large, the calculation process not only is involved a huge amount of computation, but also reinvent the same and redundant work in most of time. But if the result can be compromised with an approximate value, the workload will be exponentially reduced. With n grows continuously, the approximation is also infinitely close to the true value. Even if the n is small, the output of the Stirling's formula is accurate enough to meet system's requirements.

$$\lim_{n \to \infty} n! = \sqrt{2\pi n}\left(\frac{n}{e}\right)^n$$

$$\ln(n!) = n \ln(n) - n + O(\ln(n))$$

Its principle is to seek a limit of a infinite series called Stirling series, the specific derivation process has already exhibited in the relevant papers. Here just use it as a conclusion and understanding that stirling's approximation (or Stirling's formula) is an approximation for factorials. It is a very powerful approximation, leading to accurate results even for small values of n.

Then, the formula to calculate R() which have mentioned before can be approximated as follows:

$$\ln R(k) \approx k \ln \lambda - k \ln(k) + k - \lambda.$$

4   Result Testing

4.1   Initialization

In order to verify the correctness and accuracy of the keyword popularity analysis system, the raw data is crawled from some portal sites during the April in 2015, then extract some keyword like "stock", "internet", "accident" etc. from the data. Observe and record the frequency of each keyword's occurrence number as the system's input.

Analyze the input data with humans, decide whether the keyword is hot or non-hot in a specific day. The analysis result will be treated as the reference system. Then type the input into the system and get its output.

4.2   Verification

Adjust the state holding probability p, the initial status parameter of the system q, and θ with the different input keywords to make the output coinside the expected output from the reference system as far as possible. The above process needs to be operated repeatedly and iteratively, until the result fit the artificial analysis result or have repeated enough times.

During the verification process, we should also notice about the noise. By adjusting the input data, test the sensitivity of the noise. Analyzing the stability and accuracy of the system and balance them properly (Table 1).

Table 1. Raw data

Date	Freq	Date	Freq	Date	Freq
1	296	11	297	21	167
2	205	12	345	22	159
3	197	13	360	23	114
4	166	14	328	24	73
5	200	15	319	25	203
6	360	16	244	26	362
7	362	17	202	27	390
8	364	18	176	28	363
9	212	19	134	29	321
10	195	20	135	30	308

Table 2. Output and expected status of keyword analysis system

Date	Output	Expected	Date	Output	Expected	Date	Output	Expected
1	S_1	S_1	11	S_1	S_1	21	S_0	S_0
2	S_1	S_0	12	S_1	S_1	22	S_0	S_0
3	S_0	S_0	13	S_1	S_1	23	S_0	S_0
4	S_0	S_0	14	S_1	S_1	24	S_0	S_0
5	S_0	S_0	15	S_1	S_1	25	S_1	S_0
6	S_1	S_1	16	S_0	S_1	26	S_1	S_1
7	S_1	S_1	17	S_0	S_0	27	S_1	S_1
8	S_1	S_1	18	S_0	S_0	28	S_1	S_1
9	S_1	S_0	19	S_0	S_0	29	S_1	S_1
10	S_0	S_0	20	S_0	S_0	30	S_1	S_1

4.3 Analyze Result

When the system's parameters are all be determined after the adjusting process, a new keyword will be typed into the system, then observe whether the system works correctly (Fig. 4 and Table 2).

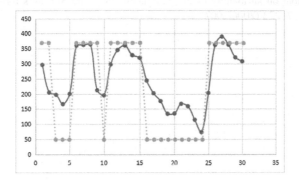

Fig. 4. Control figure

5 Conclusion

This paper introduced the finite state machine as a starting point to analyze the principle of the system which is similar to the keyword analysis system. Use their implementations for reference and improved their disadvantages. By studying the features of the popular keyword, a new system based on Hidden Markov Model has been established. Combined with the probability theory and other related mathematical tools, the paper derived a series of formulas to analyze the new system. Then improved these formulas so that they have the practical feasibility. Adjust the system's parameters by experiment and verified the accuracy of the keyword analysis system. Finally reached the goal which the system is supposed to achieve from the begining.

Acknowledgement. This work was supported by the open project of Science and Technology on Information Transmission and Dissemination in Communication Networks Laboratory (ITD-U14002 /KX142600009).

References

1. Kleinberg, J.: Bursty and hierarchical structure in streams (2001)
2. Zhou, S., ShiQian, X., ChengYi, P.: Probability theory and mathematical statistics, pp. 32–42, 149–172 (2011)
3. Allan, J., Papka, R., Lavrenko, V.: On-line new event detection and tracking. In: Proceedings of SIGIR International Conference Information Retrieval (1998)
4. Rabiner, L.R.: A tutorial on hidden markov models and selected applications in speech recognition. Proc. IEEE **77**(2), 257–286 (1989)

5. Rabiner, L.R., Juang, B.H.: An introduction to HMMs. IEEE ASSP Mag. **3**(1), 4–16 (1986)
6. Viterbi, A.J.: Error bounds for convolutional codes and an asymptotically optimum decoding algorithm. IEEE Trans. Inf. Theory **13**(2), 260–269 (1967)
7. Yang, Y., Ault, T., Pierce, T., Lattimer, C.W.: Improving text categorization methods for event tracking. In: Proceedings of SIGIR International Conference Information Retrieval (2000)
8. Li, Y.-C.: A note on an identity of the gamma function and Stirling's formula. Real Anal. Exch. **32**(1), 267–272 (2006/2007)

Base Station Location Optimization Based on the Google Earth and ACIS

Qingxi Xie[1(✉)], Xiyu Liu[1], and Xuebin Yan[2]

[1] College of Management Science and Engineering,
Shandong Normal University, Jinan, China
{sdqxxie,sdxyliu}@163.com
[2] China United Network Communications Co., Beijing, China
yanxb6@163.com

Abstract. At present, People quickly go into the era of 4 G, which requires vast amounts of 4 G base stations to be established. So How to use the algorithm to layout the base station reasonably in order to save costs for operators has become an important research content. In this context, this paper proposes a new solution–using ACIS and Google Earth techniques to establish a new Telecommunication base station site selection of the CAD system. This system on the basis of predecessors innovatively introduced the reconstructing 3 d terrain simulation system into the base station location optimization problem and used the particle swarm optimization algorithm to solve multi-objective mathematical model of the problem about base station planning problem under the condition of considering the geographic information. It can automatically produce base station primary scheme and showed the primary scheme on the reconstruction of the terrain by ACIS/HOOPS modeling techniques.

Keywords: Base station optimization · CAD system · ACIS · Google earth · PSO

1 Introduction

Telecommunication base station automatic programming system proposed in this paper is based on Windows platform. The development environment includes Microsoft visual studio, Xtreme Toolkit Pro plug-ins, ACIS/HOOPS and Google earth.

The process of solve the problem of base station planning as follows. First, use Microsoft visual studio, Xtreme Toolkit Pro, ACIS/HOOPS to build the development environment. Second, using com technology import Google earth into the development environment and accessing and transforming Google earth coordinates which include longitude, latitude, and elevation. Third, use ACIS/HOOPS technology to reconstruct Three-Dimensional Terrain according to the transformed coordinates. At the same time, establish a multi-objective mathematical model about base station planning according to geographic information and produce base station primary scheme using particle swarm algorithm. At last, it uses ACIS/HOOPS modeling techniques to display the primary scheme on the reconstructed terrain. Structure of the process is shown in Fig. 1:

© Springer International Publishing Switzerland 2016
Q. Zu and B. Hu (Eds.): HCC 2016, LNCS 9567, pp. 487–496, 2016.
DOI: 10.1007/978-3-319-31854-7_44

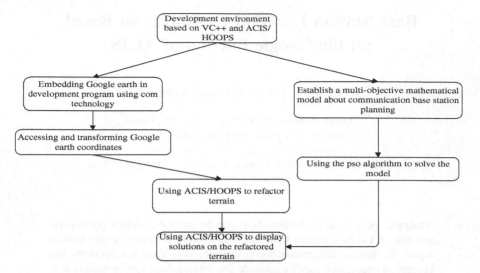

Fig. 1. Flow chart of Base station location Optimization

2 Prerequisites

2.1 Presentation of ACIS

ACIS is a three-dimensional geometric modeling engine based on object-oriented software technology. It is the products of the Spatial Company. It can provide application software system with powerful functions of geometric modelling capabilities.

ACIS is a development platform based on C++ structure graphics system, which includes a series of C++ functions and classes (including data members and methods). Developers can use these classes and functions construct a Three-Dimensional software system for end users.

Wireframe modeling, surface modeling and entity modeling method integrated in the ACIS development platform. And these modeling methods can coexist in a unified data structure. So, an ACIS entity can use one of the above methods and various to display at the same time.

ACIS can Produce, modify, and management entity with ACIS method which include Laws, Graph Theory, Boolean Operations, Surfacing Techniques, Sweeping, Blending, Analysis, SAT file Save and Restore, Part Management, History and Roll and so on.

Simple graphics such as a cone and frustum of a cone can be established by API function such as api_solid_cylinder_cone which provide by ACIS. The following code is a cone of which the bottom circle's center is (0, 0, 1) and radius is 0.2. The following code can be turned into other forms of cone and frustum of a cone if parameters be changed.

```
BODY* my_body = NULL;
outcome result = api_solid_cylinder_cone(
SPAposition(0,0,1),
```

SPAposition(0,0,1.5),
0.2,
0.2,
0.0,
NULL,
my_body);
api_rh_set_entity_rgb((ENTITY*)my_body,rgb_color(0.9412, 1.0000, 1.0000));
HA_Render_Entity((ENTITY*)my_body);

Using the ACIS ten kinds of technology repeatedly can establish Complex graphics. The left of the Fig. 2 is a candlestick; the right of the Fig. 2 is a bridge. These are all established by ACIS technology.

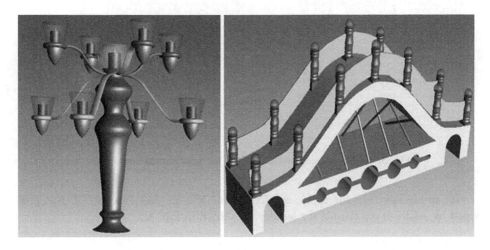

Fig. 2. Candlestick and bridge constructed by ACIS

2.2   Terrain Reconstruction

This system Uses COM technology to get Google earth's CLSID, and then embeds Google earth in development program using CLSID. The key code as follows.

Static const CLSID CLSID_ApplicationGE = {0x8097D7E9,0xDB9E,0x4AEF, {0x9B,0x28,0x61,0xD8,0x2A,0x1D,0xF7,0x84}};

m_geApplication.CreateDispatch(CLSID_ApplicationGE,NULL);

This system accesses terrain coordinates which include longitude, latitude, and elevation by API function provided by Google earth. The key code as follows.

CPointOnTerrainGE gePoint;
gePoint = m_geApplication.GetPointOnTerrainFromScreenCoords(x,y);
double dlon,dlat;
dlon = gePoint.get_Longitude();
dlat = gePoint.get_Latitude();
geoElv = gePoint.get_Altitude();

The left of Fig. 3 is the longitude, latitude, and elevation, the right of Fig. 3 is the Screen coordinates which has been transformed. This system can use Screen coordinates to reconstruct the terrain.

提取的坐标.txt - 记事本	转化后的坐标.txt - 记事本
文件(F) 编辑(E) 格式(O) 查看(V) 帮助(H)	文件(F) 编辑(E) 格式(O) 查看(V) 帮助(H)
B=117.1368314514 L=36.5667285125 H=586.619	x=-1.00 y=-0.34 h=0.0603 d=153.6351
B=117.1368109626 L=36.5681096986 H=551.620	x=-1.00 y=-0.31 h=0.0637 d=153.6351
B=117.1368082894 L=36.5695037791 H=519.053	x=-1.00 y=-0.29 h=0.0591 d=153.6351
B=117.1370588880 L=36.5709938006 H=523.093	x=-1.00 y=-0.26 h=0.0548 d=153.6351
B=117.1372056749 L=36.5724475279 H=512.063	x=-1.00 y=-0.23 h=0.0541 d=153.6351
B=117.1372094143 L=36.5738561587 H=480.158	x=-1.00 y=-0.20 h=0.0625 d=153.6351
B=117.1372113111 L=36.5752700298 H=447.851	x=-1.00 y=-0.17 h=0.0687 d=153.6351
B=117.1371920471 L=36.5766834117 H=412.318	x=-1.00 y=-0.14 h=0.0669 d=153.6351
B=117.1371934390 L=36.5781092538 H=379.669	x=-1.00 y=-0.11 h=0.0657 d=153.6351
B=117.1373017843 L=36.5795705447 H=362.594	x=-1.00 y=-0.09 h=0.0611 d=153.6351
B=117.1377166855 L=36.5811152131 H=390.571	x=-1.00 y=-0.06 h=0.0600 d=153.6351
B=117.1382460489 L=36.5826831009 H=435.556	x=-1.00 y=-0.03 h=0.0581 d=153.6351
B=117.1383989899 L=36.5841543506 H=425.091	x=-1.00 y=0.00 h=0.0539 d=153.6351
B=117.1385012572 L=36.5856163222 H=407.083	x=-1.00 y=0.03 h=0.0496 d=153.6351
B=117.1386738743 L=36.5870961943 H=399.442	x=-1.00 y=0.06 h=0.0453 d=153.6351
B=117.1388491145 L=36.5885779874 H=392.160	x=-1.00 y=0.09 h=0.0477 d=153.6351
B=117.1390586892 L=36.5900672650 H=389.980	x=-1.00 y=0.11 h=0.0508 d=153.6351
B=117.1392687910 L=36.5915570296 H=387.866	x=-1.00 y=0.14 h=0.0547 d=153.6351
B=117.1394648448 L=36.5930450405 H=383.640	x=-1.00 y=0.17 h=0.0513 d=153.6351
B=117.1395281659 L=36.5945156348 H=359.483	x=-1.00 y=0.20 h=0.0576 d=153.6351
B=117.1395437511 L=36.5959848871 H=328.055	x=-1.00 y=0.23 h=0.0604 d=153.6351
B=117.1396546284 L=36.5974704415 H=310.849	x=-1.00 y=0.26 h=0.0545 d=153.6351
B=117.1399127432 L=36.5989731526 H=315.809	x=-1.00 y=0.29 h=0.0511 d=153.6351
B=117.1401941421 L=36.6004767856 H=324.316	x=-1.00 y=0.31 h=0.0506 d=153.6351
B=117.1405393872 L=36.6019829869 H=342.543	x=-1.00 y=0.34 h=0.0502 d=153.6351
B=117.1406021132 L=36.6034711892 H=317.916	x=-1.00 y=0.37 h=0.0498 d=153.6351
B=117.1406761431 L=36.6049645005 H=294.904	x=-1.00 y=0.40 h=0.0493 d=153.6351
B=117.1408770030 L=36.6064650288 H=291.154	x=-1.00 y=0.43 h=0.0469 d=153.6351

Fig. 3. The extracted coordinates and the transformed coordinates

It can use api_face_spl_apprx, api_face_plane and api_loft_faces which was provided by ACIS to reconstruct the terrain. As shown in Fig. 4.

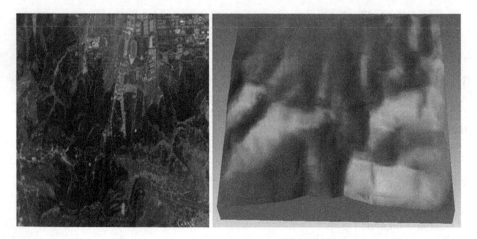

Fig. 4. The actual terrain and the reconstructed terrain

2.3   Particle Swarm Optimization Algorithm

Particle swarm optimization algorithm is an intelligent optimization algorithm which originates from a simulation about a simple social model. It is a kind of representative method of swarm intelligence which has been proposed because of the behavioral pattern of birds group. Some scholars found that the birds' behavior is often unpredictable in the process of flight. They often suddenly spread out, change direction, gathered themselves together but they keep the consistency as a whole and always keep the most suitable distance between individuals. Scholars found that there is a kind of social information sharing mechanism in biological groups in their process of the research on biological groups' behavior. This information sharing mechanism provides advantages for the evolution of the group and it is the basis of Particle swarm optimization algorithm.

Particle swarm optimization algorithm find the global optimal solution by Coordinate between individuals. It takes advantage of the information sharing between the biological groups. Assume the following scenario: A flock of birds search for food randomly in an area. At the beginning, all the birds don't know the specific location of food. But, these birds know the distance from their current position to the food. So how the birds find food? What is its strategy? The easiest and most effective way to search for food is search in the surrounding area of a bird which is Closest to the food. Particle swarm optimization algorithm was inspired from this model and used it to solve optimization problem.

In the particle swarm optimization algorithm, a bird in the search space which is called "particle" is a potential solution for each of optimization problem. Particle swarm optimization algorithm can be abstract as one n dimensional search space and a population Consists of m particle. The first i particle's location represented as an n dimensional vector: $X_i = (x_{i1}, x_{i2}, \ldots, x_{in})$ Each individual as a particle represents a potential solution. The pros and cons of these solutions are determined by the fitness value function which is related to the objective function for the problem. $V_i = (v_{i1}, v_{i2}, \ldots, v_{in})$, is the speed of the particle i; $P_i = (p_{i1}, p_{i2}, \ldots, p_{in})$ is the best location for particle i experienced; $P_g = (p_{g1}, p_{g2}, \ldots, p_{gn})$ is the best location that the whole particle swarm search for so far. $f(x_{ij}^k)$ is the particle i's objective function of the first j dimensional in the first k iteration. So, we can get the particle's velocity and position updating formula:

$$v_{ij}^{k+1} = v_{ij}^k + c_1 \alpha (p_{ij}^k - x_{ij}^k) + c_2 \beta (p_{gj}^k - x_{ij}^k) \tag{1}$$

$$x_{ij}^k = x_{ij}^k + v_{ij}^{k+1} \tag{2}$$

In the formula, v_{ij}^k is the particle i's speed of the first j dimensional in the first k iteration; p_{ij}^k is the particle i's best location of the first j dimensional in the first k iteration; $\alpha (p_{ij}^k - x_{ij}^k)$ is the part of "cognitive" of the first j dimensional expresses the particles themselves thinking, and $\beta (p_{gj}^k - x_{ij}^k)$ is the part of "social" of the first j dimensional expresses information sharing between the particles. c_1 expresses the influence of particle velocity created by "cognitive" part, c_2 expresses the influence of particle velocity created by "social" part. They are all constant which usually take to number two. α and β are all random number evenly distributed in the interval $[0, 1]$. They are used to maintain the diversity of population. When it reaches the largest number of iterations or gets the global optimal solution that meet the requirement of error for this specific question the iteration will be end. The basic particle swarm algorithm's flow chart is Fig. 5.

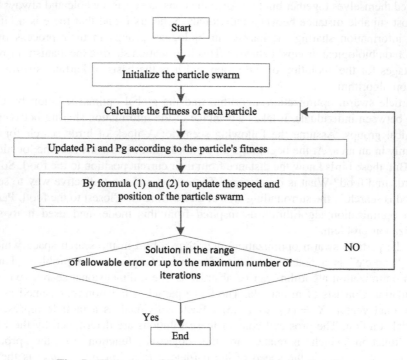

Fig. 5. Flow chart of Particle swarm optimization algorithm

3   Implementation of the Telecommunication Base Station Planning

3.1   Multi-objective Planning of Telecommunication Base Station

Telecommunication base station Select the address usually considering from Coverage, capacity and cost. The objectives are as follows:

The Objective of Coverage. Many network operators put forward an optimized goal is coverage. Coverage objective refers to the quality goals that meet the area network quality requirements. It mainly includes business quality, coverage probability and soft switching. Business quality refers to the clarity of the signal or the throughput rate of effective information. Coverage probability shows the percentage of an area covering area of total area. Soft switching rate is mainly used to reflect the effective utilization rate of resources.

The Objective of Capacity. Capacity is the key characteristics to the wireless network performance. It was used to describe the number of users that the system can meet. It is often associated with network costs. Operators minimize costs on the basis of the number of users that need to be service or maximize service users on the basis of the basic facilities budget. Features of the capacity are very dependent on available service types and their quality requirements.

The Objective of Cost. The cost of the network is an important optimization target. The cost of each station is usually fixed for the positioning of the base station or site given. But it accounts for two-thirds of the total investment. So the cost target is the chief problem that operator usually consider of. Reduce cost and save money is one of the important goals of network construction.

3.2 Particle Swarm Algorithm Coding Principle and Mathematical Model

Base station site selection should not only consider the position of the base station, but also consider the set of base station itself. Considering the base station parameters are: base station location, height of base station and transmission power and so on. So the base station information can be said with a point. That is a particle in the particle swarm. The encoding is shown below:

$$\sigma = \begin{bmatrix} Location\ of\ the base\ station \\ Height\ of\ the\ base\ station \\ Transmission\ power \end{bmatrix}$$

According to objectives of the base station planning to establish mathematical model .4 G base stations optimization deployment of Jinan southern mountains somewhere is the simulation environment. The region covers an area of 8 km * 8 km. The height of the base station is 40 to 50 m. The base station location is x, y, z screen coordinates that transformed from Longitude, latitude and elevation coordinates that provided by Google Earth. The base station transmission power is 40-50 w. Mathematical model is as follows:

$$minF_1 = |\Omega| \tag{3}$$

s.t.

$$\sum_{j \in J} p_{ij} \leq P_{max}, i \in \Omega \tag{4}$$

$$n_i \leq n_{max} * \eta^k, (x_i, y_i, z_i) \in D^k, k = \{0, 1, 2\} \tag{5}$$

$$\sum_{i=1}^{n} \left(\frac{S_i^k}{S^k}\right)^* = r^k, k = \{0, 1, 2\} \tag{6}$$

$$(x_i, y_i) \in D \qquad\qquad (7)$$

The objective function of the model (3) indicates a minimum number of the base station that meet all the constraint. The formula (4) indicates the down link power allocation. The power sum of each user in the village cannot exceed the maximum effective power of the base station. The formula (5) indicates the general user n_i cannot exceed the allowed maximum number of users. n_i's calculation is first to judgment where area that the base station belong to. Then calculated according to the distance between the user points that around the base station and base station. From the nearest user point, join them into the set of user point that the base station covers, until the number of user points up to $n_{max}\eta^k$. The formula (6) indicates coverage area must be completely covered. The preceding paragraph indicates the Preliminary selection sum of each base station's effective coverage ratio. The formula (7) indicates the scope of the decision variables. As can be seen by above method, P_{ij}, n_i can be classified as the function of (x_i, y_i, z_i), Therefore the model decision variables actually include coordinate variables only, and other variables can be as intermediate variables.

3.3   Primary Scheme Displays on the Reconstructed Terrain

It is concluded that primary scheme of base station planning by using particle swarm optimization algorithm. And then it shows the primary scheme on the reconstruction of the terrain by ACIS/HOOPS modeling techniques. In Fig. 6, use cone instead of base station. The left of Fig. 6 let the base station distributed on the terrain uniformly, and up to complete coverage of signal. However, the principle of we build base station don't usually built on top of the mountain. Because it is easy to create a "black under the tower", lead to signal blind area. And the base station should be built in the center of densely populated areas, so that it can achieve the most efficient.

Base station planning also should take Consider of the problem of population. High population density areas should be built multiple base stations so that it can meet everyone's need.

The right of the Fig. 6 is the primary scheme which created by Particle swarm optimization algorithm Particle swarm optimization algorithm. we can see that Base stations almost located in densely populated areas and the number of base stations distributed in densely populated areas has increased . It meets the general principles of the base station planning.

The terrain is 8 km * 8 km area, Coverage radius of base station signal is 1 km. The Fig. 7 is Signal overlays. The left of Fig. 7 corresponding to the left of Fig. 6, and the right of Fig. 7 corresponding to the right of Fig. 6. They are all reached full coverage. But the left of Fig. 7 does not think about the capacity obviously, and it is Easy to generate signal blind area. We can see that from the right of the Fig. 7 that Signal overlap in densely populated areas. So, it can meet the need of people. And the base station was built in the center of densely populated areas.

Fig. 6. Initial base station location and optimized base station location

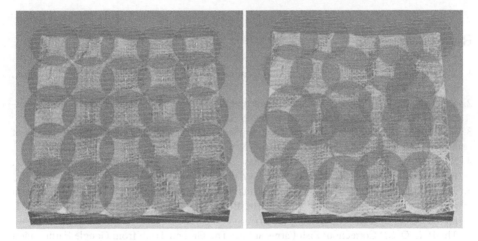

Fig. 7. Preliminary single cover and single cover optimization

4 Conclusion

With the deepening of 4 G technology, through analyze the previous base station planning mode; this paper proposes a new solution–using ACIS and Google Earth techniques to establish a new Telecommunication base station site selection of the CAD system. This system on the basis of predecessors innovatively introduced the reconstructing 3 d terrain simulation system into the base station location optimization problem and used the particle swarm algorithm to solve multi-objective mathematical model of the problem about base station planning problem under the condition of considering the geographic information. It can automatically produce base station primary scheme and showed the primary scheme on the reconstruction of the terrain by ACIS/HOOPS modeling techniques. The system has certain application value.

This paper still exist deficiencies, Particle swarm optimization algorithm is still exist a lot of limitations. When the algorithm goes into the middle state, the speed of the particles becomes smaller and smaller, until close to zero in the end. Cause particle position not update, the whole may fall into local optimum. So, the particle swarm algorithm should be improved in the future, and then apply it into the base station planning.

Acknowledgment. Project supported by National Natural Science Foundation of China (61170038), Natural science foundation of Shandong Province, China (ZR2011FM001), Technology development projects of Shandong province, China (2012G0020314), Soft science research project of Shandong Province, China (2013RZB01019), Jinan City independent innovation plan project in Colleges and Universities, China (201401202), Ministry of education of Humanities and social science research projects, China (12YJA630152), Social Science Fund Project of Shandong Province, China (11CGLJ22), outstanding youth scientist foundation project of Shandong Province, China (BS2013DX037), young star of science and technology plan project, Jinan (20120108), science and technology development project, Jinan (201211003), science and technology development project, Jinan (201305004).

References

1. Vannucci, G., DeMont, J.P.: Base station location derived from wireless terminal information. U.S. Patent No. 9,078,229, 7 July 2015
2. Kennedy, J., Eberhart, R.: Particle swarm optimization. In: Proceedings of the IEEE International Conference on Neural Networks, pp. 1942–1947 (1995)
3. Kennedy, J.: Particle swarm optimization. In: Sammut, C., Webb, G.I. (eds.) Encyclopedia of Machine Learning, pp. 760–766. Springer, New York (2010)
4. Shihai, S., et al.: Optimal location of the base station based on measured interference power. In: 2015 IEEE International on Wireless Symposium (IWS). IEEE (2015)
5. Ren, S., Li, X., Liu, X.: The 3D visual research of improved DEM data based on Google earth and ACIS. In: Zu, Q., Vargas-Vera, M., Hu, B. (eds.) ICPCA/SWS 2013. LNCS, vol. 8351, pp. 497–507. Springer, Heidelberg (2014)
6. The P. L. O. S. "Correction: Fish Farms at Sea: The Ground Truth from Google Earth." PloS one, 10(7) (2015)

Efficient Multiple-Reference Temporal Error Concealment Algorithm Based on H.264/AVC

Chen Yu[✉], Chao Cheng, Hai Jin, and Jingli Zhou

Services Computing Technology and System Lab, Cluster and Grid Computing
Lab, School of Computer Science and Technology, Huazhong University
of Science and Technology, Wuhan 430074, China
yuchen@hust.edu.cn

Abstract. Temporal error concealment at the video communication receiver recovers damaged blocks using temporal information redundancy. To enhance the quality of reconstructed image, a multiple-reference temporal error concealment algorithm based on H.264/AVC was proposed. Firstly, a pre-concealment is implemented to improve video frame; then the fractional pixel boundary matching algorithm and search algorithm are used to evaluate the candidate motion vectors from a number of reference frames, and the motion vector (MV) giving the minimum boundary matching distortion (MBMD) is selected as optimal motion vector; finally it is used to recover the damaged block and the video frame quality can be improved further. For various video sequences and different macro-block loss ratio, experimental results show that the proposed algorithm is significantly better than traditional temporal error concealment algorithms such as BMA and BM from both objectively and subjectively. At the loss ratio of 10 %, improvements of the proposed algorithm are more than $0.8 \sim 3.7$ dB compared to that of other algorithms.

Keywords: Temporal domain · Multiple-reference · Fractional pixel · Boundary matching · Search algorithm

1 Introduction

With the rapid development of multimedia and mobile communication technology, the application of video communication has become an inevitable trend. However, in wireless mobile channels, code error and data loss are always difficult to avoid, and compressed video data is very sensitive to the code error, so a small amount of errors may lead to a large number of codes' incorrect decoding. To control and reduce the effect of transmission errors, error concealment technology is used (H.264/AVC) to maximize the recovery of the damaged blocks [1, 2].

Error concealment technique at the video receiver recovers damaged blocks using temporal and spatial information redundancy in video transmission signal. When error occurs during the transmission, receiver uses the correct decoding information to improve image quality via reconstructed damaged block. Common error concealment algorithms are divided into temporal and spatial error concealment algorithms [3]. The former makes use of temporal information redundancy to estimated MV of the

© Springer International Publishing Switzerland 2016
Q. Zu and B. Hu (Eds.): HCC 2016, LNCS 9567, pp. 497–509, 2016.
DOI: 10.1007/978-3-319-31854-7_45

damaged block and this MV is used to conceal the damaged block. The latter recovers damaged block using its neighboring blocks.

The critical step of temporal error concealment is to correctly estimate MV of the damaged block. The commonly used technique is to replace the damaged motion vector with (0, 0) [4]. This technique is referred to as temporal replacement (TR). Another technique is to replace the damaged motion vector with the median of neighboring vectors [5]. To choose the proper MV among candidate vectors, a boundary matching algorithm (BMA) has been suggested in [6]. A concealment algorithm based on block matching (BM) is proposed in [7].

In H.264/AVC video standard, a more precise and flexible inter-frame prediction method is introduced [8]. E.g., multiple-reference takes the place of single-reference, accuracy prediction of 1/4 pixel and 1/8 pixel replace that of integer pixel, 4×4 integer transform replaces discrete cosine transform (DCT), etc. In [9], a multiple-reference concealment algorithm based on motion field interpolation (MFI) is suggested. In this method, all the pixels in the damaged block are interpolated one by one, but calculation of each pixel need to know the MV of all the neighboring blocks and it may causes long delay, so this method is not suitable for real-time mobile channel.

According to the new features of H.264/AVC, a multiple-reference temporal error concealment algorithm is proposed. Firstly, a pre-concealment is implemented to improve video frame; then the weighted boundary matching algorithm based on fractional pixel and search algorithm are used to evaluate the candidate motion vectors from a number of reference frames (In this paper, reference frame number is 5), and the candidate MV giving the minimum boundary matching distortion is selected as the optimal MV; finally this MV is used to recover the damaged block and the video frame quality can be improved further.

Part II discusses the multiple-reference temporal error concealment algorithm. Part III presents the experiments and discussion and the conclusions are given at last.

2   Multiple-Reference Temporal Concealment

2.1   Pre-concealment of the Damaged Macro-Block

As described previously, the BMA, BM and MFI algorithms respectively mentioned in [6, 7, 9] only use the neighboring available blocks to do boundary matching, and the concealed blocks are used to provide candidate concealments. The disadvantage is that it doesn't make full use of the information of neighboring blocks, and there is likely to cause big boundary matching distortion and unsmooth matching between the final motion compensated block (MCB) and the available blocks. To resolve the problem, a pre-concealment method is implemented to improve video frame quality and then the improved boundary matching algorithm is used to evaluate candidate MVs of the damaged block.

The idea of pre-concealment is to do simple motion vector estimation and motion compensation for every damaged block. The current damaged block is denoted by $MB_{current}$ and the block in previous frame that has the same position with $MB_{current}$ is denoted by MB_{ahead}. MB_{up} and MB_{down} denote the blocks that are above and under

$MB_{current}$. (1) If the movement of MV of MB_{ahead} is not more than 8 pixels at x and y direction, the estimated MV of $MB_{current}$ is assigned to that of MB_{ahead}. (2) Otherwise, if MB_{up} is available and isn't boundary block of the current frame, the estimated MV of $MB_{current}$ is assigned to that of MB_{up}. (3) Otherwise, if MB_{down} is available and isn't boundary block, the estimated MV of $MB_{current}$ is assigned to that of MB_{down}. (4) Otherwise, the MV of $MB_{current}$ is assigned to that of MB_{ahead}.

2.2   Set of Candidate Motion Vectors

In this paper, as shown in Fig. 1, the coding modes of the neighboring vertical and horizontal blocks.

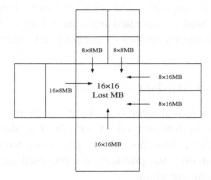

Fig. 1. Candidate motion vectors

The set of candidate motion vectors can be obtained by calculation, which is denoted by C. The motion vectors of the vertical and horizontal blocks, e.g.: the motion vectors of 8 × 8, 16 × 16, 16 × 8 and 8 × 16 coding mode as shown in Fig. 1.

- Zero motion vector [4].
- Mean motion vector [5], that is:

$$\begin{cases} mv_x = \frac{1}{N} \sum_{i=0}^{N-1} mv_x^i \\ mv_y = \frac{1}{N} \sum_{i=0}^{N-1} mv_y^i \end{cases} \tag{1}$$

- Median motion vector [5], that is:

$$\begin{cases} mv_x = Median(mv_x^i, i = 0, 1, \ldots, N-1) \\ mv_y = Median(mv_y^i, i = 0, 1, \ldots, N-1) \end{cases} \tag{2}$$

Among them, mv_x^i and mv_y^i are the coordinates x and y of the motion vectors, and N is the total number of the motion vectors of the available blocks.

2.3   1/4 Pixel Interpolation

The accuracy of the MV in H.264 is 1/4 pixel. In order to make full use of it, 1/4 pixel interpolation can be used for the reference frames. The rules of interpolation methods and H.264 standard decoding process are same [8], that is, half-pixel interpolation of the luminance signal uses six-order FIR filter and quarter-pixel interpolation of the luminance signal uses linear interpolation. Because the change of color difference signal is lower than that of luminance signal and humans' eyes are not sensitive on the color difference signal, we only use luminance signal for boundary matching. To reduce the complexity of the algorithm, the color difference signal doesn't use 1/4 pixel interpolation. It can be directly concealed from the reference frame that hasn't been interpolated by using the motion vectors of integer-pixel accuracy.

2.4   Proposed Boundary Matching Algorithm

When there exist edges or spatial sampling ratio is not high enough to cope with the rapid gray level change in the original image, the boundary matching algorithm (BMA) [6] and side matching algorithm (SMA) don't work properly when pixel values change abruptly. To overcome the problem, we proposed an improved, robust and efficient boundary matching algorithm.

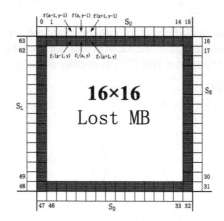

Fig. 2. Optimized boundary matching algorithm

The four neighboring blocks of damaged 16×16 block, including available blocks, concealed blocks and pre-concealed blocks, have 64 boundary integer-pixels. According to a clockwise sequence, assume that their ID are $0, 1, \ldots, 63$ from the upper-left corner. As shown in Fig. 2, the variations between the current image block and the one above it is denoted by S_U, where $f_1(x - 1, y)$, $f_1(x, y)$ and $f_1(x + 1, y)$ are the boundary integer pixel value of inside and $f(x - 1, y - 1)$, $f(x, y - 1)$ and $f(x + 1, y + 1)$ are the boundary integer pixel values of outside. S_U is defined as:

$$S_U = \sum_{i=0}^{15} \min\{Diff_1^i, Diff_2^i, Diff_3^i, Diff_4^i, Diff_5^i, Diff_6^i, Diff_7^i\} \tag{3}$$

In Eq. (3), $Diff_1$, $Diff_2$ and $Diff_3$ are the difference between inside and outside boundary integer pixel values and they are respectively defined as:

$$\begin{cases} Diff_1 = |f_1(x, y) - f(x - 1, y - 1)| \\ Diff_2 = |f_1(x, y) - f(x, y - 1)| \\ Diff_3 = |f_1(x, y) - f(x + 1, y - 1)| \end{cases} \tag{4}$$

$Diff_4$, $Diff_5$, $Diff_6$ and $Diff_7$ are the difference between the integer pixel value and sub-pixel value or the integer pixel value and quarter-pixel value. They are respectively defined as:

$$\begin{cases} Diff_4 = |f_1(x, y) - f_{\frac{1}{2}}(x - 1, y)| \\ Diff_5 = |f_1(x, y) - f_{\frac{1}{2}}(x + 1, y)| \\ Diff_6 = |f_1(x, y) - f_{\frac{1}{4}}(x - 1, y)| \\ Diff_7 = |f_1(x, y) - f_{\frac{1}{4}}(x + 1, y)| \end{cases} \tag{5}$$

In Eq. (5), $f_{1/2}(x-1,y)$ and $f_{1/2}(x + 1,y)$ are sub-pixel value and $f_{1/4}(x-1,y)$ and $f_{1/4}(x + 1,y)$ are the quarter-pixel value, they can be calculated by Eq. (6).

$$\begin{cases} f_{\frac{1}{2}}(x - 1, y) = \frac{1}{4}[f(x - 1, y - 1) + f(x, y - 1) \\ \qquad\qquad + f_1(x - 1, y) + f_1(x, y)] \\ f_{\frac{1}{2}}(x + 1, y) = \frac{1}{4}[f(x + 1, y - 1) + f(x, y - 1) \\ \qquad\qquad + f_1(x + 1, y) + f_1(x, y)] \\ f_{\frac{1}{4}}(x - 1, y) = \frac{1}{8}[3f(x - 1, y - 1) + 3f(x, y - 1) \\ \qquad\qquad + f_1(x - 1, y) + f_1(x, y)] \\ f_{\frac{1}{4}}(x + 1, y) = \frac{1}{8}[3f(x + 1, y - 1) + 3f(x, y - 1) \\ \qquad\qquad + f_1(x + 1, y) + f_1(x, y)] \end{cases} \tag{6}$$

Similarly, the variations between the current block and its left and right blocks and the one below it are denoted by S_D, S_L and S_R (as shown in Fig. 2), which are defined as:

$$S_R = \sum_{i=16}^{31} \min\{Diff_1^i, Diff_2^i, Diff_3^i, Diff_4^i, Diff_5^i, Diff_6^i, Diff_7^i\} \tag{7}$$

$$S_D = \sum_{i=32}^{47} \min\{Diff_1^i, Diff_2^i, Diff_3^i, Diff_4^i, Diff_5^i, Diff_6^i, Diff_7^i\} \tag{8}$$

$$S_L = \sum_{i=48}^{63} \min\{Diff_1^i, Diff_2^i, Diff_3^i, Diff_4^i, Diff_5^i, Diff_6^i, Diff_7^i\} \tag{9}$$

To make full use of the correctness of the neighboring blocks, a weighted method is introduced in boundary matching. The total variation SAD is defined as:

$$SAD = W_U S_U + W_D S_D + W_L S_L + W_R S_R \tag{10}$$

Among them, W_U, W_D, W_L and W_R are the weighted values of the boundary matching variations. According to status of the neighboring blocks, W_U, W_D, W_L and W_R can be assigned to one of the three values, which are 1, 1/4 and 1/8. (1) If it comes from correctly decoded information block, chooses 1, (2) If the concealed block, chooses 1/4; (3) If the pre-concealed block (Sect. 2.1), chooses 1/8.

2.5 Proposed Search Algorithm

To find the MV that makes SAD obtain the minimum value in a number of reference frames more accurately and quickly, we need to set up the search range of boundary matching and take advantage of suitable search algorithm. Under ordinary conditions, search range is selected as rectangular window and full search (FS) algorithm mentioned in is used to give the global optimum solution to the motion estimation. In order to reduce the search time further, the cross search and diamond search algorithms are respectively proposed.

To improve the efficiency of searching motion vector, an efficient cross-diamond search algorithm for fast block matching motion estimation based on multiple-reference is presented in this paper. As shown in Fig. 3, four kinds of search patterns such as cross search, small diamond search, horizontal diamond search and vertical diamond search need to be used in the proposed algorithm.

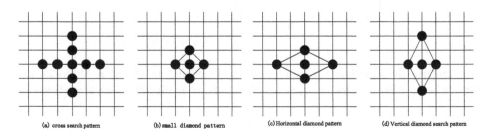

(a) cross search pattern   (b) small diamond pattern   (c) Horizontal diamond pattern   (d) Vertical diamond search pattern

Fig. 3. Four kinds of search patterns

Assume that the set of candidate motion vectors $C = \{mv_1, mv_2,..., mv_n\}$, and $mv_i = (mv_x^i, mv_y^i)$, $1 < i < n$, and the upper-left coordinate of the 16×16 damaged block is (x_0, y_0).

Step1. For each (mv_x^i, mv_y^i) of set C, the original coordinate (x_0, y_0) changes into $(4x_0 + mv_x^i, 4y_0 + mv_y^i)$ after 1/4 pixel interpolation and take it as the upper-left coordinate, we set up 16×16 block which has the same size with the damaged block. The total variations SAD between this block and the neighboring blocks of the damaged block can be work out by Eq. (10) and take the MV which makes SAD obtain the minimum value in the set of candidate motion vectors C as the candidate optimal MV of every reference frame, denoted by MV_C.

Step2. Take the pixel point of MV_C as the center point (origin of coordinate (0, 0)) and test it and its 8 nearby points which are combined as a cross (cross search pattern). Calculating boundary matching distortion by using Eq. (10), as shown in Fig. 4(a), if the minimum boundary matching distortion (MBMD) point is located at the center position, MV_C is selected as the candidate optimal MV of this current reference frame, and go to end; otherwise go to step3.

Step3. Test the two points selected from the set $\{(1, 1), (1, -1), (-1, 1), (-1, -1)\}$ and have the shortest distance with MBMD point. Then compare the two points with the MBMD point which generated in the previous step, as shown in Fig. 4(b), if the new MBMD point of the three is located at one of the coordinates of $\{(0, 1), (0, -1), (1, 0), (-1, 0)\}$, take the MV of MBMD point as the candidate optimal MV of this current reference frame, and go to end; otherwise go to step 4.

Step4. Take the two points that test in previous step and another three points on the cross to compose a small diamond. If the MBMD point of the five is in the horizontal direction, horizontal diamond pattern is selected to search the new MBMD points; if the MBMD point of the five is in the vertical direction, the vertical diamond pattern is selected. Then we judge whether the new MBMD point is the center point, if it is, go to step 6, otherwise go to step 5.

Step5. Take the new MBMD point as the center point to search optimal point, if it is in the horizontal direction of diamond in previous step, horizontal diamond pattern is selected, otherwise vertical diamond pattern is selected. In this step, if the new MBMD point is the center point go to step 6, recursively repeat this step until MBMD point located in the center position.

Step6. Take the MBMD point which generated in step4 or step5 as the center point to do search by using small diamond pattern, and the point has the minimum boundary matching distortion is selected as the candidate optimal MV of the current frame and the search process is end. Figure 4(c) shows the whole search process of the cross-diamond search algorithm.

For the 5 reference frames, the candidate MV of every reference frame can be found by above-mentioned algorithm, and its motion compensated block is denoted by B_k $(1 \leq k \leq 5)$. In these blocks, the one that makes SAD obtain the minimum value is used to recover the damaged block. $B' = \arg\min\{SAD(B_k)\}$

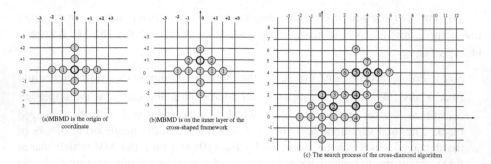

Fig. 4. The search process of the cross-diamond search algorithm.

2.6   The Concealment of Damaged Macro-Block

From the analysis above, the MV that corresponds to the block B' is the optimal MV in the whole search process and let (m_x, m_y) denote it. Assume that $Y_{M,FP}(x, y)$ is the Y component value at coordinates (x, y) after 1/4 pixel interpolation. $U_M(x, y)$ and $V_M(x, y)$ are the U and V component values at coordinate (x, y) when reference frame is not interpolated, so the concealed Y, U and V component values of the damaged block are as follows:

$$\begin{cases} Y(x,y) = Y_{M,FP}(4x + m_x, 4y + m_y) \\ U(x,y) = U_M(x + \frac{m_x}{4}, y + \frac{m_y}{4}) \\ V(x,y) = V_M(x + \frac{m_x}{4}, y + \frac{m_y}{4}) \end{cases} \tag{11}$$

In Eq. (11), x and y are in the range of $x_0 \le x < x_0 + 16$, $y_0 \le y < y_0 + 16$.

3   Simulation Results and Discussions

In the experiment, H.264/AVC standard test model JM15.0 was used to simulate the situation of packet loss of the video compression code streaming in the network transmission. In the same packet loss ratio, three temporal error concealment algorithms which are the proposed multiple-reference temporal error concealment (MTEC), boundary matching-based algorithm (BMA) and error concealment based on block matching (BM) had been compared on different sequences to show the effects.

Five different QCIF (176 × 144) coding sequences, each of 100 frames, were used: FOREMAN, MOBILE, MISS, CLAIRE and COASTGUARD. The flexible macro-block order (FMO) technique in H.264/AVC standard was used that the consecutive macro-block loss caused by packet loss was converted to dispersive macro-block loss. Each test sequence used IPPP frame format to encode and the macro-blocks in I-frame were not lost and the loss ratio of P-frames were as follows: 2 %, 5 % and 10 %. The loss ratio of 2 % means that 2 % of macro-blocks were damaged per frame. Quantization parameter (QP) is 28. We calculate the average peak signal to noise ratio (PSNR) values after damaged frames in the sequences had been concealed. We take the average value of the experimental results in 30 times as the ultimate objective evaluation criteria.

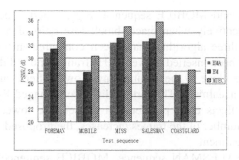

Fig. 5. The comparison of the average PSNR of three algorithms

Table 1 shows the average PSNR values of five different video sequences at the loss ratio of 2 %, 5 % and 10 %. And Fig. 5 shows the comparison of the average PSNR of three algorithms at the loss ratio 10 %. The performance of the boundary matching-based algorithm (BMA) and block matching algorithm (BM) are not as good as the proposed multiple-reference temporal error concealment algorithm (MTEC) for the damaged P-frame in different sequences. The proposed algorithm has better adaptability and it can recover the video information more clearly. For the sequence of simple scene and texture, such as MISS, the concealed PSNR of ASEC are 0.73∼3.02 dB and 0.59∼2.24 dB larger than that of BMA and BM respectively; for the sequence of more complex exercises as well as more details, such as MOBILE, the proposed algorithm has better effect of concealment. At the loss ratio of 10 %, compared with BMA, improvements are 1.22∼3.75 dB and compared with BM the values are 0.34∼2.53 dB.

Table 1. Simulation results for different macroblock loss ratio

Video sequences	Algorithms	PSNR/dB		
		2 %	5 %	10 %
FOREMAN	BMA	35.24	34.76	31.93
	BM	36.12	34.58	31.47
	MTEC	36.46	35.32	33.19
MOBILE	BMA	31.14	29.27	26.51
	BM	32.27	30.49	27.73
	MTEC	33.36	31.38	30.26
MISS	BMA	35.58	33.06	32.48
	BM	36.83	35.23	33.12
	MTEC	37.79	36.57	34.94
SALESMAN	BMA	39.56	37.85	32.69
	BM	40.14	38.42	33.03
	MTEC	40.73	39.27	35.71
COASTGUARD	BMA	32.67	29.74	27.35
	BM	32.42	28.22	25.84
	MTEC	33.59	30.56	28.08

For SALESMAN and MOBILE sequence, Figs. 6 and 7 depict PSNR of each concealed frame respectively when macro-block loss ratio of 5 % occurs. The concealed results of the three algorithms have been compared in the front 40 damaged P-frames. I-frame had been inserted in every 20 P-frames and it didn't have packet loss. The P-frames that are close to the I-frame have lower effects and they have higher PSNR values after concealment. The farther distance damaged P-frame is away from I-frame, the greater effects error proliferation causes, the lower PSNR values after concealment. As the number of the frames increases, the proposed algorithm can obtain better results of concealment.

Compared with SALESMAN sequence, MOBILE sequence has more complex exercises and intense scenes. And when the damaged P-frames are concealed by BMA, BM and the proposed MTEC algorithms respectively in different sequences. As shown in Figs. 6 and 7, for SALESMAN sequence, the downward trends of three algorithms are almost the same; and for MOBILE sequence, the decreasing rate of BMA and BM are larger than that of MTEC.

For MISS sequence, Fig. 8 compares the subjective quality of concealed image in the forty-second frame by using BMA, BM and MTEC algorithms respectively when macro-block loss ratio of 10 % occurs. As show in the Fig. 8, the proposed algorithm shows substantial improvement over the existing methods and the concealment of the subjective image quality is closest to the original image, but the quality of the three image are clear and the effect are not obvious.

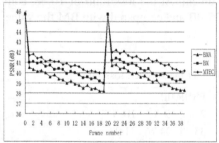

Fig. 6. PSNR of three temporal concealment algorithms for SALESMAN when macro-block loss ratio of 5 % occurs

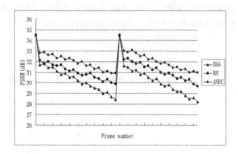

Fig. 7. PSNR of three temporal concealment algorithms for MOBILE when macro-block loss ratio of 5 % occurs

For MOBILE sequence, Fig. 9 compares the subjective quality of concealed image in the eighth frame by using BMA, BM and MTEC algorithms respectively when macro-block loss ratio of 10 % occurs. MOBILE sequence has the most complicated scenes and intense exercises, and it contains more rich information. In the Fig. 9, the difference of subjective quality of the three concealed image in MOBILE sequence is more obvious than that of MISS sequence. In MOBILE and MISS sequence, the PSNR of MTEC is 3.53 dB and 2.56 dB larger than that of BMA, while the PSNR of MTEC is 4.18 dB and 1.69 dB larger than that of BM. The proposed algorithm shows

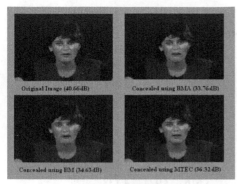

Fig. 8. The comparison of subjective quality of concealed image for MISS when macro-block loss ratio of 10 % occurs

Fig. 9. The comparison of subjective quality of concealed image for MOBILE when macro-block loss ratio of 10 % occurs

improvement over the existing methods and the concealment of the subjective image quality is closest to the original image.

Table 2 shows the average decoding time of five different video sequences at the loss ratio of 10 % and these test sequences are respectively 50, 100 and 200 frames. Figure 10 shows the comparison of the decoding time when the length of test sequence is 100 frames. When the frame number is 50, the decoding time of MTEC is little longer than that of BMA and BM, while in some special cases such as MISS sequence of 50 frames, MTEC has the least decoding time; when the frame number increases to 100 and 200, the decoding time of MTEC increases more slowly and it is $0.4 \sim 0.9$ s longer than the decoding time of BMA and BM.

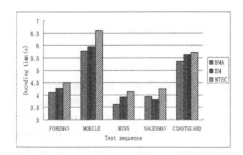

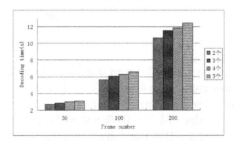

Fig. 10. The comparison of the decoding time of three algorithms

Fig. 11. The average decoding time of MTEC when using different reference number

Table 3 shows the average decoding time of two different video sequences such as MOBILE and SALESMAN when using different reference number of MTEC at the loss ratio of 10 % and these test sequences are respectively 50, 100 and 200 frames. Figure 11 shows the average decoding time of MTEC when using different reference

Table 2. Decoding time of different temporal error concealment algorithms

Video sequence	Frame number	Decoding time/s		
		BMA	BM	MTEC
FOREMAN	50	1.825	1.839	1.901
	100	4.105	4.276	4.508
	200	8.547	8.396	9.204
MOBILE	50	2.845	2.937	3.109
	100	5.769	5.942	6.593
	200	11.566	11.935	12.463
MISS	50	1.809	1.876	1.781
	100	3.616	3.924	4.138
	200	7.428	7.873	8.069
SALESMAN	50	1.792	1.674	1.930
	100	3.939	3.817	4.252
	200	7.861	7.529	8.538
COASTGUARD	50	2.562	2.746	2.837
	100	5.348	5.623	5.714
	200	10.886	11.430	11.791

Table 3. Decoding time of MTEC algorithm when using different reference number

Video sequence	Frame number	Decoding time/s		
		2	3	4
MOBILE	50	2.684	2.860	2.985
	100	5.651	6.085	6.263
	200	10.682	11.524	11.839
SALESMAN	50	1.581	1.758	1.841
	100	3.594	3.774	4.048
	200	7.146	7.872	8.094

number. It can be seen that when the reference number decreases to 4, the decoding time can reduce 4 % ~ 5 % compared to that of the 5 reference frame; when decreases to 3, the decoding time can reduce 7 % ~ 9 %; when decreases to 2, the decoding time can reduce 14 % ~ 16 % and in this case, the decoding time of MTEC is less than that of BM and BMA in Table 2, but the cost is the PSNR of these concealed image are less than that of 5 reference number.

4 Conclusion

A temporal error concealment algorithm based on multiple-reference was proposed in this paper. The proposed algorithm uses H.264/AVC new features: multiple-reference frames, 1/4 pixel interpolation, etc. In addition, it optimized the boundary matching algorithm and search method. The proposed algorithm can obtain better image quality. The experimental results show that it has strong adaptability and is significantly better than traditional H.264/AVC algorithms like BMA, SMA and BM from both objectively and subjectively.

Acknowledgement. The work is partly supported by NSFC (No. 61472149), the Fundamental Research Funds for the Central Universities (2015QN67) and the National 863 Hi-Tech Research and Development Program under grant (2015AA01A203).

References

1. Suh, J.W., Ho, Y.S.: Error concealment techniques for digital TV. IEEE Trans. Broadcast. **48**(4), 299–306 (2002)
2. Wiegand, T., Sullivan, G.J., Bjontegaard, G., et al.: Overview of the H.264/AVC video coding standard. IEEE Trans. Circuits Syst. Video Technol. **13**(7), 560–576 (2003)
3. Wang, Y., Zhu, Q.F.: Error control and concealment for video communication: a review. Proc. IEEE **86**(3), 974–997 (2003)
4. Aign, S., Fazel, K.: Temporal and spatial error concealment technique for hierarchical MPEG-2 video codec. Proc. IEEE Int. Conf. Commun. **3**, 1778–1783 (1995)
5. Haskell, P., Messerschmitt, D.: Resynchronization of motion compensated video affected by ATM cell loss. In: Proceedings of IEEE International Conference on Acoustics, Speech and Signal Processing, pp. 545–548 (2003)
6. Valente, T.S., Dufour, C., Groliere, F., Snook, D.: An efficient error concealment implementation for MPEG4 video streams. IEEE Trans. Consum. Electron. **47**(3), 568–578 (2001)
7. Kim, D., Yang, S., Jeong, J.: A new temporal error concealment method for H.264 using adaptive block sizes. In: Proceedings of IEEE International Conference on Image Processing, vol. 3, pp. III-928–III-931 (2005)
8. Draft ITU-T Recommendation and Final Draft International Standard of Joint Video Specification (ITU–T Rec. H.264 ISO/IEC 14496–10 AVC), Geneva, Switzerland, May 2003
9. Chen, B.N., Lin, Y.: Temporal error concealment using selective motion field interpolation. Electron. Lett. **42**(24), 1390–1391 (2006)

Mining and Modeling the Information Propagation in an Email Communication Network

Chao Yang$^{(\boxtimes)}$, Bin Jiang, and Lei Wang

College of Computer Science and Electronic Engineering,
Hunan University, Changsha, China
{yangchaoedu, jiangbin}@hnu.edu.cn,
stone4827321@163.com

Abstract. Information exchange among people via email service has produced a mass of communication data, which have been widely used in research about information propagation in virtual social networks. The focus of this paper is on the "Enron Email Dataset". The ideas discussed give thorough consideration to the diversity of organizational positions, the dynamic behaviors of users to select information contents and communication partners via email service. We then establish a probability selection model to analyze the impact of multiple inter-active relationships on the email communication network. On the basis, an agent-based model for modeling the information diffusion in an organization via email communication network is proposed, by relating the micro individual behaviors and the macro system evolution to address the real phenomena. Further, we conduct sensitivity analysis of the interference parameter on the evaluative network. The experimental results show that our proposed model is beneficial to uncover the implicit communication mechanisms of a real organization.

Keywords: Agent-based model · Email analysis · Information propagation · Communication network

1 Introduction

The rapid development of Internet technology has made the use of email to be one of the predominant means of communication in the information society [1]. Enterprise organizations widely use email platforms for various purposes such as scheduling tasks, issuing notices, submitting reports, data transfers and other works, which significantly improve their work efficiency. The underlying phenomena of information flows in an organization are mostly the consequence of complex organizational interactions (sending or receiving information) among numerous users.

Generally, the interactions of users in specified organizations (such as a company) are special to some extent. For example, there have obvious hierarchical differences among users positions, such as Top-level (C.E.O., President etc.), Middle-level (Director, Manager etc.) and Bottom-level (general Employees). This leads to the variance in communication mechanisms among users, as they belong to either same or different

Q. Zu and B. Hu (Eds.): HCC 2016, LNCS 9567, pp. 510–522, 2016.
DOI: 10.1007/978-3-319-31854-7_46

position levels. Furthermore, users are socially familiar with each other within the same group and usually prefer to send information to authority users of other groups. Therefore, familiarity decides the user's influence of communication within the group, and authority determines the influence outside of the group. Meanwhile, due to task requirements or the need to save time, a certain number of emails are transferred through P2MP (peer-to-multi-peer) mode, instead of P2P (peer-to-peer) mode. Meanwhile, users can also forward the received emails to other users, who may also forward them in turn. All the above mentioned reasons increase the difficulty of modeling the information propagation in a communication network.

In this paper, we propose an agent-based model which considers the above mentioned specialty for modeling information propagation in an organizational communication network, through which we compare and analyze the interaction mechanisms among users, information and network, and also their influences on system evolution. Our research consists of four steps: first, extract facts from actual email data, in order to define entities of the users and the emails as well as their relevant state variables; next, establish the virtual communication mechanisms based on agent-based model and carry out the simulations; third, analyze and compare the results of the model with the real data using social network analysis techniques; and finally conduct experiments on the agent model with different parameters set by changing features of the interaction, through which we observe and compare the different impacts of users interaction mechanisms on information propagation.

The data set we adopted is the Enron Email Dataset, which includes a large set of email messages and is made public by a legal investigation concerning the Enron organization. This data set is available from the site http://www.cs.cmu.edu/~enron/, which contains email data from January, 2000 to June, 2002 [2]. We utilize the emails of 151 people with their sender/receiver links, and we also get the files which describe the organizational positions of these 151 staffs in the Enron organization.

The rest of this paper is organized as follows: Sect. 2 briefly reviews the related research works on email communication network; Sect. 3 describes our proposed agent-based model through the ODD protocol; Sect. 4 gives the simulation experiments and then discusses the results; and finally, we conclude our work and present the future works in Sect. 5.

2 Related Works

There have been lots of research works on the email communication network. In this paper, we roughly divide these contributions into two categories:

The first category analyzes topological structure of the communication network. For example, Ebel et al. study the topology of email networks from server log files and find that the resulting network exhibits a scale-free link distribution and pronounces small-world behavior. They further conclude that the spreading of email viruses is greatly facilitated in scale-free network structure compared with random architectures [3]. Diesner et al. extract communication networks from Enron corpus by refining the relations, and then apply various quantitative indicators to explore structural properties of the networks in Enron and to identify key persons across time [4]. Karagiannis et al.

study the behavioral patterns of email usage in a large-scale enterprise by focusing on pair-wise interactions; they have examined various factors that could potentially affect email replies [5]. Uddin et al. use social network analysis measures of degree-, betweenness-, closeness centrality and reciprocity for exploring a longitudinal email communication network among students [6].

The other category aims to explore how a communication network evolves dynamically over time. Among these contributions, Wu et al. introduce a model with decay in the transmission probability of information as a function of the distance between the source and the target. They find the decay of similarity among members has strong implications for the information propagation [7]. Matsuyama et al. analyze the implicit mechanisms of communications among people in Enron organization by using an agent-based simulation model. They also examine the influence of changes of the members in a group on an artificial society [8]. And, Menges et al. use an agent-based approach to model the growth of email-based social networks, in which individuals establish, maintain and allow atrophy of links through contact-lists and emails. Their approach enhances both common neighbors and preferential attachment in order to model the connection between the nodes at a deeper level [9]. Besides, Wang et al. utilize a stochastic branching model to capture the structural properties of email spreading trees, i.e., to how many people a user forwarded the email and the total coverage the email reached. The result indicates that the spreading process follows a random yet reproducible pattern, largely independent of the context [10].

3 Model Description with ODD Protocol

In this paper, we study how information propagates in an organization through multiple interaction relationships on email communication network through agent-based approach. The model description follows the ODD (Overview, Design concepts, Details) protocol for describing agent-based models [11].

3.1 Purpose

The purpose of this study is to analyze and model Enron email propagation based on the complex interaction mechanisms among the organizational members, the email content and the social network relationships via email service. We also focus on how multiple interactions impact on the evolution of information propagation network. Overall, this work provides a new attempt for the design of information diffusion mechanism, quantization of influence measurements and so on from heterogeneous group communications.

3.2 Entities, State Variables, and Scales

As shown in Table 1, our model includes two types of entities: the user and the email. The user is regarded as the individuals who disseminate information (sending or receiving emails), and the email is regarded as the carrier of information. Further, Table 2 defines and describes the relevant state variables of these two entities.

Table 1. Definition and description of entities

Entity	Description	Definition
User	The individuals who disseminate the email	Agent
Email	The carriers of the information	Information

Table 2. Definition and description of relevant state variables

State variables	Description	Variable Name
The agent position	The position of the user	*aPosition*
The partner's position	The position set of the user's potential communication partners	*apList*
The agent state	The distance between the user and the Internet	*aState*
The disseminated content	The email set that the user has disseminated	*eList*
The agent's position	The position set of users who can spread the specific email	*epList*
The disseminated number	The disseminated number of the email	*eNumber*

3.3   Process Overview and Scheduling

The overview of the simulation process mainly includes four parts. First, system initializes the type and number of agents (users) and information (emails) according to the actual email records. Then is the information spreading process, each agent acts as the executer in turn and carry out the following actions: (1) change the state, if the value of the state is zero, follow-up process will be performed; (2) select the communication way (posting a new information or forwarding an old information) and the information; (3) select the receiver; and (4) update the links status and the related parameters. Finally, the simulation will be terminated at a predefined value.

3.4   Design Concepts

Basic Principles. The main principle of this model came from the theory of "Philos Relationships", proposed by Krackhardt [12]. He has developed the concept of influence strength in and further defined the relationship as one that meets three conditions: Interaction (frequency of interaction), Affection (one feels affection for another) and Time (history of interaction). According to Krackhardt's theory, Time creates the opportunity for the exchange of information, and Interaction and Affection actively contribute to predict influence strength. Based on Krackhardt's theory, in this paper, we study the heterogeneous relationships of users from multi-dimensional influences, and then take the Interaction as Familiarity and the Affection as Authority in the history of interactions, in order to determine the probability of selecting which influence on users' interactions, and build our information propagation model.

Adaptation. Each agent is the subject who conducts the spreading behaviors. Its adaptation is represented as dynamic behaviors for selecting receivers according to their influence strength in different communication groups.

Emergence. In the model, agents select content and receivers based on a series of rules, their dynamic behaviors and interactions would lead to different evolution of the information propagation network, and emerge different distribution features.

Stochasticity. During the information propagation process, if an agent chooses to send a piece of new information, then the type of new information is randomly generated according to the agent's information spreading ability.

Collectives. The agent's behavior of participating in the information spreading would form agent groups and communication network structures, implying a direct or indirect relationship or influence among agents, which will affect the individual selection behaviors as a feedback.

Observation. The experimental data collected from the agent-based simulation includes the information items, the agents and the dissemination path among the participant agents during the entire simulation process. Therefore, a communication network and some distribution features are observed, such as the quantitative distribution of users to send or receive emails, the size distribution of email chains, the distribution of communication frequency between users in different positions and so on.

3.5 Initialization

The initialization of our agent-based model is mainly the type and number of the agent and the information. Tables 3 and 4 give the details of initialization according to the actual Enron email data, where T, M and B represent the top, middle and bottom position, respectively; and Null represents a null set.

Table 3. Agent type and distribution in Enron email data

Ability Position	T	M	B	T M	T B	M B	T M B	Null
T	0	1	0	0	0	5	10	0
M	0	0	0	0	1	13	39	2
B	0	0	8	2	0	30	37	3

Table 4. Information type and distribution in Enron email data

Type	T	M	B	TM	TB	MB	TMB
Number	1500	15000	30000	7000	6000	50000	5000

As outlined in Table 3, each type of agent is distinguished by their organizational positions and information spreading abilities. Here, the agent's information spreading ability refers to the positions collection of his potential receivers in communication event, expressed and distinguished by either complete set or subset of agent positions, which also includes the type of never spreading. And, the information types in Table 4 are represented by a collection of agent positions, which indicates that only these agents can participate in spreading this information. The figures of these two tables correspond to the actual amount of each type in Enron email dataset. Besides, the parameter λ is to a very small value 0.001 to eliminate the influence of random strengths on the result under the assumption that email delivery activities of an organization have their explicit purposes and strong relevance.

3.6 Sub Models

3.6.1 Change the State of Agent

We simulate the change of agent's state by extending the random-walk model proposed by Michaela. We employ this model because it can explain well how human groups make their decisions in uncertain environments. Meanwhile, it could simulate users' sending behavior for bursty or occasionally. At each simulation step, the agent has a state represented by an integer, namely the distance between the agent and the Internet. The agent cannot access the Internet to spread information via social media service unless his current state value is zero. As the users may use email for a period of time, therefore, we modify the original model to make the change of state not so fast, and the operations are given in Eq. (1).

$$aState_t = \begin{cases} aState_{t-1} + 1, & if\, 0 \leq r < 1/3 \\ aState_t, & if\, 1/3 \leq r < 2/3 \\ aState_{t-1} - 1, & otherwise \end{cases} \tag{1}$$

Where $aState_{t-1}$ and $aState_t$ represent the user's state at simulation step $t - 1$ and t, respectively; r is a random number in (0, 1].

3.6.2 Select the Communication Way and Information

We define two types of communication way in the model: sending new information or forwarding old information. According to the real data, the probability of sending new information and forwarding old information are set to 0.7 and 0.3 respectively. The initialization of the information is proportional to the quantitative distribution of all information in Enron data, and the type of the new information must satisfy the agent position and its information spreading abilities described in the Tables 3 and 4. The probability of selecting a piece of old information is given in Eq. (2).

$$Pr[E_k] = \frac{1/eNumber_{k,t}}{\sum_m^{|eList_{i,t}|} 1/eNumber_{m,t}} \tag{2}$$

Where E_k is the candidate information, $eList_{i,t}$ is the information set sent and received by agent A_i before simulation step t, $eNumber_{k,t}$ is the disseminated number of E_k at simulation step t.

3.6.3   Select the Information Receivers

The third sub-process explains how to select receivers through social relationships. As information could be sent by either P2P or P2MP mode, therefore, agent A_i needs first to determine the number of receivers. In the model, we set this number not more than 50, and the selection probability of each value is given in Eq. (3).

$$Pr[n] = \frac{1/n}{\sum_{k=1}^{50} 1/k}, 0 < n \leq 50 \tag{3}$$

Below, we explain how to select the information receivers in two steps. The first step is to select the recipient's group, which is discussed in two cases: (1) In the first case, if the sender's information spreading ability determines that he can only select receivers from one group; then the recipient's group is this group. (2) Or else, if the sender's ability allows him to select the receivers from different groups, then the recipients' group is determined based on sender's historic selected information list. After determining the receiver's group, the second step is to select n recipients from this selected group. The model considers and simulates two kinds of interaction mechanisms for selecting receivers: Familiarity for those participants in the same group; and Authority for those who come from different groups. These two kinds of interaction influences are quantitative calculated below:

$$Familiarity: Pr[A_j] \frac{FAT_t(A_i, A_j, T) + \lambda}{\sum_k^{|A|} (FAT_t(A_i, A_k, T) + \lambda)}, \ Authority: Pr[A_j] \frac{AUT_t(A_i, A_j, T) + \lambda}{\sum_k^{|A|} (AUT_t(A_i, A_k, T) + \lambda)}$$

$$\tag{4}$$

Where A is the set of all agents, A_j is the information receiver to be evaluated, T is one type of information ever selected by A_i, $FAT_t(A_i, A_j, T)$ is the total communication volume between A_i and A_j on information type T at simulation step t, $AUT_t(A_i, A_j, T)$ is the total information volume that A_j has received from other agents in A_i's group on information type T at simulation step t; λ is the interference parameter and its role is in twofold: (1) to ensure the denominator of formulas not be zero in the simulation process, so as to prevent floating point arithmetic overflow; (2) to adjust the impact strength of each kind of interaction by changing the value of λ, the bigger the value of λ, the smaller the strength. When λ tends to infinity, the probability of each agent to be selected tends to be the same. Namely, the agent A_i selects the receiver randomly.

3.6.4   Update the State Variables

When agent A_i sends an email E_k to agent A_j, a directed edge from A_i pointing to A_j will be added into the interaction network (if the edge already exists, then the edge's weight plus 1). The out-degree of A_i, the in-degree of A_j and the disseminated number of E_k are increased by 1. Furthermore, E_k is added into the *eList* set of the receiver A_j. In this case, if the email E_k is a piece of new information, then it should be also added into the *eList* set of the releaser user A_i.

4   Experiment and Discussion

4.1   Experiment 1: Comparison of Statistical Features of Communication Network

The results of three indexes in Table 5 describe the statistical features under different network structures: average degree of nodes, average shortest path length and average clustering coefficient. For better comparison, we also perform the simulation with random network and small-world network model. We set up the random network and small-world network by starting with a ring of 151 nodes. Each connects to its ten nearest neighbors, and then rewiring these two networks with probabilities of 1 and 0.2, respectively. It should be noted that, the network generated from our model has multiple edges. Then, the duplicate edges are also allowed in the process of rewiring in random network and small-world network. However, that is not completely in conformity with these two common models, where duplicate edges are forbidden.

Table 5.   Basic statistical characteristics of different network structures

Network type	Number of nodes (SD)	Average degree of nodes (SD)	Shortest path length (SD)	Clustering coefficient (SD)
Enron network	151	21	2.08	0.51
Our model network	151	20 (3)	2.28 (0.22)	0.60 (0.05)
Random network	151	20	1.90 (0.03)	0.12 (0.01)
WS model network	151	20	1.90 (0.01)	0.30 (0.02)

The results in Table 5 show that the communication network formed by Enron email data has a "small-world" property – short path length and high clustering coefficient. Meanwhile, the network generated by our model, with the same number of nodes, has its average degree of nodes, average shortest path length and average clustering coefficient approximate to the actual Enron data. It suggests that our model could generate a social communication network of small world as in the real world.

Further, we compare the degree distribution of nodes between Enron email network and the resultant communication network of our model, shown in Fig. 1.

The results in Fig. 1 show that our model has successfully reproduced the degree distribution of agents approximate to the actual data. Especially, we observe some nodes with large in-degrees in Fig. 1(a) and (b). By comparing with the actual data, we find that these nodes correspond to a small fraction of users who not only communicate frequently with other users of the same group, but also often receive information from users of other groups, thus forms large in-degrees. Further analysis finds that such agent with large in-degree receives information from other agents at any type of position,

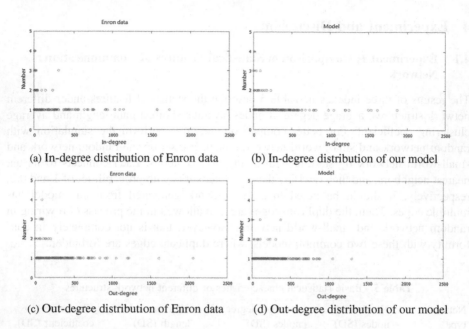

(a) In-degree distribution of Enron data   (b) In-degree distribution of our model

(c) Out-degree distribution of Enron data   (d) Out-degree distribution of our model

Fig. 1. Degree distribution of Enron data and our model

indicating a strong ability in communication with others. Thus, we conclude that those agents with strong ability of obtaining information from multi-channels are easier to form large in-degree, but the number of these agents is small.

Meanwhile, we observe a few of agents with large out-degree in Fig. 1(c) and (d). Actually, these agents conduct several large-scale information spreading behaviors. Figure 2 draws the information propagation path of once large-scale spreading action by such agents, which shows obvious center-propagation pattern via P2MP broadcast mode. And the releaser (the darkest node) finishes over 75 % of the total amount of propagation. However, the largest value of out-degree of our generated network is less than 1500. This is because that we set the number of receivers in one spreading limit to 50, and it is almost impossible for the same agent to send email to many receivers every time, thus would not form very large out-degree.

Fig. 2. Center-propagation pattern by agent with large out-degree in Enron email data

4.2   Experiment 2: Comparison of Diffusion Features of Information

As the information propagation via Email communication forms a diversity of information chains, and it actually reflects the users' behaviors and preferences in the information propagation process, we therefore compare some diffusion features of information between the Enron email data and the simulated result of our model. Below, Fig. 3 compares the distribution of the size of the information chain.

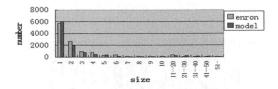

Fig. 3. the distribution of size of the information chain

As shown in Fig. 3, the size of 1 denotes that the information has not been forwarded, but only sent from the releaser to his partner in the first round propagation, while other information have been either forwarded once, or disseminated at least once with P2MP mode or several times with P2P mode. The results also show power law distribution of the size of information chain of both Enron email data ($y = 5.5e3x^{-1.41}$, R^2:0.975) and our simulated data ($y = 5.2e3x^{-1.46}$, R^2:0.987). The power law distribution in our model could be explained by the process of selecting the old information and the number of receivers. Different from a rich-get-richer phenomenon, the agent in our model prefers to select the old information with smaller disseminated number consistent with the actual records, and so is the receiver number. Such mechanism could also give rise to a power law distribution. Meanwhile, we find most information chains have small size. The average size of Enron email chain is 3.5, and 4.0 in our simulation model. This suggests that email is a typical "Narrowcasting Media". However, under certain situations, some information (especially *TMB* type information) still get a mass diffusion, and the size is more than 50. The information diffusion path of such information always emerges as center-propagation pattern and key-propagation pattern.

Figure 4 gives an example of information diffusion with key-propagation pattern in Enron email data. As shown in Fig. 4, although the releaser agent (the darkest node) only sends the information to a small number of partners in the first transmission, there exists several key agents (the lightest node) who promotes the spreading of this information in the first round forwarding, thus leading to the size of this information chain is larger than general chains. But such large chains are less in the actual data.

Furthermore, because the participants in information spreading come from different position groups, there exists communication frequency difference between each pair of *(sender, receiver)*. Such difference implies an impact of agent's attribute of positions on information propagation in an organization. Figure 5 therefore compares the distribution of information communication frequency of each pair of *(sender, receiver)* between the Enron email data and the simulated data of our model.

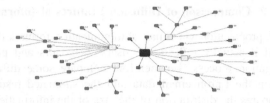

Fig. 4. The key-propagation pattern of information diffusion in Enron email data

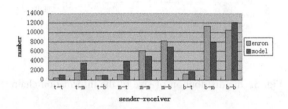

Fig. 5. The distribution of communication frequency

The results in Fig. 5 show that the *b-b*, *b-m*, *m-b* and *m-m* pairs occupy a major proportion in the actual communication of Enron email data, and our model also reproduces the similar distribution. This is because Enron email data has more participants with *Bottom* and *Middle* positions than those with *Top* positions, and staffs with *Bottom* and *Middle* positions participate in the communication more frequently than those with *Top* positions in Enron organization. Further, we find that *b-b* pairs hold the largest communication quantity of the Enron email data, mostly implemented by P2P mode with small size of information chain. Meanwhile, most of *b-m* pairs pass on information in P2MP mode, which actually expands the spreading scale of this information. To conclude, there exists diverse communications among users across the organizational positions, and our model is good at simulating these special features.

4.3   Experiment 3: Sensitivity Analysis of λ on Network Evolution

Next, we examine the effect of interaction strength on network evolution by changing the value of λ. The results are given in Table 6.

The results show that the average degree of nodes in the communication network increases with the rising λ, but the increased rate is not obvious. And, the average shortest path length decreases with the rising λ. It is because the selection of information receivers tends to be more random when λ becomes bigger, which improves the interaction probability among agents. Consequently, there are easier to form a direct path between two agents and shorten the average shortest path length of the network.

Besides, we also observe that when λ is less than 0.1, clustering coefficient decreases with the rising λ, while when λ is greater than 0.5, the clustering coefficient increases with the rising λ. We discuss such results below: (1) when λ is less than 0.1, *Familiarity* and *Authority* influence play dominant roles in the selection of communication partners.

Table 6. Sensitivity test of λ on network features

λ	Average degree of nodes (SD)	Shortest path length (SD)	Clustering coefficient (SD)
0.001	21 (0.10)	2.28 (0.22)	0.60 (0.05)
0.01	21 (0.13)	2.31 (0.20)	0.55 (0.05)
0.1	21 (0.15)	1.68 (0.13)	0.45 (0.05)
0.5	22 (0.20)	1.44 (0.15)	0.70 (0.07)
1	22 (0.20)	1.35 (0.12)	0.77 (0.06)
10	23 (0.22)	1.24 (0.09)	0.88 (0.08)
100	23 (0.30)	1.24 (0.09)	0.88 (0.07)

Under this case, the smaller the λ is, the two agents who ever communicated by *Familiarity* also have higher probability to select a common agent of them by *Authority* for spreading information, thus increasing the average clustering coefficient of the communication network. (2) When λ is greater than 0.5, the random factor is the dominant influence. Under this case, it is relatively easy for any two agents to generate a link and finally form a communication network with a higher clustering coefficient. Interestingly, the clustering feature in this case is quite different from the result of general random network, listed as the third network in Table 5. It is supposed that much detailed consideration such as the selection of information type and communication group in our random model before random linking edges limited the alternative range of attachable nodes, thus lead to a different result.

5   Conclusion and Future Work

In this paper, we have proposed an agent-based model to simulate and analyze the email content propagation in social network of Enron enterprise. We first give the definition of user and email by extracting the actual data, and extend the random-walker model to simulate the user behavior of sending email messages. Then, we make a qualitative and quantitative analysis of the interaction between the user, the email and the network, such as the impact of the cumulative propagation times of email, the familiarity influence based on the interaction among users with same position groups and the authority strength for interaction spans different groups. On this basis, we have compared the network topological characteristics and diffusion features of our model with the Enron dataset using social network analysis techniques. Although the origins of the two networks are quite different, the characteristics are quite similar to each other.

The conclusions mainly include: (1) the email communication network has a typical small-world property—short path length and high clustering coefficient; (2) most of users have relatively small out-degrees and less users have large out-degrees due to the different sending frequencies and transmission modes caused by the user's random walk behaviors; and the similar distribution of in-degrees resulted by the cumulative difference of users interaction history; (3) email is a typical narrowcasting media, and the number of communication between users at different positions has obvious differences; and (4) different intensity of interactions forms different topological structure of the email communication network, especially the average path length and the average clustering coefficient have obvious differences.

In the future work, we might try to use other reasonable models, such as Levy Flight model (a special random motion with an occasional larger step jump) on simulating more complex behavior of users. And, revise and apply the current model on other social medias, such as Sina weibo.

References

1. Uddin, S., Jacobson, M.J.: Dynamics of email communications among university students throughout a semester. Comput. Educ. **63**, 95–103 (2013)
2. Shetty, J., et al.: The Enron email dataset database schema and brief statistical report. Information Sciences Institute Technical Report, University of Southern California (2004)
3. Ebel, H., et al.: Scale-free topology of e-mail networks. Phys. Rev. E **66**(3), 1–4 (2002)
4. Diesner, J., Carley, K.M.: Exploration of communication networks from the Enron email corpus. In: Workshop on Link Analysis, Counterterrorism and Security, SIAM International Conference on Data Mining 2005, pp. 3–14 (2005)
5. Karagiannis, T., Vojnovic, M.: Behavioral profiles for advanced email features. In: 18th International Conference on World Wide Web, pp. 711–720 (2009)
6. Uddin, S., Thompson, K., Schwendimann, B., Piraveenan, M.: The impact of study load on the dynamics of longitudinal email communications among students. Comput. Educ. **72**, 209–219 (2014)
7. Wu, F., Huberman, B.A., Adamic, L.A., Tyler, J.R.: Information flow in social groups. Physica A **337**(1), 327–335 (2004)
8. Matsuyama, S., Terano, T.: Analyzing the ENRON communication network using agent-based simulation. J. Netw. **3**(7), 26–33 (2008)
9. Menges, F., et al.: Modeling and simulation of e-mail social networks: a new stochastic agent-based approach. In: 40th Conference on Winter Simulation, pp. 2792–2800 (2008)
10. Wang, D.S., Wen, Z., et al.: Information spreading in context. In: The 20th International Conference on World Wide Web, pp. 735–744 (2011)
11. Polhill, J.G., Parker, D., Brown, D., Grimm, V.: Using the ODD protocol for describing three agent-based social simulation models of land-use change. J. Artif. Soc. Soc. Simul. **11**(23) (2008)
12. Krackhardt, D.: The strength of strong ties: the importance of philos in organizations. In: Nohria, N., Eccles, R. (eds.) Networks and Organizations: Structure, Form, and Action, pp. 216–239. Harvard Business School Press, Boston (1992)

Invulnerability Analysis for SDN Based on Complex Network Theory

Jinbao Yang[1(✉)], Mei Song[1], Chumeng Zhan[2],
Xiaojuan Wang[1], and Yue Ma[3]

[1] School of Electronic Engineering, Beijing University of Posts
and Telecommunications, Beijing, China
yangjinbao@bupt.edu.cn
[2] School of Information Science and Technology, University of Science
and Technology of China, Beijing, China
[3] School of Computer, Beijing University of Posts and Telecommunications,
Beijing, China

Abstract. Based on SDN (Software Defined Network) theory, this paper constructs a topology modeling for deliberate attacks. Then this paper analyzes the network vulnerability anti deliberate attacks and topological characteristics and with the distribution coefficient, then proposed the flow uniformity scheme to enhance the invulnerability of complex network, and by verified by simulation.

Keywords: Network invulnerability · Network connectivity · Network error · Network attack, network topology simulation

1 Introduction

The current high-speed development of Internet technology and mobile communications, variety of information acquisition and transmission method, complex of data storage and sharing way, jointly gave birth to a variety of business types (such as OTT, cloud platform rental, mobile payments, etc.) coexist in a complex, symbiotic heterogeneous communication networks. The network contains wired communication network, micro, macro cellular networks, mobile Ad hoc networks, and other forms, showing a relationship between the evolution of mutual coexistence. In traditional heterogeneous network architecture, network and transport layers retain the data packet forwarding, distributed routing addressing core communication functions, while providing a specific protocol for the QoS, VLAN, traffic control and other business needs, in order to ensure a heterogeneous network communication. However, due to network control and data forwarding function is cured over a network device by a tightly coupled manner, make the interaction and coordination agreement between becoming more complex and individualized needs of the business to be set up for individual network nodes, thus further increasing the complexity of network control and management. How to design a more generic technology, fundamentally promote heterogeneous integration has been becoming the current hot spot.

As shown in Fig. 1 [1, 4], the current heterogeneous fusion technology is based on a "patch", this mode of heterogeneous converged network has become a stodgy,

© Springer International Publishing Switzerland 2016
Q. Zu and B. Hu (Eds.): HCC 2016, LNCS 9567, pp. 523–533, 2016.
DOI: 10.1007/978-3-319-31854-7_47

structure and complex system, to some extent this unable to adapt to the present stage of progress for increasing complexity. SDN (software defined network) what is based on the forward control and separation, and programming of network architecture, mainly used in the center of the cloud data, broadband transmission network scenarios, such as network data flow on the basis of centralized control and management, fundamentally improve the network control ability. Essentially understanding, SDN is a framework, a kind of network design concept, it can be introduced into the "small core, large margin" heterogeneous converged network system with IP as the core.

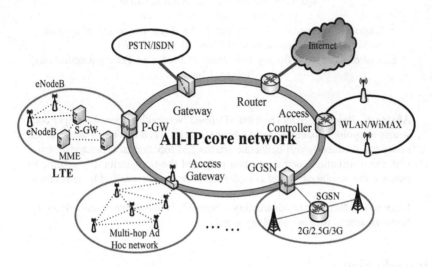

Fig. 1. The convergence of heterogeneous networks

SDN introducing the idea of the variety of heterogeneous network elements and flat structures will bring route traffic of virtual research challenges, one of which is to discuss the design of fault-tolerant algorithms comprehensiveness [2]. Due to the equipment aging, link failures, equipment maintenance, fault tolerant fault caused by damage of network isolation, and network traffic attack targeted failure caused by deliberate attacks. Virtual mapping with amplification effect: carrying a large amount of traffic node failure, because of the fault-tolerant and reliable mechanism for virtual algorithm causes the current local traffic diversion [3]. Mass flow will cause the link pressure to the around nodes, the shunt link load, on the one hand, will cause the failure of large-scale virtual map, on the other hand, overweight load will increase further link failures. How starting from the mechanism of fault tolerant fault and deliberate attacks, respectively to construct theory analysis model and design a robust anti-damage virtual mapping algorithm is the key point of this study [5].

This paper proposes a topology modeling for a deliberate attack, and then analyzed the network vulnerability anti deliberate attacks and topological characteristics and with the distribution coefficient, then proposed the flow uniformity scheme to enhance the invulnerability of complex network, and by verified by simulation.

2   Different Deliberate Attack Analysis

2.1   Deliberate Attack

Figure 2 [6] shows the two key nodes AB and five virtual request, scheme as shown. In the virtual request 1 mapping relationship is: {a → B, b → A, c → D}, link resources mapping relationship is: {ab → ($\overline{BCA}$), bc → ($\overline{AD}$)}. In the virtual request 2 mapping relationship is: {d → E, e → A}, link resources mapping relationship is: {de → ($\overline{EFBGA}$)}. In the virtual request 3 mapping relationship is: {f → A, g → L, h → K}, link resources mapping relationship is: {fg → ($\overline{AL}$), gh → ($\overline{LKJ}$), hf → ($\overline{JIBHA}$)}. In the virtual request 4 mapping relationship is: {i → F, j → M}, link resources mapping relationship is: {ij → ($\overline{FBM}$)}. In the virtual request 5 mapping relationship is: {k → N, l → O, m → P, n → Q}, link resources mapping relationship is: {kl → ($\overline{NBO}$), lm → ($\overline{OP}$), mn → ($\overline{PQ}$)}. The node A assumes the function of three virtual nodes, the node B is the middle node of the four virtual requests. When the physical node A fails, A peripheral node cannot afford the huge computation request; when the physical node B fails, the virtual request 4 don't have alternate path, then the request exit the virtual mapping; and virtual request 2 despite have the standby path $\overline{AHFE}$, but F, H nodes caused by a lack of CPU resources, cannot afford to the requests of mapping.

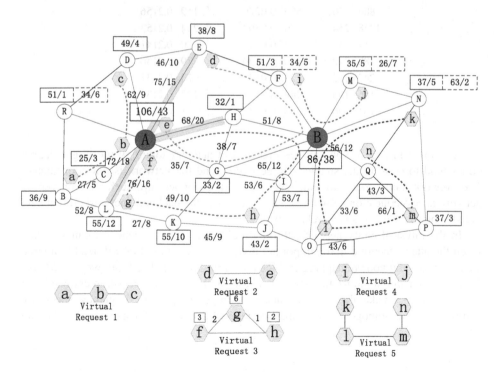

Fig. 2. The deliberate attacks problem description

2.2 Problem Analysis

Virtual mapping process random failure has robustness to the network, the network connectivity (the maximum component, etc.) is not damaged due to individual node failure. From different perspectives on the real topology node important degree of evaluation results can be seen (Table 1), evaluation of the degree value of the center node similarity is stronger, betweenness centrality and closeness centrality node assessment similar is strong, other policies' similarity is relatively weak. In node 1, for example, it is more important in the value center, but in betweenness, closeness of the relatively low ranking. This is because the node 1 tends to star topology, weak on the bridging capability. That is at the centre of the community instead of two corporate connection position. Different emphases of different strategies can't replace each other, so it is necessary to analyze the changes in network connectivity under different attack strategies, thus providing theoretical basis for invulnerability mapping algorithm design.

Table 1. The important node for different attack strategy in real

No.	Degree	No.	Betweenness	No.	Closeness
136	345	47	0.0378	47	0.2250
1	342	146	0.0348	146	0.2240
92	327	79	0.0251	126	0.2181
886	320	509	0.0226	119	0.2156
1248	254	70	0.0209	244	0.2153
4	250	117	0.0199	70	0.2141
180	242	7350	0.0190	79	0.2136
242	213	126	0.0187	73	0.2133
156	193	244	0.0177	127	0.2132
161	190	218	0.0175	6811	0.2131

As shown in Fig. 3, you can see that in real network topology the larger degree nodes tend to connect the smaller degree nodes, and the network is not coordinated. The network autonomous domain level decided to connect up, such as a university network access education network and then access to the backbone network, direct data transfer between university is relatively few.

In the physical entity network, through deliberate attacks scene we can see that, when the attack occurred in the important nodes or bridge link, this will lead to a large area of the virtual node remapping and local troubleshooting. Therefore we should take the protection and immunization measures base on the different measurement results of network nodes, make the network nodes' computing power, frequency spectrum, bandwidth more homogeneous, so that the face of deliberate attacks avoid "cascading effect".

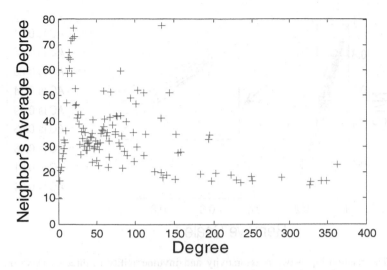

Fig. 3. The relation between degree and neighbor's average degree

3   Virtual Network in Survivability Mapping Algorithm Based on Edge Assortativity Property

As the topological properties, assortativity coefficient have a strong correlation with network invulnerability index (such as the largest connected component, network characteristic spectrum). For the further analysis of assortativity properties and network invulnerability index, first we evaluate network invulnerability in view of the different strategies under different assortativity properties; then according to conclusion of assortativity coefficient, we design the edge assortativity property determination and selection algorithm; finally this paper proposes a flow equalization scheme to improve the invulnerability of virtual network mapping.

3.1   Analysis of Assortativity Coefficient Confrontation with Survivability Effects

Assortativity coefficient is the depiction of assortative properties on the edge, when there are a lot of same attribute nodes interconnected, the network showed the assortative properties; when there are a lot of different attribute nodes interconnected, the network showed the disassortative properties. The properties of the nodes can be degree, closeness, betweenness topology indicators, it can also be CPU resources, spectrum, bandwidth, etc. This section select degree as a node property measurement, and assess the network's invulnerability with a variable assortative coefficient, where the accuracy parameter is 4. As shown in Fig. 4, with the increase of remove scale, network giant branch in 0.35 occurred the percolation phase transition; with the increase of AC (assortative coefficient), network's invulnerability becomes strong. This

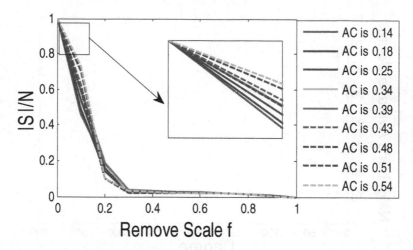

Fig. 4. The relationship between assorativity and invulnerability in directed network. (Color figure online)

is because the similar of node's degree is high, cascade effect between the nodes that have the same properties offset, making the resolution speed of giant branch slow down.

3.2 Determination and Selection of Edge Assortativity Property

In algorithm design process, as the global topological index assortativity coefficient has limitations in control of the virtual mapping process. In determining the edge assortativity property, we must clear two concepts: first, the virtual requests that has been carried, including node properties (CPU resources, spectrum resources, etc.) and link attributes (bandwidth requirements, etc.); Second, the remaining resource topology, the physical entity network's carrying capacity minus the virtual request that has already carried. The ratio between them is the criteria of a network assortativity property.

In theoretical modeling and invulnerability analysis, we find that the impact of assortativity coefficient is the amendments of edge assortativity property between the networks. Through the way of edge swap we can effectively change the value of assortativity coefficient, in virtual map, each virtual request loading is a rewiring process, can effectively change the physical network topology. When a deliberate attack occurs, the network's reloading may try to weaken the "cascade effect". Therefore, this section, first of all, based on the node capacity to choose an alternative set, and then update bearing ratio for each node, normalize the set of alternative, and finally, the node selection is converted to a random sampling without replacement problem, making low bearing ratio nodes is selected at a high probability. So as to realize the flow uniformity, specific algorithm process as shown in Fig. 5.

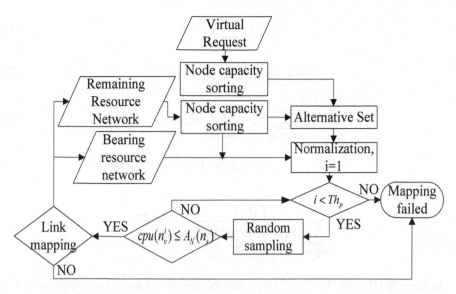

Fig. 5. The determine and select algorithm based on edge assorativity

4 Optimization Scheme

4.1 Flow Uniformity Scheme Design

(1) *Node mapping stage*

In view of the system of invulnerability mapping process method is as follows:

Objective function

$$\text{Maximize } T(n_s^a) \tag{1}$$

Constraints:

$$cpu(n_v^i) \leq A_N(n_s) \tag{2}$$

$$dis(loc(n_v^i), loc(n_s^a)) \leq R \tag{3}$$

$$n_{cr}(n_v^i) \leq A_{sp}(n_s) \tag{4}$$

$$\forall a \in N_s, \sum_{i \in N_v} g_a^i \leq 1 \tag{5}$$

$$\forall i \in N_v, \sum_{a \in N_s} g_a^i = 1 \tag{6}$$

$$\forall a \in N_s, \forall i \in N_v, g_a^i \in \{0, 1\} \tag{7}$$

$$\left| \sum_{(a,b) \in L_s} f_{ab}^{ij} - \sum_{(a,b) \in L_s} f_{ba}^{ij} \right| \geq 2 \tag{8}$$

$$\delta(n_a, n_b) = 1 \tag{9}$$

$$\frac{T(n_s)}{\sum_{\forall n_s^a \lrcorner n_s} T(n_s^a) / \underset{num}{\arg}(\forall n_s^a \lrcorner n_s)} \leq Th_1 \tag{10}$$

In formula (10) $\underset{num}{\arg}((n_s \lrcorner n_s^a) \lrcorner l_s')$ represent the number of nodes connected to the key node, Th_1 as the key source node constraint threshold, the formula represents that the mapping ability of node is same with the mapping ability of node that associated with it.

(2) *Link mapping stage*

Objective function

$$\text{Maximize } R/C \tag{11}$$

Constraints:

$$f_{ab}^{ij} \cdot B(l_v^{ij}) \leq \lambda B(l_s^{ab}) + (1 - \lambda)\gamma_{l_{ab}} W(l_s^{ab}) \tag{12}$$

$$q = \sum_{(a,b) \in L_s} f_{ab}^{ij} - \sum_{(a,b) \in L_s} f_{ba}^{ij} = \begin{cases} 1 & \text{if } g_a^i = 1 \\ -1 & \text{if } g_a^j = 1 \\ 0 & \text{otherwise} \end{cases}, \forall a \in N_s, \forall l_v^{ij} \in L_v \tag{13}$$

$$\forall l_s^{ab} \in L_s, \forall l_v^{ij} \in L_v, f_{ab}^{ij} \in \{0, 1\} \tag{14}$$

$$\forall(a,b) \in L_s, \forall M_v \subset N_v, \sum_{i,j \in CS(M_v, N_v - M_v)} f_{ab}^{ij} + f_{ba}^{ij} < CS(M_v, N_v - M_v) \tag{15}$$

$$\frac{\sum\limits_{\forall l_v \in L_v \to l_s}\left[\sum\limits_{\forall l_s \leftarrow ln_s} \lambda \cdot B(l_s) + \sum\limits_{\forall l_v \in L_v \to l_s}(1-\lambda)\gamma_{l_s}W(l_s)\right]}{\sum\limits_{\forall(n_s \leftarrow ln_s^a)\leftarrow ll_s'} A_L(l_s')\,/\,\underset{num}{\arg}((n_s \leftarrow ln_s^a)\leftarrow ll_s')} \leq Th_2 \tag{16}$$

In formula (16) $\underset{num}{\arg}((n_s \leftarrow ln_s^a)\leftarrow ll_s')$ represent the number of links connected to the key node's neighboring nodes, Th_2 as the key intermediate node constraint threshold, the formula represents the link bandwidth has been mapped is same with the available bandwidth that a neighbor has, from link mapping stage further implements the flow uniformity, making the network whose link is failure because of deliberate attack can receive as small as possible reconnection.

4.2   Simulation and Analysis

In this section simulation, we will use the GT-ITM tool generates the underlying physical network topology and virtual network requests. The CPU resources of each physical node is evenly distributed from 50 to 100, the physical link bandwidth available resources is evenly distributed from 50 to 100. Unit cost CPU resources and bandwidth resources obey uniform distribution of [1, 3]. Virtual network requests subject to parameters [4, 14] Poisson process. The number of virtual nodes obey parameters [5, 15] integer uniform distribution, the location information of each virtual node obey integer uniform distribution. The connection probability of each pair of nodes is 0.5. CPU resource request of virtual node obey 0–20 integer uniform distribution, the bandwidth request of virtual boundary obey 0 to 50 integer uniform

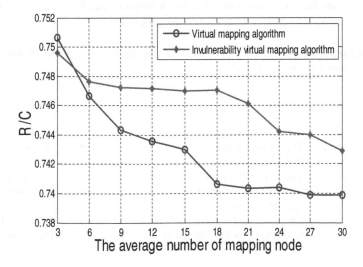

Fig. 6. The invulnerability virtual network mapping algorithm based on different nodes pressure

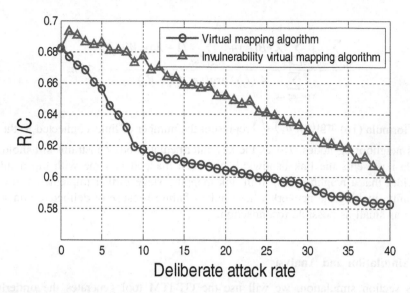

Fig. 7. The invulnerability virtual network mapping algorithm based on different attack rate

distribution. The distance between the virtual node to the physical node limit LL obey integer uniform distribution from 1 to 10. According to the location information and distance limitations can get a set of mappable physical node.

As shown in Fig. 6, it can be seen from the income and expenditure ratio R/C, when the average number of virtual mapping nodes increase, the node pressure increases, the improved invulnerability algorithm will have better resource utilization.

As shown in Fig. 7, it can be seen from the income and expenditure ratio R/C, when the average number of virtual mapping nodes increase, the improved invulnerability algorithm increases the tolerance of deliberate attacks, and when the node pressure increases, it will have better resource utilization.

Acknowledgment. This work was supported in part by the National Natural Science Foundation of China under Grant No. 61471055.

References

1. Anderson, T., et al.: The NEBULA future internet architecture. In: Galis, A., Gavras, A. (eds.) FIA 2013. LNCS, vol. 7858, pp. 16–26. Springer, Heidelberg (2013)
2. Jacobson, V., Smetters, D.K., Thornton, J.D., et al.: Networking named content. In: Proceedings of the 5th International Conference on Emerging Networking Experiments and Technologies, pp. 1–12. ACM (2009)
3. Seskar, I., Nagaraja, K., Nelson, S., Raychaudhuri, D.: MobilityFirst future internet architecture project. In: Proceedings of the 7th Asian Internet Engineering Conference, pp. 1–3 (2011)

4. Anand, A., Dogar, F., Han, D., Li, B., Lim, H., Machado, M., et al.: XIA: an architecture for an evolvable and trustworthy Internet. In: Proceedings of the 10th ACM Workshop on Hot Topics in Networks, pp. 14–15 (2011). CABO: Concurrent Architectures are Better than One [OL]. http://www.nets-find.net/Funded/Cabo.Php

5. Yap, K.-K., et al.: Blueprint for introducing innovation into wireless mobile networks. In: Proceedings of the SIGCOMM VISA Workshop, New Delhi, India (2010)

6. Xia, Y., Fan, J., Hill, D.: Cascading failure in Watts-Strogatz small-world networks. Physica A **389**(6), 1281–1285 (2010)

Outcome Anticipation and Appraisal During Risk Decision Making in Heroin Addicts

Jing Yang[2], Jitao Qin[1], Hanshu Cai[1], Quanli Han[3], Entan Ma[4],
Guosheng Zhao[4], and Bin Hu[1(⊠)]

[1] School of Information Science and Engineering,
Lanzhou University, Lanzhou, China
{qinjtl3, caihshl3, bh}@lzu.edu.cn
[2] Department of Child Psychology,
Lanzhou University Second Hospital, Lanzhou, China
Yangdoctor2007@126.com
[3] Gansu Provincial Drug Rehabilitation Administration Bureau, Lanzhou, China
1255934614@qq.com
[4] Municipal People's Hospital of Gansu Linxia, Linxia, China
{hcmaentan, Suini97}@163.com

Abstract. The gambling task is a valid predictor of various risk-taking behaviors. However, the neural underpinnings of risk processing in addiction are yet unclear. The present event related potential (ERP) study examined electrophysiological correlates associated with different stages of risky reward processing in risk-taking behavior. Ten female heroin addicts (HA) and ten female normal controls (NC) performed a simple two-choice gambling task. Behaviorally, whereas HA exhibited a risk-increase pattern, NC showed a risk-neutral pattern. During the anticipation stage, an increased stimulus-preceding negativity was elicited by high-risk compared to low-risk choices in HA and NC. Furthermore, HA as compared to NC exhibited a diminished P300 to both gains and losses.

Keywords: Risk-taking · Heroin addicts · Stimulus-preceding negativity · P300

1 Introduction

Opiate, such as heroin, is a kind of addictive drug threatening public health greatly today, especially in northwest of China. Addiction can be considered as a maladaptive decision making behavior, because addicts will seek rewarding effect from drugs, in spite of the possibility that many aversive consequences will be induced by drug taking. Impaired risk decision making function might be an important cause of the development, maintenance and relapse in addiction behavior.

In risk decision making, individuals will perceive risk of their choice; followed by predict the outcome; and then regulate their subsequent choice accordingly [1].

© Springer International Publishing Switzerland 2016
Q. Zu and B. Hu (Eds.): HCC 2016, LNCS 9567, pp. 534–543, 2016.
DOI: 10.1007/978-3-319-31854-7_48

Existing evidence shows HA have distorted representation of probability in gain and loss frames. The neural mechanisms of encoding risk may be caused by the brain structures, including insular and amygdala, which could be impaired by repeated drug exposes. Converging evidence has demonstrated that reward processing is not a homogenous construct, but can be parsed at least into distinct anticipation and outcome-appraisal stages [2–4]. With its fine-grained temporal resolution, event-related potential (ERP) technique is uniquely suitable to investigate in detail the time course of reward processing in risk decision making since it can permit the separation of neural events occurring very closely in time [5], such as reward anticipation and outcome appraisal [6, 7]. Outcome processing involves anticipation and appraisal stages. It was reported that heroin addicts had blunt experience of positive and negative outcome, such as anhedonia. This may reflect the malfunction in some cortical region and subcortical structure, such as orbital frontal cortex, medial prefrontal cotex, ventral tegmental area, and nucleusaccumbens.

Electrophysiological method is useful to investigate HA' outcome in anticipation and appraisal, because of its good temporal resolution. Reward anticipation can be indexed by the stimulus-preceding negativity(SPN) [8], a slow negative-going wave that progressively increases in amplitude prior to the presentation of feedback. This component is thought to primarily originate in the insular cortex [9, 10] and constitutes an index for anticipatory, dopaminergically mediated brain response [7, 11]. The SPN has hemispheric asymmetry, with greater right hemispheric response. That relates the specificity of right insular in risk representation.

In contrast, outcome appraisal can be indexed by P300 [12, 13]. The P300 is a positive deflection typically occurring between 300–600 ms after feedback presentation with a parietal distribution and has been associated with attentional resources involved in stimulus evaluation based on motivational significance [14, 15]. When processing positive and negative stimulus, drug users have lower P300 amplitude than healthy controls. It may reflect mesolimbic system hyposensitivity in addicts.

As far as we know, there are few research in the dynamic differences of reward circuits on process in HA and the NC. The present study sought to address this issue. To this end, we examined the reward processing in HA as compared to NC while they subjectively anticipated and experienced rewards. HA and NC made a choice between a low-risk option and a high-risk option during a simple gambling task. Behaviorally, we predicted that HA would tend to make high-risk decision compared to NC. More importantly, we also predicted that reduced sensitivity to risk in decision making could be represented in the anticipation stage as indexed by the SPN and in the outcome-appraisal stage as indexed by the P300. According to the arousal theory, HA compared to NC would exhibit reduced risk effect for these ERP components. On the other hand, if the motivational theory is correct, we expected that larger ERP components would be observed for positive rewards but smaller ERP components would be obtained for negative rewards in HA relative to NC.

2 Materials and Methods

2.1 Participants

Ten female drug addicts were recruited from the Gansu Compulsory Isolated Detox-ification Center, meeting DSM-5 opioid use disorder diagnostic criteria. Ten female controls were recruited from community. There are no significant differences between both group in age (mean and SD: 31.5 ± 10.6, 29.2 ± 7.32, respectively, $t(18) = -.86$, $p = .40$)and education(mean and SD: 8.40 ± 2.60, 10.10 ± 2.96, respectively, $t(18) = 1.37$, $p = .19$). All subjects were right handed with normal or corrected-to-normal vision. And all of them had no history of psychiatric or neurological disease, according to general questionnaire they filled in. Every participants were compensated 40 Yuan (RMB) for their participation, and additional rewards would be paid based on their performance in the task.

2.2 Stimuli and Procedure

The participants were seated comfortably in a dimly lit and sound-attenuating chamber approximately 80 cm away from computer screen. Each trial began with two options (the numeral 9 and 99, indicating the gambling points), which appeared on either side of a fixation point. The participants then selected one of the two alternatives by pressing a button, corresponding to the location of the chosen option with either their left or right index finger. This pair of options remained on the screen until the participants made a choice. Following their responses, a fixation point was presented in the center of the screen for 2000 ms and, thereafter, a number (either positive or negative) appeared for 1000 ms to indicate how many points they won or lost on the trial. Each trial finished with an inter-trial interval varying randomly from 900 to 1100 ms (Fig. 1). The task consisted of 400 trials divided into five blocks (80 trials each), and a short break was given between blocks. A practice block with 10 practice trials was used before the formal experiment, in order to familiarize participants with the procedure.

Since risk can be interpretable in terms of the mean squared deviation from the expected outcome [16], the option "9" was defined as the low-risk option that yielded either a gain of 9 points or a loss of 9 points, whereas the option "99" was defined as the high-risk option that yielded either a gain of 99 points or a loss of 99 points. Moreover, the probabilities of the outcomes of each option were equivalent, making the expected value of each option zero. Before the formal experiment, the participants were encouraged to use any strategy they wanted to maximize the amount of points. The higher the points they earned, the more bonus money they would receive. However, information regarding the conversion from points to money was not provided until the end of the experiment [1].

2.3 EEG Recording and Data Analysis

Brain electrical activity was recorded at 64 scalp sites using in electrodes mounted in an elastic cap (Brain Product, Munchen, Germany), with references on the left and right mastoids, and a ground electrode on the medial frontal aspect. The EEG were amplified

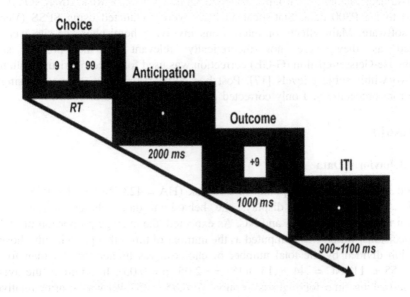

Fig. 1. Schematic representation of a simple two-choice gambling task. ITI = intertribal interval.

using a .05–100 Hz bandpass and continuously digitized at 500 Hz/channel in DC acquisition mode. All inter-electrode impedance was maintained below 20 kΩ. Offline, the data was referenced to the average of the left and right Mastoids (average mastoid reference), and bandpass filtered with low and high cutoffs of .1 and 30 Hz, respectively. Eye movement artifacts (such as eye movements and blinking) were excluded offline. Trials with amplifier clipping and peak-to-peak deflection exceeding ± 80 uV were excluded from the average. Approximately 30 % of all trails were excluded from averaging, because of ocular and movements artifacts.

The continuous EEG signals were filtered twice using different parameters with low-pass at 20 Hz for SPN analysis and band-pass of 0.1 and 30 Hz for P300 analysis to minimize the possible interferences from the SPN. Both the filtered EEG data were segmented into epochs that were time-locked to feedback onset. For the SPN, epoch began 2000 ms prior to and ended 500 ms post feedback onset, with the activity from −2000 to −1800 ms serving as the baseline; for P300, epoch included 200 ms pre-feedback activity and extended 1000 ms post-feedback, with the activity from −200 to 0 ms serving as the baseline. According to the grand average waveforms and topographic maps, the SPN was scored as the mean amplitude from −200 to 0 ms (i.e., the 200 ms window immediately before feedback onset) at lateral electrode sites (FT9/10), where the SPN was maximal. P300 was scored as the mean voltage from 340 to 440 ms post feedback onset at Pz due to a posterior distribution.

All the ERP data were analyzed in separate repeated-measures analysis of variance (RMANOVA). The SPN data were analyzed using group (HA vs. NC) as between-subject factor, while risk (9 vs. 99) and hemisphere (left vs. right) are used as within-subject factors. A Group × Valence (gain vs. loss) × Risk RMANOVA was applied to the P300 data. Statistical analyses were conducted using SPSS (Version 19.0) software. Main effects or interactions involving hemisphere or site were not reported as they were not theoretically relevant to the present study. Greenhouse-Geisser epsilon (G-GE) correction was used for all comparisons with more than two within-subject levels [17]. Post hoc comparisons were corrected using the Bonferroni procedure and only corrected p values were reported.

3 Results

3.1 Behavioral Data

HA and NC earned similar points in this task (HA = 423, NC = 216, $t(18) = -.68$, $p = .50$). Figures 2 and 3 displays the behavioral data (choice proportion and decision-making time) of HA and NC. As expected, the average proportion of making risky decisions, which was computed as the number of times that participants chose the 99 option divided by the total number of choices, was higher for HA than for NC (HA = .55 ± .11, NC = .44 ± .13, $t(18) = -2.05$, $p = 0.05$). In addition, the average decision-making time for high-risk option (796.95 ± 357.46) was shorter relative to low-risk option (910.83 ± 413.86) for HA reaching significance ($t(9) = 2.42$, $p = 0.03$). Also, the average decision-making time for high-risk option (1179.48 ± 657.86) was shorter relative to low-risk option (1262.79 ± 682.41) for NC reaching significance ($t(9) = 2.37$, $p = .04$). Importantly, there was a significant effect of group for average decision-making time (F $(1,18) = 11.30$, $p = 0.003$).

3.2 Electrophysiological Data

SPN. Figure 4 displayed grand average ERP waveforms following decision making until feedback onset and topographic maps of the SPN ($-200 - 0$ ms). Figure 5 displayed the mean amplitude of SPN for HA and NC at FT9 and FT10. Consistent with previous research [8], both groups showed a typical SPN that developed gradually as a relative negativity after the choice and reached its maximum immediately prior to the feedback onset. Moreover, the SPN appeared to be more pronounced at lateral electrode sites. Although group effect failed to produce satisfied result, there was a significant main effect of left and right hemisphere ($F(1,18) = 10.55$, $p = .004$),and a significant main effect of risk ($F(1,18) = 7.21$, $p = .01$).

P300. Grand average ERP waveforms at Pz elicited by gains and losses is presented in Fig. 6. Figure 7 displayed the mean amplitude of P300. The topographic maps for P300, from 340 to 440 ms, is also shown in Fig. 4. There was a significant main effect of risk (F $(1, 18) = 31.33$, $p < .001$), with a larger P300 following high-risk versus low-risk outcomes. The P300 was also enhanced for gains compared to losses, reflected in a significant main effect of valence (F $(1, 18) = 22.66$, $p < .001$). Importantly, there was a significant main effect of group (F $(1, 18) = 2.68$, $p = .02$), indicating that the P300 was reduced for HA as compared to NC.

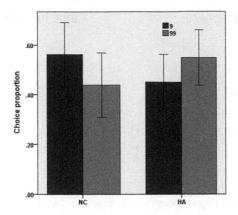

Fig. 2. Behavioral data (choice proportion). Standard errors are also depicted.

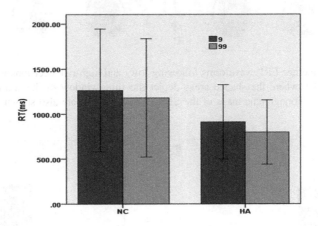

Fig. 3. Behavioral data (decision-making time). Standard errors are also depicted.

4 Discussion

The present study explored the electrophysiological correlates of reward processing in a risky decision-making task. Our results indicated that heroin abuse can modulate the effect of risk (magnitude of gain/loss) on behavioral choice, with HA trend to choose more high-risk option compared with NC. This may reflect malfunction of risk processing in HA. In addition, both HA and NC spent more time on low-risk option relative to high-risk option. The SPN was enhanced after high-risk relative to low-risk decisions, which was consistent with previous research [11, 18]. The SPN has been thought as an electrophysiological index of anticipatory, dopaminergically mediated activity [8]. In most previous SPN studies, participants performed a time-estimation task where they did not know whether they would receive positive or negative feedback [19–21], and thus it was unclear that whether the SPN was associated with reward

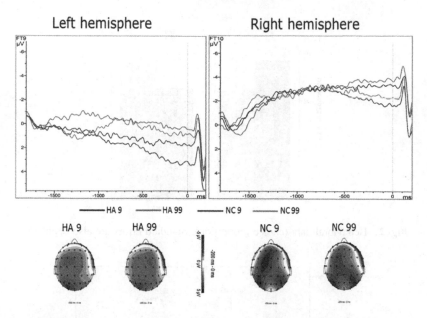

Fig. 4. Grand average ERP waveforms following low- and high-risk decisions for HA and NC at FT9 and FT10, where the shaded areas depict the time window of the stimulus-preceding negativity (SPN). Topographic maps of the SPN ($-200 - 0$ ms) are also shown.

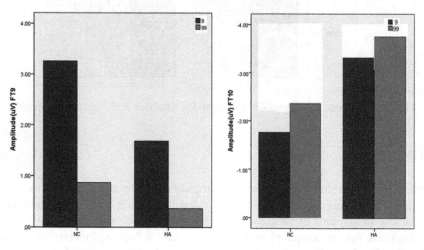

Fig. 5. ERP component data (stimulus preceding negativity) for heroin addicts (HA) and normal controls (NC). The ERP data were averaged across the electrodes selected for analysis.

anticipation or loss anticipation. Both HA and NC present the partial lateralization effect, that is average magnitude of right brain greater than the left brain. In addition, the average magnitude of high-risk option is bigger than the average magnitude of low-risk option for both HA and NC, which indicating that both of them hope to obtain

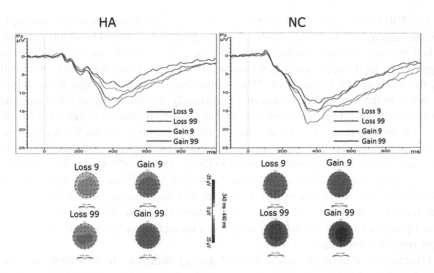

Fig. 6. Grand average ERP waveforms for gains and losses by risk at Pz, where shaded areas depicts the P300 time window. Scalp maps (340–440 ms) show the topography for the P300 by risk.

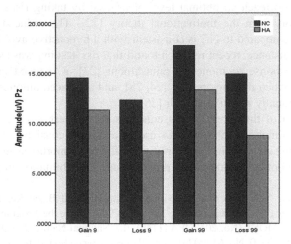

Fig. 7. ERP component data (P300) for heroin addicts (HA) and normal controls (NC). The ERP data were averaged across the electrodes selected for analysis.

high anticipation. More importantly, HA have lower SPN amplitude in right electrode. Given insular is a main source of SPN and the essential role of insular in risk representation, HA' risk processing may impaired by repeated drug exposure. However, the high and low risk level (99 and 9) effect has no difference between the two groups. This suggests the HA reserve, at least partly, the risk processing capacity which can distinguish the risk level, but the risk processing function abnormality may be general.

The P300 is thought to reflect the allocation of attentional resources involved in stimulus evaluation based on motivational significance [14]. The P300 amplitude evoked by outcomes are smaller in HA than NC, no matter the outcome valence and magnitude, which suggests the HA cannot process the choice outcomes sufficiently, and the malfunction is universal. More importantly, the two groups have different sensitivity to the magnitude of outcome. Specifically, the difference in P300 amplitude between high reward (gain 99) and low reward (gain 9) is smaller in HA than NC. But there has no difference in statistical result and p value is very small, this may be a sample limitation. Similar pattern appeared in high and low loss condition. This results suggested the HA cannot process outcome in the magnitude effectively. To sum up, the HA cannot appraise the reward and loss resulted from their own choice in a suitable way. Maybe they are insensitive to the reward and loss result, and this is because of their reward system were damaged. More importantly, this insensitive lead to the reward produced by the non-drug reward is not enough for addicts, so they will prefer to get reward from drugs.

Overall, our findings revealed that risk-taking behaviors in addiction were consistently reflected in the anticipation stage and in the outcome-appraisal stage. All the data indicated that HA would choose more high-risk than NC in order to be rewarded. HA compared to NC may have a hypoactive brain system, and consequently, they need higher stakes to perceive differences in riskiness. In real life, HA tend to seek more intense sensation to reach an optimal level of arousal by taking risks. Our ERP data lend some support from the motivational theory [22]. The reduced P300 for loss outcomes in HA compared to NC is consistent with a hypoactive avoidance system in risk-tasking. For instance, recent research found that risk-tasking was associated with a deficient brain response to monetary punishment [23], a reduced negative bias, a blunted response when making an error [24, 25], and a reduced autonomic response in the face of emotionally negative stimuli [26].

One limitation of the current study concerns the modest sample size (10 heroin addicts and 10 normal controls) and our use of a sample consisting of enforced isolation with the outside world. Therefore, it is of great importance to include heroin addicts who have not been compulsory drug addiction rehabilitation in future research.

Acknowledgements. This work was supported by the National Basic Research Program of China (973 Program) (No. 2014CB744600, No. 2011CB711000), the Program of International S&T Cooperation of MOST (No. 2013DFA11140), the National Natural Science Foundation of China (grant No. 61210010, No. 61300231), and Natural Science Foundation of Gansu Province, China (1208RJZA127)

References

1. Zheng, Y., Liu, X.: Blunted neural responses to monetary risk in high sensation seekers. Neuropsychologia, **71**, 173–180 (2015)
2. Berridge, K.C., Robinson, T.E.: Parsing reward. Trends Neurosci. **26**(9), 507–513 (2003)
3. Knutson, B., et al.: Dissociation of reward anticipation and outcome with event-related fMRI. Neuroreport, **12**(17), 3683–3687 (2001)

4. Waugh, C.E., Gotlib, I.H.: Motivation for reward as a function of required effort: dissociating the 'liking' from the 'wanting' system in humans. Motiv. Emot. **32**(4), 323–330 (2008)
5. Luck, S.J.: An Introduction to the Event-related Potential Technique. MIT press (2014)
6. Foti, D., Hajcak, G.: Genetic variation in dopamine moderates neural response during reward anticipation and delivery: evidence from event-related potentials. Psychophysiology, **49**(5), 617–626 (2012)
7. Zheng, Y., et al.: Contextual valence modulates the neural dynamics of risk processing. Psychophysiology, **52**(7), 895–904 (2015)
8. Brunia, C.H., et al.: Waiting to perceive: reward or punishment? Clin. Neurophysiol. **122**(5), 858–868 (2011)
9. Brunia, C., et al.: Visual feedback about time estimation is related to a right hemisphere activation measured by PET. Exp. Brain Res. **130**(3), 328–337 (2000)
10. Kotani, Y., et al.: The role of the right anterior insular cortex in the right hemisphere preponderance of stimulus-preceding negativity (SPN): an fMRI study. Neurosci. Lett. **450**(2), 75–79 (2009)
11. Mattox, S.T., Valle-Inclán, F., Hackley, S.A.: Psychophysiological evidence for impaired reward anticipation in Parkinson's disease. Clin. Neurophysiol. **117**(10), 2144–2153 (2006)
12. Kamarajan, C., et al.: Brain signatures of monetary loss and gain: outcome-related potentials in a single outcome gambling task. Behav. Brain Res. **197**(1), 62–76 (2009)
13. Yeung, N., Sanfey, A.G.: Independent coding of reward magnitude and valence in the human brain. J. Neurosci. **24**(28), 6258–6264 (2004)
14. Donchin, E., Coles, M.G.: Is the P300 component a manifestation of context updating. Beh. Brain Sci. **11**(3), 357–427 (1988)
15. Nieuwenhuis, S., Aston-Jones, G., Cohen, J.D.: Decision making, the P3, and the locus coeruleus–norepinephrine system. Psychol. Bull. **131**(4), 510 (2005)
16. Markowitz, H.: Portfolio selection. J. Financ. **7**(1), 77–91 (1952)
17. Jennings, J.R., Wood, C.C.: The e-adjustment procedure for repeated-measures analyses of variance. Psychophysiology (1976)
18. Poli, S., et al.: Stimulus-preceding negativity and heart rate changes in anticipation of affective pictures. Int. J. Psychophysiol. **65**(1), 32–39 (2007)
19. Chwilla, D.J., Brunia, C.H.: Event-related potentials to different feedback stimuli. Psychophysiology, **28**(2), 123–132 (1991)
20. Kotani, Y., et al.: Effect of positive and negative emotion on stimulus-preceding negativity prior to feedback stimuli. Psychophysiology, **38**(6), 873–878 (2001)
21. Ohgami, Y., et al.: Effects of reward and stimulus modality on stimulus-preceding negativity. Psychophysiology, **41**(5), 729–738 (2004)
22. Joseph, J.E., et al.: Neural correlates of emotional reactivity in sensation seeking. Psychol. Sci. **20**(2), 215–223 (2009)
23. Kruschwitz, J.D., et al.: Nothing to lose: processing blindness to potential losses drives thrill and adventure seekers. Neuroimage, **59**(3), 2850–2859 (2012)
24. Santesso, D.L., Segalowitz, S.J.: The error-related negativity is related to risk taking and empathy in young men. Psychophysiology, **46**(1), 143–152 (2009)
25. Zheng, Y., et al.: Sensation seeking and error processing. Psychophysiology, **51**(9), 824–833 (2014)
26. Lissek, S., et al.: Sensation seeking and the aversive motivational system. Emotion, **5**(4), 396 (2005)

Multi-resource Allocation for Virtual Machine Placement in Video Surveillance Cloud

Xianda Yang$^{(\boxtimes)}$, Haitao Zhang, Huadong Ma, Wensheng Li, Guangping Fu, and Yi Tang

Beijing Key Lab of Intelligent Telecommunication Software and Multimedia, Beijing University of Posts and Telecommunications, Beijing 100876, China
yxda2014@gmail.com, fkrystism@gmail.com, piggy200800@gmail.com, {zht,mhd,wenshli}@bupt.edu.cn

Abstract. Video surveillance cloud is an emerging cloud computing paradigm which can provide the elastic resource management ability for surveillance video processing tasks. The video processing tasks usually require extensive computing resources, and different tasks have different resource configuration requirements. It is challenging to find the optimal fine-grained resource configuration for various video processing tasks. In this paper, we study how to map the heterogeneous virtual machine requests to the heterogeneous physical machines. First, we design a video surveillance cloud platform architecture. The cloud platform can be seamlessly integrated with the video surveillance systems that comply with the ITU standard. Second, we propose a multi-resource virtual machine allocation algorithm named Dominant Resource First Allocation (DRFA). Our aim is to maximize the resource utilization in heterogeneous cloud computing environment. By computing the dominant resource under multiple resource dimensions, our proposed algorithm DRFA can make full advantage of the heterogeneous physical resources. Finally, we implement the cloud platform and develop some typical video surveillance services on the cloud platform. The experimental results show that our resource allocation approach outperforms other widely used approaches.

Keywords: Resource allocation · Video surveillance cloud · Virtual machine placement · Cloud computing

1 Introduction

In recent years, video surveillance systems are widely deployed all over the world. On the one hand, IP cameras are the widely used premises units for the current video surveillance systems, and allow users to easily obtain the surveillance video via Internet. On the other hand, the astonishing amount of video data generated by surveillance cameras provide many opportunities for the research and development of video surveillance services [1]. Intelligent video analysis is the typical value-added service in video surveillance systems. One intelligent video analysis task can automatically analyze the surveillance video stream and send out the results when some objects or events are detected. However, the video processing requirements of users are

© Springer International Publishing Switzerland 2016
Q. Zu and B. Hu (Eds.): HCC 2016, LNCS 9567, pp. 544–555, 2016.
DOI: 10.1007/978-3-319-31854-7_49

resource-consuming and ever-changing. Video surveillance cloud is an emerging cloud computing application paradigm to provide the elastic resource management ability for the complex surveillance video processing tasks such as video transcoding, video synopsis and people counting [2].

In the video surveillance cloud, by leveraging virtualization technology, a physical machine (PM) can host multiple virtual machines (VM) concurrently, and each VM can independently run multiple video processing tasks. The major challenges to map suitable physical servers to VM can be summarized as follows.

- **Multidimensional.** Assigning a VM to a PM requires certain amount of CPU, memory, network bandwidths. Once performance bottleneck of one resource appears in advance, the idle power wastage in other resources goes up.
- **Dynamic.** Resource allocation is a dynamic process. If the data center emphatically figure out peak pressure in particular moment, large amount of resources will be idle after that moment. Low server utilization is one of the most important factors that decrease the power efficiency of data centers.
- **Heterogeneous.** The heterogeneous feature appears in any data center. This feature is caused by not only the asynchronous hardware upgrading and eliminating but also the dynamic resource allocation process. In addition to server heterogeneity, VM requests reveal heterogeneous feature too.

In this paper, we study how to map the heterogeneous virtual machine requests to the heterogeneous physical machines. First, we design a video surveillance cloud platform architecture to efficiently process the large-scale live surveillance video. The cloud platform can be seamlessly integrated with the video surveillance systems that comply with the ITU standard [3]. Second, we propose a multi-resource allocation algorithm DRFA to maximize the resource utilization in heterogeneous cloud environment. The algorithm is based on the concept of dominant resource under the multiple resource dimensions. Finally, we implement the video surveillance cloud platform and obtain the experimental data from the real large-scale video surveillance system. The experimental results show that our proposed approach can take full advantage of the heterogeneous cloud resources and outperforms the other widely used approaches.

The remainder of the paper is organized as follows. In Sect. 2, we present the system architecture. Section 3 details the multi-resource allocation problem and the algorithm. The experiment result and analysis will be presented in Sect. 4. In Sect. 5, we discuss the related work. Finally, Sect. 6 concludes the paper.

2 System Architecture

As a typical cloud application paradigm, video surveillance cloud represents one industrial cloud platform specialized for video processing. Global Eye system in Shanghai, China, is a large-scale video surveillance system. The system collects the massive surveillance video data every day [4]. Utilizing cloud computing technology, various video surveillance applications can be published on cloud to meet both enterprises and individual users' elastic demands [5].

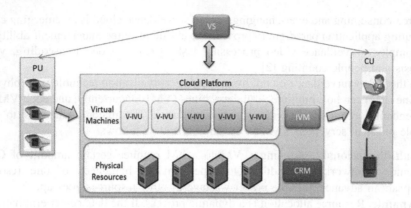

Fig. 1. System architecture.

In this section, we first present our cloud-based video surveillance system, and then give the details of the main cloud platform workflows.

2.1 Overview

We design a cloud-based video surveillance system which utilizes the virtualization technology to support the large scale surveillance video processing and provides the services finally. The video surveillance function modules comply with the ITU standard [3]. As shown in Fig. 1, the system can be divided into several parts and the functions of each part are presented as follows:

Cloud Platform: Cloud platform is the core part for the video surveillance cloud. The ultimate goal of cloud platform is to provide the available virtual machines. We implement our video surveillance cloud platform by the further development of the open source cloud platform Openstack. But the original built-in resource scheduling policy does not work well in the video surveillance cloud scenario. The algorithm is shown in the next section.

VIVU: Virtual Intelligent Visual Unit (VIVU) is the VM which incorporates a specific video processing program to complete the assigned tasks. The configuration of each VIVU is diverse, and depends on the performance trait and scale of some specific video processing task. For each VIVU, CRM manages its life cycle, but the transition between the states in the life cycle is triggered by IVM.

CRM: Cloud Resource Manager (CRM) manages the PMs and the lifecycle of VIVU in data center. CRM can provide three types of interactive modes: one is the command line interface for the operation staff, one is the restful API for other application callers and another is a Web page interface for general users.

IVM: Intelligent Visual Manager (IVM) is responsible for managing the video processing function components, such as video transcoding, video synopsis and object intrusion detection. When the video surveillance system sends a video processing request, IVM will trigger CRM to generate the VMs and deploy the corresponding video processing components on the VMs. The main tasks of IVM include: Firstly, receive and analyze the task request from the VS. Secondly, manage a set of VIVU (each one undertakes some specific video processing subtask). Thirdly, collect the processing results from VIVU and send the results to users.

CU: Customer Unit (CU) provides the integral video surveillance service interface for users. As the highly customizable software, CU can be implemented in different platforms such as PC, and mobile phone. In cloud-based video surveillance system, it initiates the workflow request, receives and presents the instant video processing results from the cloud platform.

PU: In cloud-based video surveillance system, Premises Unit (PU) is typically the IP camera which collects the surveillance video data from the monitoring region. PU can send the live video stream to other components through Internet.

VS: Visual Surveillance (VS) system is a centralized video surveillance management unit, and focuses on video application technology, which is used to remotely capture video and present it to the end user in a user-friendly manner, based on a managed broadband network with ensured quality, security and reliability. In addition, VS can send the task requests to the cloud platform for utilizing the cloud resources to efficiently process the surveillance video.

2.2 System Workflow

In this paper, we focus on the video surveillance cloud platform workflow. The other video surveillance function operations can comply with the traditional video surveillance systems [3]. The main workflow of video surveillance cloud platform includes cloud service deployment and cloud service running. The details of each workflow are as follows.

- **Cloud service deployment workflow:** CU initiates a video surveillance service which involves the video processing operation. VS receives the request from CU and forwards it to IVM. Then, IVM sends the resource request to CRM. When CRM receives the resource request from IVM, it will prepare ample IDLE VIVUs to execute the tasks. If no IDLE VIVU exists, CRM creates the relevant VIVU according to the resource request amount. This operation calls the allocation schedule module in cloud platform and changes the state of VIVU to INITING. After the preparation, CRM responds the IP address of VIVU to IVM. After IVM component gets the IP address, it assigns the video processing task to VIVU. Then VIVU transform the state to WORKING. In the process of task executing, IVM component monitors the state of VIVU. After a series of operations, the cloud service deployment workflow is over.
- **Cloud service running workflow:** For the video processing task in cloud platform, the source data is the live video data transmitted from PUs or the video data stored in VS. So the video processing tasks can be divided into online tasks and offline tasks. The VIVU, which performs the online task, receives the real-time video stream from

PUs, and can process the streaming video data instantly, e.g. object intrusion detection. The obtained results will be sent to CU directly or to VS for storage. The VIVU of the offline task can download and process the video files stored in the VS, and then uploads the results back to the VS, e.g., video synopsis. When the video processing task finishes, the VIVU changes its state to IDLE and waits for the new task. The task running process is not preemptive. If the VIVU maintains the IDLE state for a certain time, CRM will destroy it to prevent the waste of resources.

Actually, if some components consume one resource more, we will allocate more resource specified to it. We can see that, when many tasks arrive, a large number of virtual machine will be created to support the specific applications. Hence, with the placement of the virtual machines in the physical servers, the multi-resource allocation is a more serious problem in video surveillance cloud.

3   Multi-resource Allocation

As previously described, our interest scenario is the heterogeneous requests for a certain amount of multi-dimensional resources in video surveillance cloud.

3.1   Problem Formulation

We model the resource allocation in a video surveillance cloud platform with hetero-geneous servers. We consider a large cloud data center with limited physical resources. The multiple dimension resource can be classified as CPU, memory, storage, network bandwidth and so on. In this paper, our objective is to make full advantage of existing resources and maximize the resource utilization.

To formulate the problem, we use a quantity of properties that facilitates the rep-resentation of the resource allocation mechanism. We assume there are M PMs in data center and each independent PM can be formed as

$$pi = (pi_{r1}, \ldots, pi_{rj}, \ldots, pi_{rn}), \ r_j \in R,$$

then all the PMs will make up an $M*N$ matrix $P = (p_1, p_2, \ldots, p_m)^T$. For each row vector p_i in matrix P, its element pi_{rj} represents the current capacity of j-th corre-sponding resource type r_j in R. $R = (r_1, r_2, \ldots r_n)$ is a resource type set which contains several resource types abstracted from PM. In the process of allocation, the total remaining amount of each resource in video cloud can be calculated by

$$t_j = \sum_{i=1}^{m} pi_{rj}, \ p_i \in P, \ r_j \in R$$

All the t_j are integrated to a new vector: *total remaining amount vector* $T = (t_1, t_2, \ldots, t_n)^T$. Due to the dynamic nature of resource allocation, T is always changing along with the VM placement. Of particular note is that if one resource in a PM has dried up then other resource in the PM is not involved in the calculation of *total remaining amount vector*.

To build a complete P-V mapping model, we assume that there are K VM requests $V = (v_1, v_2, \ldots, v_n)^T$ to require physical resource from the numerous upper applications or users. The same as the resource description mode of physical server, each VM request can be identified as

$$vi = (vi_{r1}, \ldots vi_{rj}, \ldots vi_m), \ r_j \in R.$$

Hence, vi_{rj} denotes the amount of required resource r_j for VM to build a complete executable context.

For every VM request v_i, to analyze the concrete request situation aiming at the whole data center, we need to calculate the proportion of request amount and the total amount. We can get another relevant vector $vi^* = \left(vi_{r1}^*, \ldots, vi_{rj}^*, \ldots, vi_m^* \right)$ called *VM Request Proportion Vector* through the ratio

$$vi_{rj}^* = \frac{vi_{rj}}{t_j}, \ vi_{rj} \in vi, \ t_j \in T.$$

Simultaneously, each PM have their own *PM Resource Proportion Vector* $pi^* = \left(pi_{r1}^*, \ldots, pi_{rj}^*, \ldots, pi_m^* \right)$.

3.2   Algorithm

In this section, we present our proposed algorithm DRFA aiming at the heterogeneous cloud platform with the multi-resource VM request. To archive the target, we introduce the concept of dominant resource.

Algorithm 1. Dominant Resource First Allocation

INPUT: *pmList, vmQueue*
OUTPUT: *allocation*
1:   while *vmQueue is not empty* do
2:       *vm = vmQueue.first;*
3:       *r* = argmax(*vm.requestRatioVector*);
4:       *candidateSet* = find all pm which dominant resource type is r
5:       *candidate* = $\emptyset$;
6:       if *candidateSet* $\neq$ $\emptyset$ then
7:             *candidate = BestMatch(vm,candidateSet);*
8:       else
9:             *candidate = RANDOM(vm,pmList);*
10:   end if
11:   *allocation = (candidate,vm);*
12: end while
13: return *allocation.*

The algorithm DRFA is illustrated by Algorithm 1. In detail, the algorithm is designed as a loop program which is going to iterate all of the VM requests in the *vmQueue* (line 1). Following the FIFO principle, we choose the first *vm* request to conduct mapping (line 2) and determine which resource is dominant resource on the basis of *requestRatioVector*. For every *vm* planning to mapping, the operation is provided in two steps: firstly search for qualified candidate physical server sct (line 4) according to the dominant resource concept, secondly achieve the suitable *pm* with optimal match based on the match criteria (line 7). After the first step, if get no expected return value, we select one at random in the *pm* list as candidate (line 9). Finally, we allocate the resource from candidate to *vm* (line 11).

- **Dominant Resource** [7]. The heavily demanded resource required by VM named *VM Dominant Resource* should be $\bar{r}_j^*$ which meets the formula requirements

$$\bar{r}_j^* = argmax\left(vi_{rj}^{i*}\right), j \in [1, m].$$

and *PM Dominant Resource* $\bar{p}_i^*$ should be calculated as

$$\bar{p}_i^* = argmax\left(pi_{rj}^{i*}\right), j \in [1, m].$$

Actually, from the perspective of the entire data center, VM request is not only related to the PM remaining resource amount individually, but also the total available resource amount in data center. In detail, one kind of ample resource in a specific server cannot represent that the resource has advantages in whole data center, and perhaps it is scarce compared to other resources. With regard to this, consider the total resource is more able to grasp the characteristics of the heterogeneous resources in data center. Taking into account the *PM Dominant Resource* and *VM Dominant Resource* will be more suitable to the multidimensional, heterogeneous and dynamic feature of data center.

Algorithm 2. Best Match

INPUT: *candidateSet, vm*
OUTPUT: *candidate*
1: *minDistance* = +∞;
2: for ∀*pm* ∈ *candidateSet* do
3:     *distance* = *DISTANCE(pm,vm)*;
4:     if *minDistance* > *distance* then
5:         *minDistance* = *distance;*
6:         *candidate* = *pm;*
7:     end if
8: end for
9: return *candidate.*

- **Multi-Dimension Resource Matching Metric.** In order to find an ideal option for placing VM, we use matching criteria for candidate set in Algorithm 2 *Best Match*. The request distance is defined as the Euclidean distance of VM's request proportion vector and PM's resource proportion vector, but only if VM and PM have the same dominant resource type. The distance is calculated as:

$$DISTANCE(vi, pi) = \sqrt[2]{\sum_{j=1}^{n} \left(vi_{rj}^* - pi_{rj}^* \right)^2}, \; pi_{rj}^* \in pi^*, \; vi_{rj}^* \in vi^*$$

The smaller the request distance, the better the matching degree between vm_i and pm_i. We select pm_i with smallest distance as appropriate target node to allocate resource. In detail, if the distance value is zero, this means the resource in pm_i is exactly meet the request of vm_i.

4 Experimental Evaluation

4.1 Platform Implementation

Before proceeding any further, the platform implementation details and experimental environment is introduced in advance. Our cloud-base video surveillance system is based on two-node architecture Openstack [6].

In order to better meet the virtual machine placement scenario, we use the instance types shown in Table 1 and physical servers shown in Table 2. The instance types are all the standard types corresponding to our video processing tasks. The physical servers

Table 1. Cloud instance type

No.	Instance type	vCPU	Memory	Bandwidth
1	Standard Tiny	1 core	2 GB	1 M
2	Standard Medium1	2 core	4 GB	10 M
3	Standard Medium2	4 core	8 GB	4 M
4	Standard Medium3	4 core	8 GB	10 M
5	High-memory	8 core	16 GB	10 M
6	High-bandwidth	8 core	16 GB	20 M
7	High-CPU1	16 core	16 GB	10 M
8	High-CPU2	16 core	16 GB	20 M

Table 2. Physical Servers Type

No.	CPU	Memory	Bandwidth	Amount
1	64 core	128 GB	100 M	2
2	64 core	64 GB	50 M	2
3	32 core	64 GB	50 M	2
4	32 core	32 GB	50 M	2
5	16 core	32 GB	50 M	1

are emptied to wait the new requests. For the video processing task, we collect the live surveillance video stream from Global Eye video surveillance system in Fuzhou, China. For experiments, we randomly choose one task type to create VM and do the PM-VM mapping until that the physical resource cannot support any VM more. Each experiment, we replicate 20 times and calculate the mean value.

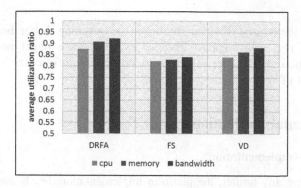

Fig. 2. Average resource utilization ratio.

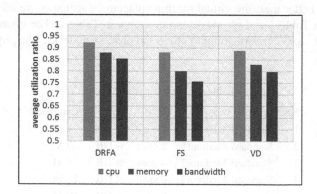

Fig. 3. Average resource utilization ratio.

4.2   Experimental Results

To evaluate the performance of our DRFA algorithm, we analyse the result by two metrics. First is the average resource utilization ratio of all physical servers. The second metric is the total amount of VM when all PMs are full. To confirm the advantage of our approach in the heterogeneous cloud scenario, we conduct the research of two other practical solutions.

FilterScheduler. FilterScheduler is the default scheduler policy in Openstack. It supports filtering and weighting to make informed decisions [6]. By weight calculation, the physical server with more memory will be selected as candidate.

VectorDot. VectorDot is proposed in [8]. The metric of VectorDot is to select PM with minimum value of the regular dot product of two vectors:

$$dotproduct(A, B) = \sum_{1 \leq i \leq |A|}^{n} a_i * b_i.$$

$A = (a_1, a_2, \ldots, a_n)$ means the physical server's load vector and $B = (b_1, b_2, \ldots, b_n)$ means the VM's resource requirements as a fraction of one PM's total capacity.

In the first experiment, we mix all task types and the daily VM requests, so all the instance types are uniform distribution. All physical servers shown in Table 2 participate in the resource allocation. We can find the result shown in Fig. 2. Through our algorithm, the average utilization ratio of each type of resource is higher than FilterScheduler and VectorDot. The average utilization ratio of memory and bandwidth are both over 90 percent.

In the second experiment, we just use the video processing task in our video surveillance cloud platform. For the task, the instance type is intensively used the 5–8 types in Table 1. All the physical servers can reveal the heterogeneous feature of servers in data center too. The result shown in Fig. 3 can reflect that the average utilization ratio of our approach is higher than those of other two policies. It means that our algorithm can make full advantage of the heterogeneous features of VM and PM. For the second experiment, we calculate the VM amount for video processing. The result is given in Fig. 4, and shows that cloud platform based on our algorithm can provide more VM than other two approaches. This is more important for a cloud platform to show the throughput. In the end, our algorithm improves system's throughput and can maximize the resource utilization.

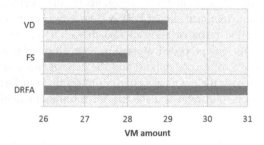

Fig. 4. VM amount in second experiment.

5 Related Work

In this section, we review a variety of relevant approaches about mapping VMs to physical servers in cloud.

The resource allocation problem can be attributed to the classical bin-packing problem in general case. To this regard, Urgaonkar et al. [9] did some research on maximizing the number of applications that can be hosted on a cloud platform. In addition to this, several open source softwares adopt simple algorithms to solve the problem. A round-robin scheduler is used in Eucalyptus [10] to select PMs. Openstack [6] uses its FilterScheduler to decide which PM is suitable and its default algorithm is select the PM with largest memory capacity. Farahnakian et al. [11] presented a VM management framework to minimize energy consumption and SLA violations, and its solution is just based on CPU. Actually, the single resource metric cannot meet the resource allocation task.

Some work considers the multi-dimensional feature. Singh et al. [8] designed an agile data center based on virtualization technologies. In order to deal with multi-dimensional resource constraints, they proposed a novel load balancing algorithm called VectorDot for multi-dimensional knapsacks. All of the above approaches pay more attention to the multi-dimension feature and lay within the range of virtualization technology without its cost. In consideration of the heterogeneous feature, Wang, W. et al. [12] does a systematic study on heterogeneous feature and generalizes the notion of Dominant Resource Fairness [7] from a single server to multiple heterogeneous servers. Nevertheless, this method is to address the job scheduling problem and achieve the max-min fair allocation.

6   Conclusion

In this paper, we design a video surveillance cloud platform to address the large scale surveillance video processing issues. Based on our cloud platform, we can provide several video processing services such as video transcoding, video synopsis, video forwarding, object intrusion detection and license plate recognition. In order to meet the multi-resource VM requests in the heterogeneous data center, we propose the multi-resource allocation approach named DRFA. Our aim is to maximize the resource utilization ratio within the resource allowed. To this end, we utilize the concept of dominant resource. With our proposed algorithm, our cloud platform can make full advantage of both the heterogeneous request and the heterogeneous physical resources. The experiment results over the practical system confirm that our DRFA algorithm has the higher resource utilization ratio and the higher throughout than the other widely used policies.

Acknowledgments. This work is supported by the National High Technology Research and Development Program of China under Grant No. 2014AA015101; Key Technologies R&D Program of China under Grant No. 2013BAK01B02; National Natural Science Foundation of China (No. 61300013 and 61190114); Doctoral Program Foundation of Institutions of Higher Education of China (No. 20130005120011); Special Fund of Internet of Things Development of Ministry of Industry and Information Technology.

References

1. Zhao, X.M., Ma, H.D., Zhang, H.T., Tang, Y., Kou, Y.: HVPI: extending Hadoop to support video analytic applications. In: 2015 IEEE 8th International Conference on Cloud Computing, pp. 789–796 (2015)
2. Ma, H.D., Zeng, C.B., Ling, C.X.: A reliable people counting system via multiple cameras. ACM Trans. Intell. Syst. Technol. 3(2), 31:1–31:22 (2012)
3. Architectural requirements for visual of surveillance. ITU-T H.626 (2011)
4. Zhao, X.M., Ma, H.D., Zhang, H.T., Tang, Y., Fu, G.P.: Metadata extraction and correction for large-scale traffic surveillance videos. In: 2014 IEEE International Conference on Big Data, pp. 412–420 (2014)
5. Gao, Y.H., Ma, H.D., Zhang, H.T., Kong, X.Q., Wei, W.Y.: Concurrency optimized task scheduling for workflows in cloud. In: 2013 IEEE Sixth International Conference on Cloud Computing, pp. 709–716 (2013)
6. OpenStack. http://www.openstack.org/
7. Wang, W., Liang, B., Li, B.: Multi-resource fair allocation in heterogeneous cloud computing systems. IEEE Trans. Parallel Distrib. Syst. 26(10), 2822–2835 (2015)
8. Singh, A., Korupolu, M., Mohapatra, D.: Server-storage virtualization: integration and load balancing in data centers. In: 2008 International Conference for High Performance Computing, Networking, Storage and Analysis, pp. 1–12 (2008)
9. Urgaonkar, B., Rosenberg, A.L., Shenoy, P.: Application placement on a cluster of servers. Int. J. Found. Comput. Sci. 18(05), 1023–1041 (2007)
10. Eucalyptus (2015). https://www.eucalyptus.com/
11. Farahnakian, F., Liljeberg, P., Pahikkala, T., Plosila, J., Tenhunen, H.: Hierarchical VM management architecture for cloud data centers. In: 2014 IEEE 6th International Conference on Cloud Computing Technology and Science, pp. 306–311 (2014)
12. Wang, W., Liang, B., Li, B.: Multi-resource fair allocation in heterogeneous cloud computing systems. IEEE Trans. Parallel Distrib. Syst. 26(10), 2822–2835 (2015)

Exploring User Mobile Shopping Activities Based on Characteristic of Eye-Tracking

Jing Zhu[2], Xue Han[2], Rong Ma[2], Xiaowei Li[2], Tong Cao[2],
Shuting Sun[1], and Bin Hu[1,2(✉)]

[1] School of Information Science and Engineering,
Shandong Normal University, Jinan, China
{sunsht14, bh}@lzu.edu.cn
[2] School of Information Science and Engineering,
Lanzhou University, Lanzhou, China
{zhujing, hanxl3, marong, lixwei, caot14, bh}@lzu.edu.cn

Abstract. This study aims to investigate user visual attention level in their mobile shopping activities based on our eye-tracking experiment, which may potentially contribute to the development in mobile commerce website design. We found that the distribution of products information in a page may have a great impact on visual search behavior and reaction time. Reaction time is normally at a minimum when target element is put on the top left. Conversely, it tends to increase when target element is put on the bottom right. Moreover, visual attention focus between computer based web pages and mobile ones is also different based on our research in characteristics of eye-tracking. Previous study has reported that user focus is mostly on higher position entries in a search engine result page, however in our research, users concern the items displayed at the central area more than the top. This is probably because that the size of a mobile shopping page is not as big as a computer based web page, also with more limited information. This finding may be a hint to enhance mobile commerce website design.

Keywords: Eye-tracking · Mobile shopping · Mobile commerce website design

1 Introduction

With the development of Internet, online shopping has become a fashion purchase habit. Furthermore, against the backdrop of growing 4G technology, mobile commerce and mobile shopping has attracted increasing attention. Estimates from CNNIC 2015 suggest that netizens who shop online account for 55.7 percent of Chinese total number of netizens respectively, while those shop on mobile commerce websites make up 42.4 percent [1].

Figures 1 and 2 show that the proportion of consumers who had online shopping experiences and who had mobile commerce websites shopping experiences. It becomes clearly that online shopping, specifically mobile shopping has really attracted a lot of attention. Therefore, the ability to investigate user visual attention level in their mobile shopping activities could offer several benefits to both end-users and mobile commerce website designers.

© Springer International Publishing Switzerland 2016
Q. Zu and B. Hu (Eds.): HCC 2016, LNCS 9567, pp. 556–566, 2016.
DOI: 10.1007/978-3-319-31854-7_50

Previous studies have used eye-tracking to understand how people view and interact with computer based web pages, generally speaking, most of them focused on the area about web search behavior and image viewing behavior.

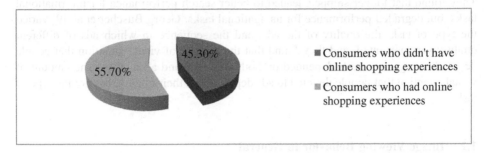

Fig. 1. The proportion of consumers who had online shopping experiences

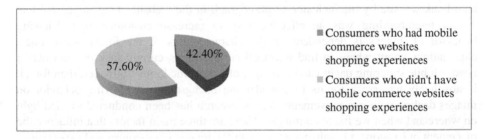

Fig. 2. The proportion of consumers who had mobile commerce websites shopping experiences

1.1 Web Search Behavior in General

When it comes to web search behavior, researchers try hard to answer 3 questions: How do users interact with the list of ranked results of WWW search engines? How many of the results do users evaluate before clicking on a link or reformulating the search? Do they read the abstracts sequentially from top to bottom, or do they skip links? Laura A. Granka et al. [2] investigated how users interacted with the results page of a WWW search engine using eye-tracking. They found that the mean time users fixated on a presented abstract at the displayed results is almost equal for the first two links. Meanwhile, after the analysis, they concluded that users did tend to scan the list from top to bottom. Silversteint et al. [3] attempted to use eye movements to infer the relevancy of documents in the retrieval phase of an information search. The researchers linked relevancy judgments to increases in pupil diameter, as a larger diameter typically signifies high interest in the content matter. And numerous works have developed well-known terms to describe typical gaze distributions on search engine result pages, such as the "golden triangle" [4] or the "F-shaped pattern" [5]. Smith, C. L et al. [6] found that search success was same for both good and degraded systems, but the users altered their strategies depending on the quality of the engine results. Joachims et al. [7]

showed that the way in which users examined a search engine result page was influenced by the position and relevance of the results. Users have a bias towards result entries at higher positions on the search engine result page. Cutrell et al. [8] looked in more detail at how eye movements were influenced by the snippets for search results. They found that longer snippets leaded to better search performance for informational tasks, but degraded performance for navigational tasks. Georg Buscher et al. [9] varied the type of task, the quality of the ads, and the sequence in which ads of different quality were presented, and they found that the amount of visual attention that people devoted to organic results depended on both task type and ad quality. The amount of visual attention that people devoted to ads depended on their quality, but not the type of task.

1.2   Image Viewing Behavior in General

Generally speaking, images play an important role in E-commerce websites. Ulrike Steinbrück et al. [10] found a significant positive effect on perceived trustworthiness of an e-bank website by the inclusion of photograph in the website. They suggested that virtual re-embedding was an effective way to increase customer trust. Viewing behavior of images is dependent on the characteristics of the image itself, one's expectations about where to find information, and one's current task or information need. Mobile shopping pages can be thought of as specific kinds of images, therefore, it is absolutely necessary for us to consider the background of viewing behavior on images dealing with eye movements. Much research has been conducted to shed light on where and when we fixate on images. There are three main factors that influence the placement of fixations: (1) salience of areas in the image; (2) memory and expectations about where to find information; and (3) task and information need at hand. [11] Henderson et al. [12] showed that salience of area was typically computed based on low-level image characteristics, particularly color, intensity, edge density, and edge orientation. They also pointed out that the first fixation was typically placed on the most salient spot, and memory and expectations also played important roles in subsequent fixations. Goldberg et al. [13] investigated eye movement on Web portals during search tasks. They found that header bars were almost not viewed before focusing the main part of the page. As a result, they suggested placing navigation bars on the left side of a page. Soussan Djamasbi et al. [14] focused on online survey and participants' eye-movement to prove that generation Y (age 18–31) may prefer pages that included a main large image, images of celebrities, little text, and a search feature. Jonathan Ling et al. [15] focused on the effect of color on the presentation of information in a navigation bar, and they show that higher contrasts between text and background color led to faster searching. LI Mi et al. [16] focused on the characteristics of visual search on Web page on cognitive science, and they found that people had paid more attention to search on the peripheral area than on the central area of Web page by vision.

In summary, previous studies have done a lot of research on computer based web pages by eye-tracking. However, when we turn the angle to mobile ones, there are few research results. For our study, we want to: (1) investigate user visual attention level in their mobile shopping activities based on our eye-tracking experiment; and (2) see if we could find any differences of visual attention focus between computer based web pages and mobile ones in characteristics of eye-tracking.

2   Methods

2.1   Participants

28 participants completed the experimental tasks. Due to the inability of some participants to be precisely calibrated, complete eye movement data was recorded for 22 of the participants, consisted of 8 females and 14 males. The mean age of participants was 24 years 11 months, with a standard deviation of 3 years 1 month. All participants spoke Chinese as their mother tongue, and had trichromatic and normal or corrected to normal vision. All participants reported a high familiarity with online shopping, with 21 users indicating that they shop on mobile commerce websites frequently.

2.2   Apparatus

The experiment was performed on a 17″ LCD monitor at a screen resolution of 1024 × 768 pixels. Eye tracking was performed using the Eye link II eye tracker. The eye tracker had an accuracy of 0.5° and a sampling rate of 500 Hz. Before starting the tasks, we performed a 9 point calibration of the eye tracker for each participant.

2.3   Experimental Design and Procedure

In this study, one training task and five experimental tasks were conducted by each participant. Every task included two parts, one was to search a special target element on a mobile shopping page, and the other was to choose the most appealing goods on the searching result list pages. More specifically, for each task, participants were asked to search a target element on the mobile shopping page first. Each target element was put on the top left, bottom left, top right, bottom right or central area of the pages arbitrarily, which was composed of a short phrase or a special picture. Participants had to press the space key as soon as possible when they saw the target element. After that, a searching result list page contained five items would show on monitor, participants were asked to choose the most appealing goods by pressing the number key 1, 2, 3, 4 or 5 on keyboard. All experimental materials were captured from mobile shopping pages, and displayed on monitor at a screen resolution of 400 × 710 pixels.

Each participant completed demographic and consent, then received an explanation of the experiment. After one training task, the eye tracker began to work, followed by a short calibration procedure. Five experimental tasks were then presented in a fixed order. The experiment took about 10 min per participant.

Figure 3 showed the experimental procedure. From this figure, it became clearly that the experimental procedure included five steps.

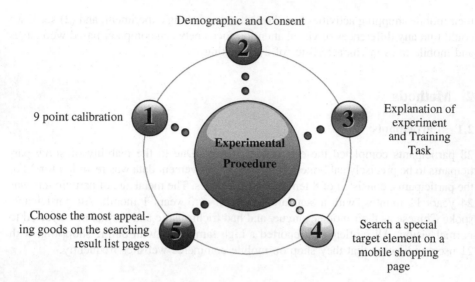

Fig. 3. The experimental procedure

2.4   Measures

Gaze data that recorded with EyeLink eye tracker was processed by EyeLink Data Viewer. In this study, we paid close attention to three types of gaze data.

One type of gaze data that caught our attention was scan path. Scan path can reproduce the visual search process of the participants clearly. In this study, we used typical chart of scan path to describe eye tracking when the participants searched the target information.

Fixation is the second type of gaze data that we focused on. Previous studies have defined fixation as a gaze longer than 300 ms, [17] and fixation was always linked to intense cognitive processing. Similar to prior research, in this study, we translated the cumulative fixation data for all participants into heat maps. In a heat map, areas without color were not fixated upon, green indicate a decreasing level of fixation, while red indicates a high level of fixation. Correspondingly, areas with red were the areas that the participants fixated the most on a page.

In addition, data was gathered on the reaction time. Reaction time was a period, after the page was presented, until participants found the target information on specific areas of interest on a page. The shorter the searching time, the more efficient searching result.

3   Results

3.1   Analysis of Scan Path

In the first part of our experiment, we divided the mobile shopping pages into a total of 5 areas of interest, which lied at top left, bottom left, top right, bottom right and central area of the pages. We put the target element on corresponding areas of interest arbitrarily and asked participants to search.

Figure 4 showed the eye movement contrails of scan path on mobile shopping pages. It became clear that the major gaze regions mainly concentrated on the peripheral area of pages, rather than the central area. Moreover, the feature was independent of the location of the target element, that is to say, even if the target element located on the central of the mobile shopping page, the major gaze regions also concentrated on the peripheral area of the pages. Furthermore, we can see that, when target element was put on the top left area, the number of fixations was at a minimum, and when target element was put on the central areas, the number of fixations was at a maximum. Therefore, we could draw a conclusion from Fig. 1, nearly all participants followed the searching habit, searching from top to bottom, or left to right.

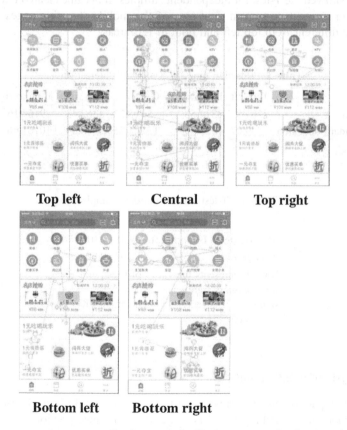

Fig. 4. The eye movement contrails of scan path. Circle represented a fixation, the bigger the circle was, the loner the fixation duration last. Arrowed segments between each two circles were saccades, which depicted the scan path.

3.2   Analysis of Reaction Time

In the first part of our experiment, we compared reaction time in 5 areas of interest. Analysis of variance (ANOVA) was used to assess the effect of location in terms of differences in reaction time, and post hoc analysis tested for differences in performance between combinations.

Table 1 showed the mean and standard deviation of the reaction time for 5 areas of interest. Moreover, the figures in Table 1 indicated that, when target element was put on top left, reaction time required was at a minimum (3.2 s), and when target element was put on the bottom right areas, reaction time required was at a maximum (9.1 s). Furthermore, we sorted the reaction time from short to long, the sequence was top left, bottom left, top right, center and bottom right area.

A one-way ANOVA showed that there was an effect of location combination, $F_{(4,105)} = 3.06$, $p = 0.02 < 0.05$.

Table 2 showed the T-test for independent samples. It became cleared that when we put the target element on bottom right area of the mobile shopping pages it showed significantly different from top left and bottom left areas.

Table 1.   Reaction time for 5 areas of interest (ms)

	Top left	Bottom left	Center	Top right	Bottom right
Mean	3261.51	3314.53	8795.23	4362.43	9164.16
Standard deviation	769.27	2525.59	13248.35	5348.54	10161.66

Table 2.   T-test for independent samples

		t	sig
Bottom right	Bottom left	7.05	0.01
Bottom right	Top left	12.07	0.00

Note: *t* represents the value of t-test, and *sig* represents significance, there is a significant difference between samples if sig < 0.05.

3.3   Analysis of Fixation and Heat Maps

In the second part of our experiment, participants were asked to choose the most appealing goods in a searching result list page. As mentioned previously, fixation was defined as a gaze longer than 300 ms, and heat maps were translated by cumulative fixation data for all participants.

Figure 5 showed images of the heat maps. In general, the highest rated pages had focused, bright red hot spots, located at the second and the third item of the list. On the lowest rated pages, fixation was much more scattered, suggested that nothing immediately drew the attention of the participants.

In addition, Fig. 6 showed the choice times of each item in our experiment, and the figures in this figure added to growing evidence that links ranked 2 and 3 get more attention.

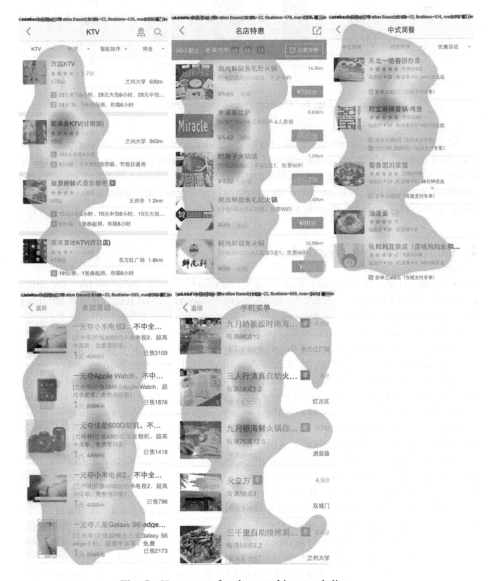

Fig. 5. Heat maps for the searching result list page

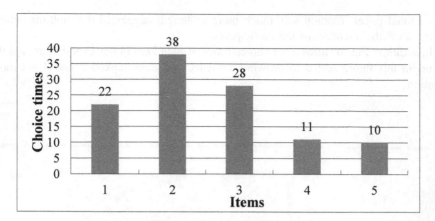

Fig. 6. Choice times of each item

More specifically, fixation on the highest rated pages appeared on the prices, the names of stores and others' comments. However, images did not get as much attention. It was not surprising that the prices, the name, score and distance of the store received attention, particularly as these were the principal factors when participants choose the most appealing goods on mobile commerce websites.

4   Conclusion and Discussion

Overall, our study investigates user visual attention level in their mobile shopping activities based on our eye-tracking experiment. Moreover, we find some differences between computer based web pages and mobile ones in characteristics of eye-tracking.

Previous studies have drawn a conclusion that visual search behavior would be guided by the physical location of the display [16, 17]. In this study, our findings are in general accord with previous research. We find that the distribution of products information in a page may have a great impact on visual search behavior and reaction time (Figure 1 and Table 1). We further find that reaction time is normally at a minimum when target element is put on the top left area. Conversely, it tends to increase when target element is put on the bottom right area. The sequence of reaction time is in line with people's reading habits, reading from top to bottom, or left to right.

For most people, the central region of a page is always the first point of fixation. Interestingly, the reaction time becomes longer when the target element appears at the central area in this study. GODIJN R et al. Some scholars come up with a theory "Inhibition-of-Return" for the reason. As the central region of a page has already been browsed, the participants will inhibit themselves back to the central area, and give more priority to the peripheral area. Therefore, it is recommended that, when mobile commerce website designers put the principal contents in the central area of a mobile shopping page, we need to use a small group of types set in larger size or brighter text colors or more striking images than the other areas of the page to help end-users search for information.

Moreover, the reaction time required is at a minimum when target element is put on the top left area of a mobile shopping page, on which mobile commerce website designers should put much more principal information, so that the efficiency of searching will be significantly enhanced. For example, most mobile commerce website designers tend to place navigation on this area, it is quite advisable. On the contrary, the reaction time required is at a maximum when target element is put on the bottom right area It is recommended that mobile commerce website designers should better not place any important information on this area where is easily overlooked.

Previous study has reported that user focus is mostly on higher position entries in a search engine result page, which displayed ten or more results per page [7], however in our research, we find that links ranked 2 and 3 in a searching result list page always get more attention, and the choice times are more than others. In our study there were just five results contained per mobile shopping page, so we can believe that users concern the items displayed at the central area more than the top. This is probably because the size of a mobile shopping page is not as big as a computer based web page, also with more limited information. It is recommended that, when sellers sell their products on mobile commerce websites, the central area is the golden position, where would get more attention come along with more profit.

We further find that the prices, the names of stores and others' comments get much attention when participants choose the most appealing goods in a searching result list page. Conversely, images did not get as much attention. Online consumers, especially end-users of a mobile commerce website who use cyberspace for transactions normally reserved for the storefront are always prefer to choose their familiar sellers and quality merchandises with better commentary. Moreover, users shop on a mobile commerce website just would like to save cost. Therefore, the price is the primary factor considered when users make a purchase decision. Consequently, sellers should focus on improving the quality of products and service rather than display striking images to attract attention.

5 Future Work

In addition to further evaluations of the eye tracking data itself, we are currently gathering characteristics of user mobile shopping activities. For example, what is the relationship between a purchase decision and the characteristic of eye-tracking? Do users tend to choose the merchandise which cost a relatively longer watching time? These will require us to assess user behavior more detailed in the future.

Acknowledgement. This work was supported by the National Basic Research Program of China (973 Program) (No.2014CB744600), the National Natural Science Foundation of China (grant No.60973138, grant No.61003240), the International Cooperation Project of Ministry of Science and Technology (No.2013DFA11140), the National Basic Research Program of China (973 Program) (No.2011CB711000).

References

1. The 35th survey report from CNNIC: Personal Application of Internet. http://tech.sina.com. cn/i/2015-02-03/doc-iawzunex9713411.shtml
2. Granka, L.A.: Eye-tracking analysis of user behavior in WWW search. In: Proceedings of the 27th Annual International ACM SIGIR Conference on Research and Development in Information Retrieval, pp. 478–479 (2004)
3. Silverstein, C., Henzinger, M., Marais, J., Moricz, M.: Analysis of a very large AltaVista query log. Technical report, Hewlett Packard Laboratories, Number SRC-TN 1998-014, 19 October 1998
4. Hotchkiss, G., Alston, S., Edwards, G.: Eye tracking study (2006). Accessed 18 Jan 2010
5. Nielsen, J.: F-Shaped pattern for reading Web content (2006). Accessed 18 Jan 2010
6. Smith, C.L., Kantor, P.B.: User adaptation: good results from poor systems. In: Proceedings SIGIR 2008, pp. 147–154 (2008)
7. Joachims, T., Granka, L., Pan, B., Hembrooke, H., Gay, G.: Accurately interpreting clickthrough data as implicit feedback. In: Proceedings SIGIR 2005, pp. 154–161 (2005)
8. Cutrell, E., Guan, Z.: What are you looking for? An eye-tracking study of information usage in web search. In: Proceedings CHI 2007, pp. 407–416 (2007)
9. Georg, B., Susan, D., Edward, C.: The good, the bad, and the random: an eye-tracking study of ad quality in web search. In: Proceedings of the 33rd International ACM SIGIR Conference on Research and Development in Information Retrieval, pp. 42–49 (2010)
10. Steinbrück, U., Schaumburg, H., Duda, S., Krüger, T.: A picture says more than a thousand words -photographs as trust builders in e-commerce websites. In: Short Talk: User Studies – Lessons for HCI, pp. 748–749 (2002)
11. Buscher, G., Cutrell, E., Morris, M.R.: What do you see when you're surfing? Using eye tracking to predict salient regions of web pages. In: Proceedings of the SIGCHI Conference on Human Factors in Computing Systems, pp. 21–30 (2009)
12. Henderson, J.M.: Human gaze control during real-world scene perception. Trends Cogn. Sci. 7(11), 498–504 (2003)
13. Goldberg, J.H., Stimson, M.J., Lewenstein, M., Scott, N., Wichansky, A.M.: Eye tracking in web search tasks: design implications. In: Proceedings of the 2002 Symposium on Eye Tracking Research & Applications, pp. 51–58 (2002)
14. Djamasbi, S., Siegel, M., Tullis, T.: Generation Y, web design, and eye tracking. Int. J. Hum. Comput. Stud. 68(5), 307–323 (2010)
15. Ling, J., van Schaik, P.: The effect of text and background colour on visual search of web pages. Displays 23, 223–230 (2002)
16. Mi, L., Ning, Z., Shengfu, L.V.: A study about the characteristics of visual search on web pages. J. Front. Comput. Sci. Technol. 3, 649–655 (2009)
17. Djamasbi, S., Tullis, T., Hsu, J., Mazuera, E., Osberg, K., Bosch, J.: Gender preferences in web design: usability testing through eye tracking. In: Proceedings of the 13th Americas Conference on Information Systems, pp. 1–8 (2007)

Frequency Domain and Time Domain Study of a Novel Compact CPW Fed Monopole UWB Antenna with L Shaped Slots for Band Notched Characteristics

Jinning Zhao, Rong Ma, Bin Hu[✉], Guoping Gao, Lele He,
and Xiaolong Tian

School of Information Science and Engineering,
Lanzhou University, Room 404, FeiYun Lou, 222 TianShui Road,
Lanzhou 730000, Gansu Province, People's Republic of China
bh@lzu.edu.cn

Abstract. In this paper, the design, simulation and fabrication of a CPW fed monopole UWB antenna with band-notched function suitable for UWB application are presented and investigated. The band–notched characteristic is achieved by inserting two L shaped slots symmetrically in the radiation element. Experimental results show that the proposed antenna meets the requirement of VSWR < 2 in the working bandwidth of 3.1–10.6 GHz except the stop band (5.0–5.9 GHz) for avoiding the WLAN band. The study of transfer function (magnitude of S_{21} and group delay) and time domain characteristic (fidelity and power spectrum density (PSD)) verify the band-notched function of the antenna. The proposed antenna have compact size, good radiation characteristics, ultra wide band-width and good time-domain behaviors, which satisfy the requirement of the current wireless communications systems.

Keywords: UWB antenna · L shaped slot · Band notched · Frequency domain · Time domain

1 Introduction

Recently, ultra-wideband (UWB) technology has given rise to much interest in designing wideband antennas [1]. It is mainly because the UWB technology has much attractive features such as wide bandwidth, low cost, small size, easy fabrication and omni-directional radiation pattern. Since the Federal Communications Commission (FCC) released unlicensed band from 3.1 to 10.6 GHz for radio communication in 2002, UWB antennas have been widely investigated by both industry and academia. Printed monopole antennas have received so much attention in UWB application as they exhibit very attractive merits such as wide impedance bandwidth, simple structure and omni-directional radiation pattern. Recently, several printed monopole antennas have been proposed to cover the frequency band defined by the FCC from 3.1 to 10.6 GHz for UWB applications [2–4].

© Springer International Publishing Switzerland 2016
Q. Zu and B. Hu (Eds.): HCC 2016, LNCS 9567, pp. 567–577, 2016.
DOI: 10.1007/978-3-319-31854-7_51

In general, UWB antenna covers the frequency range from 3.1 to 10.6 GHz. However, this frequency range includes the WLAN band of 5.15–5.825 GHz for IEEE 802.11a. To avoid the possible interference between the UWB band and the WLAN band, it is necessary to filter the WLAN band that disturbs the UWB system. Compared with the method that integrating a filter with the antenna, a antenna with band-notched characteristic can be a better choice to overcome this problem because it is a simple way. A large numbers of antennas with band-notched characteristic have been reported, and various methods have been used to obtain this function. The most popular methods are adding stubs on the radiation patch and the micro-strip line [5, 6] or introducing parasitic strips near the radiation elements, micro-strip line and the ground plane [7–10]. In addition, dielectric resonator technology is also often used to achieve band-notched characteristic [11]. But they are all too complex. Etching slots on the patch or on the ground plane is a traditional and simple method to create notched band [12]. The design of the band-notched UWB antenna is still a major challenge nowadays.

In this paper, a compact CPW fed monopole UWB antenna is proposed and investigated. The band-notched characteristic is achieved by two symmetrical L shaped slots inserted in the radiation element. By adjusting the location and length of the slots, the band-notched function can be realized. Details of the antenna design, simulation and measurement results are presented and discussed in the next sections.

2   Antenna Design and Results

Figure 1 shows the geometry and photograph of the proposed monopole antenna. The antenna is fabricated on a substrate with the relative dielectric constant of 2.78 and the thickness of 0.8 mm. Total size of the antenna is W × L. The radiation element is a U shaped circular disc which is fed by coplanar waveguide (CPW) structure. The width and gap of the CPW feed line are fixed with W1 and g to achieve 50 Ω characteristic

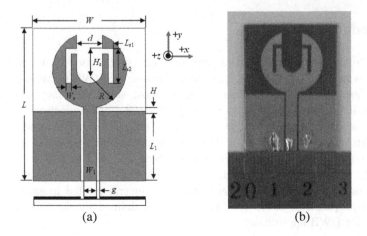

(a)   (b)

Fig. 1. The geometry and photograph of the proposed antenna, (a) geometry, (b) photograph.

impedance. In order to avoid the interference between UWB band and WLAN band, two L shaped slots are inserted symmetrically in the radiation element. The slots destroy the surface current on the radiation element so that the antenna makes negative response at the notched frequency. The location, length and width of the slots are adjusted to obtain a stop band at the designed frequency. Detailed dimensions of the antenna are shown in Table 1.

Table 1. The dimensions of the proposed antenna. All dimensions are in millimeters.

Parameter	W	L	W_1	L_1	g	H
Value	26	35	3	16	0.6	0.8
Parameter	R	d	H_s	W_s	L_{s1}	L_{s2}
Value	8.6	6	5	1.2	2.5	8

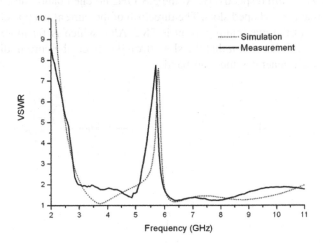

Fig. 2. The measured and simulated VSWR of the proposed antenna.

An antenna prototype is constructed and investigated with the parameters given in Table 1. The simulation of the antenna is carried out by CST Microwave Studio software based on the method of finite integration technology (FIT), and the measurement is implemented by using Agilent E8363B Vector Network Analyzer. Figure 2 shows the measured and simulated VSWR of the proposed antenna respectively. It is clearly seen that the band notched characteristic is obtained by inserting L shaped slots into the antenna. Simulation and measurement results of the band notched antenna agree well with each other. Measured frequency range of VSWR < 2 is from 2.9 GHz to 11 GHz except the notched band from 5.0 to 5.9 GHz. The measured notched band of VSWR > 2 is a little wider than the simulated one. This difference is mainly caused by the fabrication error, the SMA connector and the numerical error. Both the measured and simulated results are suitable for UWB antenna with 5 GHz notched band.

In order to study the band notched characteristics of the antenna, parameters Ls2 and Ws which define the length and the width of the L shaped slots are studied. The Ls1 is fixed at 2.5 mm in the parameter study. Figure 3 shows the effect of changing Ls2 on VSWR. It can be seen the notched frequency decreases when increasing the length of the slot. The VSWR of the notched frequency decreases when decreasing the length of the slot. So both the notched frequency and the peak VSWR of the notched band should be considered when selecting the length of the slot.

The effect of the width of the slot Ws on the band-notched characteristics is shown in Fig. 4. The width of the L shaped slots Ws shows less influence on the VSWR. The bandwidth of the notched frequency shows a little increase when increasing Ws. It is promising to control the notched band by varying the length and the width of the slots.

The simulated surface current distributions of the proposed antenna at 3.5 GHz, 5.8 GHz (notched-band) and 8.8 GHz are plotted in Fig. 5(a), (b) and (c) respectively. At the frequencies of 3.6 GHz and 8.8 GHz, the current distribution focus on the microstrip line and the bottom part of the monopole antenna. The maximum current is 13.0 A/m and 11.5 A/m respectively. At the 5.8 GHz notched band, the current mainly distributes around the L shaped slots. The direction of the current is opposite around the L shaped slots and the maximum current is 58.2 A/m, which is far more than that at the operation band. It is evident that the slots strongly affects the current distribution of the antenna, which generates the stop band.

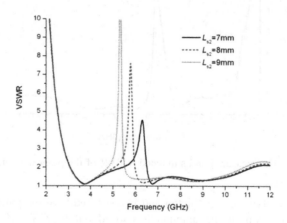

Fig. 3. The effect of changing L_{s2} on VSWR.

Simulated radiation patterns in the x-z, x-y and y-z planes are plotted in Fig. 6(a), (b) and (c) respectively. It can be seen that the x-z plane (H-plane) radiation patterns are approximately omni-directional over the entire operation frequencies, and the radiation is relatively stable (variation less than 10 dB) at different frequencies. The x-y plane and y-z plane (E-plane) radiation patterns at 4 GHz and 7 GHz are as same as that of a dipole antenna, while it becomes butterfly-shaped at 10 GHz. So the E-plane pattern is monopole-like and the number of lobes rises with the increase of the frequency, which means the antenna becomes more directional. Figure 7 shows the peak gain against

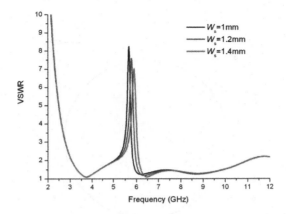

Fig. 4. The effect of changing W_s on VSWR.

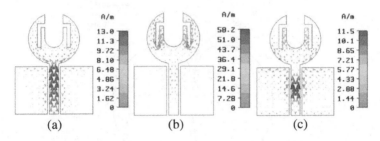

(a)   (b)   (c)

Fig. 5. Simulated current distribution of the proposed antenna in different frequencies, (a) 3.6 GHz, (b) 5.8 GHz, (c) 8.8 GHz.

frequency of the proposed antenna. It is evident that the peak gain is relatively flat over the operation band and the variation is from 2.2 to 3.56 dBi, while a large drop is observed at the notched-frequency. The minimum value of the peak gain is in the vicinity of 5.5 GHz (−4.15 dBi). The antenna gain, which corresponds well with the VSWR, presents that the antenna successfully performs the band-notch function at 5 GHz WLAN band.

3   Transfer Function and Time Domain Study

3.1   Transfer Function Measurement

Since the UWB systems use short pulses to transmit signals, it is very important to study the transfer function and time domain characteristics for evaluating the antenna's performance and designing the transmitting pulse signals. In our study, the UWB antenna is viewed as a filter with magnitude (antenna gain) and phase response. The phase response and group delay are related to the antenna gain response. The group delay is able to clearly show any nonlinearity that presented in the phase response, which indicates the degree of the distortion. For UWB applications, the magnitude of

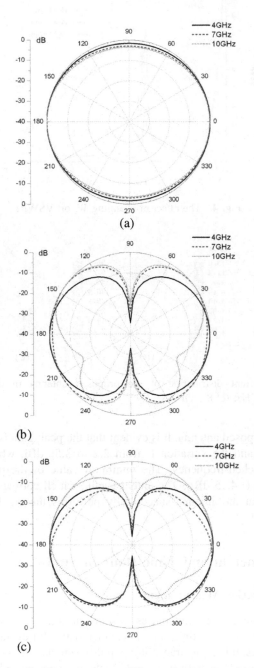

Fig. 6. The simulated radiation patterns at different frequencies. (a) *x-z* plane (*H*-plane); (b) *x-y* plane (*E*-plane); (c) *y-z* plane (*E*-plane).

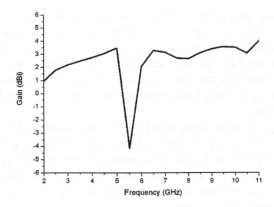

Fig. 7. Peak gain against frequency of the proposed antenna.

the transfer function should be as flat as possible and the phase response should be linear, meanwhile, the group delay is required to be constant over the entire band as well.

The transfer function was measured by the Agilent E8363B Vector Network Analyzer as shown in Fig. 8. It should be noted that the measurement was carried out in real environment with reflecting objects in surrounding area. A pair of the proposed antennas are used as the transmitting and receiving antenna respectively. The transmitter and receiver are positioned side by side (x directions opposite) with the distance of 10 cm. Considering the antenna system as a two-port network, the transmission scattering parameter S21 which indicates the transfer function is measured. In order to evaluate the transfer function in direction z, the transmitter and receiver are positioned face to face (z directions opposite) in our experiment.

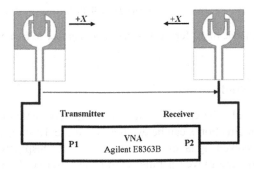

Fig. 8. The schematic diagram of transfer function measurement (side by side mode).

The measured magnitudes of S_{21} in face to face mode and side by side mode are shown in Fig. 9. It can be seen that the attenuation is more than 20 dB in the notched band, and the magnitude outside of the notched-band in 3.1 GHz–10.6 GHz is relative flat.

So it reveals that the antenna has notched characteristic in x and z directions. Stable band-notched characteristic of the proposed UWB antenna is obtained.

Measured phases of S_{21} for the antenna system in two different mode are shown in Fig. 10. In Fig. 10, the dash line represents the measured phase in side by side mode and the solid line represents the measured phase in face to face mode. It can be seen that the phase response is nearly linear in the operation frequency band, while it distorts in 5 GHz notched band.

The measured group delay is given in Fig. 11. The variation of the group delay for both face to face mode and side by side mode are within 1.0 ns across the whole UWB band except the notched band, in which the maximum group delay is nearly 8 ns. The group delay of the antenna system corresponds well with the magnitude and phase response of the transfer function. So it proves that the antenna has good time-domain characteristic and small pulse distortion.

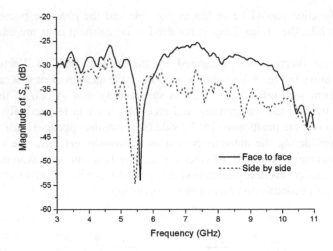

Fig. 9. Measured magnitude of S_{21} for the antenna system in face to face mode and side by side mode.

3.2   Time Domain Study

Time domain study is also based on the measurement schematic diagram as shown in Fig. 8, so the pulse in direction x can be evaluated. Figure 12 shows the excited signal, radiated signal and received signal of the proposed antenna respectively. In order to see clearly, the waveforms are moved parallel along the abscissa. It can be seen that the radiated signal and received signal distort compared with the excited signal, so we can study the fidelity and the normalized power spectrum density (PSD) to evaluate the characteristics of signal transmitting and receiving in side by side mode.

Figure 13 shows the normalized power spectrum density (PSD) of the excited signal, radiated signal and received signal respectively. It can be seen that all the pulses comply with FCC's emission mask. Reduction of the bandwidth of the radiated and

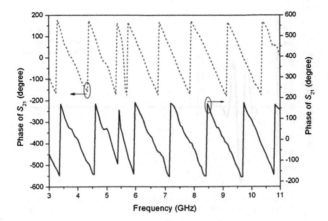

Fig. 10. Measured phase of S_{21} for the antenna system in face to face mode and side by side mode.

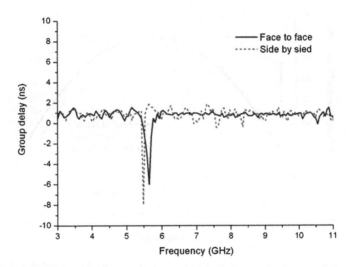

Fig. 11. Measured group delay of the antenna system in face to face mode and side by side mode.

received pulse's PSD can be seen compared with the PSD of the excited pulse. The PSD of radiated and received signal show a similar result and decreased in the notched band, which confirms the transfer function results.

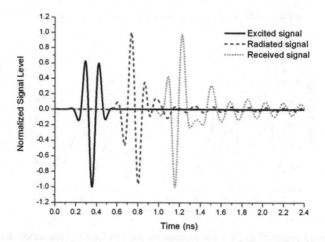

Fig. 12. The pulse waveforms of the antenna system in side by side mode.

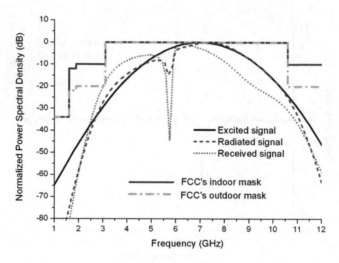

Fig. 13. The normalized power spectrum density (PSD) of pulses for the antenna system in side by side mode.

4 Conclusion

A novel band-notched CPW fed monopole antenna with two L shaped slots inserted to the radiation element is investigated in this paper. The study of VSWR, current distribution and gain show that the antenna has band-notched characteristic at 5 GHz WLAN band. Monopole-like radiation pattern of the proposed antenna is observed. Transfer function and time domain study results confirm that the proposed antenna have band-notched characteristics in the WLAN band, which is suitable for the UWB signal communication.

Acknowledgment. This work was supported by the National Basic Research Program of China (No. 2014CB744600), the International Cooperation Project of Ministry of Science and Technology (No. 2013DFA11140), the National Natural Science Foundation of China (No. 61401183 and No. 61210010), and the Fundamental Research Funds for the Central Universities (lzujbky-2014-53).

References

1. Lim, E.G., Wang, Z., Lei, C.-U., Wang, Y., Man, K.: Ultra wideband antennas—past and present. IAENG Int. J. Comput. Sci. **37**, 304–314 (2010)
2. Shaalan, A.A.M., Ramadan, M.I.: Design of a compact hexagonal monopole antenna for ultra-wideband applications. J. Infrared Milli Terahz Waves **31**, 958–968 (2010)
3. Moghadasi, M.N., Dadashzadeh, G.R., Abdollahvand, M., Zehforoosh, Y., Virdee, B.S.: Planar triangular monopole antenna with multioctave bandwidth. Microwave Opt. Technol. Lett. **53**, 10–14 (2011)
4. Srifi, M.N., Podilchak, S.K., Essaaidi, M., Antar, Y.M.M.: Compact disc monopole antennas for current and future ultrawideband (UWB) application. IEEE Trans. Antennas Propag. **59** (12), 4470–4480 (2011)
5. Pan, C.Y., Chiu, K.Y., Duan, J.H., Jan, J.Y.: Band-notched ultra-wideband planar monopole antenna using shunt open-circuited stub. Microwave Opt. Technol. Lett. **53**(7), 1535–1537 (2011)
6. Zhu, F., Gao, S., Ho, A.T.S., Al Hameed, A., See, C.H., Brown, T.W.C., Li, J., Wei, G., Xu, J.: Multiple band-notched UWB antenna with band-rejected elements integrated in the feed line. IEEE Trans. Antennas Propag. **61**(8), 3952–3960 (2013)
7. Mullick, T.U., Ershad, M.E., Matin, M.A., Rahman, A.: Design of UWB antenna with a band-notch at 5 GHz. In: Proceedings of the LAPC, Loughborough, U.K., pp. 1–4 (2012)
8. Wang, J., Wang, Z., Yin, Y., Liu, X.: UWB monopole antenna with triple band-notched characteristic based on a pair of novel resonators. Prog. Electromagn. Res. C **49**, 1–10 (2014)
9. Ojaroudi, M., Ojaroudi, N.: Ultra-wideband small rectangular slot antenna with variable band-stop function. IEEE Trans. Antennas Propag. **62**(1), 490–494 (2014)
10. Li, Y., Li, W., Mittra, R.: Miniaturized CPW-fed UWB antenna with dual-frequency rejection bands using stepped impedance stub and arc-shaped parasitic element. Microwave Opt. Technol. **56**(4), 783–787 (2014)
11. Abedian, M., Rahim, S.K.A., Danesh, S., Khalily, M., Noghabei, S.M.: Ultrawideband dielectric resonator antenna with WLAN band rejection at 5.8 GHz. IEEE Antennas Wirel. Propag. Lett. **12**, 1523–1526 (2013)
12. Li, G., Long Li, H.Z., Liang, C.: A nesting-L slot antenna with enhanced circularly polarized bandwidth and radiation. IEEE Antennas Wirel. Propag. Lett. **13**, 225–228 (2014)

Flow Field Analysis of Cutter Head for Cutter Suction Dredgers

Min Zhang$^{(\boxtimes)}$, Shidong Fan, and Haoyu Zhang

School of Energy and Power Engineering,
Wuhan University of Technology, Wuhan 430063, China
zhm@whut.edu.cn, fsd1963@263.net, 1569999@163.com

Abstract. For a cutter suction dredger, exploring slurry formation mechanism plays an important role for improving the dredger's efficiency and performance. In order to optimize the dredger's working parameters, the flow field is simulated for the cutter head of a cutter suction dredger in this study. First, Cutter's 3D model is constructed by 3D Modeling software after necessary parameters are collected according to the designing 2D geometric drawing and related empirical contour curves. Then import the model to CFD for analysis, numerically simulate the cutter's flow field in different working conditions so as to achieve the velocity and pressure distribution in and around the cutter head. And based on the simulation result, the optimized working point can be found in terms of equipment service life, environment protection and energy consumption.

Keywords: Flow field · Cutter head · Cutter suction dredger · Slurry density

1 Introduction

Cutter suction dredger is increasingly widely used worldwide for its wide depth range, good soil adaptability and high working efficiency, and it can continuously complete dredging, discharging and slurry treatment processes one time. [1] Slurry formation around the suction mouth is related to several factors including the soil property, dredger's structural and operational parameters. And constructional parameters are type of the cutter, suction mouth's shape and position and others. The operational ones are composed of cutter rotational speed, swing speed and pump rotational speed and so forth.

Sand or soil is cut down and mixed with water into slurry as result of the cutter's rotation and stir. Sands will be crushed into particles in different sizes, some with large diameters will settle to the water stream bottom, the particles of small sizes will flow into the water. So the volume of the sand entering water is related with the sand crushing degree. The slurry will be partly or fully sucked into the suction mouth depending on the suction force. The movement of the particles can be simplified as spiral movement for the combination of the diffuse movement by the centrifugal force caused by the rotating cutter head and the forward movement approaching the suction mouth because of the pump's suction [2].

© Springer International Publishing Switzerland 2016
Q. Zu and B. Hu (Eds.): HCC 2016, LNCS 9567, pp. 578–587, 2016.
DOI: 10.1007/978-3-319-31854-7_52

Most dredgers are manually operated and the productivity mainly depends on the dredger operator's working experience, physical and mental status and knowledge level. So the dredger operator is difficult to keep high productivity, stable working process for long time. And on the other hand, the dredger's performance is totally different in diffident working conditions and by different operators. For a typical dredger, the cutting and transporting capacity need to cooperate so as to achieve higher productivity, less energy waste, long dredger service life and better environment friendliness. So first it's necessary to optimize the cutter's operational parameters, but little has know about the working mechanism including the slurry formation and spillage generation inside of the cutter. Some researcher designed testing experiments to explore the flow field regarding the cutter as a black box, but just measured some data on the velocity and pressure in different locations in and around the cutter. And the experiment costs long time and the measured data's integrity, continuity and repeatability should be improved. With the rapid developing of computer-aided design and simulation, computational fluid dynamics problem can be solved by CFD software. Then for operational parameter optimization and cutter performance evaluation can be supported by constructing CFD model and simulation in CFD software.

And the purpose of this study is to simulate the flow field of the cutter and analyze the optimized operational parameters for a typical cutter and provide reasonable operation advice for dredger operation.

2 Flow Field Modeling of Cutter Head

2.1 3D Modeling of Cutter Head

The major part of cutter head for cutter suction dredger is composed of cutter hub, cutter ring, cutter arm and cutter teeth. Cutter's designing parameters have significant influence on cutting performance and efficiency, and the important parameters are the ring diameter, speed of revolutions per minute, rated power, etc. In the research, a typical 6-arm cutter is modeled. The cutter hub and ring can be constructed by direct stretching or rotating method in CAD software referring to the 2D geometric drawing. And for the cutter arm, the mathematical reference equation method is generally used to describe its complicated space cure for its contours. To setup a cartesian coordinate system, geometrical center on the cutter ring's upper surface is defined as the original point O, the upper surface as the plane XOY, cutter axial direction as the axis Z. The outer and inside contours can be described as below Eqs. (1) and (2) [3].

$$\begin{cases} X = \dfrac{d_1}{2} \sin \Omega_2 \sin \theta - B \sin \phi \\ Z = h \sin \theta + (k_1 D - B \cos \phi) k_2 \cos \theta + (k_1 D - B \cos \phi) k_2 \\ Y = (k_1 D - B \cos \phi) \cos \theta + k_2 h \sin \theta + (0.5 - k_1) D \end{cases} \quad (1)$$

$$\begin{cases} X = \dfrac{d}{2}\sin \Omega_1 \sin \theta \\ Y = k_1 D \cos \theta + k_2 \sin \theta + (0.5 - k_1)D \\ Z = H \sin \theta - k_1 k_2 D \cos \theta + k_1 k_2 D \end{cases} \qquad (2)$$

D is the cutter's external diameter,
d_1 is the hub's external diameter,
k_1 is the cutting coefficient,
k_2 is the cutter's shape coefficient,
H is the height of the cutter's external contour peak,
θ is the parametric variable,
Ω_1 the cornerite of the external contour,
Ω_2 the cornerite of the internal contour.

The equations for contours can be obtained by cutter's 2D geometric drawing and some measuring results. The main parts of the cutter can be modeled in 3D CAD software as shown in Fig. 1.

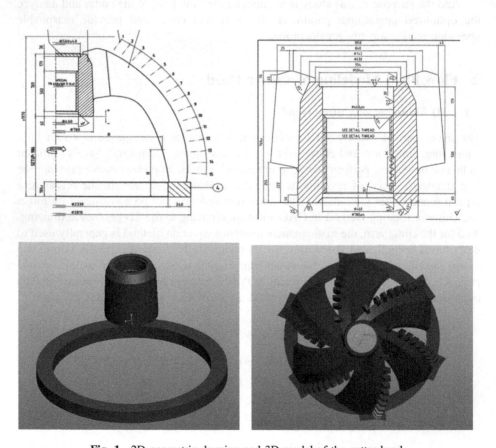

Fig. 1. 2D geometric drawing and 3D model of the cutter head

2.2 Cutter Flow Field Modeling and Analysis

Considering cutter height and ring's diameter, a cylinder computing domain with 6000 mm diameter and 15000 mm height is setup for the cutter head, and a 220 mm diameter kidney-shape suction mouth is added according to the specific size of the studied cutter dredger. Then partition the constructed 3D cutter model into meshes in Fluent preprocessor Gambit. Balancing computer hardware performance and computing precision and time, the flow field of the cutter is divided into cutter water field, cutter near-water-field and cutter remote-water-field, and the three water areas are divided by the adaptive mixed tetrahedral unstructured meshes. Finally the cutter water area is divided into 795142 meshes, cutter near-water-field into 475567 meshes and cutter remote-water-field into 434160 meshes.

Since slurry flow field inside the cutter head is complicated, and velocity is always changing, it is generally considered to be turbulence when solve the flow field with CFD. The comparatively mature two-equation k-ε model is generally used to simulate turbulence [4, 5]. After analyzing several models, the standard k-ε equations are chosen for closing the control equations. Turbulent kinetic energy equation is Eq. (3) and turbulent diffusion equation is Eq. (4).

$$\frac{\partial}{\partial t}(\rho k) + \frac{\partial}{\partial x_i}(\rho k u_i) = \frac{\partial}{\partial x_j}\left[\left(\mu + \frac{\mu_t}{\sigma_k}\right)\frac{\partial k}{\partial x_j}\right] + G_k + G_b - \rho\varepsilon - Y_M + S_k \qquad (3)$$

$$\frac{\partial}{\partial t}(\rho\varepsilon) + \frac{\partial}{\partial x_i}(\rho\varepsilon u_i) = \frac{\partial}{\partial x_j}\left[\left(\mu + \frac{\mu_t}{\sigma_\varepsilon}\right)\frac{\partial\varepsilon}{\partial x_j}\right] + C_{1\varepsilon}\frac{\varepsilon}{k}(G_k + C_{3\varepsilon}G_b) - C_{2\varepsilon}\rho\frac{\varepsilon^2}{k} + S_\varepsilon \quad (4)$$

$C_{1\varepsilon}, C_{2\varepsilon}, C_{3\varepsilon}$ are coefficients of constant terms of the equation,

G_k, G_b are the velocity gradient and the turbulent kinetic energy generated by the buoyancy respectively,

S_k, S_ε are user-defined functions,

Y_M is the fluctuation of the pulsation expansion,

$\mu = \rho C_u \frac{k^2}{\varepsilon}$ is turbulence viscosity coefficient.

The governing equation is discretized by the most frequently used finite volume method and solved by Euler mode. In CFD process, residual value is adopted to judge the computing result convergence with 10^{-4} as the precision.

The dredging water surface is connected to the atmosphere with one standard atmospheric pressure, so cutter depth pressure can be converted into standard atmospheric pressure [6], which constitutes the boundary conditions of the pressure entry in the cutter flow field. As a continuous process, the fluid flows into the computing domain and outside the exit of the computing domain, so the boundary conditions for the entry match that of exit. The exit velocity is set as 4.6 m/s according to actual engineering experience. During dredging the flow field is very complicated and inside slurry is unsteady flow. In order to conveniently computing, all water domain is considered as still, the cutter working domain is processed as rotating, and cutter working process is simplified as steady flow [7].

The initial conditions for each computing domain can be set referring to actual dredging parameters. The fluid media in near-water-area and remote-water-area can be choose with water-liquid which is built and optional in Fluent, and its value can be set one standard atmosphere pressure. For the fluid media in cutter water area, water or slurry can be chosen, and 2 types of slurry marked with mud1 and mud2 as shown in Table 1 can be selected for simulation.

Table 1. Fluid media parameters

	Density(kg/m^3)	Dynamic viscosity($kg/m.s$)
water-liquid	998.2	0.001
mud 1	1200	0.0032
mud 2	1400	0.009

3 Influence Analysis of Different Parameters on the Cutter Flow Field

Slurry density in the cutter keeps changing with dredging parameters when the cutter suction dredger is working. Based on CFD theory, slurry in the flow field is treated as homogeneous flow. The economic operating parameters can be achieved by changing the dredging parameters and analyzing its influence on the cutter flow field. In the study slurry with 2 slurry densities and 6 cutter rotational speeds as shown in Table 2, similar with actual dredging project, are selected for analyzing. And each density and each rotational speed can be named one working condition (WC).

Table 2. Simulating working conditions

RPM	12 r/m	18 r/m	24 r/m	30 r/m	36 r/m	42 r/m
Density						
1200 kg/m³	WC1	WC2	WC3	WC4	WC5	WC6
1400 kg/m³	WC7	WC8	WC9	WC10	WC11	WC12

In order to compare pressure distribution chart and velocity vector chart on cutter flow field under different slurry densities and cutter rotational speeds, 4 locations' pressure and velocity are targeted, and these locations, marked with 1#, 2#, 3#, 4#, are the connection between cutter arm and cutter ring's upper surface, the inside of arm, the suction mouth inlet and the streamline of rejection fluid. The targeted locations are shown in Fig. 2.

 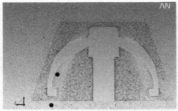 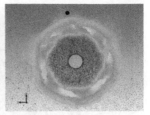

Fig. 2. 4 targeted locations in cutter flow field

3.1   Influence Analysis of Slurry Density on the Cutter Flow Field

Slurry density is set as 1200 kg/m^3 and 1400 kg/m^3, cutter flow field is numerically simulated in different cutter rotational speeds, then the pressure distribution chart and velocity vector chart can be achieved in Fluent, and the pressure values of the targeted 1# and 2# can be also achieved as listed in Tables 3 and 4. For the computing results are too many to be demonstrated in this paper, part of them is selected to show as in Fig. 3.

The pressure and velocity values in targets can be used to analyze the performance of the cutter, such as productivity, service life, energy efficiency and environmental friendliness. Generally, the pressure value is related with energy consumption and cutter structure strength, and the velocity is related with energy consumption and environment friendliness.

Table 3. 1#, 2#'s pressure with slurry density of 1200 kg/m^3

Target	Pressure value(× 10^{6}Pa)					
	12 r/m	18 r/m	24 r/m	30 r/m	36 r/m	42 r/m
1#	27.45	59.31	97.86	160.77	229.21	306.36
2#	13.77	30.38	50.5	81.38	115.87	145.79

Table 4. 1#, 2#'s pressure with slurry density of 1400 kg/m^3

Target	Pressure value(× 10^{6}Pa)					
	12 r/m	18 r/m	24 r/m	30 r/m	36 r/m	42 r/m
1#	32.2	71.59	121.41	191.91	273.88	372.18
2#	16.28	36.61	62.16	96.16	135.53	183.41

The above data demonstrates that pressure of target 1# and 2# keeps increasing with the increase of the cutter rotational speed under 2 kinds of slurry, and the pressure increases more in 1400 kg/m^3 than 1200 kg/m^3. This shows that cutter working with slurry density of 1400 kg/m^3 will withstand greater pressure load and requires higher constructional strength.

On the other hand, the velocity values of the targeted locations can be also achieved in Fluent as listed in Tables 5 and 6.

By comparing Target 1# and 3# speeds changing with cutter rotational speed, the speeds at the connection of cutter ring and arm and at suction mouth inlet in different cutter rotational speeds is nearly the same at 1400 kg/m^3 and in 1200 kg/m^3.

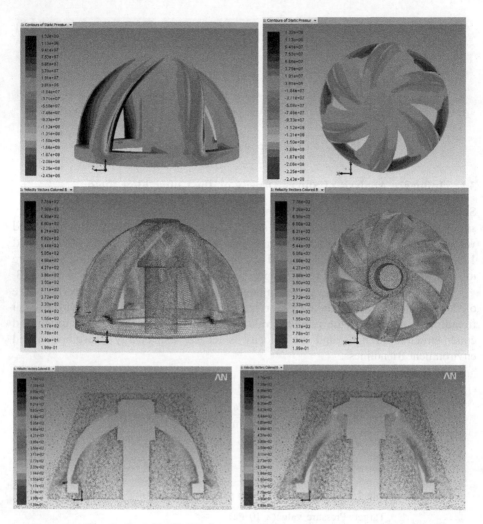

Fig. 3. Pressure distribution and velocity vector charts in WC9

Furthermore, it can be observed that the cutter slurry-rejection streamline velocity is much faster in 1400 kg/m³ than in 1200 kg/m³ by comparing Target 4's speed changing with the rotational speed rising in 2 densities.

By comparing every targeted location's pressure and velocity in 2 densities, as with both densities the velocities of the cutter suction mouth inlet and connection between the ring and the blade are essentially unchanged, but fluid ejection velocity of 1400 kg/m³ is much faster than that of 1200 kg/m³, which means more fluid will be ejected out of the cutter in 1400 kg/m³ and will result in energy waste and water pollution. In addition, the cutter has to withstand stronger pressure load and need higher structural strength in 1400 kg/m³, and it doesn't conform to the principle of dredger's economic operation.

Table 5. Targets' velocity with slurry density of 1200 kg/m³

Target	Velocity value(× 100 m/s)					
	12 r/m	18 r/m	24 r/m	30 r/m	36 r/m	42 r/m
1#	2.5	3.75	4.73	6.16	7.34	8.2
2#	1.75	2.57	3.38	4.31	5.2	5.85
3#	0.99	1.48	1.99	2.44	2.88	3.42
4#	0.86	1.33	1.63	2.04	2.44	2.89

Table 6. Targets' velocity with slurry density of 1400 kg/m³

Target	Velocity value(× 100 m/s)					
	12 r/m	18 r/m	24 r/m	30 r/m	36 r/m	42 r/m
1#	2.48	3.79	4.81	6.19	7.37	8.58
2#	1.75	2.64	3.55	4.35	5.17	6.01
3#	1.02	1.53	2.02	2.51	3.01	3.51
4#	0.86	1.51	1.93	2.45	2.89	3.33

From above analysis, slurry in 1200 kg/m³ is more suitable for the cutter in term of slurry spillage, cutter structural strength and water pollution.

3.2 Influence Analysis of Cutter Rotational Speed on the Cutter Flow Field

From 3.1 analysis, it can be concluded that 1200 kg/m³ is more suitable for the cutter, so cutter flow field from WC1 to WC6 is numerically simulated and the pressure distribution chart and velocity vector chart can also be obtained. Figure 4 is just selected to show part results.

From Table 7 it can be found that the pressure values increase with the increase of the cutter rotational speed. And arm inside's pressure has a small increase when the cutter rotational speed increases over 24 rpm, but increase amplitude of the pressure on the intersection of arm ring upper surface and cutter arm is higher, this shows that in this working condition when the rotational speed rises up to and over 24 rpm then flowing of the fluid inside of the cutter can be improved but at the same time the cutter's strength load has been greatly increased, which accelerates the cutter deforming. And Pressure values for all the targeted locations can be obtained in Fluent as shown in Table 8.

The velocity in target 1# keeps increasing significantly higher than that of the suction mouth inlet when the cutter rotational speed increases over 24 rpm, which means that the cutter rotational speed increase over 24 rpm fails to improve the fluid mixing and the cutter can't play an better role in slurry suction, and it doesn't match the economic principle in dredging engineering. Meanwhile, slurry rejection speed in Target 4# is obviously higher, which indicates that with the cutter rotational speed increasing over 24 rpm more fluid is rejected outward the cutter, leading to more energy consumption and water pollution.

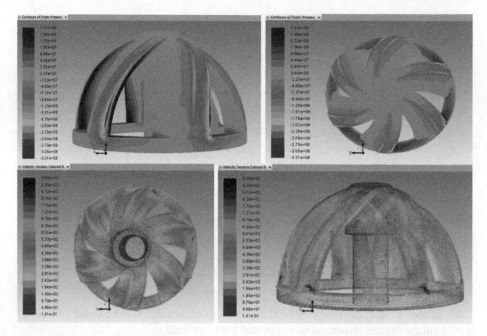

Fig. 4. Pressure distribution and velocity vector charts in WC4 at 1200 kg/m³

Table 7. Pressure values for target 1# and 2#

Target	Pressure value(× 10⁶Pa)					
	12 r/m	18 r/m	24 r/m	30 r/m	36 r/m	42 r/m
1#	27.45	59.31	97.86	160.77	229.21	306.36
2#	13.77	30.38	50.5	81.38	115.87	145.79

Table 8. Velocity values for 4 targets(m/s)

Target	Velocity value(× 100 m/s)					
	12 r/m	18 r/m	24 r/m	30 r/m	36 r/m	42 r/m
1#	2.5	3.75	4.73	6.16	7.34	8.2
2#	1.75	2.57	3.38	4.31	5.2	5.85
3#	0.99	1.48	1.99	2.44	2.88	3.42
4#	0.86	1.33	1.63	2.04	2.44	2.89

At the same time the velocity difference between the target 1# and suction mouth inlet keeps increasing with the cutter rotational speed increasing, and the difference increase is obvious when the cutter rotational speed is over 24 rpm. So when the cutter rotational speed reaches 24 rpm, the speed increase can't help suck more fluid to the suction mouth, which means 24 rpm is more suitable considering dredger's economic operation.

4 Conclusion

By analyzing simulation result in 2 densities, the velocities of the cutter suction mouth inlet and connection between the ring and the blade are essentially unchanged, but fluid ejection velocity of 1400 kg/m^3 is much faster than that of 1200 kg/m^3, which means more fluid will be ejected out of the cutter in 1400 kg/m^3 and will result in energy waste and water pollution. Furthermore, from point of structural strength, the cutter has to withstand stronger pressure load and need higher structural strength in 1400 kg/m^3. By comparing cutter field flow simulation results with slurry density of 1200 kg/m^3 and different rotational speeds, rotational speed up to 24 rpm can improve fluid flowability in inner blade, but also increase cutter strength load and accelerate cutter deformation. And rotational speed over 24rmp fails to further improve fluid mixing in the cutter and suck the mixture around the cutter, and fluid rejection velocity is much faster in the near outer space of the cutter, which means rotational speed increase over 24rmp will lead to more fluid ejection out of the cutter, more energy waste and water pollution.

From above simulation and analysis, it can be concluded that the optimized working condition for this cutter is under slurry density of 1200 kg/m^3 and rotational speed of 24 rpm. For density of 1400 kg/m^3 not only aggravates pressure load, requires higher structural strength but also leads to more energy consumption and water pollution. And with the density of 1200 kg/m^3 at 24 rpm for the cutter can improve the fluid flowability, eject a certain amount of slurry out of the cutter and to some content limit the increasing strength load so as to prolong cutter or the dredger's service life and save energy consumption.

In future research, the discharging pipe and pumps will also be studied with the cutter as a whole system.

Acknowledgment. The research has been supported by the National Natural Science Foundation of China (No. 51179144).

References

1. Jianzhong, T.: Research on Optimization and Control of Dredging Operations for Cutter Suction Dredgers, pp. 1–3. Zhejiang University, Hanzhou (2007)
2. Wenliang, Z., Zhang Dexin, N.: Three dimensional modeling for the Dredger cutter-head. Ship & Ocean Eng. **2007**(01), 45–48
3. den Burger, M.: Mixture forming in a cutterhead. In: Proceedings of CEDA Dredging days, Amsterdam (1997)
4. Piller, M., Nobile, E., Thomas, J.: DNS study of turbulent transport at low Prandtl numbers in a channel flow. J. Fluent Mech. **2002**(458), 419–441
5. Wissink, J.G.: DNS of separating low reynolds number flow in a turbine cascade with incoming wakes. Int. J. Heat Fluid Flow **24**(4), 626–635 (2003)
6. Yuan, F., Fusheng, N.: Numerical simulation of 2-D water flow in and around cutter of a Dredger. China Harbour Eng. **04**, 4–5 (2011)
7. Laccarno, G.: Prediction of the turbulent flow in a diffuser with commercial CFD codes. In: Annual Research Briefs, Center for Turbulence Research, USA, pp. 271–278 (2000)

Searching Parameter Values in Support Vector Machines Using DNA Genetic Algorithms

Wenke Zang[1]([⊠]) and Minghe Sun[2]

[1] School of Management Science and Engineering, Shandong Normal
University, Jinan 250014, China
wenke.zang@utsa.edu
[2] Department of Management Science and Statistics, The University of Texas
at San Antonio College of Business, San Antonio, TX 78249-0632, USA
minghe.sun@utsa.edu

Abstract. A novel DNA encoding genetic algorithm, called SVM-DNAGA, is proposed to search for optimal values for the parameters in support vector machines. With this algorithm, the training process of support vector machines can converge quickly and the performance of the support vector machines can improve. The parameters in the support vector machines are encoded into chromosomes using DNA encoding. DNA genetic operations, including selection, transgenosis and frameshift mutation, are used in SVM-DNAGA. Four datasets are used in the computational experiments to verify the effectiveness of SVM-DNAGA. Compared with other commonly used classifiers, SVM-DNAGA obtains very good results.

Keywords: Support Vector Machine · Genetic algorithms · SVM-DNAGA · Classification · Data mining

1 Introduction

Supported Vector Machine (SVM), developed by Vapnik [1] as a machine learning technique, is an effective method for classification. SVMs have many unique advantages over other classification techniques such as the construction of nonlinear and high dimensional classification functions using kernels and good generalization capabilities. However, there still exist some knots for SVMs [2]. It has been experimentally observed that the construction of a perfect classifier without predetermined appropriate configuration is often impossible. The most typical problem for SVMs is that there are no established unified criteria to select kernel functions and there is no theoretical model to determine the parameters, or sometimes called super parameters, in the SVM model and in the kernel functions. These parameters have great impact on the performance of SVMs. Searching for a good set of values for the parameters is not an easy task. At present, the parameters are often determined through repeated experiments. Although some systematic methods, such as grid search, have been used, more efficient searching methods need to be developed.

Genetic algorithms (GA) [3], as heuristic searching techniques that mimic the natural selection process, have been successively applied to numerous difficult

© Springer International Publishing Switzerland 2016
Q. Zu and B. Hu (Eds.): HCC 2016, LNCS 9567, pp. 588–598, 2016.
DOI: 10.1007/978-3-319-31854-7_53

optimization problems. Inspired by the biological background of DNA computing [4], researchers believe that the abundant DNA genetic operations can promote GA to simulate the biological expression mechanisms and, thus, to improve the GA performance [5]. Hence, researchers studied DNA genetic algorithms (DNA-GA) and applied them to optimization problems in business and engineering, among others [6].

This study proposes a DNA-GA algorithm to search for a set of good values for the parameters in the SVM given a kernel function has been selected. The algorithm can move quickly to a set of good parameter values and can improve the classification performance of the SVM. Four datasets from the UCI repository [7] are used to test the performance of the proposed algorithm and four standard classification methods are used to compare the results. Results show that the DNA-GA algorithm is very effective as compared with these four standard classification methods. The main contribution of this study is the use of the searching capability of DNA-GA to improve the convergence speed in the training of the SVM.

2 SVMs and Parameters

The primal and dual formulations of SVMs are briefly introduced and the necessities for searching good parameter values are discussed in this section. More detailed treatments of the theory and techniques of SVMs are available in other publications [1].

2.1 SVM for Classification

For two-class classification, a SVM constructs a classification function representing a hyperplane such that the classification margin between the two classes is maximized. An observation or a data point i in the dataset is represented by $(\mathbf{x}_i, y_i)$ for $i = 1, \ldots, m$ with $\mathbf{x}_i$ representing the input vector and y_i representing the class membership or desired output. For a two-class classification problem, y_i has two possible values, i.e., $y_i = 1$ representing one class and $y_i = -1$ representing the other. Assume the dataset cannot be linearly separated and a nonlinear classification function is constructed. The classification function to be constructed has the form in (1) in the following:

$$g(\mathbf{x}) = \mathbf{w}^T \varphi(\mathbf{x}) + b. \tag{1}$$

In (1), $\mathbf{w}$ and b are the parameters in the classification function that need to be estimated, and $\varphi(\mathbf{x})$ maps an input vector from the input space to a vector in a higher dimensional feature space. The parameters $\mathbf{w}$ and b, also called the primal variables, are estimated by solving the quadratic programming (QP) model, called the primal formation, in (2) in the following:

$$\begin{cases} \min & \dfrac{1}{2}\|\mathbf{w}\|^2 + C\sum_{i=1}^{m}\xi_i \\ s.t. & y_i(\mathbf{w}^T\mathbf{x}_i + b) \geq 1 - \xi_i, \quad i = 1, \ldots, m. \end{cases} \tag{2}$$

In (2), C is a regularization parameter that determines the relative weights of the two terms in the objective function and ξ_i represents the classification error of observation i. The optimal solution to this QP model is a saddle point of the Lagrangian function:

$$L(\mathbf{w}, b, \boldsymbol{\alpha}) = \frac{\|\mathbf{w}\|^2}{2} - \sum_{i=1}^{m} \alpha_i (y_i(\mathbf{w}^T \varphi(\mathbf{x}_i) + b) - 1), \tag{3}$$

where α_i is the Lagrangian multiplier, also called the dual variable, of observation i, and $\boldsymbol{\alpha}$ is a vector of all α_i for $i = 1, \ldots, m$. The Lagrangian function is minimized with respect to $\mathbf{w}$ and b and maximized with respect to α_i for $i = 1, \ldots, m$. Taking partial derivatives of the Lagrangian function with respect to $\mathbf{w}$ and b, setting the partial derivatives to 0, and representing $\mathbf{w}$ and b with α_i for $i = 1, \ldots, m$, the dual formulation of the QP model in (2) is obtained. The dual formulation, also a QP model, is shown in (4) in the following:

$$\begin{cases} \max & \sum_{i=1}^{m} \alpha_i - \frac{1}{2} \sum_{i,j=1}^{m} \alpha_i \alpha_j y_i y_j (\varphi(\mathbf{x}_i) \cdot \varphi(\mathbf{x}_j)) \\ s.t. & \sum_{i=1}^{m} \alpha_i y_i = 0, \ 0 \leq \alpha_i \leq C, \ i = 1, \ldots, m \end{cases} \tag{4}$$

The Lagrangian multipliers α_i for $i = 1, \ldots, m$ are determined by solving this dual formulation. The dual formulation is usually easier to solve than the primal formulation. Because the QP model in (2) or (4) is usually solved using numerical methods, the solution process is usually called the training or learning process of the SVM model.

2.2   The Regularization Parameter

The first term in the objective function of the primal formulation (2) represents the maximization of the classification margin and the second term represents the minimization of the sum of the classification errors. The value of C balances the two terms in the objective function of the primal formulation (2). Because the second term represents the contribution of the sum of classification errors to the objective function, C is a penalty factor for misclassification of the observations in the dataset. A larger value of C represents a greater impact of the misclassified observations on the objective function, and vice versa. If the value of C is too large, too much emphasis will be attached to the minimization of the classification errors. As a result, the model may be over trained, or called "over learning" by learning the patterns of the individual observations. If the value of C is too small, not enough attention will be given to the misclassified observations and the model may be under trained, or called "under learning". In either case, the trained model may not have good generalization capabilities. Therefore, a good value of C is very important for any application of SVM for classification.

2.3   Kernel Functions

Since the input vectors $\mathbf{x}_i$ for $i = 1, \ldots, m$ appear only in the objective function of the dual formulation (4) in the form of inner product of the nonlinear mappings, i.e., $\varphi(\mathbf{x}_i) \cdot \varphi(\mathbf{x}_j)$, the actual mapping $\varphi(\mathbf{x}_i)$ is not needed and is not necessarily explicitly known as long as the inner product is known. The inner product is obtained through the use of kernel functions,

$$K(\mathbf{x}_i, \mathbf{x}_j) = \varphi(\mathbf{x}_i) \cdot \varphi(\mathbf{x}_j). \tag{5}$$

Therefore, the use of kernel functions is essential to SVMs and nonlinear classification functions are constructed in high dimensional feature spaces through the use of kernel functions. The kernel functions used in the literature include linear, polynomial, Gaussian and multilayer perceptron kernel functions. The Gaussian kernel function is also called the radial basis function (RBF) [8].

Even the data in the two classes are not linearly separable in the original input space, they, or at least more observations, may become linearly separable in the higher dimensional feature space.

With the use of kernel functions, the dual formulation of the SVM model in (4) becomes that in (6) in the following:

$$\begin{cases} \max & \sum_{i=1}^{m} \alpha_i - \frac{1}{2} \sum_{i,j=1}^{m} \alpha_i \alpha_j y_i y_j K(\mathbf{x}_i, \mathbf{x}_j) \\ s.t. & \sum_{i=1}^{m} \alpha_i y_i = 0, \ 0 \leq \alpha_i \leq C, \ i = 1, \ldots, m \end{cases} \tag{6}$$

Vapnik [1] found that the values of the parameters of the kernel functions are critical factors affecting the performance of the SVM. The parameters implicitly determine the distribution of the data after they are mapped to the new high dimensional feature space. Changing the kernel parameters in fact changes the mapping of the data, and then changes the distribution of the mapped data in the high dimensional feature space. If the values of the parameters are inappropriate, the SVM will not achieve the expected learning results.

The Gaussian kernel function is widely used in practice. It has the form in (7):

$$K(\mathbf{x}_i, \mathbf{x}_j) = e^{-\gamma \|\mathbf{x}_i, \mathbf{x}_j\|^2}, \tag{7}$$

where γ is the parameter of the Gaussian kernel. The expression $\|\mathbf{x}_i, \mathbf{x}_j\|$ denotes the distance between two input vectors $\mathbf{x}_i$ and $\mathbf{x}_j$. If $\mathbf{x}_i$ is very close to $\mathbf{x}_j$, then $\|\mathbf{x}_i, \mathbf{x}_j\|$ is close to 0 and the value of $K(\mathbf{x}_i, \mathbf{x}_j)$ is close to 1. Otherwise, if $\mathbf{x}_i$ and $\mathbf{x}_j$ are far away, then $\|\mathbf{x}_i, \mathbf{x}_j\|$ is large and the value of $K(\mathbf{x}_i, \mathbf{x}_j)$ is close to 0.

The parameter γ in (7) determines the width of the Gaussian kernel and is often called the width parameter. As stated earlier, the value of γ affects the distribution of the data in the high dimensional feature space and determines the performance of the SVM [9]. As for C, the value of γ is usually determined in practice through repeated experiments.

3   SVM Based on DNA-GA

Appropriate parameter values and kernel functions are critical to the performance of the SVM model for classification. This study proposes a DNA-GA algorithm, called SVM-DNAGA, to search for good values for the parameters in the SVM. Specifically, the algorithm simultaneously searches for good values for the regularization parameter C in (2), (4) or (6) and the width parameter of the RBF kernel γ in (7). The DNA-GA algorithm can also be used for searching parameter values if other kernel functions are used in the SVM. The fitness function used in the DNA-GA algorithm is defined as the reciprocal of the objective function of the primal formulation in (2), i.e.,

$$f(C,\gamma) = \frac{1}{\frac{1}{2}\|\mathbf{w}\|^2 + C\sum_{i=1}^{m}\xi_i}. \tag{8}$$

In the DAN-GA algorithm, a selection operation, a transgenosis operation and two frameshift mutation operations are used. These operations are discussed in detail in this section. The DNA-GA is incorporated into the training process of the SVM in searching for good values for the parameters C and γ. By finding good values of these parameters, the training process may converge quickly and the constructed classification function may perform better.

3.1   DNA Encoding and Decoding

The basic elements of biological DNA are nucleotides with four bases: Adenine (A), Guanine (G), Cytosine (C) and Thymine (T). A triplet code of nucleotide bases specifies a codon which assists in genetic information transmission in the formation of specific amino acids. A DNA strand, also called a chromosome or an individual, which is the main carrier of genetic information, consists of combinations of the four bases and can represent different genes. Thousands DNA strands with specific features constitute the DNA soup which is also called the DNA population. In the following, T represents the number of individuals in the DNA soup.

From the biological DNA structure, an artificial DNA computation model can be exploited for practical optimization problems. A single DNA strand is like a string consisting of a combination of the four different symbols, A, G, C, and T. Mathematically, a string composed of the four symbols A, G, C and T is used to encode a parameter of an optimization problem. Based on the DNA model, features of the biological DNA can be introduced into GA and new DNA-GA algorithms can be developed. In the SVM-DNAGA, a string or a section of a chromosome is used to encode one parameter and a chromosome is used to encode all the parameters. Specifically, a chromosome represents the values of the parameters C and γ in this study.

The length of the DNA chromosome L is variable and is determined by the number of parameters it represents, N, and the precision required for the parameter values. Hence, the length of a DNA string, called a DNA segment, representing one parameter is $l = L/N$. For easy reference, S_t is used to represent the tth chromosome in the DNA soup and $f(S_t)$ is used to represent the corresponding fitness value defined in (8). Before computing $f(S_t)$, S_t is decoded into the values of the parameters that it represents. Hence, each S_t, for $t = 1, \ldots, T$, represents a set of trial values of the encoded parameters C and γ in this study. The notations $f(S_t)$ and $f(C, \gamma)$ are used interchangeably.

3.2 DNA Genetic Operators

Three, i.e., selection, transgenosis and mutation, DNA genetic operators are used in the SVM-DNAGA algorithm. The selection and transgenosis operations make the individuals of the population resemble each other as the genetic process continues. If individuals become similar in early generations, the solution process may be trapped in local optimal points due to the lack of diversity. The mutation operation can help maintain the population diversified and avoid convergence to local optima. These DNA genetic operations are described as follows.

3.2.1 The Selection Operation

The selection operation is the process of stochastically selecting individuals from the population according to their fitness values and the selected individuals form part of the DNA soup of the new generation. The relative cumulative fitness values are adopted in the selection operation. The relative cumulative fitness value of a DNA strand S_t is represented by P_t and is defined as in (9) in the following,

$$P_t = \sum_{t'=1}^{t} f(S_t) / \sum_{t'=1}^{T} f(S_t). \tag{9}$$

DNA strands are selected at random in the selection operation. A random number r is generated first and S_t is selected only if $P_t > r$. Selection according to their relative cumulative fitness values gives those DNA strands with low fitness values the chance to be chosen so as to maintain the diversity of the DNA soup. However, the DNA strand with the largest fitness value may also be left out. To prevent this from happening, the elitism strategy [10] is adopted. With the elitism strategy, the DNA strand with the largest fitness value is directly passed on to the next generation. Therefore, the genetic information can be retained for the DNA strand with the largest fitness value. The elitism strategy can prevent the best individual from losing during evolution.

3.2.2 The Transgenosis Operation

The transgenosis operation operates on a pair of chromosomes, called Parent A and Parent B, and produces two new chromosomes, called Offspring A and Offspring B. The chromosomes in the DNA soup are sorted first in the descending order of their fitness values. The one on the top is designated Parent A and the one at the bottom is designated Parent B for the first pair. The second on the top and the second at the bottom form the second pair, and so on. The operation on one DNA segment, e.g., the first one, is performed through the following steps:

(1) Randomly choose a nucleotide at position η in the rear half of the DNA segment in Parent A, i.e., $\eta \in [[l/2+1],l]$. Denote the fragment from $\eta+1$ to l of the DNA segment in Parent A by Rs and denote the number of nucleotides in Rs by n_{Rs}.

(2) Move Rs from the end of the DNA segment in Parent A to the front of the DNA segment in Parent B to form the DNA segments in Middle A and Middle B.

(3) Randomly generate a fragment Rs' with n_{Rs} nucleotides and paste it to the end of the DNA segment in Middle A to form the DNA segment in Offspring A.

(4) Cut off the fragment with n_{Rs} nucleotides at the end of the DNA segment in Middle B to form the DNA segment in Offspring B.

3.2.3   The Mutation Operations

Frameshift mutation operators are employed in the SVM-DNAGA algorithm. In a biological DNA chromosome, there are two types of frameshift mutations [11]. One is the deletion mutation in which a fragment of bases is removed from and the other is the insertion mutation in which a fragment of bases is inserted into a sequence. Accordingly, two frameshift mutations, i.e., deletion and insertion, are used in the SVM-DNAGA algorithm. Each of the two frameshift mutations is executed according to a pre-specified probability P_m. For each chromosome in the DNA soup, the following steps are performed:

(1) A random number r is generated and the deletion mutation operation is performed only if $P_m > r$.

(2) A second random number r is then generated and the insertion mutation operation is performed only if $P_m > r$.

3.3   The Local Search Strategy

A local search method is incorporated into the SVM-DNAGA algorithm to improve the local search ability and speed up the convergence of the algorithm. After the fitness evaluation, the best chromosome S_{best} and its fitness value $f(S_{best})$ are recorded. If no significant improvement is made in the best fitness value in consecutive G_L generations, the local search is triggered. Since the best chromosome S_{best} carries better genes than other chromosomes, the codons in S_{best} may be slightly disturbed to form new chromosomes in the DNA soup. These new chromosomes form the neighborhood of S_{best}.

The local search method has the following steps:

(1) Randomly generate T chromosomes in the neighborhood of S_{best} and calculate the fitness value for each of them.

(2) Use S_t' to represent the chromosome with the largest fitness value, $f(S_t')$, among the newly generated chromosomes.

(3) If $f(S_t') \geq f(S_{best})$, replace S_{best} with S_t' in the DNA soup.

3.4   The SVM-DNAGA Algorithm

The SVM-DNAGA algorithm executes until a termination criterion is met. Two termination criteria are used. The selection, transgenosis and mutation operations, and possibly also the local search, are executed in that order in one generation. One termination criterion is for the execution to stop after reaching a pre-specified maximum number of generations G_{max}. The other is for the execution to stop when the changes in the best fitness value stay within a pre-specified value δ for a pre-specified number of generations G_{end}. The steps of the SVM-DNAGA algorithm are described as follows:

Step 1.   Initialization. Set the parameters of the SVM-DNAGA algorithm including the length of a chromosome L, the probabilities of the transgenosis and mutation operations, the size of DNA soup T, the maximum number of generations G_{max}, and so on. Initialize the DNA soup by randomly generating T chromosomes.

Step 2.   DNA decoding and SVM training. For each chromosome in the current DNA soup, decode it to obtain the corresponding values for the parameters C and γ, train the SVM with these parameter values, and compute the fitness value (8).

Step 3.   Local search. Perform local search described in Sect. 3.3 if the condition for the local search is met.

Step 4.   Termination. If any of the termination criteria is satisfied, record the best chromosome and then Stop. Otherwise, continue.

Step 5.   The selection operation. Apply the selection operation described in Sect. 3.2.1 to chromosomes in the current DNA soup. The selected chromosomes form the new DNA soup. Randomly generate chromosomes and add them to the new DNA soup until the total number of chromosomes reaches T.

Step 6.   The transgenosis operation. Execute the transgenosis operation described in Sect. 3.2.2 to the chromosomes in the new DNA soup.

Step 7.   The mutation operations. Apply the frameshift mutation operations described in Sect. 3.2.2 to the chromosomes in the new DNA soup.

Step 8.   Go back to Step 2.

Note that the termination criteria are checked in Step 4. If any of the termination criteria is satisfied, the operations in Steps 5, 6 and 7 do not need to be executed. The classification function constructed with the SVM trained with the parameter values represented by the best chromosome is then used to classify observations.

4   Experiments and Analysis

Four, i.e., the Wine, Heart, Vowel and Glass, datasets from the UCI Machine Learning Repository [7] are used for the computational experiments. These four datasets have been frequently used to verify the effectiveness of classification algorithms [12]. The characteristics of these datasets are shown in Table 1. Each dataset is randomly and roughly equally split into a training set and a test set. For each dataset, 50 runs are performed, each with a different seed for the random number generator.

Table 1. Characteristics of the datasets

Dataset	Number of case	Number of classes	Number of attributes
Wine	178	3	13
Heart	270	2	13
Vowel	990	11	13
Glass	214	7	9

The size of the initial DNA soup is set to $T = 30$. The length of the chromosomes is set to $L = 30$. The maximum number of generations is set to $G_{max} = 150$. The probabilities of the transgenosis and the mutation operations are set to $P_c = 0.01$ and $P_m = 0.01$, respectively. The pre-specified value in the change of fitness values and the number of generations for the second termination criterion are set to $\delta = 0.00001$ and $G_{end} = 5$, respectively. The number of generations without significant change in the best fitness values to trigger the local search is set to $G_L = 3$.

Four well-known classification algorithms from WEKA [13], a software package for machine learning, are used for comparison purpose. These four classification algorithms are k nearest neighbor (KNN) [14], naive Bayes (NB), C4.5 and SVM. For the SVM for comparison, the parameter values are determined empirically.

4.1   Results

The Wine Dataset. For the 50 runs, the best values of the parameters were obtained at the 5th generation on the average for this dataset. The final values of the parameters in the SVM are $C = 89.9474$ and $\gamma = 1.2272$, respectively. The correct classification rate is 100 % that is better than those obtained with the other four classifiers.

The Heart Dataset. The Statlog Heart dataset used in this study is modified from the UCI Heart Disease dataset. The best chromosome is found after the evolution of 28 generations on the average. The best parameter values in the SVM are $C = 71.5857$ and $\gamma = 0.0046866$, respectively. Among the 135 observations in the test set, 117 of them were classified correctly. The classification rate is 86.67 % that is higher than those obtained with the other classifiers used for comparison.

The Vowel Dataset. This dataset was already split into a training set with 528 observations and a testing set with 462 observations. The best chromosome is found at the 15th generation on the average among the 50 runs. The best parameter values obtained are $C = 56.0765$ and $\gamma = 0.843378$, respectively. With these parameter values, 400 out of 462 observations in the testing set are classified correctly, resulting in a classification rate of 86.58 % that is higher than those obtained with NB, C4.5 and SVM but is lower than that obtained with KNN.

The Glass Dataset. The training set has 109 observations and the test set has 104 observations for this dataset. For the 50 runs, the best parameter values were found at the 42nd generation on the average. The best values of the parameters are $C = 0.4$ and $\gamma = 2.76$, respectively. The classification rate is 78.57 % that is higher than those obtained with the other classifiers.

4.2   Analysis

The classification results are summarized in Tables 2 and 3. Table 2 lists the classification rates and Table 3 lists the standard deviations of the classification rates of the 50 runs for each dataset and for each classifier. As can be seen from Table 2, the classification results obtained with SVM-DNAGA are better than those obtained with KNN, NB, C4.5 or SVM except for the Vowel dataset. These results show the effectiveness of the SVM-DNAGA algorithm. The best result for each dataset is highlighted in Table 2. The lowest standard deviation is highlighted for each dataset in Table 3. As can be seen in Table 3, SVM-DNAGA obtained the lowest standard deviation for the Wine, Heart and Vowel datasets, while C4.5 obtained the lowest standard deviation for the Glass dataset. This fact shows that SVM-DNAGA is more stable in obtaining good solutions than other classifiers.

Table 2. Classification rates

Dataset	Classification rates (%)				
	KNN	NB	C4.5	SVM	SVM-DNAGA
Wine	99.29	63.74	81.52	71.41	**100.00**
Heart	85.24	76.35	82.57	74.39	**86.58**
Vowel	**99.29**	63.74	81.52	71.41	86.67
Glass	70.56	48.60	66.82	56.08	**78.57**

Table 3. Standard deviations of classification rates

Dataset	KNN	NB	C4.5	SVM	SVM-DNAGA
Wine	6.38	2.12	1.97	2.28	**1.91**
Heart	10.63	5.36	5.32	3.54	**2.32**
Vowel	21.60	36.51	20.01	19.35	**15.84**
Glass	8.58	13.72	**4.70**	6.01	4.89

5   Conclusions

A novel DNA-GA approach, called SVM-DNAGA, is developed to search for parameter values in SVMs. Specifically, SVM-DNAGA is used to search for the best values for the regularization parameter C of the SVM model and the width parameter γ of the RBF kernel. The values of these parameters are encoded into DNA chromosomes in SVM-DNAGA. Genetic operators are then applied to these chromosomes so as to search for good values of these parameters. Genetic operators used in SVM-DNAGA include the selection, transgenosis and mutation operators. A local search strategy is also used to intensify the search in the neighborhood of a local best chromosome. The genetic operators and the SVM-DNAGA algorithm are described in detail. Since SVM-DNAGA is a general approach, it can be used in searching for the best parameter values when other types of kernel functions, such as the polynomial, are used in the SVM.

Four datasets from the UCI Machine Learning Repository are used in the computational experiments and four well known classification methods are used for comparison. Experimental results show that SVM-DNAGA is very effective and stable in finding good values for these parameters.

Acknowledgments. This research project was completed while the first author was working as a visiting researcher at the University of Texas at San Antonio. This research project is partially supported by the National Natural Science Foundation of China (No. 61472231), the Jinan Youth Science & Technology Star Project (No. 20120108), the soft science research project on Shandong province national economy and social informatization development (No. 2015EI013).

References

1. Vapnik, V.: The Nature of Statistical Learning Theory. Springer, New York (1995)
2. Sonar, R., Deshmukh, P.: Multiclass classification: a review. Int. J. Comput. Sci. Mob. Comput. **3**(4), 65–69 (2014)
3. Goldberg, D.: Genetic Algorithms in Search, Optimization and Machine Learning. Addison-Wesley, Reading (1989)
4. Adleman, L.: Molecular computation of solution to combinatorial problems. Science **266**(11), 1021–1024 (1994)
5. Ding, Y., Ren, L., Shao, S.: DNA computation and soft computation. J. Syst. Simul. **13**(z1), 198–201, 213(2001)
6. Dai, K., Wang, N.: A hybrid DNA based genetic algorithm for parameter estimation of dynamic systems. Chem. Eng. Res. Des. **90**(12), 2235–2246 (2012)
7. Bache, K., Lichman, M.: UCI machine learning repository (2013). http://archive.ics.uci.edu/ml
8. Zuo, R., Carranza, E.: Support vector machine: a tool for mapping mineral prospectively. Comput. Geosci. **37**, 1967–1975 (2011)
9. Xiao, Y., Wang, H., Xu, W.: Parameter selection of Gaussian kernel for one-class SVM. IEEE Trans. Cybern. **45**(5), 927–939 (2015)
10. Cheng, W., Shi, H., Xin, X., Li, D.: An elitism strategy based genetic algorithm for streaming pattern discovery in wireless sensor networks. IEEE Commun. Lett. **15**(4), 419–421 (2011)
11. Streisinger, G., Okada, Y., Emrich, J., Newton, J., Tsugita, A., Terzaghi, E., Inouye, M.: Frameshift mutations and the genetic code. Cold Spring Harb. Perspect. Biol. **31**, 77–84 (1966)
12. Mendialdua, I., Arruti, A., Jauregi, E., Lazkano, E., Sierra, B.: Classifier subset selection to construct multi-classifiers by means of estimation of distribution algorithms. Neurocomputing **157**, 46–60 (2015)
13. Hall, M., Frank, E., Holmes, G., Reutemann, B., Witten, I.: The WEKA data mining software: an update. ACM SIGKDD Explor. Newsl. **11**(1), 10–18 (2009)
14. Aha, D., Kibler, D., Albert, M.: Instance-based learning algorithms. Mach. Learn. **6**(1), 37–66 (1991)

HCOpt: An Automatic Optimizer for Configuration Parameters of Hadoop

Xiong Zhang, Linxi Zeng, Xuanhua Shi[✉], Song Wu, Xia Xie, and Hai Jin

Services Computing Technology and System Laboratory,
Big Data Technology and System Laboratory, Cluster and Grid Computing Laboratory,
School of Computer Science and Technology, Huazhong University of Science and Technology,
Wuhan 430074, China
xhshi@hust.edu.cn

Abstract. MapReduce is an efficient tool for data-intensive applications. Hadoop, an open-source implementation of MapReduce, has been widely adopted and experienced by some enterprises and scientific computing communities. However, when users intend to run a MapReduce program in Hadoop, they have to set a number of configuration parameters to make sure the program runs efficiently. Users often run into performance problems because they are unaware of how to set these parameters. To address these performance problems, we focus on the optimization opportunities presented by the high configurability of Hadoop, and propose an automation tool named HCOpt for performance optimization of Hadoop configuration parameters. HCOpt uses a Profile Engine to collect monitoring information from running MapReduce programs, a Prediction Engine to estimate the performance of a given Hadoop configuration and a genetic-based search algorithm to find an optimized configuration in the large search space. Our evaluation shows that HCOpt reduces the job completion time of Hadoop applications by up to 20 % when compared to applications run with configuration parameters that suggested by the rule-based optimization.

Keywords: Mapreduce · Hadoop performance optimization · Automatic

1 Introduction

We are in the age of information explosion, and there has been a growing large scale data processed by some enterprises and scientific computing communities. MapReduce [1] is a relatively young framework that first proposed by Google for large-scale data processing. Apache Hadoop [2] is an open-source implementation of MapReduce framework that follows the design laid out in the original paper. The main problem MapReduce addresses is processing large amount of data that requires lots of processing capability. MapReduce handles this problem by parallelizing and distributing the load over a number of commodity machines that are in clusters where the clusters are highly scalable [3]. The other major property that MapReduce addresses is the automatic fault tolerance capability.

Q. Zu and B. Hu (Eds.): HCC 2016, LNCS 9567, pp. 599–610, 2016.
DOI: 10.1007/978-3-319-31854-7_54

A number of enterprises use Hadoop in production deployments for applications, such as Web indexing data mining, report generation, log file analysis, financial analysis, scientific simulation, and bioinformatics research. MapReduce frameworks are well suited to run on cloud computing platforms. For programs written in this model, the run-time system automatically parallelizes the processing across large-scale cluster of machines and handles machine failures.

To run the program as a job in Hadoop, a job configuration object is created; and the parameters of the job are specified. Apart from the job configuration parameters, there are a large number of other parameters whose values have to be specified before the job can be run in a MapReduce framework like Hadoop. More than 190 parameters are specified to control the behavior of a MapReduce job in Hadoop. Even though the programming in MapReduce has emerged as a model for developing data-intensive processing applications, the configuration design-space of MapReduce has not been studied in detail. Users often run into performance problems because they are unaware of how to set these parameters, or because they do not even know the existence of these parameters.

The objective of this research is to propose an automation tool for performance optimization of Hadoop configuration parameters. In this paper, we present the design and implementation of HCOpt, which is composed of a Profile Engine to collect detailed and statistical information from unmodified MapReduce programs, a Prediction Engine that uses a lightweight simulator to estimate the performance of Hadoop configuration parameters and a genetic algorithm to find an optimized solution in large search spaces. We evaluate the effectiveness of HCOpt on representative MapReduce programs from various application domains, such as WordCount and Sort.

The rest of this paper is organized as follows: Sect. 1 discusses the background knowledge of this work and then discusses the related work in Sect. 2. The design and implementation of the HCOpt system is described in detail in Sect. 3. Section 4 describes how the system is evaluated and presents the results. Finally, we conclude the paper and propose our future work in Sect. 5.

2   Related Work

In this section, we describe current approaches that users take when they want to make their MapReduce job running faster in Hadoop.

2.1   Rule-Based Optimization in Hadoop

When users are asked to find good configuration settings for MapReduce jobs, they have to rely on their experiences, intuition, knowledge of the data that will be processed, rules of thumb from human experts or turning manuals, or even guess to complete the task. For example, *mapred.reduce.tasks* is set to be roughly 0.9 times the total number of reduce slots in the cluster. The rationale is to ensure that all reduce tasks run in one wave while leaving some slots free for executing failed or slow tasks. It is important to note that rule-based optimizer still requires information from past job execution to work effectively. For example, to set *io.sort.record.percent* requires calculating the average map output record size based on the number of records and sizes of the map output produced during a job execution.

Information collected from previous job executions is also used by performance analysis and diagnosis tools for identifying performance bottlenecks. Hadoop Vaidya [4] and Hadoop Performance Monitoring UI [5] execute a small set of predefined diagnostic rules to diagnose various performance problems, and offer targeted advice. Unlike our optimizers, the recommendations given by these tools are qualitative instead of quantitative. For example, if the ratio of spilled records to total map output records exceeds a user-defined threshold, then Vaidya will suggest to increase *io.sort.mb*, but without specifying how much to increase. On the other hand, our cost-based approach automatically suggests concrete configuration settings to use.

2.2 MapReduce Program Optimization

A MapReduce program has semantics similar to a *Select-Project-Aggregate* (SPA) in SQL with *user-defined functions* (UDFs) for the selection and projection (map) and the aggregation (reduce). This equivalence is used in recent work to perform semantic optimization of MapReduce programs [6–9]. Manimal performs static analysis of MapReduce programs written in Java in order to extract selection and projection clauses. This information is used to perform optimizations like the use of B-Tree indexes, avoiding reads of unneeded data, and column-aware compression [7]. Manimal uses rule-based optimization mentioned before. MRShare performs multi-query optimization by running multiple SPA programs in a single MapReduce job [8]. MRShare proposes a simplified cost model for this application. SQL joins over MapReduce have been proposed in the literature [6], but cost-based optimization is either missing or lacks Prediction Engine.

In summary, previous work related to MapReduce optimization targets semantic optimizations for MapReduce programs that correspond predominantly to SQL specifications. In contrast, we support simply to arbitrarily complex MapReduce programs expressed in whatever programming language the user or application finds convenient. We concentrate more on the optimization opportunities presented by the high configurability of Hadoop.

3   Design and Implementation

3.1   Design

HCOpt is composed of three major components: a Profile Engine, a Prediction Engine with a lightweight MapReduce simulator and a genetic-based Search Engine. As shown in Fig. 1, when users run a MapReduce program which can be written in various programming languages, Predicted Engine will turn on for collecting the monitoring information from running job, and generating a job profile file, then the Prediction Engine uses a lightweight simulator to simulate the execution of tasks in the MapReduce job and estimate job completion time. However, even with a lightweight Prediction Engine, exhaustively iterating through all possible candidates is infeasible due to the large space of configuration parameters. Therefore, we have developed a genetic-based search algorithm that allows HCOpt to guide the Prediction Engine through the search space intelligently.

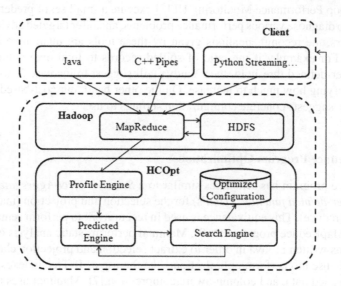

Fig. 1. Architecture of HCOpt

3.2 HCOpt Implementation

Profile Engine. A MapReduce Job executes as Map tasks and Reduce tasks. Map task execution consists of the phases: read (reading map inputs), map (map function processing), collect (buffering map outputs before spilling), spill (sorting, combing, compressing, and writing map outputs to local disk), and merge (merging sorted spill files). Reduce task execution consists of the phases: shuffle (transferring map outputs to reduce tasks, with decompression if needed), merge (merging sorted map outputs), reduce (reduce function processing), and write (writing reduce outputs to the distributed file-system). Additionally, both map and reduce tasks have setup and cleanup phases.

The BTrace [10] dynamic instrumentation tool is used in our current implementation of the Profile Engine which is written in Java. To collect monitoring data for a program running in Hadoop, the Profile Engine uses ECA rules (also specified in Java) to dynamically instrument the execution of selected Java classes within Hadoop. This process intercepts the corresponding Java class bytecodes as they are executed, and injects additional bytecodes to run the associated actions in the ECA rules.

The space of possible events in the ECA rules corresponds to events arising during program execution such as entry or exit from functions, memory allocation, and system calls to the operating system. If the condition associated with the event holds when the event fires, then the associated action is invoked. An action can involve, for example, getting the duration of a function call, examining the memory state, or counting the number of bytes transferred.

A MapReduce job profile is a vector in which each field captures some unique aspects of dataflow or costs during job execution at the task level or the phase level within tasks. The fields in a profile belong to one of four categories:

Dataflow Fields: capture the number of bytes and records (key/value pairs) flowing through the different tasks and phases of a MapReduce job execution. An example field is the number of map output records.

Cost Fields: capture the execution time of tasks and phases of a MapReduce job execution. An example field is the number of map output records.

Dataflow Statistics Fields: capture statistical information about the dataflow, e.g., the average number of records outputted by map tasks per input record (Map selectivity) or the map function per input record.

Obviously, the Dataflow and Cost fields in the profile of a job j help to understand j's behavior. On the other hand, the Dataflow Statistics and Cost Statistics fields in j's profile are used by the Prediction Engine to predict the behavior of hypothetical jobs that run the same MapReduce program as j.

Prediction Engine. Given the profile of a job $j = <p, d, r, c1>$ that runs a MapReduce program p over input data d and cluster resources r using configuration $c1$, what the performance of program p will be if p runs over the same input data and cluster resources but using configuration $c2$? That is, how job $j' = <p, d, r, c2>$ will perform, and which configuration is better for this MapReduce program? Prediction Engine is used to answer these questions.

As shown in Fig. 2, our Prediction Engine draws the idea of MRPerf [1]. The information available on an input dataset d includes d's size, the block layout of files that comprise d in the distributed file-system, and whether d is stored compressively. The information available on cluster resources r includes the number of nodes and network topology of r, the number of Map and Reduce task execution slots per node, and the maximum memory available per task slot. In the case of traditional Hadoop simulator such as MRPerf, users are responsible for providing this information, while the only thing users need to do in HCOpt is turning on the Profile Engine while running a MapReduce program in Hadoop.

As there is no benefit of using HCOpt's Prediction Engine if finding an optimized configuration takes an inordinate amount of time, we decide to trade absolute accuracy for speed. Given that the main objective of the simulator is to score candidates for comparison, the goal of our Prediction Engine is not to be an accurate predictor of completion time but instead to correctly identify performance differences between MapReduce programs that runs with different configurations. To enable fast scoring for

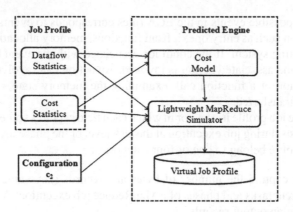

Fig. 2. Architecture of predicted engine

each candidate, we use a simplified execution model instead of attempting a full-system simulation. For example, when we predict the completion time of read phase in map task, we use the following formula (the description of the formula parameters is in Table 1):

Table 1. Description of formula parameters

Formula parameter	Description
map_read	running time of read phase in Map task
splitSize	data size of Map input split, 64 MB by default
hdfs_cost	the cost for reading a byte of input data from HDFS
uncompressCost	the cost for uncompressing a byte from input split
reduce_input_byte	the size of Reduce task input data
map_out_byte	the size of Map task output data
map_out_compressRatio	Map task output compression ratio
reduce_time	the running time of reduce phase in Reduce task
reduce_cpuCost	the cost for processing a byte by reduce function

$$map\_read = splitSize \times hdfs\_cost + splitSize \times uncompressCost \qquad (1)$$

Taking into account that map tasks as well as reduce tasks in MapReduce job are mutual independence, and parallel executions without any IPC (*Inter-Process Communication*), so we can calculate the running time of reduce phase in Reduce task by the following formulas:

$$reduce\_input\_byte = map\_out\_byte / map\_out\_compressRatio \qquad (2)$$

$$reduce\_time = reduce\_input\_bytes \times reduce\_cpuCost \qquad (3)$$

The Prediction Engine executes the following two steps to answer the question mentioned before: (1) estimating a virtual job profile for the hypothetical job *j'*, (2) using the virtual profile to simulate how *j'* will execute.

In step (1), the overall estimation process has been broken down into smaller steps: First, estimating dataflow and cost fields; second, estimating dataflow statistics fields; last, estimating cost statistics fields. By default, the Prediction Engine makes a cluster node homogeneity assumption which says that the CPU and I/O (both local and remote) costs per phase of MapReduce job execution are equal across all the nodes in the clusters r.

After step (1), we get a virtual job profile containing detailed dataflow and cost information estimated at the task and phase level for the hypothetical job j'. The Prediction Engine uses a Task Scheduler Simulator, along with the models and information on the cluster resources r, to simulate the scheduling and execution of map and reduce tasks in j'. The Task Scheduler Simulator is a pluggable component. Our current implementation is a lightweight and discrete event simulation of Hadoop's default FIFO scheduler. Finally, we can compute the estimated job completion time according to the output of our Prediction Engine.

Search Algorithm. More than 190 parameters are specified to control the behavior of a MapReduce job in Hadoop. To efficiently identify an approximate solution, we first decrease the dimensionality of the subspaces and then choose a genetic-based search algorithm (GA) to generate possible candidates for the Prediction Engine to evaluate.

MapReduce gives a natural clustering of parameters into two clusters: parameters that predominantly affect map task execution and parameters that predominantly affect reduce task execution. The two subspaces for map tasks and reduce tasks respectively can be optimized independently.

Some parameters have small and finite domains, e.g., Boolean. At the other extreme, we have to narrow down the domain of any parameter whose domain is unbounded. In these cases, the HCOpt relies on information from the job profile and the cluster resources.

GA is a search technique inspired by evolutionary biology for finding solutions to optimization and search problems. It is natural to map value selection for a Hadoop parameter to GA's gene representation, and to apply operations during the GA's evolution process. To represent each possible candidate of configuration parameters, we use a bit string with the length of n. The binary value of the string represents the value of the parameter.

Algorithm 1 shows the execution flow of our Search Engine: First, we initialize a population of candidates (Hadoop configuration). It then goes through the evolution process of selection and reproduction until it terminates. After the evaluation, we choose 1/3 configurations with which the given MapReduce program runs faster than the left candidates which will be filtered out. In the reproduction step, mutation, swap, or crossover operations are applied at random to the candidate population to create off-spring, i.e., the next generation of candidates. When the number of candidates recovers as original, we repeat the process of selection and reproduction until the iterations is T or the difference between the average fitness values of two generational populations becomes less than μ. In this paper, $\mu = 5\%$, $M = 30$, and $T = 50$. The core idea of our algorithm is making the candidates better and better by selection and reproduction to approach the optimal solution of the problem.

Algorithm 1. The genetic-based search algorithm

Require: *initialize()* initializes the population with random individuals, *select()* selects good solutions by using Elitist Strategy selection, *crossover()* creates new individuals by recombining the selected population, *mutation()* creates new individuals by using mutation to the selected population, and *distance()* returns the difference between the fitness value of generational populations.

```
 1:  P(0) ← initialize()
 2:  //P(0) is the initial population
 3:  t ← 0
 4:  do
 5:      for num in [0..M - 1] do
 6:      //M is the number of candidates
 7:          Evaluate fitness of individuals in P(t)
 8:      end for
 9:      P(t) ← select( P(t) )
10:  //sort and select the top 1/3M candidates
11:      P_C(t) ← crossover( P(t) )
12:      P_M(t) ← mutation( P(t) )
13:      P(t + 1) ← P(t) ∪ P_C(t) ∪ P_M(t)
14:      t ← t + 1
15:  while t ≤ T or distance(P(t), P(t-1) ) < μ
16:  return P(t)
```

Assuming the number of candidates in a generational population is M and the maximum iterations is N, as we use a quick sort algorithm to sort the candidates according to the fitness value during each iteration, the time complexity of this algorithm is $O(N*M*\log(M))$.

4   Evaluation

There are two main goals of our evaluation, demonstrating the effectiveness of HCOpt and confirming the accuracy of Prediction Engine. The evaluation environment consists of four nodes cluster (one node for master-node, and the others for slave-nodes). Each node in the cluster is equipped with 16 quad-core 2.40 GHz Xeon processors, 16 GB of memory and 1 TB of disk, runs RHEL5 with kernel 2.6.18, and is connected with 1 Gigabit Ethernet.

4.1   HCOpt vs. Rule-Based Optimization

To evaluate the efficiency of HCOpt, we run the WordCount and Sort MapReduce programs using the Hadoop default configuration, configuration parameter settings suggested by the rule-based optimization and HCOpt.

Figure 3 shows the completion time of WordCount and Sort running with the Hadoop default configuration, rule-based optimization and HCOpt suggested configuration settings. Note that the MapReduce programs running with rule-based optimization configuration run faster than that with Hadoop default configuration overall, but in some case the superiority are not obvious. While these results show that HCOpt reduces the job completion time by 29–44 % (up to 20 %) when compared to the applications run in configuration parameters suggested by the rule-based optimization. In the case of Word-Count, it even reduces the completion time by 54.3 %.

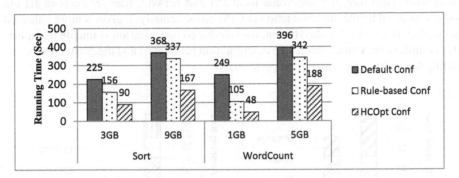

Fig. 3. Running time for MapReduce jobs run with Hadoop Default, Rule-based Optimization, and HCOpt suggested configuration

We call the WordCount job which runs with rule-based optimization configuration as JR (see Table 2), and which runs suggested by HCOpt as JH.

Table 2. Rule-based optimization and HCOpt suggested configuration parameters

Conf. parameter	Rule-based	HCOpt
io.sort.factor	88	87
io.sort.mb	298	268
io.sort.record.percent	0.44	0.16
io.sort.spill.percent	0.80	0.84
mapred.compress.map.output	true	false
mapred.inmem.merge.threshold	1000	366
mapred.job.reduce.input.buffer.percent	0.1	0.50
mapred.job.shuffle.input.buffer.percent	0.01	0.54
mapred.job.shuffle.merge.percent	0.66	0.65
mapred.output.compress	false	false
mapred.reduce.tasks	6	12
min.num.spills.for.combine	9999	9999
Use of the Combiner	true	false

Figure 4 shows a detail map and reduce time breakdown for JR and JH. As we can see, the map tasks in JH run faster than the map tasks in JR. Setting higher for *io.sort.mb* and *io.sort.spill.percent* in JR leads to a small number of spills. The data from each spill are processed by the Combiner and the Compressor in JR, resulting in high data reduction. However, the Combiner and the Compressor cause high CPU contention, negatively affecting all the compute operations in JR's map tasks. On the contrary, JR chooses to disable both the use of the Combiner and compressor. Consequently, the configuration suggested by HCOpt causes an increase in the amount of intermediate data spilled to disk and shuffled to the reducers. HCOpt also chooses to increase the number of reduce tasks in JR to 12 due to the increase in shuffled data, improving the degree of parallelism. Therefore, the additional local I/O and network transfer costs in JH are counterbalanced by the huge reduction in CPU costs; actually, it gives a more balanced usage of all resources. Unlike HCOpt, the rule-based optimization is unable to capture such complex interactions among the configuration parameters and the cluster resources, leading to significantly suboptimal performance.

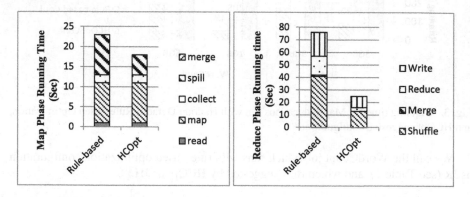

Fig. 4. Map and reduce timeline for WordCount (1 GB) running with Rule-based Optimization and HCOpt suggested configuration settings

4.2   Accuracy of Prediction Engine

We compare the Prediction Engine's output to the results obtained from running on real hardware. The bars in Fig. 5 show the completion time predicted by HCOpt and the actual completion times. As can be seen, the simulation-based predicted completion time

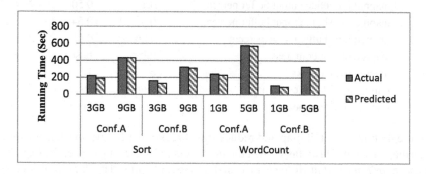

Fig. 5. Actual vs. predicted (by Prediction Engine) running times for representative MapReduce programs running with different input data and configuration

has slight difference from the actual ones. The difference ranges from 3.8 %–15 % for the Sort program, 7.3 %–20 % for the WordCount program. As mentioned in Sect. 3.2, the goal of our Prediction Engine is not to be an accurate predictor of completion time but instead to correctly identify performance differences between MapReduce programs that running with different configurations. As seen in Fig. 6, predicted times follow the trends of the actual completion time.

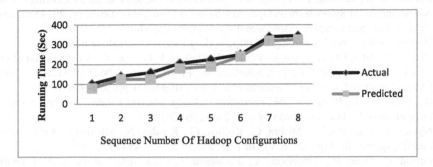

Fig. 6. Actual vs. predicted (by Prediction Engine) running times for WordCount (1 GB) running with different configurations

5 Conclusion and Future Work

In this paper, we introduce an automation tool named HCOpt for performance optimization of Hadoop configuration parameters. We focus on the optimization opportunities presented by the high configurability of Hadoop.

We propose a Profile Engine to collect detailed statistical information from unmodified MapReduce programs. The Profile Engine can be used to collect profiles online while MapReduce jobs are executed on the production cluster. We also propose a Prediction Engine with a lightweight MapReduce simulator for the fine-grained cost estimation needed by the Search Engine which is used to find an optimized configuration for a given MapReduce program.

A promising direction for future work is to make our system applicable to optimize the execution of jobs which comes from a higher-level system like Hive [11] or Pig [12]. Several new research challenges arise when we consider the full space of optimization opportunities provided by these systems. These systems submit several jobs together in the form of job workflows. Workflows exhibit data dependencies that introduce new challenges in enumerating the search space of configuration parameters. In addition, the optimization space now grows to include logical decisions such as selecting the best partitioning function, join operator, and data layout.

Acknowledgments. This paper is partly supported by the NSFC under grant No. 61433019 and No. 61370104, International Science & Technology Cooperation Program of China under grant No. 2015DFE12860, and Chinese Universities Scientific Fundunder grant No. 2015MS077.

References

1. Dean, J., Ghemawat, S.: MapReduce: simplified data processing on large clusters. In: Proceedings of the 6th on Symposium on Operating Systems Design & Implementation (OSDI), pp. 137–150 (2004)
2. Apache hadoop. http://hadoop.apache.org
3. Ghemawat, S., Gobioff, H., Leung, S.T.: The Google file system. In: Proceedings of the Nineteenth ACM Symposium on Operating Systems Principles (SOSP), pp. 29–43 (2003)
4. Vaidya. hadoop.apache.org/mapreduce/docs/r0.21.0/vaidya.html
5. Hadoop Performance Monitoring UI. http://code.google.com/p/hadoop-toolkit/wiki
6. Blanas, S., Patel, J.M., Ercegovac, V., Rao, J., Shekita, E.J., Tian, Y.: A comparison of join algorithms for log processing in MapReduce. In: Proceedings of the 2010 ACM SIGMOD International Conference on Management of Data (SIGMOD), pp. 975–986 (2010)
7. Bu, Y., Howe, B., Balazinska, M., Ernst, M.: HaLoop: efficient iterative data processing on large clusters. VLDB Endowment 3(1–2), 285–296 (2010)
8. Nykiel, T., Potamias, M., Mishra, C., Kollios, G., Koudas, N.: MRShare: sharing across multiple queries in MapReduce. VLDB Endowment 3(1–2), 494–505 (2010)
9. Olston, C., Reed, B., Silberstein, A., Srivastava, U.: Automatic optimization of parallel dataflow programs. In: Proceedings of USENIX 2008 Annual Technical Conference, (ATC), pp. 267–273 (2008)
10. A Instrumentation Tool for Java. https://kenai.com/projects/btrace
11. Thusoo, A., Sarma, J.S., Jain, N., Shao, Z., Chakka, P., Anthony, S., Murthy, R.: Hive - a warehousing solution over a MapReduce Framework. VLDB Endowment 2(2), 1626–1629 (2009)
12. Olston, C., Reed, B., Srivastava, U., Kumar, R., Tomkins, A.: Pig Latin: a not-so-foreign language for data processing. In: Proceedings of the 2008 ACM SIGMOD International Conference on Management of Data (SIGMOD), pp. 1099–1110 (2008)

With Negative Emotion to Enrich Public Product Experiences Design for Children Hospital

Xuan Zhang[1(✉)], Wenjun Hou[2,3], Xiangang Qin[3], and Ni Xiao[1,2,3]

[1] Automation School, Beijing University of Posts and Telecommunications, Beijing, China
1275542183@qq.com
[2] Digital Media and Design Art, Beijing University of Posts and Telecommunications,
Beijing, China
hou1505@163.com
[3] Network System and Network Culture Key Laboratory of Beijing, Beijing, China
1229537579@qq.com

Abstract. This paper demonstrates how to enrich children's product experiences by purposefully involving negative emotions in user-product interaction. This approach is derived from a framework of rich experience, which explains how and under what circumstances children's negative emotions make a product experience richer and enjoyable. The approach contains the following three steps: (1) Which experience can be enriched with the negative emotions in children hospital. (2) Under what circumstances the negative emotions of children are likely to be awakened. (3) How to transform the negative emotions of public product design in children hospital to make the caring user experiences. The solution to the problem is as follows, (1) Study on the children's arousal, preference and dominance to the negative emotions. (2) To investigate children hospital design and children's behavior. (3) Several product concepts of the children toys design with negative emotions to enrich product experiences.

Keywords: Design approach · Emotional design · Negative emotion · Public product experiences design

1 Introduction

Consider the following new product concepts: (1) Children hospitals just use the equipment for adults to monitor, diagnose and treat children. The best condition is to reduce the size. (2) The indifferent design of the hospital's public product makes children produce a lot of negative emotions. (3) Children's poor emotional control ability brings a big trouble with medical treatment process. These concepts may seem strange at first glance. Indeed, by eliciting negative emotions their purpose seems even contrary to that of experience design: to provide people with pleasurable product experiences. However, we believe that these concepts illuminate a promising new direction in experience design. Several authors have published a number of guidelines for experience- driven design. Although diverse, these existing approaches aim to provide guidance in designing products that stimulate positive emotions and experiences. For example,

© Springer International Publishing Switzerland 2016
Q. Zu and B. Hu (Eds.): HCC 2016, LNCS 9567, pp. 611–621, 2016.
DOI: 10.1007/978-3-319-31854-7_55

Jordan (2000) suggested four sources of product pleasure, Norman [1] discussed three cognitive levels of pleasurable product experiences, Desmet [2] proposed nine sources of product appeal, and Arrasvuori et al. [3] surveyed and categorized 22 different ways for products to elicit playfulness. But in paper Steven and Pieter [4] outline an approach that is different in purpose and even opposite in its consideration of emotions. It is different in purpose because it aims to create rich experiences rather than pleasure, playfulness or positive appeal, and opposite in its consideration of emotions because it conceives negative emotions at the basis of these rich product experiences.

There are a few reasons why we focus on negative emotions in this paper, instead of on highly positive ones. Firstly, some of the most interesting and enjoyable things in life are not simply positive or negative. It is difficult to durably elicit strong positive emotions with everyday products. Such emotions are usually only evoked by personal goal achievements or by highly favorable life events (e.g., Lazarus [5]), in which products normally play a supportive role at best (Desmet) [6]. Products are in some cases able to elicit certain strong positive emotions, but unattainable to most people, such as the satisfaction evoked by living in a big house. Secondly, negative emotions can have beneficial mental and bodily effects on the experiencing individual, which can lead to a positive overall experience. One participant in a rage that her teacher's evaluation is not right at the beginning, she was more focused on the showing ability on his own. Another participant said that the sadness she felt when saying goodbye to her grandparents had a positive effect, because it made her realize their importance in her life (Fokkinga & Desmet) [7].

Considering most traditional emotional design for the children is based on positive emotion, but most of the time the child is very lively and cheerful, easy to be excited. But sometimes crying, sometimes laughing, really be the most changeful. Not only can we directly design to encourage children's positive emotions, but also use negative emotions through the transformation model of the perception and attitude to enrich user experiences. Such not only can appropriately guide the growth of children, but also make children more positive interaction.

2 Related Work

2.1 Evaluation of Children's Negative Emotion in Hospital

The measurement of emotions [7] generally involves several aspects of emotional reactions, including the user's subjective experience, facial expression, physiological response. In the understanding, the commonly methods are the following:

Subjective experience: the self-report method allows users to assess their own emotional experience, such as borrowing 7 point scale or 5 point scale allows users to assess their own subjective feelings, from the emotional three-dimensional (pleasure, arousal and dominance). Pleasure: see the picture feel happy or unhappy. Arousal: see the picture feel excited, raised spirit, or not. Dominance: see the pictures feel like living in a dominant or dominated position.

Behavioral responses: can use emotional assessment scale, such as user study members of the first video to record the user's behavior, and then according to emotional behavior scale of user behavior is evaluated.

Physiological responses: physiological reaction generally the naked eye is difficult to see, only with professional instruments to measure the user's various physiological indicators of change.

2.2 Behavior and Psychological Characteristics of Children Patients

Children's psychological development is obvious in different stages, so the response to disease is not the same. Easy frightened, cry and spasm in the neonatal period; easy to produce fear and antagonism after admission in patients with early childhood; preschool children with emotional attachment to family, emotion is more complex, personality is also formed; school-age children entering school have fear, solitary secluded, fear, sadness, anxiety, etc. In general, the characteristics of children patients are small age, lack of profound understanding of disease, have problems to communicate their own disease with the medical staff and psychological activities rapidly change with the treatment situation [8].

However, because their attention transfer fast, relatively straightforward and simple expression of their feelings and not good at conceal the illness, it's easy to lead them to adapt to the new environment as long as the emotional design based on the characteristics of their mental activity.

3 Design Interview Hospital Children Using Emotions Card Method

In this section, to make evaluation more accurate and credible, the procedures are organized in the same way as those of Hanna, Risden, and Alexander, who created a document with guidelines for evaluation with children and this is still one of the very few and most often cited articles on this subject [16].

First the set-up and planning is discussed, followed by the way to make introductions and how to conduct the evaluation itself. Second, evaluation results t is considered. Than the article ends with a short discussion of the negative emotions of children have significant correlation in public product design.

3.1 Set-up and Planning

The number of children: Several researchers have shown that the first three to five test participants are enough to find 80 % of the problems. At least five and preferably more than five children will uncover much higher percentages of problems. Furthermore, using five or more participants also gives a much clearer impression of the severity of problems.

Selecting children: Especially when the budget for testing is small and therefore not many children can be included in the user evaluation, it is crucial to get as much information out of each child as possible. Including only children who will experience many problems and verbalize them as well is a good way to optimize children's input. In this paper, we choose preschool children (0–6) who go to the children hospital to receive an infusion for the first time, with the obvious negative emotion.

Using a protocol: Although it helps to put some essential things about how the test will proceed on paper for the evaluation, it is not advisable to refer too strictly to this protocol when introducing the children to the test. It should be something that you use in a very natural way.

The observer training: Before we make the observation plan of the design interview, in order to find more potential design requirements, we should not only clarify the object and behavior, but also understand the motivation behind the behavior. For the same user, we display the use scenario and asked the feeling, through observation and guidance of the designer, the object of the experiment clear their own needs and form a stable emotional experience.

3.2 Using the Emotion Card Method

We proposed the Emotion Card Method to make children express more problems explicitly. It is essentially a box with picture cards symbolizing different types of problems that children can encounter while the treatment process. These picture cards were used to explain the purpose of the evaluation and served as a reminder during the evaluation [17] (Fig. 1).

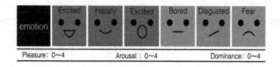

Fig. 1. Emotion card method

Finally, the picture cards could be used by less articulate children to express problems clearly in a non-verbal way by putting a picture card in the box. An experiment showed that children indicated more problems explicitly with the picture cards than without the picture cards, without decreasing the number of verbalized problems. Furthermore the children liked to use the picture cards.

3.3 During the Interview

In paper Steven and Pieter [4] mentioned if a designer is mostly concerned with the user's subjective experience of a situation, transformation of perception might be the most relevant to consider. In contrast, if a designer is mainly interested in changing a user's behavior, a focus on attitude transformation might be more worthwhile.

Situational Interview Based on Emotional Subjective Experience. To extract the different emotional experience factors in the context of the interaction between the children and infusion, let children express their feelings before the interaction, during the interaction and after the interaction. These emotional experiences may propose different design requirements for product design. Extract which has the common characteristics of the children's emotional experiences, ignoring some characteristics of the less impact to the user experiences. Scene (a) is the description of the situation before the interaction, scene (b) is the description of the situation during the interaction, and scene (c) is the description the situation during and after the interaction (Fig. 2).

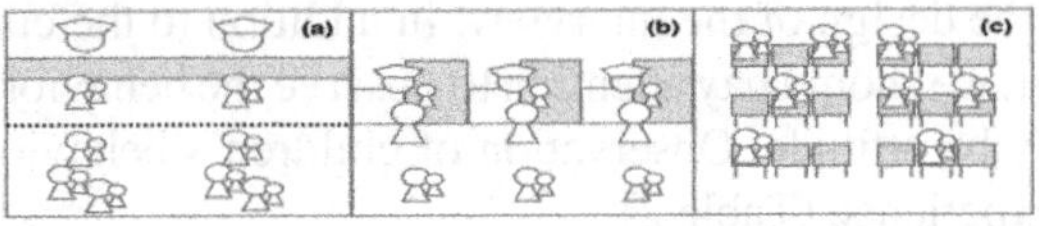

Fig. 2. Situations of infusion: (a) Check window, (b) Injection platform, (c) Transfusion room.

Table 1. The perception of children emotion experience in the process of transfusion

	Perception	Emotion	Number	Percentage
Before	The first time to hospital	Fear	5	71.4 %
	Repeated transfusion	Disgust	3	42.9 %
	Parents' depression	Disgust	3	42.9 %
	Unwell disease problems	Disgust	2	28.6 %
During	Nothing to do during the infusion	Bored	7	100 %
	The pain of an injection	Fear	2	28.6 %
	Pain of transfusion	Angry	2	28.6 %
	Don't know the meaning of infusion	Sad	1	14.3 %
	Forced to sit still	Angry	1	14.3 %
	Seeing other children crying	Fear	1	14.3 %
After	Exhausted after transfusion	Disgust	7	100 %
	The wound is still in pain	Sad	1	14.3 %

We have in-depth interviewed with 7 children, aged between 3–6. According to the above results, we can understand the emotional experience changes of children in different processes of infusion. The interview of our children's emotional experience includes the perception experience and attitude experience, the perception is the subjective feeling of the hospital objective environment, and the attitude is the behavior of the children's subjective emotions.

Through self-reporting method, children describe their mood at that time, and make details about perception experience. As is follow some important findings: (1) Stronger negative experiences are produced before the infusion, while more during the infusion. (2) Before the infusion, children's most fear comes from the strangeness of the hospital and also due to the disease problems or parents' depression. (3) During the infusion, children's most fear comes from the pain experience of injection, followed with all negative experience produced by boring and endless seating still and nothing to do.

(4) When leaving the hospital, all of the children felt exhausted and have a disgusted emotional experience self-reporting.

Behavior Observation Based on Interview Scene. When the perception of the objective environment is not enough to enhance the emotional experience, we can also considering the children's subjective emotional experience. Emotional psychology research shows emotional therapy can help children understand and control their emotions to obtain a positive emotional experience and expression.

In the course of the design of the interview, in addition to the children's subjective emotional self-report, we should pay attention to observe the behavior of children, which is influenced directly by attitude. Observation of children's behavior is to observe the children's attitude experience (Table 2).

Table 2. The Attitude of children emotional experience in the process of transfusion

	Attitude	Emotion	Number	Percentage
Before	Look around	Fear	7	100 %
	Weep and snuggle	Disgust	3	42.9 %
	Held by the parents go back and forth	Fear	1	14.3 %
During	Held by the parents in their seats	Disgust	5	71.4 %
	Look around	Bored	5	71.4 %
	Move transfusion fixing plate	Disgust	4	57.3 %
	Playing games	Bored	3	42.9 %
	Crying and twisting	Angry	2	28.6 %
	Fall asleep	Bored	1	14.3 %
After	Tightly holding the parents hand	Disgust	5	71.4 %
	Not to speak or speak little	Sad	5	71.4 %
	Softly weeping	Angry	2	28.6 %

From the Table 3 data statistics we can predict the following facts: (1) First time to hospital, all of the children always look around because of fear and half or less weep and snuggle. This makes parents much more troubles to take care of them and queue. (2) With the increase of infusion time, children's behavior problems become more and more exposed. (3) Majority of children had to be held by parents in their seats. Because it is boring, most children need toys to distract attention, otherwise it will be crying constantly. Parents pointed out that in this process, let children fall asleep is the best solution. (4) After the transfusion, the children's behavior problems were reduced, but the mood is still very low.

3.4 Research Results

When we integrate the data of the two lists, and pay more attention to the emotional experience of the two aspects, we will have more findings. According to the severity of the emotional behavior problems, to sort negative emotions, respectively, is angry, fear, disgust, sad, bored. During the infusion, the main negative emotions of the children are disgust. In the framework of the emotional experience, each kind of emotional experience is generated by a certain perception experience or attitude experience, and then shows the behavior problem (Fig. 3).

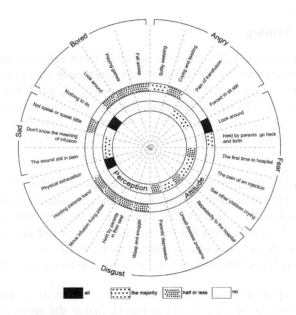

Fig. 3. The aspect of theoretical conceptualization of emotional experience in hospital

From the above, we can know that the emotional experience of children's hospital can be improved from two aspects: perception experience and attitude experience. If a designer is mostly concerned with the user's subjective experience of a situation, transformation of perception might be the most relevant to consider. In contrast, if a designer is mainly interested in changing a user's behavior, a focus on attitude transformation might be more worthwhile. Because of the problem of children's behavior in the process of hospital treatment, the doctors and parents have brought considerable troubles, so in this design background we should pay more attention to the transformation of attitude, improve the negative emotion experience and the behavior of children.

4   Framework and Approach to Children Negative Emotional Experience Design

In the view of the functional theory of emotion [15], emotion is an important internal supervision system, which has the effect of evaluating things and driving behavior, and different events are different, but people's expectation of emotional reaction influences their behavior. So we can be sure that the emotional therapy is feasible and necessary. In emotional therapy, we should focus on the attitude experience rather than the perception experience. The purpose of the treatment is to help children understand and control their emotions, to obtain the right emotional experience and expression. Therefore, according to the general pattern of emotional impact on children's behavior problems, emotional therapy can be started from the following aspects of the specific operation: (1) Emotional venting; (2) Positive associations; (3) Self-suggestion; (4) Roles play.

4.1 Emotional Venting

Behavior problems in children's emotions are often under pressure, so the emotional therapy should be the first to let the children to opening their heart. Let the children send their own grievances, sadness, discontent and resentment, so that it can reach the psychological balance. The way to vent emotions can be diverse, can be verbal, so that children try to speak their own discontent, let the children in the form of diary record their feelings, but also to provide children with the place, items, in the fight, fall, smashing the hearts of children in the process of bad mood.

Positive Association. Because of the behavior problems of children in the family environment and school environment, the cognition of the environment is negative, lack of the power to stimulate the positive trend. Therefore, to provide children with positive situation, so that children in accordance with their own hearts of the target will be the ideal state to associate and express it, to wake up the hearts of the children of a beautiful state of mind, to mobilize their enthusiasm for improving mood and behavior.

Self-suggestion. By guiding the behavior problems of children to carry out self-suggestion, establish the bridge between reality and ideal, change the views of their own and the environment, and then establish a reasonable emotional reaction mechanism, so that children's pessimistic negative emotions, and thus fully mobilize their enthusiasm and potential. Note that, in the process of self-suggestion, based on the reality of the environment, try to make children find hope from the reality of the environment, instead of experience the incapable of action between the strong contrast.

Roles Play. As a major task or behavior in childhood is a game, it can be combined with the development of children to play a role in children's behavior. Using social imitation, role experience, group interaction, positive reinforcement, etc., to promote children's emotional and behavior to overcome their weaknesses, and strive to promote the consolidation and migration of new experiences and behavior in practice.

4.2 Approach to Negative Emotional Experience Design for Children Hospital

The above method can alleviate the negative emotions of children with behavior problems and let the children find the motivation to adapt to the environment. The rich experience qualities specifically were developed by using these methods for five different negative emotion.

Table 3 shows the overview of the five rich qualities with the three elaborated steps and a short description of emotional therapy. Designers can use this overview as a guideline for experimenting with the different emotions and rich experiences and come up with conceptual ideas for a product or product feature that afford rich experiences.

Table 3. The attitude of children's emotion experience in the process of transfusion

Rich quality	Negative emotion	Step 1 – Emotion selection (attitude experience)	Step 2 – Emotion elicitation	Step 3 – Emotion therapy
The sadistic	Angry	Softly weeping / Crying and twisting	Advantage (Physical / material / skill / cognitive)	Emotional venting / Self suggestion
The thrilling	Fear	Look around / Held by parents back and forth	Danger(physical, psychological, or social)	Positive association / Self suggestion
The grotesque	Disgust	Weep and snuggle / Held by parents in their seats / Move infusion fixing plate / Holding parents hand	Repulsive object or concept	Positive association / Roles play
The sentimental	Sad	Not speak or speak little	Virtue against the odds or expectations	Positive association / Roles play
The eerie	Bored	Look around / Playing game / Fall asleep	Uncertain or uncanny threats	Roles play

4.3   The Application of the Approach

This section illustrates how the information in Table 1 can be used to design product concepts, by showing one short design cases that were carried out by the first author to explore the usefulness and applicability of the emotional therapy with several rich inter-action qualities (Fig. 4).

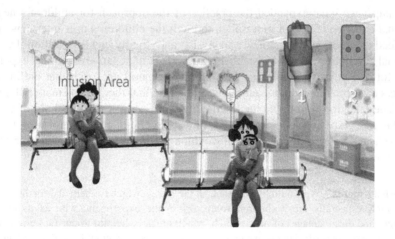

Fig. 4. Transfusion chair design for children's hospital

The design interview above found that infusion is the most painful process, forced to sit in the seat with nothing to do for a long time. Parents often hold them weeping and snuggle. At the same time children in the process of infusion have to wear a fixed plate of infusion to prevent the wound from being accidentally touched, but children could not help but move the fixed plate. So the first step in the approach was to find a quality that adds engagement and positive association to the experience of infusion.

In this case, the grotesque quality seemed suitable, because it gives the user more focus and energy (transformation of attitude). The next step was to find a specific way to elicit disgust through a repulsive object or concept (Table 3). The repulsive object can occur at different moments in the interaction, for example before, during or after the infusion, and the designer can also use the original negative emotions. In this context uncomfortable sitting posture of infusion and fixed plates are repulsive object or concept to stimulate children's disgust. The resulting concept was 'Connection'. This concept is a light switch that people wear on the fixing plate, which have four buttons to control the light feedback around the infusion bottle. The color of the light is constant of four species: red, yellow, blue, green. Through light and sound feedback, children greet each other: (1) If one children press one color button on the fixed plate, the lamp of the infusion bottle of particular can be lit with a piece of encouraging sound, like "You are so brave, can I make friends with you?" (2) When children press the button of another color, it will light another part of the children's lamp, saying another words. (3) When children press a button to light their own lamps, the light will form a beautiful love shape around the infusion bottle. To take the last step in the approach, the concept uses positive association and roles play: The infusion process is not boring. You can contact the other children through the button. Each color represents a part of friends, establishing social relationships by greeting.

5   Discussion

In this paper we have expanded the practice of the approach for children's negative emotional experience design in hospital, through the children's user interviews to get the effective emotional experience analysis, and finally get inspiration from the emotional psychology theory to establish a framework of negative emotional experience design for 3–6 years old children. Apart from a general approach that outlines how designers can combine negative emotions and emotional therapy to create rich experiences. The intention of introducing the quality was to lower the threshold of working with the rich experience approach, by offering certain combinations of negative emotions and emotional therapy which we think are interesting and useful for product experiences.

Acknowledgements. We would like to thank all the people who have helped us in the course of our research, especially the 7 children volunteers in the experiment, who let us know the advantages and disadvantages of our research, which are very helpful to our future research. In addition, our work described in this paper was fully supported by a grant from Beijing University of Posts & Telecommunications, Beijing (Project no. Z151100003015165).

References

1. Norman, D.A.: Emotional Design: Why We Love (or Hate) Everyday Things. Basic Civitas Books, New York (2004)
2. Desmet, P.M.A.: Product emotion. In: Schifferstein, H.N.J., Hekkert, P. (eds.) Product Experience, pp. 379–398. Elsevier, San Diego (2008)

3. Arrasvuori, J., Boberg, M., Korhonen, H.J.: Understanding playfulness: An overview of the revised playful experience (PLEX) framework. Paper Presented at the 7th Conference on Design and Emotion, Chicago, IL (2010)
4. Fokkinga, S.F., Desmet, P.M.A.: Ten ways to design for disgust, sadness, and other enjoyments: A design approach to enrich product experiences with negative emotions. Int. J. Des. 7(1), 19 (2013)
5. Lazarus, R.S.: Emotion and Adaptation. Oxford University Press, New York (1991)
6. Desmet, P.M.A.: Designing emotions (Doctoral Dissertation). Delft University of Technology, Delft, The Netherlands (2002)
7. Fokkinga, S.F., Desmet, P.M.A.: Meaningful mix or tricky conflict? A categorization of mixed emotional experiences and their usefulness for design. In: Brassett, J., Hekkert, P., Ludden, G., Malpass, M., McDonnell, J. (eds.) Proceedings of the 8th International Design and Emotion Conference, 11–14 September 2012, Central Saint Martin College of Art & Design, London, UK (2012b)
8. Liang, M.: Emotion analysis and psychological intervention of the children with infusion in outpatient department of Pediatrics in the theory of emotion cognition. J. Math. Med. 25(5) (2012)
9. Shu, W., Zhang, K.: The emotional design of children's medical devices. J. Changsha Acad. Railway Sci. (Soc. Sci. Ed.) 15(4) (2014). Journal of Changsha Railway University
10. Anonymous: Bit by bit like eating. China News Weekly (28) (2008)
11. Wang, K.: Research on the design strategy of medical products based on the theory of emotional design. Art Sci. Technol. 6, 211–212 (2013)
12. PHILPS's CT scanner for children. http://www.rxart.net/projects/ct-scanner-for-advocate-hope-childrens-hospital
13. Ellsworth, P.C., Scherer, K.R.: Appraisal processes in emotion. In: Davidson, R.J., Scherer, K.R., Goldsmith, H.H. (eds.) Handbook of Affective Sciences, pp. 572–595. Oxford University Press, New York (2003)
14. Frijda, N.H.: The Emotions. Cambridge University Press, Cambridge (1986)
15. Apter, M.J.: Reversal Theory: The Dynamics of Motivation, Emotion, and Personality, 2nd edn. One World, Oxford (2007)
16. Fokkinga, S.F., Desmet, P.M.A.: Darker shades of joy: the role of negative emotion in rich product experiences. Des. Issues 28(4), 42–56 (2012a)
17. Barendregt, W., Bekker, M.M.: Guidelines for user testing with children. Department of Industrial Design, Eindhoven University of Technology
18. Zhao, Y., Zhang, J., Han, J., Ren, F., Cai, R.: The establishment of image database of Chinese children's emotion evaluation (7-14 years old, Shanghai). Department of children and adolescent health, Xinhua Hospital Affiliated to Shanghai Key Laboratory of Environment and Children's Health, Medicine School, Shanghai Jiao Tong University, Shanghai (200092), R749.94.A. Chin. J. Child Health Care (6) (2009)
19. Jiang, J., Li, Y.: Emotional therapy: a new perspective on the correction of children's behavior problems. Northeast Normal Univ. J. (Philos. Soc. Sci. Ed.) (3) (2006)

An Efficient Multi-service Resource Scheduling Algorithm in Cognitive Relay System

Yanan Zhang[✉], Yong Zhang, Yajun Zhang, Xu Si, and Baoling Liu

Beijing Key Laboratory of Work Safety Intelligent Monitoring,
School of Electronic Engineering, Beijing University of Posts
and Telecommunications, Beijing, People's Republic of China
{zhangyanan,yongzhang,zhangyajun,
xusi,blliu}@bupt.edu.cn

Abstract. Relay is one of the key techniques in LTE-Advanced, which can expand the network coverage, increase the system capacity and improve the cell-edge performance and the fairness among users. Based on the current resource scheduling researches with relay technology, this paper investigates a resource scheduling algorithm called QoS (Quality of Service)-based Two Hop Proportional Fair (QTHPF), which can efficiently guarantee the multi-service QoS performance in a cognitive LTE-Advanced relay system. Our basic idea is to establish the optimized frequency lists corresponding to different services and to introduce the multi-service utility function to calculate scheduling priority. Extensive simulation results confirm that the proposed algorithm improves the fairness, QoS performance and system throughput, and reduces the channel switching frequency.

Keywords: LTE-Advanced · Relay · Resource scheduling · Multi-service

1 Introduction

In LTE-Advanced system, relay technology is introduced to improve cell-edge throughput and expand cell coverage, while providing temporary network deployment and mobile service [1, 2]. However, the introduction of relay technology has increased new transmission links, exacerbating the competition for wireless spectrum resource. Here comes a problem for us to solve as how to optimize the traditional cellular network scheduling strategy to take the most advantages of relay transmission technology.

Up to now, there are a number of previous studies on resource allocation in relay system. A collaborative algorithm based on the market game theory has been proposed to solve the problem of resource allocation in the LTE-Advanced relay network [3]. To meet the multi-service QoS demand, [4] presents a multi-user multi-service scheduling scheme in the two-hop cooperative relay network, which introduces AU-Function as an optimization objective. In [5], the author puts forward an improved partial proportional fairness algorithm (IPPT). [6] takes into consideration the communication node selection [7] and the relay power control to minimize network power in OFDMA relay system. Meanwhile, investigates an algorithm to resolve the problem of the user fairness and QoS. In DF (Decode-and-Forward) relay-assisted SC-FDMA (Single Carrier-Frequency

Division Multiple Access) system, with the greedy heuristic thinking, the resource allocation algorithm can maximize system capacity and reduce complexity. However, most of above algorithms rarely consider distinguishing QoS levels of various different services especially in the multi-service hybrid transmission system.

In this paper, we investigate an efficient multi-service resource scheduling algorithm, namely QTHPF, in cognitive relay system to achieve both QoS requirement and fairness, optimizing system overall performance. The proposed algorithm establishes the optimized frequency list based on frequency priority in descending order, which is divided into four parts in accordance with the proportion that four types of service traffic account for total traffic in the system. Afterwards, we design the multi-service utility function, taking the application layer factors, like time delay, jitter and packet loss rate into consideration. In the two sub-slots of communication stage, the multi-service utility function is introduced to calculate the scheduling priority of sub-channel users.

The rest of our paper is organized as follows. Section 2 introduces the system model, including the network structure and transmission model. In Sect. 3, there is a detailed description of the proposed resource scheduling algorithm. Later in Sect. 4, we analyze simulation results to evaluate the performance of our algorithm. Finally, we draw a conclusion in Sect. 5.

2 System Model

2.1 Network Structure

The system scenario is shown in Fig. 1. The system consists of Primary Base Stations (PBSs) and Secondary Base Stations (SBSs) corresponding to Primary Users (PUs) and Secondary Users (SUs). The centralized primary system and secondary system coexist in the same geographic area. Besides, we assume that there are no relay nodes in the authorized network. Cognitive relay nodes in the cognitive system assist in the communication between base stations and users. In this paper, we adopt the Overlay spectrum sharing mechanism.

The transmission links of cognitive network are divided into two categories, namely direct-passing links and relay links. And relay links are subdivided into the first-hop link (SBS-SR link) and the second-hop link (SR-SU link). Meanwhile, cognitive users are also divided into direct-passing users and relay users. To communicate with the base station, the users can choose whether to pass directly or to forward via a suitable relay node, depending on the routing policy. This paper employs the routing selection strategy based on the geographic location information, in which the users select the nearest base station or relay node as a routing criterion.

Relay nodes, working in TDD (Time Division Duplex) mode, cannot send and receive data at the same time, so the two-hop transmission signal must be scheduled to two different time slots. In this mode, relay nodes transmit data in DF method, and all data is processed in real-time.

As shown in Fig. 2, in a multi-carrier mobile communication system, system resource in the time domain is divided into several time slots and in the frequency domain is divided into a plurality of sub-channels. Each time slot is divided into two

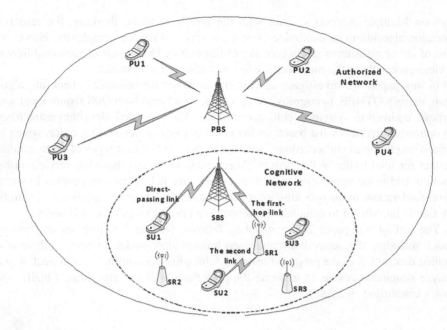

Fig. 1. The model of cognitive relay system

sub-slots, one sub-slot and one sub-channel constituting a basic time-frequency resource block. We take each time slot as a scheduling period, namely TTI (Transmission Time Interval), during which a time-frequency resource block can only be dispatched to one user. In the first sub-slot, the base station transmits data packets to a user or a relay node. And in the second sub-slot, the user receives data packets from the base station or the relay node.

It is assumed that all channel conditions of communication links are known, ignoring interference within the cell and the fast-moving user node. Within a scheduling period TTI, the relay node chosen by the user according to the routing policy is fixed. All system resource is uniformly scheduled by the scheduler according to the predefined scheduling strategy. The proposed algorithm adopts a scheme in which routing policy and resource scheduling mechanism are separated, and only scheduling aspects are considered.

2.2 Transmission Model

We define $U_D = \{1, 2, \cdots, M_D\}$, $U_R = \{1, 2, \cdots, M_R\}$, $U_R = \{1, 2, \cdots, M_R\}$ and $N_n = \{1, 2, \cdots, N\}$ to be the set of direct-passing users, relay users, relay nodes and available sub-channels. In the i-th (i = 1,2) sub-slot, the channel capacity of the direct-passing user m_D in sub-channel n can be written as:

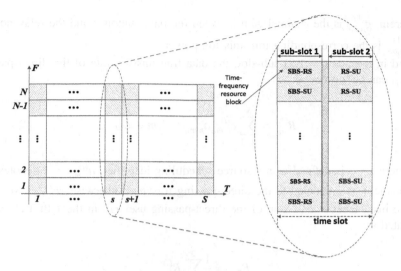

Fig. 2. The time-frequency structure model

$$c_{n,m_D}^{(i)} = B_n log_2 \left(1 + \frac{g_{n,b,m}^{(i)} \cdot p_{n,b,m}^{(i)}}{\Gamma \sigma^2} \right), \quad \forall m \in U_D \tag{1}$$

Whereby, B_n is the bandwidth of each sub-channel, $g_{n,b,m}^{(i)}$ is the channel gain between the base station and the direct-passing user, $p_{n,b,m}^{(i)}$ is the corresponding transmission power, $\Gamma = -\ln(5 \cdot BER)/1.5$ is SNR tolerance under certain error rate, BER is the bit error rate required by the system, σ^2 is the additive white Gaussian noise power.

And in the second sub-slot, the channel capacity of the relay user m_R in sub-channel n is expressed by

$$c_{n,m_R}^{(2)} = B_n log_2 \left(1 + \frac{g_{n,r,m}^{(2)} \cdot p_{n,r,m}^{(2)}}{\Gamma \sigma^2} \right), \quad \forall m \in U_R \tag{2}$$

In (2), $g_{n,r,m}^{(2)}$ is the channel gain between the relay node r and the user m_R, and $p_{n,r,m}^{(2)}$ is the corresponding transmission power.

In the first sub-slot, the channel capacity of the relay node r in sub-channel n can be calculated as (3).

$$c_{n,r}^{(1)} = B_n log_2 \left(1 + \frac{g_{n,b,r}^{(1)} \cdot p_{n,b,r}^{(1)}}{\Gamma \sigma^2} \right), \quad \forall r \in R_n \tag{3}$$

Herein, $g_{n,b,r}^{(1)}$ is the channel gain between the base station b and the relay node r, and $p_{n,b,r}^{(1)}$ is the corresponding transmission power.

And in the i-th (i = 1,2) sub-slot, the data transmission rate of the direct-passing user m_D can be written as:

$$R_{m_D}^{(i)} = \sum_{n=1}^{N} c_{n,m_D}^{(i)} a_{n,m_D}^{(i)}, \quad \forall m \in U_D \tag{4}$$

Where $a_{n,m_D}^{(i)}$ is defined as a resource scheduling identifier. $a_{n,m_D}^{(i)} = 1$ denotes that sub-channel n is scheduled to the direct-passing user m_D, otherwise, $a_{n,m_D}^{(i)} = 0$.

The instantaneous data rate of the direct-passing user m_D in the τ th TTI can be calculated as:

$$R_{m_D} = \frac{1}{2} \sum_{i=1}^{2} R_{m_D}^{(i)} \tag{5}$$

The data transmission rate of the relay user m_R in the second sub-slot is expressed by:

$$R_m^{(2)} = \sum_{n=1}^{N} c_{n,m_R}^{(2)} a_{n,m_R}^{(2)}, \quad \forall m \in U_R \tag{6}$$

The data transmission rate of the relay node r in the second sub-slot is expressed by:

$$R_r^{(2)} = \sum_{m \in I_r} R_m^{(2)}, \quad \forall m \in U_R \tag{7}$$

With (7), I_r is the set of relay users served by the relay node r.

The data transmission rate of the relay node r in the first sub-slot can be written as:

$$R_r^{(1)} = \sum_{n=1}^{N} c_{n,r}^{(1)} a_{n,r}^{(1)}, \quad \forall r \in R_n \tag{8}$$

Meanwhile, the data transmission rate of the relay user m_R in the first sub-slot can be calculated as (9).

$$R_m^{(1)} = \frac{R_m^{(2)}}{R_r^{(2)}} R_r^{(1)}, \quad \forall m \in U_R \tag{9}$$

The instantaneous data rate of the relay user m_R in the τ th TTI can be expressed as:

$$R_{m_R} = min\left\{R_m^{(1)}, R_m^{(2)}\right\} \quad, \quad \forall m \in U_R \tag{10}$$

3 Analysis on the Proposed Resource Scheduling Scheme

In this section, we introduce the design of the QoS-based Two Hop Proportional Fair (QTHPF) algorithm in cognitive relay system, which can achieve scheduling fairness and improve multi-service QoS performance.

This paper considers a carrier scheduling algorithm, so we make a reasonable assumption that the system equally assigns transmission power to each sub-channel, and then does resource scheduling. And a complete scheduling time slot contains two stages, spectrum sensing stage and communication stage, in multi-relay-based resource scheduling model of cognitive LTE-Advanced system. In the sensing stage, based on the frequency point sensing strategy of proactive spectrum environment, SUs periodically sense the authorized spectrum in the optimized spectrum sensing time slot. And in the communication stage, according to the proposed scheduling algorithm, frequency points are uniformly assigned to each SU within a cell by the base station scheduler.

Step1: Establishing the optimized frequency lists corresponding to different services

The base station prioritizes for all the available frequency by receiving sensing results of cognitive users, i.e., interference probability P_n and free time T_n of each frequency, then selecting several optimal frequency points to form the optimized frequency list according to the descending order of T_n/P_n. At each scheduling time slot, based on frequency priority in descending order, we divide the optimized frequency list into four parts in accordance with the proportion that four types of service traffic account for total traffic in the system, namely the conversational service optimized frequency list, the streaming service optimized frequency list, the interactive service optimized frequency list and the back-office service optimized frequency list. Meanwhile the data packet is also grounded in accordance with the service. For each type of service, its optimized frequency list corresponds to its data packet. In the communication stage, if an authorized user is present or channel quality cannot meet the current service requirement, SUs will immediately switch to the remaining highest priority frequency in the optimized frequency list corresponding to the service.

Step2: Resource scheduling for all users in the second sub-slot

In the second sub-slot of communication stage, scheduling priority of the user m in the sub-channel n is:

$$QM_{m,n,t}^2 = \begin{cases} Q_m \cdot c_{n,m_D}^{(2)}(t)\Big/R(m,t), & m \in U_D \\ Q_m \cdot c_{n,m_R}^{(2)}(t)\Big/R(m,t), & m \in U_R \end{cases} \tag{11a}$$

$$m^* = \arg\max_m QM^2_{m,n^*,t} \tag{11b}$$

Therein, the average data rate of the user m can be updated as (12).

$$R(m,t) = \sum_{n \in C(k)} R(m,n,t) \tag{12}$$

$R(m,n,t)$ denotes the average data rate of the user m in the sub-channel n at the moment in time t. And $C(k)$ is the set of all sub-channels.

$$R(m,n,t) = \begin{cases} \left(1 - \frac{1}{T_c}\right)R(m,n,t-1) + \frac{1}{T_c}R_m(t), & m = m^* \\ \left(1 - \frac{1}{T_c}\right)R(m,n,t-1), & m \neq m^* \end{cases} \tag{13a}$$

$$R_m(t) = \begin{cases} R_{m_D}(t), & m \in U_D \\ R_{m_R}(t), & m \in U_R \end{cases} \tag{13b}$$

In this algorithm, taking QoS requirement and multi-user QoS priority into account, the multi-service utility function is introduced to calculate scheduling priority. Utility function Q_m for user m is expressed as:

$$Q_m = \exp\left(\frac{\tau^*_m}{\tau^*_m - \tau_m}\right) \cdot \exp\left(\frac{\varphi^*_m}{\varphi^*_m - \varphi_m}\right) \cdot \frac{\omega_m}{\omega^*_m} \tag{14}$$

Where τ_m is the current time delay and τ^*_m is a preset time delay threshold value, φ_m is the current state of buffer, and φ^*_m is a preset buffer size, ω_m is the current packet loss rate, and ω^*_m is a preset threshold value of packet loss rate.

In the optimized frequency list of every sort of service, we randomly choose a sub-channel n^* and calculate scheduling priority $QM^2_{m,n^*,t}$ of all users, by (11), within the current time slot on the sub-channel n^*. Afterwards, the sub-channel n^* is scheduled to the user m^* with the largest scheduling priority. At the moment, the time-frequency resource block may be dispatched to the second hop of the two-hop user or to the direct-passing user, until all sub-channels are scheduled or the needs of all service are met. With the scheduling result in the second sub-slot, we calculate the data rate $R_r^{(2)}$ of each relay node on its second-hop transmission link.

Step3: Resource scheduling for all relay nodes and direct-passing users in the first sub-slot

In the first sub-slot of communication stage, scheduling priority of the direct-passing user m_D in the sub-channel n is:

$$QM^1_{m_D,n,t} = Q_m \cdot c^{(1)}_{n,m_D}(t) \Big/ R(m,t), \qquad m \in U_D \tag{15}$$

For the relay node r, its multi-service utility function is expressed by the utility function's algebraic average of all relay users serviced by this relay node.

Therefore, scheduling priority of the relay node r in the sub-channel n is:

$$QM^1_{r,n,t} = \left(\frac{1}{\|I_r\|}\sum_{m\in I_r} Q_m\right) \cdot \beta_r \cdot c^{(1)}_{n,r}(t) \Big/ \overline{R_r}, \quad r \in R_n, m \in U_R \qquad (16)$$

Here, the factor β_r is introduced to balance channel capacity between two-hop transmission links of relay users. $\overline{R_r}$ is the average data transmission rate of relay nodes. And they are calculated as follows:

$$\beta_r = R^{(2)}_r \Big/ R^{(1)}_r \qquad (17a)$$

$$\overline{R_r} = \frac{1}{\|I_r\|}\sum_{m\in I_r} R(m,t), \quad m \in U_R \qquad (17b)$$

To sum up, in the first sub-slot, resource scheduling priority in the sub-channel n is:

$$QM^1_{s,n,t} = \begin{cases} Q_s \cdot c^{(1)}_{n,s}(t) \Big/ R(s,t), & s \in U_D \\ \left(\frac{1}{\|I_s\|}\sum_{m\in I_s} Q_m\right) \cdot \beta_s \cdot c^{(1)}_{n,s}(t) \Big/ \overline{R_s}, & s \in R_n, m \in U_R \end{cases} \qquad (18a)$$

$$s^* = \arg\max_s QM^1_{s,n^*,t} \qquad (18b)$$

In the optimized frequency list of every sort of service, we randomly choose a sub-channel n^* and calculate the scheduling priority $QM^1_{s,n^*,t}$ of all relay nodes (if a relay node simultaneously serves many types of service users, we only refer to the highest priority service) and direct-passing users, by (18), within the current time slot on the sub-channel n^*. Then, the sub-channel n^* is scheduled to the user s^* with the largest scheduling priority. If $\beta_r \leq 1$, the relay node will stop competing for carrier resource. The entire process is completed when all sub-channles are scheduled or the needs of all service are met. Furthermore, the following indicators, $R^{(1)}_r$, R_{m_D}, R_{m_R}, $R(m,t)$, $\overline{R_r}$, need to be updated.

4 Simulation Results and Analysis

In this section, we will explain several performance advantages of the proposed QTHPF algorithm in the cognitive relay system, compared with the classical THPF (Two Hop Proportional Fair) algorithm, over system throughput, QoS performance, the

Table 1. Simulation parameters

Parameter	Value/description
Cell Radius	600 m
System Frequency	2 GHz
BS Tx Power	46 dBm
Number of Sub-channels	128
Sub-channel Bandwidth	5 MHz
Noise Spectral Density	−174 dBm/Hz
Relay Tx Power	38 dBm
Subframe Duration	1 ms
Path Loss Index	SBS-SR:2, other:4
Number of multipath channel taps	6
Window Length	100
Standard Deviation of Shadow Fading	7 dB

average switching frequency and fairness. SUs periodically sense the authorized spectrum in the center frequency, namely 2 GHz, to establish the optimized frequency list. As a comparison, THPF schedules SUs to the frequency with the highest priority, not considering the priority of multiple services. Simulation parameters are summarized in Table 1.

4.1 System Throughput Comparison

From Fig. 3, firstly, system throughput of two scheduling algorithms increases with traffic load, then leveling off due to system bandwidth constraint when the load reaches 0.7. The proposed algorithm has a better system throughput performance than THPF. Especially as traffic load gets heavier, this advantage is becoming increasingly

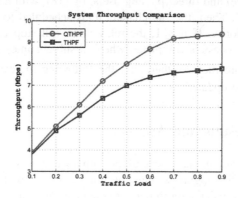

Fig. 3. The system throughput comparison

apparent. It is because QTHPF algorithm takes the channel state into account and utilizes multi-user diversity gain to improve inter-carrier frequency-selective gain.

4.2 QoS Performance Comparison

Delay and packet loss rate are two important evaluation indexes of QoS. From Figs. 4 and 5, we can clearly know QTHPF can achieve remarkable performances in these two areas. Because QTHPF divides optimized frequency lists of different service models and utilizes the multi-service utility function to distinguish QoS levels. As we can see, both delay and packet loss rate increase with traffic load. With the gradual increase of load, data packet needs to wait in a longer queue. At the same time, the router has no time to deal with them, the part of which will be discarded. When the load reaches 0.4, due to network congestion, delay and packet loss rate of the entire network grow even more rapidly.

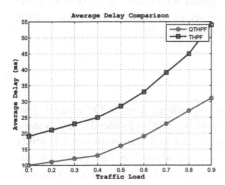
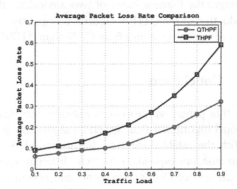

Fig. 4. The average delay comparison   **Fig. 5.** The average packet loss rate comparison

4.3 Average Switching Frequency Comparison

Figure 6 shows the comparison of the average switching frequency between QTHPF and THPF, from which we find out the proposed algorithm shows a superior performance, especially when the traffic load is larger. Because the QTHPF algorithm effectively avoids that packets with higher priority are scheduled to the disturbed and unstable frequency, reducing switching frequency and system overhead, while THPF fails to consider channel allocation strategies for the different service priority.

4.4 Fairness Comparison

Here, Jain fairness index is used to evaluate the performance of two scheduling algorithms in fairness. The simulation result is showed in Fig. 7. And in our algorithm

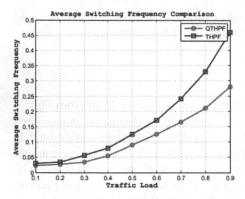

Fig. 6. The average switching frequency comparison

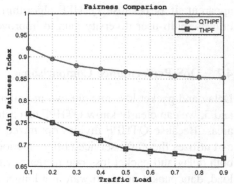

Fig. 7. The fairness comparison

design, the fairness index of two algorithms decreases with traffic load. However, the reduction of the QTHPF algorithm is greatly improved as traffic load increases, and the improvement is as much as 67 % than THPF when load is 0.9.

5   Conclusion

In this paper, we propose a resource scheduling algorithm, namely QoS-based Two Hop Proportional Fair (QTHPF) algorithm, in cognitive LTE-Advanced relay system. With the establishment of the optimized frequency list and the multi-service utility function corresponding to four different services, this algorithm can guarantee the multi-service QoS requirements and optimize system overall performance. From simulation results, compared to THPF, QTHPF has a better performance in terms of system throughput, delay, the average packet loss rate, the average switching frequency and fairness, in particular, when the traffic load increases.

Acknowledgment. This work is supported by the State Major Science and Technology Special Projects under Grant No. 2014ZX03004002.

References

1. Abdallah, A., Serhal, D., Fakih, K.: Relaying techniques for LTE-advanced. In: Proceedings of European Wire-less 2015, 21th European Wireless Conference. VDE (2015)
2. Zhiguo, D., Leung, K.K., Goeckel, D.L.: A relay assisted cooperative transmission protocol for wireless multiple access systems. IEEE Trans. Commun. **58**(8), 2425–2435 (2010)
3. Egena, O., Omar, A.: Collaborative algorithm for resource allocation in LTE-advanced relay networks. In: 2014 9th International Symposium on Communication System, Networks & Digital Sign Processing (CSNDSP), pp. 938–942 (2014)

4. Yinglei, T., Mei, S., Fang, N., Guangquan, C., Junde, S.: Cooperative OFDMA resource allocation for Multi-QoS guarantee: a cross-layer utility scheduling approach. In: 2009 Joint Conferences on Pervasive Computing (JCPC), pp. 267–272 (2009)
5. Jiansong, M., Lin, M., Kai, L., Yan, W., Shuying, W.: Improved partial proportional fair scheduling algorithm for OFDMA relay system. In: 2014 4th IEEE International Conference on Information Science and Technology (ICIST), pp. 49–53 (2014)
6. Jingon, J., Sumei, S.: Network-power-saving resource allocation algorithm with hybrid communication mode for OFDMA relay networks. In: 2011 IEEE 22nd International Symposium on Personal Indoor and Mobile Radio Communication (PIMRC), pp. 1850–1854 (2011)
7. Seunghoon, N., Mai, V., Tarokh, V.: Relay selection methods for wireless cooperative communications. In: 2008 42nd Annual Conference on Information Sciences and System, CISS 2008, pp. 859–864 (2008)

A Novel Load Balancing Algorithm Based on Improved Particle Swarm Optimization in Cloud Computing Environment

Yongfei Zhu[1], Di Zhao[2], Wei Wang[3], and Haiwu He[2(✉)]

[1] Network Operation System, Huawei Technologies Co., Ltd.,
Beijing, China
zhuyongfei@huawei.com
[2] Computer Network Information Center, Chinese Academy of Sciences,
Beijing 100190, China
zhaodi@sccas.cn, haiwuhe@cstnet.cn
[3] Department of Information Security, Beijing Jiaotong University,
Beijing 100044, China
wangweil@bjtu.edu.cn

Abstract. In the area of cloud computing load balancing, the Particle Swarm Optimization (PSO) algorithm is neoteric and now praised highly, but recently a more neoteric algorithm which deploys the classifier into load balancing is presented. Besides, an algorithm called red-black tree which is aiming at improving the efficiency of resource dispatching is also praised. But the 3 algorithms all have different disadvantages which cannot be ignored. For example, the dispatch efficiency of PSO algorithm is not satisfying; although classifier and red-black tree algorithm improve the efficiency of dispatching tasks, the performance in load balancing is not that good, as a result the improved PSO algorithm is presented. Some researches are designed to get the advantages of new algorithm. First of all, the time complexity and performance for each algorithm in theory are computed; and then actual data which are generated in experiments are given to demonstrate the performance. And from the experiment result, it can be found that for the speed of algorithm itself PSO is the lowest, and the improved PSO solve this problem in some degree; improved PSO algorithm has the best performance in task solving and PSO is the second one, the red-black and Naive Bayes algorithm are much slower; PSO and improved PSO algorithm perform well in load balancing, while the other two algorithms do not do well.

Keywords: Cloud computing · Load balancing · Particle swarm optimization · Bayesian classifier · Red-black tree

1   Introduction

The area of Cloud computing is getting more hot, at the same time, a more intensive task waiting to be processed, how to allocate cloud tasks reasonably so that the nodes in the cloud computing environment can have a balanced load become more critical, this task allocation strategy is called load balancing. Of course, the research on load

© Springer International Publishing Switzerland 2016
Q. Zu and B. Hu (Eds.): HCC 2016, LNCS 9567, pp. 634–645, 2016.
DOI: 10.1007/978-3-319-31854-7_57

balancing has never stopped, after summarizing, the dynamic load balancing technology is considered more in line with the cloud computing environment, the development of dynamic load balancing technology is becoming more and more vigorous. But from the direction of the current study, the use of dynamic load balancing algorithm is very different, the load balancing algorithm currently used is divided into two categories as below.

First, the complex algorithm hasn't been applied to the load balancing field, such as feedback load balancing strategy, load balancing algorithm based on load weights [7], load balancing algorithm based on red-black tree, greedy strategy.

Second, the complex algorithm is applied to load balancing, such as load balancing strategy based on particle swarm optimization algorithm, load balancing strategy based on ant colony optimization algorithm, load balancing strategy based on Bayesian Classifiers [1] and so on.

Experiment has proved that the load balancing degree of PSO algorithm is relatively high. It is in line with the load balancing strategy in the needs of balance degree. And Bayesian Classifier algorithm belongs to another way. The experiments show that their running speed is considerable, red-black tree algorithm is with its simple, efficient node ordering by attention. These three algorithms have their own disadvantages. PSO algorithm, the time complexity of its own operation is too high. Bayesian Classifier algorithm, because in the process of using data to make classifier training, the amount of data is not large enough thus lead to inaccurate classification results, and thus lead to load balancing degree can not be satisfactory. Unfortunately for the red-black tree algorithm in load balancing and task execution speed, the performance is not satisfactory. According to the above list the advantages and disadvantages of the three algorithms, we think the PSO algorithm can be improved and with the red-black tree algorithm combined to produce an improved PSO algorithm (the RB-PSO, in some places below use algorithm RB-PSO instead of improved PSO algorithm) and in the algorithm execution speed and load balancing degree have made a good progress.

2 Related Work

2.1 Particle Swarm Optimization Algorithm

Load balancing in the cloud computing environment cannot directly apply the standard Particle-Swarm-Optimization algorithm, because it is just suitable for solving a continuous problem. The computing nodes in the cloud computing environment can be abstracted as a discrete graph, and the standard Particle-Swarm-Optimization algorithm can not be competent.

For discrete Particle-Swarm-Optimization algorithm, there is still space for improvement. The convergence rate of discrete Particle-Swarm-Optimization algorithm is very fast in the global search, and the latter part of the algorithm's iteration should focus on the ability of local search [5], which is the improvement in the algorithm level. Foreign scholars Hesam Izakian has a theory of discrete Particle-Swarm-Algorithm and applies it to grid computing [6]. In load balancing, the similarity of grid computing and cloud computing is very low. According to comparisons, among the ACO, Genetic

Algorithm, FPSO, CPSO and DPSO, Izakian finds DPSO has the best performance. Therefore, it can be applied to the load balancing of cloud computing, to accelerate the convergence of local search, and a brand new DPSO algorithm.

The formula for the discrete Particle-Swarm-Optimization (DPSO) is involved:

$$V_k^{t+1}(i,j) = V_k^t(i,j) + c_1 r_1 (pbest_k^t(i,j) - X_k^t(i,j)) + c_2 r_2 (gbest_k^t(i,j) - X_k^t(i,j)) \quad (1)$$

$$X_k^t(i,j) = \begin{cases} 1 & if \ V_k^{t+1}(i,j) = \max(V_k^{t+1}(i,j)) \\ 0 & otherwise \end{cases} \quad (2)$$

Equation (1) is the velocity update for the k particles. c_1, c_2 are the fixed coefficient, it means the current particle optimal value and the proportion of the particle population's optimal value. The research shows that when $c_1 + c_2 = 4.1$ the optimal solution can be obtained, and the general situation is defined as $c_1 = c_2 = 2$ (*pbest, gbest, V, X*, what are the representatives). X indicates the position of the particle, and the $pbest_k^t$ represents the best position of the first k particle, which is the position matrix; the $gbest_k^t$ is similar to the $pbest_k^t$, but only the best position matrix of the global.

Equation (2) is the of particle position update, we can see that all of the particles that have the maximum speed will run on this node. The particle swarm optimization in load balancing can be understood in this way. We have given the N particles, the particles should contain the information of T tasks (which should be distributed at present), and the information of the existing M computing nodes. Of course, the information of computing nodes still need through the heartbeat mechanism return and during its return remained a reverberation time T state (hypothesis does not consider correct the load of nodes). The speed of each particle is updated by using the formula, and the current state of the particle is obtained by the formula. Until the end of the iteration, the optimal solution is selected. Here is a simple calculation of the time complexity of the algorithm between each of the two beats, assuming that the number of iterations for I times, then the time complexity is: $I*(N + 0.5*I)*T^2*M + T*M^2$ which can be divided into two parts. First of all, it calculates the complexity of velocity updating needs, that is each particle in each computing node for each of the tasks required for each iteration complexity multiplied by the particle number N, number of iterations I, task number T and the number of computing nodes M, as the basic unit here is $(N + 50)*T$, N as the times of optimal solution compared in the population, $0.5*I$ is the average number of particles I times iteration and its own comparison, T is to calculate the number of nodes in which each task is assigned to.

2.2   Bayesian Classifier Algorithm

Cai Song puts forward a new idea in his article, by using the method of classifier, the nodes in the cloud computing environment can be divided, and the classifier is trained in advance or at runtime. The authors use the Naive Bayesian Classifier, which is assumed that all eigenvalues of sample are independent. Experiments have proved that when the hypothesis is established, the Naive Bayesian Classifier is more accurate than other classifiers. For complex classifiers, such as decision tree, neural network and so on, the author has avoided it due to the realization of the difficulty. But in fact, in the cloud computing environment, we select the nodes with three properties, the CPU processing capacity of node, the RAM of node and the BW of node. The coupling between these three properties is relatively small, that is, between the three properties, there is no relevant nearly, so that the accuracy and time for classification of the Bayesian Classifier should be more appropriate. In addition, pre-defined classification should be applied before the true load balancing, using a training sample to train the classifier which is need. When the load is balancing, we use the load node to classify the information returned.

Under the cloud computing environment, the most important attributes of nodes or features of nodes are as the follows. The idle ratio for CPU processing power of computing nodes is $CP = P_{free}/P_{total}$, the idle ratio for RAM computing nodes is $CRAM = RAM_{free}/RAM_{total}$, the idle ratio for BW of computing nodes is $CBW = BW_{free}/BW_{total}$. These three attributes are all the current state of the computing nodes, through the cloud computing heartbeat return to get node state. Now assume that these three properties are not relevant, easy to know, this assumption is quite correct, the error is small. The classifier is designed by a set of training samples for training, recorded as $TSC = \{TS_1, TS_2, TS_3, \ldots, TS_n\}$ are divided into four categories, while S_1 is idle state, S_2 is the light load state, S_3 is the minor overload state, and S_4 is the overload state.

The formula and principle of Naive Bayesian's theorem is not too much to explain here. We use the Naive Bayesian theorem to divide the computing nodes into four categories.

After the cloud computing node is assigned, we apply the hash algorithm for cloud tasks and then it is needed to be assigned to a specific queue, as shown in Fig. 1.

2.3   The Red-Black Tree Algorithm

In the field of load balancing in cloud computing, load balancer is required to know the heartbeat mechanism of nodes under the state of load to make dynamic feedback, and there is a certain time interval between every two beats. So the performance of load balancing will be studied in the heartbeat time interval. In the nodes of the load balancing, they maintain the information of computing node that through the heart returns. And in the field of load balancing, the red-black tree should be a more suitable way. Specific practice is to arrange a session for computing nodes in cloud computing environment, but also through the heartbeat mechanism return to the nodes of load balance, using the load state, organizing the computing nodes which are under the cloud computing environment with the way of red-black tree.

Assuming that the computing nodes have N, the time complexity of the insertion of a node is $O(\lg N)$, so the time complexity of the N node is $N*O(\lg N)$. After the organization of the node, because the red-black tree is with sorting function, so it can be divided. Assume that the node is organized according to computing capacity of red-black tree, then we select the first 25 % of the nodes as the highest priority queue, and 40 % of tasks will be assigned to the node in the queue, the form of distribution is the same as the form of classifier algorithm, that were randomly selected the computing

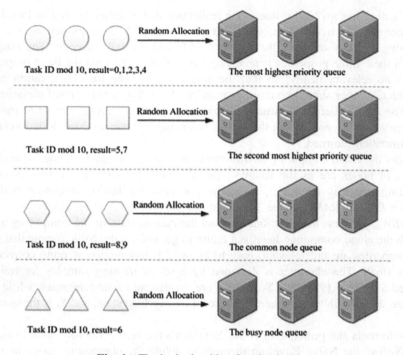

Fig. 1. The hash algorithm for cloud tasks.

code within the queue, assign the tasks. The node of the first 25 %–50 % is as a priority queue, 30 % of the task will be randomly assigned to this queue. The node of the first 50 %–75 % node is as a common queue, 20 % of the task will be randomly assigned to this queue, the remaining nodes will be organized as a busy queue, 10 % of the task will be randomly assigned to this queue. The algorithm is shown in Fig. 2.

3 Load Balancing Based on Improved PSO Algorithm

3.1 Improved PSO Algorithm

Referred to above, in terms of existing technology, PSO algorithm is the industry recognized outstanding load-balancing algorithm, the performance of the PSO algorithm is often regarded as the best. For example, compared with ACO, annealing algorithm, its running speed and load balance tends to be better.

In the first section, the PSO algorithm has been improved by the discrete PSO algorithm, which is designed for discrete computing nodes in cloud computing environment. However, the time complexity of the algorithm is linear with the number of tasks and the number of cloud computing nodes assigned by Broker. And because the division operation of the linear growth, which was a way that cost lots of time in the processing of CPU, resulting in very slow speed of the algorithm. With N cloud tasks,

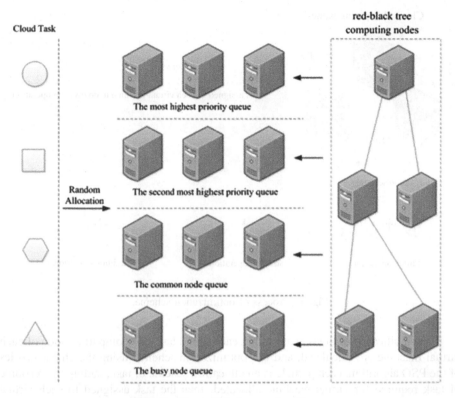

Fig. 2. The red-black tree algorithm.

M virtual machine, for each particle, its time complexity is $O(N*M)$, and for specific data, it can do more intuitive expression of the problem, $N = 5000$, $M = 20$, so that is 5000 cloud tasks and 20 virtual machines, it is necessary to carry out the division for 100000 times, the slow speed of operation can be imagined.

The solution for PSO algorithm is as below: Using the flowtime of the summation process instead of the original flowtime, using the improved makespan to replace the original. In the first place, we have mentioned that flowtime is the sum of the time required to perform the task of the whole, and the makespan is for each machine, makespan is represent one of the machines which cost the longest time to finish the task. In this way, we first start to take addition operation for M times, based on the ETC we have mentioned, a cloud background calculation for each resource node should add cloud tasks assigned in which the consumption of resources, then each machine to do division to conclude the time of each computing nodes need to complete the last task, greatly reducing the time complexity. After that, adding the time of each machine's division time, it is called flowtime, and the maximum value is makespan. The process of optimization scheme is shown in Fig. 3.

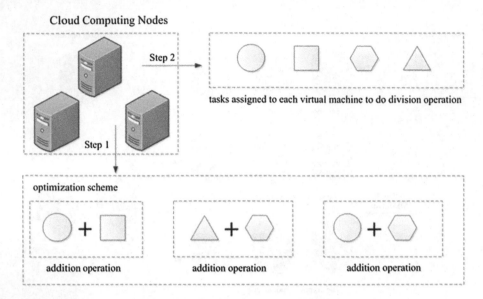

Fig. 3. Process of optimization scheme.

The significance of the scheme is that each cloud task and computing node of each virtual machine are calculated, and our optimization scheme, using the characteristics of the PSO algorithm, each particle is an allocation scheme of task, adding the resource of task required for virtual machine allocated, then the task assigned to each virtual machine to do division. In this way, from the division of linear growth to now the addition operation of linear growth, the speed lifts of course.

3.2 Combined with the Red-Black Tree Algorithm

Even to make the change, as shown above, the time complexity of the algorithm itself reduces to linear additive, but the execution time of this algorithm is slower than red-black tree algorithm and Bayesian Classifier algorithm in theory. (Here assuming that the training time of Bayes Classifier is not in consideration of the time complexity). One advantage of taking into account the PSO algorithm for load balancing of levels are higher, and red-black tree algorithm itself does not undertake optimized on balance degree of load, thus the algorithm combined improved PSO algorithm with red-black tree algorithm that can accelerate speed and optimize the load balancing.

In introducing the red-black tree algorithm mentioned above, red-black tree nodes divide into four queues to assign tasks, but in the process of assigning tasks the algorithm uses random way, so their balanced level performance is not satisfactory. Here combined with improved PSO algorithm in terms of balance ensures on the one hand, on the other hand the linear addition of the PSO algorithm is required to further shorten the time (need some form of synchronization, so that four groups of PSO's flowtime (flowtime explanation see above) is the total execution time of the algorithm).

4 Simulation Experiment and Comparison of Results

The system environment of the experiment is CentOS Linux 6.5, the dual core CPU, 1 GHz, RAM 4G, the experimental operating environment for the CloudSim [9] simulator, version 3.0.3. The PSO algorithm, Bayesian Classifier algorithm, the red-black tree algorithm and improved Particle-Swarm-Optimization (IPSO) algorithm were compared in algorithm execution time and the load balance degree. The following experiments are computing nodes in the 20 cloud computing environment, or become a virtual machine, virtual machine CPU for single core, MIPS size is {21, 73, 194, 319, 294, 209, 141, 335, 448, 208, 356, 200, 30, 100, 31, 95, 413, 82, 221, 458}, the size of RAM is {206, 46, 54, 26, 241, 88, 35, 97, 130, 131, 146, 144, 68, 77, 225, 243, 232, 161, 91, 57}, the size of the BW is {9, 5, 1, 3, 2, 8, 6, 2, 9, 9, 9, 4, 4, 5, 5, 5, 3, 2, 5, 4}, the computing nodes are heterogeneous. The length cloud task is 30, and the number is from 100 to 700. Cloud tasks can be understood as the isomorphism.

4.1 The Comparison of Running Time of Algorithms

The time complexity of PSO algorithm is very large for theoretically analyzing. In this case, the Bayesian Classifier is used to neglect the time consumed by the training samples. But because of the process of the actual test, it is unable to find a large and accurate training sample, using the simulation data of MATLAB for training, and the accuracy is not high. The red-black tree algorithm's time complexity should be the most satisfactory. Improved Particle-Swarm-Optimization (IPSO) algorithm is a algorithm which combines the PSO algorithm and the red-black tree algorithm, not only in the level of PSO algorithm is improved, and the node that is using a red-black tree algorithm to sort out. In each part using the PSO, compared to PSO have considerable promotion.

In the experiment, we found that the speed of PSO algorithm is too slow, and it can't be compared with the other three algorithms, so we zoom it in there. The comparison list of Bayesian Classifier algorithm, improved PSO algorithm, the red-black tree algorithm is as shown in Fig. 4.

Due to the PSO algorithm spending a long time, it cannot be compared with the red-black tree algorithm and Bayesian Classifier algorithm in column chart, now only compare the PSO algorithm with the improved PSO algorithm.

As can be seen from Table 1, the improved PSO algorithm is much faster than before, and the PSO algorithm is much slower than the improved PSO algorithm in the computation speed.

4.2 Comparison of Algorithm in the Load Balancing

The following algorithm is compared in the load balancing. As the CloudSim simulator does not provide the statistics of the execution of each cloud computing node in the process of task processing, the standard deviation of cloud computing nodes while handle the cloud task is used to judge the balance degree of cloud computing nodes.

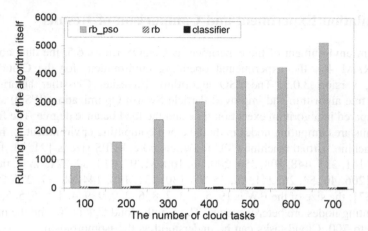

Fig. 4. The comparison of running time.

Table 1. The comparison of running time.

#Cloud task	50	100	150	200	250	300
PSO	304803	321575	329195	342916	355112	367308
RB_PSO	814	1601	2417	3469	4222	5146

The smaller the standard deviation, the more balanced the time of each node to handle the cloud task, that is, the algorithm can assign tasks according to the performance of the nodes, and the load is more balanced. For the convenience of description, we use rb_pso or RB-PSO instead of improved PSO, as a PSO algorithm with red-black tree algorithm. According to the data from the experimental results, we draw a column chart as follows.

As can be seen from Fig. 5, in the improved PSO algorithm and PSO algorithm, the standard deviation of cloud task execution between the cloud computing nodes is very small, and not grow with the growth of cloud tasks. The reason is that the PSO algorithm is designed to search for the optimal solution, because the purpose of finding the optimal solution is to make the flowtime minimum, and the load of the nodes is balanced.

Bayesian Classifier algorithm and the red-black tree algorithm have only optimized the running speed, without considering the problems of load balancing. Within a node taken randomly assigned, it makes the cloud task distribution more uneven. It is not difficult to see from the Fig. 5, red-black tree algorithm is better than the Bayesian Classifier algorithm in load balancing, the reason should be that the training problem of Bayesian Classifier. Because we can't find enough of practical data as the training sample, and using simulated data to generate data as the training set, leads to inaccurate classification of Bayesian Classifier, which reflects the uneven distribution in the cloud task that is why the load balancing is not good.

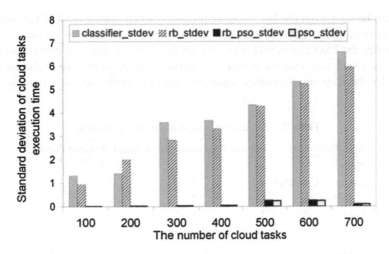

Fig. 5. The standard deviation of cloud tasks execution time.

4.3   Comparison of Processing Speed of the Algorithm in Cloud Tasks

The following is to compare the processing velocity of four algorithms after the allocation of the cloud tasks, here is the flowtime of the cloud task, that is, the time of the last task finished. Vm of Cloudsim uses spaceshared, that is, each virtual machine executes a cloud task at a time, and the rest of cloud tasks which is assigned to this virtual machine, waiting in the queue to be executed. Bayesian Classifier algorithm needs to specify the CPU, RAM and BW when the virtual machine is initialized. The following icon will do a comparison of the flowtime of the cloud tasks assigned by these four algorithms, In order to facilitate the description, we use rb_pso or RB-PSO instead of the improved PSO algorithm.

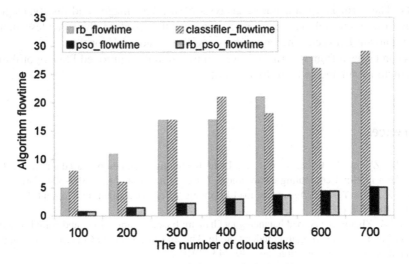

Fig. 6. The processing speed of algorithms.

As can be seen from the Fig. 6, the improved PSO algorithm and PSO algorithm in the flowtime of cloud tasks have obvious advantages compared with the other two, the reason is that the PSO algorithm is aimed at the flowtime to select the best combination, so that the cloud task execution time is relatively good. There are a distinct disadvantage for the Bayesian Classifier algorithm and the simple red-black tree algorithm.

Table 2. The comparison of different algorithms.

Algorithm name	running time	processing speed	balance degree
PSO	1	4.7	5
Bayesian Classifier	4.5	3	1
Red-black tree	5	3	1
Improved PSO	3	5	5

5 Conclusion

Through the analysis of the time complexity and the results of the experiments, the conclusions are as follows: the time complexity of PSO algorithm is high, and is proportionate to the number of cloud tasks. But the advantages is the balance degree of the computing nodes, and it is good. Operation time of the classifier itself is not high, but this is without considering the time consumed by using the training samples of training. In addition, the classification accuracy is low due to lack of training samples, and the allocation strategy of cloud task is not good enough, so that the degree of load balancing is not optimistic. The running speed of red-black tree algorithm is good, but there is a big problem of it in the cloud task management and balance degree. Finally, for the improved PSO algorithm, it combines the excellence in balance degree and the flowtime of cloud task by PSO algorithm. And by cutting makespan and collocation red-black tree to reduce the running time of itself, the algorithm is remarkable in all aspects. The form is a comparative analysis of the advantages and disadvantages of each algorithm, the full mark is 5, and 5 points for the standard, the value less than 5 is the comparison between other algorithms and the standard algorithm.

As can be seen from the Table 2, we can find that the improved PSO algorithm has an absolute advantage in these four algorithms.

References

1. Cai, S., Zhang, J., Chen, J., Pan, J.: Load balancing technology based on naive Bayes algorithm in cloud computing environment. J. Comput. Appl. **34**(2), 360–364 (2014)
2. Feng, X., Pan, Y.: DPSO resource load balancing in cloud computing. Comput. Eng. Appl. **49**(6), 105–108 (2013)
3. Zhang, Z., Zhang, X.: A load balancing mechanism based on ant colony and complex network theory in open cloud computing federation. In: The 2nd International Conference on Industrial Mechatronics and Automation, pp. 240–243 (2010)

4. Chen, Z.: Resource allocation for cloud computing base on ant colony optimization algorithm. J. Qingdao Univ. Sci. Technol. (Nat. Sci. Ed.) **33**(6), 619–623 (2012)
5. Liu, J., Yang, R., Sun, S.: The analysis of binary particle swarm optimization. J. Nanjing Univ. (Nat. Sci.) **47**(5), 504–514 (2011)
6. Izakian, H., Ladani, B.T., Abraham, A., Snasel, V.: A discrete particle swarm optimization approach for grid job scheduling. Int. J. Innovative Comput. Inf. Control **6**(9), 1–15 (2010)
7. Zhang, Y., Wei, Q., Zhao, Y.: Load balancing algorithm based on load weights. Appl. Res. Comput. **29**(12), 4711–4713 (2012)
8. Li, J., Sun, L., Zhang, Q., Zhang, C.: Application of native Bayes classifier to text classification. J. Harbin Eng. Univ. **24**(1), 71–74 (2003)
9. Calheiros, R.N., Ranjan, R., Beloglazov, A., De Rose, C.A.F., Buyya, R.: CloudSim: a toolkit for modeling and simulation of cloud computing environments and evaluation of resource provisioning algorithms. Softw. Pract. Experience **41**(1), 23–50 (2011)

Multi-matched Similarity: A New Method for Image Retrieval

Zhun Zhong[1], Lichuan Geng[2], Song Zhi Su[1],
Guoxi Wu[2], and Shao Zi Li[1(✉)]

[1] Department of Cognitive Science, Xiamen University,
Xiamen 361005, China
szlig@xmu.edu.cn
[2] UAVLARS Collaborative Innovation Center, Xuchang University,
Xuchang 461000, China

Abstract. In Bag-of-Words (BoW) based image retrieval, soft assignment (SA) assigns R-nearest visual words to a feature, which significantly enhances the performance of image retrieval. However, it requires to calculate the weight of each visual word according to the distance from feature to visual word. This method sometimes loses its power when the codebook size is small, since a smaller codebook will cause larger quantization error and lead the distance to be more imprecise. In this paper, instead of depending on distance, we present a novel method to calculate the similarity between features by counting the number of identical visual words assigned to them. We describe how to create the inverted index, and weight the score between matched features. We evaluate the proposed Multi-Matched Similarity (MMS) method on Holidays and Ukbench datasets. Experimental results demonstrate that our method significantly improves the retrieval performance and outperforms the SA approach on both datasets.

Keywords: Image retrieval · Soft assignment · Inverted index · Multi-matched

1 Introduction

This paper considers the task of specific object retrieval from an image database. Given a query image in which an object has been specific, and the goal is to retrieve the images from a database containing the same object. It is a more challenging problem than whole-image retrieval, since the object may be occluded, scale variant, illumination variant or different viewpoints in returned images.

A rapid growth of research in image retrieval has been witnessed in recent years, and countless of models have been proposed. Among them, the Bag-of-Words model [1, 2] has established itself as the state-of-the-art for object image retrieval. This model maps the local descriptors to "visual words", where the local descriptor is extraction of interest regions from an image, represent by a high-dimensional feature vector (e.g. SIFT [3] or its variants [4]), and produce a single vector that represents the image for recognition. The "visual words" are offline obtained by constructing a codebook through unsupervised clustering with the local descriptors from the training database,

© Springer International Publishing Switzerland 2016
Q. Zu and B. Hu (Eds.): HCC 2016, LNCS 9567, pp. 646–654, 2016.
DOI: 10.1007/978-3-319-31854-7_58

e.g. k-means algorithm. To improve efficiency, approximate k-means [5] and hierarchical k-means [6] were used. Then each of the cluster center is regarded as a visual word in the codebook. Inspired by text retrieval, each local descriptor is mapped to the nearest visual word and represents each image as a histogram of visual words. Finally, images are ranked using various indexing methods [1, 7].

In most of the Bag-of-Words model method, each local descriptor is assigned to the nearest visual word (hard-assignment). If two local descriptors are assigned to the same visual word, they are considered identical. On the contrary, local descriptors assigned to different visual words are considered completely different. Then the features' similarity is measured as one if they are assigned to the same visual word or zero otherwise. This hard assignment and measure method lead to errors in effect. It is reflected in two aspects. On the one hand, the codebook is a discrete space of the local descriptor, and different descriptors may be mapped to the same visual word, it is unreasonable to consider them as identical. On the other hand, the descriptor may undergo extensive deviations which would be caused by many reasons (such as image noise, illumination variant, non-affine changes, etc.). These varieties could result in changing the local descriptor value and assigning the similar local descriptor to different visual words. Then it would consider the greatly similar features as completely different. To address these issues, soft assignment (SA) [8] and multiple assignment (MA) [9] have been used. Soft assignment is usually used in histogram comparison [10]. It is an approach that treats the value from continuous space as a weighted combination of nearby bins. Inspired by this approach, [8] maps each local descriptor to a weighted set of words. The local descriptor is represented by an R-vector which is L1 normalized. R is the number of the R-nearest visual words to the feature, allowing the inclusion of features were lost in the quantization stage of previous systems. This method costs more storage while constructing the inverted index architecture. Similarly, [9] uses the similar approach to improve the accuracy of the search with the price of more storage and query time. [11] proposes an asymmetric multiple assignment strategy to reduce the probability of missing matching descriptor pairs in case of mismatched visual word assignment. Moreover, [11] performs multiple assignment for the query only, not for the images in the database. Therefore, the inverted file's memory usage is unchanged and the query step is more effective than [8, 9]. [12] combines their proposed method with multiple assignment only applied on query side. To enhance the robustness to illumination changes, and thus improve recall, [12] adopts a large multiple assignment value on the side of color feature. [13] employs the multiple assignment of [8], instead of using soft weighting they use the weights obtained from the Hamming distance as in the case of a single assignment. All of these above methods improved the performance of image retrieval and being used widely especially SA and MA [14, 15]. However, all of them use weighting strategy to the R-nearest visual words according to the distance from feature to visual word. It sometimes loses its power when the codebook size is small, since a smaller codebook will cause larger quantization error and lead the distance to be more imprecise.

In this paper, we propose a novel similarity measure method based on soft assignment called "Multi-Matched Similarity" (MMS). The key idea is to calculate the similarity between features by counting the number of identical visual words assigned to them. Each local descriptor is assigned to R-nearest visual words, and is represented by an R-vector. This vector stores the visual word IDs. After that, the inverted index is created by the nearest visual words. In query step, we use our proposed method to calculate the similarity between the features whose nearest visual words are the same. Finally, the image retrieval results are ranked by the sum of scores. Experiments are performed on Holidays and Ukbench datasets. We demonstrate that the proposed method greatly enhances the retrieval accuracy, and efficiently in terms of both memory and time.

This paper is organized as follows. In Sect. 2, we firstly review the soft assignment, and then the Multi-Matched Similarity method is described. We examine the performance of our proposed method in comparison to the BoW based method in Sect. 3. Finally, the conclusions are drawn in Sect. 4.

2 Proposed Method

Firstly we give a brief summary of the soft assignment in this section. Then we describe our method in detail.

2.1 Weighting Strategy of Soft Assignment

In conventional soft assignment [8], given an D-dimensi-onal descriptor extracted from a keypoint, it is assigned to the R-nearest visual words. After that, the weight assigned to each visual word is calculated by the expression of $w = exp - \frac{d^2}{2\sigma^2}$, where d is the distance between the local descriptor and the visual word, and σ is a scale parameter. After computing the weight of each visual word, local descriptor is represented by an R-vector. When features x and y are matched, the similarity between them is calculated by their scalar product $w_x.w_y$, where w_x and w_y are their weight R-vectors respectively.

2.2 Multi-matched Similarity

Idea and Benefits of Our Method: In our proposed method, we utilize the soft assignment strategy to assign R-nearest visual words (cluster centers) to the local descriptor. When calculating the similarity between features, we only consider the couple of features whose nearest visual words are identical. Then we compare the other $(R - 1)$-nearest visual words by counting the number of the same visual words between them. The similarity between features is positively related to it. This is the difference from conventional soft assignment. Futermore, MMS measures the similarity between features without relying on the distance from feature to visual word.

Similarity for Features: Assume that a total of N images are contained in an image database, denoted as $I = \{I_i\}_1^N$. Each image I_i has a set of D-dimensional local features, $\{\mathcal{F}_j\}_{j=1}^{d_i}$, where d_i is the number of local features. Given a codebook $\{\mathcal{W}_i\}_{i=1}^K$ of size K, we assign each descriptor to R-nearest visual words. Each feature is represented by an R-vector. In this way, the descriptor $\mathcal{F}_j$ is denoted as $\mathcal{F}_j = (\mathcal{V}_{j,1}, \mathcal{V}_{j,2}, \mathcal{V}_{j,3}..., \mathcal{V}_{j,r})$, $r = 1,...R$, where $\mathcal{V}_{j,r}$ is the rth-nearest visual word ID. For two features $\mathcal{F}_i$ and $\mathcal{F}_j$, we formulate the similarity between them as,

$$\text{Sim}(\mathcal{F}_i, \mathcal{F}_j) = \begin{cases} pIDF(\mathcal{V}_{i,1})^2 * e^m, & where\ \mathcal{V}_{i,1} = \mathcal{V}_{j,1} \\ 0, & \textbf{otherwise} \end{cases}. \tag{1}$$

Where $pIDF(\mathcal{V}_{i,1})$ [16] denotes the weighting of visual word $\mathcal{V}_{i1}$, m is the number of the matched visual words between $\mathcal{F}_i$ and $\mathcal{F}_j$.

2.3 MMS for Image Retrieval

Inverted Index: A majority of research in the BoW based image retrieval community employ an ONE-dimensional inverted index [5, 6, 16], in which each entry corresponds to a visual word defined in the codebook. In this paper, we adopt this strategy to create the inverted index. Instead of using all the soft visual words as [8], we only use nearest visual words to create the inverted index. Given a codebook $\{\mathcal{W}_i\}_{i=1}^{K}$ of size K, the inverted index is represented as $\mathcal{W} = \{\mathcal{W}_1, \mathcal{W}_2, ..., \mathcal{W}_k\}$, $k = 1, ..., K$. Each entry $\mathcal{W}_k$ contains a list of indexed features. In each entry, image ID, and R-nearest visual word ID are stored. An example of our inverted index is illustrated in Fig. 1.

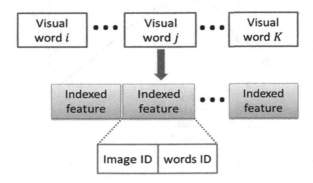

Fig. 1. Inverted index structure of our method, only the nearest visual words are used to create the inverted index. Image ID and ($R\psi \subseteq \leftarrow 1$) nearest visual words ID are stored in the inverted index per feature.

Given a query feature, it is assigned to R-nearest visual words. An entry $\mathcal{W}_k$ in the inverted index is identified according to the nearest visual word. The indexed features are treated as the candidate of the query feature. Then, we calculate the features' similarity by Eq. 1.

Visual Words Weighting: In this paper, we employ the $pIDF$ [16] to weight each visual word. This weighting method counts for the term-frequency in each images, helping to alleviate the visual word burstiness phenomenon. In fact, it can also be replaced by IDF [17] or other weighting methods [18, 19].

Table 1. Datasets used in our experiments

Datasets	Holidays	Ukbench	Flickr60k
𝕴Images	1,491	10,200	67,714
#Queries	500	10,200	N/A
#Descriptors	4,455,091	19,415,079	140,211,550

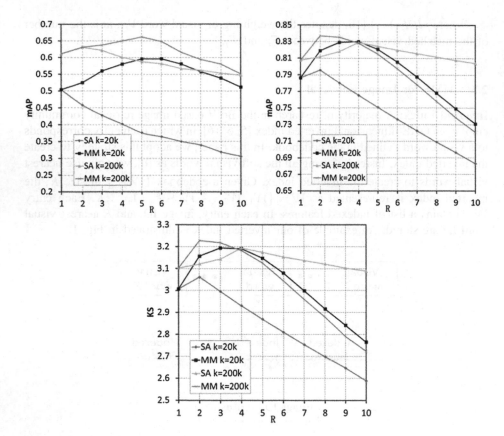

Fig. 2. Comparison of different parameter settings of R for the MMS and SA on the Holidays and Ukbench datasets.

Image Similarity: Given a query image I_x, assume that it contains d_x number of features $\{\mathcal{F}_i\}_{i=1}^{d_x}$. Then each query feature is assigned to R-vector according to the codebook. After that, we calculate the similarity between the query feature and the indexed candidate features. The similarity score between two images I_x and I_y is,

$$Sim_{image}(I_x, I_y) = \frac{\sum_{i=1}^{d_x} \sum_j Sim(\mathcal{F}_i, \mathcal{F}_j)}{||I_x|| \, ||I_y||}. \tag{2}$$

Where d_x denotes the number of features of I_x, j is the feature ID of I_y which nearest visual word is equal to $\mathcal{F}_i$'s, $\|.\|$ is the normalization factor.

3 Experiments

In this section, we use three public available datasets to evaluate our proposed method: the Holidays [17], Ukbench [6], and FLICKR60k [17] in our experiments (see Table 1 for an overview).

Table 2. Comparison of baseline, SA and MMS, where we set the parameter $R = 3$ for SA and MMS.

Method	Holidays		Ukbench			
	mAP		mAP		KS	
	20 k	200 k	20 k	200 k	20 k	200 k
Baseline [16]	0.503	0.611	0.786	0.807	3.01	3.10
SA	0.427	0.622	0.780	0.818	2.995	3.143
MMS	0.560	0.650	0.829	0.835	3.194	3.217

Table 3. Inverted file memory cost per feature, where we set the parameter $R\psi = 3$ for SA and MMS.

Method	Baseline [16]	SA	MMS
Image id	16 bits	16*R bits	16 bits
Visual word	N/A	N/A	16*(R-1) bits
Distance	N/A	16*R bits	N/A
Total	16 bits	32*R bits	16*R bits

Table 4. Average query time (s) on Holidays and Ukbench datasets, where we set the parameter $R = 3$ for SA and MMS.

Method	Holidays		Ukbench	
	20 k	200 k	20 k	200 k
Baseline [16]	0.195	0.012	0.193	0.183
SA	0.482	0.018	0.589	0.29
MMS	0.212	0.013	0.212	0.198

3.1 Datasets

Holidays: This dataset consists of 1491 images from personal holiday photos including a large variety of scene types (natural, man-made, water and fire effects, etc.) and images are of high resolution. This dataset contains 500 queries, most of which have 1–2 ground truth images. Mean average precision (mAP) is employed to measure the retrieval accuracy.

Ukbench: This object recognition benchmark contains 10200 images in total. Each image is taken as the query. For this dataset, we give both the mAP and the average number recall of the top four results denoted by KS (Kentucky Score) to measure the performance.

Flickr 60 k Dataset: The dataset is retrieved arbitrary images from Flickr and is used to learn the quantization centroids in our experiments.

3.2   Experiment Settings

Baseline: In this paper, we adopt the *pIDF* [16] method based on BoW as the baseline approach. We set the parameter p = 2.5 all over the paper.

Local descriptors: We use the Hessian-Affine detector to extract local features and 128-D SIFT [3] descriptors are computed for our experiments.

Codebook: We use the Approximate K-means (AKM) method to create the codebook. Codebook used for Holidays and Ukbench is trained on SIFT features from the independent Flickr60k dataset. We set the codebook sizes of k = 20000 and k = 200000 over the experiments. Quantization employs the approximate nearest neighbors (ANN) indexing structure.

Soft Assignment: We use the soft assignment method in [8] to compare with MMS. We set the parameter $\sigma^2 = 6500$.

3.3   Evaluation

The goal here is to evaluate the performance of MMS. Firstly, we test the sensitivity of MMS to different parameter settings of R. Then, we compare the performance of MMS with the baseline and soft assignment (SA) method. Finally, we discuss the complexity of MMS.

The Impact of Parameter *R*: The goal here is to evaluate the performance for different parameter settings of R. Results evaluated on Holidays and Ukbench datasets are summarized in Fig. 2. It can be seen from the figure that MMS significantly improves the retrieval performce, and performs better than SA approach on both datasets. The best results could obtained when the value of R is between 2 to 5. Assigning more than 5 nearest visual words does not improve the performance, which might since these additional visual words lead to more confusion during matching. Therefore, as a trade off between retrieval quality and extra computational cost and memory requirements, we use R = 3 in all following experiments.

Comparison with Baseline and SA: We compare our proposed MMS with baseline and SA, the results are show in Table 2. From Table 2, SA has a slightly better performance than baseline when the codebook size of k = 200000. However, SA does not work when the codebook size is small (k = 20000). MMS significantly outperforms baseline and SA especially on holidays datasets, and clearly outperforms SA when the codebook size of k = 20000 on both datasets.

Complexity: First, we discuss the memory cost of baseline, SA and MMS in Table 3. For each feature, 16 bits are allocated to store image ID in the baseline. In SA, each feature is assigned to R visual words, thus each feature requires to be stored R^{th} times, and the distance to the center needs to be stored in addition. MMS adds 16*(R-1) bits for the (R-1) nearest visual words ID. The MMS saves memory cost half than SA in total.

Second, the average query time on Holidays and Ukbench datasets is presented in Table 4. We run our experiments on a 2.60-GHz CPU of a quad-Core computer with 16 GB memory. From Table 4, the SA approach is the most time-consuming, since more features are indexed in the inverted file, and each query feature needs to query R^{th} times. MMS is more efficient than the SA due to the less indexed features and query rounds, and the query time of our approach is close to baseline since the comparing nearest visual words procedure is efficiently.

4 Conclusion

In this paper, we present a Multi-Matched Similarity measure method for image retrieval. The experiments show that our method significantly improves the retrieval performance and outperforms the SA approach on Holidays and Ukbench datasets. Moreover, MMS is more efficient than SA in terms of both memory and time.

Acknowledgements. This work is supported by the Nature Science Foundation of China (No. 61202143, No. 61572409), the Natural Science Foundation of Fujian Province (No. 2013J05100), the Collaborative Innovation Special Foundation of Xuchang University (No. XCUXT2014-08).

References

1. Sivic, J., Zisserman, A.: Video Google: a text retrieval approach to object matching in videos. In: 2003 Proceedings of the Ninth IEEE International Conference on Computer Vision, pp. 1470–1477. IEEE (2003)
2. Csurka, G., Dance, C., Fan, L., Willamowski, J., Bray, C.: Visual categorization with bags of keypoints. In: Workshop on Statistical Learning in Computer Vision, ECCV, vol. 1, pp. 1–2 (2004)
3. Lowe, D.G.: Distinctive image features from scale invariant keypoints. Int. J. Comput. Vision **60**(2), 91–110 (2004)
4. Mikolajczyk, K., Schmid, C.: Scale & affine invariant interest point detectors. Int. J. Comput. Vision **60**(1), 63–86 (2004)
5. Philbin, J., Chum, O., Isard, M., Sivic, J., Zisserman, A.: Object retrieval with large vocabularies and fast spatial matching. In: 2007 IEEE Conference on Computer Vision and Pattern Recognition, CVPR 2007, pp. 1–8. IEEE (2007)
6. Nister, D., Stewenius, H.: Scalable recognition with a vocabulary tree. In: 2006 IEEE Computer Society Conference on Computer Vision and Pattern Recognition, vol. 2, pp. 2161–2168. IEEE (2006)

7. Zhang, X., Li, Z., Zhang, L., Ma, W.-Y., Shum, H.-Y.: Efficient indexing for large scale visual search. In: 2009 IEEE 12th International Conference on Computer Vision, pp. 1103–1110. IEEE (2009)
8. Philbin, J., Chum, O., Isard, M., Sivic, J., Zisserman, A.: Lost in quantization: improving particular object retrieval in large scale image databases. In: 2008 IEEE Conference on Computer Vision and Pattern Recognition, CVPR 2008, pp. 1–8. IEEE (2008)
9. Jegou, H., Harzallah, H., Schmid, C.: A contextual dissimilarity measure for accurate and efficient image search. In: 2007 IEEE Conference on Computer Vision and Pattern Recognition, CVPR 2007, pp. 1–8. IEEE (2007)
10. Bishop, C.M., et al.: Pattern Recognition and Machine Learning, vol. 1. Springer, New York (2006)
11. Jégou, H., Douze, M., Schmid, C.: Improving bag-of-features for large scale image search. Int. J. Comput. Vision 87(3), 316–336 (2010)
12. Tolias, G., Avrithis, Y., Jégou, H.: To aggregate or not to aggregate selective match kernels for image search. In: 2013 IEEE International Conference on Computer Vision (ICCV), pp. 1401–1408. IEEE (2013)
13. Zheng, L., Wang, S., Liu, Z., Tian, Q.: Packing and padding: coupled multi-index for accurate image retrieval (2014). arXiv preprint arXiv:1402.2681
14. Jégou, H., Douze, M., and Schmid, C.: On the burstiness of visual elements. In: 2009 IEEE Conference on Computer Vision and Pattern Recognition, CVPR 2009, pp. 1169–1176. IEEE (2009)
15. Zheng, L., Wang, S., Tian, Q.: Lp-norm IDF for scalable image retrieval. IEEE Trans. Image Process. 23, 3604–3617 (2014)
16. Zheng, L., Wang, S., Tian, Q.: Coupled binary embedding for large-scale image retrieval. IEEE Trans. Image Process. 23(8), 3368–3380 (2014)
17. Zheng, L., Wang, S., Liu, Z., Tian, Q.: Lp-norm IDF for large scale image search. In: 2013 IEEE Conference on Computer Vision and Pattern Recognition (CVPR), pp. 1626–1633. IEEE (2013)
18. Jegou, H., Douze, M., Schmid, C.: Hamming embedding and weak geometric consistency for large scale image search. In: Forsyth, D., Torr, P., Zisserman, A. (eds.) ECCV 2008, Part I. LNCS, vol. 5302, pp. 304–317. Springer, Heidelberg (2008)
19. Robertson, S.E., Walker, S.: Some simple effective approximations to the 2-poisson model for probabilistic weighted retrieval. In: Croft, B.W., van Rijsbergen, C.J. (eds.) Proceedings of the 17th Annual International ACM SIGIR Conference on Research and Development in Information Retrieval, pp. 232–241. Springer-Verlag New York, Inc., New York (1994)
20. Singhal, A.: Modern information retrieval: a brief overview. IEEE Data Eng. Bull. 24(4), 35–43 (2001)

Design and Implementation of Reader Function Module of Aquatic Products Traceability System Based on EPC

Xing Guo and Peihua Yang[✉]

School of Logistic Engineering, Wuhan University of Technology, Wuhan, China
guoxing1967@sohu.com, 377430365@qq.com

Abstract. In order to ensure the quality and safety of aquatic products and make aquatic products industry chain fully traceable, fresh aquatic products with high-quality is taken as traceable objects in this paper, the EPC technology is applied to aquatic products traceability system, and function module of reader device in aquatic products traceability system is designed according to the analyzing about the framework of the system and some theories related to EPC. The reader function module is verified by a real case. So the input and output of tag information of EPC in a supply chain of aquatic products is realized and it is significant for the further improve of aquatic products traceability system.

Keywords: EPC tag · EPC reader device · Aquatic products traceability system · Reader function module

1 Introduction

In recent years, environmental pollution is becoming more and more serious, and the abuse of drugs or additives in aquatic products industry is overflowed around world, so the safe quality of aquatic products traceability are paid increasing attention. At the same time, the application of EPC technology is booming popularized in some industries, which is very suitable for the single-product management of rare aquatic products. Besides, data collection and identification can be achieved successfully without artificial interference through EPC technology. Therefore, creating a great traceability system of aquatic products is becoming more and more important with EPC technology applied in it. Thus, fresh aquatic products with high-quality is taken as traceable objects in this paper, the EPC reader function modules based on the aquatic products is designed according to the analyses of traceability process of aquatic products and application of EPC.

2 The Correlative Theories of EPC

The EPC tag generally is composed of three parts, tag chip with principals and information of EPC, the external coupling element tag antenna that attached to the reader and the packaging substrate for physical carrier which to package the former together. EPC saves EPC codes with index function into the EPC tag through the reader device in the

© Springer International Publishing Switzerland 2016
Q. Zu and B. Hu (Eds.): HCC 2016, LNCS 9567, pp. 655–660, 2016.
DOI: 10.1007/978-3-319-31854-7_59

specific application, and the label is affixed to the corresponding items. Then it reads the EPC codes of the tag through the corresponding reader, so as to check the related information of products from EPC codes. The EPC tag is not only the EPC code, the carrier of the additional function information. It also can communicate with EPC readers to exchange information in a data access without touch. The functions of tags to achieve are as follows [1]:

(1) Tags can be encoded with EPC in the factory, including 24 bit KILL password and other data;
(2) To be able to read and write the data of tag correctly by the reader device;
(3) Tags must be selected in a group of related tags by the reader's device through consultation;
(4) Tags can be destroyed alone.

The reader device is also known as interrogator, communicator, and scanner; it can not only read but also change the information of the electronic tag.

The reader device is composed of two modules: RF signal processing module and base band signal processing module [2]:

RF Signal Processing Module: one function is to modulate the order that the reader send to the tag by antenna to reach the electronic tag, then the electronic tag reacts to the emitted radio frequency signal and sends echo signal back to reader; another function is to analyze the echo signal by the reader device to extract the data sent back from the electronic tags.

Base Band Signal Processing Module: one function is to initialize the message of the EPC tag; another function is to read information of the EPC tag. The EPC encoding information of the EPC tag attached to a single item or a package transportation unit can be identified by the EPC reader, in this way, the information collection, traceability and management of the supply chain identification can be realized.

Another important function of the reader is to disable the EPC tag. When consumers don't want their goods to be tracked continually, a "KILL" order can disable the function of the label. The destruction of the label is also a kind of safety method. Meanwhile, if you want to erase the label, you have to use password of destruction, and if the label is destroyed, it can be not reused any more. As a result, we should be very careful to use this function [3].

3   Aquatic Products Traceability System and EPC Application

3.1   Application Background

This paper pays attention to trace the information about fresh aquatic products supply chain of high-quality, so the information of aquatic products in processing is not considered. It mainly focuses on information of aquatic products during breed period, logistics period and sales period [4]. The system is mainly divided into three layers in logic: data acquisition layer, information transmission layer, and application layer.

3.2   The Role of EPC in Aquatic Products Traceability

The traceability process of aquatic products traceability system takes the label as information carrier, the label not only can reflect the basic properties and using attributes of the products, but also can check message of the supply chain to acquaint the details about products through the encoding information of labels. Aquatic products should be inspected and quarantined to ensure the products quality in any segment, and scanning EPC codes can decide the responsible host, which ensure the traceability of whole entire supply chain [5].

Combined with the analysis of the aquatic products tracing process and the characteristics of retroactive objects — fresh aquatic products of high-quality, the business process of aquatic products supply chain can be obtained. The specific process of supply chain is as followed: take the fry into pond to breed (the situation of tank transference and reversed pond of fry can't be taken into account in this process), arrange related personnel to fish, sort and distribute corresponding aquatic products to the corresponding sales center according to the order when farming enterprises received orders, after received aquatic products, the aquatic products are being inspected, quarantined, unloaded and inputted label information and so on, and then the aquatic products is put on the shelves for sale by sales center, the situation of aquatic products on the hands of consumers won't be discussed. Its specific implementation steps are shown in Fig. 1:

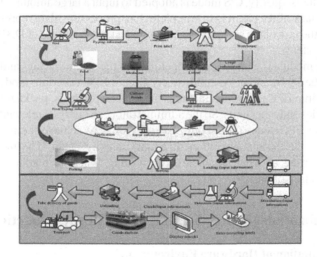

Fig. 1. The supply identification flow chart of aquatic products

4   The Design of EPC Reader Function Module

The information traceability needs EPC reader device to read the information of label, its working content mainly focus on the following objects of the entire supply chain which includes: the supplies of aquatic products' feed, drugs, seeds, other raw materials, aquatic products breeding on breeding incubator, transportation of delivery center and the sell to consumers in wholesale prices about fresh aquatic products with high quality:

(1) Raw materials: the EPC reader device connected with the computer on the site reads the unique ID number of label and checks it according to the created EPC codes of the selected raw materials, then the EPC will be encoded into the electronic tag. In the end, the whole data will be written into the local database.

(2) Aquatic products: using the EPC reader which can write the EPC Codes into the tag to identify the uniqueness of aquatic products. The user can query all information concerning the whole process on breeding stage of aquatic products by taking the EPC codes as an index.

(3) Transport unit: The EPC tags are attached to the transport vehicles on distribution to identify the transport vehicles uniquely. The relation between transport vehicles and delivery note is established. Encoding on the label to use EPC reader device to read the data of tag, we can realize the traceability in distribution process.

(4) Sales unit: a product information screen is installed on each kind of shelf in the supermarkets or other sales places, and a EPC tag reader is mounted on it, the customers can query the product's details as long as they take the aquatic products that affixed EPC label within the effective range of the screen reader.

EPC tag, the operation implementation of the information carrier, is mainly based on the EPC reader function system throughout the entire supply chain process. According to the characteristics of the aquatic products industry chain and the need of the tracing products' quality, C/S mode is adopted to input a large amount of information into label. The task of the client is to complete data processing, data representation and user interface; the task of the server is to complete the core functions of DBMS (database management system).

EPC reader module is mainly for the operation of the electronic tags and the communication with the server of background. According to EPC encoding mode, EPC codes will be written into EPC tag, which includes the aquatic products, packaging box, transportation vehicles and other units. So the administrator can query its relevant information by inputting the EPC codes on tracing platform, so as to achieve the monitoring and management of the various operation of aquatic supply chain. The module mainly includes: the setting of label parameter, the writing function, reading function and destruction function of tag.

5 The Realization and Application of the Reader Function Module

5.1 The Adaptation of Hardware Environment

The hardware options of EPC reader device's function module concerning aquatic products traceability system include EPC tags, tag reader, as well as server. The selection of corresponding RFID tag and RFID reader should be designed based on the characteristics of each link with the aquatic products supply chain, the adaptation of EPC tag and tag reader are shown as follows:

EPC Tags: they are attached to the items to record its information and the identification of the original item which has storage information.

(1) Aquatic products label: to record the aquatic products individual's specific information, anti- corrosion features, which can be recycled.

(2) Packaging unit label: to record the specific list of the goods within the packaging unit, they can be recycled.

EPC Reader: link the fore-end information carrier of the entire RFID system with the channel supported by database in the background.

Portable reader can be used in the site to read the tag information and can meet the requirements of single-product. PDA multi-function reader device is selected as hand-held reader in this system to collect and read the data.

5.2 The Settings of Performance Parameter

The function module of EPC reader device is mainly responsible for controlling and adjusting the reader, besides, it can record into the data or output from data through electronic tag; and the Reader module can totally control the reader mainly through the API function which is provided by the reader manufacturers. The performance parameters of the reader used in the experiment are as follows:

Performance Index: (1) Product model: JT-HF68, (2) Working frequency: 13.56 MHz, (3) Communication interface: USB, off-line, (4) Reader distance: 0 ~ 70 mm, (5) Serial communication baud rate: 9600BPS ~ 115200BPS, (6) Dimensions: 143 mm × 110 mm × 28 mm.

Parameters Configuration: It is necessary to set the corresponding parameters of the label before operating the reader.

1. Working mode setting: It is better to operate label (including reading and writing tags) in master-slave mode. Master-slave operation mode refers to the operation of reader device which is solely completed by the host; adjacent discriminant: reader device to achieve the data filtering of tag ID.

2. Communication mode setting: Communication interface type: according to the difference of communication interface between the reader and the controller, Wiegand or RS-485, RS-232 interface can be selected. The interface settings of input interface in the system is mainly to choose the RS-232, the parameters refer to initial value of the baud rate can only be set to 9600.

3. Reader parameter setting: device number, power, read card mode, antenna type and frequency band, the parameter values are 0, 147, multiple EPC tags, single antenna, frequency hopping (1, 11, 31, 41, 21) respectively.

5.3 The Application of EPC Reader in Aquatic Products Traceability

The label can be operated by the reader after completing the adaptation of hardware environment and the setting of performance parameters.

The system label ID, namely, EPC encoding is generated automatically based on a certain encoding rules. Click the "fast-written card" button, you can write information into the label successfully, at the same time, there will be a sound of "BEE", and it will tell you that "label has been written, please change a new label", edit box will add one automatically after done, for example, encoding of 112131.010203.140520001 is written into the first label, the information will be written successfully after clicking the "fast-written card" button, and now it will be a sound of "BI", and it show that the label has been written, please replace the new label.

6   Conclusion

According to the research and application of EPC tag technology and EPC reader technology, the EPC reader function module of aquatic products traceability system is designed based on C/S model after analyzing the overall framework of aquatic products traceability system and the process of tag identification about aquatic products supply chain in this paper, and the developing example is verified by simulation. Then the operation of EPC tags in the aquatic products supply chain is realized by EPC reader device, such as parameter setting, writing data, reading label information and destruction function, thus the information tracing of aquatic products in the whole supply chain can be realized. The establishment of reader device function module of aquatic products supply chain tracing platform based on EPC encoding is of great significance to promote the development and establishment of China's aquatic products industry and the improvements of the traceability system concerning about aquatic products market.

References

1. Xiaoxiao, L.: Research of label encoding program of food supply chain security traceability based on the EPC-256. Food Ind. Technol. **06**, 52–54+58 (2014)
2. Peets, S., Gasparin, C.P., Blackburn, D.W.K., Godwin, R.J.: RFID tags for identifying and verifying agrochemicals in food traceability systems. Precision Agric. **10**, 382–394 (2009)
3. Kang, Y.S.: LEE Y H. Development of generic RFID traceability services. Comput. Ind. **64**, 609–623 (2013)
4. Randrup, M., Haiping, W., Jørgensen, B.M.: On the track of fish batches in three distribution networks. Food Control **26**(2), 439 (2012)
5. Zhou, H., Zhang, L.Z.: Studies and application of aquatic processing products supply chain traceability system. Key Eng. Mater. **419**, 860–864 (2010)

P System Based Quantum Genetic Algorithm to Solve the Problem of Clustering

Caiping Hou and Xiyu Liu[✉]

College of Management Science and Engineering, Shandong Normal University, Jinan, China
{sdnuhcp,sdxyliu}@163.com

Abstract. In recent years, the quantum genetic algorithm is drawing attention from scholars. The algorithm is a probabilistic optimization method of combining the quantum computing and genetic algorithms. How to design a more effective way to improve the performance of the quantum genetic algorithm is more worth studying. As is known to all, the P system can search for the optimal clustering partition with the help of its parallel computing advantage effectively. In this paper, we attempt to utilize the P system to optimize the quantum genetic algorithm (PQGA) and then to alleviate the drawbacks in the k-means clustering method. The algorithm can improve the parallelism of the quantum genetic algorithm and short the average running time of the algorithm effectively. This algorithm is of particular interests to when dealing with large and heterogeneous data sets and when being faced with an unknown number of clusters, which due to that it can obtain the optimal number of clusters as well as providing the optimal cluster centroids. In this paper, we use the real datasets in UCI to validate the performance of PQGA. The experimental results show that PQGA is promising and effective.

Keywords: Quantum genetic algorithm · Quantum computing · P system

1   Introduction

With the development of the quantum computation theory, the quantum genetic algorithm has been drawn extensive attention. Quantum genetic algorithm (QGA) uses qubits coding to represent chromosome and the chromosomal gene can represent the superposition of multiple states, so that the diversity of the population increases. In addition, we can update the chromosome through the operations of the quantum rotation gate, so that the target can be optimized. We can also optimize the objectives. Compared with the traditional genetic algorithm, QGA converges to the global optimal solution rapidly when in smaller populations. Apart from inheriting the advantages of traditional genetic algorithms, QGA also has its own unique advantages, e.g. the smaller population size, the faster convergence [1]. We can see that the quantum genetic algorithm has great research value.

Membrane computing (known as P systems) is a class of distributed parallel computing models; it focuses on the communication in the membranes, cells, tissues or other structures of organisms. Compared to these benefits of membrane computing, the

© Springer International Publishing Switzerland 2016
Q. Zu and B. Hu (Eds.): HCC 2016, LNCS 9567, pp. 661–667, 2016.
DOI: 10.1007/978-3-319-31854-7_60

P system is in a maximally parallel way and can find the best candidate individuals in a shorter time, which must be effective to choose the optimal clustering center.

2   The Quantum Genetic Algorithm

Unlike the two-state (0/1) representation in conventional computing, the smallest information representation in quantum computing is called qubits (Q-bit). The state of Q-bit may be "0" state, "1" state or any superposition of the two. So the state of Q-bit can be represented as follows:

$$|\psi> = \alpha|0> \beta|1>$$

where α and β are complex numbers that specify the probability amplitudes of the corresponding states. Normalization of the state to the unity guarantees as follows: $|\alpha|^2 + |\beta|^2 = 1$, where, $|\alpha|^2$ represents a quantum state observation probability value is 0 and $|\beta|^2$ represents a quantum state observation probability value is 1. 0 and 1 represent the states of spin-up and spin-down, respectively [2].

In the evolutionary computing, the Q-bit representation has a better characteristic of population diversity than other representations, because it can represent linear superposition of states probabilistically [3].

P system is the biological model of Membrane Computing [4]. Membrane computing approaches are suitable used to solve combinatorial problems because of the vast parallelism (The parallelism lessens the time complexity of clustering process). In this work, we proposed a new quantum genetic algorithm based on P System named PQGA to improve the performance of the quantum genetic algorithms by combining the parallelism of P system in Membrane Computing. Algorithms are completed in two stages. Stage 1: genetic operation happens within the membrane; Stage 2: genetic operation happens outside the membrane.

3   The Implementation Process of PQGA

Representation of Chromosome in PQGA: Before coding the chromosomes, the range of K (number of clusters) $[K_{min}; K_{max}]$ should be defined first, where $K_{min} \geq 2$ and $K_{max} \leq N$ (N is the number of instances). In this paper, the range of K is set to $[2, \sqrt{N} + 1]$.

Given N, we are also aware of the number of binary string length B to denote a pattern ID, that is, $2^{B-1} < N \leq 2^B$. When coding the chromosome, a number $\hat{k}$ is randomly generated first, where $\hat{k} \in [K_{min}; K_{max}]$. Thus, the Q-bit string length of this chromosome is $\hat{k} \times B$. In PQGA, the length of a Q-bit individual depends on the number $\hat{k}$, and the $\hat{k}$ is a random number ranging in $[K_{min}; K_{max}]$. And after several iterations, PQGA may find the number of centroids in the best partition.

Fitness Function of PQGA: Genetic algorithm evaluates the candidate by the size of the value of the fitness function. Genetic algorithms can determine the chance of candidate solutions into the next generation of genetic based on the value of the fitness function. It is about whether the excellent characteristics of the population can be continued [5].

Best cluster center is to make clustering objective function obtained by the minimum sample point. Based on this, we can define the fitness function as: $f = {}^{a}/_{E}$, where E is the objective function of clustering. The smaller the value of the fitness function f is, the better the effect of clustering is. That a is a constant, which plays a regulatory role in preventing some of the best individual prematurely eliminated.

After encoding n individuals of the initial population into quaternary sequence, we sort the fitness values by the fitness function value. Choose the individuals with the smallest (worst) and the largest (optimal) fitness value (2 individuals in total) as elite individuals and put the remaining (N–2) individuals into the P system.

P Processing: After the operation, the two elite individuals remain in the areas between the basic outer membrane and the surface membrane. The remaining (N–2) individuals are put into m basic membranes equally, which forms a P system.

In order to make the running time of each membrane relative to the average of the running time, we define the number of the membranes as: $Z = \left\lfloor \sqrt{N-2} \right\rfloor$. Where N is the total number of individuals of initial population, Z the square root of (N–2) (round down). When N is large enough, we can get the square root of N directly. Using this way to define the number Z can maintain similar elite individuals between intramembrane and extramembrane which can reduce the overall convergence time.

Selection Operator in PQGA: Selection operator determines the direction of evolution. In this paper, we adopt elitism strategy and choose the fitness function as selection operator. Outside the membrane, we adopt the elitism strategy as well. The elite selection guarantees that the best chromosome in a certain generation would not be lost in the evolutionary process [6].

Crossover Operators in PQGA: PQGA uses a special crossover operation which can change the lengths of parental chromosomes. For each chromosome, the crossover point is randomly chosen according to its own string length. A random integer between 1 and its length is generated as the crossover point for each chromosome. Then two points perform crossover operation. Due to this change, the partition solution denoted by the chromosome is changed accordingly. Thus, the search space is larger and the optimal solution could be found.

Mutation Operator in PQGA: In the traditional genetic algorithm, mutation operation is a very important operation. But in quantum genetic algorithm, the quantum mutation is primarily as a secondary action and its role is to improve the capacity of local optimization and to prevent "premature" of the algorithm. These changes take place according to quantum rotation gate operation defined below.

Quantum Rotation Gate Operation in PQGA: In the QGA, the chromosome update mainly by quantum rotation gates, which is the most basic operations for qubits. Quantum rotation gate $U(\theta)$ is designed as:

$$U(\theta) = \begin{bmatrix} \cos\theta & -\sin\theta \\ \sin\theta & \cos\theta \end{bmatrix}$$

where, θ is the angle of rotation. Use the following quantum rotation gate to update the population.

$$\begin{bmatrix} \alpha_i' \\ \beta_i' \end{bmatrix} = U(\theta) \times \begin{bmatrix} \alpha_i \\ \beta_i \end{bmatrix} = \begin{bmatrix} \cos\theta & -\sin\theta \\ \sin\theta & \cos\theta \end{bmatrix} \begin{bmatrix} \alpha_i \\ \beta_i \end{bmatrix}$$

According to the rotation operation in the above-mentioned, a quantum gate $U(\theta_i)$ is a function of $\theta_i = s(\alpha_i,\beta_i) \times \Delta\theta_i$, where $s(\alpha_i,\beta_i)$ is the sign of θ_i which determines the direction and $\Delta\theta_i$ is the magnitude of rotation angle. The lookup table of $\Delta\theta_i$ is shown in Table 1, where b_i and r_i are the ith bit of the best solution b and a binary solution of a, respectively. In this paper, we increase/delete the r's Q-bits randomly if the length of r is less/more than the length of b. Because b is the best solution in this algorithm, the use of quantum gate rotation is to emphasize the searching direction towards b.

Table 1. The lookup table of rotation angle

r_i	b_i	$\mathscr{F}(r) < F(b)$	$\Delta\theta_i$	$s(\alpha_i, \beta_i)$			
				$\alpha_i\beta_i > 0$	$\alpha_i\beta_i < 0$	$\alpha_i = 0$	$\beta_i = 0$
0	0	False	0	0	0	0	0
0	0	True	0	0	0	0	0
0	1	False	0	0	0	0	0
0	1	True	0.05π	-1	$+1$	± 1	0
1	0	False	0.01π	-1	$+1$	± 1	0
1	0	True	0.025π	$+1$	-1	0	± 1
1	1	False	0.005π	$+1$	-1	0	± 1
1	1	True	0.025π	$+1$	-1	0	± 1

If the value of $\Delta\theta_i$ is too small, it will have an impact on the convergence rate, otherwise it may cause prematurity. The quantum rotation gate operation can ensure the convergence of the algorithm.

The Implementation: The procedure of PQGA can be summarized as follows:

(1) Initialize a population with N individuals (seen as chromosomes) using qubits representation.
(2) Collapse the qubits representation into the binary representation and then the real-coded representation; calculate and sort the fitness of each individual.

(3) Choose the two individuals with the best and worst value as elite individual. The remaining (N–2) individuals are put into the P system. Set maximum evolution generation inside the membrane as T1.
(4) Conduct quantum genetic operations in each membrane and look up table of rotation angle (refer to Table 1), and then perform rotation gate operation.
(5) Repeat step (4) until the termination criteria inside the membrane is met. Z elites are released outside and step to next round operation together with the initial 2 elite individuals. And maximum evolution generation outside the membranes is set as T2.
(6) Conduct quantum genetic operations on elite individuals and then perform rotation gate operation.
(7) Repeat step (6) till the termination criteria outside the membranes is met and finally optimal solution is generated, which is the optimal clustering center.

4 Experiment Results and Analysis

First, we test PQGA's effectiveness using the dataset of Iris in UCI. Then, we use the three datasets from famous UCI (including the Iris, Wine and Glass) machine learning repository to compare the performance and the effectiveness of PQGA with QGA. In both the experiments, we empirically set the size of population to 100. The largest population evolution algebraic G is set as 300, which is to say that the maximum evolution general inside T1 and outside T2 is 150. The parameters of the mutation operator is set as $p_m = 0.01$. And the crossover probability is set as Pr = 0.05. The number of membranes is 15(Z = 15). These algorithms are implemented in Matlab7.1.

After 50 repetitions on Iris, the results are shown in Table 2.

Table 2. The average cluster centers and the difference

Data sets	Average cluster centers	Error sum of squares with actual value
PQGA	(5.0013 3.4113 1.4698 0.2439)	0.0436
	(5.8962 2.7245 4.2312 1.2995)	
	(6.6038 2.9978 5.5236 2.0402)	
QGA	(5.0032 3.4021 1.4739 0.2501)	0.0962
	(5.8691 2.7112 4.3142 1.3672)	
	(6.7101 3.0517 5.6324 2.0549)	

Actually, the actual cluster center location of Iris dataset is as follows: (5.00 3.42 1.46 0.24), (5.93 2.77 4.26 1.32), (6.58 2.97 5.55 2.02). In the experiments, we use PQGA and QGA to find the average cluster centers of Iris. The average cluster centers and the error sum of squares with actual value got from PQGA is smaller than QGA, which indicates the cluster center derived from PQGA is closer to the actual cluster centers than QGA [7].

We can see from the results from Table 3 that PQGA obtains the exact K for all the three UCI datasets. For the average best fitness value, PQGA gets the higher value than

PGA does. In each dataset, the standard deviation that PQGA obtains is similar to those of PGA. Therefore, with the same stability [8], the better fitness that PQGA gets means the better performance PQGA makes. By using the UCI real datasets, the effectiveness of PQGA is proved. And the effectiveness of PQGA is better than that of PGA.

Table 3. Comparison between PQGA and QGA

Data sets	PQGA			QGA		
	Clusters	Average best fitness value	Standard deviation	Clusters	Average best fitness value	Standard deviation
Iris	3	12.035	3.012	5	8.824	3.381
Wine	3	11.923	2.217	10	7.216	2.937
Glass	2	63.214	2.134	2	41.192	2.339

5   Conclusions

In this paper, a new quantum genetic algorithm for cluster based on P system (PQGA) is proposed. The string length of the chromosomes can change during the crossover operation. So the value of the fitness function will be changed. Thereby, the cluster centers also will change. After repeated verifications, the PQGA performs pretty well when the population size is large enough.

Acknowledgment. Project supported by National Natural Science Foundation of China (61170038, 61472231, 61502283), Jinan City independent innovation plan project in Colleges and Universities, China (201401202), Ministry of education of Humanities and social scienc-e research project, China (12YJA630152), Social Science Fund Project of Shandong Province, China (11CGLJ22).

References

1. Farag, M.A., El-Shorbagy, M.A., El-Desoky, I.M., et al.: Genetic algorithm based on k-means clustering technique for multi-objective resource allocation problems. Br. J. Appl. Sci. Technol. **8**, 80–96 (2015)
2. Liang, C.Y., Bai, H., Cai, M.J., et al.: Advances in quantum genetic algorithm. Jisuanji Yingyong Yanjiu **29**(7), 2401–2405 (2012)
3. Paun, G.: Computing with membranes. J. Comput. Syst. Sci. **61**(1), 108–143 (2000)
4. Escuela, G., Gutierrez-Naranjo, M.A.: An application of genetic algorithms to membrane computing. In: Proceedings of Eighth Brainstorming Week on Membrane Computing, pp 101–108 (2010)
5. Jiang, Y., Peng, H., Huang, X., et al.: A novel clustering algorithm based on P systems. Int. J. Innov. Comput. Inf. Control **10**(2), 753–765 (2014)
6. Wang, K., Wang, N.: A protein inspired RNA genetic algorithm for parameter estimation in hydrocracking of heavy oil. Chem. Eng. J. **167**(1), 228–239 (2011)

7. Sardana, M., Agrawal, R.K., Kaur, B.: Clustering in conjunction with quantum genetic algorithm for relevant genes selection for cancer microarray data. In: Li, J., Cao, L., Wang, C., Tan, K.C., Liu, B., Pei, J., Tseng, V.S. (eds.) PAKDD 2013 Workshops. LNCS, vol. 7867, pp. 428–439. Springer, Heidelberg (2013)
8. Zhou, R., Cao, J.: Quantum novel genetic algorithm based on parallel subpopulation computing and its application. Artif. Intell. Rev. 41(3), 359–371 (2014)

A High Efficient Recommendation Algorithm Based on LDA

Demin Hu[(✉)] and Linshan Chen

School of Optical-Electrical and Computer Engineering,
University of Shanghai for Science and Technology, Shanghai 200093, China
deminhu@usst.edu.cn, linshan_chen@163.com

Abstract. As for the low recommendation degree of the traditional collaborative filtering recommendation algorithm, a high efficient recommendation algorithm was put forward based on LDA. A new interest layer is added between the user layer and the project layer to produce the user - interest - item interest model. The interest information was extracted by expanded LDA, which makes use of the evaluation rank of the user on the project. Moreover, because of the constant change of the users' interests, pagerank algorithm is adopted, which takes account of the time characteristic, to support the random walk style to extend interests. Then items are recommended and user ratings are predicted according to the interest information. The experiments improve that the improved algorithm has better effect on recommendation by comparing with traditional SVD, LDA algorithms.

Keywords: LDA · Recommendation algorithm · Interest model · Interest extension

1 Introduction

With the rapid development of information technology, the issue of information overload becomes more and more serious. The users cannot get useful message from hundreds of complex information timely which leads to the decrease availability of the information recommendation system. As an important approach of information filtering, recommendation system is able to solve the present problem of information overload [1]. Among all the recommendation system, collaborative filtering recommendation algorithm is now the most widespread and successful one used in the recommendation system, which does not depend on the main content of the project, but relies on the interactive information between the user and the project. Hence, collaborative filtering recommendation is appropriate for various application scenarios and is widely researched by scholars. However, traditional filtering recommendation algorithm has the disadvantages of data sparse, low accuracy of similarity, data cold-start and low effective of recommendation etc. [2].

According to the problem of the collaborative filtering recommendation algorithm, many researches have been done to improve it. Aim at improving the recommendation efficiency and quality while processing big data, Feng et al. [3] raise a method which

© Springer International Publishing Switzerland 2016
Q. Zu and B. Hu (Eds.): HCC 2016, LNCS 9567, pp. 668–675, 2016.
DOI: 10.1007/978-3-319-31854-7_61

uses genetic algorithm to combine clustering k-means algorithm and collaborative filtering recommendation to improve it. As for the problem of low similarity, Wen et al. [4] propose an idea to correct the Tanimoto coefficient and integrate the relationship among common criteria in the traditional similarity methods, which can improve the efficiency and accuracy. But in the traditional recommendation model, association between the user and the project is weak, which results in low recommendation accuracy. Therefore, this paper proposes a user - interest - item interest model, by adding extended probabilistic topic model (LDA) to extract the user's interest information, and then produce the project according to the information, thereby improving the accuracy of recommendation algorithm.

Some symbols will appear in this paper. The followings are the descriptions of them:

α: Hyper-parameter in the LDA model
β: Hyper-parameter in the LDA model
Θ_u: Interest probability distribution vector of user μ
ϕ_t: Project probability distribution vector of created by interest t
K: Total number of interests
N: Total number of projects
M: Total number of users
W(u, i): Score value of project i from user u
C^{NK}:   N*M dimension matrix, $C^{NK}_{i,j}$ is the number that project I_i gives to interest t_j
C^{MK}:   M*K dimension matrix, $C^{MK}_{i,j}$ is the number of interest t_j among all the consumptive project by user u_i.

2   Description of the LDA Model

In order to extract user's interest by using LDA model, we can match user, interest and project respectively with the text, subject and word in the model. Through mapping the high dimension user collection to low dimension Latent Semantic Space, user is identified as a mixture of interest and interest is the distribution in the project space. The extracted information includes probability distribution of the user interest, the probability distribution of interest in the project and the distribution information of interest. It can be seen that the extraction process of interest information is the derivation process of latent variable while the process of generating consumption project is reversed. Because the amount of project is limited, the LDA model is appropriate to be used in this environment.

Since calculating the accurate value of the latent variable θ_u and ϕ_t is difficult in the model, Griffiths et al. proposes a very effective Gibbs sampling method which estimates the value of latent variable. Gibbs sampling is a kind of Markov chain Monte Carlo algorithm. It can be used to estimate the value of latent variable θ_u and ϕ_t. In the beginning, a random interest is given to all the consumption project of the users as the initial status of Markov chain. Secondly, each consumption project i_n of each user is iterated, under the situation that the other consumption is fixed the probability $P(t_n = k|i_n)$ of each interest is calculated in the present project according to the following function (1). Thirdly, start random sampling based on this distribution condition and get a new interest in the present project, and then calculate the next project. When all these projects have been updated, the next round of iteration will begin. Eventually, sampling finished when the Markov chain reaches the convergence condition.

$$P\left(t_i \middle| i_n, \alpha, \beta, T_{-n}\right) \propto \frac{C_{t,-n}^{MK} + \alpha}{\sum\limits_{K=1}^{K} C_{k,-n}^{MK} + K\beta} \cdot \frac{C_{t,w,-n}^{NK} + \beta}{\sum\limits_{j=1}^{N} C_{t,j,-n}^{NK} + N\beta} \tag{1}$$

In the function (1), $C_{t,-n}^{MK}$ represents the number of the project generated by total projects subtracting the present project i_n. $C_{t,w,-n}^{NK}$ represents the number of project W generated by interest t of all the user's consumption project subtracting the present project i_n.

The value of θ_u and ϕ_t can be estimated according to the posterior probability of situation of user's interest distribution and interest distribution in the project.

$$\Theta_{i,j} = P\left(t_i \middle| u_j, \alpha\right) = \frac{C_{i,j}^{MK} + \alpha}{\sum\limits_{K=1}^{K} C_{i,k}^{MK} + K\alpha} \tag{2}$$

$$\phi_{q,p} = P(i_p | t_q, \beta) = \frac{C_{q,p}^{MK} + \beta}{\sum\limits_{j=1}^{N} C_{q,j}^{MK} + N\beta}. \tag{3}$$

3   Extended Recommendation Algorithm (IxLDA)

The algorithm can be divided into the following two stages:

1. Off-line phase: according to the user's history score records, it uses the extend LDA algorithm to extract user's latent interest θ_u calculates association diagram of the user's interest and then presents the incidence matrix of interest. It combines time response with PageRank to extend interest.
2. Online phase: predict user's possible consumption project and the criteria the user will give it by using the extend interest.

3.1   Extend LDA

However, LDA only use the number of consumption project to determine whether the user is interested in the project while extracting interest. It is not an effective way. Actually, when a user expense some project at the beginning, the amount of consumption time is limited. It cannot represent the user's interest. Consequently, determining the user's interest only by using the consumption time is not an effective and accurate way.

In this paper, it supplies a gap of the above problem by using grade evaluation of user for the project. If the user gives negative comments on the same project after several times' consumptions, it seems that the user has no interest in the project. However, if the customer provides positive comments on the same project after several times' purchase, it shows that the user is interested in the project. Hence, a user's grade evaluation of a project can better help to identify the customer's interest.

According to the above comments, we can know that the project production process is related with not only to the consumption amount ϕ_t while generating a project, but also the comments of the user. Hence, the following extend LDA model is proposed, shows in the Fig. 1.

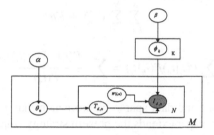

Fig. 1. Extend LDA model

In the above picture, each consumed project is represented as an observable variables, and hollow dot θ, Φ, t represent latent variables. The outer rectangle represents the probability subject distribution θ_u which is generated by repeated sampling for user number M. The inter rectangle represents that each user M_u is constituted of a group of consumption objects i and interest t which is extracted from subject distribution θ_u. And each consumption item I can be recognized as probability distribution ϕ_t which is generated by interest t in the project. θ_u and ϕ_t are Dirichlet distribution determined by hyperparameter α and β.

It can be seen from the figure that the generating process of a project is related to the overall evaluation W(u, i) of the project.

Based on considering the evaluation of the project, we can re-sampling with Gibbs sampling by the following function:

$$P(t_n = k|i_n, \alpha, \beta, T_{-n}) \propto \frac{C_{k,-n}^{MK} + \alpha}{\sum_{v=1}^{K} C_{v,-n}^{MK} + K\alpha} \cdot \frac{W(i,u) \cdot C_{k,i,-n}^{NK} + \beta}{\sum_{j=1}^{N} W(j,u) \cdot C_{k,j,-n}^{NK} + N\beta} \tag{4}$$

Accordingly, the new interest distribution of the user can be calculated as the following function:

$$\tilde{\phi}_{q,p} = P(i_p | t_q, \beta) = \frac{W(i, u)C_{q,p}^{MK} + \beta}{\sum\limits_{j=1}^{N} W(j, u)C_{q,j}^{MK} + N\beta}. \tag{5}$$

3.2 Extend Recommendation Algorithm

Since the user's interest is changing over the time, the association between interests is needed to be calculated by using the following function:

$$\pi_i = P(t_i) = \frac{\sum\limits_{m=1}^{M} C_{mi}^{MK} + \alpha}{\sum\limits_{k=1}^{K} \sum\limits_{m=1}^{M} C_{mk}^{MK} + K\alpha} \tag{6}$$

$$\eta_{i,j} = P(t_j | t_i) = \sum_{n=1}^{N} P(t_j | i_n)P(i_n | t_i) = \sum_{n=1}^{N} (\frac{P(t_j) \cdot P(i_n | t_j)}{P(i_n)} \cdot P(i_n | t_i)) \tag{7}$$

Because the cold-start and data sparse phenomenon may happen while extracting single user's interest, the paper extends the present strategy which uses only the interest of single user to that which recognizes these interests change with time. By using a PageRank algorithm with time feedback, the paper extends the interest by the way of random walk. The iteration function is as following:

$$\theta_i^{(n+1)} = (1 - \alpha) \cdot e + \alpha \cdot \theta_i^{(n)} \psi \, Weight(t) \tag{8}$$

α is damping factor, set a value of 0.85.

$$Weight(t) = \frac{d}{t}, t = \begin{cases} 1.0, & t \le 1\text{Month} \\ 1.8, & 1\text{Month} < t \le 1\text{Year} \\ 0.6, & \ge 1\text{Year} \end{cases} \tag{9}$$

Ranking it according to the Intimacy between the project and the user. Based on the interest distribution of user on some projects, calculate the project probability of the extended user. The function is described as following:

$$P(i_j | u_i) = \sum_{k=1}^{K} (P(i_j | t_k)P^{(z)}(i_k | u_i)) = \sum_{k=1}^{K} (\tilde{\phi}_{j,k} \theta_{i,k}^{(z)}) \tag{10}$$

In function (10), $\theta_{i,k}^{(z)}$ represents the interest distribution vector calculated by function (10). The function to predict the evaluation as user gives to the project can be seen in the below:

$$\hat{r} = \bar{r}_u + \frac{\sum_{x \in Neighbor(u)} sim(y,x) \cdot (r_{u,x} - \bar{r}_x)}{\sum_{x \in Neighbor(u)} sim(y,x)}.\tag{11}$$

4 Experiment Result and Analysis

In this section, we evaluate the proposed method (predict users preference by content type) and compare it with some baseline methods.

4.1 Experiment

This experiment uses a real dataset of Movielens. In the experiment, each user's consumption record can be divided into training set and test set. It randomly chooses a fixed ratio of project into the training set and the rest will be recognized as the test set.

4.2 Baseline Method

In order to compare the effectiveness of the proposed method in this paper, the method of dimension-decreasing SVD and LDA is used as the baseline method.

4.3 Evaluation Indicators

In the process of testing, only the situation of none-zero record is considered. the training set is used as the input and real data set is predicted. In order to evaluate the level of content type which is generated by different method, we trade off the following two baseline method. Recall and MAE are the evaluation standards of the ranking.

Recall: the recall rate of the recommending record. It is the rate of project which is recommended to a right user in all the test dataset.

$$Recall = \frac{Number\ of\ right\ recommdation}{Total\ number\ of\ test\ dataset}\tag{12}$$

MAE: Average absolute error, the lower the value of MAE, the higher the recommendation quality.

$$MAE = \frac{\sum_{<u,y> \in Test} \left| r_{u,y} - \hat{r}_{u,y} \right|}{CountT}\tag{13}$$

In function (13), CountT is the total number of user's evaluation; $r_{u,y}$ is the predicting evaluation value; $r_{u,y}$ is the real evaluation value a user u gives to project y.

The parameter in LDA is sett as: a = 50/K, b = 0.01, K = 300. In the data set Movielens, there are 100,000 grade evaluation records from 943 users to 1682 movies. Here we use 80 % of the data set as the training set, and the rest 20 % as the test set.

In this part, it compares the recommended effectiveness of IxLDA and baseline algorithms (SVD, LDA). Each divided training data set is used to train the recommendation algorithm and the test data set is to verify the recommendation result. In the following line charts, they demonstrate the result of the comparison. Figures 2 and 3 show the experiment result of Recall and average absolute error (MAE) while using different data division methods.

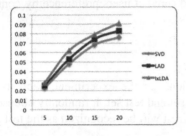   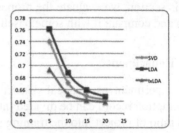

Fig. 2. Recall   **Fig. 3.** Average absolute error

From the line charts above, it can be seen that, the proposed method in this paper is better than the other baseline algorithms for predicting TOP-N recommendation and right evaluating rate.

5 Conclusion

In this paper, an improved algorithm is proposed to compensate the shortcomings of the initial algorithm, such as the low recommendation accuracy and effectiveness. It uses an extended LDA algorithm to extract user's interest information with higher accuracy and propose a user-interest-project three level model. Through this kind of hierarchy, we can better understand why a user chooses the project and it benefits the effectiveness of recommendation. However, user's interest may change along with time flying. In order to improve this part, we extend the interest information in the algorithm and calculate the interest information with a time based PageRank algorithm. It solves the problem of overfitting and cold-start. At last, through comparing this algorithm with some baseline algorithms, it verify the fact that the proposed algorithm in this paper is better and effective.

Acknowledgments. The work is supported by the National Science Foundation of China (NSFC) under Grant No. 61202376 and 61572325, Shanghai Natural Science Foundation under Grant No. 15ZR1429100, Innovation Program of Shanghai Municipal Education Commission under Grant No. 13YZ075, Shanghai Key Science and Technology Project in Information Technology Field under Grant No. 14511107902, Shanghai Leading Academic Discipline Project under Grant No. XTKX2012, and Shanghai Engineering Research Center Project under Grant No. GCZX14014 and C14001.

References

1. Xu, H.L., Wu, X., Li, X.D., Yan, B.P.: Comparison study of internet recommendation system. J. Soft. **20**(2), 350–362 (2009)
2. Hongwei, M., Guangwei, Z., Peng, L.: Survey of collaborative filtering algorithms. J. Comput. Syst. **30**(7), 1282–1285 (2009)
3. Zhiming, F., Yidan, S., Hua, Q., Hai, D.: Recommendation algorithm of combining clustering with collaborative filtering based on genetic algorithm. J. Comput. Technol. Dev. **41**(5), 68–71 (2014)
4. Junhao, J., Shan, S.: Improved collaborative filtering recommendation algorithm of similarity measure. J. Comput. Sci. (2014)

A Novel Particle Swarm Optimization Algorithm for Permutation Flow-Shop Scheduling Problem

Yucheng Jia, Jianhua Qu[✉], and Lin Wang

College of Management Science and Engineering,
Shandong Normal University, Jinan, China
{jiayucheng2014,qujh1978,moanfly}@163.com

Abstract. Obtaining the optimal schedule for permutation flow-shop scheduling problem (PFSP) is very important for manufacturing systems. A lot of approaches have been applied for PFSP to minimize makespan, but current algorithms cannot be solved to guarantee optimality. In this paper, based on Particle Swarm Optimization (PSO), a novel PSO (NPSO) is proposed for PFSP with the objective to minimize the makespan. To make original PSO suitable for discrete problems, some improvements and relative techniques for original PSO, such as, Particle representation based on PPS, different crossover and mutation of genetic algorithm (GA) used to avoid premature. Many classical problems have been used to evaluate the performance of the proposed NPSO. Through several comparisons between NPSO and PSO, we obtain that the NPSO is clearly more efficacious than original PSO for PFSP to minimize makespan.

Keywords: PSO · PFSP · GA · NPSO · Particle Position Sequence (PPS)

1 Introduction

Flow-shop scheduling problems frequently arise in industrial processes, good manufacturing systems, which is taking significant effect in production planning and manufacturing systems [1]. Many different approaches have been applied to solve PFSP, but these algorithms problems cannot guarantee optimality. In order to change this situation, this paper focuses on the effectiveness of proposed algorithm and finding global optimal solution.

To solve PFSP, researchers have done a lot of valuable researches which can be classified into three categories [2]. The first category is the precision methods. This method can obtain the precise solution, but it need waste a lot of time that it isn't suitable for very big scale PFSPs. Zhanke Yu proposed an improved branch and bound algorithm [3]. The second one is the constructive methods. These kinds of methods design the scheduling rules through local information, and finally construct the whole solution of PFSP. Leisten [4] compared some constructive heuristics to arrive at the conclusion that the well-known Nawaz–Enscore–Ham (NEH) heuristic outperforms all others. Even though these methods can quickly find the solutions, their final solutions are almost local optimal, not global optimal [2]. The third one is the Meta heuristic algorithms. Nowadays several heuristic techniques have been proposed for solving the PFSP characterized as

© Springer International Publishing Switzerland 2016
Q. Zu and B. Hu (Eds.): HCC 2016, LNCS 9567, pp. 676–682, 2016.
DOI: 10.1007/978-3-319-31854-7_62

either construction or improvement in [5]. The metaheuristics that are frequently applied to the FJSP are tabu search and GA, SA, PSO. Liu, Y.-F. and Liu, S.-Y. [6] presented a hybrid discrete artificial bee colony algorithm for PFSP. Zhang et al. [7] proposed an improved GA representation which reduces the computational time and produces competitive results with new upper bounds for some standard benchmark instances. Tamer F. Abdelmaguid [8] offered a tabu search approach utilizing the proposed neighborhood search to solve flexible job shop scheduling.

In recent years, there have been a lot of reported works focused on the modification PSO and other optimization algorithms to solve continuous optimization problems, but it's being used to solve PFSP does not have rich literatures and cannot guarantee optimality. As is all know that each approach has its own character, one popular way is combining several algorithms together to propose an algorithm for PFSP nowadays. This combination utilizes the advantages of each algorithm and overcome disadvantages of each algorithm, which has been proved to be more effective and efficient in most cases. Therefore, in this paper, according to the discrete characteristic of PFSP, we try to propose a NPSO to solve this problem effectively.

This paper aims to solve the PFSP with the makespan criterion using a particle swarm optimization with the genetic algorithm. The rest of this paper is organized as follows: Sect. 2 introduces the mathematical model of PFSP and the original PSO. Section 3 presents some improvements about PSO and proposes NPSO for PFSP. Section 4 shows the experimental results and comparisons between NPSO and other several algorithms. Section 5 concludes the paper.

2   PFSP Formulation and Original PSO and GA

2.1   PFSP Formulation

In with PFSP the least makespan criterion, there are n jobs that should be sequentially processed on a series of machines $m_1 m_2 \ldots m_m$. The pre-conditions are:

(1)   The processing sequence of all jobs on each machine is same.
(2)   The processing sequence of each job on all machines is same.
(3)   Each machine can just process at most one job at any time.
(4)   Each job must complete processing without preemption and delay

It is possible to number machines and operations in such a way that the machine path is $m_1, m_2, \ldots m_m$ and operation O_{ij} is the ith operation of job J_j, which is performed by machine m_i with fixed processing time $T_{ij}, i = 1, 2, \ldots, m, j = 1, 2, \ldots, n$.

The objective is to find the sequence of jobs minimizing the maximum flow time, which is called makespan. Let $C(K, J_j)$ denote the completion time of job J_j on machine K, and let $\{J_1, J_2, J_3 \ldots J_j\}$ denote a permutation of jobs, then the completion time for an n-job on m-machine flow-shop problem model is calculated as follow:

$$C\left(1, J_1\right) = t(1, J_1); \tag{1}$$

$$C\left(i, J_1\right) = C\left(i - 1, J_1\right) + t(1, J_1), (i = 2, 3, 4 \ldots, n) \tag{2}$$

$$C(1, J_j) = C(i, J_{j-1}) + t(1, J_j), (j = 2, 3, 4 \ldots, m) \tag{3}$$

$$C(i, J_j) = \max[C(i-1, J_j), C(i, J_{j-1})] + t_{ij}, (i = 2, 3, 4 \ldots, n, j = 2, 3, 4 \ldots, m) \tag{4}$$

The following relation calculates the makespan:

$$C_{MAX} = C(i, J_j) \tag{5}$$

2.2 Original PSO

PSO is an evolutionary computation technique developed by Dr. Eberhart and Dr. Kennedy in 1995. For a particle i, its position can be described by a D-dimensional vector $X_i = (x_{i1} x_{i2} \ldots x_{id})$ and its velocity is also a D-dimensional vector. The position at which the particle i has achieved its personal best fitness, the $P_{best} = (p_{i1} p_{i2} \ldots p_{id})$ is the best previous position yielding the best fitness value for the ith particle; and $p_g = (p_{i1}, p_{i2}, \ldots p_{id})$ is the global best particle found by all particles so far. For particle i, the velocity and position are updated as follows:

$$v_{ij}(t+1) = w * v_{ij}(t) + c_1 * r_1 * (p_{best}(t) - x_{ij}(t)) + c_2 * r_2 * (p_g(t) - x_{ij}(t)); \tag{6}$$

$$x_{ij}(t+1) = x_{ij}(t) + v_{ij}(t+1); \tag{7}$$

Where w is a parameter called the inertia weight, t represents iterative number, c_1, c_2 are learning factors. r_1, r_2 are random numbers between (0, 1). Some improvements of PSO have focused on the parameter, such as.

2.3 GA

Mutations designed to let the genetic algorithm explore a wider region of the solution space, which avoid the genetic approach caught in premature convergence towards low-quality solutions. It consists in randomly choosing a pairs of gene on different position and swaps their position to get a novel chromosome.

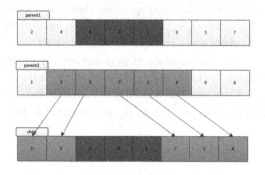

Fig. 1. Crossover

Crossover operators recombine the genes of two selected chromosomes to generate a new chromosome to include in the next generation. The process of crossover is illustrated in Fig. 1.

3   A Novel Particle Swarm Optimization to Solve PFSP

It is evident that original PSO is suitable for solving the consecutive problem, but, PFSP is find a descent sequence, which is discrete problem [15]. Therefore, the key problem to solve PFSP is particle encoding. In order to overcome this shortcoming, the particle representation based on Particle Position Sequence (PPS) is presented.

Particle i, its position can be described as $X_i = (x_{i1}x_{i2} \ldots x_{id})$, which the position vector x_{ij} are randomly produced and updated by Eq. (6)*(7). Therefore, the position vector must have a sequence. The paper presents a Two-dimensional vector to represent the particle. The first dimension denotes the jobs, N = 1, 2...n, the second dimension denotes particle position. $X_i = (x_{i1}x_{i2} \ldots x_{id})$, Fig. 2 shows the format of the Two-dimensional vector.

N	1	2	3	....	....	n-1	n
position	Xi1	Xi2	Xi3	....	....	Xi(n-1)	Xin

Fig. 2. The format of the Two-dimensional

Even though PSO can quickly find the solutions, their final solutions are often fell into local optimal. To avoid falling into local optimum, GA has been applied to avoid the shortcoming of poor local search ability in PSO.

This paper adapts the GA to optimize PSO, which includes two obvious improvements. Firstly, personal best sequence X characterized by an objective function value f(X), a neighbor sequence X' is selected from the crossover (global best as parent1 and personal best as parent2) and calculate the value of its objective function as f (X'). If f(X) > f (X'), the novel sequence X' replace the X. Secondly, global best sequence Y characterized by an objective function value f(Y), neighbor sequence Y' is selected from the mutation and calculate the value of its objective function as f (Y'). If f(Y) > f (Y'), the sequence Y' replace the sequence Y as global best.

- Step 1: Set the parameters; initialize a population of particles with random positions.
- Step 2: Calculate each particle's fitness value of initialization population, and let first generation P_i as P_{best}, and choose the particle with the best fitness value of all the particles as the P_g.
- Step 3: Update P_g and P_{best} by mutation and crossover.
- Step 4: Update the position of particles base on Eqs. (6) and (7), evaluate the fitness values of all particles.
- Step 5: Compare current fitness value of each particle with its P_{best} value. If the current value is small, then replace P_{best} with the current position and fitness value.

- Step 6: Calculate fitness value of all the particles, chose the best fitness value compare with P_g, if the best fitness value is smaller than $P_g(gbest)$, then replace $P_g(gbest)$ with the current position and fitness value, k = k+1.
- Step 7: Check the stop criteria, then output P_g, and its objective value; otherwise, go back to Step 3.

4 Numerical Experiments

To illustrate the effectiveness and performance of NPSO algorithm for PFSP to minimize makespan, computational simulation base on practical data is carried out including rec1–rec9. The NPSO algorithms are coded in matlab with the machine is hp431 Intel i3-2310 M@2.10 GHz/2 GB.

Swarm population size as PS = 50, learning factors as c1 = c2 = 2, the number of iteration N = 300. The average values (AVG), minimum value (MIN), maximum value (MAX), are calculated as the statistics to test the performance of NPSO. C* is the optimal makespan or lower bound value known so far.

To further show the effectiveness of the proposed NPSO algorithm, the results of NPSO and standard PSO are compared as shown in Table 1. It can be seen that NPSO can obtain the lower smaller and lower bound makespan than NEH and original PSO for PFSP, which means that the improvements about original PSO is successful.

Table 1. Comparison of PSO and NPSO Algorithms used to solve the instances.

Problem	C*	NEH		MAX	MIN	AVG
Rec1	1278	1381	PSO	1407	1297	1297.7
			NPSO	1347	1278	1279.1
Rec2	1359	1458	PSO	1460	1369	1376.7
			NPSO	1420	1359	1366.9
Rec3	1081	1213	PSO	1270	1088	1116
			NPSO	1258	1086	1096.9
Rec4	1293	1488	PSO	1493	1308	1318.6
			NPSO	1477	1293	1319.4
Rec5	1235	1381	PSO	1396	1250	1295.5
			NPSO	1338	1235	1242.8
Rec6	1195	1385	PSO	1364	1195	1214.2
			NPSO	1314	1195	1209.3
Rec7	1234	1360	PSO	1388	1239	1258
			NPSO	1352	1234	1251.6
Rec8	1206	1401	PSO	1403	1211	1215
			NPSO	1389	1206	1217.9
Rec9	1230	1366	PSO	1396	1233	1256.2
			NPSO	1350	1230	1253.8

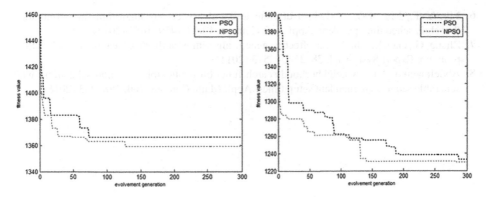

Fig. 3. Convergence rate of PSO and NPSO (rec5 and rec9)

In order to display convergence process of algorithms, two PFSP instances' convergence rate contrast figure used by NPSO algorithm and PSO be shown in Fig. 3. The simulation solution clearly shows that NPSO algorithm's convergence speed is faster than PSO to find the optimal solutions.

5 Conclusion

The objectives of this paper are to find a solution to minimize makespan. We adopted NPSO algorithm for PFSP to minimize makespan. The improvements include original PSO suitable for discrete problems, the utilization of GA avoid falling into local optima. In order to test the performance of these algorithms, 9 problems were adopted to prove. The results of NPSO on 9 problems have shown the ability of the improvement and effective of NPSO than original PSO.

Acknowledgment. This work was supported by: Science-Technology Program of the Higher Education Institutions of Shandong Province, China (No. J12LN22) and Research Award Foundation for Outstanding Young scientists of Shandong Province, China (No. BS2012DX041) and the National Natural Science Foundation of China (Grant No. 61472231).

References

1. Li, X., Yin, M.: A hybrid cuckoo search via Levy flights for the permutation flow shop scheduling problem. Int. J. Prod. Res. **51**(16), 4732–4754 (2013)
2. Qiu, C.H., Wang, C.: An immune particle swarm optimization algorithm for solving permutation flowshop problem. Key Eng. Mater. **419**, 133–136 (2010)
3. Zhanke, Yu., Mingfang, N., Zeyan W.: Improved branch and bound algorithm. J. Comput. Appl. (2011). s2
4. Leisten, R.: Flowshop sequencing problems with limited buffer storage. Int. J. Prod. Res. **28**(11), 2085–2100 (1990)
5. Murata, T., Ishibuchi, H., Tanaka, H.: Genetic algorithms for flow-shop scheduling problems. Comput. Ind. Eng. **30**(4), 1061–1071 (1996)

6. Liu, Y.-F., Liu, S.-Y.: A hybrid discrete artificial bee colony algorithm for permutation flowshop scheduling problem. Appl. Soft Comput. **13**(3), 1459–1463 (2013)
7. Zhang, G., Gao, L., Shi, Y.: An effective genetic algorithm for the flexible job-shop scheduling problem. Expert Syst. Appl. **38**, 3563–3573 (2011)
8. Abdelmaguid, T.F.: A neighborhood search function for flexible job shop scheduling with separable sequence-dependent setup times. Appl. Math. Comput. **260**, 188–203 (2015)

Customer Satisfaction Analysis Based on SVM

Zhenni Jiang, Wenke Zang[✉], and Xiyu Liu

School of Management Science and Engineering,
Shandong Normal University, Jinan, Shandong, China
1179480219@qq.com, zwker@163.com, xyliu@sdnu.edu.cn

Abstract. The current intense market competition environment force many enterprises take more and more attention to customer demands, and adopt effective methods to evaluate the importance of customer satisfaction. In order to analysis the customer's actual need, enterprises need to use the effective data analysis method to analyze customer satisfaction. The economic development of e-commerce era has made the original offline entity transactions convert into online transactions. The way of traditional survey is no longer suitable for the analysis of customer satisfaction. For the lafite wine which sells on the tmall market, the author collected the data of many shops, adopted the method of SVM (support vector machine), analyzed the main factors that affect customer satisfaction, and find their own shortcomings at the end. This method improved the precision of the analysis of customer satisfaction, and can help policymakers understand the demand of customers.

Keywords: SVM · Customer satisfaction · Customer relationship management

1 Introduction

Customer satisfaction [1, 3] is the production of free competition in the market economy. In recent years, with the development of the national economy and the accelerated pace of life, people's daily habits are changing, such as consumer shopping. Due to the rapid development of e-commerce, consumers are increasingly inclined to carry out shopping on the internet. In this environment, who can seize the opportunity to retain customers, who will win the victory of the war. This paper is mainly based on the main background of China's e-commerce network environment to make the customer satisfaction analysis. In this paper, we take into account the characteristics of information in the era of e-commerce, and change the traditional way of questionnaire, interviews and other low efficiency, direct take use of online customer data records. Using SVM data analysis method, the key factors that affect customer satisfaction are analyzed, and some suggestions are put forward to improve the service quality, improve the customer's purchasing power, and enhance the competitiveness and profitability of the enterprise. We collected the sales data of tmall Wine Lafite on shop, and understood the corresponding classification methods through the relevant literature. In this paper, we use the SVM classification method, according to the customer data for a simple classification, and pick out a few stores from the classification to compare, and find out the difference. The data in experiment were collected from real stores.

© Springer International Publishing Switzerland 2016
Q. Zu and B. Hu (Eds.): HCC 2016, LNCS 9567, pp. 683–688, 2016.
DOI: 10.1007/978-3-319-31854-7_63

The simulation experiment is finished in the MATLAB 2014a. Finally, the experiment get the key factors that affecting customer satisfaction.

2 Related Knowledge

Customer relationship management theory [2] is the enterprises use the corresponding information technology and Internet technology to coordination the sales between enterprises and customers, and the interaction of marketing and service, so as to enhance their management style, and provide customers innovative personalized customer interaction and service process. It's processing as follows Fig. 1:

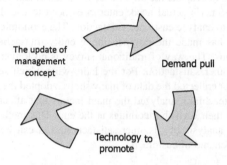

The update of management concept

Demand pull

Technology to promote

Fig. 1. The development process of CRM

Customer satisfaction is the customer's perception of a commodity or a service effect after comparison with his expectations of feeling in the heart, such as pleasure or disappointment. Heart state corresponds to the degree of customer satisfaction and satisfaction, this is the customer satisfaction, it is the level of customer satisfaction quantification. The structure of customer satisfaction is Maslow's hierarchy of needs.

Support vector machine (SVM) [4] method is based on statistical learning theory of VC dimension theory and structure risk minimum principle. It depends on the complexity of the limited samples of information in the model (i.e. on a particular learning accuracy of training samples) and learning ability (neither error any ability to identify sample) to search the best compromise. Because of SVM concerns of the VC dimension, so we also know that using SVM to solve the problem is relation with the dimensions of the samples, so the SVM is very suitable for solving the problem of text classification.

A linear function is a real function. But our classification problem is discrete output values. This paper use the 0 to represent the sample not belong to the classifier C_1, and use the 1 to represent the sample belong to the classifier C_1 [5].

For example, we have a linear function $g(x) = wx + b$. When we have samples need to distinguish, we can get the $g(x_i)$. If $g(x_i) > 0$, the sample belong to C_1. If $g(x_i) < 0$, the sample belong to C_2. The optimal classification line in the case of linear separable is as follows Fig. 2:

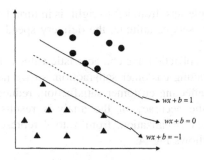

$wx + b = 1$

$wx + b = 0$

$wx + b = -1$

Fig. 2. The optimal classification line in the case of linear separable

3   The Analysis of Customer Satisfaction Based on SVM

The data in this paper was collected from 178 Lafite wine stores. Considering the actually difficult, we can't get the enough data from one store. This paper choose the stores which have the larger sale data, so the results of the study has a certain credibility. The data format and impact factor as follows Table 1.

Table 1. Data format and impact factor

Number	Name	The tupe of data	Length
1	Taste	Data	10
2	Packaging	Data	10
3	Postage	Data	10
4	Price	Data	10
5	Description service	Data	10
6	Service attitude	Data	10
7	The delivery speed	Data	10
8	Month record	Data	10
9	Cumulative assessment	Data	10

The process of the study is to use the MATLAB 2014a and libsvm toolbox to analyze the data. The collected data was made into a.mat file. The data of 178 stores were collected, and the data of the first ten samples were displayed because of the space limitation. The partial sample data sets are as follows Fig. 3:

	1	2	3	4	5	6	7	8	9
1	0.7200	0.7200	20	139	4.8000	4.8000	4.7000	1054	797
2	0.7100	0.5800	0	259	4.8000	4.8000	4.7000	2054	13955
3	0.7200	0.7500	20	789	4.8000	4.8000	4.7000	586	896
4	0.6800	0.5800	0	119	4.8000	4.8000	4.8000	694	2940
5	0.7300	0.6000	20	349	4.8000	4.8000	4.7000	437	1923
6	0.6800	0.7600	0	399.8600	4.8000	4.8000	4.8000	337	1157
7	0.7200	0.7700	20	649	4.8000	4.8000	4.7000	356	1780
8	0.7200	0.7900	0	538	4.8000	4.8000	4.8000	369	1451
9	0.7000	0.5800	20	339	4.8000	4.8000	4.7000	252	4910
10	0.6400	0.7300	0	87	4.8000	4.8000	4.7000	420	1709

Fig. 3. Partial data sample

The attributes of sample sets, from left to right, is in turn: taste, packaging, postage, price, description service, service attitude, the delivery speed, month record, cumulative assessment.

In the process of data collection, the characteristic value is nine, but not all of these are important factors affecting customer satisfaction, so we need to analyze the data, find out the key factors affecting customer satisfaction, reduce the dimension of data analysis, and improve the accuracy of the analysis results. We draw the fractal dimension of the test data visualization, from 1 to 9 represent the nine attribute in Table 1. The result as follows Fig. 4:

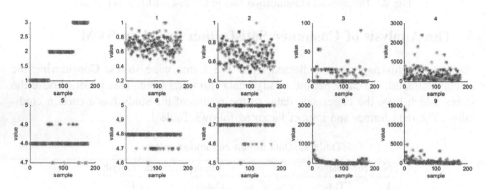

Fig. 4. Data visualization

(1) First of all, we classified 178 stores into three categories, when all the feature vectors are analyzed. By constantly trying, we get the highest classification accuracy when c = 3, g = 3. The experiment results are as follows Fig. 5:

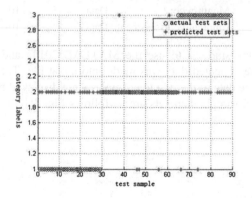

Fig. 5. The actual and prediction classification in test sets

(2) Selecting three aspects which is description service, service attitude, delivery speed to analysis. By constantly trying, we get the highest classification accuracy when c = 2, g = 3. The experiment results are as follows Fig. 6:

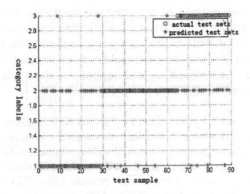

Fig. 6. The actual and prediction classification in test sets

The accuracy is 42.6966 % (38/89) (classification). We can get that the accuracy rate is relatively lower than before. At the same time, it also cannot effectively explain the customer satisfaction.

(3) In the end, we analyzed the characteristics of the main factors e.g. taste, packaging and price in the visual analysis. Using the same method, we can get the highest classification accuracy when c = 3, g = 5. We can get the experiment results are as follows Fig. 7:

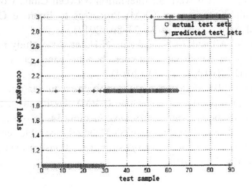

Fig. 7. The classification results in test sets

The accuracy is 89.8876 % (80/89) (classification). The accuracy rate close to 90 %. So we can get the taste, packaging and price are the main factors that affect customer satisfaction.

4 Conclusion

The paper analysis the data for the sales data of Lafite stores based on support vector machine (SVM) technology. At the same time, we use the MATLAB2014a to realize the simulation. All factors that may affect customer satisfaction were considered.

Finally, the general classification of customer satisfaction is analyzed by means of visual form, and we get the several key factors affecting customer satisfaction that are taste, packaging and price. This method can improve the accuracy of customer satisfaction analysis, which can help decision makers to understand the customer's evaluation more accurately and provide a good support for the implementation of CRM (Customer Relationship Management).

Acknowledgment. This work was supported by National NSF of China (61170038), NSF of Shandong, China (ZR2011FM001), Technology development projects of Shandong, China (2012G0020314), Soft scienceresearch project of Shandong, China (2013RZB01019), Jinan City independent innovation plan project in Colleges and Universities, China (201401202), Ministry of education of Humanities and social science research projects, China (12YJA630152), Social Science Fund Project of Shandong, China (11CGLJ22), outstanding youth scientist foundation of Shandong, China (BS2013DX037), young star of science and technology plan project, Jinan (20120108), science and technology development project, Jinan (201211003), science and technology development project, Jinan (201305004).

References

1. Xiao, Y., Liu, B., Luo, D., et al.: Multi-agent system for customer relationship management with SVMs tool. Int. J. Intell. Inf. Database Syst. **4**(2), 121–136 (2010)
2. Al-nsour, S., Alryalat, H., Alhawari, S.: Integration between Cloud Computing Benefits and Customer Relationship Management (CRM) Processes to Improve Organization's Performance. Int. J. Cloud Appl. Comput. **4**(2), 73–86 (2014)
3. Mohammadhossein, N., Ahmad, M.N., Zakaria, N.H., et al.: A study towards the relation of customer relationship management customer benefits and customer satisfaction. Int. J. Enterp. Inf. Syst. (IJEIS) **10**(1), 11–31 (2014)
4. Turker, M., Koc-San, D.: Building extraction from high-resolution optical spaceborne images using the integration of support vector machine (SVM) classification, Hough transformation and perceptual grouping. Int. J. Appl. Earth Obs. Geoinf. **34**, 58–69 (2015)
5. Yu, L., Wang, S., Lai, K.K.: Developing an SVM-based ensemble learning system for customer risk identification collaborating with customer relationship management. Front. Comput. Sci. China **4**(2), 196–203 (2010)

Numerical Algorithm of Non-circular Gear's Tooth Profile Based on Jarvis March

Botao Li[(✉)], Jiquan Hu, Dingfang Chen, Bo Li,
Hongxiang Zhang, and Jun He

Institute of Intelligent Manufacturing and Control,
Wuhan University of Technology, Wuhan 430063, Hubei, China
177011047@qq.com, cadcs@126.com

Abstract. According to Jarvis March method and characteristics of non-circular gear's tooth profile, a numerical algorithm of non-circular gear's tooth profile based on Jarvis March has been proposed. This method can calculate the non-circular gear's tooth profile with the help of improved Jarvis March method. And improve efficiency and accuracy by simplify shaper cutter model and envelope process. So this method can calculate the non-circular gear's tooth profile accurately and efficiently. In order to detect the correctness and efficiency of this method, the method has been used to calculate the tooth profile's curve data of non-circular gear. In the end, good results have been obtained and indirectly verify the correctness and efficiency of this method.

Keywords: Non-circular gear · Jarvis March method · Tooth profile

1 Introduction

The curve data of non-circular gear's tooth profile plays an important role in non-circular gear's design, manufacture, precision testing and other areas. However, every teeth profile on non-circular gear are different due to the particularity of the non-circular gear's pitch curve [1, 2]. Although in theory, only need to do is to obtain envelope's mathematical equations and get the tooth profile. But the theory is too complex to understand and the result is too difficult to get [3–5]. So, for now, the calculation of the non-circular gear's tooth profile generally relies on numerical method. But these method [6, 7] need to scan a huge point set of data to find points located on the curve of non-circular gear's tooth profile, and sort them in tooth profile's direction. So the balance of time and accuracy in these methods can be difficult to handle. Using these methods improperly can easily take lots of time in calculating curve data to get high accuracy tooth profile [1, 8].

In order to overcome the contradiction in time and accuracy, this paper presents a numerical algorithm of non-circular gear's tooth profile based on Jarvis March method, which can improve efficiency and accuracy by using Jarvis March method and pruning method in the calculation of non-circular gear's tooth profile curve data.

Q. Zu and B. Hu (Eds.): HCC 2016, LNCS 9567, pp. 689–694, 2016.
DOI: 10.1007/978-3-319-31854-7_64

2   Jarvis March Introduction

Convex Hull is a computer graphics concept. As shown in the Fig. 1, suppose Q is the set of all points on the plane, then the Q'S convex hull is the minimum convex polygon which has all points on or in it. In Fig. 1 is the point set Q's convex hull where $Q = \{p_0, p_1, p_2, \cdots p_m\}$.

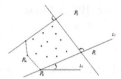

Fig. 1. Q's convex hull

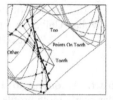

Fig. 2. One tooth's envelope diagram

Jarvis March is one of the most commonly used convex hull algorithm. It uses a strategy called "rotational sweep", to get a point set's convex hull. As shown in Fig. 1. It can be seen that Jarvis March has advantages in draw a polygonal area with a set of points. And maybe, these advantages can be used in calculating non-circular gear's tooth profile.

Figure 2 is part of envelope diagram of a tooth of a non-circular gear. Assume Q is the intersection set which formed by the curve of non-circular gear's tooth profile in Fig. 2. Then the tooth's profile is formed by subset of Q and the envelope line between those points. It has a lot of similarities with the calculation of the convex. By comparing Fig. 1, can see the both the calculation of the convex hull and the calculation of the non-circular gear's tooth profiles need to calculate the profile of a point set. So in some extent, they are similar. But the calculation of non-circular gear's tooth profile and the convex hull has something not in comment. The profile in the calculation of convex hull is the smallest flange type which all point on or in it. But in the calculation of non-circular gear's tooth profile, the profile means non-circular gear's tooth profile which is formed by enveloping lines' and points on it. So the tooth profile is neither Closed nor formed by straight line. In order to correctly and effectively calculate non-circular gear's tooth profile, Jarvis March method must be improved based on the similarities and deviations between a convex hull and a non-circular gear's tooth profile.

3   Calculation of the Tooth Profile

In envelope method, non-circular gear's tooth profile model was enveloped many times by a same shaper cutter in a unit time. More times cutter envelopes, denser the envelope line will be, and the result of tooth profile's accuracy will be higher. But to envelope more frequently will surely increase the size of intersection set rapidly and reduce Jarvis March's efficiency. So the pruning conditions need to be found to removing large number of unnecessary intersection points from intersection set in order to improve the efficiency of Jarvis March Method. And here are two aspects in which intersection set will be simplified:

Simplified the Intersection Set by Simplify the Cutter Model. In the pure rolling process between cutter model and non-circular gear's pitch curve model, only some part of the cutter are related to a tooth profile, and most parts of the cutter are not. But those unnecessary parts produced a large number of meaningless intersections in the process of rolling. So, in order to simplifying the intersection set, cutter model needed to be simplified in first place.

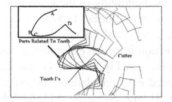   

Fig. 3. The simplification of cutter model   **Fig. 4.** Tooth I's envelope process

Assume the left profile of tooth I in Fig. 3 need to be calculated. In Fig. 3, it's obvious that not all parts of the cutter are related to the left profile of tooth I, only the parts of which envelope the tooth I's profile are, and other parts of the cutter model are unnecessary in calculation of the tooth I's left profile. So in Fig. 3, the other parts can be excluded from the model of the cutter and leave only A, B, C, and D to calculate the profile. Thus greatly reduces the intersections generate from non-related parts of cutter model, and only left intersections generate by part A, B, C and D. And that's one aspect to simplify the intersection set.

Simplify the Intersection Set by Simplify the Envelope Process. Likewise, as shown in Fig. 4, in the pure rolling process between cutter model and non-circular gear's pitch curve model, most of process have nothing to do with the current profile and only little part process is related to the profile. But intersections can be produced in any process. So, to simplify the intersection set, the envelope process need to be simplified.

   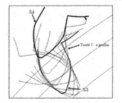

Fig. 5. The beginning of the envelope   **Fig. 6.** The ending of the envelope

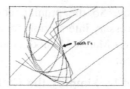

Fig. 7. The final simplified intersection set

Based on the envelope motion model of pitch curve and cutter in Fig. 5, the position S2 can be set in which the cutter's tooth top and the gear's root are tangent. Similarly, in Fig. 6, position S3 can be set in which the cutter's root and the tooth I's top are tangent. When get S2 and S3, can see that, the beginning of the tooth profile's envelope is the last position before S2 in which the cutter first doesn't have intersection on S2's C part when cutter is rolling. In Fig. 5, it is S1. And the envelope's ending position is the position after S3 in which the first position in which the cutter first don't have intersection on S3's D part when cutter is rolling. In Fig. 6, it is S4. So, in the calculation of the tooth I's left profile, the only needed is to calculate the intersections generate by the simplified cutter rolling between S1 and S4, even S1 and S4 are excluded. That's the other aspect to simplify the intersection set.

And the final result is shown in Fig. 7, in which both the cutter model and the envelope process are simplified. In the end, a simplified intersection set can be used in Jarvis March method.

Let Q be the set of all intersection points in Fig. 7. In order to use Jarvis March method, a start point needs to be found in Q. In original Jarvis March method, only needs to find the point with minimum horizontal and vertical coordinate to be start point. In fact, because the convex hull is closed, any point on the convex hull's vertex is ok. But, the non-circular gear's tooth profile is a non-closed curve, so one of the curve's endpoints is needed to become the start point in Jarvis March method. It can be seen in Fig. 6 that, the endpoint close to addendum is in the middle of the S3's D part, it's difficult to calculate the point's position. On the other hand, in Fig. 5 the endpoint close to the root is on the right endpoint of S2's part B, it's easy to obtain. So, the right endpoint of B in position S2 is the start point in Jarvis March method, donated as p_0.

After Q and p_0 was gotten, Jarvis March method still can't be used to draw a non-circular gear's tooth profile. Because Jarvis March is suitable for draw a convex hull, but a tooth profile unlike a convex hull it's neither convex nor closed. As shown in the Fig. 8, for example, p_0, p_1 and p_2 are three points on the tooth profile. If use original Jarvis March method, draw a line through p_0 and rotating it counterclockwise until the line through another point. In Fig. 8, the point is p_2, and skipped p_1 which is also on the tooth profile. That is not right, so improvements need to be made in Jarvis March method to meet to calculate the profile of non-circular gear's tooth.

Look at Fig. 8 again, it can be seen that although the line through p_0 rotating and encounter p_2 first, but p_0 and p_2 are not on the same enveloping line, in consequence, missed p_1. So in the improved Jarvis March method, the second point is not only the first encountered by the line but also required that, both first point and the second points are on the same enveloping line. And here are improved Jarvis March method's steps:

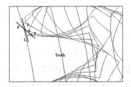

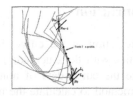

Fig. 8. Use Jarvis March to get tooth profile.   **Fig. 9.** Improved Jarvis March method

1. As shown in Fig. 9. Suppose the set of points on the tooth profile is CK(Q). And p_0 is the start point of tooth profile. Therefore, $p_0 \in$ CK(Q).
2. Suppose L_0 is a line which parallel to the B part of the cutter in position S2 of Fig. 5 and through p_0. Set p_0 as the rotating center of L_0 and counterclockwise. Until L_0 through another point which and p_0 on the same enveloping line, named as p_1, and $p_1 \in$ CK(Q).
3. Draw a line which parallel to L_0's original position and through p_1, named L_1. Then set p_1 as the rotating center of L_1 and counterclockwise, Until L_1 through another point which and p_1 on the same enveloping line, named as p_2. As the same, $p_2 \in$ CK(Q).
4. Repeat steps 2 and 3 until find a point pm which is on the D part of the cutter in position S3 of Fig. 6. Then p_m is the end point on tooth profile and $p_m \in$ CK(Q). At this time, CK(Q) is the result.

4 Experiment

Here is a non-circular gear which is part of our group's development, a decollator use non-circular gear instead of cam, will be used as an example in the detection of non-circular gear tooth profile and to explain the correctness and effectiveness of the improved Jarvis March method.

Frist, according to the motion of the partition, the parameters of the non-circular gears will be calculated. And here are those parameters: Module m = 2; Tooth number z = 20; Pressure angle α = 20° and Addendum modification $h_a^* = 1$. And the pitch curve equations are as follows:

$$y = \begin{cases} 30 & x \in [0,\ pi] \\ 66/(2.35416833 - 0.520835^*cos(2^*x)) & x \in [pi,\ 2^*pi] \end{cases}$$

When parameters and equations were set, cutter model and non-circular gear's pitch curve model can be established. Then pure rolling them to get non-circular gear's envelope diagram. After that, get every tooth profile's point set from enveloping lines' intersections. And use improved Jarvis March method to get every tooth profile of this non-circular gear. At last, compare the theoretical tooth profile data calculated by improved Jarvis March method and the actual tooth profile data detect by the three coordinate measuring instruments. Then the accuracy of the detected gear's tooth profile can be detected. The test results show that the theoretical data matches the actual data, showing the correctness of this method.

5 Conclusion

The calculation of the curve data of non-circular gear's tooth profile has a lot of similarities with the calculation of the convex hull. So Jarvis March can be used to calculate the curve data of non-circular gear's tooth profile. In order to use Jarvis March method to calculate the non-circular gear's tooth profile, Jarvis March need to be improved to meet the characteristics of the non-circular gear, so that it can draw the non-circular gear's tooth profile correctly. The tooth profile data obtained by this method is applied to the detection of non-circular gears in the decollator, and got satisfactory results. It's proved that this method is correct and effective.

Acknowledgments. This research is supported by Science and technology support program of Hubei Province under Grant No. 2014BAA024. The authors also would like to express appreciation to the anonymous reviewers for their helpful comments on improving the paper.

References

1. Xutang, W., Guihai, W.: Non-circular Gears and Non-uniform Transmission. Mechanical Industry Press, Beijing (1997)
2. Jing, L.: The Theory and Application of Conjugate Curve Engagement Angle Function. Science Press, Beijing (2005)
3. Bair, B.W.: Computer aided design of elliptical gears. J. Mech. Des. **124**(12), 787–793 (2002)
4. Jiangang, L., Xutang, W., Shimin, M.: Numerical calculation of tooth profile of non-circular gear. J. Xi'an Jiao Tong Univ. **39**, 75–78 (2005)
5. Weiming, T., Jun, A., Jiu, C.: Mathematical model of tooth profile curve of non-circular gears with asymmetric teeth. J. Foshan Univ. Nat. Sci. Ed. **20**, 22–26 (2002)
6. Minghui, F., Ge, L., Yun, Z.: Research on the algorithm of non-circular gear based on MATLAB. Agric. Mechanization Res. **32**, 57–60 (2010)
7. Peng, H., Ge, L., Ninghui, C.: Method of feature point of non-circular gear tooth profile based on the tangent line of nodes. J. Zhejiang Sci-Tech Univ. **29**, 240–244 (2012)
8. Chuanyu, W., Yuzhen, J., Leiying, H.: Research on calculation method of tooth profile of non-circular gear based on envelope feature. China Mech. Eng. **19**(15), 1796–1799 (2008)

Vibration Response and Research of Energy Harvesting of the Piezoelectric Cantilever

Hongjun Liu$^{(\boxtimes)}$, Dingfang Chen, Lijie Li, and Bo Li

Research Institute of Intelligent Manufacture and Control,
Wuhan University of Technology, Wuhan, China
whutlhj@163.com, cadcs@126.com

Abstract. Through modeling, simulation and testing of its output characteristics, this paper focuses on the study of the piezoelectric cantilever vibration energy harvester. First of all, potential function and output response of the system are obtained by calculation of the mechanical and electrical equation of the electromechanical coupling model of the piezoelectric cantilever vibration energy harvester. Then, ANSYS is used to simulate the structure and output response characteristics of the piezoelectric cantilever vibration energy harvester. At last, a experiment is made to prove the rationality, feasibility and correctness of the theoretical analysis and simulation of this paper. The work can be a foundation for the future study.

Keywords: Energy harvester · PZT-5A · Runge-Kutta · ANSYS · Output voltage

1 Introduction

Since the micromachining, micro-electronics and wireless sensing technology are developing rapidly, the radio frequency identification systems, embedded systems, wireless sensors and wireless sensor networks are widely used in the formation of their daily lives. But it requires appropriate power supply components to be small size, high integration, long life and even unattended or without replacement. Piezoelectric vibration energy harvester as a new type of power supply can convert the ubiquitous vibration mechanical energy into useful electrical energy, which can be a steady stream of power for micro devices [1]. The cantilever has a simple structure, flexibility, energy transfer ability, ease of processing, etc., thus become an ideal choice for piezoelectric energy harvesting device [2]. This study uses a cantilever structure. Firstly, the electromechanical coupling model is established according to the mechanical structure of the piezoelectric cantilever vibration energy harvester. The mechanical and electrical equations of the system are obtained by the Newton's second law and Kirchhoff's law. The method of Runge-Kutta is used to complete the numerical solution and analysis of potential function of the system. This paper can also get the output displacement and output voltage of the piezoelectric cantilever vibration energy harvester. And its simulation of the structure and output characteristics are completed by ANSYS. Finally, a experiment is made to prove the rationality, feasibility and correctness of the modeling, theoretical analysis and simulation.

© Springer International Publishing Switzerland 2016
Q. Zu and B. Hu (Eds.): HCC 2016, LNCS 9567, pp. 695–701, 2016.
DOI: 10.1007/978-3-319-31854-7_65

2 Piezoelectric Cantilever Vibration Energy Harvester

2.1 Basic Structure

This paper studies the piezoelectric cantilever vibration energy harvester, which is mainly based on piezoelectric effect of piezoelectric material. The basic structure of the energy harvester of double-crystal piezoelectric cantilever is shown in Fig. 1 [3]. The geometry of the free end of the mass is shown in Fig. 2, which consists of a support layer (Cu), a piezoelectric composite cantilever composed of upper and lower layers of the piezoelectric sheet (PZT-5A) and a mass (Ni) on the free end. The piezoelectric layers on the upper and lower surfaces of the support are in the same size. When inspired by the external excitation P(t), piezoelectric cantilever will vibrate and achieve electrical energy by piezoelectric effect.

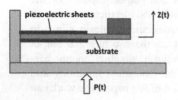

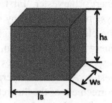

Fig. 1. Structure of the piezoelectric cantilever vibration energy harvester

Fig. 2. Geometries of the mass

2.2 Electro-Mechanical Coupling Model

In Fig. 1, the structure of the piezoelectric cantilever energy harvester contains variables of mechanical and electrical. Its Electromechanical coupling model can be equivalent to "spring - mass - damper - piezoelectric" system (Fig. 3). According to the Newton's second law, can get the dynamics equation [4]:

$$M_{eq} \ddot{Z}(t) + C_{eq} \dot{Z}(t) + K_{eq} Z(t) = kP(t) + k_v V(t) \tag{1}$$

Where M_{eq}, C_{eq} and K_{eq} represents equivalent quality, equivalent damping and equivalent stiffness of the mechanical structure. k is the correction factor of the lateral vibration cantilever lumped parameter model, $k_v V(t)$ is the output voltage of the piezoelectric sheet, V(t) is the piezoelectric coupling force, k_v is the coupling constant, P(t) is the external excitation, Z(t) is the displacement of the equivalent quality,

$$M_{eq} = M + 33m/140 \tag{2}$$

$$C_{eq} = 2M_{eq}\xi_r \omega_r \tag{3}$$

$$K_{eq} = \frac{6E_b J}{(l_b - l_B)^2 [2(l_b - l_B) + 1.5l_B]} \tag{4}$$

$$k_v = e_{31} \psi_r' \omega_b \frac{t_b + t_e}{2} \tag{5}$$

M is the quality of the mass on the free end of the cantilever, $M = \rho_B l_B \omega_B h_B$, m is the quality of the piezoelectric composite cantilever, $m = \rho_b l_b \omega_b t_b + 2\rho_e l_e \omega_e t_e$, ω_r is the natural frequency of the piezoelectric cantilever's mechanical part, $\omega_r = \sqrt{K_{eq}/M_{eq}}$, ξ_r is the mechanical damping ratio, J is the moment of inertia.

$$J = 2\left[\frac{\omega_b t_e^3}{12} + \omega_b t_e \left(\frac{t_e + t_b}{2}\right)^2\right] + \frac{E_b \omega_b t_b^3}{12E_e} \tag{6}$$

E_b is the young's modulus of the cantilever substrate; E_e is the young's modulus of the piezoelectric material PZT-5A; e_{31} is the piezoelectric coefficient; ψ_r' is the spatial derivatives of the mechanical vibration mode vector; ρ_B, l_B, ω_B, h_B, ρ_b, l_b, ω_b, t_b, ρ_e, l_e, ω_e, t_e is the density, length, width, height of the mass, beamand piezoelectric sheet.

Considering the ratio of quality of the cantilever and quality of the mass on the free end, a correction factor (k) is introduced, which can improve the prediction accuracy. The mathematical expression of the correction factor is:

$$k = \frac{(M/m)^2 + 0.603(M/m) + 0.08955}{(M/m)^2 + 0.4637(M/m) + 0.05718} \tag{7}$$

According to Kirchhoff's law, the circuit equation of the circuit part of the piezoelectric cantilever vibration energy harvester is:

$$k_v \dot{Z}(t) = \frac{1}{2} C_P \dot{V}(t) + \frac{V(t)}{R_L} \tag{8}$$

C_P is the equivalent capacitance of the circuit, $C_P = \frac{\varepsilon_{33}^S \omega_b l_b}{t_e}$, R_L is the resistance of the circuit, ε_{33}^S is the permittivity, $\varepsilon_{33}^S = \varepsilon_{31}\varepsilon_0$, ε_{31} is the relative permittivity, ε_0 is the absolute vacuum permittivity.

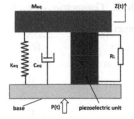

Fig. 3. Electromechanical coupling model

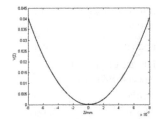

Fig. 4. Potential function

2.3   Analysis of the Potential Function

In order to effectively characterize the changes of the mechanical energy of piezoelectric cantilever vibration energy harvester, the potential of the system can be as the elastic potential energy of the equivalent model without considering the influence of gravity.

When $Z = Z_0$, the potential energy can be expressed as follow [3]: $V(Z_0) = \int_0^{Z_0} K_{eq} Z dZ$. The trend chart of the potential function V(Z) can be obtained by integrating, as shown in Fig. 4.

2.4   Numerical Calculation and Simulation

In this paper, the structural material parameters and geometry of the piezoelectric cantilever vibration energy harvester are selected by a review of the relevant literature, as shown in Tables 1 and 2 [5]. Research and analyze the output displacement and the output voltage of the piezoelectric cantilever vibration energy harvester by using classical fourth-order Runge-Kutta for solving differential equations of higher order. The bandwidth of the frequency is 0 – 200 Hz and the intensity D = 1 of the random excitation P(t) while simulat, which obey the Gaussian. While the other parameter values are as follow: $\psi_r' = 0.0513$, $\xi_r = 0.0178$, $R_L = 10\,\text{M}\Omega$. The output displacement Z(t) and the output voltage V(t) can be obtained through the simulation analysis of the differential Eqs. (1) and (8), shown in Figs. 5 and 6. The analysis shows that, the system has large amplitude with a higher output voltage when the excitation frequency of the external environment is equal or close to the natural frequency of the piezoelectric cantilever vibration energy harvester.

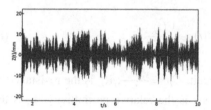

Fig. 5. Output displacement

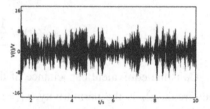

Fig. 6. Output voltage

Table 1. Material parameters of each structure

Parameter	Value
Material of piezoelectric sheets: PZT-5A	
E_e/GPa	66
ρ_e/kg·m^{-3}	7800
ε_{31}	1500
ε_0	8.854
e_{31}/PC·N^{-1}	−190
Material of the base: Cu	
E_b/GPa	100
ρ_b/kg·m^{-3}	7165
Material of the mass: Ni	
ρ_B/kg·m^{-3}	8900

Table 2. Geometries of each structure

Geometry	Value
l_b, l_e/mm	60
ω_b, ω_e/mm	10
t_e	0.2
t_b	0.5
l_B	8
ω_B	10
h_B	4

3 Finite Element Analysis

The modeling, static analysis, modal analysis and harmonic response analysis of the piezoelectric cantilever vibration energy harvester will be completed by using the finite element software ANSYS. In order to reduce the computational burden of finite element analysis, the electrode layer of the geometric model is usually not considered and its thickness is smaller than any other structural layers. The way to reduce the degree of computational complexity and get relevant results is simplifying the device and determining the relevant parameters of the model during finite element analysis. Creating a finite element model, meshing, definition of electrode and one end of the model fixing can be completed by GUI interface operation, as shown in Figs. 7 and 8.

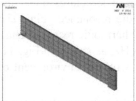

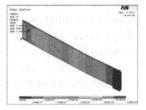

Fig. 7. Finite element model and meshing   **Fig. 8.** Define electrode and fix the end   **Fig. 9.** Stress distribution of the piezoelectric cantilever

3.1 Static Analysis

The main purpose of static analysis is to calculate the structural response under the effect of fixed load, do not consider the effect of inertia and damping and the load does not change over time. When the static force, which is 0.1 N, is applied to the free end of the piezoelectric cantilever, the maximum stress at the root of the cantilever can be obtained, which is 23.3 MPa and less than the allowable stress of the piezoelectric material, as shown in Fig. 9.

3.2 Modal Analysis

Modal Analysis is to analyze the natural vibration characteristics of structure primarily. The vibration of the structure can be represented by a linear combination of each vibration mode, which have different natural frequency. The first mode has the minimum frequency. The natural frequency of each mode becomes higher with the increase of the order, and the value of each natural frequency is in large difference. Figure 10 shows each vibration mode of the cantilever without thinking about the damping and other influence in the environment.

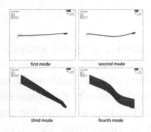

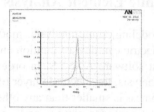

Fig. 10. Mode shape of the piezoelectric cantilever

Fig. 11. Output voltage of the structure under different vibration frequency

3.3 Harmonic Response Analysis

Harmonic response analysis is used to analyze the response of structures under the excitation of different frequency, especially the response at the resonance point. The voltage values under different parameters can be obtained by harmonic response analysis when the range of the frequency is set from 0 Hz to 100 Hz, as shown in Fig. 11. The figure shows that, the piezoelectric structure may be in working environment of first-order resonance to obtain the maximum output power.

4 Experiment

The making of piezoelectric cantilever vibration energy harvester which is in the same size of material parameters and structures as shown in Tables 1 and 2 can verify the theoretical analysis and simulation results of the second part of this paper. The cooper thin film electrode are pasted on two surfaces of the piezoelectric cantilever, as shown in Fig. 12. The exciter is the center of the experimental platform. The sinusoidal signal, produced by the signal generator GFG-8016G, driving the exciter after amplified by the amplifier AV-2218. The positive and negative electrode are connected with the oscilloscope, which can show the output voltage. The acceleration signal remains constant during the experience. The oscilloscope records the peak of the output voltage while the range of the frequency vary from 0 Hz to 200 Hz, than draw the graph of the output voltage on the excitation frequency changes, shown in Fig. 14. Figure 14 shows the natural frequency of the piezoelectric cantilever vibration energy harvester is 48 Hz and the peak of the output voltage value is 9.23 V when the frequency of the input signal is consistent with the natural frequency while the cantilever is working in resonance case. The theoretical analysis, output response of the simulation and experiment remain the same by comparing Figs. 12 and 14, which can prove the rationality, feasibility and correctness of the theoretical analysis and simulation of the second part of this paper (Fig. 13).

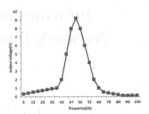

Fig. 12. Energy harvester   **Fig. 13.** Output voltage   **Fig. 14.** Frequency response chart of the output voltage

5 Conclusions

The electromechanical coupling model of the piezoelectric cantilever vibration energy harvester established in this paper is rationality and its mechanical and electrical equation are calculated to get the potential function and output response characteristics of the system. ANSYS is also feasible to simulate the piezoelectric cantilever of its structure and output response characteristics. The experiment proves the correctness of the electromechanical coupling model and the theoretical analysis and the simulation.

Acknowledgement. This research was supported by The National Natural Science Fund (51175395), and Independent innovation fund for graduate students of WHUT (155218002).

References

1. Xiaozhen, D., Jinkui, Z., Xianggao, P.: Study on electricity generating mechanism of micro cantilever. China Mech. Eng. **16**(suppl1), 41–43 (2005)
2. Priya, S., Inman, D.J.: Energy Harvesting Technologies. Dongnan University Press, Nanjing (2010). (in Chinese) (translated by Huang J Q, Huang Q A)
3. Chen, Z.S., Yang, Y.M.: Stochastic resonance mechanism for wideband and low frequency vibration energy harvesting based on piezoelectric cantilever beams. Acta Phys. Sin. **60**(7), 1–7 (2011). (in Chinese). Article ID 074301
4. Shu, S., Shuqian, C.A.O.: Dynamic modeling and analysis of a bistable piezoelectric cantilever power generation system. Acta Phys. Sin. **61**(21), 201505 (2012)
5. Roundy, S., Wright, P.K., Rabaey, J.: A study of low level vibrations as a power source for wireless sensor nodes. Comput. Commun. **26**, 1131–1144 (2003)

Information Propagation Model for Social Network Based on Information Characteristic and Social Status

Lin Liu, Mingchun Zheng$^{(\boxtimes)}$, and Yuqin Xie

School of Management Science and Engineering,
Shandong Normal University, Jinan, Shandong, China
{liulincn8, zhmc163, sdnuxyq}@163.com

Abstract. In this paper, we investigate the propagation process of social public opinion on social network and the influence factors of this process and how do they work. We propose a novel information diffusion model considering the characteristics of information and the social status of network individuals. And we provide an individual choice for diffusion considering the perception of conformity by entropy of information and the perception of blindness by authority. In the process of simulating information propagation, we regulate the influence factors of the diffusion process and find how they work. The simulation experiment results show that: (1) the model can reflect the psychological characteristics of individuals; (2) the related departments need to intervene the diffusion of public opinion on the dangers timely.

Keywords: Social-network · Influence factors · Characteristic of information · Intervention of public opinion

1 Introduction

With the development of internet technology, the network society has become a branch of our real society. The SN (social networks) attract more and more users and became a very important way of usual communication and emotional expression and life service like Facebook, QQ, micro blog and so on [1]. But on these platforms there are some existences we should be vigilant like malicious diffusion, rumor induction, etc. So our study about the process of information diffusion and the mechanism of opinion evolution has important significance for network security, social security and network public opinion monitoring [2].

There are two main kinds of models, the Discrete View Model and the Continuous View Model. Previous proposed many typical models such as Sznzjd model [3] and Galam model [4] which study the mutual influence between the adjacent individuals, the later one has HK model [5] and Deffuant model [6] which consider that the individual only communicates with people who have similar views. And there are other kind, such as CODA model [7] which separate inner psychological activity and external behavior performance. These models have a good description of the process of the evolution of viewpoints but cannot describe the individuals' psychological differences when they accepted different information.

© Springer International Publishing Switzerland 2016
Q. Zu and B. Hu (Eds.): HCC 2016, LNCS 9567, pp. 702–707, 2016.
DOI: 10.1007/978-3-319-31854-7_66

We study the propagation of information in social networks, in view of the above problem, providing an individual communication model based on information characteristic and the individual social status, providing an individual spread behavior strategy. And considering the perception of conformity by entropy of information and the perception of blindness by authority, the model defined a new opinion evolution model. In simulation experiments, we study the influence factors of the information diffusion process and their influence mechanism. Firstly, we construct the topology based on the social network characteristics. Secondly, we provide a new opinion evolution model based on information characteristic. Then we study the information diffusion process in simulation experiments and explain the phenomenon.

2 Network Topology Model

We structure our BA network following the growth and preferential attachment mechanism and referencing Liu Yanhang's method [8]: the individual who just come into the social network would prefer making network connection with the one who has more power. With the grow process will make new connection on the basis of degree with probability of and will make new connection on the basis of recommendation of neighbor node with probability of, that is our call 'friend's friend is friend'. In this paper we make the grow process run twice and the probability to structure a social network topology with 500 nodes on the multi-agent simulation software, the degree distribution is shown in Fig. 1 as following and nearly a power distribution (1.0848, −1.7085).

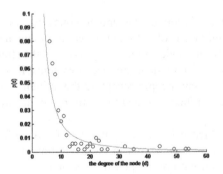

Fig. 1. The degree distribution of the nodes

3 Information Propagation Model

In our model, we simplify the complex social attributes to social status which will decide the thinking and the behavior. According to social experience and the theory of Social Status, we use the number of neighbors to measure one's social status. In our topological network, the degree of node reflects the status using the symbol d.

The normal nodes with small degree pay more attention to the information amusing than the responsibility of diffusion behavior. And the leader nodes are on the contrary, more responsibility and less amusing. According to 2–8 theorem and our experimental statistics, we define reasonably that the nodes with $d < 10$ are ordinary-nodes and the nodes with $10 < d < 30$ are elite-nodes and the nodes with $d > 30$ are leader-nodes. The information characteristic is another critical factor influencing the diffusion behavior. In this paper, we simplify it to the factor *information_amusement* $\in [0, 1]$. How the two factors influence individual diffusion strategy is our working point. The people always have a behavior standard call behavior threshold using symbol s and they will make an action when their viewpoint named v beyond the threshold s. We define the s which is about information characteristic *information_amusement* and social status d.

$$s = random\_normal\left(s_d, \frac{1}{5}\right) \tag{1}$$

$$s_d = \begin{cases} 1 - information\_amusement & d < 10 \\ \dfrac{1 + information\_amusement}{3} & 10 \le d \le 30 \\ \dfrac{2 - information\_amusement}{3} & d > 30 \end{cases} \tag{2}$$

Based on previous studies [10], we provide a new viewpoint evolution model.

$$v = \alpha v' + (1 - \alpha)(\beta Q + (1 - \beta)E) \tag{3}$$

In our model the evolution of viewpoint concerns two aspects, the previous viewpoint v' and the influence of information environment include the overall state influence E and the authority nodes influence Q. The α is the strength of self-confidence expressing what degree the individual influenced by himself or environment. Because of the social nature of human, people accepting the influence of the environment will consider the overall state influence E and the authority nodes influence Q, and the β is the adjustment.

The overall state influence E is a very important factor to forming a viewpoint and can reflect the consistency of viewpoint in the environment. In this paper, we use the conception of information entropy proposed by Shannon.

$$H(X) = -\sum_{i=1}^{n} p(x_i) \log_b p(x_i) \tag{4}$$

(3) is the information entropy, $X = \{x_1, x_2, \ldots, x_n\}$, $p(x_i)$ is the probability of x_i. We know that the information can have two state positive or negative. So

$$H(X) = -p(x_1) \log_2 p(x_1) - p(x_2) \log_2 p(x_2) \tag{5}$$

$p(x_i)$ is the proportion of the positive nodes in neighbors and $p(x_2)$ is about the negative nodes.

$$p(x_1) = \frac{num\_positive}{num\_positive + num\_negative} \qquad (6)$$

$$p(x_2) = \frac{num\_negative}{num\_positive + num\_negative} \qquad (7)$$

And we make the overall state influence E

$$E = \begin{cases} v^+ (1 - H(X)) & num\_positive > num\_negative \\ 0 & num\_positive = num\_negative \\ v^- (1 - H(X)) & num\_positive < num\_negative \end{cases} \qquad (8)$$

v^+ is the mean viewpoint of positive nodes, v^- is the mean viewpoint of negative nodes. We define the authority nodes influence $Q = v_{max-d}$. And now, we got our Network Topology model and Behavior Threshold model and Viewpoint Evolution model.

4   Simulation Experiment and Analysis

We make simulation experiments using our Behavior Threshold model and Viewpoint Evolution model in a 500 nodes BA network structured on the multi-agents simulation software and record the process of information propagation. Repeat the experiment, observe the results and analysis.

4.1   The Influence of Information Characteristic

In our real society there are all kinds of information and the information characteristic can make difference to information propagation. We set different information characteristic *information_amusement* and unified the rest of the parameters. Repeat experiments and record the scope of influence at the 50 tick and the result as shown in Fig. 2.

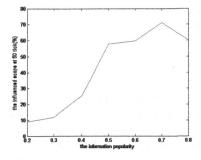

Fig. 2. The influence of information characteristic ($\alpha = 0.5$, $\beta = 0.5$, d of initial node $= 20$)

4.2   The Process of Information Propagation Under Authority Intervention

In our social networks people have great freedom of speech and complex information diffusion behaviors, so there are lots of rumors and not real crisis information flooding the network which can make serious interference to social and economic life. At this point, the government or other authority institutions should monitor the information and make timely intervention to guide the public to improve the recognition of this kind of information.

In simulation experiments, we set that the initial information is the hazard information and the government has a warning line w. The government will screen the information whose scopes have reached the warning line w. Repeat experiments at a set of warning lines $w = 0.1, 0.2, 0.3, 0.4, 0.5$ and the results are shown as following in Fig. 3.

From the experiments above we know that setting an appropriate warning line w is very important for the authority institution to monitor the network. The authority institution can set different monitoring levels based on the process of propagation and harmfulness especially in the case of cost constraints.

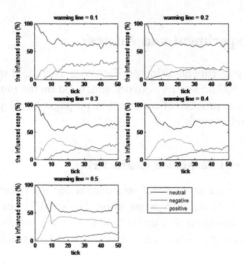

Fig. 3. The process of information propagation ($\alpha = 0.5$, $\beta = 0.5$, d of initial node $= 20$, information_amusement $= 0.5$)

5   Conclusion

In this paper, we proposed a new Information Propagation model which consisted of the Behavior Threshold model and the Viewpoint Evolution mode and we simulated the process of information propagation on our social network topology. We studied the influencing factors of the process and their working mechanism. Specifically, the Behavior Threshold model considered the information characteristic and the social status and the Viewpoint Evolution mode considered the confidence and the sense of conformity and authority. The simulation experiments revealed that: (1) the scope of influence will be wider with higher status of the initial node, higher information popularity. (2) The simulation experiments about the process of information propagation under the authority intervention by setting warming lines can provide a good reference for monitoring network security.

In the future work, we plan to study the influence of network structure by adjusting the connection probability p. And we will study about the dynamic network structure and the dynamic information propagation model and the mutual influence mechanism between them.

Acknowledgment. This paper was supported by: the National Natural Science Foundation of China (No. 61472231), Shandong Provincial Natural Science Foundation of China (No. IR2012MF013), National Social Science Foundation of China (No. 14BTQ049).

References

1. China Internet Network Information Center (CNNIC): The 35th statistical report on the development of Chinese internet (2015)
2. Wang, H., Han, J.-H., Deng, L., Cheng, K.-Q.: Dynamics of rumor spreading in mobile social networks. Acta Physica Sinica **11**, 106–117 (2013)
3. Martins, A.C.R.: Continuous opinions and discrete actions in opinion dynamics problems. Int. J. Mod. Phys. C **19**(04), 617–624 (2011)
4. Sznajd-Weron, K., Sznajd, J.: Opinion evolution in closed community. Hsc Res. Rep. **11**(06), 1157–1165 (2000)
5. Deffuant, G., Neau, D., Amblard, F., et al.: Mixing beliefs among interacting agents. Adv. Complex Syst. **3**(01n04), 87–98 (2011)
6. Holme, P., Kim, B.J.: Growing scale-free networks with tunable clustering. Phys. Rev. E: Stat., Nonlin. Soft Matter Phys. **65**(2Pt2), 95–129 (2002)
7. Martins, A.C.R.: Opinion evolution in closed community. Int. J. Mod. Phys. C **19**(04), 617–624 (2011)
8. Liu, Y.-H., Li, F.-P., Sun, X., Zhu, J.-Q.: Social network model based on the transmission of information. J. Commun. **04**, 1–9 (2013)

Examination Data Analysis and Evaluation Platform Based on Cloud Computing

Quan Li[1](✉), Wenchao Jiang[2](✉), Sui Lin[3], Xigang Gao[1], Aobing Sun[2],
Guohui Luo[3], and Zhiwei Xu[2]

[1] Guangdong Moring Star Technology Co., Ltd., Guangzhou 510530, China
{85711585,76575839}@qq.com
[2] Guangdong Electronics Industry Institute, Dongguan 523808, China
jiangwenchao@gdut.edu.cn, myheart112@sina.com
[3] Computer School, Guangdong University of Technology, Guangzhou 510006, China
425606051@qq.com

Abstract. To increase the efficiency and accuracy of obtaining, storing and analysis of examination data, this paper developed an examination data analysis and evaluation platform based on cloud computing technologies. First of all, the examination data base was constructed based on data OLAP. Then, an examination analysis system was developed according to the application experience from the users. Finally, an education and examination data analysis and evaluation platform was developed based on cloud computing technology. The practical applications from more than 100 cities in 16 provinces showed that this platform can increase the efficiency of the examination data obtaining, storing, analysis, and evaluation for the education management department, school, teacher and student. Currently, this platform has owned more 40 % market share of the education and examination data services in China.

Keywords: Education and examination · Big data · Cloud computing · Analysis and evaluation

1 Introduction

Accurate education evaluation can help the government to make correct decisions during examination and education reform. Based on scientific analysis approaches focused on big amount of examination data, education evaluation can judge whether or not efficient and scientific the education actions, education process, and education results are [1, 2]. The main tasks of education evaluation include student evaluation, teacher evaluation, teaching evaluation, courses evaluation, school evaluation and education policies evaluation etc. [3, 4].

Chinese Ministry of Education has paid high attentions to education evaluation. But, most schools in China still use only scores to evaluate whether the students are excellent or not. Actually, many aspects of data about the students and educations including score, interesting and home background etc. were recorded and stored in data bases in China. However, we never did some works to mine the inner information hiding in the data.

© Springer International Publishing Switzerland 2016
Q. Zu and B. Hu (Eds.): HCC 2016, LNCS 9567, pp. 708–713, 2016.
DOI: 10.1007/978-3-319-31854-7_67

Furthermore, scientific evaluation indicators are still not well defined and advanced information technologies were not utilized.

The development of information technologies, especially the network and database technologies, make it possible that going over examination papers through machine and network [5]. The examination data obtained, collected and stored in database provide great chances to analysis the relations among scores, interesting, behaviors and home background etc. in large scales. Cloud computing technologies make it possible the obtaining, collecting, storing, processing, mining and querying the big data in examination and education area [6].

This paper constructed the examination data base based on data warehouse technology, designed an examination system according to the application experience from the users, developed an education and examination data analysis and evaluation platform based on cloud computing technologies. The practical applications from more than 100 cities in 16 provinces showed that this platform can increase the efficiency and accuracy of the examination data obtaining, storing, analysis, and evaluating for the education management department. Our platform has owned more 40 % market share of the education and examination data services in China.

The remainder of this paper is organized as following. Section 2 presented the platform architecture, and Sect. 3 presented the details of the platform realization. Platform application and conclusion instances are given in Sect. 4.

2   Platform Architecture

Cloud based examination data analysis and evaluation platform architecture was designed as three parts: one data center, two kinds of applications and three sub-systems. The function modules of the whole platform were showed in Fig. 1.

(1) Data center. Data center stored all the examination data collected from all schools in different cities.
(2) Two kinds of applications. One kind of application was called center application which was mainly oriented to data managers. The main tasks of center application include examination database management, data collection and storage, data classification and analysis, report generation etc.
(3) Sub-system. The whole platform was constructed as three sub-systems according to different functions which were separately examination data management system, paper correcting system and evaluation system.

In Fig. 1, IaaS was composed of infrastructure and system software. The function of IaaS was storing and managing the examination data based on distributed technologies such as HDFS. PaaS was composed of data warehouse and all kind of data process tools. Data warehouse was responsible of data format transferring, data mining and evaluation generation engine. SaaS was oriented to different platform users such as education management department, school, teacher, parents and students etc. The main functions of SaaS include information querying, history information analysis, report generation, evaluation mining etc.

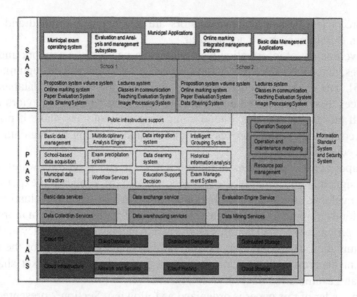

Fig. 1. Function modules of the platform

3 Platform Implementation

3.1 Database Construction

Examination database was constructed based on OLAP as analysis-oriented, and the analysis action was driven only by data. As shown in Fig. 2, OLAP can be described as a multiple dimension graph which was composed of four levels: original data, data warehouse, middle level and presentation level. The original data come from the school examination and feedback information from the students, teachers, parents and education management department etc. The data warehouse stored the data which was classified and cleaned base on ODS technology. The middle level was responsible of the data processing, mining and analysis based on OLAP and WEB technologies. The data querying and indexing was realized in presentation level.

To collect correct data, the answer card must be designed carefully. The data collection process include data scanning, data transferring, data proofread and data storage etc. The answer card was designed using Office Word, and the users can design their own card style according to the different kinds of examination. Anyway, the student ID, pages number, label of absent and the zone of subjective item and objective item must be set. The answer card was scanned into an image and stored in the local database or uploaded to the remote server through FTP protocol. Teachers need only input the RUL of the corresponding examination to correct the papers.

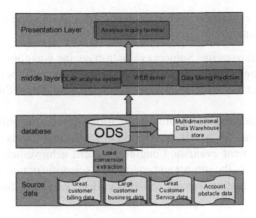

Fig. 2. Education and examination data warehouse

3.2 Multiple Dimension Analysis Model

To evaluate the examination results from different viewpoint, the analysis model was defined into five dimensions, e.g. human viewpoint, material viewpoint, teaching method viewpoint, teaching technology viewpoint and teaching result viewpoint. The different attributes belonging to different viewpoint can also be defined according to the real test need. The users can analysis the teaching effect from different viewpoint according to their examination purpose. The analysis action include Drill-up, Drill-down, Slice, Dice and Pivot. Detailed analysis work-flow was shown in Fig. 3.

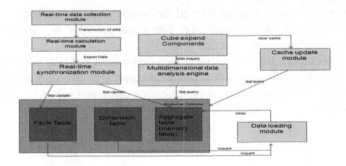

Fig. 3. Multidimensional data analysis

3.3 Evaluation Indicator Defining

Evaluation indicator defining decided whether the evaluation system was scientific or not. The evaluation indicators were classified into two levels. The first level is static indicator which include general statistical analysis of the examination scores, general classification according to scores, ranking of the students etc. The second level of indicator is dynamic indicator which was the deep analysis and evaluation based on the first level indicators. Based on the evaluation indicators, three evaluation engines were constructed: subject evaluation engine, content evaluation engine and student achievement evaluation engine.

(1) Subject evaluation engine. Subject evaluation engine was composed of two dimensions which were ability and content separately. Content dimension can reflect the basic knowledge and basic technique the student can obtain through studying this subject.

(2) Content evaluation engine. Content evaluation engine can define the objective of a subject, and it was the details description of the course standards.

(3) Student achievement evaluation engine. Student achievement evaluation engine was the evidence of the subject and course was scientific or not. Usually, the student achievement evaluation was defined as excellent, good and pass.

3.4   Evaluation Report Generation

Evaluation report was a conclusion report which can help the users to analysis teaching quality, reform the teaching technique, find the insufficient in the teaching process etc. Evaluation report includes student report, teacher report and department report. Taking the education management department as an example shown in Fig. 4, the evaluation report can provide accurate information to allocation of the education resources.

(1) Student report. Student report show the detailed information of the examination for every student. The ranking of each courses, the superiority and the inefficiency, the suggestions etc. were all given in the report. Because our platform were mainly used in China, only Chinese version was developed. One example of the student report was shown in Fig. 4.

(2) Teacher report. Teacher report showed the comparison information of each course from different school, zone and city. The statistical table was given to find the deficiency in the teaching process.

(3) Department report. Here, department included school and education management department. The information of department report was also shown in table format which reflect the comparison among different department respect to certain course or subject.

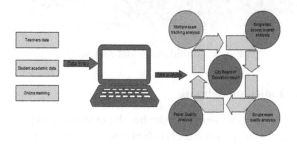

Fig. 4. Services for education managers

4   Conclusion

Based on the data collection in education and examination area, this paper constructed an examination data base based on data warehouse technology, designed an examination analysis system according to the application experience from the users, and developed an analysis and evaluation platform based on cloud computing technologies. The practical applications from more than 100 cities in 16 provinces showed that this platform can increase the efficiency and accuracy of the examination data obtaining, storing, analysis, and evaluation for the users including education management department, schools, teachers and students. Our examination data analysis and evaluation platform has owned more 40 % market share of the education and examination data services in China.

Acknowledgement.   This paper was supported by National Science and technology support program (NO. 2015BAK19B03), Guangzhou Science and technology support program (2014XYD-007). Guangdong Innovative Research Team Program (No. 201001D0104726115).

References

1. Liu, F., Yang, T.-T., Chen, S.-G., Liu, J.-D., Zhang, S.-G., Chen, P., He, J.-T., He, B.-S.: Hierarchical clustering based teaching reform courses examination data analysis approach applied in China Open University System. In: 2014 Seventh International Symposium on Computational Intelligence and Design, pp. 377–381 (2014)
2. Hsu, M.-J., Ho, C.-P.: Creating a knowledge discovery model using MOEX's examination database for in-depth analysis and reporting. In: 2012 IEEE Symposium on Robotics and Applications (ISRA), pp. 705–707 (2012)
3. Saadatdoost, R., Sim, A.T.H., Jafarkarimi, H.: Application of self organizing map for knowledge discovery based in higher education data. In: 2011 International Conference on Research and Innovation in Information Systems (ICRIIS), pp. 1–6 (2011)
4. Sheriff, C.I., Geetha, A.: eLog — teaching and data management system: seemless data capture and analysis of education data. In: 2013 IEEE International Conference on MOOC Innovation and Technology in Education (MITE), pp. 310–314 (2013)
5. Baker, R.S.: Educational data mining: an advance for intelligent systems in education. IEEE Intell. Syst. 29(3), 78–82 (2014)
6. Banumathi, A., Pethalakshmi, A.: A novel approach for upgrading Indian education by using data mining techniques. In: 2012 IEEE International Conference on Technology Enhanced Education (ICTEE), pp. 1–5 (2012)

Linear Magnetostrictive IDM Actuator Based on Composite Cantilever Beam

Quanguo Lu$^{(\boxtimes)}$, Qin Nie, and Yameng Xu

Institute of Micro/Nano Actuation and Control,
Nanchang Institute of Technology, Nanchang 330099, China
Luqg2010@126.com, 1134598717@qq.com

Abstract. According to the weight and vibration of power cable will affect the motion precision unavoidably in the moving process of linear piezoelectric IDM actuator, and the mobile speed and load capacity of linear piezoelectric IDM actuator is not ideal, This article used giant magnetostrictive alloy Terfenol-D as the driving source, researching a novel linear magnetostrictive IDM actuator based on the composite cantilever beam. Combined with 3D modeling software SoildWorks and finite element analysis software COMSOL Multiphysics to process magnetic-structure coupling simulation analysis, and analyzed the reason for the largest deformation position of the composite cantilever beam is not located in the center of symmetry plane but biased towards the counterweight block some distance, from the simulation results, more pieces and small size Terfenol-D slices interval onto the elastic sheet composited the cantilever beam has a very large deformation, so we can know that the magnetostrictive IDM actuator has bigger output force, the load capacity is stronger, and it has a very broad application prospect.

Keywords: Magnetostrictive · IDM · Composite cantilever beam · Terfenol-D · Finite element analysis

1 Introduction

Impact drive mechanism (IDM) actuator is a kind of driving mechanism which working under the action of sawtooth driving signal, and can realize the precise linear displacement by the combination of inertia impact force and friction force [1]. The existing linear IDM actuator generally adopted the piezoelectric materials as driving element [2], has the characteristics of small volume [3], low cost [4], large motion route [5], and has been applied to the precision drive fields preliminary. However, the piezoelectric IDM drive mode is the voltage signal drive. In the movement process of piezoelectric IDM actuator, it needs the power supply cable to provide the electric energy, the weight and the vibration of the power supply cable will have a great influence on the motion accuracy. In addition, the piezoelectric materials exist the problems of small deformation and small output force, which makes the linear piezoelectric IDM actuator is not ideal in the aspects of moving speed and load capacity.

© Springer International Publishing Switzerland 2016
Q. Zu and B. Hu (Eds.): HCC 2016, LNCS 9567, pp. 714–719, 2016.
DOI: 10.1007/978-3-319-31854-7_68

Rare earth giant magnetostrictive material is a new type of functional material, which is driven by magnetic field. As the typical representative of rare earth giant magnetostrictive material, Terfenol-D is a new type of magnetostrictive alloy, the preparation is according to a certain proportion of the rare earth element terbium (Tb), dysprosium (Dy) and metal element iron (Fe), with the characteristics of large strain, high precision, large output force, faster response speed and higher reliability, it is the ideal material for the structure of precision actuator.

In the present actuators which adopt the Terfenol-D as driving source, the magnetic coil is directly contacted with the drive block. The vibration of the power cable will influence the motion precision, so the reliability of the actuators is poor. Aiming at the shortage of the existing technology, this paper aims to provide a new type of linear IDM actuator based on the composite cantilever beam, and can be bidirectional driven and continuously moving, without carrying the power supply cable.

2 Structure Design and Working Principle

2.1 Structure Design

Structure of the linear magnetostrictive IDM actuator includes the coils, barrel, drive block, counterweight block and the cantilever composite beams composed of flexure strip and Terfenol-D. The coil is wound in the peripheral surface of the barrel, and the drive block is arranged inside the barrel body, and the drive block is clearance fit with the barrel. Composite cantilever beam comprises two pieces of flexure strips, and a plurality of Terfenol-D slices, two flexure strips are correspondingly arranged, one end of the composite cantilever beam is fixed on the drive block, and the other end is connected with the counterweight block, Terfenol-D slices are interval pasted in the outer side of the two flexure strips, the maximum magnetostrictive direction of the Terfenol-D slices is consistent with the length direction of composite cantilever beam, the structure of composite cantilever beam is shown in figure below (Figs. 1 and 2).

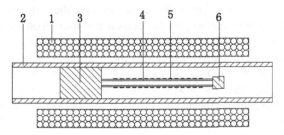

1. Coils 2. Barrel 3. Drive Block 4. Flexure Strip
5. Terfenol-D 6. Counterweight Block

Fig. 1. Vertical cutaway view of linear magnetostrictive IDM actuator

Flexure Strip

Terfenol-D

Fig. 2. Schematic diagram of composite cantilever beam

2.2 Working Principle

Terfenol-D slice stretches along the length direction of the cantilever beam in the magnetic field generated by the electrify coils, driving the cantilever beam to bend, and the bending degree of the cantilever beam increases with the increase of Terfenol-D slice elongation. The Terfenol-D slice restores to the original state after cutting the current off and the magnetic field disappears. The sawtooth wave current is a slow rise and fast drop or fast rise slow drop current signal. As shown in Fig. 3.

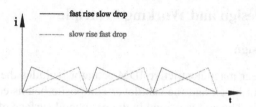

Fig. 3. Schematic diagram of current signal

The driving process of the linear magnetostrictive IDM actuator is shown as below:

(a) Assuming that the coil is connected to a slow rise and fast drop current signal.
(b) With the current signal increases slowly, the Terfenol-D slices elongate slowly, and drive the two flexure strips bending outward slowly and symmetrically, the bending degree of the two flexure strips increases with the elongation increase of Terfenol-D slices, and the elongation of Terfenol-D slices increases with the increase of magnetic field strength, as shown in Fig. 4, flexure strips drive the counterweight block move towards the left slowly, but because the existence of friction on the internal surface of the barrel and drive blocks, so the drive block remains motionless.
(c) When the current gradually increases to the maximum value and then decreases rapidly to zero, Terfenol-D slices quickly became shorter, driving the flexure strips to recover quickly, the counterweight block is rapidly moving to the right. Due to the friction force between the driving block peripheral surface and the cylinder inner peripheral surface is not sufficient to overcome the inertia impact force, the driving block moves a small step towards the left.

When the coil is continuously passed through the slow rise fast drop current signal, the drive block continuously moves towards the left. Based on the same principle, when the coil is connected to a fast rise slow drop current signal, the drive block will move towards the right.

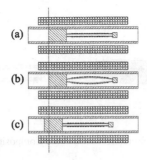

Fig. 4. Working principle diagram of linear magnetostrictive IDM actuator

3   Magnetic-Structure Coupling Simulation Analysis

In order to further research the linear magnetostrictive IDM actuator, in here, the magnetic-structure coupling simulation analysis of the actuator is carried out with the 3D modeling software SoildWorks and the finite element analysis software COMSOL Multiphysics. The three-dimensional structure of the linear magnetostrictive IDM actuator which was modeled by SoildWorks is shown in Fig. 5.

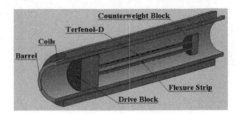

Fig. 5. 3D Structure diagram of linear magnetostrictive IDM actuator

The simulation of magnetic-structure coupling is carried out by combining the Magnetic Fields modules and the Solid Mechanics. The thickness of Terfenol-D is set as 0.2 mm, the plane size of Terfenol-D is set as a square with length as 1 mm, and the gap between two pieces of Terfenol-D is set as 2 mm. The barrel, counterweight block and the flexure strips adopts non-magnetic material. Taking into account the calculation speed of the software and computer memory, the simulation number of Terfenol-D slices is set as 12, the grid division diagram are shown in the following figures (Figs. 6 and 7).

Select reference edge in the coils structure, the current signal is applied to the reference edge. The current is set as 2 A, the turn number is set as 2000. One end of the composite cantilever beam is fixed with the driving block. The simulation results are shown in the following figures. The maximum von Mises stress is 3.3461×10^5 N/m^2, the maximum Magnetic flux density norm is 0.177 T, the average maximum deflection displacement is 8.3501×10^{-4} mm.

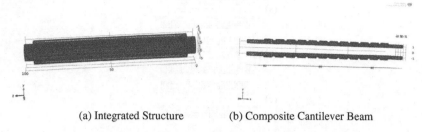

(a) Integrated Structure   (b) Composite Cantilever Beam

Fig. 6. Schematic diagram of grid division

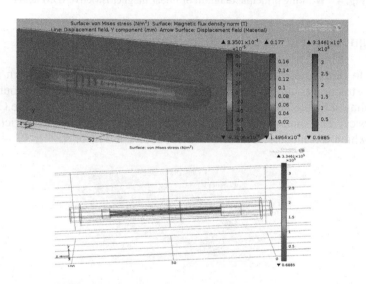

Fig. 7. Schematic diagram of simulation results

As shown above, the maximum deformation location of composite cantilever beam is not located in middle symmetry plane, but biased towards the counterweight block some distance, there may exists two reasons, one reason is that due to the quality of the counterweight block is less than the drive block, so the mass center of composite cantilever beam, the counterweight block and the drive block is not located in the symmetry plane, the other reason is because the boundary displacement conditions of the connecting position between cantilever composite beam and the driving block is set as 0, this constraint transfer effect leads to maximum deformation displacement bias the counterweight block a distance.

In addition, we can see that the deflection displacement of the composite cantilever beam is very large, and the two pieces of composite cantilever beam have been bonded together under the current drive condition of 2000 turn and 2 A. It shows this new type of linear magnetostrictive IDM actuator has a very wide range of application.

4   Conclusion

This article designed a new type of linear magnetostrictive IDM actuator based on composite cantilever beam, using giant magnetostrictive material Terfenol-D as the driving source, through three-dimensional modeling software SoildWorks to build the structure model driver, using the finite element analysis software COMSOL Multiphysics carry out magnetic-structure simulation analysis, we can conclude from the analysis results, the maximum deformation position of the composite cantilever beam is not located in the middle symmetry plane, but bias the counterweight block at a distance, but the deformation is very large, we can infer the output force is very impressive, this new magnetostrictive IDM actuator will has a wide range of application.

Acknowledgements. This work is supported by the National Natural Science Foundation of China (Grant No. 51165035). Science and Technology Fund of Jiangxi Province of Higher Education (KJLD14094), Youth Science Fund of Jiangxi Province (20133BAB21004), and the Young scientist cultivation plan of Jiangxi Province (20112BCB23025).

References

1. Wang, S., Xia, X., Chen, J.: Design and analysis on micro displacement magnifying mechanism with flexible hinges. Hydraulics Pneumatics Seals **1**, 17–20 (2011)
2. Moon, S.-J., Lim, C.-W., Kim, B.-H.: Structural vibration control using linear magnetostrictive actuators. J. Sound Vib. **302**(5), 875–891 (2007)
3. Zheng, B., Chang, C.-J., Gea, H.-C.: Topology optimization of energy harvesting devices using piezoelectric materials. Struct. Multidiscip. Optim. **38**(1), 17–23 (2009)
4. Gong, J., Xu, Y., Ruan, Z.: Simulation on generating capacity for energy harvesting device with piezoelectric bimorph cantilever. J. Vib. Meas. Diagn. **34**(8), 658–663 (2014)
5. Gao, W., Sato, S.J., Arai, Y.: A linear-rotary stage for precision positioning. Precis. Eng. **34**(2), 301–306 (2011)

A Universal Rapid Modeling Method on Virtual Human for Virtual Reality

Taotao Li, Xiongbing Fang[✉], Rui Lin, and Jiejie Chen

Information Technology Research and Development,
China Ship Development and Design Center, Wuhan, China
taotaoliwhut@163.com, cadcs@126.com

Abstract. Aiming to satisfy the various modeling demand for virtual human in virtual reality field, a universal method which is used for virtual human rapid modeling is systematically put forward, combining the advantage of modular and universal modeling method. Based on the analysis result of custom-made marine virtual human modeling demand, one vivid marine virtual human is created through modular modeling method and personalized feature modeling by universal modeling method, validating the characteristic of the advanced universal rapid virtual human modeling method which includes feasibility, high efficiency and universality.

Keywords: Virtual human modeling · Universality · Rapid modeling

1 Introduction

Virtual human is the geometric and behavior characteristics presentation of Realistic agents in the virtual space generated by computers [1, 2]. With the rapid development of computer and virtual reality technology, Virtual human is so widely applied to product animation, interactive virtual reality ergonomic three dimensional movie and other fields in which highly customized and personalized virtual human is eagerly demanded in explosive growth trends [3–5]. Shortcomings such as high modeling challenge long period and rich experience highly needed are shown in traditional modeling method for virtual human, so extensive research has been conducted by the researchers at home and abroad. Dekker et al. carried out the advanced 3D scanning modeling method which can produce virtual human models highly matched to realistic agents. While the fancy price of 3D scanner restricts its extension in virtual human modeling application.

Given the problems above, based on modularized virtual human modeling method and the function powerful virtual human modeling method, one universal and rapid modeling method for virtual human is creatively explored and realized following the leading edge in virtual human modeling technology.

2 Universal Rapid Modeling Method and Process of Virtual Human

The virtual human universal rapid modeling process is mainly constituted by two parts that are the modularized virtual human modeling in the modular modeling method and

© Springer International Publishing Switzerland 2016
Q. Zu and B. Hu (Eds.): HCC 2016, LNCS 9567, pp. 720–725, 2016.
DOI: 10.1007/978-3-319-31854-7_69

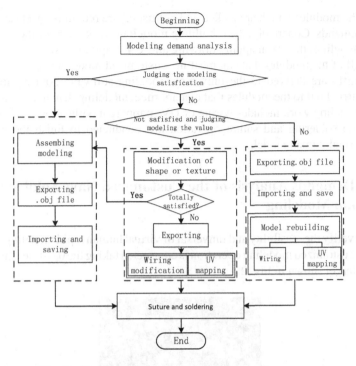

Fig. 1. The block diagram of universal modeling process

personalization characteristic modeling in universal modeling method. The universal modeling method and process are shown in Fig. 1.

Step1: First the demand of customized virtual human modeling is analyzed and then the model database has been traversed to find it that if the modules in the database can meet all of the modeling demands. If the conclusion of the judgment is positive, then the Step2 will be executed, otherwise the Step3 will be executed.

Step2: All of the modules which highly meet the modeling demands are chosen to rapidly assembled to generate the customized virtual human model and then all of the models are derived to the universal VR modeling method.

Step3: All of the modules that can not meet the modeling demands are compared to the customized to judge it that if they have some reference values in the shape or texture aspects. If the conclusion of the judgment is positive, then the Step4 will be executed, and otherwise the Step5 will be executed.

Step4: The modifications in shape or texture are implemented to the modules which is not totally satisfied the modeling demand but useful in texture or shape aspects, judging it that if the modified modules meet the modeling demands. If the conclusion of the judgment is positive, then the Step2 will be executed, otherwise the Step6 will be executed.

Step5: The modules which are lacked and not useful are rebuilt to meet the modeling demands. Concretely, the rebuilding modeling work includes the model shape modeling, the UV mapping drawing and UV mapping vest.

Step6: All of the modules that can meet the customized modeling demands totally or partly are derived to the universal modeling software. And modification is carried out to the modules that can not meet modeling demands totally and the modeling work includes wiring or UV mapping modification.

Step7: The soldering and suture operation are conducted to finish the continuous virtual human model.

3   The Demands Analysis of the Customized Navy Soldier Virtual Human Modeling

Aiming to verify the feasibility and universal of virtual human rapid modeling suggested above, the customized modeling operation is conducted taking the 07-style Chinese navy soldier as target shown in Fig. 2.

Fig. 2.   The customized modeling prototype of Chinese navy soldier

Based on the virtual human modular modeling theory the navy soldier virtual human is divided into modules including head trunk limbs shako coat trousers and boots. Compared to the customized navy virtual human modeling target to analyze and raise the modeling demand in all of the modeling modules. The modeling demand and method of different modules are shown in Table 1.

Table 1.   Navy virtual human modeling requirements analysis table

Item	Judgement	Modeling method
Somato	Matched	Modeling in modular method
Boots	Matched	Modeling in modular method
Shako	Totally not matched	Modeling in universal method
	Not valuable	
Coat Trousers	Shape matched	Modeling in universal and modular method
	Texture not matched	
	Valuable	

4   The Modular Modeling Method of Virtual Human

Modular modeling method is one new modeling theory in virtual human field based on modular modeling technology in which all of the character virtual human parts including body and costume are divided in modular pattern. In the virtual human modeling process in modular modeling method, totally or partly coincident fundamental module model should be searched and chosen from the database closely combining the navy soldier modeling demand shown in Table 1. And all of the modules can be assembled rapidly to generate one preliminary human model which is very similar to the customized navy soldier model. The main modeling steps and process of the preliminary modeling which is highly matched is shown in Fig. 3.

Fig. 3.   The rapid modeling process of virtual human based on modular method

5   The Personalized Character Modeling of Virtual Human Based on Universal Method

In the foundation of realization of virtual human modeling resource transfer, the modeling method of shako coat trousers is researched respectively, according to the navy soldier modeling demand analysis shown in Table 1.

5.1   The Transfer of Virtual Human Resource

To satisfy the application demand in virtual reality and make it comfortable to realize the individual copyreader, the virtual human model should be converted in document format which can be identified in the virtual reality field. The universal modeling method which is universal and widely used in VR field is chosen as the transfer target from modular models.

5.2   Modeling and Mapping of Shako

As is shown in Table 1, appropriate shape and texture cap model do not exist in the modular modeling database, so the shako shape and texture should be created totally in the VR universal modeling software. The modeling process including four steps is shako modeling in shape drawing of UV mapping UV mapping vest and cockade modeling shown in Fig. 4.

Fig. 4. The rebuilding process of shako based on universal modeling method

5.3 The Modeling of Coat and Trousers

The models generated in modular method can fit the shape demand, while its texture goes against to the demand. Thus the wiring modification and UV mapping rebuilding in VR universal software based on the geometric models exported models of coat and trousers is conducted. The armband and badge model should be created solely and merged with the coat model. The final coat and trousers model effect pictures are shown in Fig. 5.

Fig. 5. The scenograph of navy coat and trousers

5.4 The Construction of the Continuous Virtual Human Model

Till now, the modeling work of all modules in the navy soldier including shako coat trousers boots and body models has been done. While the current navy virtual human is one assembled model which is combined by different modules, distinguish to the continuous virtual human. At last the integrative and continuous virtual human navy soldier is created.

Fig. 6. The integrative model in wireframe

Fig. 7. The scenograph of virtual human

As is shown in Fig. 6, the last virtual human model is integrative, indicating that the continuous navy virtual human has been finished after the operation of suture and soldering at the port place between connected two modules. And comparing the Fig. 7 to the Fig. 2, the continuous model is highly lifelike to the modeling target, verifying the universal rapid model method is feasible and universal.

6 Conclusion

(1) Based on the modular virtual human modeling method and the powerfully modeling functional universal modeling method, one universal and rapid modeling method has been put forward to virtual human. As to the normal virtual human modeling method, it can be finished in 2–3 days much shorter than the 15 days current situation. Just as it is shown that the universal rapid modeling method is much efficient and universal, creatively changing the traditional virtual human modeling current situation which is lowly efficient heavy workload and high cost in shortcomings.

(2) Taking the 07-style Chinese navy soldier as modeling target, practical operation is applied as to the three possible conditions in the practical project, finishing the modeling target and comparing the traditional virtual human modeling method, the modeling advantage such as highly efficient, low price is highlighted.

Acknowledgment. This research was supported by China Ship Development and Design Center project. Project number is: China Ship Development and Design Center: YF15-03-47 YFA14-03-41.

References

1. Badler, N.I., Phillips, C.B., Webber, B.L.: Simulating Humans: computer Graphics, Animation, and Control. Oxford University Press, London (1999)
2. Shihong, X., Zhaoqi, W.: The research development of virtual human combination. Sci. Chin. **39**(5), 483–498 (2009)
3. Jinfeng, H., Wei, T., Gang, Z., et al.: Standard for applications of virtual reality in man-machine engineering. Chin. J. Ship Res. (6), 49–53, 60 (2008)
4. Yumei, Z., Xinqi, W., Jun, Z.: Evaluation of overall warship operability and maintainability based on the technology of virtual reality. Chin. J. Ship Res. **2**, 6–12 (2013)
5. Jia, L.: Research on the maintainability verification system of ship based on virtual reality technology. Chin. J. Ship Res. **2**, 70–73 (2008)

Cognitive Radio Enabled Channel Access
for Public Bus Network

Xia Liu[✉], Zhimin Zeng, Caili Guo, and Chunyan Feng

Beijing Key Laboratory of Network System Architecture and Convergence,
Beijing University of Posts and Telecommunications, Beijing, China
{liuxiabupt,zengzm,guocaili,cyfeng}@bupt.edu.cn

Abstract. Public bus network plays a significant role to enable public vehicle communications and allow for the exchange of safety and other types of information. The wireless access in vehicular environments protocol has been standardized over the 5.9 GHz as dedicated short range communications spectrum. Under the wireless access in vehicular environments standard mechanism, public bus nodes are not allowed to use service channels during control channel interval. This causes half of the service channel intervals to remain idle, which makes not sufficient spectrum for reliable exchange of information in public bus network. To alleviate this problem, we propose a system that employs cognitive network principles to increase the spectrum allocated and it outperforms in channel utilization and robust delivery of data. Simulation results confirm that the proposed scheme raised the spectrum utilization by 50 % compared to the performance under the wireless access in vehicular environments standard, which improves reliability for data transmission.

Keywords: Public bus network · Cognitive radio · Channel access

1 Introduction

Intelligent transportation system (ITS) as an optimum way to improve public traffic efficiency and safety has enjoyed a tremendous growth in the last decade. A huge amount of applications (e.g., vehicular traffic collision warning, traffic condition prediction, automatic charging) have been implemented with the increase of people's demand to the safe, efficient and green way to traffic in public transportation [1]. Public bus network turns to the key supported technologies of the intelligent public transport system [2]. Public bus network is composed by public buses and hence it is a distributed network that does not rely on a central administration for communication among buses and between buses and fixed road infrastructure. In order to guarantee the vehicular communication, Federal Communication Commission (FCC) allocated 75 MHz at 5.9 GHz frequencies as DSRC (dedicated Short Range Communications) spectrum to be used exclusively for vehicle to vehicle and vehicle to infrastructure communications. Under the WAVE (wireless access in vehicular environments) standard [3], the operating spectrum is divided into seven channels with a 10 MHz bandwidth to each one, including six service channels (SCHs) and one control channel (CCH). CCH serves as transmitting

© Springer International Publishing Switzerland 2016
Q. Zu and B. Hu (Eds.): HCC 2016, LNCS 9567, pp. 726–731, 2016.
DOI: 10.1007/978-3-319-31854-7_70

management and safety messages while all data transmission is supposed to be handled by SCHs. The WAVE standard for vehicular communication defines the sync interval with default length of 100 ms which constitutes of 50 ms control channel interval and 50 ms service channel interval. Recent researches have confirmed that the control channel can encounter large data contention [4] through the studying of packet reception rate and safety message access delay while the SCHs remain underutilized for half of each sync interval.

Several protocols have been proposed based on the WAVE standard to improve the performance in vehicular network. The extended SCH interval scheme has been proposed in [5] to improve the reliability of safety applications in throughput and end to end delay. Vehicular network based on cognitive radio (CR) have been investigated in some preliminary works [6–8]. CR based architecture is proposed to solve the afore-mentioned possible spectrum resource starvation in vehicular network. However the demand of different applications will become prominent in public bus network. Large amount of channel access requested would generate along with the number of passengers on a bus [9]. In addition to the channel access conflicts caused by buses gathered in the same site. There are high requirements in end-to-end delay, packet dropped ratio and fairness of the channel access for safety applications in public bus network. Therefore, reliable transmission and congestion control are very important in public bus network though the requirements for buses and passengers applications (web search, online games, etc.).

This paper presents a system that represents a cognitive public bus network to face spectrum scarcity for public bus communication in urban areas. The rest of this paper is organized as follows. Simulation confirmed that the proposed cognitive public bus network raises the spectrum utilization by 50 % compared to the network based on WAVE and improves the reliability for data transmission.

2 Cognitive-Public Bus Network Architecture

Public bus network mainly realize the vehicle-to-vehicle and vehicle-to-road side unit (RSU) communication. As shown in Fig. 1, RSUs as a road infrastructure would be laid along the bus stops, such as public transport management center. At the same time, public bus network affords internet services for passengers as well as providing safety applications. Public bus network is generally different from vehicular network in the following aspects. Under the complex urban or suburban wireless environment, it was influenced by many factors, such as buildings, crossroads, traffic lights, etc. The nodes (public buses) in public bus network send data by the pre-scheduled repetitive paths. In addition, the nodes are easy to master all the RSUs information and to predict other nodes paths.

Different with the user applications in traditional vehicular network, there are a large number of passengers on a bus. It means that a bus might be subjected to multiple requests at any time. In order to guarantee the communication of bus, our system imple-ments a cognitive network to offer bus on the road spectrum from the 5.8 GHz ISM band that is underused. We describe the notion of cognitive radio public bus network

(CRPBN) deals with a changing spectrum environment while protecting the transmission of the primary users. For the sake of adapting to dynamic spectrum environment, the CRPBN use energy detection algorithm to identify spectrum hole and switch to the underused band for data transmission between cog-buses when the dedicated spectrum is not enough. The application of cognitive radio in public bus network is enabled by the physical layer described in IEEE 802.11p. The physical layer modulation scheme is based on orthogonal frequency division multiplexing (OFDM). The signal bandwidth is reduces to 10 MHz, and the sub-carrier interval decreased to 156.25 kHz in order to against inter-symbol interference and the Doppler spread effect.

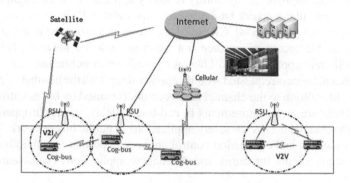

Fig. 1. Proposed system topology

3   Proposed Cognitive-Public Bus Network Mac Protocol

The proposed cognitive radio-enabled multi-channel access protocol (CRMA) is adopted for the cog-public bus network in the 5.9 GHz dedicated band. The primary users (PUs) are the providers with safety-related messages for emergency or police cars, while the public buses with non-safety information as second users. The primary provider has persistent opportunity to deliver its data until terminate. This means that the PUs have outstanding priority in channel negotiation. The cognitive public buses will only be able to transmit data if there exists spectrum holes in the dedicated band. Based on the proposed CRMA protocol for the cog-public bus network, the emergency or police cars can transmit its data for more than one sync interval in order to guarantee the safety-related messages transmission. As Fig. 2 shows, this scheme leaves conduct channel sensing and contention within the CCH intervals. The public bus in this scheme as the secondary providers will sense the channel within CCH intervals to find the appropriate CCH for data transmission dynamically.

When the 5.9 GHz dedicated band was completely occupied by vehicles, the proposed cognitive radio-enabled access enhanced protocol (CRAE) is adopted for the cog-public bus network. The cog-public bus will turn to detect the 5.8 GHz band white space for data transmission between public buses. At this time, the primary users become the authorized user in 5.8 GHz. Figure 3 shows the examples to explain the operations of the proposed CRAE protocol for cog-public bus network. It is noted that the data transmission are intense competitive within the six SCHs. Assuming that the public bus provide fail in the channel contention while the other vehicles win, the pair of public bus will not be allowed to switch to any of six SCHs during the SCH interval to conduct data transmission. Based on the design of proposed CRAE protocol, the public bus failed to transfer with in dedicated bands will turn to detect spectrum holes at 5.8 GHz band taking advantage of energy detection algorithm. If there are remain bands at 5.8 GHz frequencies, the pair of public buses will turn to it for communication.

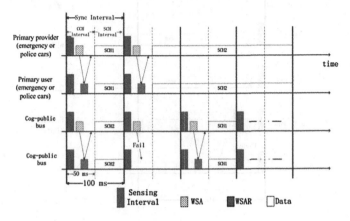

Fig. 2. CRMA scheme for cog-public bus network

4 Performance Evaluation

The performance of the proposed CRMA and CRAE schemes was carried out through simulation and results were compared with the WAVE protocol. The parameters defined in the WAVE are adopted in the simulations. The sync interval, CCH interval and SCH interval respectively are 50 ms, 50 ms. The number of CCH is defined one and the number of SCHs is six. Figure 4 illustrates the ratio of spectrum utilization with the proposed CRMA and CRAE schemes compared with cog-public bus network and WAVE based public bus network. The arrival rate is assumed for both primary and secondary providers. Due to the application of cognitive radio technology, public bus network protocol could use the 5.9 GHz dedicated spectrum dynamically. And the cog-public bus network makes it possible to use the spectrum holes at 5.8 GHz ISM band with continuously occupy one channel to communicate until data transmission completion. Therefore, the spectrum efficiency compared with no cognitive radio technology can improve at least 50 %. The enhanced ratio of channel utilization from CRAM and CRAE scheme is shown in the curves with circles in Fig. 4. And Fig. 5 illustrates the packet lose rare, with the increase of the arrival rate, packet loss rate has a trend to decline. Due to the emergency communication increase in the number of packages sent per unit time, the packet loss rate decline.

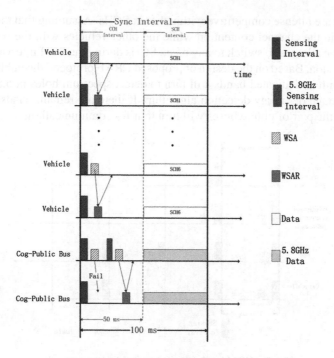

Fig. 3. CRAE scheme for cog-public bus network

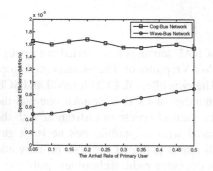

Fig. 4. Spectral efficiency

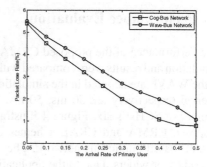

Fig. 5. Packet lose rare

5   Conclusion

In this paper, the CRPBN system is proposed to improve the quality of the transmission for public bus network. As cognitive radio-enabled access protocol CRMA and CRAE protocols are proposed to enhance the channel utilization of WAVE standard for public bus communication. Based on the analysis for cognitive radio-enabled public bus network, the proposed scheme can be further increase the spectrum utilization and improve public bus network reliability by opportunistically using spectrum.

Acknowledgements. This work was supported in part by the Chinese National Nature Science Foundation under Grant 61571062, the Fundamental Research Funds for the Central Universities under Grant 2014ZD03-01, and Beijing Higher Education Young Elite Teacher Project under Grant 96254006.

References

1. Alsabaan, M., Alasmary, W., Albasir, A., Naik, K.: Vehicular networks for a greener environment: a survey. IEEE Commun. Surv. Tutor. **3**, 1372–1388 (2013)
2. Acer, U., Giaccone, P., Hay, D., Neglia, G., Tarapiah, S.: Timely data delivery in a realistic public bus network. Trans. Veh. Tech. **61**, 1251–1265 (2012)
3. IEEE trial-use standard for wireless access in vehicular environments (wave) - multi-channel operation, IEEE Std 1609.4-2006
4. Wang, Z., Hassan, M.: How much of DSRC is available for non-safety use? In: 5th ACM International Workshop on Vehicular Internetworking, pp. 23–29. ACM Press, (2008)
5. Wang, S.Y., Chou, C.L., Liu, K.C., Ho, T.W., Hung, W.J., Huang, C.F., Hsu, M.S., Chen, H.Y., Lin, C.C.: Improving the channel utilization of ieee 802.11p/1609 networks. In: Wireless Communications and Networking Conference (WCNC), pp. 1–6. IEEE Press, Budapest (2009)
6. Al-Ali, A., Chowdhury, K., Felice, M.D., Paavola, J.: Querying spectrum databases and improved sensing for vehicular cognitive radio networks. In: IEEE International Conference on Communications (ICC), pp. 1379–1384. IEEE Press, Sydney (2014)
7. Li, H., Irick, D.K.: Collaborative spectrum sensing in cognitive radio vehicular ad hoc networks: belief propagation on highway. In: 71st of IEEE Vehicular Technology Conference (VTC), pp. 1–5. IEEE Press, Taiwan (2010)
8. Doost-Mohammady, R., Chowdhury, K.R.: Design of spectrum database assisted cognitive radio vehicular networks. In: 7th International ICST Conference on Cognitive Radio Oriented Wireless Networks and Communications (CROWNCOM), pp. 1–5. IEEE Press, Stockholm (2012)
9. Acer, U., Giaccone, P., Hay, D., Neglia, G., Tarapiah, S.: Timely data delivery in a realistic bus network. In: 2011 Proceedings INFOCOM, pp. 1251–1265. IEEE Press, Shanghai (2012)

An Improved Registration Mechanism
for Network Mobility

Xuejun Ma[✉] and Shufen Liu

College of Computer Science and Technology, Jilin University, Changchun, China
jlmxj08@163.com, liusf@jlu.edu.cn

Abstract. Network Mobility is mainly to solve the mobility problems of the whole local area network, which is composed of a number of network nodes. When the number of Mobile Nodes is huge, part of Mobile Nodes could not communicate because the Mobile Node Prefixes carried by the Request extension are limited. New TLV is proposed to extend the Request extension and the Acknowledgement extension, the former represents a batch of Mobile Node Prefixes that the Mobile Router registered to the Home Agent, the latter represents a batch of Mobile Node Prefixes that the Home Agent replied to the Mobile Router. The Mobile Router batch encapsulation and registration request mechanism to the Home Agent is proposed. Simulation results show that the application of our method, the Mobile Router can make Mobile Node Prefixes batch encapsulated and registered to the Home Agent, all Mobile Nodes can be in mobile communication.

Keywords: Network Mobility · Mobile Node · Mobile Router · Home Agent · New TLV

1 Introduction

The Mobile IP protocol supports host mobility, but with the development of various wireless and mobile technologies today, the movement of the army, planes, ships, the provision of Internet access from these mobile platforms, making it necessary to also support the mobility of complete networks. In order to meet this demand, the Internet Engineering Task Force (IETF) has developed the Network Mobility (NEMO) Basic Support Protocol, it providing continuous network connectivity to a group of hosts moving together, enabling network mobility [1–4].

Mobile IPv4 is a communication protocol that the Mobile Node moves from one network to another, the Mobile Node does not perceive movement process, its IP address unchanged at a fixed IP address [5]. NEMO is an extension of Mobile IPv4. NEMO sends Request extension through Mobile Router to the Home Agent, the Home Agent replies Acknowledgement extension to the Mobile Router, and then establish a tunnel between the Mobile Router and the Home Agent for Mobile Nodes through the Home Agent communication [6]. Architecture overview of NEMO and the tunnel in NEMO is shown in Fig. 1.

© Springer International Publishing Switzerland 2016
Q. Zu and B. Hu (Eds.): HCC 2016, LNCS 9567, pp. 732–738, 2016.
DOI: 10.1007/978-3-319-31854-7_71

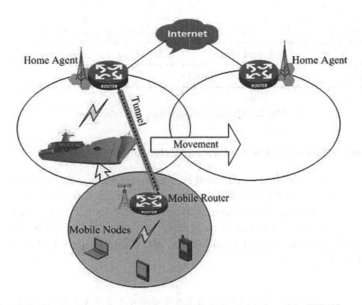

Fig. 1. Architecture overview of NEMO and the tunnel in NEMO

When the Mobile Router sends Request extension to the Home Agent, the Mobile Node Prefix list is carried by the Request extension. If the number of prefixes is huge, the Request extension cannot carry the whole prefixes, leads part of Mobile Nodes cannot communicate through the Home Agent. Require creating batch encapsulation and registration request mechanism between the Mobile Router and the Home Agent, so that Mobile Router can carry the complete Mobile Node Prefixes when sending Request extension to the Home Agent.

2   The Related Technologies

Mobile IPv4 has no solution for explicit registration of the Mobile Networks served by the Mobile Router. The Mobile Router uses the mobile network extensions to claim certain Mobile Network Prefixes are authorized to the Home Agent. Here, we will introduce the mobile network extensions in detail.

2.1   Mobile Network Request Extension

When registration, the Mobile Network Request is sent to the Home Agent from the Mobile Router, it includes the Mobile Network Prefixes which need to be registered. When several Mobile Networks need to be registered, each is included in a separate Mobile Network Request extension, with its own Type, Length, Sub-Type, Prefix Length, and Prefix. The format is shown in Fig. 2.

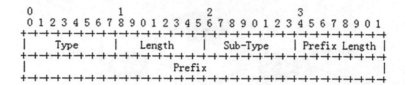

Fig. 2. Mobile Network Request extension

2.2 Mobile Network Acknowledgement Extension

The Mobile Network Acknowledgement is sent to the Mobile Router from the Home Agent, it includes the prefixes which the Home Agent accept forwarding from the corresponding Mobile Router. When several Mobile Networks need to be acknowledged explicitly, each is included in a separate Mobile Network Acknowledgement extension, with its own Type, Sub-Type, Length, Prefix, and Prefix Length fields. The format is shown in Fig. 3.

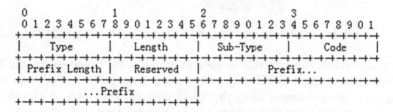

Fig. 3. Mobile Network Acknowledgement extension

As mentioned above, the disadvantage of the existing technologies is that when the number of Mobile Node Prefixes is huge, the encapsulation cache of the Mobile Router is fixed, thus limits the Mobile Router to send a complete list of Mobile Node Prefixes. There must be a part of the Mobile Node prefixes cannot be encapsulated into the Request extension, caused the un-encapsulated Mobile Nodes cannot communicate by the Home Agent. When the number of Mobile Node Prefixes is large, it will also result in Mobile Router instant memory waste.

3   The Improved Registration Mechanism for Network Mobility

An improved registration mechanism is proposed between the Mobile Router and the Home Agent: the Mobile Router batch encapsulating the Mobile Node Prefixes and sends the Request extension to the Home Agent, the Home Agent batch processing the Request extension of the Mobile Router. This makes the Mobile Router can send a complete list of Mobile Node Prefixes, reach to all Mobile Node Prefixes registered and kept alive, so that all Mobile Nodes can be in mobile communication via the Home Agent.

3.1   New TLV

Batch encapsulations are distinguished by the New TLV (Type-New, Length-New, Value-New), it is carried in the Request extension and the Acknowledgement extension. The New TLV is generated by the Mobile Router, of which the Type-New is 254, Length-New is 4, Value-New is the data of 4 bytes. Each Value-New represents a batch of registered data. The format is shown in Fig. 4.

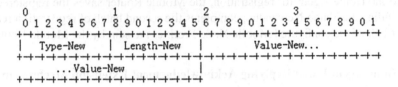

Fig. 4. New TLV

After adding the New TLV, the Request extension and Acknowledgement extension have the corresponding changes, the format is shown in Figs. 5 and 6.

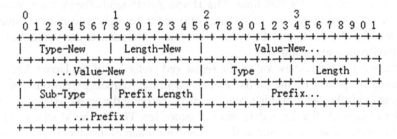

Fig. 5. New TLV Request extension

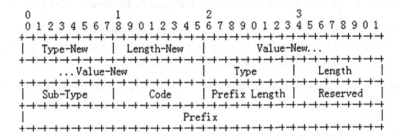

Fig. 6. New TLV Acknowledgement extension

3.2   Mobile Router Batch Sending Request Extension Mechanism

When the Mobile Router meets the requirements of sending the Request extension to the Home Agent, the Mobile Router traverses the configured Mobile Node Prefixes.

1. Encapsulates the New TLV Request extension. The Value-New value is generated by the Mobile Router of a 4 bytes data, and each generated value is not the same. Mobile Router sends the Request extension carrying the New TLV to the Home Agent, the Mobile Router saves the registration data including the Value-New value, completes a batch of registration request.
2. If there arc still un-encapsulated Mobile Node Prefixes, the Mobile Router generates a new Value-New value, encapsulates the New TLV Request extension and sends it to the Home Agent for registration, the Mobile Router saves the registered data including the Value-New value, completes the second batch of registration request.
3. Until all of the configured Mobile Node Prefixes are sent by the Mobile Router.

3.3 Home Agent Batch Replying Acknowledgement Extension Mechanism

The Home Agent receives the Request extension sent by the Mobile Router, parsing the New TLV in the Request extension, to find if its own internal recorded the Value-New value of the registration data of this Mobile Router.

1. If there is no Value-New value, records the prefix list and Value-New value that is allowed to register for this time. The Home Agent sends the Acknowledgement extension carrying the prefix list that is allowed to be registered and the same New TLV to the Mobile Router, the Value-New value is the same as the Value-New value of the Request extension.
2. If there is the Value-New value, the registered prefix list of the Home Agent local records is updated by the prefix list carried in the Request extension. The Home Agent sends the Acknowledgement extension carrying the prefix list that is allowed to be registered after the update and the same New TLV to the Mobile Router, the Value-New value is the same as the Value-New value of the Request extension.

3.4 Mobile Router Response the Acknowledgement Extension Mechanism

The Mobile Router receives the Acknowledgement extension from the Home Agent, parsing the New TLV in the Acknowledgement extension, and judging whether the Value-New value is in the saved sending Value-New list.

1. If there is the Value-New value, parsing the prefix list carried by the Acknowledgement extension, updates the local registered prefix list of the corresponding Value-New value.
2. If there is no Value-New value, then do nothing.

4   Evaluation

In accordance with the batch encapsulation and registration thought and method above, the simulation system is constructed and simulated by using multiple computers under the laboratory environment, and complete the required function evaluation and performance analysis.

The structure of the message is the base head + prefix list + authentication extension. Which, the base head occupies 24 bytes; the authentication extension using the MD5-Hash authentication, occupies 22 bytes. In the test, the buffer is 1024 bytes, and has 512 prefixes, each of which takes 8 bytes.

4.1 The Existing Registration Process

Using the existing technology, only 122 Mobile Nodes in the simulation process can be in mobile communications via the Home Agent.

The prefix list stored in the buffer can take up $1024 - 24 - 22 = 978$ bytes. Each prefix occupies 8 bytes, it can send $978/8 = 122$ prefixes. Each registration will cover the previous, sends the same prefix list, leading to $512 - 122 = 390$ prefixes not registered. The registration request process is shown in Fig. 7.

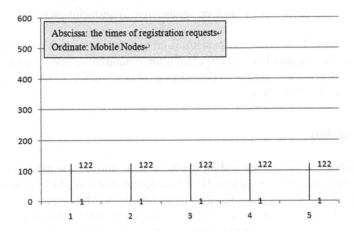

Fig. 7. The existing registration process

4.2 The Improved New TLV Batch Encapsulation and Registration

Using the New TLV batch encapsulation and registration request mechanism, the configuration of all Mobile Nodes in the simulation process can be in mobile communications through the Home Agent.

Because the new TLV takes 6 bytes, so the prefix list stored in the buffer can take up $1024 - 24 - 22 - 6 = 972$ bytes. The sending prefix is still 8 bytes, it can send $972/8 = 121$ prefixes. After the addition of the New TLV, each Value-New value represents a batch of registration, although the buffer is only 1024, but all prefixes can be registered to the Home Agent after 5 times of registration. The first 4 times to carry the same number of prefixes, the last time to register with only $512 - 121*4 = 28$ prefixes, but the parsing process is the same. The registration request process is shown in Fig. 8.

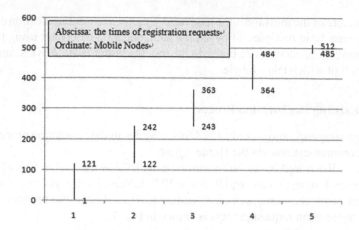

Fig. 8. New TLV batch encapsulation and registration process

Using the New TLV batch encapsulation and registration request mechanism, when the Mobile Router encapsulates message that is only required for once, the encapsulation and registration process is similar to the existing registration process, the cost is to send 6 bytes more of the New TLV.

5   Conclusion

The registration mechanism of adding the New TLV into the Request extension and Acknowledgement extension, enable the Mobile Router can make Mobile Node Prefixes batch encapsulated and registered to the Home Agent, the Mobile Router not only can send a complete list of Mobile Node Prefixes, make all Mobile Nodes through the Home Agent communication, but also reduce the instant memory cost of the encapsulation.

References

1. Devarapalli, V., Wakikawa, R., Petrescu, A., Thubert, P.: Network Mobility (NEMO) Basic Support Protocol, January 2005
2. Bernardos, C.J., Soto, I., Calderón, M.: Internet Protoc. J. **10**(2), 16–27 (2007)
3. Ryu, S., Park, K.-J., Choi, J.-W.: Enhanced fast handover for network mobility in intelligent transportation systems. IEEE Trans. Veh. Technol. **63**(1) (2014)
4. Humayun Kabir, Md., Mukhtaruzzaman, M., Atiquzzaman, M.: Efficient route optimization scheme for nested-NEMO. J. Netw. Comput. Appl. **36**, 1039–1049 (2013)
5. Postel, J.: Internet Protocol, September 1981
6. Droms, R.: Dynamic Host Configuration Protocol, March 1997
7. Droms, R., Bound, J., Volz, B., Lemon, T., Perkins, C.E., Carney, M.: Dynamic Host Configuration Protocol for IPv6 (DHCPv6), July 2003
8. Stallings, W.: Mobile IP, The Internet Protoc. J. **4**(2) (2001)
9. Perkins, C.E.: IP Mobility Support for IPv4, August 2002

The Study of Cross Networks Alarm Correlation
Based on Big Data Technology

Yi Man[1(✉)], Zhipeng Chen[2], Jianbin Chuan[1], Mei Song[1],
Ningning Liu[3], and Yanning Liu[4]

[1] School of Electronic Engineering, Beijing University of Posts and Telecommunications,
Beijing 100876, China
manyi@bupt.edu.cn, cjb1990524@163.com
[2] BOCO Inter-Telecom, Beijing 100093, China
Chenzhipeng@boco.com.cn
[3] Neusoft, Shenyang 110179, China
[4] Tianjin University, Tianjin, China

Abstract. Cross network alarm correlation is an important basis for fault root
cause analysis. Based on big data association analysis algorithm, this paper puts
forward a new analysis method of cross network of the network element (NE)
alarm correlation. Meanwhile, in order to overcome the disadvantages of previous
alarm correlation which is based on topology and rules, a kind of correlation
strategy of pan NE relation is put forward. The validity of the new method of
alarm correlation analysis is verified by the test of the actual data coming from
operator.

Keywords: Big data · Alarm correlation · Cross network · OSS

1 Introduction

In network management system, the number of alarms in devices is extremely huge, in
fact, the number of network failures hidden in these alarms is much less, so it is a very
meaningful topic to reduce the amount of alarms on which we must focus attention.
Operators currently through the artificial summary of a number of rules can further
reduce the number of alarms, but there are many subjective factors in manual way to
produce the omission, deviation and other issues.

In the research field, some alarm correlation analysis methods, which come from
different computer fields, such as artificial intelligence, graph theory, neural networks,
information theory and automatic control theory, have been proposed. The most
common method is rule based reasoning, fault propagation model, encoding, Bayesian
network and so on. For examples, An OPTICS clustering method [1] is presented to
divide the time cluster in the timeline of alarm, and then the correlation analysis of time
cluster is carried out by using APR correlation analysis. A method of alarm correlation
analysis [2, 3] is presented based on the entity relationship model, but it is a complex
and arduous process of building up a professional knowledge model in this method. In
order to improve the processing efficiency, an improved FP-growth algorithm [4] is

© Springer International Publishing Switzerland 2016
Q. Zu and B. Hu (Eds.): HCC 2016, LNCS 9567, pp. 739–745, 2016.
DOI: 10.1007/978-3-319-31854-7_72

presented which is applied in alarm correlation analysis and data mining. An implemented architecture [5, 6] is presented according to correlation judgment mechanism based on rule model and alarm correlation analysis based on rule engine. A resolution based on artificial neural network [7] is presented to promote the performance of identifying fault in an SDH-based environment. In conclusion, the method based on rule or entity relationship needs to establish a complex knowledge system in advance, which is not realistic in the new field of management, such as the 4G management in which operators have not a lot of experience. Because of computational constraints or business problems, the algorithm based on the data mining do not involve cross NE, cross network alarm correlation analysis.

2   Cross Network Alarm Correlation Analysis Based on Pan NE Relation

2.1   Method Improvement

Based on network topology of NE, the traditional process approach is formed multi NE relationship set in advance, and then superimposed time relationship on the partition NE space so as to carry out the shopping basket model based on alarm clustering. Finally, the correlation analysis is carried out by using correlation analysis model. But the relationship between the NE is divided into many levels. Obviously, topological relation is not the only factor affected the network faults, but only one of them. Furthermore, there is no unified management for other NE relationship in the network management system in the present, not even appeared in the existing IT system. So any default rules will limit the completeness of cross NE alarm correlation analysis. And that is to say, the best rule is no rule, applying with data of its own rules to describe among NE alarm topology is a pan element relation.

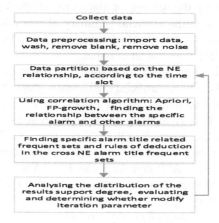

Fig. 1. The process of the alarm correlation analysis

In Fig. 1, the transformation of traditional data mining process is mainly in the third step: Data preparation, Instead of using the preset conditions defined cross NE set, but the way of combination of any NE, this method will produce large number of pending analysis NE. However, due to the use of large data processing technology, the performance of the operator's current alarm correlation problem scale is able to meet the needs of the requirements.

2.2 Selection of Algorithm

Apriori algorithm gets the results through multiple iterations and can be characterized as building K maximum frequent sets, scanning the database for k + 1 times, taking up less memory, and finishing statistical process through the IO. Therefore, Apriori algorithm is running slowly in most of the cases. FP-growth algorithm only scans the database two times, but the FP tree must be compressed into memory, and thus it takes a lot of memory, so it generally uses distributed mode to run fast, however, in the case of sparse data set, FP-growth algorithm is often less efficient than Apriori because the generation of FP tree is much more luxuriant. But this situation does not exist in the alarm correlation analysis. In practice, the two algorithms have been applied, and the advantages of FP-growth algorithm in speed is for all to see.

In the implementation of the algorithm, the single version and the parallel distributed version are both used. Mahout is an open source and scalable machine learning software library of Apache that is designed to be a parallel machine learning tool when the data size is far greater than the single processing capability. In this alarm correlation analysis, we use mahout to implement the FP-Growth algorithm in an efficient and scalable way, and in order to solve the problem of insufficient memory for single processor, the algorithm is converted to the HDFS based on Hadoop or YARN for large-scale data processing. The required data type of Mahout is no longer a complete nominal type of data, it can be a numerical attribute.

2.3 Algorithm Practice

The required alarm data fields for analysis are shown in Table 1.

Table 1. Alarm analysis data structure

Event time	Cancel time	NE type	Severity class	Alarm title	NE label	Sub alarm type	Service influence

Experimental data is the full network alarm data of 1 province of China Mobile. The total number of alarm data for 2 month is 50424759, including 1211624 NE. Segmenting the data by combining 10 min fixed time slot with 2 min sliding window strategy, the results are obtained for 3551197 alarm title frequent sets (min support degree 0.1) in Table 2.

Table 2. The example for alarm frequent sets of multi NE

Id	Level	Num	Confidence	Sets
11744	3	8657	0.985542	0. Alarm when the times of attempting to log in reaches the max
				−78087178.PDH 2M Physical interface loss of signal (LOS)
				1698491989.PDH 2M Physical interface loss of signal (LOS)
36287	3	8055	0.917008	671279061. Synchronized loss
				−1696050529.BTS-EXTERNAL [9] EXT-ALARM (Default) [9]
				0. Alarm when the times of attempting to log in reaches the max
28022	4	8053	0.916781	−151098320.PWE3-CES Alarm of the client signal's failure (CSF)
				671279061. Synchronized loss
				0. Alarm when the times of attempting to log in reaches the max
				0. The interrupt of Network cell's connection

Analysis of the results, we can draw out the distribution map of the support degree which shown in Fig. 2.

1. The median is a digital feature that describes the location of the data center, and the median of support degree is 0.16, thus it is to say, nearly half of the data's support degree is concentrated in 0.1–0.16;
2. The median and mean number are different, so the data is skewed distribution;
3. Support degree > 0.5, the distribution of frequency is relatively dense, and the stability of data is low.

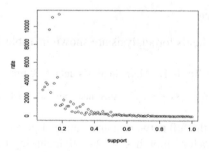

Fig. 2. The distribution map of the support degree

The data point begin to be dense when the support degree is about 0.5 at the scattered point diagram above. In view of 0.5 is an intermediate value, then we select support degree = 0.5 as the key value.

Operating speed of different algorithm in different environment is shown in Table 3. We can clearly see the advantages of the distributed algorithm.

Table 3. Operating speed of different algorithm in different environment

Method	Hardware	Task	Time
FP-growth distributed algorithm	4 nodes PC server cluster	Correlation mining for 8000 NEs	4 h
FP-growth distributed algorithm	143 nodes PC server cluster	Correlation mining for 8000 NEs	20 min
APR single point algorithm	1 node, mem: 128 M, CPU: 32 cores	Correlation mining for 8000 NEs	Unable to complete

3 Analysis System Structure

The method of alarm correlation analysis of cross network in this paper is applied to the design and implementation of network alarm data mining system, the overall architecture of this system is shown in Fig. 3:

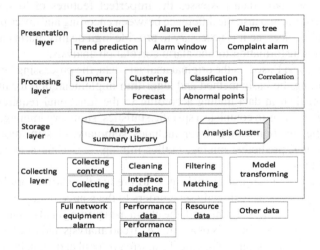

Fig. 3. General architecture of network alarm data mining

Network alarm data mining includes data collecting layer, storage layer, processing layer, presentation layer, and thus it's a typical full architecture of data analysis system based on big data processing technology.

Data source: Data analysis and mining, which is based on alarm data, mainly involved in the main data types of network maintenance management, the full network alarm data including equipment alarm, performance alarm data. Note that the full network data includes voice traffic, flow data, transmission, etc. Performance alarm is generated by real-time monitoring system according to certain rules. Also it needs to access the user's complaint data so as to proceed the correlation analysis of alarm and user's complaint. Obviously, analysis of alarm and performance data is inseparable from the NE resource allocation information, so it is necessary to access to NE configuration information from integrated resource management system. Considering completeness and accuracy, we also need some other type information data which is based on the data mining of business analysis. The above information belongs to the acquisition data at the same segment of time which required by the same subject of analysis and data mining.

Collecting layer: The collecting layer is responsible for collecting the raw data from source system one by one, and also transforming the raw data to the data type model required by the algorithm. The main functions of this layer include interface adapting, collecting, filtering, cleaning, matching, model transforming. And also it is need to have a unified control capability of collection.

Storage layer: The storage layer is responsible for preserving the original collecting data, the intermediate results of analysis and processing and the data of analysis conclusions. Data storage model adopts hybrid storage model. It provides distributed storage model, i.e., the HDFS based on Hadoop or YARN, for those original and analysis data which has huge scale or complex processing. And in order to support flexible query requirements, it puts to use MySQL database for the final result or the raw data of small scale. As the raw alarm data possesses the imperfect features of loss, discordance, exception, repetition, and also the difference between encoding and description of alarm data in different devices, so it is necessary to provide high quality alarm data by extraction and model transformation for the alarm correlation analysis.

Processing layer: Based on the original analysis data, the processing layer is responsible for providing the basic method and algorithm implementation for miscellaneous analysis of statistical in data mining according to the functional requirements of the presentation layer, so as to complete a specific statistics, summary, mining, results evaluation, etc. The function of this layer includes summary, classification, clustering, correlating mining, predictive mining, outlier mining, etc. Thus it involves a lot of specific algorithms.

The purpose of the alarm data analysis is to predict the alarm, correlate the alarm and merge the alarm, so as to directly send orders to the source fault of trigger alarm to reduce the number of orders. To this end, the alarm data mining analysis includes a multi dimension and granularity analysis of alarm, i.e., trend analysis and forecast of the faults from the alarm time series, and achieving the alarm protocol and reducing the alarm rate by digging out the source fault of trigger alarm from concurrent correlation, transfer correlation, sequence correlation and analysis of principal and subordinate relationship of alarm. Alarm data mining analysis will find the correlation between the alarm and performance alarm, the correlation between the complaint and the alarm, and finally form the alarm tree.

Presentation layer: The final results of alarm analysis are presented to the comprehensive monitoring personnel and related users in graphical way. The presentation of concrete results includes the statistics result in the form of pie chart and column chart, the trend forecast result in the form of curve graph, the alarm correlation tree result in the form the tree diagram, etc. And it also can present the alarm correlation of equipment performance, the management of alarm and complaint and others in the form of list.

In order to obtain the self-learning ability from the history of alarm analysis rule in the future, it can support expert intervening alarm results as well.

4 Conclusions

Applying data mining technology to the alarm correlation analysis, we can convert the inherent understanding of computability which is formed from previous data analysis and mining, so the problem that is incalculable in the past now can be solved. And also we can abandon the previous compromise on algorithm due to the limitations of the computable. Based on this idea, the cross network alarm correlation analysis which supported by the relationship of pan NE is presented in this paper. It can be expected to find more interesting and useful conclusions by continuing to apply this idea in the field of data analysis and mining. The conclusion of this paper is applied to the practical operation and maintenance work of the operators, and implemented in the support system.

Acknowledgements. This work is supported by the "National Natural Science Foundation of China" program "Research on Green-oriented Cognitive Cross-domain Mobile Communication Network Architecture and Cooperative Technologies (No. 61372117)".

References

1. Tao, H.: The design and implementation of alarm correlation analysis module for power communication network, Beijing University of Posts and Telecommunications, December 2013
2. Liangfeng, D.: The research of alarm relativity analysis method in multiple specialty network, Beijing University of Posts and Telecommunications, May 2008
3. Xin, D., Luoming, M.: Application of alarm correlation model for fault diagnosis in communication networks. J. Beijing Univ. Posts Telecommun. **29**(3), 66–69 (2006)
4. Yuanchao, L.: Research on alarm correlation application in communication networks, Tianjin University of Technology, January 2012
5. Xiuli, M., Hongxia, W., Lingyun, Z.: Research on the implementation of alarm dependency analysis in network faults management system. Trans. Shenyang Li Gong Univ. **28**(3), 9–14 (2009)
6. Yuxin, Y., Xiaoqiang, X., Hui, F.: A network fault monitoring algorithm based on alarm correlation. Comput. Know. Technol. **8**(19), 4715–4717 (2012)
7. Gardner, R.D., Harle, D.A.: Alarm correlation and network fault resolution using the kohonen self-organising map. In: IEEE Global Telecommunications Conference, November 1997

The Quality Control and Management
of Component-Oriented Software Development

Chun Shan[1(✉)], Wei Zhang[2], and Shaohua Teng[2]

[1] Guangdong Polytechnic Normal University, Guangzhou, China
shanchun2002@126.com
[2] Guangdong University of Technology, Guangzhou, China
{weizhang,shteng}@gdut.edu.cn

Abstract. The software components is discussed and component-oriented software development is shown in the paper. A group of game engine component is developed, and two games are produced by game engines. Then the quality control and management of components and software are discussed in this paper. The system of evaluating software quality is developed and applied in practice software development.

Keywords: Software component · Quality model · Quality control · Development method

1 Introduction

The purpose of software reuse is to speed develop the software production of quality at low cost. The software reuse can create new software from existing software according to the relevant characteristics of the software. These characteristics include: development experience, design experience, design decisions, architecture, requirements, design, coding, testing, and documentation, etc.

Caper Jones [1] lists 10 parts of software reuse, including: project planning, cost estimation, architecture, demanding model and specification, designing, source code, user documentation and technical documentation, user interface, data, and test cases.

In general, when developing a new software, in order to find the reuse parts about the existing software, the analysis of requirement is asked.

As the reuse technology becomes even more practical and matured,the software development of reuse-based has been widely applied in system software development, and component-oriented is a kind of typical reusable software.

2 The Introduction of Component-Oriented

Software component is used to develop a new software. Component has relatively independent functions, clear interface specification, and all kinds of replaceable basic component.

© Springer International Publishing Switzerland 2016
Q. Zu and B. Hu (Eds.): HCC 2016, LNCS 9567, pp. 746–751, 2016.
DOI: 10.1007/978-3-319-31854-7_73

Definition: a software component is an independent software unit which encapsulates the design and implementation, and provides the uniform external interface. Some components can form a larger whole component through the interfaces.

Based on the above definition, software component is a binary function unit which can be delivered and released independently according to component model (or standard interface). Components from different enterprises can be assembled into an application software.

The software component specification is as follows:

Component :: = < component specification, component implement>

Component specification :: = < interface, structure>

Interface :: = < exposed interface function set, embed interface function set, service function set>

Service :: = < outward provide function set, outward request function set>

Structure :: = < unit component structure > | < composite component structure>

Unit component structure :: = < component implementation reference>

Composite component structure :: = < referenced component type, instance statement, instance connection, mapping>

There are 3 standard component model, they are as follows:

OMG: CORBA/CCM

Microsoft: MTS/COM, DCOM, COM+

Sun: Java/EJB.

3   The Quality Control and Component Management

The qualities of components vary from the different standards and requirements. In general, we can analyze the component through the component classification, component development, component's use; where the quality model of component and application effects could be used to evaluate the quality of the component.

3.1   The Classification of Components

Based on the function, the component can be divided into applied system-oriented special component, application system domain-oriented shared components, computer system-oriented basic components.

The components can be divided into applicational component, business component, and data component based on the hierarchy.

The application layer separates the business layer from external impact in order to uniformly present the request of business logic. The application components include: (1) present the information of user, provide the interactive user's mechanism; (2) deal with user interface events who trigger the process of business logic; (3) manage the data interface with other external systems, such as inputting and outputting; (4) generate reporting table and execute batch files; (5) manage the collaborating layer and mapping layer (if the presentation layer exists sublayer), convert the input action of user to the request that can be understood by the business layer. (6) offer various forms of helps for application interaction. (7) pay attention to customer's interest and benefit (where the business layer pay attention to enterprise's interest and benefit), such as session data and user preferences, etc. (8) separate the application layer from business layer, uniformly define business logic.

The common application components include:

(1) multi-granular application components; (2) user task components (contain a single task); (3) batch components; (4) subtask components.

The business layer is composed of controlling logic layer and business object layer, and it is responsible for the following work:

(1) ensure the application of business rules; (2) ensure that data integrity and consistency; (3) handle the business requests.

The data layer converts the logic view in business layer into the actual physical storage, all of these works are accomplished by the collaborating layer and mapping layer. The data layer is responsible for the following work:

(1) ensure that the data are stored correctly; (2) implement the data access; (3) separate business logic from accessing data (4) convert the logic view in business layer into actual physical data storage.

3.2 The Component-Based Software Development

Software component technology includes: component model, architecture, analysis and design, implementation technologies, and component-based application system construction and implementation technology, etc. When the component technology is applied to a specific application system development, it is often called component-based software development (CBD). CBD includes component acquisition, component model, component description language, component classification and retrieval, component assembly and component standardization, etc.

In general, there are three kinds of component-based software development models: (1) project-based software development; (2) commercial off the shelf (COTS) software development; and (3) product line engineering.

The project-based software development is shown in Fig. 1(a):

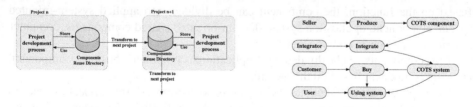

Fig. 1. (a) Project-based software development (b) COTS software development

COTS software development is shown in Fig. 1(b).

The software product line is a software development system that has a common architecture and reusable components. Both of them establish a software platform to support the specific field.

The ideal CBD structure is shown in Fig. 2(a). Under a distributed environment, CBD can be distributed into three layers, which are object design layer, domain component implementation layer, and system assembly layer. Object design mainly analyzes the common and individual behavior in the application, and it constructs many independent functional particles. These particles are all varies of system classes and basic object classes written by user. Domain component implementation layer is the core of the work, and mainly package one or more class files into reuse entities. These entities are some functional blocks that possess independent domain business logic and provide uniform services through a standard interface, this layer achieves the customization of interface, tables and graphics. The system assembly layer assembles and couple components according to the requirements. CBD in a distributed environment is shown in Fig. 2(b).

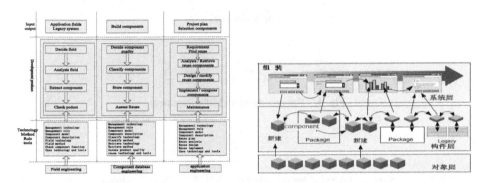

Fig. 2. **(a).** The ideal CBD architecture **(b).** CBD for a distributed environment

3.3   The Production and Management of Component

The production and management of component includes requirement analysis, design, implement, test, release, management and maintenance, as showed in Fig. 3. In order to get a high-quality and portable component, the quality control of software is very important.

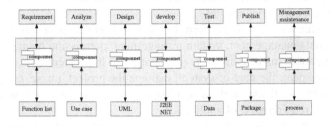

Fig. 3.   The production and management of component

3.4   The Quality and Model of Component

Software quality is defined as all features related to the requirement ability of software, which is specified and implied [2].

ISO/IEC 9126 document [2] describes the features of software quality from external quality, internal quality, and using quality. In ISO/IEC 9126, external and internal quality includes functionality, reliability, efficiency, portability, ease of use, maintenance, and 27 child features. Using quality includes efficiency, safety, productivity and satisfaction, on this basis, Yang [1] proposes reliability indicators, as showed in Fig. 4.

The features of software quality also applies to the software component, these features are usually referred to as basic quality of software component. Because of the particularity of component, Yang [1], and Guo [2] propose the reusability of component, which includes interface maturity, easy to assemble, independence, versatility, evolution compatibility, and compliance. The internal and external quality model of software component is shown in Fig. 5.

Fig. 4. The quality model of component

Fig. 5. The internal and external quality model of component

3.5   The Software Quality Evaluation Platform

Based on the quality features of software component, we develop a software quality evaluation platform. The platform contains the storage of quality problems of software, classification management, and statistics. It realizes to easy and fast search for quality problems, generate the statistics charts, and also providing data support for quality evaluation during software development.

Software quality evaluation platform includes 5 modules: user information, statistical analysis, data management, system management, permission management.

User information: manage the basic information of the current user.

Data management: the core of system, manage the project, phase, target, template, etc. Target includes all the features of component quality, it also can be extended according to the requirements of application.

Statistical analysis: select a set of targets, then perform statistical analysis, generate statistical results such as reports, charts, etc.

System management: software system configuration and maintenance, manages the information of user, management system log, manage system menu.

Permission management: manage the assignment of user permission according to the requirements. In this system, the users are divided into 5 classes: system manager, project manager, project operator, supervisor, general user.

4   The Application

Based on component technology, we develop a game engine in android platform based on OPEN GLES, the functional module of this engine is comprised of 8 components: rendering engine, physics engine, collision detection engine, sound engine, animation engine, script engine, AI engine, scene management engine, etc. All components are developed in Java, and the functional modules can be replaced or added as required.

We develop two games through these engine components. It is shown in Fig. 6. Both of the two games are high quality in testing.

Fig. 6. (a)(b) The game developed through engine components

5   Conclusions

Based on the technology of component, a component-based software development method is described in the paper, a group of engine components is developed, and instantiate two games are implemented. On this basis, quality control and management technology is proposed, meanwhile, we develop a quality evaluation platform, then apply it to the component-based software development.

Acknowledgments. This research was partly supported by Guangdong Provincial Science & Technology Project (Grant No. 2012B091000173, 2013B010401034, 2013B090200017, 2013B010401029), Guangzhou City Science & Technology Project (Grant No. 2012J5100054, 2013J4500028, 201508010067), and Key Laboratory of the Ministry of Guangdong Province project (Grant No. 15zk0132).

References

1. Chunhe, Y., Haihua, Y., Maozhong, J., Zhongyi, G.: Software component quality metrics, computer engineering and design, **27**(3), 411–414 (2006)
2. GB/T 16260—ISO/IEC 9126, quality modes, software-product quality (2001)
3. Shuhang, G., Yuqing, L., Maozhong, J.: Some issues about trusted components research. Comput. Sci. **34**(5), 243–246 (2007)

Research on Building and Analysis for Attribute Model in Quality Evaluation of Domain Software

Jian Su, Lu Han, Yue Li, Shufen Liu, Zhilin Yao, and Tie Bao[✉]

College of Computer Science and Technology, Jilin University, Changchun 130012, China
{sujian14,yuel13}@mails.jlu.edu.cn,
{hanlu,liusf,yaozl,baotie}@jlu.edu.cn

Abstract. This paper looks into how to select attributes for domain software quality evaluation and put forward a method to build the attribute model of domain software. It also conducts an analysis into the correlation between the change in attributes and the change in software quality evaluation based on the model. Domain software pays more attention to domain features of the software. Based on quality evaluation need, a structured attribute model was built by selection of general, domain and application attributes. Based on the attribute model, an analysis on the impact of change in attributes on software quality evaluation can be conducted. At last, a case is used to demonstrate the process of analyzing how the change in the weight of a single attribute would impact on software quality evaluation. The building method of attribute model put forward in this paper focuses on general and domain attributes of domain software meanwhile looks into the trend of software quality evaluation variation based on the attribute model, thus provides better support for domain software quality evaluation.

Keywords: Software engineering · Quality evaluation · Attribute model · Impact analysis

1 Introduction

With fast development of software technology and deepening trend of industry informationization, the society is more and more dependent on software which plays a crucial role in production management, device control, business collaboration and procedure support in many fields thus draws people's attention to its quality. Software quality is the most important reference in software selection and service quality evaluation. Studies in software engineering and relevant technology have been dedicated to improving software quality and quality evaluation thus becomes an important issue. Software quality refers to how much the software is consistent with the desired functions and satisfied needs, therefore a full evaluation of software quality often needs to set up a multi-layer attribute model as reference based on which the software quality is then evaluated.

Selection of attributes and construction of the model is the foundation for software quality evaluation, so the attribute model and relevant studies are taken. Mohammadi and others [1] provided a first attempt to identify software quality attributes, which

© Springer International Publishing Switzerland 2016
Q. Zu and B. Hu (Eds.): HCC 2016, LNCS 9567, pp. 752–758, 2016.
DOI: 10.1007/978-3-319-31854-7_74

contribute to trustworthiness. Based on a survey of the literature, they provided a structured overview on software quality attributes and their contribution to trustworthiness. To study the problem of multiple attribute decision making in which the decision making information values are triangular fuzzy number, a relative entropy decision making method for software quality evaluation is proposed [2]. Using Analytical Network Process (ANP), the aim of Ref. [3] is to determine the relationships among quality and environmental attributes and relative priorities of attributes. The results are presented as a guide for green software developers. In Ref. [4], Monga et al. studied various attributes or factors that affect the reusability of software. The most common factors are identified and their impact is analyzed. Montagud et al. [5] presented a systematic literature review with the objective of identifying and interpreting all the available studies from 1996 to 2010 that present quality attributes and/or measures for software product line. Muhammad et al. identify a list of quality attributes which are specific to the integrated environmental modelling, and further discuss how quality attributes are linked with the environmental models and how they affect the quality of those models. Mahdavi-Hezavehi et al. aim at assessing methods for handling variability in quality attributes of service-based systems, collecting evidence about current research that suggests implications for practice, and identifying open problems and areas for improvement. Lence and others presented a software product line approach that permits modeling the variability of quality attributes using feature models, and generating configurations of their software architecture depending on the particular concerns required by each application. The quality view and the tradeoff view to the Quality-driven Architecture Design and quality Analysis (QADA) framework were introduced, and it is easier to understand how the requirements on software quality are mapped onto the system architecture. Main objective of Ref. is to determine whether, with the use of modeling tools, we can simplify and automate the definition process of a software product line, improving the selection process of reusable assets. In Ref., Chen et al. established the evaluation attributes of comprehensive categorical, and analysis the assessment model computational logic by AHP, establish corresponding assessment method. This method can analysis and evaluate the domain software reliability, and propose sensitivity analysis.

In conclusion, relevant studies by far focus mainly on the definition, categorization and weights of general attributes or on software attributes of certain applications and certain environment. It hasn't paid much attention to the attribute model and domain attributes of the software with absence of construction method and follow-up research on the model. This paper looks into how to construct a comprehensive attribute model based on domain attributes and studies the impact of attributes on software quality evaluation based on the constructed model.

2   Construction of Attribute Model

Compared to general software, evaluation of domain software quality pays more attention to its domain attributes, meaning how much the software is consistent with the domain needs. Thus, apart from general attributes, it is more important to inspect attributes relevant to the domain. In Fig. 1, the attribute model of domain software should be built up based on 3 aspects, which are general, domain and application attributes, each of which also needs to be broken down into more specific groups and attribute indicators as needed.

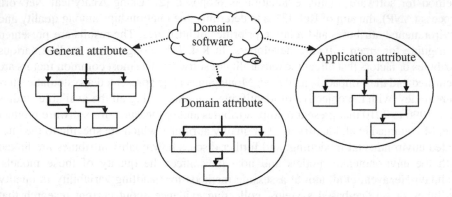

Fig. 1. Attributes to be inspected for domain software and grouping

(1) General Attributes. General attributes refer to aspects that generally need to be inspected in software quality evaluation, such as availability, reliability, safety, timeliness, maintainability etc., which can be organized in multi-layer structure. For example, reliability attributes can be divided into groups of system reliability and function reliability, while the former can further contain specific inspection indicators like test coverage and code defect rate, etc.

(2) Domain Attributes. Domain attributes refer to aspects to be inspected that are closely linked to domain attributes and are of greater significance to software quality. In application of domain software in certain domain, users are more concerned about whether the software can be closely connected to domain features and it's inspected based on 3 sub-aspects, which are domain knowledge, domain business and domain coding. Domain knowledge refers to whether the software supports modeling of main entities and entity relation in the domain and interaction, domain business refers to whether the software is able to standardize and support main business procedures of the domain and domain coding refers to whether the software seals and supports main coding standards of the domain.

(3) Application Attributes. Application attributes refer to aspects to be inspected that are closely linked to application details, which are mainly actual needs in the application of domain software. For example, in an actual application, the selection of attributes should consider specific laws and regulations and business procedures of the application institute and would be subject to limitation of evaluation cost and technology condition in the application which has much impact on the quality evaluation as well.

Based on the needs of quality evaluation, through selection of attributes on the above 3 aspects, a comprehensive attribute model can be built for domain software.

For example, Fig. 2 shows that the attribute model can be constructed with a tree-shape layered structure. Details of weights of the model can be defined by methods like AHP and domain experts and users should also be involved in this process. In the process of quality evaluation, the attribute model can be used as a reference in defining what evidence is related to specific attribute target, thus extracts and analyzes such evidence to evaluate the quality. The evidence mainly comes from various products in the software life cycle, for example, implementation codes, models and software documentations.

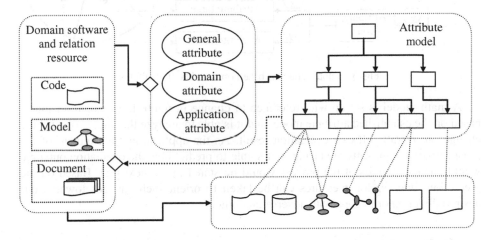

Fig. 2. Construction of attribute model and relevant evidence for evaluation

3 Impact Analysis of Attributes

Attribute model is the foundation of software quality evaluation. In the general evaluation process, a layer-structured attribute model needs to be set up at the first place followed by assigning weights to the sub-branches and defining arithmetic logic. Then an overall evaluation is conducted for the domain software with combination of measurement value related to the attribute target. As shown in Fig. 3, an established attribute model has explicit weights for all sub-branches thus each attribute or attribute target would have some impact on overall evaluation result, and the extent of the said impact depends on the proportion of the weights in the overall evaluation. However, the weights here do not always maintain the same value and domain software's focus may vary by application unit or utilization stage. All these factors may lead to change in evaluation demand and further to change in attribute model. For example, quality evaluation on the information management software of a power plant may select different attributes and assign different weights in the model in different types of power station, i.e. powered by coal, water or nuclear, as well as in different utilization stage, i.e. stages of construction, trial production and official production.

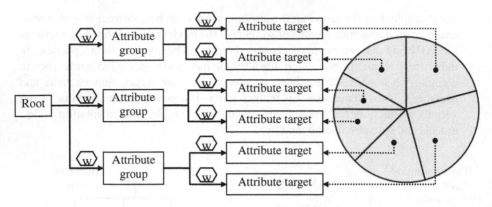

Fig. 3. Impact analysis based on weights of attributes

A math model is set up with reference to change in multi-dimensional attributes based on the established attribute model and it is able to analyze the impact of attribute change on overall software evaluation result. As the application environment of the prospective domain software changes, it's able to predict how the evaluation outcome would change. Details of the process would be stated in the next part. Based on the prediction, intervention measures can be taken to orient such changes towards our desired direction or to cope with adverse outcome.

4   A Case of Application

A detailed case of application in this section is used to illustrate the impact analysis process that's based on attribute model. In the case, quality evaluation is conducted for specific domain software and as is shown in Table 1, an attribute model is set up and weights are assigned to the sub-branches. Attribute models are divided into 3 groups, i.e. general, domain and application attributes, each of which contains specific attribute targets. Among them, both general and domain attribute groups contain 2 attribute targets, while the application attribute group contains only one. For convenience in illustration, we do not involve specific evidence measurement here. Instead the evaluation score of each attribute target is given. Overall quality evaluation scores are calculated by summing up weights of each sub-branch.

Table 1. Score and weights of nodes in different layers of the attribute model

Root node name (total)	Attribute group node		Attribute target node		
	Weight	Name (score)	Weight	ID (score)	Effect to root
Root (7.2)	0.4	General attribute (8.5)	0.5	GA1 (8)	20 %
			0.5	GA2 (9)	20 %
	0.4	Domain attribute (6)	0.5	DA1 (7)	20 %
			0.5	DA2 (5)	20 %
	0.2	Application attribute (7)	1	AA1 (7)	20 %

Attribute weights are constant for established attribute model. As the application conditions of domain software change, focuses in the evaluation may also change and attribute weights may need some adjustment which may involve changes in multiple attributes. In this case, it may have complex impact on overall evaluation, but we only conduct impact analysis on a single-dimension attribute as shown in Fig. 4. The curves there stand for impact of change in each attribute's weight on the overall evaluation (AA1 and DA1 share one curve since they show the same value). In the current model, all 5 attributes have equally 20 % impact on overall evaluation, thus the curves intersect at the coordinate (20, 7.2). In this case, only change in single-dimension attribute is analyzed, hence a simple curve. While analyzing impact of change in multi-dimensional attributes on overall evaluation, the same method can be employed, however, the curves would turn out to be more complex.

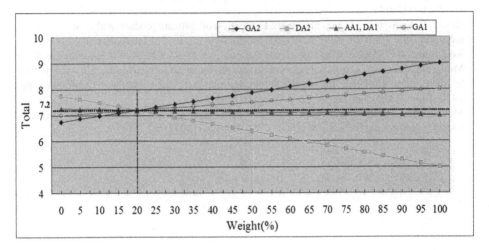

Fig. 4. Trend of change in overall evaluation based on single dimension attribute change

5   Conclusion

This paper looks into the construction of attribute model used for domain software quality evaluation in the perspective of problems in the current quality evaluation. It also conducts an impact analysis that's based on attribute model and illustrates the process of the analysis with a case. The methods put forward here help to build a comprehensive attribute model for domain software with stress on not only the general attribute but also the domain and application attributes of the software. Full coverage of the domain attributes of software provides solid support for accurate analysis of software quality. This paper puts forward a simpler impact analysis, while coming studies should take into account the impact of changes of multi-dimensional attributes on software quality evaluation in complex conditions and build up a more advanced trend model to provide better support for analyzing domain software quality.

Acknowledgements. This work was supported by the National Natural Science Foundation of China (Grant No. 61472160), the National Key Technology Research and Development Program of China (Grant No. 2014BAH29F03) and the Jilin Province Science and Technology Development Program (Grant No. 20140204072GX).

References

1. Mohammadi, N.G., Paulus, S., Bishr, M., Metzger, A., Koennecke, H., Hartenstein, S., Pohl, K.: An analysis of software quality attributes and their contribution to trustworthiness. In: 3rd International Conference on Cloud Computing and Services Science, pp. 542–552. INSTICC, Aachen (2013)
2. Li, Q.X., Zhao, X.F., Lin, R., Chen, B.Y.: Relative entropy method for fuzzy multiple attribute decision making and its application to software quality evaluation. J. Intell. Fuzzy Syst. **26**, 1687–1693 (2014)
3. Koçak, S.A., Alptekin, G.I., Bener, A.B.: Evaluation of software product quality attributes and environmental attributes using ANP decision framework. In: 3rd International Workshop on Requirements Engineering for Sustainable Systems, pp. 37–44. CEUR-WS, Karlskrona (2014)
4. Monga, C., Jatain, A., Gaur, D.: Impact of quality attributes on software reusability and metrics to assess these attributes. In: 4th IEEE International Advance Computing Conference, pp. 1430–1434. IEEE Computer Society, Gurgaon (2014)
5. Montagud, S., Abrahão, S., Insfran, E.: A systematic review of quality attributes and measures for software product lines. Softw. Qual. J. **20**, 425–486 (2012)

Architecture of Demand Forecast for Online Retailers in China Based on Big Data

Luona Song[1(✉)], Tingjie Lv[1], Xia Chen[1], and Junjun Gao[2]

[1] School of Economics and Management,
Beijing University of Posts and Telecommunications, Beijing 100876, China
songlona@bupt.edu.cn, lutingjie@buptsem.cn, cxbupt@263.net
[2] SHU-UTS SILC Business School, Shanghai University, Shanghai 200444, China
gaojunjun@shu.edu.cn

Abstract. The paper designs a demand forecast system for online retailers based on big data and the theory of consumer behavior on the purpose of improving regional forecasting accuracy as well as shortening the forecasting periods. The necessity and the urgency of strengthening e-commerce enterprises' forecasting abilities are emphasized from the perspective of enterprises and consumers. Analysis and design process make use of the concepts of Engel-Kollat-Blackwell Model to put forward a framework composed of four phased prediction, which are the Initial Demand, the Possible Demand, the Core Demand and the Effective Demand. The further discussion then details how online retailers could implement this big-data-based system to cope with various shopping scenarios, such as the New Arrival periods and the November 11 Singles' Day shopping spree. By restating theoretical innovation in the field of demand forecasting research, the paper concludes with an outlook of potential improvement of the architecture and the direction of related practices.

Keywords: Demand forecasting · Online retailers · Big data · Consumer behavior · EKB model

1 Introduction

With the mushroom growth of e-commerce and the rapid development of modern logistics, an increasing number of retail brands begin to use the Internet for online sales activities. It is undeniable that online shopping has dramatically expanded the served markets of retailers and enriched consumer alternatives at a super low-cost. However, apart from the increase of transaction efficiency and sales, online retailers from different shopping platforms are confronted with intense competition. On the purpose of fast response, retailers have to allocate their inventories scientifically and rationally. Furthermore, regional differences of consumption [1] and the change of satisfaction factors of online shoppers [2] require companies focusing on regional demand. Therefore, accurate and effective demand forecasting becomes the key to set up online brand superiority.

Currently, Tmall and JD.com are the two leading online retail platforms of the country. Nevertheless, Tmall still forecasts monthly demand which is far from market

© Springer International Publishing Switzerland 2016
Q. Zu and B. Hu (Eds.): HCC 2016, LNCS 9567, pp. 759–764, 2016.
DOI: 10.1007/978-3-319-31854-7_75

requirement. Although JD.com implements weekly plans to improve response speed
further, the sales forecast results are unsatisfactory. For offline sales prediction, most of
the research is focused on the monthly demand [3] and the prediction range is often
decided by the data type [4] miss considering the effect of regional differences on
demand. Hence, it is extremely urgent to carry out the research of e-commerce demand
forecast deeply and systematically.

The paper builds a demand forecasting system realizing accurate regional demand
and short cycle predictions, based on massive traceable data captured by the internet
when consumers shop online. Consumer online behavior is the central focus and all
possible influential factors and details are highlighted. Furthermore, demand fluctuations
caused by large-scale promotion and the New Arrival are analyzed during the establishment of the system.

2   The Framework of E-Commerce Demand Forecasting

The paper focuses on the future short-term demand of Durable Consumption Goods
(DCG) sold by various online retailers. According to EKB Model, consumer decision-
making process comprises of five parts that are Problem Recognition, Information
Search, Alternative Evaluation, Product Selection and the Results [1]. For each part,
online shoppers express distinct attitudes and behaviors. Hence, we set weekly demand
of a single product in a regional warehouse as forecast target and design the following
four-stage demand forecasting system (Fig. 1).

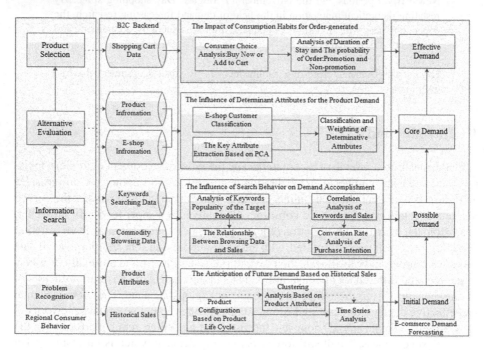

Fig. 1. The framework of e-commerce demand forecasting

2.1   The Initial Demand: Based on Problem Recognition and Historical Sales Data

The Initial Demand is the beginning of this forecasting process which describes the objective demand of a certain products during the coming week. Whenever consumers realize the existence of gaps between their actual state and ideal state, Problem Recognition happens and consumers have to take action closing them [1]. As long as the products have been displayed on the web page, they all have the possibility to be searched, be browsed and be purchased by their target consumers.

It is noteworthy that the adequacy of historical sales data will directly affect the forecast results. So in this stage, the enterprises should divide products into different categories based on product life cycle. For instance, the Initial Demand of common products can be estimated by simple quantitative prediction methods. After predicting the Initial Demand, we considers that if the goods fail to appear in consumers' search interface that means there is no click or browse, consumers are not likely to obtain the product information and order further. So after obtaining the Initial Demand, the search behavior of consumers becomes the focus of the next step.

2.2   The Possible Demand: Based on Information Search

The Possible Demand discusses the consumer attention on target product over a period of time by observing their searching and browsing behaviors. Once problem recognition happens, consumers need to use information to solve the problem. In the era of online shopping, shoppers are capable of getting product information widely and conveniently. Product searching and browsing both belong to the product information search and will leave digital footprint which could obtained by platform providers and other third-party (Table 1).

Table 1. Related data generated by key words searching behavior, adapted from Tmall Data Cube (2015).

Name	Definition
Search popularity	A corresponding index result from data processing of the population searching the keyword
Search index	A corresponding index result from data processing of searching times
Click rate	A corresponding index result from data processing of clicks
Click index	The rate of click on to enter product pages after searching the keyword
Transaction index	A corresponding index result from data processing of orders after searching the keyword
Conversion rate	The conversion rate contributed by the keyword

So far, the second stage of demand forecasting considers the influence of information search behavior on product sales. However, it is important to note that searching keywords, clicking and browsing product information are just the prelude to a real consumers purchase intention. Therefore, in order to get the real demand, further discussion details consumer's purchase intention, the key attributes affecting product selection and different consumers' types.

2.3   The Core Demand: Based on Determinate Attributes

The Core Demand represents all final decisions of choosing the target product after evaluating all alternative brands and products. After searching information, consumers usually get a set of alternatives and carry out a comprehensive evaluation on several determinate attributes [1]. With the purpose of fulfilling consumer demands, online shopping platform providers usually provide all kinds of statistics data which might be used by their members in the process of purchase decision, including the network evaluation scores and stars, sales ranking and reputation evaluation. And the above attributes can be broadly divided into two categories. The First is product information and the second is called store information.

2.4   The Effective Demand: Based on Consumption Habits

The Effective Demand means the actual orders that come in the following week and this result supports Inventory Decision of online retailers directly. The result of the Core Demand calculation basically determines the product demand for a period of time in the future, but this predicted result is not precise enough. Because the influence of shopping habits after selecting the target product does not come into careful consideration. According to the online stores page design, consumers have two options after choosing their target products. One is the "buy now" bottom, in this case, the core demand 100 % translate into orders. While the other one is "add to cart", in this case, when the order will be submit is unknown and the realization of the Core Demand will change over time.

3   The Implement of E-Commerce Demand Forecasting

3.1   Setting the Initial Demand

Normal products demand forecasting can choose moving average method, exponential smoothing method or time series analysis. Since new products are lack of historical data, we need the historical data of other products for reference. The CBR technology might be a proper method focusing on product attributes. By calculating the matching rate and fitness of the past cases and the current case, the CBR technology solves new problems using the solution of past cases. Firstly, principal component analysis (PCA) is used to determine the key attributes of the target product, and then we take a number of key attributes as the input for clustering analysis. Next, we could find the most similar sequences comparing with the new products through similarity search, and finally get the Initial Demand of the new products [3].

3.2   Estimating the Possible Demand

For qualitative data collected at this stage, enterprises could allocate the hot search keywords into different areas according to online buyers' registration information. Moreover, keyword search directly affects browse and click of the product interface, so the relationship between browsing behavior and sales need to be studied. In addition, during the particular time of the network promotion, such as November 11 Singles' Day shopping spree, promotional efforts will response on consumer search behavior and relevance of the sales and keywords search will spike. Furthermore, the product concern brought by search behavior may lag expression before the arrival of sales season. At the same time, sales during the quarter, search behavior and the relationship between sales also need to focus on.

3.3 Identifying the Core Demand

For information consumer needs to evaluate the alternatives, analysts should analyze its relevance to sales through the relevant methods and select key attributes which significantly influence consumer decision making. In addition, the consumer in evaluating alternatives will show the commonness and characteristics. Different types of consumers in evaluating alternatives have different dominant properties. Enterprises can divide regional consumer into different consumer types through the study of area consumer preferences. Moreover, they may speculate decisive attributes of different types of consumers and then give weight to key attributes depending on the type and the relationship with the sales. This step can adopt the method of multiple linear regression (MLR) and add the multiple related variables into account.

3.4 Forecasting the Effective Demand

In spite of "buy now" behavior, once the goods add in the shopping cart, consumers can either submit the order after purchasing other goods or give up the purchase with the passage of time. However, when it comes to shopping cart behavior, the study of Shopping cart goods and actual sales conversion has not been found yet. Hence, the Effective Demand forecasting method has yet to be discussed. In addition, the number of products added in the shopping cart may increase dramatically over time before the promotion season. This indicates that shopping cart conversion rate is different between the sales promotion and normal seasons and further analysis need to consider time periods.

4 Conclusions

This paper focuses on the reality problem of online demand forecasting dilemma, and fills the research gap by providing ideas and systematic framework. At the same time, the prediction model and methods are also introduced which guarantees the prediction system not divorcing from reality as well as provides directions for subsequent research. Of course, deficiencies and limitations still exist in this study. For instance, the specific function of each module is relatively brief and rationality is in doubt because of the deletion of statistical data.

The following research could start from several aspects. First of all, based on the current research of demand forecasting system, scholars can organize investigation on online enterprises to understand and evaluate practicability of this system. Meanwhile, according to the results of investigation, scholars could make use of feedback to modify and perfect this system. In addition, for each part of this system, analysis of influence factors and forecasting modelling can be performed under the e-commerce environment to further refine the influence of online search behavior, alternative evaluation behavior and shopping cart behavior on the actual demand of products.

Acknowledgement. This work was supported by National Basic Research Program of China (973 Program) (2012CB315805).

References

1. Solomon, M.R.: Consumer Behavior, pp. 282–293. China Renmin University Press, China (2009)
2. Pan, X.: Study of value-based B2C management model. Mod. Econ. Inform., (15) (2011)
3. Wu, D., Li, S., Li, H., Liu, B.: Integrated forecasting model of cosmetic based on CBR. J. Beijing Univ. Aeronaut. Aeronaut. (Soc. Sci. Ed.), (01) (2012)
4. Cao, Y.: Sales forecasting of cars based on ANFIS system and consumption demand factors. Auto Ind. Res., (11) (2013)

iLearning: Mobile Training Platform

Wei Tong[1] and Peng Gong[2(✉)]

[1] Anhui Wonder University of Information Engineering, Hefei, China
[2] Department of Computer Science, Shandong University, Weihai, China
gongpeng@sdu.edu.cn

Abstract. The paper proposes a mobile training platform – iLearning, which makes people able to conduct all kinds of learning on the centralized training, professional training, newbie training, and emergency training without leaving their jobs. The mobile training platform iLearning is based on Android technical design. The thesis presents the logical structure and technical architecture of this mobile training platform, iLearning, and designs programs for testing the networking structure and each function module of the mobile training platform. By testing, this platform can continuously release different training courses aimed at different needs of people and let people learn professional knowledge and skills in a simple and economical manner.

Keywords: Mobile training · Android · Networking engineering

1 Introduction

Mobile learning is a kind of learning which is not restricted by time and space with the help of mobile terminal (MT) and can provide omnipresent learning experience for people. Mobile training platform system iLearning is a professional service based on Android technical design with the help of third-party mobile applications and Internet database applications.

The developed mobile training platform iLearning mainly applies technologies such as Android UI, Android data storage, and VPDN networking. It solves problems such as design, database storage and network communications of mobile training platform interfaces. The paper introduces the logical and technical architecture of the mobile training platform iLearning and programs for testing the networking structure and each function module of iLearning.

2 Logical Structure of the System

There are three categories of users for the mobile learning system of iLearning: administrator, customer and trainee. Their functions are as follows:

Copyright owner, platform administrator and course developer of iLearning, responsible for the management and maintenance of the system. Be able to establish customer archives and grant some customers or some trainees the right of using professional

© Springer International Publishing Switzerland 2016
Q. Zu and B. Hu (Eds.): HCC 2016, LNCS 9567, pp. 765–771, 2016.
DOI: 10.1007/978-3-319-31854-7_76

courses, be able to release new courses, track and check the learning process and learning results of some customers or some trainees and issue a report of the trainee learning for some customers.

Customers, as trainees and the community personnel of iLearning, can check the learning processes and learning results of trainees of their own enterprises, can read statistical statements and check their costs and balance of iLearning accounts, and can make the online payment to purchase new courses or add, modify and delete trainees of their own enterprises.

Trainees, as trainees and the community personnel of iLearning, can do self-learning, self-tests, feedback their grades and suggestions on courses, share their learning notes, discuss some courses, and invite other trainees to learn.

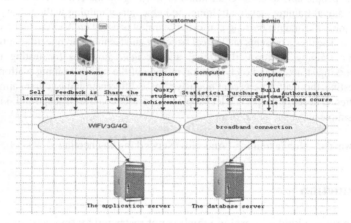

Fig. 1. Logical structure of iLearning system

3   System Design

The design of mobile training platform system iLearning should integrate mobile terminal users and the mobile training platform system iLearning organically together on the premise of protecting original hardware & software investment and establish a mobile application system with strong functions, services in various forms and the convenient use. Thus, the overall idea of the establishment of mobile training platform system iLearning is:

1. Comprehensive connection: realize connections of the mobile training platform system iLearning carried with one person anytime and anywhere. Employees of the company can conduct fully mobile connections with the existing business application systems.
2. Support for the mainstream intelligent mobile terminal: with the development of mobile training platform iLearning, MT will expand in more directions.

3.1 System Architecture

According to the system logical structure shown in Fig. 1, the mobile training platform system iLearning can be divided into three major parts – foreground, communications and background:

Foreground (Mobile Domain): The mobile phone platform used by trainees (classified into Android platform and IOS platform). It includes the rights management, customer information, trainee information, authorized release, course topics, course content, learning tests, learning feedback, learning records, sharing and statement inquiry.

Communications (Access Domain): The communication channel between APP and Internet background.

Background (Internal Domain): The Internet website platform used by administrators and customers. It includes the main interface of trainee identification, warm tips, course list, course topics, course content, learning tests, learning feedback, learning records, sharing and network synchronization (Fig. 2).

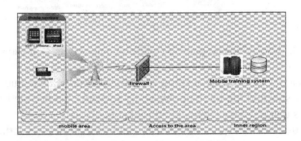

Fig. 2. Technical architecture of mobile training system — iLearning

3.2 VPDN Networking Program

To strengthen the security of mobile security release platform, mobile training platform iLearning adopts VPDN (Virtual Private Dialup Network) and the VPN technique. GRE (Generic Routing Encapsulation) is a protocol of bearing the third tunnel. Currently, the most common VPN networking method is applicable to establish the enterprise internal virtual private network (Intranet VPN and Extranet VPN). The technical process of establishing GRE VPN connections is:

(1) Establish a GRE tunnel from the user side to China Unicom.
(2) MS (Mobile Station, i.e. Intelligent Mobile Terminal) makes a request of Activate PDP. PDP messages carry the information about APN, user name and password, etc.
(3) After SGSN (Serving GPRS Support Node, Serving GPRS Support Node) gets the authentication from HLR (Home Location Register), it acquires GGSN IP from DNS of China Unicom and makes a request of setting up GTP (GPRS Tunneling Protocol) tunnel.

(4) After getting an access to the user information from SGSN, GGSN sends an authentication request to AAA Server, then AAA Server conducts the authentication on the terminal user and the IP address will be assigned by GGSN/AAA Server.

(5) Communications between MS and the user server.

Lease VPDN circuit based on the private line method from China Unicom. In other words, open a 10 M private line from the core-network computer room of China Unicom. This private line relies on the backbone transmission network of China Unicom, which is connected up to GGSN mobile gateway device of China Unicom. Meanwhile, set a router in the data center computer room (Fig. 3).

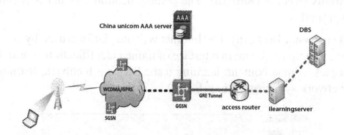

Fig. 3. Networking program of mobile training system — iLearning

Obviously, such a networking method essentially eliminates connections between the router of user side and the Internet physically by using the private line technology, which guarantees that the data of client end is absolutely safe.

AAA Server used for safety certification and authentication is set at the side of China Unicom while at the user side, GRE tunnel is established through the router and GGSN device of China Unicom. IP addresses of mobile users shall be temporarily assigned by AAA Server and GGSN.

4   System Function Module

4.1   System Background Function

Trainee Information. Trainee's Chinese name, English name, nickname, customer, age, gender, photo, profile, title and rank in the enterprise, learning credits, learning level in the system, etc. Learning administrators can add, modify and delete some trainees.

Android system provides a standard SQLite database, which fully supports database statements and can store a relatively large-scale data (including video and audio). In addition, the data can be standardized and stored according to the information of trainees and customers.

Authorized Release. According to the payment records of customers/trainees, learning administrators can release which courses allocated to which trainees of which customers to learn, and meanwhile specify deadlines of learning each course. Authorized release can be carried out singly and also in batches.

Subjects of Courses. The Chinese names of the courses, English names of the courses, ICON, concrete types, applicable levels, brief introduction, dates of announcement, dates of modification, and so on.

Units of courses define the structure of the courses. The manager of learning can define several units to form a course. Content of courses refers to the concrete component parts of the course unit. The manager of learning can define which content to be included, such as texts, graphs, audio and video.

Learning Tests. The manager of learning can define the test after learning for each course. The functions and characteristics are similar to those of the test before learning (Fig. 4).

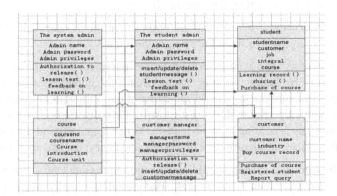

Fig. 4. UML diagram of background function module of iLearning system

4.2   Foreground Functions of the System

Main Interface for Identification of Trainee. The system can identify the trainee according to the mobile phone number and automatically show the personalized main interface according to the authority of the trainee.

Table of the Course. The system lists the subjects of course to be learned for each trainee according to the subject of course defined by the manager. The trainee can also check by himself or herself what other courses in the system can be learned (which the client has not paid for), and decide whether to pay by himself or herself and learn the course.

Content of the Course. The trainee can click on a certain subject of course, get to the content of course under it, and click to choose the unit of course to learn. The system can record the trainee's stopping position of the unfinished learning of last time. The trainee can continue to learn the unfinished course starting from the stopping position of the unfinished learning of last time. The trainee can learn a certain course repeatedly, but cannot copy and relay the content of course.

5 Testing of System

With regard to the mobile training of iLearning, for operating the example used for testing, it is required to construct a computer network composed of multiple computers as well as other network equipment, which adopts the cluster technology and load balancing technology, and is connected to the Internet.

The content of testing for iLearning training system is divided into sections as follows: testing of functions, performance testing, flexibility testing, stability testing, and safety testing. The details of various testing indicators are as follows:

Function Indicator: It is required for the system to support 1,000 end users with the maximum number of concurrent users being 50.

Performance Indicator: When the mobile phone is in the 3G network environment, the time length for logging in should not be greater than 3 s.

Flexibility Indicator: The various configuration parameters for the mobile phone training system can be configured. It is ensured that if the core process is not changed, the changes in most subsystems should not cause the modification of program codes. The system supports the user to develop custom-made software both at the client-side and at the server-side according to its own business needs and expand the server equipment under the unified mechanism of safe access and encrypted transmission.

Stability Indicator: The system should satisfy the requirement of stable and reliable operation for 24 h a day and 7 days a week. The cumulative malfunction time in each year shall not be greater than 1 h. The system shall be tested for malfunction time when running continuously for 72 h (Table 1).

Table 1. Testing environment of iLearning mobile training system

System resource	Quantity	Description and instruction
Database server	2	Cluster database environment
Network or sub-net	1	Conduct the testing in a Gigabit access network
Application server	3	Load balancing application server
Database	1	Dual-server cluster database environment
Testing PC at the client side	10	
Intelligent phones for testing at the client side	20	
Special configuration requirements included	No	No
Testing storage	1	SAN storage system with a capacity of more than 2 TB
Testing the development PC	3	

6 Conclusion

This article makes a detailed introduction to the design and realization of the iLearning system. After the testing of the designed functions of the system, all the testing indicators can meet the expected requirements. The iLearning mobile training system based on the Android technology realizes the functions of course learning, test of learning, feedback on learning, record of learning, communication sharing, check on reports, network synchronization, and others. At the client-side, trainees can learn by themselves anywhere.

References

1. IETF. RFC2501. Mobile Ad Hoc networking (MANET)
2. Rubin, L., Hua, X., Liu, Y.-C., Ju, H.-J.: A Distributed Stable Backbone Maintenance Protocol for Ad Hoc Wireless Networks. [EB/OL]. [2009212]
3. Jingjing, G.: Study and Realization of the Mobile Learning System Based on J2ME. Beijing University of Posts and Telecommunications (2012)
4. Xiaokang, L.: Learning System at the Hand Held End Based on Android. Xidian University (2012)

Capacity and Spectrum Utilization of Spatial, Temporal, and Joint Time-Space Spectrum Sharing

Yao Tang[1](✉) and Qian Li[2]

[1] Beijing University of Posts and Telecommunications,
Beijing 100876, People's Republic of China
TangyaoBupt@126.com
[2] Research Center for Development and Strategy, China Electronics Technology
Group Corporation, Beijing 100041, People's Republic of China
liqian_bupt@163.com

Abstract. In cognitive radio networks (CRNs), efficient spectrum utilization can be achieved in both the time and space domains through temporal spectrum sharing and spatial spectrum sharing, respectively. Joint temporal and spatial spectrum sharing has been considered to decrease the outage probability, but the capacity and spectrum utilization of spectrum sharing techniques has not been examined. Thus in this paper, the capacity and spectrum utilization of temporal, spatial, and joint time-space spectrum sharing are derived. Results are presented which show that joint time-space spectrum sharing has better performance in terms of capacity and spectrum utilization.

1 Introduction

Efficient spectrum utilization is one of the most important issues in cognitive radio networks (CRNs) [1]. These networks allow for dynamic spectrum sharing to address the spectrum scarcity problem by exploiting spectrum holes, which are the available spectrum bands for secondary users (SUs) [1]. Current studies divide dynamic spectrum sharing into two categories [2], respectively.

Spectrum underlay always allows secondary users (SUs) to access the spectrum subject to interference constraints [3]. Thus, it can be considered as spatial spectrum sharing. However, SUs are required to limit their transmit power to satisfy interference constraints even when the spectrum is idle, so their achievable capacity is limited. Further, if an SU is very close to the primary transmitter (PT), the co-channel interference from the PT will not allow the SU to communicate. Therefore, SUs in different geographic region may have different spatial spectrum sharing opportunities.

Spectrum overlay allows secondary users to utilize the spectrum when it is idle. This is determined by a technique called spectrum sensing [1]. Thus, spectrum overlay can be considered as temporal spectrum sharing. However, temporal spectrum sharing can vary considerably depending on the behavior of

© Springer International Publishing Switzerland 2016
Q. Zu and B. Hu (Eds.): HCC 2016, LNCS 9567, pp. 772–778, 2016.
DOI: 10.1007/978-3-319-31854-7_77

the primary users [2]. If the spectrum is always busy (such as with TV channels), there will be no spectrum access opportunities for secondary users. In addition, the accuracy of spectrum sensing depends on the distance between the PU and SU. If an SU is far from the PU, the detected signal may be too weak for the SU to be able to make a decision. Thus, these SUs will not have temporal spectrum sharing opportunities, and therefore temporal spectrum sharing is restricted by primary user behavior and the spectrum sensing capabilities of the SUs, which depends on their geographic positions.

To overcome the disadvantages of the two spectrum sharing techniques and utilize the spectrum more efficiently, joint temporal and spatial spectrum sharing has been proposed [2,4]. It was shown that joint spatial and temporal spectrum sharing can lower the outage probability compared to the separate spectrum sharing techniques [4]. However, the capacity and spectrum utilization of these spectrum sharing techniques has not yet been studied. Therefore, in this paper we first derive closed-form expressions for the capacity and spectrum utilization of temporal spectrum sharing, spatial spectrum sharing, and joint time-space spectrum sharing. Results are presented which show that joint time-space spectrum sharing has better performance in terms of capacity and spectrum utilization efficiency.

2   Spectrum Sharing Model

Consider a network with multiple primary users (PUs) and secondary users (SUs) located in a circular area of radius R as shown in Fig. 1(a) A primary transmitter (PT) is located in the center of the circle and has transmit power P_0. The PUs are assumed to be uniformly distributed around the PT (with density μ_p), within the primary exclusive region (PER) [3]. Assume that the PT is present in a frequency band with probability p_p, and absent with probability $1 - p_p$. For a cognitive radio network (CRN), SUs dynamically share the available licensed spectrum of the PUs, and are assumed to be uniformly distributed in the area outside the PER with a density of μ nodes per unit area. All SUs have maximum transmit power P_S. The SUs are divided into different groups and each group is connected to a wireless access point (AP). Orthogonal frequency division multiple access (OFDMA) is assumed to mitigate the interference from other SUs. Therefore, the interference between SUs is negligible and controllable compared to the interference from the PT.

A path loss channel model is considered. Given a distance $d(r, \theta)$ between a transmitter and user, the channel power gain is $g = A \min \{1, 1/d^\alpha\}$ [3], where A is a frequency dependent constant and α is the path loss exponent.

A primary exclusive region (PER) is used to limit the proximity of cognitive transmitters in order to guarantee PU performance. The PER radius is [2]

$$R_1 = \left(\frac{P_0}{\sigma^2 (2^{C_0} - 1)} \right)^{1/\alpha}, \tag{1}$$

where σ^2 is the noise power spectral density at the PU.

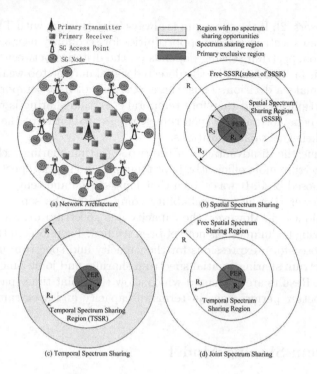

Fig. 1. The spectrum sharing model [4].

3 Spatial Spectrum Sharing

As shown in Fig. 1(b), with spatial spectrum sharing SUs must employ power control to limit the interference to the PUs. However, if an SU is too close to the PT, the interference from the PT will significantly degrade the performance of the SU. Therefore a threshold distance R_2 can be determined within which an SU should not use spatial spectrum sharing to avoid this interference, which is given by [2]

$$R_2 = \sqrt{\frac{A_{th}}{\pi P_0^{2/\alpha} P_S^{2/\alpha}} \left(P_0^{2/\alpha} - P_S^{2/\alpha} \right)}, \qquad (2)$$

where A_{th} is the minimum coverage requirement of the AP in the CRN [2]. Since only an SU with a distance at least R_2 from the PU can perform spatial spectrum sharing, R_2 can be considered as a lower bound on the spatial spectrum sharing region (SSSR) radius.

When an SU is sufficiently far from the PUs, the interference will be minimal so that transmit power control is not needed. Thus there exists a distance R_3 beyond which SUs can perform spatial spectrum sharing without power control, and this distance is a lower bound on the radius of a region called the free spatial spectrum sharing region (Free-SSSR). R_3 can be expressed as [2]

$$R_3 = \left(\frac{2\pi P_S \mu}{(\alpha - 2)\beta I_{th}} \right)^{\frac{1}{\alpha - 2}} + R_1 \tag{3}$$

where $I_{th} = \frac{P_0/r_p^\alpha}{2^{C_0} - 1} - \sigma^2$ is the PU interference constraint, and β is the PU outage probability threshold. From the above analysis, spatial spectrum sharing opportunities exist in the SSSR at a distance R_2 from the PT, while SUs can share the spectrum freely without transmit power constraints in the Free-SSSR at a distance R_3 from the PT.

3.1 Capacity with Spatial Spectrum Sharing

For an SU employing spatial spectrum sharing, a communication outage will occur when the SU is the region between the PER and SSSR where no spectrum sharing opportunities exist, or it is in the SSSR but the data rate falls below a threshold C_S. SUs located in the SSSR but outside the Free-SSSR ($R_1 \leq d \leq R_3$) must employ power control. The transmit power limit in this case is [4]

$$P_S' = \min \left\{ \frac{(\alpha - 2)\beta I_{th}(R_3 - R_1)^{\alpha - 2}}{2\pi \mu}, P_S \right\}, \tag{4}$$

and the corresponding outage probability is

$$\zeta_{spa} = \frac{R_2^2 - R_1^2}{R^2 - R_1^2} + \frac{R_3^2 - R_2^2}{R^2 - R_1^2} \Pr \left(\log \left(1 + \frac{P_S' D_0}{P_0 d^{-\alpha} + \sigma^2} \right) \leq C_s \right)$$
$$+ \frac{R^2 - R_3^2}{R^2 - R_1^2} \Pr \left(\log \left(1 + \frac{P_S D_0}{P_0 d^{-\alpha} + \sigma^2} \right) \leq C_s \right) \tag{5}$$

where $D_0 = d_{ss}^{-\alpha}$ is the path loss from the AP to the SU.

If the capacity of the CRN with spatial spectrum sharing is defined as the number of supported SUs whose communication is not interrupted, then it can be calculated as

$$C_{spa} = n \int_{R_2}^{R} \int_{0}^{2\pi} (1 - \zeta_{spa})(r, \theta) \, \omega(r, \theta) d\theta dr \tag{6}$$

where $n = \mu \pi (R^2 - R_1^2)$ is the total number of SUs in the system.

3.2 Spectrum Utilization with Spatial Spectrum Sharing

IF the spectrum utilization is defined as the ratio of the area with temporal spectrum sharing opportunities to the total area, then it can be expressed as

$$Opp_{spa} = \frac{\pi (R^2 - R_2^2)}{\pi R^2} = 1 - \frac{A_{th} \left(P_0^{2/\alpha} - P_S^{2/\alpha} \right)^2}{\pi P_0^{2/\alpha} P_S^{2/\alpha} R^2}. \tag{7}$$

4   Temporal Spectrum Sharing

Typically, as long as an SU is outside the PER, it can perform temporal spectrum sharing (i.e. detect the spectrum status based on spectrum sensing), and opportunistically use the available spectrum if the PU is idle. However, the sensing capability is greatly affected by the distance between the SU and PU. If the SU is far from the PU, the received signal will be very weak and lead to a high probability of spectrum sensing error. Therefore, a geographic region should be established beyond which a SU cannot employ temporal spectrum sharing, i.e. a temporal spectrum sharing region (TSSR) as shown in Fig. 1(c).

Assume that the SU employs energy detector based spectrum sensing. Since the TSSR is closely related to the sensing capability, it could be expressed as follows [2]

$$R_4 = \left(\frac{P_0 N}{\sigma^2 (A + B + C)} \right)^{\frac{1}{\alpha}},$$ (8)

where $A = Q^{-1}(\xi_f) \sqrt{N}$, $B = \left(Q^{-1}(\xi_m) \right)^2$, $C = Q^{-1}(\xi_m) \sqrt{N + 2A + B}$, N is the number of samples used for spectrum sensing, and ξ_m and ξ_f are the required missed detection probability p_m and false alarm probability p_f, respectively.

4.1   Capacity with Temporal Spectrum Sharing

For a SU employing temporal spectrum sharing, an outage occurs when it is outside the TSSR, or it is inside the TSSR but the data rate is below the threshold C_S. In addition, an SU transmits with probability $p_{tem} = (1 - p_p)(1 - p_f) + p_p p_m$. Therefore, the outage probability is

$$
\begin{aligned}
\zeta_{tem} = \; & \frac{R^2 - R_4^2}{R^2 - R_1^2} \\
& + \frac{R_4^2 - R_1^2}{R^2 - R_1^2} \Pr \left(p_{tem} \log \left(1 + \frac{P_S D_0}{p_p p_m P_0 r^{-\alpha} + \sigma^2} \right) \le C_s \right)
\end{aligned}
$$ (9)

where $D_0 = d_{ss}^{-\alpha}$ represents the path loss from the AP to the SU.

Similar to the capacity with spatial spectrum sharing, the capacity with temporal spectrum sharing is

$$C_{tem} = n \int_{R_1}^{R_4} \int_0^{2\pi} (1 - \zeta_{tem}) (r, \theta) \, w(r, \theta) d\theta dr.$$ (10)

4.2   Spectrum Utilization with Temporal Spectrum Sharing

Define the spectrum utilization as the ratio of the area with temporal spectrum sharing opportunities to the total area, which is

$$Opp_{tem} = \frac{\pi R_4^2}{\pi R^2} = \frac{\left(\frac{P_0 N}{A+B+C} \right)^{\frac{2}{\alpha}}}{R^2}.$$ (11)

5   Joint Spatial and Temporal Spectrum Sharing

With either spatial or temporal spectrum sharing, there always exist regions where the SUs cannot share the spectrum. This motivates the use of joint spatial and temporal spectrum sharing which combines the TSSR and the Free-SSSR, as shown in Fig. 1(d). As shown in the figure, the SUs can either use temporal spectrum sharing in TSSR or spatial spectrum sharing in Free-SSSR, which means that the joint spatial and temporal spectrum sharing provides all SUs with spectrum sharing opportunities, thus the spectrum utilization is 1.

5.1   Outage Probability

With joint spatial and temporal spectrum sharing, an outage occurs when a node is in the TSSR and the data rate falls below a threshold C_S, or a node is in the Free-SSSR and its data rate falls below C_S. Thus the outage probability is

$$\zeta_{joint} = \frac{R_3^2 - R_1^2}{R^2 - R_1^2} \Pr\left(p_{tem} \log\left(1 + \frac{P_S D_0}{p_p p_m P_0 r^{-\alpha} + \sigma^2}\right) \leq C_s\right)$$
$$+ \frac{R^2 - R_3^2}{R^2 - R_1^2} \Pr\left(\log\left(1 + \frac{P_S D_0}{P_0 r^{-\alpha} + \sigma^2}\right) \leq C_s\right) \tag{12}$$

and the corresponding capacity is

$$C_{joint} = n \int_{R_1}^{R} \int_0^{2\pi} (1 - \zeta_{joint})(r, \theta)\, \omega(r, \theta) d\theta dr. \tag{13}$$

6   Performance Results

In this section, the capacity and the spectrum utilization of temporal, spatial, and joint time-space spectrum sharing is examined. The parameters employed are $\alpha = 4$, $P_S = 30$ dBm, $\sigma^2 = 10^{-6}$, $\mu = 0.01$, $A_{th} = \pi \cdot 30^2$, $C_0 = 0.1$, $R = 350$, and $\beta = 0.02$. The capacity with primary network interference is shown in Fig. 2. When P_0 is very small, the capacity of temporal spectrum sharing is close to 0. As P_0 increases, this capacity increases while the capacity with spatial spectrum sharing and joint spatial and temporal spectrum sharing decreases. The capacity of joint spatial and temporal spectrum sharing is higher than when just one technique is employed, and it is always around 400.

Figure 3 shows the influence of the primary network on the spectrum utilization. The spectrum utilization with joint temporal and spatial spectrum sharing is 1 as there always exists an area where the SUs can share the licensed spectrum. The spectrum utilization of spatial spectrum sharing decreases as the primary transmit power P_0 increases because the SSSR area shrinks due to the increase in the primary network interference. The spectrum utilization with temporal spectrum sharing is close to 0 when P_0 is very small because the SUs cannot detect the primary signal. It increases to 1 as the primary transmit power P_0 increases as this helps the SUs detect the primary signal.

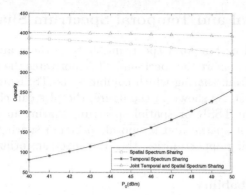

Fig. 2. The capacity of three spectrum sharing techniques vs. P_0.

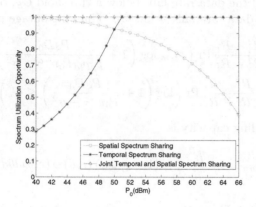

Fig. 3. The effect of the primary network on the spectrum utilization vs. P_0.

References

1. Wang, B., Liu, K.J.R.: Advances in cognitive radio networks: a survey. IEEE J. Sel. Top. Sig. Process. **5**(1), 5–23 (2011)
2. Li, Q., Feng, Z.Y., Li, W., Gulliver, T.A.: Joint temporal and spatial spectrum sharing in cognitive radio networks: a region-based approach with cooperative spectrum sensing. In: Proceedings of IEEE Wireless Communications and Networking Conference, Shanghai, China (2013)
3. Mai, V., Devroye, N., Tarokh, V.: On the primary exclusive region of cognitive networks. IEEE Trans. Wirel. Commun. **8**(7), 3380–3385 (2009)
4. Li, Q., Feng, Z.Y., Li, W., Gulliver, T.A., Zhang, P.: Joint spatial and temporal spectrum sharing for demand response management in cognitive radio enabled smart grid. IEEE Trans. Smart Grid **5**(4), 1993–2001 (2014)

Intrusion Detection Technology Based on Rough Set Attribute Reduction Theory

Wuqi Wang[1(✉)], Zhimin Yang[2], and Mingtao Zhang[1]

[1] Zhejiang Institute of Security Technology, Wenzhou, Zhejiang, China
wwq571@126.com, zjutzmt@163.com
[2] Shangdong University, Jinan, Shandong, China
yangzhimin@sdu.edu.cn

Abstract. There are diverse and complex network attack forms in the world, although the attack forms cannot be predicted by the information system in advance, the system call sequence is stable and consistent. In this paper, the rough set attribute reduction theory is used to establish the normal behavior system call short sequence set forecasting model of network operating system, and the changes of the system call sequence are studied. When the network is attacked, the prediction model can automatically detect the degree that the system call sub-sequence deviates from the normal sequence, so as to detect the abnormal behavior or attack events.

Keywords: Rough set · System call sequence · Intrusion detection technology

1 Introduction

When the network suffers from the attack, many an invasion behavior happens chronologically. System call is the function interface between the program and the operating system kernel. Users can use the interface to realize the device management, so as to ensure functions such as I/O system, process management, communication and storage. It is an effective intrusion detection method to detect whether the system is attacked by analyzing system call sequence.

2 System Call Sequence Analysis

System call sequence has local stability in the operation of the program. If the normal system call sequence is divided into several short sequences as the object of the intrusion detection unit and then the appropriate algorithm is used to generate the legitimate behavior sequence patterns. Once the system is under attack or abnormal, system call sequence will be a significant change, deviating from the normal legitimate behavior sequence, then it can be identified as an invasion.

Sequence detection analysis belongs to abnormal intrusion detection. The objective of system call sequence detection analysis is to explore the inner-correlation among different data items in the data records by means of correlation analysis and to find the correlations between different data records by means of sequence analysis. There are

© Springer International Publishing Switzerland 2016
Q. Zu and B. Hu (Eds.): HCC 2016, LNCS 9567, pp. 779–786, 2016.
DOI: 10.1007/978-3-319-31854-7_78

some legal rules in the system call sequence in these different data records. Identifying the rules is the key to intrusion detection.

3 Rough Set Theory

In rough set theory, knowledge is considered as a kind of ability to classify abstract objects or real ones. Classification can be considered as a kind of knowledge according to the characteristics of the object of the discussion. Suppose the domain U ($U \neq \Phi$) is a finite set of objects, and any subset of X ($X \subseteq U$) called X is a concept or category of U (Φ is also considered as a concept). Any concept family of U is known as the abstract knowledge of U, which is called knowledge for short. U in any concept known as the abstract knowledge of U, referred to as knowledge for short. A division of ζ is defined as: $\zeta = \{X1, X2, \ldots, Xn\}$; $Xj \subset U$, $Xi \neq \Phi$, $Xi \cap Xj \neq \Phi$, as for $i \neq j$, $i, j = 1, 2, \ldots, n$; $\cup Xi = U$. A group division on U is called a knowledge base about U.

Definition 1. Quadruples $S = (U, A, V, f)$ is a knowledge representation system, where U: object of non-empty finite set, is called domain; A: non empty finite set of properties; $V = \cup a \in Ava$, Va a range of attribute a; f: U × A→V is an information function, which gives each attribute of each object an information value, namely:

$$\forall a \in A, x \in U, f(x, a) \in V_a. \tag{1}$$

Suppose $A = C \cap D$, $C \cup D = \Phi$, C is known as the condition attribute values, and D is called the decision attribute values. Knowledge representation system with conditional attributes and decision attributes is called decision table.

Suppose R is an equivalence relation on U, U/R represents R of all the equivalence classes of R(U).[x]R contains the elements of x∈U R equivalence. A knowledge base is a relational system $K = (U, R)$, where U is the discourse domain, R is a family of equivalence relations on U.

Definition 2. Given knowledge expression system is that $S = (U, A, V, f)$, according to each subset of $X \subseteq U$ and attribute subset $R \subseteq A$, two subsets are:

$$\underline{R}X = \cup\{Y \in U/ind(R)|Y \subseteq X\} = \{x \in U|[x]_R \subseteq X\} \tag{2}$$

$$\overline{R}X = \{Y \in U/ind(R)|Y \cap X \neq \emptyset\} = \{x \in U|[x]\_R \cap X \neq \emptyset\} \tag{3}$$

It is respectively called X's lower approximation set and the upper approximation set. Here, $\underline{R}X$ represents a lower approximate set, all "must" of U under R can belong to X's equivalence class elements set; $\overline{R}X$ represents an upper approximate set, all "may" of U under R is included in the X's equivalence class elements set.

$bn_R(X) = \overline{R}X - \underline{R}X$ is defined as X's R domain boundaries, which shows "not sure" under R belongs to the set of equivalence class elements X or $-X$; $pos_R(X) = \underline{R}X$ is called X's R positive region which is the same as $\overline{R}X$; $neg_R = U - \overline{R}X$ is called X's negative domain, which is a set of "must not belong to" X's equivalence elements under R.

Obviously:

$$\bar{R}X = pos_R(X) \cup bn_R(X) \tag{4}$$

Attribute reduction refers to keep the information system classification or decision-making ability unchanged. Delete attribute focuses on redundancy attributes of irrelevant or unimportant attributes and gets the best attributes. Attribute reduction is one of the cores of rough set theory.

Definition 3. Suppose R is a family of equivalence relations, $R \in R$, if ind(R) = ind(R−{R}), R is an unnecessary one of R; otherwise, necessary.

Definition 4. Suppose $Q \subseteq R$, if Q is independent and ind(Q) = ind(R), then Q is a reduction of R, which has multiple reduces, which can be denoted as red(R); a set composed of all the necessary relationship is R 'score, denoted as core(R) and core (R) = ∩red(R).

The core is a set of knowledge features, which can't be removed in the attribute collection. The removal of any attributes in the core will result in the desence of the classification ability of the information system. The core is the intersection of all the reductions, and each reduction contains the information of core, which can be empty. Suppose the equivalence relations between P and Q are U, Q's positive region is denoted as PosP(Q). That is

$$Pos_p(Q) = \cup_{X \in U/Q} \underline{P}X \tag{5}$$

The positive region of Q's P is the object set that all the information of U, according to the classification U/P, which can be accurately divided into the relationship Q of the equivalence class. Suppose P and Q are equivalence relation family, $R \in P$, if

$$Pos_{ind(P)}(ind(Q)) = Pos_{ind(P-\{R\})}(ind(Q)). \tag{6}$$

R is known as Q's unwanted one of P; or R is known as Q's necessary one of P. If each R of P is required for Q, it is known that P is independent on Q (it is also denoted as $Pos_{ind(P)}(ind(Q)) = PosP(Q)$).

Definition 5. Suppose $P' \subseteq P$, P' is the reduction of P's Q if and only if P' is P's Q independent sub-family and PosP'(Q) = PosP (Q), P's reduction of Q is referred to as relative reduction for short; All the Q of P necessary relationship constitutes the set, P's Q nuclear, referred to as a relative core and denoted as coreQ(P), and coreQ(P) = redQ(P).

Definition 6. In the domain of U, the degree of dependence of the attribute set D to R is defined as follow:

$$r(R, D) = |pos_R(D)|/|U| \tag{7}$$

$r(R, D)$ shows that after the attribute can be divided into U, any sample of x in the domain of U can be correctly classified into the probability of decision attributes, which shows condition attribute set R has the decision-making ability to the decision attribute.

Definition 7. In the domain of U, the attribute $c \in C$, the importance of attribute c can be defined as follow:

$$Sig(c, R, D) = r(R, D)r(R - \{c\}, D). \tag{8}$$

The larger the value of Sig(c,R,D) is, the larger the value of the attribute set C is, if the value is 0, and then the attribute C can be deleted.

The idea is that the position of the k-th system is forecasted by using rough set theory, and the first k−1 position is considered as a conditional attribute set, and the k-th location is regarded as the decision attribute, as is to establish information system decision table. The reduction method of rough set theory is able to ensure that minimal rule set predicting the k-th system call position are obtained, and then the actual process is detected. Using rough set attribute reduction theory to describe the normal model of the minimum prediction rule set can improve the detection speed, and realize on-line real-time detection.

4 Intrusion Detection Model

Suppose X is a set of M (L) of all system calls that can be generated by a process in normal operation. A window with a length of k(k < L) slides along each sequence of the M(L) in turn, a series of a length of k is made up of short sequence set, a collection of normal system call sequence set, namely the domain U, is composed of all the short sequence.

As for each short sequence in U, the former k−1 system calls are composed of a general position property set C, and the k-th system call is the last position attribute, which constitutes the decision attribute set {d}. Property set C and V, the value range of {d}, which is the collection of all the system calls (usually there are not more than 180 system calls in UNIX operating system).

The purpose of establishing the normal program behavior model is to predict the k-th system calls, according to the former k−1 system calls M (L), i.e. find the condition attribute set C, and then determine the minimal decision rule set of the decision attribute d. Examples are as follows.

A system call sequence M(L): …open write close open write close open write close…, the system call sequence described a definite normal process, the sliding window size is 3 (i.e. k = 3), a sub-sequence set U is obtained as shown in Table 1.

Table 1. Normal system call sequence set

U	c_1	c_2	c_3
u_1	open	write	close
u_2	write	close	open
u_3	close	open	write

There are the conditional attribute C and the decision attribute {d} in the sequence fragment ui, among them, $C = \{c1, c2\}, \{d\} = \{c3\}$. Judging from the instance, if you have C2, you can infer c3. SoM(L) normal behavior prediction rule set can be reduced to M(2, {c2}), namely $\{c2 = open \Rightarrow c3 = write, c2 = write \Rightarrow c3 = close, c2 = close \Rightarrow c3 = open\}$.

Once the normal model of the process behavior is got, the intrusion detection system can judge whether the running state is normal or not according to the short sequence. If running process sequence and short sequences of normal model appear inconsistent, the system can carry out anomaly detection via maximum vote Max-voting strategy. The specific process is as follows.

Step1: A window of step-size of 1, the length of k slides on the target system call sequence, and sequence set consists of multiple short sequences of fixed length k;

Step2: The results of prediction, which most commonly occurs, are selected for the prediction of the k−1 system calls, based on the short sequences;

Step3: If there is more than one rule and short sequence matching in the rule base, vote one for the result of prediction, the largest number of votes for results of prediction was chosen as a final decision, namely the k-th attribute value.

Step4: If the forecast result is the same as the k-th system call of the short sequence, the prediction is successful;

Step5: If the forecast result is different from that of the k-th system call of the short sequence, the prediction fails.

The ratio of unsuccessful system call sequence matching can be shown as

$$\eta_{Lm} = \frac{m}{\left(N - \frac{(L+1)}{2}\right)L}. \tag{9}$$

Among them, N is the length of the current system call sequence, m the number of short sequence of the unsuccessful match, η intrusion alarm threshold. When η is greater than or equal to ηLm, the system is considered as an abnormal one; otherwise, a normal one. The calculation is easy to be realized.

5 Case Analysis

In the process of sending and receiving e-mails, a normal system call sequence is S: ……open, read, mmap, mmap, open, getrlimit, mmap, open, getrlimit, mmap, open, read, getrlimit,……, when $L = 3$, a M (L) model is established to construct a decision table, as shown in Table 2.

$$U/\{c1\} = \{\{u1, u6, u10\}\{u2\}\{u3, u4, u8\}\{u5, u9\}\{u7\}\}$$
$$U/\{c2\} = \{\{u1, u10\}\{u2, u3, u7\}\{u4, u8\}\{u5, u9\}\{u6\}\}$$
$$U/\{c3\} = \{\{u1, u2, u6\}\{u3, u7, u10\}\{u4, u8\}\{u5\}\{u9\}\}$$
$$U/D = U/\{d\} = \{\{u1, u5\}\{u2, u6, u9\}\{u3, u7\}\{u4, u10\}\{u8\}\}$$
$$U/C = U/\{c1, c2, c3\} = \{\{u1\}\{u2\}\{u3\}\{u4, u8\}\{u5\}\{u6\}\{u7\}\{u9\}\{u10\}\}$$

Table 2. Decision table of system call sequence

U	C			D
	c1	c2	c3	d
u_1	open	read	mmap	mmap
u_2	read	mmap	mmap	open
u_3	mmap	mmap	open	getrlimit
u_4	mmap	open	getrlimit	mmap
u_5	open	getrlimit	mmap	open
u_6	getrlimit	mmap	open	getrlimit
u_7	mmap	open	getrlimit	mmap
u_8	open	getrlimit	mmap	open
u_9	getrlimit	mmap	open	read
u_{10}	mmap	open	read	getrlimit

Then there is:

$$POSc(D) = \{u1, u2, u3, u5, u6, u7, u9, u10\}$$
$$U/C - \{c1\} = \{\{u1\}\{u2\}\{u3, u7\}\{u4, u8\}\{u5\}\{u6\}\{u9\}\{u10\}\}$$
$$POSC - \{c1\}(D) = \{u1, u2, u3, u5, u6, u7, u9, u10\}$$
$$U/C - \{c2\} = \{\{u1, u6\}\{u2\}\{u3\}\{u4, u8\}\{u5\}\{u7\}\{u9\}\{u10\}\}$$
$$POSC - \{c2\}(D) = \{u2, u3, u5, u7, u9u10\}$$
$$U/C - \{c3\} = \{\{u1, u10\}\{u2\}\{u3\}\{u4, u8\}\{u5, u9\}\{u6\}\{u7\}\}$$
$$POSsC - \{c3\}(D) = \{u2, u3, u6, u7\}$$

The dependence of D on C
$r(C, D) = |POSc(D)|/|U| = 8/10 = 0.8$, In the same way:

$$r(C - \{c1\}, D) = |POSC - \{c1\}(D)|/|U| = 8/10 = 0.8;$$
$$r(C - \{c2\}, D) = |POSC - \{c2\}(D)|/|U| = 6/10 = 0.6;$$
$$r(C - \{c3\}, D) = |POSC - \{c3\}(D)|/|U| = 4/10 = 0.4$$

The important degree of each attribute in the condition attribute set C:

$$Sig(c1, C, D) = r(C, D) - r(C - \{c1\}, D) = 0.8 - 0.8 = 0;$$
$$Sig(c2, C, D) = r(C, D) - r(C - \{c2\}, D) = 0.8 - 0.6 = 0.2;$$
$$Sig(c3, C, D) = r(C, D) - r(C - \{c3\}, D) = 0.8 - 0.4 = 0.4$$

Therefore the important degree of the condition attribute c1 opposite decision attribute D is 0, c1 can be deleted directly, the minimum prediction rule set can be obtained by means of rough set attribute reduction and decision reduction. It is shown in Table 3 as follows.

Table 3. Minimum rule set

U	C		D
	c2	c3	d
u_1	read	mmap	mmap
u_2	mmap	mmap	open
u_3	mmap	open	getrlimit
u_4	open	getrlimit	mmap
u_5	getrlimit	mmap	open
u_6	mmap	open	getrlimit
u_7	open	getrlimit	mmap
u_8	getrlimit	mmap	open
u_9	mmap	open	read
u_{10}	open	read	getrlimit

A test system call sequence T is given: ......read, mmap, mmap, open, getrlimit, mmap, open, swapon, read, getrlimit, ..., the voting results are shown in Table 4, based on our model, one can judge abnormality.

Table 4. The voting results of M (L) model

C2	C3	D	Vote
mmap	mmap	open	1
mmap	open	getrlimit	2
open	getrlimit	mmap	1
getrlimit	mmap	open	1
mmap	open	swapon	0
open	swapon	read	0
swapon	read	getrlimit	0

Table 4 shows that test sequence T's length N = 10, L = 3, generating a total of seven sub-sequences, which has 3 sub-sequences with the vote for 0, namely m = 3 which is substituted into the formula (9), unsuccessful ratio of the system call sequence matching is obtained η_{Lm} = 12.5 %.

In conclusion, the intrusion detection model M(L) with good performance, better detection efficiency, can adapt to real-time on-line detection.

6 Summary

Diversity and complexity of application service have inevitable connection with timing and stability of system call sequence. That system call sequence of the process operation is to describe the process of the normal operation of the state, is a kind of effective intrusion detection technology.

Rough set reduction theory is applied in the research, a system call short sequence analysis method is proposed and rules extraction of intrusion detection technology are used, a prediction model of intrusion detection is established. According to the first $k-1$ position of the process system calls, the k-th position is predicted by means of rough set attribute reduction. Rough set attribute reduction theory is able to get a set of minimal rule set predicting the position of the k-th system, so as to use this set of rules to detect the actual process.

Of course, rough set theory applied in the intrusion detection system, must be further studied: how to reduce the intersection of normal behavior and abnormal behavior to cut down the rate of false positives; rough set theory is combined with other uncertain analysis methods to establish better real-time intrusion detection system, better structural robustness and higher accuracy.

Acknowledgment. This project is supported by the research program of educational technology in Zhejiang Province, JB 146; Zhejiang Institute of Security Technology, AF 201503.

References

1. Guoyin, W., Yiyu, Y., Hong, Y.: A survey on rough set theory and applications. Chin. J. Comput. **7**(32), 1229–1246 (2009)
2. Tengfei, Z., Jianmei, X., Xihuai, W.: Algorithms of attribute relative reduction in rough set theory. Acta Electronica Sinica. **11**(33), 2080–2083 (2005)
3. Guojun, Z.: Research on Relative-Attribute Reduction Algorithm and Decision-Making Method Based on Rough Set. Huazhong University of Science and Technology, Wuhan (2010)
4. Danqing, D.: Algorithms and Key Technologies of Intrusion Detection System. A Dissertation Submitted for the Degree of Doctor of Philosophy Central South University, May 2007
5. Huixian, S.: Research on Analysis Model of Process Behavior. Master thesis submitted to University of Electronic Science and Technology of China, April 2013

Magnetorheological Control for Seismic Response of Container Crane

Yangyang Wang[✉], Gongxian Wang, Yi Yang, and Jiquan Hu

School of Logistic Engineering, Wuhan University of Technology, Wuhan 430063, China
{jandy_wyy,alex_to,hjq580818}@126.com, wgx@whut.edu.cn

Abstract. This paper develops a new vibration control system on the basis of a seesaw mechanism with magnetorheological dampers to improve the seismic performance of container cranes. This mechanism fixed on the portal beam of the crane is connected with the portal leg by braces. So the seismic responses of container crane can be controlled easily by adjusting the force of MR dampers. The magnification factors of deformation and damping force with control system configuration is delivered. The time history of the portal legs displacements of without control, semi-active control, Passive-off and Passive-on control are presented. Simulation results exhibit that the seismic reduction effectiveness of semi-active control is best.

Keywords: Container crane · MR damper · Seesaw mechanism · Seismic response

1 Introduction

Crane is one of the most important equipment in the port operation. With the rapid development of the economic, large scale cranes are needed more than ever, as a result of that the cranes are more vulnerable to earthquake loads. For example, the 1995 Kobe Earthquake clearly exposed the destructive effects of earthquake motions on cranes. The modern container crane with the high center of gravity and large gauge is easy to swing. The connections between the leg and the portal beam are prone to buckling and being instability under earthquakes, which is the main form of destruction [1]. The destruction produced by horizontal loads make the earthquakes destructive so physical model of the crane was subjected to uniaxial horizontal loading through the critical axis vibration [2]. Michael Jordan [3] presented the method that the friction dampers are located at the bottom of each lower diagonal brace.

Semi-active control has been widely used in many successful engineering applications and has demonstrated significant achievements. A semi-active control strategy to a two-span continuous beam bridge equipped with MR dampers is proposed, the results indicate that this method is well capable of controlling the seismic responses and reducing the damage index of the pier simultaneously [4]. A Lyapunov-based control

© Springer International Publishing Switzerland 2016
Q. Zu and B. Hu (Eds.): HCC 2016, LNCS 9567, pp. 787–793, 2016.
DOI: 10.1007/978-3-319-31854-7_79

approach for MR dampers is presented, the effectiveness of the proposed approach integrated in building structures is verified [5]. MR damper is very effect in reducing vibration amplitudes of buildings and bridge structures. However, there is no relevant literature report on the seismic control of the container crane.

The aim of this study is to improve the seismic performance of container crane. For this purpose, a new vibration control system on the basis of a seesaw mechanism with MR dampers is proposed; semi-active control algorithm is adopted to change the output state of MR dampers to control the seismic responses of container crane. The result shows that the control effect is obvious, and has a great potential for engineering applications.

2   Seesaw Seismic Mitigation System Using MR Dampers

The proposed vibration control system, which is installed in the end face of portal beam, is connected between the tension rod and portal leg, as presented in Fig. 1. A couple of MR dampers are installed in the seesaw member, which is pin-supported. By introducing pre-tension in rods, the influence on seismic mitigation induced by the brace buckling problem is negligible, only tensile force appears in bracing members.

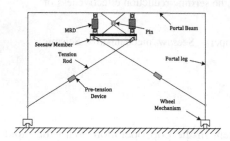
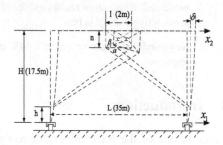

Fig. 1. Vibration control system   **Fig. 2.** Schematic representation

Kang JD [7] presented the relation between the horizontal displacement of the portal frame and the damper displacement can be expressed as.

$$\delta_d = f_s \delta \tag{3}$$

Where δ_d represents damper displacement, δ stands for the horizontal displacement of the portal frame, the magnification factor is $f_s = 2\left(1 - \frac{\xi}{\cos \alpha}\right)\left(\frac{\cos \alpha \cos \beta}{\sin (\alpha + \beta)}\right)$. In order not to affect the normal operation of the container crane after installing the mitigation device, the connecting point of the rod must keep a certain distance from the ground, so it can't be directly connected to the wheel mechanism. x_1, x_2 respectively represents the horizontal displacement of the portal beams and wheel mechanism. Since the surrounded area of the deformation of the leg is a triangle, the following relation is obtained.

$$\delta \approx \left(1 - \frac{h}{H}\right)x_2 + \frac{h}{H}x_1 \tag{4}$$

Because $\frac{h}{H}x_1$ is very small, Eq. 4 is expressed simply as follow.

$$\delta \approx \left(1 - \frac{h}{H}\right)x_2 \tag{5}$$

Simultaneously, H and h exist the following geometric relations.

$$\frac{h}{H} = 1 - \frac{(L + l)\tan \alpha}{2H} \tag{6}$$

Therefore, two sets of MR damping devices are installed on the crane, the displacement magnification factor is expressed as.

$$f_s \approx 4\left(1 - \frac{\xi}{\cos \alpha}\right)\left(\frac{\cos \alpha \cos \beta}{\sin (\alpha + \beta)}\right)\left(\frac{(L + l)\tan \alpha}{2H}\right) \tag{7}$$

Where ξ signifies the rod deformation factor, α represents the horizontal angles of brace, β denotes the angle between the connection member and the center pin, L stands for crane gauge, H denotes the height of the portal legs, and h denotes the distance between the connection point of the brace and the wheel mechanism, and l is the width of seesaw mechanism, n is the height of seesaw mechanism, as shown in Fig. 2.

Considering Eq. 7, the value of f_s decreases for the increase of ξ. When $\xi = 0$, that is, the brace is a rigid body, f_s can give the maximum value, in which the cases of $\beta = 20°$, $40°$. Figure 3 presents the variation of the seesaw system magnification factor f_s with respect to α and ξ.

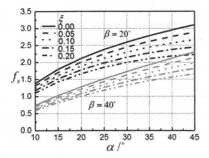

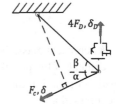

Fig. 3. Magnification factor   **Fig. 4.** Analysis of force

Under the seismic loads, analysis of forces acting on a portal frame with MR dampers can be described as a mathematical model, as represented in Fig. 4. Because of the small rotary angle of the damper during work, the relation between the horizontal control force of mitigation device and the force of a single MR damper can be expressed as

$$F_c(t) = f_d F_d(t) \tag{8}$$

where f_d denotes the magnification factor of the control force, which is

$$f_d = 4\left(\frac{\cos \alpha \cos \beta}{\sin (\alpha + \beta)}\right) \tag{9}$$

3   Equation of Motion for the Crane with Seesaw System

Since the destructive effect of earthquakes is a result of horizontal vibrations, the establishment of the horizontal mathematical model of the crane can meet the seismic
response analysis [7]. Figure 5 shows a schematic diagram of a typical container crane.
Since the upper structure of the crane acts as rigid body under the earthquake loadings.
Now the track jump is not taking into consideration, the single degree-of-freedom
dynamic model of the crane is established (Fig. 6).

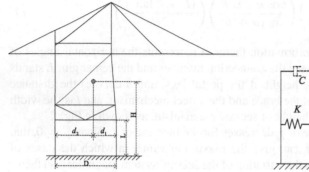

Fig. 5. Schematic diagram of container crane   **Fig. 6.** Dynamic model

Using the Lagrange method, the equation of motion of a container crane system
which is subjected to external disturbance can be obtained as follow:

$$M\ddot{x}(t) + C\dot{x}(t) + Kx(t) = -M\ddot{x}_g(t) \tag{10}$$

where M, C, K represent mass, damping and stiffness respectively, $x(t)$ denotes the horizontal displacement of the portal beams, $\ddot{x}_g(t)$ is the earthquake acceleration excitation.

The equation of motion of a container crane system with seesaw system with MR
dampers is expressed as

$$M\ddot{x}(t) + C\dot{x}(t) + Kx(t) = -M\ddot{x}_g(t) + F_c(t) \tag{11}$$

where $F_c(t)$ represents the control force of the seesaw system.

4   Analysis on Semi-active Control Effect of Seesaw System

The state vector is expressed as $Z = \begin{bmatrix} X^T & \dot{X}^T \end{bmatrix}^T$, Eq. 11 is converted into state model

$$Z(t) = A\dot{Z}(t) + BF_c(t) + D\ddot{x}_g(t) \tag{12}$$

Where $A = \begin{bmatrix} 0 & I \\ -M^{-1}K & -M^{-1}C \end{bmatrix}$, $B = \begin{bmatrix} 0 \\ -M^{-1}B_s \end{bmatrix}$, $D = \begin{bmatrix} 0 \\ -M^{-1}M\Gamma \end{bmatrix}$ and where $I \in R$ is a unit matrix.

The optimal control algorithm based on state feedback is developed to determine the optimal control force

$$F_c(t) = -R^{-1}B^T P(t)Z(t) \tag{13}$$

With reference to the optimal active control force $F_c(t)$ and considering the actual control situation of MR damper, the following bound optimal semi-active control algorithm is adopted [6]

$$F_d(t) = \begin{cases} F_{max}, & F_c(t)\gamma < 0 \ and \ |F_c(t)| > F_{max} \\ \frac{F_c(t)}{f_s}, & F_c(t)\gamma < 0 \ and \ F_{min} < |F_c(t)| < F_{max} \\ F_{min}, & other \end{cases} \tag{14}$$

Where F_{max}, F_{min} denote the control force of MR damper in the maximum and minimum magnetic field, respectively. γ denotes the relative velocity between the connection of the rod and portal beam.

In the calculation of optimal control force $F_c(t)$, the weight matrix Q and R are two important control parameters, how to select the optimal weight matrix Q and R are key to get good control effect. Q and R are expressed as respectively

$$Q = \eta \begin{bmatrix} K & 0 \\ 0 & M \end{bmatrix}, \quad R = \mu I \tag{15}$$

where K denotes the stiffness matrix of the container crane, M denotes the mass matrix of the container crane, I denotes the unit matrix. Modeled crane subjected to the ground motion of the El Centro earthquake (1940), whose peak ground acceleration was equal to 620 gal, has been simulated. Earthquake ground motion is used as input to a crane system taking advantage of without control, semi-active control, Passive-off and Passive-on control respectively. Where $\eta = 100$, $\mu = 1 \times 10^{-6}$ are the weight matrix, giving active optimal control force $F_c(t)$. For the case of $\alpha = 28°$, $\beta = 20°$ displacement magnification coefficient is $f_s = 2.51$, control magnification coefficient is $f_d = 4.58$, the selected maximum and minimum damping force of a MR damper are respectively 700 kN and 35 KN. The displacement responses of the structure under the horizontal earthquake loading are obtained by MATLAB software.

Figure 7 shows that the displacement amplitude is effectively suppressed by the semi-active control of the crane using seesaw system with MR dampers. The peak response of portal leg deformation is decreased by 40.9 %. The results show that the damping effect of the mitigation device based on semi-active control is better than that of the Passive-off and Passive-on control. At the same time, portal leg deformation of the crane is respectively 0.470 m, 0.369 m, 0.434 m, 0.278 m. The analysis shows that the proposed seesaw system with MR damper can effectively improve the seismic performance of crane under semi-active control.

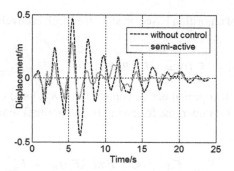

Fig. 7. Time history response of displacement under EI earthquake

5   Summary

This paper presented seesaw system with MR dampers to suppress seismic response of container crane. First, the magnification factor of the proposed vibration control system was derived. Results of the case study revealed that the magnification factor is influenced by the values of, β, ξ.

By introducing MR dampers in this system, semi-active control was adopted as control method to adjust the force of MR dampers. To conform the applicability of this method, seismic response analyses were conducted for crane taking advantage of without control, semi-active control, Passive-off and Passive-on control. The results of analyses demonstrated that the proposed system can reduce the seismic response of the frames. And compared to other passive control methods, the damping effect is best.

Acknowledgements.   This work was supported by the ministry of transport applied basic research project (2014329811050) and Study on seismic performance evaluation and dynamic behavior of jumbo container cranes (51275369). We are grateful to our partner company for their support of our research.

References

1. Loh, CH., Tsai, K.C., Kashiwazaki, A.: Study on the dynamic behavior of container cranes under strong earthquakes, pp. 279–284. Ishikawajima-Harima Heavy Industries Co. (1998)
2. Kanayama, T., Kashiwazaki, A.: A study on the dynamic behavior of container cranes under strong earthquakes. Seismic Eng. **364**, 276–284 (1998)
3. Jordan, M., Oritatsu, Y.: Seismic protection of quay cranes. Ports, pp. 1–11 (2009)
4. Songjian, S., Nan, J., Zhongxian, L.: Semi-active control strategy for continuous beam bridges based on damage to the piers subjected to strong earthquake. J. Earthq. Eng. Eng. Vibr. **33**, 140–145 (2013)

5. Ha, Q.P., Kwok, N.M., Nguyen, M.T., Li, J., Samali, B.: Mitigation of seismic responses on building structures using MR dampers with Lyapunov-based control. Struct. Control Health Monit. **15**, 604–621 (2008)
6. Xu, Z.D., Guo, Y.Q.: Neuro-fuzzy control strategy for earthquake excited nonlinear magnetorheological structures. Soil Dyn. Earthq. Eng. **28**, 717–727 (2008)
7. Kang, J.D., Tagawa, H.: Seismic response of steel structures with seesaw systems using viscoelastic dampers. Earthq. Eng. Struct. Dyn. **42**, 779–794 (2013)

An ERP Study of Attentional Bias to Drug Cues in Heroin Dependence by Using Dot-Probe Task

Zhijie Wei[1], Hanshu Cai[1], Qinglin Zhao[1(✉)], Quanli Han[2], Entan Ma[3], Guosheng Zhao[3], and Hong Peng[1]

[1] School of Information Science and Engineering, Lanzhou University, Lanzhou, China
{weizhj13,caihsh13,qlzhao,pengh}@lzu.edu.cn
[2] Gansu Provincial Drug Rehabilitation Administration Bureau, Lanzhou, China
1255934614@qq.com
[3] Municipal People's Hospital of Gansu Linxia, Linxia, China
{Hcmaentan,Suini97}@163.com

Abstract. Electroencephalogram (EEG) contains a wealth of information of the brain cognitive activities. Previous studies have provided that the behavioral data of reaction time (RT) is the main evidence of the attentional bias (AB) to drug cues in the heroin dependence. It is the primary method of measuring AB among the addicts. In this paper, RT is used to test the AB of the heroin addict towards heroin-related cues by using the dot-probe task. Meanwhile, event-related potentials (ERPs) are used to compare the differences between heroin addicts and normal controls. The heroin-related dot-probe task is performed on the heroin addicts (n = 22) and health normal controls (n = 22). The results show that heroin addicts have more expeditious response when the dot located on the heroin-related picture (valid) compared with on the neutral picture (invalid). Meanwhile, it is opposite to controls. At onset of the images, the average amplitude of P1 and P2 show obvious differences between addicts and controls at FCz. When at onset of the dot, an increased N2 is elicited under the valid condition compared with the invalid condition, which appeared in heroin addicts and controls. The latency of P3 of the controls is longer than that of addicts at Pz. These findings suggest that heroin addicts have differences when processing heroin-related cues compared to controls.

Keywords: Heroin dependence · Attentional bias · Dot-probe task · ERPs

1 Introduction

The drug addiction is a chronically relapsing disorder, which always begins with recreational use and develops into obsessive drug taking. Many evidences suggest that drug-related cues are a critical factor to drug taking and drug relapse in following treatment [1]. Drug-related cues which increase the craving will capture the attention of drug addicts. The viewpoint of AB to drug-related stimuli [2] is supported by previous study based on cognitive and behavioral theories of addiction. The incentive-sensitization model of Robinson and Berridge [3] postulates that the drug-related cues will

© Springer International Publishing Switzerland 2016
Q. Zu and B. Hu (Eds.): HCC 2016, LNCS 9567, pp. 794–799, 2016.
DOI: 10.1007/978-3-319-31854-7_80

conspicuously grab the attention and make the addicts use drugs again. At present, the study of AB in heroin addict mainly uses behavioral [4] and neurophysiologic measures [5]. However, the effect of heroin to the brain is not clear. The ultimate aim of this paper is to understand the AB of the heroin addicts with behavioral data and find differences between addicts and controls in the ERP data. The components of ERP are associated with drug-related cues in many different substances abuse. For example, Franken [5] holds the viewpoint that heroin addicts exhibits a larger amplitude of slow positive wave (SPW) component than the neutral pictures to heroin-related pictures. An early component P1 is useful to the visual task, and it is related to the attentional capture. Previous studies have shown that the drug-related cues can induce larger P2 component among the drug addicts compared with the controls. A number of studies have provided evidence suggesting that the latency of the P3 component reflects the time of stimulus evaluation in choice reaction tasks. We assumed that heroin addicts and controls have different course of processing to the heroin-related cues.

This paper is aimed at examining the influence of the heroin-related pictures to heroin addicts by using a dot-probe paradigm, which investigates the AB of heroin addicts. In the dot-probe task, the target stimulus will appear on the position of the drug-related or neutral pictures after that two pictures disappear. The drug addicts have faster reaction time to the target stimulus when the target stimulus appear at the position of drug-related cues than it appear at the position of neutral cues [2]. However, the dot-probe task is complex and the reaction time may be influenced by different exterior objective conditions. So, the ERP is used to research the differences between addicts and controls. It is predicted in this paper that an expeditious response to the dot was elicited under the valid condition compared with the invalid condition for heroin addicts but not for controls. Compared with the controls, the addicts will exhibit obvious discrepancies in ERP amplitude and latency.

2 Methods

2.1 Participants

Twenty-two male heroin addicts were recruited from a compulsory isolated detoxification center (Linxia Hui Autonomous Prefecture, China). Twenty-two male health control subjects were recruited from the local residents. Five subjects including three heroin addicts and two normal controls were excluded because of excessive artifacts in the electroencephalographic (EEG) signal. All addicts were matched to the diagnostic standard which is used for opioid substance dependence. The diagnostic standard is a part of the "Handbook of Diagnosis and Statistics of Mental Disorder" 5th edition (DSM-V). All participants are right-handed, and they have normal or corrective vision and don't have history of color blindness. Participants will be excluded if they rely on other drugs, mental illness, epilepsy, obvious head injury. The average age of addicts was 37.53 (S.D. = 7.65) years old and controls was 37.40 (S.D. = 6.17) years old. There is no significant difference in age (P = 0.955, by t-test) between the two groups. They volunteered for the task and signed the informed consent. The education years of addicts were 2.89 (S.D. = 2.75) and controls were 7.30 (S.D. = 3.47). Therefore, there was significant difference in the education background (P < .005, by t-test) between the two groups. However, there is no research proving that the education level is related to AB. The average time of drug-using was 3.54 years (S.D. = 3.21), and the average dose of drug-using was 2.34 g (S.D. = 1.63) per week. All the participants are paid for compensation after the completion of the task.

2.2   The Dot-Probe Task

In the dot-probe task, two stimuli, include one heroin-related picture and one neural scenery picture, were showed on each trial. When the pair of pictures disappeared, a target stimulus will replace one of them. Participants were asked to respond to the target stimulus as fast as possible (Fig. 1). Twenty-nine heroin addicts were recruited to evaluate the relevancy between 60 pictures (30 heroin-related and 30 neural) and heroin by using a 9 scale (0 means no relationship and 9 means great relationship). We selected 10 heroin-related pictures (mean = 7.91, S.D. = .11) and 10 neural scenery pictures (mean = 1.42, S.D. = .23) to make a comparison. The two sets pictures had significant discrepancy (t_{18} = 79.50, p < .005). The two sets pictures were matched in brightness, contrast and color.

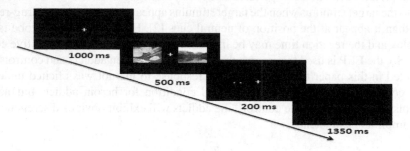

Fig. 1.   Illustration of the experimental sequence.

The task consisted of 4 blocks and the first block was used to practice. The format of basic trial was same across all blocks. Following a 1000 ms presentation of a fixation cross (2 cm × 2 cm) at the center of the screen, a pair of pictures were presented for 500 ms. The pictures were the cues. The two pictures were presented respectively in the right and left side of the fixation cross with equal distance (15 cm center to center). The target stimulus will appear for 200 ms in the location where one of the images disappeared. The target stimulus consisted of two dots with the center distance of 5 mm and the semidiameter of each dot is 1 mm. The pair of dots was oriented either horizontally (..) or vertically (:) and appeared at a distance of 8 cm either to the left or to the right of the fixation. Participants had to determine the orientation of the dots by pressing one of two prespecified buttons by using two fingers of their right hand. A new trial began 1350 ms after the target stimulus offset. Special feedback signal presented when participants didn't respond or wrongly responded to the target stimulus. One block consisted of 80 trials. The participants' eyes were 80 cm away from the monitor. They were asked to accomplish 20 practice trials. After that there were 240 main trials.

2.3   Collection and Offline Analysis of ERP Data

The tool for analysis and recording system is produced by German company "Brain Products". We selected 64 leads electrode cap whose setup referred to 10–20 international recording system. We used software, such as "the Vision Recorder" to record EEG data and "the BrainVision Analyzer 2.0" to analyze data offline. The scalp resistance was controlled below 10 KΩ. The sample rate was 1000 Hz, and the filter setting was 0.1–100 Hz online. The EEG data which exceeding ±80 μV would be removed from further analysis. The electrooculogram (EOG) was corrected by independent component analysis (ICA) method. Bilateral mastoid electrodes were used to serve as the reference electrodes. The offline EEG signals were filtered with a band-pass filter of 0.1 to 30 Hz for the ERPs. Statistical analyses were conducted by "SPSS (Version 19.0)" software. The ERP data and behavioral data were mainly analyzed in separate repeated-measures analysis of variance (RMANOVA).

3   Results

3.1   Behavioral Reaction Time Data

The data which was generated by wrong response was deleted, as well as when the reaction time (RT) was less than 200 ms. The Group (addicts vs. controls) acted as the between-subject factor. The Site (valid vs. invalid) acted as the within-subject factor. There was 2×2 mixed design. The results showed that both no effect of Group ($F_{1,37} = .02$, $P = 0.88$) and no effect of Site ($F_{1,37} = .001$, $P = 0.97$). However, there was a significant interaction between Group and Site ($F_{1,37} = 6.50$, $P = 0.015$). The simple effect test showed that there were marginally significant effects of Site in the addicts (valid: 496.98 ms, invalid: 504.34 ms, $F_{1,37} = 3.26$, $P = 0.079$) as well as in the controls (valid: 508.18 ms, invalid: 501.03 ms, $F_{1,37} = 3.24$, $P = 0.080$). That is to say, the addicts have a swifter response in the valid condition than in the invalid condition, but the result is exactly opposite in the controls (see Fig. 2a).

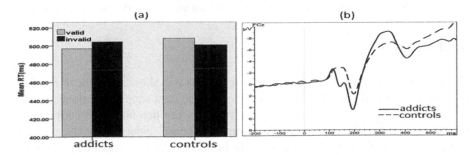

Fig. 2. (a) Results of behavioral data. (b) ERPs at FCz, time-locked the onset of the images and averaged across all conditions.

3.2 ERPs to Image-Pairs Onset

Grand average ERP waveforms at FCz were elicited by the pictures (see Fig. 2b), the average amplitude of P1 (the first major positive voltage deflection in the ERP occurring 130–155 ms after the cue) of the heroin addicts was evidently larger than that of the controls (addicts: 0.14 μV, controls: −2.75 μV, t_{37} = 2.95, P = 0.006). The average amplitude of P2 (the following major positive voltage deflection occurring 170–205 ms after the cue) of the addicts was also larger than that of the controls (addicts: 3.37 μV, controls: 0.68 μV, t_{37} = 2.06, P = .046).

3.3 ERPs to Dot Onset

Grand average ERP waveforms at Pz were elicited by the dot (see Fig. 3). There was also a 2 × 2 mixed design. The Group acted as between-subject factor and the Site acted as within-subject factor. There was a significant main effect of Site with a larger N2 (the major negative voltage deflection occurring 220–275 ms after target onset) under valid condition versus invalid condition ($F_{1,37}$ = 5.90, P = .02), but no main effect of Group ($F_{1,37}$ = 2.10, P = .16). There were no effect of Group and Site for P3 (the major positive deflection occurring 300–450 ms after target onset). However, there was a marginally significant main effect of Group for latency of P3 ($F_{1,37}$ = 3.25, P = .08).

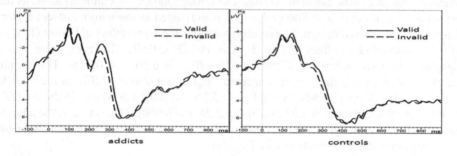

Fig. 3. ERPs at Pz, time-locked to the onset of the dot and averaged across all conditions.

4   Discussion

Behavioral studies have showed that the drug addicts will show AB to the drug-related cues by using the dot probe task [2]. The behavioral data support the prediction that heroin addicts distribute more attention resource to the heroin-related cues than the neural cues. However, the controls have rapid response under the invalid condition compared with under the valid condition. The heroin-related cues capture little attention compare with the neutral cues to the controls. The AB means that the drug-related cues are more likely to capture their attention and elicit the conditioned response which is important to maintain compulsive drug taking. It leads to relapse easily when they see or touch the opioid-related cues. The AB is related to the addict demand for addictive substances.

No matter the time is locked to the moment of images onset or the dots onset, we have discovered obvious discrepancies in the component of ERPs between heroin addicts and normal controls. When the time is locked to the moment of images onset, the early components P1 and P2 of the heroin addicts is significantly larger than that of the normal controls on the parietal region. This paper speculates that the heroin-related pictures can lead to larger early component for heroin addicts. When the time is locked to the moment of dot onset, the N2 and P3 are induced by the dot at the occipital region. The average amplitude of N2 is significantly larger under the valid condition than under invalid condition for heroin addicts and controls. The cues influence the component of latter target stimuli. The latency of P3 of the heroin addict is obviously shorter than the normal control's. The latency of the P3 shows that the heroin addicts have much shorter time to process P3. The latency of P3 reflects the time of stimulus evaluation and the heroin addicts can faster process the target stimulus than controls because the addicts are familiar with the heroin-related cues.

Acknowledgements. This work was supported by the National Basic Research Program of China (973 Program) (No.2014CB744600, No.2011CB711000), the Program of International S&T Cooperation of MOST (No.2013DFA11140), the National Natural Science Foundation of China (grant No.61210010, No.61300231), and Natural Science Foundation of Gansu Province, China (1208RJZA127).

References

1. Tiffany, S.T.: A cognitive model of drug urges and drug-use behavior: role of automatic and nonautomatic processes. Psychol. Rev. **97**(2), 147 (1990)
2. Lubman, D., et al.: Attentional bias for drug cues in opiate dependence. Psychol. Med. **30**(01), 169–175 (2000)
3. Robinson, T.E., Berridge, K.C.: The neural basis of drug craving: an incentive-sensitization theory of addiction. Brain Res. Rev. **18**(3), 247–291 (1993)
4. Franken, I.H., et al.: Selective cognitive processing of drug cues in heroin dependence. J. Psychopharmacol. **14**(4), 395–400 (2000)
5. Franken, I.H., et al.: Neurophysiological evidence for abnormal cognitive processing of drug cues in heroin dependence. Psychopharmacology **170**(2), 205–212 (2003)

A 3D Streaming Scheme for Fly-Through
in Large Scale P2P DVEs

Guisong Yang[1(✉)], Xingyu He[1], Huifen Xu[1], Wei Wang[1,2(✉)],
Chunxue Wu[1], and Linhua Jiang[1]

[1] Shanghai Key Lab of Modern Optical System,
University of Shanghai for Science and Technology, Shanghai, People's Republic of China
gsyang@usst.edu.cn
[2] Guangdong, Electronic Industry Institute Dongguan,
Dongguan, People's Republic of China
yanwang_neu@126.com

Abstract. Peer-to-peer (P2P) has become a powerful tool to deal with real-time transmission of large scale 3D scenes (i.e., P2P 3D streaming) in various distributed virtual environments (DVEs) based applications. However, there are still some issues worth further study to improve the performance of P2P 3D streaming. This paper thus designs a P2P 3D streaming scheme for fly-through in DVEs. The main work of this paper is a hybrid strategy to discover desired scenes sources (i.e., nodes which provide scenes that are required by others). Finally, outline future work is discussed.

Keywords: P2P · 3D Streaming · Fly-through · DVEs

1 Introduction

Distributed virtual environments (DVEs) [1, 2] (e.g., virtual city [3] and Massively Multiuser Online Games (MMOG) [3, 4]) are cyberspaces that inspired by both virtual reality and Internet, allowing users from different physical locations to roam or interact with others on the Internet. Originally, when a user tries to enter a VE, he/she is required to build the entire 3D virtual world (models and textures that allow rendering of scenes, and virtual representations of users are called avatars) at the client, by pre-installing of CD-ROM or downloading of 3D content progressively (i.e., 3D streaming [5]) via Internet. However, with the scale of a VE become more and more gigantic, "bottleneck" likely happen when massive clients download the same huge VE in a client/server (C/S) model simultaneously, because of limited bandwidth and CPU capacity.

The P2P 3D streaming [5] is proposed to relieve the bottleneck. The basic rationale of P2P 3D streaming can be described as: since users have overlapped visibility within the DVE, in other words, they have date requests for the same areas; nearby users can thus exchange 3D contents mutually to reduce request scenes from a server. Hence, P2P improves the scalability greatly when compared with C/S, because it's bandwidth and computing resources increases as the users increasingly join in the P2P overlay. In the implementation of P2P 3D streaming, there are some essential steps like search and selection of scenes source (a node providing 3D contents that are required by others) no

© Springer International Publishing Switzerland 2016
Q. Zu and B. Hu (Eds.): HCC 2016, LNCS 9567, pp. 800–805, 2016.
DOI: 10.1007/978-3-319-31854-7_81

matter what kind of P2P 3D streaming scheme is used. However, there are still some problems without good solutions, and we try to break through them here by a scheme to realize P2P 3D Streaming for Flythrough a large-scale VE.

The rest of this paper is organized as follows. Section 2 gives a brief overview of related work on 3D streaming. Section 3 describes the framework of a designed P2P-DVE and the general procedure of P2P 3D streaming for fly-through a large-scale VE. A series of strategies for searching and selecting appropriate nodes to deliver 3D data in the P2P-DVE and how to deliver scenes are introduced in Sect. 4 respectively. Finally, Sect. 5 concludes this paper and outline future work.

2   Related Work

2.1   Works on 3D Streaming

In this section, we present the representative researches on 3D streaming. Given limited visibility and occlusion among objects, a viewer can only observe a portion of a whole VE. To save disk space and waiting time, viewers are allowed to just download visible scenes at their current viewpoint for rendering immediately, and then progressively download newly visible scenes as their viewpoints move. One of the most popular approaches for 3D streaming is the *area of interest* (AOI) [6–8], which is a circular area with the viewer's visibility distance as its radius and viewpoint as its center, all objects within AOI can be regarded as visible scenes.

As there might be still huge scenes within an AOI in a crowed area of a VE, the *level of detail* (LOD) [9, 10] has been utilized for streaming of objects; the typical continuous LOD method is the *progressive mesh* (PM) [9] and its improvement. After processed by the PM, a 3D model can be divided into a *base mesh* that represents the lowest resolution for viewing, and a series of *PM increment pieces* that can restore the model to its original resolution progressively in terms of requirement. To determine the number of PM increments required for rendering, the *optimal resolution model* is described in [8].

FLoD [5] and its subsequent work [11] (it is noted as EFLoD for abbreviation here) are representative researches on P2P 3D streaming for real-time walkthrough of DVE; it gains encouraging advantageous performance over the C/S model. Both LODDT [12] and HyperVerse [13] focus on P2P 3D streaming for interactive flythrough of DVE. However, the performance of these schemes is not validated in a dynamic P2P overlay with high churn [14] (i.e., nodes join/leave with continuously), but the stability is a critical metric to evaluate a P2P 3D streaming scheme.

2.2   Works on Scenes Sources Discovery

There are two main ways to discover scenes sources, one is *data query* of FLoD and the other is *active data exchange* proposed in EFLoD. The main process of data query can be described as follows: a requester sends queries of required pieces to its AOI neighbors for response, if all of required pieces cannot be obtain from the AOI neighbors, the requester is allowed to request scenes from a server. However, some flaws exist: (a) in most cases, we can collect all required pieces with help of only a portion of AOI neighbors, so it is unnecessary to deliver queries to all of AOI neighbors. In other words, delivering redundant piece queries spends unnecessary time and bandwidth. (b) A requester only searches scenes sources from its AOI neighbors and the server, and those scenes sources outside of the AOI are omitted. In some cases, the incomplete searching may spend longer time to find a scenes source.

In the active data exchange way, a viewer sends its data availability incrementally to it AOI neighbors periodically; especially, a viewer distributes full information of data availability to its all new AOI neighbors; then, this viewer asks for pieces from its AOI neighbors who posse them. However, active data exchange cannot guarantee all required pieces be found in theory.

Although there might be more than one scene sources for a given piece request, only one of them is selected to deliver this piece. In FLoD, a requester selects a node from the set of scenes sources randomly to deliver a piece, and the maximum piece request a node could process at a moment is limited to be five. The random scenes source selection makes each scenes source have equal opportunity to serve piece requests, this could avoid overload nodes to an extent; nevertheless, it may cause request contention when multiple nearby viewers request same data at the same time.

3   Framework of 3D Streaming

We introduce two notions here, one is the *AOIv*, which is an abbreviation of the AOI on viewing, it represents *how far area a given avatar can view* in the 2D-Plane, it often looks like a ellipse; and the other one is the *AOIn*, which is an abbreviation of the AOI on nodes, it represents *how large area those nodes within it are interested by a given avatar,* it is a circle like the classic AOI. According to the spatial relation of viewers in the VE, if an avatar locates in the AOIn of another avatar, the former is treated as the latter's AOIn neighbor (or neighbor for abbreviation) (Fig. 1).

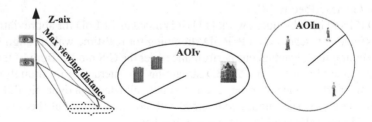

Fig. 1. Some geometrical notions in flythrough. (a) Observing areas projection for different viewpoint on a plane which is perpendicular to the VE ground; (b) AOIv; (c) AOIn

To determine an avatar's visible scenes efficiently, the ground of a VE is partitioned as fixed-size square *cells*; each cell is assigned with a unique ID and a *scenes description file* which gives a description for each object whose 2D-projection within it. If projection of an object intersected with two adjacent cells, this object is assigned to one of the two cells who have a bigger projection area. With the scenes description file, by judging the spatial relation of cells and the AOIv (i.e., a cell is overlapped by the AOIv or not) in the 2D-plane, a viewer could know objects located in his/her AOIv.

4   Scenes Sources Discovery

4.1   Scenes Source Discovery

A three-stage scenes source discovery strategy including three stages is proposed here, data availability exchange, data availability query and data query from sever.

Data Availability Exchange. Given a requester A if its neighbors receive A's position update message, they notify A about their incremental scenes availability instantly; for a new neighbor, the difference is its all scenes availability would be sent to A. A *then* requests pieces from its neighbors who possess this piece. In some case, the first stage cannot guarantee all required pieces are found. For example, A fails to receive some scenes availability messages due to reasons of network (e.g., nodes are connected via UDP, some packets might be lost due to unstable network or network congestion), however, neighbors who sent the message does not know such failure. Then, the data availability query is invoked.

Data Availability Query. A scenes source prioritized discovery strategy is utilized to realize the data availability query in our paper. We do not follow the query way in FLoD because of aforementioned flaws. In our way, it should be noted that: (a) all nodes only focus on scenes within its AOI in a very short time; bss) the limited size of AOI makes A's neighbors do not have the same interesting areas with A totally. More overlapped area means more same interesting area, so if A sends specified area' pieces queries to those neighbors just located in this specified area firstly, there will be less overhead for finding scenes sources than sending pieces queries to all AOI neighbors. Here, the detail process is introduced (Fig. 2).

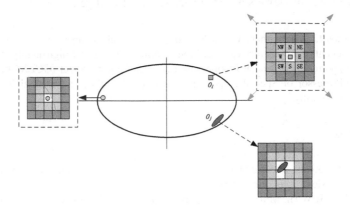

Fig. 2. Data availability query in three cases

(a) A sends queries of O_i to those neighbors within the adjacent eight cells, notes N, NE, NW, W, SW, S, SE and E. If the desired scenes source cannot be found in this step once, the searching scope will be expanded to adjacent sixteen cells, the similar process will be continues until a certain of cells outside the AOIn.

(b) If the object crosses more than one cell, these cells are combined as one "cell", then ask for pieces from those neighbors in the adjacent eight cells, the following process is similar with the first case.

(c) If the object located in border cell of AOIn, in other words, some cells in the set of eight adjacent cells outside the AOIn, in this case, A will expand its searching scope outward which is similar with the first case.

Data Query from Server. A threshold T_{sl} is arranged as the maximum duration for scenes source searching, if time spent on searching scenes source longer than T_{sl}, the scenes source searching will be ceased, and then the server is treated as the scenes source. Such an operation avoids a viewer spending too time to search a scenes source, just with workload of server growing slightly.

5 Conclusions

Various DVEs are interesting topics, however, there are still issues hindering popularization of DVE, especially, the bottleneck problem caused by the conflict between the limited resource and increasing 3D contents. In order to address these obstacles that are hard to handle in C/S, a P2P 3D streaming scheme for fly-through in large-scale DVEs is proposed, which consists of a series of strategies to realize delivery of massive 3D contents with favorable user experience.

We will implement a series of experiments to evaluate our methods in a P2P network. Our research has just found a way to the real-time fly-through of DVEs, leaving questions unsolved yet, e.g., current work only focus on scenes streaming when viewers roam without churn (viewers are assumed stay in the DVE always), however, viewers might leave or join the DVE randomly. How to attack more negative factors while keeping smooth experience of viewers have not been resolved well yet.

Acknowledgment. The authors would like to appreciate all anonymous reviewers for their insightful comments and constructive suggestions to polish this paper in high quality. The research was partly supported by Shanghai Engineering Research Center Project (GCZX14014) and the program for Professor of Special Appointment (Eastern Scholar) at Shanghai Institutions of Higher Learning jointly.

References

1. Singhal, S., Zyda, M.: Networked Virtual Environments: Design and Implementation. Addison-Wesley Professional (1999)
2. Ng, B., Lau, R.W.H.: Multi-server support for large scale distributed virtual environments. IEEE Trans. Multimedia **7**(6), 1054–1065 (2005)
3. http://secondlife.com
4. http://earth.google.com

5. Hu, S.Y., Huang, T.H., Chang, S.C., Sung, W.L., Jiang, J.R., Chen, B.Y.: Flod: a framework for peer-to-peer 3D streaming. In: Proceedings of INFOCOM 2008, pp. 2047–205. IEEE (2008)
6. Falby, J., Zyda, M., Pratt, D., Mackey, R.: NPSNET: hierarchical data structures for real-time three-dimensional visual simulation. Comput. Graphics 17(1), 65–69 (1993)
7. Chim, J., Lau, R.W.H., Leong, H.V., Si, A.: CyberWalk: a web based distributed virtual walkthrough scenes. IEEE Trans. Multimedia 5(4), 503–515 (2003)
8. Li, F.W.B., Lau, R.W.H., Kilis, D., Li, L.W.F.: Game-on-demand: an online game engine based on geometry streaming. ACM Trans. Multimedia Comput. Commun. Appl. 7(3), 408–417 (2011). Article No. 19
9. Hoppe, H.: Progressive mesh. In: Proceedings of SIGGRAPH 1996, pp. 99–108. ACM(1996)
10. Teler, E., Lischinski, D.: Streaming of complex 3D scenes for remote walkthroughs. Comput. Graphics Forum 20(3), 17–25 (2007)
11. Sung, W.L., Hu, S.Y., Jiang, J.R.: Selection strategies for peer-to-peer 3D streaming. In: Proceedings of NOSSDAV 2008, pp. 15–20. ACM (2008)
12. Royan, J., Gioia, P., Cavagna, R., Bouville, C.: Network-based visualization of 3D landscapes and city models. IEEE Comput. Graphics Appl. 27(6), 70–79 (2007)
13. Botev, J., Esch, M., Schloss, I.S.H., Sturm, P.: Hyperverse: Simulation and testbed reconciled. Int. J. Adv. Media Commun. 4(2), 167–181 (2010)
14. Stutzbach, D., Rejaie, R.: Understanding Churn in peer-to-peer networks. In: Proceedings of IMC 2006, pp. 189–202. ACM (2006)

Construction of Online Teaching Application Platform Based on Cloud Computing

Hongyu Zhao[1(✉)], Hong Zhang[2], Ping Zhang[2], and Weidong Xiao[2]

[1] Chinese Association for Artificial Intelligence,
No 10 West Tucheng Road, Haidian District, Beijing 100876, China
zhaohy@caai.cn
[2] Logistics Academy, No 23 Taiping Road, Haidian District, Beijing 100858, China
wengweilu@126.com, zhang_web@sina.com, 13366021927@163.com

Abstract. Based on the analysis of the development of online teaching, this paper proposes the overall conception of online teaching application platform based on cloud computing, describes the basic framework of the platform, and introduces the main tasks of the platform. In addition, an in-depth analysis is given on the construction of cloud data center, cloud storage platform, search engine and search navigation for teaching resources, online teaching management as well as management service cloud platform. Several key issues in the construction of the platform are also discussed.

Keywords: Cloud computing · Online teaching application platform · Construction

1 Introduction

After more than ten years of construction, great process has been made in online teaching applications. Many colleges and universities have established online teaching application platform and resources with their own teaching and training characteristics.

At the same time, there remain some problems.

1. The construction of the platform is strictly within each college and university itself. There are quite a number of online teaching application platforms, but their resource settings tend to lack commonality and openness, which means that their resources cannot be shared;
2. The construction is not standardized. Poor platform compatibility means they cannot be interconnected;
3. Network environments vary greatly, platform software and hardware development is not balanced, and configurability is poor [1].

If these problems are not addressed, the benefits of modern education technology cannot be brought into full play to meet the needs of the students in learning.

© Springer International Publishing Switzerland 2016
Q. Zu and B. Hu (Eds.): HCC 2016, LNCS 9567, pp. 806–812, 2016.
DOI: 10.1007/978-3-319-31854-7_82

2 Model and Build of Cloud-Based Online Teaching Application Platform

2.1 Basic Framework

Cloud-based Online Teaching Application Platform contains all necessary hardware and software computing resources for online teaching. These computing resources, after virtualization, are to be provided for the faculty and students. Cloud-based architecture of the platform is composed of the physical resource pools, basic management, application interface and application online teaching [1] (Fig. 1).

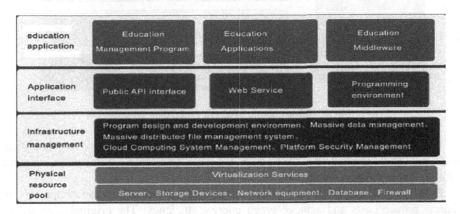

Fig. 1. Architecture of online teaching application platform based on cloud computing

2.2 Build Individualized Teaching and Cloud Data Centers

With the advent of the era of big data, the amount of data generated by Online Teaching Application Platform has been surging. Traditional data centers simply cannot stand the impact of big data, let alone helping students effectively utilize large data in online learning. At the same time the utilization and flexibility of data centers are on the decline. In particular, when it comes to the needs to meet teachers' individualized teaching demand as well as students' personalized learning demand, the system cannot satisfy the demand for access at peak pressure. Nor is it unable to give full play to the efficiency of hardware resources at pressure trough.

Cloud data centers, based on traditional data centers, are the service-oriented new data centers whose infrastructure can be dynamically expanded. Platform management uses cloud infrastructure to mobilize resources more dynamically and manage equipment and resources in a more intelligent and humanistic way.

Cloud data center infrastructure mainly consists of three levels (Fig. 2) [2]. Resource pool includes computing, storage and network resources, as well as database, middleware and other resources. Resources in resource pool are dynamically mobilized through the management system, according to the needs of remote users. When users need a new application, they will first send a request to the management subsystem of online teaching application platform, requiring to call the server resources, storage resources, bandwidth resources and software resources necessary for supporting the applications. Management subsystem obtains resources from the resource pool to allocate to student users who then access the acquired resources through the application platform. According to the pressure caused by each user application on the resources, management subsystem can also dynamically adjust the allocation of resources to avoid application crashes during peak access.

Fig. 2. Infrastructure of cloud-based data centers

For data centers of Online Teaching Application Platform to achieve "cloudification", we should implement a "three-step" strategy: data center optimization, resource pooling and intelligent management [2].

Firstly, it is necessary to integrate existing infrastructure resources to improve efficiency, reduce costs and achieve green energy efficiency. The original architecture should be simplified to reduce deployment complexity and realize simplified management.

Secondly, virtualization of data center resources involves virtualization of servers, storage devices and the network, which enables us to put physical basic resources together to form a virtual pool of resources that can be shared, with the aim to use these resources more flexibly and cost-effectively. Resource pooling can ensure flexible use and allocation of resources. Through the use of virtualization technology, it can decouple application and the underlying hardware and make sure that the construction of the data center is not tied to any particular hardware realization.

Finally, in the operation, maintenance and management of cloud-based data centers, it is necessary to build a corresponding cloud management platform to meet the service demands of data centers in the cloud era by performing the functions such as user management, user support, service management, operation and maintenance management, resource management, security management, disaster management, and monitoring management.

2.3 Build Virtual Classroom Teaching, Courseware Teaching and Cloud Storage Platform

Virtual classroom teaching and courseware teaching, by breaking the constraints of time and space, can meet the needs of the students in their self-study for teaching resources which are the basis for virtual classrooms, courseware production and teaching practice [2]. Teaching resources include such types as text, image, animation, sound and video, and are enormously large in number. With the extensive application of e-learning, the amount of data in teaching resources has witnessed an exponential growth, which means the need for more investment, including additional hardware and room environment equipment, increasing operation and maintenance costs and rising labor costs. Moreover, repetitive resource construction has resulted in the rapid growth of junk information, resulting in a waste of storage space. These problems have not only unnecessarily increased investment in education resources, but also hindered the improvement of teaching quality. Hence it is paramount to integrate teaching resources to the maximum extent and range, for the purpose of reducing teaching cost, improving teaching quality, and accelerating the development of online teaching.

Cloud storage platform, based on clustering applications, grid technology and distributed file systems, aims to put together a number of different types of storage devices through application software so that they can work collaboratively to provide data storage and business access for online teaching application platform [1]. Cloud storage platform infrastructure, from the bottom up, is divided into four layers: storage, basic management, application interface and access (Fig. 3) [2].

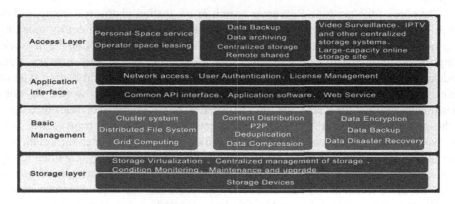

Fig. 3. Infrastructure of cloud storage platform

"Storage" offers a variety of storage services for users. Data of all services are stored in a unified cloud storage system to form a massive data pool. "Basic management" provides for the upper management a unified view of public administration for different services. Through public data management including a unified user management, security management, copy management and strategy management, the underlying storage is seamlessly connected to upper layer applications. "Application interface" is the part in cloud storage platform that can be flexibly extended and directly operated by customers. To satisfy different customer demands, different application interfaces can pop out to provide corresponding services. "Access" is the layer where any authorized user at any place, through any networked terminal equipment, can enjoy cloud storage service if they log oncloud storage platform using standard public application interface.

2.4 Build Search Engines and Search Navigation Platform for Teaching Resources

With the forms of teaching becoming more and more diverse and teaching contents needing constant updates and changes, teaching information resources has grown exponentially. The vast amount of resources, while providing rich information resources for students and teachers, poses a challenge to quick acquisition of the needed information. Effectively finding the most-needed information has become a complex and complicated task. Therefore, development of high-performance search engines and providing high-quality teaching resources navigation services has increasingly attracted the attention of users including students and the faculty [3].

Teaching Resources search navigation platform allows for a vertical search and navigation of educational information resources. As an online search engine system with catalog indexing, it can provide macro and micro view for online teaching information resources and offer corresponding access to teachers and students; provide a convenient and efficient information gathering, organizing and publishing platform for resource content administrators; and offer system management functions such as user management, data mining, resource monitoring, and resource assessment to system administrators.

The core of the teaching Resources search & navigation platform is composed of Web crawler, data indexing engine, page evaluation system, and directory indexing engine. Web crawlers migrate from one page to another, and by traversing the network, they can acquire educational teaching resources in a broad and deep manner. Data indexing engine analyzes collected pages, extracts the URL link and coding type of relevant pages, and information contained in page contents like key words, keyword position, generation time, size, and links between pages. Then based on relevance algorithm and page evaluation system, the engine gets the relevance of a page against each keyword in the page content and in the hyperlinks, and uses the related information to create web page index database. Contents Index engine forms category classification by manual work. Teachers, students and other users can gradually enter the topics of interest along the hierarchical classification directory, and then find the required information.

The Navigation system has multiple databases including directory navigation classification library, theme navigation search library, query index database, keyword library, Chinese sub word bank, and the library for value-added search services.

2.5 Build Online Teaching Management and Management Service Cloud Platform

With the growth of online teaching and education reform in universities and colleges, the number of students is on the sharp rise, posing a enormous challenge to the educational administration of online teaching. Educational administration has become increasingly heavy and complex. Large amounts of data, such as students' general information, course information, performance information, and faculty information, should be dealt with, which puts forward higher requirements not only for education administrators, but also for the data processing capacity and speed of education management subsystem [4].

An open cloud solution that can integrate various infrastructures is the key to the construction of teaching management service cloud platform. The so-called openness refers to using existing hardware in the process of building network application systems and servers, without the need for a full update, thus minimizing the cost. The so-called integration means that cloud platform can take full advantage of existing infrastructure and integrate heterogeneous platforms and devices without relying on one vendor's technology and products.

Construction of cloud platforms vary for different situations. When building a cloud environment, we need to assess the status of the network and resources, look for suitable approaches, develop a strategic cloud plan, conduct load test with non-critical work, and then gradually expand the range of applications.

3   Discussion

There several key issues in the construction of the platform we should pay more attention.

1. Avoid Attaching Full Importance to the Construction of Hardware Facilities While Neglecting Software Development. The ultimate goal of cloud-based online teaching application platform is to promote teaching. If attention is paid only to the construction of the platform's hardware systems like the networks, servers, and storage, while the development and use of related software is neglected, online teaching resources cannot be fully and effectively used, leaving us to face the awkward situation of having insufficient software to match the capacity of hardware.

2. Avoid Overemphasizing Form While Neglecting Application. Construction of Online Teaching Application Platform should focus on applications. In the process we should try to prevent the occurrence of the following phenomena summarized as "seven fewer, one more": fewer online courses, fewer informative resources beyond courses, fewer open teaching systems, fewer communication channels between management staff, the faculty and students, fewer capacity of information resources, fewer basic data, fewer contents for entertainment and leisure, but more constraints on the interaction between resources and information.

3. Pay Attention to Platform Openness. If the openness is not fully considered during the platform's design, information exchange and collaboration based on the platform will be a problem. Even if the majority of students can connect to each other through the platform, the lack of open, distributed management will make it difficult to achieve information sharing, distributed computing and collaborative research between the students in different areas. Besides, if there are more limits when the platform performs a variety of applications, the exchange, cognitive and guide functions will not be fully realized.

4. Pay Attention to the Standards and Specifications When Constructing Online Teaching Application Platform. In the construction of the platform, the network infrastructure protocol, the database interfaces for the information systems, share and exchange of data, and evaluation of teaching all require unified standards and specifications. Integration of resources is the bottle neck for Online Teaching Application

Platform. Only after this problem is completely resolved, can we make full use of the existing resources on online teaching application platform, integrate related resources on existing platforms, promote information consistency between platform systems and achieve interconnection, interoperability and share of data between different platforms. Only after the standards and specifications of remote platforms are finally set up, can cloud-based online teaching application platform truly benefit the majority of students, and enter the track of healthy development.

4   Conclusion

Online Teaching Application Platform based on Cloud Computing is a new stage in network education. It can preventing platform data loss, avoiding platform virus infection, facilitating unified management and professional protection of platforms, reducing the construction cost of online teaching application platform. It also can satisfy the learning desire and meet personalized learning requirements for students, therefore it has high economic and social benefits as well as good promotion prospects. Meanwhile it will play a positive role in changing the traditional mode of education, promoting college education reform, accelerating the development of college network education, and improving modern education management.

References

1. Zhao, H.: Grid computing and web education, Educational Technology, April 2007
2. Zhao, H.: Building Distance Education System based on Cloud Computing (2013)
3. Zhao, H.: Distant education based on web2.0 (2010)
4. Developing Applications for HUE[EB/OL], 27 September 2010
5. Yang, L., Zhao, H.: The Top-level Design Method on Informatization, ICPCA6//SWS3 (2011)

Aquatic Product Traceability Bar Code Generation Based on Barcode and Print Services to Verify

Qiaohong Zu and Rui Ma[✉]

School of Logistics Engineering, Wuhan University of Technology,
Wuhan 430063, People's Republic of China
965465631@qq.com

Abstract. In order to combine the demand of people's quality and safety of aquatic products and the practical needs of the enterprise, in this paper, taken one of the aquaculture farms and processing plants as a pilot exercise, the internationally used GS1 traceability standard is researched, the one-dimensional barcode GS1 Databar and two-dimensional barcode QR Code are chosen as the traceability information carrier. Set the links of the aquatic product breeding phase and processing phase as the main line, a full traceability pattern, both horizontally and vertically, is built in this paper. Databar GS1 and Code QR are used in the process of aquatic product breeding and processing, and the application of the barcode printing service technology and the bar code automatic generation printing service technology in the aquatic product traceability system is verified to achieve the real-time synchronization of the bar code in the process of aquatic production and processing, and ensure the authenticity and safety of the relevant information.

Keywords: Aquatic product traceability · Barcode technology · Database

1 Introduction

The bar code technology, set light, machine, electricity and computer as a whole, is a High-tech technology which is developed and widely applied in the middle of the twentieth Century. It is an important method and means to automatically collect data and enter into a computer and it can realize the fast and accurate acquisition and transmission of information. The bar code technology has been organically connected with the information system of all walks of life. It provides the technical means for the realization of the logistics and information flow. It can effectively improve the efficiency of supply chain management. At the same time, the quality of aquatic products has caused the attention of the relevant persons. In this paper, the application of bar code technology in water product traceability is studied.

© Springer International Publishing Switzerland 2016
Q. Zu and B. Hu (Eds.): HCC 2016, LNCS 9567, pp. 813–819, 2016.
DOI: 10.1007/978-3-319-31854-7_83

2   Bar Code Technology in Aquatic Product Traceability System

2.1   Bar Code Technology

The implementation of the GS1 global traceability standard can be used in any technology, but the best practice is to use the bar code on the box or on the pallet and exchange basic business information through electronic information [1]. Through the bar code technology can realize the fast, accurate access and transmission of information. Bar code technology is a more mature practical technology with the advantages of information acquisition speed, large collection of information, simple operation, high reliability, low cost and so on. It has broad prospects for development in the field of food safety traceability.

2.1.1   Characteristics of GS1 Data Bar

Now all the trade items reader can read GS1 Data bar barcode and process GS1 application identifier. Compared with other one-dimensional bar code, Data bar GS1 is a new code symbol standard. Because of its higher density, it can be used to identify more characters in a limited space, so that all the information of the products can be compiled into the bar code. Therefore, bar Data barcode is mainly used in small or difficult identifiable products, random measurement of fresh food and available space is not sufficient to provide all the information of the project in the field of logistics unit [2]. Bar Data code use series linear code system of the GS1 system which mainly divided into Databar-14 series, limited bar Data and expanded Data bar [3].

2.1.2   Characteristics of QR Code

Quick Response Code (QR Code) was invented by the Japanese company Denso-Wave in 1994 and it is currently one of the most popular two-dimensional bar code. Code QR is square and it is composed of a dark color module that represents a binary '1' and a light color that represents a binary '0'. At the same time, three of which lies in the four corners of the square, with smaller printed on the back of the square shaped pattern for fast locating reader software.

2.2   GS1 Traceability Standard

GS1 traceability standard is based on the GS1's global identity system, which is based on the product, supply chain transaction parties, trading position, enterprise receiving or delivery of the logistics unit, a warehouse or storage of goods for the sole identification. It can realize the information record and share of all links in the process of the up and down step and the supply chain [4].

GS1 system is composed of the coding system, the data carrier which can automatically identify and the electronic data exchange standard protocol. And the coding system is composed of GTIN, GLN, sscc, GIAI, GRAI, GSRN, attribute code. It is a data carrier based on barcode and RFID tags, and the information is exchanged through the electronic data interchange (EANCOM), and the form of EDI packet is transmitted.

GS1 system has the advantages of systematic, global unity, scientific and expansibility. It solves the problem that the information encoding is not the only one in the supply chain. It avoids the waste of resources caused by the system which is not compatible, optimizes the efficiency of the whole supply chain management, and provides a fast data communication solution for the trade partners. By providing a common framework to achieve seamless of logistics and information flow, it provides the necessary foundation for the field of food safety traceability, and also brings us a lot of benefits.

2.3   The Advantages of Databar and Code QR's Combination

GS1 Databar, which is designed by GS1, is a new type of bar code, and it is widely used in the field of the traceability which can store more information in less space. QR code has good characters information storage capacity, and with the popularity of mobile phone built-in QR code recognition and decoding software, QR code is more and more used in mobile client products traceability query field. Based on the above advantages, we carry out the aquatic products traceability label design, combined with GS1 Databar in the one-dimensional bar code and QR Code the two-dimensional bar code.

3   Aquatic Product Traceability System Based on Bar Code

3.1   The Overall Scheme Design

In this paper, combining with some breeding and processing of aquatic products enterprise actual demand, the paper combines the bar code technology and the information technology, and realizes the quality and safety of aquatic products by building a aquatic product traceability system based on bar code technology.

GS1 Databar's storage is a special code structure of traceable yards or batch number. And GS1 Databar and aquatic products traceability system Web terminal are mainly used in combination. In the process of aquatic product traceability queries, it needs to be matched with the data from the database to complete the relevant information of aquatic products. This method, based on the aquatic product traceable system's web queries, has a strong dependence on the database and network. What's stored in QR Code is the key links in the process of encryption and processing of the Chinese character information, and mainly combined with aquatic products in the mobile phone client. In the process of aquatic product traceability queries, only through the mobile client of QR code for correct reading and decryption, can be directly to obtain information of Chinese characters on aquatic product traceability. This method cannot rely on the database and the network to complete the search method based on the mobile client scan code (Fig. 1).

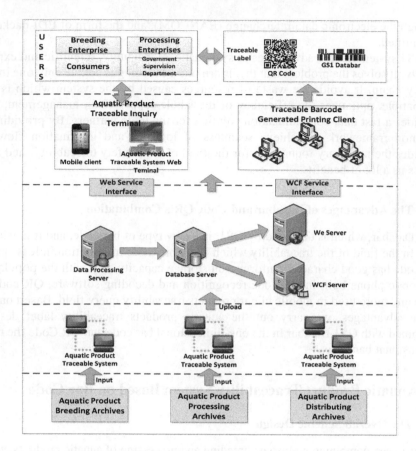

Fig. 1. Overall plan of aquatic product traceability system based on bar code technology

3.2 Databar and QR Code's Hybrid Applications

The Databar and QR Code are mixed in the process of stage of breeding and stage of aquatic product. It mixes the combination of bar code technology and aquatic product traceability system, so that all aspects of the information collection and entry of aquatic products can be more efficient and more convenient. So we can improve the traceability of aquatic products.

3.3 The Design of Aquatic Product Traceability

3.3.1 Service Oriented System Architecture Design

SOA services package the components or elements of the specific operation level. They provide users with standardized external interface, reused, stateless, independent technology. Its biggest feature is the use of complex business or technical logic, focusing on what provides, while hiding the internal details. It focuses on the purpose and not implementation. This paper is based on the principles of constructing SOA and

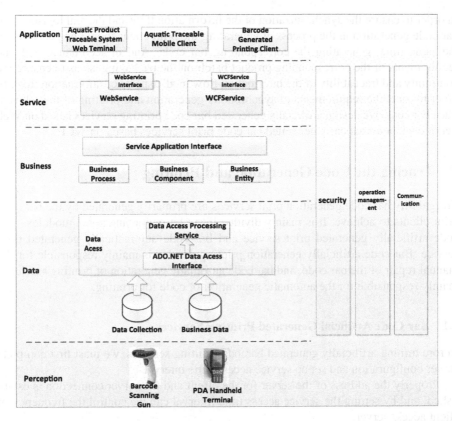

Fig. 2. Overall framework of service oriented aquatic product traceability system

combined with the actual needs of the whole chain traceability of aquatic product. It also built the overall framework of the service to orient aquatic product traceability system.

The overall framework of the service oriented aquatic product traceability system is designed as the five layer-Perception layer, Data layer, Business layer, Service layer and Application layer.

The overall architecture of the system is based on the idea of service oriented, which can make the relative coupling between the various service functions. It will make the system more flexible and the service communicate through the simple, standard, neutral interface, but does not involve the underlying specific programming and internal structure. The system will have better expansibility and generality, so it can greatly reduce the cost of service application development.

3.3.2   The Design of Printing Service for the Generation of Barcode

In the process of aquatic product's breeding and processing, the relevant information of each link is entered into the system. And the system will generate the corresponding batch number of each link according to the certain structure and rules of the encoding.

In order to ensure the synchronization of the information flow and the real logistics, the bar code generation in the process of generating the print client should be generated at the same time, generating the corresponding bar code. And in accordance with the requirements of the corresponding product batch on the packaging, so as to ensure the continuity and traceability of the information flow in all aspects of information flow. In order to meet the requirements of synchronous generation and printing of the relevant trace bar code, we design artificially generated bar code printing services based on Web Service and automatically generated bar code print services based on WCF.

4   Tracing the Code Generation and Printing

Traceability bar code generation print services are primarily generated by the bar code print clients to achieve. It is mainly divided into two major functional modules - bar code artificially generated print service and bar code automatically generated print service. Bar code artificially generation printing service is mainly responsible for the manual repair of the bar code, and bar code automatic generation of printing service is mainly responsible for the automatic generation of code for printing.

4.1   Bar Code Artificial Generated Printing Services

Before turning artificially generated barcode printing services, we must first complete server configuration and set up service access time interval.

Properly the address of the server for the client and the server connection is established, and by setting the service access time interval can we control the frequency of client access server.

After the configuration is complete, enter the bar code to generate the print service main interface. Bar code artificial generated printing services mainly include Databar, generator, breeding QR Code generator, processing QR Code generator. DataBar generator is mainly responsible for the corresponding feed batch number, drug batch number, fry batch number, processing raw material batch number and retroactive processing code DataBar bar code generation and printing. Breeding QR Code generator and processing QR Code generator are mainly responsible for breeding and processing traceable bar code's generated printing.

In this section, we select processing traceable Databar bar code generation printing, breeding traceable QR bar code generation printing and processing traceable QRbar code generation printing to take examples of verification.

4.2   Bar Code Automatic Generated Printing Services

Bar code automatic generated printing service is mainly dependent on WCF technology. The service truly realized the server automatically send the generated printing bar code command to the generated printing bar code client. New process trade code or traceable bar code is generated when generated bar code prints in real time. When starting the bar code automatic generated printing service, first of all, we need to enter the account of the printing device to log in, and determine which printing equipment to complete the bar code printing work. After starting up the service, when the aquatic product traceability system Web end inputs the aquatic products, processing and other information, the database will generate a corresponding new process trade code or traceable code. Bar code generation and printing client will automatically generate the corresponding QR Code or Databar code's synchronized generated printing.

The bar code generation print client will monitor the generated printing bar code, and generate the corresponding print records. At the same time, the bar code's printing content, printing equipment, printing number printing time and other information will be stored in the data table dbo.CodePrint in the database. As shown in Fig. 2. By using bar code's automatic generated printing services, the generated bar code will be printed no more than 500 ms, and has a higher response than the artificial printing bar code.

5   Conclusion

In this article, through traceability system of aquatic products related technology research and implementation, we achieve the real-time synchronization of the bar code in the process of aquatic production and processing mainly based on bar code's artificial generated printing services and bar code's automatic generated printing services to ensure the authenticity and safety of the relevant information.

References

1. BS ISO/IEC 24724-2011: Information technology. Automatic identification and data capture technology. GS1 data bar code symbol specification
2. Wen, X.: Application of GS1 system in food safety tracing. Food Saf. Guide **06**, 75–77 (2009)
3. JIS X0509-2012: Information technology. Automatic identification and data acquisition technology. GS1 Databar code symbol specification
4. Wu, H.: The basis of modern logistics information management-GS1 system. Space Stand. **02**, 37–40 (2009)

Research and Application on Aquatic Products Traceability System Based on EPC Coding

Qiaohong Zu[✉] and Xiaochang Liu

School of Logistics Engineering, Wuhan University of Technology, Wuhan 430063, China
zuqiaohong@foxmail.com, 623365479@qq.com

Abstract. Through the analysis of the class of aquatic products business processes and information in the process of supply chain, using EPC coding technology, database technology and anti-counterfeiting technology, we designed traceability system coding scheme and anti-counterfeiting traceability solution, establish the traceability system on aquatic products through-out the supply chain. It is proved that the method is feasible. We realize the automatic and efficient data acquisition and can improve the safety of the product.

Keywords: EPC code · Aquatic product traceability · Security encryption

1 Introduction

Food safety is a hot area of current research, aquatic products as an important part in the food category its security problem is getting more and more attention by people. The quality and safety of aquatic products directly related to people's health and life safety. Establish and improve the aquatic product traceability system and ensure the quality and safety of aquatic products, has become a top priority for the sustainable development of aquatic products industry. In this paper, aquatic products are as the research object. In order to meet the enterprise's intelligent information management, consumers of aquatic safety information query, facilitate the government to carry out regulatory work. We take the water product as the research object, starting from the supply chain each link, using technology to achieve the security of aquatic retroactive.

2 EPC-Based Aquatic Products Traceability System

Electronic Product Code (EPC) is a product electronic coding system developed by the United States Auto-ID Center. This system will replace the bar codes in the radio frequency identification system. EPC consists of the title description area and three data zones. Title Description data area is 64 or 96. The first date area stores manufacturer code; the second one stores the product code; the third one stores the unique product serial number. EPC is compatible with Global trade product code (GTIN) and other Global trade product code (GTIN) and other codes EPC is very similar to GTIN and VIN.EPC is an advanced, comprehensive and complex system, which is committed to

© Springer International Publishing Switzerland 2016
Q. Zu and B. Hu (Eds.): HCC 2016, LNCS 9567, pp. 820–826, 2016.
DOI: 10.1007/978-3-319-31854-7_84

becoming a global, open label standard for each single product. Compared with the bar code, the application of EPC technology is more flexible and has greater information capacity, anti-environmental pollution and stronger anti-interference ability.

A large number of data is stored in the database shared by many users. Whether it is a consumer or enterprise, query or update the information in the process of tracing is the operation of the database, if the database is designed unreasonably, the access speed will slow down and maintenance data will be difficult. Therefore, before starting to write an application code, we should think about how to design a reasonable and efficient database. This system is based on three principles of stable, reliable, safe, scalable [1].

According to some rules, the data is generated by the EPC encoding. In the production and sale of aquatic products, the staff need to check these EPC encoding. Right EPC encoding will be written to the electronic label. Data is entered into the database, and detailed information. Data is copied to a database, and details linked. In retrospective query process, Users can get all the information stored in the database through the whole process of EPC code as an index. Users can get all the information stored in the database In EPC code as an index.

3   System Design

3.1   Overall System Architecture Design

By using EPC technology and RFID, this system can manage aquatic products supply chain processes. To achieve this purpose, first, we want to achieve the acquisition and modification of data. Second. We want to store and manage data that we collected. Finally, we want to achieve information analysis and other functions. In logic system is mainly divided into: data acquisition layer, information transmission layer, application layer system.

Data collection layer: information is mainly from the farm, distribution and marketing chain links.

Data transport layer: the collected information is stored in the database through this layer. Data is stored in the database to ensure data security.

System application layer: system application layer is mainly to achieve the application of the various segments of the enterprise and the management of traceability information. Users can add, delete, change, check the data through the application layer, the layer is a direct manifestation of the query.

3.2   System Function Module Design

The ultimate goal of the system is the final trace. In this paper, we use the B/S model of the three tier architecture (presentation layer, business logic layer, data access layer). In the process of the supply chain, the user's working interface is realized through the Web browser. Users can operate in any place and do not need to install any special software. As the aquatic supply chain involves many enterprises, different enterprises can view the information is different, in order to give different users in the system to assign different roles and permissions (Fig. 1).

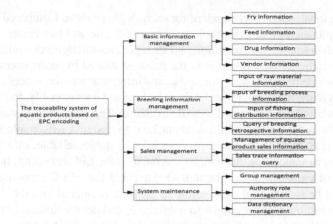

Fig. 1. Function module diagram of water product traceability system

Basic Information Maintenance Module: The module is mainly to maintain information about the fish, feed, drugs, vendor. Users can increase, delete, change or check the data, and realize the basic maintenance.

Breeding Retrospective Information Management: As the source of the whole course quality, there are many security problems in the process of breeding. For example, the quality of feed, drug residues, etc. Therefore, the management of aquaculture needs to be traced back to the process of information management and query.

Breeding Information Management: The management of raw material information, procurement process information, fishing and distribution information and traceability information.

Sales Information Management: This is the end of the supply chain information. This stage is a good and fresh water product sales management and traceability, mainly including the sales of product information management and sales retrospective information query.

System management includes the data dictionary, user authority, system settings, and other parameters set up.

3.3 EPC Application

In consideration of the special nature of water product, the business process of water supply chain is given. The specific applications of EPC in each process are as follows:

(1) Application of raw materials: According to the encoding rules, EPC encoding is generated based on the information about feed, fry and breeding process. After checking, encoding is written into electronic tags, and the information is stored in the database. Raw material storage process.

(2) Application of aquatic products: In the breeding process, EPC encoding is generated based on the information about the name, origin, variety, and batch. Through the EPC encoding as an index, the user can query the information of water product culture stage.

(3) Identification of transport units: In the delivery process, the EPC tag is the only label on the transport vehicle. Through the label and encoding, we can establish contact with the vehicle delivery, to achieve traceability in distribution process.

(4) Sales unit identification application: After delivery of water to the destination, the sales quality inspection personnel to check the order information and the information into the database. As a result, the manager and the consumer can check the product details through the relevant equipment. At checkout, the sales information is recorded and the tag is recovered.

4   Design of Water Product Tracing Scheme

4.1   Association Scheme Design of Tracing Information

To achieve the full track of the water product, first of all, we need to identify the product with encoding. Through the analysis mentioned above, aquatic product is different from the general domestic animals. In the whole supply chain process, it is usually carried out in batches as a unit to manage the tracking. In the design of this paper, the relationship between the various links to achieve the association between the various links. In the water product traceability system, the ultimate goal is to achieve the individual's retrospective. But in the process of breeding, logistics and sales, the realization of the function of the unit is batch. The following table is detailed information of each batch of encoding. As the index information, encoding series of data contact data stored in the database, to realize the coherence of all stages of the entire supply chain [3].

4.2   EPC Encoding Project Design

Liability subject of the traceability system uses a general encoding structure. Universal identifier EPC scheme is independent of any specification or labeling scheme and is independent of the EPC global standard tag data. The capacity of the 96 encoding has been large enough to meet the needs of the water product traceability. From the cost point of view, the cost of the label to be reduced, so the overall consideration of the 96 encoding structure is the most suitable.

According to the above analysis, the supply chain process of the water supply chain is after being recovered, Fish from the distribution center was sent to the sales store from the distribution center. Since the goal is to achieve the individual's back, then the label will need to identify the individual water products.

Manager Code: To consider the cost of the problem, the manager of the code only records breeding base, distribution center and the Sales Department and never records information in the process of breeding and distribution. To solve this problem, we have all these details stored in the central database. As long as we are able to identify the farms, logistics centers and sales departments, we can identify the identity of the information stored in the central database through these logos.

Object Classification Code: There are six digits of the object classification code. The object classification code is used to identify the type of aquatic products, feed, drug type, freight unit, etc. And the details of these objects are stored in the central database.

Serial Number: there are nine digits of the serial number, the first six of the sequence number is the date, the date format is YYMMDD, and the three bit is randomly generated sequence number used to uniquely identify the product.

In this paper, seed, feed, medicine, aquatic products, single product transportation vehicles using EPC Tags.

4.3 Security Anti-counterfeiting Scheme Design

As far as the current research is concerned, the problem of data security has been paid more attention. The tag is unique, so it has the ability to secure the security. But there are some areas that rely solely on the label encoding itself is not sufficient to meet the requirements of security. We need to increase other means to improve its security level.

The physical method of tag anti forgery is mainly physical separation method and kill label method. The physical separation method is mainly used to block the transmission of electromagnetic wave in the label without the need to read. Kill the label method is mainly in the label application cycle after the completion of the label service method, also called "kill tag". This method generally adapts to the low cost and the use of more frequent tags. Considering the actual demand of water product and the cost, the system chooses the appropriate physical encryption. The method is mainly used to kill the tag, when the execution of the method of killing the tag, the tag automatically destroyed, not to use.

Encryption technology is to study the preparation of passwords and password. This technique is closely to transmit information and ensure that the data in the transmission process will not be leaked [5]. Encryption technology is mainly related to the sender and receiver, information and encryption, algorithm and key three elements. Data encryption technology is based on the key algorithm, is generally in accordance with the characteristics of the key algorithm for classification. At present, the algorithm is divided into two categories: symmetric cryptography algorithm and asymmetric key algorithm.

In this paper, we have a large amount of data to be encrypted. In general, the asymmetric algorithm is slower than the symmetric algorithm, so we adopt a symmetric encryption algorithm for the characteristics of the system. At the same time, considering the problem of label cost, the more complex the algorithm is, the higher the requirements of the label. Considering the speed and cost, the DES algorithm is used to encrypt the information in the electronic tag. The formation of encrypted information is stored in the tag. After the DES algorithm is encrypted, the label information is enhanced in order to further strengthen the authenticity of the information. The principle of encoding encryption security is to generate the corresponding encoding, and then write the text information into the tag chip. The data transmission between the tag and the reader is transmitted in encrypted form, which ensures the security of data transmission. In this way, even if the molecules do not send the appropriate information in the label, it will not read any useful information, in order to achieve the purpose of preventing information leakage and tampering of information. At the same time in order to store the information of the goods and the encrypted encoding, need to establish the corresponding database. The global unique identifier TID also needs to be stored in the database. Encoding is read by the tag reader, through the tag in the EPC encoding as the index to achieve the information in all aspects of the association and query, to achieve traceability of goods.

4.4 Database Design

Information digitization is the basis of the water product traceability system, and also the basic guarantee for the realization of the system. Although the system is used as the carrier of electronic tags as retrospective information, for the limited capacity of the label, the information on the label is only an index and cannot store all the information about the water. Any information must be stored in the database, the user uses the label information to connect the database to the water product detailed inquiry. Therefore, we must pay attention to the design of the database in order to realize the traceability of the entire supply chain. In this paper, through the analysis of the characteristics of the water supply chain and the user's needs, we have carried out the detailed design of the database.

B/S model of the water product traceability platform is the ultimate display platform. Different roles, different permissions are assigned to the corresponding users. For example, the users of the breeding enterprise can operate the information of the breeding stage through the platform.

5 Summary

In this paper, the application of EPC encoding technology, based on the particularity of the aquatic product, the function and application of EPC tags are analyzed and designed. Based on the structure model of aquatic product supply chain, the role of the breeding base, logistics and sales center as the main factors in the process of tracing back to the process is analyzed. The traceability of the information content in each link of the supply chain is determined. The overall structure and functional modules of the traceability query system are designed. In the system implementation of the program, the encoding program is analyzed in detail. Information security and database design. An example is developed and the simulation is verified.

References

1. Current situation and construction of industrial technology system of large freshwater fish in China, Ge Xianping, "Chinese fisheries", 05 May 2010
2. Ling, J., Da Liu, M., Zhu, Y.: Based on IOT tobacco security and quality traceability system. Food Ind. **12**, 247–250 (2014)

3. Animal husbandry and feed science. Anim. Husb. Feed Sci. **12**, 131–144 (2013)
4. Wu, M.: Research on DES and RSA Hybrid Encryption Algorithm. Harbin Institute of Technology, Harbin (2013)
5. Lu, A., Yang, J., Li, F., Zhang, B., Joan, C.: A comparative study on several kinds of lightweight encryption algorithms. Mod. Electron. Technol. **12**, 37–41 (2014)

The Information Encryption Design and Application of the Aquatic Product Tracing Process

Qiaohong Zu and Lian Liu[✉]

School of Logistic Engineering,
Wuhan University of Technology, Wuhan, China
zuqiaohong@foxmail.com, 1098814367@qq.com

Abstract. In recent years, aquatic product quality and safety problems occur frequently make aquatic product traceability is increasingly important, and the problems of data security exposure in the tracing process also must be resolved. In this paper, the research object is based on the system of aquatic product traceability system, and two kinds of encryption technology (symmetric encryption and asymmetric encryption technology) has been introduced. After considering the features of the information in the tracing process and the advantages and disadvantages of the two encryption technologies, three specific data encryption scheme in the three major data processing of aquatic product traceability have been designed. And the encryption scheme has been programmed to realize, which is proved to be feasible.

Keywords: Aquatic product traceability · Encryption technology · MD5 algorithm · DES algorithm · QR code

1 Introduction

The rapid development of information and communications technology lead human into a new era of big data. The popularization of the Internet makes information becomes ubiquitous. However we are also faced with unprecedented information security issues while we are enjoying the boon of convenience and quick access to information. In order to improve the safety and reliability of the information, encryption technology has been increasingly used as an effective way to protect data security in the field of information security.

After a comprehensive analyze of the current existing aquatic traceability system, the phenomenon that information encryption is weak or no encryption has been found. Therefore, in order to improve information security of the data communication and storage in the bar code and prevent the communication data from random tampering, theft or tracing code being random forged, this paper is aimed at the above problems. The related encryption technologies are further studied and Aquatic traceability encryption algorithm is designed and the relevant applications are carried out to provide comprehensive security for aquatic traceability.

© Springer International Publishing Switzerland 2016
Q. Zu and B. Hu (Eds.): HCC 2016, LNCS 9567, pp. 827–834, 2016.
DOI: 10.1007/978-3-319-31854-7_85

2 Encryption Technology

Encryption technology is the most commonly used means of security measures, which mainly convert the original clear data into unreadable messy code through the encryption algorithm before transmission, and then restore the plaintext data after reaching the destination through certain means to protect data from being stolen or tampered with arbitrarily [1].

Algorithm and cipher code are the two core elements of encryption technology. Algorithm is a procedure of combining an ordinary text (plaintext) and a string of numbers (cipher code) to produce unintelligible messy code (ciphertext), the cipher code is a algorithm of using for data encoding and decoding. Corresponding to the keys divided into two big classes of symmetric and asymmetric keys, data encryption algorithm is mainly divided into symmetric encryption algorithm and the non-symmetric encryption algorithm. The biggest difference between them is that the former uses the same encryption and decryption keys, but the latter uses the different keys. Therefore encryption key of asymmetric encryption algorithm can be made public [2].

2.1 Symmetric Encryption Method

Symmetric encryption algorithm which has been applied early time has mature technology and the advantage of a fast speed of encryption and decryption, a small amount of computation, the open algorithm and difficult to crack when using long key. However, the problem of symmetric encryption algorithm is that its security is completely determined by the secrecy of the key. In order to guarantee the uniqueness of the key, the number of the key is increased by the geometric progression which cause the key management being more difficult and costly. There are some commonly used symmetric encryption algorithm such as DES encryption algorithm, AES encryption algorithm, RC5 algorithm, etc.

2.2 Asymmetric Encryption Method

Different from symmetric encryption which uses the same key encryption and decryption, asymmetric encryption algorithm has public key and private key. Its working principle is to generate a pair of public key and private key firstly. The public key can be made public. When using the private key to encrypt the information or data, others can only use this key to decrypt the corresponding public key and vice versa. When using public key to encrypt the information or data, others can only use this public key to decrypt the corresponding private key [3]. As asymmetric encryption algorithm avoids the problem of sharing common key, so it is more secure and very suitable for public media or network data encryption. However the algorithm is more complex, which makes its encryption speed slow comparing to symmetric encryption, so asymmetric encryption algorithm are generally used to encrypt small amounts of data, such as digital signatures, encryption, rather than large files. There are some commonly used asymmetric encryption algorithm such as RSA algorithm, DSA, Elgamal algorithm, etc.

In this paper, the encryption scheme is based on the data characteristics of different stages of the aquatic product tracing process and under the consideration of the advantages and disadvantages of the two encryption algorithms.

3 Design of Data Encryption Scheme in the Process of Tracing

In the process of aquatic product tracing, to ensure the security of data communication and the security of the information stored in the bar code, prevent the communication data from being tampered with, steal casually, it requires the use of appropriate data encryption technology to encrypt the related information. The related algorithm design mainly from three aspects of the user login encryption, data encryption and communication QRCode encryption in this paper.

3.1 User Login Encryption

In the water product traceability system, only the users who have the appropriate permissions are allowed to add, modify, delete and query the related information to ensure the authenticity and safety of the relevant information in the aquatic product traceability system, therefore, users need to enter the correct user name and corresponding password to enter the system. To ensure the security of user passwords, there is no explicit text storing user passwords directly in the database. Instead, it is stored in the corresponding data table in the form of a cipher text encrypted with MD5 algorithm. Thus effectively prevent the user password is stolen or tampered by others (Fig. 1).

MD5 algorithm is the most widely used one in hash algorithms, it is a function that can compress a message of any length to a 128 bit message digest, the algorithm principle is shown in the following diagram [4]:

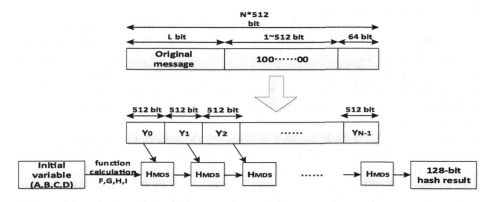

Fig. 1. The schematic diagram of MD5 algorithm

(1) Data filling: By adding a number 1 and appropriate number of 0 after the original message, we could make the length 64 less than the multiple of 512. The filling scope ranges in the digit from 1 to 512.

(2) Adding length: By adding a length of 64 digit after the filling message, we could make the final length exact multiple of 512.

(3) Initialization variable: Use 4 variables (A, B, C, D) to calculate the message digest. Initialize the four 32 bit registers to Hexadecimal values: A = 01234567h, B = 89abcdefh, C = fedcba98h, D = 76543210h.

(4) Data processing: Through 4 auxiliary functions, processing the message grouped in 512 byte blocks, the 4 auxiliary functions are shown below:

$$F(X, Y, Z) = (X \& Y)|((\sim X)\&Z) \tag{1}$$

$$G(X, Y, Z) = (X \& Z)|(Y\&(\sim Z)) \tag{2}$$

$$H(X, Y, Z) = X^{\wedge}Y^{\wedge}Z \tag{3}$$

$$I(X, Y, Z) = Y^{\wedge}(X|(\sim Z)) \tag{4}$$

Of which & means AND operation, | means OR operation, $\sim$ means NO operation, $\wedge$ means XOR operation.

(5) Output: After all the 512 byte blocks is processed, the ABCD cascade will be output as a result of the MD5 hash.

The biggest characteristic of MD5 algorithm is its non-reversibility, even though understand the MD5 algorithm in detail, it cannot return a message encrypted with the MD5 algorithm, at the same time, the MD5 algorithm can transform any length of the string into a large integer of 128 bits, so it has a good compressibility. Moreover so long as to make any changes to the original information, the resulting MD5 hash value will be very different, so the MD5 algorithm has good resistance to modify and impact, MD5 algorithm is often applied to digital signature, message origin authentication, etc. based on the above advantages.

In order to guarantee the user's account security, the MD5 algorithm is used to encrypt the password of the system users in this paper. In the specific program implementation, as the System.Web.Security class under the .NET platform directly provides the MD5 encryption method which has been compiled, so directly invoking System.Web.Security.HashPassword ForStoringInConfigFile (password, "MD5") method can complete the user password MD5 encryption. In this system, in order to enhance the security of MD5 algorithm, MD5 ciphertext is taken a further optimized processing by the MD5 method which is called by the system, that is, splicing 16 bit ciphertext and 32 bit ciphertext into a new 40 bit ciphertext using MD5 algorithm according certain rules. The splicing rule is: 16 bit MD5 ciphertext + the posteriori 8 bit of the 32 bit MD5 ciphertext + the posteriori 8 bit of the 16 bit MD5 ciphertext + the front 8 bit of the 32 bit MD5 ciphertext. The optimized MD5 encryption algorithm further increase the crack difficulty through the Stitching rules which have been defined by the system, and improve the security of user password.

When the system needs to verify the user password, it only need to compute the clear text of the users entered password into the MD5 hash value, and Splice the result according to the predefined rules, then compare with the corresponding ciphertext stored in the database, in this way, the system can complete the authentication of user identity in case of not know the real password of the user, so that ensure the user's account security effectively.

3.2 Communication Data Encryption

The data exist a risk of being stolen, tampered or eavesdropping when communicating between the client and server, so it is necessary to select the appropriate encryption technology to encrypt the communication data. In this paper, DES encryption algorithm is adopted to encrypt the communication data. DES encryption algorithm is one of the most widely used algorithms in symmetric encryption algorithm. It is a typical block algorithm based on key encryption, which is composed of three core elements: Key, Data and Mode, and Key is the 64 bits key (actually only 56 bits are used for the algorithm, and the other 8 bits are used for even-odd check.). Data is the 64 bit that need to encrypt or decrypt. Mode refers to the two operate mode of encrypt or decrypt. The algorithm principle is: divide the 64 bit plaintext data block into two half block of 32 bits to build Fiestel structure, and process the half data block and the scheduling generated Sub key using Fiestel function, and OXR the result with the another half block, then merge and exchange order with the original half block group, after 16 iterated operation like this, conduct inverse displacement of the final output half block

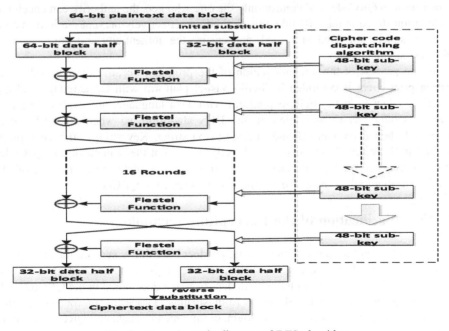

Fig. 2. The schematic diagram of DES algorithm

(The inverse function of the initial permutation), therefore obtain the 64 bit data block [5]. The principle diagram of DES algorithm is as follows:

In the process of the realization of the specific program, the DES encryption and decryption method which has been compiled in the System.Web.Security class is directly called to realize the communication data encryption and decryption. Only need to use the same key between the server and the client, encrypt the data with the key in the communication source, then decrypt the data after receiving the encrypted data in the receiving terminal, you can get the clear text data from the transmission. Because the security of DES algorithm does not depend on the algorithm's security, but depends on the key. Therefore, in order to further improve the security of communication data, it needs to update the key synchronously at both data communication terminals (server and client) to ensure the secure transmission of communication data (Fig. 2).

3.3 Tracing QRCode Encryption

As the identification and tracing credential of the aquatic products, the tracing barcode has stored the breeding and processing phases information of the aquatic products, the key information of the barcode will be easily to be forged or tampered with if there is any protection, and the consumers cannot get the true tracking information of the aquatic products. Because the QRCode has the function of optimizing the Chinese character information processing, so the Key information of each link in the cultivation and processing stage of aquatic product can be store in the QRCode in the form of Chinese characters directly to facilitate the mobile client scan and query.

This paper uses the DES encryption algorithm to encrypt the Chinese character information in QRCode, and control only the one who gets the authority can check the information stored in the QRCode, this method can effectively prevent the information is freely stolen, tampered or forged, and ensure the authenticity and uniqueness of QRCode simultaneously.

In the process of the implementation of the program, because the bar code generation print client is compiled in Studio Visual platform with C# language and the aquatic product is in the Eclipse platform with Java language, and both of the two languages offer classes to implement the DES algorithm, so when the QRCode is generated, the system can call the Encrypt (Text string, Key string) DES encryption method in System.Web.Security class directly to encrypt the content of the QRCode, and call the decryptDES(Text string, Key string) to complete the decryption of the QRCode content when using the mobile client to scan the QRCode.

4 Case Verification of the Encryption Technology

In order to protect the safety of the aquatic product traceability system, the encryption technology is used in many aspects such as user login, communication data and QRCode to effectively prevent the system data from the data stored in the QRCode and the information stored in the database from stealing, tampering or forging. In this section, the encryption scheme of user login, communication data and QRCode specific applications are given to verify.

4.1   User Login Encryption Scheme Instance Verification

As mentioned above, the user login password is encrypted by MD5 encryption algorithm, and splice the MD5 ciphertext according to the rules: "16 bit MD5 ciphertext + the posteriori 8 bit of the 32 bit MD5 ciphertext + the posteriori 8 bit of the 16 bit MD5 ciphertext + the front 8 bit of the 32 bit MD5 ciphertext", then, the final result is stored in the corresponding user table in the database.

No matter how long the user password is, the length of the cipher text is always 40 bit after being treated by the MD5 encryption algorithm according to some rules. Take the user name "aa" as an example, its Passwords plaintext is "19900812", the ciphertext is "9E8130BBD0F579E6A9AF00A5D0F579E6536564EC" the first 16 bits ciphertext of the "9E8130BBD0F579E6" corresponds to the plaintext "19900812", "A9AF00A5" and "536564EC" correspond to the first 8 bit and the last 8 bit, "D0F579E6" is the ciphertext's last 8 bit after the calculation of MD5 algorithm. When users enter a user name and password to log into the system, the system only need to encrypt the password by MD5 algorithm, and then compare the obtained results with the ciphertext stored in the data table, and the verification of the user's password can be completed.

4.2   Communication Data Encryption Scheme Instance Verification

For the aquatic product traceability system, data requires frequent communication between the client and server when making a service call or callback, therefore, in order to ensure the security of the communication data and prevent data from illegal eavesdropping or tampering when transmission, DES encryption algorithm is used to encrypt communication data in this paper. Now, the example that the server-side transfers the Dataset of retrospective batch number which the data bar code has not printed is taking to verify the data communication encryption scheme.

In this example, because the DataSet object can not be transmitted directly by the Web service, and therefore the DataSet object should be serialized first. First, transform retrospective batch number which have stored unprinted Databar into Byte arrays, then, encrypt the byte array with DES encryption algorithm, and the encrypted results can be seen by calling the Web method interface released by Web services. From the resultant picture, the retrospective batch number sequences become a piece of irregular array messy code, in this way, secure transmission of communication data has been effectively guaranteed.

4.3   QRCode Encryption Scheme Instance Verification

In order to protect the security of the information stored in the QRCode, and prevent the QRCode counterfeiting, we use the DES algorithm to encrypt the Chinese character information in QRCode, and generate the corresponding encryption QRCode in this paper. Now, we'll verify QRCode encryption scheme using a processing retrospection QRCode as a example.

According to the example, the information stored in the QRCode is the Chinese characters plaintext before encryption, the information which provides the name of Aquaculture processing plant, the processing time, the delivery time and related raw material details (raw material name and fishing time point) is encrypted into a meaningless string by the DES algorithm using the assigned key "123". When using a mobile client to scan the encrypted QRCode, if you fail to enter the correct password to decrypt, you can only get the messy code, rather than the related retrospection information, and thus ensure the authenticity and uniqueness of QRCode.

5   Conclusion

Problems and shortcomings of the data encryption in the retrospective process of the aquatic product are analysed in order to illustrate the important of the data encryption, symmetric and asymmetric encryption method are introduced in detail in this paper, and a primary solution of encryption is proposed, then, a detailed encryption plan is designed in the three important data processing and transmission stages and related encryption algorithms are provided, finally, three examples are given to verify the schemes.

References

1. Liu, Y.: Analysis of application of data encryption technology in computer security. Inf. Commun. **02**, 160–161 (2012)
2. Jiang, W.: Brief comments on the principle and application of information encryption technology. Comput. Era **05**, 10–11 (2011)
3. Zhuo, X., Zhao, F., Zeng, D.: Study on asymmetric encryption technology. J. Sichuan Univ. Sci. Eng. (Nat. Sci. Ed.) **05**, 562–564 (2010)
4. Rabah, K.: Theory and implementation of data encryption standard: a review. Inf. Technol. J. **44**, 210–211 (2010)
5. Penchalaiah, N., Seshadri, R.: Effective comparison and evaluation of DES and Rijndael Algorithm (AES). Int. J. Comput. Sci. Eng. **25**, 88–89 (2010)

The Design of the Tracing of Aquatic Products Production Based on PDA

Qiaohong Zu and Yinglie Lv[✉]

Wuhan University of Technology,
Heping Road No. 1040, Wuchang District, Wuhan 430063, Hubei, China
{22836099,1293711149}@qq.com

Abstract. This paper mainly studies the key technology of aquatic product traceability system based on PDA mode, and finally designs a scheme of the system. To achieve this scheme, a B/S and C/S hybrid architecture is being built. C/S, the client side, is the aquatic product traceability system based on PDA. Its function is to fulfill the operation of information and communicate with the remote server. B/S, the server side, adopts integrated management approach of SQLServer database, knowledge base, logical application, etc. At the same time, A logic scheme under the hybrid is being designed. Through these we can trace the information related to the supply chain, which verifies the application of key technologies to achieve a retrospective, and improve system stability, fluency and latency. This paper has done a thorough and useful reference and exploration for the future application of PDA.

Keywords: PDA · Producing traceable · C/S and B/S hybrid architecture · Webservice

1 Introduction

The Internet of Things technology development is in full swing. Research scope gradually extends to all areas of the national economy life. Mobile devices are increasingly added to the Internet of Things and the use of intelligent terminal for information collection is becoming an important means of field data acquisition, data processing and data transmission. In the field of aquaculture, The desire of getting access to data collection, feedback and information sharing in any time, any place by using intelligent terminal is significantly intense. Now the smart terminal equipment-PDA makes it possible.

The direction of the paper is regarding aquaculture and production traceability. By analyzing the overall need from the perspective of industrial application of PDA, we can use some key technologies to solve the problems in real process. The main work of this paper is building a hybrid architecture of B/S and C/S system based on PDA and designing a logic program under the framework.

© Springer International Publishing Switzerland 2016
Q. Zu and B. Hu (Eds.): HCC 2016, LNCS 9567, pp. 835–841, 2016.
DOI: 10.1007/978-3-319-31854-7_86

2   The Related Technology of the Tracing of Aquatic Products Production Based on PDA

2.1   Function and Operating System of PDA

The full name of PDA is Personal Digital Assistan. This intelligent handhold terminal combines computer, telephone, SMS, software installation, fax, network, and other functions in one [1]. Now the PDA is usually refers to the palm computer in general sense. It has the advantages of using Wi-Fi to connect with the internet, installing system such as GPRS, Bluetooth, WiFi and other modules and building in Microsoft embedded operating system which is open. [2] As the important equipment for collecting information in the future, PDA is moving forward to the convenient operating system, abundant entertainment and multimedia, longer using cycle, more portable volume and weight, powerful communication and so on. The paper studies the tracing of aquatic products which is based on the operating system of WinCE- a kind of electronic equipment operating system based on handhold computer. This operating system is suitable for many kinds of embedded products and widely used in PDA, POS and set-top boxes. Its application can be divided into many modules, so people can design the related modules according to their own needs. It also has such characters as multitask, multithread and real-time preemptive priority. [3] A lot of software support this operating system, including the Studio.NET Visual and C++ and the use of Builder Platform. All of these tools greatly simplify the working strength and the difficulties in development, shorten the time and labor costs, and improve the efficiency.

2.2   PDA Wireless Communication Technology

A suitable wireless communication mode is important when developing the tracing of aquatic products production based on PDA. It must be able to achieve the communication among the PDA, terminal services and barcode printer, namely, the wireless communication mode of PDA can achieve in various real time environments. The PDA which is based on the project platform can carry three kinds of wireless communication modules, that is, Bluetooth, GPRS and WiFi. All of these have their own advantages and disadvantages. After the PDA is equipped with these three modules, a special link protocol is designed and then we can achieve wireless transmission in a short distance [4, 5].

2.3   Framework for Service Oriented Architecture

For a complete application system, its not enough to only understand the PDA itself. When PDA communicates with server and bar code printer, Service Web and WCF network communication services enable the server to dynamically push bar code printing. Web Service network communication is mainly responsible for the connection of PDA terminal and PDA through the wireless WiFi. It transfers the data collected by PDA into the server in real-time, then the sever updates the database. As a result, the operator in system center can readily see the change of data and take the corresponding measures. All of these form a "wireless" interactive process. Since the biggest advantage of Service Web is to realize the mutual access of the program in different platforms, systems and languages through a series of standard protocols and data definition format, and it can also cross the network firewall, most of the communication services are through XML Web Service when the PDA communicate with servers. Each method that be used in PDA will be wrote in the server B/S framework system, using the Service Web to package and publish.

WCF network service is mainly responsible for the pushing in service side. In the aquatic product traceability system, the server can push the bar code machine for real-time dynamic printing by using WCF technology. When the program is written into the Winform application, the configuration of the IIS host and the Winform application host can achieve duplex communication, that is, the method of server side callback client. So when PDA put the new data into SQLCE and simultaneously into the server database SQLServer, the method of WCF will automatically callback client which is already configured, then driving the method performs in Winform application and finally achieve the purpose of printing.

3 The Overall Design of the Traceability System Based on PDA

3.1 The Design of C/S and B/S Hybrid Architecture

Analysis and Selection of C/S and B/S Hybrid Architecture Platform

C/S Architecture Model. C/S architecture, namely, the client/server architecture. It can base on any communication protocol, and assign tasks to the client or server reasonably. It's widely used in the mobile terminal because of saving system resources and convenient operation. To build a C/S architecture we should install a client in the PC or mobile terminal. It is a platform for users to communicate with the remote server.

B/S Architecture Model. B/S architecture, that is, the browser/server mode. It is a network structure model after the rise of WEB. WEB browser is the most important utility software in client. In the traditional sense, it is an improvement of the C/S architecture. In B/S architecture, some task is displayed and provided to users in the front end of the browser, Others are at the back end, the remote server, to respond to the user's operation and feedback in the way needed.

In contrast to the C/S architecture we can find that the browser in B/S mode can only handle simple transactional logic, but can't allocating the resource to two computers properly in real-time. A large part of the work must be transferred from the server concentratively. Consuming the system resources greatly, the pressure of the server will be great and the processing power will be affected by the amount of data. As a result, the system in this paper uses the optimized C/S model, which integrates the B/S client technology. In the research of the system, the server is built on the PC The application of the tracing of aquatic products system which is based on C/S is conducted on the client and the development based on B/S is proceed on the server.

Build the Overall Structure of the System Platform. The research in the paper builds a system of tracing aquatic products which is centered on PDA smart terminal and a comprehensive information platform of back-office service side. Furthermore, the data transfer through cross-platform can be accomplished by converting the mode of database. C/S client is the aquatic products production system based on PDA. In the traceability system, each PDA operator can operates the information from the purchase, breeding, fishing, quarantine, processing, and distribution to sales through the friendly interface. To some extent, the B/S server has become a pivot for processing and feedback of the data collected by mobile terminal PDA. Its purpose is to make unified management of SQLServer database, knowledge base and logic application in server. The overall structure of the system platform is shown in Fig. 1.

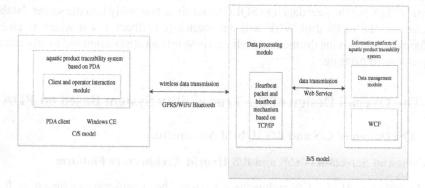

Fig. 1. The overall structure of the system platform

3.2   Design of the Whole System Framework

In addition to studying on the key technologies and related theories of the aquatic products production system, we should solve such problems as "many to many", "one to many", "many to one" and other complicated relation problems which appeared in the tracing of supply chain during the process of designing. Whether it is reverse or forward, consumers hope that they can monitor and query all pertinent information about upstream at the end of the experience. For thousands of products, we need to use a special way to identify them, and make each of them the only one. In this way, no matter how complex the supply chain is, the "only" will make logical relationship of the supply chain more careful, but not confused.

In the logic design of the system we introduced the concept of "business batch number". Its meaning is to lock every aquatic product, no matter which part it is, And to identify the specific information of the aquatic product. For example, in the breeding process, managers use a specific encoding (2 bit header + 6 bit stocking date + 2 bit pond number + 2 bit net cage number + 2 bit serial) number to identify it when a fish is caught in a fish pond. The parameters in encoding can guarantee the uniqueness of the product. Then small arrows are used to pointed to the batch number related to other links so we can know the relationship between the upstream and downstream. Finally, we can trace any information in the procurement of raw materials by using this specific batch number in the breeding management module.

3.3 Communication Between PDA and Web Service

In my research, wince, the operating system in PDA, is provided by Microsoft. Although there is a interacting across heterogeneous platform with the operating system of Windows in server side, the method we use is packaged by Microsoft and based on HTTP protocol. We can achieve cross-platform communication simply by accessing the API interface in server side and parsing data packaged by SOAP protocol and XML format. Communication between PDA and Web Service is shown in Fig. 2.

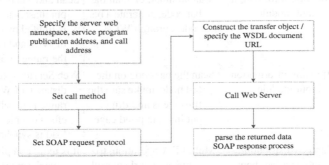

Fig. 2. The process to realize communication between PDA and Web service

4 Realization and Analysis of the Aquatic Products Production System Based on PDA

4.1 Realization of the Construction Scheme of B/S in Server Side

The aquatic products production system in sever side allows the operator to inspect and handle node information in the whole supply chain through accessing to the browser-the B/S side. There are two aspects of the system. On one hand, the operator in the information center can add, delete, modify and check the node date of the current supply chain directly. On the other hand, when the data which comes out from PDA needs to be processed, modified or deleted, that is, the data of SQLCE gets into the SQLServer database synchronously, operator can send a request through the B/S system at that time, and then synchronous information will be bound in the page. Finally the data can be easily modified and deleted.

4.2 Analysis of the Application Effect of the System

In the design of the aquatic products production system based on PDA, we must contin-uously test the whole system of its stability, operability, etc. We integrate the B/S system and C/S system throughout the testing process, and test the function of functional module. The purpose of the test is to verify the consistency of the output results with the results anticipated and with the same parameter inputs. The whole testing process is under WiFi environment. The test results are shown in Table 1.

Table 1. Test results of the functional test of the aquatic products production system in server side

Test times	Test projects	Input and operation	Result
120	Login module	Enter the corresponding parameter, trigger the access server operation	After the encryption of the data decryption, the server can get response data, and log in successfully
100	Purchase information input module	Manual input, or scan the bar code, generate a bar code Through WCF	Scan and Tie the bar code of purchasers in sever WCF is limited by the distance of Wifi, and is feasible in the range of 50 m
100	Breeding information input module	Scan the bar code on the last node, make sure the fries feeds and drugs put into the pond cage	Web Service is limited by the distance of WiFi, 50 m range is feasible, and the effect of upload and download is synchronized
100	Capture/distribution information input module	Multi PDA operation, to achieve a single or bulk upload and download, And call the WCF technology to produce the bar code in the process of distribution or catch	It is more complicated in asynchronous and heartbeat packet processing, also affected by the network WiFi, when packet loss rate control in 5 %, in the case of a single PDA in laboratory, the information is fully synchronized.

In the system performance, the stability, fluency, delay, memory occupancy rate and energy consumption in server side and PDA side are the most direct experience to users. In functional testing, the overall stability of the two systems is well performed, the switch between the modules is smooth, and no thread blocking, card screen and system collapse appear at PDA terminal. After using the application of the WebService service, the memory usage of the PDA system is greatly reduced.

In the area of time-delay, test results are shown in Fig. 3.

On the basis of the WCF and WebService which is simultaneous deployed, there is some redundancy and delay in the network. The average delay is over 1220 ms, but still within the acceptable range.

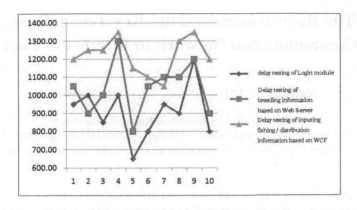

Fig. 3. Delay testing of the system in three modules

5 Summary

This paper mainly studies the key technology of aquatic product traceability system based on PDA mode, and finally designs a scheme of the system. To achieve this scheme, a B/S and C/S hybrid architecture is being built and a logic structure about the "uniqueness" which solves the requirement for the "uniqueness" in the process of the tracing is being designed. Finally, the consumer can trace the information "forward" or "backward" at any node in the supply chain. So the practical value of the application is achieved. These have cemented the foundation of solving the key technologies of the aquatic products production system based on PDA and achieving the value of tracing.

References

1. Trushenski, J.: New and ongoing society initiatives to craft a lasting partnership between AFS and all things aquaculture. Fisheries **6**, 285 (2013)
2. Draper, D.: Managing patron-driven acquisitions (PDA) records in a multiple model environment. Tech. Serv. Q. **2**, 153–165 (2013)
3. Mo, D.Y., Tseng, M.M., Cheung, R.K.: Design of inventory pools in spare part support operation systems. Int. J. Syst. Sci. **6**, 1296–1305 (2014)
4. Reza, A.W., Dimyati, K., Noordin, K.A., Kausar, A.S.M.Z., Sarker, M.S.: A comprehensive study of optimization algorithm for wireless coverage in indoor area. Optimization Lett. **8**(1), 145–157 (2014)
5. Cropf, R.A.: Information Communication Technologies and the Virtual Public Sphere: Impacts of Network Structures on Civil Society (2011)

The Requirement and the Key Technologies
of Communication Network in Internet of Energy

Wei Zhang[✉], Jianqi Li, Jing Zhou, and Ziwei Hu

Information and Communication Research Department,
State Grid Smart Grid Research Institute, Changping District, Beijing 102209, China
{wei.zhang,lijianqi,zhoujing,huziwei}@sgri.sgcc.com.cn

Abstract. Energy is the material basis of human development, Energy Internet, considered as a possible solution of energy sustainability is becoming a hot research topic and mainstream technology, in this change, Information and communication technology will play an important role. In this paper, first we analyses the current business requirement of energy internet, then predict the possible business in the energy internet. At last, we analyses the key technology in the communication network of energy internet.

Keywords: Energy internet · Communication · Standard · Technology

1 Introduction

Energy is the material basis of human being development, but some energy, such as fossil fuel, it is not inexhaustible, to deal with the problem such as climate change, energy sustainability should be paying much more attention. To solve the energy problem, it is not simply increase the supply of energy, improve the utilization rate of energy. And we need a complete revolution, this revolution couple the energy stream and information stream, and build a brand new energy system, and create the innovation mode of the energy utilization.

The introduction of Energy internet concept provides a new way to solve above problem. By now, there is not a unified concept for internet of energy, in academia, they think the internet of energy should be the concept of "peer-to-peer Sharing" [1, 2], in Energy internet, it includes not only electric power system, but it should include the natural gas system, transportation system (such as electric vehicle) and some other more generalized energy system. But in the view of enterprise, such as state grid, it puts forward the concept of global energy internet, and it defines the global energy internet as "By utilize the ultra-high voltage power network as the backbone network (channel), convey the cleaning energy as the leading task, global interconnected and strong smart electric power network".

There are lot kinds of energy, and electric power is just one of them, but electric power is much cleaner than them, it will be a trend to replace the fossil fuel with the electric power. And the transfer efficiency has much more advantage compare to other energy. And it is easy to transmission and transaction. So, in this paper, the energy will be limited to electric power, and its business requirement will be based on the business of state grid company.

In the December of 2013, the president of state grid company, Liu zhenya published a paper "smart grid carry the third industrial revolution", in this paper, he pointed out, "future smart grid is the energy internet with the character of strong rack, extensive interconnected, highly smart, open and interactive", smart grid will be the energy internet that support the third industrial revolution [3], the development of information and communication technology will be the key factor and the main problem of future energy internet.

To build the global energy internet, it needs the next-generation information and communication infrastructure with the character of open, ubiquitous, smart, interaction, trustworthy. Realize the change from the support the power grid business only, To not only support power grid business internal, but also serve the public external.

The research to energy internet is just at the beginning, but there are some prototypes like FREEDM, E-Energy, related paper can refer to [4, 5]. In this paper, we focus on the communication requirement of energy internet, and predict the new business and its requirement to communication network. By now, the communication technology can meet the requirement of global interconnection, but the energy internet has its own requirement to communication technology, this paper will give our analyses on these key technologies.

2 Communication Requirement of Energy Internet

To build the energy internet, it involves the integration of several modules, such as power and electron technology, communication technology, smart control and management technology [6]. Communication technology is the basic support technology of energy internet. But its communication network can't scrap it and start all over again. Because current communication infrastructure has invest a lot of money, and its technology is familiar to the public. And the replacement will need huge money and bring the delay. Compatible with the current infrastructure, and update the service step by step, it is a better choice. Refer to the internet development experience, at the beginning, the internet was deployed at the public telephone network. By use the elastic organization principle, evolution step by step, now it forms the current internet. Similarly, the information and communication infrastructure of energy internet, it has to utilize current power grid basis, and realize its special function, and try to make a breakthrough on efficiency and durability [2].

2.1 The Overall Requirement to Communication Network in Energy Internet

The information and communication network of energy internet will evolve from the information and communication network of power grid. Different from the public network of the service provider like China mobile and China Unicom, which provide the service for voice and data, the primary goal of communication network in energy internet is to ensure the safety production of power grid. Then serve the information construction of state grid company.

The information and communication network of energy internet will inherit all the business of communication network in power grid. And provide downward compatibility, the communication and information infrastructure of energy internet should have following basic requirement [2]: two-way communication, has the inter-operation ability toward the advanced application of energy internet, realize end-to-end secure communication, and has the ability to against the potential attack.

Because the research to the energy internet is at the beginning, so the business discussion of energy internet can't break away from the current business of power grid. It should include all the business of current power grid, but also the special business of energy internet.

2.2 Current Business in the Information and Communication Network of Energy Internet

In the information and communication network of current power grid, it includes all the application such as production, business and management information. According to the business mode, it will be divided into two categories, production business and non-production business. These businesses will exist in the energy internet for a long time.

The production business includes operation control business and operation information business. Operation control business, such as protection, stabilization business, and they don't require too much bandwidth, but they are very sensitive to the reliability and real-time.

Non-production business, such as video conference, office automation, administrative telephone, 95598 service, and they need high bandwidth, some business, such as VoIP, video-conferencing, they have high requirement to network delay.

2.3 The New Business of Information and Communication Network in Energy Network

2.3.1 Energy Access Business of Energy Internet

The energy terminal in energy internet will say goodbye to the mode of accept electric power or sent out the electric power only step by step. And generally they will have the information port, and have the ability to interact with the power grid. With the support of energy access business. The energy terminal has the ability to join the schedule of power grid. And they can interact with the energy terminal nearby. In this precondition, the power grid should provide the function including authority, authentication and accounting. The business interface even became the information channel between the energy terminals.

2.3.2 Energy Interconnect Business in Energy Internet

The energy interconnect business include the new power generation unit, such as the distributed renewable energy resources, large-scale new energy base. And also include the flexible access of user side unit, such as electric vehicle, smart electrical equipment. Intelligent electricity village. And also include the power transmission business in transmission network and distribution network. Finally large scale energy basis can transmit the energy cross-region. And distributed micro grid realizes the flexibly energy configuration of local network. And combine the information stream, energy stream, business stream into one stream. And implement flexible and high efficiency global coordination mechanism across the power generation, power transmission, power distribution and power utilization in energy internet. Flexibly construct the micro-grid. And implement self-organization of power grid. These kinds of business information will also include in the information and communication network in energy internet.

2.3.3 Data and Decision-Making Business in Energy Internet

Energy internet will be the data network of electric power. The massive data in power grid will upload to related business system. So each business system will highly depend on the information system for data aware, data transmission, data pre-processing and data sharing. And big data digging of data information also need robust platform to do calculation. And make the decision based on the data. And change the decision-making method by the experience of power grid production and management. So, in the future, there is huge data information in the information and communication network of energy internet. And used for decision-making.

2.3.4 Energy Transaction Business of Energy Internet

In the future, the energy transaction will be on the open platform. And do the fair transaction between the user side and power generation side. And implement the carbon transaction on the energy transaction platform. And value-added business such as energy credits. Surely, this kind of transaction information will include in the information and communication network of energy internet.

2.3.5 Data-Value Business of Energy Internet

The data in the energy internet will be the important asset, there are plentiful data in the energy internet, and user data can show the clean energy deployment, resident consumption ability, migration of population, national economic development and etc. and has plentiful internal value. At the same time, electric power user data can form the plentiful user smart service. So it is necessary to use cloud-computing and big data technology, to do data value digging related job and open the data service step by step, and contribute more to the society by using big data value of power grid.

2.3.6 Public Service in Energy Internet

Energy internet will use its power grid rack asset, site, internet of things and its sensing terminal, and use its information and communication network, to construct the public service platform. Provide service and the robust base platform and application for sensing network, smart home, smart building and smart city, and provide the plentiful public service for society. In the future, the information and communication network of energy internet will reserve the public service interface for these services. And carry the public service information.

3   The Key Communication Technology to Build Energy Internet

To construct energy internet or the global energy internet, first we need to migrate the traditional internet technology and its super fusion ability to current energy system. So each kind of energy can open and share to each other, and came into one kind of integration structure with effectiveness, stability, flexibility and scalability. And its communication network, can't break away from current communication technology, such as wire communication technology (optical fiber, Ethernet etc.), wireless communication technology (GPRS, wifi, 3G/4G/5G, Zigbee), power line communication technology. Now, traditional internet technology can meet the requirement of global interconnect. But there are still some problem need to be addressed, such as network quality of service, security and reliable transmission of power grid control information, sensitive information transmission across the country. Specifically, we need to solve following key technologies.

3.1   Satellite Communication Technology for Wide-Area Power Grid and Distributed Energy Base

Because the introduction like wind power in the sea, it is very expensive to pave seabed optical fiber. And, some other large-scale energy base, it is always at remote area, transportation and communication is not convenient. It is necessary to introduce satellite communication technology [7], as the supplement of current communication technology. And satellite can provide accurate location and time service. Satellite communication can cover wide area, one satellite can cover 1/3 earth area. And the communication capacity is big, and it can provide thousands of telephone channels between two points at the same time, transmission quality is good, radio wave is stable. Easy to build the network and it is convenient to achieve seamless global connection. It is regarded as one of important global emergency communication.

3.2   Coherent Optical Communication Technology that Support Large Capacity Long-Distance Power Transmission

Coherent optical communication [8] system use the technology of coherent modulation, heterodyne detection, efficiently changes the sensitivity of signal receiving. Improved the unrepeatered transmission performance of optical fiber communication. Coherent optical communication has the good performance of wavelength selection, further reduce the gap of frequency, and improve the transmission capacity by multiplex more wavelengths.

Some energy base in energy internet, due to its limitation of location, it may need the communication of cross-ocean, cross-desert, in this kind of environment, relay device is easy to damage, and replacement and maintenance costs are expensive.

Compare to current optical fiber technology, Coherent optical technology can provide more capacity and transmit much long distance without relay. And it can be used for global communication that support energy internet. By the promotion of transmission distance, to support cross-ocean, cross-continent transmission. By the promotion of transmission capacity by using dense wave technology, to improve big range regulate and control of energy internet information.

3.3 Programmable Network Technology for Dynamic Resource Allocation of Energy Internet

Current information and communication network of power grid, its architecture refers to internet architecture. But with the development of application. Its extensibility, security, mobility and quality of service, became the problem that need to be solved immediately.

Refer to the idea of SDN [9] and some other programmable network technology. By use its advantage like flexible, efficiency and configurable. Design the high performance, open, secure and extensible communication network; provide the support for energy access, energy transmission, and energy dispatch.

3.4 Ubiquitous Sensing Network Technology for Friendly Access of Distributed Energy

Sensing network is the important component of energy internet. Sensor can do the signal perception and transmission in wide area network node. In order to ensure the energy internet run safely and reliably, need a lot of sensors, these sensors can monitor and control energy internet status.

In the energy internet, there are still some key sensing technology need to be solved, for distributed energy, there are some technologies like cooperative monitor, sensing system for multi-dimension detection, sensing array, sensing network data fusion technology. Need to research on low power consumption module design with highly integration on power taking, power saving, sensing and communication. And realize the friendly and ubiquitous access of distributed energy and ubiquitous calculation.

4 Conclusion

Information and communication technology has become the driving force of each industry, and bring a lot of new operation and commercial mode. Internet has provide enough technology experience to the information and communication network of energy internet, but compare to the goal of energy internet, current research result can't meet its requirement. There are still a lot of problems need to be solved, and bring the unprecedented challenge to it.

This paper first analyses the current communication requirement of energy internet, and predict the new business and its requirement to the communication network of energy internet. At last, we analyzed several key technologies to build the communication network of energy internet. Research on the basic technology of energy internet, it has not only the academic significance, but also has the strategic significance.

Acknowledgement. This research is coordinated with Information and Communication Department of State Grid. The authors thank the department managers and staff workers for their time and opinions.

References

1. Cao, J., Kun, M., Jiye, W.: Energy internet and energy router. China Sci. Inf. Sci. **44**(6), 714–727 (2014)
2. Cao, J., Wan, Y., et al.: Information and communication architecture of smart grid. J. Comput. (2013)
3. Liu, Z.: Smart grid carry the third industrial revolution. State Grid (2014)
4. Jiye, W., Kun, M., Junwei, C., et al.: A survey for information and communication technology of energy internet. Comput. Res. Dev. **52**(5), 1109–1126 (2015)
5. Cao, J., Yang, M., et al.: Energy internet—the integration of information and energy. South Power Grid Technol. 8(4) (2014)
6. Cha, Y., Tao, Z., Zhuo, H., et al.: Key technology analysis of energy internet. China Sci. Inf. Sci. **44**(6), 702–713 (2014)
7. Min, L., Lvxi, Y., Gong, Z.: A survey for satellite mobile antenna development. Telecommun. Sci. (2006)
8. Ran, Z.: Research on modulation formats and automatic polarization control technology of coherent optical communication system, Master thesis of BUPT (2009)
9. Tootoonchian, A., Gorbunov, S., Ganjali, Y., et al.: On controller performance in software-defined networks. In: Hot-ICE, San Jose, USA (2012)

Environmental Incidents Detection from Chinese Microblog Based on Sentiment Analysis

Yang Zhou[1,2], Tingting Lu[3], Tingshao Zhu[1,4(✉)], and Zhenxiang Chen[3]

[1] Institute of Psychology, Chinese Academy of Sciences, Beijing, China
tszhun@psych.ac.cn
[2] Chinese Academy of Sciences, Beijing, China
[3] University of Jinan, Shandong 250022, China
[4] Institute of Computing Technology, Chinese Academy of Sciences, Beijing, China

Abstract. Environmental incidents affect the stable development of economy and society. If environmental incidents can be detected timely through microblog, it will be possible to reduce risk factors and improve social stability. Microblog has now become an important platform for generating and propagating incidents on the Web, it is an ideal field to detect incidents. However, since the texts of microblog messages are very short and unstructured, it is a challenging task to detect incidents from microblogs. Due to the diversity of Chinese microblogs, the results identified by Dynamic Query Expansion (DQE) always contain a considerable number of unrelated events. This paper proposes to filter microblogs by calculating emotion values via Sentiment Analysis (SA), thus to improve the accuracy of detection. Experimental results demonstrated that DQE + SA can be more accurate and effective to detect environmental incidents.

Keywords: Sentiment analysis · Event detection · Dynamic query expansion · Microblog

1 Introduction

Environmental incidents occur frequently in nowadays China. Currently, incidents are mainly detected by manual, so it's difficult to discover and cope with them promptly. Therefore, environmental incidents detection is significant for keeping the social order and protecting the public security.

Microblog has now become a main channel for more and more people exchanging information. It is an important platform for generating and propagating events. Compared with traditional media, microblog has the following features: (1) Dynamic. Message on microblog is restricted to 140 Chinese characters and not constrained by any traditional language grammar. (2) Timeliness. With the popularity of mobile devices, microblog becomes to be a real-time information platform when incidents occur. (3) Emotional. Emotional expression occupies a large proportion of microblog contents. There are more affective words in microblog than in traditional media.

The dynamic feature of microblog makes it difficult to detect events based on fixed keywords. Due to the emotional feature of microblog, we analyze the emotions

© Springer International Publishing Switzerland 2016
Q. Zu and B. Hu (Eds.): HCC 2016, LNCS 9567, pp. 849–854, 2016.
DOI: 10.1007/978-3-319-31854-7_88

of microblog content besides the textual content, in order to improve both precision and accuracy.

Detecting environmental incidents by Dynamic Query Expansion (DQE) could address the challenge of microblog's dynamic. DQE iteratively expands keywords based on initial keywords determined by experts, generates specific keywords and a set of microblogs which related to environmental incidents. However, we found that DQE also generates quite a few microblogs that unrelated to our targeted domain. In this paper, we combine dynamic query expansion with sentiment analysis to improve the performance of incident detection. After obtaining microblog messages may related to environmental incidents by DQE, we analyze the results by fine-grained sentiment analysis and filter out unrelated microblogs.

The major contributions of this paper are as follows:

- This is the first event detection study that applies dynamic query expansion to Chinese microblog. Moreover, we improve its performance according to the features of Chinese microblog.
- Our approach makes use of fine-grained sentiment analysis, which has been shown to be efficient in improving the detection performance.
- We propose approach of DQE + SA for detecting incidents from microblogs, which outperforms the DQE method on both precision and recall.

2   Related Work

Although much research have been conducted for event detection on microblog, most of them focus on general interests events instead of specific domains like earthquake, anthrax outbreaks, environmental incidents, terrorism and so on.

Methods for general interest event detection generally apply clustering techniques on text stream [3], Jianshu et al. detected event with clustering of wavelet-based signals.

Specific events detection are typically based on fixed keywords. Takeshi Sakaki et al. classified microblogs by keywords. Hassan et al. created keyword graph at first, then detected events by keyword graph. Hamed et al. [1] identified meaningful candidates for event descriptions.

Due to microblogs' unstructured and dynamic characteristics, it is insufficient for detecting events just by fixed keywords. Liang et al. proposed unsupervised approach for detecting events in targeted domain.

Currently, sentiment analysis in event detection is divided into two categories: coarse-grained sentiment analysis and fine-grained sentiment analysis. Coarse-grained sentiment analysis only distinguish positive and negative. Fine-grained sentiment analysis distinguish more detailed type. Plaban et al. [4] applied ADTboost.MH to news sentences, generating six types of emotion. Cuneyt et al. [2] detected emotion and public opinion changes over time by emotional lexicon, which include eight types.

In addition, most of studies of sentiment analysis in event detection focus on general interest events [2]. We lack the research focused on targeted-domain event detection combining with sentiment analysis.

3 Methods

3.1 Data Collection

We obtain microblog data through Sina Weibo API. Because Chinese texts have no separators, the word segmentation is needed. We use the Language Technology Platform (LTP) of HIT-SCIR [5] as a segmentor.

After word segmentation, for the purpose of improving the proportion of the effective keywords and the efficiency in the next work, we need filter the stop words not containing meaningful information.

3.2 Dynamic Query Expansion

DQE (Dynamic Query Expansion) obtains the dynamic keywords by dynamic expanding microblog messages. A set of keywords related to specific domain need to be specified by domain experts in advance. We define the weight of the initial keywords as 1, and the weight is on behalf of the correlation between keywords and the targeted domain. We set microblogs containing any keyword as the expanded messages. Because the other words of messages is considered to describe the same event with the initial keywords, the weight of those should be updated. According to the document frequency-inverse document frequency (DF-IDF), we calculate the weight of words, and the calculation method is as follow:

$$W_i = \{j{:}t_i \in d_j\} \times \log \frac{|D|}{\{j{:}t_i \in d_j\}} \tag{1}$$

j is the number of messages including keywords and $|D|$ is the total number of messages.

We choose the words with high weight as the expanded keywords, and expand messages according to the expanded keywords. DQE expand keywords based on containment between words and messages, stop the iteration until the expanded keywords and the last round ones changes less than the threshold.

DQE was mainly used in Twitter. Considering the diversity of Chinese semantics, it is easy to find uncorrelated events if we expand the microblog messages with one keyword. If the post is forwarded many times, the content of it could be detected even though it has nothing to do with environmental incidents. Therefore, we modify the condition of the DQE in the first round, after several tests, we found that the deviation of event detection results could be reduced if we limited at least two keywords in expanded messages in the first round of expansion.

3.3 Sentiment Analysis

Emotional words include 27,476 words from Chinese affective lexicon. In addition, Sina Weibo provides some default emoticons, we classify the emoticons then import them into affective lexicon as a basis for sentiment analysis. Chinese affective vocabulary is based on the six sentiment categories proposed by Ekman. On the basis of Ekman, we add "good" into lexicon for more detailed classification. The final results are seven categories: happy, good, anger, sorrow, fear, evil and surprise.

We aim to detect environmental incidents caused by public dissatisfactory. So the emotions of messages related to environmental incidents should be negative. We could filter out messages which sentiment are positive. To verify this hypothesis, we choose 70 messages randomly associated with labeled event and get the output of seven categories of emotions. We compare the results with the same amount of unrelated messages. As shown in Fig. 1: Happy has the most significant difference. Messages related to environmental incidents do not contain any words of "happy", which is consistent with our common sense. Therefore, we set "the number of emotional words which belong to the category of happy must be zero" as a filter condition. In other words, we'll filter out all messages containing "happy" words from expanded messages.

4 Experiments

4.1 Dataset and Labels

This paper detects environmental incidents of Qingdao from January 1, 2015 to July 31, 2015. Microblogs of 120,000 Qingdao active users posted in 2015 were downloaded.

We detected environmental incidents day by day to estimate whether any event has occurred or not. There are 60,000–80,000 microblog posts one day on average.

Our environmental incidents results were validated against the labeled data set. Labeled set is organized by staff of Qingdao Environmental Protection Bureau, and the sources are as follows: Qingdao News, China Daily, Qingdao TV live online, QTV2 life online, City News, and Qingdao Morning Post. The principle of labeled event sets is: Choose the environmental incidents from the sources at first. Because not all of environmental incidents are reflected in microblog, we just choose labeled event sets reflected in microblog (the number of related microblog messages is more than 4). The number of labeled event is 23.

4.2 DQE

The initial keywords of DQE specified by domain experts are: denounce, pollution, violation and so on. Because of the multiple semantic of Chinese microblog, we limit two or more keywords instead of one or more in first round of expansion. We apply the improved DQE in the microblog from January 1, 2015 to July 31, 2015. Running time on data of one day is about 53 s.

We detected 135 events, including 15 labeled events and the recall is 65.22 %. When we calculate precision of the result, we found that the labeled events provided by Qingdao Environmental Protection Bureau are not all environmental incidents. We ask authoritative experts in Qingdao Environmental Protection Bureau to decide whether the events not contained in labeled events are meaningful or not. After identification by experts, there are 75 meaningful events, so the precision is 55.56 %.

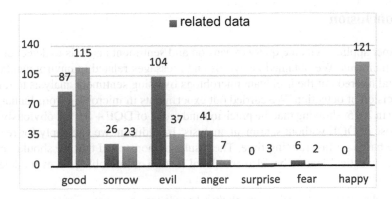

Fig. 1. Comparison of emotion value

4.3   DQE + SA

In order to compare the results of DQE with DQE + SA, we used the same initial keywords, the same microblog data and the same labeled set. Running time on data of one day is about 63 s.

The results of sentiment analysis are applied to the DQE dynamic expansion process. We analyze the emotion value of microblogs in each expanded microblog set, and filter out microblogs containing emotion words of happy type from expanded set, and then continue to the next step of keywords expansion.

We finally detected 113 events using DQE + SA method, including 17 labeled events. The recall is 0.74. There are 88 meaningful events, the precision is 0.78 and the F-measure is 0.76. The comparison of DQE and DQE + SA is shown as Fig. 2 and we can find that the precision and recall of DQE + SA are obviously better than those of DQE without sentiment analysis.

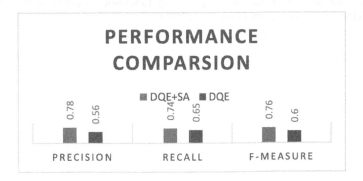

Fig. 2. Comparison of DQE + SA and DQE

5   Conclusion

This paper applies dynamic query expansion and sentiment analysis to detect environmental incidents. We obtained keywords and messages related to environmental incidents and filtered out the irrelevant microblogs by using sentiment analysis to improve the precision of detection. We carried out experiments in microblog from January to July in 2015, showing that the precision and recall of DQE + SA are obviously better than those of DQE without sentiment analysis. In addition, we can apply for real-time purpose based on fast running time. The results demonstrated that we should not only focus on statistical feature but also emotional feature of microblogs in event detection.

Acknowledgements. The authors gratefully acknowledges the generous support from National High-tech R&D Program of China (2013AA01A606), National Basic Research Program of China (2014CB744600), and Key Research Program of Chinese Academy of Sciences (CAS) (KJZD-EWL04).

References

1. Abdelhaq, H., Sengstock, C., Gertz, M.: Eventweet: Online localized event detection from twitter. Proc. VLDB Endowment **6**(12), 1326–1329 (2013)
2. Akcora, C.G., Bayir, M.A., Demirbas, M., Ferhatosmanoglu, H.: Identifying breakpoints in public opinion. In: Proceedings of the First Workshop on Social Media Analytics. pp. 62–66. ACM (2010)
3. Becker, H., Naaman, M., Gravano, L.: Beyond trending topics: Real-world event identification on twitter. ICWSM **11**, 438–441 (2011)
4. Bhowmick, P.K., Basu, A., Mitra, P.: Classifying emotion in news sentences: when machine classification meets human classification. Int. J. Comput. Sci. Eng. **2**(1), 98–108 (2010)
5. Che, W., Li, Z., Liu, T.: LTP: a chinese language technology platform. In: Proceedings of the 23rd International Conference on Computational Linguistics: Demonstrations. pp. 13–16. Association for Computational Linguistics (2010)

The Research Review of Spiking Neural Membrane System

Wei Bi[✉] and Wenke Zang

College of Management Science and Engineering,
Shandong Normal University, Jinan, China
{dreampower001, zwker}@163.com

Abstract. Membrane computing is a new branch of natural computing. In recent years, with the rapid development, membrane systems are divided into three categories: Cell-type membrane systems, Tissue membrane system, Neuronal membrane system. Spiking neural membrane system (Spiking Neural P Systems) is a special type of neuronal membrane system, referred to as SN P system, which is a new branch of membrane computing. It not only has the scientific significance of the computer, but also in terms of biological modeling and simulation have potential applications. In this paper, the concept and principles of spiking neural membrane system, the current species and varieties spiking neural membrane system are analyzed, some research progress theory expounded.

Keywords: Membrane computing · Spiking neural membrane systems · Types and varieties

1 Introduction

Membrane Computing is a new branch of natural computing, aiming to abstract computational model from the structure function of living cells and collaboration of tissues and organs in cell populations.

As of now, there are three types of membrane computing model: the cell type, tissue type and neuronal membrane system. Neuronal membrane system is focus of the membrane computing theory research. The membrane system cells are made of neurons, and their thinking are derived from biological nervous system. Neuronal membrane system has two types: basic neuronal membrane system and pulse neuronal membrane system. Spiking neural membrane system (abbreviated as SN P system) is a membrane computing in a new class of biological computing device. Based on the biological phenomena that neurons transmit pulse to other neurons via synapses, Lonescu and Păun in 2006 first proposed this kind of model and demonstrate the versatility of the model calculation. That is to say it has a computing power equal to Turing machine. Spiking neural membrane system is very different with the conventional model: some of the information is no longer used to represent sequences of different objects, but in a different sequence of the same object represented trigger time. Therefore, in this new computing model, the time is not only as a computing resource as in complex theory, but as a way of encoding information and a data support.

© Springer International Publishing Switzerland 2016
Q. Zu and B. Hu (Eds.): HCC 2016, LNCS 9567, pp. 855–860, 2016.
DOI: 10.1007/978-3-319-31854-7_89

The model can simulate some of the mechanisms and characteristics of biological neural membrane systems, by the concern of many scholars. Neuronal membrane systems research focuses on spiking neural computing systems [1].

This article will introduce the concepts of spiking neural membrane system and its basic principles, study progress of spiking neural membrane system to be introduced, and analyzes the application of research progress.

2   The Concept or the Principle of Spiking Neural Membrane System

2.1   Biological Background of Spiking Neurons

Neural cells are structural and functional units of the nervous system of higher animals, it is also known as neurons. Neuronal can be divided into two parts: cell bodies and projections. Cell body is similar to other cellular structures and projections are issued by the cell body, which are divided into two types: dendrites and axons. Dendrites are thick and short, repeated branch, tapering. Axons generally has only one, slender and uniform, less midway branch, and the end to form many branches, each inflated spherical tip portion, called synaptosome [2]. That bridge between synaptosome and dendrites of neighboring neurons is the synapse. Synapses can change information with each other through the synapse. Neurons which send signals are called presynaptic neuron, and which receive signal is called postsynaptic neurons.

The nervous system is a huge, complex network structure. The basic unit which neurons transmit information is spike. Spike can be divided into electrical impulses and chemical pulses according to the material transmitted by spike. It can be divided excitation pulse and pulse suppression according to the nature of spike. Pulse transmission process between neurons: When a neuron has fully pulse stimulation, this neuron will sent neuronal electrical or chemical pulses to the synaptosome via the axon, and then synaptosome sent these pulses to neighboring neurons.

2.2   Formal Definition Spiking Neural Membrane System

This article describes the general form of spiking neural membrane system and it is the calculation model which use extended rule. The model can have input and provides an output, the rules can be issued more than one pulse.

A degree $m \geq 1$ extended spiking neural membrane systems, specifically construct is as follows:

$\Pi = (O, \sigma_1, \ldots, \sigma_m, syn, in, out)$,

Where:

(1) $O = \{a\}$ is the set of single letter, and 'a' denotes a pulse.
(2) $\sigma_1, \ldots, \sigma_m$ representation m neurons of system Π, neurons σ_i expressed as $\sigma_i = (n_i, R_i)$, $1 \leq i \leq m$, where:

(a) $n_i \geq 0$ represents the number of pulses in the calculation of the beginning of neurons σ_i included;

(b) R_i represent a finite set of neurons σ_i constitute all rules, including the following two form Rules.

① $E/a^c \rightarrow a^p$; d, E is positive regular expression on 'a', $c \geq p \geq 1$, $d \geq 0$.

② $a^s \rightarrow \lambda$, $s \geq 1$, for Ri each type ① rule $E/a^c \rightarrow a^p$; d, there $area^s \notin$ L (E).

(3) syn $\subseteq \{1,2,...,m\} \times \{1,2,...,m\}$ indicates the connection relationship between neurons, have $(i, i) \notin$ syn, have been established for each $1 \leq i \leq m$.

(4) in, out $\in \{1,2,..., m\}$ denote the input and output neurons [3]. The neurons rules are divided into two kinds: firing rules and forgetting rules. Where in the form of $E/a^c \rightarrow a$; d is called the standard rules of firing rules. In the form of $E/a^c \rightarrow a^p$; d, p ≥ 1 is called extended firing rules. In the form of rules $a^s \rightarrow \lambda$ is called the forgotten rules. If the rule $E/a^c \rightarrow a^p$; d satisfy $E = a^c$, then it can be abbreviated as $E/a^c \rightarrow a^p$; d.

If a neuron containing a forgotten rules $a^s \rightarrow \lambda$, then for this neuronal any firing rule $E/a^c \rightarrow a^p$; dare required to meet $a^s \notin$ L (E) (i.e., a neuron cannot trigger the firing rules and forgetting rules at the same time).

Excitation rule $E/a^c \rightarrow a^p$; d is used as follows: at some time point, provided neurons σ_i contains k pulses, if k satisfies two conditions: a^k is a sentence of language L (E) represented by the regular expression E (i.e. $a^k \in$ L(E) and $k \geq c$), then you can use the neuron firing rules $E/a^c \rightarrow a^p$; d. If the neurons σ_i use excitation rules in tth step $E/a^c \rightarrow ap$; d, $d \geq 1$,after this rule, c pulses will be consumed (neurons σ_i remaining k-c pulses). After d units of time, the neuron will produce p new pulse, and immediately sends p pulses to all neurons connected to it respectively. In addition, within this period of time that begin to use of this rule to send a new impulse, neurons is in the refractory period, it will not receive and send any pulses, and this state of neurons is called the closed state (relatively, the state that neurons can receive and transmit pulse condition is called open state). For example neurons σ_i use excitation rules $E/ac \rightarrow ap$; d in tth step, the neurons in the t, t + 1, ..., t + d−1 steps are closed, and in the t + d steps, neuronal recover to open.

Forgotten rule $as \rightarrow \lambda$ is used as follows: When neurons σ_i contains exactly s pulse, it can use the forgotten rules $as \rightarrow \lambda$. Note that at this time all the neurons firing rules cannot be used. When the neurons use this forgotten rule, it will consume s pulse, but no new pulse.

In each time unit, if the neurons σ_i can use the rules, then it must use someone in a rule R_i. Because for two excitation rules, their intersection is the empty set. Therefore, in a neuron, there may be multiple rules used and in this case, only one to be selected to use non-deterministically. Note: By definition, when there is firing rules can be used, the forgetting rules cannot be used; and vice versa.

Therefore, each neuron, the use of the rule is serial, that is to say a rule is used at most in each neuron in each step. But neurons are run in parallel with each other. It is worth noting that the rules can use or not depends on the total number of pulses that neurons located in the rules.

3 Research Progress Spiking Neural Membrane System

3.1 Category of Spiking Neural Membrane System

At present, after studied by a number of experts and scholars, type or variant publication referred to spiking neural membrane system includes the following more than ten species:

1. Standard spiking neural membrane system (standard SN P systems)
2. The extended spiking neural membrane system (extended SN P systems)
3. SNP systems with exhaustive use of rules
4. The asynchronous spiking neural membrane system (asynchronous SN P systems)
5. Spiking neural P systems with anti-spikes
6. Spiking neural P systems with astrocyte-like control.

In addition to spiking neural membrane system described above, there are a number of other species: attenuation of pulses and pulse bounded spiking neural membrane systems, asynchronous spiking neural membrane system with catalyst, having overcome environmental impact Robust type of time-independent spiking neural membrane system, having a plurality of output neuron spiking neural membrane systems, parallel execution using the minimum rules spiking neural membrane systems, Spiking neural P systems along the axon, sequential SN P systems [4].

3.2 Research Process of Spiking Neural Membrane System

January 2007, GhPăun proposed 26 open questions about the spiking neural membrane systems at seminar on membrane computing, and soon it became a hotspot of scholars from various countries, and it has aroused widespread concern of scholars.

At present, SNP systematic theoretical research is popular. Most theoretical results mainly involves the following aspects: the ability to produce the number or languages, the ability to identify the number or language, small general problem of system, the paradigm system, calculates effect, and spiking neural membrane system or a variant based on a number of different types with different biological context presented so on.

With respect to the theoretical researches, applications research is purposes to a lot less. Currently, as a means to generate numbers, spiking neural membrane system, the results of the system is the distance between the first two pulses when the time is output to the environment. Garcia-Amau et al. further proved that standard spiking neural membrane system also has computing completeness under the conditions that even without the use of delay and forgetting rules. Spiking neural membrane system is also capable of generating the language as a means. When we definite the time the output neuron output and not output the pulse value are labeled "1" and "0", it can generate a binary language alphabet {0,1}, but it cannot produce all of the limited language. After using the mapping between the binary alphabet and pluralism of the alphabet, spiking neural membrane system has generated recursively enumerable family of languages in any language.

Chinese Academy of Sciences Professor Chen Haiming studied the language generation capacity of spiking neural computing systems, proving spiking neural computing system can generate recursively enumerable language, and discussing its relationship with the limited language and a regular language. In other articles, experts and scholars studied the use of spiking neural membrane system, and spiking neural membrane systems are simulated by numerical calculation of addition, subtraction, multiplication and issue arbitrary binary natural number divisible. He studied the computing capacity of spiking neural computing systems from language of generating capacity, small versatility and effectiveness of the three aspects. More further, simulation study in computing theory, application and simulation are several types of computing power spiking neural membrane systems, small versatility, logic and arithmetic operations to achieve formal verification methods and content models. Among the many articles, there are many articles, experts and scholars elaborated the versatility of the system, demonstrated its ability to solve problems [5]. Liang Jiarong introduced the self-synaptic spiking neural membrane system and how the system generates a special number set [6]. CaiRongtai analyzed how neurons pulse encodes the input stimulus by pulse sequence and how the input pulse train is converted to an output pulse sequence. And it gives the image reconstruction examples based on this way of working. XueJie, solved oriented with improved spiking neural membrane systems in Hamilton path problem [7].

Although the spiking neural membrane system has been a lot of research, but still left many open questions: (1) Under the standard rules, SNP systems with exhaustive use of rules problems common rules; (2) the use of spiking neural membrane system portray context-free language problems; (3) the use of SAT problem solving precomputed resource is allowed to be used or not, and so on.

4 Summary and Outlook

Spiking neural membrane system is an important branch of membrane computing. Since put forward, it has been rapidly developed and the nervous system is a hot current of membrane computing theory research. The membrane system cells are used in neuronal cells, and the idea comes from the biological nervous system. In this paper, the biological background of spiking neural membrane system and standard formula were expressed in detail and summarizes the types and variations of up to more than ten kinds of experts proposed spiking neural membrane systems. These new systems type and variant can solves a lot of problems for a lot of difficult problems to provide new research ideas. Because the time of putting forward is late, spiking neural membrane system research is still in its initial stage. Both directions spiking neural computing systems, computing completeness and computational effectiveness still need to continue to improve, in particular, the application of spiking neural system needs to have a breakthrough. We expect more researchers can work in this regard.

Acknowledgments. This work was supported by National Natural Science Foundation of China (61170038), Natural science foundation of Shandong Province, China (ZR2011FM001), Technology development projects of Shandong province, China (2012G0020314), Soft science research project of Shandong Province, China (2013RZB01019), Jinan City independent innovation plan project in Colleges and Universities, China (201401202), Ministry of education of Humanities and social science research projects, China (12YJA630152), Social Science Fund Project of Shandong Province, China (11CGLJ22), outstanding youth scientist foundation project of Shandong Province, China (BS2013DX037).

References

1. Wang, J.: Computing power research of spiking neural membrane system biologically inspired. Huazhong University of Science and Systems Analysis and Integration, Wuhan (2013)
2. Wang, K.: Application problems research neuronal and cell type P system. West China University Computer Software and Theory, Chengdu (2011)
3. Hu, H.: Spiking Neural membrane system with Self-study Synapses. Guangxi University computer software and theory, Nanning (2013)
4. Peng, X., Fan, X.-P., Liu, J., Wen, H.: Homogeneous Spiking Neural membrane system with Anti-pulse. Computer Systems, Shenyang (2013)
5. Keqin, J., Yufang, H., Jinbang, X., Zhihua C., Jinbang, X.: Small Universal Sequential Spiking Neural P Systems based on Minimum Spike Number. In: Pre-Proceedings of the Second Asian Conference on Membrane Computing, Chengdu (2013)
6. Liang, J.-R., Hu, H., Li, R.: Generatation a Self-synaptic Spiking Neural membrane systems and Special number set. Guangxi University, Nanning (2013)
7. Xue, J., Liu, X.: Solving directed hamilton path problem in parallel by improved SN P system. In: Zu, Q., Hu, B., Elçi, A. (eds.) ICPCA/SWS 2012. LNCS, vol. 7719, pp. 689–696. Springer, Heidelberg (2013)

Ant Colony Optimization for Power Line Routing Problem

Qianqian Feng, Feng Qi$^{(\boxtimes)}$, and Xiyu Liu

College of Management Science and Engineering,
Shandong Normal University, No.88 East of Wenhua Road,
Jinan 250014, Shandong, People's Republic of China
qfsdnu@126.com

Abstract. In recent years, intelligent algorithms have developed so fast and have obtained many achievements. Since ant colony optimization (ACO) algorithm was proposed, lots of improvements have been made. And it was applied to many problems, such as travel salesman problem (TSP), quadratic assignment problem (QAP), robot path planning, and so on. In this paper, a modified ant colony optimization based on the meta-heuristic ant colony algorithm is applied to solve power line path routing problem.

Keywords: Ant colony optimization · Least cost path · Power line routing

1 Introduction

Electric transmission line routing is one of the most difficult problems in electrical engineering. As lots of criteria like slope, residential areas, avoidance areas etc. should be considered, finding the best route is a very complex process. The manual design of a new electric transmission line like using paper maps, aerial photography, and field visits lacks the detailed analytical and consistent methodology needed to defend why the route is selected. Consequently, the routes often need to be reworked multiple times resulting in schedule delays and cost overruns.

The actual terrain information (slopes, geographic restrictions, obstacles, etc.) is not always suitably associated with nodes and lines. Using the vector maps can cause lots of difficulties in routing process. So the rasterized map is used where each cell represents an elementary area and position. And the line is a set of cells with links between neighboring cells in a particular sequence [1]. In the raster map, the cells are assigned values which indicate the difficulties of passing through them considering various criteria [2, 3]. The EPRI-GTC overhead electric transmission line siting methodology introduced a "least cost path" analysis which is used to create a line connecting the start and end point by considering the minimum accumulative cost path [4]. In the total weighted surface raster map, genetic algorithm is applied to find the route with the minimum accumulative cost in the previous studies [5]. In this paper, ant colony optimization is used to find the best route for electric power line.

Q. Zu and B. Hu (Eds.): HCC 2016, LNCS 9567, pp. 861–866, 2016.
DOI: 10.1007/978-3-319-31854-7_90

2 Ant Colony Optimization

Ant colony optimization (ACO) was first proposed by Marco Dorigo. ACO takes inspiration from the foraging behavior of real ants. These ants leave message which is called pheromone on the ground where they have traversed in order to mark the favorable path that should be followed by other ants in the same colony. Other ants perceive the pheromone and tend to follow paths where pheromone concentration is higher. Through this kind of positive feedback mechanism, ants are able to find the best route from food to their nest in a fairly effective way. So ACO has been developed to provide heuristic solutions for more kinds of optimization problems.

In order to better understand the basic principle of ACO, this paper uses a model to describe it. ACO was first used to solve the well-known traveling salesman problem (TSP). In TSP, there is a set of cities and the distance between each of them is known. The goal is to find the shortest tour that allows each city to be visited once and only once. In ACO, the problem is tackled by simulating a number of artificial ants moving on a complete graph. In the graph, each vertex represents a city and each edge represents a connection between two cities.

3 Ant Colony Optimization Used in Power Line Routing Problem

To simplify the routing process, the raster map is used. The studied area is divided into $N_R * N_C$ small square grids. Each grid represents an elementary area and the position where it is by assuming that the cost of pass through this grid is uniformly distributed along the path in this grid.

The least cost path analysis is based on the definition of a so called cost surface, which is a raster map where all the grids are assigned values representing the difficulties of passing through them. This cost is expected to be relevant to various criteria, such as slopes, obstacles, geographic terrain and so on. And this cost surface raster map was acquired according to the previous studies [2–4]. In the cost raster map, assigned values ranging from 1 to 9 reflect the suitability of each grid cell. A value of 1 identifies an area of greatest suitability, and a value of 9 identifies an area of least suitability. And the values between them mean moderate suitability as is shown in Fig. 1. In this cost raster map, we need to find a path with least accumulated costs connecting the start point and the end point. In Fig. 1, the path with the least accumulated cost is the grids with green background having a cost of $20(4 + 2 + 1 + 3 + 3 + 4 + 1 + 2 = 20)$.

Point (i, j) means the grid which is in row i and column j. For each grid except for the grids on the edge of this map, it has eight adjacent grids that can be reached directly as illustrated in Figs. 2 and 3.

Supposing that the coordination of the next point is (g, h), it can be defined as:

$$\begin{cases} g = i + di[v] \\ h = j + dj[v] \end{cases} v = 0, 1, \ldots, 7 \tag{1}$$

					Start
1	3	3	2	5	4
2	4	2	6	9	2
7	5	2	5	1	3
6	4	3	3	4	7
1	6	9	5	3	2
2	1	3	2	4	2

End

Fig. 1. The path with the least accumulated costs

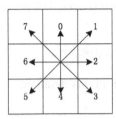

Fig. 2. The next step feasible point set

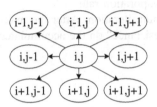

Fig. 3. The eight adjacent grids

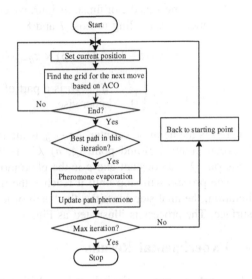

Fig. 4. The flow chart of the algorithm

where v corresponds to one of the eight grids in Fig. 3, di and dj are one dimensional arrays, di = {−1, −1, 0, 1, 1, 1, 0, −1} and dj = {0, 1, 1, 1, 0, −1, −1, −1}.

As the ant can't visit the grids it has already visited, so we create a tabu list $tabu_k$ to store the grids it has already visited and the grids in it should be excluded from the next feasible point set. The ant k at point (i, j) chooses the next point (g, h) to be visited the next step according to probability given by Eq. 6.

$$
p_{ij \to gh}^k = \begin{cases} \dfrac{[\tau_{ij \to gh}]^\alpha \cdot [\eta_{gh}]^\beta}{\sum\limits_{(x,y) \in allowed_k} [\tau_{ij \to xy}]^\alpha \cdot [\eta_{gh}]^\beta}, & \text{if } (g,h) \in allowed_k; \\ 0, & \text{otherwise.} \end{cases} \tag{2}
$$

where $allowed_k$ is the point set that ant k at point (i, j) can get to, $\tau_{ij \to gh}$ is the pheromone level between point (i, j) and (g, h) and it is a constant with a small value at the beginning, α and β are the parameters to show the importance of pheromone level and η_{gh} respectively, η_{gh} is the visibility of the point (g, h), which is inversely proportional to the cost of passing through point (g, h).

In this path finding process, the ant sometimes can't get to the end point. In order to acquire more feasible solutions, there will be two groups of ants beginning its exploring from the start point and the end point separately. The numbers of the two groups of ants are equal, and each ant chooses the next grid according to the probability given by Eq. 6. There are some principles the ants will follow: (1) For ant k, if allowed$_k$ is void before it get to the end, it will die and can't generate a feasible path; (2) If an ant reaches its own destination, its path is a feasible solution; (3) If one ant and another ant from the other group are next to each other, link the two paths and a new path is generated.

When all the ants die or finish its tour, we call one iteration is over. The pheromone will be updated according to Eqs. 7 and 8.

$$\tau_{ij \to gh}(t+1) = (1 - \rho) \times \tau_{ij \to gh}(t) + \Delta\tau_{ij \to gh}(t), (0 < \rho < 1) \tag{3}$$

$$\Delta\tau_{ij \to gh} = \begin{cases} \frac{Q}{C^{ib}}, & ij \to gh \text{ is a part of the best path in this iteration;} \\ 0, & \text{otherwise.} \end{cases} \tag{4}$$

where t is the iteration counter, $\Delta\tau_{ij \to gh}$ is the increase of pheromone level on the path between point (i, j) and point (g, h), C^{ib} is the minimum accumulated cost in this iteration, Q is a constant and ρ is the pheromone evaporation rate.

The process will stop until it reaches the maximum iteration. After the maximum iteration, the final step identifies the "path of least resistance" on the accumulated cost surface. The process is illustrated as Fig. 4.

4   Experimental Results

This least cost path analysis based on ACO was implemented in C ++. The proposed algorithm is tested several times to determine the proper parameter.

In this algorithm, α and β are parameters to control the relative importance of pheromone level versus visibility. ρ is the evaporation rate and it regulates the influence of the pheromone laid on the path. High value of α will make the algorithm result in stagnation behavior very quickly without finding good results. So does high value of ρ. When one parameter is tested, the others are held constant. Through a set of experiments, the results are consistent with our understanding of the algorithm. The experimental optimal set of parameter is that, $\alpha = 1$, $\beta = 3$, $\rho = 0.6$ and $Q = 200$. The population size of the ants and iteration times need to be determined. So the algorithm is run several times on an area with 250 * 250 grids and the results are shown in Table 1.

Though the results in the experiments may differ from each other, they are very close to the least cost path (1035). As the number of iterations increase, the results are getting closer to the best result although it is not so strictly linear. And the results are quite satisfactory. In this area, we can choose the end and start point arbitrarily and the path connecting them will be obtained. After obtaining the result, the path will be drawn in a simulated 3D map as is shown in Fig. 5.

Table 1. Values of the algorithm

Experiment Number	Values		
	Population	Iteration	Accumulated costs
1	50	50	1135
2		250	1104
3		500	1098
4		1000	1086
5	100	50	1107
6		250	1093
7		500	1082
8		1000	1060
9	250	250	1075
10		500	1069
11		1000	1055
12		2000	1042
13	500	250	1079
14		500	1072
15		1000	1060
16		2000	1049
17	1000	250	1074
18		500	1062
19		1000	1048
20		2000	1045

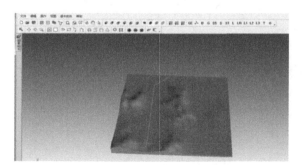

Fig. 5. A path showed in a simulated 3D map

5 Summary

In this paper, an algorithm based on ACO is proposed and applied to solving power line routing problem. As is known to everyone, the whole routing process is rather complicated and lots of factors should be considered. So in some particular problems, specific factors should be taken into account. Anyway, the ant colony algorithm used in this problem is proved quite efficient. With the help of this study, new alternative route will be proposed and will be much helpful for the researchers to find the best route in a raster map.

Acknowledgments. This work was supported by the Natural Science Foundation of China (NO.61502283), Outstanding Young Scientist Research Award Fund of Shandong Province, China (NO.BS2013DX037).

References

1. Monteiro, C., Ramírez-Rosado, I.J., Miranda, V., et al.: GIS spatial analysis applied to electric line routing optimization. IEEE Trans. J. Power Delivery **20**(2), 934–942 (2005)
2. Bahmani, H.F., Hosseini, M., Shabannejad, F.: An AHP based way to evaluate appropriate points for installing power towers and finding the best way for power transmission lines by GA Algorithm. Department of Artificial, Iran (2011)
3. Eroğlu, H., Aydin, M.: Optimization of electrical power transmission lines' routing using AHP, Fuzzy AHP and GISTurk. J. Electr. Eng. Comput. Sci. **23**(5), 14–18 (2015). https://journals.tubitak.gov.tr/
4. EPRI-GTC Overhead Electric Transmission Line Siting Methodology. EPRI, Palo Alto, CA, and Georgia Transmission Corporation, Tucker, GA, 1013080 (2006)
5. Eroglu, H., Aydin, M.: Genetic algorithm in electrical transmission lines path finding problems. In: 8th IEEE International Conference on Electrical and Electronics Engineering, pp. 112–116 (2013)

Research on the Tracing of Aquatic Products Production Based on PDA

Xing Guo and Songsen Lin(✉)

School of Logistics Engineering, Wuhan University of Technology,
Wuhan 430063, People's Republic of China
{2633283313,1585369972}@qq.com

Abstract. The communication design of PDA client and server in C/S architecture is mainly studied in this paper. The data synchronization and cross platform sharing is achieved by using *SQLCE* and *SQL Server* technology, and then the communication and data processing functions among PDA, server and bar code printing is realized in aquatic products traceability system. Finally, the information intelligence tracing of aquatic product is realized in supply chain.

Keywords: PDA · Production traceability · Data processing · Data synchronization

1 Introduction

In our country, the infrastructure of the pond aquaculture is weak, and fishery management is also lack of effective management policies and regulations. All these eventually lead to a lot of serious hazards in the quality and safety of aquatic products. The technical support for fry feeding and safety protection can be provided with the study on intelligent perception of ecological environment in different condition [1]. It is urgent to establish an aquaculture system with the function of remote and automatic control, which can deal with the occurrence of unexpected situations by monitoring the aquatic products breeding site in real time [2]. It is just the occasion of the PDA terminal acquisition equipment [3].

Operators can use PDA in all aspects of the workplace from collecting, processing and querying to feedback of aquatic product information with dynamic linkage with barcode printer to implement print function. Finally, the traceability of the entire aquaculture supply chain can be realized.

2 Design of Aquatic Products Production Tracing System Based on PDA

In this paper, the theory was researched about the retrospect of aquatic production based on PDA. Upon this, the overall system architecture was designed. The system includes the C/S system, communication between PDA and server. To a certain extent the whole system will verify the feasibility of the theory and system design.

© Springer International Publishing Switzerland 2016
Q. Zu and B. Hu (Eds.): HCC 2016, LNCS 9567, pp. 867–872, 2016.
DOI: 10.1007/978-3-319-31854-7_91

2.1   The Overall Program Design of Traceability System

When the operator is in the process of fishing, the operators who hold the field intelligent terminal PDA will set the fishing batch number according to the information such as the current fishing date, pond number, cage number and random serial number. After that, the fishing batch number, the type of fries and other information will be inputted to the *SQLCE* database in PDA side at the same time. When all information is inputted, PDA releases the data into server using Web Service through wireless *GPRS/WIFI* and other networks(the distance of wireless *WIFI* data transmission can reach to 100 m [4]). Operators in monitoring center will see the updated data information through the water product information platform, meanwhile, the new data which is inputted in the server database through the Web Service communication, it will trigger the bar code printing subsystem to print bar code through the WCF service. The system overall scheme design is shown in Fig. 1.

2.2   PDA Client and Server Communication Scheme Design

The communication between PDA and Web is mainly based on the Web Service communication technology, and the SOAP protocol is based on *HTTP*. Thus, the problem of firewall is solved in the process of Web transmission based on wireless *WIFI*. *XML* data format guarantee that data exchange under different platforms can be carried out normally. And by using wireless *WIFI* can transmit amounts of the data for free [5]. The PDA client and server communication process design is shown in Fig. 2:

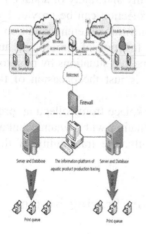

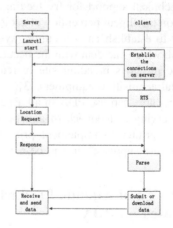

Fig. 1. Overall design drawing of system   **Fig. 2.** PDA client and server communication process design

3 The Key Technology Research of an Aquatic Products Traceability System Based on PDA Mode

After the design of overall scheme and function module of the system are completed, some technical matters of PDA and server communication in the process of producing water products should be solved to achieve all kinds of function of the aquatic product traceability system which is based on PDA mode. This chapter will put great emphasis on the study of the data synchronization technology between SQLCE database in PDA side and SQL Server database in server-side.

3.1 The Data Synchronization Technology Between *SQLCE* and *SQL* Server

Data synchronization is the process of realizing the data sharing and the real-time transmission synchronization in different terminal-platform's database, and that can ensure the integrity and consistency of data between systems. Synchronization Service For ADO.NET is one of the latest synchronization technology between mobile terminals and large systems.

3.1.1 Remote Data Access Technology-RDA

RDA synchronization technology is the primary data synchronization technology of SQLCE and SQL Server PDA. When the PDA interacts with server for the first time, the information of SQL server data table can be downloaded to SQLCE, if the format of shared datasheet has the same gauge outfit and field type.

3.1.2 The Function of Push and Pull in Server-Side

RDA data push mechanism consists of three parts:

Pull. The client database requests data from the server database, that means to access the remote SQL Server database, then download the data and store it in a table of the local SQL Compact Edition database, real-time tracking the change of the local table.

Push. The changes of the datasheet which is specified are submitted in the SQLCE database SQL Server database. At the same time, if the Pull method is called before Push method, the TrackOn parameter in it must be set.

SubmitSQL. The submitted SQL statement can run at the server of SQL Server. Meanwhile, the SQL statement can execute the function such as "CRUD" and also can execute the stored procedures, but the data will not be returned.

RDA synchronization technology is mainly used in programming appliance, its core object is the SQLCERemoteDataAccess. After the object was instantiated, the above three methods- Push, Pull, SubmitSQL can be called. Before these three methods were used, it is needed to confirm the path on the PDA and establish the database, and then connect server database and PDA database.

The Codes as follows:

```
SQLCEEngineeng = new SQLCEEngine(VariantClass.localConnectionString);
eng.CreateDatabase();
eng.Dispose();
public class VariantClass
{
 public static string strConn = @"Provider=SQLOLEDB;"
                    + @"Data Source=10.141.109.143;"
                    + @"Database=DB_AqucticTracing;"
                    + @"Uid=sa;Password=whut123;";
    public static string internetUrl =
@"http://10.141.109.143:8004/SQLCEWeb/SQLCEsa35.dll";
    public static string dataFileName = "/Program Files/pdacode/localDB_pda.sdf";
    public static string localConnectionString = @"Data Source=" + dataFileName;
    public static string internetLogin = "";
     public static string internetPassword = "";}
```

The Pull method which is needs to provide at least three parameters is called to request data from the server. That means four parameters are used when the second overloaded method is called in the application. Each one represents the name of local table which receives data, *SQL* statement, datasheet username and password which are needed to link server database, the *TrackingOn*, a setting datasheet name. The datasheet is used in the *Push* method, but data error message will be placed in the *Error Table* when data conflict was happened.

Code instance:

```
string strSQL = "SELECT * FROM Culti_Fry";
rda.Pull("Culti_Fry",strSQL,VariantClass.strConn, RdaTrackOption.TrackingOn,
"cultiErr");
```

The corresponding *SQLCERemoteDataAccess.Push* is used to push data into server database. The virtual datasheet must be established before the data was pushed into the server *SQL Server*, but this datasheet format should be consistent with the server's datasheet format, otherwise it cannot be imported to the database, and the format of each field in the datasheet must be matched to the server's datasheet.

4 The Implementation of Aquatic Products Production Tracing System Based on PDA

4.1 Design of Framework for C/S in PDA Port

The corresponding username and password are needed to judge whether the user has logging authority just like server's functions in the aquatic products production tracing system which is based on *WinCe* system. Considering that PDA is applied in the field, the purpose is to collect and transmit the corresponding data, and the core thought is convenient and quick which can help operators record, read and transmit the data in a high efficiency. So its contents and interfacial effects do not need to be displayed so fine just like the effects in server-end.

4.2   Implementation of Data Transmission and Collection in Service

4.2.1   Communication Between PDA and Server

When the water product production tracing system uses PDA to guide information into the database, what should be achieved is that the data can completely return to the server with short delay time through *WIFI* based on the *Web Service*. The data can be displayed in real time when it is browsed through webpage.

The PDA is used for information inputting, but the communication between the PDA and the server is only the first half operation of the system to achieve the PDA as functionally-orientation. The original intention of the design system is to generate the bar code in the bar code printer, and to complete the process of generating the information from the PDA terminal to the bar code. Bar code will be assigned to the goods in each link of the supply, so that the uniqueness of aquatic products is identified.

4.2.2   The Implementation of Communication Among PDA, Server and Barcode Generator

This section is different from the communication function between PDA and server in the previous section, it adds the bar code printing function which is based on *WCF services*, and then the whole process of information inputted to bar code printing is becoming more and more real-time and dynamic. When PDA is used as the guide and operator input one or a number of aquatic product information, the information is not only able to access to the server *SQL Server* database synchronously, but also water product production traceability system in *B/S* end can display synchronously in real time, and achieve the function of printing dynamically in synchronous driving bar code printer.

As shown in Fig. 3, it's a *DataBar* code which is dynamically printed by the bar code printing subsystem when *SQL Server* datasheet data were increased. The one-dimensional bar code is generated in accordance with the following number. And as shown in Fig. 4, it is a *DataBar* code printed by synchronously driving. The *DataBar* code is truncated to store a certain length of one-dimensional bar code. The bar code

0115031102013001

Fig. 3. PC screenshot of examples

Fig. 4. PC screenshot of bar code barcode printing subsystem

system and *DataBar* code will not be introduced in this paper, it just explain the WCF service can drive bar code to be printed, and finally realize the printing function when PDA drives the bar code printing subsystem through interactive server.

5 Summary

The water product production tracing system based on PDA is researched in the context of the internet of things technology and the popularizing of PDA intelligent terminal. The key technology of *SQLCE* and *SQL Server* data synchronization which will be used in water product production tracing based on PDA is analyzed, and the application environment of water product production tracing system based on PDA is also analyzed in this paper. According to the specific application environment, the overall implementation scheme of the system and the architecture of C/S system are designed. The communication between PDA-end and the server of the aquatic product production tracing system is also designed. The RDA synchronization technology in the process of data exchange between PDA and server and the cross platform sharing of the database are studied. The water product production tracing system in PDA-end under the C/S framework is realized, and the communication and data processing among PDA, server and bar code printing in SOA is also realized. Finally, the tracing in aquatic products breeding and production of the whole supply chain is implemented.

References

1. Ge, X.P., Miu, L.H.: The research progress in freshwater fish industry development present situation and the system in China. Qual. Stand. Chin. Fish. **03**, 22–31 (2011)
2. Trushenski, J.: New and ongoing society initiatives to craft a lasting partnership between AFS and all things aquaculture. Fisheries **38**(6), 285 (2013)
3. Draper, D.: Managing Patron-Driven Acquisitions (PDA) Records in a Multiple Model Environment. Techn. Serv. Q. **30**(2), 153–165 (2013)
4. Reza, A.W., Dimyati, K., Noordin, K.A., Kausar, A.S.M.Z., Sarker, S.: A comprehensive study of optimization algorithm for wireless coverage in indoor area. Optim. Lett. **8**(1), 145–157 (2014)
5. Bluetooth and WIFI wireless connection which is the most needed for mobile devices. Comput. Netw. **14**, 31 (2012)

A Dynamic Channel Allocation Algorithm in Random Access Process for LTE System

Jianing Li$^{(\boxtimes)}$, Baoling Liu, and Hui Tian

Key Laboratory of Universal Wireless Communication,
Beijing University of Posts and Telecommunications,
Beijing 100876, People's Republic of China
{ljn,blliu,tianhui}@bupt.edu.cn

Abstract. Random access technology is necessary in media access control of telecommunication system. Its function is directly related to the performance of the whole system. How to use time and frequency resource of LTE system effectively and reduce access delay as far as possible is the focus of this paper.

This paper proposes a dynamic random access channel allocation algorithm for competitive conditions. The algorithm focuses on improving the utilization of time and frequency resource in LTE system and avoiding waste caused by idle resource.

Keywords: LTE · Random access · Dynamic channel allocation · Utilization of channels · Access delay

1 Introduction

Nowadays, with wireless techniques developing rapidly, when 3G technology can not meet people's need anymore, LTE emerged as the times require.

As quasi 4G technology, LTE has the advantages of high spectrum utilization, [1–3] low communication delay and high transmission speed, achieving a good transition from 3G to 4G. LTE system can fulfill the access for multi-user and satisfy the QoS requirements for multi-traffic [4].

Random access technology is a key technology in media access control of LTE system [5]. The algorithms on channel allocation focus on improving the utilization of time and frequency resource. This paper presents a dynamic channel allocation algorithm which has relatively good performance and can achieve high channel utilization and low access delay whether in light traffic or heavy traffic situation.

2 Design and Analysis of the Algorithm

2.1 Design of Dynamic Channel Allocation Algorithm

The algorithm assumes that the number of users that arrives in each frame follows Poisson distribution whose mean is λ. In the algorithm, a record window consists of three frames and collision users in this window will send access request in the first frame of the next window. Since the first frame of the new window will deal with the

© Springer International Publishing Switzerland 2016
Q. Zu and B. Hu (Eds.): HCC 2016, LNCS 9567, pp. 873–878, 2016.
DOI: 10.1007/978-3-319-31854-7_92

requests not only from the new users, but also from the collision users of the last window, the number of channels in this frame has different adjustment compared to the other two frames of each window (i.e. the second and third frame).

Specific processes of the algorithm is as follows:

(1) The initialization of LTE system: Set the initial access probability, the initial number of channels and the initial number of access users to 1.
The following steps are given in Fig. 1

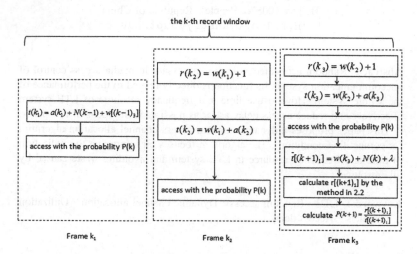

Fig. 1. Steps of the dynamic channel allocation algorithm.

The meaning of each variable in the figure is as follows:

$t(k_1/k_2/k_3)$:   the number of users intended to access in the first, second or third frame of the k-th record window

$\bar{t}[(k+1)_1]$:   the number of users estimated to be intended to access in the first frame of the k + 1-th record window

$a(k1/k2/k3)$:   the number of users arriving in the first, second or third frame of the k-th record window

$w(k_1/k_2/k_3)$:   the number of users failed to send access request in the first, second or third frame of the k-th record window

$w[(k-1)_3]$:   the number of users failed to send access request in the third frame of the k-1-th record window

$r(k_1/k_2/k_3)$:   the number of channels in the first, second or third frame of the k-th record window

$r[(k+1)_1]$:   the number of channels in the first frame of the k + 1-th record window

$P(k/k+1)$:   the access probability of the k-th or k + 1-th record window

$N(k-1/k)$:   the number of collision users in the k-1-th or k-th record window
In the k-th record window (The window consists of three frames, which are Frame k_1, Frame k_2 and Frame k_3.)

In Frame k1,

(2)   Take the users arriving in this frame, the collision users in the k-1th window and the users failed to send access request in the third frame of the k-1-th window as the access users of this frame.

(3)   Users select channels randomly and access with probability P. Users failed to send out access request will send access request again with probability P in the next frame.

In Frame k_2,

(4)   Take the number of users who failed to send access request in Frame k1 plus 1 as the number of channels in the frame.

(5)   Repeat(3).

In Frame k3,

(6)   Take the number of users who failed to send access request in Frame k2 plus 1 as the number of channels in the frame.

(7)   Repeat(3).

(8)   At the end of Frame k3, estimate the number of users in the next frame (i.e. the first frame in the k + 1-th window).

The method of estimating: the number of users failed to send access request in the frame + the number of collision users + arrival rate λ

(9)   Calculate the number of channels in the first frame of the k + 1-th window according to the status of the k-th window.

The specific calculating method will be introduced in the next chapter.

(10) The access probability of the k + 1-th window: the number of channels calculated in (9) / the number of users estimated in (8)

In the k + 1-th record window,

(11) Return to (2).

2.2   Dynamic Distribution of Random Access Channels

As the description in Sect. 2.1, at the last frame of each record window, the number of channels in the first frame of the new record window will be determined. The users in the first frame of the new window include the collision users in the last window. Compared to other frames, the traffic is heavier, and thus a suitable method to calculate the number of new channels is needed.

After considering various factors, the new channel-number calculation formula is obtained.

$$R(k+1) = \left\lfloor I \times 2^{N(k)/3} + 0.5 \times R(k) + 0.5 \times (N(k) + S(k)) + 0.5 \right\rfloor \qquad (2-1)$$

The meaning of each variable in the formula is as follows:

R(k + 1): the number of channels allocated to the new window

I: Collision indicator. When a collision occurs in the window, I is 1. Or I is 0.

N(k): the number of collision users in the current window

R(k): the number of current channels in the window

S(k): the number of users who send access request successfully.

Because the bandwidth of the LTE system are limited, the maximum number of channels is set to Rm. And the minimal number of channels is 1.

2.3 Analysis of the Algorithm Performance

The utilization ratio of channels is the primary performance indicator in the simulation.

In order to verify the practicality of the algorithm, backoff algorithm and channel status are not considered in the following simulation.

As shown in Fig. 2, it is the utilization ratio of channels in LTE system when the number of users that arrives in each frame follows Poisson distribution whose mean is 0.5. The simulation select 150 record windows to observe the channel utilization ratio in different record windows. The fixed-channel algorithm is selected to compare and the fixed numbers of channels are 2, 6, 10.

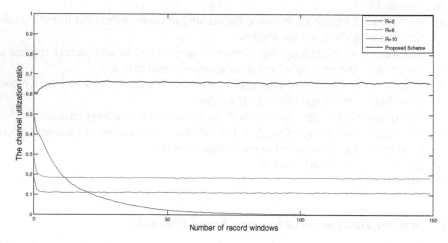

Fig. 2. Channel utilization ratio of dynamic channel allocation algorithm and fixed channel algorithm ($\lambda = 0.5$).

When the number of channels is two, with the frames increasing, the collision users are more and more, which results in the channel utilization ratio reducing to zero. When the number of channels is 6 or 10, the system can hold the current traffic easily. But the channel utilization ratio is very low.

As we can see from the figure, the channel utilization ratio stably maintains between 60 % and 70 %, much higher than the channel utilization ratio of fixed channel system, which reflects good adaptability and superior performance of the dynamic channel allocation algorithm.

As shown in Fig. 3, it is the utilization ratio of channels when the mean of Poisson distribution is 2.

When the number of fixed channels is two, the collision happens frequently and the system channel utilization ratio falls sharply to 0. When the number of fixed channels is six, because of user cumulativeness, more and more users come later, which leads to

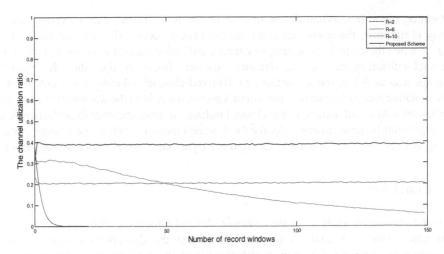

Fig. 3. Channel utilization ratio of dynamic channel allocation algorithm and fixed channel algorithm ($\lambda = 2$).

more collisions and channel utilization ratio declining. As for 10 fixed channels, the system can satisfy the need of users to access. But most of channels are empty and the channel utilization ratio is low.

Since the traffic is heavier now, it is difficult to predict the number of users in the new frame for dynamic channel allocation algorithm. So the prediction performance is not as good as that of light traffic. But the channel utilization ratio remains at around 40 %, much better than the fixed channels condition.

It is the average user access delay when $\lambda = 2$ that is shown in Fig. 4. Among three bar charts, the middle one is the user's average access delay of the dynamic channel

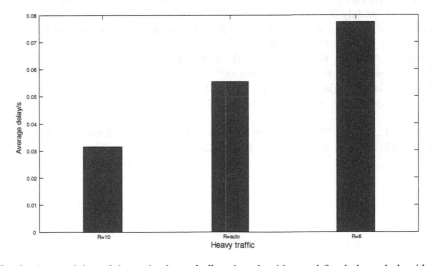

Fig. 4. Access delay of dynamic channel allocation algorithm and fixed channel algorithm.

allocation algorithm. When the number of channels is 10, the user's average access delay is minimal, the users can complete the fastest access. But we can know from Fig. 3, when there are 10 channels, its channel utilization ratio is only 20 %, half of the channel utilization ratio of the dynamic channel allocation algorithm. In terms of average access delay, the advantages of 10-fixed-channel scheme is not noteworthy. The dynamic channel allocation algorithm's access delay is in the acceptable range, and combined with its advantage in the channel utilization ratio, the overall performance of the algorithm is quite superior. As for the 6-fixed-channel scheme, the average access delay is large. Its performance is far from the dynamic channel allocation algorithm.

3 Conclusion

It is the simulation analysis of the dynamic channel allocation algorithm proposed in this paper. From the analysis we can inform that the dynamic channel allocation algorithm can maintain fair channel utilization ratio. Its performance is far superior to the fixed channel strategy. In terms of access delay, the dynamic channel allocation algorithm can also perform well. Overall, the dynamic channel allocation algorithm can predict the number of users to arrive and assign resource of channels rationally to adapt to changes in the system. Compared to the fixed channel scheme, it has a great advantage.

Acknowledgments. This work is supported by the National High Technology Research and Development Program of China (863 Program) (No.2013AA013603).

References

1. Dahlman, E., Parkvall, S., Skold, J.: 3G Evolution, HSPA and LTE for Mobile Broadband, pp. 21–37, 28 July 2010
2. Lescuyer, P., Lucidarme, T.: Evolved Packet System (EPS): The LTE and SAE Evolution of 3G UMTS, 43–52, 7 March 2008
3. Sesia, S., Toufik, I., Baker, M.: LTE, The UMTS Long Term Evolution: From Theory to Practice, pp. 77–94. Wiley, New York (2009)
4. Sun, L., Gao, Y., Tian, H., Xu, H., Zhang, P.: An adaptive random access protocol for OFDMA system. In: Vehicular Technology Conference, VTC-2007, pp. 1827–1831. Fall (2007)
5. Xunwei, L., Hui, L., Ming, Z.: 3GPP Long Term Evolution: Architecture and Specification, pp. 31–121. Posts & Telecom Press, Beijing (2010)

Research and Implementation of Scene Effect Based on Particle System in Virtual Maintenance Platform

Li Jia[1], Junzhong Sun[1], Yi Xie[1], Feng Shi[1], and Han Sun[2(✉)]

[1] Navy Submarine Academy, Qingdao, Shandong, China
lijiavr@126.com, sunjunzhong@vip.sohu.com,
{datou1977,25345}@163.com
[2] School of Logistic Engineering, Wuhan University of Technology, Wuhan, Hubei, China
234918954@qq.com

Abstract. The particle system generating principal was presented in this paper. According to the characteristics of fire effect, the mathematical model to achieve fire effect was established based on the particle system; Combined with hierarchical structure particle system, the tree structure chart of the fire effect was constructed and framework of the implementation process was built up. Under texture blending principal, the real fire effect was realized finally through C++ programming language.

Keywords: Scene effect · Particle system · OSG

1 Outline

Particle effect scene mainly stands for the simulation of rain, snow, fog or spark implemented by particle system which can control the particle's size, color, length of lifecycle, speed downwards, amount as well as the wind direction and wind power through relative parameters to obtain diverse particle systems. In order to enhance the performance ability of particle system and because a large number of nature phenomena are extremely complex in selves, some applications must adopt the particle system possessing hierarchical structure, that is, particles on a certain layer are the sub-particle system of the next layer. When father system changes, its subsystem and particles in the subsystem change therewith. Subsystem has inheritance to the father system which makes the same group of particles have similar attribute change and motion law. Therefore, a hierarchical structure can be used to globally control the external motion of complex fuzzy object composed by many particle systems.

In this thesis, it is easy to control the whole system's physical process by using particle system bearing hierarchical structure. Take the gunpowder explosion simulation for example, during the explosion process, every separated fragment gains certain initial conditions when it leaves its parent, such as mass, speed, direction and so on. Under the circumstance of ignoring air resistance and other factors, these separated fragments and their parent satisfy the law of conservation of mass and energy. And then, each fragment satisfies this condition too after experiencing another explosion. It is pretty difficult to model the fire effect naturally and conveniently without adopting hierarchical structure.

© Springer International Publishing Switzerland 2016
Q. Zu and B. Hu (Eds.): HCC 2016, LNCS 9567, pp. 879–883, 2016.
DOI: 10.1007/978-3-319-31854-7_93

2   Analysis of Fire Effect

2.1   Characteristics of Fire Effect

Below are the show details and characteristics of fire effect:

- Affected by wind and changing its shape fantastically with the shape of emission source;
- With ever-changing color. The frame color changes in the wake of comburent material and even the same flame changes its color still;
- Displaying various sizes. Along with different continuous time and speed, the size is different;
- Gradually disappearing;
- With smoke effect.

2.2   Mathematical Modeling of Fire Effect

Using a circle parallel to the XOZ plane of the world coordinate system as the flame's particle emitter. Assuming the circle center and radius respectively are: (O_x, O_y, O_z), r, its equation is:

$$(x - o_x)^2 + (z - o_z)^2 = r^2 \tag{1}$$

The initial position of the new particle produced by the particle emitter is:

$$\begin{aligned} x &= o_x + rand() \times r \\ y &= o_y \\ z &= o_z + rand() \times r \end{aligned} \tag{2}$$

Describe velocity direction via spherical coordinate system. Set ϕ as the included angle between the unit velocity vector and the positive z axis of the world coordinate system and set θ as the included angle between the projection of the unit velocity vector in the XOY plane and the positive x axis, then:

$$\begin{aligned} v_x &= \sin\phi \cos\theta \\ v_y &= \sin\phi \sin\theta \\ v_z &= \cos\phi \end{aligned} \tag{3}$$

ϕ and θ can be defined as follows by random functions:

$$\begin{aligned} \phi &= m\phi + rand() \times v\phi \\ \theta &= m\theta + rand() \times v\theta \end{aligned} \tag{4}$$

In the equations, mean values mφ and mθ usually take for 90 degrees in most applications, but variances vφ and vθ depend on the specific application, usually take for about 10 degrees.

3   Basic Principle of Particle System Based on OSG

3.1   Principle of OSG Particle System

The authors referred to the particle SDK in the OSG and the specific logical structure is shown in Fig. 1.

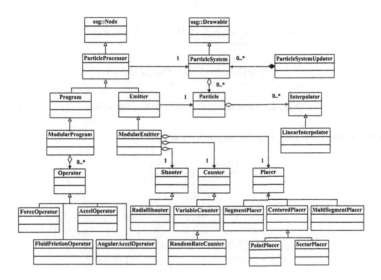

Fig. 1. Structure chart of the OSG particle system

The main programming idea is as follows:

Firstly, create a particle template. Particle template is namely a particle object which contains the particle's various attributes.

Secondly, create a particle system object and set its acquiescent status attribute including texture, mix and light. Add the particle template to the particle system.

Thirdly, create a Modular Emitter and define three modules simultaneously, they are Counter, Placer and Shooter. The Placer can be Segment Placer, Centered Placer or Multi Segment Placer.

Then in order to introduce the impact of the gravity, this thesis introduces the Program inherited from the Particle Processor which can be used to adjust the particle's attribute. Take the Modular Program for example; it can define some particles actions.

Lastly, add the Particle System Updater to update the particles continuously.

3.2 Design Process

Fire effect design creates two particle systems: one is the fire, another is the smoke. The scene tree structure of the fire effect design is shown in Fig. 2 which mainly contains the initial settings of the relevant attributes of fire and smoke. The relevant attributes of fire include shape, size, color, lifetime, velocity, mass, radius and so on.

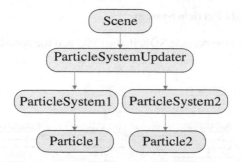

Fig. 2. Tree structure chart of the fire effect

Figure 3 is the flow chart of the fire effect scene:

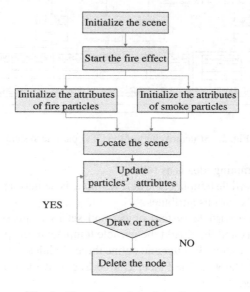

Fig. 3. Flow chart of the fire effect scene

The fire effect scene is designed through the method of stratified particle system. Positioning of the scene relies on a certain point in the scene world coordinate obtained via collect algorithm. Obtaining the intersection point coordinate via menu (view/fine-detail information) and retyping it into the "emitter position" in the attribute dialog box of fire particle and smoke particle.

Dialog box of the fire effect changes some characteristics of the fire effect on the basis of the particle's relevant attributes which includes the particle's lifecycle, initial size, terminate size, initial color, terminate color and the emitter's position.

3.3 Texture Fusion

Located by the PointPlacer, the relative positions of fire and smoke are: (0,0,0) and (0,0,1). In the scene, we can obtain the intersection points' position in the world coordinate system by utilizing option nodes thus to locate more fire effects. Meanwhile, texture fusion mode is needed to get more authentic fire effect. Therefore, it is necessary to designate the absolute path as: the AppDir+ "data\\models\\images\\smoke.rgb".

The terminate effect can be saved as .osg format, but the saving path of the models must be on the same layer as images' where the texture is stowed. Remember to put the texture into the "images" when modeling, that is, only the relative paths of osg model file and "images folder" remain unchanged cannot the texture be missed. Fire effects without and with texture are respectively shown in Figs. 4 and 5:

Fig. 4. Fire effect without texture   **Fig. 5.** Fire effect with texture

4 Summarize

According to the characteristics of fire effect, the mathematical model to achieve fire effect was established based on the particle system; Combined with hierarchical structure particle system, the tree structure chart of the scene effect was constructed and framework of the implementation process was built up. Under texture blending principal, the real fire effect was realized finally through C++ programming language.

References

1. Stam, J.: Interacting with smoke and fire in real time. Commun. ACM **43**(7), 77–83 (2000)
2. Physically-Based Modeling and Real-Time Simulation of Fluids. http://www.dart.rst.ucf.edu/grouPs/deghheses/chen.html
3. Reeves, W.T.: Particle systems – a technique for modeling a class of fuzzy objects. Comput. Graph. **17**(3), 359–376 (1983)
4. Zhou, K., Zhong, R., Lin, S., et al.: Real-time smoke rendering using compensated ray marching. ACM Trans. Graph. **27**(3), 12 (2008)
5. Martz, P.: OpenSceneGraph Quick Start Guide[M/OL]. Skew Matrix Software LLC, New York (2007). http://www.lulu.com/content/1164927

Research on Data Processing Algorithm of Data Fusion Simulator

Mingyang Liu, Shufen Liu, Songyuan Gu[✉], Quan Zhang, and Zhanjian Zhu

College of Computer Science and Technology, Jilin University, Changchun, China
{liumingyangjlu,gusongyuan614}@163.com,
liusf@mail.jlu.edu.cn, zhangquan328@126.com,
zhuzj10@mails.jlu.edu.cn

Abstract. A data processing algorithm of data fusion simulator is proposed in this paper to solve the problem that it is difficult to process the information of target tracks from detectors of mother ship to data fusion simulator. The proposed algorithm is utilized to execute fusion process, form main track list and send comprehensive situation of mother ship imitatively, thereby the value of global correlation decision can be acquired, furthermore, the correlativity between tracks can also be acquired. Finally the difficulty in data processing of data fusion simulator is solved.

Keywords: Data fusion · Simulation technology · Simulator · Track processing

1 Introduction

Multi-sensor information resources in different time and space are taken advantage of sufficiently in this paper, and computer technology is utilized to obtain multi-sensor observation information according to time order, the information would be analyzed, integrated, assigned and utilized automatically under certain rules, to acquire coincident interpretation and description, accordingly the missions of decision-making and estimating can be accomplished [1, 2]. Data processing procedure of data fusion simulator is analyzed in detail, and related algorithm is represented for correlativity judgement and data fusion. Memberships of sensor resolution and difference between tracks are obtained from resolution of sensors, then the value of global correlation decision can be acquired, furthermore, the correlativity between tracks can also be acquired. Weight sum method is used to calculate the fused tracks in this paper, which results in the better approximation to sensors with high precision for weighted fused data.

2 Processing Procedure of Data Fusion Simulators

The major function of data fusion simulator is to receive target track information from detectors of mother ship, execute fusion process, form main track list and send comprehensive situations of mother ship imitatively. The major procedures are as follow: (a) main track list initialization. Including cleaning up of main track list and initialization

Q. Zu and B. Hu (Eds.): HCC 2016, LNCS 9567, pp. 884–889, 2016.
DOI: 10.1007/978-3-319-31854-7_94

of flag bit; (b) original tracks reading. Receive the track information from each sensor, then write the information into main track list and modify the flag bit of main track list; (c) original tracks preprocessing. The preprocessing method is to forecast the tracks through polynomial fitting; (d) temporal and space alignment [3]. Forecast the tracks in main track list, unify the tracks from each simulator into identical time; (e) correlativity judgement. Mainly including attribute correlativity, location correlativity and speed correlativity. If exists irrelevance, an irrelevant processing should be executed; on the contrary a relevant processing should be done if relevant; (f) track fusion [4]. Extrapolate the track to the time of system tracks when receives a set of local tracks, and fuse this track with system tracks through weighted fusion to acquire estimation of current state. Repeat this processing method when receives another set of tracks; (g) main track list updating. Write the fused track information into main track list as the reference value of next track fusion; (h) track quality updating. Add 1 on value of track quality when fuses data successfully, the value of track quality is up to 7.

The major procedures of algorithm of data fusion simulator are shown as Fig. 1 below.

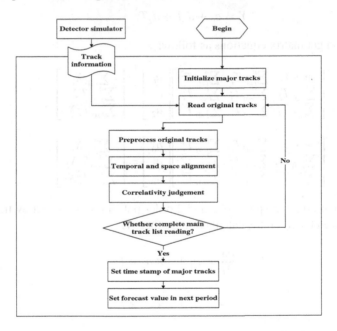

Fig. 1. Major procedures of algorithm of data fusion simulator

3   Data Process Algorithm of Data Fusion Simulator

3.1   Major Tracks Initialization

Write forecast value of last period into major tracks as the reference value for correlativity judgement in this period. Then generate forecast time stamp in next period. Make preparations for temporal and space alignment.

3.2 Temporal and Space Alignment

First execute temporal alignment, then analyze historical speed information of tracks, fit latest 3 historical points to generate 2 order polynomial by means of least square method, forecast value of original track is the value of 2 order polynomial with the time value of major tracks. Location forecast value is the integral sum of last period location and differential interval which is generated by original tracks' time value and major tracks' time value using 2 order polynomial.

For the convenience of forecasting [5], transform speed and location information of original tracks into rectangular coordinates and forecast. Then retransform the forecast value into polar coordinates and write back to original tracks.

It is able to fit $(X_1, T_1), (X_2, T_2), (, T_3)$ and $(Y_1, T_1), (Y_2, T_2), (Y_3, T_3)$ respectively depend on the least square method. Historical speed forecast procedures are as follow:

$$X = a_0 + a_1 T + a_2 T^2 \tag{1}$$

$$Y = a_0 + a_1 T + a_2 T^2 \tag{2}$$

So we can get matrix equations as follow:

$$\begin{bmatrix} n+1, & \sum_{i=0}^{n} T_I, & \sum_{i=0}^{n} T_i^2 \\ \sum_{i=0}^{n} T_I, & \sum_{i=0}^{n} T_i^2, & \sum_{i=0}^{n} T_i^3 \\ \sum_{i=0}^{n} T_i^2 & \sum_{i=0}^{n} T_i^3 & \sum_{i=0}^{n} T_i^4 \end{bmatrix} \begin{bmatrix} a_0 \\ a_1 \\ a_2 \end{bmatrix} = \begin{bmatrix} \sum_{i=0}^{n} X_i \\ \sum_{i=0}^{n} T_i X_i \\ \sum_{i=0}^{n} T_i^2 X_i \end{bmatrix} \tag{3}$$

$$\begin{bmatrix} n+1, & \sum_{i=0}^{n} T_I, & \sum_{i=0}^{n} T_i^2 \\ \sum_{i=0}^{n} T_I, & \sum_{i=0}^{n} T_i^2, & \sum_{i=0}^{n} T_i^3 \\ \sum_{i=0}^{n} T_i^2 & \sum_{i=0}^{n} T_i^3 & \sum_{i=0}^{n} T_i^4 \end{bmatrix} \begin{bmatrix} a_0 \\ a_1 \\ a_2 \end{bmatrix} = \begin{bmatrix} \sum_{i=0}^{n} X_i \\ \sum_{i=0}^{n} T_i X_i \\ \sum_{i=0}^{n} T_i^2 X_i \end{bmatrix} \tag{4}$$

Calculate a_0, a_1, a_2 respectively, and 2 order polynomials needed by track forecast can be obtained based on the calculation. So there is

$$V_x = \frac{\partial X}{\partial T} = a_1 + 2 \times a_2 \times T \tag{5}$$

$$V_y = \frac{\partial Y}{\partial T} = a_1 + 2 \times a_2 \times T \tag{6}$$

Forecast the location based on speed:

$$X = X_0 + \int_0^1 V_X \tag{7}$$

$$Y = Y_0 + \int_0^1 V_Y \tag{8}$$

3.3   Correlativity Judgement

This procedure mainly judges whether targets from different sensors originate from the same one, tracks requiring to perform correlativity judgement are the original tracks didn't be correlated with any major tracks. Correlativity of attributes and types would be judged based on the following rules: tracks with different attributes and types are irrelative, oppositely are correlative. Jude it as correlative if attributes and types are unknown. Employ tracks correlativity formula to perform correlativity judgement of locations and speeds. Correlativity judgement method of locations and speeds of tracks is as follow [6]: assume the tracks originating from different sensors are

$$
R_i = \begin{bmatrix} r_{i1} \\ r_{i2} \\ \cdots \\ r_{in} \end{bmatrix}, i = 1, 2, \ldots , \tag{9}
$$

Corresponding resolutions are

$$
\Delta R_i = \begin{bmatrix} \delta_{i1} \\ \delta_{i2} \\ \cdots \\ \delta_{in} \end{bmatrix}, i = 1, 2, \ldots , \tag{10}
$$

where $r_{ik}, k = 1, 2, \ldots , n$ represent tracks' features, such as distance, direction, course and speed. n represents the amount of features, there are 4 features here, they are speed, course, direction and distance. $\delta_{ik}, k = 1, 2, \ldots , n$ represents the resolution of features. Assume senor A's precision is higher than B's, so

$$
\delta_{Ak} < \delta_{Bk}, k = 1, 2, \ldots , n \tag{11}
$$

Regard this as a hypothesis, let H represents the hypothesis, the following formula can be obtained

$$
H = \begin{cases} 1 \\ 0 \end{cases} \tag{12}
$$

where 1 represents the two tracks originate from the same target, 0 represents the two tracks originate from different targets.

Define the statistical distance between two curves as

$$
d_{ij=}^2 \begin{cases} \left\| R_j - R_i \right\|, when\ i \neq j \\ \left\| \Delta_i \right\|, when\ i = j \end{cases} \tag{13}
$$

Thus, there is

$$
\begin{cases}
d_{11} = \sqrt{\Delta_1^T \Delta_1} \\
d_{12} = \sqrt{(R_2 - R_1)^T (R_2 - R_1)} \\
d_{21} = d_{12} \\
d_{22} = \sqrt{\Delta_2^T \Delta_2}
\end{cases}
\tag{14}
$$

Similarity measure between elements is as follow:

$$
u_{ij} = \frac{1/d_{ij}^{2/(m-1)}}{\left[\sum_{x=1}^{c} (1/d_{xj})^{2/(m-1)} \right]} \forall i, j = 1, 2
\tag{15}
$$

Where c represents targets amount, membership of resolution can be obtained from formulas (14) and (15), u_{ij} represents membership of difference of the two tracks R_i and R_j. Global correlation decision D_x is made by sensor with lowest precision, thus, there is

$$
D_x = \begin{cases} 1, u_{12} > u_{22} \\ 0, u_{12} < u_{22} \end{cases}
\tag{16}
$$

Formula of correlativity between tracks of sensors is shown below:

$$
H = \begin{cases} 1, D_x = 1 \\ 0, D_x = 0 \end{cases}.
\tag{17}
$$

3.4   Track Fusion

Function of track fusion [7] is to confirm whether tracks originating from different sensors belong to the same target, and group their covariance matrices and state estimations together.

Processing method of track fusion is that, when receives a set of local tracks, extrapolate the track to the time of system tracks and fuse this track with system tracks to acquire estimation of current state and form system tracks. Repeat this processing method when receives another set of track.

Consequently, track fusion's algorithm procedures are shown below:

Calculate weighted factor above all for the successfully judged tracks, utilize the acquired weighted factor to perform fusions of location and speed, the attribute and type set as the value of correlativity judgement.

Assume tracks' corresponding detectors are $X_1, X_2, \ldots, X_n$, corresponding precisions are $P_1, P_2, \ldots, P_n$, calculate fused detector value $\bar{X}$ through weighted fusion, weighted coefficient is proportional to the precision of sensor, then we can obtain:

$$
\bar{X} = \sum_{i=1}^{n} \frac{P_i}{\sum_{i=1}^{n} P_i} X_i
\tag{18}
$$

Let weighted factor be α, original track's value be a, major track before fusion be b, then value after fusion b' is

$$b' = \alpha \times a + (1 - \alpha) \times b \tag{19}$$

Calculation method of weighted factor is as follow:

$$\alpha = \frac{\delta_m/\delta_0}{n + \delta_m/\delta_0} \tag{20}$$

where δ_m is error of major track, δ_0 is error of original track, n is the amount of correlativity information source of major track, i.e. weighted factor shows a linear relationship with sensor's precision. Above all, process the speeds and locations, we can obtain

$$V_m = (1 - \alpha) \times V_0 + \alpha \times V_m \tag{21}$$

$$P_m = (1 - \alpha) \times P_0 + \alpha \times P_m \tag{22}$$

Where V_m is speed of major track before processing, V_0 is speed of original track, P_m is location of major track before processing (decomposed into XY direction), P_0 is location of original track (decomposed into XY direction), α is the weighted factor.

4   Conclusion

Data fusion problem confronting data processing in simulation system is considered sufficiently in this paper, and practicable solutions are proposed. Data fusion simulator' major function and processing procedures of the algorithm has been introduced, and the weighted data fusion algorithm based on precision of sensor has been represented.

References

1. Hao, R.Z., Yang, R.P.: Current research status of multi-sensor data fusion technology and its military applications. Ordnance Ind. Autom. **4**, 007 (2007)
2. Zhu, Z.: Current research status and its development direction of multi-sensor data fusion technology. Ship Electron. Eng. **2**, 003 (2009)
3. Zhang, Y., Dong, P., Gao, H.: Time-space alignment method for radar netting. Fire Control Radar Technol. **2**, 003 (2013)
4. Zhang, K.S., Li, X.R., Chen, H., et al.: Multi-sensor multi-target tracking with out-of-sequence measurements. In: Proceedings of the 6th International Conference on Information Fusion, pp. 672–679. IEEE, USA (2003)
5. Wu, X., Guan, H., Yin, L.: The data fusion and tracks prediction of multiple radar system. J. Math. Pract. Theor. **40**, 160–173 (2010)
6. Dong, Y.: Track matching based on correlation theory. Ship Electron. Eng. **5**, 024 (2012)
7. Huang, X., Wu, Q.: Weighted fusion method for out of sequence measurement problem. Jisuanji Gongcheng yu Yingyong (Computer Engineering and Applications) **48**(30), 157–161 (2012)

Library Mobile Service Innovation Under Html5 Environment

Qing Lu[✉]

Library of Nanchang Institute of Technology, Nanchang, China
33152327@qq.com

Abstract. This article analyzed the development and present situation of the library mobile service, pointed out the deficiencies of present model. On the basis of describing the HTML5 functional characteristics, a mobile service model based on HTML5 is proposed.

Keywords: HTML5 · Library · Mobile services

1 Development and Present Situation of Library Mobile Service

The "2015 thirty-sixth China Internet development statistics report" released by China Internet Network Information Center (CNNIC) shows that as of June 2015, the scale of China's mobile phone users has reached 0.594 billion, and the proportion of the overall internet users increased to 88.9 %. With the promote of large screen and application experience, the trend that mobile phone as the major internet terminal is more obvious [1]. Library, as an important part of social cultural service system, should conform to the trend of the times, so as to give users a better and more convenient service experience, simultaneously strengthen the mobile internet development application in the library. At present, there are a variety of mobile services in the library, but there are some defects. Therefore, the development of the mobile Internet application based on HTML5 will be the main service mode in the future.

Early in the early 21st century, foreign library field had been keen on the influence of mobile internet technology to the library, and began to study mobile internet technology and mobile phone application in library. University of Toyama, in 2000, launched the bibliographic query system based on i-mode phone, to provide users with bibliographic query, appointments, reminders and renew and other aspect services [2]. University of Tokyo, in 2001, launched a library bibliographic query system, the same year, the Helsinki Finland Technology University Library began to use mobile phone text messaging service, Sogang University of South Korea launched a mobile library to query the library information also. In 2005, the Sims American Library of Louisiana College SMS put out the first SMS reference services in American [3]. In 2003, library of Beijing Institute of Technology launched the first domestic SMS notification, books reminder, lectures information push and other mobile phone service. In July 2006, the Hunan Institute of Science and Technology launched the first domestic library WAP website.

© Springer International Publishing Switzerland 2016
Q. Zu and B. Hu (Eds.): HCC 2016, LNCS 9567, pp. 890–894, 2016.
DOI: 10.1007/978-3-319-31854-7_95

At present, there are three main mobile service methods, the SMS (Short Message Service), WAP (Wireless Application Protocol) and Native App (Application Native). These three ways are also the development context of mobile communication technology (as shown in Fig. 1).

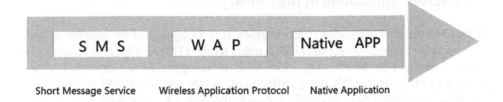

Fig. 1. Development context of library mobile service model

Early mobile communication technology is mainly refer to the short message service, so SMS service has been developed and improved, and the mobile service of the library is based on the SMS. WAP website is the most widely used mobile service model, service content mainly includes information retrieval, database utilization, electronic books, electronic journals etc. Native App client software service is a kind of services developing with the mobile internet and smart mobile terminal equipment, that the library in the need to create a more interactive performance and better service experience, the service content is extracted from the WAP. Now the mainstreams of mobile services in the domestic and international are WAP and Native APP, SMS is the auxiliary.

2   Lack of Current Mobile Services

SMS has a unique advantage in the give back reminder and the notice of appointment books to the library. But because of the length of the message is limited, there exists interaction energy difference and the difficulty of realizing the complex information retrieval. WAP is an global unity open protocol standard which provides internet content and advanced value-added services to mobile terminals. The biggest characteristic is the flexibility of system structure and the openness of protocol. It can develop interactive service interface, but the display effect of WAP is often different from the terminal, and the interaction is bad [4]. Compared with rich service provided by the library, it is inferior. App Native, or client, is a software that can be used in the smart phone terminal, has the advantages of efficient sources mining and integration, personalized customization and push, easy access and rapid spread, features rich and interesting. But the development of App Native is based on smart phones, and there are many kinds of smart phone operating system, the version is updated quickly, so the App Native development cycle is long and difficult, it is also necessary to download from store or market application market, which limits the development of its development model [5]. Therefore, it is necessary to establish a more open and popular mobile service system, it needs a kind of more efficient and common development technology, HTML5 technology, a variety of new features and cross platform features are catering to this need, so that bring forth the new through the old library's mobile service model is possible.

3   HTML5: New Opportunities for the Development of Mobile Internet Application in the Library

HTML5 is the next generation of the internet. It is a language of the internet content construction. The broad sense of HTML5 refers to the HTML, CSS3, JavaScript, and a series of new API (as shown in Fig. 2). HTML5 technology hopes to reduce the browser to plug in Flash such as Microsoft, Silverlight, Adobe and so on, and provide more standard sets which can effectively enhance the network application. Specifically, HTML5 adds a number of new syntax features that are the new features and functionality that will bring change to the mobile application development model of library.

HTML5	Web Workers	
CSS 3	Web Sockets Protocol/API	CSSOM View Module
DOM Level 3 Events	Indexed Database	Cross-Origin Resource Sharing
SVG 1.1	File API	RDFa
WAI-ARIA 1.0	Geolocation	Microdata
MathML 2.0	Server-Sent Events	WOFF
ECMAScript 5	Element Traversal	HTTP 1.1part a to part 7
2D Context	Media Fragments	TLS 1.2(updated)
WebGL	XMLHttp Request	IRI(updated)
Web Storage	Selectors API	

Fig. 2. System of HTML5

3.1   New Tag Elements: Semantic Features

HTML5 canceled a number of outdated HTML4 tags, introduced <article>, <header>, <aside>, <nav>, <section>, <footer> and other structured semantic labels, and greatly simplify the declaration of the character set, strengthen the structural semantics of web documents, so that the HTML page is more easy to load and more suitable for SEO, just like the label elements head and title, when some mobile devices in the analysis to these labels to make special tips or more humane display. Html5 also has a substantial increase in the function of the form, a variety of different form elements to correspond to different input requirements. These elements are more suitable for customization of mobile platforms. HTML5 also introduces micro data, so that machine can identify the method using to label contents. The new tag element technology in the structure of the improvement not only improves the readability of the web page but also reduce the burden of the form design staff.

3.2   Multimedia Technology: Web Multimedia Features

Html5 added <video>, <audio> tags used to embed audio and video playback functions in web pages, without the support of flash and other embedded plug-ins. In mobile devices, the original application for audio and video and text pictures mixed content (such as MicroBlog) processing is quite inconvenient and inefficient, and its different elements of the material need to use different components to deal with, while in the HTML5 page, audio and video can be freely embedded, do not need to take special treatment for individual material.

3.3 Offline Storage Technology: Local Storage Characteristics

Offline data caching, on-line state detection and localization, the 3 ways of storage are a bit like the integration of the old technology cookie and the client database. But it's better than cookie because it supports multiple windows stores, and it has better security and performance, even after the browser is closed it can be saved. To save data to a user's browser means you can simply create a number of application features such as, save user information, cache data, load the user's application status. This makes the development of HTML5 based on the APP has a shorter start-up time and faster network speed.

3.4 2D/3D Image Rendering Technology: Three-Dimensional, Graphics and Special Effects

Canvas is one of the most powerful API, in the past, through the FLASH and other plug-ins to achieve the books and animation now only use JavaScript can achieve. Canvas has a variety of rendering paths, rectangles, circles, characters and the method of adding images. It provides a good technical support for drawing all kinds of 2D graphics, graphics and animation. And based on the 3D function of SVG, WebGL and the CSS3, the user will marvel at the amazing visual effects in the browser.

3.5 Devices and Applications API: Device Compatibility Features

HTML5 provides unprecedented data and application access to open interfaces. So that the external application can be directly connected with the data directly in the browser, such as video can be directly linked to the microphones and camera. There are geographic location aware API, motion sensing event, general sensor API, etc., they provide a simplified operation interface for App Web mail, camera, phone, SMS, geographic location, file storage and other terminal functions.

4 Library Mobile Application Service Based on HTML5 Standard

In the HTML5 environment, the development of App Web need not use the third party plug-ins to achieve a wealth of interactive operations and multi-threaded processing, which makes the App Web to complete the more complex operation tasks. Compared to the previous mobile service mode in the library, the Web App model based on HTML5 will be more ideal for mobile application development.

4.1 Develop Personalized Mobile Service Projects

HTML5, a new label more simplified grammar and clearer structure includes can be traced to the same origin with the HTML development plan, the development threshold greatly reduced. So the library can be less with the aid of software companies, and can target to develop more features, more personalized service projects. Web supports natural thermal updates, users no longer need to feel trouble for upgrade the client. Innovative mobile web applications based on HTML5 B/S architecture will be more and more, leading the mobile library services developing toward to the business environment cloud, business display terminal, business deployment collaboration, business content correlation, business forms model.

4.2 Construction of Interactive Mobile Service Model

With the development of network and new technology, there is more new products and interactive mode and more people pay attention to the interactive experience. The biggest feature of HTML5 is that you can really change the user's interaction with the document, type <canvas>, and HTML5's drawing labels allow you to do more interactive and animated, as we use the flash to achieve. HTML5's device compatibility features makes a more user interaction. Bring the library users a better experience, so that they enjoy the interactive process.

4.3 Create Three-Dimensional Mobile Service Space

Modern popular browsers all support HTML5 (Firefox, Chrome, Safari, IE9, and Opera), even old IE6 can support. Users can also access Web App based on Html5 design in the mobile terminals such as phone, MP4, handheld reader, tablet. And the HTML5 excellent three-dimensional, graphics and special effects added a wealth of interactive and content display elements for mobile applications, multimedia features make the user can on-demand a large number of audio and video resources at any time on the mobile phone, local storage characteristics support the offline reading of library literature, and then create a three-dimensional mobile service space at anytime and anywhere.

References

1. China Internet Network Information Center. 2015 thirty-sixth China Internet network development status report. https://www.cnnic.net/
2. Xiaocheng, Z.: Research on mobile library services based on 3G technology. Nanchang University (2012)
3. Stahr, B.: Text message reference service: five years later. Ref. Librarian 1–2, 9–19 (2010)
4. Rui, L.: Research on the mobile library system of the University, Liaoning Normal University (2013)
5. Min, L., Qiongchao, W.: Mobile internet development and application under the HTML5 environment. Libr. J. 6, 108–110 (2015)

Predicting Mass Incidents from Weibo

Wenwen Li[1,2], Yang Zhou[1,2], Tingting Lu[3], and Tingshao Zhu[1,4(✉)]

[1] Institute of Psychology, Chinese Academy of Sciences, Beijing, China
tszhun@psych.ac.cn
[2] University of Chinese Academy of Sciences, Beijing, China
[3] University of Jinan, Jinan 250022, Shandong, China
[4] Institute of Computing Technology, Chinese Academy of Sciences, Beijing, China

Abstract. The outbreak of mass incidents severely affects the stability of society. If we can predict mass incidents in advance, we may find the solution to avoid the confliction in time. Some of the existing approaches rely on emotional modeling. Much research has been conducted on microblog incident detection using statistical models, like LASSO regression method, Dynamic Query Expansion (DQE) and so on. In this paper, we propose to combine sentiment analysis and statistical methods, and uses LASSO regression method for mass incidents prediction. Experiments on Qingdao demonstrated that our proposed approach achieves a good performance.

Keywords: Mass incidents · Event forecasting · Sentiment analysis · Dynamic query expansion · LASSO

1 Introduction

Mass incidents are considered as that certain number of people gathering and expressing their opinions in a non-institutionalized way due to popular dissatisfaction. As mass incidents cannot be completely avoided, it is important to predict mass incidents in advance and take actions to solve conflictions timely, in order to improve the social stability and public satisfaction.

Nowadays, Hundreds of millions of users are willing to express their views, opinions and feelings on microblog. Microblog has its own advantages in reporting and propagating major events, because it is convenient, effective and interactive. Messages released by users reflect the focus of people to some extent, some signs of mass incidents on microblog platform should be able to be detected before it happens, so it inspires us to predict mass incidents from Weibo, the most popular microblogging service in China.

Existing microblog events prediction methods mainly rely on the statistical features of messages or word frequency. Although sentiment analysis has already been taken into account, it is still difficult to do so, since microblog is very messy and entertainment news and babbles occupy large part. Some methods use statistical feature like keywords, word frequency and so on. More specifically, Dynamic Query Expansion (DQE) expands seed keywords of certain domain iteratively, finally obtain new keywords that are related to targeted incidents. In this paper, we take DQE results as statistical features,

© Springer International Publishing Switzerland 2016
Q. Zu and B. Hu (Eds.): HCC 2016, LNCS 9567, pp. 895–900, 2016.
DOI: 10.1007/978-3-319-31854-7_96

the values of negative emotions as emotional feature, and use LASSO regression method to predict the mass incidents.

2   Related Work

People can aware forthcoming events by the event forecasting method from huge Weibo data. It could help people response quickly to impending event. Event predicting has been applied to many areas, such as forecasting upcoming international political crisis, earthquake, terrorism [4] and disease outbreak [1, 4] etc.

There are already a number of studies focusing on the event forecasting. Radinsky et al. built predictive models for generalizing the events by a probabilistic model. Develop general techniques for summarizing the temporal dynamics of textual content and identifying outbreak. Amodeo et al. built time-series model to predict forthcoming events based on documents order by publication date. Radinsky et al. extracted generalized templates in the form of "x causes y" from past news and applied on predicting events. Given many existing methods cannot naturally modelling the implicit heterogeneous network structure in social media, [3] presented Non-Parametric Heterogeneous Graph Scan (NPHGS) for event detection and forecasting. Ramakrishnan et al. set fixed keywords as feature and uses LASSO regression to predict events. L. Zhao proposed DQE method, iteratively expand initial keywords and finally obtained expansion keywords related to events. Proposed the prediction model of civil unrest, sets the fixed term of LASSO as static feature and the expansion keywords generated by DQE as dynamic feature. However, these methods only take into account the statistical features of the content of the text, without considering the semantic. Nguyen et al. proposed to detect emergencies with emotional features, but it is difficult to detect or predict events in specific areas.

3   Model

As shown in Fig. 1, DQE iteratively expands initial keywords to get final keywords and Weibo messages related to mass incidents. We set the number of Weibo messages including expansion keywords as statistical features and negative emotions by sentiment analysis as emotional feature. We use both statistical and emotional features, then apply LASSO regression method to build predictive model.

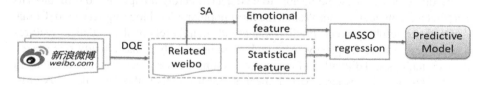

Fig. 1. The flowchart of predictive model

3.1   Statistical Features

The data crawled from Sina Weibo need to be preprocessed. Word segmentation with LTP of HIT [2] is used at first, due to Chinese words is not separate by default. We filter out stop words to remove any meaningless information.

Initial keywords are provided by specific domain experts. Based on containment relationship between words and Weibo messages, DQE expands initial keywords iteratively to obtain a number of related Weibo messages and update keywords ranked by DF-IDF (document frequency-inverse document frequency). DF-IDF differs from TF-IDF in that DF-IDF focuses on the number of Weibo messages including keywords rather than word frequency.

Since we focus on mass incidents caused by public dissatisfactory, we don't consider expansion Weibo containing positive emotions, to filter out Weibo message which has nothing to do with mass incidents and improve the effectiveness of the results.

Denote D as the statistical feature and k as the number of keywords. Define the statistical feature as $D^{t,i}, i = (1, 2, \ldots, k)$. $D^{t,i}$ is the number of Weibo messages containing the i-th expansion keyword at time t.

3.2   Emotional Feature

We analyze emotions on Weibo messages generated by DQE. Emotional words including 27476 words from Chinese affective lexicon. In addition, microblog platform provides some default emoticons, which we can add into affective lexicon. Chinese affective lexicon are classify as 20 categories: happy, peace, respect, praise, believe, love, anger, sorrow, disappointment, guilt, miss, panic, fear, shame, irritancy, hate, blame, jealous, suspect and surprise. Psychology professionals analyzed affective lexicon and determined negative emotions related to mass incidents, including: anger, sorrow, disappointment, irritancy, hate and suspect. So we defined the sum of these emotions' value as emotional feature S^t, representing emotional value on the t-th day.

3.3   LASSO Regression

LASSO (Least Absolute Shrinkage and Selection Operator) is a regression method by minimizing the sum of the squares of error. By means of least square method, unknown data can be easily obtained and minimize the sum of the squares of the error between real data and calculated data. LASSO is formulated as follows:

$$\arg\min \left\| q^1 S^t + q^2 D^{t,1} + q^3 D^{t,2} + \ldots + q^{k+1} D^{t,k} - Y^t \right\|_2^2 + \rho \left\| q^l \right\|_1 \qquad (1)$$

$Y^t = 1$ if mass incidents happen on next day; $Y^t = 0$, otherwise. ρ is the regularization parameter to prevent the model overfitting the training data. $q^l (l \in [1, k])$ is coefficient of regression that need to be measured.

4 Experiment

To evaluate the performance of our approach, we make the prediction of environmental mass incidents in Qingdao. In order to reduce the interference of advertising and other noise information, we only pay attention to active users who have posted more than 500 messages. Qingdao has 120,000 active users, and our task is to predict whether one mass incident may occur next day. We download 120,000 active users' data from January 1, 2015 to May 31, 2015, which produces 60,000 pieces of Weibo posts every day. We used the data from January 1, 2015 to April 30, 2015 as training data, the data from May 1, 2015 to May 31, 2015 as testing data. The experiment results were validated against labeled events set which was provided by Qingdao Environmental Protection Bureau. If any event happens next day, it is labelled as "1", or "0" otherwise.

First of all, 16 keywords related to environmental incidents were defined by domain experts, such as "pollution" and "emission". We applied DQE to Weibo data based on these 16 keywords, obtained the expanded keywords based on containment relationship between words and Weibo messages. The statistical features is the number of Weibo messages containing any of expanded words.

The emotional feature is the emotional value calculating the sum of anger, sadness, frustration, boredom, disgust, skepticism value about Weibo messages related to environmental mass incidents. In particular, emotional value is the count of emotional words in expansion Weibo messages. We use both statistical and emotional feature to train LASSO regression model to predict the likelihood of events in May 2015 t. As the maximum number of keywords in DQE is 14, so we can select 1 to 14 statistical features.

Figure 2 shows the performance of varying number of statistical features, the change of accuracy is not obvious, but precision, recall and F-measure rises with the numbers of statistical feature increasing, so we chose 14 statistical features. In this case, the accuracy is 0.81, the precision is 0.5, and the recall is 1 which means we can predicted all four labeled events. Such as the residents pull the banner to boycott Rubber Factory in May 24, 2015, the event forecasting results in May 23, 2015 is "1". There are some days got the result "1" while there is no mass incidents occur next day, but these days do exist some events which many people concerned and have discontent. There is no doubt that these events are worth paying attention by government, though they won't develop into mass incidents for some reason. In actual application, the relevant staff said the events we got the wrong results "1" still valuable. They can take timely measures to deal with the events aroused public concern and dissatisfaction. Given this, the model has practical usage although the precision is not good enough.

For comparison, if we do not use any emotional feature in predictive model, the accuracy is 0.77, the precision is 0.3, and the recall is 0.75. If we do not use any statistical features in predictive model, the accuracy is 0.81, the precision is 0.38, and the recall is 0.75. Figure 3 illustrates that the predictive model with both emotional and statistical features has better performance for predicting.

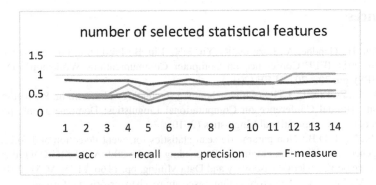

Fig. 2. Number of selected statistical features (Color figure online)

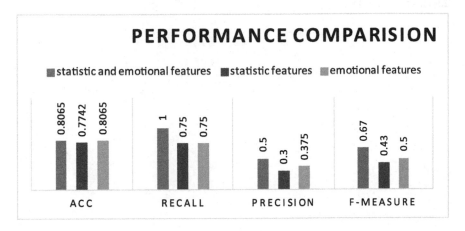

Fig. 3. Performance comparison (Color figure online)

5 Conclusion

This paper take into account not only the impact of statistical features like the number of related Weibo data, but also the relevance of public sentiment, to predict whether mass incidents happen or not based on statistical features and emotional feature. Experimental result on environmental mass incidents in Qingdao shows that the proposed model works with a fairly good performance.

Acknowledgements. The authors gratefully acknowledges the generous support from National High-tech R&D Program of China (2013AA01A606), National Basic Research Program of China (2014CB744600), and Key Research Program of Chinese Academy of Sciences (CAS) (KJZD-EWL04).

References

1. Achrekar, H., Gandhe, A., Lazarus, R., Yu, S.H., Liu, B.: Predicting flu trends using twitter data. In: 2011 IEEE Conference on Computer Communications Workshops (INFOCOM WKSHPS), pp. 702–707. IEEE (2011)
2. Che, W., Li, Z., Liu, T.: LTP: a Chinese language technology platform. In: Proceedings of the 23rd International Conference on Computational Linguistics: Demonstrations, pp. 13–16. Association for Computational Linguistics (2010)
3. Chen, F., Neill, D.B.: Non-parametric scan statistics for event detection and forecasting in heterogeneous social media graphs. In: Proceedings of the 20th ACM SIGKDD International Conference on Knowledge Discovery and Data Mining, pp. 1166–1175. ACM (2014)
4. Cheong, M., Lee, V.C.: A microblogging-based approach to terrorism informatics: exploration and chronicling civilian sentiment and response to terrorism events via twitter. Inf. Syst. Front. 13(1), 45–59 (2011)

A Modified Spectral Clustering Algorithm Based on Density

Yue Li[1], Xiyu Liu[1(✉)], and Xuebin Yan[2]

[1] College of Management Science and Engineering, Shandong Normal University,
East of Wenhua Road No. 88, Jinan 250014, Shandong, China
{liyuemoon11,sdxyliu}@163.com
[2] China United Network Communications Co., Beijing, China
yanxb6@163.com

Abstract. Spectral clustering is a clustering method based on algebraic graph theory. The clustering effect by using spectral method depends heavily on the description of similarity between instances of the datasets. During creating a similarity matrix W, the raw spectral clustering is often based on Euclidean distance, but it is impossible to accurately reflect the complexity of the data distribution. This paper constructed a new matrix S based on density as the similarity matrix, and proposed K-Means based on density to converge the global optimization. Making it find the spatial distribution characteristics of complex data. Experimental results show that it can improve the clustering accuracy and avoid falling into local optimum.

Keywords: Spectral clustering · K-Means · Density clustering

1 Introduction

Clustering is an important research field in data mining. It aims to divide a dataset into natural groups so that data points in the same group are similar while data points in different groups are dissimilar to each other [1].

Most of the clustering algorithms were designed to cluster the data in convex spherical sample space; they can't guarantee global optimization [2]. Spectral clustering addresses this deficiency. The purpose of spectral clustering is to find the partition of a graph so that the linkages between groups are minimized and the linkages within groups are maximized.

During creating the similarity matrix, the raw spectral clustering is often based on Euclidean distance, but it is impossible to accurately reflect the complexity of the data distribution [3]. Inspired by density clustering, this paper proposed to construct the similarity matrix based on data density and improved the K-Means by density to guarantee global optimization of clusters.

2 The Modified Spectral Clustering Algorithm Based on Density

It is known that spectral clustering is based on dividing the spectrum theory. Compared with other classical clustering technology, it can find clustering in the sample space with

© Springer International Publishing Switzerland 2016
Q. Zu and B. Hu (Eds.): HCC 2016, LNCS 9567, pp. 901–906, 2016.
DOI: 10.1007/978-3-319-31854-7_97

randomly distributed clustering structure, and eventually converges to the global optimal solution. According to the feature vector data, spectral clustering constructs a more simple data space in the implementation process. Recently, the spectral clustering has been applied to many fields, such as image and video segmentation, speech recognition, text mining and so on [4].

2.1 Classical Spectral Clustering

The spectral clustering algorithm takes the datasets as the vertex set V of the figure [5], the similarity set between each point as the edge set E. Constructed the dataset as a graph G = (V, E), and take the adjacency matrix of figure as a similarity matrix W. Then add up the elements of each column in the W get n (the number of nodes) numbers, put them on the diagonal (the other place is zero), to form a new degree matrix D. Where $d_{ij} = \sum_{j=1}^{n} w_{ij}$.

Order L = D − W. L is the Laplacian Matrix. Calculate the former k eigenvalues of L and corresponding eigenvectors. Finally, the k eigenvectors are arranged together to form an n × k matrix; regard every line of the matrix as a vector of the k dimension space (Reduction from the high-dimensional space to a low dimensional space). Then the new datasets can be clustered by the K-Means algorithm, and the category that each row of results belongs is the original nodes in the graph G respectively belong.

In a nutshell, the spectral clustering algorithm has three main processes: The first step: calculate feature values and feature vectors of the sample similarity matrix; the second step: select the appropriate feature vector; the third step: use the classical clustering algorithms (such as K-Means) to cluster the feature vector.

2.2 The Similarity Matrix Based on Density

For any two points, smaller the distance is the more similar. However, Euclidean distance can't describe the similarity between datasets in every case. In the process of creating a similarity matrix W, the classical spectral clustering usually calculated the similarity by Gaussian kernel based on Euclidean distance, but it can't reflect the complexity of the data distribution accurately.

The main idea of this improvement is shown as follows: if two data points are distributed in the same class, so they are density-reachable, the similarity between them is less than or equal to the density threshold; Otherwise, they are not density-reachable.

Suppose the number of data points in the dataset is n, the dataset can be expressed as X = (x1, x2,…, xn). Dist (xi, xj) denotes the Euclidean distance between data xi and xj, SEps (xi) denotes all points that within the density threshold to xi. The process of the algorithm is as follows:

Step 1: Set the starting point and the final point: start = xi, terminal = xj.

Step 2: Calculate the Euclidean distance between the point in SEps (start) and the terminal point. Choose the minimum distance: MinDist = Min {Dist (xp, terminal) | xp belongs to SEps (start)}.

Step 3: if MinDist < Dist (start, xj), then set the starting point as: start = xk, return Step 2; Otherwise, go to the next step.

Step 4: Exchange the starting point and final point: exchange = start, start = terminal, terminal = exchange, return Step 2.

Step 5: Set the density coefficient between xi and xj as mij = 1/MinDist. Then, the similarity matrix S can be constructed as follows:

$$S_{ij} = m_{ij} \times \exp\left(\frac{- \parallel x_i - x_j \parallel^2}{2\delta^2} \right)$$ (1)

2.3 K-Means Algorithm Based on Density

The classical K-Means algorithm is sensitive to the initial clustering center [6]. This improvement is designed to take data points in highest density area as the initial center as much as possible, as well as the distance between each other as far as possible. We need avoid taking two or more points relatively close to each other in high density area, because that can lead to duplication check. In order to avoid the interference of the noise data, this paper takes the farthest k objects in the high density area as the initial clustering center.

The improved K-Means algorithm based on density is described below.

Input: The dataset N, K (the number of clusters), neighborhood radius ε, and MinPts (the minimum number of objects in the neighborhood).

Output: The k clusters.

Step 1: Calculate the distance between objects in the dataset, i.e. d (i,j).

Step 2: Calculate the number of data objects in neighborhood of the data object respectively. If it is greater than the minimum number MinPts, then add the corresponding object to the set H (the set of points that in high density area).

Step 3: Find out the data object k1 that the number of objects in its neighborhood is the largest among the set H. That is to say k1 is in the highest density area. Then delete the objects k1 from H, and put k1 to the set C (the set of initial clustering centers).

Step 4: Calculated the distance between k1 and all the data objects in the set H, find out the data object k2 who is farthest from the k1. Then delete the objects k2 from H, and put k2 to the set C.

Step 5: Find out the data object k3 from the set H that is farthest from the k1 and k2. It is equivalent to that the sum of distance between k3 and k1, k2 is largest among all the objects in the set H. Then delete the objects k3 from H, and put k3 to the set C.

Step 6: Continue to find out the data object ki (i ≤ k) who is furthest from the set C among all data objects in the set H until to i = k or the set H is empty.

Step 7: If i = k, it means that the first k initial clustering center have been found, then go to next step. Otherwise, the number of objects in the set C is smaller than k and the set H is empty, then it need to continue find out the objects in the set N-C who is furthest from the set C, until i = k.

Step 8: Take the objects in set C as the initial clustering centers, using the K-Means algorithm to cluster the dataset N.

2.4 The Modified Spectral Clustering Algorithm Based on Density

The basic framework of the Modified Spectral Clustering Algorithm (shorthand for SC-D) is similar to other classical spectral clustering. The process of SC-D can be described as follows:

Step 1: Similar to the classical spectral clustering, construct the initial similarity matrix W by using the Gaussian kernel function based on Euclidean distance to measure the similarity between the sample points. The dataset can be expressed as $X = (x_1, x_2, \ldots, x_n)$, the similarity between data can be expressed as follows (σ is scale parameter).

$$w_{ij} = \exp\left(\frac{-||x_i - x_j||^2}{2\delta^2}\right) \tag{2}$$

Step 2: Calculate the density coefficient matrix M by using the method that described in Sect. 2.2. Construct the density similarity matrix S: S = M * W.

Step 3: Construct Laplacian Matrix $L = D^{-1/2}SD^{-1/2}$, where D is a diagonal matrix, the diagonal elements dij can be expressed as:

$$d_{ij} = \sum_{j=1}^{n} s_{ij} \tag{3}$$

Figure out the former k largest eigenvector of Laplacian matrix xi; construct a low-dimensional quantum space as X:

$$X = (x1, x2, \ldots, xk) \tag{4}$$

Step 4: Transform every row vector of X into a unit vector to construct matrix N:

$$n_{ij} = \frac{x_{ij}}{\sqrt{\sum_j x_{ij}^2}} \tag{5}$$

Step 5: Take every line of the matrix N as a single point in the subspace. Then execute the algorithm described in Sect. 2.3 to cluster the points in the subspace.

Step 6: If the line n of the matrix N is divided into the class j, then the corresponding data object is divided into the class j.

3   Test and Analysis

We coded the algorithm with MATLAB 7.10.1(R2010a) in windows 7 system, and selected datasets from UCI. The detail of the datasets is showed in Table 1. In order to evaluate the quality of the clustering results, we used Clustering Accuracy (ACC) and the Normalized Mutual Information (NMI). A larger ACC indicates a better clustering performance. The higher the NMI score, the better the clustering quality.

Table 1. The detailed information of benchmark data

Dataset	Instances	Features	Classes
Wine	178	13	3
Iris	150	4	3
Ionosphere	351	34	2
Glass	214	9	6

We have compared the performance of our method with Classical spectral clustering and K-Means algorithm. Each part of the experiments was repeated 20 times, and then takes the average of NMI and ACC. The results are shown in Tables 2 and 3.

Table 2. The test results—ACC

Clustering methods	Wine	Iris	Ionosphere	Glass
SC-D	73.0337	90.6667	72.4986	52.8037
SC	71.7977	90	72.1368	49.3458
K-Means	66.3512	81.89	71.1245	48.4412

Table 3. The detailed information of benchmark data

Clustering methods	Wine	Iris	Ionosphere	Glass
SC-D	0.4122	0.7632	0.2135	0.3893
SC	0.4021	0.5825	0.1969	0.3553
K-Means	0.4004	0.6168	0.1869	0.3541

From Table 2, we can see that the clustering results of ACC the glass dataset is least, and the iris dataset is best. The main reason is that the performance of the algorithm is relative to the datasets. From Table 3, we can see that the clustering results of NMI the ionosphere dataset is least, The disadvantages become obvious as the size of the dataset increase. But compare to other method, SC-D shows out instability and accuracy.

4   Conclusion

In this paper we have presented a novel spectral clustering method based on density. The density similarity measure can help us find out the spatial distribution characteristics of complex data more accurate. However, algorithm remains to be further improved to deal with large quantities of data. The experimental results verified the improved spectral clustering method has better performance than other clustering methods.

Acknowledgment. This work is supported by National Natural Science Foundation of China (61170038, 61472231 and 61502283), Jinan City independent innovation plan project in Colleges and Universities, China (201401202), Ministry of education of Humanities and social science research project, China (12YJA630152), Social Science Fund Project of Shandong Province, China (11CGLJ22).

References

1. Sun, J.G., Liu, J., Zhao, L.Y.: Clustering algorithms research. J. Softw. **19**(1), 48–61 (2008)
2. Kwok, W., Sun, H.: Multi-directional interpolation for spatial error concealment. IEEE Trans. Consum. Electron. **39**(3), 455–460 (1993)
3. Jia, H., Ding, S., Xu, X., Nie, R.: The latest research progress on spectral clustering. Neural Comput. Appl. **24**, 1477–1486 (2014)
4. Yan, J., Cheng, D., Zong, M., Deng, Z.: Improved spectral clustering algorithm based on similarity measure. In: Luo, X., Yu, J.X., Li, Z. (eds.) ADMA 2014. LNCS, vol. 8933, pp. 641–654. Springer, Heidelberg (2014)
5. Wang, Z.: Density sensitive hierarchical clustering algorithm research. Lanzhou University of Technology (2013)
6. Fu, D., Zhou, C.: The improved K-Means algorithm based on density and implementation. J. Comput. Appl. **11**, 432–434 (2011)

The Development of Miniature Piezoelectric Vibration Energy Harvesting System

Zhibiao Li[⊠], Gang Tang, and Min Hu

Jiangxi Provincial Key Laboratory of Precision Drive and Control,
Nanchang Institute of Technology, Nanchang 330099, China
123284289@qq.com

Abstract. The miniature piezoelectric vibration energy harvesting system has received wide attention, which is promising to have good prospect of applications in self-powered wireless sensor network. In the paper we reviewed the work carried out by researchers in the last decades, and analyzed the future trend.

Keywords: Piezoelectric · Vibration · Energy harvesting device · Miniature electromechanical system

1 Introduction

With the fast development in manufacture techniques of miniature mechanics, integrated circuit and the wireless technology, devices are now gradually tending to be miniature, portable, wireless and low power consuming, and the power supplies with better performance, higher quality, bigger capacity and longer lifetime are required for the devices with the features mentioned above. At present, the principal means to power these devices are still batteries which are usually with shorter lifetime, limited capacity for power and require regular replacement. Therefore, it gives rise to a hot research focus on how to supply energy effectively and conveniently to solve the bottle-neck problem.

Currently, regarding the power supplying for miniature devices, energy harvester can convert energy from environment into electrical energy and replace the conventional power source for micro devices. Vibration energy harvesting devices can be categorized in terms of operation modes into the piezoelectric, the electromagnetic and the electrostatic ones, among which the piezoelectric ones surpass the rest for their less complicated structure, higher energy density, longer cycle life and the advantage of being easier to be miniaturized.

In the paper we reviewed the work of the piezoelectric energy harvester carried out by researchers in the last decades, and analyzed the future trend.

2 Researches for Piezoelectric Energy Harvesters

2.1 Materials for Piezoelectric Energy Harvesting Devices

Piezoelectric materials have comparatively large influences on the performance of the device. At present, researches are mainly focusing on the following materials.

© Springer International Publishing Switzerland 2016
Q. Zu and B. Hu (Eds.): HCC 2016, LNCS 9567, pp. 907–912, 2016.
DOI: 10.1007/978-3-319-31854-7_98

- PZT: Piezoelectric ceramic material PZT, which is featured with good piezoelectric performance and stable temperature, is widely used in piezoelectric vibration energy harvesting devices. Despite this, however, it is rather fragile as it has been proved by Lee in Korean Academy of Science and Technology that fatigue breaking would easily happen when PZT material is subjected to high frequency periodic vibration. Therefore, the main purpose of the research is turned to developing PZT material with more flexibility for the devices [1].
- PVDF: PVDF is another type of piezoelectric polymer material with good flexibility often used on piezoelectric energy harvesting devices. In 2004, Lee developed an energy harvesting device with a PVDF film and PEDOT/PSS electrodes. The experiments showed that the piezoelectric system is with good fatigue resistance and is able to supply more energy in its lifetime [2].
- Piezoelectric Composite Fabrics: Piezoelectric Composite Fabrics with very good flexibility can be applied to the energy harvesting devices. In 2003, Mohammadi developed a material of composite fabrics. The test showed that the transducer made of this material is able to harvest a maximum voltage of 350 V and electrical power of 120 mW [3].
- The Relaxor-type Ferroelectrics: A new type of piezoelectric materials, such as the relaxor-type ferroelectric unimorphs (PMN, PZN, PMN-PT, PZN-PT), has been regarded as the ones more suitable for energy harvesting devices, for the features of large electromechanical coupling coefficient and the piezoelectric coefficient as well as a high strain level. The horizontal electromechanical coupling coefficient of this type of materials is at least 90 % larger than that of the PZT materials. In 2009, Sun in Pittsburgh University, developed a piezoelectric energy harvesting device with PMN-PT unimorph material [4, 5].

2.2   The Structure of the Device

The parameters of the structure play important parts in generating electrical power. In order to harvest high electrical power and converting efficiency through a certain vibration, the researchers have designed several types of piezoelectric vibrators and optimized parameters of the structure.

2.2.1   Structure of the d31

Nowadays, most devices are designed with a structure of the d31 with plate-type electrodes, which means that the external force is vertical to the direction of the piezoelectric voltage. The experiments were initiated by Roundy and his team in 2003, and the power generated from piezoelectric cantilever d31 converting model was theoretically analyzed. It is concluded that the device has a lower resonance frequency in d31 converting model, thus easily resonates in normal environment [6].

Ordinary energy harvesting system in use usually has only one piezoelectric material called unimorph structure. The model of analyzing piezoelectric unimorph structure is established by Cho and his team in 2005. This model shows that the electromechanical coupling coefficient relates to the remaining stress, the thickness of the foundation base and piezoelectric layer and the size of electrodes' coverage area. When the coverage of the electrode film reaches 42 %, the electromechanical coupling coefficient of the system is the maximum [7]. In 2006, Johnson and his team in Pittsburgh University of USA, designed an energy harvesting device with a piezoelectric unimorph cantilever [8].

Another structure often used is the bimorph structure which has an upper and a lower piezoelectric layer linked together. Sodano and his team established a mathematical model to predict how a piezoelectric bimorph cantilever can harvest energy and then proved this model through experiments.

Most piezoelectric energy harvesting devices are designed with a rectangle cantilever structure. To increase the output electrical power of the device, researchers have set down to improve the structure. Baker and his team, who analyzed via finite element method the distribution of the rectangle cantilever structure in vibration, discovered that the stress concentrates at the fixed ends near the cantilever which should be replaced by a triangle cantilever structure in order to make the stress evenly distributed and increase the output electrical power. The experiments showed 30 % increase to the output electrical power.

2.2.2 Structure of d33 Converting Model

Another working model of piezoelectric effect is called d33 structure, which has interdigital electrodes. The external stress and the mechanical deformation are in the same direction as the voltage. Compared with d31, this model has twice the piezoelectric coefficient. Therefore, d33 has higher converting efficiency. Jong and his team from Korean Academy of Science and Technology have created a MEMS piezoelectric energy harvesting device based on d33 model, as is shown in Fig. 1. The fabricated energy harvester generated an electrical power of 1.1 uW with 4.4 V from a vibration with an acceleration of 0.39 g [9].

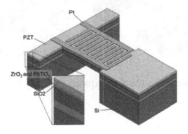

Fig. 1. Structure of d_{33} model

2.3 Researches on Frequency Matching and Widening

There are two frequency matching ways, the active regulation and the passive regulation. Figure 2 shows the active regulation frequency matching device which was designed by Roundy and his team in 2005 [10]. However, the results of theoretical analysis and experiments showed that the active regulation method is not suitable for frequency matching for the reason that it results a system generating even less output electrical power due to the power loss in the regulation itself.

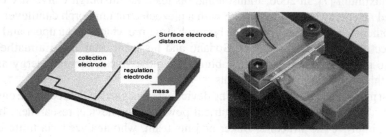

Fig. 2. Structure of the active regulation energy harvesting device

In 2006, Leland from University of California of USA and his team gained a resonance frequency matching through adding axial preloading stress to the beam. The frequency regulation range of the system expands by 24 %. In vibration within the driving frequency range between 200–250 Hz, the sample device can generate 300–400 uW output electrical power.

In 2008, Liu and his team designed an energy harvesting device with multiple operation frequency, as is shown in Fig. 3. This system consists of three cantilevers of the same size but with difference natural frequency due to their different masses at the free ends. The test showed that the device is able to generate stable output electrical power within a large vibration frequency range [11].

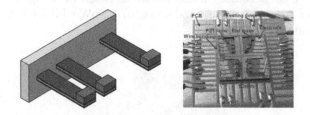

Fig. 3. Structure of multiple frequency energy harvesting device

3   Future Trends

For the reason that piezoelectric technology in generating electrical power can make the device to meet the requirement of adaptive power supply, piezoelectric energy harvesting system is to replace the traditional batteries or cable to supply power to wireless sensors and MEMS devices during the development of wireless sensor network and miniature electromechanical system. Nevertheless, there is no successful piezoelectric vibration energy harvesting product. It is also true that the electrical power harvested from low frequency source in natural environment is too weak to supply power to most electronics. Therefore, to increase the output electrical power, more research should be done on piezoelectric materials to design a structure with more efficiency and develop new electric circuit technology for electrical power storage. As follows are the aspects that claim further study on miniature vibration energy harvesting system:

- Piezoelectric Materials: Currently, the majority of the researches are focusing on improving energy converting efficiency by optimizing the geometrical structure and electrical circuit of the device yet only small portion of the researches are concerning improving the system performance by using piezoelectric materials. PVDF and PZT materials are most frequently reported in devices but very few devices use relaxor-type ferroelectric materials (PMN, PZN, PMN-PT and PZN-PT) which usually have large electromechanical coupling coefficient and piezoelectric parameters. Therefore, relaxor-type materials deserve further study.
- Prediction on the Device's Life: In order to give the device a longer life, a life prediction is necessary. At present, the research focus still lies on the issue how the voltage, structure fatigue and environmental factors like temperature and humidity will affect the performance of the piezoelectric materials. There are inadequate researches on how the operating frequency, acceleration and working cycle influence the system's life. Therefore, future researches should lay more weight on the impacts acceleration and frequency give to device's life.
- Optimization of the Structure Performance: According to the above analysis of the researches conducted home and abroad, the devices especially the MEMS devices are with low voltage and electrical power performances, which result in a low possibility of widely applying and industrializing the devices. Therefore, there is still much to be done to improve the output performance through a small-scale optimization of the structure and performance of the device.

4   Conclusions

Piezoelectric vibration energy harvesting system which can convert vibration energy existing in the surroundings by using the piezoelectric effect of the materials into electrical power for electronics has become a global hot research issue. The factors affecting the output performance of the device include the piezoelectric material, the piezoelectric vibrator, etc. At present, as devices with piezoelectric vibration energy harvesting system, especially the devices which are able to harvest energy from the low frequency source in natural environment, have not been successfully produced, the research of this part proves rather weak. However, it is believed that as the researches on piezoelectric materials are deepening and the piezoelectric structure is further optimized, the piezoelectric vibration energy harvesting system will be widely applied and industrialized in the near future.

Acknowledgement. The author would like to acknowledge the financial support for this research from the Science and technology support project of Jiang Xi Province and Nanchang city (No. 20151BBE50113, 2014HZZC009), and the Youth Foundation of Nanchang Institute of Technology (2014KJ010).

References

1. Lee, C.S., Joo, J., Han, S., et al.: Poly (vinylidene fluoride) transducers with highly conducting poly (3,4-ethylenedioxythiophene) electrodes. Synth. Met. **152**(1–3), 49–52 (2005)
2. Lee, C.S., Joo, J., Han, S., et al.: Multifunctional transducer using poly (vinylidene fluoride) active layer and highly conducting poly (3,4-ethylenedioxythiophene) electrode: actuator and generator. Appl. Phys. Lett. **85**(10), 1841–1843 (2004)
3. Mohammadi, F., Khan, A., Cass, R.: Power generation from piezoelectric lead zirconate titanate fiber composites, pp. 263–270 (2003)
4. Zhang, S., Lebrun, L., Jeong, D.-Y., et al.: Growth and characterization of Fe-doped $Pb(Zn_{1/3}Nb_{2/3})O_3$-$PbTiO_3$ single crystals. J. Appl. Phys. **93**(11), 9257–9262 (2003)
5. Sun, C., Qin, L., Li, F.: Piezoelectric energy harvesting using single crystal $Pb(Mg1/3Nb2/3)$ O 3-xPbTiO3 (PMN-PT) device. J. Intell. Mater. Syst. Struct. **20**(5), 559 (2009)
6. Roundy, S.: Energy scavenging for wireless sensor nodes with a focus on vibration to electricity conversion. University of California (2003)
7. Cho, J., Anderson, M., Richards, R., et al.: Optimization of electromechanical coupling for a thin-film PZT membrane: II. Experiment. J. Micromech. Microeng. **15**(10), 1804–1809 (2005)
8. Johnson, T., Charnegie, D., Clark, W., et al.: Energy harvesting from mechanical vibrations using piezoelectric cantilever beams, p. 61690D (2006)
9. Park, J.C., Park, J.Y., Lee, Y.-P.: Modeling and characterization of piezoelectric d33-mode MEMS energy harvester. J. Microelectromech. Syst. **19**(5), 1215–1222 (2010)
10. Roundy, S., Zhang, Y.: Toward self-tuning adaptive vibration-based microgenerators, pp. 373–384 (2005)
11. Liu, J.Q., Fang, H.B., et al.: A MEMS-based piezoelectric power generator array for vibration energy harvesting. Microelectron. J. **39**, 802–806 (2008)

Voxelization Algorithm Based on STL Model

Kaiwei Sun[1(✉)], Jiarui Hou[2], Song Zhao[2], Yiqiao Dong[2],
Runan Luo[2], Qing Guo[2], and Liang Ma[2]

[1] School of Mechanical Engineering,
Zhejiang University, Hangzhou 310027, China
363113891@qq.com
[2] School of Mechanical Engineering,
Hebei University of Technology, Tianjin 300401, China

Abstract. Voxelization is a frequently-used modeling method in rapid prototyping. This paper was aimed to come up a voxel-based method for STL model
generated by CAD software. Mainly through solving process to study voxel data
of intersection between lines and triangular patches. Experimental results show
that the algorithm has better time advantage; especially for handling rule model,
the algorithm of this paper can highlight the good applicability.

Keywords: STL models · Linear intersection · Voxelization

1 Introduction

Voxelization has become a common modeling approach because it can realize the
modeling of material objects and make STL data file visual. So far, scholars at home
and abroad have studied many voxelization methods. There are voxelization algorithm
based on z-buffer, voxelization algorithm based on octree and voxelization algorithm
based on Euclidean distance measure mesh model, etc. Reference [1] uses function of
normal vector as distance standard to disperse polygon models. Reference [2] uses
Scale-space Theory to obtain antialiasing voxel models of points, lines and triangular
patches. Reference [3] uses Distance Fields and Distance Transform to generate voxel
models, aiming at segmenting gray-scale volume data into voxel models.

It is useful to convert surface data to voxels and this process of voxelization
products a set of values on a regular three dimensional grid [4]. Thus, if a more efficient
arithmetic can be promoted, the practical applicability of voxelization will be promoted
to a large extent.

2 Intersection Theory

2.1 Intersection Between Lines and Triangles

See Fig. 1, assuming the line L with one point $m(m_1, m_2, m_3)$ and the direction vector
$\overrightarrow{N_L}(n_1, n_2, n_3)$ intersects with the given triangle T at intersection $O(x, y, z)$. $\overrightarrow{N_P}(np_1,$
$np_2, np_3)$ is the normal vector of the given triangle T. $V(v_1, v_2, v_3)$ is one vertex of the
given triangle T.

© Springer International Publishing Switzerland 2016
Q. Zu and B. Hu (Eds.): HCC 2016, LNCS 9567, pp. 913–918, 2016.
DOI: 10.1007/978-3-319-31854-7_99

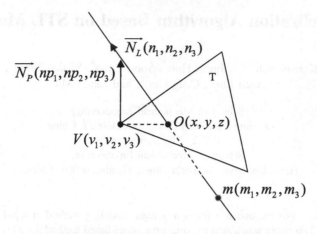

Fig. 1. Intersection sketch map of line and triangle.

Using parameter equation, the following equation is obtained.

$$
\begin{aligned}
x &= m_1 + n_1 \times t \\
y &= m_2 + n_2 \times t \\
z &= m_3 + n_3 \times t
\end{aligned}
\tag{1}
$$

$\overrightarrow{N_P}(np_1, np_2, np_3)$ is perpendicular to segment OV, thus, the following equation is obtained.

$$
np_1(x - v_1) + np_2(y - v_2) + np_3(z - v_3) = 0
\tag{2}
$$

Here, $\overrightarrow{N_P}(np_1, np_2, np_3)$ can be solved by the following equation.

$$
\begin{aligned}
np_1 &= \overrightarrow{np_{AB}}.y \cdot \overrightarrow{np_{AC}}.z - \overrightarrow{np_{AB}}.z \cdot \overrightarrow{np_{AC}}.y; \\
np_2 &= -(\overrightarrow{np_{AB}}.x \cdot \overrightarrow{np_{AC}}.z - \overrightarrow{np_{AB}}.z \cdot \overrightarrow{np_{AC}}.x); \\
np_3 &= \overrightarrow{np_{AB}}.x \cdot \overrightarrow{np_{AC}}.y - \overrightarrow{np_{AB}}.y \cdot \overrightarrow{np_{AC}}.x;
\end{aligned}
\tag{3}
$$

Obtain $\overrightarrow{np_{AC}}$ and $\overrightarrow{np_{AB}}$ from three vertexes of the triangle.
By solving the Eqs. (1) and (2), the intersection is obtained.

$$
\begin{aligned}
t =& ((v_1 - m_1) \cdot np_1 + (v_2 - m_2) \cdot np_2 + (v_3 - m_3) \cdot np_3)/ \\
& (np_1 \cdot n_1 + np_2 \cdot n_2 + np_3 \cdot n_3)
\end{aligned}
\tag{4}
$$

If the denominator $(np_1 \cdot n_1 + np_2 \cdot n_2 + np_3 \cdot n_3)$ of Formula (3) is not equal to, then it indicates that the respective planes that line and triangle lie are parallel to each other, which condition needs discussed further more. When the denominator is not equal to, we can get coordinate figure (x, y, z) of intersection O after substituting t to Formula (1).

However, there may appear two cases in this situation; (1) The intersection is inside of the given triangle; (2) The intersection is outside of the given triangle. Thus, the relationship between the intersection and the triangle should be judged before going to the next process. The judgment method is described in Sect. 2.2.

2.2 Intersection Judgment

(1) Area judgment method. See Fig. 2(a), there are four triangles $\triangle abc, \triangle aob, \triangle aoc,$ $\triangle boc$ and suppose their areas are $S_{\triangle abc}, S_{\triangle aob}, S_{\triangle aoc}, S_{\triangle boc}$ respectively. If their relationship satisfies the following equation, the given point O is inside of triangle $\triangle abc$. Otherwise, point O is outside of the triangle $\triangle abc$.

$$S_{\triangle abc} = S_{\triangle aob} + S_{\triangle aoc} + S_{\triangle boc}$$

(2) Angle judgment method. See Fig. 2(b), the relationship of $\triangle aob, \triangle aoc, \triangle boc$ satisfies the following equation, the given point O is inside of triangle $\triangle abc$. Otherwise, point O is outside of the triangle $\triangle abc$.

$$\angle aob + \angle boc + \angle aoc = 360°$$

(3) Vector product method. See Fig. 2(c), if point O locates at the same side of all segments, along the edges of triangle $\triangle abc$ clockwise (or anticlockwise), the given point O is inside of triangle $\triangle abc$. Otherwise, point O is outside of the triangle $\triangle abc$.

Area judgment method is the most intuitive and easiest method. And the core problem is solving the area of triangle. Above all, area judgment method is selected in this paper to judge whether the intersection is inside of the given triangle or not.

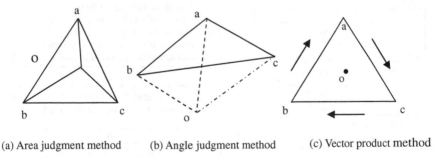

(a) Area judgment method   (b) Angle judgment method   (c) Vector product method

Fig. 2. Intersection judgment method.

3 Voxelization Algorithm Based on STL Model

3.1 Basic Algorithm Flow

When using two-value voxelization, all voxel values can be showed by 0 or 1. This is the simplest and commonest voxelization form [5]. One simpler voxelization method is that intersecting surface triangular patches of three-dimensional model and voxel grids.

If one voxel has intersection with any triangular patches, then assigning this voxel 1, otherwise assigning this voxel 0.

A intersection method has been promoted to realize voxelization algorithm in this paper: Intersection between lines and triangular patches. This method simplifies the intersection process. Though it lowers accuracy requirement of voxel model, it can enhance the speed of algorithm, as described next.

Saving model data, established by CAD software, as STL format firstly. Algorithm reads-in STL format file, whose contents record all geometrical informations of each triangular patch, including the plane's normal vector and three vertex coordinates. Show three-dimensional model with OpenGL graphics library after reading and establish a minimum bounding box to contain the whole model. Divide rectangles based on X-Y plane in the bounding box into grids. Each grid is a square and its side length exactly is the side length of voxel cube. Regard bottom left vertex (whose x, y coordinate value are both the minimum among four vertexes) of each square as datum point and draw forth line segment perpendicular to X-Y plane through the vertex. The line segment will end up at position in which Z-axis coordinate value is maximum of whole bounding box and get a line segment parallel to Z-axis in space. Get the intersection through the relationship between this line segment and each triangular patch. The intersection we got can be used as a basis for drawing the voxel. Find the corresponding voxel cube and get the three-dimensional dispersion model. Thus we can achieve the visualization of the voxel model. At this point we have completed the algorithm that we came up before. The detail flow chart as Fig. 3 shows.

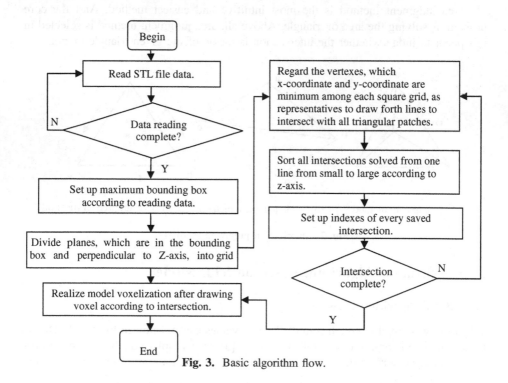

Fig. 3. Basic algorithm flow.

3.2   The Experimental Results

The voxelization algorithm has been implemented using Visual C++ [6]. Three test results are provided in Fig. 4 to verify this algorithm.

In Fig. 4, the first model is spherical model. We can find that after the voxelization process, the voxel model we gained can restore the original model preferably; The second one is a ring. It can still get a good voxelization effect, even there is void in the center of those models; The third model is a bowl shaped model. The expression of the edge of model part is not complete, but the contour has been able to show.

It can be seen from the cases in Fig. 4 the algorithm proposed in this paper can meet the requirements of fidelity. As for the regular model, this algorithm has a good applicability. The algorithm can generate voxelization results fast. Compared to the voxelization method which bases on the depth buffer, it can reflect the advantage of running efficiency in the same model.

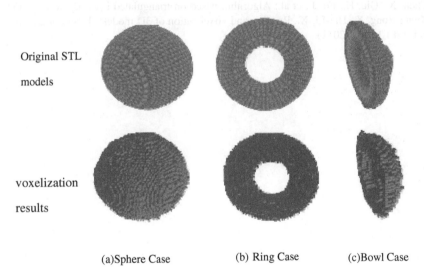

Original STL

models

voxelization

results

(a)Sphere Case   (b) Ring Case   (c)Bowl Case

Fig. 4. Three original models and their voxelization results

4   Conclusion

Based on the theories of the three-dimensional model data processing and reading and displaying the model, we achieved the voxelization of models and got the voxelization results of the STL models through the theory of intersection between lines and triangular patches. At the last part, we showed several voxel models got from experiments and made the corresponding description for them. Thus we completed our algorithm. We have saw that our algorithm can achieve fast generate voxelization results in the premise of satisfying certain precision. This can improve the running efficiency of the algorithm.

Acknowledgments. This paper is supported by Scientific Research Funding of School of Mechanical Engineering, Hebei University of Technology and Scientific Research Funding of Hebei University of Technology.

References

1. Karabassi, E.-A., Papaioannou, G., Theoharis, T.: A fast depth-buffer-based voxelization algorithm. J. Graph. Tools **4**(4), 5–10 (2013). Taylor & Francis
2. Prakash, C.E., Manohar, S.: Volume rendering of unstructured grids - a voxelization approach. Comput. Graph. **19**(5), 711–726 (2009)
3. Jones, M.W., Satherley, R.: Voxelisation: modeling for volume graphics. In: Girod, B., Greiner, G., Niemann, H., Seidel, H.-P. (eds.) Vision, Modeling, and Visualization, pp. 319–326. IOS Press, Amsterdam (2000)
4. Passalis, G., Kakadiaris, I.A., Theoharis, T.: Efficient hardware voxelization. In: Proceedings of the CGI 2004, pp. 374–377 (2004). ISSN: 1530-1052
5. Chen, X., Qiu, H., Fu, J., et al.: Algorithm based on triangulated irregular network (TIN)
6. Xiang-Rong, X., Hai-Li, X.: Reading and voxelization of 3D models. J. Nantong Univ. (Nat. Sci. Ed.) **1**, 006 (2011)

A Novel Web Text Classification Model Based on SAS for e-commerce

Wei Sun, Laisheng Xiang, Xiyu Liu$^{(\boxtimes)}$, and Dan Zhao

College of Management Science and Engineering,
Shandong Normal University, Jinan, China
{weizifighting, sdxyliu, 13793195081}@163.com

Abstract. In this paper, we establish a model to analysis business enterprise customer query information for text classification to help e-commerce companies control the user's spending habits, and help users to find their needed goods. This study accesses to customer inquiry data and preprocesses these text data firstly. Then, it applies the improved TF-IDF principle to obtain the text feature vectors. Finally, this study establishes the classification model combining the Naive Bayes text classification and the semi-supervised EM iterative algorithm and uses various criteria to evaluate the model. When facing multi-class text classification feature selection, keyword weights prone to great volatility. This study improves the keyword weight calculation formula to perfect the classification results. The experimental results show that classification has good classification effect.

Keywords: Text classification · Electronic commerce · Improved TF-IDF · Naive Bayes text classification · EM iteration · SAS

1 Introduction

The rapid development of Internet technology makes the Electronic commerce (briefly called EC) become a new business model at the same time. EC greatly facilitates our life and also produces some problems. On the one hand, electricity companies provide customers with more and more kinds of goods, but also makes the customers be difficult to find the most interested product; On the other hand, a large number of information which may conclude great commercial value becomes potential information in the network.

Forrest Research statistics indicated that more than 80 percent of the data exists in unstructured form [1], and are generally in the form of text. So, text mining is particularly important. Text classification plays an important role in text mining.

This study establishes a new model to classify electronic commerce customers query information in order to help e-commerce companies control the user's spending habits, and help customers to find their needed goods. This study accesses to customer inquiry data and pre processes these text data firstly. Then, it applies the improved TF-IDF principle to obtain the text feature vectors. Finally, this study establishes the classification model combining the Naive Bayes [2] text classification and the semi-supervised EM iterative algorithm and uses various criteria to evaluate the model.

© Springer International Publishing Switzerland 2016
Q. Zu and B. Hu (Eds.): HCC 2016, LNCS 9567, pp. 919–924, 2016.
DOI: 10.1007/978-3-319-31854-7_100

When facing multi-class text classification feature selection, keyword weights prone to great volatility. This study improves the keyword weight calculation formula to perfect the classification results.

2   Text Preprocess

The structured data sets can be read directly from a relational database. Text needs to eliminate the noise data and be converted to a structured form firstly. Before classify the text, it is important to select the feature vectors since the model is sensitive to the feature selection. This study adopt the improved TF-IDF method to select the feature vectors.

$$TF_{ij} = \frac{\left(\sum_{D_1=1}^{n} c_{D_1} * l_{D_1} \right)}{\sum_{D_2=1}^{s} l_{D_2}} \tag{1}$$

In (1), c_{D_1} reflects the number that the text i appeared in the document D_1, l_{D_1} means the length pf the document D_1, n is the number of document which concludes the text i, l_{r_2} reflects the length of the document r_2, s is the number of document concluded in the class.

$$IDF_j = \log_2\left(\frac{N}{df_j} + 1 \right) \tag{2}$$

In (2), N is the total number of the document, df_j is the number of document which included the j-th term.

Through the (1) and (2), the weight of the text is that:

$$w_{ij} = \frac{TF_{ij}}{|v|} * IDF_i \tag{3}$$

In (3), $|v|$ is the total number of all word appeared.

3   The Description of the Model

3.1   The Frame of the Model

This study adopts a semi-supervised learning method and addresses the problem of learning accurate text classifiers from limited numbers of labeled examples. When naive Bayes is given just a small set of labeled training data and the accuracy may be great influenced by the noise data. This study apply the EM to naive Bayes. After the use of the two algorithm, two classifiers (prior probability classifier and conditional probability classifier) are produced. When there is a new inquiry into the system, the model first calculates the posterior probability of the text and takes the most likelihood category.

Assumptions: each word in a document is independent in the context, and the probability of word generated is none business of its context in the document (Fig. 1).

Assume that the document is produced by the multinomial distribution. And on the premise of a given category c_j, the probability of document d_i can be calculated by the following formula.

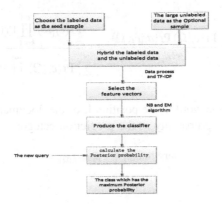

Fig. 1. The model calculate process

$$\Pr(d_i|c_j) = \Pr(|d_i|)(|d_i|!) \prod_{t=1}^{|v|} \frac{\Pr(w_t|c_j;\Omega)}{N_{ti}!} \tag{4}$$

In (4), $|v|$ is the sum number of all word, N_{ti} is the number of the w_t appeared in the document d_i.

The probability of w_t can calculate as follows:

$$\Pr(w_t|c_j;\Omega) = \frac{\sum_{i=1}^{|D|} N_{ti} \Pr(c_j|d_i)}{\sum_{s=1}^{|v|} \sum_{i=1}^{|D|} N_{si} \Pr(c_j|d_i)} \tag{5}$$

In (5), $|D|$ means the number of all documents. If the document d_i belongs to the class c_j, the $\Pr(c_j|d_i) = 1$.

In order not to make the denominator become zero, the formula (5) is smoothed as follow:

$$\Pr(w_t|c_j;\Omega) = \frac{\lambda + \sum_{i=1}^{|D|} N_{ti} \Pr(c_j|d_i)}{\lambda * |v| + \sum_{s=1}^{|v|} \sum_{i=1}^{|D|} N_{si} \Pr(c_j|d_i)} \tag{6}$$

In general, $0 < \lambda < 1$. Finally the prior probability of the class is that:

$$Pr(c_j|\Omega) = \frac{\sum\limits_{i=1}^{|D|} Pr(c_j|d_i)}{|D|} \qquad (7)$$

Through (4), (5), (6), and (7) the posteriori probability is:

$$Pr(c_j|d_i; \Omega) = \frac{Pr(c_j|\Omega) Pr(d_i|c_j; \Omega)}{Pr(d_i; \Omega)} = \frac{Pr(c_j|\Omega) \prod\limits_{k=1}^{|d_i|} Pr(w_{d_i,k}|c_j; \Omega)}{\sum\limits_{r=1}^{|c|} Pr(c_r|\Omega) \prod\limits_{k=1}^{|d_i|} Pr(w_{d_i,k}|c_r; \Omega)} \qquad (8)$$

In (8), $w_{d_i,k}$ means the word in the position k of the document. Take the class with the maximum posteriori probability as the prediction category.

$$\arg \max c_j \in c_{Pr(c_j|d_i;\Omega)}. \qquad (9)$$

3.2   The EM Algorithm

EM is a class of iterative algorithms for maximum likelihood or maximum a posteriori estimation in problems with incomplete data [4, 5]. The EM consists of two steps the expectation step and the maximization step.

Step 1: using the formula (8) to build a classifier f in the document set D.

Step 2: calculate the posterior probability of the unlabeled text belonging to every category.

Step 3: according to the document posterior probability, a new classifier is construct. The new classifier given by the following formula:

The prior probability:

$$Pr(c_j|\Omega_T) = \frac{\sum\limits_{i=1}^{|D|} Pr(c_j|d_i; \Omega_{T-1})}{|D|}$$

The conditional probability:

$$Pr(w_t|c_j; \Omega_T) = \frac{\lambda + \sum\limits_{i=1}^{|D|} N_{ti} Pr(c_j|d_i; \Omega_{T-1})}{\lambda|v| + \sum\limits_{s=1}^{|v|} \sum\limits_{i=1}^{|D|} N_{si} Pr(c_j|d_i; \Omega_{T-1})}$$

Step 4: Repeat step 2 and 3 until the final classifier parameters are no longer change or only small changes in the position.

3.3   The Evaluation of the Model

All of the classification model is essentially a process map, so the evaluation of the model is the model accuracy and speed.

$$a_i = c_{ii} \tag{10}$$

In (10), a_i means the number of the text that has been assigned to the correct class

$$b_i = \sum_{j=1}^{i-1} c_{ij} + \sum_{j=i+1}^{|c|} c_{ij} \tag{11}$$

In (11), b_i means the number of the text which should belong to the class of c_i and is not assigned to the class of c_i.

$$e_i = \sum_{k=1}^{i=1} c_{ki} + \sum_{k=i+1}^{|c|} c_{ki} \tag{12}$$

In (12), e_i reflects the number of the text which should not belong to the class of c_i and is assigned to the class of c_i.

$$d_i = \sum_{j=1}^{i-1}\sum_{k=1}^{i-1} c_{kj} + \sum_{j=1}^{i-1}\sum_{k=i+1}^{|c|} c_{kj} + \sum_{j=i+1}^{|c|}\sum_{k=1}^{i-1} c_{kj} + \sum_{j=i+1}^{|c|}\sum_{k=i+1}^{|c|} c_{kj} \tag{13}$$

In (13), d_i reflects the number of the text which should not belong to the class of c_i and is also not assigned to the class of c_i.

$$precision = \frac{\sum_{i=1}^{|C|} a_i}{\sum_{i=1}^{|C|} a_i + \sum_{i=1}^{|C|} b_i} \tag{14}$$

$$recall = \frac{\sum_{i=1}^{|c|} a_i}{\sum_{i=1}^{|c|} a_i + \sum_{i=1}^{|c|} e_i} \tag{15}$$

The higher the precision and the recall means the model is better. The experiment results has shown our model behaves well Fig. 2.

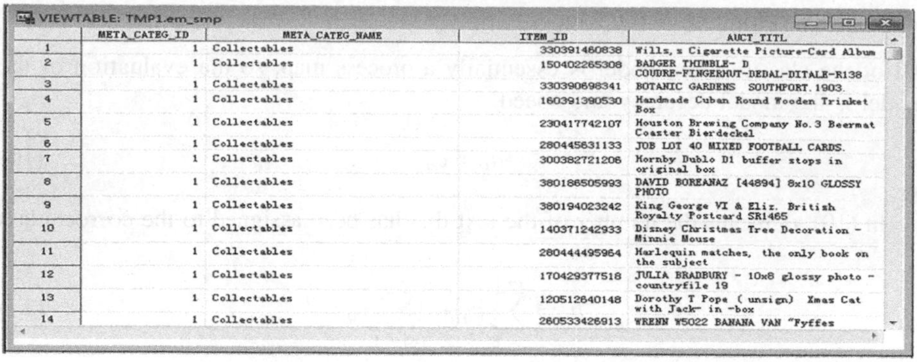

VIEWTABLE: TMP1.em_smp

	META_CATEG_ID	META_CATEG_NAME	ITEM_ID	AUCT_TITL
1	1	Collectables	330391460838	Wills, s Cigarette Picture-Card Album
2	1	Collectables	150402265308	BADGER THIMBLE- D COUDRE-FINGERHUT-DEDAL-DITALE-R138
3	1	Collectables	330390698341	BOTANIC GARDENS SOUTHPORT. 1903.
4	1	Collectables	160391390530	Handmade Cuban Round Wooden Trinket Box
5	1	Collectables	230417742107	Houston Brewing Company No. 3 Beermat Coaster Bierdeckel
6	1	Collectables	280445631133	JOB LOT 40 MIXED FOOTBALL CARDS.
7	1	Collectables	300382721206	Hornby Dublo D1 buffer stops in original box
8	1	Collectables	380186505993	DAVID BOREANAZ [44894] 8x10 GLOSSY PHOTO
9	1	Collectables	380194023242	King George VI & Eliz. British Royalty Postcard SR1465
10	1	Collectables	140371242933	Disney Christmas Tree Decoration - Minnie Mouse
11	1	Collectables	280444495964	Harlequin matches, the only book on the subject
12	1	Collectables	170429377518	JULIA BRADBURY - 10x8 glossy photo - countryfile 19
13	1	Collectables	120512640148	Dorothy T Pope (unsign) Xmas Cat with Jack- in -box
14	1	Collectables	260533426913	WRENN W5022 BANANA VAN "Fyffes

Fig. 2. The experiment results

4 Conclusion

This paper has presented a novel model to classify the customer query for the e-commerce. And the classification not only can help users find the commodity which you need quickly, but also can help the enterprises to control the user's spending habits. We have presented an hybrid algorithm that takes advantage of the two algorithms and experimental results has shown better performance.

Acknowledgement. Project supported by National Natural Science Foundation of China (61170038, 61472231), Jinan City independent innovation plan project in College and Universities, China (201401202), Ministry of education of Humanities and social science research project, China (12YJA630152), Social Science Fund Project of Shandong Province, China (11CGLJ22), outstanding youth scientist foundation project of Shandong Province, China (BS2013DX037).

References

1. Feigenbaum, E.A., McCorduck, P.: The Fifth Generation: Artificial Intelligence and Japan's Challenge to the World. Addison-Wesley, Boston (1983)
2. Chen, J., Huang, H., Tian, S., et al.: Feature selection for text classification with Naïve Bayes. Expert Syst. Appl. **36**(3), 5432–5435 (2009)
3. Greenshtein, E., Park, J.: Application of non parametric empirical Bayes estimation to high dimensional classification. J. Mach. Learn. Res. **10**, 1687–1704 (2009)
4. Luxburg, U.V.: A tutorial on spectral clustering. Stat. Comput. **17**(4), 395–416 (2007)
5. Nigam, K., Mccallum, A.K., Thrun, S., et al.: Text Classification from labeled and unlabeled documents using EM. Mach. Learn. **39**(2–3), 103–134 (2000)

Online Social Network User Behavior Analysis — With RenRen Case

Wenqian Wang[✉] and Yinghong Ma[✉]

College of Management Science and Engineering, Shandong Normal University, Jinan, China
{wenqiansuk,yinghongma71}@163.com

Abstract. This paper investigated typical user behaviors in RenRen and used a clustering algorithm that assigns users to groups through a distance measure that is computed based on the values of user feature vector. The user feature vector consists of four attributes and we got six user groups from the clustering process. By analyzing the six different user behavior patterns, we considered some strategies for providers to improve their service quality.

Keywords: RenRen · Clustering · User behavior · Strategy

1 Introduction

Exploring user habit and psychology hidden behind the user behavior is very important in the research of online social networks. For example, some users are enthusiastic to express themselves by updating status and uploading as many logs or photos as they can, whereas there are users that act like free-riders [1] and just want to enjoy the contents that made publicly available. When tapping into user behavior, [2] analyzed a large online community system and investigated the relationship and engagement between users and groups of users. In [3] it showed that the user behavior can improve the accuracy of a web search ranking algorithm. User behavior models have also been extensively studied from a community of users with a single behavior to multiple classes of users [2, 3].

Our work differs fundamentally from the aforementioned references. We investigated user behaviors of a concrete online social network and based on users personal and social attributes to assigns them to different groups. In Sect. 2, we compared several clustering algorithms and expounded the clustering algorithm. In Sect. 3 we defined user feature vector based on personal attributes and social attributes and then applied K-means algorithm to get the final results. In Sect. 4, we analyzed characteristics of user behaviors and think strategies to improve the service quality of RenRen. Finally we give the conclusion and future directions.

2 Analyze Clustering Algorithm

We compare different clustering algorithms: the density-based approach such as DBSCAN; partition clustering algorithm; and agglomerative hierarchical clustering algorithm etc. [4]. For DBSCAN, when the amount of data increases, it requires large

© Springer International Publishing Switzerland 2016
Q. Zu and B. Hu (Eds.): HCC 2016, LNCS 9567, pp. 925–929, 2016.
DOI: 10.1007/978-3-319-31854-7_101

memory support and the I/O consumption is great. For agglomerative hierarchical clustering algorithm, it has high time and space complexity O(n2). And it cannot be separated by the way of the split to the previous state [5]. Considered the characteristics of user behavior attributes and the distinction of algorithms, we choose K-means as the clustering algorithm and the Euclidean distance as the distance measure.

For a given D dimensional space R^d, an evaluation function $E:\{p:p \in C\} \to R^+$ is defined in R^d. Give each cluster a quantitative evaluation and then input object set C in R^d and one integer k. Output one division of $C:C_1, C_2, \ldots C_k$ which makes the evaluation function E minimize. We used the mean square error as the evaluation function and it is defined as $E = \sum_{i=1}^{k} \sum_{p \in c_i} |p - m_i|^2$.

E is the sum of squared error of all the objects and p is point in R^d which represents a given data, m_i is the mean value of cluster C_i (p and m_i are multidimensional), $|p - m_i|^2$ represents the distance between the data object and the centroid.

Algorithm flow:

(1) Select K initial centroids: for example, $c[0] = data[0], \ldots, c[k-1] = data[k-1]$;
(2) For $data[0], \ldots, data[n]$, compare with $c[0], \ldots, c[k-1]$ respectively and if the difference between it and $c[i]$ is the least, it is marked as i;
(3) For all the points marked as i, recalculate $c[i] = \{$the sum of all the $data[j]$ which marked as i the number of points which marked as i..
(4) Repeat 2 and 3 until all the change values of $c[i]$ less than the defined threshold. (The threshold in this paper is defined as 10^{-5}).

3   Users Behavior in RenRen

3.1   Users' Behavior Data Preprocessing

Define the user feature vector as a one-dimensional vector of length four, where each position contains information about the referred user: $user_i = [f_1, f_2, f_3, f_4]$. The four features are detailed:

(1) Number of uploads (f_1): f_1 represents the number of uploaded status, logs and photos by user. It indicates the potential of a user as a content producer.
(2) Number of watches (f_2): f_2 represents how many videos, logs, albums or other Internet information have been watched by the user. It could indicate the potential of the user as a content consumer.
(3) Age (f_3): We consider user age as the time elapsed between its join date and last login.
(4) Number of comments (f_4): f_4 represents the number of comments which other people give for their status and logs. It indicates the popularity of the user and his willingness to interact with others.

Calculate the correlation coefficient between each two attributes (Table 1). All the correlation coefficients are less than 0.5 which indicates their correlations are low enough to put these four attributes as the representative features of user behavior vector. These four features are of different units and magnitudes. To ensure the distance is computed with features of equal weight, we normalized the data by the maximum value of each feature so that every feature ranges from 0 to 1.

Table 1. The correlation coefficients

Correlation coefficient	f_1	f_2	f_3	f_4
f_1	1.000	0.385	0.207	0.459
f_2	0.385	1.000	0.167	0.306
f_3	0.207	0.167	1.000	0.200
f_4	0.459	0.306	0.200	1.000

3.2 Cluster User Behavior According to Feature Vector

We used an error value J to measure the effect of clustering under different number of clusters (k) in which J is represented by the sum distances from every point to their centroids in each cluster.

$$J = \sum_{j=1}^{n} \alpha \left(data[j] - c[i] \right)^2.$$

n is the total number of points which marked as i and α is a parameter ($0 < \alpha < 1$). The smaller the error value, the better the clustering effect. Through the experiment of iterating different k values, the J values are obtained and presented in Fig. 1. When k reaches 6, the cluster error value is obviously decreased, and it changes a little when k value increased. So we choose 6 as the number of cluster. Then we work on 2390 user behavior vectors and get result as Table 2.

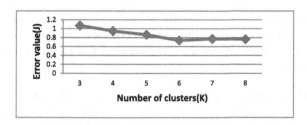

Fig. 1. Corresponding error value J calculated under different k

3.3 Clustering Results and Analysis

Present above results as Fig. 2: the horizontal coordinates are created clusters and the percentage of users assigned to each cluster; the vertical coordinate is the intergroup relative feature value. We can analysis the behavior of different groups:

Table 2. Results of clustering

Attribute values and proportion / Groups	center	f_1	f_2	f_3	f_4	proportion	features
Group 1	U_0	0.819	0.476	0.722	0.559	26.47%	Upload lots, watch and communicate less,
Group 2	U_1	1.399	0.883	0.749	2.008	15.55%	Upload and communicate lots but watch less,
Group 3	U_2	0.153	0.143	0.593	0.073	34.03%	All values are less,
Group 4	U_3	1.367	1.613	0.715	5.736	5.88%	Upload and watch less and communicate lots,
Group 5	U_4	6.972	2.440	0.725	3.773	4.20%	All values are large,
Group 6	U_5	1.737	2.639	0.746	0.891	13.87%	Upload and watch lots but communicate less.

Group 1: They like show their daily life by uploading status, logs and photos but they are not much interested in Internet resources and they get less comment from their friends. They do not usually communicate with others. They prefer to be a kind of pure content producer and they are 26.47 % of all users.

Group 2: They upload a lot but browse Internet resources less. The contents uploaded by them can be commended by more people. It reflects they are more popular and they are more enthusiastic in communication. They have 15.55 % of all and we can call them content producer & energetic communicator.

Group 3: All the attribute values of this group are quiet low. Most of them abandoned their accounts after they registered. It represents the largest fraction of users (34.03 %). This group of users is inactive user.

Group 4: The users are unwilling to upload status or photos as well as pay attention to web information. They are more enthusiastic to communicate with their friends. They are pure energetic communicators. The proportion of this group of users is relatively low, is about 5.88 %.

Group 5: Uploads, watches and communication number are all large in this group. They not only produce and consume contents, but also frequently communicate with friends. They are active users but only with a low proportion (4.2 %).

Group 6: Compared to communicate with others, they are more willing to show themselves and browse web information. They have both characteristics of content producers and consumers, so we name them producer & consumer (13.87 %).

The user age is roughly equal distributed among clusters. It does not affect the clustering result of user behavior so that we can delete this attribute to reduce the occupancy of the data storage space and improve the clustering efficiency.

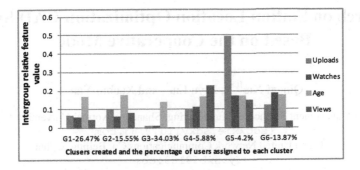

Fig. 2. Relative feature values for the six clusters created

4 Consider Implementation Strategies

Identifying different user behaviors is helpful to improve business and resource management in social networks. For example, for pure content producers, they show their lives but get no more attention. So in order to improve their initiative in interacting with others, something can be done to search and introduce them some friends with same interests through the key words of the contents they have uploaded. For content producer & consumer, considering they are less willing to communicate with others, we can support them expansive display platforms as well as more attractive network resources. For pure energetic communicator, they are interested in neither display platform nor web resources, so more energetic should be put in improving the quality of interaction services.

In this article, we identified six distinct behaviors of RenRen users. Generally, one can use the methodology we presented to assign users to groups with similar behavior. For future directions we could investigate more online social network user behavior and explore their difference. More work should be done to study the influence of user behaviors to the structure of network.

References

1. Feldman, M., Papadimitriou, C., Chuang, J.: Free-riding and whitewashing in peer-to-peer systems. IEEE J. Sel. Areas Commun. **24**, 1010–1019 (2006)
2. Backstrom, L., Kumar, R., Marlow, C., Novak, J.: Preferential behavior in online groups. In: Proceedings of the ACM Web Search and Data Mining, Stanford, CA, USA, February 2008
3. Cha, M., Kwak, H., Rodriguez, P., Ahn, Y.-Y., Moon, S.: I tube, you tube, everybody tubes: analyzing the world's largest user generated content video system. In: Proceedings of the ACM Internet Measurement Conference (IMC), San Diego, CA, USA, October 2007
4. Gong, X., Ning, Q., Zhou, A.: Clustering in very large databases based on distance and density. J. Comput. Sci. Technol. **18**(1), 67–76 (2013)
5. Zhou, Y., Peng, F., Zhou, J.: Complex surface fitting based on interpolation and approximation. J. Eng. Graph. **4**, 47–54 (2014)

Research on Station Location Optimization CAD System Based on the Cooperative Mode

Qingxi Xie[1(✉)], Xiyu Liu[1], and Xuebin Yan[2]

[1] College of Management Science and Engineering, Shandong Normal University, Jinan, China
{sdqxxie,sdxyliu}@163.com
[2] China United Network Communications Co, Beijing, China
yanxb6@163.com

Abstract. Currently, the mobile communications business has become a major driving force of China's information communication industry. This means that a wireless communication network needs to provide better quality of service. An excellent base location planning is the basis of building high quality wireless communications network. Early period, the way of dependent on experience and field measurements manner is costly and inefficient. Under this background we propose a new idea – station Location optimization CAD System based on the HOOPS cooperative mode. This station Location optimization CAD System effectively takes advantage of CAD technology and geographic information systems and it makes Rapid configuration technology and multi-target solution techniques Cooperative based on HOOPS flow.

Keywords: CAD · HOOPS flow · Base station planning · Cooperative

1 Introduction

Optimization of the base station location problem has become an important research content. Research on GIS and CAD technology integration to solve the problem of communication base station planning is very little. This article bases on an in-depth analysis of the communication base station planning on actual demand, Combine the advantages of CAD technology and related geographic information system, Research on communication base station planning CAD system key technologies. It makes Rapid configuration technology and multi-target solution techniques Cooperative based on HOOPS flow.

2 The Key Technology and Collaborative Strategies

Technical innovation of this system includes entities' rapid prototyping technology, Multi-objective modeling and solving technology, and software systems' distributed Collaborative integration technology.

© Springer International Publishing Switzerland 2016
Q. Zu and B. Hu (Eds.): HCC 2016, LNCS 9567, pp. 930–935, 2016.
DOI: 10.1007/978-3-319-31854-7_102

2.1 Entities' Rapid Prototyping Technology

The technology is mainly used to achieve fast configuration of complex entities which are related to the base station planning. By analyzing the base station Programming, it involves three types of entities. They are Base Station Entities, Topography entity, and building entities. For the three entities were established corresponding member database. When reproducing base planning area in the computer three entities to call up the respective part and combined by the member database. Their mutual relations and function in Specific software systems as shown in Fig. 1.

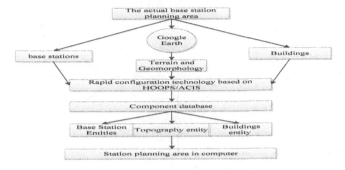

Fig. 1. Rapid configuration function relationship diagram

(a) Base Station Entities: Given the complexity of the base station configuration, it chooses 2–3 kinds of typical base station to design. It uses Boolean operations of ACIS to achieve complex entities configuration.

(b) Topography entity: It includes mountains, rivers and other geographical elements. This configuration part must be based on the entity's geographic information data base planning area. Therefore we need the help of Google Earth to export geographical data of planning area. And then it will be converted to CAD modeling data. The system uses masked, stakeout and other technologies of ACIS to generate terrain entities.

(c) Buildings entity: General buildings have a greater impact on the base station planning. Therefore, when considering the characteristics of the area of the base station planning, the location, height and width of the building should be taken into account. Given the general characteristics of the building, it can be based on bones or homotopic mapping method of ASIC technology to automatically generate.

One of the most critical technology consists of two parts: First, this system completes the seamless integration of Google Earth. And it uses Google Earth's open API for secondary development and gets geographic information of planning area. The second is entity component assembly technology based on boundary detection technology.

2.2 Multi-objective Modeling and Solving Technology

The technology is used to solve the problem of how to establish a Multi-objective mathematical model of base station plan in consideration of geographic information. And it is used to solve the problem of Problem solving of multi-objective model and evaluate the Solutions. New multi-objective mathematical model is the key issues that need to be focus on to solve in this project. It needs the support of the relevant base plan technology. Multi-objective mathematical model can be solved by the membrane computing, DNA computing, and quantum evolutionary computation algorithms. The most important feature of such algorithms is all have good parallelism. This is important to the multi-objective optimization problem. Evaluation of Model Solution is mainly through reducing base position in the planning area by Model Solution. And then Combined with the actual GIS data to determine it whether meets the actual situation. Their mutual relations and function in Specific software systems as shown in Fig. 2.

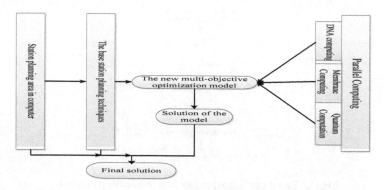

Fig. 2. Relations and function of multi-objective modeling and solving

2.3 Software Systems Distributed Collaborative Integration Technology

The technology is used to complete the integration of Sects. 2.1 and 2.2 parts, and achieve the distributed and Cooperative Mechanism based on hoops. It also includes the integrated display the final solution of, save, and modify functions. Reflect the specific software system, it consists of eight modules. Their mutual relations and function in Specific software systems as shown in Fig. 3.

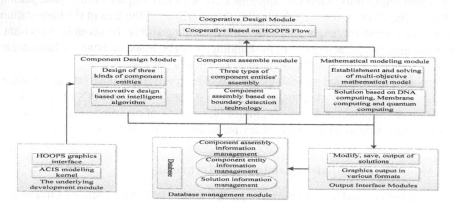

Fig. 3. Software systems' distributed collaborative integration relationship diagram

(a) Component design module: Mainly to achieve the design of three entities component based on innovative design approach of intelligent computing.

(b) Component assemble module: The module's function is to implement the assembly of three types of entities Component.

(c) Mathematical modeling module: The module's function is to complete the establishment of a new multi-objective mathematical model by composing communication base station planning techniques and solve the model by DNA computing, Membrane Computing and quantum computing. Finally, it produces the final solution.

(d) Database management module: It is mainly used for data management functions based on topic database. It includes component assembly information management, information management component entity and information management solutions.

(e) The underlying development module: It is mainly used to implement and development various functions of the underlying geometry engine and it provides more convenient implementation tools for other modules. It includes the application of ACIS/HOOPS and other tools.

(f) Cooperative Design Module: It implements the Cooperative Design function base on the network environment. It includes data transfer mechanism, resource sharing methods, the role of management and other key technologies.

(g) Output Interface Modules: It is mainly used to implement conversion interface between SAT entity files and other international mainstream three-dimensional format and save modify, output of solutions.

3   Implement of Key Technology

3.1   Implement of Rapid Configuration

In this system, it major reconstructs two kinds of base stations. The following Fig. 4 shows the two kinds of base stations.

Fig. 4. Two kinds of base station

This system uses Google Earth to obtain geographical information. Then it will be converted to CAD modeling data. The system uses masked, stakeout and other technologies of ACIS to generate terrain entities. The following Fig. 5 is a dialog that about Google Earth.

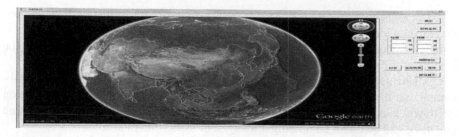

Fig. 5. Google Earth dialog

Through this dialog, you can navigate to your terrain that will be reconstructed. You can get the segment terrain's longitude, latitude, elevation and other geographical information. You can save it in a txt file. You also can change the longitude, latitude, elevation and other geographic information into the screen a three-dimensional coordinate system x, y, z coordinates and save it in the database. This system will import the information that saved in the database into the hoops flow. Now it can reconstruct the terrain. The left of the figure is the actual terrain and the right of the figure is the reconstructed terrain (Fig. 6).

Fig. 6. The actual terrain and the reconstructed terrain

3.2 The Base Station Solver Program Display

In the Fig. 7, the left is base station layout that divided equally. The right is base station layout that has used parallel algorithms.

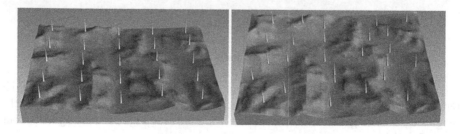

Fig. 7. Base station layout

4 Conclusions

With the deepening of 4 G technology, through analyze the previous base station planning mode, we propose a new idea– station Location optimization CAD System based on the HOOPS cooperative mode. This station Location optimization CAD System effectively takes advantage of CAD technology and geographic information systems and it makes Rapid configuration technology and multi-target solution techniques Cooperative based on HOOPS flow. It has a strong practical significance to Research and Application such a system.

There are still shortcomings in this system. For example interface design is not beautiful and preselected program is single.

Acknowledgment. Project supported by National Natural Science Foundation of China (61170038), Natural science foundation of Shandong Province, China (ZR2011FM001), Technology development projects of Shandong province, China (2012G0020314), Soft science research project of Shandong Province, China (2013RZB01019), Jinan City independent innovation plan project in Colleges and Universities, China (201401202), Ministry of education of Humanities and social science research projects, China (12YJA630152), Social Science Fund Project of Shandong Province, China (11CGLJ22), outstanding youth scientist foundation project of Shandong Province, China (BS2013DX037), young star of science and technology plan project, Jinan (20120108), science and technology development project, Jinan (201211003), science and technology development project, Jinan (201305004).

References

1. Vannucci, G., DeMont, J.P.: Base station location derived from wireless terminal information. U.S. Patent No. 9,078,229. 7 July 2015
2. The PLOS: Correction: fish farms at sea: the ground truth from Google Earth. PloS ONE **10**(7), e0134745 (2015)
3. Shao, S., et al.: Optimal location of the base station based on measured interference power. In: 2015 IEEE International Wireless Symposium (IWS). IEEE (2015)
4. Ren, S., Li, X., Liu, X.: The 3D visual research of improved DEM data based on Google Earth and ACIS. In: Zu, Q., Vargas-Vera, M., Hu, B. (eds.) ICPCA/SWS 2013. LNCS, vol. 8351, pp. 497–507. Springer, Heidelberg (2014)
5. Slavin, R.E.: Cooperative Learning: Theory, Research, and Practice, vol. 14. Allyn and Bacon, Boston (1990)
6. Yoshikawa, H.: General design theory and a CAD system. Man-Machine Communication in CAD/CAM (1981)
7. Chern, J.-H., et al.: Multilevel metal capacitance models for CAD design synthesis systems. IEEE Electron Device Lett. **13**(1), 32–34 (1992)

One Level Membrane Structure P System Based Particle Swarm Optimization

Wei Xu and Xiyu Liu[✉]

College of Management Science and Engineering, Shandong Normal University, Jinan, China
{muxixi_w,sdxyliu}@163.com

Abstract. Particle swarm optimization algorithm is an excellent algorithm for solving optimization problems. As to improve the accuracy of the PSO, we used a way to combining related theories of membrane computing, to overcome the premature convergence. One Level Membrane Structure P-System based particle swarm optimization is proposed in a P system frame in this paper. This proposed OLMS-PSO can effectively improve the convergence rate and convergence speed compare with formal PSO.

Keywords: Membrane · Particle swarm optimization · P system · OLMS

1   Introduction

Particle swarm optimization algorithm (PSO) has become a powerful tool to solve complexity problems for its versatility and simple algorithm formula. It has been widely used in many fields, such as production plan and scheduling, spacecraft design, multi-dimensional optimization problem, neural network training, fuzzy control system designs, etc. Membrane computing (MC), as a new branch of natural computing was proposed by Păun in 1998 [2], and has been applied in broad fields such as graph theory, finite state problems, combinatorial problem [3], etc.

This paper combines these two above to form a new and efficient algorithm. Some researches on combining P systems with PSO have been done in recent years. In our research, PSO is introduced into the framework of membrane computing model.

2   PS, PSO and PS-PSO

2.1   PSO

Membrane system is a new class of distributed parallel computing devices, it is inspired from the cell-structures and introduced by Păun [4]. Membrane computing is based on P systems and is motivated by the way of nature computing at the cellular level.

The membrane structure is a hierarchical arrangement of membranes that are embedded in the skin membrane separating the inner membranes from external environment. Each region contains a multi-set of objects and a set of evolution rules. The result of the computation is obtained in the output membrane or emit from the skin

© Springer International Publishing Switzerland 2016
Q. Zu and B. Hu (Eds.): HCC 2016, LNCS 9567, pp. 936–941, 2016.
DOI: 10.1007/978-3-319-31854-7_103

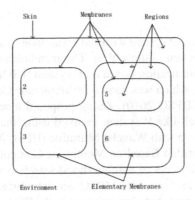

Fig. 1. Membrane structure

membrane [5]. The membrane structure of a cell-like P system is shown in Fig. 1, which can be formalized as follows:

$$\prod = (O, T, \mu, \omega_1, \cdots, \omega_m, (R_1, \rho_1), \cdots, (R_m, \rho_m)) \qquad (1)$$

(1) O is the alphabet of objects; (2) $T \subseteq O$ is the output alphabet; (3) μ is a membrane structure with m membranes and the regions labeled by the elements of a given set H. m is called the degree of Π; (4) wi $\in V^*$ ($1 \leq i \leq m$) are the multisets of objects associated with the m regions of μ; (5) Ri ($1 \leq i \leq m$) are the finite sets of multiset rewriting rules associated with the m regions of μ.

2.2 PSO

Particle swarm optimization (PSO) is a swarm intelligence based metaheuristic algorithm proposed by Kennedy and Eberhart [1]. High decentralization, cooperation amongst the particles and simple implementation make PSO efficiently applicable to optimization problems.

In PSO, each individual in the swarm, called a particle. It has three main components, particles, social and cognitive components and the velocity of the particles. Cognitive learning is represented by personal best and social learning is represented by the global best value. The pBest solution is the best solution the particle has ever achieved in its history, the gBest value is the best position the swarm has ever achieved. The swarm guides the particle using parameter gBest. Together cognitive and social learning are used to calculate the velocity of particles to their next position. Each particle updates its speed and position, according to the following iterative formula, and produces a new particle of the next generation.

$$v_{id}^{t+1} = wv_{id}^{t} + c_1 r_1 (p_{id}^{t} - x_{id}^{t}) + c_2 r_2 (p_{gd}^{t} - x_{id}^{t}) \qquad (2)$$

$$x_{id}^{t+1} = x_{id}^{t} + v_{id}^{t+1}. \qquad (3)$$

2.3   PS-PSO

The first attempt to hybridize P system with PSO was done by Zhou et al. in 2010. They used it for continuous function optimization. The membrane algorithm proposed was named Particle Swarm Optimization Based on P system (PSOPS). Yang et al. came up with another combination, which was named as Membrane Computing Based Particle Swarm Optimization (MCBPSO 2010). Zhang proposed a new variant of membrane algorithm, which was a cell-like P system evolved using the update rules of Hybrid Particle Swarm Optimization with Wavelet Mutation (HPSOWM 2012).

The Bio-Inspired Algorithm Based on Membrane Computing (BIAMC 2013) was de-signed by Xiao, using concept of neighborhood search to avoid premature convergence. Later in 2013, the algorithm MO-MPSO was introduced by Wang et al. with an idea of using horizontal hybrid mutation operator in the PSO.

3   Design of OLMS-PSO

Inspired by P system's simplicity and the limitations of PSO algorithm, we proposed Particle Swarm Optimization based on One Level Membrane Structure (OLMS-PSO). It puts particles in different membranes of P system, and implements the evolution rules of PSO separately in different membrane.

We divide the membranes into two kinds, according to their function. One is called main membrane, others is auxiliary membrane. There is one main membrane together with several auxiliary membranes. Particles in auxiliary membranes have the responsibility to explore (global search), while the particles in main membrane are responsible for the development (partial optimization).

Particles in auxiliary membranes have to be as far as possible to keep the population diversity for the purpose of exploring, in order to search the whole space. For the reason of development, particles in main membrane will search optimal solution after receiving the message from the auxiliary membranes carefully. Membranes use communication rules to exchange information between membranes and membranes.

Each particle's position is seen as an object in the membrane, and will be organized in multisets in P system. The evolutionary rules of PSO, as well as communication-like rules of P systems will be responsible to evolve the system and select the best individuals.

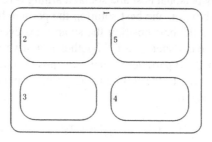

Fig. 2.   OLMS-PSO

The pseudocode of the OLMS-PSO algorithm is shown in Fig. 3, where each step is described in detail as follow:

(1) A membrane structure $[_1[_2]_2[_3]_3[_4]_4[_5]_5]_1$ is built (Fig. 2), with 5 regions contained in the skin membrane (main membrane), denoted by 1. (2) Initialize the position and velocity of the particle in each membrane and find individual optimal value and the global optimal value in every membrane. (3) Each of the compartments 1 to 5 implements the evolution rules of PSO independently. (4) And through communication rules the best fit 10 particles in auxiliary 2 to 5 will be sent into main membrane 1. (5) After receive 40 particles from auxiliary membranes, the worst 40 particles will be discarded into environment, and with the best fit 10 particle being send to compartment membrane 2–5 to affect the next generation update.

Membrane structure is shown in Fig. 2, the P system can be expressed as the following multiple groups:

$$\prod = (O, T, \mu, \omega_1, \cdots, \omega_5, (R_1, \rho_1), \cdots, (R_5, \rho_5)) \qquad (4)$$

where O is the alphabet, T is output alphabet, μ is a membrane structure, w_1–w_5 are multisets in the membranes, n_1–n_6 are numbers of particles in membrane. R_i is the rule corresponding to membrane i, ρ_i is the priority of rules in membrane i.

Begin
(i)   Initialize membrane structure
(ii)   Assign individuals to each membrane
(iii)   *for* t=1:generation num
            for i=1:5
            perform PSO in i membrane
             IN membrane 2-5
            communicate the best 10 particle to membrane 1
             IN membrane 1
            Drop the worst 40 particles to environment
            sort and select the best 10 particles retune to 2-5
            end
            t←t+1
            end
(iv)   Output optimal solution
End

Fig. 3. Pseudocode of OLMS-PSO

4   Experiments and Results

Three benchmark functions are used to test the performance of the algorithm proposed: Rosenbrock, Rastrigin and Ackley function. We use the standard PSO algorithm and the proposed algorithm to solve these three test functions respectively by using MATLAB2012. Parameters are set as follows: particle population size is 100, function dimension d = 3, evolution generations t = 1000, learning factor $c_1 = 1$, $c_2 = 2$, standard PSO inertia weight w = 2. (Only two results' figs are given.)

$$f_1 = \sum_{i=1}^{n-1} (100(x_{i+1} - x_i^2)^2) + (x_i - 1)^2) \qquad f_2 = \sum_{i=1}^{n} (x_i^2 - 10\cos(2\pi x_i) + 10)$$

$$f_3 = -c_1 \times \exp(-c_2 \sqrt{\frac{1}{l} \times \sum_{i=1}^{D} x_i^2}) - \exp(\frac{1}{l} \sum_{i=1}^{D} \cos(c_3 x_i)) + c_1 + e;$$

$$(c_1 = 20, c_2 = 0.2, c_3 = 2\pi)$$

We take those 10 times test average to be the experiment result. It can be seen in the image curve trend that OLMS-PSO algorithm has faster convergence speed. In 160 generations, the novel PSO algorithm has basically found out the optimal value of bench functions. While formal PSO algorithm has found out the optimal value in about 400–600 generations. Fitness, corresponding to OLMS-PSO, on Rosenbrock Function, Rastrigin function, Ackley Function are nearly 0 while fitness corresponding to PSO are: 2.43, 6.12, 2.62. It shows that the new algorithm has played a very positive role in the development phase, improved the convergence precision of the algorithm. Therefore, OLMS-PSO algorithm has higher optimizing efficiency than the standard PSO algorithm (Figs. 4 and 5).

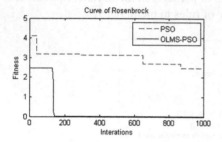
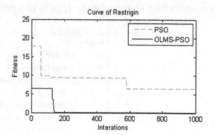

Fig. 4. Rosenbrock function   **Fig. 5.** Rastrigin function

5 Conclusion

This paper proposed an improved PSO algorithm OLMS-PSO, which introduced membrane computing knowledge into PSO algorithm. Experiments show that this new algorithm has stronger optimization ability compare to PSO formal algorithm. The optimal solution is more accurate, and has faster convergence speed than that of the formal original PSO (an easy to converge one). But it is also noted that this algorithm is in its infancy, more researches are needed to make it perfect.

Acknowledgment. This work was supported by the Natural Science Foundation of China (No. 61170038), Natural Science Foundation of China (No. 61472231), University Innovation Project of Jinan, China (No. 201401202), Humanities and Social Science Project of Ministry of Education, China (No. 12YJA630152), Social Science Fund Project of Shandong Province, China (No. 11GGLJ22), Outstanding Young Scientist Research Award Fund of Shandong Province, China (No. BS2013DX037).

References

1. Kennedy, J., Eberhart, R.: Particle swarm optimization. In: Proceedings of IEEE International Conference on Neural Networks, vol. 4, pp. 1942–1948. IEEE (1995)
2. Păun, G.: Computing with membranes. TUCS report 208. Turku Center for Computer Science (1998)
3. Paun, G., Rozenberg, G., Salomaa, A.: Handbook of Membrane Computing, pp. 35–40. Oxford University Press, Oxford (2009)
4. Zhang, G., Gheorghe, M., Pan, L., et al.: Evolutionary membrane computing: a comprehensive survey and new results. Inf. Sci. **279**, 528–551 (2014)
5. Păun, G.: Computing with membranes. J. Comput. Syst. Sci. **61**(1), 108–143 (2000)

A Personalized Sensitive Label-Preserving Model and Algorithm Based on Utility in Social Network Data Publishing

Yuqin Xie$^{(\boxtimes)}$, Mingchun Zheng$^{(\boxtimes)}$, and Lin Liu

College of Management Science and Engineering,
Shandong Normal University, Jinan, China
{sdnuxyq,zhmcl63,liulincn8}@163.com

Abstract. As the need for social network data publishing continues to increase, the trade-off between privacy and utility in publishing tabular data is becoming an important and challenging issue. Existing anonymization approaches, which measure utility loss with number of changes to the graph build with social network data, may over alter the graph structure properties. In the paper, we address this problem. We propose a personalized sensitive label-preserving model based on utility. First, a novel metric is proposed that calculates the changes on social network topological feature. Second, an efficient nodes segmentation anonymization algorithm based the metric is designed. Experimental evaluation shows that our approach effectively improves the utility preservation as compared to the number-of-change metric with adding nodes or edges.

Keywords: Social networks · Privacy · Anonymization · Data utility · Topological structure similarity

1 Introduction

With the rapid growth of social networks, network operators are increasingly publish and sharing social network data. However, social network data contains sensitive information about the personal user, publishing social network data raises privacy concerns [1]. Thus, how to protect individual's privacy with the same time preserve the utility of social network data becomes a challenging topic.

To address the users' labels privacy preserving in social network data publishing, various anonymization methods [2–4] have been proposed. But in such methods there is excessive anonymity of node label. As almost all possible sensitive attribute values were anonymized by the same degree. And they try to achieve anonymity with minimal changes [4] made to the social network graph. Then this will surely cause excessive anonymous and information loss. In this paper, to solve this problem we focus on the re-identification attack [5] based on the user nodes degree as background knowledge, then propose a personalized graph anonymization model based on utility.

The rest of the paper is organized as follows. Section 2 briefly provides some background knowledge of the problem to be solved and reviews related works about social network data anonymization. Section 3 details the novel utility measure model.

© Springer International Publishing Switzerland 2016
Q. Zu and B. Hu (Eds.): HCC 2016, LNCS 9567, pp. 942–947, 2016.
DOI: 10.1007/978-3-319-31854-7_104

Then presents the node segmentation algorithm based on the proposed utility metric. Section 4 reports the experiment results. Finally, Sect. 5 concludes the paper.

2 Related Knowledge

In this section, we first present the models for the social network and adversary. We also introduce the related work and the terminology that will be used in this paper.

2.1 Social Network Data Model

Vertex-labeled graph model which the vertices are labeled is the basis for this article. We introduce the vertex-labeled graph model proposed by Yin [6], and supplement its definition and description. In this model, this paper further put all attributes' diverse values as attribute nodes based on the simple model G(V, E), then the edge between user node and attribute node indicates that the user has this attribute value.

Definition 1 (Vertex-Labeled Graph Model). A vertex-labeled graph is an undirected graph which models the social network contain relationship between users and user attributes. Formal definition [7] is as follows:

$$G = \{VU, VA, EU, EA\}$$

VU is a set of n labeled vertices representing individuals in the social network; VA is a set of attribute nodes representing all possible values of the attributes; EU is a set of m unlabeled edges describing the relationship between the individuals; EA is a collection of correspondence between attribute nodes and user, each of which represents one side of a user with this attribute value. Figure 1 shows an example of a social network graph.

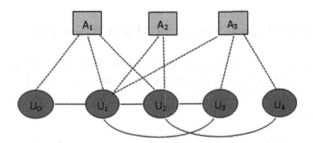

Fig. 1. Social-attribute network

2.2 Privacy Adversary Model and Related Conceptual Definition

Definition 2 (Structural Re-identification Attack (SRA) [5]). Given a social network G, its published graph G*, a target entity t ∈ VU and the attacker background knowledge F(t), the attacker performs the structural re-identification attack by searching for all the vertices in G* that could be mapped to t, i.e., VF (t) = {v ∈ V * |F(v) = F(t)}. If |VF (t)| < < |V*|, then t has a high probability to be re-identified.

Definition 3 (k-degree Anonymity [5]**).** Given a graph G = (V, E) with V = {v_1, v_2,..., v_n} and $d(v_i) = |\{u ∈ V : (u, v_i) ∈ E\}|$, the degree sequence of G is defined to be the sequence ($d(v_1)$, $d(v_2)$, ..., $d(v_n)$). k-degree anonymous if for every vertex $v_i ∈ V$, there exist at least k other vertices in G with the same degree as v_i.

Definition 4 (Attribute Similarity). The attribute value sequence of the node v_j is expressed an n-dimensional Boolean vector [8]: $B_j = \left(b_j^1, b_j^2, ..., b_j^n\right)$, b_j^i is equal to or 1, when $b_j^1 = 0$, then the node v_j does not have the first attribute value, as user attributes distribution is sparse in social network. In this paper the attribute similarity of two user vertices is measured by the cosine similarity, Therefor this paper designed attribute similarity function of user node VU_i and VU_j:

$$(VU_i, VU_j)_{AS} = \frac{B_i \cdot B_j}{\|B_i\| \cdot \|B_j\|}.$$

Definition 5 (Attribute Value Sensitivity Function). The sensitivity of the label nodes is established by membership function usually. We use a trapezoidal distribution membership function which range [0, 1] to determine the attribute value sensitivity and preserving threshold ρ:

$$sensitivity(x) = \begin{cases} 0, x < a \\ \dfrac{x-a}{b-a}, a \le x \le b \\ 1, x > b \end{cases}$$

Critical points a, b is the threshold mentioned before, for the convenience of the experiment, this article sets threshold based on experience. But for the practical application, it should be performed by statistics and analysis.

3   The Sensitive Label-Preserving Model Based Utility

In our work, we aim at improving the utility of the graph G* anonymized from the original graph G while achieving high privacy protection to resist the re-identification attack, upon the user nodes degree as background knowledge. Our model is divided into two modules:

3.1   Generating Sensitive Attribute Vertices Anonymization Set

In sensitive label preserving problem, to remain high utility we consider using two layer networks to divide the original graph into two sets which one is nodes connecting sensitive attribute value node(s) and the other one is the rest of nodes:

The upper virtual network graph D(VU, VA,EA) is used to pick out a set of sensitive attribute anonymize vertices SV = {sv_1, sv_2, ..., sv_t}, every sv_i ∈SV means sensitivity (sv_i) >=ρ.

The lower distributed network $D(VU, EU)$ has an expectation for finding out the key (or bridging) nodes set $KV = \{kv_1, kv_2, \ldots\}$ by network centrality analysis in social network analysis. In the simulation experiments, we use two indicators: node degree, node betweenness centrality to dig the central nodes:

a. The degree of a node vu_i is the number of nodes directly connected to the point, indicated by $d(vu_i)$;

b. Node betweenness of vu_t is defined: $C_B(vu_t) = \sum\limits_{i \in VU} \sum\limits_{j \neq i \in VU} \frac{\delta_{ij}(VU_t)}{\delta_{ij}}$.

3.2 Graph Utility Measurement

This paper try design a new utility assessment function D_{change}, where variant APL and CC represent respectively the average path length and clustering coefficient of graph G, while APL* and CC* are two parameters measuring the topology features of G*; The function TC captures the change degree of social network structure, and formula IL say attributes information loss.

$$D_{change} = a \cdot (TC) + b \cdot (IL)$$

$$s.t. \begin{cases} TV = \alpha \cdot \frac{APL^* - APL}{APL} + \beta \cdot \frac{CC^* - CC}{CC}; \\ IL = \frac{|SV \cap KV|}{|VU|}; \\ a + b = 1; \\ \alpha + \beta = 1; \\ \forall a, b, \alpha, \beta \neq 0; \end{cases}$$

3.3 Improved Algorithm Based on K-Degree Anonymization

Specific algorithm steps are as follows:

Input: Graph G(VU,VA, EU,EA),k, F,ρand KV
Output: K- degree anonymized graph G*.
1) For each user-node vu in VU
2) Mse←sensitivity(vu);   // Generate node attribute sensitivity matrix
3) IF sensitivity(vu)>ρ
4) SV←vu   // node vu is a sensitive node
5) End For;
6) M← $SU - KV$ // Generated anatomy node sequence set M
7) For each user-node m in M
8) v1,v2←new node()   / divide the current node into two new nodes
9) For each social edge e in of m
10) Distributebydegree(e,v1,v2) //assign e to meet k-degree anonymous
11) For each attribute b of m
12) Distributebysafy(b, v1,v2)
13) End For;
14) Return G*;

4 Simulation Experiment

In this section, we report the empirical result that we conducted to evaluate the performance of our proposed approach. All of the experiments have been implemented using MATLAB 2010a. The experiments were conducted on a PC having an Intel Duo 2.13 GHz processor and 2 GB RAM with Windows7. A real data sets is used in our tests, namely Last.fm-dataset [http://mtg.upf.edu/node/1671]. The datasets is 13 M. We sampled subgraphs from these datasets with the changing from 500 to 1000 respectively by software Gephi.

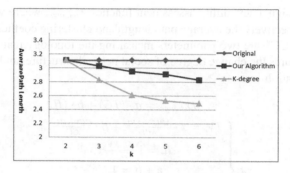

Fig. 2. The impact on APL

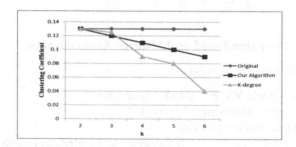

Fig. 3. The impact on CC

Figures 2 and 3 reflects the different impacts on the social network representative structure indicators: the APL and the CC, between our improved k-degree algorithm by node segmentation and the original k-degree algorithm with edges addition. In the Average Path Length evaluation (Fig. 2), it is shown that when the k requirement increases, the amount of distortion also increases, and our node segmentation algorithm can be more close to the straight line in the graph, For clustering coefficient (Fig. 3), the state is same.

5 Conclusion

Privacy and utility are two main components of a good privacy protection scheme. In this paper, we propose a novel utility-oriented social network anonymization approach in this paper to achieve high privacy protection and low utility loss. Experimental evaluation on real dataset shows our approach outperforms the existing k-degree approaches in terms of the utility with the same privacy preserving.

Acknowledgements. This work is supported by the Natural Science Foundation of China (NO. 61402266), Natural Science Foundation of Shandong Province, China (ZR2012MF013), Social Science Foundation of China (14BTQ049).

References

1. Ninggal, M.I.H., Abawajy, J.H.: Utility-aware social network graph anonymization. J. Netw. Comput. Appl. **56**, 137–148 (2015)
2. Yuan, M., Chen, L., Yu, P.S., et al.: Protecting sensitive labels in social network data anonymization. IEEE Trans. Knowl. Data Eng. **25**(3), 633–647 (2013)
3. Fung, B.C.M., Jin, Y., Li, J.: Preserving privacy and frequent sharing patterns for social network data publishing. In: 2013 International Conference on Advances in Social Networks Analysis and Mining (ASONAM), pp. 479–485. IEEE Computer Society (2013)
4. Lee, B., Fan, W., Squicciarini, A.C., et al.: The relativity of privacy preservation based on social tagging. Inf. Sci. **288**, 87–107 (2014)
5. Liu, K., Terzi, E.: Towards identity anonymization on graphs. In: Proceedings of the 2008 ACM SIGMOD (2008)
6. Yin, Z., Gupta, M., Weninger, T., Han, J.: LINKREC: a unified framework for link recommendation with user attributes and graph structure. In: Rappa, M. (ed.) Proceedings of the 19th International Conference on World Wide Web, pp. 1211–1212. ACM Press, New York (2010)
7. Fu, Y.-Y., Zhang, M., Feng, D.-G.: Attribute privacy preservation in social networks based on node anatomy. J. Softw. **25**(4), 768–780 (2014)
8. Wang, Y., Long, X., Zheng, B., Lee, K.C.K.: High utility K-anonymization for social network publishing. Knowl. Inf. Syst. **41**(3), 697–725 (2014)

The Simulation and Optimization for Re-entrant Manufacturing System

Chenjie Zhang[✉] and Hu Sun[✉]

Wuhan University of Technology, Heping Road No. 1040,
Wuchang District, Wuhan 430063, Hubei, China
mixinman@163.com, 525090277@qq.com

Abstract. Due to necessary requirement of product processing, the re-entrant manufacturing system, which has re-entrant property, is different from general manufacturing system or reworking. The frequency of re-entry is far more than general manufacturing system, which will lead to the WIP (work-in-process) competing for one equipment in different phrases of production. The production load of the equipment fluctuates randomly, so that it's impossible to make precise prediction on arriving time of WIP. Since the semiconductor manufacturing system is a typical representative of re-entrant manufacturing, the paper taking Mini-fab as an example to simulate, makes research on re-entrant manufacturing system and analyzes the quantity of output and the WIP under different feed rates by means of modeling and ExtendSim simulation.

Keywords: Re-entrant manufacturing system · Mini-fab model · ExtendSim · Simulation

1 Introduction

The Re-entrant manufacturing system refers that WIP repeatedly passes through the same work station at different stage of the process flows in production manufacturing system. The complex re-entrant wafer manufacturing system is a special type of production which developed with manufacturing of semiconductor chips, the films, and new type displays LCD since 1980s.

Traditional manufacturing system consists of Job-shop and Flow-shop. The products have a wide range, small amount, short production path and randomness in the type of Job-shop, while the type of Flow-shop has the property of single type, mass production, fixed production path and no backflow. Due to re-entrant property, the production of wafer is different from either Flow-shop or Job-shop, which was classified into third type manufacturing by Kumar. Represented by chips manufacturing, the production of re-entrant manufacturing system has the property of huge scale, multiple re-entrant characteristics, complex production process, expensive, and hybrid production. With the development of technology and the sharply rise in microelectronics industry, researches on scheduling problem and application in re-entrant manufacturing system have become a hotspot in controlling science and engineering field.

© Springer International Publishing Switzerland 2016
Q. Zu and B. Hu (Eds.): HCC 2016, LNCS 9567, pp. 948–953, 2016.
DOI: 10.1007/978-3-319-31854-7_105

Many scholars have made deep research on re-entrant manufacturing system, and gained tremendous theoretical achievements on production scheduling method, it's hard to apply the theory to practical scheduling problems due to complexity of re-entrant manufacturing system. Many problems need deeper study. The paper taking advantage of Mini-fab model, made research on re-entrant manufacturing system, set forth the way to modelling re-entrant manufacturing system, and analyzed the output of specific product by ExtendSim simulation software.

2   ExtendSim Simulation of Re-entrant Manufacturing System

In early days, for small scale, single or few variety re-entrant manufacturing system, research mainly were done from the perspective of Flow-shop. With the development of the products' variety and amount, scheduling problem brought by re-entrance was becoming more and more serious, thus most research was based on traditional Job-shop. The traditional re-entrant system model has queuing network model, fluid model, and Petri net model. Though performing well in modelling real system, the calculating time might be longer with the production scale rising, which even leads to dimension disaster.

ExtendSim, multifunctional, repeatable and extensible, interactive, visible, and connective, is convenient to build simulation model for discrete event. The simulation result seems closer to reality with the ability to modelling tiny details.

Semiconductor wafer manufacturing system is an extreme complex system, which mainly contains three features:

(1) Large scale of raw material exists in the manufacturing system.
(2) Production machine is a lot and the process needs huge amount of steps.
(3) The system has high re-entrant property, that is, raw material enters into the same machine many times in the process of production.

Mini-Fab model contains all important features in re-entrant manufacturing system, such as re-entrant process, different production time, producing in large scale and so on. The paper chooses Mini-Fab as research object, creates a system containing 3 work stations (Station A, B, C) and 6 production steps (Step 1–6), among which step 4–6 are re-entrant processes. Station A is diffusion center, working for step 1 and step 5. Station B is ion implantation center, working for step 2 and step 4. Station C is exposure center, workin for step 3 and step 6. Product A_1 is a kind of continuous Mini-Fab model. The production process is shown as the following Fig. 1 and the elapsed time of each step is shown in the following Table 1.

Table 1. The producing routine of product A_1

A	Step 1: 1 h	Step 4: 0.5 h
B	Step 2: 2 h	Step 5: 1 h
C	Step 3: 0.5 h	Step 6: 1 h

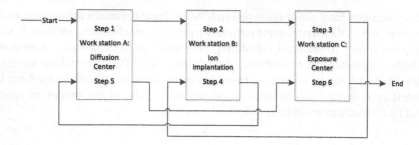

Fig. 1. The re-entrant manufacturing system

For the sake of convenience, hypotheses are as follows:

(1) The yield rate of unit products is 100 %, that is, no sub-quality product needs re-production.
(2) The system operates 24 h continuously every day.
(3) The time of shipment, load and unload, the adjustment of the equipment, and maintenance time and downtime of equipment are ignored.

According to Table 1, we can conclude that total production time of product A_1 is 6 h, among which re-entrant step 4–6 takes 2.5 h in all. Assuming that the input rate is 6 units per day, and the average interval is 4 h. The system operates from null state, and the total simulation operating time is 20 days.

The simulation objects include producing machines, product transportation channel and information flows. The simulation process include raw material input, production, re-entrant production, finished products output, and output statistics. For the sake of convenience, it is supposed that WIP operates continuously in the process, which means no storing, upload and download or carrying process exist, and no sub-quality product is produced during the production processes.

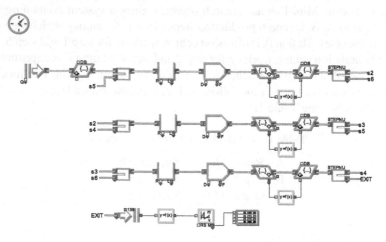

Fig. 2. ExtendSim simulation model of product A_1

The Mini-Fab model simulated by ExtendSim simulation software according to the assumptions above is shown as the Fig. 2.

3   Analysis on ExtendSim Simulation

3.1   Analysis on Output

The computational result is shown in the following Fig. 3. The system operates from null state, so there is no output at the beginning. The system starts to have product output at approximately 450 min and the output rate increases sharply from then on. When it comes to 4300 min, that is, the 3rd day, the output rate is approaching to a stable status. The output is 5.7 units per day, almost the same as the input 6 units per day. And it can be regarded as material conservation.

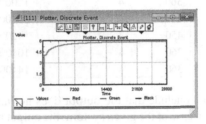

Fig. 3. The result of A_1's ExtendSim simulation

Later the research was extended to various input rates, that is the input rate is 2, 5, 8, 12 units per day. A "Math" module is added in the simulation model to observe the WIP number in the system perpetually. The amount of output and WIP vary as time goes by, the constantly line chart of output and WIP number of each case are as Figs. 4, 5, 6 and 7. The input rate, output and WIP amount are represented by λ, α, β (units per day) respectively. Time and input interval are represented by t(min) and Δt(min). Product comes out at t1(min), corresponding initial output is $\alpha1$ (units per day). The system comes into stability at t2(min) and the corresponding output is $\alpha2$ (units per day). The input-output of each case is shown in Table 2.

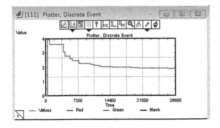

Fig. 4. Simulation result when λ is 2

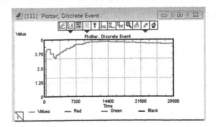

Fig. 5. Simulation result when λ is 5

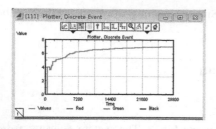

Fig. 6. Simulation result when λ is 8

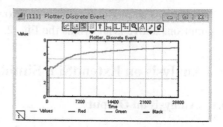

Fig. 7. Simulation result when λ is 12

Table 2. Overview of input-output

λ(units per day)	Δt(min)	t1(min)	α1(units per day)	t2(min)	α2(units per day)
2	720	360	4	12000	2
5	288	360	4	10800	4.8
6	240	450	3.2	4200	5.7
8	180	360	4	10800	6.5
12	120	360	4	14400	6.7

From Table 2, we can conclude that the output does not necessarily increase with the increasing input rate. In case of the given system, the output becomes more and more unsatisfying when the input is over 6 units per day.

3.2 Analysis on WIP

When λ is 2, the amount of output and WIP is shown in Fig. 8. The WIP and output come into stability almost at the same time, and the WIP amount is approaching to 1. Thus it is easy to speculate that most equipment in the system is in idle mode and the utilization is low. When λ is 4, the amount of output and WIP is shown in Fig. 9. The WIP and output come into stability almost at the same time as well, and the WIP is nearly the same as the output. It is speculated that the system is in relatively saturation state. When λ is 8, the amount of output and WIP is shown in Fig. 10. As time goes by, the WIP amount increases at first, and then decreases, and approaches to continuously increasing status. We can conclude that input rate is too fast when input rate is 8 units per day, and the system cannot produce correspondent product.

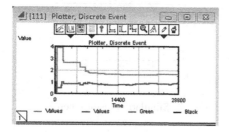

Fig. 8. Output and WIP when λ is 2

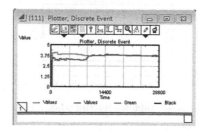

Fig. 9. Output and WIP when λ is 4

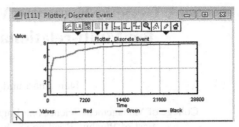

Fig. 10. Output and WIP when λ is 8   **Fig. 11.** Output after adjustment

The capacity of whole system is limited, so there exists a bottleneck problem. The production times of work station A, B, C are different. Since the work load is the heaviest, work station B is the bottleneck in the system. The adjustment is made on work station B, and then when input rate added to 8 units per day, the stable output rise to 8 units per day from 6.5 units per day, shown as (Fig. 11). The efficiency of the system is promoted prominently.

4 Summary

Mini-Fab model is a hot research area. The paper did research on general continuous re-entrant manufacturing system by ExtendSim simulation, and got the result according with the reality. After research on different output rate with different input rate (λ is 2, 5, 6, 8, 12 units per day), finds are that:

(1) The output does not necessarily increase with the input. When input rate is more than 6 units per day, the input-output ratio becomes more and more unsatisfying.
(2) The capacity of the system is limited, as the input rate increases, bottleneck problem comes into being, which will limit the output amount.
(3) Bottleneck problem is critical in promoting system performance. The adjustment to bottleneck can increase the output and decrease the WIP effectively.

References

1. Lin, D., Lee, C.K.: A review of the research methodology for the re-entrant scheduling problem. Int. J. Prod. Res. **8**(49), 2221–2242 (2011)
2. Dong, M., He, F.: A new continuous model for multiple re-entrant manufacturing system. Eur. J. Oper. Res. **7**(2), 659–668 (2012)
3. Jianyou, X., Yin, Y., et al.: A memetic algorithm for the re-entrant permutation flowshop scheduling problem to minimize the makespan. Appl. Soft Comput. **11**(24), 277–283 (2014)
4. Jing, C., Huang, W., Tang, G.: Minimizing total completion time for re-entrant flow shop scheduling problems. Theoret. Comput. Sci. **412**, 6712–6719 (2011)
5. Armbruster, D., Ringhofer, C.: Thermalized kinetic and fluid models for re-entrant supply chains. SIAM J. Multiscale Model. Simul. **3**(1), 782–800 (2005)
6. Wu, H.H., Yeh, M.L.: A DBR scheduling method for manufacturing environments with bottleneck re-entrant flows. Int. J. Prod. Res. **44**(5), 883–902 (2006)

A Genetic K-means Membrane Algorithm for Multi-relational Data Clustering

Dan Zhao and Xiyu Liu[✉]

College of Management Science and Engineering, Shandong Normal University,
East of Wenhua Road no.88, Jinan 250014, Shandong, China
{13793195081, sdxyliu}@163.com

Abstract. Most structured data are stored in relational databases containing multiple semantically linked relations. Mining interrelated data in relational databases is important in many real-world applications. This paper proposed a genetic K-means membranes clustering algorithm (GKM), which combine membrane computing and genetic K-means algorithm to solve the problem of clustering on multi-relational data set. In this paper, we design a tissue-like P system with two-level membranes structure, each membranes searches the best threshold by the evolution rules and communication rules. The algorithm makes full use of the parallelism of P system, the good convergence of genetic algorithm and the local search ability of K-means algorithm, and achieves good partitioning for a data set. Experimental results show that the proposed algorithm has better convergence accuracy and computational efficiency.

Keywords: Tissue-like P system · Membrane computing · Multi-relational clustering · Genetic algorithm · K-means algorithm

1 Introduction

In the real world, a lot of data is multi relational, that is, the data is composed of many different types of entities, and all kinds of entity attribute is not the same. And the entities are connected through a variety of relationships. Ignoring the multi relationship characteristics of the data, and still using the traditional method of data mining to mine the data will get inaccurate conclusions. Therefore, in order to improve the accuracy of mining results, the multi relationship characteristics of the data must be properly handled.

K-means is one of most popular unsupervised learning methods due to its simplicity and effectiveness. However, k-means has several drawbacks. To overcome these, evolutionary clustering algorithms have been considered in recent years. GA-based clustering methods were first reported in the literature [1], and have two approaches to express the solution of a clustering problem: point-based schemes [2] and center-based schemes [3]. GA follows the evolution process of biology, through the population reproduction and exchange generation after generation, it can search to more than one local extremum, which increases the chance of find the global optimal solution.

© Springer International Publishing Switzerland 2016
Q. Zu and B. Hu (Eds.): HCC 2016, LNCS 9567, pp. 954–959, 2016.
DOI: 10.1007/978-3-319-31854-7_106

Membrane computing (P systems) was initiated by Gh. Paun, as a new branch of natural computing. P systems have several interesting features: non-determinism, programmability, extensibility, readability, they are easy to communicate, etc., and many variants have been proposed. Most P systems variants have proved to be powerful and effective [4].

Inspired by the membrane computing, the characteristics and the advantages of the P system are applied to the multi-relational clustering. This paper proposes a genetic K-means membranes clustering algorithm, which gives full play to the parallel computing ability of P system to improve the convergence speed and calculation efficiency of the algorithm.

2 Similarity Measure

The process of clustering to objects in target tables in relational database is called the multi-relation clustering. The main task for multi-relation clustering is to calculate the similarity of two random objects in target table. The similarity of two random objects in the target table should be presented as the sum of their inside-class distance and all their outside-class distance.

In relational database, if target table is T_0, and there are n non-target table, denoted as $T_1, T_2, ..., T_n$, then the similarity between two random objects m_1 and m_2 in T_0 is denoted as:

$$d(m_1, m_2) = \alpha_0 d_{T_0}(m_1, m_2) + \alpha_1 d_{T_1}(m_1, m_2) + ... + \alpha_n d_{T_n}(m_1, m_2) \qquad (1)$$

Where, $d_{T0}(m_1, m_2)$ is the inside-class distances between m_1 and m_2 decided by the attributes in T0, while $d_{T_1}(m_1, m_2), d_{T_2}(m_1, m_2), ..., \alpha_n d_{T_n}(m_1, m_2)$ are the outside-class distances between m_1 and m_2 decided by the attributes in $T_1, T_2, ..., T_n$, α_0 is the pertinence between the target table and itself, values for 1. $\alpha_1, \alpha_2, ..., \alpha_n$ are the pertinence of T_0 to $T_1, T_2, ..., T_n$.

After obtaining the similarity of two random objects in the target table, this paper mainly uses genetic k-means membranes clustering method to do the clustering of the objects in the target table.

3 Genetic K-means Membranes Clustering Algorithm

3.1 A Tissue-like P System Designed for the GKM Algorithm

This chapter uses tissue-like P system, which has symporter/reverse transfer rules. Its environment as the output cell is initially empty. In the process of operation, the optimal object is stored in the environment, and the optimal object is transferred to each basic membrane to promote the evolution in the basic membrane (Fig. 1).

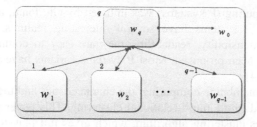

Fig. 1. The membrane structure of the tissue-like P system and its communication channels.

3.1.1 Object's Fitness

In this paper, the sum of the Euclidean distance of each data point in the data set to its corresponding cluster centers is used as the evaluation criteria of the object. The object's evaluation criteria B are calculated as follows:

$$B(C_1, C_2, \ldots, C_K) = \sum_{i=1}^{K} \sum_{x_j \in C_i} \|x_j - C_i\| \qquad (2)$$

Where, $x_1, x_2, \ldots, x_n$ is the data points of the corresponding cluster, n is the number of the data points. Generally, the smaller the B value is, the better the object is. The fitness function of the object is defined as the reciprocal of the B value, that is, f = 1 / B.

3.1.2 Evolutionary Rules

(1) k-means rule. K-means rule derives from the idea of k - means algorithm [5]. Let $x_1, x_2, \ldots, x_n$ is a data point set and $z_1, z_2, \ldots, z_K$ is the clustering center. If the distance from the point xi to the cluster center z_j is less than the distance from the point xi to the other cluster centers, the point xi is classified into the cluster C_j. When all the points are attributed to the corresponding cluster, the new cluster center Z_i^* is the average value of all points in the cluster.

$$z_i^* = \frac{1}{n_i} \sum_{x_j \in C_i} x_j, i = 1, 2, \ldots k \qquad (3)$$

Where, Z_i^* is a new cluster center of the cluster Ci, and n_i is the number of points belonging to the cluster C_i.

(2) Selection rule. Selection rule simulates the natural selection in nature. According to the object's fitness value, it selects the more adaptive object from the object set. In this paper, we use the roulette wheel method widely used. $\sum f_i$ represent the fitness value sum of the object set, and f_i said the fitness value of object i in the object set. The probability that the object is selected is the proportion of its fitness value.

(3) Cross rule. Cross rule selects two objects. They cross with a certain probability, and exchange information with each other, so as to generate two new objects. The crossover position is random, and this paper uses the single point crossover. If the object's length is L, then the crossover point is a random integer in the range of [1, L-1]. Two objects are exchanged at the right of the crossover point to produce two new objects.

(4) Mutation rule. Each object mutates according to a fixed mutation probability. Mutation methods are as follows:

δ is a random real number between [0, 1], which is in accordance with the statistics law of uniform distribution. Before the mutation, variation the value of the mutation position is υ, after variation, the value becomes:

$$\upsilon \pm 2 \times \delta \times \upsilon, \upsilon \neq 0$$
$$\upsilon \pm 2 \times \delta, \upsilon = 0$$

Where, Take " + " or " $-$ " With equal probability.

3.1.3   Communication Rules

Communication rule realizes information exchange mechanism between the membrane and membrane, and realizes the exchange and sharing of optimal objects between the basic membrane and the basic membrane as well as the basic membrane and the environment. It promotes the evolution of the object set in each membrane.

In each iteration, basic membrane 1,..., basic membrane q-1 select m optimal objects and transfer them to the membrane q. Membrane q selects m optimal objects from the (q-1) × m objects, and transfers them to the basic membrane 1,..., basic membrane q-1 to replace the worst m objects of them. At the same time the membrane q communicates with the environment, and transfers the optimal object to the environment. If the optimal object in the membrane q is better than that of the object in the environment, the object in the environment is replaced by the best object in the membrane q. Otherwise, the object is discarded. The environment always only holds an object, which is the optimal object to date. In each iteration, the environment communicates with the membrane 1,..., membrane q-1, and transfers the optimal object to the membrane 1,..., membrane q-1 to replace the worst object of them. Make sure that there is the optimal object in each membrane.

3.1.4   Halting and Output

For simplicity, the Tissue-like P system uses the halt condition of maximum number of execution steps. Upon halting, the global best object stored in the skin membrane is regarded as the final computing result, the best cluster centers found.

3.2   The GKM Algorithm

(1) Generate a set of initial objects for membrane 1,..., membrane q-1, and set related control parameters.

(2) Apply the evolution rules (crossover rule, mutation rule, selection rule and k-means rule) for each object in the membrane 1,…, membrane q-1.
(3) Apply the communication rule.
(4) If the end condition is met, the object in the environment outputs, that is, the final optimal clustering center, otherwise repeat steps (2)−(4).

4 Experimental Results

To verify the effectiveness of genetic K-means membranes clustering algorithm (GKM), GKM was compared with K-means and genetic K-means (G-K-means). There algorithms are implemented in the multi-relational database Movie. The experiment is carried out in a computer with a Pentium IV CPU and 1 G RAM, Windows XP. Use the B values to evaluate the clustering results.

The parameters of the P system were set to: q = 5, that is, there are four basic membrane; The object number in membrane 1,…, membrane q-1 is 100; The certain probability is 0.8; The mutation probability is 0.001. The iteration number of these three algorithms is 100 times.

Table 1. The comparison results of B values for GKM, K-means and G-K-means.

Runs	K-means		G-K-means		GKM	
	B	Time	B	Time	B	Time
Runs = 1	2857.058973	16.485	2800.023654	15.869	2800.095478	13.387
Runs = 2	2803.244504	16.406	2800.131595	15.639	2799.92506	13.369
Runs = 3	2800.435165	16.397	2800.023266	15.687	2800.076397	13.401
Runs = 4	2842.79271	16.839	2800.069109	15.586	2799.872639	13.789
Runs = 5	2841.357386	17.021	2800.257654	15.724	2799.859928	13.524
Runs = 6	2800.464892	16.235	2800.270766	15.736	2800.160963	13.432
Runs = 7	2800.412324	16.354	2800.131387	15.698	2799.948129	13.478
Runs = 8	2800.756731	16.218	2799.936141	15.902	2799.980222	13.692
Runs = 9	2800.251323	16.379	2800.185716	15.579	2800.010378	13.579
Runs = 10	2800.328663	16.412	2800.046778	15.628	2799.982711	13.428
max	2857.058973	17.021	2800.270766	15.902	2800.160963	13.789
min	2800.251323	16.218	2799.936141	15.579	2799.859928	13.369
mean	2814.710267	16.4746	2800.107607	15.7048	2799.991191	13.5079
variance	516.1447066		0.011680139		0.009447882	

Table 1 shows the results of three algorithms independent running 10 times on the data set Movie. As can be seen from the results, the optimal result of GKM is better than the other two algorithms, and its worst result is a bit worse than the optimal result of G-K-means, but better than the optimal result of K-means. The average of GKM is better than the other two algorithms. In terms of variance, compared with algorithm K-means and G-K-means, the variance of GKM is the smallest, which is superior to other two algorithms. Compared with other two algorithms, GKM have obvious advantage in running time. In a word, the clustering performance of GKM is superior to K-means and G-K-means.

5 Conclusion

In this paper, we propose an innovative solution inspired by P systems techniques, the genetic K-means membranes clustering algorithm. In this algorithm, each membrane completes the local optimization by performing selection, crossover, mutation rule and K-means rule, and completes the global optimization by communication rule. Finally, the surface membrane output the global optimal object. This algorithm combines the parallelism of P system, the good convergence of genetic algorithm and the local search ability of K-means algorithm, and gives full play to the advantage of the above three computing models. Experimental results show that the proposed algorithm has better convergence accuracy and computational efficiency.

Acknowledgment. Project supported by National Natural Science Foundation of China (61170038,61472231), Jinan City independent innovation plan project in College and Universities, China (201401202), Ministry of education of Humanities and social science research project, China (12YJA630152), Social Science Fund Project of Shandong Province, China (11CGLJ22), outstanding youth scientist foundation project of Shandong Province, China (BS2013DX037).

References

1. Chang, D., Zhang, X., Zheng, C.: A genetic algorithm with gene rearrangement for k-means clustering. Pattern Recogn. **42**, 1210–1222 (2009)
2. Maulik, U., Bandyopadhyay, S.: Genetic algorithm based clustering technique. Pattern Recogn. **33**, 1455–1465 (2000)
3. Bandyopdhyay, S., Saha, S.: GAPS: a clustering method using a new point symmetry-based distance measure. Pattern Recogn. **40**, 3430–3451 (2007)
4. Peña-Cantillana, F., Díaz-Pernil, D., Christinal, H.A., et al.: Implementation on CUDA of the smoothing problem with tissue-like P systems. Nat. Comput. Simul. Knowl. Discovery, 184 (2013)
5. Wang, J., Wang, J., Ke, Q., et al.: Fast approximate k-means via cluster closures. In: Baughman, A.K., Gao, J., Pan, J.-Y., Petrushin, V.A. (eds.) Multimedia Data Mining and Analytics, pp. 373–395. Springer International Publishing, Switzerland (2015)

Power Lines Optimization Algorithm for Membrane Computing Based on Google Earth and ACIS

Dan Zhao, Xiyu Liu[✉], and Wei Sun

College of Management Science and Engineering,
Shandong Normal University, East of Wenhua Road No.88, Jinan, Shandong 250014, China
{13793195081,sdxyliu,weizifighting}@163.com

Abstract. CAD technology is an important part of electronic information technology, which is promoting the renewal and transformation of traditional industries and disciplines. The development of CAD technology can help us to solve many practical problems. This paper designed a power location optimization system, which apply CAD technology into the application of power line location and optimization. We achieved the real terrain reconstruction based on Google Earth and ACIS. Combining with be membrane computing and ant colony optimization (ACO), we proposed a power lines optimization algorithm, MACO, which solved power line location and optimization problem in the new terrain that we constructed.

Keywords: Path optimization · Evolution–communication P system · ACIS · Google earth · Ant colony optimization (ACO)

1 Introduction

The location of power line is related to the stable development of power industry. So it becomes more urgent to apply the high efficiency and low cost computer technology to the location and optimization of power line.

CAD technology is promoting the renewal and transformation of traditional industries and disciplines. The development of CAD technology has brought new opportunities that can solve many practical problems [1]. Google Earth not only provides users with a kind of 3D visual model of the Earth, but also provides us with three-dimensional coordinates of the ground. ACIS is an open software architecture, which affords a platform of geometry model for us to design various three-dimensional modeling. This paper achieves a 3D visual application program based on ACIS and the Google Earth.

Ant colony optimization (ACO) is a probabilistic algorithm used to find the optimal path in the graph [2]. Power line optimization is a discrete, nonlinear, multi constraint problem. The complex nonlinear process can be mapped into ant colony to search the shortest path to food. Therefore, an ant colony optimization (ACO) algorithm can be used to solve the nonlinear problem. Membrane computing (P systems) was initiated by Gh. Păun [3], as a new branch of natural computing. P systems have several interesting features: non-determinism, programmability, extensibility, readability, they are easy to

© Springer International Publishing Switzerland 2016
Q. Zu and B. Hu (Eds.): HCC 2016, LNCS 9567, pp. 960–965, 2016.
DOI: 10.1007/978-3-319-31854-7_107

communicate, etc., and many variants have been proposed. Most P systems variants have proved to be powerful and effective.

This paper designed a power location optimization system, which fully apply all of the above techniques. This system provided the important reference for the actual power line location, which saved a lot of resources on the topographic survey and measurement.

2   Related Works

2.1   Extraction and Transformation of Coordinates from Google Earth

Earth Google contains the coordinate information of each location. We use three major class libraries (IApplicationGE, ICameraInfoGE, IPointOnTerraGE) to extract the coordinates information from the Google Earth. First, the latitude, longitude and altitude coordinates are obtained by using three functions gePoint.get_Longitude (), gePoint.get_Latitude (), and gePoint.get_Altitude (). Then the extracted coordinates information is stored in a text file.

The geodetic coordinates can't be directly used for three-dimensional terrain simulation, and need to be further transformed into screen coordinates. Obtain the screen coordinates to the geodetic coordinates of all control points on the selected terrain in a certain sequence. Finally, screen coordinates are saved to a text file, which are used to generate 3 d terrain.

2.2   Terrain Reconstruction

We simulate reproducing the specified region based on ACIS and screen coordinates information, and use HOOPS as the display platform.

(1) Read the screen coordinates of the control points in order, and place them in the points set of declarations.
(2) Use the function api_mk_fa_spl_fit () provided by the ACIS to simulate generating a surface for the specified region.
(3) Use the function api_face_plane () provide by the ACIS to simulate a square plane with the same length and width of the specified region, which is used as the bottom of the whole three-dimensional terrain.
(4) Use the function api_loft_faces () provided by the ACIS to fitting together the generated two faces, forming a three-dimensional overall configuration.
(5) Use the function api_rh_set_entity_rgb () coloring for the face with the parameter to control the color. Function HA_Render_Entity () is used to display the three-dimensional overall configuration.

2.3   MACO: Power Lines Optimization Algorithm Based on Membrane Computing and Ant Colony Optimization (ACO)

We uses an evolution–communication P system proposed by Cavaliere [4], which contains two types of rules: evolution rules (classical evolution rules without

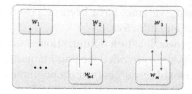

Fig. 1. The membrane structure of the evolution–communication P system

communication targets) and symport/antiport rules (for communication). We construct an evolution–communication P system of degree $q \geq 1$. Figure 1 shows the membrane structure of the system.

2.3.1 Evolutionary Rules

The evolution of objects in the system is achieved only within the m basic membranes. In this work, the differential evolution mechanism considered relies on evolution rules. The evolution rule is ACO rule. ACO rule derives from the idea of ant colony optimization algorithm [5].

(1) Generate M ants, put it hem in the beginning.
(2) Calculate the transition probability Pk according to the formula (1). Choose the next point according to the probability Pk. Join the selected points into its taboo table.
(3) Calculate the best solution to the current iteration. Update the pheromone on the path according to the formula (2).

$$p_{ij \to gh}^{k} = \begin{cases} \dfrac{\tau_{ij \to gh}^{\alpha}}{\sum\limits_{(x,y) \in allowed_{k}} \tau_{ij \to xy}^{\alpha}}, & \text{if } (x,y) \in allowed_{k}; \\ 0, & \text{otherwise.} \end{cases} \tag{1}$$

Where, $allowed_k$ is the point set which the ant k can reach, which contain the point in the point set allowed (i,j) removing the point ant k have walked. Indicates the pheromone between point (i,j) and point (g,h). Its initial value is a small constant, and will be changed gradually with the operation of the algorithm. α indicates the important degree of pheromone.

$$\tau_{ij \to gh}(t+1) = (1-\rho) \times \tau_{ij \to gh}(t) + \Delta\tau_{ij \to gh}(t), (0 < \rho < 1) \tag{2}$$

$$\Delta\tau_{ij \to gh} = \begin{cases} \dfrac{1}{L^{ib}}, & ij \to gh \text{ in the optimal path of this iteration}; \\ 0, & otherwise. \end{cases} \tag{3}$$

Where, L^{ib} is the length of the best solution for this iteration, ρ is the factor of the pheromone evaporation.

2.3.2 Communication Rules

Communication rules realize the communication of objects, which enable communication channels connecting basic membranes and skin membranes. Basic membranes have two types of communication rules, which exchange objects to and from skin membranes:

(1) Rule $[O^i_{lbest}]_i \rightarrow O^i_{lbest}$, where is the best object in basic membrane i, for i = 1,2,…,m. The rule transmits its best object into the skin membrane and updates the global best object. The updating strategy is

$$O_{gbest} = \begin{cases} O^i_{lbest}, \, if \, f(O^i_{lbest}) < f(O_{gbest}) \\ O_{gbest}, \, Otherwise \end{cases} \tag{4}$$

(2) Rule $O_{gbest} \rightarrow [O_{gbest}]_i$, where is the global best object in the skin membrane, and i = 1,2,…,m.

The rule indicates that the global best object, in the skin membrane is communicated into basic membrane i. The communicated global best object will participate in the evolution of objects in the next computing step.

2.3.3 Halting and Output

For simplicity, the evolution–communication P system uses the halt condition of maximum number of execution steps. Upon halting, the global best object stored in the skin membrane is regarded as the final computing result, the best path found.

3 Implementation of the Power Location Optimization System

In this paper, we designed a power location optimization system, which has its own unique features and technology. Combining the software of VS, ACIS, HOOPS and Earth Google, it has the function of extraction and transformation of coordinates, 3D visualization of terrain, path optimization and so on.

3.1 Extraction, Transformation and Preservation of Coordinates from Earth Google

We embedded Google earth into the system environment. The system can operate on Google earth, and joined some functions, such as Google earth's latitude and longitude positioning, coordinate obtain, transformation and storage.

First, entering the latitude and longitude of Ji'nan generate a positioning interface, which is easy to find a region, and save the time of dragging Google earth to find a certain region. That is, as long as we know the latitude and longitude coordinates of the target region, it will be accurate to find the region. Then we chose a region from Shandong Normal University to Zhonggong town. Note that, obtaining the coordinates information from Google earth is limited, and each time we can only extract the 4900 points coordinates. Because the number of control points is relatively small, and we choose the

B=116.9516330524 L=36.4659671420 H=288.761 end	x=-1.000 y=-1.00 h=0.0253 d=107.6867
B=116.9515565154 L=36.4669333597 H=276.896 end	x=-1.000 y=-0.99 h=0.0242 d=107.6867
B=116.9517025513 L=36.4680408502 H=299.370 end	x=-1.000 y=-0.98 h=0.0262 d=107.6867
B=116.9517356187 L=36.4690759696 H=304.420 end	x=-1.000 y=-0.97 h=0.0267 d=107.6867
B=116.9517686663 L=36.4701106584 H=309.468 end	x=-1.000 y=-0.96 h=0.0271 d=107.6867
B=116.9518017066 L=36.4711448838 H=314.513 end	x=-1.000 y=-0.95 h=0.0275 d=107.6867
B=116.9518347410 L=36.4721786670 H=319.556 end	x=-1.000 y=-0.94 h=0.0280 d=107.6867
B=116.9518677460 L=36.4732120165 H=324.598 end	x=-1.000 y=-0.93 h=0.0284 d=107.6867
B=116.9519007570 L=36.4742449008 H=329.636 end	x=-1.000 y=-0.92 h=0.0289 d=107.6867
B=116.9518294774 L=36.4752163275 H=318.601 end	x=-1.000 y=-0.91 h=0.0279 d=107.6867
B=116.9517011397 L=36.4761556332 H=298.771 end	x=-1.000 y=-0.90 h=0.0262 d=107.6867
B=116.9516149532 L=36.4771207064 H=285.445 end	x=-1.000 y=-0.89 h=0.0250 d=107.6867
B=116.9516430747 L=36.4781515846 H=289.752 end	x=-1.000 y=-0.88 h=0.0254 d=107.6867
B=116.9516712028 L=36.4791820738 H=294.057 end	x=-1.000 y=-0.87 h=0.0257 d=107.6867
B=116.9516993021 L=36.4802121948 H=298.361 end	x=-1.000 y=-0.86 h=0.0261 d=107.6867
B=116.9518873673 L=36.4812200573 H=296.501 end	x=-1.000 y=-0.85 h=0.0260 d=107.6867
B=116.9515806707 L=36.4821768552 H=280.012 end	x=-1.000 y=-0.84 h=0.0245 d=107.6867
B=116.9514737814 L=36.4831349047 H=263.504 end	x=-1.000 y=-0.83 h=0.0231 d=107.6867
B=116.9513667374 L=36.4840942416 H=246.973 end	x=-1.000 y=-0.82 h=0.0216 d=107.6867

Fig. 2. The terrain coordinates and the screen coordinates

region is relatively large, the accuracy of three-dimensional terrain is not enough, which is different from the actual terrain. So we divide the selected terrain into ten blocks according to the vertical coordinates, extract the terrain coordinates respectively, and then integrate the ten blocks. The terrain coordinates and the screen coordinates is shown in the Fig. 2 below.

3.2 Terrain Reconstruction and 3D Visualization of Terrain with ACIS

We simulate reproducing the specified region based on ACIS and screen coordinates, the actual terrain and the 3D simulated terrain is shown in Fig. 3.

Fig. 3. The actual terrain and the 3D simulated terrain

3.3 Location and Optimization of Power Line by MACO Algorithm and Show This Optimized Path

We locate and optimize the power line by MACO algorithm on the 3D simulated terrain. We input two points on the 3D simulated terrain, respectively, as the starting point and end point, and the optimized path can be displayed on the 3D simulated terrain. The process of implementation is shown in Figs. 4 and 5:

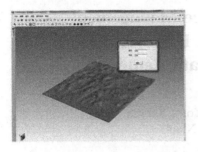

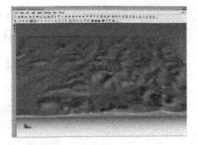

Fig. 4. Input the starting point and end point   **Fig. 5.** The optimized path by MACO

4 Conclusion

In this paper, we designed a power location optimization system, which implement the power line location and optimization by the MACO algorithm on 3D visualization terrain.

However, there are still many shortcomings, need to improve and enhance. Such as the precision of the 3D simulated terrain is still needed to strengthen, and the show of the power path on the actual terrain also needs further consideration. Further work will be done to perfect the research.

Acknowledgment. Project supported by National Natural Science Foundation of China (61170038,61472231), Jinan City independent innovation plan project in College and Universities, China (201401202), Ministry of education of Humanities and social science research project, China (12YJA630152), Social Science Fund Project of Shandong Province, China (11CGLJ22), outstanding youth scientist foundation project of Shandong Province, China (BS2013DX037).

References

1. Li, W.D., et al.: Collaborative computer-aided design—research and development status. Comput. Aided Des. **37**(9), 931–940 (2005)
2. Li, B.H., et al.: Parallel ant colony optimization for the determination of a point heat source position in a 2-D domain. Appl. Therm. Eng. **91**, 994–1002 (2015)
3. Păun, Gh, Pérez-Jiménez, M.J.: Membrane computing: brief introduction, recent results and applications. BioSystems **85**, 11–22 (2006)
4. Juayong, R.A.B., Adorna, H.N.: Relating computations in non-cooperative transition P systems and evolution-communication P systems with energy. Fundamenta Informaticae **136**(3), 209–217 (2015)
5. Mandloi, M., Bhatia, V.: Congestion control based ant colony optimization algorithm for large MIMO detection. Expert Syst. Appl. **42**(7), 3662–3669 (2015)

Information Resource Management and Control Platform Based on Cloud Computing in Data Centers

Hongyu Zhao[1](✉), Chunlan You[2], Xueyan Zhang[3],
and Weidong Xiao[2]

[1] Chinese Association for Artificial Intelligence,
No 10 West Tucheng Road, Beijing 100876, Haidian District, China
zhaohy@caai.cn
[2] Logistics Academy, No 23 Taiping Road,
Beijing 100858, Haidian District, China
{qcxyycl,13366021927}@163.com
[3] Graduate School of the Academy of Medical Sciences,
No 27 Taiping Road, Beijing 100850, Haidian District, China
1955029742@qq.com

Abstract. Based on the analysis of the current status and development of domestic and foreign information resource management and control platforms, we propose to apply cloud computing to the resource management and control platform in data centers. The application can enhance the utilization efficiency of information resources, facilitate information sharing, and improve the accuracy and intensity of information resource management and control.

Keywords: Cloud computing · Data center · Information resource management and control platform

1 Introduction

At present governments all over the world attach great importance to the development of information resource management and control platform in data centers (referred to as the platform thereafter). The new generation of cloud-based large-scale data centers has played an important part in the implementation and deployment of cloud computing strategy by national governments and enterprises. In early 2011 the European Union provided funding worth \$ 21.4 million to IBM and 15 European partners, and launched a project named "Vision Cloud—Virtualized Storage Services for the Future Internet".

Over the past 30 years, the US government, in particular the Department of Defense (DOD) has established a large number of data centers. From 1998 to 2010 the number of data centers witnessed an annual growth rate of 14 %, but the utilization rate of the computing capacity was only 27 %. With the rapid development of cloud computing technology and the increasing tightening of IT budgets, information resource management and control in data centers has attracted the attention of the US government and DOD, and gradually become a focus of information technology development.

© Springer International Publishing Switzerland 2016
Q. Zu and B. Hu (Eds.): HCC 2016, LNCS 9567, pp. 966–971, 2016.
DOI: 10.1007/978-3-319-31854-7_108

In the Federal Cloud Computing Strategy released by the US government and the military in 2011 and Cloud Computing Strategy (DOD), the strategic role of cloud computing in national policies was defined for the first time. Since then the "cloud first" policy began to be implemented, and $80 billion was invested to utilize cloud computing technology to integrate government data centers.

Most of the data centers in China are operated in traditional patterns, lacking the ability to solve such problems as low utilization efficiency of information resources, poor information sharing, and weak accuracy and intensity in information resource management and control. Only since 2012 did cloud-based data centers begin to be constructed, therefore the cloud-based platform is just in its infancy.

2 Cloud-Based Information Resource Management and Control Platform in Data Centers

2.1 Provision and Deployment of Virtual Resources

The platform is characterized by unified deployment, centralized management and control, and distributed use. On the basis of resource virtualization technology, it is possible to realize automatic deployment of resources, centralized monitoring, dynamic optimization, energy saving and low consumption with the use of cloud computing technology.

2.2 Virtual Resource Scheduling

Resource scheduling is the process of adjusting resources in the data center information resources by following rules for resource use. Different information resources correspond to different computing tasks, and each computing task corresponds to one or more processes in the operating system. The purpose of resource scheduling is to assign users to the appropriate resources, so as to meet users' needs with the minimal task completion time and the highest resource utilization rate. The ultimate goal of resource scheduling is to optimize time span, service quality, load balance, and cost efficiency. However there are various cloud infrastructures from different vendors, making it difficult to reach agreement on a uniform international standard for management and scheduling of resources. Various scheduling algorithms are also seen on the market based on different scheduling infrastructures and scheduling models.

2.3 Virtual Machine Migration

The platform is provided to users in the form of virtual machines which make it possible to dynamically cut and allocate resources and through which the users perform tasks. There are a large number of virtual machines on the platform, and the number and load of the virtual machines will constantly change according to the needs of users and applications. Static resource allocation tends to result in a waste of resources or insufficient resources, while artificial dynamic resource adjustments will cause significant time lag. Therefore, it is important to realize dynamic adjustment of virtual machine resources.

Virtual machine live migration is generally used in a virtual environment. The so-called live migration of virtual machines means that the virtual machine migrates from one virtual platform server to another without shutting down or suspending its services. Currently major virtual platform vendors such as Citrix, VMware and Microsoft have all presented its own virtual machine live migration technology.

Cloud-based data centers typically contain a large number of computing nodes and node failures often occur. As a result, failure of virtual machines is the norm. Therefore, it is important to work through virtual machine live migration so that the virtual machine can be seamlessly transferred from the failed physical machine to a stable one and new nodes can be rapidly deployed to replace the failed ones, with the ultimate goal of fault isolation and the availability of the computing environment.

3 Model and Build the Cloud-Based Data Center Information Resource Management and Control Platform

3.1 Basic Framework

The platform is mainly realized through virtual resource management technique (as shown in the following figure). Virtual resource management is composed of four parts: resource provision, virtual machine deployment, resource scheduling, and virtual machine migration. Additionally, through resource virtualization and user-oriented scheduling optimization, resource management and control is achieved.

3.2 Technical Program

In the construction of the platform, the basic functions to be performed include storage architecture, resource model, resource discovery, resource provision, virtual machine deployment, scheduling strategy, monitoring and evaluation of resource status, energy management, data security, and QOS support. The approach to realize resource management and control is resource virtualization and user-oriented scheduling optimization.

3.3 Basic Functions of the Platform

The basic function of the platform is to accept the resource request from cloud users and allocate the specific resources to the requesters, reasonably schedule appropriate resources, and facilitate the running of tasks requested by users. The platform provides four basic control services, namely resource discovery, resource monitoring, resource storage and resource scheduling. Resource discovery can discover suitable virtual resources in the data center for users and automatically find and use the relevance between virtual resources and physical resources; resource monitoring can automatically monitor the status and performance of the underlying hardware resources;

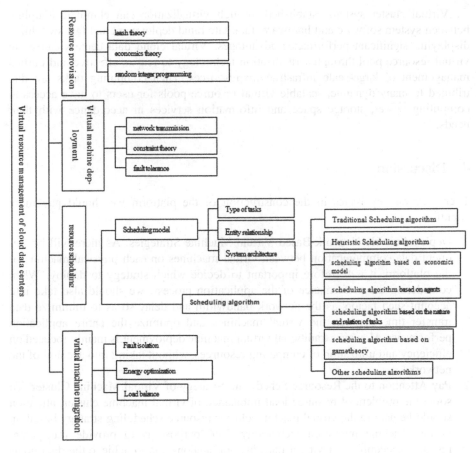

Fig. 1. Virtual resource management in cloud-based data center information resource management and control platform

resource scheduling can use different strategies to allocate the required resources to corresponding user tasks. Provision of virtual resources and deployment of virtual machine resources are the basis for resource management (Fig. 1).

3.4   Extensions of the Platform

The platform realizes a unified data management and control of information resources by shielding differences among low-level physical equipment through virtualization technology and abstracting for low-level architecture in cloud data centers.

The emergence of virtual machines makes it possible for all computing tasks to be encapsulated within a virtual machine. Because virtual machine can be isolated, it is possible to complete the migration of virtual machine computing tasks and optimize resources through dynamic migration of virtual machines.

Virtual cluster system established through virtualization can eliminate coupling between system software and hardware, facilitate rapid deployment and fast switching, displaying significant performance advantages. Virtual cloud data centers can build virtual resource pool through virtualization technology to realize effective and unified management of large-scale infrastructure resources. Then computing tasks are distributed to many dynamic, scalable virtual resource pools for users to have access to computing power, storage space and information services in accordance with their needs.

4 Discussion

There several key issues in the construction of the platform we should pay more attention.

1. Deploy Suitable Network-Based Virtual Machine Strategies. As there will be frequent data communication between virtual machines on each physical machine of the platform, it is therefore important to decide which strategy to deploy. When considering the performance of the application process, we should also take into account such factors as the network bandwidth and delay so as to minimize data transfer time between the virtual machines and optimize the entire application performance. However traditional virtual machine deployment is mainly focused on efficiency and utilization of computing resources, without taking into account of the networks.

2. Pay Attention to the Resource Scheduling Strategy of Virtual Machine Cluster. To solve the problem of resource load imbalance of virtual machine cluster, attention should be paid to the virtual machine cluster resource scheduling strategy based on virtual machine migration technology. The purpose is to provide transparent resource scheduling for virtual machine applications and to achieve the dual goals of load balancing for virtual machine clusters and energy saving. Efforts should also be made to realize load balancing based on dynamic resource allocation in the virtual machine cluster model, real-time monitoring of resource use on virtual machines and physical machines, resources re-allocation for virtual machines running on the same physical machine, with the goal of load balancing for local virtual machines. Meanwhile hot migration of virtual machines is to be performed between physical machines to achieve global load balancing to optimize resources allocation for virtual machines, with the ultimate goal of achieving global load balancing for virtual machine clusters.

3. Choose Agent-based Scheduling Algorithm. Cloud resource scheduling algorithm can draw on the outcomes from grid computing and distributed computing, and pay attention to the characteristics of cloud computing resource scheduling. Resource scheduling based on agent-based scheduling algorithm will package each resource node into an "agent", so that resource management system becomes a multi-level set of Agent systems. Scheduling is therefore simplified to match computing tasks between the Agents, adjust according to the changes of the Agents and continue to allocate the subtasks in the agents.

5 Conclusion

Cloud-based data center information resource management and control platform allows different algorithms for different resource scheduling models. What we are using is the time optimal algorithm. Time optimal algorithm intends to complete tasks within budget as quickly as possible. It will estimate the completion time of a task for each resource by taking into account of the previous allocated tasks and completion rates, sort the resources in ascending order based on the completion time, and then extract resources in order from the queue. If the cost of the task is less than or equal to its budget, the task is assigned to the resource. The platform realizes a unified data management and control of information resources by shielding differences among low-level physical equipment through virtualization technology and abstracting for low-level architecture in cloud data centers. It will play a positive role in changing the traditional mode of information resources management and control method in data center.

References

1. Yu, Y.: Data Center in Cloud Time. Electronics Industry Press, August 2012
2. Zheng, Y.: Construction and Management of Cloud Data Center. Tsinghua University Press, September 2013
3. Editorial Committee: Intelligence Cloud Data Center, Electronics Industry Press, April 2013
4. Zhao, H.: Building Distance Education System based on Cloud Computing (2013)
5. Yang, L., Zhao, H.: The top-level design method on informatization. In: ICPCA6/SWS3 (2011)

Author Index

Printed in the United States
by Bookmasters

Printed in the United States
By Bookmasters